Readings In
Western Civilization

Readings In
Western Civilization

Selected and Edited by

GEORGE H. KNOLES
Stanford University

and RIXFORD K. SNYDER
Stanford University

J. B. LIPPINCOTT COMPANY
Chicago   Philadelphia   New York

COPYRIGHT, 1951, BY J. B. LIPPINCOTT COMPANY

PRINTED IN THE UNITED STATES OF AMERICA

Preface

The editors in preparing this book have provided a collection of readings to accompany college courses in the History of Western Civilization. We have not sought to produce a substitute for a textbook, but to furnish what a textbook cannot offer, namely, extensive illustrative source materials to amplify and to enrich the text and other readings. We have not hesitated to draw upon the rich heritage in the fields of religion, literature, science, and the arts for these selections in our search to find suitable readings to illuminate some of the more significant aspects of the development of Western Civilization.

An effort has been made to select materials which lend themselves to use in class discussion. It is this emphasis upon usability in discussion rather than full coverage of all phases of a culture that has led to this particular collection of readings. We have found in our teaching that some of our finest results flowed from class discussion of the issues raised in these sources. Wherever possible we have included fairly long selections to allow a fuller acquaintance with the works chosen. All of the selections appear in the language of the authors or translators; in many cases we have followed spelling and printing styles of these authors or translators. We have not condensed nor abstracted materials. We have, however, been rigorous in our selections and have omitted much; we have indicated the omissions in the usual manner.

The materials are arranged generally in chronological order; there are some departures from this plan to permit a logical progression within a given section. There is no special virtue in our organization of the sections, and individual instructors will find that assignments can be made to suit their own courses or textbook arrangements.

The editors have not thought it necessary to furnish elaborate explanatory and interpretive settings for the documents, believing that this can be done better by the textbook. On the other hand, they think it helpful to give students adequate directions to assist them in making full use of the readings. The notes preceding each selection direct the students' attention to the significant points or conclusions in the reading. We have not sought to spoon-feed the students; rather we have told them what to look for with the thought that not only will they gain a better insight into the authors' intentions, but will also be better prepared to carry on an intelligent class discussion.

The editors are indebted to many persons for their helpfulness in the preparation of this volume. Particularly we wish to thank our former colleague, Professor Max Savelle, now of the University of Washington, who reviewed our plan and made valuable suggestions during the early stages of our work. Professor William Carroll Bark, of Stanford University, has given us the benefit of his critical judgment of the selections and scheme of the book for which we owe a debt of gratitude. To Mrs. Justin Truman Reid and to Mrs. Walter Scott Perry we are indebted for assistance in the preparation of the typescript.

GEORGE HARMON KNOLES
RIXFORD KINNEY SNYDER

STANFORD UNIVERSITY

CONTENTS

The Ancient Near East

Greek Civilization

Roman Civilization

The Decline of Classical Civilization

Civilization in the Middle Ages

Renaissance and Reformation

Civilization in the Seventeenth and Eighteenth Centuries

The Revolutionary Era and the Conservative Reaction

Industrialism, Liberalism, and Democracy in the Nineteenth Century

Social and Cultural Trends in the Nineteenth Century

Nationalism, Imperialism, and the War of 1914–1918

Economic, Social, and Political Changes in the Twentieth Century

Contemporary Civilization

The Ancient Near East

Properly speaking, the Near East is not a part of the area in which Western Civilization originated and developed. Nevertheless, the region between the western borders of India and the eastern shores of the Mediterranean Sea, including the valley of the Nile, provided the setting for the earliest civilizations, and these first ventures of mankind into more mature methods of living and thinking furnished the background for subsequent cultural developments in the Mediterranean world. Beginning in the millennium 4000–3000 B.C. and extending down through the centuries when Greece and Rome were first emerging, successive civilizations developed and flourished in Egypt, Mesopotamia, Palestine, and Persia. For the most part they were characterized by political absolutism which in turn gave rise to imperial rule over neighboring peoples. This phase of their culture inevitably required the development of legal principles, many of which were codified from time to time. For a variety of reasons, too, the peoples of the Ancient Near East were deeply concerned with religious ideas and with the ceremonies which developed to give expression to them. From these peoples, then, the western world gained certain legalistic and religious concepts which were to influence its civilization materially. A proper approach to the history of Western Civilization should therefore begin with a study of the Ancient Near East.

Hammurabi

The Amorite, Hammurabi (1950–1900 B.C.), succeeded in constructing an empire in Mesopotamia with Babylon as his capital city. In an effort to unify his conquests the king codified and systematized the various and conflicting laws and customs of his lands. This code, cut in a diorite shaft nearly eight feet high, was discovered early in the twentieth century by French archaeologists at Susa, in Persia, to which place it had been carried from Babylon by unknown persons. Provisions of this code continued in use for centuries and exerted considerable influence on Arabic and Islamic law. Comparisons of this code with selections from the Mosaic code to be found in the early books of the Bible will prove informative. In reading the following selections from Hammurabi's compilation, note regulations concerning (1) trial by ordeal, (2) scheduling of fines and punishments on the basis of social classes, (3) slavery and problems arising therefrom, (4) marriage, divorce, alimony, and the protection of children, and (5) business, agriculture, and the professions.

From: THE CODE OF HAMMURABI

1. If a man has accused another of laying a *nêrtu* (death spell?) upon him, but has not proved it, he shall be put to death.

2. If a man has accused another of laying a *kišpu* (spell) upon him, but has not proved it, the accused shall go to the sacred river, he shall plunge into the sacred river, and if the sacred river shall conquer him, he that accused him shall take possession of his house. If the sacred river shall show his innocence and he is saved, his accuser shall be put to death. He that plunged into the sacred river shall appropriate the house of him that accused him.

3. If a man has borne false witness in a trial, or has not established the statement that he has made, if that case be a capital trial, that man shall be put to death.

6. If a man has stolen goods from a temple, or house, he shall be put to death; and he that has received the stolen property from him shall be put to death.

8. If a patrician has stolen ox, sheep, ass, pig, or ship, whether from a temple, or a house, he shall pay thirtyfold. If he be a plebeian, he shall return tenfold. If the thief cannot pay, he shall be put to death.

14. If a man has stolen a child, he shall be put to death.

15. If a man has induced either a male or female slave from the house of a patrician, or plebeian, to leave the city, he shall be put to death.

21. If a man has broken into a house he shall be killed before the breach and buried there.

22. If a man has committed highway robbery and has been caught, that man shall be put to death.

23. If the highwayman has not been caught, the man that has been robbed shall state on oath what he has lost, and the city or district governor in whose territory or district the robbery took place shall restore to him what he has lost.

25. If a fire has broken out in a man's house and one who has come to put it out has coveted the property of the householder and appropriated any of it, that man shall be cast into the self-same fire.

26. If a levy-master, or warrant-officer, who has been detailed on the king's service, has not gone, or has hired a substitute in his place, that levy-master, or warrant-officer, shall be put to

C. H. W. Johns, *Babylonian and Assyrian Laws, Contracts and Letters,* Charles Scribner's Sons, New York, 1904, 44–66. Courtesy of Charles Scribner's Sons.

death and the hired substitute shall take his office.

27. If a levy-master, or warrant-officer, has been assigned to garrison duty, and in his absence his field and garden have been given to another who has carried on his duty, when the absentee has returned and regained his city, his field and garden shall be given back to him and he shall resume his duty.

28. If a levy-master, or warrant-officer, has been assigned to garrison duty, and has a son able to carry on his official duty, the field and garden shall be given to him and he shall carry on his father's duty.

36. The field, garden, or house, of a levy-master, warrant-officer, or tributary shall not be sold.

37. If a man has bought field, garden, or house, of a levy-master, a warrant-officer, or tributary, his title-deed shall be destroyed and he shall lose his money. He shall return the field, garden, or house to its owner.

42. If a man has hired a field to cultivate and has caused no corn to grow on the field, he shall be held responsible for not doing the work on the field and shall pay an average rent.

48. If a man has incurred a debt and a storm has flooded his field or carried away the crop, or the corn has not grown because of drought, in that year he shall not pay his creditor. Further, he shall post-date his bond and shall not pay interest for that year.

53, 54. If a man has neglected to strengthen his dike and has not kept his dike strong, and a breach has broken out in his dike, and the waters have flooded the meadow, the man in whose dike the breach has broken out shall restore the corn he has caused to be lost. [54.] If he be not able to restore the corn, he and his goods shall be sold, and the owners of the meadow whose corn the water has carried away shall share the money.

55. If a man has opened his runnel for watering and has left it open, and the water has flooded his neighbor's field, he shall pay him an average crop.

100. [If an agent has received money of a merchant, he shall write down the amount] and [what is to be] the interest of the money, and when his time is up, he shall settle with his merchant.

102, 103. If the merchant has given money, as a speculation, to the agent, who during his travels has met with misfortune, he shall return the full sum to the merchant. [103.] If, on his travels, an enemy has forced him to give up some of the goods he was carrying, the agent shall specify the amount on oath and shall be acquitted.

104. If a merchant has given to an agent corn, wool, oil, or any sort of goods, to traffic with, the agent shall write down the money value, and shall return that to the merchant. The agent shall then take a sealed receipt for the money that he has given to the merchant.

107. If the principal has overcharged the agent and the agent has [really] returned to his principal whatever his principal gave him, and if the principal has disputed what the agent has given him, that agent shall put his principal on oath before the elders, and the merchant, because he has defrauded the agent, shall pay to the agent sixfold what he misappropriated.

108. If the mistress of a beer-shop has not received corn as the price of beer or has demanded silver on an excessive scale, and has made the measure of beer less than the measure of corn, that beer-seller shall be prosecuted and drowned.

109. If the mistress of a beer-shop has assembled seditious slanderers in her house and those seditious persons have not been captured and have not been haled to the palace, that beer-seller shall be put to death.

110. If a votary, who is not living in the convent, open a beer-shop, or enter a beer-shop for drink, that woman shall be put to death.

117. If a man owes a debt, and he has given his wife, his son, or his daughter [as hostage] for the money, or has handed someone over to work it off, the hostage shall do the work of the creditor's house, but in the fourth year he shall set them free.

122. If a man has given another gold, silver, or any goods whatever, on deposit, all that he gives shall he show to witnesses, and take a bond and so give on deposit.

123. If he has given on deposit without witnesses and bonds, and has been defrauded where he made his deposit, he has no claim to prosecute.

125. If a man has given anything whatever on deposit, and, where he has made his deposit,

something of his has been lost together with something belonging to the owner of the house, either by house-breaking or a rebellion, the owner of the house who is in default shall make good all that has been given him on deposit, which he has lost, and shall return it to the owner of the goods. The owner of the house shall look after what he has lost and recover it from the thief.

128. If a man has taken a wife and has not executed a marriage-contract, that woman is not a wife.

129. If a man's wife be caught lying with another, they shall be strangled and cast into the water. If the wife's husband would save his wife, the king can save his servant.

132. If a man's wife has the finger pointed at her on account of another, but has not been caught lying with him, for her husband's sake she shall plunge into the sacred river.

138. If a man has divorced his wife, who has not borne him children, he shall pay over to her as much money as was given for her bride-price and the marriage-portion which she brought from her father's house, and so shall divorce her.

139. If there was no bride-price, he shall give her one mina · of silver, as a price of divorce.

140. If he be a plebeian, he shall give her one-third of a mina of silver.

141. If a man's wife, living in her husband's house, has persisted in going out, has acted the fool, has wasted her house, has belittled her husband, he shall prosecute her. If her husband has said, "I divorce her," she shall go her way; he shall give her nothing as her price of divorce. If her husband has said, "I will not divorce her," he may take another woman to wife; the wife shall live as a slave in her husband's house.

142. If a woman has hated her husband, and has said, "You shall not possess me," her past shall be inquired into, as to what she lacks. If she has been discreet, and has no vice, and her husband has gone out, and has greatly belittled her, that woman has no blame, she shall take her marriage-portion and go off to her father's house.

143. If she has not been discreet, has gone out, ruined her house, belittled her husband, she shall be drowned.

145. If a man has married a votary, and she has not granted him children, and he is determined to marry a concubine, that man shall marry the concubine, and bring her into his house, but the concubine shall not place herself on an equality with the votary.

148. If a man has married a wife and a disease has seized her, if he is determined to marry a second wife, he shall marry her. He shall not divorce the wife whom the disease has seized. In the home they made together she shall dwell, and he shall maintain her as long as she lives.

151. If a woman, who is living in a man's house, has persuaded her husband to bind himself, and grant her a deed to the effect that she shall not be held for debt by a creditor of her husband's; if that man had a debt upon him before he married that woman, his creditor shall not take his wife for it. Also, if that woman had a debt upon her before she entered that man's house, her creditor shall not take her husband for it.

152. From the time that that woman entered into the man's house they together shall be liable for all debts subsequently incurred.

153. If a man's wife, for the sake of another, has caused her husband to be killed, that woman shall be impaled.

159. If a man, who has presented a gift to the house of his prospective father-in-law and has given the bride-price, has afterward looked upon another woman and has said to his father-in-law, "I will not marry your daughter"; the father of the girl shall keep whatever he has brought as a present.

160. If a man has presented a gift to the house of his prospective father-in-law, and has given the bride-price, but the father of the girl has said, "I will not give you my daughter," the father shall return double all that was presented him.

168. If a man has determined to disinherit his son and has declared before the judge, "I cut off my son," the judge shall inquire into the son's past, and, if the son has not committed a grave misdemeanor such as should cut him off from sonship, the father shall [not] disinherit his son.

170. If a man has had children borne to him by his wife, and also by a maid, if the father in his lifetime has said, "My sons," to the chil-

dren whom his maid bore him, and has reckoned them with the sons of his wife; then after the father has gone to his fate, the children of the wife and of the maid shall share equally. The children of the wife shall apportion the shares and make their own selections.

175. If either a slave of a patrician, or of a plebeian, has married the daughter of a free man, and she has borne children, the owner of the slave shall have no claim for service on the children of a free woman. And if a slave, either of a patrician or of a plebeian, has married a free woman and when he married her she entered the slave's house with a marriage-portion from her father's estate, be he slave of a patrician or of a plebeian, and from the time that they started to keep house, they have acquired property; after the slave, whether of a patrician or of a plebeian, has gone to his fate, the free woman shall take her marriage-portion, and whatever her husband and she acquired, since they started house-keeping. She shall divide it into two portions. The master of the slave shall take one half, the other half the free woman shall take for her children.

177. If a widow, whose children are young, has determined to marry again, she shall not marry without consent of the judge. When she is allowed to remarry, the judge shall inquire as to what remains of the property of her former husband, and shall intrust the property of her former husband to that woman and her second husband. He shall give them an inventory. They shall watch over the property, and bring up the children. Not a utensil shall they sell. A buyer of any utensil belonging to the widow's children shall lose his money and shall return the article to its owners.

186. If a man has taken a young child to be his son, and after he has taken him, the child discover his own parents, he shall return to his father's house.

188, 189. If a craftsman has taken a child to bring up and has taught him his handicraft, he shall not be reclaimed. If he has not taught him his handicraft that foster child shall return to his father's house.

195. If a son has struck his father, his hands shall be cut off.

196. If a man has knocked out the eye of a patrician, his eye shall be knocked out.

197. If he has broken the limb of a patrician, his limb shall be broken.

198. If he has knocked out the eye of a plebeian or has broken the limb of a plebeian, he shall pay one mina of silver.

199. If he has knocked out the eye of a patrician's servant, or broken the limb of a patrician's servant, he shall pay half his value.

200. If a patrician has knocked out the tooth of a man that is his equal, his tooth shall be knocked out.

201. If he has knocked out the tooth of a plebeian, he shall pay one-third of a mina of silver.

206. If a man has struck another in a quarrel, and caused him a permanent injury, that man shall swear, "I struck him without malice," and shall pay the doctor.

215. If a surgeon has operated with the bronze lancet on a patrician for a serious injury, and has cured him, or has removed with a bronze lancet a cataract for a patrician, and has cured his eye, he shall take ten shekels of silver.

216. If it be plebeian, he shall take five shekels of silver.

217. If it be a man's slave, the owner of the slave shall give two shekels of silver to the surgeon.

218. If a surgeon has operated with the bronze lancet on a patrician for a serious injury, and has caused his death, or has removed a cataract for a patrician, with the bronze lancet, and has made him lose his eye, his hands shall be cut off.

221. If a surgeon has cured the limb of a patrician, or has doctored a diseased bowel, the patient shall pay five shekels of silver to the surgeon.

224. If a veterinary surgeon has treated an ox, or an ass, for a severe injury, and cured it, the owner of the ox, or the ass, shall pay the surgeon one-sixth of a shekel of silver, as his fee.

225. If he has treated an ox, or an ass, for a severe injury, and caused it to die, he shall pay one-quarter of its value to the owner of the ox, or the ass.

229. If a builder has built a house for a man, and has not made his work sound, and the house he built has fallen, and caused the

death of its owner, that builder shall be put to death.

237. If a man has hired a boat and boatman, and loaded it with corn, wool, oil, or dates, or whatever it be, and the boatman has been careless, and sunk the boat, or lost what is in it, the boatman shall restore the boat which he sank, and whatever he lost that was in it.

240. If a boat, on its course, has run into a boat at anchor, and sunk it, the owner of the boat that was sunk shall estimate on oath whatever was lost in his boat, and the owner of the moving vessel, which sank the boat at anchor, shall make good his boat and what was lost in it.

245. If a man has hired an ox and has caused its death, by carelessness, or blows, he shall restore ox for ox, to the owner of the ox.

250. If a bull has gone wild and gored a man, and caused his death, there can be no suit against the owner.

251. If a man's ox be a gorer, and has revealed its evil propensity as a gorer, and he has not blunted its horn, or shut up the ox, and then that ox has gored a free man and caused his death, the owner shall pay half a mina of silver.

259. If a man has stolen a watering-machine from the meadow, he shall pay five shekels of silver to the owner of the watering-machine.

261. If a man has hired a herdsman, to pasture oxen, or sheep, he shall pay him eight *gur* of corn yearly.

273. If a man has hired a laborer from the beginning of the year to the fifth month, he shall pay six *še* of silver daily; from the sixth month to the close of the year, he shall pay five *še* of silver daily.

The Bible

The Book of Exodus includes materials drawn from different ages and put together about the middle of the fourth century B.C. The chapters selected give the account of the meeting of Moses and Jahweh and the drawing up of a contract between Jahweh and the people of Israel. The Mosaic code, which in this account was made a part of the contract between Jahweh and Moses, dates from before 1000 B.C. and was largely derived from Egyptian and Babylonian codes. A comparison with the Code of Hammurabi (see above p. 3) will be profitable. Note (1) the kind of deity that is represented here, (2) the economic interests and practices of the Israelites, (3) the ethical principles stressed, (4) the terms of the contract between Jahweh and the Israelites, (5) the religious practices prescribed, (6) the boundaries Jahweh set for the future home of the Israelites, (7) the method used to seal the contract, (8) the provisions made to permit Jahweh to move from Mt. Sinai and accompany the people of Israel in their wanderings, and (9) the character of Jahweh as here described.

From: THE SECOND BOOK OF MOSES, CALLED EXODUS

In the third month, when the children of Israel were gone forth out of the land of Egypt, the same day came they into the wilderness of Sinai. For they were departed from Rephidim,

Adapted from the King James version of the Bible.

and were come to the desert of Sinai, and had pitched in the wilderness; and there Israel camped before the mount.

And Moses went up unto God, and the Lord

called unto him out of the mountain, saying, "Thus shalt thou say to the house of Jacob, and tell the children of Israel: 'Ye have seen what I did unto the Egyptians, and how I bare you on eagles' wings, and brought you unto myself. Now therefore, if ye will obey my voice indeed, and keep my covenant, then ye shall be a peculiar treasure unto me above all people: for all the earth is mine. And ye shall be unto me a kingdom of priests, and a holy nation.' These are the words which thou shalt speak unto the children of Israel."

And Moses came and called for the elders of the people, and laid before their faces all these words which the Lord commanded him. And all the people answered together, and said, "All that the Lord hath spoken we will do." And Moses returned the words of the people unto the Lord.

And the Lord said unto Moses, "Lo, I come unto thee in a thick cloud, that the people may hear when I speak with thee, and believe thee forever." And Moses told the words of the people unto the Lord. And the Lord said unto Moses, "Go unto the people, and sanctify them today and tomorrow, and let them wash their clothes, and be ready against the third day, for the third day the Lord will come down in the sight of all the people upon Mount Sinai. And thou shalt set bounds unto the people round about, saying, 'Take heed to yourselves, that ye go not up into the mount, or touch the border of it: whosoever toucheth the mount shall be surely put to death.' There shall not a hand touch it, but he shall surely be stoned, or shot through; whether it be beast or man, it shall not live: when the trumpet soundeth long, they shall come up to the mount."

And Moses went down from the mount unto the people, and sanctified the people; and they washed their clothes. And he said unto the people, "Be ready against the third day: come not at your wives."

And it came to pass on the third day in the morning, that there were thunders and lightnings, and a thick cloud upon the mount, and the voice of the trumpet exceeding loud; so that all the people that was in the camp trembled. And Moses brought forth the people out of the camp to meet with God; and they stood at the nether part of the mount. And Mount Sinai was altogether on a smoke, because the Lord descended upon it in fire; and the smoke thereof ascended as the smoke of a furnace, and the whole mount quaked greatly. And when the voice of the trumpet sounded long, and waxed louder and louder, Moses spake, and God answered him by a voice. And the Lord came down upon Mount Sinai, on the top of the mount: and the Lord called Moses up to the top of the mount; and Moses went up.

And the Lord said unto Moses, "Go down, charge the people, lest they break through unto the Lord to gaze and many of them perish. And let the priests also, which come near to the Lord, sanctify themselves, lest the Lord break forth upon them."

And Moses said unto the Lord, "The people cannot come up to Mount Sinai: for thou chargedst us, saying, 'Set bounds about the mount, and sanctify it.' "

And the Lord said unto him, "Away, get thee down, and thou shalt come up, thou, and Aaron with thee: but let not the priests and the people break through to come up unto the Lord, lest he break forth upon them."

So Moses went down unto the people, and spake unto them.

And God spake all these words, saying, "I am the Lord thy God, which have brought thee out of the land of Egypt, out of the house of bondage.

"Thou shalt have no other gods before me.

"Thou shalt not make unto thee any graven image, or any likeness of any thing that is in heaven above, or that is in the earth beneath, or that is in the water under the earth; thou shalt not bow down thyself to them, nor serve them: for I the Lord thy God am a jealous God, visiting the iniquity of the fathers upon the children unto the third and fourth generation of them that hate me; and showing mercy unto thousands of them that love me, and keep my commandments.

"Thou shalt not take the name of the Lord thy God in vain; for the Lord will not hold him guiltless that taketh his name in vain.

"Remember the sabbath day, to keep it holy. Six days shalt thou labor, and do all thy work: but the seventh day is the sabbath of the Lord thy God: in it thou shalt not do any work, thou, nor thy son, nor thy daughter, thy manservant, nor thy maidservant, nor thy cattle, nor thy stranger that is within thy gates: for in six days the Lord made heaven and earth, the sea, and all that in them is, and rested the seventh day: wherefore the Lord blessed the sabbath day, and hallowed it.

"Honour thy father and thy mother: that thy days may be long upon the land which the Lord thy God giveth thee.

"Thou shalt not kill.

"Thou shalt not commit adultery.

"Thou shalt not steal.

"Thou shalt not bear false witness against thy neighbor.

"Thou shalt not covet thy neighbour's house, thou shalt not covet thy neighbour's wife, nor his manservant, nor his maidservant, nor his ox, nor his ass, nor any thing that is thy neighbour's."

And all the people saw the thunderings, and the lightnings, and the noise of the trumpet, and the mountain smoking: and when the people saw it, they removed, and stood afar off.

And they said unto Moses, "Speak thou with us, and we will hear: but let not God speak with us, lest we die."

And Moses said unto the people, "Fear not: for God is come to prove you, and that his fear may be before your faces, that ye sin not."

And the people stood afar off, and Moses drew near unto the thick darkness where God was. And the Lord said unto Moses, "Thus thou shalt say unto the children of Israel: 'Ye have seen that I have talked with you from heaven. Ye shall not make with me gods of silver, neither shall ye make unto you gods of gold. An altar of earth thou shalt make unto me, and shalt sacrifice thereon thy burnt offerings, and thy peace offerings, thy sheep, and thine oxen: in all places where I record my name I will come unto thee and I will bless thee. And if thou wilt make me an altar of stone, thou shalt not build it of hewn stone: for if thou lift up thy tool upon it, thou hast polluted it.'"

"Now these are the judgments which thou shalt set before them:

"If thou buy a Hebrew servant, six years he shall serve: and in the seventh he shall go out free for nothing. If he came in by himself, he shall go out by himself: if he were married, then his wife shall go out with him. If his master have given him a wife, and she have borne him sons or daughters; the wife and her children shall be her master's, and he shall go out by himself. And if the servant shall plainly say, 'I love my master, my wife, and my children; I will not go out free': then his master shall bring him unto the judges; he shall also bring him to the door, or unto the door post; and his master shall bore his ear through with an awl; and he shall serve him for ever.

"And if a man sell his daughter to be a maidservant, she shall not go out as the menservants do. If she please not her master, who hath betrothed her to himself, then shall he let her be redeemed: to sell her unto a strange nation he shall have no power, seeing he hath dealt deceitfully with her. And if he hath betrothed her unto his son, he shall deal with her after the manner of daughters. If he take him another wife, her food, her raiment, and her duty of marriage, shall he not diminish. And if he do not these three unto her, then shall she go out free without money.

"He that smiteth a man, so that he die, shall be surely put to death. And if a man lie not in wait, but God deliver him into his hand; then I will appoint thee a place whither he shall flee. But if a man come presumptuously upon his neighbour, to slay him with guile; thou shalt take him from mine altar, that he may die. And he that smiteth his father, or his mother, shall be surely put to death.

"And he that stealeth a man, and selleth him, or if he be found in his hand, he shall surely be put to death.

"And he that curseth his father, or his mother, shall surely be put to death.

"And if men strive together, and one smite another with a stone, or with his fist, and he die not, but keepeth his bed: if he rise again, and walk abroad upon his staff, then shall he that smote him be quit; only he shall pay for the loss of his time, and shall cause him to be thoroughly healed.

"And if a man smite his servant, or his maid, with a rod, and he die under his hand; he shall be surely punished. Notwithstanding, if he continue a day or two, he shall not be punished: for he is his money.

"If men strive, and hurt a woman with child,

so that her fruit depart from her, and yet no mischief follow: he shall be surely punished, according as the woman's husband will lay upon him; and he shall pay as the judges determine. And if any mischief follow, then thou shalt give life for life, eye for eye, tooth for tooth, hand for hand, foot for foot, burning for burning, wound for wound, stripe for stripe.

"And if a man smite the eye of his servant, or the eye of his maid, that it perish; he shall let him go free for his eye's sake. And if he smite out his manservant's tooth, or his maid-servant's tooth; he shall let him go free for his tooth's sake.

"If an ox gore a man or a woman, that they die: then the ox shall be surely stoned, and his flesh shall not be eaten; but the owner of the ox shall be quit. But if the ox were wont to push with his horn in time past, and it hath been testified to his owner, and he hath not kept him in, but that he hath killed a man or a woman; the ox shall be stoned, and his owner also shall be put to death. If there be laid on him a sum of money, then he shall give for the ransom of his life whatsoever is laid upon him. . . .

"And if a man shall open a pit, or if a man shall dig a pit, and not cover it, and an ox or an ass fall therein; the owner of the pit shall make it good, and give money unto the owner of them; and the dead beast shall be his.

"And if one man's ox hurt another's, that he die; then they shall sell the live ox, and divide the money of it; and the dead ox also they shall divide. Or if it be known that the ox hath used to push in time past, and his owner hath not kept him in; he shall surely pay ox for ox; and the dead shall be his own.

"If a man shall steal an ox, or a sheep, and kill it, or sell it; he shall restore five oxen for an ox, and four sheep for a sheep. If a thief be found breaking up, and be smitten that he die, there shall no blood be shed for him. If the sun be risen upon him, there shall be blood shed for him: for he should make full restitution; if he have nothing, then he shall be sold for his theft. If the theft be certainly found in his hand alive, whether it be ox, or ass, or sheep; he shall restore double. . . .

"If a man deliver unto his neighbour an ass, or an ox, or a sheep, or any beast, to keep; and

it die, or be hurt, or driven away, no man seeing it: then shall an oath of the Lord be between them both, that he hath not put his hand unto his neighbour's goods; and the owner of it shall accept thereof, and he shall not make it good. And if it be stolen from him, he shall make restitution unto the owner thereof. If it be torn in pieces, then let him bring it for witness, and he shall not make good that which was torn. And if a man borrow ought of his neighbour, and it be hurt, or die, the owner thereof being not with it, he shall surely make it good. But if the owner thereof be with it, he shall not make it good: if it be a hired thing, it came for his hire.

"And if a man entice a maid that is not betrothed, and lie with her, he shall surely endow her to be his wife. If her father utterly refuse to give her unto him, he shall pay money according to the dowry of virgins.

"Thou shalt not suffer a witch to live.

"Whosoever lieth with a beast shall surely be put to death.

"He that sacrificeth unto any god, save unto the Lord only, he shall be utterly destroyed.

"Thou shalt neither vex a stranger, nor oppress him: for ye were strangers in the land of Egypt.

"Ye shall not afflict any widow, or fatherless child. If thou afflict them in any wise, and they cry at all unto me, I will surely hear their cry; and my wrath shall wax hot, and I will kill you with the sword; and your wives shall be widows, and your children fatherless.

"If thou lend money to any of my people that is poor by thee, thou shalt not be to him as a usurer, neither shalt thou lay upon him usury. If thou at all take thy neighbour's raiment to pledge, thou shalt deliver it unto him by that the sun goeth down: for that is his covering only, it is his raiment for his skin: wherein shall he sleep? and it shall come to pass, when he crieth unto me, that I will hear; for I am gracious.

"Thou shalt not revile the gods, nor curse the ruler of thy people. . . .

"And in all things that I have said unto you be circumspect: and make no mention of the name of other gods, neither let it be heard out of thy mouth. . . .

"The first of the firstfruits of thy land thou

shalt bring into the house of the Lord thy God. Thou shalt not seethe a kid in his mother's milk.

"Behold, I send an Angel before thee, to keep thee in the way, and to bring thee into the place which I have prepared. Beware of him, and obey his voice, provoke him not; for he will not pardon your transgressions: for my name is in him. But if thou shalt indeed obey his voice, and do all that I speak; then I will be an enemy unto thine enemies, and an adversary unto thine adversaries. For mine Angel shall go before thee, and bring thee in unto the Amorites, and the Hittites, and the Perizzites, and the Canaanites, the Hivites, and the Jebusites; and I will cut them off. Thou shalt not bow down to their gods, nor serve them, nor do after their works: but thou shalt utterly overthrow them, and quite break down their images.

"And ye shall serve the Lord your God, and he shall bless thy bread, and thy water; and I will take sickness away from the midst of thee. . . . I will send my fear before thee, and will destroy all the people to whom thou shalt come; and I will make all thine enemies turn their backs unto thee. And I will send hornets before thee, which shall drive out the Hivite, the Canaanite, and the Hittite, from before thee. I will not drive them out from before thee in one year; lest the land become desolate, and the beast of the field multiply against thee. By little and little I will drive them out from before thee, until thou be increased, and inherit the land. And I will set thy bounds from the Red sea even unto the sea of the Philistines, and from the desert unto the river: for I will deliver the inhabitants of the land into your hand; and thou shalt drive them out before thee. Thou shalt make no covenant with them, nor with their gods. They shall not dwell in thy land, lest they make thee sin against me: for if thou serve their gods, it will surely be a snare unto thee. . . ."

And Moses came and told the people all the words of the Lord, and all the judgments: and all the people answered with one voice, and said, "All the words which the Lord has said will we do."

And Moses wrote all the words of the Lord, and rose up early in the morning, and builded an altar under the hill, and twelve pillars, according to the twelve tribes of Israel. And he sent young men of the children of Israel, which offered burnt offerings, and sacrificed peace offerings of oxen unto the Lord. . . .

And the Lord said unto Moses, "Come up to me into the mount, and be there: and I will give thee tables of stone, and a law, and commandments which I have written; that thou mayest teach them. . . ."

And Moses went up into the mount, and a cloud covered the mount. And the glory of the Lord abode upon Mount Sinai, and the cloud covered it six days: and the seventh day he called unto Moses out of the midst of the cloud. And the sight of the glory of the Lord was like devouring fire on the top of the mount in the eyes of the children of Israel. And Moses went into the midst of the cloud, and gat him up into the mount: and Moses was in the mount forty days and forty nights.

And the Lord spake unto Moses, saying, "Speak unto the children of Israel, that they bring me an offering: of every man that giveth it willingly with his heart ye shall take my offering. And this is the offering which ye shall take of them; gold, and silver, and brass, and blue, and purple, and scarlet, and fine linen, and goats' hair, and rams' skins dyed red, and badgers' skins, and shittim wood, oil for the light, spices for anointing oil, and for sweet incense, onyx stones, and stones to be set in the ephod, and in the breastplate.

"And let them make me a sanctuary; that I may dwell among them. According to all that I show thee, after the pattern of the tabernacle, and the pattern of all the instruments thereof, even so shall ye make it.

"And they shall make an ark of shittim wood: two cubits and a half shall be the length thereof, and a cubit and a half the breadth thereof, and a cubit and a half the height thereof. And thou shalt overlay it with pure gold, within and without shalt thou overlay it, and shalt make upon it a crown of gold round about. And thou shalt cast four rings of gold for it, and put them in the four corners thereof; and two rings shall be in the one side of it, and two rings in the other side of it. And thou shalt make staves of shittim wood, and overlay them with gold. And thou shalt put the staves into the rings by the sides of the ark, that the ark may be borne with them. The staves shall be in the rings of the ark: they shall not be taken from it. And thou shalt put into the ark the testimony which I shall give thee.

"And thou shalt make a mercy seat of pure gold: two cubits and a half shall be the length thereof, and a cubit and a half the breadth thereof. And thou shalt make two cherubim of gold, of beaten work shalt thou make them, in the two ends of the mercy seat. And make one cherub on the one end, and the other cherub on the other end: even of the mercy seat shall ye make the cherubim on the two ends thereof.

"And the cherubim shall stretch forth their wings on high, covering the mercy seat with their wings, and their faces shall look one to another; toward the mercy seat shall the faces of the cherubim be.

"And thou shalt put the mercy seat above upon the ark; and in the ark thou shalt put the testimony that I shall give thee. And there I will meet with thee, and I will commune with thee from above the mercy seat, from between the two cherubim which are upon the ark of the testimony, of all things which I will give thee in commandment unto the children of Israel. . . ."

The Books of the Kings were put together shortly before the fall of the Kingdom of Judah (ca. 586 B.C.) from earlier records kept by priests and other interested writers. Following their conquest of Canaan, the Israelites gradually succumbed to the culture of the conquered. In this process Jahweh and his worship was neglected for the worship of the agricultural deities abounding in this area. The law of survival applied to the gods of the ancient orient and many lost out in the struggle. Jahweh entered into this conflict for existence and in the dramatic episodes centering around the careers of Elijah and Elisha, He emerged victorious. Henceforth there was little question in the minds of the Israelites as to who their god was to be, and the way was opened for a further refinement of Jahweh's character. In the selections note (1) the subject of the dispute between Ahab and Elijah, (2) the preparations made for the test between Elijah and the priests of Baal, (3) the extent to which apostasy had spread as indicated by the relative numbers of contenders, (4) the results of the contest, (5) Jahweh's approval of the mass murder of priests, (6) the success of Jehu's rebellion against Ahab, (7) Jehu's slaughter of the worshippers of Baal, (8) the desecration of the temple of Baal, and (9) Jehu's reward from Jahweh for his devotion.

From: THE BOOKS OF THE KINGS

And it came to pass after many days, that the word of the Lord came to Elijah in the third year, saying, "Go, show thyself unto Ahab; and I will send rain upon the earth."

And Elijah went to show himself unto Ahab. And there was a sore famine in Samaria. And Ahab called Obadiah, which was the governor of his house. (Now Obadiah feared the Lord greatly: for it was so, when Jezebel cut off the prophets of the Lord, that Obadiah took a hundred prophets, and hid them by fifty in a cave, and fed them with bread and water.)

And Ahab said unto Obadiah, "Go into the land, unto all fountains of water, and unto all brooks: peradventure we may find grass to save the horses and mules alive, that we lose not all the beasts."

So they divided the land between them to pass throughout it: Ahab went one way by himself, and Obadiah went another way by himself. And as Obadiah was in the way, behold, Elijah met him: and he knew him, and fell on his face, and said, "Art thou that my lord Elijah?"

And he answered him, "I am: go, tell thy lord, 'Behold, Elijah is here.' "

And he said, "What have I sinned, that thou wouldst deliver thy servant into the hand of Ahab, to slay me? As the Lord thy God liveth, there is no nation or kingdom, whither my lord hath not sent to seek thee: and when they said, 'He is not there'; he took an oath of the kingdom and nation, that they found thee not. And now thou sayest, 'Go, tell thy lord, "Behold, Elijah is here." ' And it shall come to pass, as soon as I am gone from thee, that the Spirit of the Lord shall carry thee whither I know not; and so when I come and tell Ahab, and he cannot find thee, he shall slay me: but I thy servant fear the Lord from my youth. Was it not told my lord what I did when Jezebel slew the prophets of the Lord, how I hid a hundred men of the Lord's prophets by fifty in a cave, and fed them with bread and water? And now thou sayest, 'Go, tell thy lord, "Behold, Elijah is here" ': and he shall slay me."

And Elijah said, "As the Lord of hosts liveth, before whom I stand, I will surely show myself unto him today."

So Obadiah went to meet Ahab, and told him: and Ahab went to meet Elijah.

And it came to pass, when Ahab saw Elijah, that Ahab said unto him, "Art thou he that troubleth Israel?"

And he answered, "I have not troubled Israel; but thou, and thy father's house, in that ye have forsaken the commandments of the Lord, and thou hast followed Baalim. Now therefore send, and gather to me all Israel unto Mount Carmel, and the prophets of Baal four hundred and fifty, and the prophets of the groves four hundred, which eat at Jezebel's table."

So Ahab sent unto all the children of Israel, and gathered the prophets together unto Mount Carmel. And Elijah came unto all the people, and said, "How long halt ye between two opinions? If the Lord be God, follow him: but if Baal, then follow him." And the people answered him not a word.

Then said Elijah unto the people, "I, even I only, remain a prophet of the Lord; but Baal's prophets are four hundred and fifty men. Let them therefore give us two bullocks; and let them choose one bullock for themselves, and cut it in pieces, and lay it on wood, and put no fire under: and I will dress the other bullock, and lay it on wood, and put no fire under: and call ye on the name of your gods, and I will call on the name of the Lord: and the God that answereth by fire, let him be God." And all the people answered and said, "It is well spoken."

And Elijah said unto the prophets of Baal, "Choose you one bullock for yourselves, and dress it first; for ye are many; and call on the name of your gods, but put no fire under."

And they took the bullock which was given them, and they dressed it, and called on the name of Baal from morning even until noon, saying, "O Baal, hear us." But there was no voice, nor any that answered. And they leaped upon the altar which was made.

And it came to pass at noon, that Elijah mocked them, and said, "Cry aloud: for he is a god; either he is talking, or he is pursuing, or he is in a journey, or peradventure he sleepeth, and must be awaked."

And they cried aloud, and cut themselves after their manner with knives and lancets, till the blood gushed out upon them. And it came to pass, when midday was past, and they prophesied until the time of the offering of the evening sacrifice, that there was neither voice, nor any to answer, nor any that regarded.

And Elijah said unto all the people, "Come near unto me." And all the people came near unto him. And he repaired the altar of the Lord that was broken down. And Elijah took twelve stones, according to the number of the tribes of the sons of Jacob, unto whom the word of the Lord came, saying, "Israel shall be thy name": and with the stones he built an altar in the name of the Lord: and he made a trench about the altar, as great as would contain two measures of seed. And he put the wood in order, and cut the bullock in pieces, and laid him on the wood, and said, "Fill four barrels with water, and pour it on the burnt sacrifice, and on the wood." And he said, "Do it the second time." And they did it the second time. And he said, "Do it the third time." And they did it the third time. And the water ran round about the altar; and he filled the trench also with water.

And it came to pass at the time of the offering of the evening sacrifice, that Elijah the prophet came near, and said, "Lord God of Abraham, Isaac, and of Israel, let it be known this day that thou art God in Israel, and that I am thy servant, and that I have done all these things at thy word. Hear me, O Lord, hear me, that this people may know that thou art the Lord God, and that thou hast turned their heart back again."

Then the fire of the Lord fell, and consumed the burnt sacrifice, and the wood, and the stones, and the dust, and licked up the water that was in the trench. And when all the people saw it, they fell on their faces: and they said, "The Lord, he is the God; the Lord, he is the God."

And Elijah said unto them, "Take the prophets of Baal; let not one of them escape." And they took them: and Elijah brought them down to the brook Kishon, and slew them there.

And Elijah said unto Ahab, "Get thee up, eat and drink; for there is a sound of abundance of rain."

So Ahab went up to eat and to drink. And Elijah went up to the top of Carmel; and he cast himself down upon the earth, and put his face between his knees, and said to his servant, "Go up now, look toward the sea." And he went up, and looked, and said, "There is nothing." And he said, "Go again seven times."

And it came to pass at the seventh time, that he said, "Behold, there ariseth a little cloud out of the sea, like a man's hand." And he said, "Go up, say unto Ahab, 'Prepare thy chariot, and get thee down, that the rain stop thee not.'"

And it came to pass in the meanwhile, that the heaven was black with clouds and wind, and there was a great rain. And Ahab rode,

and went to Jezreel. And the hand of the Lord was on Elijah; and he girded up his loins, and ran before Ahab to the entrance of Jezreel. . . .

And Ahab had seventy sons in Samaria. And Jehu wrote letters, and sent to Samaria, unto the rulers of Jezreel, to the elders, and to them that brought up Ahab's children, saying, "Now as soon as this letter cometh to you, seeing your master's sons are with you, and there are with you chariots and horses, a fenced city also, and armor; look even out the best and meetest of your master's sons, and set him on his father's throne, and fight for your master's house."

And it came to pass, when the letter came to them, that they took the king's sons, and slew seventy persons, and put their heads in baskets, and sent him them to Jezreel. So Jehu slew all that remained of the house of Ahab in Jezreel, and all his great men, and his kinsfolk, and his priests, until he left him none remaining.

And he arose and departed, and came to Samaria. And as he was at the shearing house in the way, Jehu met with the brethren of Ahaziah king of Judah, and said, "Who are ye?" And they answered, "We are the brethren of Ahaziah; and we go down to salute the children of the king and the children of the queen." And he said, "Take them alive." And they took them alive, and slew them at the pit of the shearing house, even two and forty men; neither left he any of them.

And when he came to Samaria, he slew all that remained unto Ahab in Samaria, till he had destroyed him, according to the saying of the Lord, which he spake to Elijah.

And Jehu gathered all the people together, and said unto them, "Ahab served Baal a little; but Jehu shall serve him much. Now therefore call unto me all the prophets of Baal, all his servants, and all his priests; let none be wanting: for I have a great sacrifice to do to Baal; whosoever shall be wanting, he shall not live." But Jehu did it in subtilty, to the intent that he might destroy the worshippers of Baal.

And Jehu said, "Proclaim a solemn assembly for Baal." And they proclaimed it. And Jehu sent through all Israel: and all the worshippers of Baal came, so that there was not a man left that came not. And they came into the house of

Baal; and the house of Baal was full from one end to another. And he said unto him that was over the vestry, "Bring forth vestments for all the worshippers of Baal." And he brought them forth vestments. And Jehu went, and Jehonadab the son of Rechab, into the house of Baal, and said unto the worshippers of Baal, "Search, and look that there be here with you none of the servants of the Lord, but the worshippers of Baal only."

And when they went in to offer sacrifices and burnt offerings, Jehu appointed fourscore men without, and said, "If any of the men whom I have brought into your hands escape, he that letteth him go, his life shall be for the life of him."

And it came to pass, as soon as he had made an end of offering the burnt offering, that Jehu said to the guard and to the captains, "Go in, and slay them; let none come forth." And they smote them with the edge of the sword; and the guard and the captains cast them out, and went to the city of the house of Baal. And they brought forth the images out of the house of Baal, and burned them. And they brake down the image of Baal, and brake down the house of Baal, and made it a draught house unto this day. Thus Jehu destroyed Baal out of Israel. And the Lord said unto Jehu, "Because thou hast done well in executing that which is right in mine eyes, and hast done unto the house of Ahab according to all that was in mine heart, thy children of the fourth generation shall sit on the throne of Israel."

Following Jahweh's victory over his rivals, the way was prepared for a transformation in the character of Jahweh. Two significant achievements are to be noted in connection with the Hebrew prophetic movement beginning in the eighth century B.C.: the development of the idea that Jahweh is more interested in social justice than mere sacrifice and ritual, and the development of the idea that there is only one God in the universe. The external history of the ancient orient between 800 B.C. and 500 B.C. helped immeasurably to shape the internal history of Hebrew religious thought. For one thing, Israel achieved great prosperity during the first half of the eighth century B.C., and a situation developed in which the rich became richer and the poor, poorer. The outward prosperity seemed proof that Jahweh was pleased with his people and the rich remembered Him with ever more lavish sacrifices and ritual. A second factor shaping religious thought was the rise and fall of the later empires of antiquity—Assyria, Chaldean Babylonia, and Persia. In an effort to explain the movements of these peoples involving the loss of liberty and destruction of the Hebrew kingdoms, Hebrew prophets extended the tradition of supernatural intervention in their own history to the control by Jahweh of other gods and other peoples in order to fulfill His purposes with respect to the people of Israel.

Amos, a plain, roughly dressed tender of flocks from the grasslands of the southern kingdom, appeared about 760 B.C. in the northern kingdom with a message of impending doom and disaster. The Assyrian armies, he warned, acting as the scourge of Jahweh were about to overrun the land, destroying homes, fields, and flocks because of the violence, oppression, fraud, and corruption practiced on every hand in Israel. Jahweh's pardon cannot be bought by sacrifice and ritual; but He demands justice and righteousness from His people. In reading the selection note (1) Amos's method of first pronouncing doom upon neighboring peoples before including his hearers in the prophecy, (2) the kinds of misdeeds specified in the judgment, (3) the punishments to be visited upon Israel for social injustice, (4) what Amos has Jahweh say regarding sacrifice and ritual, (5) what Jahweh demands of His people, (6) Amos's prophecy of captivity, and (7) what Jahweh's intentions are for the future of Israel after He punishes them.

From: AMOS

Amos said, "The Lord will roar from Zion, and utter his voice from Jerusalem; and the habitations of the shepherds shall mourn, and the top of Carmel shall wither."

Thus saith the Lord: "For three transgressions of Damascus, and for four, I will not turn away the punishment thereof; because they have threshed Gilead with threshing instruments of iron. But I will send a fire into the house of Hazael, which shall devour the palaces of Ben-hadad. I will break also the bar of Damascus, and cut off the inhabitant from the plain of Aven, and him that holdeth the sceptre from the house of Eden: and the people of Syria shall go into captivity unto Kir," saith the Lord.

Thus saith the Lord: "For three transgressions of Gaza, and for four, I will not turn away the punishment thereof; because they carried away captive the whole captivity, to deliver them up to Edom. But I will send a fire on the wall of Gaza, which shall devour the palaces thereof: and I will cut off the inhabitant from Ashdod, and him that holdeth the sceptre from Ashkelon, and I will turn mine hand against Ekron: and the remnant of the Philistines shall perish," saith the Lord God.

Thus saith the Lord: "For three transgressions of Tyrus, and for four, I will not turn away the punishment thereof; because they delivered up the whole captivity to Edom, and remembered not the brotherly covenant. But I will send a fire on the wall of Tyrus, which shall devour the palaces thereof."

Thus saith the Lord: "For three transgressions of Edom, and for four, I will not turn away the punishment thereof; because he did pursue his brother with the sword, and did cast off all pity, and his anger did tear perpetually, and he kept his wrath for ever. But I will send a fire upon Teman, which shall devour the palaces of Bozrah."

Thus saith the Lord: "For three transgressions of the children of Ammon, and for four, I will not turn away the punishment thereof; because they have ripped up the women with child of Gilead, that they might enlarge their border. But I will kindle a fire in the wall of Rabbah, and it shall devour the palaces thereof, with shouting in the day of battle, with a tempest in the day of the whirlwind: and their king shall go into captivity, he and his princes together," saith the Lord.

Thus saith the Lord: "For three transgressions of Moab, and for four, I will not turn away the punishment thereof; because he burned the bones of the king of Edom into lime. But I will send a fire upon Moab, and it shall devour the palaces of Kirioth: and Moab shall die with tumult, with shouting, and with the sound of the trumpet: and I will cut off the judge from the midst thereof, and will slay all the princes thereof with him," saith the Lord.

Thus saith the Lord: "For three transgressions of Judah, and for four, I will not turn away the punishment thereof; because they have despised the law of the Lord, and have not kept his commandments, and their lies caused them to err, after the which their fathers have walked. But I will send a fire upon Judah, and it shall devour the palaces of Jerusalem."

Thus saith the Lord: "For three transgressions of Israel, and for four, I will not turn away the punishment thereof; because they sold the righteous for silver, and the poor for a pair of shoes; that pant after the dust of the earth on the head of the poor, and turn aside the way of the meek: and a man and his father will go in unto the same maid, to profane my holy name: and they lay themselves down upon clothes laid to pledge by every altar, and they drink the wine of the condemned in the house of their god.

"Yet destroyed I the Amorite before them, whose height was like the height of the cedars, and he was strong as the oaks; yet I destroyed his fruit from above, and his roots from beneath. Also I brought you up from the land of Egypt, and led you forty years through the wilderness, to possess the land of the Amorite. And I raised up of your sons for prophets, and of your young men for Nazarites. Is it not even thus, O ye children of Israel?" saith the Lord. "But ye gave the Nazarites wine to drink; and commanded the prophets, saying, 'Prophesy not.'

"Behold, I am pressed under you, as a cart is pressed that is full of sheaves. Therefore the flight shall perish from the swift, and the strong shall not strengthen his force, neither shall the mighty deliver himself: neither shall he stand that handleth the bow; and he that is swift of foot shall not deliver himself: neither shall he that rideth the horse deliver himself. And he that is courageous among the mighty shall flee away naked in that day," saith the Lord.

Hear ye this word which I take up against you, even a lamentation, O house of Israel: "The virgin of Israel is fallen; she shall no more rise: she is forsaken upon her land; there is none to raise her up." For thus saith the Lord God: "The city that went out by a thousand shall leave a hundred, and that which went forth by a hundred shall leave ten, to the house of Israel."

For thus saith the Lord unto the house of Israel, "Seek ye me, and ye shall live: but seek not Beth-el, nor enter into Gilgal, and pass not to Beer-sheba: for Gilgal shall surely go into captivity, and Beth-el shall come to nought."

Seek the Lord, and ye shall live; lest he break out like fire in the house of Joseph, and devour it, and there be none to quench it in Beth-el. Ye who turn judgment to wormwood, and leave off righteousness in the earth, seek him that maketh the seven stars and Orion, and turneth the shadow of death into the morning, and maketh the day dark with night: that calleth for the waters of the sea, and poureth them out upon the face of the earth: the Lord is his name.

Forasmuch therefore as your treading is upon the poor, and ye take from him burdens of wheat: ye have built houses of hewn stone, but ye shall not dwell in them; ye have planted pleasant vineyards, but ye shall not drink wine of them. For I know your manifold transgressions and your mighty sins: they afflict the just, they take a bribe, and they turn aside the poor in the gate from their right. Therefore the prudent shall keep silence in that time; for it is an evil time.

Seek good, and not evil, that ye may live: and so the Lord, the God of hosts, shall be with you, as ye have spoken. Hate the evil, and love the good, and establish judgment in the gate: it may be that the Lord God of hosts will be gracious unto the remnant of Joseph. Therefore the Lord, the God of hosts, the Lord saith thus: "Wailing shall be in all streets; And they shall say in the highways, 'Alas! alas!' And they shall call the husbandman to mourning, and such as are skilful of lamentation to wailing. And in all vineyards shall be wailing: For I will pass through thee," saith the Lord.

"Woe unto you that desire the day of the Lord! To what end is it for you? The day of the Lord is darkness, and not light. As if a man did flee from a lion, and a bear met him; or went into the house, and leaned his hand on the wall, and a serpent bit him. Shall not the day of the Lord be darkness and not light? Even very dark and no brightness in it? I hate, I despise your feast days, and I will not smell in your solemn assemblies. Though ye offer me burnt offerings and your meat offerings, I will not accept them: neither will I regard the peace offerings of your fat beasts. Take thou away from me the noise of thy songs; for I will not hear the melody of thy viols. But let judgment run down as waters, and righteousness as a mighty stream. Have ye offered unto me sacrifices and offerings in the wilderness forty years, O house of Israel? But ye have borne the tabernacle of your Moloch and Chiun your images, the star of your god, which ye made to yourselves. Therefore will I cause you to go into captivity beyond Damascus," saith the Lord, whose name is the God of hosts.

"Are ye not as children of the Ethiopians unto me, O children of Israel?" saith the Lord. "Have not I brought up Israel out of the land of Egypt? And the Philistines from Caphtor, and the Syrians from Kir? Behold, the eyes of the Lord God are upon the sinful kingdom, and I will destroy it from off the face of the earth; saving that I will not utterly destroy the house of Jacob," saith the Lord. "For, lo, I will command, and I will sift the house of Israel among all nations, like as corn is sifted in a sieve, yet shall not the least grain fall upon the earth. All the sinners of my people shall die by the sword, which

say, 'The evil shall not overtake nor prevent us.'

"In that day will I raise up the tabernacle of David that is fallen, and close up the breaches thereof; and I will raise up his ruins, and I will build it as in the days of old: that they may possess the remnant of Edom, and of all the heathen, which are called by my name," saith the Lord that doeth this.

"Behold, the days come," saith the Lord, "that the plowman shall overtake the reaper, and the treader of grapes him that soweth seed; and the mountains shall drop sweet wine, and all the hills shall melt. And I will bring again the captivity of my people of Israel, and they shall build the waste cities, and inhabit them; and they shall plant vineyards, and drink the wine thereof; they shall also make gardens, and eat the fruit of them. And I will plant them upon their land, and they shall no more be pulled up out of their land which I have given them," saith the Lord thy God.

Amos had warned the northern kingdom that Jahweh would punish it for injustice, using the Assyrian host as a scourge of iron. The conquest of Samaria by the Assyrians in 722 B.C. seemed to fulfill this prophecy. Now was Israel being punished by Jahweh for its failure to achieve social justice. Would the southern kingdom heed this plain warning? Isaiah and Micah the Morasthite appeared in Jerusalem to sound the tocsin of impending destruction which Jahweh planned for the entire nation for its failure to heed the demands of justice. Lacking a precise definition of the corporate nature of sin, Isaiah and Micah, nevertheless, stated their conviction in bold terms that the entire community must suffer for its lapses. Although Israel would be chastised, Micah expressed a dream of universal peace that would eventually prevail. This statement represents one of the earliest professions of faith for a peaceful world and is the more significant because it emerged at a time when its fulfillment seemed utterly hopeless. In reading these selections note (1) what social and political wrongs met Jahweh's disapproval, (2) the punishment awaiting Zion and Jerusalem, (3) Micah's dream of universal peace, (4) Jahweh's contrast of how people were remembering Him and what He really desired of them, and (5) the conviction that after punishing them, Jahweh would eventually restore the people of Israel to their privileged position.

From: ISAIAH and MICAH

Hear, O heavens, and give ear, O earth: for the Lord hath spoken: "I have nourished and brought up children, and they have rebelled against me. The ox knoweth his owner, and the ass his master's crib; but Israel doth not know, my people doth not consider."

Ah sinful nation, a people laden with iniquity, a seed of evildoers, children that are corrupters! They have forsaken the Lord, they have provoked the Holy One of Israel unto anger, they are gone away backward.

Why should ye be stricken any more? ye will revolt more and more; the whole head is sick, and the whole heart faint. From the sole of the foot even unto the head there is no soundness in it; but wounds, and bruises, and putrifying sores: they have not been closed, neither bound up, neither mollified with ointment. Your country is desolate, your cities are burned with fire: your land, strangers devour it in your presence, and it is desolate, as overthrown by strangers. And the daughter of Zion is left as a cottage in a vineyard, as a lodge in a garden of cucumbers, as a besieged city. Except the Lord of hosts had left unto us a very small remnant, we should have been as Sodom, and we should have been like unto Gomorrah.

Hear the word of the Lord, ye rulers of Sodom! Give ear unto the law of our God, ye people of Gomorrah! "To what purpose is the multitude of your sacrifices unto me?" Saith the Lord: "I am full of the burnt offerings of rams, and the fat of fed beasts; and I delight not in the blood of bullocks, or of lambs or of he goats. When ye come to appear before me, who hath required this at your hand, to tread my courts? Bring no more vain oblations; incense is an abomination unto me; the new moons and sabbaths, the calling of assemblies, I cannot away with; it is iniquity, even the solemn meeting. Your new moons and your appointed feasts my soul hateth: they are a trouble unto me; I am weary to bear them. And when ye spread forth your hands, I will hide mine eyes from you: Yea, when ye make many prayers, I will not hear: your hands are full of blood. Wash you, make you clean; put away the evil of your doings from before mine eyes; cease to do evil; learn to do well; seek judgment, relieve the oppressed, judge the fatherless, plead for the widow. Come now, and let us reason together," saith the Lord, "though your sins be as scarlet, they shall be as white as snow; though they be red like crimson, they shall be as wool. If ye be willing and obedient, ye shall eat the good of the land: but if ye refuse and rebel, ye shall be devoured with the sword," for the mouth of the Lord hath spoken it. . . .

Woe unto them that decree unrighteous decrees, and that write grievousness which they have prescribed; to turn aside the needy from judgment, and to take away the right from the poor of my people, that widows may be their prey, and that they may rob the fatherless! And what will ye do in the day of visitation, and in the desolation which shall come from far? To whom will ye flee for help? And where will you leave your glory? Without me they shall bow down under the prisoners, and they shall fall under the slain. For all this his anger is not turned away, but his hand is stretched out still.

O Assyrian, the rod of mine anger, and the staff in their hand is mine indignation. I will send him against a hypocritical nation, and against the people of my wrath will I give him a charge, to take the spoil, and to take the prey, and to tread them down like the mire of the streets. Howbeit he meaneth not so, neither doth his heart think so; but it is in his heart to destroy and cut off nations not a few. For he saith, "Are not my princes altogether kings? Is not Calno as Carchemish? Is not Hamath as Arpad? Is not Samaria as Damascus? As my hand hath found the kingdoms of the idols, and whose graven images did excel them of Jerusalem and of Samaria; shall I not, as I have done unto Samaria and her idols, so do to Jerusalem and her idols?"

ISAIAH

Hear, I pray you, O heads of Jacob, and ye princes of the house of Israel; is it not for you to know judgment? Who hate the good, and love the evil; who pluck off their skin from off them, and their flesh from off their bones; who also eat the flesh of my people, and flay their skin from off them; and they break their bones, and chop them in pieces, as for the pot, and as flesh within the caldron. Then shall they cry unto the Lord, but he will not hear them: he will even hide his face from them at that time, as they have behaved themselves ill in their doings.

Thus saith the Lord concerning the prophets that make my people err, that bite with their teeth, and cry, "Peace"; and he that putteth not into their mouths, they even prepare war against him: "Therefore night shall be unto you, that ye shall not have a vision; and it shall be dark unto you, that ye shall not divine; and the sun shall go down over the prophets, and the day shall be dark over them. Then shall the seers be ashamed, and the diviners confounded: yea, they shall all cover their lips; for there is no answer of God."

But truly I am full of power by the spirit of the Lord, and of judgment and of might, to declare unto Jacob his transgression, and to Israel his sin. Hear this, I pray you, ye heads of the house of Jacob, and princes of the house of Israel, that abhor judgment, and pervert all equity. They build up Zion with blood, and Jerusalem with iniquity. The heads thereof judge for reward, and the priests thereof teach for hire, and the prophets thereof divine for money: yet will they lean upon the Lord, and say, "Is not the Lord among us? None evil can come upon us." Therefore shall Zion for your sake be plowed as a field, and Jerusalem shall become heaps, and the mountain of the house as the high places of the forest.

But in the last days it shall come to pass, that the mountain of the house of the Lord shall be established in the top of the mountains, and it shall be exalted above the hills; and people shall flow unto it. And many nations shall come, and say, "Come, and let us go up to the mountain of the Lord, and to the house of the God of Jacob; and he will teach us of his ways, and we will walk in his paths": for the law shall go forth of Zion, and the word of the Lord from Jerusalem.

And he shall judge among many people, and rebuke strong nations afar off; and they shall beat their swords into plowshares, and their spears into pruninghooks: nation shall not lift up a sword against nation, neither shall they learn war any more. But they shall sit every man under his vine and under his fig tree; and none shall make them afraid: for the mouth of the Lord of hosts hath spoken it. For all people will walk every one in the name of his god, and we will walk in the name of the Lord our God for ever and ever.

"In that day," saith the Lord, "will I assemble her that halteth, and I will gather her that is driven out, and her that I have afflicted; and I will make her that halted a remnant, and her that was cast far off a strong nation": and the Lord shall reign over them in Mount Zion from henceforth, even for ever. . . .

Hear ye now what the Lord saith: "Arise, contend thou before the mountains, and let the hills hear thy voice."

Hear ye, O mountains, the Lord's controversy, and ye strong foundations of the earth: for the Lord hath a controversy with his people, and he will plead with Israel.

"O my people, what have I done unto thee? And wherein have I wearied thee? Testify against me. For I brought thee up out of the land of Egypt, and redeemed thee out of the house of servants; and I sent before thee Moses, Aaron, and Miriam."

Wherewith shall I come before the Lord, and bow myself before the high God? Shall I come before him with burnt offerings, with calves of a year old? Will the Lord be pleased with thousands of rams, or with ten thousands of rivers of oil? Shall I give my firstborn for my transgression, the fruit of my body for the sin of my soul? He hath showed thee, O man, what is good; and what doth the Lord require of thee, but to do justly, and to love mercy, and to walk humbly with thy God? . . .

Woe is me! for I am as when they have gathered the summer fruits, as the grape gleanings of the vintage: there is no cluster to eat: my soul desired the first ripe fruit. The good man is perished out of the earth; and there is none upright among men: they all lie in wait for blood; they hunt every man his brother with a net.

That they may do evil with both hands earnestly, the prince asketh, and the judge asketh for a reward; and the great man, he uttereth his mischievous desire: so they wrap it up. The best of them is as a brier: the most upright is sharper than a thorn hedge: the day of thy watchmen and thy visitation cometh; now shall be their perplexity.

Trust ye not in a friend, put ye not confidence in a guide: keep the doors of thy mouth from her that lieth in thy bosom. For the son dishonoreth the father, the daughter riseth up against her mother, the daughter-in-law against her mother-in-law; a man's enemies are the men of his own house. Therefore I will look unto the Lord; I will wait for the God of my salvation: my God will hear me.

Rejoice not against me, O mine enemy: when I fall, I shall arise; when I sit in darkness, the Lord shall be a light unto me. I will bear the indignation of the Lord, because I have sinned against him, until he plead my cause, and execute judgment for me: he will bring me forth to the light, and I shall behold his righteousness. Then she that is mine enemy shall see it, and shame shall cover her which said unto me, "Where is the Lord thy God?" Mine eyes shall behold her: now shall she be trodden down as the mire of the streets. In the day that thy walls are to be built, in that day shall the decree be far removed. In that day also he shall come even to thee from Assyria, and from the fortified cities, and from the fortress even to the river, and from sea to sea, and from mountain to mountain. Nothwithstanding, the land shall be desolate because of them that dwell therein, for the fruit of their doings.

Feed thy people with thy rod, the flock of thine heritage, which dwell solitarily in the wood, in the midst of Carmel: let them feed in Bashan and Gilead, as in the days of old. According to the days of thy coming out of the land of Egypt will I show unto him marvelous things.

The nations shall see and be confounded at all their might: they shall lay their hand upon their mouth, their ears shall be deaf. They shall lick the dust like a serpent, they shall move out of their holes like worms of the earth: they shall be afraid of the Lord our God, and shall fear because of thee. Who is a God like unto thee, that pardoneth iniquity, and passeth by the transgression of the remnant of his heritage? He retaineth not his anger for ever, because he delighteth in mercy. He will turn again, he will have compassion upon us; he will subdue our iniquities; and thou wilt cast all their sins into the depths of the sea. Thou wilt perform the truth to Jacob, and the mercy to Abraham, which thou hast sworn unto our fathers from the days of old.

MICAH

The disasters of the eighth century had considerably weakened Israel's faith in Jahweh as its divine protector. With the Assyrian conquerors came foreign ways and foreign gods. Other conquering hordes swept over the land, first the Scythian war bands followed by Chaldean Babylonians. In 586 B.C. Nebuchadnezzar appeared before Jerusalem, breached the fortifications, burned the temples and palaces, and deported thousands to Babylon. The Babylonian captivity had many consequences. Jahweh became more of a spiritual entity, disassociated as He was from the familiar scenes of His earlier triumphs. Moreover, with the community shattered by deportation, the personal and individual aspects of religion tended to supplant religion as a community enterprise. In this selection note (1) Ezekiel's statement of individualism in religion, (2) the listing of misdeeds of a social and of a religious nature, (3) the promise of favor to those who repent and, (4) the call for a new life on the part of each man.

From: EZEKIEL

The word of the Lord came unto me again, saying, "What mean ye, that ye use this proverb concerning the land of Israel, saying,

'The fathers have eaten sour grapes,
And the children's teeth are set on edge'?

"As I live," saith the Lord God, "ye shall not have occasion any more to use this proverb in Israel. Behold, all souls are mine; as the soul of the father, so also the soul of the son is mine: the soul that sinneth, it shall die.

"But if a man be just, and do that which is lawful and right, and hath not eaten upon the mountains, neither hath lifted up his eyes to the idols of the house of Israel, neither hath defiled his neighbor's wife, neither hath come near to a menstruous woman, and hath not oppressed any, but hath restored to the debtor his pledge, hath spoiled none by violence, hath given his bread to the hungry, and hath covered the naked with a garment; he that hath not given forth upon usury, neither hath taken any increase, that hath withdrawn his hand from iniquity, hath executed true judgment between man and man, hath walked in my statutes, and hath kept my judgments, to deal truly; he is just, he shall surely live," saith the Lord God.

"If he beget a son that is a robber, a shedder of blood, and that doeth the like to any one of these things, and that doeth not any of those duties, but even hath eaten upon the mountains, and defiled his neighbor's wife, hath oppressed the poor and needy, hath spoiled by violence, hath not restored the pledge, and hath lifted up his eyes to the idols, hath committed abomination, hath given forth upon usury, and hath taken increase: shall he then live? He shall not live: he hath done all these abominations; he shall surely die; his blood shall be upon him.

"Now, lo, if he beget a son, that seeth all his father's sins which he hath done, and considereth, and doeth not such like, that hath not eaten upon the mountains, neither hath lifted up his eyes to the idols of the house of Israel, hath not defiled his neighbor's wife, neither hath oppressed any, hath not withheld the pledge, neither hath spoiled by violence, but hath given his bread to the hungry, and hath covered the naked with a garment, that hath taken off his hand from the poor, that hath not received usury nor increase, hath executed my judgments, hath walked in my statutes; he shall not die for the iniquity of his father, he shall surely live.

"As for his father, because he cruelly oppressed, spoiled his brother by violence, and did that which is not good among his people, lo, even he shall die in his iniquity.

"Yet say ye, 'Why? doth not the son bear the iniquity of the father?' When the son hath done that which is lawful and right, and hath kept all my statutes, and hath done them, he shall surely live. The soul that sinneth, it shall die. The son shall not bear the iniquity of the father, neither shall the father bear the iniquity of the son: the righteousness of the righteous shall be upon him, and the wickedness of the wicked shall be upon him. But if the wicked will turn from all his sins that he hath committed, and keep all my statutes, and do that which is lawful and right, he shall surely live, he shall not die. All his transgressions that he hath committed, they shall not be mentioned unto him: in his righteousness that he hath done he shall live. Have I any pleasure at all that the wicked should die?" saith the Lord God: "and not that he should return from his ways, and live?

"But when the righteous turneth away from his righteousness, and committeth iniquity, and doeth according to all the abominations that the wicked man doeth, shall he live? All his righteousness that he hath done shall not be mentioned: in his trespass that he hath trespassed, and in his sin that he hath sinned, in them shall he die.

"Yet ye say, 'The way of the Lord is not equal.' Hear now, O house of Israel: is not my way equal? Are not your ways unequal? When a righteous man turneth away from his righteousness, and committeth iniquity, and dieth in them; for his iniquity that he hath done shall he die. Again, when the wicked man turneth away from his wickedness that he hath committed, and doeth that which is lawful and right, he shall save his soul alive. Because he considereth, and turneth away from all his transgressions that he hath committed, he shall surely live, he shall not die. Yet saith the house of Israel, 'The way of the Lord is not equal.' O house of Israel, are not my ways equal? Are not your ways unequal? Therefore I will judge you, O house of Israel, every one according to his ways," saith the Lord God. "Repent, and turn yourselves from all your transgressions; so iniquity shall not be your ruin.

"Cast away from you all your transgressions, whereby ye have transgressed; and make you a new heart and a new spirit: for why will ye die, O house of Israel? For I have no pleasure in the death of him that dieth," saith the Lord God: "wherefore turn yourselves, and live ye."

The earlier prophets, whatever kind or degree of superiority they attributed to Jahweh, seemingly never questioned that the gods of other peoples were real; but the prophets after 600 B.C. went far beyond this position, first by asserting that Jahweh was superior to all other gods, and second by proclaiming that there were no other gods. In the writings of the unknown prophet, sometimes known as the Second Isaiah or Deutero-Isaiah, there is pictured a Jahweh of immeasurable might and lofty majesty, before whom everything on earth that lifts itself on high before Him shall be abased. Moreover, Jahweh is here described as sole God, maker of heaven and earth, and ruler of the destinies of men and nations. Such assertions of omnipotence at the very moment of Judah's destruction, which in the eyes of the world represented Jahweh's total defeat, needed explanation. Jahweh had been responsible for the defeat of Israel and Judah; indeed, He had been responsible for putting into motion the empires of antiquity to serve and fulfill His purpose. All of the forces of history were controlled by one universal will. The Second Isaiah answered another troublesome question: How was it possible for the god of a small and relatively unimportant segment of the human family to be sole God of the universe? How, if there be but one God, was it that the Jews alone knew and worshipped Him? God, who was identical with Jahweh, chose Israel and revealed Himself to it so that Israel could be the prophet of the true God to enlighten the Gentile world. In reading the selections note (1) the author's description of God's majesty, (2) his statement of monotheism, (3) the role of Israel as a messenger to the Gentiles, and (4) the nature and mission of the messiah, or anointed one of God.

From: ISAIAH

"Comfort ye, comfort ye my people," saith your God. "Speak ye comfortably to Jerusalem, and cry unto her, that her warfare is accomplished, that her iniquity is pardoned: for she hath received of the Lord's hand double for all her sins."

The voice of him that crieth in the wilderness, "Prepare ye the way of the Lord, make straight in the desert a highway for our God. Every valley shall be exalted, and every mountain and hill shall be made low: and the crooked shall be made straight, and the rough places plain: and the glory of the Lord shall be revealed, and all flesh shall see it together: for the mouth of the Lord hath spoken it."

The voice said, "Cry." And he said, "What shall I cry?"

"All flesh is grass, and all the goodliness thereof is as the flower of the field: the grass withereth, the flower fadeth: because the spirit of the Lord bloweth upon it: surely the people is grass. The grass withereth, the flower fadeth: but the word of our God shall stand for ever."

O Zion, that bringest good tidings, get thee up into the high mountain; O Jerusalem, that bringest good tidings, lift up thy voice with strength; lift it up, be not afraid; say unto the cities of Judah, "Behold your God!"

Behold, the Lord God will come with strong hand, and his arm shall rule for him: behold, his reward is with him, and his work before him. He shall feed his flock like a shepherd: he shall gather the lambs with his arm, and carry them in his bosom, and shall gently lead those that are with young.

Who hath measured the waters in the hollow of his hand, and meted out heaven with the span, and comprehended the dust of the earth in a measure, and weighed the mountains in scales, and the hills in a balance? Who hath directed the Spirit of the Lord, or being his counsellor hath taught him? With whom took he counsel, and who instructed him, and taught him in the path of judgment, and taught him knowledge, and showed to him the way of understanding? Behold, the nations are as a drop of a bucket, and are counted as the small dust of the balance: behold, he taketh up the isles as a very little thing. And Lebanon is not sufficient to burn, nor the beasts thereof sufficient for a burnt offering. All nations before him are as nothing; and they are counted to him less than nothing, and vanity.

To whom then will ye liken God? Or what likeness will ye compare unto him? . . . Have ye not known? Have ye not heard? Hath it not been told you from the beginning? Have ye not understood from the foundations of the earth? It is he that sitteth upon the circle of the earth, and the inhabitants thereof are as grasshoppers; that stretcheth out the heavens as a curtain, and spreadeth them out as a tent to dwell in; that bringeth the princes to nothing; he maketh the judges of the earth as vanity. Yea, they shall not be planted; yea, they shall not be sown; yea, their stock shall not take root in the earth; and he shall also blow upon them, and they shall wither, and the whirlwind shall take them away as stubble.

"To whom then will ye liken me, or shall I be equal?" saith the Holy One. Lift up your eyes on high, and behold who hath created these things, that bringeth out their host by number: he calleth them all by names by the greatness of his might, for that he is strong in power; not one faileth. Why sayest thou, O Jacob, and speakest, O Israel, "My way is hid from the Lord, and my judgment is passed over from my God"?

Hast thou not known? Hast thou not heard, that the everlasting God, the Lord, the Creator of the ends of the earth, fainteth not, neither is weary? There is no searching of his understanding. He giveth power to the faint; and to them that have no might he increaseth strength. Even the youths shall faint and be weary, and the young men shall utterly fall: but they that wait upon the Lord shall renew their strength; they shall mount up with wings as eagles; they shall run, and not be weary; and they shall walk, and not faint. . . .

Thus saith the Lord to his anointed, to Cyrus, whose right hand I have held, to subdue nations before him; and I will loose the loins of kings, to open before him the two-leaved gates; and the gates shall not be shut: "I will go before thee, and make the crooked places straight: I will break in pieces the gates of brass, and cut in sunder the bars of iron; and I will give thee the treasures of darkness, and hidden riches of secret places, that thou mayest know that I, the Lord, which call thee by thy name, am the God of Israel. For Jacob my servant's sake, and Israel mine elect, I have even called thee by thy name; I have surnamed thee, though thou hast not known me. I am the Lord, and there is none else, there is no God beside me; I girded thee, though thou hast not known me: that they may know from the rising of the sun, and from the west, that there is none beside me. I am the Lord, and there is none else. I form the light, and create darkness: I make peace, and create evil: I the Lord do all these things. Drop down, ye heavens, from above, and let the skies pour down righteousness; let the earth open, and let them bring forth salvation, and let righteousness spring up together; I the Lord have created it. Woe unto him that striveth with his Maker! Let the potsherd strive with the potsherds of the earth. Shall the clay say to him that fashioneth it, 'What makest thou?' Or thy work, 'He hath no hands'? Woe unto him that saith unto his father, 'What begettest thou?' Or to the woman, 'What hast thou brought forth?' "

Thus saith the Lord, the Holy One of Israel, and his Maker, "Ask me of things to come concerning my sons, and concerning the work of my hands command ye me. I have made the earth, and created man upon it; I, even my hands, have stretched out the heavens, and all their host have I commanded. I have raised him up in righteousness, and I will direct all his ways; he shall build my city, and he shall let go my captives, not for price nor reward," saith the Lord of hosts.

Thus saith the Lord, "The labor of Egypt, and merchandise of Ethiopia and of the Sabeans, men of stature, shall come over unto thee, and they shall be thine: they shall come after thee; in chains they shall come over, and they shall fall down unto thee, they shall make supplication unto thee, saying, 'Surely God is in thee; and there is none else, there is no God.' "

Verily, thou art a God that hidest thyself, O God of Israel, the Saviour. They shall be ashamed, and also confounded, all of them: they shall go to confusion together that are makers of idols. But Israel shall be saved in the Lord with an everlasting salvation: ye shall not be ashamed nor confounded world without end. . . .

Who hath believed our report? And to whom is the arm of the Lord revealed? For he shall grow up before him as a tender plant, and as a root out of a dry ground: he hath no form nor comeliness; and when we shall see him, there is no beauty that we should desire him. He is despised and rejected of men; a man of sorrows, and acquainted with grief: and we hid as it were our faces from him; he was despised, and we esteemed him not. Surely he hath borne our griefs, and carried our sorrows: yet we did esteem him stricken, smitten of God, and afflicted. But he was wounded for our transgressions, he was bruised for our iniquities: the chastisement of our peace was upon him; and with his stripes we are healed. All we like sheep have gone astray; we have turned every one to his own way; and the Lord hath laid on him the iniquity of us all. He was oppressed, and he was afflicted, yet he opened not his mouth: he is brought as a lamb to the slaughter, and as a sheep before her shearers is dumb, so he openeth not his mouth. He was taken from prison and from judgment: and who shall declare his generation? For he was cut off out of the land of the living: for the transgression of my people was he stricken. And he made his grave with the wicked, and with the rich in his death; because he had done no violence, neither was any deceit in his mouth.

Yet it pleased the Lord to bruise him; he hath put him to grief: when thou shalt make his soul an offering for sin . . . , the pleasure of the Lord shall prosper in his hand. He shall see of the travail of his soul, and shall be satisfied: by his knowledge shall my righteous servant justify many; for he shall bear their iniquities. Therefore will I divide him a portion with the great, and he shall divide the spoil with the strong; because he hath poured out his soul unto death: and he was numbered with the transgressors; and he bore the sin of many, and made intercession for the transgressors.

The Egyptians

From earliest times the Egyptians believed that moral goodness, right-doing, and righteousness pleased both gods and men, while wrong-doing displeased the gods and angered their fellow men. Moreover, evidence suggests that they believed they would be judged after death by a court presided over by a god-judge. These views underwent slow development from vague and undefined beginnings in early Egyptian history to a more certain and definite set of beliefs used in regulating many of the activities of everyday life. Religious thought developed rapidly after the downfall of the Old Kingdom (about 2500 B.C.), and ethics came to be more thoroughly integrated with religion than formerly. The cult of Osiris increased in popularity, partly because of its promise of eternal life not only to kings, but to all men and women; in time Osiris came to be identified with the supreme judge who sat in the Hall of Maāt. In addition to requiring high moral conduct on earth as a prerequisite for an afterlife, certain magic spells and rubrics were considered useful to the soul in its journey to the judgment hall. The title given to one of these collections by modern scholars is The Book of the Dead. This selection (composed about 1500 B.C.) is a part of the declaration which the soul made before Osiris and the judges. In reading it note (1) the salutation to the gods, (2) the actions which refer to the conduct of religious practices, (3) the standards of personal morality, (4) the emphasis upon social justice, and (5) the evidences of magic.

From: THE BOOK OF THE DEAD

Homage to Thee, O Great God, Lord of the city of MAĀTI, I have come unto Thee, O my Lord, and I have brought myself hither that I may gaze upon Thy beauties (or beneficence).

I know Thee, I know Thy Name, I know the name[s] of the Forty-two gods who are with Thee in this Hall of MAĀTI, who live as the warders of sinners [and] who swallow their blood on that day of reckoning up the characters (or dispositions of men) in the presence of UN-NEFER (i.e. OSIRIS). In truth 'REKHTI-MERTI-NEB-MAĀTI' is Thy Name.

Verily I have come unto Thee, I have brought unto Thee MAĀT (i.e. TRUTH, or the LAW), I have crushed for Thee SIN.

1. I have not acted sinfully towards men.
2. I have not oppressed the members of my family.
3. I have not done wrong instead of what is right.
4. I have known no worthless folk.
5. I have not committed abominable acts.
6. I have not made excessive work to be done for me on any day(?).
7. I have [not made] my name to go forth for positions of dignity.
8. I have not domineered over servants.
9. I have not belittled god [or the God].
10. I have not filched the property of the lowly man.
11. I have not done things which are the abominations of the gods.
12. I have not vilified a servant to his master.
13. I have not inflicted pain (or caused suffering).
14. I have not permitted any man to suffer hunger.
15. I have not made any man to weep.
16. I have not committed murder (or slaughter).
17. I have not given an order to cause murder.

E. A. Wallis Budge, *From Fetish to God in Ancient Egypt*, Oxford University Press, London, 1934, 296–300. Courtesy of the University College, Oxford and Christ College, Cambridge.

18. I have not made men and women to suffer calamities.
19. I have not purloined the oblations in the temples.
20. I have not defrauded the gods of [their] cakes (or offerings).
21. I have not carried off the cakes of the AAKHU (the dead?).
22. I have not committed sodomy.
23. I have not polluted [the sacred waters of the god of my city].
24. I have not made light the bushel.
25. I have not filched from, nor added to, an estate.
26. I have not encroached upon the fields [of others].
27. I have not added to the weights of the scales [to cheat the seller].
28. I have not diminished the weight of the pointer of the scales.
29. I have not snatched away milk from the mouth[s] of children.
30. I have not driven away the cattle from their pastures.
31. I have not snared the geese in the preserves of the gods.
32. I have not fished with bait made of the bodies of fish.
33. I have not stopped water when it should run.
34. I have not made a cutting in a canal of running water.
35. I have not extinguished a fire when it should burn.
36. I have not neglected the times for the chosen offerings.
37. I have not driven away the cattle from the farms of the gods.
38. I have not obstructed the god in his comings forth (or appearances in processions).
39. Hail, HEPT-SHET, coming out from KHER-ĀBA, I have not robbed.
40. Hail, ARITI-F-SHET, coming out from SEKHEM, I have not defrauded.
41. Hail, NEBA, coming out and retreating, I have not plundered sacred property.
42. Hail, SET-QESU, coming out from HENSU (HERAKLEOPOLIS), I have not uttered falsehood.
43. Hail, UADJ-NESERT, coming out from HE-T-KA-PTAH (MEMPHIS), I have not blasphemed (or cursed god or man).
44. Hail, UNEM-BESKU, coming out from the MĀBET chamber, I have not laid waste ploughed lands.
45. Hail, QERTI, coming out from AMENT, I have not uttered slanders (or words of backbiting).
46. Hail, NEB-MAĀT, coming out from the city of MAĀTI, I have not played the eavesdropper.
47. Hail, MA-ANTEF, coming out from PER-MENU, I have not lain with the woman of a man (i.e. another man's wife).
48. Hail, AN-HETEP-F, coming out from SAU-T (SAÏS), I have not acted truculently (or with unnecessary violence).
49. Hail, NEFER-TEM, coming out from HE-T-KA-PTAH (MEMPHIS), I have not spoken treasonably about the king.
50. Hail, NEHEB-KAU, coming out from his sanctuary, I have not increased my possessions except through my own property.

I am washed. I am washed. I am washed. I am washed. My purity (?) is the purity of that great BENU which is in HENSU (i.e. HANES, HERAKLEOPOLIS). For I am that Nose of the Lord of the Winds (i.e. THOTH), who maketh all mankind to live, on the day of the filling of the UDJAT (i.e. full moon) in ANNU (HELIOPOLIS) in the second month of the season of PERT, the last day [in the presence of the Lord of this land]. I have seen the fullness of the UDJAT (i.e. full moon) in ANNU. Evil shall not happen to me in this land, in the Hall of MAĀTI, because I know the name[s] of these gods who are therein [who are the followers of the Great God].

Greek Civilization

The first people to develop an outstanding civilization on the continent of Europe were the Greeks. Their ancestors had migrated from central Europe, beginning sometime around 2000 B.C., and had conquered the peoples who were already living on the peninsula that was to become their home. When the Greeks arrived on the shores of the Mediterranean, their culture was a primitive one, but it gradually matured, and by 500 B.C. these people entered what has become known as the Golden Age of Greece. They excelled in nearly every phase of human achievement, and in a period of less than 200 years prominent Greeks produced works that have placed their names for all times among the great men of human history. Politically, they developed democratic institutions which in turn made possible an environment conducive to individual expression and creation. Philosophy, in particular, appealed to them, but the search for truth and perfection was not confined to that activity; they carried it into the fields of literature, art, and, in the case of the Alexandrian Greeks, of science as well. By 300 B.C. the Greek Civilization was eclipsed and other peoples took their places of leadership in the Mediterranean world, but subsequent ages have never ceased to study what the Greeks achieved, and thus their contribution to Western Civilization has been continuous as well as profound.

Thucydides

Thucydides (about 471–400 B.C.), one of the world's greatest historians, concluded that the Peloponnesian War, which in many respects was like a civil war among the city states of the Greek world, represented a major event in world history. The Greeks had succeeded in turning back the Persian hosts, thus saving the West from engulfment in a sweeping tide of oriental influences. Victory in the Persian wars released significant creative energies among the Greeks with startling achievements, particularly in the city-state of Athens, which witnessed a flowering of culture and at the same time sought political supremacy among her neighbors. This latter ambition led to the disastrous Peloponnesian Wars which so weakened the Greek states that they became an easy prey to the armies of Alexander. Thucydides, believing that the war had a far-reaching importance, carefully recorded its history. This selection is from the author's account of a funeral oration delivered by the great Athenian leader, Pericles, in which Pericles attempted to explain some of the underlying characteristics of the Athenian spirit. In reading it note (1) the nature of the funerary ceremonies, (2) Pericles' description of Athenian democracy, and (3) the ideals of the Athenian way of life.

From: THE PELOPONNESIAN WAR

In the same winter the Athenians gave a funeral at the public cost to those who had first fallen in this war. It was a custom of their ancestors, and the manner of it is as follows:

Three days before the ceremony, the bones of the dead are laid out in a tent which has been erected; and their friends bring to their relatives such offerings as they please. In the funeral procession cypress coffins are borne in carts, one for each tribe; the bones of the deceased being placed in the coffin of their tribe. Among these is carried one empty bier decked for the missing, that is, for those whose bodies could not be recovered. Any citizen or stranger who pleases, joins in the procession: and the female relatives are there to wail at the burial. The dead are laid in the public sepulchre in the most beautiful suburb of the city, in which those who fall in war are always buried; with the exception of those slain at Marathon, who for their singular and extraordinary valour

were interred on the spot where they fell. After the bodies have been laid in the earth, a man chosen by the state, of approved wisdom and eminent reputation, pronounces over them an appropriate panegyric; after which all retire. Such is the manner of the burying; and throughout the whole of the war, whenever the occasion arose, the established custom was observed. Meanwhile these were the first that had fallen, and Pericles, son of Xanthippus, was chosen to pronounce their eulogium. When the proper time arrived, he advanced from the sepulchre to an elevated platform in order to be heard by as many of the crowd as possible, and spoke as follows:

"Most of my predecessors in this place have commended him who made this speech part of the law, telling us that it is well that it should be delivered at the burial of those who fall in battle. For myself, I should have thought that the worth which had displayed itself in

As translated by R. Crawley in *The Complete Writings of Thucydides, The Peloponnesian War,* The Modern Library, New York, 1934, 102–109. Courtesy of Random House, Inc.

deeds, would be sufficiently rewarded by honours also shown by deeds; such as you now see in this funeral prepared at the people's cost. And I could have wished that the reputations of many brave men were not to be imperilled in the mouth of a single individual, to stand or fall according as he spoke well or ill. For it is hard to speak properly upon a subject where it is even difficult to convince your hearers that you are speaking the truth. On the one hand, the friend who is familiar with every fact of the story, may think that some point has not been set forth with that fulness which he wishes and knows it to deserve; on the other, he who is a stranger to the matter may be led by envy to suspect exaggeration if he hears anything above his own nature. For men can endure to hear others praised only so long as they can severally persuade themselves of their own ability to equal the actions recounted; when this point is passed, envy comes in and with it incredulity. However, since our ancestors have stamped this custom with their approval, it becomes my duty to obey the law and to try to satisfy your several wishes and opinions as best I may.

"I shall begin with our ancestors: it is both just and proper that they should have the honour of the first mention on an occasion like the present. They dwelt in the country without break in the succession from generation to generation, and handed it down free to the present time by their valour. And if our more remote ancestors deserve praise, much more do our own fathers, who added to their inheritance the empire which we now possess, and spared no pains to be able to leave their acquisitions to us of the present generation. Lastly, there are few parts of our dominions that have not been augmented by those of us here, who are still more or less in the vigour of life; while the mother country has been furnished by us with everything that can enable her to depend on her own resources whether for war or for peace. That part of our history which tells of the military achievements which gave us our several possessions, or of the ready valour with which either we or our fathers stemmed the tide of Hellenic or foreign aggression, is a theme too familiar to my hearers for me to dilate on, and I shall therefore pass it by. But

what was the road by which we reached our position, what the form of government under which our greatness grew, what the national habits out of which it sprang; these are questions which I may try to solve before I proceed to my panegyric upon these men; since I think this to be a subject upon which on the present occasion a speaker may properly dwell, and to which the whole assemblage, whether citizens or foreigners, may listen with advantage.

"Our constitution does not copy the laws of neighbouring states; we are rather a pattern to others than imitators ourselves. Its administration favours the many instead of the few; this is why it is called a democracy. If we look to the laws, they afford equal justice to all in their private differences; if to social standing, advancement in public life falls to reputation for capacity, class considerations not being allowed to interfere with merit; nor again does poverty bar the way, if a man is able to serve the state, he is not hindered by the obscurity of his condition. The freedom which we enjoy in our government extends also to our ordinary life. There, far from exercising a jealous surveillance over each other, we do not feel called upon to be angry with our neighbour for doing what he likes, or even to indulge in those injurious looks which cannot fail to be offensive, although they inflict no positive penalty. But all this ease in our private relations does not make us lawless as citizens. Against this fear is our chief safeguard, teaching us to obey the magistrates and the laws, particularly such as regard the protection of the injured, whether they are actually on the statute book, or belong to that code which, although unwritten, yet cannot be broken without acknowledged disgrace.

"Further, we provide plenty of means for the mind to refresh itself from business. We celebrate games and sacrifices all the year round, and the elegance of our private establishments forms a daily source of pleasure and helps to banish the spleen; while the magnitude of our city draws the produce of the world into our harbour, so that to the Athenian the fruits of other countries are as familiar a luxury as those of his own.

"If we turn to our military policy, there also we differ from our antagonists. We throw open our city to the world, and never by alien acts exclude foreigners from any opportunity of learning or observing, although the eyes of an enemy may occasionally profit by our liberality; trusting less in system and policy than to the native spirit of our citizens; while in education, where our rivals from their very cradles by a painful discipline seek after manliness, at Athens we live exactly as we please, and yet are just as ready to encounter every legitimate danger. In proof of this it may be noticed that the Lacedaemonians do not invade our country alone, but bring with them all their confederates; while we Athenians advance unsupported into the territory of a neighbour, and fighting upon a foreign soil usually vanquish with ease men who are defending their homes. Our united force was never yet encountered by any enemy, because we have at once to attend to our marine and to despatch our citizens by land upon a hundred different services; so that, wherever they engage with some such fraction of our strength, a success against a detachment is magnified into a victory over the nation, and a defeat into a reverse suffered at the hands of our entire people. And yet if with habits not of labour but of ease, and courage not of art but of nature, we are still willing to encounter danger, we have the double advantage of escaping the experience of hardships in anticipation and of facing them in the hour of need as fearlessly as those who are never free from them.

"Nor are these the only points in which our city is worthy of admiration. We cultivate refinement without extravagance and knowledge without effeminacy; wealth we employ more for use than for show, and place the real disgrace of poverty not in owning to the fact but in declining the struggle against it. Our public men have, besides politics, their private affairs to attend to, and our ordinary citizens, though occupied with the pursuits of industry, are still fair judges of public matters; for, unlike any other nation, regarding him who takes no part in these duties not as unambitious but as useless, we Athenians are able to judge at all events if we cannot originate, and instead of looking on discussion as a stumbling-block in the way of action, we think it an indispensable preliminary to any wise action at all. Again, in

our enterprises we present the singular spectacle of daring and deliberation, each carried to its highest point, and both united in the same persons; although usually decision is the fruit of ignorance, hesitation of reflexion. But the palm of courage will surely be adjudged most justly to those who best know the difference between hardship and pleasure and yet are never tempted to shrink from danger. In generosity we are equally singular, acquiring our friends by conferring, not by receiving favours. Yet, of course, the doer of the favour is the firmer friend of the two, in order by continued kindness to keep the recipient in his debt; while the debtor feels less keenly from the very consciousness that the return he makes will be a payment, not a free gift. And it is only the Athenians who, fearless of consequences, confer their benefits not from calculations of expediency, but in the confidence of liberality.

"In short, I say that as a city we are the school of Hellas; while I doubt if the world can produce a man, who where he has only himself to depend upon, is equal to so many emergencies, and graced by so happy a versatility as the Athenian. And that this is no mere boast thrown out for the occasion, but plain matter of fact, the power of the state acquired by these habits proves. For Athens alone of her contemporaries is found when tested to be greater than her reputation, and alone gives no occasion to her assailants to blush at the antagonist by whom they have been worsted, or to her subjects to question her title by merit to rule. Rather, the admiration of the present and succeeding ages will be ours, since we have not left our power without witness, but have shown it by mighty proofs; and far from needing a Homer for our panegyrist, or other of his craft whose verses might charm for the moment only for the impression which they gave to melt at the touch of fact, we have forced every sea and land to be the highway of our daring, and everywhere, whether for evil or for good, have left imperishable monuments behind us. Such is the Athens for which these men, in the assertion of their resolve not to lose her, nobly fought and died; and well may every one of their survivors be ready to suffer in her cause.

"Indeed if I have dwelt at some length upon the character of our country, it has been to show that our stake in the struggle is not the same as theirs who have no such blessings to lose, and also that the panegyric of the men over whom I am now speaking might be by definite proofs established. That panegyric is now in a great measure complete; for the Athens that I have celebrated is only what the heroism of these and their like have made her, men whose fame, unlike that of most Hellenes, will be found to be only commensurate with their deserts. And if a test of worth be wanted, it is to be found in their closing scene, and this not only in the cases in which it set the final seal upon their merit, but also in those in which it gave the first intimation of their having any. For there is justice in the claim that steadfastness in his country's battles should be as a cloak to cover a man's other imperfections; since the good action has blotted out the bad, and his merit as a citizen more than outweighed his demerits as an individual. But none of these allowed either wealth with its prospect of future enjoyment to unnerve his spirit, or poverty with its hope of a day of freedom and riches to tempt him to shrink from danger. No, holding that vengeance upon their enemies was more to be desired than any personal blessings, and reckoning this to be the most glorious of hazards, they joyfully determined to accept the risk, to make sure of their vengeance and to let their wishes wait; and while committing to hope the uncertainty of final success, in the business before them they thought fit to act boldly and trust in themselves. Thus choosing to die resisting, rather than to live submitting, they fled only from dishonour, but met danger face to face, and after one brief moment, while at the summit of their fortune, escaped, not from their fear, but from their glory.

"So died these men as became Athenians. You, their survivors, must determine to have as unaltering a resolution in the field, though you may pray that it may have a happier issue. And not contented with ideas derived only from words of the advantages which are bound up with the defence of your country, though these would furnish a valuable text to a speaker even before an audience so alive to them as the present, you must yourselves realise the power of Athens, and feed your eyes upon her from day to day, till love of her fills your hearts; and then, when all her greatness shall break upon you, you must reflect that it was by courage, sense of duty, and a keen feeling of honour in action that men were enabled to win all this, and that no personal failure in an enterprise could make them consent to deprive their country of their valour, but they laid it at her feet as the most glorious contribution that they could offer. For this offering of their lives made in common by them all they each of them individually received that renown which never grows old, and for a sepulchre, not so much that in which their bones have been deposited, but that noblest of shrines wherein their glory is laid up to be eternally remembered upon every occasion on which deed or story shall fall for its commemoration. For heroes have the whole earth for their tomb; and in lands far from their own, where the column with its epitaph declares it, there is enshrined in every breast a record unwritten with no tablet to preserve it, except that of the heart. These take as your model, and judging happiness to be the fruit of freedom and freedom of valour, never decline the dangers of war. For it is not the miserable that would most justly be unsparing of their lives; these have nothing to hope for: it is rather they to whom continued life may bring reverses as yet unknown, and to whom a fall, if it came, would be most tremendous in its consequences. And surely, to a man of spirit, the degradation of cowardice must be immeasurably more grievous than the unfelt death which strikes him in the midst of his strength and patriotism!

"Comfort, therefore, not condolence, is what I have to offer to the parents of the dead who may be here. Numberless are the chances to which, as they know, the life of man is subject; but fortunate indeed are they who draw for their lot a death so glorious as that which has caused your mourning, and to whom life has been so exactly measured as to terminate in the happiness in which it has been passed. Still I know that this is a hard saying, especially when those are in question of whom you will constantly be reminded by seeing in the homes of others blessings of which once you also boasted: for grief is felt not so much for the want of what we have never known, as for the loss of that to which we have been long accustomed. Yet you who are still of an age to beget children must bear up in the hope of having others in their stead; not only will they help you to forget those whom you have lost, but will be to the state at once a reinforcement and a security; for never can a fair or just policy be expected of the citizen who does not, like his fellows, bring to the decision the interests and apprehensions of a father. While those of you who have passed your prime must congratulate yourselves with the thought that the best part of your life was fortunate, and that the brief span that remains will be cheered by the fame of the departed. For it is only the love of honour that never grows old; and honour it is, not gain, as some would have it, that rejoices the heart of age and helplessness.

"Turning to the sons or brothers of the dead, I see an arduous struggle before you. When a man is gone, all are wont to praise him, and should your merit be ever so transcendent, you will still find it difficult not merely to overtake,

but even to approach their renown. The living have envy to contend with, while those who are no longer in our path are honoured with a goodwill into which rivalry does not enter. On the other hand, if I must say anything on the subject of female excellence to those of you who will now be in widowhood, it will be all comprised in this brief exhortation. Great will be your glory in not falling short of your natural character; and greatest will be hers who is least talked of among the men whether for good or for bad.

"My task is now finished. I have performed it to the best of my ability, and in words, at least, the requirements of the law are now satisfied. If deeds be in question, those who are here interred have received part of their honours already, and for the rest, their children will be brought up till manhood at the public expense: the state thus offers a valuable prize, as the garland of victory in this race of valour, for the reward both of those who have fallen and their survivors. And where the rewards for merit are greatest, there are found the best citizens.

"And now that you have brought to a close your lamentations for your relatives, you may depart."

Plato

Plato (427?–347? B.C.), one of the greatest thinkers of all time, studied under Socrates, and from him he obtained many of his ideas. He wrote a series of dialogues, with his master as the principal character, and it is from this source that most of our knowledge of Socrates is obtained. The Crito relates some of the events that took place while Socrates was in prison for having antagonized certain elements in the Athenian population in the period following the Peloponnesian Wars. In reading the Crito note (1) Crito's message to Socrates, (2) his plan of action, (3) Socrates' reply, (4) the principal characteristics of the good man, (5) the attitude of Socrates toward democracy, and (6) what he considered his responsibility toward the city state.

As translated by Benjamin Jowett in The Dialogues of Plato, 2nd ed., 5 vols., Clarendon Press, Oxford, 1875, I, 383–396. Courtesy of the Jowett Copyright Fund.

THE CRITO

Persons of the Dialogue: *Socrates, Crito.*
Scene: The Prison of Socrates.

Socrates. Why have you come at this hour, Crito? it must be quite early?

Crito. Yes, certainly.

Soc. What is the exact time?

Cr. The dawn is breaking.

Soc. I wonder that the keeper of the prison would let you in.

Cr. He knows me, because I often come, Socrates; moreover, I have done him a kindness.

Soc. And are you only just arrived?

Cr. No, I came some time ago.

Soc. Then why did you sit and say nothing, instead of at once awakening me?

Cr. I should not have liked myself, Socrates, to be in such great trouble and unrest as you are—indeed I should not: I have been watching with amazement your peaceful slumbers; and for that reason I did not awake you, because I wished to minimize the pain. I have always thought you to be of a happy disposition; but never did I see anything like the easy, tranquil manner in which you bear this calamity.

Soc. Why, Crito, when a man has reached my age he ought not to be repining at the approach of death.

Cr. And yet other old men find themselves in similar misfortunes, and age does not prevent them from repining.

Soc. That is true. But you have not told me why you come at this early hour.

Cr. I come to bring you a message which is sad and painful; not, as I believe, to yourself, but to all of us who are your friends, and saddest of all to me.

Soc. What? Has the ship come from Delos, on the arrival of which I am to die?

Cr. No, the ship has not actually arrived, but she will probably be here today, as persons who have come from Sunium tell me that they left her there; and therefore tomorrow, Socrates, will be the last day of your life.

Soc. Very well, Crito; if such is the will of God, I am willing; but my belief is that there will be a delay of a day.

Cr. Why do you think so?

Soc. I will tell you. I am to die on the day after the arrival of the ship.

Cr. Yes; that is what the authorities say.

Soc. But I do not think that the ship will be here until tomorrow; this I infer from a vision which I had last night, or rather only just now, when you fortunately allowed me to sleep.

Cr. And what was the nature of the vision?

Soc. There appeared to me the likeness of a woman, fair and comely, clothed in bright raiment, who called to me and said: O Socrates,

"The third day hence to fertile Phthia
shalt thou go."

Cr. What a singular dream, Socrates!

Soc. There can be no doubt about the meaning, Crito, I think.

Cr. Yes; the meaning is only too clear. But, oh! my beloved Socrates, let me entreat you once more to take my advice and escape. For if you die I shall not only lose a friend who can never be replaced, but there is another evil: people who do not know you and me will believe that I might have saved you if I had been willing to give money, but that I did not care. Now, can there be a worse disgrace than this—that I should be thought to value money more than the life of friend? For the many will not be persuaded that I wanted you to escape, and that you refused.

Soc. But why, my dear Crito, should we care about the opinion of the many? Good men, and they are the only persons who are worth considering, will think of these things truly as they occurred.

Cr. But you see, Socrates, that the opinion of the many must be regarded, for what is now happening shows that they can do the greatest evil to any one who has lost their good opinion.

Soc. I only wish it were so, Crito; and that the many could do the greatest evil; for then they would also be able to do the greatest good—and what a fine thing this would be! But in reality they can do neither; for they cannot make a man either wise or foolish; and whatever they do is the result of chance.

Cr. Well, I will not dispute with you; but please to tell me, Socrates, whether you are not acting out of regard to me and your other friends: are you not afraid that if you escape from prison we may get into trouble with the informers for having stolen you away, and lose either the whole or a great part of our property; or that even a worse evil may happen to us? Now, if you fear on our account, be at ease; for in order to save you, we ought surely to run this, or even a greater risk; be persuaded, then, and do as I say.

Soc. Yes, Crito, that is one fear which you mention, but by no means the only one.

Cr. Fear not—there are persons who are willing to get you out of prison at no great cost; and as for the informers, they are far from being exorbitant in their demands—a little money will satisfy them. My means, which are certainly ample, are at your service, and if you have a scruple about spending all mine, here are strangers who will give you the use of theirs; and one of them, Simmias the Theban, has brought a large sum of money for this very purpose; and Cebes and many others are prepared to spend their money in helping you to escape. I say, therefore, do not hesitate on our account, and do not say, as you did in the court, that you will have a difficulty in knowing what to do with yourself anywhere else. For men will love you in other places to which you may go, and not in Athens only; there are friends of mine in Thessaly, if you like to go to them, who will value and protect you, and no Thessalian will give you any trouble. Nor can I think that you are at all justified, Socrates, in betraying your own life when you might be saved; in acting thus you are playing into the hands of your enemies, who are hurrying on your destruction. And further I should say that you are deserting your own children; for you might bring them up and educate them; instead of which you go away and leave them, and they will have to take their chance; and if they do not meet with the usual fate of orphans, there will be small thanks to you. No man should bring children into the world who is unwilling to persevere to the end in their nurture and education. But you appear to be choosing the easier part, not the better and manlier, which would have been more becoming in one who professes to care for virtue in all his actions, like yourself. And, indeed, I

am ashamed not only of you, but of us who are your friends, when I reflect that the whole business will be attributed entirely to our want of courage. The trial need never have come on, or might have been managed differently; and this last act, or crowning folly, will seem to have occurred through our negligence and cowardice, who might have saved you, if we had been good for anything; and you might have saved yourself, for there was no difficulty at all. See now, Socrates, how sad and discreditable are the consequences, both to us and you. Make up your mind, then, or rather have your mind already made up, for the time of deliberation is over, and there is only one thing to be done, which must be done this very night, and if we delay at all will be no longer practicable or possible; I beseech you therefore, Socrates, be persuaded by me, and do as I say.

Soc. Dear Crito, your zeal is invaluable, if a right one; but if wrong, the greater the zeal the greater the danger; and therefore we ought to consider whether I shall or shall not do as you say. For I am and always have been one of those natures who must be guided by reason, whatever the reason may be which upon reflection appears to me to be the best; and now that this chance has befallen me, I cannot repudiate my own words: the principles which I have hitherto honoured and revered I still honour, and unless we can at once find other and better principles, I am certain not to agree with you; no, not even if the power of the multitude could inflict many more imprisonments, confiscations, deaths, frightening us like children with hobgoblin terrors. What will be the fairest way of considering the question? Shall I return to your old argument about the opinions of men?—we were saying that some of them are to be regarded, and others not. Now, were we right in maintaining this before I was condemned? And has the argument which was once good now proved to be talk for the sake of talking—mere childish nonsense? That is what I want to consider with your help, Crito: —whether, under my present circumstances, the argument appears to be in any way different or not; and is to be allowed by me or disallowed. That argument, which, as I believe, is maintained by many persons of authority, was to the effect, as I was saying, that the opinions of some men are to be regarded, and of other men not to be regarded. Now you, Crito, are not going to die tomorrow—at least, there is no human probability of this—and therefore you are disinterested and not liable to be deceived by the circumstances in which you are placed. Tell me, then, whether I am right in saying that some opinions, and the opinions of some men only, are to be valued, and that other opinions, and the opinions of other men, are not to be valued. I ask you whether I was right in maintaining this?

Cr. Certainly.

Soc. The good are to be regarded, and not the bad?

Cr. Yes.

Soc. And the opinions of the wise are good, and the opinions of the unwise are evil?

Cr. Certainly.

Soc. And what was said about another matter? Is the pupil who devotes himself to the practice of gymnastics supposed to attend to the praise and blame and opinion of every man, or of one man only—his physician or trainer, whoever he may be?

Cr. Of one man only.

Soc. And he ought to fear the censure and welcome the praise of that one only, and not of the many?

Cr. Clearly so.

Soc. And he ought to act and train, and eat and drink in the way which seems good to his single master who has understanding, rather than according to the opinion of all other men put together?

Cr. True.

Soc. And if he disobeys and disregards the opinion and approval of the one, and regards the opinion of the many who have no understanding, will he not suffer?

Cr. Certainly he will.

Soc. And what will the evil be, whither tending and what affecting, in the disobedient person?

Cr. Clearly, affecting the body; that is what is destroyed by the evil.

Soc. Very good; and is not this true, Crito, of other things which we need not separately enumerate? In questions of just and unjust, fair and foul, good and evil, which are the subjects of our present consultation, ought we to follow the opinion of the many and to fear them; or the opinion of the one man who has understanding? ought we not to fear and reverence him more than all the rest of the world: and if we desert him shall we not destroy and injure that principle in us which may be assumed to be improved by justice and deteriorated by injustice;—there is such a principle?

Cr. Certainly there is, Socrates.

Soc. Take a parallel instance:—if, acting under the advice of those who have no understanding, we destroy that which is improved by health and is deteriorated by disease, would life be worth having? And that which has been destroyed is—the body?

Cr. Yes.

Soc. Could we live, having an evil and corrupted body?

Cr. Certainly not.

Soc. And will life be worth having, if that higher part of man be destroyed, which is improved by justice and depraved by injustice? Do we suppose that principle, whatever it may be in man, which has to do with justice and injustice, to be inferior to the body?

Cr. Certainly not.

Soc. More honourable than the body?

Cr. Far more.

Soc. Then, my friend, we must not regard what the many say of us: but what he, the one man who has understanding of just and unjust, will say, and what the truth will say. And therefore you begin in error when you advise that we should regard the opinion of the many about just and unjust, good and evil, honourable and dishonourable.—"Well," some one will say, "but the many can kill us."

Cr. Yes, Socrates; that will clearly be the answer.

Soc. And it is true: but still I find with surprise that the old argument is unshaken as ever. And I should like to know whether I may say the same of another proposition—that not life, but a good life, is to be chiefly valued?

Cr. Yes, that also remains unshaken.

Soc. And a good life is equivalent to a just and honourable one—that holds also?

Cr. Yes, it does.

Soc. From these premises I proceed to argue the question whether I ought or ought not to try to escape without the consent of the Athenians: and if I am clearly right in escaping, then I will make the attempt; but if not, I will abstain. The other considerations which you mention, of money and loss of character and the duty of educating one's children, are, I fear, only the doctrines of the multitude, who would be as ready to restore people to life, if they were able, as they are to put them to death—and with as little reason. But now, since the argument has thus far prevailed, the only question which remains to be considered is, whether we shall do rightly either in escaping or in suffering others to aid in our escape and paying them in money and thanks, or whether in reality we shall not do rightly; and if the latter, then death or any other calamity which may ensue on my remaining here must not be allowed to enter into the calculation.

Cr. I think that you are right, Socrates; how then shall we proceed?

Soc. Let us consider the matter together, and do you either refute me if you can, and I will be convinced; or else cease, my dear friend, from repeating to me that I ought to escape against the wishes of the Athenians: for I highly value your attempts to persuade me to do so, but I may not be persuaded against my own better judgment. And now please to consider my first position, and try how you can best answer me.

Cr. I will.

Soc. Are we to say that we are never intentionally to do wrong, or that in one way we ought and in another way we ought not to do wrong, or is doing wrong always evil and dishonourable, as I was just now saying, and as has been already acknowledged by us? Are all our former admissions which were made within a few days to be thrown away? And have we, at our age, been earnestly discoursing with one another all our life long only to discover that we are no better than children? Or, in spite of the opinion of the many, and in spite of consequences whether better or worse, shall we insist on the truth of what was then said, that injustice is always an evil and dishonour to him who acts unjustly? Shall we say so or not?

Cr. Yes.

Soc. Then we must do no wrong?

Cr. Certainly not.

Soc. Nor when injured injure in return, as the many imagine; for we must injure no one at all?

Cr. Clearly not.

Soc. Again, Crito, may we do evil?

Cr. Surely not, Socrates.

Soc. And what of doing evil in return for evil, which is the morality of the many—is that just or not?

Cr. Not just.

Soc. For doing evil to another is the same as injuring him?

Cr. Very true.

Soc. Then we ought not to retaliate or render evil for evil to any one, whatever evil we may have suffered from him. But I would have you consider, Crito, whether you really mean what you are saying. For this opinion has never been held, and never will be held, by any considerable number of persons; and those who are agreed and those who are not agreed upon this point have no common ground, and can only despise one another when they see how widely they differ. Tell me, then, whether you agree with and assent to my first principle, that neither injury nor retaliation nor warding off evil by evil is ever right. And shall that be the premise of our argument? Or do you decline and dissent from this? For so I have ever thought, and continue to think; but, if you are of another opinion, let me hear what you have to say. If, however, you remain of the same mind as formerly, I will proceed to the next step.

Cr. You may proceed, for I have not changed my mind.

Soc. Then I will go on to the next point, which may be put in the form of a question:— Ought a man to do what he admits to be right, or ought he to betray the right?

Cr. He ought to do what he thinks right.

Soc. But if this is true, what is the application? In leaving the prison against the will of the Athenians, do I wrong any? or rather do I not wrong those whom I ought least to wrong? Do I not desert the principles which were acknowledged by us to be just—what do you say?

Cr. I cannot tell, Socrates; for I do not know.

Soc. Then consider the matter in this way:—

Imagine that I am about to play truant (you may call the proceeding by any name which you like), and the laws and the government come and interrogate me: "Tell us, Socrates," they say, "what are you about? Are you not going by an act of yours to overturn us—the laws, and the whole State, as far as in you lies? Do you imagine that a State can subsist and not be overthrown, in which the decisions of law have no power, but are set aside and trampled upon by individuals?" What will be our answer, Crito, to these and the like words? Any one, and especially a rhetorician, will have a good deal to say on behalf of the law which requires a sentence to be carried out. He will argue that this law should not be set aside; and shall we reply, "Yes, but the State has injured us and given an unjust sentence." Suppose I say that?

Cr. Very good, Socrates.

Soc. "And was that our agreement with you?" the law would answer, "or were you to abide by the sentence of the State?" And if I were to express my astonishment at their words, the law would probably add: "Answer, Socrates, instead of opening your eyes—you are in the habit of asking and answering questions. Tell us,—What complaint have you to make against us which justifies you in attempting to destroy us and the State? In the first place did we not bring you into existence? Your father married your mother by our aid and begat you. Say whether you have any objection to urge against those of us who regulate marriage?" None, I should reply. "Or against those of us who after birth regulate the nurture and education of children, in which you also were trained? Were not the laws which have the charge of education, right in commanding your father to train you in music and gymnastic?" Right, I should reply. "Well, then, since you were brought into the world and nurtured and educated by us, can you deny in the first place that you are our child and slave, as your fathers were before you? And if this is true, you are not on equal terms with us; nor can you think that you have a right to do to us what we are doing to you. Would you have any right to strike or revile or do any other evil to your father or your master, if you had one, because you have been struck or reviled by him, or received some other evil at his hands? —you would not say this? And because we

think right to destroy you, do you think that you have any right to destroy us in return, and your country as far as in you lies? Will you, O professor of true virtue, pretend that you are justified in this? Has a philosopher like you failed to discover that our country is more to be valued and higher and holier far than mother or father or any ancestor, and more to be regarded in the eyes of the gods and of men of understanding? also to be soothed, and gently and reverently entreated when angry, even more than a father, and either to be persuaded, or if not persuaded, to be obeyed? And when we are punished by her, whether with imprisonment or stripes, the punishment is to be endured in silence; and if she lead us to wounds or death in battle, thither we follow as is right; neither may any one yield or retreat or leave his rank, but whether in battle or in a court of law, or in any other place, he must do what his city and his country order him; or he must change their view of what is just: and if he may do no violence to his father or mother, much less may he do violence to his country." What answer shall we make to this, Crito? Do the laws speak truly, or do they not?

Cr. I think that they do.

Soc. Then the laws will say: "Consider, Socrates, if we are speaking truly that in your present attempt you are going to do us an injury. For, having brought you into the world, and nurtured and educated you, and given you and every other citizen a share in every good which we had to give, we further proclaim to any Athenian by the liberty which we allow him, that if he does not like us when he has become of age and has seen the ways of the city, and made our acquaintance, he may go where he pleases and take his goods with him. None of us laws will forbid him or interfere with him. Anyone who does not like us and the city, and who wants to emigrate to a colony or to any other city, may go where he likes, retaining his property. But he who has experience of the manner in which we order justice and administer the State, and still remains, has entered into an implied contract that he will do as we command him. And he who disobeys us is, as we maintain, thrice wrong; first, because in disobeying us he is disobeying his parents; secondly, because we are the authors of his education; thirdly, because he has made an agreement with us that he will duly obey our commands; and he neither obeys them nor convinces us that our commands are unjust; and we do not rudely impose them, but give him the alternative of obeying or convincing us;—that is what we offer, and he does neither.

"These are the sort of accusations to which, as we were saying, you, Socrates, will be exposed if you accomplish your intentions; you, above all other Athenians." Suppose now I ask, why I rather than anybody else? They will justly retort upon me that I above all other men have acknowledged the agreement. "There is clear proof," they will say, "Socrates, that we and the city were not displeasing to you. Of all Athenians you have been the most constant resident in the city, which, as you never leave, you may be supposed to love. For you never went out of the city either to see the games, except once when you went to the Isthmus, or to any other place unless when you were on military service; nor did you travel as other men do. Nor had you any curiosity to know other States or their laws: your affections did not go beyond us and our State: we were your special favourites, and you acquiesced in our government of you; and here in this city you begat your children, which is a proof of your satisfaction. Moreover, you might in the course of the trial, if you had liked, have fixed the penalty at banishment; the State which refuses to let you go now would have let you go then. But you pretended that you preferred death to exile, and that you were not unwilling to die. And now you have forgotten these fine sentiments, and pay no respect to us, the laws, of whom you are the destroyer; and are doing what only a miserable slave would do, running away and turning your back upon the compacts and agreements which you made as a citizen. And, first of all, answer this very question: Are we right in saying that you agreed to be governed according to us in deed, and not in word only? Is that true or not?" How shall we answer, Crito? Must we not assent?

Cr. We cannot help it, Socrates.

Soc. Then will they not say: "You, Socrates, are breaking the covenants and agreements which you made with us at your leisure, not in any haste or under any compulsion or decep-

tion, but after you have had seventy years to think of them, during which time you were at liberty to leave the city, if we were not to your mind, or if our covenants appeared to you to be unfair. You had your choice, and might have gone either to Lacedaemon or Crete, both which States are often praised by you for their good government, or to some other Hellenic or foreign State. Whereas you, above all other Athenians, seemed to be so fond of the State, or, in other words, of us, her laws (and who would care about a State which has no laws?), that you never stirred out of her; the halt, the blind, the maimed were not more stationary in her than you were. And now you run away and forsake your agreements. Not so, Socrates, if you will take our advice; do not make yourself ridiculous by escaping out of the city.

"For just consider, if you transgress and err in this sort of way, what good will you do either to yourself or to your friends? That your friends will be driven into exile and deprived of citizenship, or will lose their property, is tolerably certain; and you yourself, if you fly to one of the neighbouring cities, as, for example, Thebes or Megara, both of which are well governed, will come to them as an enemy, Socrates, and their government will be against you, and all patriotic citizens will cast an evil eye upon you as a subverter of the laws, and you will confirm in the minds of the judges the justice of their own condemnation of you. For he who is a corrupter of the laws is more than likely to be a corrupter of the young and foolish portion of mankind. Will you then flee from well-ordered cities and virtuous men? and is existence worth having on these terms? Or will you go to them without shame, and talk to them, Socrates? And what will you say to them? What you say here about virtue and justice and institutions and laws being the best things among men? Would that be decent of you? Surely not. But if you go away from well-governed States to Crito's friends in Thessaly, where there is great disorder and licence, they will be charmed to hear the tale of your escape from prison, set off with ludicrous particulars of the manner in which you were wrapped in a goatskin or some other disguise, and metamorphosed as the manner is of runaways; but will there be no one to remind you that in your old age you were not ashamed to violate the most sacred laws from a miserable desire of a little more life? Perhaps not, if you keep them in a good temper; but if they are out of temper you will hear many degrading things; you will live, but how?—as the flatterer of all men, and the servant of all men; and doing what?—eating and drinking in Thessaly, having gone abroad in order that you may get a dinner. And where will be your fine sentiments about justice and virtue? Say that you wish to live for the sake of your children—you want to bring them up and educate them—will you take them into Thessaly and deprive them of Athenian citizenship? Is this the benefit which you will confer upon them? Or are you under the impression that they will be better cared for and educated here if you are still alive, although absent from them; for your friends will take care of them? Do you fancy that if you are an inhabitant of Thessaly they will take care of them, and if you are an inhabitant of the other world that they will not take care of them? Nay; but if they who call themselves friends are good for anything, they will—to be sure they will.

"Listen, then, Socrates, to us who have brought you up. Think not of life and children first, and of justice afterwards, but of justice first, that you may be justified before the princes of the world below. For neither will you nor any that belong to you be happier or holier or juster in this life, or happier in another, if you do as Crito bids. Now you depart in innocence, a sufferer and not a doer of evil; a victim, not of the laws but of men. But if you go forth, returning evil for evil, and injury for injury, breaking the covenants and agreements which you have made with us, and wronging those whom you ought least of all to wrong, that is to say, yourself, your friends, your country, and us, we shall be angry with you while you live, and our brethren, the laws in the world below, will receive you as an enemy; for they will know that you have done your best to destroy us. Listen, then, to us and not to Crito."

This, dear Crito, is the voice which I seem to hear murmuring in my ears, like the sound of the flute in the ears of the mystic; that voice, I say, is humming in my ears, and prevents me from hearing any other. And I know that anything more which you may say will be vain. Yet speak, if you have anything to say.

Cr. I have nothing to say, Socrates.

Soc. Leave me then, Crito, to fulfil the will of God, and to follow whither he leads.

Aristotle

Aristotle (384–322 B.C.) *was the student of Plato and the third member of the great intellectual triumvirate of ancient Greece. One of the problems to which Greek thinkers inevitably turned was that of human conduct and what was involved in "the good life." Aristotle gave one of the most typically Greek answers to this question of ethics and in so doing made use of the compromise position which he took in philosophy generally. The golden mean that he discussed was the ideal which Greeks customarily sought as a guide to their daily lives, both public and private. It followed naturally that Aristotle associated ethics with the state and not with religion as Christianity subsequently taught. In reading the selections from the Ethics note (1) Aristotle's method of argument, (2) what he regarded as the greatest good in life, (3) how he arrived at that conclusion, (4) how he defined happiness, (5) the formation of moral virtue, (6) the relationship between virtue and pleasure and pain, and (7) what constituted moral virtue.*

Adapted from *The Nicomachean Ethics of Aristotle,* translated by F. H. Peters, London, 1886, 1–5; 12–18; 34–52.

From: THE NICOMACHEAN ETHICS

Every art and every kind of inquiry, and similarly every act and purpose, seems to aim at some good; and so it has been well said that the good is that at which everything aims. But a difference is observable among these aims or ends. What is aimed at is sometimes the exercise of a faculty, sometimes a certain result beyond that exercise. And where there is an end beyond the act, there the result is better than the exercise of the faculty. Now since there are many kinds of actions and many arts and sciences, it follows that there are many ends also; the end of medicine is health, of ship-building, ships, of war, victory, and of economy, wealth. But when several of these are subordinated to some one art or science—as bridle-making and other arts concerned with horsemanship, and this in turn, along with all else the soldier does, to the art of war, and so on—then the end of the master-art is always more desired than the ends of the subordinate arts, since these are pursued for its sake. And this is equally true whether the end in view be the mere exercise of a faculty or something beyond that, as in the case of the sciences just mentioned.

If then in what we do there be some end which we wish for on its own account, choosing all the other ends as means to this, but not every end without exception as a means to something else (for so we should go on indefinitely, and desire would be left void and without object) this evidently will be the good or the best of all goods. And surely from a practical point of view it concerns us much to know this good; for then, like archers shooting at a target, we shall be more likely to get what we want. If this be so, we must try to indicate roughly what it is, and first of all to which of the arts or sciences it belongs. It would seem to belong to the highest art or science, that one which most of all deserves the name of master-art or master-science. Politics seems to answer this description. [Politics for Aristotle covers the whole field of human life; it must determine (a) what is the good and (b) what law can do to promote this good.] For politics prescribes which of the sciences a state needs, and which each man shall study, and how much; and to politics we see subordinated even the highest arts, such as economy [the management of a household], rhetoric, and war. Since then politics makes use of the other practical sciences, and since further it ordains what men are to do and from what to refrain, its end must include the ends or objectives of the others, and this end is the good of man. For though this good is the same for the individual as well as the state, yet the good of the state seems a larger and more perfect thing both to attain and to secure; and glad as one would be to do this service for a single individual, to do it for a people and for a number of city-states is nobler and more divine. This then is the aim of the present inquiry, which is political science.

We must be content if we can attain to so much precision in our statement as the subject will permit, for the same degree of accuracy is no more to be expected in all kinds of reasoning than in all kinds of manufacture. Now what is noble and just (with which political science deals) is so various and uncertain, that some think that these are merely conventional, and not natural, distinctions. There is a similar uncertainty also about what is good, because good things often do people harm; men have before now been ruined by wealth or have lost their lives through courage. Our subject then and our data being of this nature, we must be content if we can indicate roughly and in outline the truth; and if, in dealing with matters not subject to immutable laws, and reasoning from premises that are but probable, we can arrive at probable conclusions. The reader, on his part, should take each of my statements in the same spirit; for it is the mark of an educated man to require, in each kind of study, just so much exactness as the subject permits; it is equally absurd to accept probable reasoning from a mathematician, and to demand scientific proof from an orator.

Now each man can form a judgment about what he knows, and is called a good judge of that—that is of any special matter in which he has received special training. And the man who has received an all-round education is a good judge in general. And hence a young man is not qualified to be a student of politics; for he lacks experience of the affairs of life which form the data and the subject matter of political science. Further, since he is apt to be swayed by his passions, he will derive no benefit from a study whose aim is practical and not speculative. And it makes no difference whether he is young in years or young in character, for the young man's disqualification is not a matter of time, but is due to the fact that feeling or passion rules his life and directs all his desires. Men of this character turn the knowledge they get to no practical account, as we see with those we call incontinent; but those who direct their desires and ambitions by reason will gain much profit from a knowledge of these matters. So much, then, by way of preface as to the student, and the spirit in which he must accept what we say, and the object which we propose to ourselves. . . .

Let us return once more to the question of what this good can be of which we are in search. It seems to be different in different kinds of action and in different arts; it is different in medicine, in war, and in the other arts. What then is the good in each of these? Surely that for the sake of which all else is done. And that in medicine is health, in war is victory, in building is a house—a different thing in each case, but always the end in whatever we do and in whatever we choose. For it is always for the sake of the end that all else is done. If then there be one end of all that man does, this end will be the good achievable in action, and if there be more than one, these will be the goods achievable by action. Our argument has thus come round by a different path to the same point; this we must try to explain more clearly. We see that there are many ends. But some of these are chosen only as means, as wealth, flutes, and the whole class of instruments. And so it is plain that not all ends are final. But the best of all things must be something final. If then there be only one final end, this will be what we are seeking; or if there be more than one, then the most final of them.

Now that which is pursued as an end in itself is more final than that which is pursued as a means to something else, and that which is never chosen as a means than that which is chosen both as an end in itself and as a means, and that is strictly final which is always chosen as an end in itself and never as a means. Happiness seems more than anything else to answer this description, for we always choose it for itself, and never for the sake of something else; while honor and pleasure and reason, and all virtue or excellence, we choose partly for themselves (for, apart from any result, we should choose each of them), but partly also for the sake of happiness, supposing that they will help to make us happy. But no one chooses happiness for the sake of those things, or as a means to anything else at all.

We seem to be led to the same conclusion when we start from the idea of self-sufficiency. The final good is thought to be self-sufficing or all-sufficing. In applying this term we do not regard a man as an individual leading a solitary life, but we take account also of parents, children, wife, and in short, friends and fellow-citizens generally, since man is naturally a social being. Some limit must indeed be set for this; for if you go on to parents and descendants and friends of friends, you will never come to a stop. But this we will consider further on; for the present we will take self-sufficing to mean what by itself makes life desirable and in want of nothing. And happiness answers this description. And further, happiness is believed to be the most desirable thing in the world, and that not merely as one among other good things. If it were merely one among other good things [so that other things could be added to it] it is plain that the addition of the least of other goods must make it more desirable; for the addition becomes a surplus of good, and of two goods the greater is always more desirable. Thus it seems that happiness is something final and self-sufficing, and is the end of all that man does.

But perhaps the reader thinks that though no one will dispute the statement that happiness is the best thing in the world, yet a still more precise definition of it is needed. This will best be gained by asking, What is the function of man? For as the goodness and the excellence of the flute-player or the sculptor, or the practitioner of any art, and generally of those who have any business to do, lies in the function, so man's good would seem to lie in his function, if he possesses one. But can we suppose that, while a carpenter or a shoemaker has a function and a business of his own, man has no business and no function assigned to him as man by nature? Nay, surely as his several members, eye, hand, and foot, plainly have each its own function, so we must suppose that man also has some function over and above all of these. What then is it? Life evidently he has in common even with the plants, but we want that which is peculiar to man. We must exclude, therefore, the life of mere nutrition and growth. Next to this comes the life of sense; but this too he plainly shares with horses and cattle and all kinds of animals. There remains then the life whereby he acts—the life of his rational nature with its two aspects or divisions, one rational as obeying reason, the other rational as having and exercising reason. But as this expression is ambiguous, we must be understood to mean thereby the life that consists in the exercise of the faculties; for this seems to be more properly entitled to the name. The function of man, then, is the exercise of his soul on one side in obedience to reason, and on the other side with reason. But what is called the function of a man of any profession and the function of a man who is good in that profession are generically the same, that is to say, of a harper and of a good harper; and this holds in all cases without exception, only that in the case of the latter his superior excellence at his work is added; for we say a harper's function is to play the harp, and a good harper's function is to play the harp well. Man's function then being, as we say, a kind of life—that is, the exercise of his faculties and action of various kinds with reason—the good man's function is to do this well and nobly. But the function of anything is done well when it is done in accordance with the proper excellence of that thing. Putting all this together, then, we find that the good of man is the exercise of his faculties in accordance with excellence or virtue, or, if there be more than one, in accordance with the best and most complete virtue. But there must be a full term of years for this exercise; for one swallow or one fine day does not make a spring, nor does one day or any small space of time make a happy or virtuous man.

This, then, may be taken as a rough outline of the good; for this, I think, is the proper method: first to sketch the outline, and then to fill in the details. But it would seem that, the outline once fairly drawn, any one can carry on the work and fit in the several items which time reveals to us or aids us to discover. And this, indeed, is the way in which the arts and sciences have developed, for it requires no unusual genius to fill in the gaps. We must bear in mind, however, what was said earlier, and not demand the same degree of accuracy in all branches of inquiry, but in each case as much as the subject permits and as is proper to that kind of study. The carpenter and the geometer both look for the right angle, but in different ways; the former only wants such an approximation of it as his work requires, but the latter wants to know what constitutes a right angle, or what is its special quality—his aim is to find the truth. And so in other cases we must follow the same course, lest we spend more time on what is immaterial to our purpose than on the real business at hand. Nor must we in all cases alike demand the reason why. Sometimes it is sufficient if the undemonstrated fact be fairly pointed out, as in the case of the first principles of a science. Undemonstrated facts always form the first step or beginning of a science; and these first principles are arrived at some in one way and some in another way, some by induction, others by perception, others by some kind of training. But in each case we must attempt to apprehend them in the proper way, and do our best to define them clearly, for they have great influence upon the subsequent course of an inquiry. A good start is more than half the race, and our starting-point, once found, clears up a number of difficulties. . . .

Excellence or virtue, then, being of two kinds, intellectual and moral, intellectual excellence owes its birth and growth mainly to teaching, and so requires time and experience, while moral excellence is the result of habit or custom (*ethike*), and has accordingly received in our language [Greek] a name formed by a slight change from the word *ethos* (habit). From this it is plain that none of the moral excellencies or virtues is implanted in us by nature; for that which is by nature implanted within us cannot be altered by training. For example, a stone naturally tends to fall down-ward, and you could not train it to rise up-ward, though you tried to do so by throwing it up ten thousand times, nor could you train fire to move downward, nor accustom anything which naturally behaves in one way to behave in any other way. The virtues, then, come neither by nature nor contrary to nature, but nature gives us the capacity for acquiring them, and this is developed by training.

Again, where we do things by nature we get the power first, and put this power forth in act afterwards (as we plainly see in the case of the senses); for it is not by constantly see-ing and hearing that we acquire those facul-ties, but, on the contrary, we had the power first and then used it, instead of acquiring the power by use. But we acquire the virtues by doing the acts, as is the case with the arts. We learn an art by doing those things which we wish to do when we have learned the art; we become builders by building, and harpists by playing the harp. And so by doing just and virtuous acts we become just and virtuous, and by doing acts of temperance and courage we become temperate and courageous. This is confirmed by what happens in states; for the legislators make their citizens good by training, and this is the wish of all legislators. Those who do not succeed in this miss their aim, and it is this that distinguishes a good from a bad constitution.

Again, both virtues and vices result from and are formed by the same acts in which they manifest themselves, as is the case also with the arts. It is by playing the harp that good harpers and bad harpers alike are produced; and so it is with builders and the rest, by building well they will become good builders and bad builders by building badly. Indeed, if if were not so, they would not need anybody to teach them, but would all be born either good or bad at their trades. And it is just the same with the virtues also. It is by our con-duct in our dealings with other men that we become just or unjust, and by acting in circum-stances of danger, and training ourselves to feel fear or confidence, that we become cou-rageous or cowardly. So too with our animal appetites and the passion of anger; for by be-having in this way or in that on occasions with

which these passions are concerned, some be-come temperate and gentle, others profligate and ill-tempered. In a word, the several habits or characters are formed by the same kind of acts as those which they produce. Hence we ought to make certain that our acts be of a particular kind; for the resulting character varies as the acts vary. Instead of making a very small difference whether a man be trained from his youth up in this way or that, it makes a very great difference; indeed, it makes all the difference.

But our present study has not, like the rest, merely a theoretical aim. We are not inquiring simply to learn what excellence or virtue is, but in order to become good; for otherwise our study would be useless. We must ask therefore about these acts, and see of what kind they are to be; for, as we said, it is the acts that deter-mine our habits or character. First of all, then, that they must be in accordance with right reason is a common characteristic of them, which we shall take for granted here, reserving for future discussion the question what this right reason is, and how it is related to the other excellencies or virtues. But let it be understood before we go on, that all reasoning on matters of practice must be in outline merely, and not scientifically exact; for as we said at the beginning the kind of reasoning de-manded varies with the subject in hand, and in practical matters and questions of expediency there are no invariable laws, any more than in questions of health. And if our general conclu-sions are thus inexact, still more inexact is all reasoning about particular cases; for these fall under no system of scientifically established rules or traditional maxims, but the agent must always consider for himself what the special occasion requires, just as in medicine or navi-gation. In spite of this, however, we must try to give what help we can.

First of all then, we must observe that, in matters of this sort, to fall short and to go be-yond are both fatal. To illustrate what we can-not see by what we can see: This is plain in the case of strength and health. Too much and too little exercise alike destroy strength, and to take too much meat and drink, or to take too little, is equally ruinous to health; but the proper amount produces and increases strength and health. So it is with temperance also and courage and the other virtues. The man who shuns and fears everything and never makes a stand becomes a coward; while the man who fears nothing at all, but will face anything, becomes foolhardy. So, too, the man who takes his fill of any kind of pleasure and abstains from none, is self-indulgent; but the man who avoids all pleasures (like a boor) lacks sensibility. For temperance and courage are destroyed both by excess and defect, but are preserved by moderation.

But habits or types of character are not only produced and preserved and destroyed by the same occasions and the same means, but they will also manifest themselves in the same circumstances. This is the case with obvious things like strength. Strength is produced by taking plenty of nourishment and doing plenty of hard work, and the strong man, in turn, has the greatest capacity for these. And the case is the same with the virtues. By abstaining from pleasure we become temperate, and when we have become temperate we are best able to abstain. And so with courage. By habituating ourselves to despise danger, and to face it, we become courageous; and when we have become courageous, we are best able to face danger.

The pleasure or pain that accompanies the acts must be taken as a test of the formed habit or character. He who abstains from the pleasures of the body and rejoices in the abstinence is temperate, while he who is vexed at having to abstain is self-indulgent. And, again, he who faces danger with pleasure, or at any rate, without pain is courageous, but he to whom this is painful is a coward. For moral virtue or excellence is closely concerned with pleasure and pain. It is pleasure that moves us to do what is base and pain that moves us to refrain from what is noble. And therefore, as Plato says, man needs to be so trained from his youth as to find pleasure and pain in the right objects. This is what sound education means. Another reason why virtue has to do with pleasure and pain is that it has to do with actions and passions or affections; but every affection and every act is accompanied by pleasure or pain. This is indicated also by the use of pleasure and pain in correction; they have a

kind of curative property, and a cure is effected by administering the opposite of the disease.

Again, as we said before, every type of character or habit is essentially relative to, and concerned with, those things that form it for good or for ill; but it is through pleasure and pain that bad characters are formed—that is to say, through pursuing and avoiding them at the wrong time, or in the wrong manner, or in any other of the various ways of going wrong that may be distinguished. And hence some people go so far as to define the virtues as a kind of impassive or neutral state of mind. But they make a mistake in saying this absolutely, instead of qualifying it by the addition of the right and wrong manner, time, etc. We may lay down, therefore, that this kind of excellence [moral excellence or virtue] makes us do what is best in matters of pleasure and pain, while vice or badness has the contrary effect. The following considerations will throw additional light on the point. There are three kinds of things that move us to choose and three that move us to avoid them. On the one hand, the beautiful or noble, the advantageous, the pleasant. On the other hand, the ugly or base, the hurtful, the painful. Now the good man is apt to go right, and the bad man to go wrong about them all, but especially about pleasure; for pleasure is not only common to man and animals, but also accompanies all pursuit or objects of choice; for even the noble and advantageous appear pleasant.

Again, the feeling of pleasure has been fostered in us all from our infancy by our training, and has thus become so ingrained in our life that it can scarcely be washed out. And, indeed, we all more or less make pleasure our test in judging actions. For this reason too, then, our whole study must be concerned with these matters; since to be pleased and pained in the right or wrong way has great influence on our actions. And lastly, as Heraclitus says, it is harder to fight with pleasure than with wrath; and virtue, like art, is always more concerned with what is harder; for the harder the task, the better is success. For this reason also, then, both moral virtue or excellence and political science must always be concerned with pleasures and pains; for he that behaves rightly with regard to them will be good, and he that behaves badly will be bad. We will take it as established then, that moral virtue or excellence has to do with pleasures and pains; and that the acts which produce virtue develop it, and also, when done differently, destroy it; and that it manifests itself in the same acts which produced it.

But here we may be asked what we mean by saying that men can become just and temperate only by doing what is just and temperate. Surely, it may be said, if their acts are just and temperate, they themselves are already just and temperate, as they are grammarians and musicians if they do what is grammatical and musical. We may answer, I think firstly, that this is not quite the case even with the arts. A man may do something grammatical or write something correctly by chance, or at the prompting of another person. He will not be grammatical till he not only does something grammatical, but also does it like a grammatical person—because of his own knowledge of grammar. But secondly, the virtues are not in this point analogous to the arts. The products of art have their excellence in themselves, and so it is enough if when produced they are of a certain quality; but in the case of the virtues, a man is not said to act justly or temperately or like a just or temperate man if what he does merely be of a certain sort—he must also be in a certain state of mind when he does it. That is to say, first of all he must know what he is doing; secondly he must choose it, and choose it for himself; and thirdly his act must be the expression of a formed and stable character. Now, of these conditions, only one, the knowledge, is necessary for the possession of any art; but for the possession of the virtues, knowledge is of little or no value, while the other conditions that result from repeatedly doing what is just and temperate are not just slightly important, but all-important.

The thing that is done, therefore, is called just or temperate when it is such as the just or temperate man would do; but the man who does it is not just or temperate unless he also does it in the spirit of the just or temperate man. It is right then to say that by doing what is just a man becomes just, and temperate by doing what is temperate, while without doing thus he has no chance of ever becoming good. But most men, instead of doing thus, fly to theories and fancy that they are philosophizing and that this will make them good, like a sick man who listens attentively to what the doctor says and then disobeys all his orders. This sort of theorizing will no more produce a healthy habit of mind than this sort of treatment will produce a healthy habit of body.

Next we must consider what virtue is. Everything psychical is either (1) a passion or emotion, or (2) a power or faculty, or (3) a habit or a trained faculty; and so virtue must be one of these three. By (1) passion or emotion we mean appetite, anger, fear, confidence, envy, joy, love, hate, longing, emulation, pity, or generally that which is accompanied by pleasure or pain; (2) a power or faculty is that in respect of which we are said to be capable of being affected in any of these ways, as for instance, that in respect of which we are able to be angered or pained or to pity; and (3) a habit or trained faculty is that in respect of which we are well or ill regulated or disposed in the matter of our affections; as, for instance, in the matter of being angered, we are ill regulated if we are too violent or too slack, but if we are moderate in our anger we are well regulated. And so with the rest.

Now neither the virtues nor the vices are passions (1) because we are not called good or bad in respect of our emotions, but are called good or bad in respect of our virtues or vices; (2) because we are neither praised nor blamed in respect of our emotions (a man is not praised for being afraid or angry, nor blamed for being angry simply, but for being angry in a particular way), but we are praised or blamed in respect of our virtues or vices; (3) because we may be angered or frightened without deliberate choice, but the virtues are a kind of deliberate choice, or at least are impossible without it; and (4) because in respect of our emotions we are said to be moved, but in respect of our virtues and vices we are not said to be moved, but to be regulated or disposed in this way or in that way. For these same reasons also they are not powers or faculties; for we are not called either good or bad for being merely capable of emotion, nor are we either praised or blamed for this. And further, while nature gives us our powers or faculties, she does not make us either good or bad. This point, however, we have already treated.

If, then, the virtues be neither emotions nor faculties, it remains for them to be habits or trained faculties.

We have thus found the genus to which virtue belongs; but we want to know, not only that it is a trained faculty, but also what species of trained faculty it is. We may safely assert that the virtue or excellence of a thing causes that thing both to be itself in good condition and to perform its function well. The excellence of the eye, for example, makes both the eye and its work good; for it is by the excellence of the eye that we see well. Similarly the excellence of the horse makes a horse both good in itself and good at running and at carrying its rider and at awaiting the attack of the enemy. If this is true in every case, therefore, the virtue of man also will be the state of character which makes a man good and which makes him do his own work well.

How this is to be done we have already said, but we may exhibit the same conclusion in another way, by inquiring what the nature of this virtue is. Now, if we have any quantity, whether continuous or divisible, it is possible to take either a larger, or a smaller, or an equal amount, and that either absolutely or relatively to our own needs. By an equal or fair amount I understand a mean amount, or one that lies between excess and deficiency. By the absolute mean, or mean relatively to the thing itself, I understand that which is equidistant from both extremes, and this is one and the same for all. By the mean relatively to us I understand that which is neither too much nor too little for us; and this is not one and the same for all. For instance, if ten be larger and two be smaller, if we take six we take the mean relatively to the thing itself [or the arithmetical mean]; for it exceeds one extreme by the same amount by which it is exceeded by the other extreme. This is the mean in arithmetical proportion. But the mean relatively to us cannot be found in this way. If ten pounds of food is too much for a given man to eat, and two pounds too little, it does not follow that the trainer will order six pounds. For that also may perhaps be too much for the man in question or too little; too little for Milo [a famous Greek wrestler], too much for the beginner. The same holds true in running and wrestling. And so we say that generally a master in any art avoids what is too much and what is too little and seeks for the mean and chooses it—not the absolute but the relative mean.

Every art or science, then, perfects its work in this way, looking to the mean and bringing its work up to this standard; so that people are wont to say of a good work that nothing could be taken from it or added to it, implying that excellence is destroyed by excess or deficiency, but secured by observing the mean. And good artists do in fact keep their eyes fixed on this in all that they do. Virtue therefore, since like nature it is more exact and better than any art, must also aim at the mean—virtue of course meaning moral virtue or moral excellence; for it has to do with passions and actions, and it is these that admit of excess and deficiency and the mean. For example, it is possible to feel fear, confidence, desire, anger, pity, and generally to be affected pleasantly and painfully, either too much or too little, in either case wrongly; but to be thus affected at the right times, and on the right occasions, and toward the right persons, and with the right object, and in the right fashion, is the mean course and the best course, and these are characteristics of virtue. And in the same way our outward acts also admit of excess and deficiency, and the mean or intermediate. Virtue then is concerned with feelings or passions and with outward acts, in which excess is wrong and deficiency is also blamed, but the mean is praised and is right; and being praised and being successful are both characteristics of virtue. Virtue, therefore, is a kind of moderation or mean as it aims at the mean or moderate amount.

Again, there are many ways of going wrong (for evil is infinite in nature, to use a figure of the Pythagoreans, while good is finite or limited), but only one way of going right; so that the one is easy and the other hard—easy to miss the mark and hard to hit the mark. On this account also excess and deficiency are characteristic of vice; hitting the mean is characteristic of virtue:

"Goodness is simple, evil takes any shape."

Virtue, then, is a habit or trained faculty of choice, the characteristic of which lies in observing the mean relatively to the persons concerned, and which is guided by reason, that is, by the judgment of the prudent man. And it is a moderation, firstly, inasmuch as it comes in the middle or the mean between two vices, one on the side of excess, the other on the side of deficiency; and secondly, inasmuch as, while these vices fall short of or exceed the mean or intermediate measure in feeling and in action, it finds and chooses the mean, middling, or moderate amount. Regarded in essence, therefore, or according to the definition of its nature, virtue is a moderation or middle state, but viewed in its relation to what is best and right it is the extreme of perfection.

But it is not all actions nor all passions that admit of moderation; there are some whose very names imply badness, as malevolence, shamelessness, envy, and among acts, adultery, theft, murder. These and all other like things are blamed as being bad in themselves, and not merely in their excess or deficiency. It is impossible, therefore, to go right in them; they are always wrong. Rightness and wrongness in such things, adultery for example, does not depend upon whether it is the right woman, at the right time, and in the right way, but the mere doing of any one of them is wrong. It would be equally absurd to look for moderation or excess or deficiency in unjust, cowardly, or self-indulgent conduct; for then there would be moderation in excess or deficiency, and excess in excess, and deficiency in deficiency. The fact is that just as there can be no excess or deficiency in temperance or courage because the mean or moderate amount is, in a sense, an extreme, so in these kinds of conduct also there can be no moderation or excess or deficiency, but the acts are wrong however they be done.

It is not enough, however, to make these general statements about virtue and vice; we must go on and apply them to particulars—that is to the several virtues and vices. For in reasoning about matters of conduct general statements are too vague and do not convey as much truth as particular propositions. It is with particulars that conduct is concerned. Our statements, therefore, when applied to these particulars, should be found to hold good. These particulars then—the several virtues and vices and the several acts and affections with which they deal—we will take from the following [list].

Moderation in the feelings of fear and confidence is courage. Of those that exceed, he that exceeds in fearlessness has no name (as often happens), but he that exceeds in confidence is foolhardy, while he that exceeds in fear, but is deficient in confidence, is cowardly.

Moderation in respect of certain pleasures and also (though to a less extent) certain pains is temperance, while excess is self-indulgence or profligacy. But defectiveness in the matter of these pleasures is hardly ever found, and so this sort of people also have as yet received no name. Let us put them down as devoid of sensibility, or call them insensible.

In the matter of giving and taking money, moderation is liberality, excess and deficiency are prodigality and illiberality. But these two vices exceed and fall short in contrary ways. The prodigal exceeds in spending, but falls short in taking; while the illiberal man exceeds in taking, but falls short in spending. . . . But, besides these, there are other dispositions in the matter of money. There is a moderation which is called magnificence (for the magnificent is not the same as the liberal man; the former deals with large sums, the latter with small), and an excess which is called bad taste or vulgarity, and a deficiency which is called meanness; and these vices differ from those that are opposed to liberality. How they differ will be explained later.

With respect to honor and disgrace, there is a mean or moderation which is high-mindedness, and an excess which may be called vanity, and a deficiency which is little-mindedness. But just as we said that liberality is related to magnificence, differing only in that it deals with small sums, so here there is a virtue related to high-mindedness, and differing only in that it is concerned with small instead of great honors. A man may have a due desire for honor and also more or less than a moderate desire. He that carries this desire to excess is called ambitious, he that has a deficiency is called unambitious, while he that has the proper amount has no special name. There are also no abstract names for the characters, except "ambition" corresponding to ambitious. And on this account those who occupy the extremes lay claim to the middle place. And in common parlance too, the moderate man is sometimes called ambitious and sometimes unambitious, and sometimes the ambitious man is praised and sometimes the unambitious. Why this is so we will explain later. For the present we will continue the plan and enumerate the other types of character.

In the matter of anger also we find excess and deficiency and the mean or moderation. The characters themselves scarcely have recognized names, but as the moderate man is here called gentle, we will call his character gentleness; of those who go into extremes, we may use the term wrathful or irascible for him who exceeds, with wrathfulness or irascibility for the vice, and wrathless for him who is deficient, with wrathlessness for his character.

Besides these, there are three kinds of moderation, bearing some resemblance to one another, and yet different. They all have to do with intercourse in speech and action, but they differ in that one has to do with the truthfulness of this intercourse, while the other two have to do with its pleasantness—one of the two with pleasantness in matters of amusement, the other with pleasantness in all the relations of life. We must therefore speak of these qualities also in order that we may the more plainly see how, in all cases, moderation is praiseworthy, while the extreme courses are neither right nor praiseworthy, but blamable. In these cases also names are for the most part wanting, but we must try here as elsewhere to coin names in order to make our argument clear and easy to follow. In the matter of truth, then, let us call him who observes the mean a true or truthful person, and observance of the mean truth or truthfulness; pretence, when it exaggerates, may be called boasting, and the person a boaster; when it understates, let the names be irony and ironical. With regard to pleasantness in amusement, he who observes the mean we may call witty, and his character wittiness; excess may be called buffoonery, and the man a buffoon; while we may call the deficient person boorish, and boorishness for his character. With regard to pleasantness in the other affairs of life, he who makes himself properly pleasant may be called friendly, and his moderation friendliness; he that exceeds may be called an obsequious person if he have no ulterior motive, but a flatterer if he is looking out for his own advantage; he that is deficient in this respect, and always makes himself disagreeable, may be called a quarrelsome and surly sort of person.

Moreover, in the emotions and passions and in our conduct with regard to them there are ways of observing the mean. For example, shame is not a virtue, but yet the modest man is praised. For in these matters also we speak of this man as observing the mean, of that man as going beyond it (as the shame-faced man whom the least thing makes shy), while he who is deficient in the feeling, or lacks it altogether, is called shameless; but the term modest is applied to him who observes the mean.

Righteous indignation, again, hits the mean between envy and spite or malevolence. These have to do with feelings of pleasure and pain at what happens to our neighbors. A man is called righteously indignant when he feels pain at the sight of undeserved prosperity, but the envious man goes beyond and is pained by the sight of any one in prosperity, while the spiteful or malevolent man is so far from being pained that he actually exults in the sight of prosperous iniquity. . . .

The universal character of Aristotle's interests and the fact that he was a Greek naturally led him to a study of government, and in his Politics we have the results of his thinking in this field. In reading the selections from them note (1) his view concerning the origin of the state, (2) his classification of the forms of government and their perversions, (3) the best form of government ideally and practically, (4) the justification of his choice, and (5) his view as to how the good life could best be realized.

As translated by Benjamin Jowett in *The Politics of Aristotle,* 2 vols., Clarendon Press, Oxford, 1885, I, 1–5; 77–84; 126–131. Courtesy of the Jowett Copyright Fund.

From: THE POLITICS

Every state is a community of some kind, and every community is established with a view to some good; for mankind always act in order to obtain that which they think good. But, if all communities aim at some good, the state or political community, which is the highest of all, and which embraces all the rest, aims at good in a greater degree than any other, and at the highest good.

Some people think that the qualifications of a statesman, king, householder, and master are the same, and that they differ, not in kind, but only in the number of their subjects. For example, the ruler over a few is called a master; over more, the manager of a household; over a still larger number, a statesman or king, as if there were no difference between a great household and a small state. The distinction which is made between the king and the statesman is as follows: When the government is personal, the ruler is a king; when, according to the rules of the political science, the citizens rule and are ruled in turn, then he is called a statesman.

But all this is a mistake; for governments differ in kind, as will be evident to any one who considers the matter according to the method which has hitherto guided us. As in other departments of science, so in politics, the compound should always be resolved into the simple elements or least parts of the whole. We must therefore look at the elements of which the state is composed, in order that we may see in what the different kinds of rule differ from one another, and whether any scientific result can be attained about each one of them.

He who thus considers things in their first growth and origin, whether a state or anything else, will obtain the clearest view of them. In the first place there must be a union of those who cannot exist without each other; namely, of male and female, that the race may continue (and this is a union which is formed, not of deliberate purpose, but because, in common with other animals and with plants, mankind have a natural desire to leave behind them an image of themselves), and of natural ruler and subject, that both may be preserved. For that which can foresee by the exercise of mind is by nature intended to be lord and master, and that which can with its body give effect to such foresight is a subject, and by nature a slave; hence master and slave have the same interest. Now nature has distinguished between the female and the slave. For she is not niggardly, like the smith who fashions the Delphian knife for many uses; she makes each thing for a single use, and every instrument is best made when intended for one and not for many uses. But among barbarians no distinction is made between women and slaves, because there is no natural ruler among them: they are a community of slaves, male and female. Wherefore the poets say—

"It is meet that Hellenes should rule over barbarians";

as if they thought that the barbarian and the slave were by nature one.

Out of these two relationships between man and woman, master and slave, the first thing to arise is the family, and Hesiod is right when he says—

"First house and wife and an ox for the plough,"

for the ox is the poor man's slave. The family is the association established by nature for the supply of men's everyday wants, and the members of it are called by Charondas "companions of the cupboard," and by Epimenides the Cretan, "companions of the manger." But when several families are united, and the association aims at something more than the supply of daily needs, the first society to be formed is the village. And the most natural form of the village appears to be that of a colony from the family, composed of the children and grandchildren, who are said to be suckled with the same milk. And this is the reason why Hellenic states were originally governed by kings; because the Hellenes were under royal rule before they came together, as the barbarians still are. Every family is ruled by the eldest, and therefore in the colonies of the family the kingly form of government prevailed because they were of the same blood. As Homer says:

"Each one gives law to his children and to his
     wives."

For they lived dispersedly, as was the manner in ancient times. Wherefore men say that the Gods have a king, because they themselves either are or were in ancient times under the rule of a king. For they imagine, not only the forms of the Gods, but their ways of life to be like their own.

When several villages are united in a single complete community, large enough to be nearly or quite self-sufficing, the state comes into existence, originating in the bare needs of life, and continuing in existence for the sake of a good life. And therefore, if the earlier forms of society are natural, so is the state, for it is the end of them, and the nature of a thing is its end. For what each thing is when fully developed, we call its nature, whether we are speaking of a man, a horse, or a family. Besides, the final cause and end of a thing is the best, and to be self-sufficing is the end and the best.

Hence it is evident that the state is a creation of nature, and that man is by nature a political animal. And he who by nature and not by mere accident is without a state, is either a bad man or above humanity; he is like the

"Tribeless, lawless, heartless one,"

whom Homer denounces—the natural outcast is forthwith a lover of war; he may be compared to an isolated piece at draughts.

Now, that man is more of a political animal than bees or any other gregarious animals is evident. Nature, as we often say, makes nothing in vain, and man is the only animal whom she has endowed with the gift of speech. And whereas mere voice is but an indication of pleasure or pain, and is therefore found in other animals (for their nature attains to the perception of pleasure and pain and the intimation of them to one another, and no further), the power of speech is intended to set forth the expedient and inexpedient, and therefore likewise the just and the unjust. And it is a characteristic of man that he alone has any sense of good and evil, of just and unjust, and the like, and the association of living beings who have this sense makes a family and a state.

Further, the state is by nature clearly prior to the family and to the individual, since the whole is of necessity prior to the part; for example, if the whole body be destroyed, there will be no foot or hand, except in an equivocal sense, as we might speak of a stone hand; for when destroyed the hand will be no better than that. But things are defined by their working and power; and we ought not to say that they are the same when they no longer have their proper quality, but only that they have the same name. The proof that the state is a creation of nature and prior to the individual is that the individual, when isolated, is not self-sufficing; and therefore he is like a part in relation to the whole. But he who is unable to live in society, or who has no need because he is sufficient for himself, must be either a beast or a god: he is no part of a state. A social instinct is implanted in all men by nature, and yet he who first founded the state was the greatest of benefactors. For man, when perfected, is the best of animals, but, when separated from law and justice, he is the worst of all; since armed injustice is the more dangerous, and he is equipped at birth with arms, meant to be used by intelligence and virtue, which he may use for the worst ends. Wherefore, if he have not virtue, he is the most unholy and the most savage of animals, and the most full of lust and gluttony. But justice is the bond of men in states, for the administration of justice, which is the determination of what is just, is the principle of order in political society. . . .

We have next to consider whether there is only one form of government or many, and if many, what they are, and how many, and what are the differences between them.

A constitution is the arrangement of magistracies in a state, especially of the highest of all. The government is everywhere sovereign in the state, and the constitution is in fact the government. For example, in democracies the people are supreme, but in oligarchies, the few; and, therefore, we say that these two forms of government also are different: and so in other cases.

First, let us consider what is the purpose of a state, and how many forms of government there are by which human society is regulated. We have already said, in the first part of this treatise, when discussing household management and the rule of a master, that man is by nature a political animal. And therefore, men, even when they do not require one another's help, desire to live together; not but that they are also brought together by their common interests in proportion as they severally attain to any measure of well-being. This is certainly the chief end, both of individuals and of states. And also for the sake of mere life (in which there is possibly some noble element so long as the evils of existence do not greatly overbalance the good) mankind meet together and maintain the political community. And we all see that men cling to life even at the cost of enduring great misfortune, seeming to find in life a natural sweetness and happiness.

There is no difficulty in distinguishing the various kinds of authority; they have been often defined already in discussions outside the school. The rule of a master, although the slave by nature and the master by nature have in reality the same interests, is nevertheless exercised primarily with a view to the interest of the master, but accidentally considers the slave, since, if the slave perish, the rule of the master perishes with him. On the other hand, the government of a wife and children and of a household, which we have called household management, is exercised in the first instance for the good of the governed or for the common good of both parties, but essentially for the good of the governed, as we see to be the case in medicine, gymnastic, and the arts in general, which are only accidentally concerned with the good of the artists themselves. For there is no reason why the trainer may not sometimes practise gymnastics, and the helmsman is always one of the crew. The trainer or the helmsman considers the good of those committed to his care. But, when he is one of the persons taken care of, he accidentally participates in the advantage, for the helmsman is also a sailor, and the trainer becomes one of those in training. And so in politics: when the state is framed upon the principle of equality and likeness, the citizens think that they ought to hold office by turns. Formerly, as is natural, every one would take his turn of service; and then again, somebody else would look after his interest, just as he, while in office, had looked after theirs. But nowadays, for the sake of the advantage which is to be gained from the public revenues and from office, men want to be always in office. One might imagine that the rulers, being sickly, were only kept in health while they continued in office; in that case we may be sure that they would be hunting after places. The conclusion is evident: that governments which have a regard to the common interest are constituted in accordance with strict principles of justice, and are therefore true forms; but those which regard only the interest of the rulers are all defective and perverted forms, for they are despotic, whereas a state is a community of freemen.

Having determined these points, we have next to consider how many forms of government there are, and what they are; and in the first place what are the true forms, for when they are determined the perversions of them will at once be apparent. The words constitution and government have the same meaning, and the government, which is the supreme authority in states, must be in the hands of one, or of a few, or of the many. The true forms of government, therefore, are those in which the one, or the few, or the many, govern with a view to the common interest; but governments which rule with a view to the private interest, whether of the one, or of the few, or of the many, are perversions. For the members of a state, if they are truly citizens, ought to participate in its advantages. Of forms of government in which one rules, we call that which regards the common interests, kingship or royalty; that in which more than one, but not many, rule, aristocracy; and it is so called, either because the rulers are the best men, or because they have at heart the best interests of the state and of the citizens. But when the citizens at large administer the state for the common interest, the government is called by the generic name—a constitution. And there is a reason for this use of language. One man or a few may excel in virtue; but as the number increases it becomes more difficult for them to attain perfection in every kind of virtue, though they may in military virtue, for this is found in the masses. Hence in a constitutional government the fighting-men have the supreme power, and those who possess arms are the citizens.

Of the above-mentioned forms, the perversions are as follows:—of royalty, tyranny; of aristocracy, oligarchy; of constitutional government, democracy. For tyranny is a kind of monarchy which has in view the interest of the monarch only; oligarchy has in view the interest of the wealthy; democracy, of the needy: none of them the common good of all.

But there are difficulties about these forms of government, and it will therefore be necessary to state a little more at length the nature of each of them. For he who would make a philosophical study of the various sciences, and does not regard practice only, ought not to overlook or omit anything, but to set forth the truth in every particular. Tyranny, as I was saying, is monarchy exercising the rule of a master over the political society; oligarchy is when men of property have the government in their hands; democracy, the opposite, when the indigent, and not the men of property, are the rulers. And here arises the first of our difficulties, and it relates to the distinction just drawn. For democracy is said to be the government of the many. But what if the many are men of property and have the power in their hands? In like manner oligarchy is said to be the government of the few; but what if the poor are fewer than the rich, and have the power in their hands because they are stronger? In these cases the distinction which we have drawn between these different forms of government would no longer hold good.

Suppose, once more, that we add wealth to the few and poverty to the many, and name the governments accordingly—an oligarchy is said to be that in which the few and the wealthy, and a democracy that in which the many and the poor are the rulers—there will still be a difficulty. For, if the only forms of government are the ones already mentioned, how shall we describe those other governments also just mentioned by us, in which the rich are the more numerous and the poor are the fewer, and both govern in their respective states?

The argument seems to show that, whether in oligarchies or in democracies, the number of the governing body, whether the greater number, as in a democracy, or the smaller number, as in an oligarchy, is an accident due to the fact that the rich everywhere are few, and the poor numerous. But if so, there is a misapprehension of the causes of the difference between them. For the real difference between democracy and oligarchy is poverty and wealth. Wherever men rule by reason of their wealth, whether they be few or many, that is an oligarchy, and where the poor rule, that is a democracy. But, as a fact, the rich are few and the poor many; for few are well-to-do, whereas freedom is enjoyed by all, and wealth and freedom are the grounds on which the oligarchical and democratical parties respectively claim power in the state.

Let us begin by considering the common definitions of oligarchy and democracy, and what is justice oligarchical and democratical. For all men cling to justice of some kind, but their conceptions are imperfect and they do not express the whole idea. For example, justice is thought by them to be, and is, equality; not, however, for all, but only for equals. And inequality is thought to be, and is, justice; neither is this for all, but only for unequals. When the persons are omitted, then men judge erroneously. The reason is that they are passing judgment on themselves, and most people are bad judges in their own case. And whereas justice implies a relation to persons as well as to things, and a just distribution, as I have already said in the *Ethics,* implies the same ratio between the persons and between the things, they agree about the equality of the things, but dispute about the equality of the persons, chiefly for the reason which I have just given —because they are bad judges in their own affairs; and secondly, because both the parties to the argument are speaking of a limited and partial justice, but imagine themselves to be speaking of absolute justice. For the one party, if they are unequal in one respect, for example wealth, consider themselves to be unequal in all; and the other party, if they are equal in one respect, for example free birth, consider themselves to be equal in all. But they leave out the capital point. For if men met and associated out of regard to wealth only, their share in the state would be proportioned to their property, and the oligarchical doctrine would then seem to carry the day. It would not be just that he who paid one mina should have the same share of a hundred minae, whether of the principal or of the profits, as he who paid the remaining ninety-nine. But a state exists for the sake of a good life, and not for the sake of life only; if life only were the object, slaves and brute animals might form a state, but they cannot, for they have no share in happiness or in a life of free choice. Nor does a state exist for the sake of alliance and security from injustice, nor yet for the sake of exchange and mutual intercourse; for then the Tyrrhenians and the Carthaginians, and all who have commercial treaties with one another, would be the citizens of one state. True, they have agreements about imports, and engagements that they will do no wrong to one another, and written articles of alliance. But there are no magistracies common to the contracting parties who will enforce their engagements; different states have each their own magistracies. Nor does one state take care that the citizens of the other are such as they ought to be, nor see that those who come under the terms of the treaty do no wrong or wickedness at all, but only that they do no injustice to one another. Whereas, those who care for good government take into consideration virtue and vice in states. Whence it may be further inferred that virtue must be the care of a state which is truly so called, and not merely enjoys the name: for without this end the community becomes a mere alliance which differs only in place from alliances of which the members live apart; and law is only a convention, 'a surety to one another of justice,' as the sophist Lycophron says, and has no real power to make the citizens good and just.

This is obvious; for suppose distinct places, such as Corinth and Megara, to be brought together so that their walls touched, still they would not be one city, not even if the citizens had the right to intermarry, which is one of the rights peculiarly characteristic of states. Again, if men dwelt at a distance from one another, but not so far off as to have no intercourse, and

there were laws among them that they should not wrong each other in their exchanges, neither would this be a state. Let us suppose that one man is a carpenter, another a husbandman, another a shoemaker, and so on, and that their number is ten thousand: nevertheless, if they have nothing in common but exchange, alliance, and the like, that would not constitute a state. Why is this? Surely not because they are at a distance from one another: for even supposing that such a community were to meet in one place, but that each man had a house of his own, which was in a manner his state, and that they made alliance with one another, but only against evil-doers; still an accurate thinker would not deem this to be a state, if their intercourse with one another was of the same character after as before their union. It is clear then that a state is not a mere society, having a common place, established for the prevention of mutual crime and for the sake of exchange. These are conditions without which a state cannot exist; but all of them together do not constitute a state, which is a community of families and aggregations of families in wellbeing, for the sake of a perfect and self-sufficing life. Such a community can only be established among those who live in the same place and intermarry. Hence arise in cities family connections, brotherhoods, common sacrifices, amusements which draw men together. But these are created by friendship, for the will to live together is friendship. The end of the state is the good life, and these are the means towards it. And the state is the union of families and villages in a perfect and self-sufficing life, by which we mean a happy and honourable life.

Our conclusion, then, is that political society exists for the sake of noble actions, and not of mere companionship. Hence they who contribute most to such a society have a greater share in it than those who have the same or a greater freedom or nobility of birth but are inferior to them in political virtue; or than those who exceed them in wealth but are surpassed by them in virtue.

From what has been said it will be clearly seen that all the partisans of different forms of government speak of a part of justice only. . . .

We have now to inquire what is the best

constitution for most states, and the best life for most men, neither assuming a standard of virtue which is above ordinary persons, nor an education which is exceptionally favoured by nature and circumstances, nor yet an ideal state which is an aspiration only, but having regard to the life in which the majority are able to share, and to the form of government which states in general can attain. As to those aristocracies, as they are called, of which we were just now speaking, they either lie beyond the possibilities of the greater number of states, or they approximate to the so-called constitutional government, and therefore need no separate discussion. And in fact the conclusion at which we arrive respecting all these forms rests upon the same grounds. For if what was said in the *Ethics* is true, that the happy life is the life according to virtue lived without impediment, and that virtue is a mean, then the life which is in a mean, and in a mean attainable by every one, must be the best. And the same principles of virtue and vice are characteristic of cities and of constitutions; for the constitution is in a figure the life of the city.

Now in all states there are three elements: one class is very rich, another very poor, and a third in a mean. It is admitted that moderation and the mean are best, and therefore it will clearly be best to possess the gifts of fortune in moderation; for in that condition of life men are most ready to follow rational principle. But he who greatly excels in beauty, strength, birth, or wealth, or on the other hand who is very poor, or very weak, or very much disgraced, finds it difficult to follow rational principle. Of these two the one sort grow into violent and great criminals, the others into rogues and petty rascals. And two sorts of offences correspond to them, the one committed from violence, the other from roguery. Again, the middle class is least likely to shrink from rule, or to be over-ambitious for it; both of which are injuries to the state. Again, those who have too much of the goods of fortune, strength, wealth, friends, and the like, are neither willing nor able to submit to authority. The evil begins at home; for when they are boys, by reason of the luxury in which they are brought up, they never learn, even at school, the habit of obedience. On the other hand, the very poor, who are in the opposite

extreme, are too degraded. So that the one class cannot obey, and can only rule despotically; the other knows not how to command and must be ruled like slaves. Thus arises a city, not of freemen, but of masters and slaves, the one despising, the other envying; and nothing can be more fatal to friendship and good fellowship in states than this: for good fellowship springs from friendship; when men are at enmity with one another, they would rather not even share the same path. But a city ought to be composed, as far as possible, of equals and similars; and these are generally the middle classes. Wherefore the city which is composed of middle-class citizens is necessarily best constituted in respect of the elements of which we say the fabric of the state naturally consists. And this is the class of citizens which is most secure in a state, for they do not, like the poor, covet their neighbours' goods; nor do others covet theirs, as the poor covet the goods of the rich; and as they neither plot against others, nor are themselves plotted against, they pass through life safely. Wisely then did Phocylides pray—"Many things are best in the mean; I desire to be a middle condition in my city."

Thus it is manifest that the best political community is formed by citizens of the middle class, and that those states are likely to be well-administered, in which the middle class is large, and stronger if possible than both the other classes, or at any rate than either singly; for the addition of the middle class turns the scale, and prevents either of the extremes from being dominant. Great then is the good fortune of a state in which the citizens have a moderate and sufficient property; for where some possess much, and the others nothing, there may arise an extreme democracy, or a pure oligarchy; or a tyranny may grow out of either extreme—either out of the most rampant democracy, or out of an oligarchy; but it is not so likely to arise out of the middle constitutions and those akin to them. I will explain the reason of this hereafter, when I speak of the revolutions of states. The mean condition of states is clearly best, for no other is free from faction; and where the middle class is large, there are least likely to be factions and dissensions. For a similar reason large states are less liable to faction than small ones, because in them the middle class is large; whereas in small states it is easy to divide all the citizens into two classes who are either rich or poor, and to leave nothing in the middle. And democracies are safer and more permanent than oligarchies, because they have a middle class which is more numerous and has a greater share in the government; for when there is no middle class, and the poor greatly exceed in number, troubles arise, and the state soon comes to an end. A proof of the superiority of the middle class is that the best legislators have been of a middle condition; for example, Solon, as his own verses testify; and Lycurgus, for he was not a king; and Charondas, and almost all legislators.

These considerations will help us to understand why most governments are either democratical or oligarchical. The reason is that the middle class is seldom numerous in them, and whichever party, whether the rich or the common people, transgresses the mean and predominates, draws the constitution its own way, and thus arises either oligarchy or democracy. There is another reason—the poor and the rich quarrel with one another, and whichever side gets the better, instead of establishing a just or popular government, regards political supremacy as the prize of victory, and the one party sets up a democracy and the other an oligarchy. Further, both the parties which had the supremacy in Hellas looked only to the interest of their own form of government, and established in states, the one, democracies, and the other, oligarchies; they thought of their own advantage, of the public not at all. For these reasons the middle form of government has rarely, if ever, existed, and among a very few only. One man alone of all who ever ruled in Hellas was induced to give this middle constitution to states. But it has now become a habit among the citizens of states, not even to care about equality; all men are seeking for do·minion, or, if conquered, are willing to submit.

What then is the best form of government, and what makes it the best, is evident; and of other constitutions, since we say that there are many kinds of democracy and many of oligarchy, it is not difficult to see which has the first and which the second or any other place in the order of excellence, now that we have determined which is the best. For that which is nearest to the best must of necessity be better, and that which is furthest from it worse, if we are judging absolutely and not relatively to given conditions: I say "relatively to given conditions," since a particular government may be preferable, but another form may be better for some people.

Sophocles

Sophocles (496?–406 B.C.) lived in the period that witnessed the victory of the Greeks over the Persians and the flowering of culture in Athens. One of the great triumvirate of dramatists which included Aeschylus and Euripides, Sophocles interested himself in the perennial human question of how men react to the problems presented by life. In this great tragedy prepared for presentation at one of the annual Dionysian festivals at Athens, Sophocles portrayed the reactions of King Œdipus to the fate outlined for him by the inexorable decree of the gods. In reading this play note (1) that the chorus is used by the author as an additional character to aid in telling the story, (2) the style of writing and the form of the play, (3) evidence of religious thought, (4) the relationship between moral conduct and equivalent rewards and punishments, (5) man's role when confronted by adversity, and (6) evidence of the Greek view of life.

As translated by Thomas Francklin in *Sophocles*, New York, 1834, 238–288.

ŒDIPUS THE KING

DRAMATIS PERSONÆ

Œdipus, king of Thebes
Jocasta, wife of Œdipus
Creon, brother of Jocasta
Tiresias, a blind prophet of Thebes
A Shepherd from Corinth
A Messenger
An Old Shepherd, formerly belonging to Laius
High Priest of Jupiter
Chorus, composed of the priests and ancient men of Thebes, Theban youths, children of Œdipus, attendants, &c.

ARGUMENT

Laius, king of Thebes, having learned from the oracle of Apollo that he was destined to perish by the hand of his son, commanded his wife Jocasta to destroy her infant as soon as it came into the world. The mother accordingly gave the child to a domestic, with orders to expose him on Mount Cithæron, where he was found by one of the shepherds of Polybus, king of Corinth; who having no children, determined, by the advice of his queen, to keep the boy in ignorance of the circumstances of his birth, and educate him as his own son. When Œdipus had arrived at years of maturity, he went to consult the oracle, which terrified him with the intelligence that he would commit parricide and incest. He now therefore resolved to return to Corinth no more; and travelling towards Phocis, met Laius, and, in a dispute which ensued, slew him. As Œdipus was ignorant of the rank and quality of the man whom he had killed, he was attracted to Thebes by the report of the sphinx; the overthrow of which monster raised him to the throne, while the prophecy was completed by his nuptials with the widow of Laius, by whom he had four children. The Theban territories were at length desolated by a plague, which the oracle declared should cease when the murderer of Laius was banished from Bœotia. After a minute investigation, the dreadful secret was at length divulged; and Jocasta put a period to her existence, while Œdipus deprived himself of sight, and was, at his own request, banished from Thebes by the order of Creon, the brother of Jocasta, who then assumed the reins of government.

ACT I

Scene, Thebes before the palace of Œdipus.
Œdipus, High Priest of Jupiter
Œdi. O my loved sons! the youthful progeny
Of ancient Cadmus! wherefore sit you here,
And suppliant thus, with sacred boughs adorn'd,
Crowd to our altars? Frequent sacrifice,
And prayers, and sighs, and sorrows fill the land.
I could have sent to learn the fatal cause:
But see, your anxious sovereign comes himself
To know it all from you: behold your king,
Renowned Œdipus. Do thou, old man
(For best that office suits thy years), inform me
Why you are come. Is it the present ill
That calls you here, or dread of future woe?
Hard were indeed the heart that did not feel
For grief like yours, and pity such distress.
If there be aught that Œdipus can do
To serve his people, know me for your friend.
    Priest. O king! thou seest what numbers throng thy altars.
Here, bending sad beneath the weight of years,
The hoary priests, here crowd the chosen youth
Of Thebes, with these a weak and suppliant train
Of helpless infants: last, in me behold
The minister of Jove: far off thou seest
Assembled multitudes, with laurel crown'd,
To where Minerva's hallow'd temples rise
Frequent repair, or where Ismenus laves
Apollo's sacred shrine. Too well thou know'st,
Thy wretched Thebes, with dreadful storms oppress'd,
Scarce lifts her head above the whelming flood:
The teeming earth her blasted harvest mourns,
And on the barren plain the flocks and herds
Unnumber'd perish; dire abortion thwarts
The mother's hopes, and painful she brings forth
The half-formed infant; baleful pestilence

Hath laid our city waste; the fiery god
Stalks o'er deserted Thebes; while, with our
    groans
Enrich'd, the gloomy god of Erebus
Triumphant smiles. O Œdipus! to thee
We bend: behold these youths; with me they
    kneel,
And suppliant at thy altars sue for aid,
To thee, the first of men, and only less
Than they, whose favour thou alone canst gain,
The gods above: thy wisdom yet may heal
The deep-felt wounds, and make the powers
    divine
Propitious to us. Thebes long since to thee
Her safety owed, when, from the sphinx de-
    liver'd,
Thy grateful people saw thee, not by man
But by the gods instructed, save the land.
Now, then, thou best of kings! assist us now:
O! by some mortal or immortal aid
Now succour the distress'd! On wisdom oft
And prudent counsels, in the hour of ill,
Success awaits. O dearest prince! support,
Relieve thy Thebes; on thee, its saviour once,
Again it calls: now, if thou wouldst not see
The memory perish of thy former deeds,
Let it not call in vain; but rise, and save.
With happiest omens once, and fair success,
We saw thee crown'd: O! be thyself again,
And may thy will and fortune be the same!
If thou art yet to reign, O king! remember,
A sovereign's riches is a peopled realm;
For what will ships or lofty towers avail,
Unarm'd with men to guard and to defend
    them?
    Œdi. O my unhappy sons! too well I know
Your sad estate; I know the woes of Thebes:
And yet among you lives not such a wretch
As Œdipus; for O! on me, my children!
Your sorrows press. Alas! I feel for you,
My people, for myself, for Thebes, for all.
Think not I slept regardless of your ills;
O no; with many a tear I wept your fate,
And oft in meditation deep revolved
How best your peace and safety to restore.
The only medicine that my thoughts could find
I have administered: Menœceus' son,
The noble Creon, went by my command
To Delphi, from Apollo's shrine to know
What must be done to save this wretched land.
'Tis time he were returned; I wonder much

At his delay: if, when he comes, your king
Perform not all the god enjoins, then say
He is the worst of men.
    Priest.   O king! thy words
Are gracious; and, if right these youths in-
    form me,
Creon is here.
    Œdi.   O Phœbus! grant he come
With tidings cheerful as the smile he wears?
    Priest. He is the messenger of good; for see,
His brows are crown'd with laurel.
    Œdi.   We shall soon
Be satisfied: he comes.

        Enter Creon, Chorus.

              My dearest Creon!
O! say, what answer bear'st thou from the god?
Or good or ill?
    Cre.   Good, very good; for know,
The worst of ills, if rightly used, may prove
The means of happiness.
    Œdi.   What says my friend?
This answer gives me naught to hope or fear.
    Cre. Shall we retire, or would you that I
    speak
In public here?
    Œdi.   Before them all declare it:
Their woes sit heavier on me than my own.
    Cre. Then mark what I have heard: the god
    commands
That instant we drive forth the fatal cause
Of this dire pestilence, nor nourish here
The accursed monster.
    Œdi.   Who? what monster? how
Remove it?
    Cre.   Or by banishment, or death:
Life must be given for life; for yet his blood
Rests on the city.
    Œdi.   Whose? what means the god?
    Cre. O king! before thee Laius ruled o'er
    Thebes.
    Œdi. I know he did, though I did ne'er be-
hold him.
    Cre. Laius was slain, and on his murderers
(So Phœbus says) we must have vengeance.
    Œdi.   Where,
Where are the murderers? who shall trace the
    guilt
Buried so long in silence?
    Cre.   Here, he said,

Ev'n in this land: what's sought for may be
found;
But truth, unsearch'd for, seldom comes to
light.

Œdi. How did he fall, and where? at home,
abroad?
Died he at Thebes, or in a foreign land?

Cre. He left his palace, fame reports, to seek
Some oracle; since that we ne'er beheld him.

Œdi. But did no messenger return? Not one
Of all his train, of whom we might inquire
Touching this murder?

Cre.   One, and one alone,
Came back, who, flying, 'scaped the general
slaughter;
But nothing, save one little circumstance,
Or knew, or e'er related.

Œdi.   What was that?
Much may be learn'd from that; a little dawn
Of light appearing, may discover all.

Cre. Laius, attack'd by robbers, and oppress'd
By number, fell; such is his tale.

Œdi.   Would they,—
Would robbers do so desperate a deed,
Unbribed and unassisted?

Cre.   So indeed
Suspicion whisper'd then; but, Laius dead,
No friend was found to vindicate the wrong.

Œdi. But what strange cause could stop inquiry thus
Into the murder of a king?

Cre.   The sphinx:
Her dire enigma kept our thought intent
On present ills, nor gave us time to search
The past mysterious deed.

Œdi.   Myself will try
Soon to unveil it: thou, Apollo! well,
And well hast thou, my Creon! lent thy aid;
Your Œdipus shall now perform his part:
Yes, I will fight for Phœbus and my country,
And so I ought; for not to friends alone
Or kindred owe I this, but to myself.
Who murder'd him perchance would murder
me;
His cause is mine; wherefore, my children! rise,
Take hence your suppliant boughs, and sum-
mon here
The race of Cadmus, my assembled people.
Naught shall be left untried: Apollo leads,
And we will rise to joy, or sink for ever.

Priest. Haste then, my sons! for this we
hither came;
About it quick; and may the god, who sent
This oracle, protect, defend, and save us!
[*Exeunt.*

Chorus

STROPHE I

O, thou great oracle divine!
Who didst to happy Thebes remove,
    From Delphi's golden shrine,
And in sweet sounds declare the will of Jove;
Daughter of hope! O! soothe my soul to rest,
And calm the rising tumult in my breast.
    Look down, O Phœbus! on thy loved abode;
Speak, for thou know'st the dark decrees of
    fate,
Our present and our future state.
O Delian! be thou still our healing god!

ANTISTROPHE I

Minerva! first on thee I call,
Daughter of Jove, immortal maid;
    Low beneath thy feet we fall:
O! bring thy sister Dian to our aid.
Goddess of Thebes! from thy imperial throne
Look with an eye of gentle pity down;
    And thou, far-shooting Phœbus! once the
    friend
        Of this unhappy, this devoted land;
        O! now, if ever, let thy hand
Once more be stretched to save and to defend.

STROPHE II

Great Thebes, my sons! is now no more;
    She falls, and ne'er again shall rise;
Naught can her health or strength restore;
    The mighty nation sinks, she droops, she
    dies.
Stripp'd of her fruits behold the barren earth:
The half-form'd infant struggles for a birth;
    The mother sinks, unequal to her pain:
        While, quick as birds in airy circles fly,
        Or lightnings from an angry sky,
    Crowds press on crowds to Pluto's dark do-
    main.

ANTISTROPHE II

Behold, what heaps of wretches slain,
    Unburied, unlamented lie;

Nor parents now nor friends remain
  To grace their deaths with pious obsequy;
The aged matron and the blooming wife,
Clung to the altars, sue for added life.
  With sighs and groans united, Pæans rise;
    Re-echoed still doth great Apollo's name
    Their sorrows and their wants proclaim
  Frequent to him ascends the sacrifice.

STROPHE III

Haste, then, Minerva! beauteous maid!
  Descend in this afflictive hour;
Haste to thy dying people's aid;
  Drive hence this baneful, this destructive
    power,
Who comes not arm'd with hostile sword or
    shield,
Yet strews with many a corse the ensanguined
field.
  To Amphitrite's wide-extending bed,
    O! drive me, goddess, from thy favourite
    land;
    Or let him, by thy dread command,
  Bury in Thracian waves his ignominious
head.

ANTISTROPHE III

Father of all, immortal Jove!
  O! now thy fiery terrors send;
From thy dreadful stores above
Let lightnings blast him, and let thunders
rend.
And thou, O Lydian king! thy aid impart;
Send from thy golden bow the unerring dart;
  Smile, chaste Diana! on this loved abode,
While Theban Bacchus joins the maddening
    throng.
O god of wine, and mirth, and song!
  Now with thy torch destroy the base, in-
glorious god.   [Exeunt.

ACT II

Œdipus, Chorus, *the People assembled.*

Œdi. Your prayers are heard; and, if you
    will obey
Your king, and hearken to his words, you soon
Shall find relief: myself will heal your woes.
I was a stranger to the dreadful deed,
A stranger ev'n to the report till now;

And yet, without some traces of the crime,
I should not urge this matter; therefore hear
    me.
I speak to all the citizens of Thebes,
Myself a citizen; observe me well:
If any know the murderer of Laius,
Let him reveal it; I command you all;
But if, restrain'd by dread of punishment,
He hide the secret, let him fear no more;
For naught but exile shall attend the crime,
Whene'er confess'd: if by a foreign hand
The horrid deed was done, who points him out
Commands our thanks, and meets a sure re-
    ward;
But if there be who knows the murderer,
And yet conceals him from us, mark his fate,
Which here I do pronounce; let none receive,
Throughout my kingdom, none hold converse
    with him,
Nor offer prayer, nor sprinkle o'er his head
The sacred cup; let him be driven from all,
By all abandon'd, and by all accursed;
For so the Delphic oracle declared:
And therefore to the gods I pay this duty,
And to the dead. O! may the guilty wretch,
Whether alone, or by his impious friends
Assisted, he perform'd the horrid deed,
Denied the common benefits of nature,
Wear out a painful life and, O! if here,
Within my palace I conceal the traitor,
On me and mine alight the vengeful curse!
To you, my people! I commit the care
Of this important business; 'tis my cause,
The cause of Heaven, and your expiring coun-
    try.
Ev'n if the god had naught declared, to leave
This crime unexpiated were most ungrateful:
He was the best of kings, the best of men;
That sceptre now is mine which Laius bore:
His wife is mine; so would his children be,
Did any live; and therefore am I bound,
Ev'n as he were my father, to revenge him.
Yes, I will try to find this murderer:
I owe it to the son of Labdacus,
To Polydorus, Cadmus, and the race
Of great Agenor. O! if yet there are
Who will not join me in the pious deed;
From such may Earth withhold her annual
    store,
And barren be their bed, their life most
    wretched,

And their death cruel as the pestilence
That wastes our city; but on you, my Thebans!
Who wish us fair success, may Justice smile
Propitious, and the gods for ever bless!

Cho. O king! thy imprecation unappall'd
I hear, and join thee, guiltless of the crime,
Nor knowing who committed it. The god
Alone, who gave the oracle, must clear
Its doubtful sense, and point out the offender.

Œdi. 'Tis true; but who shall force the powers divine
To speak their hidden purpose?

Cho.   One thing more,
If I might speak.

Œdi.   Say on, whate'er thy mind
Shall dictate to thee.

Cho.   As among the gods
All-knowing Phœbus, so to mortal men
Doth sage Tiresias in foreknowledge sure
Shine forth pre-eminent: perchance his aid
Might much avail us.

Œdi.   Creon did suggest
The same expedient, and by his advice
Twice have I sent for this Tiresias; much
I wonder that he comes not.

Cho.   'Tis most fitting
We do consult him; for the idle tales
Which rumour spreads are not to be regarded.

Œdi. What are those tales? for naught
should we despise.

Cho. 'Tis said, some travellers did attack the
king.

Œdi. It is: but still no proof appears.

Cho.   And yet,
If it be so, thy dreadful execration
Will force the guilty to confess

Œdi.   O no!
Who fears not to commit the crime will ne'er
Be frighted at the curse that follows it.

Cho. Behold, he comes, who will discover
all!
The holy prophet, see! They lead him hither:
He knows the truth, and will reveal it to us.

Enter Tiresias

Œdi. O sage Tiresias! thou, who knowest all
That can be known, the things of heaven above
And earth below; whose mental eye beholds,
Blind as thou art, the state of dying Thebes,
And weeps her fate; to thee we look for aid;
On thee alone for safety we depend.

This answer, which perchance thou hast not
heard,
Apollo gave: The plague, he said, should cease,
When those who murder'd Laius were dis-
cover'd,
And paid the forfeit of their crime by death
Or banishment. O! do not then conceal
Aught that thy art prophetic, from the flight
Of birds or other omens, may disclose.
O! save thyself, save this afflicted city,
Save Œdipus, avenge the guiltless dead
From this pollution! Thou art all our hope;
Remember, 'tis the privilege of man,
His noblest function, to assist the wretched.

Tir. Alas! what misery it is to know,
When knowledge is thus fatal! O Tiresias!
Thou art undone. Would I had never come!

Œdi. What sayest thou? Whence this
strange dejection? Speak.

Tir. Let me be gone; 'twere better for us
both
That I retire in silence: be advised.

Œdi. It is ingratitude to Thebes, who bore
And cherish'd thee; it is unjust to all,
To hide the will of Heaven.

Tir.   'Tis rash in thee
To ask, and rash I fear will prove my answer.

Cho. O! do not, by the gods, conceal it from
us:
Suppliant we all request, we all conjure thee.

Tir. You know not what you ask: I'll not
unveil
Your miseries to you.

Œdi.   Know'st thou then our fate,
And will not tell it? Mean'st thou to betray
Thy country and thy king?

Tir.   I would not make
Myself and thee unhappy: why thus blame
My tender care, nor listen to my caution!

Œdi. Wretch as thou art, thou wouldst pro-
voke a stone,
Inflexible and cruel, still implored,
And still refusing.

Tir.   Thou condemn'st my warmth,
Forgetful of thy own.

Œdi.   Who would not rage,
To see an injured people treated thus
With vile contempt?

Tir.   What is decreed by Heaven
Must come to pass, though I reveal it not.

Œdi. Still 'tis thy duty to inform us of it.

Tir. I'll speak no more, not though thine anger swell
Ev'n to its utmost.

Œdi.   Nor will I be silent.
I tell thee, once for all, thou wert thyself
Accomplice in this deed; nay more, I think,
But for thy blindness, wouldst with thine own hand
Have done it too.

Tir.   'Tis well; now hear Tiresias:
The sentence, which thou didst thyself proclaim,
Falls on thyself: henceforth shall never man
Hold converse with thee, for thou art accursed;
The guilty cause of this our city's woes.

Œdi. Audacious traitor! think'st thou to escape
The hand of vengeance?

Tir.   Yes, I fear thee not;
For truth is stronger than a tyrant's arm.

Œdi. Whence didst thou learn this? Was it from thy art?

Tir. I learn'd it from thyself: thou didst compel me
To speak, unwilling as I was.

Œdi.   Once more
Repeat it then, that I may know my fate
More plainly still.

Tir.   Is it not plain already,
Or mean'st thou but to tempt me?

Œdi.   No; but say,
Speak it again.

Tir.   Again then I declare
Thou art thyself the murderer whom thou seek'st.

Œdi. A second time thou shalt not pass unpunish'd.

Tir. What wouldst thou say, if I should tell thee all?

Œdi. Say what thou wilt; for all is false.

Tir.   Know then,
That Œdipus, in shameful bonds united
With those he loves, unconscious of his guilt,
Is yet most guilty.

Œdi.   Darest thou utter more,
And hope for pardon?

Tir.   Yes, if there be strength
In sacred truth.

Œdi.   But truth dwells not in thee:
Thy body and thy mind are dark alike,
For both are blind; thy every sense is lost.

Tir. Thou dost upbraid me with the loss of that
For which thyself ere long shall meet reproach
From every tongue.

Œdi.   Thou blind and impious traitor!
Thy darkness is thy safeguard, or this hour
Had been thy last.

Tir.   It is not in my fate
To fall by thee; Apollo guards his priest.

Œdi. Was this the tale of Creon, or thy own?

Tir. Creon is guiltless, and the crime is thine.

Œdi. O riches, power, dominion, and thou far
Above them all, the best of human blessings,
Excelling wisdom, how doth envy love
To follow and oppress you! This fair kingdom,
Which, by the nation's choice and not my own,
I here possess, Creon, my faithful friend
(For such I thought him once), would now wrest from me,
And hath suborn'd this vile impostor here,
This wand'ring hypocrite, of sharpest sight
When interest prompts, but ignorant and blind
When fools consult him. Tell me, prophet! where
Was all thy art, when the abhorred sphinx
Alarm'd our city? Wherefore did not then
Thy wisdom save us? Then the man divine
Was wanting; but thy birds refused their omens;
Thy god was silent: then came Œdipus,
This poor, unlearned, uninstructed sage,
Who not from birds uncertain omens drew,
But by his own sagacious mind explored
The hidden mystery; and now thou comest
To cast me from the throne my wisdom gain'd,
And share with Creon my divided empire.
But you should both lament your ill-got power,
You and your bold compeer; for thee, this moment,
But that I bear respect unto thy age,
I'd make thee rue thy execrable purpose.

Cho. You both are angry, therefore both to blame:
Much rather should you join, with friendly zeal
And mutual ardour, to explore the will
Of all-deciding Heaven.

Tir.   What though thou rulest
O'er Thebes despotic, we are equal here;

I am Apollo's subject, and not thine;
Nor want I Creon to protect me. No;
I tell thee, king! this blind Tiresias tells thee,
Seeing thou seest not, know'st not where thou
    art,
What, or with whom. Canst thou inform me
    who
Thy parents are, and what thy horrid crimes
'Gainst thy own race, the living and the dead?
A father's and a mother's curse attend thee.
Soon shall their furies drive thee from the land,
And leave thee dark like me: what mountain
    then,
Or conscious shore, shall not return the groans
Of Œdipus, and echo to his woes?
When thou shalt look on the detested bed,
And in that haven where thou hopest to rest,
Shalt meet with storm and tempest; then what
    ills
Shall fall on thee and thine! Now vent thy rage
On old Tiresias and the guiltless Creon:
We shall be soon avenged, for ne'er did
    Heaven
Cut off a wretch so base, so vile as thou art.

    Œdi. Must I bear this from thee? Away, be-
    gone!
Home, villain, home!
    Tir.   I did not come to thee
Unsent for.
    Œdi. Had I thought thou wouldst have thus
Insulted me, I had not call'd thee hither.
    Tir. Perhaps thou hold'st Tiresias as a fool
And madman; but thy parents thought me
    wise.
    Œdi. My parents, saidst thou? Speak! who
were my parents?
    Tir. This day, that gives thee life, shall give
thee death.
    Œdi. Still dark, and still perplexing are the
words
Thou utter'st.
    Tir.   'Tis thy business to unriddle,
And therefore thou canst best interpret them.
    Œdi. Thou dost reproach me for my virtues.
    Tir.   They,
And thy good fortune, have undone thee.
    Œdi.   Since
I sav'd the city, I'm content.
    Tir.   Farewell.
Boy, lead me hence.
    Œdi.   Away with him, for here

His presence but disturbs us; being gone,
We shall be happier.
    Tir.   Œdipus! I go;
But first inform thee (for I fear thee not)
Wherefore I came: know, then, I came to tell
    thee,
The man thou seek'st, the man on whom thou
    pour'dst
Thy execrations, ev'n the murderer
Of Laius, now is here; a seeming stranger,
And yet a Theban. He shall suffer soon
For all his crimes: from light and affluence
    driven
To penury and darkness, poor and blind,
Propp'd on his staff, and from his native land
Expell'd, I see him in a foreign clime
A helpless wanderer; to his sons at once
A father and a brother; child and husband
Of her from whom he sprang. Adulterous,
Incestuous parricide! now fare thee well;
Go, learn the truth; and, if it be not so,
Say I have ne'er deserved the name of prophet.

Chorus

STROPHE I

When will the guilty wretch appear,
Whom Delphi's sacred oracle demands;
    Author of crimes too black for mortal ear,
Dipping in royal blood his sacrilegious hands?
Swift as the storm by rapid whirlwinds driven,
Quick let him fly the impending wrath of
    Heaven;
    For lo, the angry son of Jove,
    Arm'd with red lightnings from above,
Pursues the murderer with immortal hate,
And round him spreads the snares of unre-
    lenting fate.

ANTISTROPHE I

From steep Parnassus' rocky cave,
Cover'd with snow, came forth the dread com-
    mand;
    Apollo thence his sacred mandate gave,
To search the man of blood through every
    land.
Silent and sad the weary wanderer roves
O'er pathless rocks and solitary groves,
    Hoping to 'scape the wrath divine
    Denounced from great Apollo's shrine:

Vain hopes to 'scape the fate by Heaven decreed
For vengeance hovers still o'er his devoted
head.

STROPHE II

Tiresias, famed for wisdom's lore,
Hath dreadful ills to Œdipus divined;
   And as his words mysterious I explore,
Unnumber'd doubts perplex my anxious mind:
Now raised by hope, and now with fears op-
press'd,
Sorrow and joy alternate fill my breast.
    How should these hapless kings be foes,
    When never strife between them rose?
Or why should Laius, slain by hands unknown,
Bring foul disgrace on Polybus' unhappy son?

ANTISTROPHE II

From Phœbus and all-seeing Jove
Naught can be hid of actions here below;
   But earthly prophets may deceitful prove,
And little more than other mortals know.
Though much in wisdom man doth man excel,
In all that's human error still must dwell.
    Could he commit the bloody deed,
    Who from the sphinx our city freed?
O no! he never shed the guiltless blood;
The sphinx declares him wise, and innocent,
   and good.   [*Exeunt.*

ACT III

Creon, Chorus

Cre. O citizens! with grief I hear your king
Hath blasted the fair fame of guiltless Creon,
And most unjustly brands me with a crime
My soul abhors. While desolation spreads
On every side, and universal ruin
Hangs o'er the land, if I in word or deed
Could join to swell the woes of hapless Thebes,
I were unworthy, nay, I would not wish
To live another day. Alas, my friends!
Thus to be deem'd a traitor to my country,
To you, my fellow-citizens, to all
That hear me; O, 'tis infamy and shame!
I cannot, will not bear it.
  Cho.   'Twas the effect
Of sudden anger only; what he said,
But could not think.

Cre.   Who told him I suborn'd
The prophet to speak falsely? What could raise
This vile suspicion?
  Cho.   Such he had, but whence
I know not.
  Cre.   Talk'd he thus with firm com-
posure
And confidence of mind?
  Cho.   I cannot say:
'Tis not for me to know the thoughts of kings,
Or judge their actions: but, behold, he comes.

Enter Œdipus

Œdi. Ha! Creon here? And darest thou thus
  approach
My palace? thou, who wouldst have murder'd
  me,
And taken my kingdom? By the gods, I ask
  thee
(Answer me! traitor), didst thou think me fool
Or coward, that I could not see thy arts,
Or had not strength to vanquish them? What
  madness,
What strange infatuation, led thee on,
Without or force or friends, to grasp at empire,
Which only their united force can give?
What wert thou doing?
  Cre.   Hear what I shall answer,
Then judge impartial.
  Œdi.   Thou canst talk it well,
But I shall ne'er attend to thee; thy guilt
Is plain; thou art my deadliest foe.
  Cre.   But hear
What I shall urge.
  Œdi.   Say not thou art innocent.
  Cre. If self-opinion, void of reason, seem
Conviction to thee, know, thou err'st most
  grossly.
  Œdi. And thou more grossly, if thou
  think'st to pass
Unpunish'd for this injury to thy friend.
  Cre. I should not, were I guilty; but what
  crime
Have I committed? Tell me.
  Œdi.   Wert not thou
The man who urged me to require the aid
Of your all-knowing prophet?
  Cre.   True, I was;
I did persuade you: so I would again.
  Œdi. How long is it since Laius—
  Cre.   Laius? what?

Œdi. Since Laius fell by hands unknown?
Cre.   A long,
Long tract of years.
Œdi.   Was this Tiresias then
A prophet?
Cre.   Ay, in wisdom and in fame,
As now, excelling.
Œdi.   Did he then say aught
Concerning me?
Cre.   I never heard he did.
Œdi. Touching this murder, did you ne'er
    inquire
Who were the authors?
Cre.   Doubtless; but in vain.
Œdi. Why did not the same prophet then
    inform you?
Cre. I know not that, and when I'm igno-
    rant
I'm always silent.
Œdi.   What concerns thyself
At least thou know'st, and therefore shouldst
    declare it.
Cre. What is it? speak; and if 'tis in my
    power,
I'll answer thee.
Œdi.   Thou know'st, if this Tiresias
Had not combined with thee, he would not
    thus
Accuse me as the murderer of Laius.
Cre. What he declares thou best canst tell;
    of me,
What thou requirest, myself am yet to learn.
Œdi. Go, learn it, then; but ne'er shalt
    thou discover
That Œdipus is guilty.
Cre.   Art not thou
My sister's husband?
Œdi.   Granted.
Cre.   Join'd with her,
Thou rulest o'er Thebes.
Œdi.   'Tis true, and all she asks
Most freely do I give her.
Cre.   Is not Creon
In honour next to you?
Œdi.   Thou art, and therefore
The more ungrateful.
Cre.   Hear what I shall plead,
And thou wilt never think so: tell me, prince,
Is there a man who would prefer a throne,
With all its dangers, to an equal rank
In peace and safety? I am not of those

Who choose the name of king before the
    power;
Fools only make such wishes; I have all
From thee, and fearless I enjoy it all.
Had I the sceptre, often must I act
Against my will. Know, then, I am not yet
So void of sense and reason as to quit
A real 'vantage for a seeming good.
Am I not happy? am I not revered,
Embraced, and loved by all? To me they come
Who want thy favour, and by me acquire it:
What then should Creon wish for? Shall he
    leave
All this for empire? Bad desires corrupt
The fairest mind: I never entertain'd
A thought so vile, nor would I lend my aid
To forward such base purposes. But go
To Delphi; ask the sacred oracle
If I have spoke the truth: if there you find
That with the prophet I conspired, destroy
The guilty Creon: not thy voice alone
Shall then condemn me, for myself will join
In the just sentence; but accuse me not
On weak suspicion's most uncertain test.
Justice would never call the wicked good,
Or brand fair virtue with the name of vice,
Unmerited: to cast away a friend
Faithful and just, is to deprive ourselves
Of life and being, which we hold most dear:
But time, and time alone, revealeth all;
That only shows the good man's excellence:
A day sufficeth to unmask the wicked.
    Cho. O king! his caution merits your regard;
Who judge in haste do seldom judge aright.
    Œdi. When they are quick who plot against
    my life,
'Tis fit I should be quick in my defence:
If I am tame and silent, all they wish
Will soon be done, and Œdipus must fall.
    Cre. What wouldst thou have? My banish-
    ment?
    Œdi. Thy death.
    Cre. But first inform me wherefore I should
    die.
    Œdi. Dost thou rebel then? Wilt thou not
    submit?
    Cre. Not when I see thee thus deceived.
    Œdi.   'Tis fit
I should defend my own.
    Cre.   And so should I.
    Œdi. Thou art a traitor.

Cre.　　　　　What, if I should prove
I am not so?

Œdi.　　A king must be obey'd.

Cre. Not if his orders are unjust.

Œdi.　　　　　　　O Thebes!
O citizens!

Cre.　　I too can call on Thebes:
She is my country.

Cho.　　　　　O! no more, my lords!
For, see, Jocasta comes in happiest hour
To end your contest.

Enter Jocasta

Joc.　　　　　Whence this sudden tumult?
O princes! is this well, at such a time
With idle broils to multiply the woes
Of wretched Thebes? Home, home, for shame;
　　nor thus
With private quarrel swell the public ruin.

Cre. Sister! thy husband hath most basely
　　used me;
He threatens me with banishment or death.

Œdi. I do confess it; for he did conspire,
With vile and wicked arts, against my life.

Cre. O! may I never prosper, but, accursed,
Unpitied, perish if I ever did!

Joc. Believe him, Œdipus! revere the gods
Whom he contests, if thou dost love Jocasta:
Thy subjects beg it of thee.

Cho.　　　　　Hear, O king!
Consider, we entreat thee.

Œdi.　　　　　What wouldst have?
Think you I'll e'er submit to him?

Cho.　　　　　　Revere
His character, his oath, both pleading for him.

Œdi. But know you what you ask?

Cho.　　　　　　We do.

Œdi.　　　　　　What is it?

Cho. We ask thee to believe a guiltless
　　friend,
Nor cast him forth dishonour'd thus, on slight
Suspicion's weak surmise.

Œdi.　　　　　Requesting this,
You do request my banishment or death.

Cho. No, by yon leader of the heavenly host,
The immortal sun, I had not such a thought:
I only felt for Thebes' distressful state,
And would not have it by domestic strife
Imbitter'd thus.

Œdi.　　　Why, let him then depart:
If Œdipus must die, or leave his country

For shameful exile, be it so: I yield
To thy request, not his; for hateful still
Shall Creon ever be.

Cre.　　　　　Thy stubborn soul
Bends with reluctance, and when anger fires it,
Is terrible; but natures form'd like thine
Are their own punishment.

Œdi.　　　　　Wilt thou not hence?
Wilt not be gone?

Cre.　　　I go: thou know'st me not;
But these will do me justice.　　[*Exit* Creon.

Cho.　　　　　Princess! now
Persuade him to retire.

Joc.　　　　　First let me know
The cause of this dissension.

Cho.　　　　　From reports
Uncertain, and suspicions most injurious,
The quarrel rose.

Joc.　　　　Was the accusation mutual?

Cho. It was.

Joc.　　　What follow'd then?

Cho.　　　　　Ask me no more;
Enough's already known: we'll not repeat
The woes of hapless Thebes.

Œdi.　　　　　You are all blind,
Insensible, unjust; you love me not,
Yet boast your piety.

Cho.　　　　　I said before,
Again I say, that not to love my king
Ev'n as myself would mark me for the worst
Of men; for thou didst save expiring Thebes.
O! rise once more, protect, preserve thy coun-
　　try!

Joc. O king! inform me, whence this strange
　　dissension?

Œdi. I'll tell thee, my Jocasta! (for thou
　　know'st
The love I bear thee), what this wicked Creon
Did artfully devise against me.

Joc.　　　　　Speak it,
If he indeed be guilty.

Œdi.　　　　Creon says
That I did murder Laius.

Joc.　　　　Spake he this
As knowing it himself, or from another?

Œdi. He had suborn'd that evil-working
　　priest,
And sharpens every tongue against his king.

Joc. Let not a fear perplex thee, Œdipus!
Mortals know nothing of futurity,
And these prophetic seers are all impostors;

I'll prove it to thee. Know, then, Laius once,
Not from Apollo, but his priests, received
An oracle, which said it was decreed
He should be slain by his own son, the off-
    spring
Of Laius and Jocasta; yet he fell
By strangers, murder'd (for so fame reports)
By robbers in the place where three ways meet.
A son was born; but ere three days had pass'd,
The infant's feet were bored; a servant took,
And left him on the pathless mountain's top,
To perish there: thus Phœbus ne'er decreed
That he should kill his father, or that Laius
(Which much he fear'd) should by his son be
    slain.
Such is the truth of oracles: henceforth
Regard them not. What Heaven would have us
    know
It can with ease unfold, and will reveal it.

   Œdi. What thou hast said, Jocasta! much
    disturbs me:
I tremble at it.

   Joc.   Wherefore shouldst thou fear?

   Œdi. Methought I heard thee say, Laius was
    slain
Where three ways meet.

   Joc.   'Twas so reported then,
And is so still.

   Œdi.   Where happened the misfortune?

   Joc. In Phocis, where the roads unite that
    lead
To Delphi and to Daulia.

   Œdi.   How long since?

   Joc. A little time ere you began to reign
O'er Thebes, we heard it.

   Œdi.   O almighty Jove!
What wilt thou do with me?

   Joc.   Why talk'st thou thus?

   Œdi. Ask me no more; but tell me of this
    Laius,
What was his age and stature?

   Joc.   He was tall;
His hairs just turning to the silver hue;
His form not much unlike thy own.

   Œdi.   O me!
Sure I have call'd down curses on myself
Unknowing.

   Joc.   Ha! what say'st thou, Œdipus?
I tremble while I look on thee.

   Œdi.   O! much
I fear, the prophet saw too well: but say,

One thing will make it clear.

   Joc.   I dread to hear it;
Yet speak, and I will tell thee.

   Œdi.   Went he forth
With few attendants, or a numerous train,
In kingly pomp?

   Joc.   They were but five in all,
The herald with them; but one chariot there,
Which carried Laius.

   Œdi.   O! 'tis but too plain.
Who brought the news?

   Joc.   A servant, who alone
Escaped with life.

   Œdi.   That servant, is he here?

   Joc. O no: his master slain, when he return'd,
And saw thee on the throne of Thebes, with
    prayer
Most earnest he besought me to dismiss him,
That he might leave this city, where he wish'd
No longer to be seen, but to retire,
And feed my flocks: I granted his request:
For that and more his honest services
Had merited.

   Œdi.   I beg he may be sent for
Immediately.

   Joc.   He shall; but wherefore is it?

   Œdi. I fear thou hast said too much, and
    therefore wish
To see him.

   Joc.   He shall come: but, O my lord!
Am I not worthy to be told the cause
Of this distress?

   Œdi.   Thou art, and I will tell thee.
Thou art my hope; to whom should I impart
My sorrows but to thee? Know then, Jocasta!
I am the son of Polybus, who reigns
At Corinth, and the Dorian Merope
His queen; there long I held the foremost rank,
Honour'd and happy, when a strange event
(For strange it was, though little meriting
The deep concern I felt) alarm'd me much.
A drunken reveller at a feast proclaim'd
That I was only the supposed son
Of Corinth's king. Scarce could I bear that day
The vile reproach; the next, I sought my
    parents,
And ask'd of them the truth; they too, enraged,
Resented much the base indignity.
I liked their tender warmth, but still I felt
A secret anguish; and, unknown to them,
Sought out the Pythian oracle, in vain.

Touching my parents, nothing could I learn;
But dreadful were the miseries it denounced
Against me: 'twas my fate, Apollo said,
To wed my mother, to produce a race
Accursed and abhorr'd, and last to slay
My father who begat me:—sad decree!
Lest I should e'er fulfil the dire prediction,
Instant I fled from Corinth, by the stars
Guiding my hapless journey, to the place
Where thou report'st this wretched king was
    slain.
But I will tell thee the whole truth: at length,
I came to where the three ways meet; when lo!
A herald, with another man, like him
Whom thou describest, and in a chariot, met
    me.
Both strove with violence to drive me back.
Enraged, I struck the charioteer, when straight,
As I advanced, the old man saw, and twice
Smote me on the head; but dearly soon repaid
The insult on me: from his chariot roll'd,
Prone on the earth, beneath my staff he fell,
And instantly expired; the attendant train
All shared his fate. If this unhappy stranger
And Laius be the same, lives there a wretch
So cursed, so hateful to the gods as I am?
Nor citizen nor alien must receive,
Or converse or communion hold with me,
But drive me forth with infamy and shame:
The dreadful curse pronounced with my own
    lips
Shall soon o'ertake me: I have stain'd the bed
Of him whom I had murder'd; am I then
Aught but pollution? If I fly from hence,
The bed of incest meets me, and I go
To slay my father Polybus, the best,
The tenderest parent; this must be the work
Of some malignant power. Ye righteous gods!
Let me not see that day, but rest in death,
Rather than suffer such calamity.

   Cho. O king! we pity thy distress: but wait
With patience his arrival, and despair not.

   Œdi. That shepherd is my only hope:
    Jocasta!
Would he were here!

   Joc.   Suppose he were; what then?
What wouldst thou do?

   Œdi.   I'll tell thee; if he says
The same as thou dost, I am safe, and guiltless.

   Joc. What said I then?

   Œdi.   Thou saidst, he did report

Laius was slain by robbers: if 'tis true
He fell by numbers, I am innocent,
For I was unattended; if but one
Attack'd and slew him, doubtless I am he.

   Joc. Be satisfied, it must be as he first
Reported it: he cannot change the tale.
Not I alone, but the whole city heard it:
Or grant he should, the oracle was ne'er
Fulfill'd; for Phœbus said, Jocasta's son
Should slay his father; that could never be,
For, O! Jocasta's son long since is dead.
He could not murder Laius; therefore, never
Will I attend to prophecies again.

   Œdi. Right, my Jocasta! but, I beg thee,
    send
And fetch this shepherd; do not fail.

   Joc.   I will,
This moment; come, my lord! let us go in;
I will do nothing but what pleases thee.

                         [*Exeunt.*

Chorus

STROPHE I

Grant me, henceforth, ye powers divine!
  In virtue's purest paths to tread;
  In every word, in every deed,
May sanctity of manners ever shine;
  Obedient to the laws of Jove,
  The laws descended from above;
Which, not like those by feeble mortals given,
  Buried in dark oblivion lie,
  Or, worn by time, decay and die:
But bloom eternal like their native heaven!

ANTISTROPHE I

Pride first gave birth to tyranny:
  That hateful vice, insulting Pride,
  When, every human power defied,
She lifts to glory's height her votary;
  Soon stumbling, from her tottering throne
  She throws the wretched victim down.
But may the god, indulgent, hear my prayer,
  That god whom humbly I adore
  O! may he smile on Thebes once more,
And take its wretched monarch to his care!

STROPHE II

Perish the impious and profane,
  Who, void of reverential fear,
  Nor justice nor the laws revere;

Who leave their god for pleasure or for gain;
  Who swell by fraud their ill-got store;
  Who rob the wretched and the poor.
If vice, unpunish'd, virtue's meed obtain,
  Who shall refrain the impetuous soul,
  The rebel passions who control,
Or wherefore do I lead this choral train?

ANTISTROPHE II

No more to Delphi's sacred shrine
  Need we with incense now repair;
  No more shall Phocis hear our prayer,
Nor fair Olympia see her rites divine;
  If oracles no longer prove
  The power of Phœbus and of Jove.
Great lord of all! from thy eternal throne
  Behold how impious men defame
  Thy loved Apollo's honour'd name:
O! guard his rights, and vindicate thy own.
                  [*Exeunt.*

ACT IV

Jocasta, Chorus

Joc. Sages and rulers of the land! I come
To seek the altars of the gods, and there
With incense and oblations to appease
Offended Heaven. My Œdipus, alas!
No longer wise and prudent, as you all
Remember once he was, with present things
Compares the past, nor judges like himself:
Unnumber'd cares perplex his anxious mind,
And every tale awakes new terrors in him.
Vain is my counsel, for he hears me not.
First then to thee, O Phœbus! (for thou still
Art near to help the wretched), we appeal,
And suppliant beg thee now to grant thy aid
Propitious: deep is our distress; for, O!
We see our pilot sinking at the helm,
And much already fear the vessel lost.

Enter Shepherd *from Corinth*

Shep. Can you instruct me, strangers! which
  way lies
The palace of king Œdipus? himself
I would most gladly see. Can you inform me?
  Cho. This is the palace; he is now within;
Thou seest his queen before thee.
  Shep.   Ever bless'd,
And happy with the happy mayst thou live!
  Joc. Stranger! the same good wish to thee,
  for well

Thy words deserve it: but say, wherefore
  comest thou,
And what's thy news?
  Shep.   To thee, and to thy husband.
Pleasure and joy!
  Joc. What pleasure? and whence art thou?
  Shep. From Corinth: to be brief, I bring thee
  tidings
Of good and evil.
  Joc.   Ha! what mean thy words
Ambiguous?
  Shep.   Know, then, if report say true,
The Isthmian people will choose Œdipus
Their sovereign.
  Joc.   Is not Polybus their king?
  Shep. No; Polybus is dead.
  Joc.   What say'st thou? dead?
  Shep. If I speak falsely, may death seize on
  me!
  Joc. [*to one of her Attendants.*] Why fliest
  thou not to tell thy master? Hence!
What are you now, you oracles divine?
Where is your truth? The fearful Œdipus
From Corinth fled, lest he should slay the king.
This Polybus, who perish'd, not by him,
But by the hand of Heaven.

Enter Œdipus

Œdi.   My dear Jocasta!
Why hast thou call'd me hither?
  Joc.   Hear this man;
And when thou hear'st him, mark what faith is
  due
To your revered oracles.
  Œdi.   What is he,
And what doth he report?
  Joc.   He comes from Corinth,
And says, thy father, Polybus, is dead.
  Œdi. What say'st thou, stranger? Speak to
  me,
O! speak.
  Shep. If touching this thou first desirest my
  answer,
Know, he is dead.
  Œdi.   How died he? say, by treason,
Or some disease?
  Shep.   Alas! a little force
Will lay to rest the weary limbs of age.
  Œdi. Distemper then did kill him?
  Shep.   That in part,
And part a length of years that wore him down.

Œdi. Now, my Jocasta, who shall henceforth trust
To prophecies, and seers, and clamourous birds
With their vain omens? they who had decreed
That I should kill my father? He, thou seest,
Beneath the earth lies buried, while I live
In safety here, and guiltless of his blood:
Unless, perhaps, sorrow for the loss of me
Shorten'd his days, thus only could I kill
My father; but he's gone, and to the shades
Hath carried with him those vain oracles
Of fancied ill, no longer worth my care.

Joc. Did I not say it would be thus?

Œdi. Thou didst;
But I was full of fears.

Joc. Henceforth, no more
Indulge them.

Œdi. But my mother's bed—that still
Must be avoided: I must fly from that.

Joc. Why should man fear, whom chance, and chance alone,
Doth ever rule? Foreknowledge all is vain,
And can determine nothing: therefore best
It is to live as fancy leads, at large,
Uncurb'd and only subject to our will.
Fear not thy mother's bed: oft-times in dreams
Have men committed incest; but his life
Will ever be most happy who contemns
Such idle phantoms.

Œdi. Thou wert right, Jocasta!
Did not my mother live; but as it is,
Spite of thy words, I must be anxious still.

Joc. Think on thy father's death; it is a light
To guide thee here.

Œdi. It is so; yet I fear,
While she survives him.

Shep. Who is it you mean?
What woman fear you?

Œdi. Merope, the wife
Of Polybus.

Shep. And wherefore fear you her?

Œdi. Know, stranger, a most dreadful oracle
Concerning her affrights me.

Shep. May I know it,
Or must it be reveal'd to none but thee?

Œdi. O, no, I'll tell thee: Phœbus hath declared
That Œdipus should stain his mother's bed,
And dip his hands in his own father's blood;
Wherefore I fled from Corinth, and lived here,

In happiness indeed; but still thou know'st
It is a blessing to behold our parents,
And that I had not.

Shep. Was it for this cause
Thou wert an exile then?

Œdi. It was; I fear'd
That I might one day prove my father's murderer.

Shep. What if I come, O king! to banish hence
Thy terrors, and restore thy peace?

Œdi. O stranger!
Couldst thou do this, I would reward thee nobly.

Shep. Know, then, for this I came; I came to serve,
And make thee happy.

Œdi. But I will not go
Back to my parents.

Shep. Son, I see thou know'st not
What thou art doing.

Œdi. Wherefore think'st thou so?
By Heaven, I beg thee then do thou instruct me.

Shep. If thou didst fly from Corinth for this cause—

Œdi. Apollo's dire predictions still affright me.

Shep. Fear'st thou pollution from thy parents?

Œdi. That,
And that alone, I dread.

Shep. Thy fears are vain.

Œdi. Not if they are my parents.

Shep. Polybus
Was not akin to thee.

Œdi. What say'st thou? Speak;
Say, was not Polybus my father?

Shep. No;
No more than he is mine.

Œdi. Why call me then
His son?

Shep. Because long since I gave thee to him:
He did receive thee from these hands.

Œdi. Indeed!
And could he love another's child so well?

Shep. He had no children; that persuaded him
To take and keep thee.

Œdi. Didst thou buy me then,

Or am I thine, and must I call thee father?

  Shep. I found thee in Cithæron's woody
    vale.

  Œdi. What brought thee there?

  Shep.   I came to feed my flocks
On the green mountain's side.

  Œdi.   It seems thou wert
A wandering shepherd.

  Shep.   Thy deliverer,
I saved thee from destruction.

  Œdi.   How! what then
Had happen'd to me?

  Shep.   Thy own feet will best
Inform thee of that circumstance.

  Œdi.   Alas!
Why call'st thou to remembrance a misfortune
Of so long date?

  Shep.   'Twas I who loosed the tendons
Of thy bored feet.

  Œdi.   It seems, in infancy,
I suffer'd much then.

  Shep.   To this incident
Thou owest thy name.

  Œdi.   My father or my mother,
Who did it? Know'st thou?

  Shep.   He who gave thee to me
Must tell thee that.

  Œdi.   Then from another's hand
Thou didst receive me?

  Shep.   Ay, another shepherd.

  Œdi. Who was he? Canst thou recollect?

  Shep.   'Twas one,
At least so called, of Laius' family.

  Œdi. Laius, who ruled at Thebes?

  Shep.   The same: this man
Was shepherd to King Laius.

  Œdi.   Lives he still?
And could I see him?

  Shep. [*pointing to the Chorus.*] Some of
    these, perhaps,
His countrymen, may give you information.

  Œdi. [*to the Chorus.*] O! speak, my friends!
    if any of you know
This shepherd; whether still he lives at Thebes,
Or in some neighbouring country; tell me
    quick,
For it concerns us near.

  Cho.   It must be he
Whom thou didst lately send for; but the
    queen

Can best inform thee.

  Œdi.   Know'st thou, my Jocasta!
Whether the man whom thou didst order
    hither,
And whom the shepherd speaks of, be the
    same?

  Joc. Whom meant he? for I know not. Œdi-
    pus!
Think not so deeply of this thing.

  Œdi.   Good Heaven
Forbid, Jocasta! I should now neglect
To clear my birth, when thus the path is mark'd
And open to me.

  Joc.   Do not, by the gods
I beg thee, do not, if thy life be dear,
Make farther search, for I have felt enough
Already from it.

  Œdi.   Rest thou satisfied:
Were I descended from a race of slaves,
'Twould not dishonour thee.

  Joc.   Yet hear me; do not,
Once more, I beg thee, do not search this
    matter.

  Œdi. I will not be persuaded: I must search,
And find it too.

  Joc.   I know it best, and best
Advise thee.

  Œdi. That advice perplexes more.

  Joc. O! would to Heaven that thou mayst
    never know
Or who or whence thou art!

  Œdi. [*to the Attendant.*] Let some one fetch
That shepherd quick, and leave this woman
    here
To glory in her high descent.

  Joc.   Alas!
Unhappy Œdipus! that word alone
I now can speak: remember, 'tis my last.

               [*Exit* Jocasta.

  Cho. Why fled the queen in such disorder
    hence?
Sorely distress'd she seemed, and much I fear
Her silence bodes some sad event.

  Œdi.   Whate'er
May come of that, I am resolved to know
The secret of my birth, how mean soever
It chance to prove: perhaps her sex's pride
May make her blush to find I was not born
Of noble parents; but I call myself

The son of Fortune, my indulgent mother,
Whom I shall never be ashamed to own.
The kindred months, that are, like me, her
    children;
The years, that roll obedient to her will,—
Have raised me from the lowest state to power
And splendour; wherefore, being what I am,
I need not fear the knowledge of my birth.

Chorus

STROPHE

If my prophetic soul doth well divine,
Ere on thy brow tomorrow's sun shall shine,
    Cithæron! thou the mystery shalt unfold:
The doubtful Œdipus, no longer blind,
Shall soon his country and his father find,
    And all the story of his birth be told:
        Then shall we in grateful lays,
        Celebrate our monarch's praise,
And in the sprightly dance our songs tri-
umphant raise.

ANTISTROPHE

What heavenly power gave birth to thee, O
    king?
From Pan, the god of mountains, didst thou
    spring,
    With some fair daughter of Apollo join'd?
Art thou from him who o'er Cyllene reigns,
Swift Hermes, sporting in Arcadia's plains?
    Some nymph of Helicon did Bacchus find;—
        Bacchus, who delights to rove
        Through the forest, hill, and grove,
And art thou, prince, the offspring of their love?

Enter Œdipus, Shepherd from Corinth

Œdi. If I may judge of one whom yet I ne'er
Had converse with, yon old man whom I see
This way advancing, must be that same shep-
herd
We lately sent for, by his age and mien,
Ev'n as this stranger did describe him to us.
My servants too are with him; but you best
Can say, for you must know him well.
    Cho.   'Tis he,
My lord! the faithful shepherd of King Laius.
    Œdi. [to the Shepherd from Corinth.] What
        say'st thou, stranger? is it he?
    Shep.   It is.

Enter Old Shepherd

    Œdi. Now answer me, old man! look this
        way; speak;
Didst thou belong to Laius?
    O. Shep.   Sir, I did:
No hireling slave, but in his palace bred,
I serv'd him long.
    Œdi.   What was thy business there?
    O. Shep. For my life's better part I tended
        sheep.
    Œdi. And whither didst thou lead them?
    O. Shep.   To Cithæron,
And to the neighbouring plains.
    Œdi.   Behold this man;
        [pointing to the Shepherd of Corinth]
Dost thou remember to have seen him?
    O. Shep.   Whom?
What hath he done?
    Œdi.   Him who now stands before thee;
Call'st thou to mind or converse or connexion
Between you in time past?
    O. Shep.   I cannot say
I recollect it now.
    Shep.   I do not wonder
He should forget me; but I will recall
Some facts of ancient date: he must remember,
When on Cithæron we together fed
Our several flocks, in daily converse join'd,
From spring to autumn, and when winter bleak
Approach'd, retired: I to my little cot
Convey'd my sheep, he to the palace led
His fleecy care. Canst thou remember this?
    O. Shep. I do, but that is long since.
    Shep.   It is so;
But say, good shepherd, canst thou call to mind
An infant, whom thou didst deliver to me,
Requesting me to breed him as my own?
    O. Shep. Ha! wherefore ask'st thou this?
    Shep. [pointing to Œdipus] Behold him
        here,
That very child.
    O. Shep.   O! say it not; away!
Perdition on thee!
    Œdi.   Why reprove him thus?
Thou art thyself to blame, old man!
    O. Shep.   In what
Am I to blame, my lord?
    Œdi.   Thou wilt not speak
Touching this boy.

O. Shep.   Alas, poor man! he knows not
What he hath said.

Œdi.   If not by softer means
To be persuaded, force shall wring it from thee.

O. Shep. Treat not an old man harshly.

Œdi. [*to the Attendants.*]   Bind his hands.

O. Shep. Wherefore, my lord? What wouldst
    thou have me do?

Œdi. That child he talks of, didst thou give
    it to him?

O. Shep. I did, and would to Heaven I then
    had died!

Œdi. Die soon thou shalt, unless thou tell'st
    it all.

O. Shep. Say, rather, if I do.

Œdi.   This fellow means
To trifle with us, by his dull delay.

O. Shep. I do not; said I not, I gave the
    child?

Œdi. Whence came the boy? Was he thy
    own, or who
Did give him to thee?

O. Shep.   From another hand
I had received him.

Œdi.   Say, what hand? from whom?
Whence came he?

O. Shep.   Do not, by the gods! I beg thee,
Do not inquire.

Œdi.   Force me to ask again,
And thou shalt die.

O. Shep.   In Laius' palace born.

Œdi. Son of a slave, or of the king?

O. Shep.   Alas!
'Tis death for me to speak.

Œdi.   And me to hear;
Yet say it.

O. Shep. He was call'd the son of Laius;
But ask the queen, for she can best inform thee.

Œdi. Did she then give the child to thee?

O. Shep.   She did.

Œdi. For what?

O. Shep.   To kill him.

Œdi.   Kill her child! Inhuman
And barbarous mother!

O. Shep.   A dire oracle
Affrighted and constrained her to it.

Œdi.   Ha!
What oracle?

O. Shep.   Which said, her son should slay
His parents.

Œdi. Wherefore gavest thou then the infant
To this old shepherd?

O. Shep.   Pity moved me to it:
I hoped he would have soon convey'd his
    charge
To some far distant country: he, alas!
Preserved him but for misery and woe;
For, O my lord! if thou indeed art he,
Thou art of all mankind the most unhappy.

Œdi. O me! at length the mystery's un-
    ravell'd:
'Tis plain; 'tis clear; my fate is all determined.
Those are my parents who should not have
    been
Allied to me: she is my wife, ev'n she,
Whom nature had forbidden me to wed;
I have slain him who gave me life, and now
Of thee, O light! I take my last farewell,
For Œdipus shall ne'er behold thee more.

                     [*Exeunt.*

Chorus

STROPHE I

O, hapless state of human race!
How quick the fleeting shadows pass
Of transitory bliss below,
Where all is vanity and woe!
By thy example taught, O prince! we see
Man was not made for true felicity.

ANTISTROPHE I

Thou, Œdipus! beyond the rest
Of mortals wert supremely bless'd;
Whom every hand conspired to raise,
Whom every hand rejoiced to praise;
When from the sphinx thy all-preserving
    hand
Stretch'd forth its aid to save a sinking land.

STROPHE II

Thy virtues raised thee to a throne,
And grateful Thebes was all thy own:
Alas! how changed that glorious name!
Lost are thy virtues and thy fame.
How couldst thou thus pollute thy father's
    bed?
How couldst thou thus thy hapless mother
    wed?

ANTISTROPHE II

How could that bed unconscious bear
So long the vile, incestuous pair?
But Time, of quick and piercing sight,
Hath brought the horrid deed to light:
At length Jocasta owns her guilty flame,
And finds a husband and a child the same.

EPODE

Wretched son of Laius! thee
Henceforth may I never see;
But absent shed the pious tear,
And weep thy fate with grief sincere!
For thou didst raise our eyes to life and light,
To close them now in everlasting night.

[*Exeunt.*

ACT V

Messenger, Chorus

Mes. Sages of Thebes, most honour'd and
revered!
If e'er the house of Labdacus was dear
And precious to you, what will be your grief,
When I shall tell the most disastrous tale
You ever heard, and to your eyes present
A spectacle more dreadful than they yet
Did e'er behold? Not the wide Danube's waves,
Nor Phasis' stream, can wash away the stains
Of this polluted palace. The dire crimes,
Long time conceal'd, at length are brought to
light;
But those which spring from voluntary guilt
Are still more dreadful.
Cho.   Nothing can be worse
Than what we know already; bring'st thou
more
Misfortunes to us?
Mes.   To be brief, the queen,
Jocasta's dead.
Cho.   Say, by what hand?
                              Her own;
And, what's more dreadful, no one saw the
deed:
What I myself beheld, you all shall hear.
Inflamed with rage, soon as she reach'd the
palace,
Instant retiring to the nuptial bed,
She shut the door, then raved and tore her hair,
Called out on Laius dead, and bade him think

On that unhappy son who murder'd him,
And stain'd his bed: then, turning her sad eyes
Upon the guilty couch, she cursed the place
Where she had borne a husband from her hus-
band,
And children from her child: what follow'd
then
I know not, by the cries of Œdipus
Prevented, for on him our eyes were fix'd
Attentive: forth he came, beseeching us
To lend him some sharp weapon, and inform
him
Where he might find his mother and his wife;
His children's wretched mother and his own.
Some ill-designing power did then direct him
(For we were silent) to the queen's apartment:
Forcing the bolt, he rush'd unto the bed,
And found Jocasta, where we all beheld her,
Entangled in the fatal noose; which, soon
As he perceived, loosing the pendent rope,
Deeply he groan'd; and, casting on the ground
His wretched body, show'd a piteous sight
To the beholders. On a sudden thence
Starting, he pluck'd from off the robe she wore
A golden buckle, that adorn'd her side,
And buried in his eyes the sharpen'd point,
Crying, he ne'er again would look on her,
Never would see his crimes or miseries more,
Or those whom, guiltless, he could ne'er be-
hold,
Or those to whom he now must sue for aid.
His lifted eyelids then, repeating still
These dreadful plaints, he tore; while down
his cheeks
Fell showers of blood: such fate the wretched
pair
Sustain'd, partakers in calamity;
Fall'n from a state of happiness (for none
Were happier once than they) to groans and
death,
Reproach, and shame, and every human woe.
Cho. And where is now the poor unhappy
man?
Mes. "Open the doors," he cries, "and let all
Thebes
Behold his parents' murderer!" adding words
Not to be uttered: banish'd now he says
He must be, nor, devoted as he is
By his own curse, remain in this sad place.
He wants a kind conductor, and a friend
To help him now, for 'tis too much to bear.

But you will see him soon; for lo! the doors
Are open'd, and you will behold a sight
That would to pity move his deadliest foe.

Enter Œdipus

Cho. O horrid sight! more dreadful spectacle
Than e'er these eyes beheld! What madness
 urged thee
To this sad deed? What power malignant
 heap'd
On thy poor head such complicated woe?
Unhappy man! Alas! I would have held
Some converse with thee, but thy looks affright
 me:
I cannot bear to speak to thee.
 Œdi.   O me!
Where am I, and whence comes the voice I
 hear?
Where art thou, fortune?
 Cho.   Changed to misery,
Dreadful to hear, and dreadful to behold.
 Œdi. O cruel darkness! endless, hopeless
 night!
Shame, terrors, and unutterable woe!
More painful is the memory of my crimes
Than all the wounds my wild distraction made.
 Cho. Thus doubly cursed, O prince! I won-
 der not
At thy affliction.
 Œdi.   Art thou here, my friend?
I know thy voice: thou wouldst not leave the
 wretched;
Thou art my faithful, kind assistant still.
 Cho. How couldst thou thus deprive thy-
 self of sight?
What madness drove thee to the desperate
 deed?
What god inspired?
 Œdi.   Apollo was the cause;
He was, my friends, the cause of all my woes;
But for these eyes myself did quench their
 light;
I want not them. What use were they to me,
But to discover scenes of endless woe?
 Cho. 'Tis but too true.
 Œdi.   What pleasure now remains
For Œdipus? He cannot joy in aught
To sight or ear delightful. Curse on him,
Whoe'er he was, that loosen'd my bound feet,
And saved me, in Cithæron's vale, from death!
I owe him nothing; had I perish'd then,

Much happier had it been for you, my friends,
And for myself.
 Cho.   I too could wish thou hadst.
 Œdi. I should not then have murdered
 Laius; then
I had not ta'en Jocasta to my bed:
But now I am a guilty wretch, the son
Of a polluted mother, father now
To my own brother: all that's horrible
To nature is the lot of Œdipus.
 Cho. Yet must I blame this cruel act; for,
 sure,
The loss of sight is worse than death itself.
 Œdi. I care not for thy counsel or thy praise;
For with what eyes could I have e'er beheld
My honour'd father in the shades below,
Or my unhappy mother, both destroy'd
By me? This punishment is worse than death;
And so it should be. Sweet had been the sight
Of my dear children; them I could have wish'd
To gaze on; but I must never see
Or them, or this fair city, or the palace
Where I was born: deprived of every bliss
By my own lips, which doom'd to banishment
The murderer of Laius, and expelled
The impious wretch, by gods and men ac-
 cursed;—
Could I behold them after this? O, no!
Would I could now with equal ease remove
My hearing too, be deaf as well as blind,
And from another entrance shut out woe!
To want our senses, in the hour of ill,
Is comfort to the wretched. O Cithæron!
Why didst thou e'er receive me, or, received,
Why not destroy, that men might never know
Who gave me birth? O Polybus! O Corinth!
And thou, long time believed my father's pal-
 ace!
O, what a foul disgrace to human nature
Didst thou receive beneath a prince's form!
Impious myself, and from an impious race.
Where is my splendour now? O Daulian path!
The shady forest, and the narrow pass
Where three ways meet, who drank a father's
 blood,
Shed by these hands; do you not still remember
The horrid deed, and what, when here I came,
Follow'd more dreadful? Fatal nuptials! you
Produced me, you returned me to the womb
That bare me: thence relations horrible
Of fathers, sons, and brothers came: of wives,

Sisters, and mothers, sad alliance! all
That man holds impious and detestable.
But what in act is vile, the modest tongue
Should never name. Bury me, hide me, friends,
From every eye! destroy me, cast me forth
To the wide ocean! let me perish there;
Do any thing to shake off hated life.
Seize me! approach, my friends! you need not
    fear,
Polluted though I am, to touch me. None
Shall suffer for my crimes but I alone.
    Cho. In most fit time, my lord, the noble
    Creon
This way advances: he can best determine,
And best advise; sole guardian now of Thebes,
To him thy power devolves.
    Œdi.   What shall I say?
Can I apply to him for aid, whom late
I deeply injured by unjust suspicion?
                  [*Exit Messenger.*

Enter Creon

    Cre. I come not, prince, to triumph o'er thy
    woes
With vile reproach; I pity thy misfortunes:
But, O my Thebans! if you do not fear
The censure of your fellow-citizens,
At least respect the all-creating eye
Of Phœbus, who beholds you thus exposing
To public view a wretch accursed, polluted,
Whom neither earth can bear, nor sun behold,
Nor holy shower besprinkle. Take him hence,
Within the palace: those who are by blood
United should alone be witnesses
Of such calamity.
    Œdi.   O Creon! thou
The best of men, and I the worst! How kind
Thou art to visit me! O! by the gods
Let me entreat thee, since, beyond my hopes,
Thou art so good, now hear me: what I ask
Concerns thee most.
    Cre.   What is it thou desirest
Thus ardently?
    Œdi.   I beg thee banish me
From Thebes this moment, to some land re-
    mote,
Where I may ne'er converse with man again.
    Cre. My self had long since done it, but the
    gods
Must be consulted first.
    Œdi.   Their will is known

Already, and their oracle declared
The guilty parricide should die.
    Cre.   It hath;
But, as it is, 'twere better to inquire
What must be done.
    Œdi.   For such a wretch as I,
Wouldst thou again explore the will of Heaven?
    Cre. Thy hapless fate should teach us to
    believe
And reverence the gods.
    Œdi.   Now, Creon, list:
I beg thee, I conjure thee, let a tomb
Be raised, and all due honours paid to her
Who lies within. She was thy sister, Creon.
It is a duty which thou owest: for me,
I cannot hope this city now will deign
To keep me here. O Creon! let me go,
And seek the solitary mountain's top,
My own Cithæron, by my parents doom'd
Long since to be the grave of Œdipus:
There would I die, as they decreed I should.
Alas! I cannot, must not perish yet,
Till I have suffer'd evils worse than death,
For I was only saved to be unhappy;
But I must meet my fate, whate'er it be.
My sons are men, and wheresoever fortune
May place them, cannot want the means of life.
They shall not burden thee; but O, my friend!
What will become of my unhappy daughters,
With tenderest love, beneath a father's hand
Cherish'd so long? O! take them to thy care,
Thou best of men! O! might I but embrace
    them,
But shed a tear o'er their disastrous fate;
Might I be suffer'd but to touch them here;
I should rejoice, and think I saw them still.
But hark! methinks e'en now I hear the voice
Of my dear daughters. Hath the gracious
    Creon,
In pity to my woes, already brought
My children to me? Is it so?
    Cre.   It is:
Thy wishes are prevented; they are here.

Enter Daughters of Œdipus

    Œdi. May Heaven reward thee for this good-
    ness to me,
And give thee much more bliss than I have
    known!
Now, my dear children! come towards me,
    come

Towards your father and your—brother: see
These sightless eyes, pierced by my own mad
    hands;
Behold that wretched father who begat you
Unknowingly on her who gave me birth.
I cannot see you now; I can but weep
Your fate, to think what hours of wretchedness
You have to know hereafter. Whither now
Must my poor children fly? From every feast,
Joyless, with grief and shame, shall you return;
And when the time shall come when riper
    years
Should give you to the nuptial bed, who then,
Careless of fame, will let his child partake
The infamy of my abhorred race,
Sprung from a wretch accursed, who kill'd his
    father,
And from the womb that bare him did beget
You, my unhappy daughters? Such reproach
Must still be yours, to virgin solitude
Devoted ever and a barren bed.
Son of Menœceus! thou alone art left
Their father now; for O! Jocasta's dead,
And I am—nothing: do not then forsake
Thy kindred; nor, deserted and forlorn,
Suffer them still, in penury and woe,
To wander helpless, in their tender age.
Remember, they have no support but thee.
O generous prince! have pity on them; give me
Thy friendly hand in promise of thy aid.
To you, my daughters! had your early years
Permitted, I had given my last advice:
Too young for counsel, all I ask of you
Is but to pray the gods that my sad life
May not be long; but yours, my children!
    crown'd

With many days, and happier far than mine.
  Cre. It is enough: go in; thy grief transports
    thee
Beyond all bounds.
  Œdi.   'Tis hard, but I submit. .
  Cre. The time demands it; therefore go.
  Œdi.   O Creon!
Know'st thou what now I wish?
  Cre.   What is it? Speak.
  Œdi. That I may quit this fatal place.
  Cre.   Thou ask'st
What Heaven alone can grant.
  Œdi.   Alas! to Heaven
I am most hateful.
  Cre.   Yet shalt thou obtain
What thou desirest.
  Œdi.   Shall I indeed?
  Cre.   Thou shalt;
I never say aught that I do not mean.
  Œdi. Then let me go: may I depart?
  Cre.   Thou mayst;
But leave thy children.
  Œdi.   Do not take them from me.
  Cre. Thou must not always have thy will;
    already
Thou hast suffer'd for it.
  Cho.   Thebans! now behold
The great, the mighty Œdipus, who once
The sphinx's dark enigma could unfold;
Who less to fortune than to wisdom owed;
In virtue, as in rank, to all superior;
Yet fallen at last to deepest misery.
Let mortals hence be taught to look beyond
The present time, nor dare to say a man
Is happy, till the last decisive hour
Shall close his life without the taste of woe.

Plato

In the Phaedo Plato takes advantage of the incidents surrounding the death of Socrates to discuss the idea of immortality. In this dialogue he discusses his famous doctrine
of ideas. In reading the selections from the Phaedo
note (1) the moral issue involved in suicide, (2) the goal
of the true philosopher, (3) obstacles to the achievement
of this goal, (4) the discussion of immortality, (5) the
proof of immortality and the doctrine of ideas, and (6) the
similarity of Socrates' death to a Greek tragedy.

As translated by Benjamin Jowett in *The Dialogues of Plato*, 2nd ed., 5 vols., Clarendon Press, Oxford, 1875, I, 429–447; 460–461. Courtesy of the Jowett Copyright Fund.

From: THE PHAEDO

Persons of the Dialogue:
> Phaedo, who is the narrator of the
> Dialogue to
> Echecrates of Phlius.
> Socrates.
> Attendant of the Prison.
> Apollodorus.
> Simmias.
> Cebes.
> Crito.

Scene: The prison of Socrates.

Place of the Narration:—Phlius.

Echecrates. Were you yourself, Phaedo, in the prison with Socrates on the day when he drank the poison?

Phaedo. Yes, Echecrates, I was.

Ech. I should so like to hear about his death. What did he say in his last hours? We were informed that he died by taking poison, but no one knew anything more; for no Phliusian ever goes to Athens now, and it is a long time since any stranger from Athens has found his way hither; so that we had no clear account.

Phaed. Did you not hear of the proceedings at the trial?

Ech. Yes; some one told us about the trial, and we could not understand why, having been condemned, he should have been put to death, not at the time, but long afterwards. What was the reason of this?

Phaed. An accident, Echecrates: the stern of the ship which the Athenians sent to Delos happened to have been crowned on the day before he was tried.

Ech. What is this ship?

Phaed. It is the ship in which, according to Athenian tradition, Theseus went to Crete when he took with him the fourteen youths, and was the saviour of them and of himself. And they are said to have vowed to Apollo at the time, that if they were saved they would send a yearly mission to Delos. Now this custom still continues, and the whole period of the voyage to and from Delos, beginning when the priest of Apollo crowns the stern of the ship, is a holy season, during which the city is not allowed to be polluted by public executions; and when the vessel is detained by contrary winds, the time spent in going and returning is very considerable. As I was saying, the ship was crowned on the day before the trial, and this was the reason why Socrates lay in prison and was not put to death until long after he was condemned.

Ech. What was the manner of his death, Phaedo? What was said or done? And which of his friends were with him? Or did the authorities forbid them to be present—so that he had no friends near him when he died?

Phaed. No; there were several of them with him.

Ech. If you have nothing to do, I wish that you would tell me what passed, as exactly as you can.

Phaed. I have nothing at all to do, and will try to gratify your wish. To be reminded of Socrates is always the greatest delight to me, whether I speak myself or hear another speak of him.

Ech. You will have listeners who are of the same mind with you, and I hope that you will be as exact as you can.

Phaed. I had a singular feeling at being in his company. For I could hardly believe that I was present at the death of a friend, and therefore I did not pity him, Echecrates; he died so fearlessly, and his words and bearing were so noble and gracious, that to me he appeared blessed. I thought that in going to the other world he could not be without a divine call, and that he would be happy, if any man ever was, when he arrived there; and therefore I did not pity him as might have seemed natural at such an hour. But I had not the pleasure which I usually feel in philosophical discourse (for philosophy was the theme of which we spoke). I was pleased, but in the pleasure there was also a strange admixture of pain; for I reflected that he was soon to die, and this double feeling was shared by us all; we were laughing and weeping by turns, especially the excitable Apollodorus—you know the sort of man?

Ech. Yes.

Phaed. He was quite beside himself; and I and all of us were greatly moved.

Ech. Who were present?

Phaed. Of native Athenians there were, besides Apollodorus, Critobulus and his father Crito, Hermogenes, Epigenes, Aeschines, Antisthenes; likewise Ctesippus of the deme of Paeania, Menexenus, and some others; Plato, if I am not mistaken, was ill.

Ech. Were there any strangers?

Phaed. Yes, there were; Simmias the Theban, and Cebes, and Phaedondes; Euclid and Terpsion, who came from Megara.

Ech. And was Aristippus there, and Cleombrotus?

Phaed. No, they were said to be in Aegina.

Ech. Any one else?

Phaed. I think that these were nearly all.

Ech. Well, and what did you talk about?

Phaed. I will begin at the beginning and endeavour to repeat the entire conversation. On the previous days we had been in the habit of assembling early in the morning at the court in which the trial took place, and which is not far from the prison. There we used to wait talking with one another until the opening of the doors (for they were not opened very early); then we went in and generally passed the day with Socrates. On the last morning we assembled sooner than usual, having heard on the day before when we quitted the prison in the evening that the sacred ship had come from Delos; and so we arranged to meet very early at the accustomed place. On our arrival the jailer who answered the door, instead of admitting us, came out and told us to stay until he called us. "For the Eleven," he said, "are now with Socrates; they are taking off his chains, and giving orders that he is to die today." He soon returned and said that we might come in. On entering we found Socrates just released from chains, and Xanthippe, whom you know, sitting by him, and holding his child in her arms. When she saw us she uttered a cry and said, as women will: "O Socrates, this is the last time that either you will converse with your friends, or they with you." Socrates turned to Crito and said: "Crito, let some one take her home." Some of Crito's people accordingly led her away, crying out and beating herself. And when she was gone,

Socrates, sitting up on the couch, bent and rubbed his leg, saying, as he was rubbing: How singular is the thing called pleasure, and how curiously related to pain, which might be thought to be the opposite of it; for they are never present to a man at the same instant, and yet he who pursues either is generally compelled to take the other; their bodies are two, but they are joined by a single head. And I cannot help thinking that if Aesop had remembered them, he would have made a fable about God trying to reconcile their strife, and how, when he could not, he fastened their heads together; and this is the reason why when one comes the other follows: as I know by my own experience now, when after the pain in my leg which was caused by the chain, pleasure appears to succeed.

Upon this Cebes said: I am glad, Socrates, that you have mentioned the name of Aesop. For it reminds me of a question which has been asked by many, and was asked of me only the day before yesterday by Evenus the poet—he will be sure to ask it again, and therefore if you would like me to have an answer ready for him, you may as well tell me what I should say to him:—he wanted to know why you, who never before wrote a line of poetry, now that you are in prison are turning Aesop's fables into verse, and also composing that hymn in honour of Apollo.

Tell him, Cebes, he replied, what is the truth—that I had no idea of rivalling him or his poems; to do so, as I knew, would be no easy task. But I wanted to see whether I could purge away a scruple which I felt about the meaning of certain dreams. In the course of my life I have often had intimations in dreams "that I should compose music." The same dream came to me sometimes in one form, and sometimes in another, but always saying the same or nearly the same words: "Cultivate and make music," said the dream. And hitherto I had imagined that this was only intended to exhort and encourage me in the study of philosophy, which has been the pursuit of my life, and is the noblest and best of music. The dream was bidding me do what I was already doing, in the same way that the competitor in a race is bidden by the spectators to run when he is already running. But I was not certain of this;

for the dream might have meant music in the popular sense of the word, and being under sentence of death, and the festival giving me a respite, I thought that it would be safer for me to satisfy the scruple, and, in obedience to the dream, to compose a few verses before I departed. And first I made a hymn in honour of the god of the festival, and then considering that a poet, if he is really to be a poet, should not only put together words, but should invent stories, and that I have no invention, I took some fables of Aesop, which I had ready at hand and which I knew—they were the first I came upon—and turned them into verse. Tell this to Evenus, Cebes, and bid him be of good cheer; say that I would have him come after me if he be a wise man, and not tarry; and that today I am likely to be going, for the Athenians say that I must.

Simmias said: What a message for such a man! Having been a frequent companion of his I should say that, as far as I know him, he will never take your advice unless he is obliged.

Why, said Socrates,—is not Evenus a philosopher?

I think that he is, said Simmias.

Then he, or any man who has the spirit of philosophy, will be willing to die; but he will not take his own life, for that is held to be unlawful.

Here he changed his position, and put his legs off the couch on to the ground, and during the rest of the conversation he remained sitting.

Why do you say, enquired Cebes, that a man ought not to take his own life, but that the philosopher will be ready to follow the dying?

Socrates replied: And have you, Cebes and Simmias, who are the disciples of Philolaus, never heard him speak of this?

Yes, but his language was obscure, Socrates.

My words, too, are only an echo; but there is no reason why I should not repeat what I have heard: and, indeed, as I am going to another place, it is very meet for me to be thinking and talking of the nature of the pilgrimage which I am about to make. What can I do better in the interval between this and the setting of the sun?

Then tell me, Socrates, why is suicide held to be unlawful? as I have certainly heard Philolaus, about whom you were just now asking, affirm when he was staying with us at Thebes; and there are others who say the same, although I have never understood what was meant by any of them.

Do not lose heart, replied Socrates, and the day may come when you will understand. I suppose that you wonder why, when other things which are evil may be good at certain times and to certain persons, death is to be the only exception, and why, when a man is better dead, he is not permitted to be his own benefactor, but must wait for the hand of another.

Very true, said Cebes, laughing gently and speaking in his native Boeotian.

I admit the appearance of inconsistency in what I am saying; but there may not be any real inconsistency after all. There is a doctrine whispered in secret that man is a prisoner who has no right to open the door and run away; this is a great mystery which I do not quite understand. Yet I too believe that the gods are our guardians, and that we men are a possession of theirs. Do you not agree?

Yes, I quite agree, said Cebes.

And if one of your own possessions, an ox or an ass, for example, took the liberty of putting himself out of the way when you had given no intimation of your wish that he should die, would you not be angry with him, and would you not punish him if you could?

Certainly, replied Cebes.

Then, if we look at the matter thus, there may be reason in saying that a man should wait, and not take his own life until God summons him, as he is now summoning me.

Yes, Socrates, said Cebes, there seems to be truth in what you say. And yet how can you reconcile this seemingly true belief that God is our guardian and we his possessions, with the willingness to die which you were just now attributing to the philosopher? That the wisest of men should be willing to leave a service in which they are ruled by the gods, who are the best of rulers, is not reasonable; for surely no wise man thinks that when set at liberty he can take better care of himself than the gods take of him. A fool may perhaps think so—he may argue that he had better run away from his master, not considering that his duty is to remain to the end, and not to run away from the good, and that there would be no sense in his running away. The wise man will want to be ever with him who is better than himself. Now this, Socrates, is the reverse of what was just now said; for upon this view the wise man should sorrow and the fool rejoice at passing out of life.

The earnestness of Cebes seemed to please Socrates. Here, said he, turning to us, is a man who is always enquiring, and is not so easily convinced by the first thing which he hears.

And certainly, added Simmias, the objection which he is now making does appear to me to have some force. For what can be the meaning of a truly wise man wanting to fly away and lightly leave a master who is better than himself? And I rather imagine that Cebes is referring to you; he thinks that you are too ready to leave us, and too ready to leave the gods whom you acknowledge to be our good masters.

Yes, replied Socrates; there is reason in what you say. And so you think that I ought to answer your indictment as if I were in a court?

We should like you to do so, said Simmias.

Then I must try to make a more successful defence before you than I did before the judges. For I am quite ready to admit, Simmias and Cebes, that I ought to be grieved at death, if I were not persuaded in the first place that I am going to other gods who are wise and good (of which I am as certain as I can be of any such matters), and secondly (though I am not so sure of this last) to men departed, better than those whom I leave behind; and therefore I do not grieve as I might have done, for I have good hope that there is yet something remaining for the dead, and as has been said of old, some far better thing for the good than for the evil.

But do you mean to take away your thoughts with you, Socrates? said Simmias. Will you not impart them to us?—for they are a benefit in which we too are entitled to share. Moreover, if you succeed in convincing us, that will be an answer to the charge against yourself.

I will do my best, replied Socrates. But you must first let me hear what Crito wants; he has long been wishing to say something to me.

Only this, Socrates, replied Crito:—the attendant who is to give you the poison has been telling me, and he wants me to tell you, that you are not to talk much; talking, he says, increases heat, and this is apt to interfere with the action of the poison; persons who excite themselves are sometimes obliged to take a second or even a third dose.

Then, said Socrates, let him mind his business and be prepared to give the poison twice or even thrice if necessary; that is all.

I knew quite well what you would say, replied Crito; but I was obliged to satisfy him.

Never mind him, he said.

And now, O my judges, I desire to prove to you that the real philosopher has reason to be of good cheer when he is about to die, and that after death he may hope to obtain the greatest good in the other world. And how this may be, Simmias and Cebes, I will endeavour to explain. For I deem that the true votary of philosophy is likely to be misunderstood by other men; they do not perceive that he is always pursuing death and dying; and if this be so, and he has had the desire of death all his life long, why when his time comes should he repine at that which he had been always pursuing and desiring?

Simmias said laughingly: Though not in a laughing humour, you have made me laugh, Socrates; for I cannot help thinking that the many when they hear your words will say how truly you have described philosophers, and our people at home will likewise say that the life which philosophers desire is in reality death, and that they have found them out to be deserving of the death which they desire.

And they are right, Simmias, in thinking so, with the exception of the words "they have found them out"; for they have not found out either what is the nature of that death which the true philosopher deserves, or how he deserves or desires death. But enough of them: —let us discuss the matter among ourselves. Do we believe that there is such a thing as death?

To be sure, replied Simmias.

Is it not the separation of soul and body? And to be dead is the completion of this; when the soul exists in herself, and is released from the body and the body is released from the soul, what is this but death?

Just so, he replied.

There is another question, which will probably throw light on our present enquiry if you and I can agree about it:—Ought the philosopher to care about the pleasures—if they are to be called pleasures—of eating and drinking?

Certainly not, answered Simmias.

And what about the pleasures of love—should he care for them?

By no means.

And will he think much of the other ways of indulging the body, for example, the acquisition of costly raiment, or sandals, or other adornments of the body? Instead of caring about them, does he not rather despise anything more than nature needs? What do you say?

I should say that the true philosopher would despise them.

Would you not say that he is entirely concerned with the soul and not with the body? He would like, as far as he can, to get away from the body and to turn to the soul.

Quite true.

In matters of this sort philosophers, above all other men, may be observed in every sort of way to dissever the soul from the communion of the body.

Very true.

Whereas, Simmias, the rest of the world are of opinion that to him who has no sense of pleasure and no part in bodily pleasure, life is not worth having; and that he who is indifferent about them is as good as dead.

That is also true.

What again shall we say of the actual acquirement of knowledge?—is the body, if invited to share in the enquiry, a hinderer or a helper? I mean to say, have sight and hearing any truth in them? Are they not, as the poets are always telling us, inaccurate witnesses? and yet, if even they are inaccurate and indistinct, what is to be said of the other senses?—for you will allow that they are the best of them?

Certainly, he replied.

Then when does the soul attain truth?—for in attempting to consider anything in company with the body she is obviously deceived.

True.

Then must not true existence be revealed to her in thought, if at all?

Yes.

And thought is best when the mind is gathered into herself and none of these things trouble her—neither sounds nor sights nor pain nor any pleasure,—when she takes leave of the body, and has as little as possible to do with it, when she has no bodily sense or desire, but is aspiring after true being?

Certainly.

And in this the philosopher dishonours the body; his soul runs away from his body and desires to be alone and by herself?

That is true.

Well, but there is another thing, Simmias: Is there or is there not an absolute justice?

Assuredly there is.

And an absolute beauty and absolute good?

Of course.

But did you ever behold any of them with your eyes?

Certainly not.

Or did you ever reach them with any other bodily sense?—and I speak not of these alone, but of absolute greatness, and health, and strength, and of the essence or true nature of everything. Has the reality of them ever been perceived by you through the bodily organs? or rather, is not the nearest approach to the knowledge of their several natures made by him who so orders his intellectual vision as to have the most exact conception of the essence of each thing which he considers?

Certainly.

And he attains to the purest knowledge of them who goes to each with the mind alone, not introducing or intruding in the act of thought sight or any other sense together with reason, but with the very light of the mind in her own clearness searches into the very truth of each; he who has got rid, as far as he can, of eyes and ears and, so to speak, of the whole body, these being in his opinion distracting elements which when they infect the soul hinder her from acquiring truth and knowledge—who, if not he, is likely to attain to the knowledge of true being?

What you say has a wonderful truth in it, Socrates, replied Simmias.

And when real philosophers consider all these things, will they not be led to make a reflection which they will express in words something like the following? "Have we not found," they will say, "a path of thought which seems to bring us and our argument to the conclusion, that while we are in the body, and while the soul is infected with the evils of the body, our desire will not be satisfied, and our desire is of the truth? For the body is a source of endless trouble to us by reason of the mere requirement of food; and is liable also to diseases which overtake and impede us in the search after true being: it fills us full of loves, and lusts, and fears, and fancies of all kinds, and endless foolery, and, in fact, as men say, takes away from us the power of thinking at all. Whence come wars, and fightings, and factions? whence but from the body and the lusts of the body? Wars are occasioned by the love of money, and money has to be acquired for the sake and service of the body; and by reason of all these impediments we have no time to give to philosophy; and, last and worst of all, even if we are at leisure and betake ourselves to some speculation, the body is always breaking in upon us, causing turmoil and confusion in our enquiries, and so amazing us that we are prevented from seeing the truth. It has been proved to us by experience that if we would have pure knowledge of anything we must be quit of the body—the soul in herself must behold things in themselves: and then we shall attain the wisdom which we desire, and of which we say that we are lovers; not while we live, but after death; for if while in company with the body, the soul cannot have pure knowledge, one of two things follows—either knowledge is not to be attained at all, or, if at all, after death. For then, and not till then, the soul will be parted from the body and exist in herself alone. In this present life, I reckon that we make the nearest approach to knowledge when we have the least possible intercourse or communion with the body, and are not surfeited with the bodily nature, but keep ourselves pure until the hour when God himself is pleased to release us. And thus having got rid of the foolishness of the body we shall be pure and hold converse with the pure, and know of ourselves the clear light everywhere, which is no other than the light of truth." For the impure are not permitted to approach the pure. These are the sort of words, Simmias,

which the true lovers of knowledge cannot help saying to one another, and thinking. You would agree; would you not?

Undoubtedly, Socrates.

But, O my friend, if this be true, there is great reason to hope that, going whither I go, when I have come to the end of my journey, I shall attain that which has been the pursuit of my life. And therefore I go on my way rejoicing, and not I only, but every other man who believes that his mind has been made ready and that he is in a manner purified.

Certainly, replied Simmias.

And what is purification but the separation of the soul from the body, as I was saying before; the habit of the soul gathering and collecting herself into herself from all sides out of the body; the dwelling in her own place alone, as in another life, so also in this, as far as she can;—the release of the soul from the chains of the body?

Very true, he said.

And this separation and release of the soul from the body is termed death?

To be sure, he said.

And the true philosophers, and they only, are ever seeking to release the soul. Is not the separation and release of the soul from the body their especial study?

That is true.

And, as I was saying at first, there would be a ridiculous contradiction in men studying to live as nearly as they can in a state of death, and yet repining when it comes upon them.

Clearly.

And the true philosophers, Simmias, are always occupied in the practice of dying, wherefore also to them least of all men is death terrible. Look at the matter thus:—if they have been in every way the enemies of the body, and are wanting to be alone with the soul, when this desire of theirs is granted, how inconsistent would they be if they trembled and repined, instead of rejoicing at their departure to that place where, when they arrive, they hope to gain that which in life they desired—and this was wisdom—and at the same time to be rid of the company of their enemy. Many a man has been willing to go to the world below animated by the hope of seeing there an earthly love, or wife, or son, and conversing with them. And will he who is a true lover of wisdom, and is strongly persuaded in like manner that only in the world below he can worthily enjoy her, still repine at death? Will he not depart with joy? Surely he will, O my friend, if he be a true philosopher. For he will have a firm conviction that there, and there only, he can find wisdom in her purity. And if this be true, he would be very absurd, as I was saying, if he were afraid of death.

He would indeed, replied Simmias.

And when you see a man who is repining at the approach of death, is not his reluctance a sufficient proof that he is not a lover of wisdom, but a lover of the body, and probably at the same time a lover of either money or power, or both?

Quite so, he replied.

And is not courage, Simmias, a quality which is especially characteristic of the philosopher?

Certainly.

There is temperance again, which even by the vulgar is supposed to consist in the control and regulation of the passions, and in the sense of superiority to them—is not temperance a virtue belonging to those only who despise the body, and who pass their lives in philosophy?

Most assuredly.

For the courage and temperance of other men, if you will consider them, are really a contradiction.

How so?

Well, he said, you are aware that death is regarded by men in general as a great evil.

Very true, he said.

And do not courageous men face death because they are afraid of yet greater evils?

That is quite true.

Then all but the philosophers are courageous only from fear, and because they are afraid; and yet that a man should be courageous from fear, and because he is a coward, is surely a strange thing.

Very true.

And are not the temperate exactly in the same case? They are temperate because they are intemperate—which might seem to be a contradiction, but is nevertheless the sort of thing which happens with this foolish temperance. For there are pleasures which they are

afraid of losing; and in their desire to keep them, they abstain from some pleasures, because they are overcome by others; and although to be conquered by pleasure is called by men intemperance, to them the conquest of pleasure consists in being conquered by pleasure. And that is what I mean by saying that, in a sense, they are made temperate through intemperance.

Such appears to be the case.

Yet the exchange of one fear or pleasure or pain for another fear or pleasure or pain, and of the greater for the less, as if they were coins, is not the exchange of virtue. O my blessed Simmias, is there not one true coin for which all things ought to be exchanged?—and that is wisdom; and only in exchange for this, and in company with this, is anything truly bought or sold, whether courage or temperance or justice. And is not all true virtue the companion of wisdom, no matter what fears or pleasures or other similar goods or evils may or may not attend her? But the virtue which is made up of these goods, when they are severed from wisdom and exchanged with one another, is a shadow of virtue only, nor is there any freedom or health or truth in her; but in the true exchange there is a purging away of all these things, and temperance, and justice, and courage, and wisdom herself are the purgation of them. The founders of the mysteries would appear to have had a real meaning, and were not talking nonsense when they intimated in a figure long ago that he who passes unsanctified and uninitiated into the world below will lie in a slough, but that he who arrives there after initiation and purification will dwell with the gods. For "many," as they say in the mysteries, "are the thyrsus-bearers, but few are the mystics,"—meaning, as I interpret the words, "the true philosophers." In the number of whom, during my whole life, I have been seeking, according to my ability, to find a place;—whether I have sought in a right way or not, and whether I have succeeded or not, I shall truly know in a little while, if God will, when I myself arrive in the other world—such is my belief. And therefore I maintain that I am right, Simmias and Cebes, in not grieving or repining at parting from you and my masters in this world, for I believe that I shall equally find good masters and friends in another world. But most men do not believe this saying; if then I succeed in convincing you by my defence better than I did the Athenian judges, it will be well.

Cebes answered: I agree, Socrates, in the greater part of what you say. But in what concerns the soul, men are apt to be incredulous; they fear that when she has left the body her place may be nowhere, and that on the very day of death she may perish and come to an end—immediately on her release from the body, issuing forth dispersed like smoke or air and in her flight vanishing away into nothingness. If she could only be collected into herself after she has obtained release from the evils of which you were speaking, there would be good reason to hope, Socrates, that what you say is true. But surely it requires a great deal of argument and many proofs to show that when the man is dead his soul yet exists, and has any force or intelligence.

True, Cebes, said Socrates; and shall I suggest that we converse a little of the probabilities of these things?

I am sure, said Cebes, that I should greatly like to know your opinion about them.

I reckon, said Socrates, that no one who heard me now, not even if he were one of my old enemies, the comic poets, could accuse me of idle talking about matters in which I have no concern:—If you please, then, we will proceed with the enquiry.

Suppose we consider the question whether the souls of men after death are or are not in the world below. There comes into my mind an ancient doctrine which affirms that they go from hence into the other world, and returning hither, are born again from the dead. Now, if it be true that the living come from the dead, then our souls must exist in the other world, for if not, how could they have been born again? And this would be conclusive, if there were any real evidence that the living are only born from the dead; but if this is not so, then other arguments will have to be adduced.

Very true, replied Cebes.

Then let us consider the whole question, not in relation to man only, but in relation to animals generally, and to plants, and to everything of which there is generation, and the proof will be easier. Are not all things which have opposites generated out of their opposites? I mean such things as good and evil, just and unjust—and there are innumerable other opposites which are generated out of opposites. And I want to show that in all opposites there is of necessity a similar alternation; I mean to say, for example, that anything which becomes greater must become greater after being less.

True.

And that which becomes less must have been once greater and then have become less.

Yes.

And the weaker is generated from the stronger, and the swifter from the slower.

Very true.

And the worse is from the better, and the more just is from the more unjust.

Of course.

And is this true of all opposites? and are we convinced that all of them are generated out of opposites?

Yes.

And in this universal opposition of all things, are there not also two intermediate processes which are ever going on, from one to the other opposite, and back again; where there is a greater and a less there is also an intermediate process of increase and diminution, and that which grows is said to wax, and that which decays to wane?

Yes, he said.

And there are many other processes, such as division and composition, cooling and heating, which equally involve a passage into and out of one another. And this necessarily holds of all opposites, even though not always expressed in words—they are really generated out of one another, and there is a passing or process from one to the other of them?

Very true, he replied.

Well, and is there not an opposite of life, as sleep is the opposite of waking?

True, he said.

And what is it?

Death, he answered.

And these, if they are opposites, are generated the one from the other, and have their two intermediate processes also?

Of course.

Now, said Socrates, I will analyze one of the two pairs of opposites which I have mentioned to you, and also its intermediate processes, and you shall analyze the other to me. One of them I term sleep, the other waking. The state of sleep is opposed to the state of waking, and out of sleeping waking is generated, and out of waking, sleeping; and the process of generation is in the one case falling asleep, and in the other waking up. Do you agree?

I entirely agree.

Then suppose that you analyze life and death to me in the same manner. Is not death opposed to life?

Yes.

And they are generated one from the other?

Yes.

What is generated from the living?

The dead.

And what from the dead?

I can only say in answer—the living.

Then the living, whether things or persons, Cebes, are generated from the dead?

That is clear, he replied.

Then the inference is that our souls exist in the world below?

That is true.

And one of the two processes or generations is visible—for surely the act of dying is visible?

Surely, he said.

What then is to be the result? Shall we exclude the opposite process? and shall we suppose nature to walk on one leg only? Must we not rather assign to death some corresponding process of generation?

Certainly, he replied.

And what is that process?

Return to life.

And return to life, if there be such a thing, is the birth of the dead into the world of the living?

Quite true.

Then here is a new way by which we arrive at the conclusion that the living come from the dead, just as the dead come from the living; and this, if true, affords a most certain proof that the souls of the dead exist in some place out of which they come again.

Yes, Socrates, he said; the conclusion seems to flow necessarily out of our previous admissions.

And that these admissions were not unfair, Cebes, he said, may be shown, I think, as follows: If generation were in a straight line only, and there were no compensation or circle in nature, no turn or return of elements into their opposites, then you know that all things would at last have the same form and pass into the same state, and there would be no more generation of them.

What do you mean? he said.

A simple thing enough, which I will illustrate by the case of sleep, he replied. You know that if there were no alternation of sleeping and waking, the tale of the sleeping Endymion would in the end have no meaning, because all other things would be asleep too, and he would not be distinguishable from the rest. Or if there were composition only, and no division of substances, then the chaos of Anaxagoras would come again. And in like manner, my dear Cebes, if all things which partook of life were to die, and after they were dead remained in the form of death, and did not come to life again, all would at last die, and nothing would be alive—what other result could there be? For if the living spring from any other things, and they too die, must not all things at last be swallowed up in death?

There is no escape, Socrates, said Cebes; and to me your argument seems to be absolutely true.

Yes, he said, Cebes, it is and must be so, in my opinion; and we have not been deluded in making these admissions; but I am confident that there truly is such a thing as living again, and that the living spring from the dead, and that the souls of the dead are in existence and that the good souls have a better portion than the evil.

Cebes added: Your favourite doctrine, Socrates, that knowledge is simply recollection, if true, also necessarily implies a previous time in which we have learned that which we now recollect. But this would be impossible unless our soul had been in some place before existing in the form of man; here then is another proof of the soul's immortality. . . .

The lovers of knowledge are conscious that the soul was simply fastened and glued to the body—until philosophy received her, she could only view real existence through the bars of a prison, not in and through herself; she was wallowing in the mire of every sort of ignorance, and by reason of lust had become the principal accomplice in her own captivity. This was her original state; and then, as I was saying, and as the lovers of knowledge are well aware, philosophy, seeing how terrible was her confinement, of which she was herself the cause, received and gently comforted her and sought to release her, pointing out that the eye and the ear and the other senses are full of deception, and persuading her to retire from them, and abstain from all the necessary use of them, and be gathered up and collected into herself, bidding her trust in herself and her own pure apprehension of pure existence, and to mistrust whatever comes to her through other channels and is subject to variation; for such things are visible and tangible, but what she sees in her own nature is intelligible and invisible. And the soul of the true philosopher thinks that she ought not to resist this deliverance, and therefore abstains from pleasures and desires and pains and fears, as far as she is able; reflecting that when a man has great joys or sorrows or fears or desires, he suffers from them, not merely the sort of evil which might be anticipated—as, for example, the loss of his health or property which he has sacrificed to his lusts—but an evil greater far, which is the greatest and worst of all evils, and one of which he never thinks.

What is it, Socrates? said Cebes.

The evil is that when the feeling of pleasure or pain is most intense, every soul of man imagines the objects of this intense feeling to be then plainest and truest: but this is not so, they are really the things of sight.

Very true.

And is not this the state in which the soul is most enthralled by the body?

How so?

Why, because each pleasure and pain is a sort of nail which nails and rivets the soul to the body, until she becomes like the body, and believes that to be true which the body affirms to be true; and from agreeing with the body and having the same delights she is obliged to have the same habits and haunts, and is not likely ever to be pure at her departure to the world below, but is always infected by the body; and so she sinks into another body and there germinates and grows, and has therefore no part in the communion of the divine and pure and simple.

Most true, Socrates, answered Cebes.

And this, Cebes, is the reason why the true lovers of knowledge are temperate and brave; and not for the reason which the world gives.

Certainly not.

Certainly not! The soul of a philosopher will reason in quite another way; she will not ask philosophy to release her in order that when released she may deliver herself up again to the thraldom of pleasures and pains, doing a work only to be outdone again, weaving instead of unweaving her Penelope's web. But she will calm passion, and follow reason, and dwell in the contemplation of her, beholding the true and divine (which is not matter of opinion), and thence deriving nourishment. Thus she seeks to live while she lives, and after death she hopes to go to her own kindred and to that which is like her, and to be freed from human ills. Never fear, Simmias and Cebes, that a soul which has been thus nurtured and has had these pursuits, will at her departure from the body be scattered and blown away by the winds and be nowhere and nothing. . . .

When he had spoken these words, he arose and went into a chamber to bathe; Crito followed him and told us to wait. So we remained behind, talking and thinking of the subject of discourse, and also of the greatness of our sorrow; he was like a father of whom we were being bereaved, and we were about to pass the rest of our lives as orphans. When he had taken the bath his children were brought to him (he had two young sons and an elder one); and the women of his family also came, and he talked to them and gave them a few directions in the presence of Crito; then he dismissed them and returned to us.

Now the hour of sunset was near, for a good deal of time had passed while he was within. When he came out, he sat down with us again after his bath, but not much was said. Soon the jailer, who was the servant of the Eleven, entered and stood by him, saying:—To you, Socrates, whom I know to be the noblest and gentlest and best of all who ever came to this place, I will not impute the angry feeling of other men, who rage and swear at me, when, in obedience to the authorities, I bid them drink the poison—indeed, I am sure that you will not be angry with me; for others, as you are aware, and not I, are to blame. And so fare you well, and try to bear lightly what must needs be—you know my errand. Then bursting into tears he turned away and went out.

Socrates looked at him and said: I return your good wishes, and will do as you bid. Then turning to us, he said, How charming the man is: since I have been in prison he has always been coming to see me, and at times he would talk to me, and was as good to me as could be, and now see how generously he sorrows on my account. We must do as he says, Crito; and therefore let the cup be brought, if the poison is prepared: if not, let the attendant prepare some.

Yet, said Crito, the sun is still upon the hill-tops, and I know that many a one has taken the draught late, and after the announcement has been made to him, he has eaten and drunk, and enjoyed the society of his beloved: do not hurry—there is time enough.

Socrates said: Yes, Crito, and they of whom you speak are right in so acting, for they think that they will be gainers by the delay; but I am right in not following their example, for I do not think that I should gain anything by drinking the poison a little later; I should only be ridiculous in my own eyes for sparing and saving a life which is already forfeit. Please then to do as I say, and not to refuse me.

Crito made a sign to the servant, who was standing by; and he went out, and having been absent for some time, returned with the jailer carrying the cup of poison. Socrates said: You, my good friend, who are experienced in these matters, shall give me directions how I am to proceed. The man answered: You have only to walk about until your legs are heavy, and then to lie down, and the poison will act. At the same time he handed the cup to Socrates, who in the easiest and gentlest manner, without the least fear or change of colour or feature, look-ing at the man with all his eyes, Echecrates, as his manner was, took the cup and said: What do you say about making a libation out of this cup to any god? May I, or not? The man answered: We only prepare, Socrates, just so much as we deem enough. I understand, he

said: but I may and must ask the gods to pros-per my journey from this to the other world—even so—and so be it according to my prayer. Then raising the cup to his lips, quite readily and cheerfully he drank off the poison. And hitherto most of us had been able to control our sorrow; but now when we saw him drinking, and saw too that he had finished the draught, we could no longer forbear, and in spite of my-self my own tears were flowing fast; so that I covered my face and wept, not for him, but at the thought of my own calamity in having to part from such a friend. Nor was I the first; for Crito, when he found himself unable to re-strain his tears, had got up, and I followed; and at that moment, Apollodorus, who had been weeping all the time, broke out in a loud and passionate cry which made cowards of us all. Socrates alone retained his calmness: What is this strange outcry? he said. I sent away the women mainly in order that they might not misbehave in this way, for I have been told that a man should die in peace. Be quiet then, and have patience. When we heard his words we were ashamed, and refrained our tears; and he walked about until, as he said, his legs began to fail, and then he lay on his back, ac-cording to directions, and the man who gave him the poison now and then looked at his feet and legs; and after a while he pressed his foot hard, and asked him if he could feel; and he said, No; and then his leg, and so upwards and upwards, and showed us that he was cold and stiff. And he felt them himself, and said: When the poison reaches the heart, that will be the end. He was beginning to grow cold about the groin, when he uncovered his face, for he had covered himself up, and said—they were his last words—he said: Crito, I owe a cock to Asclepius; will you remember to pay the debt? The debt shall be paid, said Crito; is there any-thing else? There was no answer to this ques-tion; but in a minute or two a movement was heard, and the attendants uncovered him; his eyes were set, and Crito closed his eyes and mouth.

Such was the end, Echecrates, of our friend; concerning whom I may truly say, that of all men of his time whom I have known, he was the wisest and justest and best.

Lucretius

Lucretius (92–52 B.C.), a Roman poet, gave a classic exposition of the Hellenistic philosophy of Epicureanism in his poem, De Rerum Natura. As city-state loyalties disintegrated in the face of larger political units inherited from Alexander's day, Mediterranean peoples sought intellectual and emotional peace in philosophies of retreat and resignation. Men and women needed a philosophy which would provide them with a means of freeing their minds from the petty cares of daily life and from superstitious fears growing out of the uncertainties of existence. Lucretius found an answer in materialism based upon the atomic theories of the sixth-century, B.C., Greek philosopher-scientist, Democritus. Modifying the atomic theory to permit freedom of the human will, Lucretius developed a way of looking at life based upon the achievement of pleasure and the avoidance of pain as the highest good for man. Far from accepting an "Eat, drink, and be merry" attitude, Lucretius emphasized that man's greatest pleasure could be found in serenity of soul gained only by the elimination of all physical and mental pain and fear. In reading the selection below note (1) what Lucretius regarded as the greatest pleasures, (2) what could dispel man's fears, (3) his atomic theory, (4) means whereby freedom of the will could be reconciled, (5) evidences to support his atomic theory, (6) his view of creation and evolution, destruction and death, (7) the characteristic features of atoms, (8) his conception of infinity, and (9) his attitude toward the gods.

From: ON THE NATURE OF THINGS

It is sweet, when on the great sea the winds trouble its waters, to behold from land another's deep distress; not that it is a pleasure and delight that any should be afflicted, but because it is sweet to see from what evils you are yourself exempt. It is sweet also to look upon the mighty struggles of war arrayed along the plains without sharing yourself in the danger. But nothing is more welcome than to hold the lofty and serene positions well fortified by the learning of the wise, from which you may look down upon others and see them wandering all abroad and going astray in their search for the path of life, see the contest among them of intellect, the rivalry of birth, the striving night and day with surpassing effort to struggle up to the summit of power and be masters of the world. O miserable minds of men! O blinded breasts! in what darkness of life and in how great dangers is passed all this term of life whatever its duration! not choose to see that nature craves for itself nothing more than that the man from whose body pain holds aloof, should in mind enjoy a feeling of pleasure exempt from care and fear? Therefore in respect of the body's nature we see that but little is at

As translated by H. A. J. Munro in Lucretius, *On the Nature of Things* (De Rerum Natura), George Routledge and Sons, Ltd., London, and E. P. Dutton and Company, New York, n.d., 36–73. Courtesy of E. P. Dutton and Company.

all needed in order that such things as take away pain, should be able to spread before us many delights as well. Nor at times does nature herself want any greater solace, although there are no golden images of youths through the house holding in their right hands flaming lamps, for supply of light to the nightly banquet, though the house shines not with silver nor glitters with gold nor do the panelled and gilded roofs re-echo to the harp, what time, though these things be wanting, they spread themselves in groups on the soft grass beside a stream of water under the boughs of a high tree and at no great cost pleasantly refresh their bodies, above all when the weather smiles and the seasons of the year besprinkle the green grass with flowers. Nor do hot fevers sooner quit the body if you toss about on pictured tapestry and blushing purple, than if you must lie under a poor man's blanket. Wherefore since treasures avail nothing, in respect of our body nor birth nor the glory of kingly power advancing farther you must hold that they are of no service to the mind as well; unless may be when you see your legions swarm over the ground of the campus waging the mimicry of war, strengthened flank and rear by powerful reserves and great force of cavalry, and you marshal them equipped in arms and animated with one spirit, thereupon you find that religious scruples scared by these things fly panic-stricken from the mind; and that then fears of death leave the breast unembarrassed and free from care, when you see your fleet swarm forth and spread itself far and wide. But if we see that these things are food for laughter and mere mockeries, and in good truth the fears of men and dogging cares dread not the clash of arms and cruel weapons, if unabashed they mix among kings and kesars and stand not in awe of the glitter from gold nor the brilliant sheen of the purple robe, how can you doubt that this is wholly the prerogative of reason, when the whole of life withal is a struggle in the dark? for even as children are flurried and dread all things in the thick darkness, thus we in the daylight fear at times things not a whit more to be dreaded than those at which children shudder in the dark and fancy sure to be. This terror therefore and darkness of mind must be dispelled not by the rays of the sun and glittering shafts of day, but by the aspect and law of nature.

Now mark and I will explain by what motion the begetting bodies of matter do beget different things and after they are begotten again break them up, and by what force they are compelled so to do and what velocity is given to them for travelling through the great void: do you mind to give heed to my words. For verily matter does not cohere inseparably massed together, since we see that everything wanes and perceive that all things ebb as it were by length of time and that age withdraws them from our sight, though yet the sum is seen to remain unimpaired by reason that the bodies which quit each thing lessen the things from which they go, gift with increase those to which they have come, compel the former to grow old, the latter to come to their prime, and yet abide not with these. Thus the sum of things is ever renewed and mortals live by a reciprocal dependency. Some nations wax, others wane, and in a brief space the races of living things are changed and like runners hand over the lamp of life.

If you think that first-beginnings of things can stop and by stopping propagate new motions of things, you wander far astray from the path of true reason: since they travel about through void, the first-beginnings of things all must move on either by their own weight or haply by the stroke of another. For when during motion they have, as often happens, met and clashed, the result is a sudden rebounding in an opposite direction; and no wonder, since they are most hard and of weight proportioned to their solidity and nothing behind gets in their way. And that you may more clearly see that all bodies of matter are in restless movement, remember that there is no lowest point in the sum of the universe, and that first bodies have not where to take their stand, since space is without end and limit and extends immeasurably in all directions round, as I have shewn in many words, and as has been proved by sure reason. Since this then is a certain truth, sure enough no rest is given to first bodies throughout the unfathomable void, but driven on rather in ceaseless and varied motion they partly, after they have pressed together, rebound leaving great spaces between, while in part they are so dashed away after the stroke as to leave but small spaces between. And all that form a denser aggregation when brought together and rebound leaving trifling spaces between, held fast by their own close-tangled shapes, these form enduring bases of stone and unyielding bodies of iron and such like. But those which spring far off and rebound far leaving great spaces between, these furnish us with thin air and bright sunlight. And many more travel along the great void, which have been thrown off from the unions of things or though admitted have yet in no case been able likewise to assimilate their motions. Of this truth, even as I relate it, we have a representation and picture always going on before our eyes and present to us: observe whenever the rays are let in and pour the sunlight through the dark chambers of houses: you will see many minute bodies in many ways through the apparent void mingle in the midst of the light of the rays, and as in never-ending conflict skirmish and give battle combating in troops and never halting, driven about in frequent meetings and partings; so that you may guess from this, what it is for first-beginnings of things to be ever tossing about in the great void. So far as it goes, a small thing may give an illustration of great things and put you on the track of knowledge. And for this reason too it is meet that you should give greater heed to these bodies which are seen to tumble about in the sun's rays, because such tumblings imply that motions also of matter latent and unseen are at the bottom. For you will observe many things there impelled by unseen blows to change their course and driven back to return the way they came now this way now that way in all directions round. All you are to know derive this restlessness from the first-beginnings. For the first-beginnings of things move first of themselves; next those bodies which form a small aggregate and come nearest so to say to the powers of the first-beginnings, are impelled and set in movement by the unseen strokes of those first bodies, and they in turn stir up bodies which are a little larger. Thus motion mounts up from the first-beginnings and step by step issues forth to our senses, so that those bodies also move, which we can discern in the sunlight, though it is not clearly seen by what blows they so act.

Now what velocity is given to bodies of matter, you may apprehend, Memmius, in few words from this: when morning first sprinkles the earth with fresh light and the different birds flitting about the pathless woods through the buxom air fill all places with their clear notes, we see it to be plain and evident to all how suddenly the sun after rising is wont at such a time to overspread all things and clothe them with his light. But that heat which the sun emits and that bright light pass not through empty void; and therefore they are forced to travel more slowly, until they cleave through the waves so to speak of air. Nor do the several minute bodies of heat pass on one by one, but closely entangled and massed together; whereby at one and the same time they are pulled back by one another and are impeded from without, so that they are forced to travel more slowly. But the first-beginnings which are of solid singleness, when they pass through empty void and nothing delays them from without and they themselves, single from the nature of their parts, are borne with headlong endeavour towards the one single spot to which their efforts tend, they must sure enough surpass in velocity and be carried along much more swiftly than the light of the sun, and race through many times the extent of space in the same time in which the beams of the sun fill the heaven throughout. . . .

But some in opposition to this, being ignorant of matter, believe that nature cannot without the providence of the gods in such nice conformity to the ways of man vary the seasons of the year and bring forth crops, ay and procure all the other things, which divine pleasure the guide of life prompts men to approach, escorting them in person and enticing them by her fondlings to continue their races through the arts of Venus, that mankind may not come to an end. For when they suppose that the gods designed all things for the sake of men, they seem to me in all respects to have strayed most widely from true reason. For even if I did not know what first-beginnings are, yet this, judging by the very arrangements of heaven, I would venture to affirm, and led by many other circumstances to maintain, that the nature of the world has by no means been made for us by divine power: so great are the defects with which it stands encumbered. All which, Memmius, we will hereafter make clear to you: we will now go on to explain what remains to be told of motions.

Now methinks is the place, herein to prove this point also that no bodily thing can by its own power be borne upwards and travel upwards; that the bodies of flames may not in this matter lead you into error. For they are begotten with an upward tendency, and in the same direction receive increase, and goodly crops and trees grow upwards, though their weights, so far as in them is, all tend downwards. And when fires leap to the roofs of houses and with swift flame lick up rafters and beams, we are not to suppose that they do so spontaneously without a force pushing them up. Even thus blood discharged from our body spirts out and springs up on high and scatters gore about. See you not too with what force the liquid of water spits out logs and beams? the more we have pushed and forced them deep down and have pressed them in, many of us together, with all our might and much painful effort, with the greater avidity it vomits them up and casts them forth, so that they rise and start out more than half their length. And yet methinks we doubt not that these, so far as in them is, are all borne downwards through the empty void. In the same way flames also ought to be able, when squeezed out, to mount upward through the air, although their weights, so far as in them is, strive to draw them down. See you not too that the nightly meteors of heaven as they fly aloft draw after them long trails of flames in whatever direction nature has given them a passage? Do you not perceive stars and meteors fall to the earth? The sun also from the height of heaven sheds its heat on all sides and sows the field with light; to the earth therefore as well the sun's heat tends. Lightnings also you see fly athwart the rains: now from this side now from that fires burst from the clouds and rush about; the force of flame falls to the earth all round.

This point too herein we wish you to apprehend: when bodies are borne downwards sheer through void, at quite uncertain times and uncertain points of space they swerve a little from their equal poise: you just and only just can call it a change of inclination. If they were not used to swerve, they all would fall down, like drops of rain, through the deep void, and no clashing would have been begotten, nor blow produced among the first-beginnings: thus nature never would have produced aught.

But if haply any one believes that heavier bodies, as they are carried more quickly sheer through space, can fall from above on the lighter and so beget blows able to produce begetting motions, he goes most widely astray from true reason. For whenever bodies fall through water, and thin air, they must quicken their descents in proportion to their weights, because the body of water and subtle nature of air cannot retard everything in equal degree, but more readily give way, overpowered by the heavier: on the other hand empty void cannot offer resistance to anything in any direction at any time, but must, as its nature craves, continually give way; and for this reason all things must be moved and borne along with equal velocity though of unequal weights through the unresisting void. Therefore heavier things will never be able to fall from above on lighter nor of themselves to beget blows sufficient to produce the varied motions by which nature carries on things. Wherefore again and again I say bodies must swerve a little; and yet no more than the least possible; lest we be found to be imagining oblique motions and this the reality should refute. For this we see to be plain and evident, that weights, so far as in them is, cannot travel obliquely, when they fall from above, at least so far as you can perceive; but that nothing can swerve in any case from the straight course, who is there that can perceive?

Again if all motion is ever linked together and a new motion ever springs from another in a fixed order and first-beginnings do not by swerving make some commencement of motion to break through the decrees of fate, that cause follow not cause from everlasting, whence have all living creatures here on earth, whence, I ask, has been wrested from the fates the power by which we go forward whither the will leads each, by which likewise we change the direction of our motions neither at a fixed time nor fixed place, but where and when the mind itself has prompted? For beyond a doubt in these things his own will makes for each a beginning and from this beginning motions are willed through the limbs. See you not too, when the barriers are thrown open at a given moment, that yet the eager powers of the horses cannot start forward so instantaneously as the mind itself desires? the whole store of matter through the whole body must be sought out, in order that stirred up through all the frame it may follow with undivided effort the bent of the mind; so that you see the beginning of motion is born from the heart, and the action first commences in the will of the mind and next is transmitted through the whole body and frame. Quite different is the case when we move on propelled by a stroke inflicted by the strong might and strong compulsion of another; for then it is quite clear that all the matter of the whole body moves and is hurried on against our inclination until the will has reined it in throughout the limbs. Do you see then in this case that, though an outward force often pushes men on and compels them frequently to advance against their will and to be hurried headlong on, there yet is something in our breast sufficient to struggle against and resist it? And when too this something chooses, the store of matter is compelled sometimes to change its course through the limbs and frame, and after it has been forced forward, is reined in and settles back into its place. Wherefore in seeds too you must admit the same, admit that besides blows and weights there is another cause of motions, from which this power of free actions has been begotten in us, since we see that nothing can come from nothing. For weight forbids that all things be done by blows through as it were an outward force; but that the mind itself does not feel an internal necessity in all its actions and is not as it were overmastered and compelled to bear and put up with this, is caused by a minute swerving of first-beginnings at no fixed part of space and no fixed time.

Nor was the store of matter ever more closely massed nor held apart by larger spaces between; for nothing is either added to its bulk or lost to it. Wherefore the bodies of the first-beginnings in time gone by moved in the same way in which now they move, and will ever hereafter be borne along in like manner, and the things which have been wont to be begotten will be begotten after the same law and will be and will grow and will wax in strength so far as is given to each by the decrees of nature. And no force can change the sum of things for there is nothing outside, either into which any kind of matter can escape out of the universe or out of which a new supply can arise and burst into the universe and change all the nature of things and alter their motions.

And herein you need not wonder at this, that though the first-beginnings of things are all in motion, yet the sum is seen to rest in supreme repose, unless where a thing exhibits motions with its individual body. For all the nature of first things lies far away from our senses beneath their ken; and therefore since they are themselves beyond what you can see, they must withdraw from sight their motions also; and the more so that the things which we can see, do yet often conceal their motions when a great distance off. For often the woolly flocks as they crop the glad pastures on a hill, creep on whither the grass jewelled with fresh dew summons and invites each, and the lambs fed to the full gambol and playfully butt; all which objects appear to us from a distance to be blended together and to rest like a white spot on a green hill. Again when mighty legions fill with their movements all parts of the plains waging the mimicry of war, the glitter then lifts itself up to the sky and the whole earth round gleams with brass and beneath a noise is raised by the mighty trampling of men and the mountains stricken by the shouting re-echo the voices to the stars of heaven, and horsemen fly about and suddenly wheeling scour across the middle of the plains, shaking them with the vehemence of their charge. And yet there is some spot on the high hills, seen from which they appear to stand still and to rest on the plains as a bright spot.

Now mark and next in order apprehend of what kind and how widely differing in their forms are the beginnings of all things, how varied by manifold diversities of shape; not that a scanty number are possessed of a similar form, but because they are not all without exception one like another. And no wonder; for since there is so great a store of them that, as I have shewn, there is no end or sum, they must sure enough not be all marked by a precisely equal bulk and like shape, one with another. The race of man vouches the fact and the mute swimming shoals of the scaly tribes and the blithe herds and wild beasts and the different birds which haunt the gladdening watering spots about river-banks and springs and pools, and those which flit about and throng the pathless woods: go and take any one you like in any one kind, and you will yet find that they differ in shapes, every one from every other. And in no other way could child recognise mother or mother, child; and this we see that they all can do, and that they are just as well known to one another as human beings are. Thus often in front of the beauteous shrines of the gods a calf falls sacrificed beside the incense-burning altars, spirting from its breast a warm stream of blood; but the bereaved mother as she ranges over the green lawns knows the footprints stamped on the ground by the cloven hoofs, scanning with her eyes every spot to see if she can anywhere behold her lost youngling: then she fills with her moanings the leafy woods as she desists from her search and again and again goes back to the stall pierced to the heart by the loss of her calf; nor can the soft willows and grass quickened with dew and those rivers gliding level with their banks comfort her mind and put away the care that is on her, nor can other forms of calves throughout the glad pastures divert her mind and ease it of its care: so persistently she seeks something special and known. Again the tender kids with their shaking voices know their horned dams and the butting lambs the flocks of bleating sheep: thus they run, as nature craves, each without fail to its own udder of milk. Lastly, in the case of any kind of corn you like, you will yet find that any one grain is not so similar to any other in the same kind, but that there runs through them some difference to distinguish the forms. On a like principle of difference we see the class of shells paint the lap of earth, where the sea with gentle waves beats on the thirsty sand of the winding shore. Therefore again and again I say

it is necessary for like reasons that first-beginnings of things since they exist by nature and are not made by hand after the exact model of one, should fly about with shapes in some cases differing one from the other.

It is right easy for us on such a principle to explain why the fire of lightning has much more power to pierce than ours which is born of earthly pinewood: you may say that the heavenly fire of lightning, subtle as it is, is formed of smaller shapes and therefore passes through openings which this our fire cannot pass born as it is of woods and sprung from pine. Again light passes through horn, but rain is thrown off. Why? if not that those first bodies of light are smaller than those of which the nurturing liquid of water is made. And quickly as we see wines flow through a strainer sluggish oil on the other hand is slow to do so, because sure enough it consists of elements either larger in size or more hooked and tangled in one another, and therefore it is that the first-beginnings of things cannot so readily be separated from each other and severally stream through the several openings of any thing.

Moreover the liquids honey and milk excite a pleasant sensation of tongue when held in the mouth; but on the other hand the nauseous nature of wormwood and of harsh centaury writhe the mouth with a noisome flavour; so that you may easily see that the things which are able to affect the senses pleasantly, consist of smooth and round elements; while all those on the other hand which are found to be bitter and harsh, are held in connexion by particles that are more hooked and for this reason are wont to tear open passages into our senses and in entering in to break through the body.

All things in short which are agreeable to the senses and all which are unpleasant to the feeling are mutually repugnant, formed as they are out of an unlike first shape; lest haply you suppose that the harsh grating of the creaking saw consists of elements as smooth as those of tuneful melodies which musicians wake into life with nimble fingers and give shape to on strings; or suppose that the first-beginnings are of like shape which pass into the nostrils of men, when noisome carcasses are burning, and when the stage is fresh sprinkled with Cilician saffron, while the altar close by exhales Panchaean odours; or decide that the pleasant colours of things which are able to feast the eyes are formed of a seed like to the seed of those which make the pupil smart and force it to shed tears or from their disgusting aspect look hideous and foul. For every shape which gratifies the senses has been formed not without a smoothness in its elements; but on the other hand whatever is painful and harsh, has been produced not without some roughness of matter. There are too some elements which are with justice thought to be neither smooth nor altogether hooked with barbed points, but rather to have minute angles slightly projecting, such as can tickle rather than hurt the senses; of which class tartar of wine is formed and the flavours of elecampane. Again that hot fires and cold frost have fangs of a dissimilar kind wherewith to pierce the senses, is proved to us by the touch of each. For touch, touch, ye holy divinities of the gods, is feeling of the body, either when an extraneous thing makes its way in, or when a thing which is born in the body hurts it, or gives pleasure as it issues forth by the birth bestowing ways of Venus, or when from some collision the seeds are disordered within the body and distract the feeling by their mutual disturbance; as if haply you were yourself to strike with the hand any part of the body you please and so make trial. Wherefore the shapes of the first-beginnings must differ widely, since they are able to give birth to different feelings.

Again things which look hard and dense must consist of particles more hooked together, and be held in union because compacted throughout with branch-like elements. In this class first of all adamant rocks stand in foremost line inured to despise blows, and stout blocks of basalt and the strength of hard iron and brass bolts which cry aloud as they hold fast to their staples. Those things which are liquid and of fluid body ought to consist more of smooth and round elements; for the several drops have no mutual cohesion and their onward course too has a ready flow downwards. All things lastly which you see disperse themselves in an instant, as smoke mists and flames, if they do not consist entirely of smooth and round, must yet not be held fast by closely tangled elements, so that they may be able to pierce the body and enter into loose substances, yet not stick together: thus you may easily know, that whatever we see in this way conveyed to the senses, consists not of tangled but of pointed elements. Do not however hold it to be wonderful that some things which are fluid you see to be likewise bitter, for instance the sea's moisture: because it is fluid, it consists of smooth and round particles, and many rough bodies mixed up with these produce pains; and yet they must not be hooked so as to hold together: you are to know that though rough, they are yet spherical, so that while they roll freely on, they may at the same time hurt the senses. And that you may more readily believe that with smooth are mixed rough first-beginnings from which Neptune's body is made bitter, there is a way of separating these, and of seeing apart how the fresh water, when it is often filtered through the earth, flows into a trench and sweetens; for it leaves above the first-beginnings of the nauseous saltness, inasmuch as the rough particles can more readily stay behind in the earth.

And now that I have shewn this, I will go on to link to it a truth which depends on this and from this draws its proof: the first-beginnings of things have different shapes, but the number of shapes is finite. If this were not so, then once more it would follow that some seeds must be of infinite bulk of body. For since in one and the same small size of any first body you like the shapes cannot vary much from one another:—say for instance that first bodies consist of three least parts, or augment them by a few more; when to wit in all possible ways, by placing each in turn at the top and at the bottom, by making the right change places with the left, you shall have tried all those parts of one first body and found what manner of shape each different arrangement gives to the whole of that body, if after all this haply you shall wish still to vary the shapes, you will have to add other parts: it will next follow that for like reasons the arrangement will require other parts, if haply you shall wish still again to vary the shapes:—from all this it results that increase of bulk in the body follows upon newness of the shapes. Wherefore you cannot possibly believe that seeds have an infinite variety of forms, lest you force some to be of a monstrous hugeness, which as I have above shewn cannot be proved. Moreover I tell you barbaric robes and radiant Meliboean purple dipped in Thessalian dye of shells [and the hues which are displayed] by the golden brood of peacocks steeped in laughing beauty would all be thrown aside surpassed by some new colour of things; the smell of myrrh would be despised and the flavours of honey, and the melodies of the swan and Phoebean tunes set off by the varied play of strings would in like sort be suppressed and silenced; for something ever would arise more surpassing than the rest. All things likewise might fall back into worse states, even as we have said they might advance to better; for reversely too one thing would be more noisome than all other things to nostril, ear and eye and taste. Now since these things are not so, but a fixed limit has been assigned to things which bound their sum on each side, you must admit that matter also has a finite number of different shapes. Once more from summer fires to chill frosts a definite path is traced out and in like manner is again travelled back; for cold and heat lie on the outside and moderate warmths midway between both, filling up in succession the sum. Therefore things produced differ by finite degrees, since on each side they are marked off by points, one at one, another at the other end, molested on the one hand by flames, on the other by stiffening frosts.

And now that I have shewn this, I will go on to link to it a truth which depends on this and from this draws its proof: the first-beginnings of things which have a like shape one with the other, are infinite in number. For since the difference of forms is finite, those which are like must be infinite or the sum of matter will be finite, which I proved not to be the case, when I shewed in my verses that the minute bodies of matter from everlasting continually uphold the sum of things through an uninterrupted succession of blows on all sides. For though you see that some animals are rarer than others and discern a less fruitful nature in them, yet in another quarter and spot and in distant lands there may be many of that kind and the full tale may be made up; just as we see that in the class of four-footed beasts snake-handed elephants are elsewhere especially nu-

merous; for India is so fenced about with an ivory rampart made out of many thousands of these, that its inner parts cannot be reached, so great is the quantity of brutes, of which we see but very few samples. But yet though I should grant this point too: be there even as you will some one thing sole in its kind existing alone with a body that had birth, and let no other thing resemble it in the whole world; yet unless there shall be an infinite supply of matter out of which it may be conceived and brought into being, it cannot be produced, and, more than this it cannot have growth and food. For though I should assume this point also that birth-giving bodies of some one thing are tossed about in finite quantity throughout the universe, whence, where, by what force and in what way shall they meet together and combine in so vast a sea, such an alien medley of matter? They have methinks no way of uniting; but even as when great and numerous shipwrecks have occurred, the great sea is wont to tumble about banks, rudders, yards, prow, masts, and swimming oars, so that poop-fittings are seen floating about along every shore and utter to mortals a warning to try to shun the snares and violence and guile of the faithless sea, and never at any time to trust to it, when the winning face of calm ocean laughs treacherously; thus too if you shall once decide that certain first-beginnings are finite, different currents of matter must scatter and tumble them about through all time, so that they can never be brought into union and combine, nor abide in that union nor grow up and increase. But plain matter of fact shews that each of these results plainly takes place, that things can be brought into being and when begotten advance in growth. It is clear then that in any class you like the first-beginnings of things are infinite out of which all supplies are furnished.

Thus then neither can death-dealing motions keep the mastery always nor entomb existence for evermore, nor on the other hand can the birth and increase giving motions of things preserve things always after they are born. Thus the war of first-beginnings waged from eternity is carried on with dubious issue: now here now there the life-bringing elements of things get the mastery and are o'ermastered in turn: with the funeral wail is blended the cry which babies raise when they enter the borders of light; and no night ever followed day, nor morning, night, that heard not mingling with the sickly infant's cries wailings the attendants on death and black funeral.

And herein it is proper you should keep under seal and guard, there consigned, in faithful memory this truth, that there is nothing whose nature is apparent to sense, which consists of one kind of first-beginnings; nothing which is not formed by a mixing of seed. And whenever a thing possesses in itself in a greater degree many powers and properties, in that measure it shews that there are in it the greatest number of different kinds and varied shapes of first-beginnings. First of all the earth has in her first bodies out of which springs, rolling coolness along, replenish without fail the boundless sea, she has bodies out of which fires rise up; for in many spots the earth's crust is on fire and burns, though headstrong Aetna rages with fires of surpassing force. Then too she has bodies out of which she can raise for mankind goodly crops and joyous trees, out of which too she can supply to the mountain-ranging race of wild beasts, rivers, leaves, and glad pastures. Wherefore she has alone been named great mother of gods and mother of beasts and parent of our body.

Of her the old and learned poets of the Greeks have sung, that [borne aloft on high-raised] seat in a chariot she drives a pair of lions, teaching that the great earth hangs in the expanse of air and that earth cannot rest on earth. To her chariot they have yoked wild-beasts, because a brood however savage ought to be tamed and softened by the kind offices of parents. They have encircled the top of her head with a mural crown, because fortified in choice positions she sustains towns; adorned with which emblem the image of the divine mother is carried nowadays through wide lands in awe-inspiring state. Her different nations after old-established ritual term Idean mother, and give her for escort Phrygian bands, because they tell that from those lands corn first began to be produced throughout the world. They assign her galli, because they would shew by this type that they who have done violence to the divinity of the mother and have proved ungrateful to their parents, are to be deemed unworthy to bring a living offspring into the borders of light. Tight-stretched tambourines and hollow symbols resound all round to the stroke of their open hands, and horns menace with hoarse-sounding music, and the hollow pipe stirs their minds in Phrygian mood. They carry weapons before them, emblems of furious rage, meet to fill the thankless souls and godless breasts of the rabble with terror for the divinity of the godless. Therefore when first borne in procession through great cities she mutely enriches mortals with a blessing not expressed in words, they strew all her path with brass and silver presenting her with bounteous alms, and scatter over her a snow-shower of roses, o'ershadowing the mother and her troops of attendants. Here an armed band to whom the Greeks give the name of Phrygian Curetes, in that it haply joins in the game of arms and springs up in measure all dripping with blood, shaking with its nodding the frightful crests upon the head, represents the Dictaean Curetes who, as the story is, erst drowned in Crete that infant cry of Jove, when the young band about the young babe in rapid dance arms in hand to measured tread beat brass on brass, that Saturn might not get him to consign to his devouring jaws and stab the mother to the heart with a never-healing wound. Therefore they escort in arms the great mother, or because they mean by this sign that the godless preaches to men to be willing with arms and valour to defend their country and be ready to be a safeguard and an ornament to their parents. All which, well and beautifully as it is set forth and told, is yet widely removed from true reason. For the nature of gods must ever in itself of necessity enjoy immortality together with supreme repose, far removed and withdrawn from our concerns; for exempt from every pain, exempt from all dangers, strong in its own resources, not wanting aught of us, it is neither gained by favours nor moved by anger. And here if any one thinks proper to call the sea Neptune and corn Ceres and chooses rather to misuse the name of Bacchus than to utter the term that belongs to that liquor, let us allow him to declare that the earth is mother of the gods, if he only forbear in earnest to stain his mind with foul religion. The earth however is at all time without feeling, and because it receives into it the first-beginnings of many things, it brings them forth in many ways into the light of the sun.

And so the woolly flocks and the martial breed of horses and horned herds, though often cropping the grass from one field beneath the same canopy of heaven and slaking their thirst from one stream of water, yet have all their life a dissimilar appearance and retain the nature of their parents and severally imitate their ways each after its kind: so great is the diversity of matter in any kind of herbage, so great in every river. And hence too any one you please out of the whole number of living creatures is made up of bones, blood, veins, heat, moisture, flesh, sinews; and these things again differ widely from one another and are composed of elements of dissimilar shape. Furthermore whatever things are set on fire and burned, store up in their body, if nothing else, at least those particles, out of which they may radiate fire and send out light and make sparks fly and scatter embers all about. If you will go over all other things by a like process of reasoning, you will thus find that they conceal in their body the seeds of many things and contain elements of various shapes. Again you see many things to which are given at once both colour and taste together with smell. These properties, as there are several of them in each thing, must therefore be made up of elements of different shapes; for smell enters in where colour passes not into the frame, colour too in one way, taste in another makes its way into the senses; so that you know they differ in the particular shape of their elements. Therefore unlike forms unite into one mass and things are made up of a mixture of seed. Throughout moreover these very verses of ours you see many elements common to many words, though yet you must admit that the verses and words one with another are different and composed of different elements; not that but few letters which are in common run through them or that no two words or verses one with another are made up entirely of the same, but because as a rule they do not all resemble one the other. Thus also though in other things there are many first-beginnings common to many things, yet they make up one with the other a quite dissimilar whole; so that men and corn and joyous trees

may fairly be said to consist of different elements.

And yet we are not to suppose that all things can be joined together in all ways; for then you would see prodigies produced on all hands, forms springing up half man, half beast, and sometimes tall boughs sprouting from the living body, and many limbs of land-creatures joined with those of sea-animals, nature too throughout the all-bearing lands feeding chimeras which breathed flames from hideous mouths. It is plain however that nothing of the sort is done, since we see that all things produced from fixed seeds and a fixed mother can in growing preserve the marks of their kind. This you are to know must take place after a fixed law. For the particles suitable for each thing from all kinds of food when inside the body pass into the frame and joining on produce the appropriate motions; but on the other hand we see nature throw on the earth those that are alien, and many things with their unseen bodies fly out of the body impelled by blows: those I mean which have not been able to join on to any part nor when inside to feel in unison with and adopt the vital motions. But lest you haply suppose that living things alone are bound by these conditions, such a law keeps all things within their limits. For even as things begotten are in their whole nature all unlike one the other, thus each must consist of first-beginnings of unlike shape; not that but few are possessed of a like form, but because as a rule all do not resemble one another. Again since the seeds differ, there must be a difference in the spaces between, the passages, the connexions, the weights, the blows, the clashings, the motions; all which not only disjoin living bodies, but hold apart the lands and the whole sea, and keep the whole heaven away from the earth.

Now mark, and apprehend precepts amassed by my welcome toil, lest haply you deem that those things which you see with your eyes to be bright, because white are formed of white principles, or that the things which are black are born from black seed; or that things which are steeped in any other colour, bear that colour because the bodies of matter are dyed with a colour like to it. For there is no colour at all to the bodies of matter either like to the things or unlike. But if haply it seems to you that no impression of the mind can throw itself into these bodies, you wander far astray. For since men born blind who have never beheld the light of the sun, do yet know bodies by touch, you are to know that bodies can fall under the ken of our mind too, though stained with no colour. Again whatever things we ourselves touch in the thick darkness, we do not perceive to be dyed with any colour. And since I prove that this is the case, I will now shew that there are things linked to no colour from the beginning of time. Well any colour without any exception changes into any other; and this first-beginnings ought in nowise to do: something unchangeable must remain over, that all things be not utterly reduced to nothing. For whenever a thing changes and quits its proper limits, at once this change of state is the death of that which was before. Therefore mind not to dye with colour the seeds of things, that you may not have all things altogether returning to nothing.

Moreover if no quality of colour is assigned to first-beginnings and they are yet possessed of varied shapes out of which they beget colours of every kind and change them about by reason that it makes a great difference with what other seeds and in what position the seeds are severally held in union and what motions they mutually impart and receive, you can explain at once with the greatest ease why those things which just before were of a black colour, may become all at once of marble whiteness; as the sea, when mighty winds have stirred up its waters, is changed into white waves of the brightness of marble: you may say that when the matter of that which we often see to be black, has been mixed up anew and the arrangement of its first-beginnings has been changed and some have been added and some been taken away, the immediate result is that it appears bright and white. But if the waters of the sea consisted of azure seeds, they could in nowise become white; for however much you jumble together seeds which are azure, they can never pass into a marble colour. But if the seeds which make up the one unmixed brightness of the sea are dyed some with one, some with other colours, just as often out of different forms and varied shapes something

square and of a uniform figure is made up, in that case it were natural that as we see unlike forms contained in the square, so we should see in the water of the sea or in any other one and unmixed brightness colours widely unlike and different to one another. Moreover the unlike figures do not in the least hinder or prevent the whole figure from being a square on the outside; but the various colours of things are a let and hindrance to the whole things being of a uniform brightness.

Then too the reason which leads and draws us on sometimes to assign colours to the first-beginnings of things, falls to the ground, since white things are not produced from white, nor those which are black from black, but out of things of various colours. For white things will much more readily rise up and be born from no colour than from a white or any other colour which thwarts and opposes it.

Moreover since colours cannot exist without light and first-beginnings of things do not come out into the light, you may be sure they are clothed with no colour. For what colour can there be in total darkness? nay it changes in the light itself according as its brightness comes from a straight or slanting stroke of light. After this fashion the down which encircles and crowns the nape and throat of doves shews itself in the sun: at one time it is ruddy with the hue of bright pyropus; at another it appears by a certain way of looking at it to blend with coral-red green emeralds. The tail of the peacock when it is saturated with abundant light, changes in like fashion its colours as it faces the sun. And since these colours are begotten by a certain stroke of light, sure enough you must believe that they cannot be produced without it. And since the pupil receives into it a kind of blow, when it is said to perceive a white colour, and then another, when it perceives black or any other colour, and since it is of no moment with what colour the things which you touch are provided, but rather with what sort of shape they are furnished, you are to know that first-beginnings have no need of colours, but give forth sensations of touch varying according to their various shapes.

Moreover since no particular kind of colour is assigned to particular shapes and every configuration of first-beginnings can exist in any colour, why on a like principle are not the things which are formed out of them in every kind o'erlaid with colours of every kind? For then it were natural that crows too in flying should display a white colour from white wings and that swans should come to be black from a black seed, or of any other colour you please, uniform or diversified.

Again the more minute the parts are into which anything is rent, the more you may perceive the colours fade away by little and little and become extinct; as for instance if a piece of purple is torn into small shreds: when it has been plucked into separate threads, the purple and the scarlet far the most brilliant of colours are quite effaced; from which you may infer that the shreds part with all their colour before they come back to the seeds of things.

Lastly since you admit that all bodies do not utter a voice nor emit a smell, for this reason you do not assign to all sounds and smells. So also since we cannot perceive all things with the eye, you are to know that some things are as much denuded of colour as others are without smell and devoid of sound, and that the keen-discerning mind can just as well apprehend these things as it can take note of things which are destitute of other qualities.

But lest haply you suppose that first bodies remain stripped of colour alone, they are also wholly devoid of warmth and cold and violent heat, and are judged to be barren of sound and drained of moisture, and emit from their body no scent of their own. Just as when you set about preparing the balmy liquid of sweet marjoram and myrrh and the flower of spikenard which gives forth to the nostrils a scent like nectar, before all you should seek, so far as you may and can find it, the substance of scentless oil, such as gives out no perfume to the nostrils, that it may as little as possible meddle with and destroy by its own pungency the odours mixed in its body and boiled up with it; for the same reason the first-beginnings of things must not bring to the begetting of things a smell or sound of their own, since they cannot discharge anything from themselves, and for the same reason no taste either nor cold nor any heat moderate or violent, and the like. For as these things, be they what they may, are still liable to death, whether pliant with a soft, brittle with a crumbling, or hollow with a porous body, they must all be withdrawn from the first-beginnings, if we wish to assign to things imperishable foundations for the whole sum of existence to rest upon; that you may not have things returning altogether to nothing.

To come to another point, whatever things we perceive to have sense, you must yet admit to be all composed of senseless first-beginnings: manifest tokens which are open to all to apprehend, so far from refuting or contradicting, do rather themselves take us by the hand and constrain us to believe that, as I say, living things are begotten from senseless things. We may say in fact living worms spring out of stinking dung, when the soaked earth has gotten putridity after excessive rains; and all things beside change in the same way: rivers, leaves and glad pastures change into cattle, cattle change their substance into our bodies, and often out of these the powers of wild beasts and the bodies of the strong of wing are increased. Therefore nature changes all foods into living bodies and engenders out of them all the senses of living creatures, much in the same way as she dissolves dry woods into flames and converts all things into fires. Now do you see that it is of great moment in what sort of arrangement the first-beginnings of things are severally placed and with what others they are mixed up, when they impart and receive motions?

Then again what is that which strikes your mind, which affects that mind and constrains it to give utterance to many different thoughts, to save you from believing that the sensible is begotten out of senseless things? Sure enough it is because stones and wood and earth however mixed together are yet unable to produce vital sense. This therefore it will be proper to remember herein, that I do not assert that the sensible and sensations are forthwith begotten out of all things without exception which produce things; but that it is of great moment first how minute the particles are which make up the sensible thing and then what shape they possess and what in short they are in their motions, arrangements, positions. None of which requisites we find in woods and clods; and yet even these things, when they have so to speak become rotten through the rains, bring forth worms, because bodies of matter driven from their ancient arrangements by a new condition are combined in the same way as when living creatures are to be begotten. Next they who hold that the sensible can be produced anew out of other sensible things, in that case suppose those things, accustomed thus to have sense, to be soft; for all sense is bound up with flesh, sinews, veins; which in everything we see to be soft and formed of a mortal body. But even suppose that these things can remain eternal: they must yet I presume either have the sense of some part or else be supposed to possess a similar sense similar to the entire living creatures. But the parts cannot possibly have sense by themselves alone; for all sense of the different members has reference to something else; nor can the hand when severed from us nor any other part of the body whatever by itself maintain sensation. It remains to assume that they resemble the entire living creatures. In this case it is necessary that they should feel the things which we feel in the same way as we do, in order that they may be able on all hands to work in concert with the vital sense. How then can they be called first-beginnings of things and shun the paths of death, seeing that they are living things, and that living things are one and the same with mortal things? Nay granting they could do this, yet by their meeting and union they will make nothing but a jumble and medley of living things; just you are to know as men, cattle, and wild-beasts would be unable to beget any other thing by all their mixing with one another. But if haply they lose from their body their own sense and adopt another, what use to assign what is again withdrawn? moreover, the instance to which we had before recourse, inasmuch as we see the eggs of fowls change into living chicks and worms burst forth, when putridity has seized on the earth after excessive rains, you are to know that sensations can be begotten out of non-sensations.

But if haply any one shall say that sense so far may arise from non-sensation by a process of change, or because it is brought forth by a kind of birth, it will be enough to make plain and to prove to him that no birth takes place until a union of elements has first been effected, and that nothing changes without such a process of uniting. Above all, senses cannot exist in any body before the nature itself of the living things has been begotten, because sure enough the matter remains scattered about in air, rivers, earth, and things produced from earth, and has not met together and combined in appropriate fashion the vital motions by which the all-discerning senses are kindled into action in each living thing.

Again a blow more severe than its nature can endure, prostrates at once any living thing and goes on to stun all the senses of body and mind. For the positions of the first-beginnings are broken up and the vital motions entirely stopped, until the matter, disordered by the shock through the whole frame, unties from the body the vital fastenings of the soul and scatters it abroad and forces it out through all the pores. For what more can we suppose the infliction of a blow can do than shake from their place and break up the union of the several elements? Often too when the blow is inflicted with less violence the remaining vital motions are wont to prevail, to prevail I say and still the huge disorders caused by the blow and recall each part into its proper channels and shake off the motion of death now reigning as it were paramount in the body and kindle afresh the almost lost senses. For in what other way should the thing be able to gather together its powers of mind and come back to life from the very threshold of death rather than pass on to the goal to which it had almost run and so pass away?

Again since there is pain when the bodies of matter are disordered by any force throughout the living flesh and frame and quake in their seats within, and as when they travel back into their place, a soothing pleasure ensues, you are to know the first-beginnings can be assailed by no pain and can derive no pleasure from themselves; since they are not formed of any bodies of first-beginnings, so as to be distressed by any novelty in their motions or derive from it any fruit of fostering delight; and therefore they must not be possessed of any sense.

Again if in order that living creatures may severally have sense, sense is to be assigned to their first-beginnings as well, what are we to say of those of which mankind is specifically made? sure enough they burst into fits of shaking laughter and sprinkle with dewy tears face and cheeks and have the cunning to speak at length on the nature of things and enquire next what their own first-beginnings are; since like in their natures to the entire mortals they must in their turn be formed out of other elements, then those others out of others, so that you can venture nowhere to come to a stop: yes whatever you shall say speaks and laughs and thinks, I will press you with the argument that it is formed of other things performing the same acts. But if we see these notions to be sheer folly and madness, and a man may laugh though not made of laughing things, and think and reason in learned language though not formed of thoughtful and eloquent seeds, why cannot the things which we see to have sense be made up of a mixture of things altogether devoid of sense?

Again we are all sprung from a heavenly seed, all have that same father, by whom mother earth the giver of increase, when she has taken in from him liquid drops of moisture, conceives and bears goodly crops and joyous trees and the race of man, bears all kinds of brute beasts, in that she supplies food, with which all feed their bodies and lead a pleasant life and continue their race; wherefore with good cause she has gotten the name of mother. That also which before was from the earth, passes back into the earth, and that which was sent from the borders of ether, is carried back and taken in again by the quarters of heaven. Death does not extinguish things in such a way as to destroy the bodies of matter, but only breaks up the union amongst them, and then joins anew the different elements with others; and thus it comes to pass that all things change their shapes and alter their colours and receive sensations and in a moment yield them up; so that from all this you may know it matters much with what others and in what position the same first-beginnings of things are held in union and what motions they do mutually impart and receive, and you must not suppose that that which we see floating about on the surface of things and now born, then at once perishing, can be a property inherent in everlasting first bodies. Moreover in our verses themselves it matters much with what other elements and in what kind of order the several

elements are placed. If not all, yet by far the greatest number are alike; but the totals composed of them are made to differ by the position of these elements. Thus in actual things as well, when the clashings, motions, arrangement, position, shapes of matter change about, the things also must change.

Apply now, we entreat, your mind to true reason. For a new question struggles earnestly to gain your ears, a new aspect of things to display itself. But there is nothing so easy as not to be at first more difficult to believe than afterwards; and nothing too so great, so marvellous, that all do not gradually lessen their admiration of it. Look up at the bright and unsullied hue of heaven and the stars which it holds within it, wandering all about, and the moon and the sun's light of dazzling brilliancy: if all these things were now for the first time, if I say they were now suddenly presented to mortals beyond all expectation, what could have been named that would be more marvellous than these things, or that nations beforehand would less venture to believe could be? nothing methinks: so wondrous strange had been this sight. Yet how little, you know, wearied as all are to satiety with seeing, any one now cares to look up into heaven's glittering quarters! Cease therefore to be dismayed by the mere novelty and so to reject reason from your mind with loathing: weigh the questions rather with keen judgment and if they seem to you to be true, surrender, or if the thing is false, gird yourself to the encounter. For since the sum of space is unlimited outside beyond these walls of the world, the mind seeks to apprehend what there is yonder there, to which the spirit ever yearns to look forward, and to which the mind's immission reaches in free and unembarrassed flight.

In the first place we see that round in all directions about above and underneath, throughout the universe there is no bound, as I have shewn and as the thing of itself proclaims with loud voice and as clearly shines out in the nature of bottomless space. In nowise then can it be deemed probable, when space yawns illimitable towards all points and seeds in number numberless and sum unfathomable fly about in manifold ways driven on in ceaseless motion, that this single earth and heaven have been brought into being, that those bodies of matter so many in number do nothing outside them; the more so that this world has been made by nature, and the seeds of things chancing spontaneously to clash, after being brought together in manifold wise without purpose, without foresight, without result, have at last combined in such masses as, suddenly thrown together, became on each occasion the rudiments of great things of earth, sea, and heaven and the race of living things. Wherefore again and again I say you must admit that there are elsewhere other combinations of matter like to this which ether holds in its greedy grasp.

Again when much matter is at hand, when room is there and there is no thing, no cause to hinder, things sure enough must go on and be completed. Well then if on the one hand there is so great a store of seeds as the whole life of living creatures cannot reckon up, and if the same force and nature abide in them and have the power to throw the seeds of things together into their several places in the same way as they are thrown together into our world, you must admit that in other parts of space there are other earths and various races of men and kinds of wild beasts.

Moreover in the sum of all there is no one thing which is begotten single in its kind and grows up single and sole of its kind; but a thing always belongs to some class and there are many other things in the same kind. First in the case of living things, most noble Memmius, you will find that in this sort has been begotten the mountain-ranging race of wild beasts, in this sort the breed of men, in this sort too the mute shoals of scaly creatures and all bodies of fowls. Wherefore on a like principle you must admit that earth and sun, moon, sea, and all things else that are, are not single in their kind; but rather of a number past numbering, since the deep-set boundary-mark of life just as much awaits these and they are just as much of a body that had birth, as any class of things which here on earth abounds in samples of its kind.

If you well apprehend and keep in mind these things, nature free at once and rid of her haughty lords is seen to do all things spontaneously of herself without the meddling of the gods. For I appeal to the holy breasts of the gods who in tranquil peace pass a calm time and an unruffled existence, who can rule the

sun, who hold in his hand with controlling force the strong reins of the immeasurable deep? who can at once make all the different heavens to roll and warm with ethereal fires all the fruitful earths, or be present in all places at all times, to bring darkness with clouds and shake with noise the heaven's serene expanse, to hurl lightnings and often throw down his own temples and withdrawing into the deserts there to spend his rage in practising his bolt which often passes the guilty by and strikes dead the innocent and unoffending?

And since the birth-time of the world and first day of being to sea and earth and the formation of the sun many bodies have been added from without, many seeds added all round, which the great universe in tossing to and fro has contributed; that from them the sea and lands might increase and from them heaven's mansion might enlarge its expanse and raise its high vaults far above earth, and that air might rise up around. For all bodies from all quarters are assigned by blows each to its appropriate thing and all withdraw to their proper classes; moisture passes to moisture, from an earthy body earth increases and fires forge fires and ether ether, until nature parent of things with finishing hand has brought all things on to their utmost limit of growth. And this comes to pass when that which is infused into the life-arteries is no more than that which ebbs from them and withdraws: at this point the life-growth in all things must stop, at this point nature by her powers checks further increase. For whatever things you see grow in size with joyous increase and mount by successive steps to mature age, take to themselves more bodies than they discharge from themselves, while food is readily infused into all the arteries and the things are not so widely spread out as to throw off many particles and occasion more waste than their age can take in as nourishment. For no doubt it must be conceded that many bodies ebb away and withdraw from things; but still more must join them, until they have touched the utmost point of growth. Then piece by piece age breaks their powers and matured strength and wastes away on the side of decay. For the larger a thing is and the wider, as soon as its growth is stopped, at once it sheds abroad and discharges from it more bodies in all directions round; and its food is not readily transmitted into all its arteries and is not enough, in proportion to the copious exhalations which the thing throws off, to enable a like amount to rise up and be supplied. For food must keep all things entire by renewing them, food must uphold, food sustain all things: all in vain, since the arteries refuse to hold what is sufficient, and nature does not furnish the needful amount. With good reason therefore all things perish, when they have been rarefied by the ebb of particles and succumb to blows from without, since food sooner or later fails advanced age, and bodies never cease to destroy a thing by thumping it from without and to overpower it by aggressive blows. In this way then the walls too of the great world around shall be stormed and fall to decay and crumbling ruin. Yes and even now the age is enfeebled and the earth exhausted by bearing scarce produces little living creatures, she who produced all races and gave birth to the huge bodies of wild beasts. For methinks no golden chain let down to earth from heaven above the races of mortal beings, nor did the sea and waves which lash the rocks produce them, but the same earth bare them which now feeds them from herself. Moreover she first spontaneously of herself produced for mortals goodly corn-crops and joyous vineyards; of herself gave sweet fruits and joyous pastures; which nowadays scarce attain any size when furthered by our labour: we exhaust the oxen and the strength of the husbandmen; we wear out our iron, scarce equal to the tillage of the fields; so niggardly are they of their produce and after so much labour do they let them grow. And now the aged ploughman shakes his head and sighs again and again to think that the labours of his hand have come to nothing; and when he compares present times with times past, he often praises the fortunes of his sire and harps on the theme, how the men of old comfortably supported life on a scanty plot of ground, since the allotment of land to each man was far less of yore than now.

The sorrowful planter too of the exhausted and shrivelled vine impeaches the march of time and wearies heaven, and comprehends not that all things are gradually wasting away and passing to the grave, quite forespent by age and length of days.

Aristarchus

Aristarchus of Samos was a great astronomer of the Hellenistic age. In the third century B.C. he made one of the most accurate computations of the size of the sun and the moon and their distance from the earth. After this work had been published, he became convinced that the sun was the center around which the earth and the planets revolved. The first of the two selections is in Aristarchus' own words, while the second is quoted by Archimedes. In reading them note (1) the advanced knowledge of the nature of the universe possessed by these scientists, and (2) the rationalists' approach to investigating and analyzing the universe of reality.

From: HYPOTHESES

The moon receives its light from the sun.

The earth is in the relation of a point and center of the sphere in which the moon moves.

The distance of the sun from the earth is greater than 18 times, but less than 20 times, the distance of the moon (from the earth).

The diameter of the moon is less than

G. W. Botsford and E. G. Sihler, eds., *Hellenic Civilization*, Columbia University Press, New York, 1915, 639–640. Courtesy of Columbia University Press.

$\frac{2}{45}$ but greater than $\frac{1}{30}$ of the distance of the center of the moon from our eye.

The diameter of the sun has to the diameter of the earth a ratio greater than 19:3 but less than 43:6.

The sun has to the moon a ratio greater than 5832:1 but less than 8000:1.

[The Heliocentric Theory.] The term *world*, as it is defined by most astronomers, is here designed to signify a sphere of the heavens, whose center coincides with the center of the earth, and whose semi-diameter is the distance from the center of the earth to the center of the sun. This definition of the term *world*,

as given in the writings of other astronomers, Aristarchus of Samos refutes, and has given it a far more extensive signification; for according to his hypothesis, neither the fixed stars nor the sun are subject to any motion; but the earth annually revolves round the sun in the circumference of a circle, in the center of which the sun remains fixed. The sphere of the fixed stars, too, whose center he supposes to coincide with the sun's, is of such immense magnitude that the circle, in whose periphery the earth is supposed to revolve round the sun, bears no greater proportion to the distance of the fixed stars than the center of a sphere does to its superficies [surface].

Eratosthenes

Eratosthenes (276–196(?) B.C.), one of the great scientists of the Hellenistic age, was librarian at Alexandria, and was particularly interested in astronomy and geography. Although it was a well-known fact in his day that the earth was round, its exact size had not been determined, but Eratosthenes made the closest calculation that had yet been reached. This description of his computation is not in his own words, but was written by Cleomedes in the second century A.D. In reading this selection note (1) the understanding displayed of the universe, (2) the method used to calculate the total circumference, and (3) the results of his computation.

From: CONCERNING THE CIRCULAR MOTION OF THE HEAVENLY BODIES

Under the same meridian, he says, lie Syene and Alexandria. Since then the greatest (lines) in the universe are the meridians, the spherical lines lying under them on the earth must necessarily be the greatest. Consequently whatever extent the theory (of Eratosthenes) will demonstrate for the spherical line running through Syene and Alexandria, so extensive also will be the greatest spherical line of the earth. He then says: And it is so, that Syene lies under the summer solstice. Whenever therefore the sun, having passed into Cancer and, effecting the summer solstice, is precisely at the zenith point

of the sky, the gnomon of the sundial necessarily becomes shadowless, in accordance with the exact perpendicular of the sun standing overhead; and it is reasonable that this should happen to the extent of three hundred stadia in diameter. At Alexandria at the same hour the gnomons of the sundials cast a shadow, since this city lies more to the north than Syene. Inasmuch as these cities lie under the same meridian and the greatest spherical line, if we draw the arc from the apex of the shadow of the sundial to the base itself of the sundial which is in Alexandria, this arc will prove a

G. W. Botsford and E. G. Sihler, eds., *Hellenic Civilization*, Columbia University Press, New York, 1915, 636–637. Courtesy of Columbia University Press.

segment of the greatest spherical line in the concave sundial, since the concave surface of the sundial lies under the largest spherical line. If consequently we were to conceive straight lines extended through the earth from each of the sundials, they will meet at the centre of the earth. Since then the sundial at Syene lies perpendicularly under the sun, if we conceive in addition a straight line drawn from the sun to the apex of the style of the sundial, then the line drawn from the sun to the centre of the earth will prove *one* straight line. If then we conceive another straight line from the apex of the shadow of the gnomon drawn up to the sun from the concave dial in Alexandria, this one and the aforesaid straight line will prove to be parallel, passing from different parts of the sun to different parts of the earth. Into these (lines), which are parallel, the line drawn from the centre of the earth to the dial at Alexandria falls as a straight line, so as to render the alternate angles equal. Of these (angles) the one is at the centre of the earth

through the meeting of the straight lines which were drawn from the apex of its shadow. The other angle results through the meeting of (the lines drawn) from the apex of the dial at Alexandria and the line drawn upward from the apex of its shadow to the sun through the contact with it. Upon this is constructed the circular line which has been circumscribed from the apex of the shadow of the gnomon to its base; and upon that at the centre of the earth the (line) which passes from Syene to Alexandria. Similar then are the arcs to each other, namely, those based on equal angles. The relation therefore which the line in the concave has to its own circle is the same as the relation of the line drawn from Syene to Alexandria. The line in the concave is to be $\frac{1}{50}$ of its own circle; therefore necessarily also the distance from Syene to Alexandria must be $\frac{1}{50}$ of the largest circle of earth; and this is (a distance) of 5,000 stadia. The whole circle therefore amounts to 250,000 stadia.

Such is the computation of Eratosthenes.

Roman Civilization

While the Greeks were developing their glorious civilization in the eastern Mediterranean, the Romans were consolidating their position politically on the Italian peninsula and throughout the western Mediterranean generally. War and politics occupied much of their time and energy, and it was only natural that their civilization was dominated by these two activities. Their great men of letters wrote of the excellent qualities of Roman generals and statesmen, and inevitably Roman literature came to be an expression of the national character. When the empire was finally consolidated, and the administration established, Rome's intellectuals turned to other cultural outlets. Here, however, they were unable to create much that was original, but rather they fell back upon the cultural patterns which the Greeks had established. Thus in their epic poetry, their philosophy, their drama, and even in their art they built upon the achievements of the Greeks. Only in government, law, and engineering did the Romans excel, and in these fields the demands of imperial rule over alien peoples made it almost mandatory that they should do so. It was in construction, government, and jurisprudence, then, that the Roman world worked out its greatest contributions to Western Civilization.

Polybius

Polybius (about 205–123 B.C.) was a Greek historian who became interested in the imperial expansion of Rome while a captive in that city. He made an exhaustive study of the written sources and then sought in his Histories to interpret the facts in the light of personal travel to the sites of the events, and through practical experience in politics and warfare. He placed particular importance upon the institutions under which society lived as a determining force in the course of events. In the sixth book he discussed the Roman constitution as one of the factors contributing to Rome's imperial success. In reading the selections from it note (1) the motive of Polybius in writing this book, (2) the appeal for the student of history in the study of events, (3) the influence of Aristotle upon Polybius, (4) the elements of strength in the Roman government, (5) Polybius' feelings toward the Athenian government, (6) the fundamental attributes in every state by which it may be evaluated, (7) Roman practices to preserve the strength of the state, (8) Rome's advantage over Carthage, and (9) the author's implied forecast of Rome's future.

From: THE HISTORIES

I am aware that some will be at a loss to account for my interrupting the course of my narrative for the sake of entering upon the following disquisition on the Roman constitution. But I think that I have already in many passages made it fully evident that this particular branch of my work was one of the necessities imposed on me by the nature of my original design; and I pointed this out with special clearness in the preface which explained the scope of my history. I there stated that the feature of my work which was at once the best in itself, and the most instructive to the students of it, was that it would enable them to know and fully realise in what manner, and under what kind of constitution, it came about that nearly the whole world fell under the power of Rome in somewhat less than fifty-three years, —an event certainly without precedent. This being my settled purpose, I could see no more fitting period than the present for making a pause, and examining the truth of the remarks about to be made on this constitution. In private life if you wish to satisfy yourself as to the badness or goodness of particular persons, you would not, if you wish to get a genuine test, examine their conduct at a time of uneventful repose, but in the hour of brilliant success or conspicuous reverse. For the true test of a perfect man is the power of bearing with spirit and dignity violent changes of fortune. An examination of a constitution should be conducted in the same way: and therefore being unable to find in our day a more rapid or more signal change than that which has happened to Rome, I reserved my disquisition on its constitution for this place. . . .

What is really educational and beneficial to students of history is the clear view of the causes of events, and the consequent power of choosing the better policy in a particular case. Now in every practical undertaking by a state we must regard as the most powerful agent for success or failure the form of its constitution; for from this as from a fountainhead all con-

As translated by Evelyn S. Shuckburgh in *The Histories of Polybius*, 2 vols., Macmillan and Company, London and New York, 1889, I, 458–459; 466–467; 474–475; 494–501; 506–507. Courtesy of The Macmillan Company.

ceptions and plans of action not only proceed, but attain their consummation. . . .

I am fully conscious that to those who actually live under this constitution I shall appear to give an inadequate account of it by the omission of certain details. Knowing accurately every portion of it from personal experience, and from having been bred up in its customs and laws from childhood, they will not be struck so much by the accuracy of the description, as annoyed by its omissions; nor will they believe that the historian has purposely omitted unimportant distinctions, but will attribute his silence upon the origin of existing institutions or other important facts to ignorance. What is told they depreciate as insignificant or beside the purpose; what is omitted they desiderate as vital to the question: their object being to appear to know more than the writers. But a good critic should not judge a writer by what he leaves unsaid, but from what he says: if he detects misstatement in the latter, he may then feel certain that ignorance accounts for the former; but if what he says is accurate, his omissions ought to be attributed to deliberate judgment and not to ignorance. So much for those whose criticisms are prompted by personal ambition rather than by justice. . . .

Another requisite for obtaining a judicious approval for an historical disquisition, is that it should be germane to the matter in hand; if this is not observed, though its style may be excellent and its matter irreproachable, it will seem out of place, and disgust rather than please. . . .

As for the Roman constitution, it had three elements, each of them possessing sovereign powers: and their respective share of power in the whole state had been regulated with such a scrupulous regard to equality and equilibrium, that no one could say for certain, not even a native, whether the constitution as a whole were an aristocracy or democracy or despotism. And no wonder: for if we confine our observation to the power of the Consuls we should be inclined to regard it as despotic; if on that of the Senate, as aristocratic; and if finally one looks at the power possessed by the people it would seem a clear case of a democracy. What the exact powers of these several parts were,

and still, with slight modifications, are, I will now state.

The Consuls, before leading out the legions, remain in Rome and are supreme masters of the administration. All other magistrates, except the Tribunes, are under them and take their orders. They introduce foreign ambassadors to the Senate; bring matters requiring deliberation before it; and see to the execution of its decrees. If, again, there are any matters of state which require the authorisation of the people, it is their business to see to them, to summon the popular meetings, to bring the proposals before them, and to carry out the decrees of the majority. In the preparations for war also, and in a word in the entire administration of a campaign, they have all but absolute power. It is competent to them to impose on the allies such levies as they think good, to appoint the Military Tribunes, to make up the roll for soldiers and select those that are suitable. Besides they have absolute power of inflicting punishment on all who are under their command while on active service: and they have authority to expend as much of the public money as they choose, being accompanied by a Quaestor who is entirely at their orders. A survey of these powers would in fact justify our describing the constitution as despotic,—a clear case of royal government. Nor will it affect the truth of my description, if any of the institutions I have described are changed in our time, or in that of our posterity: and the same remarks apply to what follows.

The Senate has first of all the control of the treasury, and regulates the receipts and disbursements alike. For the Quaestors cannot issue any public money for the various departments of the state without a decree of the Senate, except for the service of the Consuls. The Senate controls also what is by far the largest and most important expenditure, that, namely, which is made by the Censors every *lustrum* for the repair or construction of public buildings; this money cannot be obtained by the Censors except by the grant of the Senate. Similarly all crimes committed in Italy requiring a public investigation, such as treason, conspiracy, poisoning, or wilful murder, are in the hands of the Senate. Besides, if any individual or state among the Italian allies requires a controversy to be settled, a penalty to be assessed, help or protection to be afforded, —all this is the province of the Senate. Or again, outside Italy, if it is necessary to send an embassy to reconcile warring communities, or to remind them of their duty, or sometimes to impose requisitions upon them, or to receive their submission, or finally to proclaim war against them,—this too is the business of the Senate. In like manner the reception to be given to foreign ambassadors in Rome, and the answers to be returned to them, are decided by the Senate. With such business the people have nothing to do. Consequently, if one were staying at Rome when the Consuls were not in town, one would imagine the constitution to be a complete aristocracy: and this has been the idea entertained by many Greeks, and by many kings as well, from the fact that nearly all the business they had with Rome was settled by the Senate.

After this one would naturally be inclined to ask what part is left for the people in the constitution, when the Senate has these various functions, especially the control of the receipts and expenditure of the exchequer; and when the Consuls, again, have absolute power over the details of military preparation, and an absolute authority in the field? There is, however, a part left the people, and it is a most important one. For the people are the sole fountain of honour and of punishment; and it is by these two things and these alone that dynasties and constitutions and, in a word, human society are held together: for where the distinction between them is not sharply drawn both in theory and practice, there no undertaking can be properly administered,—as indeed we might expect when good and bad are held in exactly the same honour. The people then are the only court to decide matters of life and death; and even in cases where the penalty is money, if the sum to be assessed is sufficiently serious, and especially when the accused have held the higher magistracies. And in regard to this arrangement there is one point deserving especial commendation and record. Men who are on trial for their lives at Rome, while sentence is in process of being voted,—if even only one of the tribes whose votes are needed to ratify the sentence has not voted,—have the

privilege at Rome of openly departing and condemning themselves to a voluntary exile. Such men are safe at Naples or Praeneste or at Tibur, and at other towns with which this arrangement has been duly ratified on oath.

Again, it is the people who bestow offices on the deserving, which are the most honourable rewards of virtue. It has also the absolute power of passing or repealing laws; and, most important of all, it is the people who deliberate on the question of peace or war. And when provisional terms are made for alliance, suspension of hostilities, or treaties, it is the people who ratify them, or the reverse.

These considerations again would lead one to say that the chief power in the state was the people's, and that the constitution was a democracy.

Such, then, is the distribution of power between the several parts of the state. I must now show how each of these several parts can, when they choose, oppose or support each other.

The Consul, then, when he has started on an expedition with the powers I have described, is to all appearance absolute in the administration of the business in hand; still he has need of the support both of people and Senate, and, without them, is quite unable to bring the matter to a a successful conclusion. For it is plain that he must have supplies sent to his legions from time to time; but without a decree of the Senate they can be supplied neither with corn, nor clothes, nor pay, so that all the plans of a commander must be futile, if the Senate is resolved either to shrink from danger or hamper his plans. And again, whether a Consul shall bring any undertaking to a conclusion or no depends entirely upon the Senate: for it has absolute authority at the end of a year to send another Consul to supersede him, or to continue the existing one in his command. Again, even to the successes of the generals the Senate has the power to add distinction and glory, and on the other hand to obscure their merits and lower their credit. For these high achievements are brought in tangible form before the eyes of the citizens by what are called "triumphs." But these triumphs the commanders cannot celebrate with proper pomp, or in some cases celebrated at all, unless the Senate concurs and grants the necessary money. As for the people, the Consuls are pre-eminently obliged to court their favour, however distant from home may be the field of their operations; for it is the people, as I have said before, that ratify, or refuse to ratify, terms of peace and treaties; but most of all because when laying down their office they have to give an account of their administration before. Therefore in no case is it safe for the Consuls to neglect either the Senate or the good-will of the people.

As for the Senate, which possesses the immense power I have described, in the first place it is obliged in public affairs to take the multitude into account, and respect the wishes of the people; and it cannot put into execution the penalty for offences against the republic, which are punishable with death, unless the people first ratify its decrees. Similarly even in matters which directly affect the senators,—for instance, in the case of a law diminishing the Senate's traditional authority, or depriving senators of certain dignities and offices, or even actually cutting down their property,—even in such cases the people have the sole power of passing or rejecting the law. But most important of all is the fact that, if the Tribunes interpose their veto, the Senate not only is unable to pass a decree, but cannot even hold a meeting at all, whether formal or informal. Now, the Tribunes are always bound to carry out the decree of the people, and above all things to have regard to their wishes: therefore, for all these reasons the Senate stands in awe of the multitude, and cannot neglect the feelings of the people.

In like manner the people on their part are far from being independent of the Senate, and are bound to take its wishes into account both collectively and individually. For contracts, too numerous to count, are given out by the Censors in all parts of Italy for the repairs or construction of public buildings; there is also the collection of revenue from many rivers, harbours, gardens, mines, and land—everything, in a word, that comes under the control of the Roman government: and in all these the people at large are engaged; so that there is scarcely a man, so to speak, who is not interested either as a contractor or as being employed in the works. For some purchase the contracts from the Censors for themselves; and others go partners with them; while others again go security for these contractors, or actually pledge their property to the treasury for them. Now over all these transactions the Senate has absolute control. It can grant an extension of time; and in case of unforeseen accident can relieve the contractors from a portion of their obligation, or release them from it altogether, if they are absolutely unable to fulfil it. And there are many details in which the Senate can inflict great hardships, or, on the other hand, grant great indulgences to the contractors: for in every case the appeal is to it. But the most important point of all is that the judges are taken from its members in the majority of trials, whether public or private, in which the charges are heavy. Consequently, all citizens are much at its mercy; and being alarmed at the uncertainty as to when they may need its aid, are cautious about resisting or actively opposing its will. And for a similar reason men do not rashly resist the wishes of the Consuls, because one and all may become subject to their absolute authority on a campaign.

The result of this power of the several estates for mutual help or harm is a union sufficiently firm for all emergencies, and a constitution than which it is impossible to find a better. For whenever any danger from without compels them to unite and work together, the strength which is developed by the State is so extraordinary, that everything required is unfailingly carried out by the eager rivalry shown by all classes to devote their whole minds to the need of the hour, and to secure that any determination come to should not fail for want of promptitude; while each individual works, privately and publicly alike, for the accomplishment of the business in hand. Accordingly, the peculiar constitution of the State makes it irresistible, and certain of obtaining whatever it determines to attempt. Nay, even when these external alarms are past, and the people are enjoying their good fortune and the fruits of their victories, and, as usually happens, growing corrupted by flattery and idleness, show a tendency to violence and arrogance,—it is in these circumstances, more than ever, that the constitution is seen to possess within itself the power of correcting abuses. For when any one of the three classes becomes puffed up, and manifests an inclination to be contentious and unduly encroaching, the mutual interdependency of all the three, and the possibility of the pretensions of any one being checked and thwarted by the others, must plainly check this tendency: and so the proper equilibrium is maintained by the impulsiveness of the one part being checked by its fear of the other. . . .

Nearly all historians have recorded as constitutions of eminent excellence those of Lacedaemonia, Crete, Mantinea, and Carthage. Some have also mentioned those of Athens and Thebes. The former I may allow to pass; but I am convinced that little need be said of the Athenian and Theban constitutions: their growth was abnormal, the period of their zenith brief, and the changes they experienced unusually violent. Their glory was a sudden and fortuitous flash, so to speak; and while they still thought themselves prosperous, and likely to remain so, they found themselves involved in circumstances completely the reverse. The Thebans got their reputation for valour among the Greeks, by taking advantage of the senseless policy of the Lacedaemonians, and the hatred of the allies towards them, owing to the valour of one, or at most two, men who were wise enough to appreciate the situation. Since fortune quickly made it evident that it was not the peculiarity of their constitution, but the valour of their leaders, which gave the Thebans their success. For the great power of Thebes notoriously took its rise, attained its zenith, and fell to the ground with the lives of Epaminondas and Pelopidas. We must therefore conclude that it was not its constitution, but its men, that caused the high fortune which it then enjoyed.

A somewhat similar remark applies to the Athenian constitution also. For though it perhaps had more frequent interludes of excellence, yet its highest perfection was attained during the brilliant career of Themistocles; and having reached that point it quickly declined, owing to its essential instability. For the Athenian demos is always in the position of a ship without a commander. In such a ship, if fear of the enemy, or the occurrence of a storm, induce the crew to be of one mind and to obey the helmsman, everything goes well; but if they recover from this fear, and begin to treat their officers with contempt, and to quarrel with each other because they are no longer all of one mind,—one party wishing to continue the voyage, and the other urging the steersman to bring the ship to anchor; some letting out the sheets, and others hauling them in, and ordering the sails to be furled,—their discord and quarrels make a sorry show to lookers on; and the position of affairs is full of risk to those on board engaged on the same voyage: and the result has often been that, after escaping the dangers of the widest seas, and the most violent storms, they wreck their ship in harbour and close to shore. And this is what has often happened to the Athenian constitution. For, after repelling, on various occasions, the greatest and most formidable dangers by the valour of its people and their leaders, there have been times when, in periods of secure tranquillity, it has gratuitously and recklessly encountered disaster. Therefore I need say no more about either it, or the Theban constitution: in both of which a mob manages everything on its own unfettered impulse—a mob in the one city distinguished for headlong outbursts of fiery temper, in the other trained in long habits of violence and ferocity. . . .

To my mind, then, there are two things fundamental to every state, in virtue of which its powers and constitution become desirable or objectionable. These are customs and laws. Of these the desirable are those which make men's private lives holy and pure, and the public character of the state civilised and just. The objectionable are those whose effect is the reverse. As, then, when we see good customs and good laws prevailing among certain people, we confidently assume that, in consequence of them, the men and their civil constitution will be good also, so when we see private life full of covetousness, and public policy of injustice, plainly we have reason for asserting their laws, particular customs, and general constitution to be bad. . . .

Now the Carthaginian constitution seems to me originally to have been well contrived in these most distinctively important particulars. For they had kings, and the Gerusia had the powers of an aristocracy, and the multitude were supreme in such things as affected them; and on the whole the adjustment of its several parts was very like that of Rome and Sparta. But about the period of its entering on the Hannibalian war the political state of Carthage was on the decline, that of Rome improving. For whereas there is in every body, or polity, or business a natural stage of growth, zenith, and decay; and whereas everything in them is at its best at the zenith; we may thereby judge of the difference between these two constitutions as they existed at that period. For exactly so far as the strength and prosperity of Carthage preceded that of Rome in point of time, by so much was Carthage then past its prime, while Rome was exactly at its zenith, as far as its political constitution was concerned. In Carthage therefore the influence of the people in the policy of the state had already risen to be supreme, while at Rome the Senate was at the height of its power: and so, as in the one, measures were deliberated upon by the many, in the other, by the best men, the policy of the Romans in all public undertakings proved the stronger; on which account, though they met with capital disasters, by force of prudent counsels they finally conquered the Carthaginians in the war.

If we look however at separate details, for instance at the provisions for carrying on a war, we shall find that whereas for a naval expedition the Carthaginians are the better trained and prepared—as it is only natural with a people with whom it has been hereditary for many generations to practise this craft, and to follow the seaman's trade above all nations in the world—yet, in regard to military service on land, the Romans train themselves to a much higher pitch than the Carthaginians. The former bestow their whole attention upon this department: whereas the Carthaginians wholly neglect their infantry, though they do take some slight interest in the cavalry. The reason for this is that they employ foreign mercenaries, the Romans, native and citizen levies. It is in this point that the latter polity is preferable to the former. They have their hopes of freedom ever resting on the courage of mercenary troops: The Romans on the valour of their own citizens and the aid of their allies. The result is that even if the Romans have suffered a defeat at first, they renew the war with undiminished forces, which the Carthaginians cannot do. For, as the Romans are fighting for country and children, it is impossible for them to relax the fury of their struggle; but they persist with obstinate resolution until they have overcome their enemies. What has happened in regard to their navy is an instance in point. In skill the Romans are much behind the Carthaginians, as I have already said; yet the upshot of the whole naval war has been a decided triumph for the Romans, owing to the valour of their men. For although nautical science contributes largely to success in sea-fights, still it is the courage of the marines that turns the scale most decisively in favour of victory. The fact is that Italians as a nation are by nature superior to Phoenicians and Libyans both in physical strength and courage; but still their habits also do much to inspire the youth with enthusiasm for such exploits. One example will be sufficient of the pains taken by the Roman state to turn out men ready to endure anything to win a reputation in their country for valour.

Whenever one of their illustrious men dies, in the course of his funeral, the body with all its paraphernalia is carried into the forum to the rostra, as a raised platform there is called, and sometimes is propped upright upon it so as to be conspicuous, or, more rarely, is laid upon it. Then with all the people standing round, his son, if he has left one of full age and he is there, or, failing him, one of his relations, mounts the rostra and delivers a speech concerning the virtues of the deceased, and the successful exploits performed by him in his lifetime. By these means the people are reminded of what has been done, and made to see it with their own eyes—not only such as were engaged in the actual transactions but those also who were not—and their sympathies are so deeply moved, that the loss appears not to be confined to the actual mourners, but to be a public one affecting the whole people. After the burial and all the usual ceremonies have been performed, they place the likeness of the deceased in the most conspicuous spot in his house, surmounted by a wooden canopy or shrine. This likeness consists of a mask made to represent the deceased with extraordinary fidelity both in shape and colour. These likenesses they display at public sacrifices adorned with much care. And when any illustrious member of the family dies, they carry these masks to the funeral, putting them on men whom they thought as like the originals as possible in height and other personal peculiarities. And these substitutes assume clothes according to the rank of the person represented: if he was a Consul or Praetor, a toga with purple stripes; if a Censor, whole purple; if he had also celebrated a triumph or performed any exploit of that kind, a toga embroidered with gold. These representatives also ride themselves in chariots, while the fasces and axes, and all the other customary insignia of the particular offices, lead the way, according to the dignity of the rank in the state enjoyed by the deceased in his lifetime; and on arriving at the rostra they all take their seats on ivory chairs in their order. There could not easily be a more inspiring spectacle than this for a young man of noble ambitions and virtuous aspirations. For can we conceive any one to be unmoved at the sight of all the likenesses collected together of the men who have earned glory, all as it were living and breathing? Or what could be a more glorious spectacle?

Besides, the speaker over the body about to be buried, after having finished the panegyric of this particular person, starts upon the others whose representatives are present, beginning with the most ancient, and recounts the successes and achievements of each. By this means the glorious memory of brave men is continually renewed; the fame of those who have performed any noble deed is never allowed to die; and the renown of those who have done good service to their country becomes a matter of common knowledge to the multitude, and part of the heritage of posterity. But the chief benefit of the ceremony is that it inspires young men to shrink from no exertion for the general welfare, in the hope of obtaining the glory which awaits the brave. And what I say is confirmed by this fact. Many Romans have volunteered to decide a whole battle by single combat; not a few have deliberately accepted certain death, some in time of war to secure the safety of the rest, some in time of peace

to preserve the safety of the commonwealth. There have also been instances of men in office putting their own sons to death, in defiance of every custom and law, because they rated the interest of their country higher than those of natural ties even with their nearest and dearest. There are many stories of this kind, related of many men in Roman history; but one will be enough for our present purpose; and I will give the name as an instance to prove the truth of my words.

The story goes that Horatius Cocles, while fighting with two enemies at the head of the bridge over the Tiber, which is the entrance to the city on the north, seeing a large body of men advancing to support his enemies, and fearing that they would force their way into the city, turned round, and shouted to those behind him to hasten back to the other side and break down the bridge. They obeyed him: and whilst they were breaking the bridge, he remained at his post receiving numerous wounds, and checked the progress of the enemy: his opponents being panic-stricken, not so much by his strength as by the audacity with which he held his ground. When the bridge had been broken down, the attack of the enemy was stopped; and Cocles then threw himself into the river with his armour on and deliberately sacrificed his life, because he valued the safety of his country and his own future reputation more highly than his present life, and the years of existence that remained to him. Such is the enthusiasm and emulation for noble deeds that are engendered among the Romans by their customs.

Again the Roman customs and principles regarding money transactions are better than those of the Carthaginians. In the view of the latter, nothing is disgraceful that makes for gain; with the former nothing is more disgraceful than to receive bribes and to make profit by improper means. For they regard wealth obtained from unlawful transactions to be as much a subject of reproach, as a fair profit from the most unquestioned source is of commendation. A proof of the fact is this: The Carthaginians obtain office by open bribery, but among the Romans the penalty for it is death. With such a radical difference, therefore, between the rewards offered to virtue among the two peoples, it is natural that the ways adopted for obtaining them should be different also.

But the most important difference for the better which the Roman commonwealth appears to me to display is in their religious beliefs. For I conceive that what in other nations is looked upon as a reproach, I mean a scrupulous fear of the gods, is the very thing which keeps the Roman commonwealth together. To such an extraordinary height is this carried among them, both in private and public business, that nothing could exceed it. Many people might think this unaccountable; but in my opinion their object is to use it as a check upon the common people. If it were possible to form a state wholly of philosophers, such a custom would perhaps be unnecessary. But seeing that every multitude is fickle, and full of lawless desires, unreasoning anger, and violent passion, the only resource is to keep them in check by mysterious terrors and scenic efforts of this sort. Wherefore, to my mind, the ancients were not acting without purpose or at random, when they brought in among the vulgar those opinions about the gods, and the belief in the punishments in Hades: much rather do I think that men nowadays are acting rashly and foolishly in rejecting them. This is the reason why, apart from anything else, Greek statesmen, if entrusted with a single talent, though protected by ten checking-clerks, as many seals, and twice as many witnesses, yet cannot be induced to keep faith: whereas among the Romans, in their magistracies and embassies, men have the handling of a great amount of money, and yet from pure respect to their oath keep their faith intact. And, again, in other nations it is a rare thing to find a man who keeps his hands out of the public purse, and is entirely pure in such matters: but among the Romans it is a rare thing to detect a man in the act of committing such a crime. . . .

That to all things, then, which exist there is ordained decay and change I think requires no further arguments to show: for the inexora-

ble course of nature is sufficient to convince us of it.

But in all polities we observe two sources of decay existing from natural causes, the one external, the other internal and self-produced. The external admits of no certain or fixed definition, but the internal follows a definite order. What kind of polity, then, comes naturally first, and what second, I have already stated in such a way, that those who are capable of taking in the whole drift of my argument can henceforth draw their own conclusions as to the future of the Roman polity. For it is quite clear, in my opinion. When a commonwealth, after warding off many great dangers, has arrived at a high pitch of prosperity and undisputed power, it is evident that, by the lengthened continuance of great wealth within it, the manner of life of its citizens will become more extravagant; and that the rivalry for office, and in other spheres of activity, will become fiercer than it ought to be. And as this state of things goes on more and more, the desire of office and the shame of losing reputation, as well as the ostentation and extravagance of living, will prove the beginning of a deterioration. And of this change the people will be credited with being the authors, when they become convinced that they are being cheated by some from avarice, and are puffed up with flattery by others from love of office. For when that comes about, in their passionate resentment and acting under the dictates of anger, they will refuse to obey any longer, or to be content with having equal powers with their leaders, but will demand to have all or far the greatest themselves. And when that comes to pass the constitution will receive a new name, which sounds better than any other in the world, liberty or democracy; but, in fact, it will become that worst of all governments, mob-rule.

With this description of the formation, growth, zenith, and present state of the Roman polity, and having discussed also its difference, for better and worse, from other polities, I will now at length bring my essay on it to an end.

Julius Caesar

Caius Julius Caesar was born in 102 B.C., during the time of growing civil strife between the Senate and the popular party in Rome. By sympathy and family ties he became associated with the latter group in its efforts to break down the walls of privilege which the Senate was seeking to preserve under the cloak of republican institutions. In 50 B.C. the conflict reached a climax when Caesar, fresh from his Gallic triumphs, sought election to the consulship while still in his province. His enemies in the Senate raised legal difficulties against his ambitions, and Pompey, as sole consul, became his principal antagonist. In 49 B.C. Caesar led his famous legions across the Rubicon River, the boundary of his province, and the civil war was on. This selection is from Caesar's Civil War and describes in his own words the outbreak of this struggle which so changed the course of history. In reading it note (1) the proposals of Caesar's friends in the Senate, (2) the methods used in rejecting them, (3) Pompey's efforts to bolster his supporters, (4) the motives Caesar attributed to his opponents, (5) the Senate's preparation for war, (6) the basis on which Caesar appealed to his troops for their support, (7) the ultimatums of the two leaders, and (8) the eloquence of Caesar's literary style when he stated his own position.

From: CAESAR'S WAR WITH POMPEIUS

When Caesar's dispatch reached the consuls, it was only the urgent representations of the tribunes that gained it a hearing by the House; the further request for a definite motion on its terms was refused, and the House passed, at the instance of the Government, to the general debate upon public affairs. Lucius Lentulus pledged his support to the Senate and Republic, provided members were ready to express themselves with boldness and determination; but any coquetting with Caesar or bidding for his favour, such as they had shown in previous years, would find him consulting his own interests without the slightest heed to their decrees. "He, as well as they," he added significantly, "had his line of retreat open to him in the favour and friendship of Caesar." Scipio spoke in similar terms. Pompeius was

resolved to stand by the Republic if supported by the Senate; but let them hesitate or shrink from decided measures, and any subsequent appeal to his aid, should they afterwards desire it, would only be made in vain. This speech of Scipio's was taken by the House as representing the actual language of Pompeius; for, although they were met within the city walls, Pompeius was at the time in the neighborhood of Rome. Other and more conciliatory measures, it should be noticed, had been previously counselled by various members present. Marcus Marcellus, for example, in addressing the House had urged that it was premature to discuss the main issue till levies had been completed throughout Italy, and armies put into commission; under whose protection they could then venture to formulate their wishes with

As translated by F. P. Long in *Caesar's Civil War with Pompeius,* Clarendon Press, Oxford, 1906, 1–11. Courtesy of the Clarendon Press.

liberty and security. Again, Marcus Calidius had a proposal that Pompeius should leave Italy and go off to his provinces, thereby removing all pretext for war; since what Caesar feared was that the retention near the capital of the two legions lately extorted from him by the Senate should look like a deliberate menace from Pompeius to himself. This proposal of Calidius was repeated, with slight verbal changes, by Marcus Caelius Rufus.

They were one and all made the object of a savage attack by the presiding consul Lentulus, and effectually silenced by his scathing satire: in fact, he even went so far as to refuse to put the motion of Calidius; whereupon Marcellus, alarmed at the growing storm of obloquy, withdrew that standing in his name. The result was that this language of the consul, backed up by the terrorizing effect of the presence of the army, together with the open threats of Pompeius's friends, succeeded in forcing the House, against the convictions of the majority, to adopt the motion of Scipio, whereby Caesar was to disband his army before a fixed date or be held guilty of open treason. This resolution being vetoed by two of the tribunes, Marcus Antonius and Quintus Cassius, the legality of such veto was immediately challenged. Extreme opinions were expressed, and the applause that greeted each speaker from the ranks of Caesar's opponents was in direct proportion to the bitter and vindictive spirit each displayed.

It was evening before the Senate broke up, and Pompeius at once summoned to a conference outside the city all who possessed a seat in the House, praising their recent action and stiffening them to face the future, while rebuking and stimulating the faint-hearted. From all parts of the country large numbers of those who had belonged to the old Pompeian armies were called out for active service, induced by hopes of plunder and high military rank; many also of those who were attached to the two legions lately transferred by Caesar now received orders to be in attendance; with the result that the city, the ascent to the Capitol, and the Comitium were soon crowded with regimental officers, centurions, and reservists. An overflowing meeting of the House was shortly afterwards held, packed with the friends of both consuls, and the supporters, not merely of Pompeius, but of all who nursed old grievances against Caesar; and these, by their threatening language and imposing numbers, intimidated the weak-kneed, strengthened the waverers, and made a free decision for most of those present impossible. An offer was made by Lucius Piso, one of the censors, and Lucius Roscius, one of the praetors, to carry a report of these proceedings to Caesar, six days only being asked for the purpose: similarly others urged that a commission be sent to lay before him the mind of the House.

To all alike objection was raised, and all alike were thwarted by speeches from the consul, from Scipio, and from Cato. Cato's opposition was due to long-standing dislike of Caesar, increased by resentment at an electoral defeat. The action of the consul Lentulus was dictated by the colossal proportions of his debts, which he looked forward to settling by the command of an army and provinces, and by the princely profits to be made out of foreign king-making: indeed, he boasted in private that he would be a second Sulla, into whose hands the supreme government would one day fall. As for Scipio, his motives were similar ambitions for a province and armies, the command of which he thought he, as a relative, would share with Pompeius: to this must be added his fears of prosecution, and also the ostentatious flattery of which he was at this time the subject, not merely from himself, but from all his most powerful contemporaries in the political and legal worlds. Finally, in the case of Pompeius, the influence of Caesar's opponents along with his inability to tolerate a rival on equal terms, had induced him completely to withdraw his old friendship and to resume intimate relations with their common antagonists, whose enmity, in the majority of cases, he had himself fastened upon Caesar in the old days of their family alliance. In addition to this, the public stigma attaching to the affair of the two legions, which, instead of marching for Asia Minor and Syria, had been diverted by him to secure his own sovereignty, drove him to work for a settlement by the sword.

It was such considerations that now caused everything to be hurried through in disorder. The delay asked for by Caesar's friends, in order to acquaint him with these developments, was steadily refused; the two tribunes of the people were allowed no opportunity either of protesting against their personal peril, or even of maintaining, in the form of the veto, that fundamental right of their office which had been left them by Lucius Sulla. The seventh day of the New Year saw them compelled to take measures for their personal safety, such as, in the case of the notorious revolutionaries of the past, had generally been adopted as their hazardous refuge only after eight months spent in multifarious political activity. Such indecent haste, in fact, was now displayed, that without more ado recourse was had to the very last weapon of Senatorial government,— the well-known "final decree,"—which no amount of effrontery in popular legislators had ever before brought to a division in the House, unless indeed Rome were all but burning, and the very existence of the country despaired of, —the decree directing consuls, praetors, tribunes, and all proconsuls near the capital to take measures for the safety of the State. This order was embodied in a decree of the House dated January 7: and thus within the first five days on which the Senate could legally be convened since Lentulus entered upon office (not reckoning the two days set down for comitial business), a decision was arrived at of extreme severity and malignity both on the question of Caesar's military command, and on the fate of two distinguished tribunes of the people. The latter at once left Rome and fled to Caesar, who was then at Ravenna, awaiting an answer to his very moderate demands, and still hoping that man's general sense of fairness would render a peaceful solution possible.

The next few days the Senate met outside the city boundary. The conduct of Pompeius tallied with the forecast given of it by Scipio. After commending the courage and firmness that the Senators had just displayed, he proceeded to lay before them an account of the military forces at his disposal, which were not less, he declared, than ten fully mobilized Roman legions. To this was added the statement that he had trustworthy intelligence that Caesar's troops looked coldly on his schemes, and could neither be induced to support his cause, nor to follow his leadership. Motions were then put before the House dealing with other requisite measures. It was proposed that enlisting should be organized throughout Italy; that Faustus Sulla should be dispatched without delay to Morocco (Mauretania); and lastly, that Pompeius should be supplied with money from the Treasury. The question was also raised of making an alliance of friendship with King Juba, but the consul Marcellus refused for the present to entertain this idea; whilst the proposal concerning Faustus was vetoed by Philippus, one of the tribunes. The rest were duly embodied in regular decrees. It was further determined to give commands of provinces to men not then in office, two of these to be consular and the rest praetorian. Of the former, Syria fell to Scipio, Gaul to Lucius Domitius. By a clandestine arrangement, Philippus and Cotta were passed over, neither of their lots being thrown in. To the remaining provinces ex-praetors were sent out; and these, without waiting for the legal confirmation of their command by the people, after offering the customary state-prayers, immediately left the capital in full military attire. The consuls, acting against all precedent, took their departure from the city, whilst inside and on the Capitol lictors were seen in attendance on men no longer in office, a sight unexampled in the history of the commonwealth. Over the whole of Italy troops were being enlisted, arms commandeered, money levied on the country towns and even plundered from the temples; in short, every distinction between the claims of the State and of religion was obliterated.

Caesar no sooner had intelligence of these proceedings than he appealed to his troops. After recounting in detail the wrongs he had suffered at the hands of his political opponents, he charged Pompeius with having allowed his mind to be misled, and his judgment to be warped by the pernicious influence these exerted upon him, owing to the petty jealousy he felt at his rival's reputation; and that, despite the fact that that rival had himself always actively supported the power and prestige of Pompeius. A further grievance was the establishment of an unwarrantable precedent in the constitution, when military force was invoked to annul and to override the tribunes' power of veto—that same veto which in past years had only been restored by a similar appeal to force.

Even Sulla, who stripped the tribunician office of all its functions, yet left it the free exercise of the veto; Pompeius, who was regarded as the restorer of their lost privileges, had actually succeeded in robbing them of what they had always enjoyed. Again, on every occasion when the well-known decree had been passed for the magistrates "to see to it that the country take no harm"—the statutory formula for summoning the Roman people to arms—it had been at a time either of the promulgation of some obnoxious legislation, of some violence offered by a tribune, or of some popular disturbance; and then only after the temples and city heights had already been seized. How such revolutionary attempts in past history had been avenged by the downfall of Saturninus and the Gracchi, he next reminded them. Yet of these circumstances not one had at this time arisen or been even thought of: no law had been promulgated, no popular legislation proposed, no disturbance taken place. He called upon them now to protect from political adversaries the honour and good name of their commander, under whose leadership for nine long years they had fought with such brilliant success the battles of their country, during which time they had gained such numberless victories, and subjugated the whole of Gaul and Germany.

The men of the Thirteenth legion, the only one present, answered with a cheer (Caesar had summoned this regiment to him when the general levy in Italy began; the concentration of the others was not yet completed), "they were ready to protect the rights of their commander and of the people's tribunes."

Assured of the temper of his troops, Caesar began his advance with this legion as far as Rimini (Ariminum), where he met the two tribunes who had lately fled to his protection: his remaining legions he ordered out of their winter quarters with instructions to follow close in his rear. At Rimini he was waited on by young Lucius Caesar, a son of one of his own generals. This young man, after first stating the primary object of his mission, went on to explain that he had a private message from Pompeius to Caesar on the subject of their personal relations. This was to the effect that "Pompeius desired to clear himself in Caesar's eyes, so that the latter should not take as an insult to himself what had solely been dictated by public exigencies; that he had always regarded the claims of public interests as prior to those of private friendship, and that Caesar similarly should now show his true greatness by sacrificing ambition and passion to the general good, and not allow resentment against opponents to go so far as to involve his country in the punishment he hoped to inflict upon them." There was more in the same strain along with excuses for the conduct of Pompeius; and a very similar appeal, in similar language, was made to Caesar by the praetor Roscius, who stated that he had it from Pompeius.

Now, although this episode had apparently but little bearing on the removal of his own grievances, yet, finding appropriate agents at hand for conveying his wishes to Pompeius, Caesar begged each of them that, as they had brought him Pompeius's terms, so they would not object to taking back his own demands to Pompeius. It was surely worth while to go to a little trouble, if by this means a great quarrel could be settled and the whole of Italy thus freed from apprehension. "Let them then understand that with him honour had always been first,—dearer than life itself. This honour had been wounded when the privilege granted him by the people of Rome had been floutingly snatched from him by opponents, and when, after being robbed of six months' command, he found himself, as he now did, dragged back to the capital, in spite of the fact that a resolution allowing his candidature at the approaching elections to be accepted in his absence had been expressly passed by the sovereign people. Though, however, he had borne without complaint, for the sake of public peace, this curtailment of his rights, yet his own modest suggestion for a general disarmament, which he made in a dispatch to the Senate, had been bluntly refused: levies were even now proceeding throughout Italy; whilst the two legions which had been detached from his command on the pretext of a Parthian war, were still detained at home: in short, the whole country was in arms. What did all this point to except his own destruction? Still, he was ready to stoop to every humiliation and to endure every injustice, if thereby he could save the commonwealth. Accordingly, these were his terms: Pompeius to take his departure to his own provinces, and both to disband their armies simultaneously with a general disarmament in Italy. That would allay the apprehension of the country, and enable elections and the whole machinery of government to be carried on by both Senate and people without coercion. Lastly, in order to facilitate the settlement by giving it fixed terms and the sanction of their sworn oath, he proposed that either Pompeius should advance to meet him, or else allow a visit from himself; for he felt confident that by talking matters over all differences could be adjusted." With this message Roscius and Lucius Caesar came to Capua, where they found the consuls and Pompeius, to whom they delivered Caesar's stipulations. After due deliberation an answer was returned by the same messengers, who thereupon brought back the written demands the other side had to make, of which the following represents the summary: "Caesar must recross the Rubicon, evacuate Rimini, and disband his army; after that, Pompeius would go to his Spanish provinces. Meanwhile until a pledge had been given that Caesar would keep his word, the consuls and Pompeius would continue to raise troops."

It was obviously a one-sided bargain to require Caesar to evacuate Rimini and retire upon his province, whilst his opponent kept both provinces and legions alike to which he had no claim: to propose that Caesar's army should be disbanded, while yet proceeding with his own levy: or again, to undertake to go to his province, without, however, fixing a date for his departure. The consequence of this last provision would have been that, supposing at the close of Caesar's consulship Pompeius had not yet left Rome, he could not justly be held guilty of any breach of faith by this refusal to quit the capital. Finally, his omission to arrange an interview or to promise any visit could but reduce the chances of peace to a minimum. Accordingly Caesar dispatched Marcus Antonius with a force of five battalions to seize Arrezo (Arretium), whilst he himself remained with two more at Rimini, where the raising of fresh troops was forthwith commenced. At the same time, with the three remaining battalions of his single legion he occupied the coast towns of Pesaro (Pisaurum), Fano (Fanum), and Ancona.

Tacitus

Tacitus was a Roman historian of the first century A.D. and one of the great writers of all time. The Annals is a brilliantly written history of the Empire from the death of Augustus to the death of Nero. His dislike of tyranny and vice inevitably colored his account, which is nevertheless outstanding for its characterizations of the principal men of the time. In reading the selections from The Annals note (1) the brief description of Roman political history prior to the reign of Augustus, (2) the purpose of Tacitus in writing The Annals, (3) his explanation for the success of Augustus, (4) evidences of prejudice against the new regime, (5) the characterization of Tiberius, and (6) the early events of his reign.

From: THE ANNALS

The first form of government that prevailed at Rome was monarchy. Liberty and the consulship were established by Lucius Junius Brutus. Dictators were created in sudden emergencies only. The jurisdiction of the decemvirs did not extend beyond two years; and the consular authority of the military tribunes soon expired. The domination of Cinna ended in a

As translated by Arthur Murphy in *The Historical Works of Tacitus*, 2 vols., Everyman's Library, J. M. Dent and Sons, Ltd., E. P. Dutton and Sons, Inc., New York, 1908, I, 4–11. Courtesy of E. P. Dutton and Sons, Inc.

short time; and that of Sylla was not of long duration. From Pompey and Crassus, the whole power of the state devolved to Julius Caesar, and, after the struggle with Lepidus and Antony, centred in Augustus; who, under the mild and well-known title of *prince of the senate,* took upon him the management of the commonwealth, enfeebled as it was by an exhausting series of civil wars. But the memorable transactions of the old republic, as well in her day of adversity as in the tide of success, have been recorded by writers of splendid genius. Even in the time of Augustus there flourished a race of authors, from whose abilities that period might have received ample justice; but the spirit of adulation growing epidemic, the dignity of the historic character was lost. What has been transmitted to us concerning Tiberius, Caligula, Claudius, and Nero, cannot be received without great mistrust. During the lives of those emperors, fear suppressed or disfigured the truth; and after their deaths, recent feelings gave an edge to resentment. For this reason, it is my intention shortly to state some particulars relating to Augustus, chiefly towards the close of his life; and thence to follow downward the thread of my narration through the reigns of Tiberius and his three immediate successors, free from animosity and partial affection, with the candour of a man who has no motives, either of love or hatred, to warp his integrity.

The fate of Brutus and Cassius being decided, the commonwealth had no longer an army engaged in the cause of public liberty. The younger Pompey received a total overthrow on the coast of Sicily; Lepidus was deprived of his legions; and Mark Antony fell on his own sword. In that situation the partisans of Julius Caesar had no leader but Octavius, who laid aside the invidious title of Triumvir, content with the more popular name of Consul, and with the tribunitian power, which he professed to assume for the protection of the people. In a little time, when he had allured to his interest the soldiery by a profusion of largesses, the people by distributions of corn, and the minds of men in general by the sweets of peace, his views grew more aspiring. By degrees, and almost imperceptibly, he drew into his own hands the authority of the senate, the functions of the magistrates, and the administration of the laws. To these encroachments no opposition was made. The true republican had perished, either in the field of battle, or by the rigour of proscriptions: of the remaining nobility, the leading men were raised to wealth and honours, in proportion to the alacrity with which they courted the yoke; and all who in the distraction of the times had risen to affluence, preferred immediate ease and safety to the danger of contending for ancient freedom. The provinces acquiesced under the new establishment, weary of the mixed authority of the senate and people; a mode of government long distracted by contentions among the great, and in the end rendered intolerable by the avarice of public magistrates; while the laws afford a feeble remedy, disturbed by violence, defeated by intrigue, and undermined by bribery and corruption.

In this state of affairs, Augustus selected Claudius Marcellus and Marcus Agrippa, to prop and strengthen his administration. The former, who was his sister's son, and still a youth, he raised to the dignity of pontiff and aedile: on the latter, by his birth obscure, but eminent for military talents, and the companion of all his victories, he conferred the honour of two successive consulships; and in a short time after, upon the untimely death of Marcellus, chose him for his son-in-law. Tiberius Nero and Claudius Drusus, the sons of his wife Livia, were adorned with the title of *imperator,* though the succession in the house of Augustus was at the time well secured by other branches of the house of Caesar. He had already adopted into the imperial family Caius and Lucius, the two sons of Agrippa; and to see them, even before they had put on the manly gown, considered as princes of the Roman youth, and marked out as future consuls, was his ardent desire; though for political reasons, he chose to disguise his sentiments. To obtain those honours for his family was the wish of his heart; while, under a show of coy reluctance, he seemed to reject them. Agrippa departed this life; and in a short time after his two sons were cut off; Lucius Caesar on his road to join the army in Spain; and Caius on his return from Armenia, where he had received a wound that impaired his health. Whether they died by their own premature fate, or the machinations of their stepmother Livia, is to this day problematical. Drusus had paid his debt to nature, leaving Tiberius the only surviving son-in-law of the emperor. The current of court favour was now directed that way. He was adopted by Augustus, declared his colleague in the government, his associate in the tribunitian power, and shown as the rising sun to the army; not, as before, by the secret arts of Livia, but with her open and avowed direction. Augustus was now in the decline of life, and Livia had gained unbounded influence over his affections. By her contrivance Agrippa Posthumus, the only surviving grandson of the emperor, was banished to the isle of Planasia. In praise of this young man much cannot be said: he was a stranger to the liberal arts, uncouth, unformed, and stupidly valuing himself on his bodily strength; yet free from vice, or the imputation of a crime.

At this time Germanicus, the immediate descendant of Drusus, was appointed to the command of eight legions on the Rhine. By the emperor's direction Tiberius adopted him as his son, though he had then issue of his own growing up to manhood. The policy, no doubt, was to guard the succession with additional securities. Augustus, in that juncture, had no war upon his hands, that in Germany excepted; which was carried on, not with a view to extension of empire, or any solid advantage, but solely to expiate the disgrace incurred by the loss of Varus and his legions. A perfect calm prevailed at Rome: the magistrates retained their ancient names; the younger part of the community were born since the battle of Actium, and the old during the civil wars: how many were then living, who had seen the constitution of their country?

The government thus overthrown, nothing remained of ancient manners, or ancient spirit. Of independence, or the equal condition of Roman citizens, no trace was left. All ranks submitted to the will of the prince, little solicitous about the present hour; while Augustus, in the vigour of health, maintained at once his own dignity, the honour of his house, and the public tranquillity. In process of time, when, worn with age, and failing under bodily infirmities, he seemed to approach the last act, a new scene presented itself to the hopes of men. Some amused themselves with ideas of ancient liberty, many dreaded the horrors of a civil war, and others wished for public commotion; the greater part discussed, with a variety of opinions, the character of the new masters at that moment impending over the state. "Agrippa was rude and savage; disgrace added to his natural ferocity; and, in point of age and experience, he was by no means equal to the weight of empire. Tiberius was matured by years; he had gained reputation in war; but the pride of the Claudian family was inveterate in his nature, and his inbred cruelty, however suppressed with art, announced itself in various shapes. Trained up in the imperial house, in the very bosom of despotism, he had been inured from his youth to the pomp and pride of consulships and triumphs. During the years which he passed in a seeming retreat, but real exile, in the isle of Rhodes, he meditated nothing so much as plans of future vengeance, clandestine pleasures, and the arts of dissimulation." To these reflections the public added their dread of a mother raging with all the impotence of female ambition: a whole people, they said, were to be enslaved by a woman, and two young men, who in the beginning would hang heavy on the state, and in the end distract and rend it to pieces by their own dissensions.

While these and other observations of a similar nature employed the public mind, the health of Augustus declined apace. The wickedness of his wife was not supposed to remain inactive. A rumour prevailed, that Augustus had gone a few months before, in a private manner, with a select party, and Fabius Maximus, his confidential friend, to the island of Planasia, on a visit to Agrippa. The meeting was said to be of the tenderest nature; tears were shed by both, and a scene of mutual affection followed. From that interview hopes were conceived, that the young prince would be once more restored to the favour and protection of his grandfather. The secret soon transpired: Fabius communicated the whole to his wife Marcia, and by her it was conveyed to Livia. Augustus knew that he had been betrayed. Maximus died soon after, perhaps by his own hand: but of that nothing can be said with certainty. At his funeral Marcia was heard, in the vehemence of distress and sorrow, to accuse herself of being accessory to the death of her husband. However that may be, Tiberius had scarcely set foot in Illyricum, when he received despatches from his mother, requiring his immediate presence. He arrived at Nola: but whether Augustus was still living, or had breathed his last, must be left in doubt. By Livia's order the avenues were closely guarded: favorable accounts were issued from time to time; and with that artifice mankind was amused, till all proper measures were concerted. At length the same report that announced the death of Augustus, proclaimed Tiberius in possession of the supreme power.

The first exploit of the new reign [A.U.C. 767, A.D. 14] was the murder of Agrippa Posthumus. A centurion of undaunted resolution attacked him by surprise. Though unprovided with arms, the young man did not easily yield: he fell after a stout resistance. Of this event Tiberius made no report to the senate, content with hinting a pretended order of his deceased father, by which the centurion, charged with the custody of Agrippa's person, was commanded to despatch him, as soon as the emperor breathed his last. Augustus, it is true, had arraigned the character and conduct of the young man in terms of asperity; he had even banished him by a decree of the senate: but it is equally true, that he never imbrued his hands in the blood of his kindred; nor is it probable that, for the security of a stepson, he would have doomed to death a descendant from himself. The stronger presumption is, that Tiberius and Livia, the former impelled by his dread of a rival, and the latter by the malice of a stepmother, were accomplices in the murder. When the assassin, in the military phrase, reported to Tiberius, that what he had given in orders was duly executed, the reply of the new emperor was, that he had given no such orders, and for what was done the centurion must answer before the Senate.

A disavowal so very extraordinary gave the alarm to Sallustius Crispus, a minister then in favour, and trusted with the secrets of the court. The warrant for the execution had passed through his hands. He dreaded a public examination; well aware that whether he disclosed the truth, or attempted to disguise it, his own danger would, in either case, be precisely the same. To ward off the blow, he remonstrated to Livia, that the secret counsels of the imperial family, the conduct of ministers, and the actions of the centurions, ought to be veiled from the public eye. By referring too much to the Senate, the prince would weaken his own authority: that men should be accountable to the sovereign only, was a branch of the imperial prerogative; and if Tiberius departed from it, he ceased to reign.

At Rome, in the meantime, all things tended to a state of abject servitude. Consuls, senators, and Roman knights, contended with emulation, who should be the most willing slaves. The higher each person's rank, the more he struggled for the foremost place in bondage. All appeared with a studied countenance. An air of gaiety might dishonour the memory of Augustus, and sadness would ill befit the opening of a new reign. A motley farce was acted; and grief and joy, distress and flattery, succeeding by turns, were curiously mixed and blended. The oath of fidelity to Tiberius was taken first by the two consuls, Sextus Pompeius and Sextus Apuleius, and by them administered to Seius Strabo and Caius Turranius; the former, praefect of the praetorian bands; the latter, controller of the corn and public stores. Their example was followed by the senate, the army, and the mass of the people.

To make everything move from the consuls, was the policy of Tiberius. He affected the appearance of republican principles, as if the constitution still subsisted, and he himself had formed no design to destroy it. The very proclamation, by which he convened the senate, professed no other authority than that of the tribunitian power conferred upon him by Augustus. The proclamation itself was short, and penned in modest terms; importing, "that the business of meeting was, to decree funeral honours to his deceased father; as to himself, he could not leave the body; that office of piety was the only function that he presumed to exercise." This was, indeed, the language of moderation; but Augustus was no sooner dead, than he assumed the supreme authority; in his character of imperator, he took upon him the whole military command; he gave the word to the praetorian guards; sentinels were stationed round the palace; the soldiers appeared under arms; the magnificence of a court was seen in all its forms; guards attended him to the forum; guards conducted him to the Senate-house; all things announced the sovereign. In his despatches to the army, he was already the successor of Augustus: he spoke the style and language of a recognised emperor, without reserve, and in the tone of power, equivocal only when he addressed the Senate.

The fact was, Tiberius dreaded Germanicus. A commander-in-chief, who had so many legions under his direction, who had formed connections with the allies of Rome, and was besides the idol of the people, might choose to seize the government, rather than linger in expectation. For this reason the fathers were to be managed.

There was at the bottom another motive: if, in appearance, he owed his elevation, not to the intrigues of an ambitious mother, or the adoption of a superannuated emperor, but to the voice of the people, it would redound more to his glory. The opportunity was also fair, to pry into the temper and dispositions of the leading senators. The event showed that his indecision was policy in disguise. He noted the words of men, he watched their looks; warped every circumstance into a crime; and, hoarding all in his memory, gathered rancour for a future day.

Vergil

Vergil (70 B.C.–19 A.D.) attracted considerable attention during the reign of Augustus with his beautiful poetry. Partially inspired by the achievements of the Augustan age and partially prompted by the great emperor, Vergil wrote his greatest work, The Aeneid. The story is that of the founding of Rome by the mythical Aeneas, but the theme is really the epic of Rome—the virtues which had made it great, and the destiny which was naturally hers. The books of the poem are concerned with the wanderings of Aeneas from Troy to the site of the city of Rome. In the sixth book the Cumaean Sibyl (guardian of the secrets of Apollo) conducted the hero into hell, and after passing through the various areas of the region, finally came to his father, Anchises, who told him of the future of Rome and the men who would contribute to its greatness. In reading this selection note (1) the character of Aeneas, (2) evidences of Greek influence on Vergil and the Romans, (3) the crimes committed by those suffering torture, (4) the souls of the great Romans waiting to be born, (5) the peculiar destiny of Rome in contrast to other states, and (6) efforts to link Rome with a glorious past.

From: THE AENEID

Now smiling hope, with sweet vicissitude,
Within the hero's mind his joys renew'd.
He calls to raise the masts, the sheets display;
The cheerful crew with diligence obey;
They scud before the wind, and sail in open sea.
Ahead of all the master pilot steers;
And, as he leads, the following navy veers.

As translated by John Dryden in *Vergil's Aeneid*, 3rd ed., London and New York, 1887, 127–156.

The steeds of Night had travel'd half the sky,
The drowsy rowers on their benches lie,
When the soft God of Sleep, with easy flight,
Descends, and draws behind a trail of light.
Thou, Palinurus, art his destin'd prey;
To thee alone he takes his fatal way.
Dire dreams to thee, and iron sleep, he bears;
And, lighting on thy prow, the form of Phorbas
    wears.
Then thus the traitor god began his tale:
"The winds, my friend, inspire a pleasing gale;
The ships, without thy care, securely sail.
Now steal an hour of sweet repose; and I
Will take the rudder and thy room supply."
To whom the yawning pilot, half asleep:
"Me dost thou bid to trust the treach'rous deep,
The harlot-smiles of her dissembling face,
And to her faith commit the Trojan race?
Shall I believe the Siren South again,
And, oft betray'd, not know the monster main?"
He said: his fasten'd hands the rudder keep,
And, fix'd on heav'n, his eyes repel invading
    sleep.
The god was wroth, and at his temples threw
A branch in Lethe dipp'd, and drunk with
    Stygian dew:
The pilot, vanquish'd by the pow'r divine,
Soon clos'd his swimming eyes, and lay supine.
Scarce were his limbs extended at their length,
The god, insulting with superior strength,
Fell heavy on him, plung'd him in the sea,
And, with the stern, the rudder tore away.
Headlong he fell, and, struggling in the main,
Cried out for helping hands, but cried in vain.
The victor daemon mounts obscure in air,
While the ship sails without the pilot's care.
On Neptune's faith the floating fleet relies;
But what the man forsook, the god supplies,
And o'er the dang'rous deep secure the navy
    flies;
Glides by the Sirens' cliffs, a shelfy coast,
Long infamous for ships and sailors lost,
And white with bones. Th' impetuous ocean
    roars,
And rocks rebellow from the sounding shores.
The watchful hero felt the knocks, and found
The tossing vessel sail'd on shoaly ground.
Sure of his pilot's loss, he takes himself
The helm, and steers aloof, and shuns the shelf.
Inly he griev'd, and, groaning from the breast,
Deplor'd his death; and thus his pain express'd:

"For faith repos'd on seas, and on the flatt'ring
    sky,
Thy naked corpse is doom'd on shores un-
    known to lie."
He said, and wept; then spread his sails before
The winds, and reach'd at length the Cumaean
    shore:
Their anchors dropp'd, his crew the vessels
    moor.
They turn their heads to sea, their sterns to
    land,
And greet with greedy joy th' Italian strand.
Some strike from clashing flints their fiery seed;
Some gather sticks, the kindled flames to feed,
Or search for hollow trees, and fell the woods,
Or trace thro' valleys the discover'd floods.
Thus, while their sev'ral charges they fulfil,
The pious prince ascends the sacred hill
Where Phoebus is ador'd; and seeks the shade
Which hides from sight his venerable maid
(Deep in a cave the Sibyl makes abode);
Thence full of fate returns, and of the god.
Thro' Trivia's grove they walk; and now be-
    hold,
And enter now, the temple roof'd with gold.
When Daedalus, to fly the Cretan shore,
His heavy limbs on jointed pinions bore
(The first who sail'd in air), 'tis sung by Fame,
To the Cumaean coast at length he came,
And here alighting, built this costly frame.
Inscrib'd to Phoebus, here he hung on high
The steerage of his wings, that cut the sky:
Then, o'er the lofty gate his art emboss'd
Androgeos' death, and off'rings to his ghost;
Sev'n youths from Athens yearly sent, to meet
The fate appointed by revengeful Crete.
And next to those the dreadful urn was plac'd,
In which the destin'd names by lots were cast:
The mournful parents stand around in tears,
And rising Crete against their shore appears.
There too, in living sculpture, might be seen
The mad affection of the Cretan queen;
Then how she cheats her bellowing lover's eye;
The rushing leap, the doubtful progeny,
The lower part a beast, a man above,
The monument of their polluted love.
Not far from thence he grav'd the wondrous
    maze,
A thousand doors, a thousand winding ways:
Here dwells the monster, hid from human view,
Not to be found, but by the faithful clew;

Till the kind artist, mov'd with pious grief,
Lent to the loving maid this last relief,
And all those erring paths describ'd so well
That Theseus conquer'd and the monster fell.
Here hapless Icarus had found his part,
Had not the father's grief restrain'd his art.
He twice assay'd to cast his son in gold;
Twice from his hands he dropp'd the forming
    mold.
   All this with wond'ring eyes Aeneas view'd;
Each varying object his delight renew'd:
Eager to read the rest—Achates came,
And by his side the mad divining dame,
The priestess of the god, Deïphobe her name.
"Time suffers not," she said, "to feed your eyes
With empty pleasures; haste the sacrifice.
Sev'n bullocks, yet unyok'd, for Phoebus
    choose,
And for Diana sev'n unspotted ewes."
This said, the servants urge the sacred rites,
While to the temple she the prince invites.
A spacious cave, within its farmost part,
Was hew'd and fashion'd by laborious art
Thro' the hill's hollow sides: before the place,
A hundred doors a hundred entries grace;
As many voices issue, and the sound
Of Sybil's words as many times rebound.
Now to the mouth they come. Aloud she cries:
"This is the time; enquire your destinies.
He comes; behold the god!" Thus while she
    said
(And shiv'ring at the sacred entry stay'd),
Her color chang'd; her face was not the same,
And hollow groans from her deep spirit came.
Her hair stood up; convulsive rage possess'd
Her trembling limbs, and heav'd her lab'ring
    breast.
Greater than human-kind she seem'd to look,
And, with an accent more than mortal, spoke.
Her staring eyes with sparkling fury roll;
When all the god came rushing on her soul.
Swiftly she turn'd, and, foaming as she spoke:
"Why this delay?" she cried—"the pow'rs in-
    voke!
Thy pray'rs alone can open this abode;
Else vain are my demands, and dumb the god."
   She said no more. The trembling Trojans
    hear,
O'erspread with a damp sweat and holy fear.
The prince himself, with awful dread pos-
    sess'd,

His vows to great Apollo thus address'd:
"Indulgent god, propitious pow'r to Troy,
Swift to relieve, unwilling to destroy,
Directed by whose hand the Dardan dart
Pierc'd the proud Grecian's only mortal part:
Thus far, by Fate's decrees and thy commands,
Thro' ambient seas and thro' devouring sands,
Our exil'd crew has sought th' Ausonian
    ground;
And now, at length, the flying coast is found.
Thus far the fate of Troy, from place to place,
With fury has pursued her wand'ring race.
Here cease, ye pow'rs, and let your vengeance
    end:
Troy is no more, and can no more offend.
And thou, O sacred maid, inspir'd to see
Th' event of things in dark futurity;
Give me what Heav'n has promis'd to my fate,
To conquer and command the Latian state;
To fix my wand'ring gods, and find a place
For the long exiles of the Trojan race.
Then shall my grateful hands a temple rear
To the twin gods, with vows and solemn
    pray'r;
And annual rites, and festivals, and games,
Shall be perform'd to their auspicious names.
Nor shalt thou want thy honors in my land;
For there thy faithful oracles shall stand,
Preserv'd in shrines; and ev'ry sacred lay,
Which, by thy mouth, Apollo shall convey:
All shall be treasur'd by a chosen train
Of holy priests, and ever shall remain.
But O! commit not thy prophetic mind
To flitting leaves, the sport of ev'ry wind,
Lest they disperse in air our empty fate;
Write not, but, what the pow'rs ordain, relate."
   Struggling in vain, impatient of her load,
And lab'ring underneath the pond'rous god,
The more she strove to shake him from her
    breast,
With more and far superior force he press'd;
Commands his entrance, and, without control,
Usurps her organs and inspires her soul.
Now, with a furious blast, the hundred doors
Ope of themselves; a rushing whirlwind roars
Within the cave, and Sibyl's voice restores:
"Escap'd the dangers of the wat'ry reign,
Yet more and greater ills by land remain.
The coast, so long desir'd (nor doubt th' event),
Thy troops shall reach, but, having reach'd,
    repent.

Wars, horrid wars, I view—a field of blood,
And Tiber rolling with a purple flood.
Simois nor Xanthus shall be wanting there:
A new Achilles shall in arms appear,
And he, too, goddess-born. Fierce Juno's hate,
Added to hostile force, shall urge thy fate.
To what strange nations shalt not thou resort,
Driv'n to solicit aid at ev'ry court!
The cause the same which Ilium once oppress'd;
A foreign mistress, and a foreign guest.
But thou, secure of soul, unbent with woes,
The more thy fortune frowns, the more oppose.
The dawnings of thy safety shall be shown
From whence thou least shalt hope, a Grecian town."
Thus, from the dark recess, the Sibyl spoke,
And the resisting air the thunder broke;
The cave rebellow'd, and the temple shook.
Th' ambiguous god, who rul'd her lab'ring breast,
In these mysterious words his mind express'd;
Some truths reveal'd, in terms involv'd the rest.
At length her fury fell, her foaming ceas'd,
And, ebbing in her soul, the god decreas'd.
Then thus the chief: "No terror to my view,
No frightful face of danger can be new.
Inur'd to suffer, and resolv'd to dare,
The Fates, without my pow'r, shall be without my care.
This let me crave, since near your grove the road
To hell lies open, and the dark abode
Which Acheron surrounds, th' innavigable flood;
Conduct me thro' the regions void of light,
And lead me longing to my father's sight.
For him, a thousand dangers I have sought,
And, rushing where the thickest Grecians fought,
Safe on my back the sacred burthen brought.
He, for my sake, the raging ocean tried,
And wrath of Heav'n, my still auspicious guide,
And bore beyond the strength decrepit age supplied.
Oft, since he breath'd his last, in dead of night
His reverend image stood before my sight;
Enjoin'd to seek, below, his holy shade;
Conducted there by your unerring aid.
But you, if pious minds by pray'rs are won,
Oblige the father, and protect the son.

Yours is the pow'r; nor Proserpine in vain
Has made you priestess of her nightly reign.
If Orpheus, arm'd with his enchanting lyre,
The ruthless king with pity could inspire,
And from the shades below redeem his wife;
If Pollux, off'ring his alternate life,
Could free his brother, and can daily go
By turns aloft, by turns descend below—
Why name I Theseus, or his greater friend,
Who trod the downward path, and upward could ascend?
Not less than theirs from Jove my lineage came;
My mother greater, my descent the same."
So pray'd the Trojan prince, and, while he pray'd,
His hand upon the holy altar laid.
Then thus replied the prophetess divine:
"O goddess-born of great Anchises' line,
The gates of hell are open night and day;
Smooth the descent, and easy is the way:
But to return, and view the cheerful skies,
In this the task and mighty labor lies.
To few great Jupiter imparts this grace,
And those of shining worth and heav'nly race,
Betwixt those regions and our upper light,
Deep forests and impenetrable night
Possess the middle space: th' infernal bounds
Cocytus, with his sable waves, surrounds.
But if so dire a love your soul invades,
As twice below to view the trembling shades;
If you so hard a toil will undertake,
As twice to pass th' innavigable lake;
Receive my counsel. In the neighb'ring grove
There stands a tree; the queen of Stygian Jove
Claims it her own; thick woods and gloomy night
Conceal the happy plant from human sight.
One bough it bears; but (wondrous to behold!)
The ductile rind and leaves of radiant gold:
This from the vulgar branches must be torn,
And to fair Proserpine the present borne,
Ere leave be giv'n to tempt the nether skies.
The first thus rent a second will arise,
And the same metal the same room supplies.
Look round the wood, with lifted eyes, to see
The lurking gold upon the fatal tree:
Then rend it off, as holy rites command;
The willing metal will obey thy hand.
Following with ease, if favor'd by thy fate,
Thou art foredoom'd to view the Stygian state:
If not, no labor can the tree constrain;

And strength of stubborn arms and steel are
    vain.
Besides, you know not, while you here attend,
Th' unworthy fate of your unhappy friend:
Breathless he lies; and his unburied ghost,
Depriv'd of fun'ral rites, pollutes your host.
Pay first his pious dues; and, for the dead,
Two sable sheep around his hearse be led;
Then, living turfs upon his body lay:
This done, securely take the destin'd way,
To find the regions destitute of day."

    She said, and held her peace. Aeneas went
Sad from the cave, and full of discontent,
Unknowing whom the sacred Sibyl meant.
Achates, the companion of his breast,
Goes grieving by his side, with equal cares
    oppress'd.
Walking, they talk'd, and fruitlessly divin'd
What friend the priestess by those words
    design'd.
But soon they found an object to deplore:
Misenus lay extended on the shore;
Son of the God of Winds: none so renown'd
The warrior trumpet in the field to sound;
With breathing brass to kindle fierce alarms,
And rouse to dare their fate in honorable arms.
He serv'd great Hector, and was ever near,
Not with his trumpet only, but his spear.
But by Pelides' arms when Hector fell,
He chose Æneas; and he chose as well.
Swol'n with applause, and aiming still at more,
He now provokes the sea gods from the shore;
With envy Triton heard the martial sound,
And the bold champion, for his challenge,
    drown'd;
Then cast his mangled carcass on the strand:
The gazing crowd around the body stand.
All weep; but most Æneas mourns his fate,
And hastens to perform the funeral state.
In altar-wise, a stately pile they rear;
The basis broad below, and top advanc'd in air.
An ancient wood, fit for the work design'd,
(The shady covert of the salvage kind,)
The Trojans found: the sounding ax is plied;
Firs, pines, and pitch trees, and the tow'ring
    pride
Of forest ashes, feel the fatal stroke,
And piercing wedges cleave the stubborn oak.
Huge trunks of trees, fell'd from the steepy
    crown
Of the bare mountains, roll with ruin down.

Arm'd like the rest the Trojan prince appears,
And by his pious labor urges theirs.
    Thus while he wrought, revolving in his
    mind
The ways to compass what his wish design'd,
He cast his eyes upon the gloomy grove,
And then with vows implor'd the Queen of
    Love:
"O may thy pow'r, propitious still to me,
Conduct my steps to find the fatal tree,
In this deep forest; since the Sibyl's breath
Foretold, alas! too true, Misenus' death."
Scarce had he said, when, full before his sight,
Two doves, descending from their airy flight,
Secure upon the grassy plain alight.
He knew his mother's birds; and thus he
    pray'd:
"Be you my guides, with your auspicious aid,
And lead my footsteps, till the branch be found,
Whose glitt'ring shadow gilds the sacred
    ground.
And thou, great parent, with celestial care,
In this distress be present to my pray'r!"
Thus having said, he stopp'd with watchful
    sight,
Observing still the motions of their flight,
What course they took, what happy signs they
    shew.
They fed, and, flutt'ring, by degrees withdrew
Still farther from the place, but still in view:
Hopping and flying, thus they led him on
To the slow lake, whose baleful stench to shun
They wing'd their flight aloft; then, stooping
    low,
Perch'd on the double tree that bears the
    golden bough
Thro' the green leaves the glitt'ring shadows
    glow;
As, on the sacred oak, the wintry mistletoe,
Where the proud mother views her precious
    brood,
And happier branches, which she never sow'd.
Such was the glitt'ring; such the ruddy rind,
And dancing leaves, that wanton'd in the wind.
He seiz'd the shining bough with griping hold,
And rent away, with ease, the ling'ring gold;
Then to the Sibyl's palace bore the prize.
Meantime, the Trojan troops, with weeping
    eyes,
To dead Misenus pay his obsequies.
First, from the ground a lofty pile they rear,

Of pitch trees, oaks, and pines, and unctuous
    fir:
The fabric's front with cypress twigs they
    strew,
And stick the sides with boughs of baleful yew.
The topmost part his glitt'ring arms adorn;
Warm waters, then, in brazen caldrons borne,
Are pour'd to wash his body, joint by joint,
And fragrant oils the stiffen'd limbs anoint.
With groans and cries Misenus they deplore:
Then on a bier, with purple cover'd o'er,
The breathless body, thus bewail'd, they lay,
And fire the pile, their faces turn'd away—
Such reverend rites their fathers us'd to pay.
Pure oil and incense on the fire they throw,
And fat of victims, which his friends bestow.
These gifts the greedy flames to dust devour;
Then, on the living coals red wine they pour;
And, last, the relics by themselves dispose,
Which in a brazen urn the priests inclose.
Old Corynaeus compass'd thrice the crew,
And dipp'd an olive branch in holy dew;
Which thrice he sprinkled round, and thrice
    aloud
Invok'd the dead, and then dismiss'd the
    crowd.
But good Æneas order'd on the shore
A stately tomb, whose top a trumpet bore,
A soldier's fauchion, and a seaman's oar.
Thus was his friend interr'd; and deathless
    fame
Still to the lofty cape consigns his name.
These rites perform'd, the prince, without
    delay,
Hastes to the nether world his destin'd way.
Deep was the cave; and, downward as it went
From the wide mouth, a rocky rough descent;
And here th' access a gloomy grove defends,
And there th' unnavigable lake extends,
O'er whose unhappy waters, void of light,
No bird presumes to steer his airy flight;
Such deadly stenches from the depths arise,
And steaming sulphur, that infects the skies.
From hence the Grecian bards their legends
    make,
And give the name Avernus to the lake.
Four sable bullocks, in the yoke untaught,
For sacrifice the pious hero brought.
The priestess pours the wine betwixt their
    horns;

Then cuts the curling hair; that first oblation
    burns.
Invoking Hecate hither to repair:
A pow'rful name in hell and upper air.
The sacred priests with ready knives bereave
The beasts of life, and in full bowls receive
The streaming blood: a lamb to Hell and Night
(The sable wool without a streak of white)
Æneas offers; and, by Fate's decree,
A barren heifer, Proserpine, to thee,
With holocausts he Pluto's altar fills;
Sev'n brawny bulls with his own hand he kills;
Then on the broiling entrails oil he pours;
Which, ointed thus, the raging flame devours.
Late the nocturnal sacrifice begun,
Nor ended till the next returning sun.
Then earth began to bellow, trees to dance,
And howling dogs in glimm'ring light advance,
Ere Hecate came. "Far hence be souls profane!"
The Sibyl cried, "and from the grove abstain!
Now, Trojan, take the way thy fates afford;
Assume thy courage, and unsheathe thy
    sword."
She said, and pass'd along the gloomy space;
The prince pursued her steps with equal pace.
    Ye realms, yet unreveal'd to human sight,
Ye gods who rule the regions of the night,
Ye gliding ghosts, permit me to relate
The mystic wonders of your silent state!
    Obscure they went thro' dreary shades, that
    led
Along the waste dominions of the dead.
Thus wander travelers in woods by night,
By the moon's doubtful and malignant light,
When Jove in dusky clouds involves the skies,
And the faint crescent shoots by fits before
    their eyes.
    Just in the gate and in the jaws of hell,
Revengeful Cares and sullen Sorrows dwell,
And pale Diseases, and repining Age,
Want, Fear, and Famine's unresisted rage;
Here Toils, and Death, and Death's
    half-brother, Sleep,
Forms terrible to view, their sentry keep;
With anxious Pleasures of a guilty mind,
Deep Frauds before, and open Force behind;
The Furies' iron beds; and Strife, that shakes
Her hissing tresses and unfolds her snakes.
Full in the midst of this infernal road,
An elm displays her dusky arms abroad:

The God of Sleep there hides his heavy head,
And empty dreams on ev'ry leaf are spread.
Of various forms unnumber'd specters more,
Centaurs, and double shapes, besiege the door.
Before the passage, horrid Hydra stands,
And Briareus with all his hundred hands;
Gorgons, Geryon with his triple frame;
And vain Chimaera vomits empty flame.
The chief unsheath'd his shining steel, pre-
par'd,
Tho' seiz'd with sudden fear, to force the
guard,
Off'ring his brandish'd weapon at their face;
Had not the Sibyl stopp'd his eager pace.
And told him what those empty phantoms
were:
Forms without bodies, and impassive air.
Hence to deep Acheron they take their way,
Whose troubled eddies, thick with ooze and
clay,
Are whirl'd aloft, and in Cocytus lost.
There Charon stands, who rules the dreary
coast—
A sordid god: down from his hoary chin
A length of beard descends, uncomb'd, un-
clean;
His eyes, like hollow furnaces on fire;
A girdle, foul with grease, binds his obscene
attire.
He spreads his canvas; with his pole he steers;
The freights of flitting ghosts in his thin bottom
bears.
He look'd in years; yet in his years were seen
A youthful vigor and autumnal green.
An airy crowd came rushing where he stood,
Which fill'd the margin of the fatal flood:
Husbands and wives, boys and unmarried
maids,
And mighty heroes' more majestic shades,
And youths, intomb'd before their fathers' eyes,
With hollow groans, and shrieks, and feeble
cries.
Thick as the leaves in autumn strow the woods,
Or fowls, by winter forc'd, forsake the floods,
And wing their hasty flight to happier lands;
Such, and so thick, the shiv'ring army stands,
And press for passage with extended hands.
Now these, now those, the surly boatman bore:
The rest he drove to distance from the shore.
The hero, who beheld with wond'ring eyes

The tumult mix'd with shrieks, laments, and
cries,
Ask'd of his guide, what the rude concourse
meant;
Why to the shore the thronging people bent;
What forms of law among the ghosts were us'd;
Why some were ferried o'er, and some refus'd.
"Son of Anchises, offspring of the gods,"
The Sibyl said, "you see the Stygian floods,
The sacred stream which heav'n's imperial
state
Attests in oaths, and fears to violate.
The ghosts rejected are th' unhappy crew
Depriv'd of sepulchers and fun'ral due:
The boatman, Charon; those, the buried host,
He ferries over to the farther coast;
Nor dares his transport vessel cross the waves
With such whose bones are not compos'd in
graves.
A hundred years they wander on the shore;
At length, their penance done, are wafted o'er."
The Trojan chief his forward pace repress'd,
Revolving anxious thoughts within his breast,
He saw his friends, who, whelm'd beneath the
waves,
Their fun'ral honors claim'd, and ask'd their
quiet graves.
The lost Leucaspis in the crowd he knew,
And the brave leader of the Lycian crew,
Whom, on the Tyrrhene seas, the tempests
met;
The sailors master'd, and the ship o'erset.
Amidst the spirits, Palinurus press'd,
Yet fresh from life, a new-admitted guest,
Who, while he steering view'd the stars, and
bore
His course from Afric to the Latian shore,
Fell headlong down. The Trojan fix'd his view,
And scarcely thro' the gloom the sullen shadow
knew.
Then thus the prince: "What envious pow'r, O
friend,
Brought your lov'd life to this disastrous end?
For Phoebus, ever true in all he said,
Has in your fate alone my faith betray'd.
The god foretold you should not die, before
You reach'd, secure from seas, th' Italian shore.
Is this th' unerring pow'r?" The ghost replied;
"Nor Phoebus flatter'd, nor his answers lied;
Nor envious gods have sent me to the deep:

But, while the stars and course of heav'n I
   keep,
My wearied eyes were seiz'd with fatal sleep.
I fell; and, with my weight, the helm
   constrain'd
Was drawn along, which yet my grip retain'd.
Now by the winds and raging waves I swear,
Your safety, more than mine, was then my care;
Lest, of the guide bereft, the rudder lost,
Your ship should run against the rocky coast.
Three blust'ring nights, borne by the southern
   blast,
I floated, and discover'd land at last:
High on a mounting wave my head I bore,
Forcing my strength, and gath'ring to the
   shore.
Panting, but past the danger, now I seiz'd
The craggy cliffs, and my tir'd members eas'd.
While, cumber'd with my dropping clothes, I
   lay,
The cruel nation, covetous of prey,
Stain'd with my blood th' unhospitable coast;
And now, by winds and waves, my lifeless
   limbs are toss'd:
Which, O, avert, by yon ethereal light,
Which I have lost for this eternal night!
Or, if by dearer ties you may be won,
By your dead sire, and by your living son,
Redeem from this reproach my wand'ring
   ghost;
Or with your navy seek the Velin coast,
And in a peaceful grave my corpse compose;
Or, if a nearer way your mother shows,
Without whose aid you durst not undertake
This frightful passage o'er the Stygian lake,
Lend to this wretch your hand, and waft him
   o'er
To the sweet banks of yon forbidden shore."
Scarce had he said, the prophetess began:
"What hopes delude thee, miserable man?
Think'st thou, thus unintomb'd, to cross the
   floods,
To view the Furies and infernal gods,
And visit, without leave, the dark abodes?
Attend the term of long revolving years;
Fate, and the dooming gods, are deaf to tears.
This comfort of thy dire misfortune take:
The wrath of Heav'n, inflicted for thy sake,
With vengeance shall pursue th' inhuman
   coast,
Till they propitiate thy offended ghost,

And raise a tomb, with vows and solemn
   pray'r;
And Palinurus' name the place shall bear."
This calm'd his cares; sooth'd with his future
   fame,
And pleas'd to hear his propagated name.
   Now nearer to the Stygian lake they draw:
Whom, from the shore, the surly boatman saw;
Observ'd their passage thro' the shady wood,
And mark'd their near approaches to the flood.
Then thus he call'd aloud, inflam'd with wrath:
"Mortal, whate'er, who this forbidden path
In arms presum'st to tread, I charge thee,
   stand,
And tell thy name, and bus'ness in the land.
Know this, the realm of night—the Stygian
   shore:
My boat conveys no living bodies o'er;
Nor was I pleas'd great Theseus once to bear,
Who forc'd a passage with his pointed spear,
Nor strong Alcides—men of mighty fame,
And from th' immortal gods their lineage came.
In fetters one the barking porter tied,
And took him trembling from his sov'reign's
   side:
Two sought by force to seize his beauteous
   bride."
To whom the Sibyl thus: "Compose thy mind;
Nor frauds are here contriv'd, nor force
   design'd.
Still may the dog the wand'ring troops
   constrain
Of airy ghosts, and vex the guilty train,
And with her grisly lord his lovely queen
   remain.
The Trojan chief, whose lineage is from Jove,
Much fam'd for arms, and more for filial love,
Is sent to seek his sire in your Elysian grove.
If neither piety, nor Heav'n's command,
Can gain his passage to the Stygian strand,
This fatal present shall prevail at least."
Then shew'd the shining bough, conceal'd
   within her vest.
No more was needful: for the gloomy god
Stood mute with awe, to see the golden rod;
Admir'd the destin'd off'ring to his queen—
A venerable gift, so rarely seen.
His fury thus appeas'd, he puts to land;
The ghosts forsake their seats at his command:
He clears the deck, receives the mighty freight;
The leaky vessel groans beneath the weight.

Slowly she sails, and scarcely stems the tides;
The pressing water pours within her sides.
His passengers at length are wafted o'er,
Expos'd, in muddy weeds, upon the miry shore.
　　No sooner landed, in his den they found
The triple porter of the Stygian sound,
Grim Cerberus, who soon began to rear
His crested snakes, and arm'd his bristling hair.
The prudent Sibyl had before prepar'd
A sop, in honey steep'd, to charm the guard;
Which, mix'd with pow'rful drugs, she cast
　　before
His greedy grinning jaws, just op'd to roar.
With three enormous mouths he gapes; and
　　straight,
With hunger press'd, devours the pleasing bait.
Long draughts of sleep his monstrous limbs
　　enslave;
He reels, and, falling, fills the spacious cave.
The keeper charm'd, the chief without delay
Pass'd on, and took th' irremeable way.
Before the gates, the cries of babes new-born,
Whom fate had from their tender mothers torn,
Assault his ears: then those whom form of laws
Condemn'd to die, when traitors judg'd their
　　cause.
Nor want they lots, nor judges to review
The wrongful sentence, and award a new.
Minos, the strict inquisitor, appears;
And lives and crimes, with his assessors, hears.
Round in his urn the blended balls he rolls,
Absolves the just, and dooms the guilty souls.
The next, in place and punishment, are they
Who prodigally throw their souls away;
Fools, who, repining at their wretched state,
And loathing anxious life, suborn'd their fate.
With late repentance now they would retrieve
The bodies they forsook, and wish to live;
Their pains and poverty desire to bear,
To view the light of heav'n, and breathe the
　　vital air:
But Fate forbids; the Stygian floods oppose,
And with nine circling streams the captive
　　souls inclose.
　　Not far from thence, the Mournful Fields
　　appear
So call'd from lovers that inhabit there.
The souls whom that unhappy flame invades,
In secret solitude and myrtle shades
Make endless moans, and, pining with desire,
Lament too late their unextinguish'd fire.

Here Procris, Eriphyle here he found,
Baring her breast, yet bleeding with the wound
Made by her son. He saw Pasiphae there,
With Phaedra's ghost, a foul incestuous pair.
There Laodamia, with Evadne, moves,
Unhappy both, but loyal in their loves:
Caeneus, a woman once, and once a man,
But ending in the sex she first began.
Not far from these Phoenician Dido stood,
Fresh from her wound, her bosom bath'd in
　　blood;
Whom when the Trojan hero hardly knew,
Obscure in shades, and with a doubtful view,
(Doubtful as he who sees, thro' dusky night,
Or thinks he sees, the moon's uncertain light,)
With tears he first approach'd the sullen shade;
And, as his love inspir'd him, thus he said:
"Unhappy queen! then is the common breath
Of rumor true, in your reported death,
And I, alas! the cause? By Heav'n, I vow,
And all the pow'rs that rule the realms below,
Unwilling I forsook your friendly state,
Commanded by the gods, and forc'd by Fate—
Those gods, that Fate, whose unresisted might
Have sent me to these regions void of light,
Thro' the vast empire of eternal night.
Nor dar'd I to presume, that, press'd with grief,
My flight should urge you to this dire relief.
Stay, stay your steps, and listen to my vows:
'Tis the last interview that Fate allows!"
In vain he thus attempts her mind to move
With tears, and pray'rs, and late-repenting
　　love.
Disdainfully she look'd; then turning round,
But fix'd her eyes unmov'd upon the ground,
And what he says and swears, regards no more
Than the deaf rocks, when the loud billows
　　roar;
But whirl'd away, to shun his hateful sight,
Hid in the forest and the shades of night;
Then sought Sichaeus thro' the shady grove,
Who answer'd all her cares, and equal'd all her
　　love.
　　Some pious tears the pitying hero paid,
And follow'd with his eyes the flitting shade,
Then took the forward way, by Fate ordain'd,
And, with his guide, the farther fields attain'd,
Where, sever'd from the rest, the warrior souls
　　remain'd.
Tydeus he met, with Meleager's race,
The pride of armies, and the soldiers' grace;

And pale Adrastus with his ghastly face.
Of Trojan chiefs he view'd a num'rous train,
All much lamented, all in battle slain;
Glaucus and Medon, high above the rest,
Antenor's sons, and Ceres' sacred priest.
And proud Idaeus, Priam's charioteer,
Who shakes his empty reins, and aims his airy
    spear.
The gladsome ghosts, in circling troops, attend
And with unwearied eyes behold their friend;
Delight to hover near, and long to know
What bus'ness brought him to the realms
    below.
But Argive chiefs, and Agamemnon's train,
When his refulgent arms flash'd thro' the shady
    plain,
Fled from his well-known face, with wonted
    fear,
As when his thund'ring sword and pointed
    spear
Drove headlong to their ships, and glean'd the
    routed rear.
They rais'd a feeble cry, with trembling notes;
But the weak voice deceiv'd their gasping
    throats.
    Here Priam's son, Deïphobus, he found,
Whose face and limbs were one continued
    wound:
Dishonest, with lopp'd arms, the youth appears,
Spoil'd of his nose, and shorten'd of his ears.
He scarcely knew him, striving to disown
His blotted form, and blushing to be known;
And therefore first began: "O Teucer's race,
Who durst thy faultless figure thus deface?
What heart could wish, what hand inflict, this
    dire disgrace?
'Twas fam'd, that in our last and fatal night
Your single prowess long sustain'd the fight,
Till tir'd, not forc'd, a glorious fate you chose,
And fell upon a heap of slaughter'd foes.
But, in remembrance of so brave a deed,
A tomb and fun'ral honors I decreed;
Thrice call'd your manes on the Trojan plains:
The place your armor and your name retains.
Your body too I sought, and, had I found,
Design'd for burial in your native ground."
    The ghost replied: "Your piety has paid
All needful rites, to rest my wand'ring shade;
But cruel Fate, and my more cruel wife,
To Grecian swords betray'd my sleeping life.
These are the monuments of Helen's love:

The shame I bear below, the marks I bore
    above.
You know in what deluding joys we pass'd
The night that was by Heav'n decreed our last:
For, when the fatal horse, descending down,
Pregnant with arms, o'erwhelm'd th' unhappy
    town,
She feign'd nocturnal orgies; left my bed,
And, mix'd with Trojan dames, the dances led;
Then, waving high her torch, the signal made,
Which rous'd the Grecians from their am-
    buscade.
With watching overworn, with cares oppress'd,
Unhappy I had laid me down to rest,
And heavy sleep my weary limbs possess'd.
Meantime my worthy wife our arms mislaid,
And from beneath my head my sword con-
    vey'd;
The door unlatch'd, and, with repeated calls,
Invites her former lord within my walls.
Thus in her crime her confidence she plac'd,
And with new treasons would redeem the past.
What need I more? Into the room they ran,
And meanly murther'd a defenseless man.
Ulysses, basely born, first led the way.
Avenging pow'rs! with justice if I pray,
That fortune be their own another day!
But answer you; and in your turn relate,
What brought you, living, to the Stygian state:
Driv'n by the winds and errors of the sea,
Or did you Heav'n's superior doom obey?
Or tell what other chance conducts your way,
To view with mortal eyes our dark retreats,
Tumults and torments of th' infernal seats."
    While thus in talk the flying hours they pass,
The sun had finish'd more than half his race:
And they, perhaps, in words and tears had
    spent
The little time of stay which Heav'n had lent;
But thus the Sibyl chides their long delay:
"Night rushes down, and headlong drives the
    day:
'Tis here, in different paths, the way divides;
The right to Pluto's golden palace guides;
The left to that unhappy region tends,
Which to the depth of Tartarus descends;
The seat of night profound, and punish'd
    fiends."
Then thus Deïphobus: "O sacred maid,
Forbear to chide, and be your will obey'd!
Lo! to the secret shadows I retire,

To pay my penance till my years expire.
Proceed, auspicious prince, with glory crown'd,
And born to better fates than I have found."
He said; and, while he said, his steps he turn'd
To secret shadows, and in silence mourn'd.
   The hero, looking on the left, espied
A lofty tow'r, and strong on ev'ry side
With treble walls, which Phlegethon
   surrounds,
Whose fiery flood the burning empire bounds;
And, press'd betwixt the rocks, the bellowing
   noise resounds.
Wide is the fronting gate, and, rais'd on high
With adamantine columns, threats the sky.
Vain is the force of man, and Heav'n's as vain,
To crush the pillars which the pile sustain.
Sublime on these a tow'r of steel is rear'd;
And dire Tisiphone there keeps the ward,
Girt in her sanguine gown, by night and day,
Observant of the souls that pass the downward
   way.
From hence are heard the groans of ghosts, the
   pains
Of sounding lashes and of dragging chains.
The Trojan stood astonish'd at their cries,
And ask'd his guide from whence those yells
   arise;
And what the crimes, and what the tortures
   were,
And loud laments that rent the liquid air.
   She thus replied: "The chaste and holy race
Are all forbidden this polluted place.
But Hecate, when she gave to rule the woods,
Then led me trembling thro' these dire abodes,
And taught the tortures of th' avenging gods.
These are the realms of unrelenting fate;
And awful Rhadamanthus rules the state.
He hears and judges each committed crime;
Enquires into the manner, place, and time.
The conscious wretch must all his acts reveal,
(Loth to confess, unable to conceal),
From the first moment of his vital breath,
To his last hour of unrepenting death.
Straight, o'er the guilty ghost, the Fury shakes
The sounding whip and brandishes her snakes,
And the pale sinner, with her sisters, takes.
Then, of itself, unfolds th' eternal door;
With dreadful sounds the brazen hinges roar.
You see, before the gate, what stalking ghost
Commands the guard, what sentries keep the
   post.

More formidable Hydra stands within,
Whose jaws with iron teeth severely grin.
The gaping gulf low to the center lies,
And twice as deep as earth is distant from the
   skies,
The rivals of the gods, the Titan race.
Here, sing'd with lightning, roll within th' un-
   fathom'd space.
Here lie th' Alaean twins, (I saw them both,)
Enormous bodies, of gigantic growth,
Who dar'd in fight the Thund'rer to defy,
Affect his heav'n, and force him from the sky.
Salmoneus, suff'ring cruel pains, I found,
For emulating Jove; the rattling sound
Of mimic thunder, and the glitt'ring blaze
Of pointed lightnings, and their forky rays.
Thro' Elis and the Grecian towns he flew;
Th' audacious wretch four fiery coursers drew:
He wav'd a torch aloft, and, madly vain,
Sought godlike worship from a servile train.
Ambitious fool! with horny hoofs to pass
O'er hollow arches of resounding brass,
To rival thunder in its rapid course,
And imitate inimitable force!
But he, the King of Heav'n, obscure on high,
Bar'd his red arm, and, launching from the
   sky
His writhen bolt, not shaking empty smoke,
Down to the deep abyss the flaming felon
   strook.
There Tityus was to see, who took his birth
From heav'n, his nursing from the foodful
   earth.
Here his gigantic limbs, with large embrace,
Infold nine acres of infernal space.
A rav'nous vulture, in his open'd side,
Her crooked beak and cruel talons tried;
Still for the growing liver digg'd his breast;
The growing liver still supplied the feast;
Still are his entrails fruitful to their pains:
Th' immortal hunger lasts, th' immortal food
   remains.
Ixion and Perithoüs I could name,
And more Thessalian chiefs of mighty fame.
High o'er their heads a mold'ring rock is plac'd,
That promises a fall, and shakes at ev'ry blast.
They lie below, on golden beds display'd;
And genial feasts with regal pomp are made.
The Queen of Furies by their sides is set,
And snatches from their mouths th' untasted
   meat,

Which if they touch, her hissing snakes she
    rears,
Tossing her torch, and thund'ring in their ears.
Then they, who brothers' better claim disown,
Expel their parents, and usurp the throne;
Defraud their clients, and, to lucre sold,
Sit brooding on unprofitable gold;
Who dare not give, and e'en refuse to lend
To their poor kindred, or a wanting friend.
Vast is the throng of these; nor less the train
Of lustful youths, for foul adult'ry slain:
Hosts of deserters, who their honor sold,
And basely broke their faith for bribes of gold.
All these within the dungeon's depth remain,
Despairing pardon, and expecting pain.
Ask not what pains; nor farther seek to know
Their process, or the forms of law below.
Some roll a weighty stone; some, laid along,
And bound with burning wires, on spokes of
    wheels are hung.
Unhappy Theseus, doom'd for ever there,
Is fix'd by Fate on his eternal chair;
And wretched Phlegyas warns the world with
    cries
(Could warning make the world more just or
    wise):
'Learn righteousness, and dread th' avenging
    deities.'
To tyrants others have their country sold,
Imposing foreign lords, for foreign gold;
Some have old laws repeal'd, new statutes
    made,
Not as the people pleas'd, but as they paid;
With incest some their daughters' bed
    profan'd:
All dar'd the worst of ills, and, what they dar'd,
    attain'd.
Had I a hundred mouths, a hundred tongues,
And throats of brass, inspir'd with iron lungs,
I could not half those horrid crimes repeat,
Nor half the punishments those crimes have
    met.
But let us haste our voyage to pursue:
The walls of Pluto's palace are in view;
The gate, and iron arch above it stands
On anvils labor'd by the Cyclops' hands.
Before our farther way the Fates allow,
Here must we fix on high the golden bough."
    She said: and thro' the gloomy shades they
    pass'd,

And chose the middle path. Arriv'd at last,
The prince with living water sprinkled o'er
His limbs and body; then approach'd the door.
Possess'd the porch, and on the front above
He fix'd the fatal bough requir'd by Pluto's
    love.
These holy rites perform'd, they took their way
Where long extended plains of pleasure lay:
The verdant fields with those of heav'n may
    vie,
With ether vested, and a purple sky;
The blissful seats of happy souls below.
Stars of their own, and their own suns, they
    know;
Their airy limbs in sports they exercise,
And on the green contend the wrestler's prize.
Some in heroic verse divinely sing;
Others in artful measures lead the ring.
The Thracian bard, surrounded by the rest,
There stands conspicuous in his flowing vest;
His flying fingers, and harmonious quill,
Strikes sev'n distinguish'd notes, and sev'n at
    once they fill.
Here found they Teucer's old heroic race,
Born better times and happier years to grace.
Assaracus and Ilus here enjoy
Perpetual fame, with him who founded Troy.
The chief beheld their chariots from afar,
Their shining arms, and coursers train'd to war:
Their lances fix'd in earth, their steeds around,
Free from their harness, graze the flow'ry
    ground.
The love of horses which they had, alive,
And care of chariots, after death survive.
Some cheerful souls were feasting on the plain;
Some did the song, and some the choir main-
    tain,
Beneath a laurel shade, where mighty Po
Mounts up to woods above, and hides his head
    below.
Here patriots live, who, for their country's
    good,
In fighting fields, were prodigal of blood:
Priests of unblemish'd lives here make abode
And poets worthy their inspiring god;
And searching wits, of more mechanic parts,
Who grac'd their age with new-invented arts:
Those who to worth their bounty did extend,
And those who knew that bounty to commend.
The heads of these with holy fillets bound,

And all their temples were with garlands
    crown'd.
  To these the Sibyl thus her speech ad-
    dress'd,
And first to him surrounded by the rest
(Tow'ring his height, and ample was his
    breast):
"Say, happy souls, divine Musaeus, say,
Where lives Anchises, and where lies our way
To find the hero, for whose only sake
We sought the dark abodes, and cross'd the
    bitter lake?"
To this the sacred poet thus replied:
"In no fix'd place the happy souls reside.
In groves we live, and lie on mossy beds,
By crystal streams that murmur thro' the
    meads:
But pass yon easy hill, and thence descend;
The path conducts you to your journey's end."
This said, he led them up the mountain's brow,
And shews them all the shining fields below.
They wind the hill, and thro' the blissful mead-
    ows go.
  But old Anchises, in a flow'ry vale,
Review'd his muster'd race, and took the tale:
Those happy spirits, which, ordain'd by Fate,
For future beings and new bodies wait—
With studious thought observ'd th' illustrious
    throng,
In nature's order as they pass'd along:
Their names, their fates, their conduct, and
    their care,
In peaceful senates and successful war.
He, when Æneas on the plain appears,
Meets him with open arms, and falling tears.
"Welcome," he said, "the gods' undoubted
    race!
O long expected to my dear embrace!
Once more 't is giv'n me to behold your face!
The love and pious duty which you pay
Have pass'd the perils of so hard a way
'Tis true, computing times, I now believ'd
The happy day approach'd; nor are my hopes
    deceiv'd.
What length of lands, what oceans have you
    pass'd;
What storms sustain'd, and on what shores
    been cast.
How have I feared your fate! but fear'd it most,
When love assail'd you, on the Libyan coast."

To this, the filial duty thus replies:
"Your sacred ghost before my sleeping eyes
Appear'd, and often urg'd this painful enter-
    prise.
After long tossing on the Tyrrhene sea,
My navy rides at anchor in the bay.
But reach your hand, O parent shade, nor shun
The dear embraces of your longing son!"
He said; and falling tears his face bedew:
Then thrice around his neck his arms he threw;
And thrice the flitting shadow slipp'd away,
Like winds, or empty dreams that fly the day.
  Now, in a secret vale, the Trojan sees
A sep'rate grove, thro' which a gentle breeze
Plays with a passing breath, and whispers thro'
    the trees
And, just before the confines of the wood,
The gliding Lethe leads her silent flood.
About the boughs an airy nation flew,
Thick as the humming bees, that hunt the
    golden dew;
In summer's heat on tops of lilies feed,
And creep within their bells, to suck the balmy
    seed:
The winged army roams the fields around;
The rivers and the rocks remurmur to the
    sound.
Æneas wond'ring stood, then ask'd the cause
Which to the stream the crowding people
    draws.
Then thus the sire: "The souls that throng the
    flood
Are those to whom, by fate, are other bodies
    ow'd:
In Lethe's lake they long oblivion taste,
Of future life secure, forgetful of the past.
Long has my soul desir'd this time and place,
To set before your sight your glorious race,
That this presaging joy may fire your mind
To seek the shores by destiny design'd."—
"O father, can it be, that souls sublime
Return to visit our terrestrial clime,
And that the gen'rous mind, releas'd by death,
Can covet lazy limbs and mortal breath?"
  Anchises then, in order, thus begun
To clear those wonders to his godlike son:
"Know, first, that heav'n, and earth's com-
    pacted frame,
And flowing waters, and the starry flame,
And both the radiant lights, one common soul

Inspires and feeds, and animates the whole.
This active mind, infus'd thro' all the space,
Unites and mingles with the mighty mass.
Hence men and beasts the breath of life obtain,
And birds of air, and monsters of the main.
Th' ethereal vigor is in all the same,
And every soul is fill'd with equal flame;
As much as earthy limbs, and gross allay
Of mortal members, subject to decay,
Blunt not the beams of heav'n and edge of day.
From this coarse mixture of terrestrial parts,
Desire and fear by turns possess their hearts,
And grief, and joy; nor can the groveling mind,
In the dark dungeon of the limbs confin'd,
Assert the native skies, or own its heav'nly
    kind:
Nor death itself can wholly wash their stains;
But long-contracted filth e'en in the soul re-
    mains.
The relics of inveterate vice they wear,
And spots of sin obscene in ev'ry face appear.
For this are various penances enjoin'd;
And some are hung to bleach upon the wind,
Some plung'd in waters, others purg'd in fires,
Till all the dregs are drain'd, and all the rust
    expires.
All have their manes, and those manes bear:
The few, so cleans'd, to these abodes repair,
And breathe, in ample fields, the soft Elysian
    air.
Then are they happy, when by length of time
The scurf is worn away of each committed
    crime;
No speck is left of their habitual stains,
But the pure ether of the soul remains.
But, when a thousand rolling years are past,
(So long their punishments and penance last,)
Whole droves of minds are, by the driving god,
Compell'd to drink the deep Lethaean flood,
In large forgetful draughts to steep the cares
Of their past labors, and their irksome years,
That, unrememb'ring of its former pain,
The soul may suffer mortal flesh again."
    Thus having said, the father spirit leads
The priestess and his son thro' swarms of
    shades,
And takes the rising ground, from thence to see
The long procession of his progeny.
"Survey," pursued the sire, "this airy throng,
As, offer'd to thy view, they pass along.

These are th' Italian names, which Fate will
    join
With ours, and graft upon the Trojan line.
Observe the youth who first appears in sight,
And holds the nearest station to the light,
Already seems to snuff the vital air,
And leans just forward, on a shining spear;
Silvius is he, thy last-begotten race,
But first in order sent, to fill thy place;
An Alban name, but mix'd with Dardan blood,
Born in the covert of a shady wood:
Him fair Lavinia, thy surviving wife,
Shall breed in groves, to lead a solitary life.
In Alba he shall fix his royal seat,
And, born a king, a race of kings beget.
Then Procas, honor of the Trojan name,
Capys, and Numitor, of endless fame.
A second Silvius after these appears;
Silvius Æneas, for thy name he bears;
For arms and justice equally renown'd,
Who, late restor'd, in Alba shall be crown'd.
How great they look! how vig'rously they wield
Their weighty lances, and sustain the shield!
But they, who crown'd with oaken wreaths ap-
    pear,
Shall Gabian walls and strong Fidena rear;
Nomentum, Bola, with Pometia, found;
And raise Collatian tow'rs on rocky ground.
All these shall then be towns of mighty fame,
Tho' now they lie obscure, and lands without
    a name.
See Romulus the great, born to restore
The crown that once his injur'd grandsire wore.
This prince a priestess of your blood shall bear,
And like his sire in arms he shall appear.
Two rising crests his royal head adorn;
Born from a god, himself to godhead born:
His sire already signs him for the skies,
And marks the seat amidst the deities.
Auspicious chief! thy race, in times to come,
Shall spread the conquests of imperial Rome—
Rome, whose ascending tow'rs shall heav'n
    invade,
Involving earth and ocean in her shade;
High as the Mother of the Gods in place,
And proud, like her, of an immortal race.
Then, when in pomp she makes the Phrygian
    round,
With golden turrets on her temples crown'd;
A hundred gods her sweeping train supply;

Her offspring all, and all command the sky.
  "Now fix your sight, and stand intent, to see
Your Roman race, and Julian progeny.
The mighty Caesar waits his vital hour,
Impatient for the world, and grasps his
    promis'd pow'r.
But next behold the youth of form divine,
Caesar himself, exalted in his line;
Augustus, promis'd oft, and long foretold,
Sent to the realm that Saturn rul'd of old;
Born to restore a better age of gold.
Afric and India shall his pow'r obey;
He shall extend his propagated sway
Beyond the solar year, without the starry way,
Where Atlas turns the rolling heav'ns around,
And his broad shoulders with their lights are
    crown'd.
At his forseen approach, already quake
The Caspian kingdoms and Maeotian lake:
Their seers behold the tempest from afar,
And threat'ning oracles denounce the war.
Nile hears him knocking at his sev'nfold gates,
And seeks his hidden spring, and fears his
    nephew's fates.
Nor Hercules more lands or labors knew,
Not tho' the brazen-footed hind he slew,
Freed Erymanthus from the foaming boar,
And dipp'd his arrows in Lernaean gore;
Nor Bacchus, turning from his Indian war,
By tigers drawn triumphant in his car,
From Nisus' top descending on the plains,
With curling vines around his purple reins.
And doubt we yet thro' dangers to pursue
The paths of honor, and a crown in view?
But what's the man, who from afar appears?
His head with olive crown'd, his hands a censer
    bears,
His hoary beard and holy vestments bring
His lost idea back: I know the Roman king.
He shall to peaceful Rome new laws ordain,
Call'd from his mean abode a scepter to sus-
    tain.
Him Tullus next in dignity succeeds,
An active prince, and prone to martial deeds.
He shall his troops for fighting fields prepare,
Disus'd to toils, and triumphs of the war.
By dint of sword his crown he shall increase,
And scour his armor from the rust of peace.
Whom Ancus follows, with a fawning air,
But vain within, and proudly popular.

Next view the Tarquin kings, th' avenging
    sword
Of Brutus, justly drawn, and Rome restor'd.
He first renews the rods and ax severe,
And gives the consuls royal robes to wear.
His sons, who seek the tyrant to sustain,
And long for arbitrary lords again,
With ignominy scourg'd, in open sight,
He dooms to death deserv'd, asserting public
    right.
Unhappy man, to break the pious laws
Of nature, pleading in his children's cause!
Howe'er the doubtful fact is understood,
'Tis love of honor, and his country's good:
The consul, not the father, sheds the blood.
Behold Torquatus the same track pursue;
And, next, the two devoted Decii view:
The Drusian line, Camillus loaded home
With standards well redeem'd, and foreign foes
    o'ercome.
The pair you see in equal armor shine,
Now, friends below, in close embraces join;
But, when they leave the shady realms of night,
And, cloth'd in bodies, breathe your upper
    light,
With mortal hate each other shall pursue:
What wars, what wounds, what slaughter shall
    ensue!
From Alpine heights the father first descends;
His daughter's husband in the plain attends:
His daughter's husband arms his eastern
    friends.
Embrace again, my sons, be foes no more;
Nor stain your country with her children's gore!
And thou, the first, lay down thy lawless claim,
Thou, of my blood, who bear'st the Julian
    name!
Another comes, who shall in triumph ride,
And to the Capitol his chariot guide,
From conquer'd Corinth, rich with Grecian
    spoils.
And yet another, fam'd for warlike toils,
On Argos shall impose the Roman laws,
And on the Greeks revenge the Trojan cause;
Shall drag in chains their Achillean race;
Shall vindicate his ancestors' disgrace,
And Pallas, for her violated place.
Great Cato there, for gravity renown'd,
And conqu'ring Cossus goes with laurels
    crown'd.

Who can omit the Gracchi? who declare
The Scipios' worth, those thunderbolts of war,
The double bane of Carthage? Who can see
Without esteem for virtuous poverty,
Severe Fabricius, or can cease t' admire
The plowman consul in his coarse attire?
Tir'd as I am, my praise the Fabii claim;
And thou, great hero, greatest of thy name,
Ordain'd in war to save the sinking state,
And, by delays, to put a stop to fate!
Let others better mold the running mass
Of metals, and inform the breathing brass,
And soften into flesh a marble face;
Plead better at the bar; describe the skies,
And when the stars descend, and when they
    rise.
But Rome, 't is thine alone, with awful sway,
To rule mankind, and make the world obey,
Disposing peace and war by thy own majestic
    way;
To tame the proud, the fetter'd slave to free:
These are imperial arts, and worthy thee."
    He paus'd and, while with wond'ring eyes
      they view'd
The passing spirits, thus his speech renew'd:
"See great Marcellus! how, untir'd in toils,
He moves with manly grace, how rich with
    regal spoils!
He, when his country, threaten'd with alarms,
Requires his courage and his conqu'ring arms,
Shall more than once the Punic bands affright;
Shall kill the Gaulish king in single fight;
Then to the Capitol in triumph move,
And the third spoils shall grace Feretrian Jove."
Æneas here beheld, of form divine,
A godlike youth in glitt'ring armor shine,
With great Marcellus keeping equal pace;
But gloomy were his eyes, dejected was his
    face.
He saw, and, wond'ring, ask'd his airy guide,
What and of whence was he, who press'd the
    hero's side:
"His son, or one of his illustrious name?
How like the former, and almost the same!
Observe the crowds that compass him around;
All gaze, and all admire, and raise a shouting
    sound:
But hov'ring mists around his brows are spread,
And night, with sable shades, involves his
    head."

"Seek not to know," the ghost replied with
    tears,
"The sorrows of thy sons in future years.
This youth (the blissful vision of a day)
Shall just be shown on earth, and snatch'd
    away.
The gods too high had rais'd the Roman state,
Were but their gifts as permanent as great.
What groans of men shall fill the Martian field!
How fierce a blaze his flaming pile shall yield!
What fun'ral pomp shall floating Tiber see,
When, rising from his bed, he views the sad
    solemnity!
No youth shall equal hopes of glory give,
No youth afford so great a cause to grieve;
The Trojan honor, and the Roman boast,
Admir'd when living, and ador'd when lost!
Mirror of ancient faith in early youth!
Undaunted worth, inviolable truth!
No foe, unpunish'd, in the fighting field
Shall dare thee, foot to foot, with sword and
    shield;
Much less in arms oppose thy matchless force,
When thy sharp spurs shall urge thy foaming
    horse.
Ah! couldst thou break thro' Fate's severe de-
    cree,
A new Marcellus shall arise in thee!
Full canisters of fragrant lilies bring,
Mix'd with the purple roses of the spring;
Let me with fun'ral flow'rs his body strow;
This gift which parents to their children owe
This unavailing gift, at least, I may bestow!"
Thus having said, he led the hero round
The confines of the blest Elysian ground;
Which when Anchises to his son had shown,
And fir'd his mind to mount the promis'd
    throne,
He tells the future wars, ordain'd by Fate;
The strength and customs of the Latian state;
The prince, and people; and forearms his care
With rules, to push his fortune, or to bear.
    Two gates the silent house of Sleep adorn;
Of polish'd iv'ry this, that of transparent horn:
True visions thro' transparent horn arise;
Thro' polish'd iv'ry pass deluding lies.
Of various things discoursing as he pass'd,
Anchises hither bends his steps at last.
Then, thro' the gate of iv'ry, he dismiss'd
His valiant offspring and divining guest.

Straight to the ships Æneas took his way,
Embark'd his men, and skimm'd along the sea,
Still coasting, till he gain'd Cajéta's bay.

At length on oozy ground his galleys moor;
Their heads are turn'd to sea, their sterns to
    shore.

Cicero

Marcus Tullius Cicero (104–43 B.C.) played a promi- nent part in the political and intellectual life of Rome during the last days of the Republic. In the period of civil strife he identified himself with the aristocratic party supporting the Republic in opposition to Julius Caesar. Cicero studied and wrote both in the fields of government and philosophy, and in The Laws he brought the two to- gether to form a well-known and very influential treatise on the origin and nature of law. Like the culture he repre- sented, Cicero lacked originality, but also like his culture, he successfully synthesized many of the ideals of Hellenic and Hellenistic culture with the practical achievements of Roman political life. Cicero promoted the classic statement of the idea of natural law which exerted so much influence on the thought of the middle ages and of the eighteenth century. In reading the selections note (1) Cicero's basic assumptions regarding the universe, God, and man, (2) evidences of Stoicism and Platonism, (3) his description of nature's endowment to humanity, (4) his arguments in favor of human equality, (5) his belief concerning the ulti- mate force behind law, (6) his rule for distinguishing a good from a bad law, (7) his effort to establish absolutes of goodness, law, justice, etc., and (8) his attitude toward man-made enactments contrary to the law of nature.

From: THE LAWS

Marcus.—But the whole subject of universal law and jurisprudence must be comprehended in this discussion, in order that this which we call civil law, may be confined in some one small and narrow space of nature. For we shall have to explain the true nature of moral justice, which must be traced back from the nature of man. And laws will have to be considered by which all political states should be governed. And last of all, shall we have to speak of those laws and customs of nations, which are framed for the use and convenience of particular coun-

tries, (in which even our own people will not be omitted,) which are known by the title of civil laws.

Quintus.—You take a noble view of the sub- ject, my brother, and go to the fountainhead, in order to throw light on the subject of our consideration; and those who treat civil law in any other manner, are not so much pointing out the paths of justice as those of litigation.

Marcus.—That is not quite the case, my Quintus. It is not so much the science of law that produces litigation, as the ignorance of it.

As translated by C. D. Yonge in *M. Tullius Cicero, On the Nature of the Gods; On Divination; On Fate; On the Re- public; On the Laws; and On Standing for the Consulship,* G. Bell and Sons, Ltd., London, 1911, 406–421; 430–435. Courtesy of G. Bell and Sons, Ltd.

But more of this by-and-by. At present let us examine the first principles of Right.

Now, many learned men have maintained that it springs from law. I hardly know if their opinion be not correct, at least according to their own definition; for "law," say they, "is the highest reason implanted in nature, which prescribes those things which ought to be done, and forbids the contrary." And when this same reason is confirmed and established in men's minds, it is then law.

They therefore conceive that prudence is a law, whose operation is to urge us to good actions, and restrain us from evil ones. And they think, too, that the Greek name for law (νόμος), which is derived from νέμω, to distribute, implies the very nature of the thing, that is, to give every man his due. The Latin name, *lex,* conveys the idea of selection, *a legendo.* According to the Greeks, therefore, the name of law implies an equitable distribution: according to the Romans, an equitable selection. And, indeed, both characteristics belong peculiarly to law.

And if this be a correct statement, which it seems to me for the most part to be, then the origin of right is to be sought in the law. For this is the true energy of nature,—this is the very soul and reason of a wise man, and the test of virtue and vice. But since all this discussion of ours relates to a subject, the terms of which are of frequent occurrence in the popular language of the citizens, we shall be sometimes obliged to use the same terms as the vulgar, and to call that law, which in its written enactments sanctions what it thinks fit by special commands or prohibitions.

Let us begin, then, to establish the principles of justice on that supreme law, which has existed from all ages before any legislative enactments were drawn up in writing, or any political governments constituted. . . . Shall we, then, seek for the origin of justice at its fountainhead? When we have discovered which, we shall be in no doubt to what these questions which we are examining ought to be referred. . . . Since, then, we wish to maintain and preserve the constitution of that republic which Scipio . . . has proved to be the best, and since all our laws are to be accommodated to the kind of political govern-

ment there described, we must also treat of the general principles of morals and manners, and not limit ourselves on all occasions to written laws; but I purpose to trace back the origin of right from nature itself, who will be our best guide in conducting the whole discussion.

Atticus.—You will do right, and when she is our guide it is absolutely impossible for us to err.

Marcus.—Do you then grant, my Atticus (for I know my brother's opinion already), that the entire universe is regulated by the power of the immortal Gods, that by their nature, reason, energy, mind, divinity, or some other word of clearer signification, if there be such, all things are governed and directed? for if you will not grant me this, that is what I must begin by establishing.

Atticus.—I grant you all you can desire. But owing to this singing of birds and babbling of waters, I fear my fellow-learners can scarcely hear me.

Marcus.—You are quite right to be on your guard; for even the best men occasionally fall into a passion, and they will be very indignant if they hear you denying the first article of that notable book, entitled "The Chief Doctrines of Epicurus," in which he says "that God takes care of nothing, neither of himself nor of any other being!"

Atticus.—Pray proceed, for I am waiting to know what advantage you mean to take of the concession I have made you.

Marcus.—I will not detain you long. This is the bearing which they have on our subject. This animal—prescient, sagacious, complex, acute, full of memory, reason, and counsel, which we call man—has been generated by the supreme God in a most transcendent condition. For he is the only creature among all the races and descriptions of animated beings who is endued with superior reason and thought, in which the rest are deficient. And what is there, I do not say in man alone, but in all heaven and earth, more divine than reason, which, when it becomes right and perfect, is justly termed wisdom?

There exists, therefore, since nothing is better than reason, and since this is the common property of God and man, a certain aboriginal rational intercourse between divine and human natures. But where reason is common, there right reason must also be common to the same parties; and since this right reason is what we call law, God and men must be considered as associated by law. Again, there must also be a communion of right where there is a communion of law. And those who have law and right thus in common, must be considered members of the same commonwealth.

And if they are obedient to the same rule and the same authority, they are even much more so to this one celestial regency, this divine mind and omnipotent deity. So that the entire universe may be looked upon as forming one vast commonwealth of gods and men. And, as in earthly states certain ranks are distinguished with reference to the relationships of families, according to a certain principle which will be discussed in its proper place, that principle, in the nature of things, is far more magnificent and splendid by which men are connected with the Gods, as belonging to their kindred and nation.

For when we are reasoning on universal nature, we are accustomed to argue (and indeed the truth is just as it is stated in that argument) that in the long course of ages, and the uninterrupted succession of celestial revolutions, there arrived a certain ripe time for the sowing of the human race; and when it was sown and scattered over the earth, it was animated by the divine gift of souls. And as men retained from their terrestrial origin those other particulars by which they cohere together, which are frail and perishable, their immortal spirits were ingenerated by the Deity. From which circumstance it may be truly said, that we possess a certain consanguinity, and kindred, and fellowship with the heavenly powers. And among all the varieties of animals, there is not one except man which retains any idea of the Divinity. And among men, themselves, there is no nation so savage and ferocious as not to admit the necessity of believing in a God, however ignorant they may be what sort of God they ought to believe in. From whence we conclude that every man must recognize a Deity, who has any recollection and knowledge of his own origin.

Now, the law of virtue is the same in God and man, and in no other disposition besides them. This virtue is nothing else than a nature perfect in itself, and wrought up to the most consummate excellence. There exists, therefore, a similitude between God and man. And as this is the case, what connexion can there be which concerns us more nearly, and is more certain?

Therefore, nature has supplied such an abundance of supplies suited to the convenience and use of men, that the things which are thus produced appear to be designedly bestowed on us, and not fortuitous productions. Nor does this observation apply only to the fruits and vegetables which gush from the bosom of the earth, but likewise to cattle and the beasts of the field, some of which, it is clear, were intended for the use of mankind, others for propagation, and others for the food of man. Innumerable arts have likewise been discovered by the teaching of nature, whom reason has imitated, and thus skilfully discovered all things necessary to the happiness of life.

With respect to man, this same bountiful nature hath not merely allotted him a subtle and active spirit, but also physical senses, like so many servants and messengers. And she has laid bare before him the obscure but necessary explanation of many things, which are, as it were, the foundation of practical knowledge; and in all respects she has given him a convenient figure of body, suited to the bent of the human character. For while she has kept down the countenances of other animals, and fixed their eyes on their food, she has bestowed on man alone an erect stature, and prompted him to the contemplation of heaven, the ancient home of his kindred immortals. So exquisitely, too, has she fashioned the features of the human face, as to make them indicate the most recondite thoughts and sentiments. For our eloquent eyes speak forth every impulse and passion of our souls; and that which we call *expression*, which cannot exist in any other animal but man, betrays all our feelings, the power of which was well known to the Greeks, though they have no name for it.

I will not enlarge on the wonderful faculties and qualities of the rest of the body, the modulation of the voice, and the power of oratory, which is the greatest instrument of influence upon human society. For these matters do not all belong to the present occasion or the present subject, and I think that Scipio has already sufficiently explained them in those books of mine which you have read.

Since, then, the Deity has been pleased to create and adorn man to be the chief and president of all terrestrial creatures, so it is evident, without further argument, that human nature has also made very great advances by its own intrinsic energy; that nature, which without any other instruction than her own, has developed the first rude principles of the understanding, and strengthened and perfected reason to all the appliances of science and art.

Atticus.—Oh ye immortal Gods! to what a distance back are you tracing the principles of justice! However, you are discoursing in such a style that I will not show any impatience to hear what I expect you to say on the Civil Law. But I will listen patiently, even if you spend the whole day in this kind of discourse; for assuredly these, which perhaps you are embracing in your argument for the sake of others, are grander topics than even the subject itself for which they prepare the way.

Marcus.—You may well describe these topics as grand, which we are now briefly discussing. But of all the questions which are ever the subject of discussion among learned men, there is none which it is more important thoroughly to understand than this, that man is born for justice, and that law and equity have not been established by opinion, but by nature. This truth will become still more apparent if we investigate the nature of human association and society.

For there is no one thing so like or so equal to another, as in every instance man is to man. And if the corruption of customs, and the variation of opinions, did not induce an imbecility of minds, and turn them aside from the course of nature, no one would more nearly resemble himself than all men would resemble all men. Therefore, whatever definition we give of man, will be applicable to the whole human race. And this is a good argument that there is no dissimilarity of kind among men; because if this were the case, one definition could not include all men.

In fact, reason, which alone gives us so many advantages over beasts, by means of which we conjecture, argue, refute, discourse, and accomplish and conclude our designs, is assuredly common to all men; for the faculty of acquiring knowledge is similar in all human minds, though the knowledge itself may be endlessly diversified. By the same senses we all perceive the same objects, and those things which move the senses at all, do move in the same way the senses of all men. And those first rude elements of intelligence which, as I before observed, are the earliest developments of thought, are similarly impressed upon all men; and that faculty of speech which is the interpreter of the mind, agrees in the ideas which it conveys, though it may differ in the words by which it expresses them. And therefore there exists not a man in any nation, who, if he adopts nature for his guide, may not arrive at virtue.

Nor is this resemblance which all men bear to each other remarkable in those things only which are in accordance with right reason, but also in errors. For all men alike are captivated by pleasure, which, although it is a temptation to what is disgraceful, nevertheless bears some resemblance to natural good; for, as by its delicacy and sweetness it is delightful, it is through a mistake of the intellect adopted as something salutary.

And by an error scarcely less universal, we shun death as if it were a dissolution of nature, and cling to life because it keeps us in that existence in which we were born. Thus, likewise, we consider pain as one of the greatest evils, not only on account of its present asperity, but also because it seems the precursor of mortality. Again, on account of the apparent resemblance between renown with honour, those men appear to us happy who are honoured, and miserable who happen to be inglorious. In like manner our minds are all similarly susceptible of inquietudes, joys, desires, and fears; nor if different men have different opinions, does it follow that those who deify dogs and cats, do not labour under superstition equally with other nations, though they may differ from them in the forms of its manifestation.

Again, what nation is there which has not a regard for kindness, benignity, gratitude, and mindfulness of benefits? What nation is there in which arrogance, malice, cruelty, and unthankfulness, are not reprobated and detested? And while this uniformity of opinions proves that the whole race of mankind is united together, the last point is that a system of living properly makes men better. If what I have said meets your approbation, I will proceed; or if any doubts occur to you, we had better clear them up first.

Atticus.—There is nothing which strikes us, if I may reply for both of us.

Marcus.—It follows, then, that nature made us just that we might share our goods with each other, and supply each other's wants. You observe in this discussion, whenever I speak of nature, I mean nature in its genuine purity, but that there is, in fact, such corruption engendered by evil customs, that the sparks, as it were, of virtue which have been given by nature are extinguished, and that antagonist vices arise around it and become strengthened.

But if, as nature prompts them to, men would with deliberate judgment, in the words of the poet, "being men, think nothing that concerns mankind indifferent to them," then would justice be cultivated equally by all. For to those to whom nature has given reason, she has also given right reason, and therefore also law, which is nothing else than right reason enjoining what is good, and forbidding what is evil. And if nature has given us law, she hath also given us right. But she has bestowed reason on all, therefore right has been bestowed on all. And therefore did Socrates deservedly execrate the man who first drew a distinction between utility and nature, for he used to complain that this error was the source of all human vices, to which this sentence of Pythagoras refers—"The things belonging to friends are common"—and that other, "Friendly equality." From whence it appears, that when a wise man has displayed this benevolence which is so extensively and widely diffused towards one who is endowed with equal virtue, then that phenomenon takes place which is altogether incredible to some people, but which is a necessary consequence, that he loves himself not more dearly than he loves his friend. For how can a difference of interests arise where all interests are similar? If there could be ever so

minute a difference of interests, then there would be an end of even the nature of friendship, the real meaning of which is such, that there is no friendship at all the moment that a person prefers anything happening to himself rather than to his friend. . . .

But in conformity with the method of philosophers (I do not mean the older sages of philosophy, but those modern ones, who have erected a magazine, as it were, of wisdom), those questions which were formerly discussed loosely and unconstrainedly, are now examined with strictness and distinctness. Nor will these men allow that we have done justice to the subject which we have now before us, unless we demonstrate in a distinct discussion that right is a part of nature. . . .

But were it the fear of punishment, and not the nature of the thing itself, that ought to restrain mankind from wickedness, what, I would ask, could give villains the least uneasiness, abstracting from all fears of this kind? And yet none of them was ever so audaciously impudent, but what he either denied that the action in question had been committed by him, or pretended some cause or other for his just indignation, or sought a defence of his deed in some right of nature. And if the wicked dare to appeal to this principle, with what respect ought not good men to treat them?

But if either direct punishment, or the fear of it, be what deters men from a vicious and criminal course of life, and not the turpitude of the thing itself, then none can be guilty of injustice, and the greatest offenders ought rather to be called imprudent than wicked.

On the other hand, those among us who are determined to the practice of goodness, not by its own intrinsic excellence, but for the sake of some private advantage, are cunning rather than good men. For what will not that man do in the dark who fears nothing but a witness and a judge? Should he meet a solitary individual in a desert place, whom he can rob of a large sum of money, and altogether unable to defend himself from being robbed, how will he behave? In such a case our man, who is just and honourable from principle and the nature of the thing itself, will converse with the stranger, assist him, and show him the way. But he who does nothing for the sake of another, and measures everything by the advantage it brings to itself, it is obvious, I suppose, how such a one will act; and should he deny that he would kill the man, or rob him of his treasure, his reason for this cannot be that he apprehends there is any moral turpitude in such actions, but only because he is afraid of a discovery, that is to say, that bad consequences will thence ensue—a sentiment this at which not only learned men but even clowns must blush.

It is therefore an absurd extravagance in some philosophers to assert, that all things are necessarily just which are established by the civil laws and the institutions of nations. Are then the laws of tyrants just, simply because they are laws? Suppose the thirty tyrants of Athens had imposed certain laws on the Athenians? Or, suppose again that these Athenians were delighted with these tyrannical laws, would these laws on that account have been considered just? For my own part, I do not think such laws deserve any greater estimation than that passed during our own interregnum, which ordained that the dictator should be empowered to put to death with impunity whatever citizens he pleased, without hearing them in their own defence.

For there is but one essential justice which cements society, and one law which establishes this justice. This law is right reason, which is the true rule of all commandments and prohibitions. Whoever neglects this law, whether written or unwritten, is necessarily unjust and wicked.

But if justice consists in submission to written laws and national customs, and if, as the same school affirms, everything must be measured by utility alone, he who thinks that such conduct will be advantageous to him will neglect the laws, and break them if it is in his power. And the consequence is, that real justice has really no existence if it have not one by nature, and if that which is established as such on account of utility is overturned by some other utility.

But if nature does not ratify law, then all the virtues may lose their sway. For what becomes of generosity, patriotism, or friendship? Where will the desire of benefiting our neighbours, or the gratitude that acknowledges kindness, be able to exist at all? For all these virtues proceed from our natural inclination to love mankind. And this is the true basis of justice, and without this not only the mutual charities of men, but the religious services of the Gods, would be at an end; for these are preserved, as I imagine, rather by the natural sympathy which subsists between divine and human beings, than by mere fear and timidity.

But if the will of the people, the decrees of the senate, the adjudications of magistrates, were sufficient to establish rights, then it might become right to rob, right to commit adultery, right to substitute forged wills, if such conduct were sanctioned by the votes or decrees of the multitude. But if the opinions and suffrages of foolish men had sufficient weight to outbalance the nature of things, then why should they not determine among them, that what is essentially bad and pernicious should henceforth pass for good and beneficial? Or why, since law can make right out of injustice, should it not also be able to change evil into good?

But we have no other rule by which we may be capable of distinguishing between a good or a bad law than that of nature. Nor is it only right and wrong which are discriminated by nature, but generally all that is honourable is by this means distinguished from all that is shameful; for common sense has impressed in our minds the first principles of things, and has given us a general acquaintance with them, by which we connect with virtue every honourable quality, and with vice all that is disgraceful.

But to think that these differences exist only in opinion, and not in nature, is the part of an idiot. For even the virtue of a tree or a horse, in which expression there is an abuse of terms, does not exist in our opinion only, but in nature; and if that is the case, then what is honourable and disgraceful, must also be discriminated by nature.

For if opinion could determine respecting the character of universal virtue, it might also decide respecting particular or partial virtues. But who will dare to determine that a man is prudent and cautious, not from his general conduct, but from some external appearances? For virtue evidently consists in perfect reason, and this certainly resides in nature. Therefore so does all honour and honesty in the same way.

For as what is true and false, creditable and discreditable, is judged of rather by their essential qualities than their external relations; so the consistent and perpetual course of life, which is virtue, and the inconsistency of life, which is vice, are judged of according to their own nature,—and that inconstancy must necessarily be vicious.

We form an estimate of the opinions of youths, but not by their opinions. Those virtues and vices which reside in their moral natures must not be measured by opinions. And so of all moral qualities, we must discriminate between honourable and dishonourable by reference to the essential nature of the things themselves.

The good we commend, must needs contain in itself something commendable; for as I before stated, goodness is not a mode of opinion, but of nature. For if it were otherwise, opinion alone might constitute virtue and happiness, which is the most absurd of suppositions. And since we judge of good and evil by their nature, and since good and evil are the first principles of nature, certainly we should judge in the same manner of all honourable and all shameful things, referring them all to the law of nature.

But we are often too much disturbed by the dissensions of men and the variation of opinions. And because the same thing does not happen with reference to our senses, we look upon them as certain by nature. Those objects, indeed, which sometimes present to us one appearance, sometimes another, and which do not always appear to the same people in the same way, we term fictions of the senses; but it is far otherwise. For neither parent, nor nurse, nor master, nor poet, nor drama, deceive our senses; nor do popular prejudices seduce them from the truth. But all kinds of snares are laid for the mind, either by those errors which I have just enumerated, which, taking possession of the young and uneducated, imbue them deeply, and bend them any way they please; or by that pleasure which is the imitator of goodness, being thoroughly and closely implicated with all our senses—the prolific mother of all evils. For she so corrupts us by her blandishments, that we no longer perceive some things which are essentially excellent, because they have none of this deliciousness and pruriency.

It follows that I may now sum up the whole of this argument by asserting, as is plain to every one from these positions which have been already laid down, that all right and all that is honourable is to be sought for its own sake. In truth, all virtuous men love justice and equity for what they are in themselves; nor is it like a good man to make a mistake, and love that which does not deserve their affection. Right, therefore, is desirable and deserving to be cultivated for its own sake; and if this be true of right, it must be true also of justice. What then shall we say of liberality? Is it exercised gratuitously, or does it covet some reward and recompense? If a man does good without expecting any recompense for his kindness, then it is gratuitous: if he does expect compensation, it is a mere matter of traffic. Nor is there any doubt that he who truly deserves the reputation of a generous and kind-hearted man, is thinking of his duty, not of his interest. In the same way the virtue of justice demands neither emolument nor salary, and therefore we desire it for its own sake. And the case of all the moral virtues is the same, and so is the opinion formed of them.

Besides this, if we weigh virtue by the mere utility and profit that attend it, and not by its own merit, the one virtue which results from such an estimate will be in fact a species of vice. For the more a man refers all his actions especially to his own advantage, the further he recedes from probity; so that they who measure virtue by profit, acknowledge no other virtue than this, which is a kind of vice. For who can be called benevolent, if no one ever acts kindly for the sake of another? And where are we to find a grateful person, if those who are disposed to be so can find no benefactor to whom they can show gratitude? What will become of sacred friendship, if we are not to love our friend for his own sake with all our heart and soul, as people say, if we are even to desert and discard him, as soon as we despair of deriving any further assistance or advantage from him? What can be imagined more inhuman than this conduct? But if friendship ought rather to be cultivated on its own account, so also for the same reason are society, equality, and justice desirable for their own sakes. If this be not so, then there can be no such thing as justice at all; for the most unjust thing of all is to seek a reward for one's just conduct.

What then shall we say of temperance, sobriety, continence, modesty, bashfulness, and chastity? Is it the fear of infamy, or the dread of judgments and penalties, which prevent men from being intemperate and dissolute? Do men then live in innocence and moderation, only to be well spoken of, and to acquire a certain fair reputation? Modest men blush even to speak of indelicacy. And I am greatly ashamed of those philosophers, who assert that there are no vices to be avoided but those which the laws have branded with infamy. For what shall I say? Can we call those persons truly chaste, who abstain from adultery merely from the fear of public exposure and that disgrace which is only one of its many evil consequences? For what can be either praised or blamed with reason, if you depart from that great law and rule of nature, which makes the difference between right and wrong? Shall corporal defects, if they are remarkable, shock our sensibilities, and shall those of the soul make no impression on us?—of the soul, I say, whose turpitude is so evidently proved by its vices. For what is there more hideous than avarice, more brutal than lust, more contemptible than cowardice, more base than stupidity and folly? Well, then, are we to call those persons unhappy, who are conspicuous for one or more of these, on account of some injuries, or disgraces, or sufferings to which they are exposed, or on account of the moral baseness of their sins? And we may apply the same test in the opposite way to those who are distinguished for their virtue.

Lastly, if virtue be sought for on account of some other things, it necessarily follows that there is something better than virtue. Is it money, then? is it fame, or beauty, or health? all of which appear of little value to us when we possess them; nor can it be by any possibility certainly known how long they will last. Or is it (what it is shameful even to utter) that basest of all, pleasure? Surely not; for it is in the contempt and disdain of pleasure that virtue is most conspicuous. . . .

Let us, then, once more examine, before we come to the consideration of particular laws,
what is the power and nature of law in general; lest, when we come to refer everything to it, we occasionally make mistakes from the employment of incorrect language, and show ourselves ignorant of the force of those terms which we ought to employ in the definition of laws.

Quintus.—This is a very necessary caution, and the proper method of seeking truth.

Marcus.—This, then, as it appears to me, has been the decision of the wisest philosophers,—that law was neither a thing contrived by the genius of man, nor established by any decree of the people, but a certain eternal principle, which governs the entire universe, wisely commanding what is right and prohibiting what is wrong. Therefore they called that aboriginal and supreme law the mind of God, enjoining or forbidding each separate thing in accordance with reason. On which account it is, that this law, which the Gods have bestowed on the human race, is so justly applauded. For it is the reason and mind of a wise Being equally able to urge us to good and to deter us from evil.

Quintus.—You have, on more than one occasion, already touched on this topic. But before you come to treat of the laws of nations, I wish you would endeavour to explain the force and power of this divine and celestial law, lest the torrent of custom should overwhelm our understanding, and betray us into the vulgar method of expression.

Marcus.—From our childhood we have learned, my Quintus, to call such phrases as this, "that a man appeals to justice, and goes to law," and many similar expressions, law, but, nevertheless, we should understand that these, and other similar commandments and prohibitions, have sufficient power to lead us on to virtuous actions and to call us away from vicious ones. Which power is not only far more ancient than any existence of states and peoples, but is coeval with God himself, who beholds and governs both heaven and earth. For it is impossible that the divine mind can exist in a state devoid of reason; and divine reason must necessarily be possessed of a power to determine what is virtuous and what is vicious. Nor, because it was nowhere written, that one man should maintain the pass of a bridge against the enemy's whole army, and that he should order the bridge behind him to be cut down, are we therefore to imagine that the valiant Cocles did not perform this great exploit agreeably to the laws of nature and the dictates of true bravery. Again, though in the reign of Tarquin there was no written law concerning adultery, it does not therefore follow that Sextus Tarquinius did not offend against the eternal law when he committed a rape on Lucretia, daughter of Tricipitinus. For, even then he had the light of reason deduced from the nature of things, that incites to good actions and dissuades from evil ones; and which does not begin for the first time to be a law when it is drawn up in writing, but from the first moment that it exists. And this existence of moral obligation is coeternal with that of the divine mind. Therefore, the true and supreme law, whose commands and prohibitions are equally authoritative, is the right reason of the Sovereign Jupiter.

Quintus.—I grant you, my brother, that whatever is just is also at all times the true law; nor can this true law either be originated or abrogated by the written forms in which decrees are drawn up.

Marcus.—Therefore, as that Divine Mind, or reason, is the supreme law, so it exists in the mind of the sage, so far as it can be perfected in man. But with respect to civil laws, which are drawn up in various forms, and framed to meet the occasional requirements of the people, the name of law belongs to them not so much by right as by the favour of the people. For men prove by some such arguments as the following, that every law which deserves the name of a law, ought to be morally good and laudable. It is clear, say they, that laws were originally made for the security of the people, for the preservation of states, for the peace and happiness of society; and that they who first framed enactments of that kind, persuaded the people that they would write and publish such laws only as should conduce to the general morality and happiness, if they would receive and obey them. And then such regulations, being thus settled and sanctioned, they justly entitled *Laws.* From which we may reasonably conclude, that those who made unjustifiable and pernicious enactments for the people, acted in a manner contrary to their own promises and professions, and established anything rather than *laws,* properly so called, since it is evident that the very signification of the word *law,* comprehends the whole essence and energy of justice and equity.

I would, therefore, interrogate you on this point, my Quintus, as those philosophers are in the habit of doing. If a state wants something for the want of which it is reckoned no state at all, must not that something be something good?

Quintus.—A very great good.

Marcus.—And if a state has no law, is it not for that reason to be reckoned no state at all?

Quintus.—We must needs say so.

Marcus.—We must therefore reckon law among the very best things.

Quintus.—I entirely agree with you.

Marcus.—If, then, in the majority of nations, many pernicious and mischievous enactments are made, which have no more right to the name of law than the mutual engagements of robbers, are we bound to call them laws? For as we cannot call the recipes of ignorant and unskilful empirics, who give poisons instead of medicines, the prescriptions of a physician, so likewise we cannot call that the true law of a people, of whatever kind it may be, if it enjoins what is injurious, let the people receive it as they will. For law is the just distinction between right and wrong, made conformable to that most ancient nature of all, the original and principal regulator of all things, by which the laws of men should be measured, whether they punish the guilty or protect and preserve the innocent. . . .

Let this, therefore, be a fundamental principle in all societies, that the Gods are the supreme lords and governors of all things,—that all events are directed by their influence, and wisdom, and Divine power; that they deserve very well of the race of mankind; and that they likewise know what sort of person every one really is; that they observe his actions, whether good or bad; that they take notice with what feelings and with what piety he attends to his religious duties, and that they are sure to make a difference between the good and the wicked.

For when once our minds are confirmed in

these views, it will not be difficult to inspire them with true and useful sentiments. For what can be more true than that no man should be so madly presumptuous as to believe that he has either reason or intelligence, while he does not believe that the heaven and the world possess them likewise, or to think that those things which he can scarcely comprehend by the greatest possible exertion of his intellect, are put in motion without the agency of reason?

In truth, we can scarcely reckon him a man, whom neither the regular courses of the stars, nor the alternations of day and night, nor the temperature of the seasons, nor the productions that nature displays for his use and enjoyment, urge to gratitude towards heaven.

And as those beings which are furnished with reason are incomparably superior to those which want it, and as we cannot say, without impiety, that anything is superior to the universal Nature, we must therefore confess that divine reason is contained within her. And who will dispute the utility of these sentiments, when he reflects how many cases of the greatest importance are decided by oaths; how much the sacred rites performed in making treaties tend to assure peace and tranquillity; and what numbers of people the fear of divine punishment has reclaimed from a vicious course of life; and how sacred the social rights must be in a society where a firm persuasion obtains the immediate intervention of the immortal Gods, both as witnesses and judges of our actions? Such is the "preamble of the law," to use the expression of Plato.

Marcus Aurelius

Marcus Aurelius (121–180 A.D.), the last of the good emperors, achieved fame both as a governor and as a student of philosophy. He attempted, with considerable success, to apply the principles of the Hellenistic philosophy of Stoicism to the problems of empire. A man of lofty ideals and fine character, he was naturally attracted by the strict ethics of Stoicism and by its emphasis on universal brotherhood. The Thoughts of Marcus Aurelius revealed these interests. In reading the selections from them note particularly (1) the basis for his belief in universal brotherhood, (2) the rules he established to govern his own daily conduct, (3) his ideas on law and political bodies, (4) his views on death, (5) his thoughts concerning the relationship between nature and man, and (6) his concept of the nature and importance of mind.

From: *THE THOUGHTS OF MARCUS AURELIUS*

Every morning repeat to thyself: I shall meet with a busybody, an ingrate, and a bully; with treachery, envy, and selfishness. All these vices have fallen to their share because they know not good and evil. But I have contemplated the nature of the good and seen that it is the beautiful; of evil, and seen that it is deformity; of the sinner, and seen that it is kindred to my own—kindred, not because he shares the same flesh and blood and is sprung from the same seed, but because he partakes of the same reason and the same spark of divinity. How then can any of these harm me? For none can involve me in the shameful save my-

As translated by John Jackson in *The Thoughts of Marcus Aurelius Antonius,* in the World's Classics, Oxford University Press, London, 1906, 8–10; 23–24; 75; 113–115. Courtesy of the Oxford University Press.

self. Or how can I be angered with my kith and kin, or cherish hatred towards them?

For we are all created to work together, as the members of one body—feet, hands, and eyelids, or the upper and nether teeth. Whence, to work against each other is contrary to nature;—but this is the very essence of anger and aversion.

This thing that I call "myself" is compact of flesh, breath, and reason. Thou art even now in the throes of death; despise therefore the flesh. It is but a little blood, a few bones, a paltry net woven from nerves and veins and arteries. Consider next thy breath. What a trifle it is! A little air, and this for ever changing: every minute of every hour we are gasping it forth and sucking it in again!

Only reason is left us. Consider thus: Thou art striken in years; then suffer it not to remain a bond-servant; suffer it not to be puppet-like, hurried hither and thither by impulses that take no thought of thy fellow-man; suffer it not to murmur at destiny in the present or look askance at it in the future.

The works of God are full of providence; the works of Fortune are not independent of Nature, but intertwisted and intertwined with those directed by providence. Thence flow all things. Co-factors, too, are necessity and the common welfare of the whole universe whereof thou art part. Now whatever arises from the nature of the whole, and tends to its well-being, is good also for every part of that nature. But the well-being of the universe depends on change, not merely of the elementary, but also of the compound. Let these dogmas suffice thee, if dogmas thou must have; but put off that thirst for books, and see thou die of good cheer, not with murmurs on thy lips, but blessing God truthfully and with all thy heart.

Bethink thee how long thou hast delayed to do these things; how many days of grace heaven hath vouchsafed thee and thou neglected. Now is the time to learn at last what is the nature of the universe whereof thou art part; what of the power that governs the universe, whereof thou art an emanation. Forget not there is a boundary set to thy time, and that if thou use it not to uncloud thy soul it will anon be gone, and thou with it, never to return again.

Let it be thy hourly care to do stoutly what thy hand findeth to do, as becomes a man and a Roman, with carefulness, unaffected dignity, humanity, freedom, and justice. Free thyself from the obsession of all other thoughts; for free thyself thou wilt, if thou but perform every action as though it were the last of thy life, without light-mindedness, without swerving through force of passion from the dictates of reason, without hypocrisy, without self-love, without chafing at destiny.

Thou seest how few things are needful for man to live a happy and godlike life: for, if he observe these, heaven will demand no more.

Abase thee, abase thee, O my soul! The time is past for exalting thyself. Man hath but a single life; and this thou hast well nigh spent, reverencing not thyself, but dreaming thy happiness is situate in the souls of others!

Why suffer the incidence of things external to distract thee? Make for thyself leisure to learn something new of good, and cease this endless round.—And here beware lest the wheel only reverse its motion. For fools, too, are they who have worn out their lives in action, yet never set before themselves a goal to which they could direct every impulse—nay, every thought.

Thou mayest search, but wilt hardly find a man made wretched through failing to read another's soul; whereas he who fails to ponder the motions of his own must needs be wretched.

Let me ever be mindful what is the nature of the universe, and what my own; how the latter is related to the former, and what part it is of what whole.—And forget not that there is none that can forbid thee to be ever, in deed and word, in harmony with the nature whereof thou art part. . . .

If the intellectual part of us is common to all, so is the reason which gives us our status as rational beings. Granted this, the reason which bids us do or not do must needs be common also. Hence it follows that there is one law; and if the law be one, we are all fellow-subjects, and, as such, members of one body-politic: that is, the universe is a species of state. —For what other conceivable political community is there, of which the whole human race can be said to be citizens?—And from this city of the universe must proceed those very faculties of intellect and reason, with our conception of law. There is no other possible source; but precisely as the earthly part of myself has been assigned me from some universal earth, and the fluid from the contrary element, while breath, warmth, and heat must each have had their proper fount, in virtue of the axiom that nothing can come from nothing any more than it can return from nothing,—so too must the intellect have had its definite origin.

Death is akin to birth in that both are mysteries of nature: in the one there is composition; in the other, decomposition: in both the antecedent and resultant elements are the same. —At all events, it is not a thing to be ashamed of, for in it there is nothing save what is consonant with the nature of rational life, and nothing that is repugnant to the laws of our being.

It is a matter of nature and necessity for men of this type to act as they do.—And, in general, remember the truth that, in a little while, both thou and he will be no more; and yet, a little while, and not so much as your names will be left. . . .

As universal Nature has given every rational being practically all her other powers, so too we are indebted to her for this: that just as she herself converts every obstacle in her path, and every attempt at resistance, to her own ends, assigns them to their proper place in destiny, and makes them part of herself, so each rational being has the power to convert any impediment into material for itself, and to use it for whatever purpose it had in view.

Trouble not thyself by pondering life in its entirety. Strive not to comprehend in one view the nature and number of the burdens that, belike, will fall to thy share. Rather, as each occasion arises in the present put this question to thyself: "Where lies the unbearable, unendurable part of this task?" Confession will put thee to the blush! Next recall to mind that neither past nor future can weigh thee down, only the present. And the present will shrink to littleness if thou but set it apart, assign it its boundaries, and then ask thy mind if it avail not to bear even this! . . .

All the objects thou prayest it may be thine to reach after many days are, even now, within thy power, if thou wilt but stretch forth thy hand to take them: in other words, if thou wilt

leave the past to itself, entrust the future to providence, and content thyself with conforming the present to holiness and justice. Holiness, that thou mayest rest content with the lot Nature assigns thee; for she bare it for thee and thee for it. Justice, that thy words may be the words of truth, free and undisguised; that thy every act may conform to law and equity; and that naught may impede thee, whether it be another's wickedness, his thoughts of thee, and his words, or the sensations of this circumscribing flesh, which, being the sufferer, may be left to look to itself. Accordingly, whensoever thou shalt draw nigh to thy journey's end, leave all else behind thee, reserve thy reverence for reason and the celestial part of thyself, and fear not because sooner or later thou must cease to live, but rather lest life by Nature's laws be yet to begin:—this do, and thou wilt be a man worthy of the universe that gave thee birth, no longer a stranger on thy native soil, no longer a dullard to whom the events of every day are marvels of the unexpected, and no longer a mere dependent on this thing or that!

God views the minds of all men in their nakedness, stripped of the casings and husks and impurities of the material. For, solely in virtue of the intellectual part of Himself, He touches directly the human intellect that emanates from Him and has flowed into these bodies of ours. So train thou thyself to do likewise, and thou shalt be quit of this sore distraction of thine. For he who has no eyes for our fleshly covering surely will not trouble himself with the contemplation of a man's house, raiment, fame, or aught else of these outer trappings and stage decorations!

There are three things whereof thou art compound: body, breath, and mind. Of these the first two are thine in so far as it is thy duty to assume their stewardship; but the third alone is thine absolutely. Wherefore, if thou wilt put away from thyself and thy mind all that others do or say, all thou thyself hast said or done, all disturbing thoughts of the future, all the vicissitudes of thy fleshly garment and its conjunct breath, with all that the circumfluent vortex whirls along, so that the intellective power, exempt and purified from the things of destiny, may dwell free and master in its own household, practising justice of action, resigned to all that chances, and speaking the truth,—if, I say, "thou wilt put aside from this reason of thine all accretions born of the fleshly affections, all time to come, and all time past, likening thyself to the Empedoclean globe— that perfect sphere rejoicing with great joy in its stability,"—and striving to live only the life thou livest, in other words the present, then the power will be thine to pass the span that is left between thee and death in calmness and cheerfulness and content with the godhead that resides within thee.

I have often marvelled how it is that every one loves himself more than the rest of human kind, yet values his own opinion of himself less than that of others. At all events, were some god or some sage to stand by a man and bid him entertain no idea, no thought, within himself without simultaneously uttering it aloud, he could not abide the ordeal for a single day. So true it is that we have more respect for our neighbours and their thoughts of us than we have for ourselves!

The Decline of Classical Civilization

Although Rome, by eclipsing the Greeks, had become the standard bearer of classical civilization, she proved to be unequal to the task of maintaining it, and gradually corruption, licentiousness, and waste began to characterize the lives of many in high places of authority. Economic maladjustments likewise began to appear in various parts of the Empire, and slowly but surely Rome's greatness began to decline. These conditions, together with the unsatisfying spiritual and moral character of the official Roman religion, furnished an ideal environment for the rapid spread of Christianity, a new religion which had emerged in the eastern Mediterranean from the bosom of the Hebrew faith. As Christianity spread westward, it brought with it certain oriental characteristics which, together with the uncertainties of life in the declining Empire, led to an increasing popularity of monasticism and a generally otherworldly outlook on life. As Rome's position gradually weakened, other powers emerged upon the Mediterranean scene to assume what Rome could no longer maintain. Thus in the East the Byzantine emperors and the followers of Mohammed inherited political and cultural leadership, while in the West the primitive Germanic peoples began their long struggle to build modern Western Civilization on the ruins of the Roman Empire.

Suetonius

Gaius Suetonius Tranquillus (about 75–150 A.D.) lived during a critical period in Roman history. Politically and culturally the empire reached its greatest development and entered into its long decline during his life. As Latin secretary to the Emperor Hadrian he had access to important archives, and as a student of human nature he was in a favorable position to gather material on the great men of the era. In The Lives of the Twelve Caesars he wrote an accurate and impartial account of the early emperors. Primarily biographical in character, they nevertheless inevitably revealed some of the factors that contributed to the decline of Rome. These selections are from the section on Nero, emperor from 54 to 68 A.D. In reading them note (1) Nero's early character and training, (2) his interest in music, (3) evidences of brutality in the life of the times, (4) Nero's depravity and extravagance, (5) the economic effects of his squanderings, (6) the political results of his superstitious fears, (7) the social and economic effects of the burning of Rome, and (8) the circumstances of his death.

From: THE LIVES OF THE TWELVE CAESARS

Nero was born at Antium nine months after the death of Tiberius, on the eighteenth day before the Kalends of January, just as the sun rose, so that he was touched by its rays almost before he could be laid upon the ground. Many people at once made many direful predictions from his horoscope, and a remark of his father, Domitius, was also regarded as an omen. For, while receiving the congratulations of his friends, he said that nothing that was not abominable and a public bane could be born of Agrippina and himself. Another manifest indication of Nero's future unhappiness occurred on his naming day. For, when Gaius Caesar was asked by his sister to give the child whatever name he liked, he looked at his uncle Claudius, who later became Emperor and adopted Nero, and said that he gave him his name. This he did, not seriously, but in jest, and Agrippina scorned the proposal, because at that time Claudius was one of the laughing-stocks of the court.

At the age of three he lost his father, being left heir to a third of his estate. But even this he did not receive in full, since his fellow heir Gaius seized all the property. Then his mother was banished too, and he was brought up at the house of his aunt Lepida almost in actual want, under two tutors, a dancer and a barber. But when Claudius became emperor, Nero not only recovered his father's property, but was also enriched by an inheritance from his step-father, Passienus Crispus. When his mother was recalled from banishment and reinstated, he became so prominent through her influence that it leaked out that Messalina, wife of Claudius, had sent emissaries to strangle him as he was taking his noonday nap, regarding him as a rival of Britannicus. An addition to this bit of gossip is, that the would-be assassins were frightened away by a snake which darted out from under his pillow. The only foundation for this tale was, that there was found in his bed near the pillow the slough of a serpent. All the same, at his mother's desire he had the skin enclosed in a golden bracelet, and wore it for a long time on his right arm. But when at last the memory of his mother grew hateful to him,

As translated by Joseph Gavorse in Suetonius, *The Lives of the Twelve Caesars*, The Modern Library, New York, 1931, 244–245; 252–253; 255–268; 273–274; 276–278. Courtesy of Random House, Inc.

he threw it away, and afterwards in the time of his extremity sought it again in vain.

While he was still a young, half-grown boy he took part in the game of Troy at a performance in the Circus with great self-possession and success. In the eleventh year of his age he was adopted by Claudius and consigned to the training of Annaeus Seneca, who was then already a Senator. They say that on the following night Seneca dreamed that he was teaching Gaius Caligula, and Nero soon proved the dream prophetic by revealing the cruelty of his disposition at the earliest possible opportunity. For merely because his brother Britannicus had, after his adoption, greeted him as usual as Ahenobarbus, he tried to convince his father that Britannicus was a changeling. Also when his aunt Lepida was accused, he publicly gave testimony against her, to gratify his mother, who was using every effort to ruin Lepida. . . .

Having gained some knowledge of music in addition to the rest of his early education, as soon as he became Emperor he sent for Terpnus, the greatest master of the lyre in those days, and after listening to him sing after dinner for many successive days until late at night, he little by little began to practice himself, neglecting none of the exercises which artists of that kind are in the habit of following, to preserve or strengthen their voices. For he used to lie upon his back and hold a leaden plate on his chest, purge himself by the syringe and by vomiting, and deny himself fruits and all foods injurious to the voice. Finally encouraged by his progress, although his voice was weak and husky, he began to long to appear on the stage, and every now and then in the presence of his intimate friends he would quote a Greek proverb meaning "Hidden music counts for nothing." And he made his début at Naples, where he did not cease singing until he had finished the number which he had begun, even though the theater was shaken by a sudden earthquake shock. In the same city he sang frequently and for several successive days. Even when he took a short time to rest his voice, he could not keep out of sight but went to the theater after bathing and dined in the orchestra with the people all about him, promising them in Greek, that when he had wetted his whistle a bit, he would ring out something good and loud. He was

greatly taken too with the rhythmic applause of some Alexandrians, who had flocked to Naples from a fleet that had lately arrived, and summoned more men from Alexandria. Not content with that, he selected some young men of the order of Knights and more than five thousand sturdy young commoners, to be divided into groups and learn the Alexandrian styles of applause, which they called "the bees," "the roof-tiles," and "the bricks." These men were noticeable for their thick hair and fine apparel. Their left hands were bare and without rings, and they played thin "claques" vigorously whenever Nero sang. The leaders of these bands were paid four hundred thousand sesterces each [$16,400.00]. . . .

While he was singing no one was allowed to leave the theater even for the most urgent reasons. And so it is said that some women gave birth to children there, while many who were worn out with listening and applauding, secretly leaped from the side of the theater, since the gates at the entrance were closed, or feigned death and were carried out as if for burial. The trepidation and anxiety with which he took part in the contests, his keen rivalry of his opponents and his awe of the judges, can hardly be credited. As if his rivals were of quite the same station as himself, he used to show respect to them and try to gain their favor, while he slandered them behind their backs, sometimes assailed them with abuse when he met them, and even bribed those who were especially proficient. . . .

Although at first his acts of wantonness, lust, extravagance, avarice, and cruelty were gradual and secret, and might be condoned as follies of youth, yet even then their nature was such that no one doubted that they were defects of his character and not due to his time of life. No sooner was twilight over than he would slip on the disguise of a cap or a wig and go to the taverns or range about the streets playing pranks, which however were very far from harmless. For he used to beat men as they came home from dinner, stabbing any who resisted him and throwing them into the sewers. He would even break into shops and rob them, setting up a market in the Palace, where he divided the booty which he took, sold it at auction, and then squandered the proceeds. In the scuffles which took place on such occasions he often ran the risk of losing his eyes or even his life, for he was beaten almost to death by a man of the senatorial order whose wife he had handled indecently. Warned by this, he never afterwards ventured to appear in public at that hour without having Tribunes follow him at a distance and unobserved. Even in the daytime he would be carried privately to the theater in a sedan, where he would take a place in the upper part of the proscenium from which he not only witnessed the brawls of the pantomimic actors but also egged them on. When they came to blows and stones and pieces of broken benches began to fly about he himself threw many missiles at the people and even broke a Praetor's head.

Little by little, however, as his vices grew stronger, he dropped jesting and secrecy and with no attempt at disguise openly broke out into worse crime.

He prolonged his revels from midday to midnight, often livening himself by a warm plunge, or, if it were summer, into water cooled with snow. Sometimes too he closed the inlets of the Naumachia and banqueted there in public, or in the Campus Martius, or in the Circus Maximus, waited on by harlots and dancing girls from all over the city. Whenever he drifted down the Tiber to Ostia, or sailed about the Gulf of Baiae, booths were set up at intervals along the banks and shores, fitted out as brothels and eating-houses, before which were matrons who played the part of bawds and hostesses, soliciting him from every side to come ashore. He also coerced his friends to give him banquets, one of whom spent four million sesterces on a dinner at which turbans were the favor, and another a considerably larger sum on one at which roses were distributed.

Besides abusing freeborn boys and seducing married women, he debauched the Vestal Virgin Rubria. The freedwoman Acte he all but made his lawful wife, after bribing some ex-consuls to perjure themselves by swearing that she was of royal birth. He castrated the boy Sporus and actually tried to make a woman of him. He married him with all the usual ceremonies, including a dowry and a bridal veil, took him to his house attended by a great throng, and treated him as his wife. And the

witty jest that some one made is still current, that it would have been well for the world if Nero's father Domitius had had that kind of wife. This Sporus, decked out with the finery of the Empresses and riding in a litter, he took with him to the assizes and marts of Greece, and later at Rome through the Street of the Images, fondly kissing him from time to time. That he even desired illicit relations with his own mother, and was kept from it by her enemies, who feared that such a relationship might give the reckless and insolent woman too great influence, was notorious, especially after he added to his concubines a courtesan who was said to look very like Agrippina. Even before that, so they say, whenever he rode in a litter with his mother, he had incestuous relations with her, which were betrayed by the stains on his clothing.

He so prostituted his own chastity that after defiling almost every part of his body, he at last devised a kind of game, in which, covered with the skin of some wild animal, he was let loose from a cage and attacked the private parts of men and women, who were bound to stakes, and when he had sated his mad lust, was dispatched by his freedman Doryphorus. For he was even married to this man in the same way that he himself had married Sporus, going so far as to imitate the cries and lamentations of a maiden being deflowered. I have heard from some men that it was his unshaken conviction that no man was chaste or pure in any part of his body, but that most of them concealed their vices and cleverly drew a veil over them; and that therefore he pardoned all other faults in those who confessed to him their lewdness.

He thought that there was no other way of enjoying riches and money than by riotous extravagance, declaring that only stingy and niggardly fellows kept a correct account of what they spent, while fine and genuinely magnificent gentlemen wasted and squandered. Nothing in his uncle Gaius so excited his envy and admiration as the fact that he had in so short a time run through the vast wealth which Tiberius had left him. Accordingly he made presents and wasted money without stint. On Tiridates, though it would seem hardly within belief, he spent eight hundred thousand sesterces a day, and on his departure presented him with more than a hundred millions. He gave the lyre-player Menecrates and the gladiator Spiculus properties and residences equal to those of men who had celebrated triumphs. He enriched the monkey-faced usurer Paneros with estates in the country and in the city and had him buried with almost regal splendor. He never wore the same garment twice. He played at dice for four hundred thousand sesterces a point. He fished with a golden net drawn by cords woven of purple and scarlet threads. It is said that he never made a journey with less than a thousand carriages, his mules shod with silver and their drivers clad in wool of Canusium, attended by a train of Mazaces and couriers with bracelets and trappings.

There was nothing however in which he was more ruinously prodigal than in building. He made a palace extending all the way from the Palatine to the Esquiline, which at first he called the House of Passage, but when it was burned shortly after its completion and rebuilt, the Golden House. Its size and splendor will be sufficiently indicated by the following details. Its vestibule was high enough to contain a colossal statue of the Emperor a hundred and twenty feet high. So large was this house that it had a triple colonnade a mile long. There was a lake in it too, like a sea, surrounded with buildings to represent cities, besides tracts of country, varied by tilled fields, vineyards, pastures and woods, with great numbers of wild and domestic animals. In the rest of the house all parts were overlaid with gold and adorned with jewels and mother-of-pearl. There were dining-rooms with fretted ceilings of ivory, whose panels could turn and shower down flowers and were fitted with pipes for sprinkling the guests with perfumes. The main banquet hall was circular and constantly revolved day and night, like the heavens. He had baths supplied with sea water and sulphur water. When the edifice was finished in this style and he dedicated it, he deigned to say nothing more in the way of approval than that he was at last beginning to be housed like a human being.

He also began a pool, extending from Misenum to the lake of Avernus, roofed over and enclosed in colonnades, into which he planned to turn all the hot springs in every part of Baiae. He likewise projected a canal to extend from Avernus all the way to Ostia, to enable the journey to be made by ship yet not by sea: its length was to be a hundred and sixty miles and its breadth sufficient to allow ships with five banks of oars to pass each other. For the execution of these projects he had given orders that the prisoners all over the empire should be transported to Italy, and that those who were convicted even of capital crimes should be punished in no other way than by sentence to this work.

He was led to such mad extravagance, in addition to his confidence in the resources of the empire, by the hope of a vast hidden treasure, suddenly inspired by the assurance of a Roman Knight, who declared positively that the enormous wealth which Queen Dido had taken with her of old in her flight from Tyre was hidden away in huge caves in Africa and could be recovered with but trifling labor.

When this hope proved false, he resorted to false accusations and robbery, being at the end of his resources and so utterly impoverished that he was obliged to postpone and defer even the pay of the soldiers and the rewards due to the veterans.

First of all he made a law, that instead of one-half, five-sixths of the property of deceased freedmen should be made over to him, if without good and sufficient reason they bore the name of any family with which he himself was connected. Further, that the estates of those who were ungrateful to their Emperor should belong to the privy purse, and that the lawyers who had written or dictated such wills should not go unpunished. Finally, that any word or deed on which an informer could base an action should come under the law against treason. He demanded the return of the rewards which he had given in recognition of the prizes conferred on him by any city in any competition. Having forbidden the use of amethystine or Tyrian purple dyes, he secretly sent a man to sell a few ounces on a market day and then closed the shops of all the dealers. It is even said that when he saw a matron in the audience at one of his recitals clad in the forbidden color he pointed her out to his agents, who dragged her out and stripped her on the spot, not only of her garment, but also of her property. He never appointed any one to an office without adding: "You know what my needs are," and "Let us see to it that no one possesses anything." At last he stripped many temples of their gifts and melted down the images of gold and silver, including those of the guardian Gods of Rome which, however, Galba soon afterwards restored.

He began his career of parricide and murder with Claudius, for even if he was not the instigator of the Emperor's death, he was at least privy to it, as he openly admitted. For he used afterwards to laud mushrooms, the vehicle in which the poison was administered to Claudius, as "the food of the Gods," as the Greek proverb has it. At any rate, after Claudius' death he vented on him every kind of insult, in act and word, charging him now with folly and now with cruelty. . . . And he disregarded many of his decrees and acts as the work of a madman and a dotard. Finally, he neglected to enclose the place where his body was burned except with a low and mean wall.

He attempted the life of Britannicus by poison, not less from jealousy of his voice (for it was more agreeable than his own) than from fear that he might sometime win a higher place than himself in the people's regard because of the memory of his father. He procured the potion from an arch-poisoner, one Locusta, and when the effect was slower than he anticipated, merely physicking Britannicus, he called the woman to him and flogged her with his own hand, charging that she had administered a medicine instead of a poison. When she said in excuse that she had given a smaller dose to shield him from the odium of the crime, he replied: "It's likely that I am afraid of the Julian law." So he forced her to mix as swift and instant a potion as she knew how in his own room before his very eyes. Then he tried it on a kid, and as the animal lingered for five hours, had the mixture steeped again and again and threw some of it before a pig. The beast instantly fell dead, whereupon he ordered that the poison be taken to the dining-room and given to Britannicus. The boy dropped dead at the very first taste, but Nero lied to his guests and declared that he was seized with the falling sickness, to which he was subject,

and the next day had him hastily and unceremoniously buried in a pouring rain. He rewarded Locusta for her eminent services with a full pardon and large estates in the country, and actually sent her pupils.

His mother offended him by too strict surveillance and criticism of his words and acts, but at first he confined his resentment to frequent endeavors to bring upon her a burden of unpopularity by pretending that he would abdicate the throne and go off to Rhodes. Then depriving her of all her honors and of her guard of Roman and German soldiers, he even forbade her to live with him and drove her from the Palace. After that he passed all bounds in harrying her, bribing men to annoy her with lawsuits while she remained in the city, and after she had retired to the country, to pass her house by land and sea and break her rest with abuse and mockery. At last terrified by her violence and threats, he determined to have her life, and after thrice attempting it by poison and finding that she had made herself immune by antidotes, he tampered with the ceiling of her bedroom, contriving a mechanical device for loosening its panels and dropping them upon her while she slept. When this leaked out through some of those connected with the plot, he devised a collapsible boat, to destroy her by shipwreck or by the falling in of its cabin. Then he pretended a reconciliation and invited her in a most cordial letter to come to Baiae and celebrate the feast of Minerva with him. On her arrival, instructing his captains to wreck the galley in which she had come, by running into it as if by accident, he detained her at a banquet, and when she would return to Bauli, offered her his contrivance in place of the craft which had been damaged, escorting her to it in high spirits and even kissing her breasts as they parted. The rest of the night he passed sleepless in intense anxiety, awaiting the outcome of his design. On learning that everything had gone wrong and that she had escaped by swimming, driven to desperation he secretly had a dagger thrown down beside her freedman Lucius Agermus, when he joyfully brought word that she was safe and sound. He then ordered that the freedman be seized and bound, on the charge of having been hired by her to kill the Emperor, and that his mother be put to death, giving out that she had committed suicide to escape the consequences of her detected guilt. Trustworthy authorities add still more gruesome details: that he hurried off to view the corpse, handled her limbs, criticizing some and commending others, and that becoming thirsty meanwhile, he took a drink. . . .

Indeed there is no kind of relationship that he did not violate in his career of crime. He put to death Antonia, daughter of Claudius, for refusing to marry him after Poppaea's death, charging her with an attempt at revolution. And he treated in the same way all others who were in any way connected with him by blood or by marriage. Among these was the young Aulus Plautius, whom he forcibly defiled before his death, saying "Let my mother come now and kiss my successor," openly charging that Agrippina had loved Plautius and that this had roused him to hopes of the throne. Rufrius Crispinus, a mere boy, his stepson and the child of Poppaea, he ordered to be drowned by the child's own slaves while he was fishing, because it was said that he used to play at being a general and an Emperor. He banished his nurse's son Tuscus, because when Procurator in Egypt, he had bathed in some baths which were built for a visit of Nero's. He drove his tutor, Seneca, to suicide, although when the old man often pleaded to be allowed to retire and offered to give up his estates, he had sworn most solemnly that he did wrong to suspect him and that he would rather die than harm him. He sent poison to Burrus, Prefect of the Guard, in place of a throat medicine which he had promised him. The old and wealthy freedmen who had helped him first to his adoption and later to the throne, and aided him by their advice, he killed by poison, administered partly in their food and partly in their drink.

Those outside his family he assailed with no less cruelty. It chanced that a comet had begun to appear on several successive nights, a thing which is commonly believed to portend the death of great rulers. Worried by this, and learning from the astrologer Balbillus that Kings usually averted such omens by the sacrifice of some illustrious person, thus bringing the danger foreboded to their own persons onto the heads of their chief men, he resolved on

the death of all the eminent men of the State, indeed, all the more firmly, and with some semblance of justice, after the discovery of two conspiracies. The earlier and more dangerous of these was that of Piso at Rome; the other was set on foot by Vinicius at Beneventum and detected there. The conspirators made their defense in triple sets of fetters, some voluntarily admitting their guilt, some even maintaining they were trying to do him a favor, saying that there was no way except by death that they could help a man disgraced by every kind of wickedness. The children of those who were condemned were banished or put to death by poison or starvation. A number are known to have been slain all together at a single meal along with their preceptors and attendants, while others were prevented from earning their daily bread. . . .

But he showed no greater mercy to the people or the walls of his capital. When some one in a general conversation said: "When I am dead, be earth consumed by fire," he rejoined "Nay, rather while I live," and his action was wholly in accord. For under cover of displeasure at the ugliness of the old buildings and the narrow, crooked streets, he set fire to the city so openly that several ex-consuls did not venture to lay hands on his household servants although they caught them on their estates with tow and firebrands, while some granaries near the Golden House, on a plot of ground he particularly desired, were demolished by engines of war and then set on fire, because their walls were of stone. For six days and seven nights destruction raged, while the people were driven for shelter to monuments and tombs. At that time, besides an immense number of apartment houses, the private houses of leaders of old were burned, still adorned with trophies of victory, and the temples of the Gods vowed and dedicated by the Kings and later in the Punic and Gallic wars, and whatever else interesting and noteworthy had survived from antiquity. Viewing the conflagration from the tower of Maecenas and exulting, as he said, in "the beauty of the flames," he sang the whole of the "Sack of Troy," dressed up in his regular stage costume. Furthermore, to gain from this calamity, too, all the spoil and booty possible, while promising the removal of the debris and dead bodies free of cost, he allowed no one to approach the ruins of his own property. And from the contributions which he not only received, but even demanded, he nearly bankrupted the provinces and exhausted the resources of individuals. . . .

When he had thus aroused the hatred of all, there was no form of insult to which he was not subjected. A lock of hair was placed on the head of his statue with the inscription in Greek: "Now there is a real contest and you must at last surrender." To the neck of another statue a sack was tied and with it the words: "I have done what I could, but you have earned the sack." People wrote on the columns that by his singing he had stirred up even the Gauls. When night came on, many men pretended to be wrangling with their slaves and kept calling out for a vindicator.

In addition he was frightened by manifest portents from dreams, auspices and omens, both old and new. He had never been in the habit of dreaming before he killed his mother. But after that he had such nightmares as: that he was steering a ship and the helm was wrenched from his hands; that he was dragged by his wife Octavia into thickest darkness; that now he was covered with a swarm of winged ants; or again, that the statues of all the heroes dedicated in Pompey's theater had surrounded him and blocked his way; that a Spanish steed of which he was very fond was changed into the form of an ape in the hinder parts of its body, and its head, which alone remained unaltered, gave forth tuneful neighs. The doors of the Mausoleum flew open of their own accord, and a voice was heard from within summoning him by name. After his domestic Gods had been adorned on the Kalends of January, they fell to the ground in the midst of the preparations for the sacrifice. . . .

At last, while his companions one and all urged him to save himself as soon as possible from the indignities that threatened him, he bade them dig a grave in his presence, proportioned to the size of his own person, collect any bits of marble that could be found, and at the same time bring water and wood for presently disposing of his body. As each of these things was done, he wept and said again and again: "What an artist the world is losing!"

While he hesitated, a letter was brought to Phaon by one of his couriers. Nero snatching it from his hand read that he had been pronounced a public enemy by the Senate, and that they were seeking him to punish him in the ancient fashion. And he asked what manner of punishment that was. When he learned that the criminal was stripped naked, fastened by the neck in a forked stake and then beaten to death with rods, in mortal terror he seized two daggers which he had brought with him, and then, after trying the point of each, put them up again, pleading that the fated hour had not yet come. Now he would beg Sporus to begin to lament and wail, and now entreat some one to help him take his life by setting him the example. Anon he reproached himself for his cowardice in such words as these: "To live despoiled, disgraced—this does not become Nero, does not become him—one should be resolute at such times—come, rouse thyself!" And now the horsemen were at hand who had orders to take him off alive. When he heard them, he quavered: "The trampling of swift-footed studs is in my ear," and drove a dagger into his throat, aided by Epaphroditus, his private secretary. He was all but dead when a Centurion rushed in, and as he placed a cloak to the wound, pretending that he had come to aid him, Nero merely gasped: "Too late!" and "This is fidelity!" With these words he was gone, his eyes so set and starting from their sockets that all who saw him shuddered with horror. First and beyond all else he had forced from his companions a promise to let no one have his head, but to contrive in some way that he be buried unmutilated. And this was granted by Icelus, Galba's freedman, who had shortly before been released from the bondage to which he was consigned at the beginning of the revolt.

He was buried at a cost of two hundred thousand sesterces and laid out in white robes embroidered with gold, which he had worn on the Kalends of January. His ashes were deposited by his nurses, Egloge and Alexandria, accompanied by his mistress Acte, in the family tomb of the Domitii on the summit of the Hill of Gardens, which is visible from the Campus Martius. In that monument his sarcophagus of porphyry, with an altar of marble from Luna standing above it, is enclosed by a balustrade of Thasian stone.

He was about the average height, his body marked with spots and malodorous, his hair light blond, his features regular rather than attractive, his eyes blue and somewhat weak, his neck overthick, his belly prominent, and his legs very slender. His health was good, for though indulging in every kind of riotous excess, he was ill but three times in all during the fourteen years of his reign, and even then not enough to give up wine or any of his usual habits. He was utterly shameless in the care of his person and in his dress, always having his hair arranged in tiers of curls, and during the trip to Greece also letting it grow long and hang down behind. And he often appeared in public in a dinner-gown, with a handkerchief bound about his neck, ungirt and unshod.

The Bible

The Gospel of Matthew was composed a few years after the writing attributed to Mark, and the author was therefore able to use the earlier work for much of the account. The outstanding feature of the later work is the emphasis it placed on the teachings of Jesus, notably in the Sermon on the Mount. The distinctive literary style of this famous passage stands out from the remainder of the Gospel and gives credence to the belief that these are the actual utterances of Jesus. In reading the Sermon on the Mount note (1) the beatitudes, (2) the moral code of Jesus, (3) His attitude toward the teaching of the prophets, (4) the similarities and the differences between His teachings and the law of Moses, and (5) any aspects of His teachings that might lead to conflict with the prevailing Jewish religious beliefs.

From: THE GOSPEL ACCORDING TO ST. MATTHEW

And seeing the multitudes, he went up into a mountain: and when he was set, his disciples came unto him: and he opened his mouth, and taught them, saying,

"Blessed are the poor in spirit:
For theirs is the kingdom of heaven.

Blessed are they that mourn:
For they shall be comforted.

Blessed are the meek:
For they shall inherit the earth.

Blessed are they which do hunger and
thirst after righteousness:
For they shall be filled.

Blessed are the merciful:
For they shall obtain mercy.

Blessed are the pure in heart:
For they shall see God.

Blessed are the peacemakers:
For they shall be called the children of
God.

Blessed are they which are persecuted
for righteousness' sake:
For theirs is the kingdom of heaven.

Blessed are ye, when men shall revile
you, and persecute you, and shall
say all manner of evil against you
falsely, for my sake.

Adapted from the King James version of the Bible.

Rejoice, and be exceeding glad: for great is your reward in Heaven: for so persecuted they the prophets which were before you.

"Ye are the salt of the earth: but if the salt have lost his savour, wherewith shall it be salted? It is thenceforth good for nothing, but to be cast out, and to be trodden under foot of men.

"Ye are the light of the world. A city that is set on a hill cannot be hid. Neither do men light a candle, and put it under a bushel, but on a candlestick; and it giveth light unto all that are in the house. Let your light so shine before men, that they may see your good works, and glorify your Father which is in heaven.

"Think not that I am come to destroy the law, or the prophets: I am not come to destroy, but to fulfil. For verily I say unto you, 'Till heaven and earth pass, one jot or one tittle shall in no wise pass from the law, till all be fulfilled.' Whosoever therefore shall break one of these least commandments, and shall teach men so, he shall be called the least in the kingdom of heaven: but whosoever shall do and teach them, the same shall be called great in the kingdom of heaven. For I say unto you, 'Except your righteousness shall exceed the righteousness of the scribes and Pharisees, ye shall in no case enter into the kingdom of heaven.'

"Ye have heard that it was said by them of old time, 'Thou shalt not kill'; and whosoever shall kill shall be in danger of the judgment. But I say unto you, 'Whosoever is angry with his brother without a cause shall be in danger of the judgment: and whosoever shall say to his brother, "Raca" [worthless], shall be in danger of the council: but whosoever shall say, "Thou fool," shall be in danger of hell fire.' Therefore if thou bring thy gift to the altar, and there rememberest that thy brother hath ought against thee; leave there thy gift before the altar, and go thy way; first be reconciled to thy brother, and then come and offer thy gift. Agree with thine adversary quickly, while thou art in the way with him; lest at any time the adversary deliver thee to the judge, and the judge deliver thee to the officer, and thou

be cast into prison. Verily I say unto thee, 'Thou shalt by no means come out thence, till thou hast paid the uttermost farthing.'

"Ye have heard that it was said by them of old time, 'Thou shalt not commit adultery.' But I say unto you, 'Whosoever looketh on a woman to lust after her hath committed adultery with her already in his heart. And if thy right eye offend thee, pluck it out, and cast it from thee: for it is profitable for thee that one of thy members should perish, and not that thy whole body should be cast into hell. And if thy right hand offend thee, cut it off, and cast it from thee: for it is profitable for thee that one of thy members should perish, and not that thy whole body should be cast into hell.' It hath been said, 'Whosoever shall put away his wife, let him give her a writing of divorcement.' But I say unto you, 'Whosoever shall put away his wife, saving for the cause of fornication, causeth her to commit adultery: and whosoever shall marry her that is divorced committeth adultery.'

"Again, ye have heard that it hath been said by them of old time, 'Thou shalt not forswear thyself, but shalt perform unto the Lord thine oaths.' But I say unto you, 'Swear not at all; neither by heaven; for it is God's throne: nor by the earth; for it is his footstool: neither by Jerusalem; for it is the city of the great King. Neither shalt thou swear by thy head, because thou canst not make one hair white or black. But let your communication be, "Yea, yea"; "Nay, nay": for whatsoever is more than these cometh of evil.'

"Ye have heard that it hath been said, 'An eye for an eye, and a tooth for a tooth.' But I say unto you, 'Resist not evil: but whosoever shall smite thee on thy right cheek, turn to him the other also. And if any man will sue thee at the law, and take away thy coat, let him have thy cloak also. And whosoever shall compel thee to go a mile, go with him twain. Give to him that asketh thee, and from him that would borrow of thee turn not thou away.'

"Ye have heard that it hath been said, 'Thou shalt love thy neighbour, and hate thine enemy.' But I say unto you, 'Love your enemies, bless them that curse you, do good to them that hate you, and pray for them which despitefully use you, and persecute you; that ye may be the children of your Father which is in heaven: for he maketh his sun to rise on the evil and on the good, and sendeth rain on the just and on the unjust.' For if ye love them which love you, what reward have ye? Do not even the publicans the same? And if ye salute your brethren only, what do ye more than others? Do not even the publicans so? Be ye therefore perfect, even as your Father which is in heaven is perfect.

"Take heed that ye do not your alms before men, to be seen of them: otherwise ye have no reward of your Father which is in heaven. Therefore when thou doest thine alms, do not sound a trumpet before thee, as the hypocrites do in the synagogues and in the streets, that they may have glory of men. Verily I say unto you, 'They have their reward.' But when thou doest alms, let not thy left hand know what thy right hand doeth: that thine alms may be in secret: and thy Father which seeth in secret himself shall reward thee openly.

"And when thou prayest, thou shalt not be as the hypocrites are: for they love to pray standing in the synagogues and in the corners of the streets, that they may be seen of men. Verily I say unto you, 'They have their reward.' But thou, when thou prayest, enter into thy closet, and when thou hast shut thy door, pray to thy Father which is in secret; and thy Father which seeth in secret shall reward thee openly. But when ye pray, use not vain repetitions, as the heathen do: for they think that they shall be heard for their much speaking. Be not ye therefore like unto them: for your Father knoweth what things ye have need of, before ye ask him. After this manner therefore pray ye:

> " 'Our Father which art in heaven,
> Hallowed be thy name.
> Thy kingdom come.
> Thy will be done
> In earth, as it is in heaven.
>
> Give us this day
> Our daily bread.
> And forgive us our debts,
> As we forgive our debtors.
> And lead us not into temptation,
> But deliver us from evil:

> For thine is the kingdom,
> And the power,
> And the glory,
> Forever. Amen.'

"For if ye forgive men their trespasses, your heavenly Father will also forgive you: but if ye forgive not men their trespasses, neither will your Father forgive your trespasses.

"Moreover, when ye fast, be not, as the hypocrites, of a sad countenance: for they disfigure their faces, that they may appear unto men to fast. Verily I say unto you, 'They have their reward.' But thou, when thou fastest, anoint thine head, and wash thy face; that thou appear not unto men to fast, but unto thy Father which is in secret: and thy Father, which seeth in secret, shall reward thee openly.

> "Lay not up for yourselves treasures upon earth,
> Where moth and rust doth corrupt,
> And where thieves break through and steal:
>
> But lay up for yourselves treasures in heaven,
> Where neither moth nor rust doth corrupt,
> And where thieves do not break through nor steal.

For where your treasure is, there will your heart be also.

"The light of the body is the eye: if therefore thine eye be single, thy whole body shall be full of light. But if thine eye be evil, thy whole body shall be full of darkness. If therefore the light that is in thee be darkness, how great is that darkness!

"No man can serve two masters: for either he will hate the one, and love the other; or else he will hold to the one, and despise the other. Ye cannot serve God and mammon.

"Therefore I say unto you, 'Take no thought for your life, what ye shall eat, or what ye shall drink; nor yet for your body, what ye shall put on.' Is not the life more than meat, and the body than raiment? Behold the fowls of the air: for they sow not, neither do they reap, nor gather into barns; yet your heavenly

Father feedeth them. Are ye not much better than they? Which of you by taking thought can add one cubit unto his stature? And why take ye thought for raiment? Consider the lilies of the field, how they grow; they toil not, neither do they spin: and yet I say unto you that even Solomon in all his glory was not arrayed like one of these.

"Wherefore, if God so clothe the grass of the field, which today is, and tomorrow is cast into the oven, shall he not much more clothe you, O ye of little faith? Therefore take no thought, saying, 'What shall we eat?' or, 'What shall we drink?' or, 'Wherewithal shall we be clothed?' (For after all these things do the Gentiles seek:) for your heavenly Father knoweth that ye have need of all these things. But seek ye first the kingdom of God, and his righteousness; and all these things shall be added unto you. Take therefore no thought for the morrow: for the morrow shall take thought for the things of itself. Sufficient unto the day is the evil thereof.

"Judge not, that ye be not judged. For with what judgment ye judge, ye shall be judged: and with what measure ye mete, it shall be measured to you again. And why beholdest thou the mote that is in thy brother's eye, but considerest not the beam that is in thine own eye? Or how wilt thou say to thy brother, 'Let me pull out the mote out of thine eye'; and, behold a beam is in thy own eye? Thou hypocrite, first cast out the beam out of thine own eye; and then shalt thou see clearly to cast out the mote out of thy brother's eye.

"Give not that which is holy unto the dogs,
   Neither cast ye your pearls before swine,
Lest they trample them under their feet,
And turn again and rend you.

Ask, and it shall be given you;
Seek, and ye shall find;
Knock, and it shall be opened unto you:

For every one that asketh receiveth;
And he that seeketh findeth;
And to him that knocketh it shall be opened.

Or what man is there of you, whom if his son ask bread, will he give him a stone? Or if he ask a fish, will he give him a serpent? If ye then, being evil, know how to give good gifts unto your children, how much more shall your Father which is in heaven give good things to them that ask him? Therefore all things whatsoever ye would that men should do to you, do ye even so to them: for this is the law and the prophets.

"Enter ye in at the strait gate: for wide is the gate, and broad is the way, that leadeth to destruction, and many there be which go in thereat: because strait is the gate, and narrow is the way, which leadeth unto life, and few there be that find it.

"Beware of false prophets, which come to you in sheep's clothing, but inwardly they are ravening wolves. Ye shall know them by their fruits. Do men gather grapes of thorns, or figs of thistles? Even so every good tree bringeth forth good fruit; but a corrupt tree bringeth forth evil fruit. A good tree cannot bring forth evil fruit, neither can a corrupt tree bring forth good fruit. Every tree that bringeth not forth good fruit is hewn down, and cast into the fire. Wherefore by their fruits ye shall know them.

"Not every one that saith unto me, 'Lord, Lord,' shall enter into the kingdom of heaven; but he that doeth the will of my Father which is in heaven. Many will say to me in that day, 'Lord, Lord, have we not prophesied in thy name? And in thy name have cast out devils? And in thy name done many wonderful works?' And then will I profess unto them, 'I never knew you: depart from me, ye that work iniquity.'

"Therefore whosoever heareth these sayings of mine, and doeth them, I will liken him unto a wise man, which built his house upon a rock: and the rain descended, and the floods came and the winds blew, and beat upon that house; and it fell not; for it was founded upon a rock. And every one that heareth these sayings of mine, and doeth them not, shall be likened unto a foolish man, which built his house upon the sand: and the rain descended, and the floods came, and the winds blew, and beat upon that house; and it fell: and great was the fall of it."

And it came to pass, when Jesus had ended these sayings, the people were astonished at his doctrine for he taught them as one having authority, and not as the scribes.

John of Patmos (not to be confused with John the Baptist or the Apostle John), probably wrote his account of the life of Jesus early in the second century A.D., thus providing us with the latest of the four Gospels. Internal evidence suggests that the writer had acquaintance with Greek philosophy, particularly the philosophy associated with the teachers at Alexandria who emphasized the great gulf existing between man and God and the necessity of an intermediary to bridge this gulf. This Gospel represented Jesus as the divine Son of God who appeared among men in the flesh, rather than the human Messiah hoped for by the Jews. In reading the selections note (1) the contrast in the style of writing compared with the earlier Gospels, (2) the use of symbolism, (3) the identification of Jesus with the Alexandrian idea of Logos [Word], the Mithraic concept of Light, and the Hebrew notion of the sacrificial Lamb, (4) the origin of Jesus and the treatment of His birth, (5) Jesus' discussion of His future while at the Last Supper, (6) the relationship between Jesus and God, (7) the emphasis given to mystic love between God and man, (8) the nature and purpose of the Holy Ghost, and (9) the contrast between Mark's and John's description of the death of Jesus.

From: THE GOSPEL ACCORDING TO ST. JOHN

In the beginning was the Word, and the Word was with God, and the Word was God. The same was in the beginning with God. All things were made by him; and without him was not any thing made that was made. In him was life; and the life was the light of men. And the light shineth in darkness; and the darkness comprehended it not.

There was a man sent from God, whose name was John. The same came for a witness, to bear witness of the Light, that all men through him might believe. He was not that Light, but was sent to bear witness of that Light. That was the true Light, which lighteth every man that cometh into the world. He was in the world, and the world was made by him, and the world knew him not. He came unto his own, and his own received him not. But as many as received him, to them gave he power to become the sons of God, even to them that believe on his name: which were born, not of blood, nor of the will of the flesh, nor of the will of man, but of God. And the Word was made flesh, and dwelt among us (and we beheld his glory, the glory as of the only begotten of the Father), full of grace and truth.

John bore witness of him, and cried, saying, "This was he of whom I spoke, 'He that cometh after me is preferred before me: for he was before me.'" And of his fulness have all we received, and grace for grace. For the law was given by Moses, but grace and truth came by Jesus Christ. No man hath seen God at any time; the only begotten Son, which is in the bosom of the Father, he hath declared him. And this is the record of John, when the Jews sent priests and Levites from Jerusalem to ask him, "Who art thou?" And he confessed, and denied not; but confessed, "I am not the Christ."

And they asked him, "What then? Art thou Elias?"

And he saith, "I am not."

"Art thou that prophet?"

And he answered, "No."

Then said they unto him, "Who art thou?

that we may give an answer to them that sent us. What sayest thou of thyself?"

He said, "I am the voice of one crying in the wilderness, 'Make straight the way of the Lord,' as said the prophet Esaias."

And they which were sent were of the Pharisees. And they asked him, and said unto him, "Why baptizest thou then, if thou be not that Christ, nor Elias, neither that prophet?"

John answered them, saying, "I baptize with water: but there standeth one among you, whom ye know not; he it is, who coming after me is preferred before me, whose shoe's latchet I am not worthy to unloose."

These things were done in Bethabara beyond Jordan, where John was baptizing.

The next day John seeth Jesus coming unto him, and saith, "Behold the Lamb of God, which taketh away the sin of the world! This is he of whom I said, 'After me cometh a man which is preferred before me: for he was before me.' And I knew him not: but that he should be made manifest to Israel, therefore am I come baptizing with water."

And John bore record, saying, "I saw the Spirit descending from heaven like a dove, and it abode upon him. And I knew him not: but he that sent me to baptize with water, the same said unto me, 'Upon whom thou shalt see the Spirit descending, and remaining on him, the same is he which baptizeth with the Holy Ghost.' And I saw, and bore record that this is the Son of God."

Again the next day after, John stood, and two of his disciples, and looking upon Jesus as he walked, he saith, "Behold the Lamb of God!"

And the two disciples heard him speak, and they followed Jesus. Then Jesus turned, and saw them following, and saith unto them, "What seek ye?"

They said unto him, "Rabbi" (which is to say, being interpreted, "Master"), "where dwellest thou?"

He saith unto them, "Come and see."

They came and saw where he dwelt, and abode with him that day: for it was about the tenth hour.

One of the two which heard John speak, and followed him, was Andrew, Simon Peter's brother. He first findeth his own brother Simon, and saith unto him, "We have found the Messias, which is, being interpreted, the Christ." And he brought him to Jesus. And when Jesus beheld him, he said, "Thou art Simon the son of Jona: thou shalt be called Cephas," which is by interpretation "a stone.". . .

Now before the feast of the passover, when Jesus knew that his hour was come that he should depart out of this world unto the Father, having loved his own which were in the world, he loved them unto the end. And supper being ended, the devil having now put into the heart of Judas Iscariot, Simon's son, to betray him, Jesus, knowing that the Father had given all things into his hands, and that he was come from God, and went to God, riseth from supper, and laid aside his garments; and took a towel, and girded himself. After that, he poureth water into a basin, and began to wash the disciples' feet, and to wipe them with the towel wherewith he was girded. Then cometh he to Simon Peter: and Peter saith unto him, "Lord, dost thou wash my feet?" Jesus answered and said unto him, "What I do thou knowest not now; but thou shalt know hereafter." Peter saith unto him, "Thou shalt never wash my feet." Jesus answered him, "If I wash thee not, thou hast no part with me." Simon Peter saith unto him, "Lord, not my feet only, but also my hands and my head." Jesus saith to him, "He that is washed needeth not save to wash his feet, but is clean every whit: and ye are clean, but not all." For he knew who should betray him; therefore said he, "Ye are not all clean." So after he had washed their feet, and had taken his garments, and was set down again, he said unto them, "Know ye what I have done to you? Ye call me Master and Lord: and ye say well; for so I am. If I then, your Lord and Master, have washed your feet; ye also ought to wash one another's feet. For I have given you an example, that ye should do as I have done to you. Verily, verily, I say unto you, 'The servant is not greater than his lord; neither he that is sent greater than he that sent him. . . .'"

When Jesus had thus said, he was troubled in spirit, and testified, and said, "Verily, verily, I say unto you that one of you shall betray me."

Then the disciples looked one on another, doubting of whom he spoke. Now there was leaning on Jesus' bosom one of his disciples, whom Jesus loved. Simon Peter therefore beckoned to him, that he should ask who it should be of whom he spoke. He then lying on Jesus' breast saith unto him, "Lord, who is it?"

Jesus answered, "He it is, to whom I shall give a sop, when I have dipped it." And when he had dipped the sop, he gave it to Judas Iscariot, the son of Simon. And after the sop Satan entered into him. Then said Jesus unto him, "That thou doest, do quickly." Now no man at the table knew for what intent he spoke this unto him. For some of them thought, because Judas had the bag, that Jesus had said unto him, "Buy those things that we have need of against the feast"; or, that he should give something to the poor. He then, having received the sop, went immediately out: and it was night.

Therefore, when he was gone out, Jesus said, "Now is the Son of Man glorified, and God is glorified in him. If God be glorified in him, God shall also glorify him in himself, and shall straightway glorify him. Little children, yet a little while I am with you. Ye shall seek me: and as I said unto the Jews, 'Whither I go, ye cannot come'; so now I say to you. A new commandment I give unto you: that ye love one another; as I have loved you, that ye also love one another. By this shall all men know that ye are my disciples, if ye have love one to another."

Simon Peter said unto him, "Lord, whither goest thou?"

Jesus answered him, "Whither I go, thou canst not follow me now; but thou shalt follow me afterwards."

Peter said unto him, "Lord, why cannot I follow thee now? I will lay down my life for thy sake."

Jesus answered him, "Wilt thou lay down thy life for my sake? Verily, verily, I say unto thee, 'The cock shall not crow, till thou hast denied me thrice.'

"Let not your heart be troubled: ye believe in God, believe also in me. In my Father's house are many mansions: if it were not so, I would have told you. I go to prepare a place for you. And if I go and prepare a place for you, I will come again, and receive you unto myself; that where I am, there ye may be also.

And whither I go ye know, and the way ye know."

Thomas saith unto him, "Lord, we know not whither thou goest; and how can we know the way?"

Jesus saith unto him, "I am the way, the truth, and the life: no man cometh unto the Father, but by me. If ye had known me, ye should have known my Father also: and from henceforth ye know him, and have seen him."

Philip saith unto him, "Lord, show us the Father, and it sufficeth us."

Jesus saith unto him, "Have I been so long time with you, and yet hast thou not known me, Philip? He that hath seen me hath seen the Father; and how sayest thou then, 'Show us the Father'? Believest thou not that I am in the Father, and the Father in me? The words that I speak unto you I speak not of myself: but the Father that dwelleth in me, he doeth the works. Believe me that I am in the Father, and the Father in me: or else believe me for the very works' sake. Verily, verily, I say unto you, 'He that believeth in me, the works that I do shall he do also; and greater works than these shall he do; because I go unto my Father.' And whatsoever ye shall ask in my name, that will I do, that the Father may be glorified in the Son. If ye shall ask any thing in my name, I will do it.

"If ye love me, keep my commandments. And I will pray the Father, and he shall give you another Comforter, that he may abide with you for ever; even the Spirit of truth; whom the world cannot receive, because it seeth him not, neither knoweth him: but ye know him; for he dwelleth with you, and shall be in you. I will not leave you comfortless: I will come to you. Yet a little while, and the world seeth me no more; but ye see me: because I live, ye shall live also. At that day ye shall know that I am in my Father, and ye in me, and I in you. He that hath my commandments, and keepeth them, he it is that loveth me: and he that loveth me shall be loved of my Father, and I will love him, and will manifest myself to him."

Judas (not Iscariot) saith unto him, "Lord, how is it that thou wilt manifest thyself unto us, and not unto the world?"

Jesus answered and said unto him, "If a man

love me, he will keep my words: and my Father will love him, and we will come unto him, and make our abode with him. He that loveth me not keepeth not my sayings: and the word which ye hear is not mine, but the Father's which sent me.

"These things have I spoken unto you, being yet present with you. But the Comforter, which is the Holy Ghost, whom the Father will send in my name, he shall teach you all things, and bring all things to your remembrance, whatsoever I have said unto you. . . ."

Pilate . . . brought Jesus forth, and sat down in the judgment seat in a place that is called the Pavement, but, in Hebrew, Gabbatha. And it was the preparation of the passover, and about the sixth hour: and he saith unto the Jews, "Behold your King!"

But they cried out, "Away with him, away with him, crucify him!"

Pilate saith unto them, "Shall I crucify your King?"

The chief priests answered, "We have no king but Caesar."

Then delivered he him therefore unto them to be crucified. And they took Jesus, and led him away. And he bearing his cross went forth into a place called the place of a skull, which is called, in the Hebrew, Golgotha, where they crucified him, and two others with him, on either side one, and Jesus in the midst. And Pilate wrote a title, and put it on the cross. And the writing was JESUS OF NAZARETH, THE KING OF THE JEWS. This title then read many of the Jews: for the place where Jesus was crucified was nigh to the city: and it was written in Hebrew, and Greek, and Latin.

Then said the chief priests of the Jews to Pilate, "Write not, 'The King of the Jews'; but that he said, 'I am King of the Jews.' "

Pilate answered, "What I have written I have written."

Then the soldiers, when they had crucified Jesus, took his garments, and made four parts, to every soldier a part; and also his coat: now the coat was without seam, woven from the top throughout. They said therefore among themselves, "Let us not rend it, but cast lots for it, whose it shall be": that the scripture might be fulfilled, which saith,

"They parted my raiment among them,
    And for my vesture they did cast lots."

These things therefore the soldiers did.

Now there stood by the cross of Jesus his mother, and his mother's sister, Mary the wife of Cleophas, and Mary Magdalene. When Jesus therefore saw his mother, and the disciple standing by, whom he loved, he saith unto his mother, "Woman, behold thy son!" Then saith he to the disciple, "Behold thy mother!" And from that hour that disciple took her unto his own home.

After this, Jesus knowing that all things were now accomplished, that the scripture might be fulfilled, saith, "I thirst." Now there was set a vessel full of vinegar: and they filled a sponge with vinegar, and put it upon hyssop, and put it to his mouth. When Jesus therefore had received the vinegar, he said, "It is finished": and he bowed his head, and gave up the ghost. . . .

The Acts of the Apostles relates the history of the early church following the death of Jesus. It was written by the author of the Gospel of Luke and carried on the story of the establishment of the Kingdom of God. The group of Apostles felt a spiritual solidarity with the departed Jesus through the Holy Spirit, which was strongly emphasized through the narrative. The author also stressed the missionary spirit implicit in the teachings of Jesus, and the efforts of His followers to spread the new faith throughout the Roman Empire. Thus The Acts of the Apostles served both as a sequel to the Gospels and as a background for the writings of Paul. In the selections note (1) the author's explanation *for the religious experiences on the day of Pentecost, (2) Peter's ideas on the relationship between Jesus and God, (3) the ceremonies observed by the Apostles and early Christians, (4) the nature of and reasons for early Christian organization, (5) the people among whom the Apostles carried on their early missionary work, (6) Saul's experience on the Damascus road, (7) the work for which Saul was selected, (8) Peter's dream and his interpretation of it to Cornelius, (9) the nature of the dispute between the teachers from Judaea and Paul and Barnabas, and (10) the settlement of this dispute at Jerusalem and the ultimate significance of this solution to Christianity.*

From: THE ACTS OF THE APOSTLES

And when the day of Pentecost was fully come, they were all with one accord in one place. And suddenly there came a sound from heaven as of a rushing mighty wind, and it filled all the house where they were sitting. And there appeared unto them cloven tongues like as of fire, and it sat upon each of them. And they were all filled with the Holy Ghost, and began to speak with other tongues, as the Spirit gave them utterance.

And there were dwelling at Jerusalem Jews, devout men, out of every nation under heaven. Now when this was noised abroad, the multitude came together, and were confounded, because that every man heard them speak in his own language. And they were all amazed and marvelled, saying one to another, "Behold, are not all these which speak Galilaeans? And how hear we every man in our own tongue, wherein we were born? Parthians, and Medes, and Elamites, and the dwellers in Mesopotamia, and in Judaea, and Cappadocia, in Pontus, and Asia, Phrygia, and Pamphylia, in Egypt, and in the parts of Libya about Cyrene, and strangers of Rome, Jews and proselytes, Cretans and Arabians, we do hear them speak in our tongues the wonderful works of God." And they were all amazed, and were in doubt, saying one to another, "What meaneth this?" Others mocking said, "These men are full of new wine."

But Peter, standing up with the eleven, lifted up his voice, and said unto them, "Ye men of Judaea, and all ye that dwell at Jerusalem, be this known unto you, and hearken to my words: for these are not drunken, as ye suppose, seeing it is but the third hour of the day. But this is that which was spoken by the prophet Joel:

' "And it shall come to pass in the last days," saith God,
"I will pour out of my Spirit upon all flesh:
And your sons and your daughters shall prophesy,
And your young men shall see visions,
And your old men shall dream dreams:
And on my servants and on my handmaidens
I will pour out in those days of my Spirit;
And they shall prophesy:
And I will show wonders in heaven above,
And signs in the earth beneath;
Blood, and fire, and vapour of smoke:
The sun shall be turned into darkness,
And the moon into blood,
Before that great and notable day of the Lord come:
And it shall come to pass,
That whosoever shall call on the name of the Lord shall be saved." '

"Ye men of Israel, hear these words: Jesus of Nazareth, a man approved of God among you by miracles and wonders and signs, which God did by him in the midst of you, as ye yourselves also know: him, being delivered by the determinate counsel and foreknowledge of God, ye have taken, and by wicked hands have crucified and slain. . . . This Jesus hath God raised up, whereof we all are witnesses. Therefore being by the right hand of God exalted, and having received of the Father the promise of the Holy Ghost, he hath shed forth this, which ye now see and hear. . . . Therefore let all the house of Israel know assuredly that God hath made that same Jesus, whom ye have crucified, both Lord and Christ."

Now when they heard this, they were pricked in their heart, and said unto Peter and to the rest of the apostles, "Men and brethren, what shall we do?" Then Peter said unto them, "Repent, and be baptized every one of you in the name of Jesus Christ for the remission of sins, and ye shall receive the gift of the Holy Ghost. For the promise is unto you, and to your children, and to all that are afar off, even as many as the Lord our God shall call." And with many other words did he testify and exhort, saying, "Save yourselves from this untoward generation."

Then they that gladly received his word were baptized: and the same day there were added unto them about three thousand souls. And they continued steadfastly in the apostles' doctrine and fellowship, and in breaking of bread, and in prayers. And fear came upon every soul: and many wonders and signs were done by the apostles. And all that believed were together, and had all things common; and sold their possessions and goods, and parted them to all men, as every man had need. And they, continuing daily with one accord in the temple, and breaking bread from house to house, did eat their meat with gladness and singleness of heart, praising God, and having favour with all the people. And the Lord added to the church daily such as should be saved. . . .

And the multitude of them that believed were of one heart and of one soul: neither said any of them that ought of the things which he possessed was his own; but they had all things common. And with great power gave the apostles witness of the resurrection of the Lord Jesus: and great grace was upon them all. Neither was there any among them that

lacked: for as many as were possessors of lands or houses sold them, and brought the prices of the things that were sold, and laid them down at the apostles' feet: and distribution was made unto every man according as he had need. And Joses, who by the apostles was surnamed Barnabas (which is, being interpreted, "the son of consolation"), a Levite, and of the country of Cyprus, having land, sold it, and brought the money, and laid it at the apostles' feet.

And by the hands of the apostles were many signs and wonders wrought among the people (and they were all with one accord in Solomon's porch. And of the rest durst no man join himself to them: but the people magnified them. And believers were the more added to the Lord, multitudes both of men and women); insomuch that they brought forth the sick into the streets, and laid them on beds and couches, that at the least the shadow of Peter passing by might overshadow some of them. There came also a multitude out of the cities round about unto Jerusalem, bringing sick folks, and them which were vexed with unclean spirits: and they were healed every one. Then the high priest rose up, and all they that were with him (which is the sect of the Sadducees), and were filled with indignation, and laid their hands on the apostles, and put them in the common prison.

But the angel of the Lord by night opened the prison doors, and brought them forth, and said, "Go, stand and speak in the temple to the people all the words of this life.". . .

And in those days, when the number of the disciples was multiplied, there arose a murmuring of the Grecians against the Hebrews, because their widows were neglected in the daily ministration. Then the twelve called the multitude of the disciples unto them, and said, "It is not reason that we should leave the word of God, and serve tables. Wherefore, brethren, look ye out among you seven men of honest report, full of the Holy Ghost and wisdom, whom we may appoint over this business. But we will give ourselves continually to prayer, and to the ministry of the word."

And the saying pleased the whole multitude: and they chose Stephen, a man full of faith and of the Holy Ghost, and Philip, and Prochurus, and Nicanor, and Timon, and Parmenas, and Nicolas a proselyte of Antioch: whom they set before the apostles: and when they had prayed, they laid their hands on them. And the word of God increased; and the number of the disciples multiplied in Jerusalem greatly; and a great company of the priests were obedient to the faith. And Stephen, full of faith and power, did great wonders and miracles among the people.

Then there arose certain of the synagogue, which is called the synagogue of the Libertines, and Cyrenians, and Alexandrians, and of them of Cilicia and of Asia, disputing with Stephen. And they were not able to resist the wisdom and the spirit by which he spoke. Then they suborned men, which said, "We have heard him speak blasphemous words against Moses, and against God."

And they stirred up the people, and the elders, and the scribes, and came upon him, and caught him, and brought him to the council, and set up false witnesses, which said, "This man ceaseth not to speak blasphemous words against this holy place, and the law: for we have heard him say that this Jesus of Nazareth shall destroy this place, and shall change the customs which Moses delivered us."

And all that sat in the council, looking steadfastly on him, saw his face as it had been the face of an angel.

Then said the high priest, "Are these things so?"

And he said, "Men, brethren, and fathers, hearken. . . . Ye stiffnecked and uncircumcised in heart and ears, ye do always resist the Holy Ghost: as your fathers did, so do ye. Which of the prophets have not your fathers persecuted? And they have slain them which showed before the coming of the Just One; of whom ye have been now the betrayers and murderers: who have received the law by the disposition of angels, and have not kept it."

When they heard these things, they were cut to the heart, and they gnashed on him with their teeth.

But he, being full of the Holy Ghost, looked up steadfastly into heaven, and saw the glory of God, and Jesus standing on the right hand of God, and said, "Behold, I see the heavens opened, and the Son of Man standing on the right hand of God."

Then they cried out with a loud voice, and stopped their ears, and ran upon him with one accord, and cast him out of the city, and stoned him: and the witnesses laid down their clothes at a young man's feet, whose name was Saul.

And they stoned Stephen, calling upon God, and saying, "Lord Jesus, receive my spirit." And he kneeled down and cried with a loud voice, "Lord, lay not this sin to their charge." And when he had said this, he fell asleep. And Saul was consenting unto his death.

And at that time there was a great persecution against the church which was at Jerusalem; and they were all scattered abroad throughout the regions of Judaea and Samaria, except the apostles. And devout men carried Stephen to his burial, and made great lamentations over him. As for Saul, he made havoc of the church, entering into every house, and haling men and women committed them to prison. Therefore they that were scattered abroad went everywhere preaching the word. . . .

And Saul, yet breathing out threatenings and slaughter against the disciples of the Lord, went unto the high priest, and desired of him letters to Damascus to the synagogues, that if he found any of this way, whether they were men or women, he might bring them bound unto Jerusalem.

And as he journeyed, he came near Damascus: and suddenly there shone round about him a light from heaven, and he fell to the earth, and heard a voice saying unto him, "Saul, Saul, why persecutest thou me?"

And he said, "Who art thou, Lord?"

And the Lord said, "I am Jesus whom thou persecutest: it is hard for thee to kick against the pricks."

And he trembling and astonished said, "Lord, what wilt thou have me to do?"

And the Lord said unto him, "Arise, and go into the city, and it shall be told thee what thou must do."

And the men which journeyed with him stood speechless, hearing a voice, but seeing no man. And Saul arose from the earth; and when his eyes were opened, he saw no man: but they led him by the hand, and brought him into Damascus. And he was three days without sight; and neither did eat nor drink.

And there was a certain disciple at Damascus, named Ananias; and to him said the Lord in a vision, "Ananias!" And he said, "Behold, I am here, Lord."

And the Lord said unto him, "Arise, and go into the street which is called Straight, and enquire in the house of Judas for one called Saul, of Tarsus: for, behold, he prayeth, and hath seen in a vision a man named Ananias coming in, and putting his hand on him, that he might receive his sight."

Then Ananias answered, "Lord, I have heard by many of this man, how much evil he hath done to thy saints at Jerusalem: and here he hath authority from the chief priests to bind all that call on thy name."

But the Lord said unto him, "Go thy way: for he is a chosen vessel unto me, to bear my name before the Gentiles, and kings, and the children of Israel: for I will show him how great things he must suffer for my name's sake."

And Ananias went his way, and entered into the house; and putting his hands on him said, "Brother Saul, the Lord, even Jesus, that appeared unto thee in the way as thou camest, hath sent me, that thou mightest receive thy sight, and be filled with the Holy Ghost."

And immediately there fell from his eyes as it had been scales: and he received sight forthwith, and arose, and was baptized. And when he had received meat, he was strengthened.

Then was Saul certain days with the disciples which were at Damascus. And straightway he preached Christ in the synagogues, that he is the Son of God. But all that heard him were amazed, and said, "Is not this he that destroyed them which called on this name in Jerusalem, and came hither for that intent, that he might bring them bound unto the chief priests?"

But Saul increased the more in strength, and confounded the Jews which dwelt at Damascus, proving that this is very Christ. And after that many days were fulfilled, the Jews took counsel to kill him: but their laying await was known of Saul. And they watched the gates day and night to kill him. Then the disciples took him by night, and let him down by the wall in a basket.

And when Saul was come to Jerusalem, he essayed to join himself to the disciples: but they were all afraid of him, and believed not that he was a disciple. But Barnabas took him, and brought him to the apostles, and declared unto them how he had seen the Lord in the way, and that he had spoken to him, and how he had preached boldly at Damascus in the name of Jesus. And he was with them coming in and going out at Jerusalem. And he spoke boldly in the name of the Lord Jesus, and disputed against the Grecians: but they went about to slay him. Which when the brethren knew, they brought him down to Caesarea, and sent him forth to Tarsus. . . .

There was a certain man in Caesarea called Cornelius, a centurion of the band called the Italian band, a devout man, and one that feared God with all his house, which gave much alms to the people, and prayed to God always. He saw in a vision, evidently about the ninth hour of the day, an angel of God coming in to him, and saying unto him, "Cornelius!"

And when he looked on him, he was afraid, and said, "What is it, Lord?"

And he said unto him, "Thy prayers and thine alms are come up for a memorial before God. And now send men to Joppa, and call for one Simon, whose surname is Peter. He lodgeth with one Simon a tanner, whose house is by the sea side: he shall tell thee what thou oughtest to do."

And when the angel which spoke unto Cornelius was departed, he called two of his household servants, and a devout soldier of them that waited on him continually; and when he had declared all these things unto them, he sent them to Joppa.

On the morrow, as they went on their journey, and drew nigh unto the city, Peter went upon the housetop to pray about the sixth hour: and he became very hungry, and would have eaten: but while they made ready, he fell into a trance, and saw heaven opened, and a certain vessel descending unto him, as it had been a great sheet knit at the four corners, and let down to the earth: wherein were all manner of fourfooted beasts of the earth, and wild beasts, and creeping things, and fowls of the air. And there came a voice to him, "Rise, Peter; kill, and eat."

But Peter said, "Not so, Lord; for I have never eaten any thing that is common or unclean."

And the voice spoke unto him again the second time, "What God hath cleansed, that call not thou common."

This was done thrice: and the vessel was received up again into heaven.

Now while Peter doubted in himself what this vision which he had seen should mean, behold, the men which were sent from Cornelius had made enquiry for Simon's house, and stood before the gate, and called, and asked whether Simon, which was surnamed Peter, were lodged there. Then called he them in, and lodged them. And on the morrow Peter went away with them, and certain brethren from Joppa accompanied him. And the morrow after they entered into Caesarea. And Cornelius waited for them, and had called together his kinsmen and near friends. And as Peter was coming in, Cornelius met him, and fell down at his feet, and worshipped him. But Peter took him up, saying, "Stand up; I myself also am a man."

And as he talked with him, he went in, and found many that were come together. And he said unto them, "Ye know how that it is an unlawful thing for a man that is a Jew to keep company, or come unto one of another nation; but God hath showed me that I should not call any man common or unclean. Therefore came I unto you without gainsaying, as soon as I was sent for: I ask therefore for what intent ye have sent for me?"

And Cornelius said, "Four days ago I was fasting until this hour; and at the ninth hour I prayed in my house, and, behold, a man stood before me in bright clothing, and said, 'Cornelius, thy prayer is heard, and thine alms are had in remembrance in the sight of God. Send therefore to Joppa, and call hither Simon, whose surname is Peter; he is lodged in the house of one Simon a tanner by the sea side: who, when he cometh, shall speak unto thee.' Immediately therefore I sent to thee; and thou hast well done that thou art come. Now therefore are we all here present before God, to hear all things that are commanded thee of God."

Then Peter opened his mouth, and said, "Of a truth I perceive that God is no respector of persons: but in every nation he that feareth him, and worketh righteousness, is accepted with him. The word which God sent unto the children of Israel, preaching Jesus Christ (he is Lord of all), that word, I say, ye know, which was published throughout all Judaea, and began from Galilee, after the baptism which John preached: how God anointed Jesus of Nazareth with the Holy Ghost and with power: who went about doing good, and healing all that were oppressed of the devil; for God was with him. And we are witnesses of all things which he did both in the land of the Jews, and in Jerusalem; whom they slew and hanged on a tree. Him God raised up the third day, and showed him openly: not to all the people, but unto witnesses chosen before of God, even to us, who did eat and drink with him after he rose from the dead. And he commanded us to preach unto the people, and to testify that it is he which was ordained of God to be the Judge of the quick and dead. To him give all the prophets witness, that through his name whosoever believeth in him shall receive remission of sins."

While Peter yet spoke these words, the Holy Ghost fell on all them which heard the word. And they of the circumcision which believed were astonished, as many as came with Peter, because that on the Gentiles also was poured out the gift of the Holy Ghost. For they heard them speak with tongues, and magnify God. Then answered Peter, "Can any man forbid water, that these should not be baptized, which have received the Holy Ghost as well as we?"

And he commanded them to be baptized in the name of the Lord. Then prayed they him to tarry certain days. . . .

Now there were in the church that was at Antioch certain prophets and teachers; as Barnabas, and Simeon that was called Niger, and Lucius of Cyrene, and Manaen, which had been brought up with Herod the tetrarch, and Saul. As they ministered to the Lord, and fasted, the Holy Ghost said, "Separate me Barnabas and Saul for the work whereunto I have called them." And when they had fasted and prayed, and laid their hands on them, they sent them away. . . .

And certain men which came down from Judaea taught the brethren, and said, "Except ye be circumcised after the manner of Moses, ye cannot be saved."

When therefore Paul and Barnabas had no small dissension and disputation with them, they determined that Paul and Barnabas, and certain other of them, should go up to Jerusalem unto the apostles and elders about this question. And being brought on their way by the church, they passed through Phenice and Samaria, declaring the conversion of the Gentiles: and they caused great joy unto all the brethren. And when they were come to Jerusalem, they were received of the church, and of the apostles and elders, and they declared all things that God had done with them. But there rose up certain of the sect of the Pharisees which believed, saying that it was needful to circumcise them, and to command them to keep the law of Moses.

And the apostles and elders came together for to consider of this matter. And when there had been much disputing, Peter rose up, and said unto them, "Men and brethren, ye know how that a good while ago God made choice among us, that the Gentiles by my mouth should hear the word of the gospel, and believe. And God, which knoweth the hearts, bore them witness, giving them the Holy Ghost, even as he did unto us; and put no difference between us and them, purifying their hearts by faith. Now therefore why tempt ye God, to put a yoke upon the neck of the disciples, which neither our fathers nor we were able to bear? But we believe that through the grace of the Lord Jesus Christ we shall be saved, even as they."

Then all the multitude kept silence, and gave audience to Barnabas and Paul, declaring what miracles and wonders God had wrought among the Gentiles by them. And after they had held their peace, James answered, saying, "Men and brethren, hearken unto me: Simeon hath declared how God at the first did visit the Gentiles, to take out of them a people for his name. And to this agree the words of the prophets. Wherefore my sentence is, that we trouble not them, which from among the Gentiles are turned to God: but that we write unto them, that they abstain from pollutions of idols, and from fornication, and from things strangled, and from blood."

Then pleased it the apostles and elders, with the whole church, to send chosen men of their own company to Antioch with Paul and Barnabas; namely, Judas surnamed Barsabas, and Silas, chief men among the brethren: and they wrote letters by them after this manner:

> The apostles and elders and brethren send greeting unto the brethren which are of the Gentiles in Antioch and Syria and Cilicia:
>
> Forasmuch as we have heard, that certain which went out from us have troubled you with words, subverting your souls, saying, "Ye must be circumcised, and keep the law": to whom we gave no such commandment: it seemed good unto us, being assembled with one accord, to send chosen men unto you with our beloved Barnabas and Paul, men that have hazarded their lives for the name of our Lord Jesus Christ. We have sent therefore Judas and Silas, who shall also tell you the same things by mouth. For it seemed good to the Holy Ghost, and to us, to lay upon you no greater burden than these necessary things; that ye abstain from meats offered to idols, and from blood, and from things strangled, and from fornication: from which if ye keep yourselves, ye shall do well.
>
> Fare ye well.

So when they were dismissed, they came to Antioch: and when they had gathered the multitude together, they delivered the epistle: which when they had read, they rejoiced for the consolation. And Judas and Silas, being prophets also themselves, exhorted the brethren with many words, and confirmed them. And after they had tarried there a space, they were let go in peace from the brethren unto the apostles. Notwithstanding it pleased Silas to abide there still. Paul also and Barnabas continued in Antioch, teaching and preaching the word of the Lord, with many others also. . . .

Paul (10 A.D.?–65 A.D.?), a Jew of the Dispersion, brought up to believe in the necessity of a strict observance of the Law (Jewish ritualism), experienced conversion to Christianity following a period of persistent activity persecuting Christians. He had become acquainted not only with oriental religious beliefs and rites but also had some contact with Greek philosophy, particularly Stoicism. Intense by nature, he became the first great Christian missionary, and established many new congregations, especially in Asia Minor and in Greece. His letters to these congregations, together with The Acts of the Apostles, give us some indication of Paul's Christianity, which appeared quite different from that presented in the Gospel of Mark. Paul elaborated, apparently for the first time, the concept of Jesus as a deity whose death upon the cross paid to God the penalty-price demanded for the wrong-doing of mankind. Man could achieve salvation only by faith and the grace of God, made available through the sacrifice of Jesus. Paul is also noted for his social ethic which is beautifully expressed in chapter 13. In the selections from this Epistle note (1) Paul's asceticism, (2) his conclusions concerning the nature and purpose of the Lord's Supper, (3) his universalism, (4) his views on charity or Christian love, (5) his doctrine of the atonement, and (6) Paul's Platonic idealism.

From: THE FIRST EPISTLE OF PAUL TO THE CORINTHIANS

Unto the Church of God which is at Corinth, to them that are sanctified in Christ Jesus, called to be saints, with all that in every place call upon the name of Jesus Christ our Lord, both theirs and ours. . . .

Now concerning virgins I have no commandment of the Lord: yet I give my judgment, as one that hath obtained mercy of the Lord to be faithful. . . . Art thou bound unto a wife? Seek not to be loosed. Art thou loosed from a wife? Seek not a wife. But and if thou marry, thou hast not sinned; and if a virgin marry, she hath not sinned. Nevertheless such shall have trouble in the flesh: but I spare you. . . .

But I would have you without carefulness. He that is unmarried careth for the things that belong to the Lord, how he may please the Lord: but he that is married careth for the things that are of the world, how he may please his wife. There is a difference also between a wife and a virgin. The unmarried woman careth for the things of the Lord, that she may be holy both in body and in spirit: but she that is married careth for the things of the world, how she may please her husband. And this I speak for your own profit; not that I may cast a snare upon you, but for that which is comely, and that ye may attend upon the Lord without distraction. But if any man think that he behaveth himself uncomely toward his virgin, if she pass the flower of her age, and need so require, let him do what he will, he sinneth not: let them marry. Nevertheless he that standeth steadfast in his heart, having no necessity, but hath power over his own will, and hath so decreed in his heart that he will keep his virgin, doeth well. . . .

Now in this that I declare unto you I praise you not, that ye come together not for the better, but for the worse. For first of all, when ye come together in the church, I hear that there be divisions among you; and I partly believe it.

For there must be also heresies among you, that they which are approved may be made manifest among you.

When ye come together therefore into one place, this is not to eat the Lord's supper. For in eating, every one taketh before other his own supper: and one is hungry and another is drunken. What? Have ye not houses to eat and to drink in? Or despise ye the church of God, and shame them that have not? What shall I say to you? Shall I praise you in this? I praise you not.

For I have received of the Lord that which also I delivered unto you, that the Lord Jesus the same night in which he was betrayed took bread: and when he had given thanks, he broke it and said, "Take, eat: this is my body, which is broken for you: this do in remembrance of me." After the same manner also he took the cup, when he had supped, saying, "This cup is the new testament in my blood: this do ye, as oft as ye drink it, in remembrance of me." For as often as ye eat this bread, and drink this cup, ye do show the Lord's death till he come. Wherefore whosoever shall eat this bread, and drink this cup of the Lord, unworthily, shall be guilty of the body and blood of the Lord. But let a man examine himself, and so let him eat of that bread, and drink of that cup. . . .

Now concerning spiritual gifts, brethren, I would not have you ignorant. Ye know that ye were Gentiles, carried away unto these dumb idols, even as ye were led. Wherefore I give you to understand, that no man speaking by the Spirit of God calleth Jesus accursed: and that no man can say that Jesus is the Lord, but by the Holy Ghost.

Now there are diversities of gifts, but the same Spirit. And there are differences of administrations, but the same Lord. And there are diversities of operations, but it is the same God which worketh all in all. But the manifestation of the Spirit is given to every man to profit withal. For to one is given by the Spirit the word of wisdom; to another the word of knowledge by the same Spirit; to another faith by the same Spirit; to another the gifts of healing by the same Spirit; to another the working of miracles; to another prophecy; to another discerning of spirits; to another divers kinds of tongues; to another the interpretation of tongues; but all these worketh that one and the selfsame Spirit, dividing to every man severally as he will.

For as the body is one, and hath many members, and all the members of that one body, being many, are one body: so also is Christ. For by one Spirit are we all baptized into one body, whether we be Jews or Gentiles, whether we be bond or free; and have been all made to drink into one Spirit. For the body is not one member, but many.

If the foot shall say, "Because I am not the hand, I am not of the body; is it therefore not of the body . . . ?" Now ye are the body of Christ, and members in particular. And God hath set some in the church, first apostles, secondarily prophets, thirdly teachers, after that miracles, then gifts of healings, helps, governments, diversities of tongues. Are all apostles? Are all prophets? Are all teachers? Are all workers of miracles? Have all the gifts of healing? Do all speak with tongues? Do all interpret? But covet earnestly the best gifts: and yet show I unto you a more excellent way.

Though I speak with the tongues of men and of angels, and have not charity, I am become as sounding brass, or a tinkling cymbal. And though I have the gift of prophecy, and understand all mysteries, and all knowledge; and though I have all faith, so that I could remove mountains, and have not charity, I am nothing. And though I bestow all my goods to feed the poor, and though I give my body to be burned, and have not charity, it profiteth me nothing. Charity suffereth long, and is kind; charity envieth not; charity vaunteth not itself, is not puffed up, doth not behave itself unseemly, seeketh not her own, is not easily provoked, thinketh no evil; rejoiceth not in iniquity, but rejoiceth in the truth; beareth all things, believeth all things, hopeth all things, endureth all things. Charity never faileth: but whether there be prophecies, they shall fail; whether there be tongues, they shall cease; whether there be knowledge, it shall vanish away. For we know in part, and we prophesy in part. But when that which is perfect is come, then that which is in part shall be done away. When I was a child, I spoke as a child, I understood as a child, I thought as a child: but when I became a man, I put away childish things. For now we see through a glass, darkly; but then face to face: now I know in part; but then shall I know even as also I am known. And now abideth faith, hope, charity, these three; but the greatest of these is charity. . . .

Moreover, brethren, I declare unto you the gospel which I preached unto you, which also ye have received, and wherein ye stand; by which also ye are saved, if ye keep in memory what I preached unto you, unless ye have believed in vain. For I delivered unto you first of all that which I also received, how that Christ died for our sins according to the scriptures; and that he was buried, and that he rose again the third day according to the scriptures: and that he was seen of Cephas, then of the twelve: after that, he was seen of above five hundred brethren at once; of whom the greater part remain unto this present, but some are fallen asleep. After that, he was seen of James; then of all the apostles. And last of all he was seen of me also, as of one born out of due time. For I am the least of the apostles, that am not meet to be called an apostle, because I persecuted the church of God. But by the grace of God I am what I am: and his grace which was bestowed upon me was not in vain; but I laboured more abundantly than they all: yet not I, but the grace of God which was with me. Therefore whether it were I or they, so we preach and so ye believed.

Now if Christ be preached that he rose from the dead, how say some among you that there is no resurrection of the dead? But if there be no resurrection of the dead, then is Christ not risen: and if Christ be not risen, then is our preaching vain, and your faith is also vain. Yea, and we are found false witnesses of God; because we have testified of God that he raised up Christ: whom he raised not up, if so be that the dead rise not. For if the dead rise not, then is not Christ raised: and if Christ be not raised, your faith is vain; ye are yet in your sins. Then they also which are fallen asleep in Christ are perished. If in this life only we have hope in Christ, we are of all men most miserable.

But now is Christ risen from the dead, and become the firstfruits of them that slept. For since by man came death, by man came also the resurrection of the dead. For as in Adam all die, even so in Christ shall all be made alive. . . .

But some man will say, "How are the dead raised up? And with what body do they come?" Thou fool, that which thou sowest is not quickened, except it die: and that which thou sowest, thou sowest not that body that shall be, but bare grain, it may chance of wheat, or of some other grain: but God giveth it a body as it hath pleased him, and to every seed his own body. All flesh is not the same flesh: but there is one kind of flesh of men, another flesh of beasts, another of fishes, and another of birds. There are also celestial bodies, and bodies terrestrial: but the glory of the celestial is one, and the glory of the terrestrial is another. There is one glory of the sun, and another glory of the moon, and another glory of the stars: for one star differeth from another star in glory. So also is the resurrection of the dead. It is sown in corruption; it is raised in incorruption; it is sown in dishonour; it is raised in glory; it is sown in weakness; it is raised in power: it is sown a natural body: it is raised a spiritual body. There is a natural body, and there is a spiritual body. . . .

Now this I say, brethren, that flesh and blood cannot inherit the kingdom of God; neither doth corruption inherit incorruption. Behold, I show you a mystery; we shall not all sleep, but we shall all be changed, in a moment, in the twinkling of an eye, at the last trump: for the trumpet shall sound, and the dead shall be raised incorruptible, and we shall be changed. For this corruptible must put on incorruption, and this mortal must put on immortality. So when this corruptible shall have put on incorruption, and this mortal shall have put on immortality, then shall be brought to pass the saying that is written, "Death is swallowed up in victory. O death, where is thy sting? O grave, where is thy victory?" The sting of death is sin; and the strength of sin is the law. But thanks be to God, which giveth us the victory through our Lord Jesus Christ. Therefore, my beloved brethren, be ye steadfast, unmovable, always abounding in the work of the Lord, forasmuch as ye know that your labour is not in vain in the Lord. . . . My love be with you all in Christ Jesus.

Augustine

Augustine (354–430 A.D.), Bishop of Hippo in North Africa, came to be the most influential Christian philosopher among the early Church Fathers. By the time Augustine appeared Christianity had undergone a rapid development from an obscure oriental sect to the official religion of the empire. Augustine gave the most satisfactory answer to the problem of the relationship of Christianity to classical culture. The Confessions, written in 397, in addition to giving an insight into the aspects of Christianity that appealed to the fourth and fifth century mind, revealed the principal steps by which Augustine found peace and happiness in Christianity. In reading the selections note (1) aspects of Augustine's youth and the influences which helped shape his character, (2) his life at Carthage and how he regarded it, (3) how he came to love philosophy, (4) his interest in Manicheanism and why he ultimately rejected its teachings, (5) what he found in Platonism and how he adapted it to Christianity, (6) his view of the role of Jesus in Christianity, and (7) his description of his conversion and of its results.

From: THE CONFESSIONS OF ST. AUGUSTINE

HOW HE WAS DRIVEN TO LEARN FROM WRONG MOTIVES, WHICH YET GOD TURNED TO GOOD

Yet in my boyhood (which my parents thought a less dangerous age than that of adolescence) I did not love learning, and I hated being driven towards it; yet I was driven, and it was well for me, though I was not doing well: for I would not learn except perforce. Now no one does well against his will, even if what he does is well. Nor were those who drove me doing well, yet was I well dealt with by Thee, O my God. For they could discern no other use for the learning, which they forced upon me, than the gratification of the insatiable craving for gilded poverty and shameful glory.

But Thou, who numberest every hair of our heads, didst turn to my profit the error of those who forced me to learn; and my own error, my reluctance to learn, Thou turnedst to my chastisement, for well did I deserve to suffer, who was so small a child, and yet so great a sinner. And so by the hands of those who did me ill, Thou wast doing me well, and by my own sin thou wast justly requiting me. For Thou hast commanded that an ill-regulated mind should be its own punishment; and it is so.

IN WHAT STUDIES HE FOUND MOST DELIGHT

But even now I cannot understand why I hated Greek, which I was taught in my earliest school-days. Because I loved Latin—the literature, I mean, not the grammar. For the first lessons of the Latin schools, in which one learns to read, write and multiply, I thought as dull and penal as Greek from first to last. Now why was this, if not from sin and vanity of life, because I was flesh and a spirit that goeth and returneth not? For certainly the first lessons, which formed in me the enduring

As translated by C. Bigg in *The Confessions of Saint Augustine*, 12th ed., Methuen and Company, Ltd., London, 1929, 52–65; 89–103; 149–152; 232–246; 278–291. Courtesy of Methuen and Company, Ltd.

power of reading books and writing what I choose, were better, because more solid, than the later, in which I was obliged to learn by heart the wanderings of Æneas, forgetting my own wanderings, and to weep for the death of Dido, who slew herself for love, while I looked with dry eyes on my own most unhappy death, wandering far from Thee, O God, my Life. For what is so pitiful as an unhappy wretch who pities not himself, who has tears for the death of Dido, because she loved Æneas, but none for his own death, because he loves not Thee!

O God, the light of my heart, Thou hidden bread of my soul, Thou mighty Husband of my mind and of the bosom of my thought, I loved Thee not. I liveth in adultery away from Thee, and all men cried unto me, Well done! well done! For the friendship of this world is adultery against Thee. Well done! well done! men cry, till one is ashamed not to be even as they. For this I had no tears, but I could weep for Dido, "slain with the sword and flying to the depths," while I was myself flying from Thee into the depths of Thy creation, earth returning to earth. And, if I was forbidden to read these tales, I grieved; because I might not read what caused me grief. Such lessons were thought more elevating and profitable than mere reading or writing. What madness is this!

But now let Thy truth, O my God, cry aloud in my soul, and say unto me Not so, not so; the earlier teaching was the better. For, lo, I would far rather forget the wanderings of Æneas, and everything of the kind, than how to read and write. Truly over the door of the grammar-school there hangs a curtain, yet is that curtain the shroud of falsehood, not the veil of mysteries. Let not those, whom no longer I fear, cry out against me, while I confess unto Thee, O my God, the promptings of my soul, and acquiesce in the condemnation of my evil ways, that I may love Thy good ways. Let not the buyers or sellers of grammar cry out against me. Because if I were to ask them whether the poet speaks the truth, when he says that Æneas came to Carthage, the unlearned would answer that they do not know, the learned that he does not.

But, if I were to ask how the name of Æneas is spelled, all who have learned spelling would answer rightly, in accordance with the convention by which men have regulated the use of the alphabet. And again, if I were to ask which it would be most inconvenient to forget, the art of reading and writing or these poetic fictions, who does not see what answer a man would be obliged to give, unless he had wholly forgotten himself? I was sinning then when, as a boy, I preferred those vanities to more useful arts, or rather when I loved the one and hated the other. "One and one two, two and two four" I thought a wearisome drone, but the wooden horse teeming with armed men, the flames of Troy, the ghost of Creusa—these were the vain delights that enchanted me.

HOW HE HATED GREEK

Why then did I hate my Greek literature, which was full of such songs? For Homer also weaves these fables with a skilful hand, nor is any vanity so delightful as his. Yet he was distasteful to me as a boy, and so I think would Virgil be to Greek boys, if they were compelled to learn him in the same way, that is to say, by dint of drudgery. The drudgery of acquiring a foreign tongue turned all the sweetness of the Grecian myths into gall. For I knew none of the words, and I was forced to master them by menaces and punishment. There was a time when I knew no Latin words, when I was an infant; but I learned them by merely attending, without fear or pain, amid caresses, laughter and joy, from nurses, friends, and playmates.

I learned them, I say, without the dread of punishment to spur me on, because my own heart was eager to bring its ideas to light, and could not do so till I had acquired some little store of phrases, not from teachers but from talkers, in whose ears I in turn was travailing to express my thoughts. It is plain, then, that the freedom of curiosity is a far better instructor in language than the compulsion of fear. Yet fear restrains the vagaries of curiosity by Thy laws, O God, Thy laws which begin with the schoolmaster's rod, and end with the martyr's fiery trial, Thy laws which have power to mingle a wholesome bitterness in our cup, calling us back to Thee, away from the fatal delights that tempted us to leave Thee.

A PRAYER FOR THE LOVE OF GOD

Hear, O Lord, my petition and suffer not my soul to faint beneath Thy chastisement. Suffer me not to faint in confessing to Thee the loving-kindness, whereby Thou didst rescue me from all my evil ways. Be Thou sweeter to me than all the allurements which I once pursued: that I may love Thee with all my strength, and clasp Thy hand with all my heart, so that I may be delivered from all temptation even unto the end.

For behold, O Lord, my King and my God, to Thy service I devote whatever useful thing I learned as a boy, my speaking, my writing, my reading, my arithmetic. For, when I learned vain things, Thou wast disciplining me, and the sin of my delight in those vanities. Thou hast forgiven. For even in them I learned many useful words, words that can be used with effect in matters that are not vain; and that is the safe path for boys to walk in.

HE DISAPPROVES OF THE WAY IN WHICH BOYS ARE TAUGHT

But woe to thee thou torrent of Use and Wont! Who can resist thee? How long wilt thou not be dried up, how long wilt thou sweep away the sons of Eve into that vast and stormy sea, which scarcely those who have embarked upon the Tree can cross in safety? Was it not in thy book that I read of Jove, the thunderer and the adulterer? Yet how could he be both? These tales were told only that the forged thunder might help and exculpate real adulterers. Which of our long-robed professors would listen patiently to a man, made out of the same dust as themselves, who should cry "These are fictions; Homer made God like man! Would he had rather made man like God." But to speak the whole truth, these fictions, for such they are, ascribe divinity to debauched men, in order that debauchery might no longer be counted debauchery, and that the libertine might seem to emulate, not the worst of men but the very Gods in heaven.

Yet, thou hellish torrent, the sons of men are tossed about in thee, and pay high fees to learn these lessons. And is it not a great disaster, when such instruction is given publicly in the market-place, in sight of the laws which promise the apt scholar a salary much higher than his fees? Thou roarest against thy rocks crying, "I teach words; I give eloquence, the power of persuasive expression." But is it so? Should we not understand these words, "shower of gold," "lap," "trick," "temples of heaven," unless Terence brought upon the stage a profligate youth, justifying his uncleanness by the example of Jove, as he gloats over a picture painted on the wall, a picture to illustrate the tale how "Jove rained into the lap of Danae a shower of gold, and so the girl was tricked?" See how he emboldens his lust by use of a divine authority!

"Aye, and what a God," he goes on, "he who shakes the temples of heaven with the crashing thunder. Was not I, poor man, to follow suit? That I did, right merrily." Certainly you need not sin in the same way to learn those words more easily, but by the words you learn to sin more boldly. I blame, not the words, which are, indeed, elect and precious vessels of thought, but the wine of error, which in them was held to our lips by drunken teachers. If we did not drink, we were beaten; nor could we appeal to any sober judge. And yet, O my God, in whose sight all my reminiscences are now free from dread, I conned these fables willingly, and, alas, with delight, and for this I was pronounced a hopeful scholar.

FURTHER STRICTURES ON THE WAY IN WHICH BOYS ARE TAUGHT LITERATURE

Suffer me also, O my God, to tell in what absurdities I frittered away my talent, which was Thy gift. One task was set me that sorely troubled my mind, that under promise of praise or of censure, and even of stripes, I should declaim the speech of Juno, wrathful and sad, because she could not drive away from Italy the Teucrian King. I had been told that Juno had never uttered the words, but we were all compelled to trace the wandering footprints of the poet's fancy, and say in bald prose what he had sung in verse. And he spoke his piece with most applause, who best acted the passions of wrath and sorrow, with due respect to the dignity of the character, and clothed the sentiments in appropriate words.

Now why did it befall me, O my true life, my God, that my recitation was applauded above those of my equals and classmates? Are not such triumphs but vapour and wind? Was there no other field in which my talent and my tongue might have found occupation? Thy praises, O Lord, Thy praises, displayed in Thy Holy Scriptures, should have propped the climbing vine of my heart; it should not have blown loose amid idle trifles, a sport for the fowls of the air. For there is more than one way of sacrificing to the fallen angels.

MEN OBEY THE LAWS OF GRAMMAR, AND DISOBEY THE LAWS OF GOD

But what wonder, if I plunged into vanities and abandoned Thy house, O my God, when I was taught to emulate men, who blushed for a barbarism or a solecism in the expression of some harmless fact, but plumed themselves on the purity and perspicacity, the fluency and brilliance of the speech, in which they revealed their own pollution. Thou seest these things, O Lord, long-suffering and plenteous in mercy and in truth, Thou seest and keepest silence. Wilt Thou keep silence for ever? Even now Thou dost pluck out of this bottomless pit the soul that seeketh Thee, and thirsteth for Thy pleasures, and saith unto Thee, "I have sought Thy face; Thy face, Lord, will I seek." For I had gone far from Thy face in the darkness of my heart.

For not by the movement of our feet, and not by spaces that can be measured, do we fly from Thee or return to Thee? Did that younger son of Thine hire horse or chariot or ship, did he fly on real wings, or walk with real legs to that far-off land where he spent in riotous living all that Thou gavest at his setting forth? In love Thou gavest, O Father; in greater love Thou forgavest the returning prodigal. A lustful heart is that far-off land, a land of darkness, far from Thy face. Behold, O Lord, behold patiently, as is Thy wont, how scrupulously men observe the covenant of letters and syllables received from the speakers of old, how carelessly they disobey the eternal covenant of everlasting life received from Thee. One who believes and teaches the time-honoured laws of pronunciation, if against the rule of grammar he says "'uman" for "human," gives more offence to his fellow-creatures than if, in violation of Thy laws, he hated the human race, to which he himself belongs. As if, forsooth, an enemy were more deadly than the hatred which regards him as an enemy, or as if a man by his malice could destroy another more utterly than he destroys his own soul.

Assuredly the laws of language are not written so deeply on our hearts as the rule of conscience: "Do not to another what thou wouldst not that he should do unto thee." How dost Thou hide Thyself, O God, Thou only great, that dwellest in high places in silence, and by an unfailing ordinance sendest penal blindness on lawless passion. A man seeking the glory of eloquence, in presence of a man who is judge, surrounded by bystanders who are men, while he inveighs against his adversary with the bitterest hatred, will be most carefully on his guard lest by a slip of the tongue he should say "men was," but will take no care at all lest, through the madness of his own soul, a man should perish from among men.

HOW THE VICES OF BOYHOOD PASS OVER INTO LATER LIFE

Such was the threshold of my moral life, such my training for this scene of strife. I was more afraid of uttering a barbarism than of envying those who did not. All these faults I confess unto Thee, O my God, but they were thought merits by those whose approbation was my standard of excellence. For I could not see the gulf of vileness in which I was cast away from Thine eyes. For in those eyes who was viler than I? nay, even the vile condemned me, for I practised innumerable deceits on my pedagogue, my masters, my parents, from love of play, from a passion for idle diversions, from a restless desire to imitate the follies of the theatre.

I even stole more than once from my father's cellar, and from the table, at the bidding of my greediness, or that I might have something to give to other boys, who sold me their play, though they loved it as much as I. And in my play I often sought to get the mastery by cheating, when I was myself mastered by the vain desire to excel. Yet what did I so detest as the very tricks which I played upon others, and what did I so angrily denounce, when I found them out? But, if I was myself found out, I would fly into a passion rather than give way.

Is this the innocence of boyhood? It is not, O Lord, it is not. I cry to Thee for pardon, O my God. As we disobeyed pedagogues and masters for nuts and balls and sparrows, so in riper years we disobey governors and kings for gold, for manors, for slaves; and so heavier penalties take the place of the cane. It was then humility, symbolised by the littleness of childhood, which Thou wast commending, when Thou saidst, "Of such is the Kingdom of Heaven."

HE GIVES THANKS TO GOD
FOR THE BLESSINGS OF BOYHOOD

And yet, O Lord my God, Thou best and most excellent Creator and Ruler of the world, I should owe Thee thanks, even though Thou hadst wished that I should never be more than boy. For I was; I was alive; I could feel; I could guard my personality, the imprint of that mysterious unity from which my being was derived; by my inner sense I could warrant the accuracy of my outer senses; I found delight in truth, even in little things and in reflections upon little things; I could not bear to make mistakes; my memory was retentive, my speech refined; friendship consoled me; pain, dishonour, ignorance I was able to avoid. Surely every part of such a creature calls for wonder and praise.

But all this is the bounty of my God and not my own; and all these capacities are good; and I am the sum of them. Truly, then, He who made me is good, and very good; and to Him will I give loud thanks for all the good that belonged to me, even as a boy. For my sin was just this, that I sought for pleasure, grandeur, reality, not in Him but in His creatures, myself and others, and thus fell headlong into sorrow, confusion, error. Thanks be unto Thee, O my God, my joy, my glory, and my confidence. Thanks be unto Thee for all Thy gifts; but do Thou keep them safe for me. For then Thou wilt keep me safe, and Thy gifts will increase and be perfected; and I shall be with Thee, for even my being is Thy gift. . . .

HOW HE WAS CAUGHT BY LOVE,
WHICH HE PURSUED

Next I went to Carthage, where debauchery bubbled around me like a frying-pan. I was not yet in love, but I loved the idea of love, and a deep-felt want made me hate myself, because I wanted less than I should. I sought something to love, loving as I say the idea of love, and hated the tranquil path, where there are no mouse-traps. For my inward man was famished for want of the inward food, Thyself, O my God, yet had I no appetite and felt no desire for the meat that perisheth not; and that not because I was full but because I was empty, and therefore disdained it. And thus my soul was sick and smitten with boils, and rushed desperately out of doors, seeking, like Job, to scrape itself with the things of sense. And yet, if these things of sense had had no soul, I could not have loved them. To love and to be loved was sweet to me, but sweeter still if I enjoyed the person that I loved.

And so I polluted the brook of friendship with the sewage of lust, and darkened its clear shining with smoke from hell, and yet, vile and disreputable as I was, my vanity was inordinate, and I aspired to be known for my fashion and my wit. Also I plunged headlong into love, whose fetters I longed to wear. O my God, my Merciful One, how good Thou wast, and with what gall didst Thou embitter that cup of sweetness! For I was beloved; I attained my wish, the bondage of clandestine fruition, and proudly riveted around myself the chain of woe; then was I scourged with the red-hot iron rods of jealousy, suspicion, fears, anger, and quarrels.

HIS LOVE FOR TRAGEDIES

The stage also bewitched me, and its manifold pictures of my misery added fuel to my fire. Why is it that men desire to be saddened by the representation of tragic misfortunes, which they do not in the least desire to suffer? Yet the spectator does desire to be saddened by them, and the sadness is the very pleasure that he seeks. Surely this is wretched folly. For in proportion as a man's emotions are less wholesome, the more deeply is he moved by the passion of tragedy. Yet, when a man actually feels this passion, we call his state misery. When he participates in it by way of sympathy, we call it pity. But now what pity can there be for the puppets of the stage? No one expects the spectator to help them; he is only asked to shed a tear, and the more tears he sheds, the more he encourages the actor of an idle tale. And, if these old-world or imaginary calamities are acted in such a way that he cannot shed a tear at all, he goes home disgusted and critical; otherwise he keeps his seat, listens with all his ears, and enjoys the luxury of weeping. Do men then delight in tears and grief? Surely not, but in joy. Or shall we say that, though misery is painful, pity is pleasant, and that because there is no pity without grief, we seek grief for the sake of pity. So that the love of grief also runs from the brook of friendship.

But whither does that brook flow? Why does it fall into a torrent of boiling pitch, into seething pools of horrid lust, where by its own free will it loses the crystal purity of its heavenly source, and is changed into the nature of that hateful flood? Are we then to banish pity? By no means. There are times, then, when we must delight in grief. But beware of uncleanness, O my soul, for fear of my God and Guardian, the God of our fathers, who is to be praised and exalted above all for evermore. Beware of uncleanness. For even now I am not pitiless. But while in the old days in the theatre I envied the lovers who enjoyed the forbidden fruits of love—though but in the mimicry of the stage—and grieved with a kind of pity when they were forced to part, and found the pity as pleasant as the joy, now I pity him who rejoices in his wicked success, and do not pity him who has lost—what?—a ruinous pleasure, a miserable happiness.

Now certainly this is a juster pity, but there is no pleasure in its grief. For, though it is the approved office of charity to grieve over the wretched, a truly pitiful man would far rather see nothing to grieve over. One who really and sincerely pities, cannot want people to be wretched, in order that he may pity them, unless there is such a thing as malevolent benevolence, which is an impossibility. Grief, then, may sometimes be right, but never desirable. And this Thou teachest us, O Lord God, who lovest the soul with a love far purer than ours, and whose pity is diviner than ours, because it feels no grief. But who is sufficient for these things? However, wretched man that I was, I loved sorrow in those days; I sought an outlet for pity in the fictitious woes of a dancer, and always that part liked me best which wrung tears from my eyes. What wonder, if the lost and wilful sheep was taken by the murrain? Thence came my delight in troubles—not such as pierce the heart, for I would not for the world have suffered what I was so eager to behold—but idle tales which glance upon the surface—yet they tore my flesh like claws, and left behind them an angry swelling and a festering sore. Is such a life worth calling life, O my God?

IN THE RHETORIC SCHOOL HE TOOK NO PART IN THE DOINGS OF THE WRECKERS

And always Thy faithful mercy hovered over me from afar. O in what wickednesses did I consume away! How did I follow my profane Curiosity, till it led me into the very depths of unbelief, into the deceitful worship of devils to whom my misdeeds were a sacrifice! And always Thou wast scourging me. I was not afraid to think of my lust, and plan a scheme for securing the deadly fruit of sin, even within the walls of Thy church during the celebration of Thy mysteries. For this Thou didst chastise me with heavy penalties, yet not as my fault deserved, O my God, my surpassing Mercy, my Refuge from the awful tormentors among whom I wandered with stubborn neck, fleeing farther and farther from Thee, loving my own ways not Thine, loving a runagate freedom.

My studies also, liberal studies they were called, drew me to look towards the Law Courts and to aspire to success at the bar, where the craftiest is the most honourable.

Such is the blindness of men, who ever glory in their blindness. And now I had reached the top of the school of rhetoric. Proud enough I was, and puffed up with conceit, yet far quieter than I had been, O Lord, Thou knowest. I would take no part at all in the wild doings of the Wreckers, a cruel and devilish name, which was looked upon as the stamp of the best set. I lived amongst them, feeling a kind of impudent shame, because I could not keep pace with them. I went about with them, and of some of them I made friends; yet I always disliked their way of going on, their "wreckings," their wanton attacks upon the shyness of freshmen, and the unprovoked affronts with which they carried on their malignant amusement. Nothing could be more like the conduct of devils, and what name could be fitter for them than Wreckers? They themselves were wrecked and broken to begin with, and the lying spirits were cozening and seducing them, while they were finding delight in flouting and deceiving others.

THE HORTENSIUS OF CICERO ROUSED IN HIM A GREAT LOVE OF PHILOSOPHY

Among such comrades in those years of indiscretion, I was studying books of rhetoric, wherein I desired to excel, seeking through the joys of vanity a flashy and reprobate success, and in the usual course I had entered upon a book by one Cicero whose tongue all men admire, though not his heart. It was the *Hortensius*, a treatise in which he extols the study of philosophy. That book changed my mind, changed my very prayers to Thee, O Lord, and altered my wishes and aspirations. From that moment vain hopes ceased to charm, and with a strange and heartfelt passion I began to long for the immortality of wisdom. Thenceforth began my upward way, and my return towards Thee. For I did not apply that book to the sharpening of my tongue, an accomplishment which it seemed hard to purchase at my mother's cost—for I was in my nineteenth year and my father had died two years before—I did not, I say, apply it to the sharpening of my tongue, for what the book itself commended was not the style but the substance of speech.

How did I burn, O my God, how did I burn to soar away from earth to Thee; yet I knew not what Thou wast doing to me. For wisdom is Thine. The love of wisdom with which those pages inspired me is called in Greek "philosophy." There are some who mislead by philosophy, tricking out their own errors with a high, attractive, and honourable title, and in this book Cicero censures and confutes nearly all these erroneous teachers of his own or earlier times. How distinctly does he preach the wholesome admonition, which Thy Spirit gives by the mouth of Thy good and pious servant: "Beware lest any man spoil you through philosophy and vain deceit, after the tradition of men, after the rudiments of the world and not after Christ. For in Him dwelleth all the fullness of the God-head bodily."

At that time, Thou knowest, O Light of my heart, these words of the Apostle were not yet known to me; yet the one point that came home to me in Cicero's book was the advice not to run after this school or that, but to love, and seek, and pursue, and clasp, and never let go Wisdom herself, wherever I found her. I was strongly moved, and kindled, and inflamed by these words; and one thing only damped my zeal, that the Name of Christ was not mentioned there. For this Name, according to Thy lovingkindness, O Lord, this Name of my Saviour, Thy Son, my infant heart had sucked in with my mother's milk, and there it still was, hidden safe away. So that any book which did not use that Name—cultivated, polished, profound as it might be—could not wholly master me.

HE DISDAINED SACRED SCRIPTURE BECAUSE OF ITS STYLE

And so I determined to read the sacred Scriptures, and find out what they were like. And behold I found a thing not known to the proud, nor laid open to children, but lowly in mien, lofty in operation, and veiled in mysteries. I was not such that I could enter into it, or bow my head at its approach. For I did not feel what I have just described, when first I read the Scriptures. They seemed to me to be far inferior to the dignity of Tully. My extravagance disliked their self-restraint, and my eye could not pierce their hidden depths. In truth it is the nature of that Book to grow with the growth of the babe. But I disdained to be a babe, and in my swelling pride fancied that I was grown-up.

HOW HE WAS CAUGHT BY THE MANICHEES

And so I fell among a sort of men vain and brain-sick, carnal and verbose, in whose mouths were snares of the Devil and lime for silly birds, made up of the syllables of Thy Name, and that of our Lord Jesus Christ, and that of the Paraclete our Comforter, the Holy Ghost. These Names were never off their lips; the sound was there, and the movement of the tongue, but the heart within was void of truth. "The Truth, the Truth," they were always saying, and often said to me, but it was not in them; they taught lies, not only of Thee who art the true Truth, but of the elements of this world, Thy creatures. But, indeed, I ought not to have heeded philosophers, even though they spoke truth about Thy works: I ought to have passed them by for love of Thee, my Father, supremely good, Thou Fairness of all that is fair. O Truth, Truth, how did the inmost marrow of my soul sigh for Thee even then, while those word-mongers were ringing the changes on Thy name in all those ponderous tomes! These were the dainty dishes wherein, when I was hungering for Thee, they served up to me the sun and moon, beautiful works indeed, but Thy works, not Thyself nor even Thy first works. For Thy spiritual world came before these material creatures, bright and heavenly though they be.

I hungered and thirsted not even for those, Thy first works, but for Thee, O Truth, in whom is no variableness, neither shadow of turning, yet still they set before me in those dainty dishes a banquet of delusions. Far better were it to love the sun we see (which to our eyes, at any rate, is real) than these fictions of a mind deceived by the eyes. And yet I fed on them because I took them for Thee, but not with appetite, because I could not find in them Thy savour. For Thou wast not those fictions, nor did they nourish, nay, they starved me. How like is food in dreams to real food! yet the dreamer is not fed, for it is a dream.

But these meats were not like Thee in any way, as Thou didst warn me even then; for they were material notions, imaginary things, far less certain than the real things, which we see with our natural eyes, in earth or sky. These the birds and beasts see as well as we; and they are far more real than those creatures of the imagination. And again, those imaginations are far more real than the infinite series of sublime nonentities which we build upon them. However, with these empty husks was I then fed, yet not fed.

But Thou, my Love, for whom I faint that I may be made strong, art neither these bodies which we see, though they be in heaven, nor those which we see not, for Thou art their Creator, nor dost Thou count them among Thy chiefest works. How far art Thou, then, from those notions that I believed in, notions of bodies which do not exist at all. For our abstract conceptions of bodies which do exist are more certain than they, and the bodies themselves are more certain still, yet Thou art none of these. Thou art not even the soul, which is the life of bodies, so that the life of bodies is better and more certain than the bodies themselves. But Thou art the life of souls, the life of lives, having life in Thyself, and never changest, O Life of my soul. Where wast Thou then? How far away from me? while I was banished far away from Thee, deprived even of the husks of the swine which I was feeding with husks. For the fables of the grammarian and the poet were far better than this deceitful stuff. Beyond a doubt verses and songs about Medea's flight through the air are more profitable than the five elements variously transformed because of the five caves of darkness, which have no existence, and slay him that believes in them. From verses and songs I can find real nutriment, and, as for Medea and her flight, even if I sang about it, I did not maintain that it was true. And when others sang about it, I did not believe them. But these absurdities I did believe.

Alas! alas! by what steps was I brought down to the depths of hell! toiling and chafing for lack of truth, and all, O my God (for unto Thee do I confess it, who hadst pity on me, even when I did not confess), all because I was seeking for Thee by the carnal senses, and not by that intelligence in which Thou madest me superior to the beasts. But Thou wast lower than my lowest depth and higher than my highest height. And so I happened upon that brazen and witless woman of whom Solomon speaks in his parable, sitting on a chair at the entrance of the door, and crying: "Eat gladly of hidden bread and drink sweet stolen water." She corrupted me because she found me rambling abroad in the lust of the eye, and ruminating such food as I had procured for myself thereby.

THE ABSURDITY OF THE MANICHEAN DOCTRINE, WHICH HE PROFESSED

For, knowing not the true Being, I was so shaken by quips and quiddities that I had no answer for these silly deceivers when they asked me what is the origin of evil? whether God is limited by a bodily form? whether he has hair and nails? whether polygamists, homicides, offerers of bloody sacrifices, can be regarded as righteous men? These doubts confused my ignorance; I turned my back on truth and thought I was looking for it, because I did not know that evil is the privation of good and next door to non-existence. How could I see this, when my eye could see nothing but bodies, and my mind nothing but materialised ideas?

I did not understand that God is a spirit, who has no parts that can be measured, whose being is not a bulk, because bulk is less in the part than in the whole, and, even if it be infinite, is less in some definite portion than in its infinity, and cannot be wholly everywhere like God, who is spirit. And I had not the least conception in what we are like God, or whether Scripture was right in saying that we are in the image of God. Nor did I know the true inner righteousness, which judges not conventionally but by the upright law of Almighty God, whereby the customs of countries and times are adapted to the countries and the times, though the law is the same everywhere and always. I did not see that by this law Abraham and Isaac and Jacob and Moses and David and all who are praised by the mouth of God were righteous; though they were counted unrighteous by foolish men, judging by man's day, and measuring the morality of the whole human race by the petty rule of their own morality, just as if one, who knew nothing about armour, should fasten a greave on his head and shoe his foot with a helmet, and then complain because they do not fit; or as if, when a holiday has been proclaimed for the afternoon, he should make a disturbance because he may not open his shop after twelve o'clock, though it was lawful in the morning; or as if in some great household, having discovered that one slave was allowed to handle things which the butler might not touch, or that things might be done in the stable which were forbidden in the dining room, he should make angry complaints, that in one house and in one family all have not the same office at the same time.

Such are they who are indignant, when they hear that some things were lawful for the righteous in old times, which are not permitted now; or that God for temporary reasons gave the ancients one commandment, us another, though we both obey the same righteousness; or when they see that in one man, in one day, in one house, different offices suit different members, that what was right just now is not right when the clock has struck, that what is done, nay, must be done, in one room is properly forbidden and punished in another. Is justice then capricious or changeable? No, but the times, over which justice presides, do not run evenly, because they are times. So men, whose days upon earth are few, quarrel with the past and accept the present, because they cannot actually see the connection between the laws that governed ages and nations of old and those that are now in operation; while they can see individuals, days, houses, in which different things at different moments are suitable to different members, parts, or persons.

All these things I neither knew nor considered; they forced themselves upon my eyes, but I could not see them. I wrote poems, in which I was not allowed to put any foot I pleased wherever I liked; each metre had its own regulations, and, even in the same line, the same foot would not suit all places. Yet the art of poetry did not make its principles to suit the case, but comprised all in one. Still I did not perceive that justice, which those good and holy men obeyed, comprises all in one in a far more excellent and admirable way; that, without changing in any degree, it yet gives out its precepts, not all at once, but with due respect to the changes of the times. And in my blindness I condemned the holy patriarchs; though they not only regulated the present by the command and inspiration of God, but moreover foretold the future as God revealed it unto them. . . .

OF FAUSTUS THE MANICHEAN, AND OF THE BLINDNESS OF PHILOSOPHERS WHO KNOW THE CREATURE YET KNOW NOT THE CREATOR

I will describe in the sight of my God the twenty-ninth year of my age. There was then at Carthage a Manichean bishop Faustus, a great snare of the devil, who entrapped many by the bait of his eloquence. This I admired; but I was beginning to distinguish the charm of words from the truth of things, which I was eager to learn, nor did I consider so much the beauty of the dish, as the kind of meat which their famous Faustus served up to me. For fame had run before him, as of one skilled in all honourable learning, and especially well versed in the liberal sciences.

And, since I was well read in the philosophers and had a good memory for their principles, I began to compare some of their doctrines with the tedious fables of the Manichees, and it struck me that probability was on the side of the philosophers, whose power reached so far that they were able to form a fair judgment of the world, although they did not find the Sovereign Lord of these His works. For Thou art great, O Lord, and hast respect unto the lowly, but the proud Thou beholdest afar off. Thou drawest near to none but the contrite in heart, nor canst Thou be found by the proud, even though by inquisitive skill they number the stars and the sand, and map out the spaces of the constellations, and track the orbits of the heavenly bodies. For it is by mind and intelligence, which Thou bestowest, that they investigate these things. Much they have found out; they have foretold even beforehand the day, the hour, the extent of eclipses of those bright luminaries, the sun and moon: their calculations did not fail, and it came to pass as they foretold: they wrote down the rules they had discovered, so that to this day they may be read, and from them may be calculated in what year, in what month, on what day of the month, at what hour of the day, in what portion of its light, sun or moon will be eclipsed, and it will come to pass just as is predicted.

And men who know not, wonder and are amazed; and men who know are boastful and lifted up; in their ungodly pride they withdraw from Thy light into the shadow of eclipse; they can foresee the eclipse of the sun, and cannot see their own. For they do not ask, as religious men should, whence comes the intelligence whereby they investigate. And when they discover that Thou didst make them, they do not give themselves up to Thee, that Thou mayest preserve what Thou didst make, nor do they sacrifice unto Thee what they have made of themselves—slaying their high thoughts like fowls of the air, and their subtleties (wherein they dart along the secret paths of the deep) like fishes of the sea, and their lusts like beasts of the field—that Thou, O God, who art a consuming fire, shouldest burn up their dead cares and renew them unto immortality.

But they know not the Way, Thy Word, by whom Thou didst create the things that are numbered, and the men who number them, and the senses by which they perceive what they number, and the intelligence whereby they number; nor do they know that of Thy Wisdom there is no number. But Thy Only Begotten Himself was made unto us wisdom and righteousness and sanctification, and was numbered amongst us, and paid tribute unto Caesar. They know not this Way, and deem that they are shining among the stars on high; and, lo, they have fallen to earth, and their foolish heart is darkened. Much that is true do they teach about creation, but the Truth, the Artificer of creation, they do not piously seek, and therefore they find not. Or if they find, they know God, yet glorify Him not as God, neither are thankful, but become vain in their imaginations: they profess themselves to be wise, claiming Thy attributes for their own, and hence, in the perversity of blindness, they ascribe to Thee those attributes that are their own, heaping lies upon Thee who art the Truth, changing the glory of the incorruptible God into an image made like to corruptible man, and to birds, and four-footed beasts and creeping things, changing Thy truth into a lie, and worshipping and serving the creature more than the Creator.

Yet I remembered many a true saying of the philosophers about creation, and I saw reason in their calculations, in the orderly sequence of times, and in the manifest attestation of the stars. This I compared with the doctrines of Manichaeus, who in his voluminous folly wrote many books on these matters. And here I could see no reason about the solstice, or the equinox, or eclipses, or whatever I had learned in books of secular philosophy. I was ordered to believe, but the ideas did not correspond with, nay, they contradicted, the rational theories established by mathematics, and indeed by the evidence of my own eyes. . . .

HOW IN THE PLATONIC BOOKS HE FOUND THE DIVINITY OF THE ETERNAL WORD, BUT NOT THE HUMILITY OF THE INCARNATE WORD

And first of all, willing to teach me how Thou dost resist the proud and givest grace to the humble, and how mercifully Thou hast made known to men the way of humility, in that Thy Word was made flesh and dwelt among men, Thou didst procure for me, through the agency of one puffed up with enormous vanity, certain books of the Platonists translated from the Greek into Latin. And therein I found, not indeed these precise words, but precisely the same truth fortified with many and divers arguments, that "in the beginning was the Word, and the Word was with God, and the Word was God, and the same was in the beginning with God; all things were made by Him, and without Him was nothing made that was made; in Him is life, and the life was the light of men, and the light shineth in darkness, and the darkness comprehended it not." Further, that the soul of man, though it bears witness to the light, is not itself that light, but God, the Word of God, is the true light that lighteth every man that cometh into the world. And that "He was in the world, and the world was made by Him, and the world knew Him not." But that "He came unto His own, and His own received Him not; but as many as received Him, to them gave He power to become the sons of God, even to them that believe on His name,"—this I could not find there.

Also I found there that God the Word "was born, not of flesh, nor of blood, nor of the will of a man, nor of the will of the flesh, but of God." But that "the Word was made flesh and dwelt among us," this I found not there. I could discover in these books, though it was expressed in other and in varying phrases, that "the Son was in the form of the Father, and thought it not robbery to be equal with God," because by nature He was that same substance. But that "He emptied Himself, taking upon Him the form of a servant, being made in the likeness of men; and, being found in fashion as a man, He humbled Himself, and became obedient unto death, even the death of the Cross; wherefore also God exalted Him from the dead, and gave Him a Name, which is above every name; that at the name of Jesus every knee should bow, of things in heaven, and things in earth, and things under the earth, and that every tongue should confess that the Lord Jesus Christ is in the glory of God the Father"—this those books do not contain.

For that, before all times and above all times, Thy only begotten Son abideth unchangeable and co-eternal with Thee, and that of His fullness all souls receive, in order that they may be blessed, and that by participation of the eternal wisdom they are renewed, in order that they may be wise, this is there. But that in due time He died for the ungodly, that Thou sparedst not Thine Only Son but deliveredst Him up for us all, this is not there. For Thou hast hidden these things from the wise, and revealed them unto babes, that they that labor and are heavy laden might come unto Him, and He might refresh them, because He is meek and lowly in heart, and the meek He guideth in judgment, and the gentle He teacheth His ways, looking upon our lowliness and troubles, and forgiving all our sins. But those who strut in the buskin of what they deem higher knowledge, will not listen to Him who saith, "Learn of me, for I am meek and lowly in heart, and ye shall find rest unto your souls," and though they know God, yet they glorify Him not as God, nor are thankful, but become vain in their imaginations, and their foolish heart is darkened; professing themselves to be wise, they became fools.

And therefore, as I read there also, they had changed the glory of Thy incorruptible nature into idols and many kinds of images, into the likeness of the image of corruptible man, and birds, and four-footed beasts and creeping things, to wit, that flesh of Egypt for which Esau lost his birthright; for Thy first-born people worshipped the head of a beast instead of Thee, turning in heart back towards Egypt, and bowing down their soul, Thy likeness, before the likeness of a calf that eateth hay. These things found I there, but I would not eat of them. For it pleased Thee, O Lord, to take away the reproach of inferiority from Jacob that the elder should serve the younger, and Thou calledst the Gentiles into Thine inheritance.

And I had come to Thee from the Gentiles; and my mind was set upon the gold which Thou willedst Thy people to carry off from Egypt, for it was Thine wherever it was. And Thou didst say unto the Athenians by the mouth of Thy Apostles that in Thee we live and move and have our being, as certain also of their own poets have said. And surely these books came from thence. But my mind was not set on the idols of the Egyptians, which they fashioned of Thy gold, changing the truth of God into a lie, and worshipping and serving the creature more than the Creator.

AUGUSTINE BEGINS MORE CLEARLY TO DISCERN DIVINE TRUTH

And, being by these books admonished to return into myself, I entered into the secret closet of my soul, guided by Thee; and this I could do because Thou wast my helper. I entered, and beheld with the mysterious eye of my soul the light that never changes, above the eye of my soul, above my intelligence. It was not the common light which all flesh can see, nor was it greater yet of the same kind, as if the light of day were to grow brighter and brighter and flood all space. It was not like this, but something altogether different from any earthly illumination. Nor was it above my intelligence in the same way as oil is above water, or heaven above earth, but it was higher because it made me, and I was lower because made by it. He who knows the truth knows that Light, and he who knows that Light knows Eternity. Love knows that Light.

O eternal Truth, and true Love, and lovely Eternity, Thou art my God; unto Thee do I sigh night and day. When first I knew Thee, Thou didst take hold of me, so that I could see there was something to be seen, though I was not yet fit to see it. And Thou didst beat back my weak sight, dazzling me with Thy splendour, and I thrilled with love and dread, and I perceived that I was far away from Thee in the land of unlikeness, as if I heard Thy voice from on high crying unto me, "I am the Food of the full-grown; become a man, and Thou shalt feed on me. Nor shalt Thou change Me into thine own substance, as thou changest the food of thy flesh, but thou shalt be changed into Mine." And I understood that Thou dost chasten man for iniquity, and hast made my soul to consume away like a spider's web. And I said, "Is truth, then, nothing, because it is not diffused through space finite or infinite?" And Thou didst cry from afar, "Nay, not so; I AM THAT I AM." And I heard as the heart heareth, and there was left no room for doubt. Sooner could I doubt my own existence than think that Truth is not, for it is clearly seen and understood by means of the things which are made.

HOW THE CREATURES ARE AND ARE NOT

And I beheld all the things that are beneath Thee, and I saw that they are neither wholly real nor wholly unreal; they are real in so far as they came from Thee, they are unreal because they are not what Thou art. For that alone is truly real which abides unchanged. It is good then for me to hold me fast by God, because if I abide not in Him, I cannot abide in myself. But He, abiding in Himself, maketh all things new. And Thou art the Lord my God, because my goods are nothing unto Thee.

ALL THAT IS, IS GOOD

And it was made clear to me that all things that are corrupted are good. They could not be corrupted, if they were chief goods, nor unless they were goods; because, if they were chief goods, they would be incorruptible, and if they were not goods at all, there would be nothing in them that could be corrupted. For corruption does harm, and it can do harm only by diminishing goodness. Either then corruption does no harm, which is impossible, or all things that are corrupted are deprived of good, and this is most certainly true. But, if they are deprived of all good, they will cease to exist. For, if they exist and can be no further corrupted, they will be better because henceforth they remain incorruptible.

Now what can be more monstrous than to maintain that, by losing all good, they have become better. If then they are deprived of all good, they will cease to exist. Therefore, so long as they exist, they are good. Therefore, all that exists is good. And so that evil, whose origin I was seeking, is not a substance; because if it were a substance, it would be good. For either it would be an incorruptible substance, that is to say, a chief good, or a corruptible substance, which could not be corrupted unless it were good. And so I saw, and saw clearly that all that Thou hast made is good; and there are no substances at all which Thou didst not make. And because Thou didst not make all things equal, each by itself is good, and the sum of all is very good; for our God made all things very good.

ALL CREATION PRAISES GOD

And to Thee there is no such thing as evil, and even to Thy creation as a whole there is not, because there is nothing beyond it that can burst in and destroy the law which Thou hast imposed upon it. In the details there are things which, because they suit not some parts, are counted evil, yet these same things suit other parts, and are good to them, and are good in themselves. And all these things which are not suitable to one another, are yet suitable to that lower half of creation called earth, which has its own windy and cloudy sky of like nature with itself.

What folly, then, would it be to think that nothing exists except this world of sense. For, if I saw this world alone, I should long indeed for a better, yet should I be bound to praise Thee for this world alone. For, that Thou art to be praised on earth, the dragons do show and all deeps, fire, hail, snow, ice, and stormy wind fulfilling Thy word; mountains and all hills, fruitful trees and all cedars; beasts and all cattle, creeping things and feathered fowl; kings of the earth and all people, princes and all judges of the earth; young men and maidens, old men and children praise Thy Name. But seeing that in heaven all Thy angels praise Thee, praise Thee, O God, in the height, and all Thy hosts, sun and moon, all stars and light, the heaven of heavens and the waters that be above the heavens praise Thy Name, seeing this, I say, I no longer desired a better world, because my thought ranged over all, and with a sounder judgment I reckoned that things above were better than things below, yet that all creation together was better than the things above.

THE SANE MIND FINDS NOTHING EVIL IN GOD'S CREATION

There is no health in those who find fault with any part of Thy creation, as there was no health in me, when I found fault with many of Thy works. And, because my soul did not dare to find fault with God, it denied that the faults it found were Thy handiwork. Thus it had wandered into the notion of two substances, and could find no rest, and talked a strange language. And, escaping from that error, it had made for itself a God extended through infinite space, and thought it to be Thee, and set it up in its heart, and became once more the temple of its own idol, abominable in Thy sight. But Thou didst soothe my brain, though I knew it not, and closed my eyes lest they should behold vanity, and thus by slow degrees my folly ceased and fell asleep. And I awoke in Thee and beheld Thee infinite, yet not in such a manner as I had supposed, and this vision was not derived from the flesh.

HOW THERE IS TRUTH AND FALSEHOOD IN CREATION

And I looked upon other things, and I saw that all that is finite owes to Thee its existence in Thee; yet it is in Thee not as it is in space, but because Thou holdest all things in the hand of Thy truth: and that all things are true in so far as they are; and that falsehood is nothing, except the existence in thought of that which is not. And I saw that everything bears fit relation, not only to its place but to its time; and that Thou, who alone art Eternal, didst not begin to work after the lapse of innumerable ages, because no time, either of past or of future, could come or go, except by Thy working and abiding.

HOW ALL THAT IS CREATED IS GOOD, THOUGH IT MAY NOT SUIT EVERYTHING

And I felt and realized that it is nothing strange, if bread, which is sweet, is a punishment to the diseased palate, and light, which is lovely to healthy eyes, is hateful to the sick. And the wicked find fault with Thy justice, as they do with the viper and the worm, yet these are good, though belonging only to the lower order of Thy creation. And there is the proper place of the wicked also, the more unlike they are to Thee; yet do they belong also to the higher order, the more they become like Thee. And I asked what wickedness was, and I found that it was no substance, but a perversity of will, which turns aside from Thee, O God, the supreme substance, to desire the lowest, flinging away its inner treasure and boasting itself an outcast.

WHAT IT IS THAT HOLDS MAN BACK FROM THE KNOWLEDGE OF THE DIVINE

And I marvelled to find that now I loved Thee, and not a phantasm in Thy stead. And I could not stand still to enjoy my God, but was swept up to Thee by Thy beauty, and again torn away from Thee by my own weight, and fell back with a groan into the world of sense; and the weight was carnal use and wont. But Thy memory dwelt with me, nor did I doubt in the least that there was One for me to cleave to, only I doubted whether I was as yet able to cleave to Him, forasmuch as the corruptible body presseth down the soul, and the earthly tabernacle weigheth down the mind that museth upon many things. Most certain I was that Thy invisible things are clearly seen from the constitution of the world, being understood through the things that are made, even Thy eternal power and Godhead.

For when I asked how I could estimate the beauty of bodies, whether celestial or terrestrial, and what rule was ready to my hand so that I could judge correctly of changeable things and say This ought to be thus, that ought to be otherwise—when I asked, I say, how it was possible for me to judge in this way, it was clear that I had found the unchangeable and true eternity of truth above my own changeable intelligence. Thus step by step was I led upwards, from bodies to the soul which perceives by means of the bodily senses, and thence to the soul's inward faculty, to which bodily sense reports external facts, and this belongs even to beasts, and thence again to the reasoning power, to whose judgment is referred the knowledge received by the bodily senses.

And when this power also within me found itself changeable, it lifted itself up to its own intelligence, and withdrew its thoughts from experience, abstracting itself from the contradictory throng of sensuous images, that it might find out what that light was wherein it was bathed, when it cried out that beyond doubt the unchangeable was better than the changeable, and how it came to know the unchangeable, which it must have known in some way or another, for otherwise it could not have preferred it so confidently to the changeable. And thus, with the flash of one hurried glance, it attained to the vision of THAT WHICH IS. And then at last I saw Thy invisible things understood by means of the things that are made, but I could not sustain my gaze; my weakness was dashed back, and I was relegated to my ordinary experience, bearing with me nothing but a loving remembrance, cherishing, as it were, the fragrance of those viands which I was not yet able to feed upon.

CHRIST THE ONLY WAY
TO SALVATION

So I cast about for some way to attain a strength that should be able to enjoy Thee; nor could I find any, until I embraced the mediator between God and man, the Man Christ Jesus, who is over all, God blessed for ever, who calleth me and saith, "I am the Way, the Truth, and the Life," who mingleth Himself with flesh, and is the food which I was as yet unable to receive, because the Word was made Flesh, that Thy all-creative wisdom might become milk for us babes. For as yet I did not humbly hold the humble Lord Jesus, nor did I know what His weakness was meant to teach us. For Thy Word, the Eternal Truth, far exalted above the higher parts of Thy creation, lifteth up His subjects towards Himself, but in the lower parts hath built for Himself a humble dwelling of our clay, that so He might pull down from themselves and win over to Himself those whom He is to make subject, lowering their pride and heightening their love, that they might not stray farther afield in self-confidence, but rather be made weak, seeing before their feet the Godhead made weak by sharing our coats of skins, and that they might cast themselves wearily upon It, and be uplifted by Its rising. . . .

HE GOES INTO THE GARDEN.
WHAT BEFELL HIM THERE

Disordered in look and mind by this desperate wrestle with my own soul in the secret chambers of my own heart, I fell upon Alypius crying out, "What has come to us? What means this tale that thou hast heard? Simple men arise and take heaven by violence, and we with all our heartless learning—see how we are wallowing in flesh and blood. Shall we stand still because they have taken the lead? Shall we not follow if we could not lead?" I scarcely knew what I said, and flung away, leaving him staring in silent astonishment. For my voice

was changed; my face, eyes, colour, tone expressed my meaning more clearly than my words.

There was a garden to our lodging, of which we were free, as indeed we were of the whole house. For our host, the master of the house, did not live there. Thither the tumult of my breast drove me, where no one could interrupt the duel into which I had entered with myself, until it should reach the issue which Thou alone couldest foresee. I was mad, unto salvation; I was dying, unto life; I knew what evil thing I was; what good thing I was soon to be I knew not. I fled then into the garden, and Alypius followed me step for step. For I had no secret wherein he did not share, and how could he leave me in such distress? We sat down, as far from the house as possible. I was groaning in spirit, shaken with a gust of indignation, because I could not enter into Thy Will and Covenant, O my God; yet all my bones were crying out that this was the way, the best of all ways, and no ship is needed for that way, nor chariot, no, nor feet, for it is not so far as from the house to the spot where we were seated.

For to go along that road, aye, and to reach the goal, is all one with the will to go; but it must be a strong and single will, not a broken-winged wish fluttering hither and thither, rising with one pinion, struggling and falling with the other. In fine, in the midst of that passionate indecision, I was doing many things which men sometimes will, yet cannot perform, because they have lost a limb, because their limbs are bound with fetters, or enfeebled by disease, or incapacitated in some other way. If I tore my hair, or beat my brow, or clasped my hands about my knees, it was because I willed to do so. Yet I might have willed in vain, if the nerves had not obeyed my bidding. Many things then I did, in which will and power to do were not the same, yet did not that one thing which seemed to me infinitely more desirable, which, before long, I should have power to will, because, before long, I should certainly will to will it. For in this the power of willing is the power of doing, and yet I could not do it. And so my body lent a ready obedience to the slightest desire of the soul, moving its limbs in instant compliance, while my soul could not aid itself in carrying out its great resolve, which needed but resolve to accomplish it.

WHY THE MIND IS NOT OBEYED WHEN IT COMMANDS ITSELF

Now whence and why is this strange anomaly? Let Thy mercy shine as the light; and suffer me to ask, if perchance I may find an answer amid the dark places of human chastisement, and the midnight of the contrition of the sons of Adam. Whence is this anomaly and why? Mind commands body, and there is instant obedience; mind commands mind, and there is rebellion. Mind commands the hand to move, and so facile is the process that you can hardly distinguish the order from its fulfilment; now the mind is mind and the hand is body. Mind commands mind to will, and, though it is one, it will not hear. Whence and why is this anomaly? I say it commands to will; and it would not command unless it did will, and yet its command is inoperative.

But it does not will wholly, and therefore it does not command wholly. For it commands, in so far as it wills, and its command is not executed, in so far as it does not will. For the will commands that there should be a will, and not another will but itself. Certainly it is not the full will that commands, hence it is not the very thing that it commands. For if it were the full will, it would not even command itself to be, because it would be already. And so this "will and will not" is no anomaly, but a sickness of the mind, which is weighed down by evil habit, and cannot rise wholly when uplifted by truth. And so there are two wills, because one of them is not whole, and one of them possesses what the other lacks.

AGAINST THE MANICHEANS, WHO, BECAUSE THERE ARE TWO CONTRARY WILLS, AFFIRM THE EXISTENCE OF TWO CONTRARY NATURES

Let them perish from Thy presence, O God, yea, and they do perish, those vain talkers and seducers of the soul, who, because they have observed that in the act of deliberation there are two wills, maintain that there are two minds of differing natures, the one good and the other bad. They themselves are bad, while they hold these bad ideas, yet will they become good, if they see the truth and assent unto the truth, that Thy Apostle may say to them, "Ye were sometimes darkness, but now are ye light in the Lord." For these Manichees, wishing to be light not in the Lord but in themselves, imagining the essence of the soul to be the essence of God, have become thicker darkness than they were, for in their dread arrogance they have gone farther away from Thee, from Thee, the true Light which lighteth every man that cometh into the world. Mark what you say, and blush for shame. Draw near unto Him and be lightened, and your faces shall not be ashamed. Who was it that willed, who was it that could not will, when I was deliberating whether I should not at once serve the Lord my God, as I had long purposed to do? Was it not I, I myself? I could not fully will, I could not fully will not. And so I was at war with myself, and dragged asunder by myself. And the strife was against my will, yet it showed not the presence of a second mind, but the punishment of the one I had. Therefore it was no more I that wrought it, but sin that dwelt in me, the punishment of a sin that was more voluntary, because I was a son of Adam. For, if there are as many opposing natures as opposing wills, there will be not two but many more.

If a man deliberates whether he shall go to their conventicle or to the theatre they cry, "See, he has two natures; the good one draws him to us, the evil drags him back. For how else shall we account for this halting between conflicting wills?" But I say that both wills are bad, that which draws him to them, not less than that which drags him back to the theatre. They naturally think it a good will which pulls in their direction. But suppose one of our people is tossed about between two wills, to go to the theatre or to go to our church—will they not be puzzled what to say? Either they must reluctantly confess that the will which carries a man to our church is as good as that which carries their own professors and adherents to theirs, or they must allow that two evil natures and two evil minds are fighting in one man, and in this case their favourite doctrine that one is good and the other evil falls to the ground, or they must be converted to the truth, and cease to deny that, when a man deliberates, one soul is agitated by opposing wills. Let them then no longer maintain that, when two wills are contending in one man, two antagonistic minds, one good and one evil, are struggling over two antagonistic substances, created by two antagonistic principles.

For Thou, O God of truth, dost reprove and confute and convict them, for both wills may be bad, as when a man deliberates whether he shall murder by poison or by knife; whether he shall seize upon this field or the other, supposing that he cannot get both; whether he shall purchase pleasure by wantonness, or keep his money through covetousness; whether he shall go to the theatre or the circus, if there are shows at both on the same day; and there may be a third course open to him, for there may be a chance of robbing a house, and even a fourth, for there may be an opportunity of committing adultery as well.

Suppose that all these objects present themselves at the same time, and are all equally desired, yet cannot all be secured together, in this case they rend the mind with four conflicting wills, or even more, if there are more objects of desire. Yet they would not say that all these are different substances. The case is the same with good wills. For I ask them whether it is good to find sober delight in reading the Apostle, or in a psalm, or in discoursing upon the Gospel. They will say that each is good. What then if all are equally delightful, and all at the same time? Are not different wills distracting the heart, when we consider which we shall prefer? All are good, but they are in conflict, till one is chosen, and the will is no longer divided between many objects but poured in its full strength upon that one. So also, when eternity attracts us from above and the pleasure of earthly goods pulls us down from below, the soul does not will either the one or the other with all its force, but it is the same soul; and the reason why it is so vexed and torn is that truth forces it to love the better, while custom will not suffer it to cast away the worse.

THE FLESH WRESTLED WITH THE SPIRIT IN AUGUSTINE

Thus was I sick and tormented, reproaching myself more bitterly than ever, rolling and writhing in my chain till it should be wholly broken, for at present, though all but snapped, it still held me fast. And Thou, O Lord, wast urgent in my inmost heart, plying with austere mercy the scourges of fear and shame, lest I should fail once more, and the remnant of my worn and slender fetter, instead of breaking, should grow strong again, and bind me harder than ever. For I kept saying within myself, "O let it be now, let it be now;" and as I spoke the word I was on the verge of resolution. I was on the point of action, yet acted not; still I did not slip back into my former indifference, but stood close and took fresh breath. I tried again, and came a little nearer and a little nearer, I could all but touch and reach the goal, yet I did not quite reach or touch it, because I still shrank from dying unto death and living unto life, and the worse, which was ingrained, was stronger in me than the better, which was untrained. And the moment, which was to make me different, affrighted me more the nearer it drew, but it no longer repelled or daunted, it only chilled me.

Trifles of trifles and vanities of vanities, my old mistresses, held me back; they caught hold of the garment of my flesh and whispered in my ear, "Can you let us go? and from that instant we shall see you no more for ever; and from that instant this and that will be forbidden you for ever." What did they mean, O my God, what did they mean by "this and that"? O let Thy mercy guard the soul of Thy servant from the vileness, the shame that they meant! As I heard them, they seemed to have shrunk to half their former size. No longer did they meet me face to face with open contradiction, but muttered behind my back, and, when I moved away, plucked stealthily at my coat to make me look back. Yet, such was my indecision, that they prevented me from breaking loose, and shaking myself free, and running after the voice that called me away; for strong habit supported them, asking me, "Do you think you can live without them?"

But the voice of Habit had lost its persuasion. For in that quarter to which I had set my face and was fain to fly, there dawned upon me the chaste dignity of Continence, calm and cheerful but not wanton, modestly alluring me to come and doubt not, holding out to welcome and embrace me her pious hands full of good examples. There might I see boys and girls, a goodly array of youth and of every age, grave widows and aged virgins, and in every one of them all was Continence herself, not barren but a fruitful mother of children, of joys born of Thee, her husband, O Lord. And she smiled upon me with a challenging smile, as if she would say, "Canst not thou do what these have done? Was it their power, was it not that of the Lord their God, that gave them strength? The Lord their God gave me unto them. Thou standest on thyself, and therefore standest not. Cast thyself on Him; fear not; He will not flinch, and thou wilt not fall. Cast thyself boldly upon Him; He will sustain thee, and heal thee." And I blushed, for still I heard the whispers of the daughters of vanity, and still I hung in the wind. And again she seemed to say, "Stop thine ears against thy unclean members upon earth, that they may be mortified. They tell thee of delights, but not according to the law of the Lord thy God." Such was the debate that raged in my heart, myself battling against myself. Alypius kept close to my side and waited in silence to see the issue of my strange agitation.

HOW BY A VOICE AND BY THE WORDS OF THE APOSTLE HE WAS WHOLLY CONVERTED

Now, when deep reflection brought forth from its secret stores the whole cloud of my misery, and piled it up in the sight of my heart, there rose a whirlwind, carrying with it a violent burst of tears. And hereupon I rose and left Alypius, till my weeping and crying should be spent. For solitude seemed fitter for tears. So I went farther off, till I could feel that even his presence was no restraint upon me. Thus it was with me, and he guessed my feelings. I suppose I had said something before I started up; and he noticed that my voice was fraught with tears. So he remained upon the bench lost in wonder. I flung myself down under a figtree, and gave my tears free course, and the floods of mine eyes broke forth, an acceptable sacrifice in Thy sight. And I cried unto Thee incessantly, not in these words, but to this purpose, "And Thou, O Lord, how long? How long, O Lord; wilt Thou

be angry for ever? O remember not our iniquities of old times." For I felt that I was held fast by them, and I went on wailing, "How long, how long? tomorrow and tomorrow? Why not now? Why not this hour make an end of my vileness?"

Thus I spoke, weeping in bitter contrition of heart, when, lo, I heard a voice from the neighbouring house. It seemed as if some boy or girl, I knew not which, was repeating in a kind of chant the words, "Take and read, take and read." Immediately, with changed countenance, I began to think intently whether there was any kind of game in which children sang those words; but I could not recollect that I had ever heard them. I stemmed the rush of tears, and rose to my feet; for I could not think but that it was a divine command to open the Bible, and read the first passage I lighted upon. For I had heard that Antony had happened to enter a church at the moment when this verse of the Gospel was being read, "Go, sell all that thou hast and give to the poor, and thou shalt have treasure in heaven; and come and follow Me," that he had taken these words home to himself, and by this oracle been converted to Thee on the spot.

I ran back then to the place where Alypius was sitting; for, when I quitted him I had left the volume of the Apostle lying there. I caught it up, opened it, and read in silence the passage on which my eyes first fell, "Not in rioting and drunkenness, not in chambering and wantonness, not in strife and envying: but put ye on the Lord Jesus Christ, and make not provision for the flesh to fulfil the lusts thereof." No further would I read, nor was it necessary. As I reached the end of the sentence, the light of peace seemed to be shed upon my heart, and every shadow of doubt melted away. I put my finger, or some other mark, between the leaves, closed the volume, and with calm countenance told Alypius. And then he revealed to me his own feelings, which were unknown to me. He asked to see what I had read. I shewed him the text, and he read a little further than I had done, for I knew not what followed. What followed was this: "Him that is weak in the faith receive." This he explained to me as applying to himself. These words of warning gave him strength, and with good purpose and resolve, following the bent of his moral character, which had always been much better than mine, without any painful hesitation, he cast in his lot with me. Immediately we went in to my mother, and to her great joy told her what had happened. But, when we explained to her how it had come to pass, she was filled with exultation and triumph, and blessed Thee, who art able to do above that we ask or think. For she saw that Thou hadst granted her far more than she had ever asked for me in all her tearful lamentations. For so completely didst Thou convert me to Thyself that I desired neither wife nor any hope of this world, but set my feet on the rule of faith, as she had seen me in her vision so many years ago. So Thou didst turn her mourning into joy, joy fuller by far than she had ventured to pray for, dearer and purer by far than that which she had hoped to find in the children of my flesh.

Augustine wrote The City of God between 413 and 426 in order to explain the tragic and incomprehensible capture of Rome by Alaric in 410. Augustine answered those who charged that the gods sent Alaric to punish the Romans for deserting the old religious worship and accepting Christianity. He placed the destruction of Rome into a cosmic plan of history designed by God. Drawing on Paul and Platonic thought, Augustine developed a theory of history in which two societies—good and evil, light and dark, the other world and this world—struggled for supremacy. In reading the selections note (1) Augustine's purpose in writing the work, (2) the nature of the two cities, (3) the significance of original sin, (4) the need of God's grace for salvation, (5) the comparison of earthly peace with eternal peace, (6) the relations between the two cities, (7) Augustine's vision of the City of God, and (8) his allegorical interpretation of the Bible.

From: *THE CITY OF GOD*

PREFACE, EXPLAINING HIS DESIGN IN UNDERTAKING THIS WORK

The glorious city of God is my theme in this work, which you, my dearest son Marcellinus, suggested, and which is due to you by my promise. I have undertaken its defence against those who prefer their own gods to the Founder of this city,—a city surpassingly glorious, whether we view it as it still lives by faith in this fleeting course of time, and sojourns as a stranger in the midst of the ungodly, or as it shall dwell in the fixed stability of its eternal seat, which it now with patience waits for, expecting until "righteousness shall return unto judgment," and it obtain, by virtue of its excellence, final victory and perfect peace. A great work this, and an arduous; but God is my helper. . . .

WHAT SUBJECTS ARE TO BE HANDLED IN THE FOLLOWING DISCOURSE

But I have still some things to say in confutation of those who refer the disasters of the Roman republic to our religion, because it prohibits the offering of sacrifices to the gods.

As translated by Marcus Dods in Philip Schaff, ed., *Select Library of the Nicene and Post-Nicene Fathers*, Charles Scribner's Sons, New York, 1899, II, 1; 21–22; 82; 93; 205; 245; 249; 262; 282–283; 401; 406–407; 412–413; 509–511. Courtesy of Charles Scribner's Sons.

For this end I must recount all, or as many as may seem sufficient, of the disasters which befell that city and its subject provinces, before these sacrifices were prohibited; for all these disasters they would doubtless have attributed to us, if at that time our religion had shed its light upon them, and had prohibited their sacrifices. I must then go on to show what social well-being the true God, in whose hand are all kingdoms, vouchsafed to grant to them that their empire might increase. I must show why He did so, and how their false gods, instead of at all aiding them, greatly injured them by guile and deceit. And, lastly, I must meet those who, when on this point convinced and confuted by irrefragable proofs, endeavor to maintain that they worship the gods, not hoping for the present advantages of this life, but for those which are to be enjoyed after death. And this, if I am not mistaken, will be the most difficult part of my task, and will be worthy of the loftiest argument; for we must then enter the lists with the philosophers, not the mere common herd of philosophers, but the most renowned, who in many points agree with ourselves, as regarding the immortality of the soul, and that the true God created the world, and by His providence rules all He has created. But as they differ from us on other points, we must not shrink from the task of exposing their errors, that, having refuted the gainsaying of the wicked with such ability as God may vouchsafe, we may assert the city of God, and true piety, and the worship of God, to which alone the promise of true and everlasting felicity is attached. Here, then, let us conclude, that we may enter on these subjects in a fresh book. . . .

THAT THE TIMES OF ALL KINGS AND KINGDOMS ARE ORDAINED BY THE JUDGMENT AND POWER OF THE TRUE GOD

Therefore that God, the author and giver of felicity, because He alone is the true God, Himself gives earthly kingdoms both to good and bad. Neither does He do this rashly, and, as it were, fortuitously,—because He is God, not fortune,—but according to the order of things and times, which is hidden from us, but thoroughly known to Himself; which same order of times, however, He does not serve as subject to it, but Himself rules as lord and appoints as governor. Felicity He gives only to the good. Whether a man be a subject or a king makes no difference; he may equally either possess or not possess it. And it shall be full in that life where kings and subjects exist no longer. And therefore earthly kingdoms are given by Him both to the good and the bad; lest His worshippers, still under the conduct of a very weak mind, should covet these gifts from Him as some great things. And this is the mystery of the Old Testament, in which the New was hidden, that there even earthly gifts are promised: those who were spiritual, understanding even then, although not yet openly declaring, both the eternity which was symbolized by these earthly things, and in what gifts of God true felicity could be found. . . .

CONCERNING THE UNIVERSAL PROVIDENCE OF GOD IN THE LAWS OF WHICH ALL THINGS ARE COMPREHENDED

Therefore God supreme and true, with His Word and Holy Spirit (which three are one), one God omnipotent, creator and maker of every soul and of every body; by whose gift all are happy who are happy through verity and not through vanity; who made man a rational animal consisting of soul and body, who, when he sinned, neither permitted him to go unpunished, nor left him without mercy; who has given to the good and to the evil, being in common with stones, vegetable life, in common with trees, sensuous life in common with brutes, intellectual life in common with angels alone; from whom is every mode, every species, every order; from whom are measure, number, weight; from whom is everything which has an existence in nature, of whatever kind it be, and of whatever value; from whom are the seeds of forms and the forms of seeds, and the motion of seeds and of forms; who gave also to flesh its origin, beauty, health, reproductive fecundity, disposition of members, and the salutary concord of its parts; who also to the irrational soul has given memory, sense, appetite, but to the rational soul, in addition to these, has given intelligence and will; who has not left, not to speak of heaven and earth, angels and men, but not even the entrails of the smallest and most contemptible animal, or the feather of a bird, or the little flower of a plant, or the leaf of a tree, without an harmony, and, as it were, a mutual peace among all its parts;—that God can never be believed to have left the kingdoms of men, their dominations and servitudes, outside of the laws of His providence. . . .

OF THIS PART OF THE WORK, WHEREIN WE BEGIN TO EXPLAIN THE ORIGIN AND END OF THE TWO CITIES

The city of God we speak of is the same to which testimony is borne by that Scripture, which excels all the writings of all nations by its divine authority, and has brought under its influence all kinds of minds, and this not by a casual intellectual movement, but obviously by an express providential arrangement. For there it is written, "Glorious things are spoken of thee, O city of God." And in another psalm we read, "Great is the Lord, and greatly to be praised in the city of our God, in the mountain of His holiness, increasing the joy of the whole earth." And, a little after, in the same psalm, "As we have heard, so have we seen in the city of the Lord of hosts, in the city of our God. God has established it for ever." And in another, "There is a river the streams whereof shall make glad the city of our God, the holy place of the tabernacles of the Most High. God is in the midst of her, she shall not be moved." From these and similar testimonies, all of which it were tedious to cite, we have learned that there is a city of God, and its Founder has inspired us with a love which makes us covet its citizenship. To this Founder of the holy city the citizens of the earthly city prefer their own gods, not knowing that He is the God of gods, not of false, i.e., of impious and proud gods, who, being deprived of His unchangeable and freely communicated light, and so reduced to a kind of poverty-stricken power, eagerly grasp at their own private privileges, and seek divine honors from their deluded subjects; but of the pious and holy gods, who are better pleased to submit themselves to one, than to subject many to themselves, and who would rather worship God than be worshipped as God. But to the enemies of this city we have replied in the ten preceding books, according to our ability and the help afforded by our Lord and King. Now, recognizing what is expected of me, and not unmindful of my promise, and relying, too, on the same succor, I will endeavor to treat of the origin, and progress, and deserved destinies of the two cities (the earthly and the heavenly, to wit), which, as we said, are in this present world commingled, and as it were entangled together. And, first, I will explain how the foundations of these two cities were originally laid, in the difference that arose among the angels. . . .

OF THE FALL OF THE FIRST MAN, THROUGH WHICH MORTALITY HAS BEEN CONTRACTED

Having disposed of the very difficult questions concerning the origin of our world and the beginning of the human race, the natural order requires that we now discuss the fall of the first man (we may say of the first men), and of the origin and propagation of human death. For God had not made man like the angels, in such a condition that, even though they had sinned, they could none the more die. He had so made them, that if they discharged the obligations of obedience, an angelic immortality and a blessed eternity might ensue, without the intervention of death; but if they disobeyed, death should be visited on them with just sentence—which, too, has been spoken to in the preceding book. . . .

OF THE LIFE OF MORTALS, WHICH IS RATHER TO BE CALLED DEATH THAN LIFE

For no sooner do we begin to live in this dying body, than we begin to move ceaselessly towards death. For in the whole course of this life (if life we must call it) its mutability tends towards death. Certainly there is no one who is not nearer it this year than last year, and tomorrow than today, and today than yesterday, and a short while hence than now, and now than a short while ago. For whatever time we live is deducted from our whole term of life, and that which remains is daily becoming less and less; so that our whole life is nothing but a race towards death, in which no one is allowed to stand still for a little space, or to go somewhat more slowly, but all are driven forwards with an impartial movement, and with equal rapidity. For he whose life is short spends a day no more swiftly than he whose life is longer. But while the equal moments are impartially snatched from both, the one has a nearer and the other a more remote goal to reach with this their equal speed. It is one thing to make a longer journey, and another to walk more slowly. He, therefore, who spends longer time on his way to death does not proceed at a more leisurely pace, but goes over more ground. . . .

THAT THE DISOBEDIENCE OF THE FIRST MAN WOULD HAVE PLUNGED ALL MEN INTO THE ENDLESS MISERY OF THE SECOND DEATH, HAD NOT THE GRACE OF GOD RESCUED MANY

We have already stated in the preceding books that God, desiring not only that the human race might be able by their similarity of nature to associate with one another, but also that they might be bound together in harmony and peace by the ties of relationship, was pleased to derive all men from one individual, and created man with such a nature that the members of the race should not have died, had not the two first (of whom the one was created out of nothing, and the other out of him) merited this by their disobedience; for by them so great a sin was committed, that by it the human nature was altered for the worse, and was transmitted also to their posterity, liable to sin and subject to death. And the kingdom of death so reigned over men, that the deserved penalty of sin would have hurled all headlong even into the second death, of which there is no end, had not the undeserved grace of God saved some therefrom. And thus it has come to pass, that though there are very many and great nations all over the earth, whose rites and customs, speech, arms, and dress, are distinguished by marked differences, yet there are no more than two kinds of human society, which we may justly call two cities, according to the language of our Scriptures. The one consists of those who wish to live after the flesh, the other of those who wish to live after the spirit; and when they severally achieve what they wish, they live in peace, each after their kind. . . .

OF THE NATURE OF THE TWO CITIES, THE EARTHLY AND THE HEAVENLY

Accordingly, two cities have been formed by two loves: the earthly by the love of self, even to the contempt of God; the heavenly by the love of God, even to the contempt of self. The former, in a word, glories in itself, the latter in the Lord. For the one seeks glory from men; but the greatest glory of the other is God, the witness of conscience. The one lifts up its head in its own glory; the other says to its God, "Thou art my glory, and the lifter up of mine head." In the one, the princes and the nations it subdues are ruled by the love of ruling; in the other, the princes and the subjects serve one another in love, the latter obeying, while the former take thought for all. The one delights in its own strength, represented in the persons of its rulers; the other says to its God, "I will love Thee, O Lord, my strength." And therefore the wise men of the one city, living according to man, have sought for profit to their own bodies or souls, or both, and those who have known God "glorified Him not as God, neither were thankful, but became vain in their imaginations, and their foolish heart was darkened; professing themselves to be wise,"— that is, glorying in their own wisdom, and being possessed by pride,—"they became fools, and changed the glory of the incorruptible God into an image made like to corruptible man, and to birds, and four-footed beasts, and creeping things." For they were either leaders or followers of the people in adoring images, "and worshipped and served the creature more than the Creator, who is blessed for ever." But in the other city there is no human wisdom, but only godliness, which offers due worship to the true God, and looks for its reward in the society of the saints, of holy angels as well as holy men, "that God may be all in all.". . .

WHAT THE CHRISTIANS BELIEVE REGARDING THE SUPREME GOOD AND EVIL, IN OPPOSITION TO THE PHILOSOPHERS, WHO HAVE MAINTAINED THAT THE SUPREME GOOD IS IN THEMSELVES

If, then, we be asked what the city of God has to say upon these points, and, in the first place, what its opinion regarding the supreme good and evil is, it will reply that life eternal is the supreme good, death eternal the supreme evil, and that to obtain the one and escape the other we must live rightly. And thus it is written, "The just lives by faith," for we do not as yet see our good, and must therefore live by faith; neither have we in ourselves power to live rightly, but can do so only if He who has given us faith to believe in His help do help us when we believe and pray. As for those who have supposed that the sovereign good and evil are to be found in this life, and have placed it either in the soul or the body, or in both, or to speak more explicitly, either in pleasure or in virtue, or in both; in repose or in virtue, or in both; in pleasure and repose, or in virtue, or in all combined; in the primary objects of nature, or in virtue, or in both,— all these have, with a marvelous shallowness, sought to find their blessedness in this life and in themselves. Contempt has been poured upon such ideas by the Truth, saying by the prophet, "The Lord knoweth the thoughts of men" (or, as the Apostle Paul cites the passage, "The Lord knoweth the thoughts of the *wise*") "that they are vain.". . .

THE REWARD PREPARED FOR THE SAINTS AFTER THEY HAVE ENDURED THE TRIAL OF THIS LIFE

But not even the saints and faithful worshippers of the one true and most high God are safe from the manifold temptations and deceits of the demons. For in this abode of weakness, and in these wicked days, this state of anxiety has also its use, stimulating us to seek with keener longing for that security where peace is complete and unassailable. There we shall enjoy the gifts of nature, that is to say, all that God the Creator of all natures has bestowed upon ours,—gifts not only good, but eternal,— not only of the spirit, healed now by wisdom, but also of the body renewed by the resurrection. There the virtues shall no longer be struggling against any vice or evil, but shall enjoy the reward of victory, the eternal peace which no adversary shall disturb. This is the final blessedness, this the ultimate consummation, the unending end. Here, indeed, we are said to be blessed when we have such peace as can be enjoyed in a good life; but such blessedness is mere misery, compared to that final felicity. When we mortals possess such peace as this mortal life can afford, virtue, if we are living rightly, makes a right use of the advantages of this peaceful condition; and when we have it not, virtue makes a good use even of the evils a man suffers. But this is true virtue, when it refers all the advantages it makes a good use of, and all that it does in making good use of good and evil things, and itself also, to that end in which we shall enjoy the best and greatest peace possible. . . .

WHAT PRODUCES PEACE, AND WHAT DISCORD, BETWEEN THE HEAVENLY AND EARTHLY CITIES

But the families which do not live by faith seek their peace in the earthly advantages of this life; while the families which live by faith look for those eternal blessings which are promised, and use as pilgrims such advantages of time and of earth as do not fascinate and divert them from God, but rather aid them to endure with greater ease, and to keep down the number of those burdens of the corruptible body which weigh upon the soul. Thus the things necessary for this mortal life are used by both kinds of men and families alike, but each has its own peculiar and widely different aim in using them. The earthly city, which does not live by faith, seeks an earthly peace, and the end it proposes, in the well-ordered concord of civic obedience and rule, is the combination of men's wills to attain the things which are helpful to this life. The heavenly city, or rather the part of it which sojourns on earth and lives by faith, makes use of this peace only because it must, until this mortal condition which necessitates it shall pass away. Consequently, so long as it lives like a captive and a stranger in the earthly city, though it has already received the promise of redemption, and the gift of the Spirit as the earnest of it, it makes no scruple to obey the laws of the earthly city, whereby the things necessary for the maintenance of this mortal life are administered; and thus, as this life is common to both cities, so there is a harmony between them in regard to what belongs to it. But, as the earthly city has had some philosophers whose doctrine is condemned by the divine teaching, and who, being deceived either by their own conjectures or by demons, supposed that many gods must be invited to take an interest in human affairs, and assigned to each a separate function and a separate department,—to one the body, to another the soul; and in the body itself, to one the head, to another the neck, and each of the other members to one of the gods; and in like manner, in the soul, to one god the natural capacity was assigned, to another education, to another anger, to another lust; and so the various affairs of life were assigned,—cattle to one, corn to another, wine to another, oil to another, the woods to another, money to another, navigation to another, wars and victories to another, marriages to another, births and fecundity to another, and other things to other gods: and as the celestial city, on the other hand, knew that one God only was to be worshipped, and that to Him alone was due that service which . . . can be given only to a god, it has come to pass that the two cities could not have common laws of religion, and that the heavenly city has been compelled in this matter to dissent, and to become obnoxious to those who think differently, and to stand the brunt of their anger and hatred and persecutions, except in so far as the minds of their enemies have been alarmed by the multitude of the Christians and quelled by the manifest protection of God accorded to them. This heavenly city, then, while it sojourns on earth, calls citizens out of all nations, and gathers together a society of pilgrims of all languages, not scrupling about diversities in the manners, laws, and institu-

tions whereby earthly peace is secured and maintained, but recognizing that, however various these are, they all tend to one and the same end of earthly peace. It therefore is so far from rescinding and abolishing these diversities, that it even preserves and adopts them, so long only as no hindrance to the worship of the one supreme and true God is thus introduced. Even the heavenly city, therefore, while in its state of pilgrimage, avails itself of the peace of earth, and, so far as it can without injuring faith and godliness, desires and maintains a common agreement among men regarding the acquisition of the necessaries of life, and makes this earthly peace bear upon the peace of heaven; for this alone can be truly called and esteemed the peace of the reasonable creatures, consisting as it does in the perfectly ordered and harmonious enjoyment of God and of one another in God. When we shall have reached that peace, this mortal life shall give place to one that is eternal, and our body shall be no more this animal body which by its corruption weighs down the soul, but a spiritual body feeling no want, and in all its members subjected to the will. In its pilgrim state the heavenly city possesses this peace by faith; and by this faith it lives righteously when it refers to the attainment of that peace every good action towards God and man; for the life of the city is a social life. . . .

OF THE ETERNAL FELICITY OF THE CITY OF GOD, AND OF THE PERPETUAL SABBATH

How great shall be that felicity, which shall be tainted with no evil, which shall lack no good, and which shall afford leisure for the praises of God, who shall be all in all! For I know not what other employment there can be where no lassitude shall slacken activity, nor any want stimulate to labor. I am admonished also by the sacred song, in which I read or hear the words, "Blessed are they that dwell in Thy house, O Lord; they will be still praising Thee." All the members and organs of the incorruptible body, which now we see to be suited to various necessary uses, shall contribute to the praises of God; for in that life necessity shall have no place, but full, certain, secure, everlasting felicity. For all those parts of the bodily harmony, which are distributed through the whole body, within and without, and of which I have just been saying that they at present elude our observation, shall then be discerned; and, along with the other great and marvellous discoveries which shall then kindle rational minds in praise of the great Artificer, there shall be the enjoyment of a beauty which appeals to the reason. What power of movement such bodies shall possess, I have not the audacity rashly to define, as I have not the ability to conceive. Nevertheless, I will say that in any case, both in motion and at rest, they shall be, as in their appearance, seemly; for into that state nothing which is unseemly shall be admitted. One thing is certain, the body shall forthwith be wherever the spirit wills, and the spirit shall will nothing which is unbecoming either to the spirit or to the body. True honor shall be there, for it shall be denied to none who is worthy, nor yielded to any unworthy; neither shall any unworthy person so much as sue for it, for none but the worthy shall be there. True peace shall be there, where no one shall suffer opposition either from himself or any other. God Himself, who is the Author of virtue, shall there be its reward; for, as there is nothing greater or better, He has promised Himself. What else was meant by His word through the prophet, "I will be your God, and ye shall be my people," than, I shall be their satisfaction, I shall be all that men honorably desire,—life, and health, and nourishment, and plenty, and glory, and honor, and peace, and all good things? This, too, is the right interpretation of the saying of the apostle, "That God may be all in all." He shall be the end of our desires who shall be seen without end, loved without cloy, praised without weariness. This outgoing of affection, this employment, shall certainly be, like eternal life itself, common to all.

But who can conceive, not to say describe, what degrees of honor and glory shall be awarded to the various degrees of merit? Yet it cannot be doubted that there shall be degrees. And in that blessed city there shall be this great blessing, that no inferior shall envy any superior, as now the archangels are not envied by the angels, because no one will wish to be what he has not received, though bound in strictest concord with him who has received; as in the body the finger does not seek to be the eye, though both members are harmoniously included in the complete structure of the body. And thus, along with his gift, greater or less, each shall receive this further gift of contentment to desire no more than he has.

Neither are we to suppose that because sin shall have no power to delight them, free will must be withdrawn. It will, on the contrary, be all the more truly free, because set free from delight in sinning to take unfailing delight in not sinning. For the first freedom of will which man received when he was created upright consisted in an ability not to sin, but also in an ability to sin; whereas this last freedom of will shall be superior, inasmuch as it shall not be able to sin. This, indeed, shall not be a natural ability, but the gift of God. For it is one thing to be God, another thing to be a partaker of God. God by nature cannot sin, but the partaker of God receives this inability from God. And in this divine gift there was to be observed this gradation, that man should first receive a free will by which he was able not to sin, and at last a free will by which he was not able to sin,—the former being adapted to the acquiring of merit, the latter to the enjoying of the reward. But the nature thus constituted, having sinned when it had the ability to do so, it is by a more abundant grace that it is delivered so as to reach that freedom in which it cannot sin. For as the first immortality which Adam lost by sinning consisted in his being able not to die, while the last shall consist in his not being able to die; so the first free will consisted in his being able not to sin, the last in his not being able to sin. And thus piety and justice shall be as indefeasible as happiness. For certainly by sinning we lost both piety and happiness; but when we lost happiness, we did not lose the love of it. Are we to say that God Himself is not free because He cannot sin? In that city, then, there shall be free will, one in all the citizens, and indivisible in each, delivered from all ill, filled with all good, enjoying indefeasibly the delights of eternal joys, oblivious of sins, oblivious of sufferings, and yet not so oblivious of its deliverance as to be ungrateful to its Deliverer.

The soul, then, shall have an intellectual remembrance of its past ills; but, so far as regards sensible experience, they shall be quite forgotten. For a skillful physician knows, indeed, professionally almost all diseases; but experimentally he is ignorant of a great number which he himself has never suffered from. As, therefore, there are two ways of knowing evil things,—one by mental insight, the other by sensible experience, for it is one thing to understand all vices by the wisdom of a cultivated mind, another to understand them by the foolishness of an abandoned life,—so also there are two ways of forgetting evils. For a well-instructed and learned man forgets them one way, and he who has experimentally suffered from them forgets them another,—the former by neglecting what he has learned, the latter by escaping what he has suffered. And in this latter way the saints shall forget their past ills, for they shall have so thoroughly escaped them all, that they shall be quite blotted out of their experience. But their intellectual knowledge, which shall be great, shall keep them acquainted not only with their own past woes, but with the eternal sufferings of the lost. For if they were not to know that they had been miserable, how could they, as the Psalmist says, for ever sing the mercies of God? Certainly that city shall have no greater joy than the celebration of the grace of Christ, who redeemed us by His blood. There shall be accomplished the words of the psalm, "Be still, and know that I am God." There shall be the great Sabbath which has no evening, which God celebrated among His first works, as it is written, "And God rested on the seventh day from all His works which He had made. And God blessed the seventh day, and sanctified it; because that in it He had rested from all His work which God began to make." For we shall ourselves be the seventh day, when we shall be filled and replenished with God's blessing and sanctification. There shall we be still, and know that He is God; that He is that which we ourselves aspired to be when we fell away from Him, and listened to the voice of the seducer, "Ye shall be as gods," and so abandoned God, who would have made us as gods, not by deserting Him, but by participating in Him. For without Him what have we accomplished, save to perish in His anger? But when we are restored by Him, and perfected with greater grace, we shall have eternal leisure to see that He is God, for we shall be full of Him when He shall be all in all. For even our good works, when they are understood to be rather His than ours, are imputed to us that we may enjoy this Sabbath rest. For if we attribute them to ourselves, they shall be servile; for it is said of the Sabbath, "Ye shall do no servile work in it." Wherefore also it is said by Ezekiel the prophet, "And I gave them my Sabbaths to be a sign between me and them, that they might know that I am the Lord who sanctify them." This knowledge shall be perfected when we shall be perfectly at rest, and shall perfectly know that He is God.

This Sabbath shall appear still more clearly if we count the ages as days, in accordance with the periods of time defined in Scripture, for that period will be found to be the seventh. The first age, as the first day, extends from Adam to the deluge; the second from the deluge to Abraham, equalling the first, not in length of time, but in the number of generations, there being ten in each. From Abraham to the advent of Christ there are, as the evangelist Matthew calculates, three periods, in each of which are fourteen generations,—one period from Abraham to David, a second from David to the captivity, a third from the captivity to the birth of Christ in the flesh. There are thus five ages in all. The sixth is now passing, and cannot be measured by any number of generations, as it has been said, "It is not for you to know the times, which the Father hath put in His own power." After this period God shall rest as on the seventh day, when He shall give us (who shall be the seventh day) rest in Himself. But there is not now space to treat of these ages; suffice it to say that the seventh shall be our Sabbath, which shall be brought to a close, not by an evening, but by the Lord's day, as an eighth and eternal day, consecrated by the resurrection of Christ, and prefiguring the eternal repose not only of the spirit, but also of the body. There we shall rest and see, see and love, love and praise. This is what shall be in the end without end. For what other end do we propose to ourselves than to attain to the kingdom of which there is no end?

I think I have now, by God's help, discharged my obligation in writing this large work. Let those who think I have said too little, or those who think I have said too much, forgive me; and let those who think I have said just enough join me in giving thanks to God. Amen.

Imperial Edict of the Byzantine Empire

The Byzantine Empire lasted for over a thousand years, and one of the reasons for its vitality, especially during the later centuries, was its relatively efficient form of government. Despotism and bureaucracy played an important role in this political system and government actively intervened in economic and social affairs to maintain a well-balanced economic life. Constantinople, or Byzantium, became the center of industry and commerce and linked the Black Sea ports and cities of Asia Minor with those of the Mediterranean world. The Book of the Prefect, an imperial edict of the ninth or tenth century, regulated the activities of the more important gilds of the Byzantine Empire. It took its name from the Prefect of Constantinople, one of the highest officials of the empire and the person responsible for enforcing the government's paternalistic policies with regard to industry and trade. In reading the passages selected note (1) the rights reserved to the imperial household, (2) the privileges of the merchants and artisans of Constantinople, (3) the regulation of disputes between various crafts, (4) attempts to protect the consumer, and (5) the opportunities offered individual craftsmen and merchants to enter or leave the various gilds.

From: THE BOOK OF THE PREFECT

PREFACE

God, after having created all things that are and given order and harmony to the universe, with his own finger engraved the Law on the tables and published it openly so that men, being well directed thereby, should not shamelessly trample upon one another and the stronger should not do violence to the weaker but that all things should be apportioned with just measure. Therefore it has seemed good for Our Serenity also to lay down the following ordinances based on the statutes in order that the human race may be governed fittingly and no person may injure his fellow.

THE BANKERS

Anyone who wishes to be nominated as a banker must be vouched for by respected and honest men who will guarantee that he will do nothing contrary to the ordinances; to wit, that he will not pare down, or cut, or put false inscriptions on *nomismata* or *miliarisia*, or set one of his own slaves in his place at his bank if he should happen to be occupied with some

As translated by A. E. R. Boak in "Notes and Documents: The Book of the Prefect," *Journal of Economic and Business History*, I (August, 1929), 600–619. Courtesy of Professor N. S. B. Gras.

temporary duties, so that no trickery may thereby enter into the business of the profession. If anyone is caught in such practices, he shall be punished by the amputation of his hand.

The money-changers shall report to the Prefect the forgers who station themselves in the squares and streets in order to prevent them from indulging in illegal practices. If they know of such and fail to report them, they shall suffer the aforementioned punishment. . . .

Each banker shall keep two assistants to sort his coins. He must go surety for these, so that if one of them is detected acting contrary to the ordinances both he and the one who appointed him shall suffer the aforesaid penalties. . . .

The bankers must not give their subordinates account books or coins and station them in the squares and streets in order to receive the profit accruing from their activities. Even on occasions of distribution of largesses or the performance of services for the emperor they shall not go away and abandon their banks. If anyone is caught doing so, he shall be beaten, shorn, and suffer confiscation.

THE SILK-GARMENT MERCHANTS

The silk-garment merchants shall buy silk garments but not any other merchandise except something for their personal needs which they may not sell to others. They shall not give foreigners any of the prohibited articles, such as red or purple silk goods of large size, so that these may not be transported to strange peoples. Whoever violates these regulations shall be flogged and suffer confiscation of goods. . . .

Whoever fails to show to the Prefect goods that are to be exported to foreign peoples so that they may receive his seal, shall suffer punishment.

Whoever is to be enrolled in the craft of the silk-garment merchants shall first be declared by five persons of the same gild in the presence of the Prefect to be worthy to be in this trade. He shall then be entered on the roll, shall open a shop, and engage in trade. He shall also pay to the corporation six *nomismata*. . . .

One who is both a silk-garment merchant and a silk weaver shall be allowed to choose one of these trades, but must give up the other. If he dares to practise both, he shall come under the punishment mentioned above.

Strangers who reside in the inns of the city must be carefully prevented from purchasing either prohibited articles of clothing or those woven in a single piece, except something for personal use and that prepared in the imperial city. Upon their departure they shall declare such articles to the Prefect so that he may know the goods that they have bought. Whoever helps them to conceal such things shall be flogged and suffer confiscation of goods.

Any silk-garment merchant who secretly or openly seeks to raise the rental of another, shall be flogged, shorn, and suffer confiscation of goods.

THE SILK WEAVERS

We forbid any prince or private person to make a purple robe of six or eight widths, but they may make ones of ten or twelve widths, provided they are true purple and of light quality, and are not in the class of those which have to be restricted by the Prefect for the use of the imperial house. They are also prohibited from making the robes with rounded bottoms reserved for the emperor, except those of medium size forming folds on the tunic and of many colors and having at least ten widths. If anyone is caught manufacturing these prohibited garments, his goods shall be confiscated and he shall be made to give up his trade.

Whoever prevents an inspector of seals or looms from entering his workshops, and whoever sells a robe valued at more than ten *nomismata* to foreigners, shall be beaten and shorn. . . .

Whoever sells a slave, a hired worker, or an overseer to persons outside the city or to foreigners, shall have his hand cut off.

The silk weavers shall buy their raw silk from the dealers. If they are caught buying it from strangers, they shall be beaten, shorn, and ousted from the business. . . .

Any weaver who knowingly takes into his service the employee of another, before the employee has done full work for the pay he has received, shall be fined the amount of pay remaining unearned. . . .

If a weaver brings a hired worker into his workshops, he shall not make a contract with him for longer than a month and shall not give him pay for more than thirty days but only so much as he can earn by working a full month. Anyone who advances pay for more than the authorized period shall lose this.

If anyone wishes to set up a workshop, he must be vouched for by five persons if he is a free man, but if he is a slave, by his own master, provided that the latter is a person of means. The sponsors shall assume the same risks as the one whom they nominate. The newly enrolled member shall pay the corporation three *nomismata*.

THE PERFUME DEALERS

Each perfume dealer shall have his own station and not try to overreach his fellows. However, they shall watch one another to prevent any from lowering their prices or selling unreasonably small quantities, or keeping in stock victualers' wares or any other sort of common goods, for an unpleasant odor does not harmonize with a pleasant one. They shall sell pepper, nard, cinnamon, wood of aloes, ambergris, musk, incense, myrrh, balsam, wild beet, balm, assafoetida, thapsia, hyssop, and all other things of use in the trade of perfumers and dyers. They shall place their show tables with the containers in a line extending from the sacred image of Christ our Lord which is by the Chalce up to the Milestone, so that these may send forth a savory aroma befitting the image and make pleasant the porches of the palace. All who are caught disobeying these ordinances shall be scourged, shorn, and banished.

Whenever wares that concern them are imported, either through the Chaldeans and Trapezuntines or from any other localities, the perfumers shall take these from the importers at the current rate for the particular variety. However, they shall not store them up for times of shortage in order to make an unreasonable profit or raise the price beyond what is necessary. The importers shall not remain here for longer than a period of three months, but

shall make their sales speedily and depart home. Whoever contravenes these regulations shall meet the penalty aforesaid. . . .

If a perfume dealer or anyone engaged in another trade is caught cheating a customer who has made a deposit on a sale by subsequently raising the price of an article, he shall be condemned to pay out of his own means the sum deposited by the customer. None of them shall have the right to buy articles weighted by a bar-balance, or victualers' wares, except such as are sold with the double scales. Whoever disobeys these regulations shall suffer the aforesaid penalty.

If a perfume dealer happens to be a victualer also, he may choose either one of these trades but must give up the other.

THE VICTUALERS

The victualers shall open their shops in the squares and streets throughout the whole city so that the necessities of life may easily be found. They shall sell meat, pickled fish, meal, cheese, honey, olive oil, green vegetables of all sorts, butter, solid and liquid pitch, cedar resin, hemp, flax, plaster, pottery vessels, bottles, nails, and all the other things sold by a bar-balance and not by twin scales. They are forbidden to engage in the trades of the perfumers, or soap-makers, or linen merchants, or tavernkeepers, or butchers even in the slightest degree. If anyone is found acting contrary to these regulations, he shall be scourged, shorn, and banished. . . .

If a victualer is caught cheating another in a purchase and raising the price agreed upon, he shall be fined ten *nomismata*. Likewise one who exhibits his wares outside his shop on the Lord's Day or on another Holy Day, shall undergo the same penalty.

The victualers shall keep watch upon the imports that pertain to them, so that, if anyone not enrolled in their gild stores these up against a time of scarcity, he may be denounced to the Prefect and called to account by him.

The victualers shall sell their goods in small quantities at a profit of two *miliarisia* on the *nomisma*. If a calculation of their authorized gains shows that they are making a large profit, they shall be scourged, shorn, and forced to give up this trade.

THE TAVERNKEEPERS

The chiefs of the tavernkeepers shall inform the Prefect whenever wine is imported so that he may decide how it shall be sold, it being the duty of the assessor to compel the tavernkeepers to make the measures and jars in which they sell the wine conform to the conditions of purchase. . . .

Tavernkeepers are forbidden to open their shops and sell wine or food before the second hour of the day (7 A.M.) on the days of high festivals or on Sundays. At night they shall close their shops and put out the fires when the second hour arrives (7 P.M.), in order to prevent the habitual daytime patrons, if they have the opportunity of returning at night, from becoming intoxicated and shamelessly engaging in fights, deeds of violence, and brawls.

If any tavernkeepers who sell wine are caught in possession of vessels not conforming to the aforesaid standard, or ones not marked with the stamp of the Prefect, they shall be flogged, shorn, and expelled from the gild.

Mohammed

The Sacred Book of the Moslems contains the words, which, according to tradition, came to the prophet Mohammed, when he was in a state of trance. These periods, when a physical change was apparent in him, began when he was forty years old, and continued for twenty-three years, until shortly before his death in 632. In all there are 114 chapters in the Koran, each the result of a revelation to the prophet. This book is the Bible of Islam, and it serves as a guide not only for religion but for social and civil matters as well. The first selection included here is entitled "The Opening" (Chapter 1) and is the most essential prayer of Islam. It is recited at all public and private worship. The second is from "The Children of Israel" (Chapter 17) and reveals some of the ethical and social teachings of Islam. The third is entitled "The Event" (Chapter 56) and is concerned with the rewards and punishments to be meted out in the hereafter to the faithful and their opponents. The last is called "Iron" (Chapter 57); it describes the greatness of Allah's creation, the necessity for personal sacrifice in the cause of Islam, and the deviation of Jews and Christians from simple monotheism to priestly institutionalized religion.

From: THE KORAN

THE OPENING

In the name of Allah, the Beneficent, the Merciful.

Praise be to Allah, Lord of the Worlds,
The Beneficent, the Merciful.

Owner of the Day of Judgment,
Thee (alone) we worship; Thee (alone) we ask for help.
Show us the straight path,
The path of those whom Thou hast favoured;

As translated by Marmaduke Pickthall in *The Meaning of the Glorious Koran*, Alfred A. Knopf, New York, 1930, 21; 284–286; 561–569. Courtesy of Alfred A. Knopf, Inc., and George Allen and Unwin, Ltd.

Not (the path) of those who earn Thine anger nor of those who go astray.

THE CHILDREN OF ISRAEL

. . . Set not up with Allah any other god (O man) lest thou sit down reproved, forsaken.

Thy Lord hath decreed, that ye worship none save Him, and (that ye show) kindness to parents. If one of them or both of them attain old age with thee, say not "Fie" unto them nor repulse them, but speak unto them a gracious word.

And lower unto them the wing of submission through mercy, and say: My Lord! Have mercy on them both as they did care for me when I was little.

Your Lord is best aware of what is in your minds. If ye are righteous, then lo! He was ever Forgiving unto those who turn (unto Him).

Give the kinsman his due, and the needy, and the wayfarer, and squander not (thy wealth) in wantonness.

Lo! the squanderers were ever brothers of the devils, and the devil was ever an ingrate to his Lord.

But if thou turn away from them, seeking mercy from thy Lord, for which thou hopest, then speak unto them a reasonable word.

And let not thy hand be chained to thy neck nor open it with a complete opening, lest thou sit down rebuked, denuded.

Lo! thy Lord enlargeth the provision for whom He will, and straiteneth (it for whom He will). Lo, He was ever Knower, Seer of His slaves.

Slay not your children, fearing a fall to poverty, We shall provide for them and for you. Lo! the slaying of them is great sin.

And come not near unto adultery. Lo! it is an abomination and an evil way.

And slay not the life which Allah hath forbidden save with right. Whoso is slain wrongfully, We have given power unto his heir, but let him not commit excess in slaying. Lo! he will be helped.

Come not near the wealth of the orphan save with that which is better till he come to strength; and keep the covenant. Lo! of the covenant it will be asked.

Fill the measure when ye measure, and weigh with a right balance; that is meet, and better in the end.

(O man), follow not that whereof thou hast no knowledge. Lo! the hearing and the sight and the heart—of each of these it will be asked.

And walk not in the earth exultant. Lo! thou canst not rend the earth, nor canst thou stretch to the height of the hills.

The evil of all that is hateful in the sight of thy Lord.

This is (part) of that wisdom wherewith thy Lord hath inspired thee (O Muhammad). And set not up with Allah any other god, lest thou be cast into hell, reproved, abandoned.

THE EVENT

In the name of Allah, the Beneficent, the Merciful.

When the event befalleth—
There is no denying that it will befall—
Abasing (some), exalting (others);
When the earth is shaken with a shock
And the hills are ground to powder
So that they become a scattered dust,
And ye will be three kinds:
(First) those on the right hand; what of those on the right hand?
And (then) those on the left hand; what of those on the left hand?
And the foremost in the race, the foremost in the race:
Those are they who will be brought nigh
In gardens of delight;
A multitude of those of old
And a few of those of later time,
On lined couches,
Reclining therein face to face.
There wait on them immortal youths.
With bowls and ewers and a cup from a pure spring.
Wherefrom they get no aching of the head nor any madness,
And fruit that they prefer
And flesh of fowls that they desire.
And (there are) fair ones with wide, lovely eyes,
Like unto hidden pearls,
Reward for what they used to do.
There hear they no vain speaking nor recrimination

(Naught) but the saying: Peace, (and again) Peace.

And those on the right hand; what of those on the right hand?

Among thornless lote-trees.
And clustered plantains,
And spreading shade,
And water gushing,
And fruit in plenty
Neither out of reach nor yet forbidden,
And raised couches;
Lo! We have created them a (new) creation
And made them virgins,
Lovers, friends,
For those on the right hand;
A multitude of those of old
And a multitude of those of later time.

And those on the left hand: What of those on the left hand?

In scorching wind and scalding water
And shadow of black smoke,
Neither cool nor refreshing.
Lo! heretofore they were effete with luxury
And used to persist in the awful sin.
And they used to say: When we are dead and have become dust and bones, shall we then, forsooth, be raised again,
And also our forefathers?
Say (unto them, O Muhammad): Lo! those of old and those of later time
Will all be brought together to the tryst of an appointed day.
Then lo! ye, the erring, the deniers,
Ye verily will eat of a tree called Zaqqûm
And will fill your bellies therewith;
And thereon ye will drink of boiling water,
Drinking even as the camel drinketh.
This will be their welcome on the Day of Judgement.
We created you. Will ye then admit the truth?
Have ye seen that which ye emit?
Do ye create it or are We the Creator?
We mete out death among you, and We are not to be outrun,
That We may transfigure you and make you what ye know not.
And verily ye know the first creation. Why, then, do ye not reflect?
Have ye seen that which ye cultivate?
Is it ye who foster it, or are We the Fosterer?

If We willed, We verily could make it chaff, then would ye cease not to exclaim:
Lo! we are laden with debt!
Nay but we are deprived!
Have ye observed the water which ye drink?
Is it ye who shed it from the raincloud, or are We the shedder?
If We willed, We verily could make it bitter. Why, then, give ye not thanks?
Have ye observed the fire which ye strike out;
Was it ye who made the tree thereof to grow, or were We the grower?
We, even We, appointed it a memorial and a comfort for the dwellers in the wilderness.
Therefore (O Muhammad), praise the name of thy Lord, the Tremendous.
Nay, I swear by the places of the stars—
And lo! that verily is a tremendous oath, if ye but knew—
That (this) is indeed a noble Qur'ân
In a Book kept hidden
Which none toucheth save the purified,
A revelation from the Lord of the Worlds.
Is it this Statement that ye scorn,
And make denial thereof your livelihood?
Why, then, when (the soul) cometh up to the throat (of the dying)
And ye are at that moment looking
—And We are nearer unto him than ye are, but ye see not—
Why then, if ye are not in bondage (unto Us),
Do ye not force it back, if ye are truthful?
Thus if he is of those brought nigh,
Then breath of life, and plenty, and a Garden of delight.
And if he is of those on the right hand,
The (the greeting) "Peace be unto thee" from those on the right hand.
But if he is of the rejecters, the erring,
Then the welcome will be boiling water
And roasting at hell fire.
Lo! this is certain truth.
Therefore (O Muhammad) praise the name of thy Lord, the Tremendous.

IRON

In the name of Allah, the Beneficent, the Merciful.

All that is in the heavens and the earth glorifieth Allah; and He is the Mighty, the Wise.

His is the Sovereignty of the heavens and the earth; He quickeneth and He giveth death; and He is able to do all things.

He is the First and the Last, and the Outward and the Inward; and He is Knower of all things.

He it is Who created the heavens and the earth in six Days; then He mounted the Throne. He knoweth all that entereth the earth and all that emergeth therefrom and all that cometh down from the sky and all that ascendeth therein; and He is with you wheresoever ye may be. And Allah is Seer of what ye do.

His is the Sovereignty of the heavens and the earth, and unto Allah (all) things are brought back.

He causeth the night to pass into the day, and He causeth the day to pass into the night, and He is Knower of all that is in the breasts.

Believe in Allah and His messenger, and spend of that whereof He hath made you trustees; and such of you as believe and spend (aright), theirs will be a great reward.

What aileth you that ye believe not in Allah, when the messenger calleth you to believe in your Lord, and He hath already made a covenant with you, if ye are believers?

He it is Who sendeth down clear revelations unto His slave, that He may bring you forth from darkness unto light; and lo! for you, Allah is Full of Pity, Merciful.

And what aileth you that ye spend not in the way of Allah, when unto Allah belongeth the inheritance of the heavens and the earth? Those who spent and fought before the victory are not upon a level (with the rest of you). Such are greater in rank than those who spent and fought afterwards. Unto each hath Allah promised good. And Allah is informed of what ye do.

Who is he that will lend unto Allah a goodly loan, that He may double it for him and his may be a rich reward?

On the day when thou (Muhammad) wilt see the believers, men and women, their light shining forth before them and on their right hands, (and wilt hear it said unto them): Glad news for you this day: Gardens underneath which rivers flow, wherein ye are immortal. That is the supreme triumph.

On the day when the hypocritical men and the hypocritical women will say unto those who believe: Look on us that we may borrow from your light! it will be said: Go back and seek for light! Then there will separate them a wall wherein is a gate, the inner side whereof containeth mercy, while the outer side thereof is toward the doom.

They will cry unto them (saying): Were we not with you? They will say: Yea, verily; but ye tempted one another, and hesitated, and doubted, and vain desires beguiled you till the ordinance of Allah came to pass; and the deceiver deceived you concerning Allah;

So this day no ransom can be taken from you nor from those who disbelieved. Your home is the Fire; that is your patron, and a hapless journey's end.

Is not the time ripe for the hearts of those who believe to submit to Allah's reminder and to the truth which is revealed, that they become not as those who received the Scripture of old but the term was prolonged for them and so their hearts were hardened, and many of them are evil-livers.

Know that Allah quickeneth the earth after its death. We have made clear Our revelations for you, that haply ye may understand.

Lo! those who give alms, both men and women, and lend unto Allah a goodly loan, it will be doubled for them, and theirs will be a rich reward.

And those who believe in Allah and His messengers, they are the loyal; and the martyrs are with their Lord; they have their reward and their light; while as for those who disbelieve and deny Our revelations, they are owners of hell-fire.

Know that the life of the world is only play, and idle talk, and pageantry, and boasting among you, and rivalry in respect of wealth and children; as the likeness of vegetation after rain, whereof the growth is pleasing to the husbandman, but afterward it drieth up and thou seest it turning yellow, then it becometh straw. And in the Hereafter there is grievous punishment, and (also) forgiveness from Allah and His good pleasure, whereas the life of the world is but matter of illusion.

Race one with another for forgiveness from your Lord and a Garden whereof the breadth is as the breadth of the heavens and the earth, which is in store for those who believe in Allah and His messengers. Such is the bounty of Allah, which He bestoweth upon whom He will, and Allah is of infinite bounty.

Naught of disaster befalleth in the earth or in yourselves but it is in a Book before We bring it into being—Lo! that is easy for Allah—

That ye grieve not for the sake of that which hath escaped you, nor yet exult because of that which hath been given. Allah loveth not all prideful boasters,

Who hoard and who enjoin upon the people avarice. And whosoever turneth away, still Allah is the Absolute, the Owner of Praise.

We verily sent Our messengers with clear proofs, and revealed with them the Scripture and the Balance, that mankind may observe right measure; and He revealed iron, wherein is mighty power and (many) uses for mankind, and that Allah may know him who helpeth Him and His messengers, though unseen. Lo! Allah is Strong, Almighty.

And We verily sent Noah and Abraham and placed the Prophethood and the Scripture among their seed, and among them there is he who goeth right, but many of them are evil-livers.

Then We caused Our messengers to follow in their footsteps; and We caused Jesus, son of Mary, to follow, and gave him the Gospel, and placed compassion and mercy in the hearts of those who followed him. But monasticism they invented—We ordained it not for them—only seeking Allah's pleasure, and they observed it not with right observance. So We give those of them who believe their reward, but many of them are evil-livers.

O ye who believe! Be mindful of your duty to Allah and put faith in His messenger. He will give you twofold of His mercy and will appoint for you a light wherein ye shall walk, and will forgive you. Allah is Forgiving, Merciful;

That the People of the Scripture [Jews and Christians] may know that they control naught of the bounty of Allah, but that the bounty is in Allah's hand to give to whom he will. And Allah is of infinite bounty.

Tacitus

I n 89 A.D. the historian Tacitus (see p. 123) spent some time in Germany, probably as an official of the imperial government. While there he observed the customs and manners of the Germanic peoples and wrote down the results in his Germania. Tacitus greatly admired the virile qualities of these primitive people, and as a moralist he inevitably stressed their virtues as an example for the luxury-loving Romans. In reading the selection note (1) German political and social institutions, (2) how they made their living, and (3) any indication that Tacitus might have been biased in his interpretation of these people.

From: THE EARLY GERMANS

Germany proper is separated from the Gauls, the Rhaetians and the Pannonians by the Rhine and the Danube, from the Sarmatians and Dacians partly by the mountains, partly by their mutual fears. The ocean washes its other boundaries, forming deep bays and embracing large islands where various tribes and their kings have become known to us through

Arthur C. Howland, *Translations and Reprints from the Original Sources of European History*, VI, no. 3. *The Early Germans* (Second Edition), University of Pennsylvania Press, Philadelphia, n.d., 4–16. Courtesy of the University of Pennsylvania Press.

the disclosures of recent war. The Rhine takes its rise in the steep and inaccessible fastnesses of the Rhaetian Alps, and, bending slightly to the west, flows into the northern ocean. The Danube, pouring down from the gently sloping ridge of Mount Abnoba, passes the borders of many nations, and finally forces its way through six outlets into the Black Sea; a seventh channel is swallowed up by the marshes.

I should say that the Germans themselves were an indigenous people, without any subsequent mixture of blood through immigration or friendly intercourse; for in ancient times it was by sea and not by land that those who wished to change their homes wandered, and the ocean, hostile, as it were, and of boundless extent on the further side, is rarely traversed by ships from our part of the world. And not to mention the danger of the terrible and unknown sea, who indeed would leave Asia or Africa or Italy to seek Germany with its wild scenery, its harsh climate, its sullen manners and aspect, unless, indeed, it were his native country? They tell in their ancient songs, the only kind of tradition and history that they have, how Tuisto, a god sprung from the earth and his son Mannus were the originators and founders of their race. Mannus is supposed to have had three sons from whose names those nearest the ocean are called *Ingaevones,* those in the middle country, *Hermiones,* and the others, *Istaevones.* Certain people assert with the freedom permitted in discussing ancient times that there were many descendants of the god, and many tribal names, such as *Marsi, Gambrivii, Suebi, Vandilii,* and that these were their true and ancient names. But the name Germany, they say, is modern and of recent application, since those who first crossed the Rhine and expelled the Gauls, and who are now called *Tungri,* were then named Germans; thus what had been a tribal, not a national name, spread little by little, so that later they all adopted the newly-coined appellation that was first employed by the conquerors to inspire fear and called themselves Germans.

They say that Hercules himself once visited them, and when about to go into battle they sing of him as the first of all heroes. They have also certain songs, by the intonation of which (*barditus,* as it is called) they excite their courage, while they divine the fortune of the coming battle from the sound itself. They inspire or feel terror according to the character of the cheering, though what harmony there is in the shouting is one of valor rather than of voices. The effect they particularly strive for is that of a harsh noise, a wild and confused roar, which they attain by putting their shields to their mouths so that the reverberation swells their deep, full voices. Ulysses, too, is thought by some to have reached this ocean in those long and fabulous wanderings of his, and to have been cast upon the shores of Germany. They say he built and named Asciburgium, a town on the banks of the Rhine still inhabited; nay even that an altar consecrated by him and inscribed with the name of his father, Laertes, has been found at the same place, and that certain monuments and tombs with Greek letters on them still exist within the confines of Germany and Rhaetia. I have no mind to argue either for or against the truth of these statements; let each one believe or reject them as he feels inclined.

I myself subscribe to the opinion of those who hold that the German tribes have never been contaminated by intermarriage with other nations, but have remained peculiar and unmixed and wholly unlike other people. Hence the bodily type is the same among them all, notwithstanding the extent of their population. They all have fierce blue eyes, reddish hair and large bodies fit only for sudden exertion; they do not submit patiently to work and effort and cannot endure thirst and heat at all, though cold and hunger they are accustomed to because of their climate.

In general the country, though varying here and there in appearance, is covered over with wild forests or filthy swamps, being more humid on the side of Gaul but bleaker toward Noricum and Pannonia. It is suitable enough for grain but does not permit the cultivation of fruit trees; and, though rich in flocks and herds, these are for the most part small, the cattle not even possessing their natural beauty nor spreading horns. The people take pride in possessing a large number of animals, these being their sole and most cherished wealth. Whether it was in mercy or wrath that the gods denied them silver and gold, I know not. Yet I would not affirm that no vein of German soil produces silver or gold; for who has examined? They do not care for their possession and use as much as might be expected. There are to be seen among them vessels of silver that have been presented as gifts to their ambassadors and chiefs, but they are held in no more esteem than vessels of earthenware; however, those nearest to us prize gold and silver because of its use in trade, and they recognize certain of our coins as valuable and choose those. The people of the interior practice barter and exchange of commodities in accordance with the simple and ancient custom. They like the old and well-known coins, those with milled edges bearing the stamp of a two-horse chariot. They are more anxious also for silver coins than for gold, not because of any special liking, but because a number of silver coins is more convenient in purchasing cheap and common articles.

Not even iron is abundant, as is shown by the character of their weapons. Some few use swords or long spears, but usually they carry javelins, called in their language *framea*, tipped with a short narrow piece of iron but so sharp and so easy to handle that as occasion demands they employ the same weapon for fighting at close range or at a distance. A horseman is content with a shield or a javelin, but the footmen, either nude or lightly clad in a small cloak, rain missiles, each man having many and hurling them to a great distance. There is no particular adornment to their weapons except that their shields are distinguished by the most carefully chosen colors. A few wear cuirasses, but hardly any have helmets of metal or leather. Their horses are noted neither for their beauty nor their speed, nor are they trained to perform evolutions, as with us. They move straight ahead or make a single turn to the right, the wheel being executed with such perfect alignment that no man drops behind the one next to him. One would say that on the whole their chief strength lies in their infantry. A picked body of these are chosen from among all the youth and placed in advance of the line where they fight mixed with the horsemen, since their swiftness makes them fully equal to engaging in a cavalry contest. Their number is fixed; there are a hundred from each canton, and from this circumstance they take their name among their own people, so that what

was at first a number is now become an appellation of honor. The main body of troops is drawn up in wedge-shaped formation. To yield ground, provided you press forward subsequently, is considered a mark of prudence rather than a sign of cowardice. They carry off the bodies of the fallen even where they are not victorious. It is the greatest ignominy to have left one's shield on the field, and it is unlawful for a man so disgraced to be present at the sacred rites or to enter the assembly; so that many after escaping from battle have ended their shame with the halter.

They choose their kings on account of their ancestry, their generals for their valor. The kings do not have free and unlimited power and the generals lead by example rather than command, winning great admiration if they are energetic and fight in plain sight in front of the line. But no one is allowed to put a culprit to death or to imprison him, or even to beat him with stripes except the priests, and then not by way of a punishment or at the command of the general but as though ordered by the god who they believe aids them in their fighting. Certain figures and images taken from their sacred groves they carry into battle, but their greatest incitement to courage is that a division of horse or foot is not made up by chance or by accidental association, but is formed of families and clans; and their dear ones are close at hand so that the wailings of the women and the crying of the children can be heard during the battle. These are for each warrior the most sacred witnesses of his bravery, these his dearest applauders. They carry their wounds to their mothers and their wives, nor do the latter fear to count their number and examine them while they bring them food and urge them to deeds of valor.

It is related how on certain occasions their forces already turned to flight and retreating have been rallied by the women who implored them by their prayers and bared their breasts to their weapons, signifying thus the captivity close awaiting them, which is feared far more intensely on account of their women than for themselves; to such an extent indeed that those states are more firmly bound in treaty among whose hostages maidens of noble family are also required. Further, they believe that the sex has a certain sanctity and prophetic gift, and they neither despise their counsels nor disregard their answers. We ourselves in the reign of the divine Vespasian saw Valaeda, who was considered for a long time by many as a sort of divinity; and formerly also Albruna and many others were venerated, though not out of servility nor as though they were deified mortals.

Among the gods they worship Mercury most of all, to whom it is lawful to offer human sacrifices also on stated days. Hercules and Mars they placate by the sacrifice of worthy animals. Some of the *Suebi* sacrifice to Isis. The reason for this foreign rite and its origin I have not discovered, except that the image fashioned like a galley shows that the cult has been introduced from abroad. On the other hand they hold it to be inconsistent with the sublimity of the celestials to confine the gods in walls made by hands, or to liken them to the form of any human countenance. They consecrate woods and sacred groves to them and give the names of the deities to that hidden mystery which they perceive by faith alone.

They pay as much attention as any people to augury and lots. The method of casting lots is uniform. They cut off a branch from a fruit-bearing tree and divide it into small wands marked with certain characters. These they throw at random on a white cloth. Then the priest of the tribe, if it is a matter concerning the community, or the father of the family in case it is a private affair, calling on the gods and keeping his eyes raised toward the sky, takes up three of the lots, one at a time, and then interprets their meaning according to the markings before mentioned. If they have proven unfavorable there can be no further consultation that day concerning that particular matter; but if they are favorable, the confirmation of auspices is further demanded. Even the practice of divination from the notes and flight of birds is known; but it is peculiar to this people to seek omens and warnings from horses also. These sacred animals are white and never defiled by labor, being kept at public expense in the holy groves and woods. They are yoked to the sacred chariot by the priest and the king or chief of the tribe, who accompany them and take note of their neighing and

snorting. In no other kind of divination is there greater confidence placed either by the common people or by the nobles; for the priests are considered merely the servants of the gods, but the horses are thought to be acquainted with their counsels. They have another sort of divination whereby they seek to know the result of serious wars. They secure in any way possible a captive from the hostile tribe and set him to fight with a warrior chosen from their own people, each using the weapons of his own country. The victory of the one or the other is accepted as an indication of the result of the war.

Concerning minor matters the chiefs deliberate, but in important affairs all the people are consulted, although the subjects referred to the common people for judgment are discussed beforehand by the chiefs. Unless some sudden and unexpected event calls them together, they assemble on fixed days either at the new moon or the full moon, for they think these the most auspicious times to begin their undertakings. They do not reckon time by the number of days, as we do, but by the number of nights. So run their appointments, their contracts; the night introduces the day, so to speak. A disadvantage arises from their regard for liberty in that they do not come together at once as if commanded to attend, but two or three days are wasted by their delay in assembling. When the crowd is sufficient they take their places fully armed. Silence is proclaimed by the priests, who have on these occasions the right to keep order. Then the king or a chief addresses them, each being heard according to his age, noble blood, reputation in warfare and eloquence, though more because he has the power to persuade than the right to command. If an opinion is displeasing they reject it by shouting; if they agree to it they clash with their spears. The most complimentary form of assent is that which is expressed by means of their weapons.

It is also allowable in the assembly to bring up accusations, and to prosecute capital offenses. Penalties are distinguished according to crime. Traitors and deserters are hung to trees. Weaklings and cowards and those guilty of infamous crimes are cast into the mire of swamps with a hurdle placed over their heads.

This difference of penalty looks to the distinction that crime should be punished publicly while infamy should be hidden out of sight. Lighter offences also are punished according to their degree, the guilty parties being fined a certain number of horses or cattle. A part of the fine goes to the king or the tribe, part to the injured party or his relatives. In these same assemblies are chosen the magistrates who decide suits in the cantons and villages. Each one has the assistance of a hundred associates as advisers and with power to decide.

They undertake no business whatever either of a public or a private character save they be armed. But it is not customary for any one to assume arms until the tribe has recognized his competence to use them. Then in a full assembly some one of the chiefs or the father or relatives of the youth invest him with the shield and spear. This is the sign that the lad has reached the age of manhood; this is his first honor. Before this he was only a member of a household, hereafter he is a member of the tribe. Distinguished rank or the great services of their parents secure even for mere striplings the claim to be ranked as chiefs. They attach themselves to certain more experienced chiefs of approved merit; nor are they ashamed to be looked upon as belonging to their followings. There are grades even within the train of followers assigned by the judgment of its leader. There is great rivalry among these companions as to who shall rank first with the chief, and among the chiefs as to who shall have the most and the bravest followers. It is an honor and a source of strength always to be surrounded by a great band of chosen youths, for they are an ornament in peace, a defence in war. It brings reputation and glory to a leader not only in his own tribe but also among the neighboring peoples if his following is superior in numbers and courage; for he is courted by embassies and honored by gifts, and often his very fame decides the issue of wars.

When they go into battle it is a disgrace for the chief to be outdone in deeds of valor and for the following not to match the courage of their chief; furthermore, for any one of the followers to have survived his chief and come unharmed out of a battle is life-long infamy and reproach. It is in accordance with their most sacred oath of allegiance to defend and protect him and to ascribe their bravest deeds to his renown. The chief fights for victory; the men of his following, for their chief. If the tribe to which they belong sinks into the lethargy of long peace and quiet, many of the noble youths voluntarily seek other tribes that are still carrying on war, because a quiet life is irksome to the Germans and they gain renown more readily in the midst of perils, while a large following is not to be provided for except by violence and war. For they look to the liberality of their chief for their war-horse and their deadly and victorious spear; the feasts and entertainments, however, furnished them on a homely but liberal scale, fall to their lot as mere pay. The means for this bounty are acquired through war and plunder. Nor could you persuade them to till the soil and await the yearly produce so easily as you could induce them to stir up an enemy and earn glorious wounds. Nay, even they think it tame and stupid to acquire by their sweat what they can purchase by their blood.

In the intervals of peace they spend little time in hunting, but much in idleness, given over to sleep and eating; all the bravest and most warlike doing nothing, while the hearth and home and the care of the fields is given over to the women, the old men, and the various infirm members of the family. The masters lie buried in sloth by that strange contradiction of nature that causes the same men to love indolence and hate peace. It is customary for the several tribesmen to present voluntary offerings of cattle and grain to the chiefs which, though accepted as gifts of honor, also supply their wants. They are particularly delighted in the gifts of neighboring tribes, not only those sent by individuals, but those presented by states as such,—choice horses, massive arms, embossed plates and armlets. We have now taught them to accept money also.

It is well known that none of the German tribes live in cities, nor even permit their dwellings to be closely joined to each other. They live separated and in various places, as a spring or a meadow or a grove strikes their fancy. They lay out their villages, not as with us in connected or closely-joined houses, but each one surrounds his dwelling with an open space, either as a protection against conflagration or because of their ignorance of the art of building. They do not even make use of rough stones or tiles. They use for all purposes undressed timber, giving no beauty or comfort. Some parts they plaster carefully with earth of such purity and brilliancy as to form a substitute for painting and designs in color. They are accustomed also to dig out subterranean caves which they cover over with great heaps of manure as a refuge against the cold and a place for storing grain, for retreats of this sort render the extreme cold of their winters bearable and, whenever an enemy has come upon them, though he lays waste the open country, he is either ignorant of what is hidden underground or else it escapes him for the very reason that it has to searched for.

Generally their only clothing is a cloak fastened with a clasp, or if they haven't that, with a thorn; this being their only garment, they pass whole days about the hearth or near a fire. The richest of them are distinguished by wearing a tunic, not flowing as is the case among the Sarmatians and Parthians, but close-fitting and showing the shape of their limbs. There are those, also, who wear the skins of wild beasts, those nearest the Roman border in a careless manner, but those further back more elegantly, as those do who have no better clothing obtained by commerce. They select certain animals, and stripping off their hides sew on them patches of spotted skins taken from those strange beasts that the distant ocean and the unknown sea bring forth. The women wear the same sort of dress as the men except that they wrap themselves in linen garments which they adorn with purple stripes and do not lengthen out the upper part of the tunic into sleeves, but leave the arms bare the whole length. The upper part of their breasts is also exposed. However, their marriage code is strict, and in no other part of their manners are they to be praised more than in this. For almost alone among barbarian peoples they are content with one wife each, excepting those few who because of their high position rather than out of lust enter into more than one marriage engagement.

The wife does not bring a dowry to the husband, but the husband to the wife. The parents and relatives are present at the ceremony and examine and accept the presents,—gifts not suited to female luxury nor such as a young bride would deck herself with, but oxen, a horse and bridle and a shield together with a spear and sword. In consideration of these offerings the wife is accepted, and she in her turn brings her husband a gift of weapons. This they consider as the strongest bond, these as their mystic rites, their gods of marriage. Lest the woman should think herself excluded from aspiring to share in heroic deeds and in the dangers of war, she is admonished by the very initiatory ceremonies of matrimony that she is becoming the partner of her husband's labors and dangers, destined to suffer and to dare with him alike in peace and in war. The yoke of oxen, the caparisoned horse, the gift of arms, give this warning. So must she live, so must she die. What things she receives she must hand down to her children worthy and untarnished and such that future daughters-in-law may receive them and pass them on to her grandchildren.

Thus they live in well-protected virtue, uncorrupted by the allurements of shows or the enticement of banquets. Men and women alike know not the secrecy of correspondence. Though the race is so numerous, adultery is very rare, its punishment being immediate and inflicted by the injured husband. He cuts off the woman's hair in the presence of her kinsfolk, drives her naked from his house and flogs her through the whole village. Indeed, the loss of chastity meets with no indulgence; neither beauty, youth, nor wealth can procure the guilty woman a husband, for no one there laughs at vice, nor is corrupting and being corrupted spoken of as the way of the world. Those tribes do better still where only the virgins marry and where the hope and aspiration of married life is done with once for all. They accept one husband, just as they have one body and one life, that they may have no thought beyond this, no further desire; that their love may be as it were not for the married state, but for the husband. To limit the number of children or to put any of the later children to death is considered a crime, and with them good customs are of more avail than good laws elsewhere.

In every household the children grow up naked and unkempt into that lusty frame and those sturdy limbs that we admire. Each mother nurses her own children; they are not handed over to servants and paid nurses. The lord and the slave are in no way to be distinguished by the delicacy of their bringing up. They live among the same flocks, they lie on the same ground, until age separates them and valor distinguishes the free born. The young men marry late and their vigor is thereby unimpaired. Nor is the marriage of girls hastened. They have the same youthful vigor, the same stature as the young men. Thus well-matched and strong when they marry, the children reproduce the robustness of their parents. An uncle shows the same regard for his sister's children as does their own father. Some tribes consider this relationship more sacred and binding than any other, and in taking hostages lay special stress upon it on the ground that they secure thus a stronger hold on the mind and a wider pledge for the family. A man's heirs and successors, however, are his own children, and no wills are made. If there are no children the next heirs are the brothers, then come the paternal and maternal uncles. The more relatives a man has and the greater the number of his connections, the more honored is his old age. Childlessness has no advantages.

A German is required to adopt not only the feuds of his father or of a relative, but also their friendships, though the enmities are not irreconcilable. For even homicide is expiated by the payment of a certain number of cattle, and the whole family accept the satisfaction, a useful practice as regards the state because feuds are more dangerous where there is no strong legal control.

No other race indulges more freely in entertainments and hospitality. It is considered a crime to turn any mortal man away from one's door. According to his means, each one receives those who come with a well-furnished table. When his food has been all eaten up, he who had lately been the host becomes the guide and companion of his guest to the next house, which they enter uninvited. There is no distinction between guests; they are all received with like consideration. No one makes any difference between friend and stranger so far as concerns the rights of hospitality. If the guest on going away asks for any gift, it is customary to grant it to him, and the host on his side feels the same freedom from constraint in making a request. They take great pleasure in presents, but they do not reckon them as favors nor do they put themselves under obligations in accepting them.

As soon as they awake from sleep, which they prolong till late in the day, they bathe, usually in warm water as their winter lasts a great part of the year. After the bath they take food, each sitting in a separate seat and having a table to himself. Then they proceed to their business, or not less often to feasts, fully armed. It is no disgrace to spend the whole day and night in drinking. Quarreling is frequent enough as is natural among drunken men, though their disputes are rarely settled by mere wrangling but oftener by bloodshed and wounds. Yet it is at their feasts that they consult about reconciling enemies, forming family alliances, electing chiefs, and even regarding war and peace, as they think that at no other time is the mind more open to fair judgment or more inflamed to mighty deeds. A race without natural or acquired cunning still continues to disclose the secret thoughts of the heart in the freedom of festivity. Therefore at such a time the minds of all are free and unconstrained. On the next day the matter is reconsidered and a particular advantage is secured on each occasion. They take counsel when they are unable to practice deception; they decide when they cannot be misled.

A liquor for drinking bearing a certain resemblance to wine is made by the process of fermentation from barley or other grain. Those next the border also buy wine. Their food is of a simple kind, wild fruit, fresh game, or curdled milk. They satisfy their hunger without elaborate preparation and without the use of condiments. In the matter of thirst they do not use the same temperance. If you should indulge their love of drink by furnishing them as much as they wanted, they might be conquered more easily by their vices than by arms.

As to games, but one and the same kind is seen in all their gatherings. Naked youths who make profession of this exhibition leap and dance among swords and spears that threaten their lives. Constant practice has given them skill, skill has given grace. Still they do not indulge in this pastime with a view to profit. The pleasure of the spectators is the reward for their recklessness, however daring. They indulge in games of chance, strange as it may seem, even when sober, as one of their serious occupations, with such great recklessness in their gains and losses that when everything else is gone they stake their liberty and their own persons on the last and decisive throw. The loser goes into voluntary slavery, Though he may be the younger and stronger of the two, he suffers himself to be bound and led away. Such is their stubbornness in a bad practice. They themselves call it honor. They sell slaves of this description to others that they may not feel the shame of such a success.

But they do not employ slaves as we do with distinct functions prescribed throughout the establishment. Each has his own domicile and rules his own house. The Lord exacts a certain amount of grain or cloth or a certain number of cattle as in the case of a tenant and this is the extent of his servitude. Other duties, those of the household, are performed by the lord's wife and children. To beat a slave or to punish him with chains and task work is rare. They occasionally kill one, not in the severity of discipline, but impetuously and in sudden wrath as they would kill an enemy, except that the deed goes without punishment. Freedmen do not rank much above slaves; they are not of much account in the household and never in the state, except only in those tribes that are ruled by kings. For there they are elevated above the free born and the nobles. The inferior position of the freedman elsewhere is the mark of the free state.

To trade with capital and to let it out at interest is unknown, and so it is ignorance rather than legal prohibition that protects them. Land is held by the villages as communities according to the number of the cultivators, and is then divided among the freemen according to their rank. The extent of their territories renders this partition easy. They cultivate fresh fields every year and there is still land to spare. They do not plant orchards nor lay off meadow-lands nor irrigate gardens so as to require of the soil more than it would naturally bring forth of its own richness and extent. Grain is the only tribute exacted from their land, whence they do not divide the year into as many seasons as we do. The terms winter, spring and summer have a meaning with them, but the name and blessings of autumn are unknown.

There is no pomp in the celebration of their funerals. The only custom they observe is that the bodies of illustrious men should be burned with certain kinds of wood. They do not heap garments and perfumes upon the funeral pile. In every case a man's arms are burned with him, and sometimes his horse also. They believe that stately monuments and sculptured columns oppress the dead with their weight; the green sod alone covers their graves. Their tears and lamentations are quickly laid aside; sadness and grief linger long. It is fitting for women to mourn, for men to remember.

Such are the facts I have obtained in general concerning the origin and customs of the Germans as a whole. . . .

Eginhard

Eginhard (about 770–840 A.D.), a monk who lived at the court of Charlemagne, survived the great emperor by a period of thirty years. During that time he wrote a short biography of the man who claimed to be the heir of the Roman emperors in the West. The work contained some errors, but is nevertheless valuable as the best contemporary account of this important monarch. In reading this biography note (1) the character of the emperor; (2) his educational training; (3) his family relationships; (4) the wars he fought and his success as a military leader; (5) his political accomplishments; (6) how he became emperor of the Romans; and (7) the general spirit of his age.

As translated by A. J. Grant in *Early Lives of Charlemagne by Eginhard and the Monk of St. Gall*, The King's Classics, Alexander Moring, Ltd., The De La More Press, London, 1905, 4–50. Courtesy of Alexander Moring, Ltd.

THE LIFE OF THE EMPEROR CHARLES

Having made up my mind to write an account of the life and conversation, and to a large extent of the actions of my lord and patron, King Charles, of great and deservedly glorious memory, I have compressed my task within the narrowest possible limits. My aim has been on the one hand to insert everything of which I have been able to find an account; and on the other to avoid offending the fastidious by telling each new incident at wearisome length. Above all, I have tried to avoid offending in this new book those who look down upon even the monuments of antiquity written by learned and eloquent men.

There are, I do not doubt, many men of learning and leisure who feel that the life of the present day must not be utterly neglected, and that the doings of our own time should not be devoted to silence and forgetfulness as wholly unworthy of record; who, therefore, have such love of fame that they would rather chronicle the great deeds of others in writings, however poor, than, by abstaining from writing, allow their name and reputation to perish from the memory of mankind. But, even so, I have felt that I ought not to hold my hand from the composition of this book, for I knew that no one could write of these events more truthfully than I could, since I was myself an actor in them, and, being present, knew them from the testimony of my own eyes; while I could not certainly know whether anyone else would write them or no. I thought it better, therefore, to join with others in committing this story to writing for the benefit of posterity rather than to allow the shades of oblivion to blot out the life of this King, the noblest and greatest of his age, and his famous deeds, which the men of later times will scarcely be able to imitate.

Another reason, and not, I think, a foolish one, occurred to me, which even by itself would have been strong enough to persuade me to write—the care, I mean, that was taken with my upbringing, and the unbroken friendship which I enjoyed with the King himself and his children from the time when first I began to live at his Court. For in this way he has so bound me to himself, and has made me his debtor both in life and death, that I should most justly be considered and condemned as ungrateful if I were to forget all the benefits that he conferred upon me and were to pass over in silence the great and glorious deeds of a man who was so kind to me; if I were to allow his life to remain as unchronicled and unpraised, as if he had never lived, when that life deserves not merely the efforts of my poor talents, which are insignificant, small and almost non-existent, but all the eloquence of a Cicero.

So here you have a book containing the life of that great and glorious man. There is nothing for you to wonder at or admire except his deeds; unless, indeed, it be that I, a barbarian, and little versed in the Roman tongue, have imagined that I could write Latin inoffensively and usefully, and have become so swollen with impudence as to despise Cicero's words when, speaking about Latin writers in the first book of the Tusculans, he says: "If a man commits his thoughts to paper when he can neither arrange them well nor write them agreeably, nor furnish pleasure of any kind to the reader, he is recklessly misusing both his leisure and his paper." The great orator's opinion would, perhaps, have deterred me from writing if I had not fortified myself with the reflection that I ought to risk the condemnation of men, and bring my poor talents into peril by writing, rather than spare my reputation and neglect this great man's memory.

THE PREFACE ENDS: THE BOOK BEGINS

The race of the Merovings from which the Franks were accustomed to choose their kings is reckoned as lasting to King Hilderich, who, by the order of Stephen, the Roman Pontiff, was deposed, tonsured, and sent into a monastery. But this race, though it may be regarded as finishing with him, had long since lost all power, and no longer possessed anything of importance except the empty royal title. For the wealth and power of the kingdom was in the hands of the Praefects of the Court, who were called Mayors of the Palace, and exercised entire sovereignty. The King, contented with the mere royal title, with long hair and flowing beard, used to sit upon the throne and act the part of a ruler, listening to ambassadors, whencesoever they came, and giving them at their departure, as though of his own power, answers which he had been instructed or commanded to give. But this was the only function that he performed, for besides the empty royal title and the precarious life income which the Praefect of the Court allowed him at his pleasure he had nothing of his own except one estate with a very small revenue, on which he had his house, and from which he drew the few servants who performed such services as were necessary and made him a show of deference. Wherever he had to go he travelled in a waggon, drawn in rustic style by a pair of oxen, and driven by a cowherd. In this fashion he used to go to the palace and to the general meetings of the people, which were held yearly for the affairs of the kingdom; in this fashion he returned home. But the Praefect of the Court looked after the administration of the kingdom and all that had to be done or arranged at home or abroad.

When Hilderich was deposed, Pippin, the father of King Charles, was performing the duties of Mayor of the Palace as if by hereditary right. For his father Charles, who put down the tyrants who were claiming dominion for themselves through all Frankland, and so crushed the Saracens, when they were attempting to conquer Gaul, in two great battles (the one in Aquitania, near the city of Poitiers, the other near Narbonne, on the river Birra), that he forced them to return into Spain—his father Charles had nobly administered the same office, and had inherited it from his father, Pippin. For the people did not usually give this honour except to such as were distinguished for the renown of their family and the extent of their wealth.

This office, then, was handed down from his father and his grandfather to Pippin, the father of King Charles, and to his brother, Carloman. He exercised it for some years conjointly with his brother Carloman on terms of the greatest harmony, still in nominal subordina-

tion to the above-mentioned King Hilderich. But then his brother, Carloman, for some unknown cause, but probably fired with love of the contemplative life, abandoned the toilsome administration of a temporal kingdom and retired to Rome in search of peace. There he changed his dress, and, becoming a monk in the monastery upon Mount Soracte, built near the church of the blessed Sylvester, enjoyed for some years the quiet that he desired, with many brethren, who joined themselves to him for the same purpose. But as many of the nobles of Frankland came on pilgrimage to Rome to perform their vows, and, unwilling to pass by one who had once been their lord, interrupted the peace that he most desired by frequent visits, he was compelled to change his abode. For, seeing that the number of his visitors interfered with his purpose, he left Mount Soracte and retired to the monastery of Saint Benedict, situated in the camp of Mount Cassino, in the province of Samnium. There he occupied what remained to him of this temporal life in religious exercises.

But Pippin, after he was made King instead of Mayor of the Palace by the authority of the Roman Pontiff, exercised sole rule over the Franks for fifteen years, or rather more. Then, after finishing the Aquitanian war, which he had undertaken against Waifar, Duke of Aquitania, and had carried on for nine consecutive years, he died at Paris of the dropsy, and left behind him two sons, Charles and Carloman, to whom by divine will the succession of the kingdom came. For the Franks called a solemn public assembly, and elected both of them to be kings, on the understanding that they should equally divide the whole kingdom, but that Charles should receive for his special administration that part which his father Pippin had held, while Carloman received the territories ruled by their uncle Carloman. The conditions were accepted, and each received the share of the kingdom that was allotted to him. Harmony was maintained between the two brothers, though not without difficulty; for many partisans of Carloman tried to break their alliance, and some even hoped to engage them in war. But the course of events proved that the danger to Charles was imaginary rather than real. For, upon the death of Carloman, his wife with her sons and some of the leading nobles fled to Italy, and, for no obvious reason, passed over her husband's brother, and placed herself and her children under the protection of Desiderius, King of the Lombards. Carloman, after ruling the kingdom for two years conjointly with Charles, died of disease, and Charles, upon the death of Carloman, was made sole king with the consent of all the Franks.

It would be foolish of me to say anything about his birth and infancy, or even about his boyhood, for I can find nothing about these matters in writing, nor does anyone survive who claims to have personal knowledge of them. I have decided, therefore to pass on to describe and illustrate his acts and his habits and the other divisions of his life without lingering over the unknown. I shall describe first his exploits both at home and abroad, then his habits and interests, and lastly the administration of the kingdom and the end of his reign, omitting nothing that demands or deserves to be recorded.

HIS EXPLOITS AT HOME AND ABROAD

Of all the wars that he waged that in Aquitania, begun, but not finished, by his father, was the first that he undertook, because it seemed easy of accomplishment. His brother was still alive, and was called upon for assistance, and, though he failed to provide the help that he promised, Charles prosecuted the enterprise that he had undertaken with the utmost energy, and would not desist or slacken in his task before, by perseverance and continuous effort, he had completely reached the end after which he strove. For he forced Hunold, who after the death of Waifar had attempted to occupy Aquitania and renew the almost finished war, to abandon Aquitania and retire into Gascony. Even there he did not allow him to remain, but crossed the Garonne, and sent ambassadors to Lupus, Duke of the Gascons, ordering him to surrender the fugitive, and threatening him with war unless he did so at once. Lupus, more wisely, not only surrendered Hunold but also submitted himself

and the province over which he presided to the power of Charles.

When the Aquitanian trouble was settled and the war finished, when, too, his partner in the kingdom had withdrawn from the world's affairs, he undertook a war against the Lombards, being moved thereto by the entreaties and the prayers of Hadrian, Bishop of the City of Rome. Now, this war, too, had been undertaken by his father at the supplication of Pope Stephen, under circumstances of great difficulty, inasmuch as certain of the chiefs of the Franks, whose advice he was accustomed to ask, so strongly resisted his wishes that they openly declared that they would leave their King to return home. But now Charles undertook the war against King Haistulf, and most swiftly brought it to an end. For, though his reasons for undertaking the war were similar to, and, indeed, the same as those of his father, he plainly fought it out with a very different energy, and brought it to a different end. For Pippin, after a siege of a few days at Pavia, forced King Haistulf to give hostages, and restore to the Romans the towns and fortresses that he had taken from them, and to give a solemn promise that he would not attempt to regain what he had surrendered. But King Charles, when once he had begun the war, did not stop until he had received the surrender of King Desiderius, whom he had worn down after a long siege; until he had forced his son Adalgis, in whom the hopes of his people seemed to be centred, to fly not only from his kingdom but from Italy; until he had restored to the Romans all that had been taken from them; until he had crushed Hruodgausus, Praefect of the Duchy of Friuli, who was attempting a revolution; until, in fine, he had brought all Italy under his rule, and placed his son Pippin as king over the conquered country. I should describe here the difficulties of the passage of the Alps and the vast toil with which the Franks found their way through the pathless mountain ridges, the rocks that soared to heaven, and the sharply-pointed cliffs, if it were not that my purpose in the present work is rather to describe Charles's manner of life than to chronicle the events of the wars that he waged. The sum of this war was the conquest of Italy, the transportation and perpetual exile of King Desiderius, the expulsion of his son Adalgis from Italy, power taken from the kings of the Lombards and restored to Hadrian, the Ruler of the Roman Church.

When this war was ended, the Saxon war, which seemed dropped for a time, was taken up again. Never was there a war more prolonged nor more cruel than this, nor one that required greater efforts on the part of the Frankish peoples. For the Saxons, like most of the races that inhabit Germany, are by nature fierce, devoted to the worship of demons and hostile to our religion, and they think it no dishonour to confound and transgress the laws of God and man. There were reasons, too, which might at any time cause a disturbance of the peace. For our boundaries and theirs touch almost everywhere on the open plain, except where in a few places large forests or ranges of mountains are interposed to separate the territories of the two nations by a definite frontier; so that on both sides murder, robbery, and arson were of constant occurrence. The Franks were so irritated by these things that they thought it was time no longer to be satisfied with retaliation but to declare open war against them.

So war was declared, and was fought for thirty years continuously with the greatest fierceness on both sides, but with heavier loss to the Saxons than the Franks. The end might have been reached sooner had it not been for the perfidy of the Saxons. It is hard to say how often they admitted themselves beaten and surrendered as suppliants to King Charles; how often they promised to obey his orders, gave without delay the required hostages, and received the ambassadors that were sent to them. Sometimes they were so cowed and broken that they promised to abandon the worship of devils and willingly to submit themselves to the Christian religion. But though sometimes ready to bow to his commands they were always eager to break their promise, so it is impossible to say which course seemed to come more natural to them, for from the beginning of the war there was scarcely a year in which they did not both promise and fail to perform.

But the high courage of the King and the constancy of his mind, which remained unshaken by prosperity and adversity, could not be conquered by their changes nor forced by weariness to desist from his undertakings. He never allowed those who offended in this way to go unpunished, but either led an army himself, or sent one under the command of his counts, to chastise their perfidy and inflict a suitable penalty. So that at last, when all who had resisted had been defeated and brought under his power, he took ten thousand of the inhabitants of both banks of the Elbe, with their wives and children, and planted them in many groups in various parts of Germany and Gaul. And at last the war, protracted through so many years, was finished on conditions proposed by the King and accepted by them; they were to abandon the worship of devils, to turn from their national ceremonies, to receive the sacraments of the Christian faith and religion, and then, joined to the Franks, to make one people with them.

In this war, despite its prolongation through so many years, he did not himself meet the enemy in battle more than twice—once near the mountain called Osning, in the district of Detmold, and again at the river Hasa—and both these battles were fought in one month, with an interval of only a few days. In these two battles the enemy were so beaten and cowed that they never again ventured to challenge the King nor to resist his attack unless they were protected by some advantage of ground.

In this war many men of noble birth and high office fell on the side, both of the Franks and Saxons. But at last it come to an end in the thirty-third year, though in the meanwhile so many and such serious wars broke out against the Franks in all parts of the world, and were carried on with such skill by the King, that an observer may reasonably doubt whether his endurance of toil or his good fortune deserves the greater admiration. For the war in Italy began two years before the Saxon war, and though it was prosecuted without intermission, no enterprise in any part of the world was dropped, nor was there anywhere a truce in any struggle, however difficult. For this King, the wisest and most high-minded of all who in that age ruled over the nations of the world, never refused to undertake or prosecute any enterprise because of the labour involved, nor withdrew from it through fear of its danger. He understood the true character of each task that he undertook or carried through, and thus was neither broken by adversity nor misled by the false flatteries of good fortune.

Whilst the war with the Saxons was being prosecuted constantly and almost continuously he placed garrisons at suitable places on the frontier, and attacked Spain with the largest military expedition that he could collect. He crossed the Pyrenees, received the surrender of all the towns and fortresses that he attacked, and returned with his army safe and sound, except for a reverse which he experienced through the treason of the Gascons on his return through the passes of the Pyrenees. For while his army was marching in a long line, suiting their formation to the character of the ground and the defiles, the Gascons placed an ambuscade on the top of the mountain—where the density and extent of the woods in the neighbourhood rendered it highly suitable for such a purpose—and then, rushing down into the valley beneath, threw into disorder the last part of the baggage train and also the rearguard which acted as a protection to those in advance. In the battle which followed the Gascons slew their opponents to the last man. Then they seized upon the baggage, and under cover of the night, which was already falling, they scattered with the utmost rapidity in different directions. The Gascons were assisted in this feat by the lightness of their armour and the character of the ground where the affair took place. In this battle Eggihard, the surveyor of the royal table; Anselm, the Count of the Palace; and Roland, Praefect of the Breton frontier, were killed along with many others. Nor could this assault be punished at once, for when the deed had been done the enemy so completely disappeared that they left behind them not so much as a rumour of their whereabouts.

He conquered the Bretons, too, who dwelt in the extreme west of France by the shores of the ocean. They had been disobedient, and he, therefore, sent against them an expedition, by which they were compelled to give hostages and promise that they would henceforth obey his orders.

Then later he himself entered Italy with an army, and, passing through Rome, came to Capua, a city of Campania. There he pitched his camp, and threatened the men of Beneventum with war unless they surrendered. But Aragis, Duke of that people, prevented this war by sending his sons Rumold and Grimold to meet the King with a large sum of money. He asked the King to receive his children as hostages, and promised that he and his people would obey all the commands of the King, except only that he would not come himself into the King's presence. Charles, considering rather the advantage of the people than their Duke's obstinacy, received the hostages who were offered him, and as a great favour consented to forego a personal interview. He kept the younger of the two children as a hostage and sent back the elder one to his father. Then he sent ambassadors to require and receive oaths of fidelity from the Beneventans and from Aragis, and so came back to Rome. There he spent some days in the veneration of the holy places, and then returned to Gaul.

Then the Bavarian war broke out suddenly, and was swiftly ended. It was caused by the pride and folly of Tassilo, Duke of Bavaria; for upon the instigation of his wife, who thought that she might revenge through her husband the banishment of her father Desiderius, King of the Lombards, he made an alliance with the Huns, the eastern neighbours of the Bavarians, and not only refused obedience to King Charles but even dared to challenge him in war. The high courage of the King could not bear his overweening insolence, and he forthwith called a general levy for an attack on Bavaria, and came in person with a great army to the river Lech, which separates Bavaria from Germany. He pitched his camp upon the banks of the river, and determined to make trial of the mind of the Duke before he entered the province. But Duke Tassilo saw no profit either for himself or his people in stubbornness, and threw himself upon the King's mercy. He gave the hostages who were demanded, his own son Theodo among the number, and further promised upon oath that no one should ever persuade him again to fall away from his allegiance to the King. And thus a war which seemed likely to grow into a very great one came to a most swift ending. But Tassilo was subsequently summoned into the King's presence, and was not allowed to return, and the province that he ruled was for the future committed to the administration not of dukes but of counts.

When these troubles had been settled, he waged war against the Slavs, whom we are accustomed to call Wilzi, but who properly— that is, in their own tongue—are called Wela- tabi. Here the Saxons fought along with the other allied nations who followed the King's standards, though their loyalty was feigned and far from sincere. The cause of the war was that the Wilzi were constantly invading and attacking the Abodriti, the former allies of the Franks, and refused to obey the King's commands to desist from their attacks. There is a gulf stretching from the western sea towards the East, of undiscovered length, but nowhere more than a hundred miles in breadth, and often much narrower. Many nations occupy the shores of this sea. The Danes and the Swedes, whom we call the Northmen, hold its northern shore and all the islands in it. The Slavs and the Aisti and various other nations inhabit the eastern shore, amongst whom the chief are these Welatabi against whom then the King waged war. He so broke and subdued them in a single campaign, conducted by him- self, that they thought it no longer wise to refuse to obey his commands.

The greatest of all his wars, next to the Saxon war, followed this one—that, namely, which he undertook against the Huns and the Avars. He prosecuted this with more vigour than the rest and with a far greater military preparation. However, he conducted in person only one expedition into Pannonia, the prov- ince then occupied by the Avars; the manage- ment of the rest he left to his son Pippin, and the governors of the provinces, and in some cases to his counts and lieutenants. These car- ried on the war with the greatest energy, and finished it after eight years of fighting. How many battles were fought there and how much blood was shed is still shown by the deserted and uninhabited condition of Pannonia, and the district in which stood the palace of the Kagan is so desolate that there is not so much as a trace of human habitation. All the nobles of the Huns were killed in this war, all their glory passed away; their money and all the treasures that they had collected for so long were carried away. Nor can the memory of man recall any war waged against the Franks by which they were so much enriched and their wealth so increased. Up to this time they were regarded almost as a poor people, but now so much gold and silver were found in the palace, such precious spoils were seized by them in their battles, that it might fairly be held that the Franks had righteously taken from the Huns what they unrighteously had taken from other nations. Only two of the nobles of the Franks were killed in this war. Eric, the Duke of Friuli, was caught in an ambuscade laid by the townsmen of Tharsatica, a maritime town of Liburnia. And Gerold, the Governor of Bavaria, when he was marshalling his army to fight with the Huns in Pannonia, was killed by an unknown hand, along with two others, who accompanied him as he rode along the line encouraging the soldiers by name. For the rest, the war was almost blood- less so far as the Franks were concerned, and most fortunate in its result, although so difficult and protracted.

After this, the Saxon war ended in a settle- ment as lasting as the struggle had been pro- tracted. The wars with Bohemia and Luneburg which followed were soon over; both of them were swiftly settled under the command of the younger Charles.

The last war of all that Charles undertook was against those Northmen, who are called Danes, who first came as pirates, and then rav- aged the coasts of Gaul and Germany with a greater naval force. Their King, Godofrid, was puffed up with the vain confidence that he would make himself master of all Germany. He looked upon Frisia and Saxony as his own provinces. He had already reduced his neigh- bours, the Abodriti, to obedience, and had forced them to pay him tribute. Now he boasted that he would soon come to Aix, the seat of the King's Court, with a mighty force. His boast, however idle, found some to believe it; it was thought that he would certainly have made some such attempt if he had not been prevented by a sudden death. For he was killed by one of his own followers, and so ended both his life and the war that he had begun.

These, then, are the wars this mighty King waged during the course of forty-seven years—for his reign extended over that period—in different parts of the world with the utmost skill and success. By these wars he so nobly increased the kingdom of the Franks, which was great and strong when he inherited it from his father Pippin, that the additions he made almost doubled it. For before his time the power of the Frankish kingdom extended only over that part of Gaul which is bounded by the Rhine, the Loire, and the Balearic Sea; and that part of Germany which is inhabited by the so-called eastern Franks and which is bounded by Saxony, the Danube, the Rhine, and the river Saal, which stream separates the Thuringians and the Sorabs; and, further, over the Alamanni and the Bavarians. But Charles, by the wars that have been mentioned, conquered and made tributary the following countries:—First, Aquitania and Gascony, and the whole Pyrenean range, and the country of Spain as far as the Ebro, which rising in Navarre and passing through the most fertile territory of Spain, falls into the Balearic Sea, beneath the walls of the city of Tortosa; next, all Italy from Augusta Praetoria as far as lower Calabria, where are the frontiers of the Greeks and Beneventans, a thousand miles and more in length; next, Saxony, which is a considerable portion of Germany, and is reckoned to be twice as broad and about as long as that part of Germany which is inhabited by the Franks; then both provinces of Pannonia and Dacia, on one side of the river Danube, and Histria and Liburnia and Dalmatia, with the exception of the maritime cities which he left to the Emperor of Constantinople on account of their friendship and the treaty made between them; lastly, all the barbarous and fierce nations lying between the Rhine, the Vistula, the Ocean, and the Danube, who speak much the same language, but in character and dress are very unlike. The chief of these last are the Welatabi, the Sorabi, the Abodriti, and the Bohemians;

against these he waged war, but the others, and by far the larger number, surrendered without a struggle.

The friendship, too, which he established with certain kings and peoples increased the glory of his reign.

Aldefonsus, King of Gallaecia and Asturica, was joined in so close an alliance with him that whenever he sent letters or ambassadors to Charles he gave instructions that he should be called "the man" of the Frankish King.

Further, his rich gifts had so attached the kings of the Scots to his favour that they always called him their lord and themselves his submissive servants. Letters are still in existence sent by them to Charles in which those feelings towards him are clearly shown.

With Aaron, the King of the Persians, who ruled over all the East, with the exception of India, he entertained so harmonious a friendship that the Persian King valued his favour before the friendship of all the kings and princes in the world, and held that it alone deserved to be cultivated with presents and titles. When, therefore, the ambassadors of Charles, whom he had sent with offerings to the most holy sepulchre of our Lord and Saviour and to the place of His resurrection, came to the Persian King and proclaimed the kindly feelings of their master, he not only granted them all they asked but also allowed that sacred place of our salvation to be reckoned as part of the possessions of the Frankish King. He further sent ambassadors of his own along with those of Charles upon the return journey, and forwarded immense presents to Charles—robes and spices, and the other rich products of the East—and a few years earlier he had sent him at his request an elephant, which was then the only one he had.

The Emperors of Constantinople, Nicephorus, Michael, and Leo, too, made overtures of friendship and alliance with him, and sent many ambassadors. At first Charles was regarded with much suspicion by them, because he had taken the imperial title, and thus seemed to aim at taking from them their empire; but in the end a very definite treaty was made between them, and every occasion of quarrel on either side thereby avoided. For the Romans and the Greeks always suspected the Frankish power; hence, there is a well-known Greek proverb: "The Frank is a good friend but a bad neighbour."

Though he was so successful in widening the boundaries of his kingdom and subduing the foreign nations he, nevertheless, put on foot many works for the decoration and convenience of his kingdom, and carried some to completion. The great church dedicated to Mary, the holy Mother of God, at Aix, and the bridge, five hundred feet in length, over the great river Rhine near Mainz, may fairly be regarded as the chief of his works. But the bridge was burnt down a year before his death, and though he had determined to rebuild it of stone instead of wood it was not restored, because his death so speedily followed. He began also to build palaces of splendid workmanship —one not far from the city of Mainz, near a town called Ingelheim; another at Nimeguen, on the river Waal, which flows along the south of the Batavian island. And he gave special orders to the bishops and priests who had charge of sacred buildings that any throughout his realm, which had fallen into ruin through age should be restored, and he instructed his agents to see that his orders were carried out.

He built a fleet, too, for the war against the Northmen, constructing ships for this purpose near those rivers which flow out of Gaul and Germany into the northern ocean. And because the Northmen laid waste the coasts of Gaul and Germany by their constant attacks he planted forts and garrisons in all harbours and at the mouths of all navigable rivers, and prevented in this way the passage of the enemy. He took the same measures in the South, on the shore of Narbonne and Septimania, and also along all the coasts of Italy as far as Rome, to hold in check the Moors, who had lately begun to make piratical excursions. And by reason of these precautions Italy suffered no serious harm from the Moors, nor Gaul and Germany from the Northmen, in the days of Charles; except that Centumcellae, a city of Etruria, was betrayed into the hands of the Moors and plundered, and in Frisia certain islands lying close to Germany were ravaged by the Northmen.

PRIVATE LIFE AND CHARACTER OF CHARLEMAGNE

I have shown, then, how Charles protected and expanded his kingdom and also what splendour he gave to it. I shall now go on to speak of his mental endowments, of his steadiness of purpose under whatever circumstances of prosperity or adversity, and of all that concerns his private and domestic life.

As long as, after the death of his father, he shared the kingdom with his brother he bore so patiently the quarrelling and restlessness of the latter as never even to be provoked to wrath by him. Then, having married at his mother's bidding the daughter of Desiderius, King of the Lombards, he divorced her, for some unknown reason, a year later. He took in marriage Hildigard, of the Suabian race, a woman of the highest nobility, and by her he had three sons—viz., Charles and Pippin and Ludovicus, and three daughters—Hrotrud and Bertha and Gisla. He had also three other daughters—Theoderada and Hiltrud and Hruodhaid. Two of these were the children of his wife Fastrada, a woman of the eastern Franks or Germans; the third was the daughter of a concubine, whose name has escaped my memory. On the death of Fastrada he married Liutgard, of the Alemannic race, by whom he had no children. After her death he had four concubines—namely, Madelgarda, who bore him a daughter of the name of Ruothild; Gersuinda, of Saxon origin, by whom he had a daughter of the name of Adolthrud; Regina, who bore him Drogot and Hugo; and Adallinda, who was the mother of Theoderic.

His mother, Bertrada, lived with him to old age in great honour. He treated her with the utmost reverence, so that no quarrel of any kind ever arose between them—except in the matter of the divorce of the daughter of King Desiderius, whom he had married at her bidding. Bertrada died after the death of Hildigard, having lived to see three grandsons and as many granddaughters in her son's house. Charles had his mother buried with great honour in the same great church of St. Denys in which his father lay.

He had only one sister, Gisla, who from

childhood was dedicated to the religious life. He treated her with the same affectionate respect as his mother. She died a few years before Charles's own death in the monastery in which she had passed her life.

In educating his children he determined to train them, both sons and daughters, in those liberal studies to which he himself paid great attention. Further, he made his sons, as soon as their age permitted it, learn to ride like true Franks, and practise the use of arms and hunting. He ordered his daughters to learn wool work and devote attention to the spindle and distaff, for the avoidance of idleness and lethargy, and to be trained to the adoption of high principles.

He lost two sons and one daughter before his death—namely, Charles, his eldest; Pippin, whom he made King of Italy; and Hruotrud, his eldest daughter, who had been betrothed to Constantine, the Emperor of the Greeks. Pippin left one son, Bernard, and five daughters—Adalheid, Atula, Gundrada, Berthaid, and Theoderada. In his treatment of them Charles gave the strongest proof of his family affection, for upon the death of his son he appointed his grandson Bernard to succeed him, and had his granddaughters brought up with his own daughters.

He bore the deaths of his two sons and of his daughter with less patience than might have been expected from his usual stoutness of heart, for his domestic affection, a quality for which he was as remarkable as for courage, forced him to shed tears. Moreover, when the death of Hadrian, the Roman Pontiff, whom he reckoned as the chief of his friends, was announced to him, he wept for him as though he had lost a brother or a very dear son. For he showed a very fine disposition in his friendships: he embraced them readily and maintained them faithfully, and he treated with the utmost respect all whom he had admitted into the circle of his friends.

He had such care of the upbringing of his sons and daughters that he never dined without them when he was at home, and never travelled without them. His sons rode along with him, and his daughters followed in the rear. Some of his guards, chosen for this very purpose, watched the end of the line of march where his daughters travelled. They were very beautiful, and much beloved by their father, and, therefore, it is strange that he would give them in marriage to no one, either among his own people or of a foreign state. But up to his death he kept them all at home, saying that he could not forego their society. And hence the good fortune that followed him in all other respects was here broken by the touch of scandal and failure. He shut his eyes, however, to everything, and acted as though no suspicion of anything amiss had reached him, or as if the rumour of it had been discredited.

He had by a concubine a son called Pippin —whom I purposely did not mention along with the others—handsome, indeed, but deformed. When Charles, after the beginning of the war against the Huns, was wintering in Bavaria, this Pippin pretended illness, and formed a conspiracy against his father with some of the leaders of the Franks, who had seduced him by a vain promise of the kingdom. When the design had been detected and the conspirators punished Pippin was tonsured and sent to the monastery of Prumia, there to practise the religious life, to which in the end he was of his own will inclined.

Another dangerous conspiracy had been formed against him in Germany at an earlier date. The plotters were some of them blinded and some of them maimed, and all subsequently transported into exile. Not more than three lost their lives, and these resisted capture with drawn swords, and in defending themselves killed some of their opponents. Hence, as they could not be restrained in any other way, they were cut down.

The cruelty of Queen Fastrada is believed to be the cause and origin of these conspiracies. Both were caused by the belief that, upon the persuasion of his cruel wife, he had swerved widely from his natural kindness and customary leniency. Otherwise his whole life long he so won the love and favour of all men both at home and abroad that never was the slightest charge of unjust severity brought against him by anyone.

He had a great love for foreigners, and took such pains to entertain them that their numbers were justly reckoned to be a burden not only to the palace but to the kingdom at large.

But, with his usual loftiness of spirit, he took little note of such charges, for he found in the reputation of generosity and in the good fame that followed such actions a compensation even for grave inconveniences.

His body was large and strong; his stature tall but not ungainly, for the measure of his height was seven times the length of his own feet. The top of his head was round; his eyes were very large and piercing. His nose was rather larger than is usual; he had beautiful white hair; and his expression was brisk and cheerful; so that, whether sitting or standing, his appearance was dignified and impressive. Although his neck was rather thick and short and he was somewhat corpulent, this was not noticed owing to the good proportions of the rest of his body. His step was firm and the whole carriage of his body manly; his voice was clear, but hardly so strong as you would have expected. He had good health, but for four years before his death was frequently attacked by fevers, and at last was lame of one foot. Even then he followed his own opinion rather than the advice of his doctors, whom he almost hated, because they advised him to give up the roast meat to which he was accustomed, and eat boiled instead. He constantly took exercise both by riding and hunting. This was a national habit; for there is hardly any race on the earth that can be placed on equality with the Franks in this respect. He took delight in the vapour of naturally hot waters, and constantly practised swimming, in which he was so proficient that no one could be fairly regarded as his superior. Partly for this reason he built his palace at Aix, and lived there continuously during the last years of his life up to the time of his death. He used to invite not only his sons to the bath but also his nobles and friends, and at times even a great number of his followers and bodyguards.

He wore the national—that is to say, the Frankish—dress. His shirts and drawers were of linen, then came a tunic with a silken fringe, and hose. His legs were cross-gartered and his feet enclosed in shoes. In winter-time he defended his shoulders and chest with a jerkin made of the skins of otters and ermine. He was clad in a blue cloak, and always wore a sword, with the hilt and belt of either gold or silver.

Occasionally, too, he used a jewelled sword, but this was only on the great festivals or when he received ambassadors from foreign nations. He disliked foreign garments, however beautiful, and would never consent to wear them, except once at Rome on the request of Pope Hadrian, and once again upon the entreaty of his successor, Pope Leo, when he wore a long tunic and cloak, and put on shoes made after the Roman fashion. On festal days he walked in procession in a garment of gold cloth, with jewelled boots and a golden girdle to his cloak, and distinguished further by a diadem of gold and precious stones. But on other days his dress differed little from that of the common people.

He was temperate in eating and drinking, but especially so in drinking; for he had a fierce hatred of drunkenness in any man, and especially in himself or in his friends. He could not abstain so easily from food, and used often to complain that fasting was injurious to his health. He rarely gave large banquets, and only on the high festivals, but then he invited a large number of guests. His daily meal was served in four courses only, exclusive of the roast, which the hunters used to bring in on spits, and which he ate with more pleasure than any other food. During the meal there was either singing or a reader for him to listen to. Histories and the great deeds of men of old were read to him. He took delight also in the books of Saint Augustine, and especially in those which are entitled the City of God. He was so temperate in the use of wine and drink of any kind that he rarely drank oftener than thrice during dinner.

In summer, after his midday meal, he took some fruit and a single draught, and then, taking off his clothes and boots, just as he was accustomed to do at night, he would rest for two or three hours. At night he slept so lightly that he would wake, and even rise, four or five times during the night.

When he was putting on his boots and clothes he not only admitted his friends, but if the Count of the Palace told him there was any dispute which could not be settled without his decision he would have the litigants at once brought in, and hear the case, and pronounce on it just as if he were sitting on the tribunal.

He would, moreover, at the same time transact any business that had to be done that day or give any orders to his servants.

In speech he was fluent and ready, and could express with the greatest clearness whatever he wished. He was not merely content with his native tongue but took the trouble to learn foreign languages. He learnt Latin so well that he could speak it as well as his native tongue; but he could understand Greek better than he could speak it. His fluency of speech was so great that he even seemed sometimes a little garrulous.

He paid the greatest attention to the liberal arts, and showed the greatest respect and bestowed high honours upon those who taught them. For his lessons in grammar he listened to the instruction of Deacon Peter of Pisa, an old man; but for all other subjects Albinus, called Alcuin, also a deacon, was his teacher—a man from Britain, of the Saxon race, and the most learned man of his time. Charles spent much time and labour in learning rhetoric and dialectic, and especially astronomy, from Alcuin. He learnt, too, the art of reckoning, and with close application scrutinised most carefully the course of the stars. He tried also to learn to write, and for this purpose used to carry with him and keep under the pillow of his couch tablets and writing-sheets that he might in spare moments accustom himself to the formation of letters. But he made little advance in this strange task, which was begun too late in life.

He paid the most devout and pious regard to the Christian religion, in which he had been brought up from infancy. And, therefore, he built the great and most beautiful church at Aix, and decorated it with gold and silver and candelabras and with wicket-gates and doors of solid brass. And, since he could not procure marble columns elsewhere for the building of it, he had them brought from Rome and Ravenna. As long as his health permitted it he used diligently to attend the church both in the morning and evening, and during the night, and at the time of the Sacrifice. He took the greatest care to have all the services of the church performed with the utmost dignity, and constantly warned the keepers of the building not to allow anything improper or dirty either to be brought into or to remain in the building. He provided so great a quantity of gold and silver vessels, and so large a supply of priestly vestments, that at the religious services not even the door-keepers, who form the lowest ecclesiastical order, had to officiate in their ordinary dress. He carefully reformed the manner of reading and singing; for he was thoroughly instructed in both, though he never read publicly himself, nor sang except in a low voice and with the rest of the congregation.

He was most devout in relieving the poor and in those free gifts which the Greeks call alms. For he gave it his attention not only in his own country and in his own kingdom, but he also used to send money across the sea to Syria, to Egypt, to Africa—to Jerusalem, Alexandria, and Carthage—in compassion for the poverty of any Christians whose miserable condition in those countries came to his ears. It was for this reason chiefly that he cultivated the friendship of kings beyond the sea, hoping thereby to win for the Christians living beneath their sway some succour and relief.

Beyond all other sacred and venerable places he loved the church of the holy Apostle Peter at Rome, and he poured into its treasury great wealth in silver and gold and precious stones. He sent innumerable gifts to the Pope; and during the whole course of his reign he strove with all his might (and, indeed, no object was nearer to his heart than this) to restore to the city of Rome her ancient authority, and not merely to defend the church of Saint Peter but to decorate and enrich it out of his resources above all other churches. But although he valued Rome so much, still, during all the forty-seven years that he reigned, he only went there four times to pay his vows and offer up his prayers.

But such were not the only objects of his last visit; for the Romans had grievously outraged Pope Leo, had torn out his eyes and cut off his tongue, and thus forced him to throw himself upon the protection of the King. He, therefore, came to Rome to restore the condition of the church, which was terribly disturbed, and spent the whole of the winter there. It was then that he received the title of Emperor and Augustus, which he so disliked at first that he affirmed that he would not have entered the church on that day—though it was the chief festival of the church—if he could have foreseen the design of the Pope. But when he had taken the title he bore very quietly the hostility that it caused and the indignation of the Roman emperors. He conquered their ill-feeling by his magnanimity, in which, doubtless, he far excelled them, and sent frequent embassies to them, and called them his brothers.

When he had taken the imperial title he noticed many defects in the legal systems of his people; for the Franks have two legal systems differing in many points very widely from one another, and he, therefore, determined to add what was lacking, to reconcile the differences, and to amend anything that was wrong or wrongly expressed. He completed nothing of all his designs beyond adding a few capitularies, and those unfinished. But he gave orders that the laws and rules of all nations comprised within his dominions which were not already written out should be collected and committed to writing.

He also wrote out the barbarous and ancient songs, in which the acts of the kings and their wars were sung, and committed them to memory. He also began a grammar of his native language.

He gave the months names in his own tongue, for before his time they were called by the Franks partly by Latin and partly by barbarous names. He also gave names to the twelve winds, whereas before not more than four, and perhaps not so many, had names of their own. Of the months, he called January Winter-month, February Mud-month, March Spring-month, April Easter-month, May Joy-month, June Plough-month, July Hay-month, August Harvest-month, September Wind-month, October Vintage-month, November Autumn-month, December Holy-month. The following are the names which he gave to the winds:—The Subsolanus (east) he called East Wind; the Eurus (east by south) East-South Wind; the Euroauster (south by east) South-East Wind; the Auster (south) South Wind; the Austro-Afric (south by west) South-West Wind; the Afric (west by south) West-South Wind; the Zephyr (west) West Wind; the

Corus (west by north) West-North Wind; the Circius (north by west) North-West Wind; Septentrion (north) North Wind; the Aquilon (north by east) North-East Wind; the Vulturnus (east by north) East-North Wind.

At the very end of his life, when already he was feeling the pressure of old age and sickness, he summoned his own son Lewis, King of Aquitania, the only surviving son of Hildigard, and then solemnly called together the Frankish nobles of his whole kingdom; and then, with the consent of all, made Lewis partner in the whole kingdom and heir to the imperial title. After that, putting the diadem on his head, he ordered them to salute him "Imperator" and Augustus. This decision of his was received by all present with the greatest favour, for it seemed to them a divine inspiration for the welfare of the realm. It added to his dignity at home and increased the terror of his name abroad.

He then sent his son back to Aquitania, and himself, though broken with old age, proceeded to hunt, as his custom was, not far from the palace of Aix, and after spending the rest of the autumn in this pursuit he came back to Aix about the beginning of November. Whilst he was spending the winter there he was attacked by a sharp fever, and took to his bed. Then, following his usual habit, he determined to abstain from food, thinking that by such self-discipline he would be able either to cure or alleviate the disease. But the fever was complicated by a pain in the side which the Greeks call pleurisy; and, as Charles still persisted in fasting, and only very rarely drank something to sustain his strength, seven days after he had taken to his bed he received holy communion, and died, in the seventy-second year of his life and in the forty-seventh year of his reign, on the fifth day before the Kalends of February, at the third hour of the day.

His body was washed and treated with the usual ceremonies, and then, amidst the greatest grief of the whole people, taken to the church and buried. At first there was some doubt as to where he should rest, since he had given no instructions during his lifetime. But at length all were agreed that he could be buried nowhere more honourably than in the great church which he had built at his own expense in the same town, for the love of our Lord God Jesus Christ and the honour of His holy and ever-virgin Mother. There he was buried on the same day on which he died. A gilded arch was raised above the tomb, with his statue, and an inscription. The inscription ran as follows:—

"Beneath this tomb lies the body of Charles, the great and orthodox Emperor, who nobly expanded the kingdom of the Franks and reigned prosperously for forty-seven years. He departed this life, more than seventy years of age, in the eight hundred and fourteenth year of our lord, in the seventh indiction, on the fifth day before the Kalends of February."

There were many prodigies to show that his end drew near, and he as well as others understood the meanings of their warnings. During all the three last years of his life there were constant eclipses of sun and moon, and a black coloured spot appeared in the sun for the space of seven days. The gallery which he had built, of great size and strength, between the palace and the church, suddenly, on Ascension Day, fell in ruins down to the foundations. Also, the wooden bridge over the Rhine near Mainz, which he had built with wonderful skill, and the labour of ten years, so that it seemed as though it would last for ever, was accidentally set on fire, and in three hours burnt so far that not a plank remained except those that were covered by the water. Further, when he was making his last expedition in Saxony against Godofrid, King of the Danes, as he was moving out of camp and beginning his march before sunrise, he suddenly saw a meteor rush across the heavens with a great blaze and pass from right to left through the clear sky. Whilst all were wondering what this sign meant, suddenly the horse that he was riding fell head foremost, and threw him so violently to the ground that the girdle of his cloak was broken, and his sword belt slipped from it. When his attendants ran up to help him they found him disarmed and disrobed. His javelin, too, which he was holding in his hand at the time of his fall, fell twenty paces and more away from him. Moreover, the palace at Aix was frequently shaken, and in houses where he lived there was a constant creaking in the fretted ceilings. The church in which he was afterwards buried was struck by lightning, and the golden apple that adorned the summit of the roof was thrown down by a thunder-stroke, and fell upon the Bishop's house, which adjoined the church. In the same church an inscription was written on the edge of the circular space which ran round the inside of the church between the upper and lower arches, saying by whom the sacred edifice had been built. And in the last line occurred the words: "Carolus Princeps." Some noticed that in the very year in which Charles died, and a few months before his death, the letters of the word "princeps" were so destroyed as to be quite invisible. But he either refused to notice or despised all these omens as though they had no connection at all with anything that concerned him. . . .

Civilization in the Middle Ages

As classical civilization declined, Europe underwent a gradual change in all aspects of life. By the year 1000 these developments had produced a new era which historians generally have called the later Middle Ages. The social and economic life of the common people centered around the institution of manorialism, while feudalism furnished one of the elements in the political organization. The idea of a universal empire for western Europe survived the collapse of Rome and persisted into modern times. The papacy and the rulers of the Holy Roman Empire vied with one another in an effort to restore such an institution under the respective leadership of each. Christianity permeated every aspect of the culture of the period. Philosophy, literature, art, and even science were brought into a harmonious synthesis with Christian doctrine, further strengthening the unity of Christendom, and offering little opportunity for variation therefrom. Occasionally, however, individuals expressed views in poetry, in government, and even in religion which deviated from the medieval synthesis. While persons within Europe were formulating new ideas and grasping for new intellectual horizons, a few men like Marco Polo were actually going out and discovering what the world beyond Europe was like.

Manorial Documents

During the Middle Ages, the manor was the basic unit of social and economic life in much of Europe. It furnished the nobility with the bulk of their income and gave to the peasants both a place to live and the means of subsistence. As early as the thirteenth century, however, the revival of trade and the reappearance of a money economy began to undermine the long-established relationship between the lord of the manor and his serfs. As a result of these changes money payments began to supplement payments in service and produce; and gradually, too, both lord and bondsman found advantages in terminating the relationship. In the following documents note (1) the methods of paying for manorial holdings, (2) the practice of summarizing the services in terms of money, (3) restrictions placed upon the villeins, (4) the lord's facilities in the manor house, (5) the statement freeing the serf, William of Wythington, (6) his privileges and obligations, and (7) the relationship between the manor and the clergy.

A DESCRIPTION OF THE MANOR OF BERNEHORNE (1307)

Extent of the manor of Bernehorne, made on Wednesday following the feast of St. Gregory the pope, in the thirty-fifth year of the reign of King Edward, in the presence of Brother Thomas, keeper of Marley, John de la More, and Adam de Thruhlegh, clerks, on the oath of William de Gocecoumbe, Walter le Parker, Richard le Knyst, Richard the son of the latter, Andrew of Estone, Stephen Morsprich, Thomas Brembel, William of Swynham, John Pollard, Roger le Glide, John Syward, and John de Lillingewist, who say that there are all the following holdings: . . .

John Pollard holds a half acre in Aldithewisse and owes 18d. at the four terms, and owes for it relief and heriot.

John Suthinton holds a house and 40 acres of land and owes 3s. 6d. at Easter and Michaelmas.

William of Swynham holds 1 acre of meadow in the thicket of Swynham and owes 1d. at the feast of Michaelmas.

Ralph of Leybourne holds a cottage and 1 acre of land in Pinden and owes 3s. at Easter and Michaelmas, and attendance at the court

in the manor every three weeks, also relief and heriot.

Richard Knyst of Swynham holds 2 acres and a half of land and owes yearly 4s.

William of Knelle holds 2 acres of land in Aldithewisse and owes yearly 4s.

Roger le Glede holds a cottage and 3 roods of land and owes 2s. 6d. Easter and Michaelmas.

Alexander Hamound holds a little piece of land near Aldewisse and owes 1 goose of the value of 2d.

The sum of the whole rent of the free tenants, with the value of the goose, is 18s. 9d.

They say, moreover, that John of Cayworth holds a house and 30 acres of land, and owes yearly 2s. at Easter and Michaelmas; and he owes a cock and two hens at Christmas of the value of 4d.

And he ought to harrow for 2 days at the Lenten sowing with one man and his own horse and his own harrow, the value of the work being 4d; and he is to receive from the lord on each day 3 meals, of the value of 5d., and then the lord will be at a loss of 1d. Thus his harrowing is of no value to the service of the lord.

And he ought to carry the manure of the

E. P. Cheney, ed., *Translations and Reprints from the Original Sources of European History*, III, no. 5, *English Manorial Documents*, University of Pennsylvania Press, Philadelphia, n.d., 8–13; 31–32. Courtesy of the University of Pennsylvania Press.

lord for 2 days with one cart, with his own 2 oxen, the value of the work being 8*d.;* and he is to receive from the lord each day 3 meals at the value as above. And thus the service is worth 3*d.* clear.

And he shall find one man for 2 days, for mowing the meadow of the lord, who can mow, by estimation, 1 acre and a half, the value of the mowing of an acre being 6*d.:* the sum is therefore 9*d.* And he is to receive each day 3 meals of the value given above. And thus that mowing is worth 4*d.* clear.

And he ought to gather and carry that same hay which he has cut, the price of the work being 3*d.*

And he shall have from the lord 2 meals for 1 man, of the value of 1½*d.* Thus the work will be worth 1½*d.* clear.

And he ought to carry the hay of the lord for 1 day with a cart and 3 animals of his own, the price of the work being 6*d.* And he shall have from the lord 3 meals of the value of 2½*d.* And thus the work is worth 3½*d.* clear.

And he ought to carry in autumn beans or oats for 2 days with a cart and 3 animals of his own, the value of the work being 12*d.* And he shall receive from the lord each day 3 meals of the value given above. And thus the work is worth 7*d.* clear.

And he ought to carry wood from the woods of the lord as far as the manor, for two days in summer, with a cart and 3 animals of his own, the value of the work being 9*d.* And he shall receive from the lord each day 3 meals of the price given above. And thus the work is worth 4*d.* clear.

And he ought to find 1 man for 2 days to cut heath, the value of the work being 4*d.*, and he shall have 3 meals each day of the value given above: and thus the lord will lose, if he receives the service, 3*d.* Thus that mowing is worth nothing to the service of the lord.

And he ought to carry the heath which he has cut, the value of the work being 5*d.* And he shall receive from the lord 3 meals at the price of 2½*d.* And thus the work will be worth 2½*d.* clear.

And he ought to carry to Battle, twice in the summer season, each time half a load of grain, the value of the service being 4*d.* And he shall receive in the manor each time 1 meal of the value of 2*d.* And thus the work is worth 2*d* clear.

The totals of the rents, with the value of the hens, is 2*s,* 4*d.*

The total of the value of the works is 2*s.* 3½*d.*, owed from the said John yearly.

William of Cayworth holds a house and 30 acres of land and owes at Easter and Michaelmas 2*s.* rent. And he shall do all customs just as the aforesaid John of Cayworth.

William atte Grene holds a house and 30 acres of land and owes in all things the same as the said John.

Alan atte Felde holds a house and 16 acres of land (for which the sergeant pays to the court of Bixley 2*s.*), and he owes at Easter and Michaelmas 4*s.*, attendance at the manor court, relief, and heriot.

John Lyllingwyst holds a house and 4 acres of land and owes at the two terms 2*s.*, attendance at the manor court, relief, and heriot.

The same John holds 1 acre of land in the fields of Hoo and owes at the two periods 2*s.*, attendance, relief, and heriot.

Reginald atte Denne holds a house and 18 acres of land and owes at the said periods 18*d.*, attendance, relief, and heriot.

Robert of Northehou holds 3 acres of land at Saltcote and owes at the said periods attendance, relief, and heriot.

Total of the rents of the villeins, with the value of the hens, 20*s.*

Total of all the works of these three villeins, 6*s.* 10½*d.*

And it is to be noted that none of the above-named villeins can give their daughters in marriage, nor cause their sons to be tonsured, nor can they cut down timber growing on the lands they hold, without license of the bailiff or sergeant of the lord, and then for building purposes and not otherwise. And after the death of any one of the aforesaid villeins, the lord shall have as a heriot his best animal, if he had any; if, however, he have no living beast, the lord shall have no heriot, as they say. The sons or daughters of the aforesaid villeins shall give, for entrance into the holding after the death of their predecessors, as much as they give of rent per year.

Sylvester, the priest, holds 1 acre of meadow adjacent to his house and owes yearly 3*s.*

Total of the rent of tenants for life, 3s.

Petronilla atte Holme holds a cottage and a piece of land and owes at Easter and Michaelmas—; also, attendance, relief, and heriot.

Walter Herying holds a cottage and a piece of land and owes at Easter and Michaelmas 18d., attendance, relief, and heriot.

Isabella Mariner holds a cottage and owes at the feast of St. Michael 12d., attendance, relief, and heriot.

Jordan atte Melle holds a cottage and 1½ acres of land and owes at Easter and Michaelmas 2s., attendance, relief, and heriot.

William of Batelesmere holds 1 acre of land with a cottage and owes at the feast of St. Michael 3d., and 1 cock and 1 hen at Christmas of the value of 3d., attendance, relief, and heriot.

John le Man holds half an acre of land with a cottage and owes at the feast of St. Michael 2s., attendance, relief, and heriot.

John Werthe holds 1 rood of land with a cottage and owes at the said term 18d., attendance, relief, and heriot.

Geoffrey Caumbreis holds half an acre and a cottage and owes at the said term 18d., attendance, relief, and heriot.

William Hassok holds 1 rood of land and a cottage and owes at the said term 18d., attendance, relief, and heriot.

The same man holds 3½ acres of land and owes yearly at the feast of St. Michael 3s. for all.

Roger Doget holds half an acre of land and a cottage, which were those of R. the miller, and owes at the feast of St. Michael 18d., attendance, relief, and heriot.

Thomas le Brod holds 1 acre and a cottage and owes at the said term 3s., attendance, relief, and heriot.

Agnes of Cayworth holds half an acre and a cottage and owes at the said term 18d., attendance, relief, and heriot. . . .

Total of the rents of the said cottagers, with the value of the hens, 34s. 6d.

And it is to be noted that all the said cottagers shall do as regards giving their daughters in marriage, having their sons tonsured, cutting down timber, paying heriot, and giving fines for entrance, just as John of Cayworth and the rest of the villeins above mentioned.

Note: Fines and penalties, with heriots and reliefs, are worth yearly 5s.

AN ENGLISH MANOR HOUSE (1256)

He received also a sufficient and handsome hall well ceiled with oak. On the western side is a worthy bed, on the ground a stone chimney, a wardrobe, and a certain other small chamber; at the eastern end is a pantry and a buttery. Between the hall and the chapel is a side room. There is a decent chapel covered with tiles, a portable altar, and a small cross. In the hall are four tables on trestles. There are likewise a good kitchen well covered with tiles, with a furnace and ovens, one large, the other small, for cakes, two tables, and alongside the kitchen a small house for baking. Also a new granary covered with oak shingles, and a building in which the dairy is contained; though it is divided. Likewise a chamber suited for clergymen and a necessary chamber. Also a henhouse. These are within the inner gate.

Likewise outside of that gate are an old house for the servants, a good stable, long and divided, and to the east of the principal building, beyond the smaller stable, a solar for the use of the servants. Also a building in which is contained a bed; also two barns, one for wheat and one for oats. These buildings are enclosed with a moat, a wall, and a hedge. Also beyond the middle gate is a good barn, and a stable for cows and another for oxen, these old and ruinous. Also beyond the outer gate is a pigsty.

FREEING OF A SERF (1278)

To all the faithful of Christ to whom the present writing shall come, Richard, by the divine permission, abbot of Peterborough and of the Convent of the same place, eternal greeting in the Lord:

Let all know that we have manumitted and liberated from all yoke of servitude William, the son of Richard of Wythington, whom previously we have held as our born bondman, with his whole progeny and all his chattels, so that neither we nor our successors shall be able to require or exact any right or claim in the said William, his progeny, or his chattels. But the same William, with his whole progeny and all his chattels, shall remain free and quit and without disturbance, exaction, or any claim on the part of us or our successors by reason of any servitude forever.

We will, moreover, and concede that he and his heirs shall hold the messuages, land, rents, and meadows in Wythington which his ancestors held from us and our predecessors, by giving and performing the fine which is called *merchet* for giving his daughter in marriage, and tallage from year to year according to our will,—that he shall have and hold these for the future from us and our successors freely, quietly, peacefully, and hereditarily, by paying to us and our successors yearly 40*s.* sterling, at the four terms of the year, namely: at St. John the Baptist's day 10*s.*, at Michaelmas 10*s.*, at Christmas 10*s.*, and at Easter 10*s.*, for all service, exaction, custom, and secular demand; saving to us, nevertheless, attendance at our court of Castre every three weeks, wardship, and relief, and outside service of our lord the king, when they shall happen.

And if it shall happen that the said William or his heirs shall die at any time without an heir, the said messuage, land, rents, and meadows with their appurtenances shall return fully and completely to us and our successors. Nor will it be allowed to the said William or his heirs to give, sell, alienate, mortgage, or encumber in any way, the said messuage, land, rents, and meadows, or any part of them, by which the said messuage, land, rents, and meadows should not return to us and our successors in the form declared above. And if this should occur later, their deed shall be declared null, and what is thus alienated shall come to us and our successors. . . .

Given at Borough, for the love of Lord Robert of good memory, once abbot, our predecessor and maternal uncle of the said William, and at the instance of the good man, Brother Hugh of Mutton, relative of the said abbot Robert, A.D. 1278, on the eve of Pentecost.

The English Barons

From the time of the Norman conquest of England in 1066, the powerful barons of the island kingdom had been kept under control by their monarchs, who had gradually succeeded in strengthening and centralizing the royal power. Beginning with the reign of the unpopular king John in 1199, however, the English nobility began to resist and to demand a restoration of their feudal privileges. Disputes with church officials, military defeats in France, and discontent among the London merchants over excessive royal expenditures all helped to weaken John's despotic rule. On June 15, 1215, he was forced to meet with his hostile barons and grant them certain feudal privileges which were written into Magna Carta. Originally the charter's provisions applied only to the small minority of freemen in England, but subsequent confirmations enhanced its importance until it came to be considered as an integral part of the English constitution, guaranteeing certain fundamental liberties. In reading Magna Carta note (1) the rights granted the English church, (2) the clauses clarifying the various feudal relationships, (3) the guarantees of legal and judicial privileges, (4) the political and civil liberties mentioned, (5) any clauses affecting Englishmen other than the nobility, and (6) methods provided for enforcing the provisions of the charter.

W. S. McKechnie, *Magna Carta* . . . , J. Maclehose and Sons, Glasgow, 1914, 216 ff. Courtesy of Hector McKechnie and J. Maclehose and Sons.

MAGNA CARTA

PREAMBLE

John, by the grace of God, king of England, lord of Ireland, duke of Normandy and Aquitaine, and count of Anjou, to the archbishops, bishops, abbots, earls, barons, justiciars, foresters, sheriffs, stewards, servants, and to all his bailiffs and liege subjects, greeting. Know that, having regard to God and for the salvation of our souls, and those of all our ancestors and heirs, and unto the honour of God and the advancement of holy Church, and for the reform of our realm, [we have granted as underwritten] by advice of our venerable fathers, Stephen, archbishop of Canterbury, primate of all England and cardinal of the holy Roman Church, Henry archbishop of Dublin, William of London, Peter of Winchester, Jocelyn of Bath and Glastonbury, Hugh of Lincoln, Walter of Worcester, William of Coventry, Benedict of Rochester, bishops; of master Pandulf, subdeacon and member of the household of our lord the Pope, of brother Aymeric, master of the Knights of the Temple in England, and of the illustrious men William Marshal, earl of Pembroke, William, earl of Salisbury, William, earl Warenne, William, earl of Arundel, Alan of Galloway, constable of Scotland, Waren Fitz Gerald, Peter Fitz Herbert, Hubert de Burgh, seneschal of Poitou, Hugh de Neville, Matthew Fitz Herbert, Thomas Basset, Alan Basset, Philip d'Aubigny, Robert of Roppesley, John Marshal, John Fitz Hugh, and others, our liegemen.

1. In the first place we have granted to God, and by this our present charter confirmed for us and our heirs for ever that the English church shall be free, and shall have her rights entire, and her liberties inviolate; and we will that it be thus observed; which is apparent from this that the freedom of elections, which is reckoned most important and very essential to the English church, we, of our pure and unconstrained will, did grant, and did by our charter confirm and did obtain the ratification of the same from our lord, Pope Innocent III, before the quarrel arose between us and our barons: and this we will observe, and our will is that it be observed in good faith by our heirs for ever. We have also granted to all freemen of our kingdom, for us and our heirs forever, all the underwritten liberties, to be had and held by them and their heirs, of us and our heirs forever.

2. If any of our earls or barons, or others holding of us in chief by military service shall have died, and at the time of his death his heir shall be full of age and owe "relief" he shall have his inheritance on payment of the ancient relief, namely the heir or heirs of an earl, £100 for a whole earl's barony; the heir or heirs of a baron, £100 for a whole barony; the heir or heirs of a knight, 100s. at most for a whole knight's fee; and whoever owes less let him give less, according to the ancient custom of fiefs.

3. If, however, the heir of any one of the aforesaid has been under age and in wardship, let him have his inheritance without relief and without fine when he comes of age.

4. The guardian of the land of an heir who is thus under age, shall take from the land of the heir nothing but reasonable produce, reasonable customs, and reasonable services, and that without destruction or waste of men or goods; and if we have committed the wardship of the lands of any such minor to the sheriff, or to any other who is responsible to us for its issues, and he has made destruction or waste of what he holds in wardship, we will take of him amends, and the land shall be committed to two lawful and discreet men of that fee, who shall be responsible for the issues to us or to him to whom we shall assign them; and if we have given or sold the wardship of any such land to anyone and he has therein made destruction or waste, he shall lose that wardship, and it shall be transferred to two lawful and discreet men of that fief, who shall be responsible to us in like manner as aforesaid.

5. The guardian, moreover, so long as he has the wardship of the land, shall keep up the houses, parks, fishponds, stanks, mills, and other things pertaining to the land, out of the issues of the same land; and he shall restore to the heir, when he has come to full age, all

his land, stocked with ploughs and "wainage,'" according as the season of husbandry shall require, and the issues of the land can reasonably bear.

6. Heirs shall be married without disparagement, yet so that before the marriage takes place the nearest in blood to that heir shall have notice.

7. A widow, after the death of her husband, shall forthwith and without difficulty have her marriage portion and inheritance; nor shall she give anything for her dower, or for her marriage portion, or for the inheritance which her husband and she held on the day of the death of that husband; and she may remain in the house of her husband for forty days after his death, within which time her dower shall be assigned to her.

8. No widow shall be compelled to marry, so long as she prefers to live without a husband; provided always that she gives security not to marry without our consent, if she holds of us, or without the consent of the lord of whom she holds, if she holds of another.

9. Neither we nor our bailiffs shall seize any land or rent for any debt, so long as the chattels of the debtor are sufficient to repay the debt; nor shall the sureties of the debtor be distrained so long as the principal debtor is able to satisfy the debt; and if the principal debtor shall fail to pay the debt, having nothing wherewith to pay it, then the sureties shall answer for the debt; and let them have the lands and rents of the debtor, if they desire them, until they are indemnified for the debt which they have paid for him, unless the principal debtor can show proof that he is discharged thereof as against the said sureties.

10. If one who has borrowed from the Jews any sum, great or small, die before that loan be repaid, the debt shall not bear interest while the heir is under age, of whomsoever he may hold; and if the debt fall into our hands, we will not take anything except the principal sum contained in the bond.

11. And if anyone die indebted to the Jews, his wife shall have her dower and pay nothing of that debt; and if any children of the deceased are left under age, necessaries shall be provided for them in keeping with the holding of the deceased; and out of the residue the debt shall be paid, reserving, however, service due to feudal lords; in like manner let it be done touching debts due to others than Jews.

12. No scutage nor aid shall be imposed on our kingdom, unless by common counsel of our kingdom, except for ransoming our person, for making our eldest son a knight, and for once marrying our eldest daughter; and for these there shall not be levied more than a reasonable aid. In like manner it shall be done concerning aids from the city of London.

13. And the city of London shall have all its ancient liberties and free customs, as well by land as by water; furthermore, we decree and grant that all other cities, boroughs, towns, and ports shall have all their liberties and free customs.

14. And for obtaining the common counsel of the kingdom anent the assessing of an aid, except in the three cases aforesaid, or of a scutage, we will cause to be summoned the archbishops, bishops, abbots, earls, and greater barons, severally by our letters; and we will moreover cause to be summoned generally, through our sheriffs and bailiffs, all others who hold of us in chief, for a fixed date, namely, after the expiry of at least forty days, and at a fixed place; and in all letters of such summons we will specify the reason of the summons. And when the summons has thus been made, the business shall proceed on the day appointed, according to the counsel of such as are present, although not all who were summoned have come.

15. We will not for the future grant to any one licence to take an aid from his own free tenants, except to ransom his body, to make his eldest son a knight, and once to marry his eldest daughter; and on each of these occasions there shall be levied only a reasonable aid.

16. No one shall be distrained for performance of greater service for a knight's fee, or for any other free tenement, than is due therefrom.

17. Common pleas shall not follow our court, but shall be held in some fixed place.

18. Inquests of *novel disseisin*, of *mort d'ancestor*, and of *darrein presentment*, shall not be held elsewhere than in their own county-courts, and that in manner following,—We, or, if we should be out of the realm, our chief

justiciar, will send two justiciars through every county four times a year, who shall, along with four knights of the county chosen by the county, hold said assizes in the county court, on the day and in the place of meeting of that court.

19. And if any of the said assizes cannot be taken on the day of the county court, let there remain of the knights and freeholders, who were present at the county court on that day, as many as may be required for the efficient making of judgments, according as the business be more or less.

20. A freeman shall not be amerced for a slight offence, except in accordance with the degree of the offence; and for a grave offence he shall be amerced in accordance with the gravity of the offence, yet saving always his "contenement"; and a merchant in the same way, saving his "merchandise"; and a villein shall be amerced in the same way, saving his "wainage"—if they have fallen into our mercy: and none of the aforesaid amercements shall be imposed except by the oath of honest men of the neighbourhood.

21. Earls and barons shall not be amerced except through their peers, and only in accordance with the degree of the offence.

22. A clerk shall not be amerced in respect of his lay holding except after the manner of the others aforesaid; further, he shall not be amerced in accordance with the extent of his ecclesiastical benefice.

23. No village or individual shall be compelled to make bridges at river banks, except those who from of old were legally bound to do so.

24. No sheriff, constable, coroners, or others of our bailiffs, shall hold pleas of our Crown.

25. All counties, hundreds, wapentakes, and trithings, except our demesne manors, shall remain at the old rents, and without any additional payment.

26. If any one holding of us a lay fief shall die, and our sheriff or bailiff shall exhibit our letters patent of summons for a debt which the deceased owed to us, it shall be lawful for our sheriff or bailiff to attach and catalogue chattels of the deceased, found upon the lay fief, to the value of that debt, at the sight of lawworthy men, provided always that nothing whatever

be thence removed until the debt which is evident shall be fully paid to us; and the residue shall be left to the executors to fulfil the will of the deceased; and if there be nothing due from him to us, all chattels shall go to the deceased, saving to his wife and children their reasonable shares.

27. If any freeman shall die intestate, his chattels shall be distributed by the hands of his nearest kinsfolk and friends, under supervision of the church, saving to every one the debts which the deceased owed to him.

28. No constable or other bailiff of ours shall take corn or other provisions from any one without immediately tendering money therefor, unless he can have postponement thereof by permission of the seller.

29. No constable shall compel any knight to give money in lieu of castle-guard, when he is willing to perform it in his own person, or if he himself cannot do it from any reasonable cause, then by another responsible man. Further, if we have led or sent him upon military service, he shall be relieved from guard in proportion to the time during which he has been on service because of us.

30. No sheriff or bailiff of ours, or other person, shall take the horses or carts of any freeman for transport duty, against the will of the said freeman.

31. Neither we nor our bailiffs shall take, for our castles or for any other work of ours, wood which is not ours, against the will of the owner of that wood.

32. We will not retain beyond one year and one day, the lands of those who have been convicted of felony, and the lands shall thereafter be handed over to the lords of the fiefs.

33. All kydells [fish-weirs] for the future shall be removed altogether from Thames and Medway, and throughout all England, except upon the sea shore.

34. The writ which is called *praecipe* shall not for the future be issued to anyone, regarding any tenement whereby a freeman may lose his court.

35. Let there be one measure of wine throughout our whole realm; and one measure of ale; and one measure of corn, to wit, "the London quarter"; and one width of cloth whether dyed, or russet, or "halberget," to wit,

two ells within the selvedges; of weights also let it be as of measures.

36. Nothing in future shall be given or taken for a writ of inquisition of life or limbs, but freely it shall be granted, and never denied.

37. If anyone holds of us by fee-farm, by socage, or by burgage, and holds also land of another lord by knight's service, we will not by reason of that fee-farm, socage, or burgage, have the wardship of the heir, or of such land of his as is of the fief of that other; nor shall we have wardship of that fee-farm, socage, or burgage, unless such fee-farm owes knight's service. We will not by reason of any small serjeanty which anyone may hold of us by the service of rendering to us knives, arrows, or the like, have wardship of his heir or of the land which he holds of another lord by knight's service.

38. No bailiff for the future shall, upon his own unsupported complaint, put anyone to his "law," without credible witnesses brought for this purpose.

39. No freeman shall be taken or [and] imprisoned or disseised or exiled or in any way destroyed, nor will we go upon him nor send upon him, except by the lawful judgment of his peers or [and] by the law of the land.

40. To no one will we sell, to no one will we refuse or delay, right or justice.

41. All merchants shall have safe and secure exit from England, and entry to England, with the right to tarry there and to move about as well by land as by water, for buying and selling by the ancient and right customs, quit from all evil tolls, except in time of war such merchants as are of the land at war with us. And if such are found in our land at the beginning of the war, they shall be detained, without injury to their bodies or goods, until information be received by us, or by our chief justiciar, how the merchants of our land found in the land at war with us are treated; and if our men are safe there, the others shall be safe in our land.

42. It shall be lawful in future for any one excepting always those imprisoned or outlawed in accordance with the law of the kingdom, and natives of any country at war with us, and merchants, who shall be treated as is above provided to leave our kingdom and to return, safe and secure by land and water, ex-

cept for a short period in time of war, on grounds of public policy—reserving always the allegiance due to us.

43. If anyone holding of some escheat, such as the honour of Wallingford, Nottingham, Boulogne, Lancaster, or of other escheats which are in our hands and are baronies, shall die, his heir shall give no other relief, and perform no other service to us than he would have done to the baron, if that barony had been in the baron's hand; and we shall hold it in the same manner in which the baron held it.

44. Men who dwell without the forest need not henceforth come before our justiciars of the forest upon a general summons, except those who are impleaded, or who have become sureties for any person or persons attached for forest offences.

45. We will appoint as justices, constables, sheriffs, or bailiffs only such as know the law of the realm and mean to observe it well.

46. All barons who have founded abbeys, concerning which they hold charters from the kings of England, or of which they have long-continued possession, shall have the wardship of them, when vacant, as they ought to have.

47. All forests that have been made such in our time shall forthwith be disafforested; and a similar course shall be followed with regard to river-banks that have been placed "in defence" by us in our time.

48. All evil customs connected with forests and warrens, foresters and warreners, sheriffs and their officers, river-banks and their wardens, shall immediately be inquired into in each county by twelve sworn knights of the same county chosen by the honest men of the same county, and shall, within forty days of the said inquest, be utterly abolished, so as never to be restored, provided always that we previously have intimation thereof, or our justiciar, if we should not be in England.

49. We will immediately restore all hostages and charters delivered to us by Englishmen, as sureties of the peace or of faithful service.

50. We will entirely remove from their bailiwicks, the relations of Gerard of Athée so that in future they shall have no bailiwick in England; namely, Engelard of Cigogné, Peter, Guy, and Andrew of Chanceaux, Guy of Cigogné,

Geoffrey of Martigny with his brothers, Philip Mark with his brothers and his nephew Geoffrey, and the whole brood of the same.

51. As soon as peace is restored, we will banish from the kingdom all foreign-born knights, cross-bowmen, serjeants, and mercenary soldiers, who have come with horses and arms to the kingdom's hurt.

52. If any one has been dispossessed or removed by us, without the legal judgment of his peers, from his lands, castles, franchises, or from his right, we will immediately restore them to him; and if a dispute arise over this, then let it be decided by the five-and-twenty barons of whom mention is made below in the clause for securing the peace. Moreover, for all those possessions, from which any one has, without the lawful judgment of his peers, been disseised or removed, by our father, King Henry, or by our brother, King Richard, and which we retain in our hand or which are possessed by others, to whom we are bound to warrant them, we shall have respite until the usual term of crusaders; excepting those things about which a plea has been raised, or an inquest made by our order, before our taking of the cross; but as soon as we return from our expedition or if perchance we desist from the expedition we will immediately grant full justice therein.

53. We shall have, moreover, the same respite and in the same manner in rendering justice concerning the disafforestation or retention of those forests which Henry our father and Richard our brother afforested, and concerning the wardship of lands which are of the fief of another, namely, such wardships as we have hitherto had by reason of a fief which anyone held of us by knight's service, and concerning abbeys founded on other fiefs than our own, in which the lord of the fee claims to have right; and when we have returned, or if we desist from our expedition, we will immediately grant full justice to all who complain of such things.

54. No one shall be arrested or imprisoned upon the appeal of a woman, for the death of any other than her husband.

55. All fines made with us unjustly and against the law of the land, and all amercements imposed unjustly and against the law of the land, shall be entirely remitted, or else it

shall be done concerning them according to the decision of the five-and-twenty barons of whom mention is made below in the clause for securing the peace, or according to the judgment of the majority of the same, along with the aforesaid Stephen, archbishop of Canterbury, if he can be present, and such others as he may wish to bring with him for this purpose; and if he cannot be present the business shall nevertheless proceed without him, provided always that if any one or more of the aforesaid five-and-twenty barons are in a similar suit, they shall be removed as far as concerns this particular judgment, others being substituted in their places after having been selected by the rest of the same five-and-twenty for this purpose only, and after having been sworn.

56. If we have disseised or removed Welshmen from lands or liberties, or other things, without the legal judgment of their peers in England or in Wales, they shall be immediately restored to them; and if a dispute arise over this, then let it be decided in the marches by the judgment of their peers; for tenements in England according to the law of England, for tenements in Wales according to the law of Wales, and for tenements in the marches according to the law of the marches. Welshmen shall do the same to us and ours.

57. Further, for all those possessions from which any Welshman has, without the lawful judgment of his peers, been disseised or removed by King Henry our father, or King Richard our brother, and which we retain in our hand or which are possessed by others, to whom we are bound to warrant them, we shall have respite until the usual term of crusaders; excepting those things about which a plea has been raised or an inquest made by our order before we took the cross; but as soon as we return, or if perchance we desist from our expedition, we will immediately grant full justice in accordance with the laws of the Welsh and in relation to the foresaid regions.

58. We will immediately give up the son of Llywelyn and all the hostages of Wales, and the charters delivered to us as security for the peace.

59. We will do towards Alexander, King of Scots, concerning the return of his sisters and

his hostages, and concerning his franchises, and his right, in the same manner as we shall do toward our other barons of England, unless it ought to be otherwise according to the charters which we hold from William his father, formerly King of Scots; and this shall be according to the judgment of his peers in our court.

60. Moreover, all these aforesaid customs and liberties, the observance of which we have granted in our kingdom as far as pertains to us towards our men, shall be observed by all of our kingdom, as well clergy as laymen, as far as pertains to them towards their men.

61. Since, moreover, for God and the amendment of our kingdom and for the better allaying of the quarrel that has arisen between us and our barons, we have granted all these concessions, desirous that they should enjoy them in complete and firm endurance for ever, we give and grant to them the underwritten security, namely, that the barons choose five-and-twenty barons of the kingdom, whomsoever they will, who shall be bound with all their might, to observe and hold, and cause to be observed, the peace and liberties we have granted and confirmed to them by this our present Charter, so that if we, or our justiciar, or our bailiffs or any one of our officers, shall in anything be at fault toward anyone, or shall have broken any one of the articles of the peace or of this security, and the offence be notified to four barons of the foresaid five-and-twenty, the said four barons shall repair to us or our justiciar, if we are out of the realm, and, laying the transgression before us, petition to have that transgression redressed without delay. And if we shall not have corrected the transgression or, in the event of our being out of the realm, if our justiciar shall not have corrected it within forty days, reckoning from the time it has been intimated to us or to our justiciar, if we should be out of the realm, the four barons aforesaid shall refer that matter to the rest of the five-and-twenty barons, and those five-and-twenty barons shall, together with the community of the whole land, distrain and distress us in all possible ways, namely, by seizing our castles, lands, possessions, and in any other way they can, until redress has been obtained as they deem fit, saving harmless our

own person, and the persons of our queen and children; and when redress has been obtained, they shall resume their old relations toward us. And let whoever in the country desires it, swear to obey the orders of the said five-and-twenty barons for the execution of all the aforesaid matters, and along with them, to molest us to the utmost of his power, and we publicly and freely grant leave to every one who wishes to swear, and we shall never forbid anyone to swear. All those, moreover, in the land who of themselves and of their own accord are unwilling to swear to the twenty-five to help them in constraining and molesting us, we shall by our command compel the same to swear to the effect foresaid. And if any one of the five-and-twenty barons shall have died or departed from the land, or be incapacitated in any other manner which would prevent the foresaid provisions being carried out, those of the said twenty-five barons who are left shall choose another in his place according to their own judgment, and he shall be sworn in the same way as the others. Further, in all matters, the execution of which is intrusted to these twenty-five barons, if perchance these twenty-five are present and disagree about anything, or if some of them, after being summoned, are unwilling or unable to be present, that which the majority of those present ordain or command shall be held as fixed and established, exactly as if the whole twenty-five had concurred in this; and the said twenty-five shall swear that they will faithfully observe all that is aforesaid, and cause it to be observed with all their might. And we shall procure nothing from anyone, directly or indirectly, whereby any part of these concessions and liberties might be revoked or diminished; and if any such thing has been procured, let it be void and null, and we shall never use it personally or by another.

62. And all the ill-will, hatreds, and bitterness that have arisen between us and our men, clergy and lay, from the date of the quarrel, we have completely remitted and pardoned to everyone. Moreover, all trespasses occasioned by the said quarrel, from Easter in the sixteenth year of our reign till the restoration of peace, we have fully remitted to all, both clergy and laymen, and completely forgiven, as

far as pertains to us. And, on this head, we have caused to be made for them letters testimonial patent to the lord Stephen, archbishop of Canterbury, of the lord Henry, archbishop of Dublin, of the bishops aforesaid, and of Master Pandulf as touching this security and the concessions aforesaid.

63. Wherefore it is our will, and we firmly enjoin, that the English Church be free, and that the men in our kingdom have and hold all the aforesaid liberties, rights, and concessions, well and peaceably, freely and quietly, fully and wholly, for themselves and their heirs, of us and our heirs, in all respects and in all places for ever, as is aforesaid. An oath, moreover, has been taken, as well on our part as on the part of the barons, that all these conditions aforesaid shall be kept in good faith and without evil intent. Given under our hand—the above-named and many others being witnesses —in the meadow which is called Runnymede, between Windsor and Staines, on the fifteenth day of June, in the seventeenth year of our reign.

Thomas Aquinas

Thomas Aquinas (1225–1274), one of Western Civilization's greatest philosophers, taught at the University of Paris where he earned the appellation, the Angelic Doctor. As a scholastic philosopher he concerned himself with the whole of human learning, including political theory. He prepared the dissertation "On The Governance of Rulers" for the edification of the King of Cyprus (about 1259). It reveals, in addition to his method, a characteristic attitude of the late Middle Ages toward the state as a divine institution for the purpose of aiding men and women in achieving the good life on earth and beatitude in heaven. In reading this selection note (1) Thomas' argument in support of government, (2) his justification of monarchy, (3) his views of tyrannicide, (4) the purposes of government, (5) obstacles to virtuous living in society, (6) duties and responsibilities of kings, and (7) similarities to the political reasoning of Aristotle and Augustine.

From: ON THE GOVERNANCE OF RULERS

MEN LIVING TOGETHER MUST BE DILIGENTLY RULED BY SOMEBODY

The first step in our undertaking must be to set forth what is to be understood by the term "king." In all things which are ordered towards some end, wherein this or that course may be adopted, some directive principle is needed through which the due end may be reached by the most direct route. A ship, for example, which moves in different directions, according to the impulse of the changing winds, would never reach its destination were it not brought to port by the skill of the pilot.

Now, man has an end to which his whole life and all his actions are ordered; for man is an intelligent agent, and it is clearly the part of an intelligent agent to act in view of an end. Men, however, adopt different methods in proceeding towards their proposed end, as the

As translated by Gerald B. Phelan in *Saint Thomas Aquinas On the Governance of Rulers (De Regimine Principum)*, revised ed., published for the Institute of Mediaeval Studies by Sheed and Ward, London and New York, 1938, 33–48; 52–61; and 95–105. Courtesy of the Pontifical Institute of Mediaeval Studies.

diversity of men's pursuits and actions clearly indicates. Consequently, man needs some directive principle to guide him towards his end.

But, the light of reason is placed by nature in every man, to guide him in his acts towards his end. Were man intended to live alone, as many animals do, he would require no other guide to his end. Then would each man be a king unto himself, under God, the highest King, inasmuch as he would direct himself in his acts by the light of reason given him from on high.

However, it is natural for man to be a social and political animal, to live in a group, even more so than all other animals, as the very needs of his nature indicate. For all other animals nature has prepared food, hair as a covering, teeth, horns, claws as means of defence, or at least speed in flight. Man, on the other hand, was created without any natural provision for these things. But, instead of them all he was endowed with reason, by the use of which he could procure all these things for himself by the work of his hands. But one man alone is not able to procure them all for himself; for one man could not sufficiently provide for life, unassisted. It is, therefore, natural that man should live in company with his fellows.

Moreover, all other animals are able to discern by inborn skill what is useful and what is injurious; just as the sheep naturally regards the wolf as his enemy. Some animals even recognize by natural instinct certain medicinal herbs and other things necessary for their life. Man, however, has a natural knowledge of the things which are essential for his life only in a general fashion, inasmuch as he has power of attaining knowledge of the particular things necessary for human life by reasoning from universal principles. But it is not possible for one man to arrive at a knowledge of all these things by his own individual reason. It is, therefore, necessary for man to live in a group so that each one may assist his fellows, and different men may be occupied in seeking by their reason to make different discoveries, one, for example, in medicine, one in this and another in that.

This point is, further, most plainly evidenced by the fact that the use of speech is a prerogative proper to man. By this means one man is able fully to express his conceptions to others. Other animals, it is true, express their feelings to one another in a general way, as a dog may express anger by barking and other animals may give vent to their feelings in various manners. So man communicates with his kind more completely than any other animal known to be gregarious, such as the crane, the ant and the bee. With this in mind, therefore, Solomon says, in Ecclesiastes, IV. 9: "It is better that two should be together than one; for they have the advantage of their company."

If, therefore, it is natural for man to live in the society of many, it is necessary that there exist among men some means by which the group may be governed. For where there are many men together, and each one is looking after his own interest, the group would be broken up and scattered unless there were also someone to take care of what appertains to the common weal. In like manner the body of a man, or any other animal, would disintegrate unless there were a general regulating force within the body which watches over the common good of all the members. With this in mind Solomon says (Prov. XI. 14): "Where there is no governor, the people shall fall."

Indeed it is reasonable that this happen, for what is proper and what is common are not identical. Things differ by what is proper to each: they are united by what they have in common. For, diversity of effects is due to diversity of causes. Consequently, there must exist something which impels towards the common good of the many, over and above that which impels towards the private good of each individual. Wherefore, also in all things that are ordained towards a single end there is something to be found which rules the rest. Thus in the corporeal universe, other bodies are regulated, according to a certain order of divine providence, by the first body, namely, the celestial body, and all bodies are controlled by a rational creature. So, too, in the individual man, the soul rules the body; and among the parts of the soul, the irascible and the concupiscible parts are ruled by the reason. Likewise, among the members of a body, one is the principal and moves all the others, as the heart or the head. Therefore, in every group there must be some governing power.

It happens, however, in certain things which

are ordained towards an end, that one may proceed in a right way and also in a wrong way. And so, too, in the government of a group there is a right way and a wrong way. Now, anything whatsoever is rightly directed when it is guided towards its proper (*convenientem*) end, wrongly when it is guided towards an improper (*non convenientem*) end. The proper (*conveniens*) end of a group of free men is different from that of a group of serfs; for the free man is one who is for his own sake (*causa sui*), the serf is one whose whole being belongs to another. If, therefore, a group of free men is governed by their ruler for the common good of the group, that government will be right and just, as is suitable to free men. If, however, the government is organized, not for the common good of the group but for the private interest of the ruler, it will be an unjust and perverted government. The Lord, therefore, threatens such rulers, saying (Ezech. XXXIV. 2): "Woe to the shepherds that feed themselves [because they seek their own interests]: should not the flocks be fed by the shepherds?" For shepherds indeed should seek the good of their flocks and every ruler, the good of the multitude subject to him. Now, if an unjust government is carried on by one man alone who seeks his own benefit from his rule, and not the good of the multitude subject to him, such a ruler is called a tyrant—a word derived from strength—because he oppresses by might instead of ruling by justice. Thus, among the ancients, all powerful men were called tyrants. But if the unjust government is carried on, not by one, but by several, especially if they be few, it is called an oligarchy, that is, the rule of a few. This occurs when a few, who differ from the tyrant only by the fact that they are more than one, oppress the people by means of their wealth. If, however, the bad government is carried on by the multitude it is called a democracy, that is, control by the populace. This comes about when the plebeian populace by force of numbers oppress the wealthy. In this way the whole people will be as one tyrant.

In like manner we must divide just governments. If the government is administered by a multitude, it is given the name of a polity: as, for instance, when a body of warriors exercises dominion over a city or a province. But, if it is administered by a few, but virtuous, men, this kind of government is called an aristocracy, that is, the best governance or governance by the best men, who for this reason are called the nobility (*optimates*). But, if a just government is in the hands of one man alone, he is properly called a king. Wherefore the Lord says by the mouth of Ezechiel (XXVII. 24): "My servant, David, shall be king over them and all of them shall have one Shepherd." From this it is clearly shown that the idea of king implies that he be one man who is chief and that he be a shepherd who seeks the common good of the multitude and not his own advantage.

Now, since men must live in a group, because they are not sufficient unto themselves to procure the necessities of life were they to remain solitary, it follows that a society will be the more perfect the more it is sufficient unto itself to procure the necessities of life. There is, indeed, to some extent sufficiency for life in one family of one household, namely, in so far as pertains to the natural acts of nourishment and the begetting of offspring and other things of this kind; it exists, furthermore, in one village with regard to those things which belong to one trade; but it exists in a city, which is a perfect community, with regard to all the necessities of life; but still more in a province because of the need of fighting together and of mutual help against enemies. So, the man who rules a perfect community, that is, a city or a province, is called a king *par excellence*: he who rules a home is called a father of a family, not a king. Still, he bears a certain resemblance to a king, on account of which, kings are sometimes called the fathers of peoples.

It is plain, therefore, from what has been said, that a king is one who rules the people of one city or province and rules them for the public good. Wherefore Solomon says (Eccles. V. 8): "The King ruleth over all the land subject to him."

IT IS MORE EXPEDIENT THAT A MULTITUDE OF MEN LIVING TOGETHER BE RULED BY ONE MAN RATHER THAN BY MANY

Having set forth these preliminary points we must now inquire what is better for a province or a city; whether to be ruled by one man or by many. Now this may be considered from the very purpose of government. For the aim of any ruler should be directed toward securing the welfare of whatever he undertakes to rule. The duty of the pilot, for instance, is to preserve his ship amidst the perils of the sea and to bring it unharmed to the port of safety. Now, the welfare and safety of a multitude formed into a society is the preservation of its unity, which is called peace, and which, if taken away, the benefit of social life is lost and moreover the multitude in its disagreement becomes a burden to itself. The chief concern of the ruler of a multitude, therefore, should be to procure the unity of peace: and it is not legitimate for him to deliberate whether he shall establish peace in the multitude subject to him, just as a physician does not deliberate whether he shall heal the sick man encharged to him. For no one should deliberate about an end which he is obliged to seek, but only about the means to attain that end. Wherefore, the Apostle, having commended the unity of the faithful people, says (Eph. IV. 3): "Be ye careful to keep the unity of the spirit in the bond of peace." The more efficacious, therefore, a government is in keeping the unity of peace, the more useful it will be. For we call that more useful which leads the better to the end. Now it is manifest that what is itself one can more efficaciously bring about unity than several: just as the most efficacious cause of heat is that which is by its nature hot. Therefore, the rule of one man is more useful than the rule of many.

Furthermore, it is evident that several persons could by no means keep a multitude from harm (*conservant*) if they totally disagreed. For a certain union is necessary among them if they are to rule at all: several men, for instance, could not pull a ship in one direction unless joined together in some fashion. Now several are said to be united according as they come closer to being one. So one man rules better than several who come near being one.

Again, whatever is in accord with nature is best: for in all things nature does what is best. Now, every natural governance is governance by one. In the multitude of bodily members there is one which moves them all, namely, the heart; and among the powers of the soul one power presides as chief, namely, the reason. Even among bees there is one queen (*rex*), and in the whole universe there is One God, Maker and Ruler of all things. And this is reasonable. For every multitude is derived from unity. Wherefore, artificial things imitate natural things, and since a work of art is better according as it attains a closer likeness to what is in nature, it necessarily follows that it is best, in the case of a human multitude, that it be ruled by one person.

This is also evident from experience; for provinces or cities which are not ruled by one person are torn with dissensions and are tossed about without peace so that the complaint seems to be fulfilled which the Lord uttered through the Prophet (Jerm. XII. 10): "Many pastors have destroyed my vineyard." But, on the contrary, provinces and cities which are ruled under one king enjoy peace, flourish in justice, and delight in prosperity. Hence, the Lord by His prophets promises to His people as a great reward that He will give them one head and that one Prince will be in the midst of them.

JUST AS THE RULERSHIP OF ONE MAN IS BEST, WHEN IT IS JUST, SO, WHEN IT IS UNJUST, IT IS THE WORST. AND THIS IS PROVED BY MANY REASONS AND ARGUMENTS

Just as the government of a king is the best, the government of a tyrant is the worst. Now democracy is the opposite of polity, since both are governments carried on by many persons, as is clear from what has been already said: while oligarchy is the opposite of aristocracy, for both are governments carried on by a few persons: and kingship is the opposite of tyranny since both are carried on by one person. It has already been shown that monarchy is the best government. If, therefore, the worst is opposed to the best, it follows that tyranny is the worst kind of government.

Further, a united force is more efficacious in producing its effect than a force which is scattered or divided. For, many persons acting together can pull a load which could not be pulled by each one taking his part separately and acting individually. Therefore, just as it is more useful for a force operating for good to be more united, in order that it may work good more effectively, so a force operating for evil is more harmful when it is one than when it is divided. Now, the power who rules unjustly works to the detriment of the public, since he diverts the common public good to his sole personal benefit. Therefore, for the same reason that, in a just government, the government is better in proportion as the ruling power is one—thus monarchy is better than aristocracy, and aristocracy than polity—so the contrary will be true of an unjust government, namely, that the ruling power will be more harmful in proportion as it is more unitary. Consequently tyranny is more harmful than oligarchy; and oligarchy than democracy.

Moreover, a government becomes unjust by the fact that the ruler, paying no heed to the public welfare, seeks his own personal advantage. Wherefore the further he departs from the public welfare the more unjust will his government be. But there is a greater departure from the public welfare in an oligarchy, in which the advantage of a few is sought, than in a democracy, in which the advantage of many is sought; and there is a still greater departure from the common welfare in a tyranny, where the advantage of only one man is sought: for a large number is closer to the complete totality than a small number, and a small number than only one. So the government of a tyrant is the most unjust.

The same conclusion is made clear to those who consider the order of Divine Providence which disposes everything for the best. For in all things, good issues from one perfect cause, from a conjunction, as it were, of all conditions favourable to the production of good, while evil results from singular defects, separately. For beauty is not in a body unless all its members are fittingly disposed; but ugliness arises when any member whatever is not fittingly disposed. Thus ugliness results in different ways from many causes: beauty from one perfect cause in one way. It is thus with all good and evil things, as if God so provided that good, arising from one cause, be stronger, while evil, arising from many causes, be weaker. It is expedient therefore that a just

government be that of one man only, that it may be stronger. But if the government should turn aside to injustice, it is more expedient that it be a government by many, so that it may be weaker and they may mutually hinder one another. Among unjust governments, therefore, democracy is more tolerable, but the worst is tyranny.

The same conclusion is most apparent if one considers the evils which come from tyrants: because, since a tyrant, despising the common good, seeks his private interest, it follows that he will oppress his subjects in different ways according as he is dominated by different passions to acquire certain goods. The one who is held down by the passion of cupidity seizes the goods of his subjects: whence Solomon says (Prov. XXIX. 4): "A just king setteth up the land: a covetous man shall destroy it." But if he be dominated by the passion of anger he sheds blood for nothing; whence it is said by Ezechiel (XXII. 27): "Her princes in the midst of her are like wolves ravening the prey to shed blood." Therefore, this kind of government is to be avoided as the Wise man admonishes (Eccli. IX. 18): "Keep thee far from the man who has the power to kill," because forsooth he kills not for justice' sake but by his power, for the lust of his will. Thus there will be no safety; everything is uncertain when there is a departure from justice nor can anything be made stable when it depends upon the will of another, much less of his caprice. Nor does he merely oppress his subjects in corporal things but he also hinders their spiritual good. For they who seek to be at the head (*praeesse*) rather than to be beneficial (*prodesse*), prevent all progress (*profectum*), suspecting all excellence in their subjects as prejudicial to their evil domination. For good men are more suspected by tyrants than bad men, and virtue in others is always a source of fear to them. So, these tyrants strive to prevent those of their subjects who have become virtuous from acquiring a spirit of magnanimity and casting off their iniquitous domination, from establishing a pact of friendship among the subjects and enjoying the benefits of peace among themselves, in order that, so long as one does not trust another, nothing can be set up against their controlling power. Wherefore, they sow discords among them, foster those that have arisen, and forbid whatever things tend to unite men in groups, as weddings, banquets, and other such things through which familiarity and confidence are begotten among men. They also strive to prevent them from becoming powerful or rich because, suspecting their subjects according to the consciousness of their own malice, they fear that the power and wealth of their subjects will become harmful to them just as they use their own power and wealth to work harm. When Job (XV. 21) says of the tyrant, "The sound of dread is always in his ears: and when there is peace [that is when no one is attempting to harm him] he always suspecteth treason." So it turns out that, when governors, who ought to lead their subjects to virtue are wickedly jealous of the virtues of their subjects, hinder it as much as they can, few virtuous men are found under the rule of tyrants. For, according to the opinion of the Philosopher, brave men are found among those among whom all brave men are honoured. And as Tullius says, "the things which are despised by everybody always languish and flourish but little." For it is natural that men, brought up in fear, should fall back into a servile spirit and become discouraged in the presence of any strenuous and manly task: and this is shown by experience in provinces that have long been ruled by tyrants. Hence, the Apostle says (Col. III. 21): "Fathers, provoke not your children to indignation, lest they be discouraged." So, considering these evil effects of tyranny, King Solomon says, (Prov. XXVIII. 12): "When the wicked reign, men are ruined," because, forsooth, through the wickedness of tyrants, subjects fall away from the perfection of virtue. And again, he says, (Prov. XXIX. 2): "When the wicked shall bear rule the people shall mourn, as though led into slavery." And again (Prov. XXVIII. 28): "When the wicked rise up men shall hide themselves," that they may escape the cruelty of the tyrant. And no wonder, because a man governing without reason according to the lust of his soul in no way differs from a beast. Whence Solomon says (Prov. XXVIII. 15): "As a roaring lion and a hungry bear, so is a wicked prince over the poor people." And therefore men hide from tyrants as from cruel beasts and it seems that to be subject to a tyrant is the same thing as to lie prostrate beneath a raging beast.

THAT IN A GOVERNMENT BY MANY, TYRANNICAL GOVERNMENT OCCURS MORE FREQUENTLY THAN IN A GOVERNMENT BY ONE: THEREFORE THE RULE OF ONE MAN IS BETTER

When a choice is to be made between two things from both of which danger impends, that one must by all means be chosen from which the lesser evil follows. Now, lesser evil follows from a monarchy if it be changed into a tyranny, than from the government of several nobles, when it becomes corrupt. For the dissension which commonly follows upon the government of several, runs counter to the good of peace, which is the principal thing in a social group; which good, indeed, is not done away with by a tyranny, unless there be an excess of tyranny which rages against the whole community, but certain goods of particular men are hindered. The rule of one man is therefore to be preferred to the rule of many, although perils follow from both. Further, that from which great dangers may more often follow is, it would seem, the more to be avoided; but the greatest dangers to the multitude follow more frequently from the rule of many than from the rule of one. For, it commonly happens that one out of the many turns from the pursuit of the common good more than does one man ruling alone. Now when any one among several leaders turns aside from the pursuit of the common good, danger of internal dissension threatens the multitude of subjects, because when the chiefs quarrel, the consequence is that dissension in the multitude follows. If, however, one man is in command, he usually, indeed, looks to the common good; or if he turn his attention away from the common good, it does not immediately follow that he turns his attention to the oppression of his subjects, which is an excess of tyranny and holds the highest degree of wickedness in government, as has been shown above. The dangers which arise from the government of many are more to be avoided, therefore, than those which arise from the government of one. Moreover, it happens that the rule of many is changed into a tyranny not less, but perhaps more, frequently than the rule of one. For once dissension arises through the rule of several, it often happens that one triumphs over the others and usurps the government of the multitude for himself alone; and this indeed may be clearly seen from what has come about in such circumstances. For the rule of almost all groups of many has ended in tyranny, as is plainly seen in the Roman Republic. When it had been administered for a long time by several magistrates, animosities, dissensions and civil wars arose and it fell into the power of the most cruel tyrants. And, in general, if one carefully considers what has happened in the past and what is happening in the present, he will discover that more men practised tyranny in lands ruled by many than in those governed by one. If, therefore, kingly rule, which is the best government, seems chiefly to be avoided because of tyranny, and on the other hand, tyranny is wont to occur not less, but more, in the rule of many than in the rule of one, it follows that it is simply more expedient to live under one king than under the rule of several.

CONCLUSION, THAT THE RULE OF ONE MAN IS SIMPLY THE BEST. IT SHOWS HOW THE MULTITUDE MUST BE DISPOSED IN REGARD TO HIM, BECAUSE THE OPPORTUNITY OF TYRANNIZING MUST BE REMOVED FROM HIM, AND THAT HE SHOULD BE TOLERATED EVEN IN HIS TYRANNY ON ACCOUNT OF THE GREATER EVIL TO BE AVOIDED

Therefore, since the rule of one man, which is the best, is to be preferred, and since it may happen that it be changed into a tyranny, which is the worst, it is clear from what has been said that diligent zeal must be exercised in order that the interests of the multitude be so safeguarded with regard to their king that they may not fall under a tyrant. First it is necessary that the man who is raised up to be king by those to whom this office belongs, should be of such character that it is improbable he should fall into tyranny. Wherefore, Daniel, commending the Providence of God with respect to the establishment of the king says (I. Kings XIII. 14): "The Lord hath sought him a man according to his own heart." Then, once the king is established, the government of the kingdom must be so arranged that opportunity to tyrannize be removed. At the same time, his power should be so tempered that he cannot easily fall into tyranny. How these things may be done we must consider in what follows. Finally, provision must be made for facing the situation should the king turn aside into tyranny.

Indeed, if there be not an excess of tyranny it is more expedient to tolerate for a while the milder tyranny than, by acting against the tyrant, to be involved in many perils which are more grievous than the tyranny itself. For it may happen that those who act against the tyrant are unable to prevail and the tyrant, thus provoked, rages the more. Even if one should be able to prevail against the tyrant, from this fact itself very grave dissensions among the people frequently ensue: the multitude may be broken up by factions either during their revolt against the tyrant, or, concerning the organization of the government, after the tyrant has been overthrown. It also happens that sometimes, while the multitude is driving out the tyrant by the help of some man, he, having received the power, seizes the tyranny, and fearing to suffer from another what he did to his predecessor, oppresses his subjects with a more grievous slavery. For this is wont to happen in tyranny, namely, that the second becomes more grievous than the one preceding, inasmuch as, without abandoning the previous oppressions, he himself thinks up fresh ones from the malice of his heart: whence, in Syracuse, when there was a time that everybody desired the death of Dionysius, a certain old woman kept constantly praying that he might be unharmed and that he might survive her. When the tyrant learned this he asked why she did it. Then she said, "When I was a girl we had a harsh tyrant and I wished for his death; when he was killed, there succeeded him one who was somewhat harsher: I was very eager to see the end of his dominion also: then we began to have a third ruler still more harsh—that was you. So if you should be taken away a worse would succeed in your place."

Now some have been of opinion that if the excess of tyranny is unbearable, it would be an act of virtue for strong men to slay the tyrant and to expose themselves to dangers of death in order to set the multitude free. An example of this occurs even in the Old Testament. For a certain Aioth (*Aod*) slew Eglon, King of Moab, who was oppressing the people of God under harsh slavery, with the dagger fastened to his thigh; and he was made a judge of the people. (Cf. Judges III. 21.) But this opinion is not in accord with apostolic teaching. For Peter admonishes us to be reverently subject to our masters, not only to the good and gentle but also to the froward (I. Petr. II. 18): "For if one who suffers unjustly bear his trouble for conscience sake, this is a grace." (*Ibid.* II. 19.) Wherefore, when many Roman emperors tyrannically persecuted the faith of Christ, a great multitude both of the nobility and of the populace was converted to the faith and they were praised, not for resisting, but for patiently and courageously bearing death for Christ. This is plainly manifested in the case of the holy legion of Thebans. Aioth (*Aod*), then, must be considered rather as having slain a foe, than as having assassinated a ruler of the people, though a tyrannical one. Hence even in the Old Testament we read that they who killed Joas, the king of Juda, although he had fallen away from the worship of God, were slain and their children spared according to the precept of the law. It would, moreover, be dangerous both for the multitude and for their rulers if certain persons should attempt on their own private presumption, to kill their governors, even tyrants. For to dangers of this kind, usually the wicked expose themselves more than the good. For the rule of a king, no less than that of a tyrant, is burdensome to the wicked because, according to the words of Solomon, "A wise king scattereth the wicked" (Prov. XX. 26). Consequently, by presumption of this kind, danger to the people from the loss of their king would be more imminent than relief through the removal of the tyrant.

Furthermore, it rather seems, that to proceed against the cruelty of tyrants is an action to be undertaken, not through the private presumption of a few, but by public authority. First of all, if to provide itself with a king belong to the right of any multitude, it is not unjust that the king set up by that multitude be destroyed or his power restricted, if he tyrannically abuse the royal power. It must not be thought that such a multitude is acting unfaithfully in deposing the tyrant, even though it had previously subjected itself to him in perpetuity; because he himself has deserved that the covenant with his subjects should not be kept, since, in ruling the multitude, he did not act faithfully as the office of a king demands. Thus did the Romans cast out from the kingship, Tarquin the Proud, whom they had accepted as their king, because of his tyranny and the tyranny of his sons; and they set up in their place a lesser power, namely, the consular power. So too Domitian, who had succeeded those most moderate Emperors, Vespasian, his father, and Titus, his brother, was slain by the Roman senate when he exercised tyranny, and all that he had wickedly done to the Romans, was justly and profitably, by a decree of the senate, declared null and void.

Thus it came about that Blessed John the Evangelist, the beloved disciple of God, who had been exiled to the island of Patmos by that very Domitian, was sent back to Ephesus by a decree of the senate.

If, however, it pertains to the right of some higher authority to provide a king for a certain multitude, a remedy against the wickedness of a tyrant is to be looked for from him. Thus when Archelaus, who had already begun to reign in Judaea in the place of Herod, his father, was imitating his father's wickedness, a complaint against him having been laid before Caesar Augustus by the Jews, his power was, first of all, diminished by depriving him of his title of king and by dividing one half of his kingdom between his two brothers; later, since he was not restrained from tyranny even by this means, Tiberius Caesar sent him into exile in Lyons, a city of Gaul.

Should no human aid whatsoever against a tyrant be forthcoming, recourse must be had to God, the King of all, who is a helper in due time in tribulation. "For, it lies within His power to turn the cruel heart of the tyrant to mildness" (Prov. IX. 10). In the words of Solomon (Prov. XXI. 1): "The heart of the king is in the hand of the Lord, whithersoever He will He shall turn it." He it was who turned into mildness the cruelty of King Assuerus, who was preparing death for the Jews. He it was who so transformed the cruel king Nabuchodonosor that he became a proclaimer of the divine power. "Therefore," he said, "I, Nabuchodonosor, do now praise and magnify and glorify the King of Heaven: because all his works are true and His ways judgments, and them that walk in pride He is able to abase" (Dan. IV. 34). Those tyrants, however, whom he deems unworthy of conversion he is able to put out of the way or reduce them to the lowest degree, according to the words of the Wise Man (Eccli. X. 17): "God hath overturned the thrones of proud princes: and hath set up the meek in their stead." He it was who, seeing the afflicting of his people in Egypt and hearing their cry, hurled the tyrant Pharaoh with his army into the sea. He it was who not only banished from his kingly throne the above mentioned Nabuchodonosor in his former pride, but also cast him from the fellowship of men and changed him into the likeness of a beast. For also His hand is not shortened that He cannot free His people from tyrants. For by Isaias He promises to give his people rest from their labour and trouble and harsh slavery in which they had formerly served; and by Ezechiel (XXXIV. 10) He says, "I will deliver my flock from their mouth," that is from the mouth of shepherds who feed themselves. But to deserve to secure this benefit from God, the people must desist from sin; because by divine permission wicked men receive power to rule as a punishment for sin, as the Lord says by the Prophet Osee (XIII. 11): "I will give thee a king in my wrath;" and it is said in Job (XXXIV. 30) that he "maketh a man that is a hypocrite to reign for the sins of the people." Sin must therefore be done away with that the scourge of tyrants may cease.

WHAT MANNER OF GOVERNMENT IS POSSIBLE FOR A KING, SEEING THAT IT IMITATES THE DIVINE PROVIDENCE; THIS METHOD OF GOVERNMENT HAD ITS ORIGIN IN THE GUIDANCE OF A SHIP; AND A COMPARISON IS SET UP BETWEEN SACERDOTAL AND ROYAL DOMINION

Just as the founding of a city or a kingdom may suitably be learned from the way the world was created, so too the way to govern may be learned from the governing of the world. Before going into that, however, we should consider that to govern is to bring the thing governed in a suitable way to its proper end. Thus a ship is said to be governed, when, through the skill of the sailor, it is brought by a direct route and unharmed to harbour. Consequently, if anything is ordained to an end outside itself (as a ship to a harbour), it is the governor's duty, not only to preserve the thing unharmed, but further to bring it to its end. If on the contrary, there should be anything whose end is not outside itself, then the governor's endeavours would merely tend to preserve the thing itself undamaged in its proper perfection. Although nothing of this kind is found in the world, except God Himself, Who is the end of all, yet the care of that which is ordained to something outside itself, is hindered by many things and in different ways. For, perhaps, one person may have the duty of preserving a thing in existence, and another the duty of bringing it to a higher state of perfection. This is clearly the case in the example of the ship, from which the idea (*ratio*) of government is derived. For it is the carpenter's duty to repair anything that is broken in the ship, but the sailor bears the anxiety of bringing the ship to port. It is the same with man. The doctor sees to it that a man's life is preserved in health, the tradesman supplies the necessities of life, the teacher takes care that he learns the truth, and the tutor sees that he lives according to reason. If a man were not ordained to any other end outside himself, the above mentioned cares would be sufficient for him.

But as long as a man's mortal life endures

there is some good extraneous to him, namely, final beatitude which is looked for after death, in the enjoyment of God, for as the Apostle says (II Cor. V. 6): "As long as we are in the body we are far from the Lord." Consequently the Christian man, for whom that beatitude has been purchased by the blood of Christ, and who in order to attain it, has received the earnest of the Holy Ghost, needs an additional spiritual care to direct him to the harbour of eternal salvation, and this care is provided for the faithful by the ministers of the Church of Christ.

We must form the same judgment about the end of society as a whole as we do concerning the end of one man. If, therefore, the end of man were some good that exists in himself, then the ultimate end of the multitude to be governed would likewise be for the multitude to acquire such good and persevere in its possession. If such an ultimate end, either of an individual man or a multitude, were a corporeal one, namely, life and health of body, to govern would then be a physician's charge. If that ultimate end were an abundance of wealth, then some financier would be king of the multitude. If the good of the knowledge of truth were of such a kind that the multitude might attain to it, the king would have the duty of teacher. But it is clear, that the end of any multitude gathered together, is to live virtuously. For, men form groups for the purpose of living well together, a thing which the individual man living alone could not attain. But a good life is a virtuous life. Therefore a virtuous life is the end for which men form groups.

The evidence for this lies in the fact that only those who render mutual assistance to one another in living well truly form part of an assembled multitude. For if men assembled merely to *live*, then animals and serfs would form a part of the civil body. And if men assembled only to acquire wealth, then all those who traded together, would belong to one city. Thus we see that only those are regarded as forming one society who are directed by the same laws and the same government, to live well. Therefore, since man, by living virtuously, is ordained to a higher end, which consists of the enjoyment of God, as we have said above, then human society must have the same end as the individual man. Therefore, it is not the ultimate end of an assembled multitude to live virtuously, but through virtuous living to attain to the possession of God. Furthermore, if it could attain this end by the power of human nature, then the duty of a king would have to include the direction of men to this end. We are supposing that he is called "king" to whom the supreme power of governing in human affairs is entrusted. Now the higher the end to which a government is ordained, the loftier is that government; for we always find that the one to whom it pertains to achieve the final end, commands those who execute the things that are ordained to that end. For example, the captain, whose business it is to regulate navigation, tells the man who builds the ship what kind of a ship he must build in order that it be suitable to navigation; and the citizen, who bears arms, tells the blacksmith what kind of arms to make. But, because a man does not attain his end which is the possession of God, by human power, but by Divine power, according to the words of the Apostle (Romans, VI. 23): "By the grace of God life everlasting," therefore the task of leading him to that end does not pertain to human government but to Divine. Consequently, government of this kind pertains to that king who is not only a man, but also God, namely, to our Lord Jesus Christ, Who by making men sons of God, brought them to the glory of Heaven.

This then is the government which has been delivered to Him and which shall not be destroyed (Cf. Dan. VII. 14), on account of which He is called, in Holy Writ, not Priest only, but King, as Jeremias says (XXIII. 5): "The king shall reign and he shall be wise." Hence a royal priesthood is derived from Him, and what is more, all those who believe in Christ, in so far as they are His members, are called kings and priests. Consequently, in order that spiritual things might be distinguished from earthly things, the ministry of this kingdom has been entrusted not to earthly kings, but to priests, and in the highest degree to the chief priest, the successor of St. Peter, the Vicar of Christ, the Roman Pontiff, to whom all the kings of Christian peoples are to be subject as to our Lord Jesus Christ Himself. For those to whom pertains the care of intermediate ends should be subject to him to whom pertains the care of the ultimate end, and be directed by his rule. Because the priesthood of the gentiles, and the whole worship of their Gods existed merely for the acquisition of temporal goods (which were all ordained to the common good of the multitude, whose care devolved upon a king), the priests of the gentiles were very properly subject to the kings. Similarly, because in the old law earthly goods were promised to a religious people (not indeed by demons but by the true God), the priests of the old law, we read, were also subject to the kings. But in the new law there is a higher priesthood by which men are guided to heavenly goods. Consequently in the law of Christ, kings must be subject to priests.

Therefore, it was a marvelous effect of Divine Providence that in the city of Rome, which God had forseen would be the principal seat of the Christian people, the custom was gradually established that the rulers of the city should be subject to the priests, for as Valerius Maximus relates: "Our City has always considered that everything should yield precedence to religion, even those things in which it aimed to display the splendor of supreme majesty. Wherefore our governments did not hesitate to minister to religion, considering that they would thus hold control of human affairs if they faithfully and constantly were submissive to Divine authority." Because it was to come to pass that the religion of the Christian priesthood should especially thrive in France, God permitted that among the Gauls too, their tribal priests, called Druids, should lay down the law of all Gaul, as Julius Caesar relates in the book which he wrote about the Gallic war.

THAT JUST AS A KING DISPOSES HIS SUBJECTS TO LIVE VIRTUOUSLY IN ORDER TO ATTAIN THEIR ULTIMATE END, HE MUST DO THE SAME TO ATTAIN THE INTERMEDIATE END, AND HERE WE NOTE THOSE THINGS WHICH DISPOSE TOWARDS A PROPER LIFE, AND THOSE WHICH HINDER, AND ALSO THE REMEDY WHICH THE KING MUST APPLY AGAINST THESE HINDRANCES

As the life by which men live well here on earth is ordained as a means to the end of that blessed life which we hope for in heaven, so too whatever particular goods are procured by man's agency, whether wealth, or profits, or health, or eloquence, or learning are ordained as a means to the end of the common good. If, then, as we have said, the person who is charged with the care of our ultimate end, ought to be over those who have charge of things ordained to that end, and to direct them by his rule, it clearly follows from what we have said that just as the king ought to be subject to the dominion and government administered by the office of priesthood, so he ought to preside over all human offices, and regulate them by the rule of his government. Now, anyone on whom it devolves to do something which is ordained to another thing as to its end, is bound to see that his work is suitable to that end; thus, for example, the armourer so fashions the sword, that it is suitable for fighting, and the builder should so lay out the house that it is suitable for habitation. Therefore, since the beatitude of heaven is the end of that virtuous life which we live at present, it pertains to the king's office to promote such good living among his people, as is suitable for the attainment of heavenly happiness, that is to say, he should command those things which lead to the happiness of Heaven, and as far as possible, forbid the contrary. What conduces to true beatitude and what hinders it are learned from the law of God, the teaching of which belongs to the office of the priest, according to the words of Malachy (II. 7): "The lips of the priest shall guard knowledge and they shall seek the law from his mouth." Wherefore, the Lord prescribes in Deut. XVII. 18, that "after he is raised to the throne of his kingdom, the king shall copy out to himself the Deuteronomy of this law, in a volume, taking the copy of the priests of the Levitical tribe, he shall have it with him and shall read it all the days of his life, that he may learn to fear the Lord his God, and keep his words and ceremonies which are commanded in the law." Therefore, the king, taught the law of God, should have for his principal concern the means by which the multitude subject to him, may live well. Now this concern is threefold: first of all, to establish a virtuous life in the multitude subject to him; second, to preserve it once-established; and third, having preserved it, to promote its greater perfection.

For an individual man to lead a good life two things are required. The first and most important is to act in a virtuous manner (for virtue is that by which one lives well); the second, which is secondary, and, as it were, instrumental, is a sufficiency of those bodily goods whose use is necessary for an act of virtue. Yet the unity of man is brought about by nature, while the unity of a society, which we call peace, must be procured through the efforts of the ruler. Therefore, to establish virtuous living in a multitude three things are necessary. First of all, that the multitude be established in the unity of peace. Second, that the multitude thus united in the bond of peace, be guided to good deeds. For just as a man can do nothing well unless unity within his members be presupposed, so a multitude of men which lacks the unity of peace, is hindered from virtuous action, by the fact that it fights against its very existence as a group. In the third place, it is necessary that there be at hand a sufficient supply of the things required for proper living, procured by the ruler's efforts. Then, when virtuous living is set up in society by the efforts of the king, it remains for him to look to its conservation.

Now there are three things which prevent permanence in public virtue. One of these arises from nature. For the good of society should not be established for one time only; it should be in a sense perpetual. Men, on the other hand, cannot abide forever because they are mortal. Even while they are alive they do not always preserve the same vigour, for the life of man is subject to many changes. So a man is not equally suited to the performance of the same duties throughout the whole span of his life. A second impediment to the preservation of public good which comes from within, consists in the perversity of the wills of man, inasmuch as they are either too lazy

to perform what the state demands, or, still further, they are harmful to the peace of society, because, by transgressing justice, they disturb the peace of their neighbours. The third hindrance to the preservation of the state comes from without, namely, when peace is destroyed through the attacks of enemies, or, as it sometimes happens, the kingdom or city is completely blotted out. In regard to these three dangers, a triple charge is laid upon the king. First of all, he must take care of the appointment of men to succeed or replace others in charge of the various offices, just as, by the providence of God, provision is made for the succession and replacement of corruptible things, which cannot last forever the same, by the generation of things to take their place. Thus just as the integrity of the universe is maintained so too, the good of the multitude subject to the king will be maintained by his care, provided he carefully attend to the appointment of new men to fill the place of those who drop out. In the second place, by his law and orders, punishments and rewards, he restrains the men subject to him from wickedness, and encourages them to works of virtue, following the example of God, Who gave His law to man and requites those who observe it with rewards, and those who transgress it with punishments. The king's third charge is to keep the multitude entrusted to him safe from the enemy. For it would be useless to prevent internal dangers if the multitude could not be defended against external dangers.

So, for the proper direction of the multitude, there remains the third duty of the kingly office, namely, that he be solicitous for its improvement. He performs this duty when, in each of the things we have mentioned, he corrects what is out of order, and supplies what is lacking, and, if any of them can be done better he tries to do it. This is why the Apostle (I. Corinth. XII. 31) exhorts the faithful to be zealous for the better gifts. These then are the duties of the kingly office. . . .

Papal Claims

In 494 Pope Gelasius I wrote a letter to the Byzantine Emperor Anastasius in which he set forth the relative power of the clergy and of royal governors. The date is significant because it was less than 20 years after the traditional fall of the Empire in the West and thus illustrates how quickly the papacy asserted its position. In reading this letter note (1) the relative position claimed for the two powers, and (2) the justification on which the claim was based.

The "Dictate of the Pope" is a statement found among the papers of Gregory VII after his death in 1085 and may have been written by him. It is generally considered to be a summary of his policies growing out of the struggle for temporal power with Emperor Henry IV. Note (1) the bases for the papal claim to supreme power, (2) the arguments supporting papal monarchy within the church, and (3) the claims to universal power in secular affairs.

In 1302, during a bitter struggle with Philip IV of France over the question of temporal sovereignty, Boniface VIII issued this bull. Note (1) the arguments upon which Boniface based his claims, (2) his use of the doctrine of the two powers, and (3) his appeal to logic as well as to scripture.

SELECTED DOCUMENTS ILLUSTRATIVE OF PAPAL CLAIMS TO SUPREME POWER

I. EXCERPTS FROM A LETTER OF POPE GELASIUS I (492–496) TO THE BYZANTINE EMPEROR ANASTASIUS

There are two powers, august Emperor, by which this world is chiefly governed: the sacred authority of the clergy and the royal power; and that of the priests is the more important inasmuch as at the Last Judgement they must render an account even for the kings themselves. . . . And if it is right that the hearts of the faithful should be obedient to all priests who administer divine matters properly, how much more should they submit to the bishop of that see which the Divine Power has decreed to be pre-eminent above all priests, and which, consequently, the devotion of the whole Church honors!

II. THE DICTATE OF THE POPE: A MEMORANDUM FOUND AMONG THE PAPERS OF POPE GREGORY VII AFTER HIS DEATH IN 1085

The Roman church was founded by God alone.

The Roman pontiff alone can rightly be called universal.

He alone can depose and reinstate bishops.

His legate, even if of lower rank, is superior in a council to all bishops, and can pass sentence of deposition against them. . . .

Reprinted from History 11, *History of Western Civilization, A Syllabus*, Stanford University Press, Stanford University, 1940, 14, with the permission of the author and of the publishers, Stanford University Press.

One ought not even to remain in the same house with those excommunicated by him.

He alone has the right under changing conditions to make new laws, to lay out new dioceses, to make an abbey of a canonry (and the reverse), to divide a wealthy bishopric and unite poor ones. . . .

All princes shall kiss the feet of the pope alone.

His name alone shall be mentioned in the churches.

His name is unique in the world.

He may depose emperors. . . .

He may ordain a cleric of any church he may wish.

He who is ordained by him may rule over another church, but may not hold a lower post; and such a one may not receive a higher rank from any bishop.

No synod shall be considered a general council without his command.

No decree and no book shall be considered canonical without his authority.

A judgement passed by him may be reversed by no one; and he himself, alone of all, may withdraw it.

He himself may be judged by no man.

No one shall dare to condemn any one who appeals to the apostolic see.

The more important cases of every church should be referred to this see.

The Roman church has never erred; nor will it err to all eternity, as Scripture bears witness. . . .

By his command and consent, subordinates may bring accusations (against their superiors). . . .

No one shall be considered catholic who is not in agreement with the Roman church.

He may absolve subjects from their oath of allegiance to wicked rulers.

III. A CONDENSATION OF THE BULL UNAM SANCTAM LAUNCHED IN 1302 AGAINST KING PHILIP IV OF FRANCE BY POPE BONIFACE VIII

That there is one holy Catholic and apostolic Church we are compelled by our faith to believe and hold, and outside of it there is neither salvation nor forgiveness of sins. The Church is one mystic body, and of this body Christ is the head, even as God is the head of Christ. In it is one Lord, one faith, and one baptism. At the time of the flood there was one ark of Noah, symbolizing the one Church, having one Noah as steersman and pilot. Outside of this all things upon the face of the earth were, as we read, destroyed. This Church we venerate and this alone. . . . It is that seamless coat of the Lord. Therefore, in this one and only Church there is one body and one head, namely, Christ and Christ's vicar, Peter and Peter's successor; for the Lord said unto Peter himself, "Feed my sheep," (and likewise) in the Gospel of John, "there is one fold, and one shepherd."

In this Church and in its power are two swords, a spiritual and a temporal. Both are in the power of the Church, the latter to be used for the Church, the former by the Church, the one by the priest, the other by the hand of kings and soldiers, but by the command and permission of the priest.

It is fitting, moreover, that one sword should be under the other, and the temporal authority subject to the spiritual power. For, according to the law of the universe, things are not brought to order directly and equally, but the lowest through the intermediate, and the inferior through the superior. We should, therefore, frankly recognize that the spiritual power excels in dignity and nobility any form whatsoever of earthly power, just as spiritual interests exceed temporal matters in importance. Therefore, if the earthly power shall err, it shall be judged by the spiritual power; if the lesser spiritual power err, it shall be judged by the higher. But if the supreme power err, it can be judged by God alone and not by man. Hence this power, although given to man and exercised by man, is not human, but rather a divine power, given by the divine lips to Peter, and founded on a rock for him and his successors.

Whoever, therefore, shall resist this power, ordained by God, resists the ordination of God. Wherefore we proclaim, assert, decree, and pronounce that it is altogether necessary to salvation for every human being to be subject to the Roman pontiff.

Dante Alighieri

Dante Alighieri (1265–1321) was a Florentine who wrote the Divina Commedia, one of the greatest literary works in the Italian language. He was also very active in the political life of the day, and was one of those who opposed the extension of the pope's secular power. When the papacy in its struggle with the Holy Roman Empire triumphed in Dante's native city, however, the great writer was forced into exile. Convinced that factional political strife should be removed from Italy, he wrote De Monarchia to espouse the cause of unity under the temporal rule of the emperor. In taking this stand, Dante was not opposed to the Church, as such, but only to some of its claims to complete supremacy in Christendom. In the following selections note (1) the question Dante proposed to investigate, (2) the three classes of men who opposed the truth he sought to establish, (3) the arguments advanced to support the supremacy of the papacy, (4) how Dante attempted to refute these claims, (5) the character of the authorities he cited in his arguments, and (6) the source and character of the claims he made for the emperor.

From: DE MONARCHIA

"He has shut the lions' mouths and they have not hurt me; inasmuch as before Him righteousness was found in me." In beginning this work I proposed to investigate three questions as far as the subject-matter would allow. For the first two questions this has been done satisfactorily in the foregoing books, I believe. We must now consider the third, the truth of which may, however, be a cause of indignation against me, since it cannot be brought forth without causing certain men to blush. But since Truth from her immutable throne demands it; and Solomon entering his forest of *Proverbs,* and marking out his own conduct, entreats that we "meditate upon truth and abhor wickedness;" and our teacher of morals, the Philosopher, admonishes us to sacrifice whatever is most precious for truth's sake: therefore, gaining assurance from the words of Daniel, wherein the power of God is shown as a shield for defenders of truth, and "putting on the breastplate of faith" according to the admonition of Paul, in the warmth of that coal taken from the heavenly altar by one of the Seraphim and touched to the lips of Isaiah, I will engage in the present conflict, and by the arm of Him who with His blood liberated us from the power of darkness, I will cast the ungodly and the liar from the arena, while the world looks on. Wherefore should I fear, when the Spirit, coeternal with the Father and the Son, says by the mouth of David, "The righteous shall be in everlasting remembrance, he shall not be afraid of evil tidings"?

The question pending investigation, then, concerns two great luminaries, the Roman Pontiff and the Roman Prince: and the point at issue is whether the authority of the Roman Monarch, who, as proved in the second book, is rightful Monarch of the world, derives from God directly, or from some vicar or minister of God, by whom I mean the successor of Peter, veritable keeper of the keys of the kingdom of heaven. . . .

As translated by Aurelia Henry in *The De Monarchia of Dante Alighieri,* Houghton Mifflin Company, Boston and New York, 1904, 135–137; 140–148; 164–182; and 196–206. Courtesy of Dr. Paul Henry Reinhardt and Houghton Mifflin Company.

In entering on this third question, let us bear in mind that the truth of the first was made manifest in order to abolish ignorance rather than contention. But the investigation of the second had reference alike to ignorance and contention. Indeed, we are ignorant of many things concerning which we do not contend: the geometrician does not know the square of the circle, but he does not contend about it; the theologian does not know the number of the angels, but he renders it no cause for quarrel; the Egyptian knows naught of the civilization of Scythia, but does not therefore make the civilization a source of strife.

Now the truth of the third question has to do with so keen a contention that, whereas ignorance generally causes the discord, here the discord causes ignorance. For it always happens to men who will things before rationally considering them that, their desire being evil, they put behind them the light of reason; as blind men they are led about by their desire, and stubbornly deny their blindness. Whence it often occurs not only that falsehood has her own patrimony, but that many men going out from her boundaries run through strange camps, where, neither understanding nor being understood at all, they provoke some to wrath, some to disdain, and not a few to laughter.

Three classes of men struggle hardest against the truth which we would establish.

First the Chief Pontiff, Vicar of our Lord Jesus Christ and successor to Peter, he to whom we should render not what is due to Christ but what is due to Peter, he, perchance in his zeal for the keys, together with some pastors of Christian flocks, and others moved solely, I believe, by their zeal for Mother Church, contradict the truth I am about to declare. They contradict it, perchance, from zeal, I repeat, not from pride.

But others in their inveterate cupidity have quenched the light of reason, and call themselves sons of the Church, although they are of their father the devil. Not only do they arouse controversy in regard to this question, but, despising the very name of the most sacred Princehood, impudently deny the first principles of this and the previous questions.

The third class, called Decretalists, utterly ignorant and unregardful of Theology and Philosophy, depending entirely on the *Decretals* (which, I grant, are deserving of veneration), and I presume trusting in the ultimate supremacy of these, derogate from the imperial power. Nor is it to be wondered at, for I have heard one of them aver and insolently maintain that ecclesiastical traditions are the foundation of faith. Let those dispel this error of thought from mortal minds whom the world doubts not to have believed in Christ, the Son of God, ere ecclesiastical traditions were, believed in Him either to come, or present, or having already suffered, and believing hoped, and hoping burned with love, and burning with love were made co-heirs with Him.

And that such mistaken thinkers may be wholly shut out from the present discussion, it must be observed that some of the Scriptures take precedence of the Church, some are equivalent to the Church, and some subordinate to it.

Those taking precedence of the Church are the Old and New Testaments, which, as the Prophet says, "were commanded for ever," and to which the Church refers in saying to the Bridegroom, "Draw me after thee."

Equivalent to the Church are those Councils so worthy of reverence, and in the midst of which no believer doubts the presence of Christ; for we have, according to Matthew's testimony, the words spoken to His disciples at His ascension into heaven: "Lo, I am with you alway, even unto the end of the world." In addition, there are the writings of the Doctors, Augustine, and others, and whosoever doubts the aid of the Holy Spirit therein has never seen their fruits, or if he has seen, has never tasted them.

Subordinate to the Church are the traditions called Decretals, which, while they must be revered for their apostolic authority, must nevertheless be held unquestionably inferior to the fundamental Scriptures, seeing that Christ rebuked the priests for not so doing. When they had inquired, "Why do thy disciples transgress the tradition of the elders?" (for they had omitted the washing of hands) Christ answered, as Matthew testifies, "Why do ye also transgress the commandment of God by your tradition?" Here the inferiority of tradition is clearly implied.

If, as we believe, traditions of the Church are subordinate to the Church, authority necessarily accrues not to the Church through traditions, but to traditions through the Church. And I repeat, those who have faith in traditions alone are excluded from this discussion. For they who would hunt down this truth must start in their search from those writings whence the authority of the Church emanates.

Others must likewise be excluded who, decked in the plumage of ravens, boast themselves white sheep of the Master's flock. In order to carry out their crimes, these sons of impiety defile their mother, banish their brethren, and scorn judgments brought against them. Why should reason be sought in behalf of these whose passions prevent them from understanding our basic principle?

There remains, then, the controversy with those only who, led by a certain zeal for their Mother the Church, are blind to the truth we are seeking. And with them, confident in that reverence which a loyal and loving son owes to father and mother, to Christ and the Church, to the Shepherd and all who profess the Christian religion, I enter in this book into combat for the preservation of truth. . . .

From the same gospel they quote the saying of Christ to Peter, "Whatsoever thou shalt loose on earth shall be loosed in heaven," and understand this saying to refer alike to all the Apostles, according to the text of Matthew and John. They reason from this that the successor of Peter has been granted of God power to bind and loose all things, and then infer that he has power to loose the laws and decrees of the Empire, and to bind the laws and decrees of the temporal kingdom. Were this true, their inference would be correct.

But we must reply to it by making a distinction against the major premise of the syllogism which they employ. Their syllogism is this: Peter had power to bind and loose all things; the successor of Peter has like power with him; therefore the successor of Peter has power to loose and bind all things. From this they infer that he has power to loose and bind the laws and decrees of the Empire.

I concede the minor premise, but the major

only with distinction. Wherefore I say that "all," the symbol of the universal, which is implied in "whatsoever," is never distributed beyond the scope of the distributed term. When I say, "All animals run," the distribution of "all" comprehends whatever comes under the genus "animal." But when I say, "All men run," the symbol of the universal only refers to whatever comes under the term "man." And when I say, "All grammarians run," the distribution is narrowed still further.

Therefore we must always determine what it is over which the symbol of the universal is distributed; then, from the recognized nature and scope of the distributed term, will be easily apparent the extent of the distribution. Now, were "whatsoever" to be understood absolutely when it is said, "Whatsoever thou shalt bind," he would certainly have the power they claim; nay, he would have even greater power, he would be able to loose a wife from her husband, and, while the man still lived, bind her to another—a thing he can in no wise do. He would be able to absolve me, while impenitent—a thing which God himself cannot do.

So it is evident that the distribution of the term under discussion is to be taken, not absolutely, but relatively to something else. A consideration of the concession to which the distribution is subjoined will make manifest this related something. Christ said to Peter, "I will give unto thee the keys of the kingdom of heaven"; that is, "I will make thee doorkeeper of the kingdom of heaven." Then He adds, "and whatsoever," that is, "everything which," and He means thereby, "Everything which pertains to that office thou shalt have power to bind and loose." And thus the symbol of the universal which is implied in "whatsoever" is limited in its distribution to the prerogative of the keys of the kingdom of heaven. Understood thus, the proposition is true, but understood absolutely, it is obviously not. Therefore I conclude that although the successor of Peter has authority to bind and loose in accordance with the requirements of the prerogative granted to Peter, it does not follow, as they claim, that he has authority to bind and loose the decrees or statutes of Empire, unless they prove that this also belongs to the office of the keys. But we shall demonstrate farther on that the contrary is true.

They quote also the words in Luke which Peter addressed to Christ, saying, "Behold, here are two swords," and they assert that the two ruling powers were predicted by those two swords, and because Peter declared they were "where he was," that is, "with him," they conclude that according to authority these two ruling powers abide with Peter's successor.

To refute this we must show the falsity of the interpretation on which the argument is based. Their assertion that the two swords which Peter designated signify the two ruling powers before spoken of, we deny outright, because such an answer would have been at variance with Christ's meaning, and because Peter replied in haste, as usual, with regard to the mere external significance of things.

A consideration of the words preceding it and of the cause of the words will show that such an answer would have been inconsistent with Christ's meaning. Let it be called to mind that this response was made on the day of the feast, which Luke mentions earlier, saying, "Then came the day of unleavened bread, when the passover must be killed." At this feast Christ had already foretold His impending passion, in which He must be parted from His disciples. Let it be remembered also that when these words were uttered, all the twelve disciples were together; wherefore a little after the words just quoted Luke says, "And when the hour was come, He sat down, and the twelve Apostles with Him." Continuing the discourse from this place he reaches the words, "When I sent you without purse, and scrip, and shoes, lacked ye anything?" And they answered, "Nothing." Then said He unto them, "But now, he that hath a purse, let him take it, and likewise his scrip: and he that hath no sword, let him sell his garment, and buy one." The meaning of Christ is clear enough here. He did not say, "Buy or procure two swords," but "twelve;" for it was in order that each of the twelve disciples might have one that He said to them, "He that hath no sword, let him buy one." And He spake thus to forewarn them of the persecution and contempt the future should bring, as though He would say, "While I was with you ye were welcomed, now shall ye

be turned away. It behooves you, therefore, to prepare for yourselves those things which before I denied to you, but for which there is present need." If Peter's reply to these words had carried the meaning ascribed to it, the meaning would have been at variance with that of Christ, and Christ would have censured him, as He did oftentimes, for his witless answers. However, He did not do so, but assented, saying to him, "It is enough," meaning, "I speak because of necessity; but if each cannot have a sword, two will suffice."

And that Peter usually spoke of the external significance of things is shown in his quick and unthinking presumption, impelled, I believe, not only by the sincerity of his faith, but by the purity and simplicity of his nature. To this characteristic presumption all those who write of Christ bear witness.

First, Matthew records that when Jesus had inquired of the disciples: "Whom say ye that I am?" before all the others Peter replied, "Thou art Christ, the Son of the living God." He also records that when Christ was telling His disciples how He must go to Jerusalem and suffer many things, Peter took Him and began to rebuke Him, saying, "Be it far from thee, Lord: this shall not be unto thee." Then Christ, turning to him, said in reproof, "Get thee behind me, Satan." Matthew also writes that on the Mount of Transfiguration, in the presence of Christ, Moses, and Elias, and the two sons of Zebedee, Peter said, "Lord, it is good for us to be here. If thou wilt, let us make here three tabernacles, one for thee, one for Moses, and one for Elias." Matthew further writes that when the disciples were on the ship in the night, and Christ walked on the water, Peter said, "Lord, if it be thou, bid me come unto thee on the water." And that when Christ predicted how all His disciples should be offended because of Him, Peter answered, "Though all men shall be offended because of thee, yet will I never be offended." And afterwards, "Though I should die with thee, yet will I not deny thee." And this statement Mark confirms, while Luke writes that, just before the words we have quoted concerning the swords, Peter had said to Christ, "Lord, I am ready to go with thee, both into prison and to death."

John tells of him, that when Christ desired

to wash his feet, Peter asked, "Lord, dost thou wash my feet?" and then said, "Thou shalt never wash my feet." He further relates how Peter smote with his sword the servant of the High Priest, an account in which the four Evangelists agree. And John tells how when Peter came to the sepulchre and saw the other disciples lingering at the door, he entered in straightway; and again when after the resurrection Jesus stood on the shore and Peter "heard that it was the Lord, he girt his fisher's coat unto him (for he was naked), and did cast himself into the sea." Lastly, he recounts that when Peter saw John, he said to Jesus, "Lord, and what shall this man do?"

It is a source of joy to have summed up this evidence of our Head Shepherd, in praise of his singleness of purpose. From all this it is obvious that when he spoke of the two swords, his answer to Christ was unambiguous in meaning.

Even if the words of Christ and Peter are to be accepted typically, they cannot be interpreted in the sense these men claim, but rather as referring to the sword concerning which Matthew writes: "Think not that I am come to send peace on earth: I came not to send peace, but a sword. For I am come to set a man at variance against his father," and what follows. This He accomplished in word and deed, wherefore Luke tells Theophilus of all "that Jesus began to do and teach." Such was the sword Christ enjoined them to buy, and Peter made answer that already they had two with them. As we have shown, they were ready for words and for works to bring to pass those things which Christ proclaimed He had come to do by the sword.

In addition, some persons affirm that the Emperor Constantine, healed of leprosy by the intercession of Sylvester, then the Supreme Pontiff, gave to the Church the very seat of Empire, Rome, together with many imperial dignities. Wherefore they argue that no one has power to assume these dignities except he receives them from the Church, to whom it is asserted they belong. And from this it would fairly follow, as they desire, that one authority is dependent on the other.

So having stated and refuted the arguments which seemed to be rooted in divine commu-

nications, it now remains to set forth and disprove those rooted in Roman deeds and human reason. We have just spoken of the first of these, whose syllogism runs thus: Those things which belong to the Church no one can rightly possess, unless granted them by the Church; and this we concede. The ruling power of Rome belongs to the Church; therefore no one can rightly possess it unless granted it by the Church. And the minor premise they prove by the facts mentioned above concerning Constantine.

This minor premise, then, I deny. Their proof is no proof, for Constantine had not the power to alienate the imperial dignity, nor had the Church power to receive it. Their insistent objection to what I say can be met thus. No one is free to do through an office assigned him anything contrary to the office, for thereby the same thing, in virtue of being the same, would be contrary to itself, which is impossible. But to divide the Empire would be contrary to the office assigned the Emperor, for as is easily seen from the first book of the treatise, his office is to hold the human race subject to one will in all things. Therefore, division of his Empire is not allowed an Emperor. If, as they claim, certain dignities were alienated by Constantine from the Empire and ceded to the power of the Church, the "seamless coat" would have been rent, which even they had not dared to mutilate who with their spears pierced Christ, the very God. Moreover, as the Church has its own foundation, so has the Empire its own. The foundation of the Church is Christ, as the Apostle writes to the Corinthians: "Other foundation can no man lay than that is laid, which is Jesus Christ." He is the rock on which the Church is founded, but the foundation of the Empire is human Right. Now I say that as the Church cannot act contrary to its foundation, but must be supported thereby, according to that verse of the *Canticles:* "Who is she that cometh up from the desert, abounding in delights, leaning on her beloved?" so the Empire cannot act in conflict with human Right. Therefore the Empire may not destroy itself, for, should it do so, it would act in conflict with human Right. Inasmuch as the Empire consists in the indivisibility of universal Monarchy, and inasmuch as an apportionment of the Empire would destroy it, it is evident that division is not allowed to him who discharges imperial duty. And it is proved, from what has been previously said, that to destroy the Empire would be contrary to human Right.

Besides, every jurisdiction exists prior to its judge, since the judge is ordained for the jurisdiction, and not conversely. As the Empire is a jurisdiction embracing in its circuit the administration of justice in all temporal things, so it is prior to its judge, who is Emperor; and the Emperor is ordained for it, not conversely. Clearly the Emperor, as Emperor, cannot alter the Empire, for from it he receives his being and state. So I say, either he was Emperor when he made the concession they speak of to the Church, or he was not. If he was not, it is plain that he had no power to grant anything with regard to the Empire. And if he was, then as Emperor he could not have done this, for the concession would have narrowed his jurisdiction.

Further, if one Emperor has power to cut away one bit from the jurisdiction of the Empire, another may do the same for like reason. And since temporal jurisdiction is finite, and every finite thing may be consumed by finite losses, the possibility of annihilating primal jurisdiction would follow. But this is inconceivable.

And since he who confers a thing has the relation of agent, and he on whom it is conferred the relation of patient, according to the Philosopher in the fourth book to *Nicomachus,* then in order for a grant to be legal, proper qualification is essential not only in the giver, but in the recipient. Indeed, it seems that the acts of agents exist potentially in a properly qualified patient. But the Church was utterly disqualified for receiving temporal power by the express prohibitive command in Matthew: "Provide neither gold, nor silver, nor brass in your purses, nor scrip for your journey," etc. For although we learn from Luke of the mitigation of this order regarding certain things, yet I am unable to find that sanction was given the Church to possess gold and silver, subsequent to the prohibition. Wherefore if the Church had not power to receive, even had Constantine power to bestow, temporal authority, the action

would nevertheless be impossible, because of the disqualification of the patient. It is demonstrated, then, that neither could the Church accept by way of possession, nor could Constantine confer by way of alienation. However, the Emperor did have power to depute to the protectorship of the Church a patrimony and other things, as long as his supreme command, the unity of which suffers no impairment, remained unchanged. And the Vicar of God had power to receive such things, not for possession, but for distribution on behalf of the Church of its fruits to the poor of Christ. We are not ignorant that thus the Apostles did.

Still further, our opponents say that Pope Hadrian called Charles the Great to the aid of himself and the Church, because of oppression by the Lombards in the reign of Desiderius their king, and that from the Pope Charles received the dignity of Empire, notwithstanding the fact that Michael held imperial sway at Constantinople. Wherefore they declare that after Charles all Roman Emperors were advocates of the Church, and must be called to office by the Church. From this would follow the relationship between the Church and Empire which they desire to prove.

To refute this argument, I answer that their premise in it is a mere nullity, for usurpation of right does not create a right. If it did, the same method would show the dependency of ecclesiastical authority on the Empire, after the Emperor Otto restored Pope Leo, and deposed Benedict, sending him in exile to Saxony. . . .

Although by the method of reduction to absurdity it has been shown . . . that the authority of Empire has not its source in the Chief Pontiff, yet it has not been fully proved, save by an inference, that its immediate source is God, seeing that if the authority does not depend on the Vicar of God, we conclude that it depends on God Himself. For a perfect demonstration of the proposition we must prove directly that the Emperor, or Monarch, of the world has immediate relationship to the Prince of the universe, who is God.

In order to realize this, it must be understood that man alone of all beings holds the middle place between corruptibility and incorruptibility, and is therefore rightly compared by philosophers to the horizon which lies between the two hemispheres. Man may be considered with regard to either of his essential parts, body or soul. If considered in regard to the body alone, he is perishable; if in regard to the soul alone, he is imperishable. So the Philosopher spoke well of its incorruptibility when he said in the second book *on the Soul*, "And this only can be separated as a thing eternal from that which perishes."

If man holds a middle place between the perishable and imperishable, then, inasmuch as every mean shares the nature of the extremes, man must share both natures. And inasmuch as every nature is ordained for a certain ultimate end, it follows that there exists for man a two-fold end, in order that as he alone of all beings partakes of the perishable and the imperishable, so he alone of all beings should be ordained for two ultimate ends. One end is for that in him which is perishable, the other for that which is imperishable.

Ineffable Providence has thus designed two ends to be contemplated of man: first, the happiness of this life, which consists in the activity of his natural powers, and is prefigured by the terrestrial Paradise; and then the blessedness of life everlasting, which consists in the enjoyment of the countenance of God, to which man's natural powers may not attain unless aided by divine light, and which may be symbolized by the celestial Paradise.

To these states of blessedness, just as to diverse conclusions, man must come by diverse means. To the former we come by the teachings of philosophy, obeying them by acting in conformity with the moral and intellectual virtues; to the latter through spiritual teachings which transcend human reason, and which we obey by acting in conformity with the theological virtues, Faith, Hope, and Charity. Now the former end and means are made known to us by human reason, which the philosophers have wholly explained to us; and the latter by the Holy Spirit, which has revealed to us supernatural but essential truth through the Prophets and Sacred Writers, through Jesus Christ, the coeternal Son of God, and through His disciples. Nevertheless, human passion would cast all these behind, were not men, like horses, astray in their brutishness, held to the road by bit and rein.

Wherefore a twofold directive agent was necessary to man, in accordance with the twofold end; the Supreme Pontiff to lead the human race to life eternal by means of revelation, and the Emperor to guide it to temporal felicity by means of philosophic instruction. And since none or few—and these with exceeding difficulty—could attain this port, were not the waves of seductive desire calmed, and mankind made free to rest in the tranquillity of peace, therefore this is the goal which he whom we call the guardian of the earth and Roman Prince should most urgently seek; then would it be possible for life on this mortal threshing-floor to pass in freedom and peace. The order of the world follows the order inherent in the revolution of the heavens. To attain this order it is necessary that instruction productive of liberality and peace should be applied by the guardian of the realm, in due place and time, as dispensed by Him who is the ever present Watcher of the whole order of the heavens. And He alone foreordained this order, that by it in His providence He might link together all things, each in its own place.

If this is so, and there is none higher than He, only God elects and only God confirms. Whence we may further conclude that neither those who are now, nor those who in any way whatsoever have been, called Electors have the right to be so called; rather should they be entitled heralds of divine providence. Whence it is that those in whom is vested the dignity of proclamation suffer dissension among themselves at times, when, all or part of them being shadowed by the clouds of passion, they discern not the face of God's dispensation.

It is established, then, that the authority of temporal Monarchy descends without mediation from the fountain of universal authority. And this fountain, one in its purity of source, flows into multifarious channels out of the abundance of its excellence.

Methinks I have now approached close enough to the goal I had set myself, for I have taken the kernels of truth from the husks of falsehood, in that question which asked whether the office of Monarchy was essential to the welfare of the world, and in the next which made inquiry whether the Roman people rightfully appropriated the Empire, and in the last which sought whether the authority of the Monarch derived from God immediately, or from some other. But the truth of this final question must not be restricted to mean that the Roman Prince shall not be subject in some degree to the Roman Pontiff, for felicity that is mortal is ordered in a measure after felicity that is immortal.

Wherefore let Caesar honor Peter as a first-born son should honor his father, so that, refulgent with the light of paternal grace, he may illumine with greater radiance the earthly sphere over which he has been set by Him who alone is Ruler of all things spiritual and temporal.

Peter Abelard

Peter Abelard (1074–1142) was a French monk, scholar, and philosopher who sought to apply logic to the teachings of the medieval church. Of a naturally skeptical frame of mind, he objected strenuously to the practice of citing numerous authorities in order to prove a religious truth. He was particularly struck by the obvious contradictions on matters of doctrine to be found in the writings of the early church fathers. In his famous work, Sic et Non, he presented one hundred and fifty-eight points of dogma, and then showed how the authorities contradicted themselves on each point. He maintained that logic could satisfactorily explain these discrepancies, thus attempting to bring reason to the support of faith. As a result of Abelard's work, theologians since his day have had to do more than merely quote authority to achieve a rational justification of faith. In reading the following summary of Sic et Non note (1) the explanations suggested for the many seeming contradictions in the writings of the church fathers, (2) the possibility of the fathers erring, (3) the position Abelard took in regard to the scriptures, (4) his statement of what he had done, (5) his opinion regarding Aristotle, and (6) the types of questions on which he found conflicting opinions.

From: SIC ET NON

There are many seeming contradictions and even obscurities in the innumerable writings of the church fathers. Our respect for their authority should not stand in the way of an effort on our part to come at the truth. The obscurity and contradictions in ancient writings may be explained upon many grounds, and may be discussed without impugning the good faith and insight of the fathers. A writer may use different terms to mean the same thing, in order to avoid a monotonous repetition of the same word. Common, vague words may be employed in order that the common people may under-

James Harvey Robinson, *Readings in European History.* . . . 2 vols., Ginn and Company, Boston, 1904, I, 450–452. Courtesy of Ginn and Company.

stand; and sometimes a writer sacrifices perfect accuracy in the interest of a clear general statement. Poetical, figurative language is often obscure and vague.

Not infrequently, apocryphal works are attributed to the saints. Then, even the best authors often introduce the erroneous views of others and leave the reader to distinguish between the true and the false. Sometimes, as Augustine confesses in his own case, the fathers ventured to rely upon the opinions of others.

Doubtless, the fathers might err; even Peter, the prince of the apostles, fell into error; what wonder that the saints do not always show themselves inspired? The fathers did not themselves believe that they, or their companions, were always right. Augustine found himself mistaken in some cases and did not hesitate to retract his errors. He warns his admirers not to look upon his letters as they would upon the Scriptures, but to accept only those things which, upon examination, they find to be true.

All writings belonging to this class are to be read with full freedom to criticise, and with no obligation to accept unquestioningly; otherwise the way would be blocked to all discussion, and posterity be deprived of the excellent intellectual exercise of debating difficult questions of language and presentation. But an explicit exception must be made in the case of the Old and New Testaments. In the Scriptures, when anything strikes us as absurd, we may not say that the writer erred, but that the scribe made a blunder in copying the manuscripts, or that there is an error in interpretation, or that the passage is not understood. The fathers make a very careful distinction between the Scriptures and later works. They advocate a discriminating, not to say suspicious, use of the writings of their own contemporaries.

In view of these considerations, I have ventured to bring together various dicta of the holy fathers, as they came to mind, and to formulate certain questions which were suggested by the seeming contradictions in the statements. These questions ought to serve to excite tender readers to a zealous inquiry into truth and so sharpen their wits. The master key of knowledge is, indeed, a persistent and frequent questioning. Aristotle, the most clear-sighted of all the philosophers, was desirious above all things else to arouse this questioning spirit, for in his *Categories* he exhorts a student as follows: "It may well be difficult to reach a positive conclusion in these matters unless they be frequently discussed. It is by no means fruitless to be doubtful on particular points." By doubting we come to examine, and by examining we reach the truth.

[The following will serve as examples of the questions Abelard raised in the *Yea and Nay:*]

Should human faith be based upon reason, or no?

Is God one, or no?

Is God a substance, or no?

Does the first Psalm refer to Christ, or no?

Is sin pleasing to God, or no?

Is God the author of evil, or no?

Is God all-powerful, or no?

Can God be resisted, or no?

Has God free will, or no?

Was the first man persuaded to sin by the devil, or no?

Was Adam saved, or no?

Did all the apostles have wives except John, or no?

Are the flesh and blood of Christ in very truth and essence present in the sacrament of the altar, or no?

Do we sometimes sin unwillingly, or no?

Does God punish the same sin both here and in the future, or no?

Is it worse to sin openly than secretly, or no?

Council of Florence

The sacraments, representing outward signs of inward grace, were, according to Christian tradition, instituted by Christ. In the first centuries of the church's development little attention was given to a scholarly interpretation of them, and neither their number nor their character was accurately expressed. With the revival of learning in the eleventh and twelfth centuries, however, and the development of skepticism in regard to contradictory Christian teaching, a renewed interest in the sacraments developed. In the twelfth century Peter Lombard in his Book of Sentences defined apparently for the first time the number of the sacraments as seven. In 1439, at the Council of Florence the sacraments were both enumerated and defined in the Decree for the Armenians. In reading this decree note (1) the number and character of the sacraments, (2) the three things necessary to make them effective, (3) the persons qualified to administer the various sacraments and the benefits derived from each, and (4) the sources from which the nature of the sacraments was derived.

From: THE DECREE FOR THE ARMENIANS

We have drawn up in the briefest form a statement of the truth concerning the seven sacraments, so that the Armenians, now and in future generations, may more easily be instructed therein.

There are seven sacraments under the new law: that is to say, baptism, confirmation, the mass, penance, extreme unction, ordination, and matrimony. These differ essentially from the sacraments of the old law; for the latter do not confer grace, but only typify that grace which can be given by the passion of Christ alone. But these our sacraments both contain grace and confer it upon all who receive them worthily.

The first five sacraments are intended to secure the spiritual perfection of every man individually; the two last are ordained for the governance and increase of the Church. For through baptism we are born again of the spirit; through confirmation we grow in grace and are strengthened in the faith; and when

we have been born again and strengthened we are fed by the divine food of the mass; but if, through sin, we bring sickness upon our souls, we are made spiritually whole by penance; and by extreme unction we are healed, both spiritually and corporeally, according as our souls have need; by ordination the Church is governed and multiplied spiritually; by matrimony it is materially increased.

To effect these sacraments three things are necessary: the things [or symbols], that is, the "material"; the words, that is, the "form"; and the person of the "ministrant," who administers the sacrament with the intention of carrying out what the Church effects through him. If any of these things be lacking, the sacrament is not accomplished.

Three of these sacraments—baptism, confirmation, and ordination—impress indelibly upon the soul a character, a certain spiritual sign, distinct from all others; so they are not

James Harvey Robinson, *Readings in European History.* . . . 2 vols., Ginn and Company, Boston, 1904, I, 348–354. Courtesy of Ginn and Company.

repeated for the same person. The other four do not imprint a character upon the soul, and admit of repetition.

Holy baptism holds the first place among all the sacraments because it is the gate of spiritual life; for by it we are made members of Christ and of the body of the Church. Since through the first man death entered into the world, unless we are born again of water, and of the spirit, we cannot, so saith Truth, enter into the kingdom of heaven. The material of this sacrament is water, real and natural—it matters nothing whether it be cold or warm. Now the form is: "I baptize thee in the name of the Father, and of the Son, and of the Holy Ghost.". . .

The ministrant of this sacrament is the priest, for baptism belongs to his office. But in case of necessity not only a priest or deacon may baptize, but a layman or a woman —nay, even a pagan or a heretic, provided he use the form of the Church and intend to do what the Church effects. The efficacy of this sacrament is the remission of all sin, original sin and actual, and of all penalties incurred through this guilt. Therefore no satisfaction for past sin should be imposed on those who are baptized; but if they die before they commit any sin, they shall straightway attain the kingdom of heaven and the sight of God.

The second sacrament is confirmation. The material is the chrism made from oil, which signifies purity of conscience, and from balsam, which signifies the odor of fair fame; and it must be blessed by the bishop. The form is: "I sign thee with the sign of the cross and confirm thee with the chrism of salvation, in the name of the Father, and of the Son, and of the Holy Ghost." The proper ministrant of this sacrament is the bishop. While a simple priest avails to perform the other anointings, this one none can confer save the bishop only; for it is written of the apostles alone that by the laying on of hands they gave the Holy Ghost, and the bishops hold the office of the apostles. We read in the Acts of the Apostles, when the apostles who were at Jerusalem heard how Samaria had received the word of God, they sent to them Peter and John; who, when they were

come, prayed that they might receive the Holy Ghost; for as yet it was fallen upon none of them,—they were only baptized in the name of the Lord Jesus. Then they laid hands upon them and they received the Holy Ghost. Now, in place of this laying on of hands, confirmation is given in the Church. Yet we read that sometimes, for reasonable and urgent cause, by dispensation from the Holy See, a simple priest has been permitted to administer confirmation with a chrism prepared by a bishop.

In this sacrament the Holy Ghost is given to strengthen us, as it was given to the apostles on the day of Pentecost, that the Christian may confess boldly the name of Christ. And therefore he is confirmed upon the brow, the seat of shame, that he may never blush to confess the name of Christ and especially his cross, which is a stumbling-block to the Jews and foolishness to the Gentiles, according to the apostle. Therefore he is signed with the sign of the cross.

The third sacrament is the eucharist. The material is wheaten bread and wine of the grape, which before consecration should be mixed very sparingly with water; because, according to the testimony of the holy fathers and doctors of the Church set forth in former times in disputation, it is believed that the Lord himself instituted this sacrament with wine mixed with water, and also because this corresponds with the accounts of our Lord's passion. For the holy Pope Alexander, fifth from the blessed Peter, says, "In the offerings of sacred things made to God during the solemnization of the mass, only bread and wine mixed with water are offered up. Neither wine alone nor water alone may be offered up in the cup of the Lord, but both mixed, since it is written that both blood and water flowed from Christ's side."

Moreover the mixing of water with the wine fitly signifies the efficacy of this sacrament, namely, the union of Christian people with Christ, for water signifies "people," according to the passage in the Apocalypse which says, "many waters, many people." And Julius, second pope after the blessed Sylvester, says: "According to the provisions of the canons the cup of the Lord should be offered filled with wine mixed with water, because a people is signified by the water, and in the wine is manifested the blood of Christ. Therefore when the wine and water are mixed in the cup the people are joined to Christ, and the host of the faithful is united with him in whom they believe."

Since, therefore, the holy Roman Church, instructed by the most blessed apostles Peter and Paul, together with all the other churches of the Greeks and Latins in which glowed the light of sanctity and of doctrine, has from the beginning of the nascent Church observed this custom and still observes it, it is quite unseemly that any region whatever should depart from this universal and rational observance. We decree, therefore, that the Armenians likewise shall conform themselves with the whole Christian world, and that their priests shall mix a little water with the wine in the cup of oblation.

The form of this sacrament is furnished by the words of the Saviour when he instituted it, and the priest, speaking in the person of Christ, consummates this sacrament. By virtue of these words, the substance of the bread is turned into the body of Christ and the substance of the wine into his blood. This is accomplished in such wise that the whole Christ is altogether present under the semblance of the bread and altogether under the semblance of the wine. Moreover, after the consecrated host and the consecrated wine have been divided, the whole Christ is present in any part of them. The benefit effected by this sacrament in the souls of those who receive it worthily is the union of man with Christ. And since, through grace, man is made one body with Christ and united in his members, it follows that through this sacrament grace is increased in those who partake of it worthily. Every effect of material food and drink upon the physical life, in nourishment, growth, and pleasure, is wrought by this sacrament for the spiritual life. By it we recall the beloved memory of our Saviour; by it we are withheld from evil, and strengthened in good, and go forward to renewed growth in virtues and graces.

The fourth sacrament is penance. The material, as we may say, consists in the acts of penitence, which are divided into three parts.

The first of these is contrition of the heart, wherein the sinner must grieve for the sins he has committed, with the resolve to commit no further sins. Second comes confession with the mouth, to which it pertains that the sinner should make confession to his priest of all the sins he holds in his memory. The third is satisfaction for sins according to the judgment of the priest, and this is made chiefly by prayer, fasting, and almsgiving. The form of this sacrament consists in the words of absolution which the priest speaks when he says, "I absolve thee," etc.; and the minister of this sacrament is the priest, who has authority to absolve either regularly or by the commission of a superior. The benefit of this sacrament is absolution from sins.

The fifth sacrament is extreme unction, and the material is oil of the olive, blessed by a bishop. This sacrament shall not be given to any except the sick who are in fear of death. They shall be anointed in the following places: the eyes on account of the sight, the ears on account of the hearing, the nostrils on account of smell, the mouth on account of taste and speech, the hands on account of touch, the feet on account of walking, and the loins as the seat of pleasure. The form of this sacrament is as follows: "Through this holy unction and his most tender compassion, the Lord grants thee forgiveness for whatever sins thou hast committed by the sight,"—and in the same way for the other members. The minister of this sacrament is a priest. The benefit is even the healing of the mind and, so far as is expedient, of the body also. Of this sacrament the blessed apostle James says: "Is any sick among you? Let him call for the elders of the church and let them pray over him, anointing him with oil in the name of the Lord: and the prayer of faith shall save the sick, and the Lord shall raise him up; and if he have committed sins, they shall be forgiven him."

The sixth sacrament is ordination. The material for the priesthood is the cup with the wine and the paten with the bread; for the deaconate, the books of the Gospel; for the subdeaconate, an empty cup placed upon an empty paten; and in like manner, other offices are conferred by giving to the candidates those things which pertain to their secular ministrations. The form for priests is this: "Receive the power to offer sacrifice in the Church for the living and the dead, in the name of the Father, and of the Son, and of the Holy Ghost." And so for each order the proper form shall be used, as fully stated in the Roman pontifical. The regular minister of this sacrament is a bishop; the benefit, growth in grace, to the end that whosoever is ordained may be a worthy minister.

The seventh sacrament is matrimony, the type of the union of Christ and the Church, according to the apostle, who saith, "This is a great mystery; but I speak concerning Christ and the church." The efficient cause of marriage is regularly the mutual consent uttered aloud on the spot. These advantages are to be ascribed to marriage: first, the begetting of children and their bringing up in the worship of the Lord; secondly, the fidelity that husband and wife should each maintain toward the other; thirdly, the indissoluble character of marriage, for this typifies the indissoluble union of Christ and the Church. Although for the cause of adultery separation is permissible, for no other cause may marriage be infringed, since the bond of marriage once legitimately contracted is perpetual.

Thomas Aquinas

Thomas Aquinas (1225–1274) accepted, as did other scholastic philosophers of his day, the challenge to Christian learning resulting from the large-scale introduction of Greek and Arabic science to the West at the moment when Peter Lombard, Gratian, and others had produced a definitive formulation of truth revealed by God in the Scriptures. By the thirteenth century, Latin learning had been absorbed without detriment to the church; could the same task be accomplished for Greek and Arabic learning? Many churchmen recoiled from the problem of attempting a reconciliation of these apparent irreconcilables; but to their eternal credit such scholars as Albert Magnus and his pupil, Thomas Aquinas, convinced that there could be no real conflict between revealed truth and rational truth, took the whole of knowledge as their province and systematically brought it into subjection to Christian theology. The great achievement of Thomas was in demonstrating that the truths of Christianity were not inconsistent with the secular learning of the Greeks and Arabs. In his greatest work, the Summa Theologica, from which the following selection is taken, Thomas raised 631 questions and answered each by quoting from authorities and by the use of logic. Contrary opinions were elaborated, followed by a harmonizing conclusion. In the Summa, Thomas answered 10,000 objections to his conclusions, no mean accomplishment in any age. In the selection entitled "Whether God Exists" note (1) Thomas' method which was characteristic of the scholastics, (2) the objections raised to the existence of God, (3) the proof submitted from authority, and (4) the proof submitted by logic.

As translated by the Fathers of the English Dominican Province in The "Summa Theologica" of St. Thomas Aquinas, Benziger Brothers, New York, 1911, Part I, First Number, Q. II, 19–27. Courtesy of Benziger Brothers.

WHETHER GOD EXISTS

FIRST ARTICLE.

WHETHER THE EXISTENCE OF GOD IS SELF-EVIDENT?

We proceed thus to the First Article:—

Objection 1. It seems that the Existence of God is self-evident. Those things are said to be self-evident to us the knowledge of which is naturally implanted in us, as we can see in regard to first principles. But the Damascene says that, *the knowledge of God is naturally implanted in all.* Therefore the Existence of God is self-evident.

Obj. 2. Further, those things are said to be self-evident which are known as soon as the terms are known, which the Philosopher says is true of the first principles of demonstration. Thus, when the nature of a whole and of a part is known, it is at once recognized that every whole is greater than its part. But as soon as the signification of the word 'God' is understood, it is at once seen that God exists. For by this word is signified that thing than which nothing greater can exist. But that which exists actually and mentally is greater than that which exists only mentally. Therefore, because as soon as the word 'God' is understood it exists mentally, it also follows that it exists actually. Therefore the proposition that God exists is self-evident.

Obj. 3. Further, the existence of Truth is self-evident; for whoever denies the existence of Truth concedes that Truth does not exist. Now, if Truth does not exist, then the proposition 'Truth does not exist' is true. But if there is anything true, there must be Truth. God is Truth itself: *I am the way, the truth, and the life.* Therefore the proposition that God exists is self-evident.

On the contrary, No one can mentally admit the opposite of what is self-evident; as is clear from the Philosopher, concerning the first principles of demonstration. The opposite of the proposition 'God is' can be mentally admitted: *The fool hath said in his heart, There is no God.* Therefore, that God exists is not self-evident.

I answer that, A thing can be self-evident in either of two ways; on the one hand, self-evident in itself, though not to us; on the other, self-evident in itself, and to us. A proposition is self-evident because the predicate is included in the notion of the subject, as 'Man is an animal,' for animal is contained in the formal idea of man. If, therefore, the essence of the predicate and subject be known to all, the proposition will be self-evident to all; as is clear with regard to the first principles of demonstration, the terms of which are common things that no one is ignorant of, such as being and non-being, whole and part, and such like. If there are some to whom the essence of the predicate and subject are unknown, the proposition will be self-evident in itself, but not to those who do not know the meaning of the predicate and subject of the proposition. Therefore, it happens, as Boethius says, that there are some mental concepts self-evident only to the learned, as that incorporeal substances are not in space. Therefore I say that this proposition, 'God exists,' of itself is self-evident, for the predicate is the same as the subject; because God is His Own Existence. For as much as we do not know the Essence of God, the proposition is not self-evident to us; but needs to be proved by such things as are more evident to us, though less evident in their nature—namely, by effects.

Reply Obj. 1. To know that God exists in a general and indefinite way is implanted in us by nature, inasmuch as God is man's beatitude. For man naturally desires happiness, and what is naturally desired by a man must be naturally known to him. This, however, is not to know absolutely that God exists; as to know that someone is approaching is not the same as to know that Peter is approaching, even though it is Peter who is approaching; for many there are who imagine that man's perfect good (which is happiness) consists in riches, and others in pleasures, and others in something else.

Reply Obj. 2. Perhaps not everyone who hears this word 'God' may understand it to signify something than which nothing better can be imagined, seeing that some have believed God to be a body. Yet, granted that everyone understands that by this word 'God' is signified something than which nothing greater can be imagined, nevertheless, it does not therefore follow that he understands that what the word signifies exists actually, but only that it exists mentally. Nor can it be argued logically that it actually exists, unless it be admitted that there exists something than which nothing greater can be imagined; and this precisely is not admitted by those who hold that God does not exist.

Reply Obj. 3. The existence of truth in a general way is self-evident, but the existence of a Primal Truth is not self-evident to us.

SECOND ARTICLE.

WHETHER IT CAN BE DEMONSTRATED THAT GOD EXISTS?

We proceed thus to the Second Article:—

Objection 1. It seems that the existence of God cannot be demonstrated; for it is an article of Faith that God exists. But what is of Faith cannot be demonstrated, because a demonstration produces knowledge; whereas Faith is of the unseen. (Heb. xi, 1). Therefore it cannot be demonstrated that God exists.

Obj. 2. Further, the essence is the middle term of demonstration. But we cannot know in what God's essence consists, but solely in what it does not consist, as the Damascene says. Therefore we cannot demonstrate that God exists.

Obj. 3. Further, if the existence of God were demonstrated, this could only be from His effects. But the effects are not proportionate to Him, since He is infinite and His effects are finite; and between the finite and infinite there is no proportion. Therefore, since a cause cannot be demonstrated by an effect not proportionate to it, it seems that the existence of God cannot be demonstrated.

On the contrary, The Apostle says: *The invisible things of God are clearly seen, being understood by the things that are made.* But this would not be unless the existence of God could be demonstrated through the things that are made; for the first thing we must know of anything is, whether it exists.

I answer that, Demonstration can be made in two ways: One is through the cause, and is called *a priori,* and this is to argue from what is prior absolutely. The other is through the effect, and is called a demonstration *a posteriori;* this is to argue from what is prior relatively only to us. When an effect is better known to us than its cause, from the effect we proceed to the knowledge of the cause. From every effect the existence of a proportionate cause can be demonstrated, so long as its effects are better known to us. Since every effect depends upon its cause, if the effect exists, the cause must have pre-existed. Hence the existence of God, in so far as it is not self-evident to us, can be demonstrated from those of His effects which are known to us.

Reply Obj. 1. The existence of God and other like truths about God, which can be known by natural reason, are not articles of Faith, but are preambles to the articles; for Faith presupposes natural knowledge, even as grace presupposes nature, and perfection something that can be perfected. Nevertheless, there is nothing to prevent a man, who cannot grasp its proof, accepting, as a matter of Faith, something in itself capable of being known and demonstrated.

Reply Obj. 2. When the existence of a cause is demonstrated from an effect, this effect takes the place of the definition of the cause in proof of the cause's existence. This is especially the case in regard to God, because, in order to prove the existence of anything, it is necessary to accept as a middle term the meaning of the word, and not its essence, for the question of its essence follows on the question of its existence. The names given to God are derived from His effects; consequently, in demonstrating the existence of God from His effects, we may take for the middle term the meaning of the word 'God.'

Reply Obj. 3. From effects not proportionate to the cause no perfect knowledge of that cause can be obtained. Yet from every effect the existence of the cause can be clearly demonstrated, and so we can demonstrate the existence of God from His effects; though from them we cannot perfectly know God as He is in His Own Essence.

THIRD ARTICLE.

WHETHER GOD EXISTS?

We proceed thus to the Third Article:—

Objection 1. It seems that God does not exist; because if one of two contraries be infinite, the other would be altogether destroyed. But the word 'God' means that He is infinite goodness. If, therefore, God existed, there would be no evil discoverable; but there is evil in the world. Therefore God does not exist.

Obj. 2. Further, it is superfluous to suppose that what can be accounted for by a few principles has been produced by many. But it seems that everything that appears in the world can be accounted for by other principles, supposing God did not exist. For all natural things can be reduced to one principle, which is nature; and all things that happen intentionally can be reduced to one principle, which is human reason, or will. Therefore there is no need to suppose God's existence.

On the contrary, It is said in the person of God: *I am Who am* (Exod. iii. 14).

I answer that, The existence of God can be proved in five ways.

The first and more manifest way is the argument from motion. It is certain and evident to our senses that some things are in motion. Whatever is in motion is moved by another, for nothing can be in motion except it have a potentiality for that towards which it is being moved; whereas a thing moves inasmuch as it is in act. By 'motion' we mean nothing else than the reduction of something from a state of potentiality into a state of actuality. Nothing, however, can be reduced from a state of potentiality into a state of actuality, unless by something already in a state of actuality. Thus that which is actually hot as fire, makes wood, which is potentially hot, to be actually hot, and thereby moves and changes it. It is not possible that the same thing should be at once in a state of actuality and potentiality from the same point of view, but only from different points of view. What is actually hot cannot simultane-

ously be only potentially hot; still, it is simultaneously potentially cold. It is therefore impossible that from the same point of view and in the same way anything should be both moved and mover, or that it should move itself. Therefore, whatever is in motion must be put in motion by another. If that by which it is put in motion be itself put in motion, then this also must needs be put in motion by another, and that by another again. But this cannot go on to infinity, because then there would be no first mover, and, consequently, no other mover—seeing that subsequent movers only move inasmuch as they are put in motion by the first mover; as the staff only moves because it is put in motion by the hand. Therefore it is necessary to arrive at a First Mover, put in motion by no other; and this everyone understands to be God.

The second way is from the formality of efficient causation. In the world of sense we find there is an order of efficient causation. There is no case known (neither is it, indeed, possible) in which a thing is found to be the efficient cause of itself; for so it would be prior to itself, which is impossible. In efficient causes it is not possible to go on to infinity, because in all efficient causes following in order, the first is the cause of the intermediate cause, and the intermediate is the cause of the ultimate cause, whether the intermediate cause be several, or one only. To take away the cause is to take away the effect. Therefore, if there be no first cause among efficient causes, there will be no ultimate cause, nor any intermediate. If in efficient causes it is possible to go on to infinity, there will be no first efficient cause, neither will there be an ultimate effect, nor any intermediate efficient causes; all of which is plainly false. Therefore it is necessary to put forward a First Efficient Cause, to which everyone gives the name of God.

The third way is taken from possibility and necessity, and runs thus. We find in nature things that could either exist or not exist, since they are found to be generated, and to corrupt; and, consequently, they can exist, and then not exist. It is impossible for these always to exist, for that which can one day cease to exist must at some time have not existed. Therefore, if everything could cease to exist, then at one time there could have been nothing in existence. If this were true, even now there would be nothing in existence, because that which does not exist only begins to exist by something already existing. Therefore, if at one time nothing was in existence, it would have been impossible for anything to have begun to exist; and thus even now nothing would be in existence—which is absurd. Therefore, not all beings are merely possible, but there must exist something the existence of which is necessary. Every necessary thing either has its necessity caused by another, or not. It is impossible to go on to infinity in necessary things which have their necessity caused by another, as has been already proved in regard to efficient causes. Therefore we cannot but postulate the existence of some being having of itself its own necessity, and not receiving it from another, but rather causing in others their necessity. This all men speak of as God.

The fourth way is taken from the gradation to be found in things. Among beings there are some more and some less good, true, noble, and the like. But 'more' and 'less' are predicated of different things, according as they resemble in their different ways something which is in the degree of 'most,' as a thing is said to be hotter according as it more nearly resembles that which is hottest; so that there is something which is truest, something best, something noblest, and, consequently, something which is uttermost being; for the truer things are, the more truly they exist. What is most complete in any genus is the cause of all in that genus; as fire, which is the most complete form of heat, is the cause whereby all things are made hot.

Therefore there must also be something which is to all beings the cause of their being, goodness, and every other perfection; and this we call God.

The fifth way is taken from the governance of the world; for we see that things which lack intelligence, such as natural bodies, act for some purpose, which fact is evident from their acting always, or nearly always, in the same way, so as to obtain the best result. Hence it is plain that not fortuitously, but designedly, do they achieve their purpose. Whatever lacks intelligence cannot fulfil some purpose, unless it be directed by some being endowed with intelligence and knowledge; as the arrow is shot to its mark by the archer. Therefore some intelligent being exists by whom all natural things are ordained towards a definite purpose; and this being we call God.

Reply Obj. 1. As Augustine says: *Since God is wholly good, He would not allow any evil to exist in His works, unless His omnipotence and goodness were such as to bring good even out of evil.* This is part of the infinite goodness of God, that He should allow evil to exist, and out of it produce good.

Reply Obj. 2. Since nature works for a determinate end under the direction of a higher agent, whatever is done by nature must needs be traced back to God, as to its first cause. So also whatever is done designedly must also be traced back to some higher cause other than human reason or will, for these can suffer change and are defective; whereas things capable of motion and of defect must be traced back to an immovable and self-necessary first principle.

French Epic

The Song of Roland *is a French legendary epic dating from the time of Charlemagne. It is based on historical fact, however, for in 778 the emperor invaded Spain but was forced to withdraw when word reached him of a Saxon revolt in the north. During the retreat through the Pyrenees, a part of his force was ambushed in a narrow defile and annihilated. These events have been idealized in the poem into a heroic description of feudal loyalty and of the virtues of the feudal warrior. Twelve vassals, of whom*

Roland was one, are depicted as the leaders of the finest section of the Frankish army. In the face of overwhelming odds and only to assure vengeance and not for personal security, Roland finally sounded his horn and gave the alarm to the main body of the Franks. The poem lifts medieval feudalism out of its legalistic, contractual pattern, and makes of it a living, personal relationship which involved much more than the mechanical fulfillment of obligations. The lines present in a vivid and moving manner the loyalty and devotion implicit in vassalage and homage—a loyalty suggestive of modern patriotism to one's country. In reading the passage note (1) the description of the highly personalized relationship between Roland and his sword, Durendal, (2) evidences of the close comradeship between Roland and Oliver, (3) indications of the devoted vassalage to Charlemagne, (4) the activities of the archbishop, (5) the number of pagans slain by the Franks, (6) the description of the forces of the Saracen king, Marsilies, (7) the tragic deaths of the companions of Roland and Oliver, (8) evidences of the crusading zeal aroused against the pagans, (9) the discussion between Roland and Oliver about sounding the olifant and the meaning of vassalage, (10) the treachery of Guenes and his disgrace, (11) the death of Oliver, and (12) the final deeds of the archbishop and Roland on the field of battle.

From: THE SONG OF ROLAND

CIV

Common the fight is now and marvellous.
The count Rollanz no way himself secures,
Strikes with his spear, long as the shaft endures,
By fifteen blows it is clean broken through;
Then Durendal he bares, his sabre good
Spurs on his horse, is gone to strike Chernuble,
The helmet breaks, where bright carbuncles grew,
Slices the cap and shears the locks in two,
Slices also the eyes and the features,
The hauberk white, whose mail was close of woof,
Down to the groin cuts all his body through
To the saddle; with beaten gold 'twas tooled.
Upon the horse that sword a moment stood,
Then sliced its spine, no join there any knew,
Dead in the field among thick grass them threw.

After he said: "Culvert, false step you moved,
From Mahumet your help will not come soon.
No victory for gluttons such as you."

CV

The count Rollanz, he canters through the field,
Holds Durendal, he well can thrust and wield,
Right great damage he's done the Sarrazines
You'd seen them, one on other, dead in heaps,
Through all that place their blood was flowing clear!
In blood his arms were and his hauberk steeped,
And bloodied o'er, shoulders and neck, his steed.
And Oliver goes on to strike with speed;
No blame that way deserve the dozen peers,
For all the Franks they strike and slay with heat,

Charles Scott Moncrieff, *The Song of Roland Done into English in the Original Measure*, Chapman and Hall, Ltd., London, 1919, 44–78. Courtesy of the estate of Charles Scott Moncrieff and Chapman and Hall, Ltd.

Pagans are slain, some swoon there in their
　　seats,
Says the Archbishop: "Good baronage indeed!"
"Monjoie" he cries, the call of Charles repeats.
　　　　　　　　　　　　　　　　AOI.

CVI

And Oliver has cantered through the crush;
Broken his spear, the truncheon still he thrusts;
Going to strike a pagan Malsarun;
Flowers and gold, are on the shield, he cuts,
Out of the head both the two eyes have burst,
And all the brains are fallen in the dust;
He flings him dead, sev'n hundred else
　　amongst.
Then has he slain Turgin and Esturgus;
Right to the hilt, his spear in flinders flew.
Then says Rollant: "Companion, what do you?
In such a fight, there's little strength in wood,
Iron and steel should here their valour prove.
Where is your sword, that Halteclere I knew?
Golden its hilt, whereon a crystal grew."
Says Oliver: "I had not, if I drew,
Time left to strike enough good blows and
　　true."
　　　　　　　　　　　　　　　　AOI.

CVII

Then Oliver has drawn his mighty sword
As his comrade had bidden and implored,
In knightly wise the blade to him has shewed;
Justin he strikes, that Iron Valley's lord,
All of his head has down the middle shorn,
The carcass sliced, the broidered sark has torn,
The good saddle that was with gold adorned,
And through the spine has sliced that pagan's
　　horse;
Dead in the field before his feet they fall.
Says Rollant: "Now my brother I you call;
He'll love us for such blows, our Emperor."
On every side "Monjoie" you'd hear them roar.
　　　　　　　　　　　　　　　　AOI.

CVIII

That count Gerins sate on his horse Sorel,
On Passe-Cerf was Gerers there, his friend;
They've loosed their reins, together spurred
　　and sped,

And go to strike a pagan Timozel;
One on the shield, on hauberk the other fell;
And their two spears went through the carcass
　　well,
A fallow field amidst they've thrown him dead.
I do not know, I never heard it said
Which of the two was nimbler as they went.
Esperveris was there, son of Borel,
And him there slew Engelers of Burdel.
And the Archbishop, he slew them Siglorel,
The enchanter, who before had been in hell,
Where Jupiter bore him by a magic spell.
Then Turpin says: "To us he's forfeited."
Answers Rollanz: "The culvert is bested.
Such blows, brother Olivier, I like well."

CIX

The battle grows more hard and harder yet,
Franks and pagans, with marvellous onset,
Each other strike and each himself defends.
So many shafts bloodstained and shatterèd,
So many flags and ensigns tatterèd;
So many Franks lose their young lustihead,
Who'll see no more their mothers nor their
　　friends,
Nor hosts of France, that in the pass attend.
Charlès the Great weeps therefor with regret.
What profits that? No succour shall they get.
Evil service, that day, Guenes rendered them,
To Sarraguce going, his own to sell.
After he lost his members and his head,
In court, at Aix, to gallows-tree condemned;
And thirty more with him, of his kindred,
Were hanged, a thing they never did expect.
　　　　　　　　　　　　　　　　AOI.

CX

Now marvellous and weighty the combat,
Right well they strike, Olivier and Rollant,
A thousand blows come from the Archbishop's
　　hand,
The dozen peers are nothing short of that,
With one accord join battle all the Franks.
Pagans are slain by hundred, by thousand,
Who flies not then, from death has no warrant,
Will he or nill, foregoes the allotted span.
The Franks have lost the foremost of their
　　band,
They'll see no more their fathers nor their clans,

Nor Charlemagne, where in the pass he stands.
Torment arose, right marvellous, in France,
Tempest there was, of wind and thunder black,
With rain and hail, so much could not be
    spanned;
Fell thunderbolts often on every hand,
And verily the earth quaked in answer back
From Saint Michael of Peril unto Sanz,
From Besençun to the harbour of Guitsand;
No house stood there but straight its walls
    must crack:
In full mid-day the darkness was so grand,
Save the sky split, no light was in the land.
Beheld these things with terror every man,
And many said: "We in the Judgement stand;
The end of time is presently at hand."
They spake no truth; they did not understand;
'Twas the great day of mourning for Rollant.

CXI

The Franks strike on; their hearts are good
    and stout.
Pagans are slain, a thousandfold, in crowds,
Left of five score are not two thousands now.
Says the Archbishop: "Our men are very proud,
No man on earth has more nor better found.
In Chronicles of Franks is written down,
What vassalage he had, our Emperour."
Then through the field they go, their friends
    seek out,
And their eyes weep with grief and pain pro-
    found
For kinsmen dear, by hearty friendship bound.
King Marsilies and his great host draw round.
                                        AOI.

CXII

King Marsilies along a valley led
The mighty host that he had gatherèd.
Twenty columns that king had numberèd.
With gleaming gold their helms were jewellèd.
Shone too their shields and sarks embroiderèd.
Sounded the charge seven thousand trumpets,
Great was the noise through all that country
    went.
Then said Rollanz: "Olivier, brother, friend,
That felon Guenes hath sworn to achieve our
    death;
For his treason no longer is secret.

Right great vengeance our Emperour will get.
Battle we'll have, both long and keenly set,
Never has man beheld such armies met.
With Durendal my sword I'll strike again,
And, comrade, you shall strike with Halteclere.
These swords in lands so many have we held,
Battles with them so many brought to end,
No evil song shall e'er be sung or said."
                                        AOI.

CXIII

When the Franks see so many there, pagans,
On every side covering all the land,
Often they call Olivier and Rollant,
The dozen peers, to be their safe warrant.
And the Archbishop speaks to them, as he can:
"My lords barons, go thinking nothing bad!
For God I pray you fly not hence but stand,
Lest evil songs of our valour men chant!
Far better 't were to perish in the van.
Certain it is, our end is near at hand,
Beyond this day shall no more live one man;
But of one thing I give you good warrant:
Blest Paradise to you now open stands,
By the Innocents your thrones you there shall
    have."
Upon these words grow bold again the Franks;
There is not one but he "Monjoie" demands.
                                        AOI.

CXIV

A Sarrazin was there, of Sarraguce,
Of that city one half was his by use,
'Twas Climborins, a man was nothing proof;
By Guenelun the count an oath he took,
And kissed his mouth in amity and truth,
Gave him his sword and his carbuncle too.
Terra Major, he said, to shame he'ld put,
From the Emperour his crown he would re-
    move.
He sate his horse, which he called Barbam-
    usche,
Never so swift sparrow nor swallow flew,
He spurred him well, and down the reins he
    threw,
Going to strike Engelier of Gascune;
Nor shield nor sark him any warrant proved,
The pagan spear's point did his body wound,
He pinned him well, and all the steel sent
    through,

From the hilt flung him dead beneath his foot.
After he said: "Good are they to confuse.
Pagans, strike on, and so this press set loose!"
"God!" say the Franks, "Grief, such a man to
lose!"

AOI.

CXV

The count Rollanz called upon Oliver:
"Sir companion, dead now is Engeler;
Than whom we'd no more valiant chevalier."
Answered that count: "God, let me him
avenge!"
Spurs of fine gold into his horse drove then,
Held Halteclere, with blood its steel was red,
By virtue great to strike that pagan went,
Brandished his blade, the Sarrazin upset;
The Adversaries of God his soul bare thence.
Next he has slain the duke Alphaïen,
And sliced away Escababi his head,
And has unhorsed some seven Arabs else;
No good for those to go to war again.
Then said Rollanz: "My comrade shews anger,
So in my sight he makes me prize him well;
More dear by Charles for such blows are we
held."
Aloud he's cried: "Strike on, the chevaliers!"

AOI.

CXVI

From the other part a pagan Valdabron.
Warden he'd been to king Marsilion,
And lord, by sea, of four hundred dromonds;
No sailor was but called his name upon;
Jerusalem he'd taken by treason,
Violated the Temple of Salomon,
The Patriarch had slain before the fonts.
He'd pledged his oath by county Guenelon,
Gave him his sword, a thousand coins thereon.
He sate his horse, which he called Gramimond,
Never so swift flew in the air falcon;
He's pricked him well, with sharp spurs he had
on,
Going to strike e'en that rich Duke, Sanson;
His shield has split, his hauberk has undone,
The ensign's folds have through his body gone,
Dead from the hilt out of his seat he's dropt:
"Pagans, strike on, for well we'll overcome!"

"God!" say the Franks, "Grief for a brave
baron!"

AOI.

CXVII

The count Rollanz, when Sansun dead he saw,
You may believe, great grief he had therefor.
His horse he spurs, gallops with great effort,
Wields Durendal, was worth fine gold and
more,
Goes as he may to strike that baron bold
Above the helm, that was embossed with gold,
Slices the head, the sark, and all the corse,
The good saddle, that was embossed with gold,
And cuts deep through the backbone of his
horse;
He's slain them both, blame him for that or
laud.
The pagans say: " 'Twas hard on us, that
blow."
Answers Rollanz: "Nay, love you I can not,
For on your side is arrogance and wrong."

AOI.

CXVIII

Out of Affrike an Affrican was come,
'Twas Malquiant, the son of king Malcud;
With beaten gold was all his armour done,
Fore all men's else it shone beneath the sun.
He sate his horse, which he called Salt-Perdut,
Never so swift was any beast could run.
And Anséis upon the shield he struck,
The scarlat with the blue he sliced it up,
Of his hauberk he's torn the folds and cut,
The steel and stock has through his body thrust.
Dead is that count, he's no more time to run.
Then say the Franks: "Baron, an evil luck!"

CXIX

Swift through the field Turpin the Archbishop
passed;
Such shaven-crown has never else sung Mass
Who with his limbs such prowess might com-
pass;
To th' pagan said: "God send thee all that's
bad!
One thou hast slain for whom my heart is sad."
So his good horse forth at his bidding ran,

He's struck him then on his shield Toledan,
Until he flings him dead on the green grass.

CXX

From the other part was a pagan Grandones,
Son of Capuel, the king of Capadoce.
He sate his horse, the which he called Mar-
more,
Never so swift was any bird in course;
He's loosed the reins, and spurring on that
horse
He's gone to strike Gerin with all his force;
The scarlat shield from's neck he's broken off,
And all his sark thereafter has he torn,
The ensign blue clean through his body's gone,
Until he flings him dead, on a high rock;
His companion Gerer he's slain also,
And Berenger, and Guiun of Santone;
Next a rich duke he's gone to strike, Austore,
That held Valence and the Honour of the
Rhone;
He's flung him dead; great joy the pagans
shew.
Then say the Franks: "Of ours how many fall."

CXXI

The count Rollanz, his sword with blood is
stained,
Well has he heard what way the Franks com-
plained;
Such grief he has, his heart would split in
twain:
To the pagan says: "God send thee every
shame!
One hast thou slain that dearly thou'lt repay."
He spurs his horse, that on with speed doth
strain;
Which should forfeit, they both together came.

CXXII

Grandonie was both proof and valiant,
And virtuous, a vassal combatant.
Upon the way there, he has met Rollant;
He'd never seen, yet knew him at a glance,
By the proud face and those fine limbs he had,
By his regard, and by his contenance;
He could not help but he grew faint thereat,
He would escape, nothing avail he can.

Struck him the count, with so great virtue, that
To the nose-plate he's all the helmet cracked,
Sliced through the nose and mouth and teeth
he has,
Hauberk close-mailed, and all the whole car-
cass,
Saddle of gold, with plates of silver flanked,
And of his horse has deeply scarred the back;
He's slain them both, they'll make no more
attack:
The Spanish men in sorrow cry, "Alack!"
Then say the Franks: "He strikes well, our
warrant."

CXXIII

Marvellous is the battle in its speed,
The Franks there strike with vigour and with
heat,
Cutting through wrists and ribs and chines
indeed,
Through garments to the lively flesh beneath;
On the green grass the clear blood runs in
streams.
The pagans say: "No more we'll suffer, we.
Terra Major, Mahummet's curse on thee!
Beyond all men thy people are hardy!"
There was not one but cried then: "Marsilie,
Canter, o king, thy succour now we need!"

CXXIV

Marvellous is the battle now and grand,
The Franks there strike, their good brown
spears in hand.
Then had you seen such sorrowing of clans,
So many a slain, shattered and bleeding man!
Biting the earth, or piled there on their backs!
The Sarrazins cannot such loss withstand.
Will they or nill, from off the field draw back;
By lively force chase them away the Franks.
AOI.

CXXV

Their martyrdom, his men's, Marsile has seen,
So he bids sound his horns and his buccines;
Then canters forth with all his great army.
Canters before a Sarrazin, Abisme,
More felon none was in that company;
Cankered with guile and every felony,

He fears not God, the Son of Saint Mary;
Black is that man as molten pitch that seethes;
Better he loves murder and treachery
Than to have all the gold of Galicie;
Never has man beheld him sport for glee;
Yet vassalage he's shown, and great folly,
So is he dear to th' felon king Marsile;
Dragon he bears, to which his tribe rally.
That Archbishop could never love him, he;
Seeing him there, to strike he's very keen,
Within himself he says all quietly:
"This Sarrazin great heretick meseems,
Rather I'ld die, than not slay him clean,
Ne'er did I love coward nor cowardice."

AOI.

CXXVI

That Archbishop begins the fight again,
Sitting the horse which he took from Grossaille;
—That was a king he had in Denmark slain;—
That charger is swift and of noble race;
Fine are his hooves, his legs are smooth and
straight,
Short are his thighs, broad crupper he displays,
Long are his ribs, aloft his spine is raised,
White is his tail and yellow is his mane,
Little his ears, and tawny all his face;
No beast is there, can match him in a race.
That Archbishop spurs on by vassalage,
He will not pause ere Abisme he assail;
So strikes that shield, is wonderfully arrayed,
Whereon are stones, amethyst and topaze,
Esterminals and carbuncles that blaze;
A devil's gift it was, in Val Metase,
Who handed it to the admiral Galafes;
So Turpin strikes, spares him not anyway;
After that blow, he's worth no penny wage;
The carcass he's sliced, rib from rib away,
So flings him down dead in an empty place.
Then say the Franks: "He has great vassalage,
With the Archbishop, surely the Cross is safe."

CXXVII

The count Rollanz calls upon Oliver:
"Sir companion, witness you'll freely bear,
The Archbishop is a right good chevalier,
None better is neath Heaven anywhere;
Well can he strike with lance and well with
spear."

Answers that count: "Support to him we'll
bear!"
Upon that word the Franks again make yare;
Hard are the blows, slaughter and suffering
there,
For Christians too, most bitter grief and care.
Who could had seen Rollanz and Oliver
With their good swords to strike and to slaugh-
ter!
And the Archbishop lays on there with his
spear.
Those that are dead, men well may hold them
dear.
In charters and in briefs is written clear,
Four thousand fell, and more, the tales declare.
Gainst four assaults easily did they fare,
But then the fifth brought heavy griefs to bear.
They all are slain, those Frankish chevaliers;
Only three-score, whom God was pleased to
spare,
Before these die, they'll sell them very dear.

AOI.

CXXVIII

The count Rollant great loss of his men sees,
His companion Olivier calls, and speaks:
"Sir and comrade, in God's Name, That you
keeps,
Such good vassals you see lie here in heaps;
For France the Douce, fair country, may we
weep,
Of such barons long desolate she'll be.
Ah! King and friend, wherefore are you not
here?
How, Oliver, brother, can we achieve?
And by what means our news to him repeat?"
Says Oliver: "I know not how to seek;
Rather I'ld die than shame come of this feat."

AOI.

CXXIX

Then says Rollanz: "I'll wind this olifant,
If Charlès hear, where in the pass he stands,
I pledge you now they will return, the Franks."
Says Oliver: "Great shame would come of that;
And a reproach on every one, your clan,
That shall endure while each lives in the land,
When I implored, you would not do this act;
Doing it now, no praise from me you'll have:

So wind your horn, but not by courage rash,
Seeing that both your arms with blood are splashed."
Answers that count: "Fine blows I've struck them back."

AOI.

CXXX

Then says Rollant: "Strong it is now, our battle;
I'll wind my horn, so the King hears it, Charlès."
Says Oliver: "That act were not a vassal's.
When I implored you, comrade, you were wrathful.
Were the King here, we had not borne such damage.
Nor should we blame those with him there, his army."
Says Oliver: "Now by my beard, hereafter
If I may see my gentle sister Alde,
She in her arms, I swear, shall never clasp you."

AOI.

CXXXI

Then says Rollanz: "Wherefore so wroth with me?"
He answers him: "Comrade, it was your deed:
Vassalage comes by sense, and not folly;
Prudence more worth is than stupidity.
Here are Franks dead, all for your trickery;
No more service to Carlun may we yield.
My lord were here now, had you trusted me,
And fought and won this battle then had we,
Taken or slain were the king Marsilie.
In your prowess, Rollanz, no good we've seen!
Charlès the great in vain your aid will seek—
None such as he till God His Judgement speak;—
Here must you die, and France in shame be steeped;
Here perishes our loyal company,
Before this night great severance and grief."

AOI.

CXXXII

That Archbishop has heard them, how they spoke,

His horse he pricks with his fine spurs of gold,
Coming to them he takes up his reproach:
"Sir Oliver, and you, Sir Rollant, both,
For God I pray, do not each other scold!
No help it were to us, the horn to blow,
But, none the less, it may be better so;
The King will come, with vengeance that he owes;
These Spanish men never away shall go.
Our Franks here, each descending from his horse,
Will find us dead, and limb from body torn;
They'll take us hence, on biers and litters borne;
With pity and with grief for us they'll mourn;
They'll bury each in some old minster-close;
No wolf nor swine nor dog shall gnaw our bones."
Answers Rollant: "Sir, very well you spoke."

AOI.

CXXXIII

Rollant hath set the olifant to his mouth,
He grasps it well, and with great virtue sounds.
High are those peaks, afar it rings and loud,
Thirty great leagues they hear its echoes mount.
So Charlès heard, and all his comrades round;
Then said that King: "Battle they do, our counts"
And Guenelun answered, contrarious:
"That were a lie, in any other mouth."

AOI.

CXXXIV

The Count Rollanz, with sorrow and with pangs,
And with great pain sounded his olifant:
Out of his mouth the clear blood leaped and ran,
About his brain the very temples cracked.
Loud is its voice, that horn he holds in hand;
Charlès hath heard, where in the pass he stands,
And Neimès hears, and listen all the Franks.
Then says the King: "I hear his horn, Rollant's;
He'd never sound, but he were in combat."
Answers him Guenes: "It is no battle, that.
Now are you old, blossoming white and blanched,
Yet by such words you still appear infant.

You know full well the great pride of Rollant;
Marvel it is, God stays so tolerant.
Noples he took, not waiting your command;
Thence issued forth the Sarrazins, a band
With vassalage had fought against Rollant;
He slew them first, with Durendal his brand,
Then washed their blood with water from the
    land;
So what he'd done might not be seen of man.
He for a hare goes all day, horn in hand;
Before his peers in foolish jest he brags.
No race neath heav'n in field him dare attack.
So canter on! Nay, wherefore hold we back?
Terra Major is far away, our land."

                      AOI.

CXXXV

The count Rollanz, though blood his mouth
    doth stain,
And burst are both the temples of his brain,
His olifant he sounds with grief and pain;
Charlès hath heard, listen the Franks again.
"That horn," the King says, "hath a mighty
    strain!"
Answers Duke Neimes: "A baron blows with
    pain!
Battle is there, indeed I see it plain,
He is betrayed, by one that still doth feign.
Equip you, sir, cry out your old refrain,
That noble band, go succour them amain!
Enough you've heard how Rollant doth com-
    plain."

CXXXVI

That Emperour hath bid them sound their
    horns.
The Franks dismount, and dress themselves
    for war,
Put hauberks on, helmets and golden swords;
Fine shields they have, and spears of length
    and force
Scarlat and blue and white their ensigns float.
His charger mounts each baron of the host;
They spur with haste as through the pass they
    go.
Nor was there one but thus to's neighbour
    spoke:
"Now, ere he die, may we see Rollant, so

Ranged by his side we'll give some goodly
    blows."
But what avail? They've stayed too long below.

CXXXVII

That even-tide is light as was the day;
Their armour shines beneath the sun's clear
    ray,
Hauberks and helms throw off a dazzling
    flame,
And blazoned shields, flowered in bright array,
Also their spears, with golden ensigns gay.
That Emperour, he canters on with rage,
And all the Franks with wonder and dismay;
There is not one can bitter tears restrain,
And for Rollant they're very sore afraid.
The King has bid them seize that county
    Guene,
And charged with him the scullions of his
    train;
The master-cook he's called, Besgun by name:
"Guard me him well, his felony is plain,
Who in my house vile treachery has made."
He holds him, and a hundred others takes
From the kitchen, both good and evil knaves;
Then Guenè's beard and both his cheeks they
    shaved,
And four blows each with their closed fists
    they gave,
They trounced him well with cudgels and with
    staves,
And on his neck they clasped an iron chain;
So like a bear enchained they held him safe,
On a pack-mule they set him in his shame:
Kept him till Charles should call for him again.

                      AOI.

CXXXVIII

High were the peaks and shadowy and grand,
The valleys deep, the rivers swiftly ran.
Trumpets they blew in rear and in the van,
Till all again answered that olifant.
That Emperour canters with fury mad,
And all the Franks dismay and wonder have;
There is not one but weeps and waxes sad
And all pray God that He will guard Rollant
Till in the field together they may stand;
There by his side they'll strike as well they can.
But what avail? No good there is in that;

They're not in time; too long have they held
    back.
                        AOI.

CXXXIX

In his great rage on canters Charlemagne;
Over his sark his beard is flowing plain.
Barons of France, in haste they spur and strain;
There is not one that can his wrath contain
That they are not with Rollant the Captain,
Whereas he fights the Sarrazins of Spain.
If he be struck, will not one soul remain.
—God! Sixty men are all now in his train!
Never a king had better Capitains.
                        AOI.

CXL

Rollant regards the barren mountain-sides;
Dead men of France, he sees so many lie,
And weeps for them as fits a gentle knight:
"Lords and barons, may God to you be kind!
And all your souls redeem for Paradise!
And let you there mid holy flowers lie!
Better vassals than you saw never I.
Ever you've served me, and so long a time,
By you Carlon hath conquered kingdoms wide;
That Emperour reared you for evil plight!
Douce land of France, o very precious clime,
Laid desolate by such a sour exile!
Barons of France, for me I've seen you die,
And no support, no warrant could I find;
God be your aid, Who never yet hath lied!
I must not fail now, brother, by your side;
Save I be slain, for sorrow shall I die.
Sir companion, let us again go strike!"

CXLI

The count Rollanz, back to the field then hieing
Holds Durendal, and like a vassal striking
Faldrun of Pui has through the middle slicèd,
With twenty-four of all they rated highest;
Was never man, for vengeance shewed such
    liking.
Even as a stag before the hounds goes flying,
Before Rollanz the pagans scatter, frightened.
Says the Archbishop: "You deal now very
    wisely!
Such valour should he shew that is bred
    knightly,

And beareth arms, and a good charger rideth;
In battle should be strong and proud and
    sprightly;
Or otherwise he is not worth a shilling,
Should be a monk in one of those old ministers,
Where, day by day, he'ld pray for us poor
    sinners."
Answers Rollant: "Strike on; no quarter give
    them!"
Upon these words Franks are again beginning;
Very great loss they suffer then, the Christians.

CXLII

The man who knows, for him there's no prison,
In such a fight with keen defence lays on;
Wherefore the Franks are fiercer than lions.
Marsile you'd seen go as a brave baron,
Sitting his horse, the which he calls Gaignon;
He spurs it well, going to strike Bevon,
That was the lord of Beaune and of Dijon,
His shield he breaks, his hauberk has undone,
So flings him dead, without condition;
Next he hath slain Yvoerie and Ivon,
Also with them Gerard of Russillon.
The count Rollanz, being not far him from,
To th' pagan says: "Confound thee our Lord
    God!
So wrongfully you've slain my companions,
A blow you'll take, ere we apart be gone,
And of my sword the name I'll bid you con."
He goes to strike him, as a brave baron,
And his right hand the count clean slices off;
Then takes the head of Jursaleu the blond;
That was the son of king Marsilion.
Pagans cry out: "Assist us now, Mahom!
God of our race, avenge us on Carlon!
Into this land he's sent us such felons
That will not leave the fight before they drop."
Says each to each: "Nay let us fly!" Upon
That word, they're fled, an hundred thousand
    gone;
Call them who may, they'll never more come
    on.
                        AOI.

CXLIII

But what avail? Though fled be Marsilies,
He's left behind his uncle, the alcaliph
Who holds Alferne, Kartagene, Garmalie,

And Ethiope, a cursèd land indeed;
The blackamoors from there are in his keep,
Broad in the nose they are and flat in the ear,
Fifty thousand and more in company.
These canter forth with arrogance and heat,
Then they cry out the pagans' rallying-cheer;
And Rollant says: "Martyrdom we'll receive;
Not long to live, I know it well, have we;
Felon he's named that sells his body cheap!
Strike on, my lords, with burnished swords and
    keen;
Contest each inch your life and death between,
That ne'er by us Douce France in shame be
    steeped.
When Charles my lord shall come into this
    field,
Such discipline of Sarrazins he'll see,
For one of ours he'll find them dead fifteen;
He will not fail, but bless us all in peace."
                                        AOI.

CXLIV

When Rollant sees those misbegotten men,
Who are more black than ink is on the pen
With no part white, only their teeth except,
Then says that count: "I know now very well
That here to die we're bound, as I can tell.
Strike on, the Franks! For so I recommend."
Says Oliver: "Who holds back, is condemned!"
Upon those words, the Franks to strike again.

CXLV

Franks are but few; which, when the pagans
    know,
Among themselves comfort and pride they
    shew;
Says each to each: "Wrong was that Emperor."
Their alcaliph upon a sorrel rode,
And pricked it well with both his spurs of gold;
Struck Oliver, behind, on the back-bone,
His hauberk white into his body broke,
Clean through his breast the thrusting spear
    he drove;
After he said: "You've borne a mighty blow.
Charlès the great should not have left you so;
He's done us wrong, small thanks to him we
    owe;
I've well avenged all ours on you alone."

CXLVI

Oliver feels that he to die is bound,
Holds Halteclere, whose steel is rough and
    brown,
Strikes the alcaliph on his helm's golden mount;
Flowers and stones fall clattering to the ground,
Slices his head, to th' small teeth in his mouth;
So brandishes his blade and flings him down;
After he says: "Pagan, accurst be thou!
Thou'lt never say that Charles forsakes me now;
Nor to thy wife, nor any dame thou'st found,
Thou'lt never boast, in lands where thou wast
    crowned,
One pennyworth from me thou'st taken out,
Nor damage wrought on me nor any around."
After, for aid, "Rollant!" he cries aloud.
                                        AOI.

CXLVII

Oliver feels that death is drawing nigh;
To avenge himself he hath no longer time;
Through the great press most gallantly he
    strikes,
He breaks their spears, their buckled shields
    doth slice,
Their feet, their fists, their shoulders and their
    sides,
Dismembers them; whoso had seen the sight
Dead in the field one on another piled,
Remember well a vassal brave he might.
Charlè's ensign he'll not forget it quite;
Aloud and clear "Monjoie" again he cries.
To call Rollanz, his friend and peer, he tries:
"My companion, come hither to my side.
With bitter grief we must us now divide."
                                        AOI.

CXLVIII

Then Rollant looked upon Olivier's face;
Which was all wan and colourless and pale,
While the clear blood, out of his body sprayed,
Upon the ground gushed forth and ran away.
"God!" said that count, "What shall I do or
    say?
My companion, gallant for such ill fate!
Ne'er shall man be, against thee could prevail.
Ah! France the Douce, henceforth art thou
    made waste

Of vassals brave, confounded and disgraced!
Our Emperour shall suffer damage great."
And with these words upon his horse he faints.
                                        AOI.

CXLIX

You'd seen Rollant aswoon there in his seat,
And Oliver, who unto death doth bleed,
So much he's bled, his eyes are dim and weak;
Nor clear enough his vision, far or near,
To recognise whatever man he sees;
His companion, when each the other meets,
Above the helm jewelled with gold he beats,
Slicing it down from there to the nose-piece,
But not his head; he's touched not brow nor
      cheek.
At such a blow Rollant regards him keen,
And asks of him, in gentle tones and sweet:
"To do this thing, my comrade, did you mean?
This is Rollanz, who ever held you dear;
And no mistrust was ever us between."
Says Oliver: "Now can I hear you speak;
I see you not: may the Lord God you keep!
I struck you now: and for your pardon plead."
Answers Rollanz: "I am not hurt, indeed;
I pardon you, before God's Throne and here."
Upon these words, each to the other leans;
And in such love you had their parting seen.

CL

Oliver feels death's anguish on him now;
And in his head his two eyes swimming round;
Nothing he sees; he hears not any sound;
Dismounting then, he kneels upon the ground,
Proclaims his sins both firmly and aloud,
Clasps his two hands, heavenwards holds them
      out,
Prays God himself in Paradise to allow;
Blessings on Charles, and on Douce France he
      vows,
And his comrade, Rollanz, to whom he's bound.
Then his heart fails; his helmet nods and bows;
Upon the earth he lays his whole length out:
And he is dead, may stay no more, that count.
Rollanz the brave mourns him with grief pro-
      found;
Nowhere on earth so sad a man you'd found.

CLI

So Rollant's friend is dead; whom when he sees
Face to the ground, and biting it with's teeth,
Begins to mourn in language very sweet:
"Unlucky, friend, your courage was indeed!
Together we have spent such days and years;
No harmful thing twixt thee and me has been.
Now thou art dead, and all my life a grief."
And with these words again he swoons, that
      chief,
Upon his horse, which he calls Veillantif;
Stirrups of gold support him underneath;
He cannot fall, whichever way he lean.

CLII

Soon as Rollant his senses won and knew,
Recovering and turning from that swoon.
Bitter great loss appeared there in his view:
Dead are the Franks; he'd all of them to lose,
Save the Archbishop, and save Gualter del
      Hum;
He is come down out of the mountains, who
Gainst Spanish men made there a great ado;
Dead are his men, for those the pagans slew;
Will he or nill, along the vales he flew,
And called Rollant, to bring him succour soon:
"Ah! Gentle count, brave soldier, where are
      you?
For by thy side no fear I ever knew.
Gualter it is, who conquered Maëlgut,
And nephew was to hoary old Droün;
My vassalage thou ever thoughtest good.
Broken my spear, and split my shield in two;
Gone is the mail that on my hauberk grew;
This body of mine eight lances have gone
      through;
I'm dying. Yet full price for life I took."
Rollant has heard these words and understood,
Has spurred his horse, and on towards him
      drew.
                                        AOI.

CLIII

Grief gives Rollanz intolerance and pride;
Through the great press he goes again to strike;
To slay a score of Spaniards he contrives,
Gualter has six, the Archbishop other five.

The pagans say: "Men, these, of felon kind!
Lordings, take care they go not hence alive!
Felon he's named that does not break their
    line,
Recreant, who lets them any safety find!"
And so once more begin the hue and cry,
From every part they come to break the line.
AOI.

CLIV

Count Rollant is a noble and brave soldier,
Gualter del Hum's a right good chevalier,
That Archbishop hath shewn good prowess
    there;
None of them falls behind the other pair;
Through the great press, pagans they strike
    again.
Come on afoot a thousand Sarrazens,
And on horseback some forty thousand men.
But well I know, to approach they never dare;
Lances and spears they poise to hurl at them,
Arrows, barbs, darts and javelins in the air.
With the first flight they've slain our Gualtïer;
Turpin of Reims has all his shield broken,
And cracked his helm; he's wounded in the
    head,
From his hauberk the woven mail they tear,
In his body four spear-wounds doth he bear;
Beneath him too his charger's fallen dead.
Great grief it was, when that Archbishop fell.
AOI.

CLV

Turpin of Reims hath felt himself undone,
Since that four spears have through his body
    come;
Nimble and bold upon his feet he jumps;
Looks for Rollant, and then towards him runs,
Saying this word: "I am not overcome.
While life remains, no good vassal gives up."
He's drawn Almace, whose steel was brown
    and rough,
Through the great press a thousand blows he's
    struck:
As Charlès said, quarter he gave to none;
He found him there, four hundred else among,
Wounded the most, speared through the mid-
    dle some,

Also there were from whom the heads he'd cut:
So tells the tale, he that was there says thus,
The brave Saint Giles, whom God made mar-
    vellous,
Who charters wrote for th' Minster at Loüm;
Nothing he's heard that does not know this
    much.

CLVI

The count Rollanz has nobly fought and well,
But he is hot, and all his body sweats;
Great pain he has, and trouble in his head,
His temples burst when he the horn sounded;
But he would know if Charles will come to
    them,
Takes the olifant, and feebly sounds again.
That Emperour stood still and listened then:
"My lords," said he, "Right evilly we fare!
This day Rollanz, my nephew shall be dead:
I hear his horn, with scarcely any breath.
Nimbly canter, whoever would be there!
Your trumpets sound, as many as ye bear!"
Sixty thousand so loud together blare,
The mountains ring, the valleys answer them.
The pagans hear, they think it not a jest;
Says each to each: "Carlum doth us bestead."
AOI.

CLVII

The pagans say: "That Emperour's at hand,
We hear their sound, the trumpets of the
    Franks;
If Charlès come, great loss we then shall stand,
And wars renewed, unless we slay Rollant;
All Spain we'll lose, our own clear father-land."
Four hundred men of them in helmets stand;
The best of them that might be in their ranks
Make on Rollanz a grim and fierce attack;
Gainst these the count had well enough in
    hand.
AOI.

CLVIII

The count Rollanz, when their approach he
    sees
Is grown so bold and manifest and fierce
So long as he's alive he will not yield.

He sits his horse, which men call Veillantif,
Pricking him well with golden spurs beneath,
Through the great press he goes, their line to
  meet,
And by his side is the Archbishop Turpin.
"Now, friend, begone!" say pagans, each to
  each;
"These Frankish men, their horns we plainly
  hear;
Charle is at hand, that King in Majesty."

CLIX

The count Rollanz has never loved cowards,
Nor arrogant, nor men of evil heart,
Nor chevalier that was not good vassal.
That Archbishop, Turpins, he calls apart:
"Sir, you're afoot, and I my charger have;
For love of you, here will I take my stand,
Together we'll endure things good and bad;
I'll leave you not, for no incarnate man:
We'll give again these pagans their attack;
The better blows are those from Durendal."
Says the Archbishop: "Shame on him that holds
  back!
Charle is at hand, full vengeance he'll exact."

CLX

The pagans say: "Unlucky were we born!
An evil day for us did this day dawn!
For we have lost our peers and all our lords.
Charles his great host once more upon us
  draws,
Of Frankish men we plainly hear the horns,
"Monjoie" they cry, and great is their uproar.
The count Rollant is of such pride and force
He'll never yield to man of woman born;
Let's aim at him, then leave him on the spot!"
And aim they did: with arrows long and short,
Lances and spears and feathered javelots;
Count Rollant's shield they've broken through
  and bored,
The woven mail have from his hauberk torn,
But not himself, they've never touched his
  corse;
Veillantif is in thirty places gored,
Beneath the count he's fallen dead, that horse.
Pagans are fled, and leave him on the spot;
The count Rollant stands on his feet once more.
                                        AOI.

CLXI

Pagans are fled, enangered and enraged,
Home into Spain with speed they make their
  way;
The count Rollanz, he has not given chase,
For Veillantif, his charger, they have slain;
Will he or nill, on foot he must remain.
To the Archbishop, Turpins, he goes with aid;
He's from his head the golden helm unlaced,
Taken from him his white hauberk away,
And cut the gown in strips, was round his
  waist;
On his great wounds the pieces of it placed,
Then to his heart has caught him and em-
  braced;
On the green grass he has him softly laid,
Most sweetly then to him has Rollant prayed:
"Ah! Gentle sir, give me your leave, I say;
Our companions, whom we so dear appraised,
Are now all dead; we cannot let them stay;
I will go seek and bring them to this place,
Arrange them here in ranks, before your face."
Said the Archbishop: "Go, and return again.
This field is yours and mine now; God be
  praised!"

CLXII

So Rollanz turns, through the field, all alone,
Searching the vales and mountains, he is gone;
He finds Gerin, Gerers his companion,
Also he finds Berenger and Otton,
There too he finds Anséis and Sanson,
And finds Gerard the old, of Rossillon;
By one and one he's taken those barons,
To the Archbishop with each of them he comes,
Before his knees arranges every one.
That Archbishop, he cannot help but sob,
He lifts his hand, gives benediction;
After he's said: "Unlucky, Lords, your lot!
But all your souls He'll lay, our Glorious God,
In Paradise, His holy flowers upon!
For my own death such anguish now I've got;
I shall not see him, our rich Emperor."

CLXIII

So Rollant turns, goes through the field in
  quest;
His companion Olivier finds at length;

He has embraced him close against his breast,
To the Archbishop returns as he can best;
Upon a shield he's laid him, by the rest;
And the Archbishop has them absolved and
　blest:
Whereon his grief and pity grow afresh.
Then says Rollanz: "Fair comrade Olivier,
You were the son of the good count Reinier,
Who held the march by th' Vale of Runïer,
To shatter spears, through buckled shields to
　bear,
And from hauberks the mail to break and tear,
Proof men to lead, and prudent counsel share,
Gluttons in field to frighten and conquer,
No land has known a better chevalier."

CLXIV

The count Rollanz, when dead he saw his
　peers,
And Oliver, he held so very dear,
Grew tender, and began to shed a tear;
Out of his face the colour disappeared;
No longer could he stand, for so much grief,
Will he or nill, he swooned upon the field.
Said the Archbishop: "Unlucky lord, indeed!"

CLXV

When the Archbishop beheld him swoon,
　Rollant,
Never before such bitter grief he'd had;
Stretching his hand, he took that olifant.
Through Rencesvals a little river ran;
He would go there, fetch water for Rollant.
Went step by step, to stumble soon began,
So feeble he is, no further fare he can,
For too much blood he's lost, and no strength
　has;
Ere he has crossed an acre of the land,
His heart grows faint, he falls down forwards
　and
Death comes to him with very cruel pangs.

CLXVI

The count Rollanz wakes from his swoon once
　more,
Climbs to his feet; his pains are very sore;
Looks down the vale, looks to the hills above;
On the green grass, beyond his companions,

He sees him lie, that noble old baron;
'Tis the Archbishop, whom in His name
　wrought God;
There he proclaims his sins, and looks above;
Joins his two hands, to Heaven holds them
　forth,
And Paradise prays God to him to accord.
Dead is Turpin, the warrior of Charlon.
In battles great and very rare sermons
Against pagans ever a champion.
God grant him now His Benediction!
　　　　　　　　　　　　AOI.

CLXVII

The count Rollant sees the Archbishop lie dead,
Sees the bowels out of his body shed,
And sees the brains that surge from his fore-
　head;
Between his two arm-pits, upon his breast,
Crossways he folds those hands so white and
　fair.
Then mourns aloud, as was the custom there:
"Thee, gentle sir, chevalier nobly bred,
To the Glorious Celestial I commend;
Ne'er shall man be, that will Him serve so well;
Since the Apostles was never such prophet,
To hold the laws and draw the hearts of men.
Now may your soul no pain nor sorrow ken,
Finding the gates of Paradise open!"

CLXVIII

Then Rollanz feels that death to him draws
　near,
For all his brain is issued from his ears;
He prays to God that He will call the peers,
Bids Gabriel, the angel, t' himself appear.
Takes the olifant, that no reproach shall hear,
And Durendal in the other hand he wields;
Further than might a cross-bow's arrow speed
Goes toward Spain into a fallow-field;
Climbs on a cliff; where, under two fair trees,
Four terraces, of marble wrought, he sees.
There he falls down, and lies upon the green;
He swoons again, for death is very near.

CLXIX

High are the peaks, the trees are very high.
Four terraces of polished marble shine;

On the green grass count Rollant swoons there-
    by.
A Sarrazin him all the time espies,
Who feigning death among the others hides;
Blood hath his face and all his body dyed;
He gets afoot, running towards him hies;
Fair was he, strong and of a courage high;
A mortal hate he's kindled in his pride.
He's seized Rollant, and the arms, were at his
    side,
"Charlè's nephew," he's said, "here conquered
    lies.
To Araby I'll bear this sword as prize."
As he drew it, something the count descried.

CLXX

So Rollant felt his sword was taken forth,
Opened his eyes, and this word to him spoke:
"Thou'rt never one of ours, full well I know."
Took the olifant, that he would not let go,
Struck him on th' helm, that jewelled was with
    gold,
And broke its steel, his skull and all his bones,
Out of his head both the two eyes he drove;
Dead at his feet he has the pagan thrown:
After he's said: "Culvert, thou wert too bold,
Or right or wrong, of my sword seizing hold!
They'll dub thee fool, to whom the tale is told.
But my great one, my olifant I broke;
Fallen from it the crystal and the gold."

CLXXI

Then Rollanz feels that he has lost his sight,
Climbs to his feet, uses what strength he might;
In all his face the colour is grown white.
In front of him a great brown boulder lies;
Whereon ten blows with grief and rage he
    strikes;
The steel cries out, but does not break outright;
And the count says: "Saint Mary, be my guide!
Good Durendal, unlucky is your plight!
I've need of you no more; spent is my pride!
We in the field have won so many fights,
Combating through so many regions wide
That Charlès holds, whose beard is hoary
    white!
Be you not his that turns from any in flight!
A good vassal has held you this long time;
Never shall France the Free behold his like."

CLXXII

Rollant hath struck the sardonyx terrace;
The steel cries out, but broken is no ways.
So when he sees he never can it break,
Within himself begins he to complain:
"Ah! Durendal, white art thou, clear of stain!
Beneath the sun reflecting back his rays!
In Moriane was Charlès, in the vale,
When from heaven God by His angel bade
Him give thee to a count and capitain;
Girt thee on me that noble King and great.
I won for him with thee Anjou, Bretaigne,
And won for him with thee Peitou, the Maine,
And Normandy the free for him I gained,
Also with thee Provence and Equitaigne,
And Lumbardie and all the whole Romaigne,
I won Baivere, all Flanders in the plain,
Also Burguigne and all the whole Puillane,
Costentinnople, that homage to him pays;
In Saisonie all is as he ordains;
With thee I won him Scotland, Ireland, Wales,
England also, where he his chamber makes;
Won I with thee so many countries strange
That Charlès holds, whose beard is white with
    age!
For this sword's sake sorrow upon me weighs,
Rather I'd die, than it mid pagans stay.
Lord God Father, never let France be shamed!"

CLXXIII

Rollant his stroke on a dark stone repeats,
And more of it breaks off than I can speak.
The sword cries out, yet breaks not in the least,
Back from the blow into the air it leaps.
Destroy it can he not; which when he sees,
Within himself he makes a plaint most sweet:
"Ah! Durendal, most holy, fair indeed!
Relics enough thy golden hilt conceals:
Saint Peter's Tooth, the Blood of Saint Basile,
Some of the Hairs of my Lord, Saint Denise,
Some of the Robe, was worn by Saint Mary.
It is not right that pagans should thee seize,
For Christian men your use shall ever be.
Nor any man's that worketh cowardice!
Many broad lands with you have I retrieved
Which Charles holds, who hath the great white
    beard;
Wherefore that King so proud and rich is he."

CLXXIV

But Rollant felt that death had made a way
Down from his head till on his heart it lay;
Beneath a pine running in haste he came,
On the green grass he lay there on his face;
His olifant and sword beneath him placed,
Turning his head towards the pagan race,
Now this he did, in truth, that Charles might
    say
(As he desired) and all the Franks his race;—
'Ah, gentle count; conquering he was slain!'—
He owned his faults often and every way,
And for his sins his glove to God upraised.
                      AOI.

CLXXV

But Rollant feels he's no more time to seek;
Looking to Spain, he lies on a sharp peak,
And with one hand upon his breast he beats:
"*Mea Culpa!* God, by Thy Virtues clean
Me from my sins, the mortal and the mean,
Which from the hour that I was born have
    been
Until this day, when life is ended here!"
Holds out his glove toward God, as he speaks;
Angels descend from heaven on that scene.
                      AOI.

CLXXVI

The count Rollanz, beneath a pine he sits;
Turning his eyes towards Spain, he begins
Remembering so many divers things:
So many lands where he went conquering,
And France the Douce, the heroes of his kin,
And Charlemagne, his lord who nourished him.
Nor can he help but weep and sigh at this.
But his own self, he's not forgotten him,
He owns his faults, and God's forgiveness bids:

"Very Father, in Whom no falsehood is,
Saint Lazaron from death Thou didst remit,
And Daniel save from the lions' pit;
My soul in me preserve from all perils
And from the sins I did in life commit!"
His right-hand glove, to God he offers it
Saint Gabriel from 's hand hath taken it.
Over his arm his head bows down and slips,
He joins his hands: and so is life finish'd.
God sent him down His angel cherubin,
And Saint Michael, we worship in peril;
And by their side Saint Gabriel alit;
So the count's soul they bare to Paradis.

CLXXVII

Rollant is dead; his soul to heav'n God bare,
That Emperour to Rencesvals doth fare.
There was no path nor passage anywhere
Nor waste ground no ell nor foot to spare
Without a Frank or pagan lying there.
Charles cries aloud: "Where are you, nephew
    fair?
Where's the Archbishop and that count
    Oliviers?
Where is Gerins and his comrade Gerers?
Otès the Duke, and the count Berengiers
And Ivorie, and Ive, so dear they were?
What is become of Gascon Engelier,
Sansun the Duke and Anséis the fierce?
Where's old Gerard of Russillun; oh, where
The dozen peers I left behind me here?"
But what avail, since none can answer bear?
"God!" says the King, "Now well may I despair,
I was not here the first assault to share!"
Seeming enraged, his beard the King doth tear.
Weep from their eyes barons and chevaliers,
A thousand score, they swoon upon the earth;
Duke Neimes for them was moved with pity
    rare.

Thomas Aquinas

Thomas Aquinas (see note on page 249) in *Of Cheating* and *Of the Sin of Usury* was concerned with ethical problems raised within Christendom resulting from the revival of trade, industry, and town life culminating in the urban civilization of the thirteenth century. The new capitalism, fostered by the revival of trade, came under the close scrutiny of the church and many practices of the burghers were condemned outright. Many prime capitalistic virtues ran counter to the spiritual principles of Christianity and its founder. In Of Cheating Thomas raised and answered such questions as "Is it lawful to sell a thing for more than its worth?" and "Is it lawful in trading to sell a thing at a higher price than was paid for it?" In reading this selection, note (1) the basis for Thomas's conclusion that it is unlawful to sell a thing for more than its worth, (2) obligations of sellers and buyers relating to things exchanged, (3) the various categories of trade and what kinds of trade are just and what kinds are unjust, and (4) Thomas's method of argument compared with the method of present-day economists.

In Of Sin and Usury, Thomas drew some fine distinctions between just and unjust practices, yet it can be observed that in treating economic practices he made a serious effort to harmonize the traditional anti-capitalistic views of Christianity with the newer demands of the expanding middle classes coming into prominence for the first time in 800 years. In reading this selection note (1) Thomas's answer and explanation to the question of whether usury (lending money for profit) is sinful, (2) how he dealt with the problem of practices designed to circumvent the churchs' prohibitions against usury, (3) under what circumstances proceeds from usury are lawfully acquired, (4) what a man should do with profits made by usury, and (5) the relative degree of guilt in lending and borrowing at usurious rates.

From: OF CHEATING and OF THE SIN OF USURY

OF CHEATING, WHICH IS COMMITTED IN BUYING AND SELLING

We must now consider those sins which relate to voluntary commutations. First, we shall consider cheating, which is committed in buying and selling: secondly, we shall consider usury, which occurs in loans. In connection with the other voluntary commutations no special kind of sin is to be found distinct from rapine and theft.

Under the first head there are four points of inquiry: (1) Of unjust sales as regards the price; namely, whether it is lawful to sell a thing for more than its worth? (2) Of unjust sales on the part of the thing sold. (3) Whether the seller is bound to reveal a fault in the thing sold? (4) Whether it is lawful in trading to sell a thing at a higher price than was paid for it?

FIRST ARTICLE.

WHETHER IT IS LAWFUL TO SELL A THING FOR MORE THAN ITS WORTH?

We proceed thus to the First Article:—

Objection 1. It seems that it is lawful to sell a thing for more than its worth. For in the commutations of human life, civil laws determine that which is just. Now according to

As translated by the Fathers of the English Dominican Province in The "Summa Theologica" of St. Thomas Aquinas, R. and T. Washbourne, Ltd., London, 1918, Part II, Second Number, QQ. LXXVII–LXXVIII, 317–341. Courtesy of Benziger Brothers.

these laws it is just for buyer and seller to deceive one another: and this occurs by the seller selling a thing for more than its worth, and the buyer buying a thing for less than its worth. Therefore it is lawful to sell a thing for more than its worth.

Obj. 2. Further, That which is common to all would seem to be natural and not sinful. Now Augustine relates that the saying of a certain jester was accepted by all: *You wish to buy for a song and to sell at a premium*, which agrees with the saying of Prov. XX. 14: *It is naught, it is naught, saith every buyer: and when he is gone away, then he will boast.* Therefore it is lawful to sell a thing for more than its worth.

Obj. 3. Further, It does not seem unlawful if that which honesty demands be done by mutual agreement. Now, according to the Philosopher, in the friendship which is based on utility, the amount of the recompense for a favour received should depend on the utility accruing to the receiver: and this utility sometimes is worth more than the thing given, for instance if the receiver be in great need of that thing, whether for the purpose of avoiding a danger, or of deriving some particular benefit. Therefore, in contracts of buying and selling, it is lawful to give a thing in return for more than its worth.

On the contrary, It is written: *All things . . . whatsoever you would that men should do to you, do you also to them.* But no man wishes to buy a thing for more than its worth. Therefore no man should sell a thing to another man for more than its worth.

I answer that, It is altogether sinful to have recourse to deceit in order to sell a thing for more than its just price, because this is to deceive one's neighbor so as to injure him. Hence Tully says: *Contracts should be entirely free from double-dealing; the seller must not impose upon the bidder, nor the buyer upon one that bids against him.*

But, apart from fraud, we may speak of buying and selling in two ways. First, as considered in themselves, and from this point of view, buying and selling seem to be established for the common advantage of both parties, one of whom requires that which belongs to the other, and vice versa, as the Philosopher states. Now whatever is established for the common advantage, should not be more of a burden to any one party than to another, and consequently all contracts between them should observe equality of thing and thing. Again, the quality of a thing that comes into human use is measured by the price given for it, for which purpose money was invented, as stated in *Ethic. V.* Therefore, if either the price exceed the quantity of the thing's worth, or, conversely, the thing exceed the price, there is no longer the equality of justice: and consequently, to sell a thing for more than its worth, or to buy it for less than its worth, is in itself unjust and unlawful.

Secondly we may speak of buying and selling, considered as accidentally tending to the advantage of one party, and to the disadvantage of the other: for instance, when a man has great need of a certain thing, while another man will suffer if he be without it. In such a case the just price will depend not only on the thing sold, but on the loss which the sale brings on the seller. And thus it will be lawful to sell a thing for more than it is worth in itself, though the price paid be not more than it is worth to the owner. Yet if the one man derive a great advantage by becoming possessed of the other man's property, and the seller be not at a loss through being without that thing, the latter ought not to raise the price, because the advantage accruing to the buyer, is not due to the seller, but to a circumstance affecting the buyer. Now no man should sell what is not his, though he may charge for the loss he suffers.

On the other hand if a man find that he derives great advantage from something he has bought, he may, of his own accord, pay the seller something over and above: and this pertains to his honesty.

Reply Obj. 1. As stated above, human law is given to the people among whom there are many lacking virtue, and it is not given to the virtuous alone. Hence human law was unable to forbid all that is contrary to virtue; and it suffices for it to prohibit whatever is destructive of human intercourse, while it treats other matters as though they were lawful, not by approving of them, but by not punishing them. Accordingly, if without employing deceit the seller disposes of his goods for more than their worth, or the buyer obtains them for less than their worth, the law looks upon this as licit, and provides no punishment for so doing, unless the excess be too great, because then even human law demands restitution to be made, for instance if a man be deceived in regard of more than half the amount of the just price of a thing.

On the other hand the Divine law leaves nothing unpunished that is contrary to virtue. Hence, according to the Divine law, it is reckoned unlawful if the equality of justice be not observed in buying and selling: and he who has received more than he ought must make compensation to him that has suffered loss, if the loss be considerable. I add this condition, because the just price of things is not fixed with mathematical precision, but depends on a kind of estimate, so that a slight addition or subtraction would not seem to destroy the equality of justice.

Reply Obj. 2. As Augustine says: *This jester, either by looking into himself or by his experience of others, thought that all men are inclined to wish to buy for a song and sell at a premium. But since in reality this is wicked, it is in every man's power to acquire that justice whereby he may resist and overcome this inclination.* And then he gives the example of a man who gave the just price for a book to a man who through ignorance asked a low price for it. Hence it is evident that this common desire is not from nature but from vice, wherefore it is common to many who walk along the broad road of sin.

Reply Obj. 3. In commutative justice we consider chiefly real equality. On the other hand, in friendship based on utility we consider equality of usefulness, so that the recompense should depend on the usefulness accruing, whereas in buying it should be equal to the thing bought.

Second Article.

Whether a Sale is Rendered Unlawful Through a Fault in the Thing Sold?

We proceed thus to the Second Article:—

Objection 1. It seems that a sale is not rendered unjust and unlawful through a fault in the thing sold. For less account should be taken of the other parts of a thing than of what belongs to its substance. Yet the sale of a thing does not seem to be rendered unlawful through a fault in its substance: for instance, if a man sell instead of the real metal, silver or gold produced by some chemical process, which is adapted to all the human uses for which silver and gold are necessary, for instance in the making of vessels and the like. Much less therefore will it be an unlawful sale if the thing be defective in other ways.

Obj. 2. Further, Any fault in the thing, affecting the quantity, would seem chiefly to be opposed to justice which consists in equality. Now quantity is known by being measured: and the measures of things that come into human use are not fixed, but in some places are greater, in others less, as the Philosopher states. Therefore, just as it is impossible to avoid defects on the part of the thing sold, it seems that a sale is not rendered unlawful through the thing sold being defective.

Obj. 3. Further, the thing sold is rendered defective by lacking a fitting quality. But in order to know the quality of a thing, much science is required that is lacking in most buyers. Therefore a sale is not rendered unlawful by a fault (in the thing sold).

On the contrary, Ambrose says: *It is manifestly a rule of justice that a good man should not depart from the truth, nor inflict on anyone an unjust injury, nor have any connection with fraud.*

I answer that, A threefold fault may be found pertaining to the thing which is sold. One, in respect of the thing's substance: and if the seller be aware of a fault in the thing he is selling, he is guilty of a fraudulent sale, so that the sale is rendered unlawful. Hence we find it written against certain people: *Thy silver is turned into dross, thy wine is mingled with water:* because that which is mixed is defective in its substance.

Another defect is in respect of quantity which is known by being measured: wherefore if anyone knowingly make use of a faulty measure in selling, he is guilty of fraud, and the sale is illicit. Hence it is written: *Thou shalt not have divers weights in thy bag, a greater and a less: neither shall there be in thy house a greater bushel and a less,* and further on: *For the Lord . . . abhorreth him that doth these things, and He hateth all injustice.*

A third defect is on the part of the quality, for instance, if a man sell an unhealthy animal as being a healthy one: and if anyone do this knowingly he is guilty of a fraudulent sale, and the sale, in consequence, is illicit.

In all these cases not only is the man guilty of a fraudulent sale, but he is also bound to restitution. But if any of the foregoing defects be in the thing sold, and he knows nothing about this, the seller does not sin, because he does that which is unjust materially, nor is his deed unjust, as shown above. Nevertheless he is bound to compensate the buyer, when the defect comes to his knowledge. Moreover what has been said of the seller applies equally to the buyer. For sometimes it happens that the seller thinks his goods to be specifically of lower value, as when a man sells gold instead of copper, and then if the buyer be aware of this, he buys it unjustly and is bound to restitution: and the same applies to a defect in quantity as to a defect in quality.

Reply Obj. 1. Gold and silver are costly not only on account of the usefulness of the vessels and other like things made from them, but also on account of the excellence and purity of their substance. Hence if the gold and silver produced by alchemists has not the true specific nature of gold and silver, the sale thereof is fraudulent and unjust, especially as real gold and silver can produce certain results by their natural action, which the counterfeit gold and silver of alchemists cannot produce. Thus the true metal has the property of making people joyful, and is helpful medicinally against certain maladies. Moreover real gold can be employed more frequently, and lasts longer in its condition of purity than counterfeit gold. If, however, real gold were to be produced by alchemy, it would not be unlawful to sell it for the genuine article, for nothing prevents art from employing certain natural causes for the production of natural and true effects, as Augustine says of things produced by the art of the demons.

Reply Obj. 2. The measures of saleable commodities must needs be different in different places, on account of the difference of supply: because where there is greater abundance, the measures are wont to be larger. However in each place those who govern the state must determine the just measures of things saleable, with due consideration for the conditions of place and time. Hence it is not lawful to disregard such measures as are established by public authority or custom.

Reply Obj. 3. As Augustine says the price of things saleable does not depend on their degree of nature, since at times a horse fetches a higher price than a slave; but it depends on their usefulness to man. Hence it is not necessary for the seller or buyer to be cognisant of the hidden qualities of the thing sold, but only of such as render the thing adapted to man's use, for instance, that the horse be strong, runs well and so forth. Such qualities the seller and buyer can easily discover.

THIRD ARTICLE.

WHETHER THE SELLER IS BOUND TO STATE THE DEFECTS OF THE THING SOLD?

We proceed thus to the Third Article:

Objection 1. It seems that the seller is not bound to state the defects of the thing sold. For since the seller does not bind the buyer to buy, he would seem to leave it to him to judge of the goods offered for sale. Now judgment about a thing and knowledge of that thing belong to the same person. Therefore it does not seem imputable to the seller if the buyer be deceived in his judgment, and be hurried into buying a thing without carefully inquiring into its condition.

Obj. 2. Further, it seems foolish for anyone to do what prevents him carrying out his work. But if a man states the defects of the goods he has for sale, he prevents their sale: wherefore Tully pictures a man as saying: *Could anything be more absurd than for a public crier, instructed by the owner, to cry: "I offer this unhealthy house for sale"?* Therefore the seller is not bound to state the defects of the thing sold.

Obj. 3. Further, Man needs more to know the road of virtue than to know the faults of things offered for sale. Now one is not bound to offer advice to all or to tell them the truth about matters pertaining to virtue, though one should not tell anyone what is false. Much less therefore is a seller bound to tell the faults of what he offers for sale, as though he were counselling the buyer.

Obj. 4. Further, If one were bound to tell the faults of what one offers for sale, this would only be in order to lower the price. Now sometimes the price would be lowered for some other reason, without any defect in the thing sold: for instance, if the seller carry wheat to a place where wheat fetches a high price, knowing that many will come after him carrying wheat; because if the buyers knew this they would give a lower price. But apparently the seller need not give the buyer this information. Therefore, in like manner, neither need he tell him the faults of the goods he is selling.

On the contrary, Ambrose says: *In all contracts the defects of the saleable commodity must be stated; and unless the seller make them known, although the buyer may have acquired a right to them, the contract is voided on account of the fraudulent action.*

I answer that, It is always unlawful to give anyone an occasion of danger or loss, although a man need not always give another the help or counsel which would be for his advantage in any way; but only in certain fixed cases, for instance when someone is subject to him, or when he is the only one who can assist him. Now the seller who offers goods for sale, gives the buyer an occasion of loss or danger, by the very fact that he offers him defective goods, if such defect may occasion loss or danger to the buyer:—loss, if, by reason of this defect, the goods are of less value, and he takes nothing off the price on that account:—danger, if this defect either hinder the use of the goods or render it hurtful, for instance, if a man sells a lame for a fleet horse, a tottering house for a safe one, rotten or poisonous food for wholesome. Wherefore if suchlike defects be hidden, and the seller does not make them known, the sale will be illicit and fraudulent, and the seller will be bound to compensation for the loss incurred.

On the other hand, if the defect be manifest, for instance if a horse have but one eye, or if the goods, though useless to the buyer, be useful to someone else, provided the seller take as much as he ought from the price, he is not bound to state the defect of the goods, since perhaps, on account of that defect the buyer might want him to allow a greater rebate than he need. Wherefore the seller may look to his own indemnity, by withholding the defect of the goods.

Reply Obj. 1. Judgment cannot be pronounced save on what is manifest: for a man judges according to his knowledge. Hence if the defects of the goods offered for sale be hidden, judgment of them is not sufficiently left with the buyer unless such defects be made known to him. The case would be different if the defects were manifest.

Reply Obj. 2. There is no need to publish beforehand by the public crier the defects of the goods one is offering for sale, because if he were to begin by announcing its defects, the bidders would be frightened to buy, through ignorance of other qualities that might render the thing good and serviceable. Such defect ought to be stated to each individual that offers to buy: and then he will be able to compare the various points one with the other, the good with the bad: for nothing prevents that which is defective in one respect being useful in many others.

Reply Obj. 3. Although a man is not bound, strictly speaking, to tell everyone the truth about matters pertaining to virtue, yet he is so bound in a case when, unless he tells the truth, his conduct would endanger another man in detriment to virtue: and so it is in this case.

Reply Obj. 4. The defect in a thing makes it of less value now than it seems to be: but in the case cited, the goods are expected to be of less value at a future time, on account of the arrival of other merchants, which was not foreseen by the buyers. Wherefore the seller, since he sells his goods at the price actually offered him, does not seem to act contrary to justice through not stating what is going to happen. If, however, he were to do so, or if he lowered his price, it would be exceedingly virtuous on his part: although he does not seem to be bound to do this as a debt of justice.

FOURTH ARTICLE.

WHETHER, IN TRADING, IT IS LAWFUL TO SELL A THING AT A HIGHER PRICE THAN WHAT WAS PAID FOR IT?

We proceed thus to the Fourth Article:—

Objection 1. It seems that it is not lawful, in trading, to sell a thing for a higher price than we paid for it. For Chrysostom says on

Matth. XXI. 12: *He that buys a thing in order that he may sell it, entire and unchanged, at a profit, is the trader who is cast out of God's temple.* Cassiodorus speaks in the same sense in his commentary on Ps. LXX. 15, *Because I have not known learning,* or *trading* according to another version: *What is trade,* says he, *but buying at a cheap price with the purpose of retailing at a higher price?* and he adds: *Such were the tradesmen whom Our Lord cast out of the temple.* Now no man is cast out of the temple except for a sin. Therefore suchlike trading is sinful.

Obj. 2. Further, It is contrary to justice to sell goods at a higher price than their worth, or to buy them for less than their value, as shown above. Now if you sell a thing for a higher price than you paid for it, you must either have bought it for less than its value, or sell it for more than its value. Therefore this cannot be done without sin.

Obj. 3. Further, Jerome says: *Shun, as you would the plague, a cleric who from being poor has become wealthy, or who, from being a nobody has become a celebrity.* Now trading would not seem to be forbidden to clerics except on account of its sinfulness. Therefore it is a sin in trading, to buy at a low price and to sell at a higher price.

On the contrary, Augustine commenting on Ps. LXX. 15, *Because I have not known learning,* says: *The greedy tradesman blasphemes over his losses; he lies and perjures himself over the price of his wares. But these are vices of the man, not of the craft, which can be exercised without these vices.* Therefore trading is not in itself unlawful.

I answer that, A tradesman is one whose business consists in the exchange of things. According to the Philosopher, exchange of things is twofold; one, natural as it were, and necessary, whereby one commodity is exchanged for another, or money taken in exchange for a commodity, in order to satisfy the needs of life. Suchlike trading, properly speaking, does not belong to tradesmen, but rather to housekeepers or civil servants who have to provide the household or the state with the necessaries of life. The other kind of exchange is either that of money for money, or of any commodity for money, not on account of the necessities of life, but for profit, and this kind of exchange, properly speaking, regards tradesmen, according to the Philosopher. The former kind of exchange is commendable because it supplies a natural need: but the latter is justly deserving of blame, because, considered in itself, it satisfies the greed for gain, which knows no limit and tends to infinity. Hence trading, considered in itself, has a certain debasement attaching thereto, in so far as, by its very nature, it does not imply a virtuous or necessary end. Nevertheless gain which is the end of trading, though not implying, by its nature, anything virtuous or necessary, does not, in itself, connote anything sinful or contrary to virtue: wherefore nothing prevents gain from being directed to some necessary or even virtuous end, and thus trading becomes lawful. Thus, for instance, a man may intend the moderate gain which he seeks to acquire by trading for the upkeep of his household, or for the assistance of the needy: or again, a man may take to trade for some public advantage, for instance, lest his country lack the necessaries of life, and seek gain, not as an end, but as payment for his labour.

Reply Obj. 1. The saying of Chrysostom refers to the trading which seeks gain as a last end. This is especially the case where a man sells something at a higher price without its undergoing any change. For if he sells at a higher price something that has changed for the better, he would seem to receive the reward of his labour. Nevertheless the gain itself may be lawfully intended, not as a last end, but for the sake of some other end which is necessary or virtuous, as stated above.

Reply Obj. 2. Not everyone that sells at a higher price than he bought is a tradesman, but only he who buys that he may sell at a profit. If, on the contrary, he buys not for sale but for possession, and afterwards, for some reason wishes to sell, it is not a trade transaction even if he sell at a profit. For he may lawfully do this, either because he has bettered the thing, or because the value of the thing has changed with the change of place or time, or on account of the danger he incurs in transferring the thing from one place to another, or again in having it carried by another. In this sense neither buying nor selling is unjust.

Reply Obj. 3. Clerics should abstain not only from things that are evil in themselves, but even from those that have an appearance of evil. This happens in trading, both because it is directed to worldly gain, which clerics should despise, and because trading is open to so many vices, since *a merchant is hardly free from sins of the lips*. There is also another reason, because trading engages the mind too much with worldly cares, and consequently withdraws it from spiritual cares; wherefore the Apostle says: *No man being a soldier to God entangleth himself with secular businesses*. Nevertheless it is lawful for clerics to engage in the first mentioned kind of exchange, which is directed to supply the necessaries of life, either by buying or by selling.

OF THE SIN OF USURY, WHICH IS COMMITTED IN LOANS.

We must now consider the sin of usury, which is committed in loans: and under this head there are four points of inquiry: (1) Whether it is a sin to take money as a price for money lent, which is to receive usury? (2) Whether it is lawful to lend money for any other kind of consideration, by way of payment for the loan? (3) Whether a man is bound to restore just gains derived from money taken in usury? (4) Whether it is lawful to borrow money under a condition of usury?

First Article.

Whether it is a Sin to Take Usury for Money Lent?

We proceed thus to the First Article:—

Objection 1. It seems that it is not a sin to take usury for money lent. For no man sins through following the example of Christ. But Our Lord said of Himself: *At My coming I might have exacted it*, i.e. the money lent, *with usury*. Therefore it is not a sin to take usury for lending money.

Obj. 2. Further, According to Ps. XVIII. 8, *The law of the Lord is unspotted*, because, to wit, it forbids sin. Now usury of a kind is allowed in the Divine law, according to Deut. XXIII. 19, 20: *Thou shalt not fenerate to thy brother money, nor corn, nor any other thing, but to the stranger*: nay more, it is even prom-

ised as a reward for the observance of the Law, according to Deut. XXVIII. 12: *Thou shalt fenerate to many nations, and shalt not borrow of any one*. Therefore it is not a sin to take usury.

Obj. 3. Further, In human affairs justice is determined by civil laws. Now civil law allows usury to be taken. Therefore it seems to be lawful.

Obj. 4. Further, The counsels are not binding under sin. But, among other counsels we find: *Lend, hoping for nothing thereby*. Therefore it is not a sin to take usury.

Obj. 5. Further, It does not seem to be in itself sinful to accept a price for doing what one is not bound to do. But one who has money is not bound in every case to lend it to his neighbour. Therefore it is lawful for him sometimes to accept a price for lending it.

Obj. 6. Further, Silver made into coins does not differ specifically from silver made into a vessel. But it is lawful to accept a price for the loan of a silver vessel. Therefore it is also lawful to accept a price for the loan of a silver coin. Therefore usury is not in itself a sin.

Obj. 7. Further, Anyone may lawfully accept a thing which its owner freely gives him. Now he who accepts the loan, freely gives the usury. Therefore he who lends may lawfully take the usury.

On the contrary, It is written: *If thou lend money to any of thy people that is poor, that dwelleth with thee, thou shalt not be hard upon them as an extortioner, nor oppress them with usuries*.

I answer that, To take usury for money lent is unjust in itself, because this is to sell what does not exist, and this evidently leads to inequality which is contrary to justice.

In order to make this evident, we must observe that there are certain things the use of which consists in their consumption: thus we consume wine when we use it for drink, and we consume wheat when we use it for food. Wherefore in suchlike things the use of the thing must not be reckoned apart from the thing itself, and whoever is granted the use of the thing, is granted the thing itself; and for this reason, to lend things of this kind is to transfer the ownership. Accordingly if a man wanted to sell wine separately from the use of the wine, he would be selling the same thing twice, or he would be selling what does not exist, wherefore he would evidently commit a sin of injustice. In like manner he commits an injustice who lends wine or wheat, and asks for double payment, viz. one, the return of the thing in equal measure, the other, the price of the use, which is called usury.

On the other hand there are things the use of which does not consist in their consumption: thus to use a house is to dwell in it, not to destroy it. Wherefore in such things both may be granted: for instance, one man may hand over to another the ownership of his house while reserving to himself the use of it for a time, or vice versa, he may grant the use of the house, while retaining the ownership. For this reason a man may lawfully make a charge for the use of his house, and, besides this, revendicate the house from the person to whom he has granted its use, as happens in renting and letting a house.

Now money, according to the Philosopher was invented chiefly for the purpose of exchange: and consequently the proper and principal use of money is its consumption or alienation whereby it is sunk in exchange. Hence it is by its very nature unlawful to take payment for the use of money lent, which payment is known as usury: and just as a man is bound to restore other ill-gotten goods, so is he bound to restore the money which he has taken in usury.

Reply Obj. 1. In this passage usury must be taken figuratively for the increase of spiritual goods which God exacts from us, for He wishes us ever to advance in the goods which we receive from Him: and this is for our own profit not for His.

Reply Obj. 2. The Jews were forbidden to take usury from their brethren, i.e. from other Jews. By this we are given to understand that to take usury from any man is evil simply, because we ought to treat every man as our neighbour and brother, especially in the state of the Gospel, whereto all are called. Hence it is said without any distinction in Ps. XIV. 5: *He that hath not put out his money to usury,* and: *Who hath not taken usury.* They were permitted, however, to take usury from foreigners, not as though it were lawful, but in order to avoid a greater evil, lest, to wit, through avarice to which they were prone according to Is. LVI. II, they should take usury from the Jews who were worshippers of God.

Where we find it promised to them as a reward, *Thou shalt fenerate to many nations,* etc., fenerating is to be taken in a broad sense for lending, as in Eccles. XXIX. 10, where we read: *Many have refused to fenerate, not out of wickedness,* i.e. they would not lend. Accordingly the Jews are promised in reward an abundance of wealth, so that they would be able to lend to others.

Reply Obj. 3. Human laws leave certain things unpunished, on account of the condition of those who are imperfect, and who would be deprived of many advantages, if all sins were strictly forbidden and punishments appointed for them. Wherefore human law has permitted usury, not that it looks upon usury as harmonizing with justice, but lest the advantage of many should be hindered. Hence it is that in civil law it is stated that *those things according to natural reason and civil law which are consumed by being used, do not admit of usufruct, and that the senate did not (nor could it) appoint a usufruct to such things, but established a quasi-usufruct,* namely by permitting usury. Moreover the Philosopher, led by natural reason, says that *to make money by usury is exceedingly unnatural.*

Reply Obj. 4. A man is not always bound to lend, and for this reason it is placed among the counsels. Yet it is a matter of precept not to seek profit by lending: although it may be called a matter of counsel in comparison with the maxims of the Pharisees, who deemed some kinds of usury to be lawful, just as love of one's enemies is a matter of counsel. Or again, He speaks here not of the hope of usurious gain, but of the hope which is put in man. For we ought not to lend or do any good deed through hope in man, but only through hope in God.

Reply Obj. 5. He that is not bound to lend, may accept repayment for what he has done, but he must not exact more. Now he is repaid according to equality of justice if he is repaid as much as he lent. Wherefore if he exacts more for the usufruct of a thing which has no other use but the consumption of its substance, he exacts a price of something non-existent: and so his exaction is unjust.

Reply Obj. 6. The principal use of a silver vessel is not its consumption, and so one may lawfully sell its use while retaining one's ownership of it. On the other hand the principal use of silver money is sinking it in exchange, so that it is not lawful to sell its use and at the same time expect the restitution of the amount lent. It must be observed, however, that the secondary use of silver vessels may be an exchange, and such use may not be lawfully sold. In like manner there may be some secondary use of silver money; for instance, a man might lend coins for show, or to be used as security.

Reply Obj. 7. He who gives usury does not give it voluntarily simply, but under a certain necessity, in so far as he needs to borrow money which the owner is unwilling to lend without usury.

SECOND ARTICLE.

WHETHER IT IS LAWFUL TO ASK FOR ANY OTHER KIND OF CONSIDERATION FOR MONEY LENT?

We proceed thus to the Second Article:—

Objection 1. It seems that one may ask for some other kind of consideration for money lent. For everyone may lawfully seek to indemnify himself. Now sometimes a man suffers loss through lending money. Therefore he may lawfully ask for or even exact something else besides the money lent.

Obj. 2. Further, As stated in *Ethic.* V. one is in duty bound by a point of honour, to repay anyone who has done us a favour. Now to lend money to one who is in straits is to do him a favour for which he should be grateful. Therefore the recipient of a loan, is bound by a natural debt to repay something. Now it does not seem unlawful to bind oneself to an obligation of the natural law. Therefore it is not unlawful, in lending money to anyone, to demand some sort of compensation as a condition of the loan.

Obj. 3. Further, Just as there is real remuneration, so is there verbal remuneration, and remuneration by service, as a gloss says on Isa. XXXIII. 15: *Blessed is he that shaketh his hands from all bribes.* Now it is lawful to accept service or praise from one to whom one has lent money. Therefore in like manner it is lawful to accept any other kind of remuneration.

Obj. 4. Further, Seemingly the relation of gift to gift is the same as of loan to loan. But it is lawful to accept money for money given. Therefore it is lawful to accept repayment by loan in return for a loan granted.

Obj. 5. Further, The lender, by transferring his ownership of a sum of money removes the money further from himself than he who entrusts it to a merchant or craftsman. Now it is lawful to receive interest for money entrusted to a merchant or craftsman. Therefore it is also lawful to receive interest for money lent.

Obj. 6. Further, A man may accept a pledge for money lent, the use of which pledge he might sell for a price: as when a man mortgages his land or the house wherein he dwells. Therefore it is lawful to receive interest for money lent.

Obj. 7. Further, It sometimes happens that a man raises the price of his goods under guise of loan, or buys another's goods at a low figure; or raises his price through delay in being paid, and lowers his price that he may be paid the sooner. Now in all these cases there seems to be payment for a loan of money: nor does it appear to be manifestly illicit. Therefore it seems to be lawful to expect or exact some consideration for money lent.

On the contrary, Among other conditions requisite in a just man it is stated that he *hath not taken usury and increase.*

I answer that, According to the Philosopher, *a thing is reckoned as money if its price can be measured by money.* Consequently, just as it is a sin against justice, to take money, by tacit or express agreement, in return for lending money or anything else that is consumed by being used, so also is it a like sin, by tacit or express agreement to receive anything whose price can be measured by money. Yet there would be no sin in receiving something of the kind, not as exacting it, nor yet as though it were due on account of some agreement tacit or expressed, but as a gratuity: since, even before lending the money, one could accept a gratuity, nor is one in a worse condition through lending.

On the other hand it is lawful to exact compensation for a loan, in respect of such things as are not appreciated by a measure of money, for instance, benevolence, and love for the lender, and so forth.

Reply Obj. 1. A lender may without sin enter an agreement with the borrower for compensation for the loss he incurs of something he ought to have, for this is not to sell the use of money but to avoid a loss. It may also happen that the borrower avoids a greater loss than the lender incurs, wherefore the borrower may repay the lender with what he has gained. But the lender cannot enter an agreement for compensation, through the fact that he makes no profit out of his money: because he must not sell that which he has not yet and may be prevented in many ways from having.

Reply Obj. 2. Repayment for a favour may be done in two ways. In one way, as a debt of justice; and to such a debt a man may be bound by a fixed contract: and its amount is measured according to the favour received. Wherefore the borrower of money or any such thing the use of which is its consumption is not bound to repay more than he received in loan: and consequently it is against justice if he be obliged to pay back more. In another way a man's obligation to repayment for favour received is based on a debt of friendship, and the nature of this debt depends more on the feeling with which the favour was conferred than on the greatness of the favour itself. This debt does not carry with it a civil obligation, involving a kind of necessity that would exclude the spontaneous nature of such a repayment.

Reply Obj. 3. If a man were, in return for money lent, as though there had been an agreement tacit or expressed, to expect or exact repayment in the shape of some remuneration of service or words, it would be the same as if he expected or exacted some real remuneration, because both can be priced at a money value, as may be seen in the case of those who offer for hire the labour which they exercise by work or by tongue. If on the other hand the remuneration by service or words be given not as an obligation, but as a favour, which is not to be appreciated at a money value, it is lawful to take, exact, and expect it.

Reply Obj. 4. Money cannot be sold for a greater sum than the amount lent, which has to be paid back: nor should the loan be made with a demand or expectation of aught else but of a feeling of benevolence which cannot be priced at a pecuniary value, and which can be the basis of a spontaneous loan. Now the obligation to lend in return at some future time is repugnant to such a feeling, because again an obligation of this kind has its pecuniary value. Consequently it is lawful for the lender to borrow something else at the same time, but it is unlawful for him to bind the borrower to grant him a loan at some future time.

Reply Obj. 5. He who lends money transfers the ownership of the money to the borrower. Hence the borrower holds the money at his own risk and is bound to pay it all back: wherefore the lender must not exact more. On the other hand he that entrusts his money to a merchant or craftsman so as to form a kind of society, does not transfer the ownership of his money to them, for it remains his, so that at his risk the merchant speculates with it, or the craftsman uses it for his craft, and consequently he may lawfully demand as something belonging to him, part of the profits derived from his money.

Reply Obj. 6. If a man in return for money lent to him pledges something that can be valued at a price, the lender must allow for the use of that thing towards the repayment of the loan. Else if he wishes the gratuitous use of that thing in addition to repayment, it is the same as if he took money for lending, and that is usury; unless perhaps it were such a thing as friends are wont to lend to one another gratis, as in the case of the loan of a book.

Reply Obj. 7. If a man wish to sell his goods at a higher price than that which is just, so that he may wait for the buyer to pay, it is manifestly a case of usury: because this waiting for the payment of the price has the character of a loan, so that whatever he demands beyond the just price in consideration of this delay, is like a price for a loan, which pertains to usury. In like manner if a buyer wishes to buy goods at a lower price than what is just, for the reason that he pays for the goods before they can be delivered, it is a sin of usury;

because again this anticipated payment of money has the character of a loan, the price of which is the rebate on the just price of the goods sold. On the other hand if a man wishes to allow a rebate on the just price in order that he may have his money sooner, he is not guilty of the sin of usury.

THIRD ARTICLE.

WHETHER A MAN IS BOUND TO RESTORE WHATEVER PROFITS HE HAS MADE OUT OF MONEY GOTTEN BY USURY?

We proceed thus to the Third Article:—

Objection 1. It seems that a man is bound to restore whatever profits he has made out of money gotten by usury. For the Apostle says: *If the root be holy, so are the branches.* Therefore likewise if the root be rotten so are the branches. But the root was infected with usury. Therefore whatever profit is made therefrom is infected with usury. Therefore he is bound to restore it.

Obj. 2. Further, It is laid down: *Property accruing from usury must be sold, and the price repaid to the persons from whom the usury was extorted.* Therefore, likewise, whatever else is acquired from usurious money must be restored.

Obj. 3. Further, That which a man buys with the proceeds of usury is due to him by reason of the money he paid for it. Therefore he has no more right to the thing purchased than to the money he paid. But he was bound to restore the money gained through usury. Therefore he is also bound to restore what he acquired with it.

On the contrary, A man may lawfully hold what he has lawfully acquired. Now that which is acquired by the proceeds of usury is sometimes lawfully acquired. Therefore it may be lawfully retained.

I answer that, As stated above, there are certain things whose use is their consumption, and which do not admit of usufruct, according to law. Wherefore if suchlike things be extorted by means of usury, for instance money, wheat, wine and so forth, the lender is not bound to restore more than he received (since what is acquired by such things is the fruit not of the thing but of human industry), unless indeed the other party by losing some of his own goods be injured through the lender retaining them: for then he is bound to make good the loss.

On the other hand there are certain things whose use is not their consumption: such things admit of usufruct, for instance house or land property and so forth. Wherefore if a man has by usury extorted from another his house or land, he is bound to restore not only the house or land but also the fruits accruing to him therefrom, since they are the fruits of things owned by another man and consequently are due to him.

Reply Obj. 1. The root has not only the character of matter, as money made by usury has; but has also somewhat the character of an active cause, in so far as it administers nourishment. Hence the comparison fails.

Reply Obj. 2. Further, Property acquired from usury does not belong to the person who paid usury, but to the person who bought it. Yet he that paid usury has a certain claim on that property just as he has on the other goods of the usurer. Hence it is not prescribed that such property should be assigned to the persons who paid usury, since the property is perhaps worth more than what they paid in usury, but it is commanded that the property be sold, and the price be restored, of course according to the amount taken in usury.

Reply Obj. 3. The proceeds of money taken in usury are due to the person who acquired them not by reason of the usurious money as instrumental cause, but on account of his own industry as principal cause. Wherefore he has more right to the goods acquired with usurious money than to the usurious money itself.

FOURTH ARTICLE.

WHETHER IT IS LAWFUL TO BORROW MONEY UNDER A CONDITION OF USURY?

We proceed thus to the Fourth Article:—

Objection 1. It seems that it is not lawful to borrow money under a condition of usury. For the Apostle says that they *are worthy of death . . . not only they that do these sins, but they also that consent to them that do them.* Now he that borrows money under a condition of usury consents in the sin of the usurer, and gives him an occasion of sin. Therefore he sins also.

Obj. 2. Further, For no temporal advantage ought one to give another an occasion of committing a sin: for this pertains to active scandal, which is always sinful, as stated above. Now he that seeks to borrow from a usurer gives him an occasion of sin. Therefore he is not to be excused on account of any temporal advantage.

Obj. 3. Further, It seems no less necessary sometimes to deposit one's money with a usurer than to borrow from him. Now it seems altogether unlawful to deposit one's money with a usurer, even as it would be unlawful to deposit one's sword with a madman, a maiden with a libertine, or food with a glutton. Neither therefore is it lawful to borrow from a usurer.

On the contrary, He that suffers injury does not sin, according to the Philosopher, wherefore justice is not a mean between two vices, as stated in the same book. Now a usurer sins by doing an injury to the person who borrows from him under a condition of usury. Therefore he that accepts a loan under a condition of usury does not sin.

I answer that, It is by no means lawful to induce a man to sin, yet it is lawful to make use of another's sin for a good end, since even God uses all sin for some good, since He draws some good from every evil, as stated in the *Enchiridion.* Hence when Publicola asked whether it were lawful to make use of an oath taken by a man swearing by false gods (which is a manifest sin, for he gives Divine honour to them) Augustine answered that he who uses, not for a bad but for a good purpose, the oath of a man that swears by false gods, is a party, not to his sin of swearing by demons, but to his good compact whereby he kept his word. If, however, he were to induce him to swear by false gods, he would sin.

Accordingly we must also answer to the question in point that it is by no means lawful to induce a man to lend under a condition of usury: yet it is lawful to borrow for usury from a man who is ready to do so and is a usurer by profession; provided the borrower have a good end in view, such as the relief of his own or another's need. Thus too it is lawful for a man who has fallen among thieves to point out his property to them (which they sin in taking) in order to save his life, after the example of the ten men who said to Ismahel: *Kill us not: for we have stores in the field.*

Reply Obj. 1. He who borrows for usury does not consent to the usurer's sin but makes use of it. Nor is it the usurer's acceptance of usury that pleases him, but his lending, which is good.

Reply Obj. 2. He who borrows for usury gives the usurer an occasion, not for taking usury, but for lending; it is the usurer who finds an occasion of sin in the malice of his heart. Hence there is passive scandal on his part, while there is no active scandal on the part of the person who seeks to borrow. Nor is this passive scandal a reason why the other person should desist from borrowing if he is in need, since this passive scandal arises not from weakness or ignorance, but from malice.

Reply Obj. 3. If one were to entrust one's money to a usurer lacking other means of practising usury; or with the intention of making a greater profit from his money by reason of the usury, one would be giving a sinner matter for sin, so that one would be a participator in his guilt. If, on the other hand, the usurer to whom one entrusts one's money has other means of practising usury, there is no sin in entrusting it to him that it may be in safer keeping, since this is to use a sinner for a good purpose.

Marco Polo

Marco Polo (1254–1324) was a Venetian who, as a young lad, accompanied his father and uncle on an overland trip to the capital of the great Tartar ruler, Kublai Khan. Like so many ventures of the time, their journey had a religious as well as an economic purpose. While making an earlier visit to Cathay, the elder Polos had promised the emperor that they would return to his court with a group of Christian missionaries to convert the Chinese. Only two Dominican friars were induced to accompany the three Polos on the second venture, however, and the difficulties of the long and arduous journey soon caused the clergymen to turn back. Thus, only the commercial aspects of the trip were carried out. For nearly 20 years the Venetians lived in the Far East, and during that time the young Marco became a great favorite of the emperor. He served him as a public official, visiting many parts of the Kublai Khan's vast empire. When he finally returned to Europe, he dictated The Book of Ser Marco Polo, which described European trading adventures in the Far East fully two centuries before the voyages of Columbus and Magellan. Indeed, Columbus, prior to embarking upon his epoch-making voyage, carefully read Marco's account, making critical marginal notes about points which to him seemed relevant to his own venture. In reading the selections from this work note (1) the activities of the Great Khan, (2) the facilities for trade in the places described, (3) the variety of articles offered for sale, (4) the customs of the people in the different regions, (5) the religion of the inhabitants, (6) the references to Zipangu (Japan), (7) the comments concerning the China Sea, (8) the descriptions of Java, Sumatra, and Ceylon, and (9) the comments about the tomb of Adam.

From: THE BOOK OF SER MARCO POLO

THE WAY THE YEAR OF THE GREAT KAAN IS DISTRIBUTED

On arriving at his capital of Cambaluc [Peking], he stays in his palace there three days and no more; during which time he has great court entertainments and rejoicings, and makes merry with his wives. He then quits his palace at Cambaluc, and proceeds to that city which he has built, as I told you before, and which is called Chandu, where he has that grand park and palace of cane, and where he keeps his gerfalcons in mew. There he spends the summer, to escape the heat, for the situation is a very cool one. After stopping there from the beginning of May to the 28th of August, he takes his departure (that is the time when they sprinkle the white mares' milk as I told

As translated by Sir Henry Yule in The Book of Ser Marco Polo the Venetian Concerning the Kingdoms and Marvels of the East, third ed., 2 vols., John Murray, London, 1903, I, 410–415; II, 170–171; 185–193; 253–256; 258–260; 263–265; 272–274; 284–286; 316–320. Courtesy of John Murray and Charles Scribner's Sons.

you), and returns to his capital Cambaluc. There he stops, as I have told you also, the month of September, to keep his Birthday Feast, and also throughout October, November, December, January, and February, in which last month he keeps the grand feast of the New Year, which they call the White Feast, as you have heard already with all particulars. He then sets out on his march towards the Ocean Sea, hunting and hawking, and continues out from the beginning of March to the middle of May: and then comes back for three days only to the capital, during which he makes merry with his wives, and holds a great court and grand entertainments. In truth, 'tis something astonishing, the magnificence displayed by the Emperor in those three days; and then he starts off again as you know. . . .

CONCERNING THE CITY OF CAMBALUC, AND ITS GREAT TRAFFIC AND POPULATION

You must know that the city of Cambaluc hath such a multitude of houses, and such a vast population inside the walls and outside, that it seems quite past all possibility. There is a suburb outside each of the gates, which are twelve in number; and these suburbs are so great that they contain more people than the city itself. . . . In those suburbs lodge the foreign merchants and travellers, of whom there are always great numbers who have come to bring presents to the Emperor, or to sell articles at Court, or because the city affords so good a mart to attract traders. [There are in each of the suburbs, to a distance of a mile from the city, numerous fine hostelries for the lodgment of merchants from different parts of the world, and a special hostelry is assigned to each description of people, as if we should say there is one for the Lombards, another for the Germans, and a third for the Frenchmen.] And thus there are as many good houses outside of the city as inside, without counting those that belong to the great lords and barons, which are very numerous.

You must know that it is forbidden to bury any dead body inside the city. If the body be that of an Idolater it is carried out beyond the city and suburbs to a remote place assigned for the purpose, to be burnt. And if it be of one belonging to a religion the custom of which is to bury, such as the Christian, the Saracen, or what not, it is also carried out beyond the suburbs to a distant place assigned for the purpose. And thus the city is preserved in a better and more healthy state.

Moreover, no public woman resides inside the city, but all such abide outside in the suburbs. And 'tis wonderful what a vast number of these there are for the foreigners; it is a certain fact that there are more than 20,000 of them living by prostitution. And that so many can live in this way will show you how vast is the population. . . .

To this city also are brought articles of greater cost and rarity, and in greater abundance of all kinds, than to any other city in the world. For people of every description, and from every region, bring things (including all the costly wares of India, as well as the fine and precious goods of Cathay itself with its provinces), some for the sovereign, some for the court, some for the city which is so great, some for the crowds of Barons and Knights, some for the great hosts of the Emperor which are quartered round about; and thus between court and city the quantity brought in is endless. . . .

Round about this great city of Cambaluc there are some 200 other cities at various distances, from which traders come to sell their goods and buy others for their lords; and all find means to make their sales and purchases, so that the traffic of the city is passing great. . . .

CONCERNING THE CITY OF SINJU AND THE GREAT RIVER KIAN

You must know that when you leave the city of Yanju, after going 15 miles south-east, you come to a city called Sinju, of no great size, but possessing a very great amount of shipping and trade. The people are Idolaters and subject to the Great Kaan, and use paper-money.

And you must know that this city stands on the greatest river in the world, the name of which is Kian. It is in some places ten miles wide, in others eight, in others six, and it is more than 100 days' journey in length from one end to the other. This it is that brings so much trade to the city we are speaking of; for on the waters of that river merchandise is perpetually coming and going, from and to the various parts of the world, enriching the city, and bringing a great revenue to the Great Kaan.

And I assure you this river flows so far and traverses so many countries and cities that in good sooth there pass and repass on its waters a great number of vessels, and more wealth and merchandise than on all the rivers and all the seas of Christendom put together! It seems indeed more like a Sea than a River. Messer Marco Polo said that he once beheld at that city 15,000 vessels at one time. And you may judge, if this city, of no great size, has such a number, how many must there be altogether, considering that on the banks of this river there are more than sixteen provinces and more than 200 great cities, besides towns and villages, all possessing vessels?

Messer Marco Polo aforesaid tells us that he heard from the officer employed to collect the Great Kaan's duties on this river that there passed up-stream 200,000 vessels in the year, without counting those that passed down! [Indeed as it has a course of such great length, and receives so many other navigable rivers, it is no wonder that the merchandise which is borne on it is of vast amount and value.] And the article in largest quantity of all is salt, which is carried by this river and its branches to all the cities on their banks, and thence to the other cities in the interior.

The vessels which ply on this river are decked. They have but one mast, but they are of great burthen, for I can assure you they carry (reckoning by our weight) from 4000 up to 12,000 cantars each.

. . . You must know that the vessels on this river, in going up-stream have to be tracked, for the current is so strong that they could not make head in any other manner. Now the tow-line, which is some 300 paces in length, is made of nothing but cane. 'Tis in this way: they have those great canes of which I told you before that they are some fifteen paces in length; these they take and split from end to end [into many slender strips], and

then they twist these strips together so as to make a rope of any length they please. And the ropes so made are stronger than if they were made of hemp.

[There are at many places on this river hills and rocky eminences on which the idol-monasteries and other edifices are built; and you find on its shores a constant succession of villages and inhabited places. . . .]

DESCRIPTION OF THE GREAT CITY OF KINSAY, WHICH IS THE CAPITAL OF THE WHOLE COUNTRY OF MANZI

When you have left the city of Changan and have travelled for three days through a splendid country, passing a number of towns and villages, you arrive at the most noble city of Kinsay [Hang-chow], a name which is as much as to say in our tongue, "The City of Heaven," as I told you before.

And since we have got thither I will enter into particulars about its magnificence; and these are well worth the telling, for the city is beyond dispute the finest and the noblest in the world. In this we shall speak according to the written statement which the Queen of this Realm sent to Bayan the conqueror of the country for transmission to the Great Kaan, in order that he might be aware of the surpassing grandeur of the city and might be moved to save it from destruction or injury. I will tell you all the truth as it was set down in that document. For truth it was, as the said Messer Marco Polo at a later date was able to witness with his own eyes. And now we shall rehearse those particulars.

First and foremost, then, the document stated the city of Kinsay to be so great that it hath an hundred miles of compass. And there are in it twelve thousand bridges of stone, for the most part so lofty that a great fleet could pass beneath them. And let no man marvel that there are so many bridges, for you see the whole city stands as it were in the water and surrounded by water, so that a great many bridges are required to give free passage about it. [And though the bridges be so high the approaches are so well contrived that carts and horses do cross them.]

The document aforesaid also went on to state that there were in this city twelve guilds of the different crafts, and that each guild had 12,000 houses in the occupation of its workmen. Each of these houses contains at least 12 men, whilst some contain 20 and some 40, —not that these are all masters, but inclusive of the journeymen who work under the masters. And yet all these craftsmen had full occupation, for many other cities of the kingdom are supplied from this city with what they require.

The document aforesaid also stated that the number and wealth of the merchants, and the amount of goods that passed through their hands, was so enormous that no man could form a just estimate thereof. And I should have told you with regard to those masters of the different crafts who are at the head of such houses as I have mentioned, that neither they nor their wives ever touch a piece of work with their own hands, but live as nicely and delicately as if they were kings and queens. The wives indeed are most dainty and angelical creatures! Moreover it was an ordinance laid down by the King that every man should follow his father's business and no other, no matter if he possessed 100,000 bezants.

Inside the city there is a Lake which has a compass of some 30 miles: and all round it are erected beautiful palaces and mansions, of the richest and most exquisite structure that you can imagine, belonging to the nobles of the city. There are also on its shores many abbeys and churches of the Idolaters. In the middle of the Lake are two Islands, on each of which stands a rich, beautiful and spacious edifice, furnished in such style as to seem fit for the palace of an Emperor. And when any one of the citizens desired to hold a marriage feast, or to give any other entertainment, it used to be done at one of these palaces. And everything would be found there ready to order, such as silver plate, trenchers, and dishes [napkins and table-cloths], and whatever else was needful. The King made this provision for the gratification of his people, and the place was open to every one who desired to give an entertainment. [Sometimes there would be at these palaces an hundred different parties; some holding a banquet, others celebrat-

ing a wedding; and yet all would find good accommodation in the different apartments and pavilions, and that in so well ordered a manner that one party was never in the way of another.]

The houses of the city are provided with lofty towers of stone in which articles of value are stored for fear of fire; for most of the houses themselves are of timber, and fires are very frequent in the city.

The people are Idolaters; and since they were conquered by the Great Kaan they use paper-money. [Both men and women are fair and comely, and for the most part clothe themselves in silk, so vast is the supply of that material, both from the whole district of Kinsay, and from the imports by traders from other provinces.] And you must know they eat every kind of flesh, even that of dogs and other unclean beasts, which nothing would induce a Christian to eat.

Since the Great Kaan occupied the city he has ordained that each of the 12,000 bridges should be provided with a guard of ten men, in case of any disturbance, or of any being so rash as to plot treason or insurrection against him. [Each guard is provided with a hollow instrument of wood and with a metal basin, and with a time-keeper to enable them to know the hour of the day or night. And so when one hour of the night is past the sentry strikes one on the wooden instrument and on the basin, so that the whole quarter of the city is made aware that one hour of the night is gone. At the second hour he gives two strokes, and so on, keeping always wide awake and on the look out. In the morning again, from the sunrise, they begin to count anew, and strike one hour as they did in the night, and so on hour after hour.

Part of the watch patrols the quarter, to see if any light or fire is burning after the lawful hours; if they find any they mark the door, and in the morning the owner is summoned before the magistrates, and unless he can plead a good excuse he is punished. Also if they find any one going about the streets at unlawful hours they arrest him, and in the morning they bring him before the magistrates. Likewise if in the daytime they find any poor cripple unable to work for his livelihood, they take him to one of the hospitals, of which there are many, founded by the ancient kings, and endowed with great revenues. Or if he be capable of work they oblige him to take up some trade. If they see that any house has caught fire they immediately beat upon that wooden instrument to give the alarm, and this brings together the watchmen from the other bridges to help to extinguish it, and to save the goods of the merchants or others, either by removing them to the towers above mentioned, or by putting them in boats and transporting them to the islands in the lake. For no citizen dares leave his house at night, or to come near the fire; only those who own the property, and those watchmen who flock to help, of whom there shall come one or two thousand at the least.]

Moreover, within the city there is an eminence on which stands a tower, and at the top of the tower is hung a slab of wood. Whenever fire or any other alarm breaks out in the city a man who stands there with a mallet in his hand beats upon the slab, making a noise that is heard to a great distance. So when the blows upon this slab are heard, everybody is aware that fire has broken out, or that there is some other cause of alarm.

The Kaan watches this city with especial diligence because it forms the head of all Manzi; and because he has an immense revenue from the duties levied on the transactions of trade therein, the amount of which is such that no one would credit it on mere hearsay.

All the streets of the city are paved with stone or brick, as indeed are all the highways throughout Manzi, so that you ride and travel in every direction without inconvenience. Were it not for this pavement you could not do so, for the country is very low and flat, and after rain 'tis deep in mire and water. [But as the Great Kaan's couriers could not gallop their horses over the pavement, the side of the road is left unpaved for their convenience. The pavement of the main street of the city also is laid out in two parallel ways of ten paces in width on either side, leaving a space in the middle laid with fine gravel, under which are vaulted drains which convey the rain water into the canals; and thus the road is kept ever dry.]

You must know also that the city of Kinsay has some 3000 baths, the water of which is supplied by springs. They are hot baths, and the people take great delight in them, frequenting them several times a month, for they are very cleanly in their persons. They are the finest and largest baths in the world; large enough for 100 persons to bathe together.

And the Ocean Sea comes within 25 miles of the city at a place called Ganfu, where there is a town and an excellent haven, with a vast amount of shipping which is engaged in the traffic to and from India and other foreign parts, exporting and importing many kinds of wares, by which the city benefits. And a great river flows from the city of Kinsay to that sea-haven, by which vessels can come up to the city itself. This river extends also to other places further inland.

Know also that the Great Kaan hath distributed the territory of Manzi into nine parts, which he hath constituted into nine kingdoms. To each of these kingdoms a king is appointed who is subordinate to the Great Kaan, and every year renders the accounts of his kingdom to the fiscal office at the capital. This city of Kinsay is the seat of one of these kings, who rules over 140 great and wealthy cities. For in the whole of this vast country of Manzi there are more than 1200 great and wealthy cities, without counting the towns and villages, which are in great numbers. And you may receive it for certain that in each of those 1200 cities the Great Kaan has a garrison, and that the smallest of such garrisons musters 1000 men; whilst there are some of 10,000, 20,000, and 30,000; so that the total number of troops is something scarcely calculable. The troops forming these garrisons are not all Tartars. Many are from the province of Cathay, and good soldiers too. But you must not suppose they are by any means all of them cavalry; a very large proportion of them are footsoldiers, according to the special requirements of each city. And all of them belong to the army of the Great Kaan.

I repeat that everything appertaining to this city is on so vast a scale, and the Great Kaan's yearly revenues therefrom are so immense, that it is not easy even to put it in writing, and it seems past belief to one who merely hears it told. But I *will* write it down for you.

First, however, I must mention another thing. The people of this country have a custom, that as soon as a child is born they write down the day and hour and the planet and sign under which its birth has taken place; so that every one among them knows the day of his birth. And when any one intends a journey he goes to the astrologers, and gives the particulars of his nativity in order to learn whether he shall have good luck or no. Sometimes they will say *no*, and in that case the journey is put off till such day as the astrologer may recommend. These astrologers are very skilful at their business, and often their words come to pass, so the people have great faith in them.

They burn the bodies of the dead. And when any one dies the friends and relations make a great mourning for the deceased, and clothe themselves in hempen garments, and follow the corpse playing on a variety of instruments and singing hymns to their idols. And when they come to the burning place, they take representations of things cut out of parchment, such as caparisoned horses, male and female slaves, camels, armour suits of cloth of gold (and money), in great quantities, and these things they put on the fire along with the corpse, so that they are all burnt with it. And they tell you that the dead man shall have all these slaves and animals of which the effigies are burnt, alive in flesh and blood, and the money in gold, at his disposal in the next world; and that the instruments which they have caused to be played at his funeral, and the idol hymns that have been chaunted, shall also be produced again to welcome him in the next world; and that the idols themselves will come to do him honour.

Furthermore there exists in this city the palace of the king who fled, him who was Emperor of Manzi, and that is the greatest palace in the world, as I shall tell you more particularly. For you must know its demesne hath a compass of ten miles, all enclosed with lofty battlemented walls; and inside the walls are the finest and most delectable gardens upon earth, and filled, too, with the finest fruits.

There are numerous fountains in it also, and lakes full of fish. In the middle is the palace itself, a great and splendid building. It contains 20 great and handsome halls, one of which is more spacious than the rest, and affords room for a vast multitude to dine. It is all painted in gold, with many histories and representations of beasts and birds, of knights and dames, and many marvellous things. It forms a really magnificent spectacle, for over all the walls and all the ceiling you see nothing but paintings in gold. And besides these halls the palace contains 1000 large and handsome chambers, all painted in gold and divers colours.

Moreover, I must tell you that in this city there are 160 *tomans* of fires, or in other words 160 *tomans* of houses. Now I should tell you that the *toman* is 10,000, so that you can reckon the total as altogether 1,600,000 houses, among which are a great number of rich palaces. There is one church only, belonging to the Nestorian Christians.

There is another thing I must tell you. It is the custom for every burgess of this city, and in fact for every description of person in it, to write over his door his own name, the name of his wife, and those of his children, his slaves, and all the inmates of his house, and also the number of animals that he keeps. And if any one dies in the house then the name of that person is erased, and if any child is born its name is added. So in this way the sovereign is able to know exactly the population of the city. And this is the practice also throughout all Manzi and Cathay.

And I must tell you that every hosteler who keeps an hostel for travellers is bound to register their names and surnames, as well as the day and month of their arrival and departure. And thus the sovereign hath the means of knowing, whenever it pleases him, who come and go throughout his dominions. And certes this is a wise order and a provident. . . .

The position of the city is such that it has on one side a lake of fresh and exquisitely clear water (already spoken of), and on the other a very large river. The waters of the latter fill a number of canals of all sizes which run through the different quarters of the city, carry away all impurities, and then enter the

Lake; whence they issue again and flow to the Ocean, thus producing a most excellent atmosphere. By means of these channels, as well as by the streets, you can go all about the city. Both streets and canals are so wide and spacious that carts on the one and boats on the other can readily pass to and fro, conveying necessary supplies to the inhabitants.

At the opposite side the city is shut in by a channel, perhaps 40 miles in length, very wide, and full of water derived from the river aforesaid, which was made by the ancient kings of the country in order to relieve the river when flooding its banks. This serves also as a defence to the city, and the earth dug from it has been thrown inwards, forming a kind of mound enclosing the city.

In this part are the ten principal markets, though besides these there are a vast number of others in the different parts of the town. The former are all squares of half a mile to the side, and along their front passes the main street, which is 40 paces in width, and runs straight from end to end of the city, crossing many bridges of easy and commodious approach. At every four miles of its length comes one of those great squares of 2 miles (as we have mentioned) in compass. So also parallel to this great street, but at the back of the market places, there runs a very large canal, on the bank of which towards the squares are built great houses of stone, in which the merchants from India and other foreign parts store their wares, to be handy for the markets. In each of the squares is held a market three days in the week, frequented by 40,000 or 50,000 persons, who bring thither for sale every possible necessary of life, so that there is always an ample supply of every kind of meat and game, as of roebuck, red-deer, fallow-deer, hares, rabbits, partridges, pheasants, francolins, quails, fowls, capons, and of ducks and geese an infinite quantity; for so many are bred on the Lake that for a Venice groat of silver you can have a couple of geese and two couple of ducks. Then there are the shambles where the larger animals are slaughtered, such as calves, beeves, kids, and lambs, the flesh of which is eaten by the rich and the great dignitaries.

Those markets make a daily display of every kind of vegetables and fruits; and among the latter there are in particular certain pears of enormous size, weighing as much as ten pounds apiece, and the pulp of which is white and fragrant like a confection; besides peaches in their season both yellow and white, of every delicate flavour.

Neither grapes nor wine are produced there, but very good raisins are brought from abroad, and wine likewise. The natives, however, do not much care about wine, being used to that kind of their own made from rice and spices. From the Ocean Sea also come daily supplies of fish in great quantity, brought 25 miles up the river, and there is also great store of fish from the lake, which is the constant resort of fishermen, who have no other business. Their fish is of sundry kinds, changing with the season; and, owing to the impurities of the city which pass into the lake, it is remarkably fat and savoury. Any one who should see the supply of fish in the market would suppose it impossible that such a quantity could ever be sold; and yet in a few hours the whole shall be cleared away; so great is the number of inhabitants who are accustomed to delicate living. Indeed they eat fish and flesh at the same meal.

All the ten market places are encompassed by lofty houses, and below these are shops where all sorts of crafts are carried on, and all sorts of wares are on sale, including spices and jewels and pearls. Some of these shops are entirely devoted to the sale of wine made from rice and spices, which is constantly made fresh, and is sold very cheap.

Certain of the streets are occupied by the women of the town, who are in such a number that I dare not say what it is. They are found not only in the vicinity of the market places, where usually a quarter is assigned to them, but all over the city. They exhibit themselves splendidly attired and abundantly perfumed, in finely garnished houses, with trains of waiting-women. These women are extremely accomplished in all the arts of allurement, and readily adapt their conversation to all sorts of persons, insomuch that strangers who have once tasted their attractions seem to get bewitched, and are so taken with their blandishments and their fascinating ways that they never can get these out of their heads. Hence it comes to pass that when they return home they say they have been to Kinsay or the City of Heaven, and their only desire is to get back thither as soon as possible.

Other streets are occupied by the Physicians, and by the Astrologers, who are also teachers of reading and writing; and an infinity of other professions have their places round about those squares. In each of the squares there are two great palaces facing one another, in which are established the officers appointed by the King to decide differences arising between merchants, or other inhabitants of the quarter. It is the daily duty of these officers to see that the guards are at their posts on the neighbouring bridges, and to punish them at their discretion if they are absent.

All along the main street that we have spoken of, as running from end to end of the city, both sides are lined with houses and great palaces and the gardens pertaining to them, whilst in the intervals are the houses of tradesmen engaged in their different crafts. The crowds of people that you meet here at all hours, passing this way and that on their different errands, is so vast that no one would believe it possible that victuals enough could be provided for their consumption, unless they should see how, on every market-day, all those squares are thronged and crammed with purchasers, and with the traders who have brought in stores of provisions by land or water; and everything they bring in is disposed of.

To give you an example of the vast consumption in this city let us take the article of *pepper;* and that will enable you in some measure to estimate what must be the quantity of victual, such as meat, wine, groceries, which have to be provided for the general consumption. Now Messer Marco heard it stated by one of the Great Kaan's officers of customs that the quantity of pepper introduced daily for consumption into the city of Kinsay amounted to 43 loads, each load being equal to 223 lbs.

The houses of the citizens are well built and elaborately finished; and the delight they take in decoration, in painting and in architecture, leads them to spend in this way sums of money that would astonish you.

The natives of the city are men of peaceful character, both from education and from the example of their kings, whose disposition was the same. They know nothing of handling arms, and keep none in their houses. You hear of no feuds or noisy quarrels or dissensions of any kind among them. Both in their commercial dealings and in their manufactures they are thoroughly honest and truthful, and there is such a degree of good will and neighbourly attachment among both men and women that you would take the people who live in the same street to be all one family.

And this familiar intimacy is free from all jealousy or suspicion of the conduct of their women. These they treat with the greatest respect, and a man who should presume to make loose proposals to a married woman would be regarded as an infamous rascal. They also treat the foreigners who visit them for the sake of trade with great cordiality, and entertain them in the most winning manner, affording them every help and advice on their business. But on the other hand they hate to see soldiers, and not least those of the Great Kaan's garrisons, regarding them as the cause of their having lost their native kings and lords.

On the Lake of which we have spoken there are numbers of boats and barges of all sizes for parties of pleasure. These will hold 10, 15, 20, or more persons, and are from 15 to 20 paces in length, with flat bottoms and ample breadth of beam, so that they always keep their trim. Any one who desires to go a-pleasuring with the women, or with a party of his own sex, hires one of these barges, which are always to be found completely furnished with tables and chairs and all the other apparatus for a feast. The roof forms a level deck, on which the crew stand, and pole the boat along whithersoever may be desired, for the Lake is not more than 2 paces in depth. The inside of this roof and the rest of the interior is covered with ornamental painting in gay colours, with windows all round that can be shut or opened, so that the party at table can enjoy all the beauty and variety of the prospects on both sides as they pass along. And truly a trip on this Lake is a much more charming recreation than can be enjoyed on land. For on the one side lies the city in its entire length, so that the spectators in the barges, from the distance at which they stand, take in the whole prospect in its full beauty and grandeur, with its numberless palaces, temples, monasteries, and gardens, full of lofty trees, sloping to the shore. And the Lake is never without a number of other such boats, laden with pleasure parties; for it is the great delight of the citizens here, after they have disposed of the day's business, to pass the afternoon in enjoyment with the ladies of their families, or perhaps with others less reputable, either in these barges or in driving about the city in carriages.

Of these latter we must also say something, for they afford one mode of recreation to the citizens in going about the town, as the boats afford another in going about the Lake. In the main street of the city you meet an infinite succession of these carriages passing to and fro. They are long covered vehicles, fitted with curtains and cushions, and affording room for six persons; and they are in constant request for ladies and gentlemen going on parties of pleasure. In these they drive to certain gardens, where they are entertained by the owners in pavilions erected on purpose, and there they divert themselves the livelong day, with their ladies, returning home in the evening in those same carriages. . . .

DESCRIPTION OF THE ISLAND OF CHIPANGU [JAPAN], AND THE GREAT KAAN'S DESPATCH OF A HOST AGAINST IT

Chipangu is an Island towards the east in the high seas, 1500 miles distant from the Continent; and a very great Island it is.

The people are white, civilized, and well-favoured. They are Idolaters, and are dependent on nobody. And I can tell you the quantity of gold they have is endless; for they find it in their own Islands, [and the King does not allow it to be exported. Moreover] few merchants visit the country because it is so far from the main land, and thus it comes to pass that their gold is abundant beyond all measure.

I will tell you a wonderful thing about the Palace of the Lord of that Island. You must know that he hath a great Palace which is entirely roofed with fine gold, just as our churches are roofed with lead, insomuch that

it would scarcely be possible to estimate its value. Moreover, all the pavement of the Palace, and the floors of its chambers, are entirely of gold, in plates like slabs of stone, a good two fingers thick; and the windows also are of gold, so that altogether the richness of this Palace is past all bounds and all belief.

They have also pearls in abundance, which are of a rose colour, but fine, big, and round, and quite as valuable as the white ones. [In this Island some of the dead are buried, and others are burnt. When a body is burnt, they put one of these pearls in the mouth, for such is their custom.] They have also quantities of other precious stones.

Cublay, the Grand Kaan who now reigneth, having heard much of the immense wealth that was in this Island, formed a plan to get possession of it. For this purpose he sent two of his Barons with a great navy, and a great force of horse and foot. These Barons were able and valiant men, one of them called Abacan and the other Vonsainchin, and they weighed with all their company from the ports of Zayton and Kinsay, and put out to sea. They sailed until they reached the Island aforesaid, and there they landed, and occupied the open country and the villages, but did not succeed in getting possession of any city or castle. And so a disaster befel them, as I shall now relate.

You must know that there was much ill-will between those two Barons, so that one would do nothing to help the other. And it came to pass that there arose a north wind which blew with great fury, and caused great damage along the coasts of that Island, for its harbours were few. It blew so hard that the Great Kaan's fleet could not stand against it. And when the chiefs saw that, they came to the conclusion that if the ships remained where they were the whole navy would perish. So they all got on board and made sail to leave the country. But when they had gone about four miles they came to a small Island, on which they were driven ashore in spite of all they could do; and a large part of the fleet was wrecked, and a great multitude of the force perished, so that there escaped only some 30,-000 men, who took refuge on this Island.

These held themselves for dead men, for they were without food, and knew not what to do, and they were in great despair when they saw that such of the ships as had escaped the storm were making full sail for their own country without the slightest sign of turning back to help them. And this was because of the bitter hatred between the two Barons in command of the force; for the Baron who escaped never showed the slightest desire to return to his colleague who was left upon the Island in the way you have heard; though he might easily have done so after the storm ceased; and it endured not long. He did nothing of the kind, however, but made straight for home. And you must know that the Island to which the soldiers had escaped was uninhabited; there was not a creature upon it but themselves.

Now we will tell you what befel those who escaped on the fleet, and also those who were left upon the Island. . . .

WHAT FURTHER CAME OF THE GREAT KAAN'S EXPEDITION AGAINST CHIPANGU

You see those who were left upon the Island, some 30,000 souls, as I have said, did hold themselves for dead men, for they saw no possible means of escape. And when the King of the Great Island got news how the one part of the expedition had saved themselves upon that Isle, and the other part was scattered and fled, he was right glad thereat, and he gathered together all the ships of his territory and proceeded with them, the sea now being calm, to the little Isle, and landed his troops all round it. And when the Tartars saw them thus arrive, and the whole force landed, without any guard having been left on board the ships (the act of men very little acquainted with such work), they had the sagacity to feign flight. [Now the Island was very high in the middle, and whilst the enemy were hastening after them by one road they fetched a compass by another and] in this way managed to reach the enemy's ships and to get aboard of them. This they did easily enough, for they encountered no opposition.

Once they were on board they got under weigh immediately for the great Island, and landed there, carrying with them the standards and banners of the King of the Island; and in this wise they advanced to the capital. The garrison of the city, suspecting nothing wrong, when they saw their own banners advancing supposed that it was their own host returning, and so gave them admittance. The Tartars as soon as they had got in seized all the bulwarks and drove out all who were in the place except the pretty women, and these they kept for themselves. In this way the Great Kaan's people got possession of the city.

When the King of the great Island and his army perceived that both fleet and city were lost, they were greatly cast down; howbeit, they got away to the great Island on board some of the ships which had not been carried off. And the King then gathered all his host to the siege of the city, and invested it so straitly that no one could go in or come out. Those who were within held the place for seven months, and strove by all means to send word to the Great Kaan; but it was all in vain, they never could get the intelligence carried to him. So when they saw they could hold out no longer they gave themselves up, on condition that their lives should be spared, but still that they should never quit the Island. And this befel in the year of our Lord 1279. The Great Kaan ordered the Baron who had fled so disgracefully to lose his head. And afterwards he caused the other also, who had been left on the Island, to be put to death, for he had never behaved as a good soldier ought to do.

But I must tell you a wonderful thing that I had forgotten, which happened on this expedition.

You see, at the beginning of the affair, when the Kaan's people had landed on the great Island and occupied the open country as I told you, they stormed a tower belonging to some of the islanders who refused to surrender, and they cut off the heads of all the garrison except eight; on these eight they found it impossible to inflict any wound! Now this was by virtue of certain stones which they had in their arms inserted between the skin and the flesh, with such skill as not to show at all externally. And the charm and virtue of these stones was such that those who wore them could never perish by steel. So when the Barons learned this they ordered the men to be beaten to death with clubs. And after their death the stones were extracted from the bodies of all, and were greatly prized. . . .

CONCERNING THE FASHION OF THE IDOLS

Now you must know that the Idols of Cathay, and of Manzi, and of this Island, are all of the same class. And in this Island as well as elsewhere, there be some of the Idols that have the head of an ox, some that have the head of a pig, some of a dog, some of a sheep, and some of divers other kinds. And some of them have four heads, whilst some have three, one growing out of either shoulder. There are also some that have four hands, some ten, some a thousand! And they do put more faith in those Idols that have a thousand hands than in any of the others. And when any Christian asks them why they make their Idols in so many different guises, and not all alike, they reply that just so their forefathers were wont to have them made, and just so they will leave them to their children, and these to the after generations. And so they will be handed down for ever. And you must understand that the deeds ascribed to these Idols are such a parcel of devilries as it is best not to tell. So let us have done with the Idols, and speak of other things.

But I must tell you one thing still concerning that Island (and 'tis the same with the other Indian Islands), that if the natives take prisoner an enemy who cannot pay a ransom, he who hath the prisoner summons all his friends and relations, and they put the prisoner to death, and then they cook him and eat him, and they say there is no meat in the world so good!—But now we *will* have done with that Island and speak of something else.

You must know the Sea in which lie the Islands of those parts is called the Sea of Chin, which is as much as to say "The Sea over against Manzi." For, in the language of those Isles, when they say *Chin*, 'tis Manzi they mean. And I tell you with regard to that Eastern Sea of Chin, according to what is said by the experienced pilots and mariners of those parts, there be 7459 Islands in the waters frequented by the said mariners; and that is

how they know the fact, for their whole life is spent in navigating that sea. And there is not one of those Islands but produces valuable and odorous woods like the lignaloe, aye and better too; and they produce also a great variety of spices. For example in those Islands grows pepper as white as snow, as well as the black in great quantities. In fact the riches of those Islands is something wonderful, whether in gold or precious stones, or in all manner of spicery; but they lie so far off from the main land that it is hard to get to them. And when the ships of Zayton and Kinsay do voyage thither they make vast profits by their venture.

It takes them a whole year for the voyage, going in winter and returning in summer. For in that Sea there are but two winds that blow, the one that carries them outward and the other that brings them homeward; and the one of these winds blows all the winter, and the other all the summer. And you must know these regions are so far from India that it takes a long time also for the voyage thence.

Though that Sea is called the Sea of Chin, as I have told you, yet it is part of the Ocean Sea all the same. But just as in these parts people talk of the Sea of England and the Sea of Rochelle, so in those countries they speak of the Sea of Chin and the Sea of India, and so on, though they all are but parts of the Ocean.

Now let us have done with that region which is very inaccessible and out of the way. Moreover, Messer Marco Polo never was there. And let me tell you the Great Kaan has nothing to do with them, nor do they render him any tribute or service. . . .

CONCERNING THE GREAT ISLAND OF JAVA

When you sail from Chamba, 1500 miles in a course between south and south-east, you come to a great Island called Java. And the experienced mariners of those Islands who know the matter well, say that it is the greatest Island in the world, and has a compass of more than 3000 miles. It is subject to a great King and tributary to no one else in the world. The people are Idolaters. The Island is of surpassing wealth, producing black pepper, nutmegs, spikenard, galingale, cubebs, cloves, and all other kinds of spices.

This Island is also frequented by a vast amount of shipping, and by merchants who buy and sell costly goods from which they reap great profit. Indeed the treasure of this Island is so great as to be past telling. And I can assure you the Great Kaan never could get possession of this Island, on account of its great distance, and the great expense of an expedition thither. The merchants of Zayton and Manzi draw annually great returns from this country. . . .

When you leave Chamba and sail for 700 miles on a course between south and southwest, you arrive at two Islands, a greater and a less. The one is called Sondur and the other Condur. As there is nothing about them worth mentioning, let us go on five hundred miles beyond Sondur, and then we find another country which is called Locac. It is a good country and a rich; [it is on the mainland]; and it has a king of its own. The people are Idolaters and have a peculiar language, and pay tribute to nobody, for their country is so situated that no one can enter it to do them ill. Indeed if it were possible to get at it, the Great Kaan would soon bring them under subjection to him.

In this country the brazil which we make use of grows in great plenty; and they also have gold in incredible quantity. They have elephants likewise, and much game. In this kingdom too are gathered all the porcelain shells which are used for small change in all those regions, as I have told you before.

There is nothing else to mention except that this is a very wild region, visited by few people; nor does the king desire that any strangers should frequent the country, and so find out about his treasure and other resources. . . .

CONCERNING THE ISLAND OF JAVA
THE LESS
THE KINGDOM OF FERLEC AND
BASMA

When you leave the Island of Pentam and sail about 100 miles, you reach the Island of Java the Less. For all its name 'tis none so small but that it has a compass of two thousand

miles or more. Now I will tell you all about this Island.

You see there are upon it eight kingdoms and eight crowned kings. The people are all Idolaters, and every kingdom has a language of its own. The Island hath great abundance of treasure, with costly spices, lignaloes and spikenard and many others that never come into our parts.

Now I am going to tell you all about these eight kingdoms, or at least the greater part of them. But let me premise one marvellous thing, and that is the fact that this Island lies so far to the south that the North Star, little or much, is never to be seen!

Now let us resume our subject, and first I will tell you of the kingdom of Ferlec.

This kingdom, you must know, is so much frequented by the Saracen merchants that they have converted the natives to the Law of Mahommet—I mean the townspeople only, for the hill-people live for all the world like beasts, and eat human flesh, as well as all other kinds of flesh, clean or unclean. And they worship this, that, and the other thing; for in fact the first thing that they see on rising in the morning, that they do worship for the rest of the day.

Having told you of the kingdom of Ferlec, I will now tell of another which is called Basma.

When you quit the kingdom of Ferlec you enter upon that of Basma. This also is an independent kingdom, and the people have a language of their own; but they are just like beasts, without laws or religion. They call themselves subjects of the Great Kaan, but they pay him no tribute; indeed they are so far away that his men could not go thither. Still all these Islanders declare themselves to be his subjects, and sometimes they send him curiosities as presents. There are wild elephants in the country, and numerous unicorns, which are very nearly as big. They have hair like that of a buffalo, feet like those of an elephant, and a horn in the middle of the forehead, which is black and very thick. They do no mischief, however, with the horn, but with the tongue alone; for this is covered all over with long and strong prickles [and when savage with any one they crush him under their knees and then rasp him with their tongue]. The head resembles that of a wild boar, and they carry it ever bent towards the ground. They delight much to abide in mire and mud. 'Tis a passing ugly beast to look upon, and is not in the least like that which our stories tell of as being caught in the lap of a virgin; in fact, 'tis altogether different from what we fancied. There are also monkeys here in great numbers and of sundry kinds; and goshawks as black as crows. These are very large birds and capital for fowling.

I may tell you moreover that when people bring home pygmies which they allege to come from India, 'tis all a lie and a cheat. For those little men, as they call them, are manufactured on this Island, and I will tell you how. You see there is on the Island a kind of monkey which is very small, and has a face just like a man's. They take these, and pluck out all the hair except the hair of the beard and on the breast, and then they dry them and stuff them and daub them with saffron and other things until they look like men. But you see it is all a cheat; for nowhere in India nor anywhere else in the world were there ever men seen so small as these pretended pygmies. . . .

THE SAME CONTINUED: THE HISTORY OF SAGAMONI BORCAN [GAUTAMA BUDDHA] AND THE BEGINNING OF IDOLATRY

Furthermore you must know that in the Island of Seilan there is an exceeding high mountain; it rises right up so steep and precipitous that no one could ascend it, were it not that they have taken and fixed to it several great and massive iron chains, so disposed that by help of these men are able to mount to the top. And I tell you they say that on this mountain is the sepulchre of Adam, our first parent; at least that is what the Saracens say. But the Idolaters say that it is the sepulchre of Sagamoni Borcan, before whose time there were no idols. They hold him to have been the best of men, a great saint in fact, according to their fashion, and the first in whose name idols were made.

He was the son, as their story goes, of a great and wealthy king. And he was of such an holy temper that he would never listen to any worldly talk, nor would he consent to be king. And when the father saw that his son would not be king, nor yet take any part in affairs, he took it sorely to heart. And first he tried to tempt him with great promises, offering to crown him king, and to surrender all authority into his hands. The son, however, would none of his offers; so the father was in great trouble, and all the more that he had no other son but him, to whom he might bequeath the kingdom at his own death. So, after taking thought on the matter, the King caused a great palace to be built, and placed his son therein, and caused him to be waited on there by a number of maidens, the most beautiful that could anywhere be found. And he ordered them to divert themselves with the prince, night and day, and to sing and dance before him, so as to draw his heart towards worldly enjoyments. But 'twas all of no avail, for none of those maidens could ever tempt the king's son to any wantonness, and he only abode the firmer in his chastity, leading a most holy life, after their manner thereof. And I assure you he was so staid a youth that he had never gone out of the palace, and thus he had never seen a dead man, nor any one who was not hale and sound; for the father never allowed any man that was aged or infirm to come into his presence. It came to pass however one day that the young gentleman took a ride, and by the roadside he beheld a dead man. The sight dismayed him greatly, as he never had seen such a sight before. Incontinently he demanded of those who were with him what thing that was? and then they told him it was a dead man. "How, then," quoth the king's son, "do all men die?" "Yea, forsooth," said they. Whereupon the young gentleman said never a word, but rode on right pensively. And after he had ridden a good way he fell in with a very aged man who could no longer walk, and had not a tooth in his head, having lost all because of his great age. And when the king's son beheld this old man he asked what that might mean, and wherefore the man could not walk? Those who were with him replied that it was through old age the man could walk no longer, and had lost all his teeth. And so when the king's son had thus learned about the dead man and about the aged man, he turned back to his palace and said to himself that he would abide no longer in this evil world, but would go in search of Him Who dieth not, and Who had created him.

So what did he one night but take his departure from the palace privily, and betake himself to certain lofty and pathless mountains. And there he did abide, leading a life of great hardship and sanctity, and keeping great abstinence, just as if he had been a Christian. Indeed . . . [if] he had but been so, he would have been a great saint of Our Lord Jesus Christ, so good and pure was the life he led. And when he died they found his body and brought it to his father. And when the father saw dead before him that son whom he loved better than himself, he was near going distraught with sorrow. And he caused an image in the similitude of his son to be wrought in gold and precious stones, and caused all his people to adore it. And they all declared him to be a god; and so they still say.

They tell moreover that he hath died fourscore and four times. The first time he died as a man, and came to life again as an ox; and then he died as an ox and came to life again as a horse, and so on until he had died fourscore and four times; and every time he became some kind of animal. But when he died the eighty-fourth time they say he became a god. And they do hold him for the greatest of all their gods. And they tell that the aforesaid image of him was the first idol that the Idolaters ever had; and from that have originated all the other idols. And this befel in the Island of Seilan in India.

The Idolaters come thither on pilgrimage from very long distances and with great devotion, just as Christians go to the shrine of Messer Saint James in Gallicia. And they maintain that the monument on the mountain is that of the king's son, according to the story I have been telling you; and that the teeth, and the hair, and the dish that are there were those of the same king's son, whose name was Sagamoni Borcan, or Sagamoni the Saint. But the Saracens also come thither on pilgrimage in great numbers, and *they* say that it is the sepulchre of Adam our first father, and that

the teeth, and the hair, and the dish were those of Adam.

Whose they were in truth, God knoweth: howbeit, according to the Holy Scripture of our Church, the sepulchre of Adam is not in that part of the world.

Now it befel that the Great Kaan heard how on that mountain there was the sepulchre of our first father Adam, and that some of his hair and of his teeth, and the dish from which he used to eat, were still preserved there. So he thought he would get hold of them somehow or another, and despatched a great embassy for the purpose, in the year of Christ, 1284. The ambassadors, with a great company, travelled on by sea and by land until they arrived at the Island of Seilan, and presented themselves before the king. And they were so urgent with him that they succeeded in getting two of the grinder teeth, which were passing great and thick; and they also got some of the hair, and the dish from which that personage used to eat, which is of a very beautiful green porphyry. And when the Great Kaan's ambassadors had attained the object for which they had come they were greatly rejoiced, and returned to their lord. And when they drew near to the great city of Cambaluc, where the Great Kaan was staying, they sent him word that they had brought back that for which he had sent them. On learning this the Great Kaan was passing glad, and ordered all the ecclesiastics and others to go forth to meet these reliques, which he was led to believe were those of Adam.

And why should I make a long story of it? In sooth, the whole population of Cambaluc went forth to meet those reliques, and the ecclesiastics took them over and carried them to the Great Kaan, who received them with great joy and reverence. And they find it written in their Scriptures that the virtue of that dish is such that if food for one man be put therein it shall become enough for five men: and the Great Kaan averred that he had proved the thing and found that it was really true.

So now you have heard how the Great Kaan came by those reliques; and a mighty great treasure it did cost him! The reliques being, according to the Idolaters, those of that king's son.

Renaissance and Reformation

By the fifteenth century the civilization of the Middle Ages was undergoing a profound change. One of the important influences bringing this about was the age of exploration which opened up new intellectual and geographical horizons to the people of Europe. Scholars began to study with renewed interest the writings of classical authors, and new humanistic and secular influences affected Europeans. Gradually men strove for greater individual expression, independent of the patterns which had formerly been so well established. Men began to think more intently in terms of pleasant living in the world about them, rather than the means of achieving the hereafter. One of the fields of cultural expression where this was most apparent was in art. Renaissance sculptors, painters, and architects created a new age of beauty that has not been surpassed by any subsequent period. In literature, too, a new interest in secular themes developed, and occasionally this trend went so far as to ridicule organized Christianity. This development, together with the growing individualism and the study of the early Christian dogma by some of the humanists, finally resulted in a revolt against the Catholic Church, itself, the institution which had been so influential in achieving the cultural unity of the Middle Ages. Before the challenge was over, new churches had been established, which protested against both the teachings and the practices of the Catholic Church, and the Age of the Reformation had forever broken the unity of Christendom.

Christopher Columbus

Christopher Columbus (1451–1506) was a native of Genoa who at an early age took up the life of a sailor. In 1492 he made his famous voyage under the sponsorship of Ferdinand and Isabella of Spain. This expedition was the climax of years of ambition on Columbus' part to reach the Orient via the route to the west. This letter was written on the return voyage to Gabriel Sanchez, an officer of the Spanish royal treasury. In reading it note (1) references which indicate Columbus' belief that he had arrived in the east, (2) his description of the islands he visited and other evidences of a scientific interest, (3) the articles he mentioned suited to trade, (4) his observation concerning facilities for commerce in the islands, (5) the customs and beliefs of the natives, (6) the opportunities he saw for missionary activity, and (7) any indication of imperial motives.

From: A LETTER TO GABRIEL SANCHEZ

As I know that it will afford you pleasure that I have brought my undertaking to a successful result, I have determined to write you this letter to inform you of everything that has been done and discovered in this voyage of mine.

On the thirty-third day after leaving Cadiz I came into the Indian Sea, where I discovered many islands inhabited by numerous people. I took possession of all of them for our most fortunate King by making public proclamation and unfurling his standard, no one making any resistance. To the first of them I have given the name of our blessed Saviour, trusting in whose aid I had reached this and all the rest; but the Indians call it Guanahani. To each of the others also I gave a new name, ordering one to be called Sancta Maria de Concepcion, another Fernandina, another Hysabella, another Johana; and so with all the rest. As soon as we reached the island which I have just said was called Johana, I sailed along its coast some considerable distance toward the west, and found it to be so large, without any apparent end, that I believed it was not an island, but a continent, a province of Cathay. But I saw neither towns nor cities lying on the seaboard, only some villages and country farms, with whose inhabitants I could not get speech, because they fled as soon as they beheld us. I continued on, supposing I should come upon some city or country houses. At last, finding that no discoveries rewarded our further progress, and that this course was leading us toward the north, which I was desirous of avoiding, as it was now winter in these regions, and it had always been my intention to proceed southwards, and the winds also were favorable to such desires, I concluded not to attempt any other adventures; so, turning back, I came again to a certain harbor, which I had remarked. From there I sent two of our men into the country to learn whether there was any king or cities in that land. They journeyed for three days, and found innumerable people and habitations, but small and having no fixed government, on which account they returned. Meanwhile I had learned from some Indians whom I had seized at this place, that this country was really an island. Consequently, I continued along toward the east, as much as 322 miles, always hugging the shore, where was the very extremity of the island. From there I saw another island to the eastwards, distant 54 miles from this Johana, which I named Hispana, and proceeded to it, and directed my course for 564 miles east by north as it were, just as I had done at Johana.

The island called Johana, as well as the others in its neighborhood, is exceedingly fertile. It has numerous harbors on all sides, very safe and wide, above comparison with any I have ever seen. Through it flow many very broad and health-giving rivers; and there are in it numerous very lofty mountains. All these islands are very beautiful, and of quite different shapes, easy to be traversed, and full of the greatest variety of trees reaching to the stars. I think these never lose their leaves, as I saw them looking as green and lovely as they are wont to be in the month of May in Spain. Some of them were in leaf, and some in fruit; each flourishing in the condition its nature required. The nightingale was singing and various other little birds, when I was rambling among them in the month of November. There are also in the island called Johana seven or eight kinds of palms, which as readily surpass ours in height and beauty as do all the other trees, herbs, and fruits. There are also wonderful pine-woods, fields, and extensive meadows, birds of various kinds, and honey, and all the different metals except iron.

In the island, which I have said before was called Hispana, there are very lofty and beautiful mountains, great farms, groves and fields, most fertile both for cultivation and for pasturage, and well adapted for constructing buildings. The convenience of the harbors in this island, and the excellence of the rivers, in volume and salubrity, surpass human belief, unless one should see them. In it the trees, pasture-lands, and fruits differ much from those of Johana. Besides, this Hispana abounds in various kinds of spices, gold, and metals. The inhabitants of both sexes of this and of all the other islands I have seen, or of which I have any knowledge, always go as naked as they came into the world, except that some of the women cover parts of their bodies with leaves or branches, or a veil of cotton, which they prepare themselves for this purpose. They are all, as I said before, unprovided with any sort of iron, and they are destitute of arms, which are entirely unknown to them, and for which they are not adapted; not on account of

any bodily deformity, for they are well made, but because they are timid and full of terror. They carry, however, canes dried in the sun in place of weapons, upon whose roots they fix a wooden shaft, dried and sharpened to a point. But they never dare to make use of these, for it has often happened, when I have sent two or three of my men to some of their villages to speak with the inhabitants, that a crowd of Indians has sallied forth; but, when they saw our men approaching, they speedily took to flight, parents abandoning their children, and children their parents. This happened not because any loss or injury had been inflicted upon any of them. On the contrary, I gave whatever I had, cloth and many other things, to whomsoever I approached, or with whom I could get speech, without any return being made to me; but they are by nature fearful and timid. But, when they see that they are safe, and all fear is banished, they are very guileless and honest, and very liberal of all they have. No one refuses the asker anything that he possesses; on the contrary, they themselves invite us to ask for it. They manifest the greatest affection toward all of us, exchanging valuable things for trifles, content with the very least thing or nothing at all. But I forbade giving them a very trifling thing and of no value, such as bits of plates, dishes, or glass, also nails and straps; although it seemed to them, if they could get such, that they had acquired the most beautiful jewels in the world. For it chanced that a sailor received for a single strap as much weight of gold as three gold solidi; and so others for other things of less price, especially for new blancas, and for some gold coins, for which they gave whatever the seller asked; for instance, an ounce and a half or two ounces of gold, or thirty or forty pounds of cotton, with which they were already familiar. So, too, for pieces of hoops, jugs, jars, and pots they bartered cotton and gold like beasts. This I forbade, because it was plainly unjust; and I gave them many beautiful and pleasing things, which I had brought with me, for no return whatever, in order to win their affection, and that they might become Christians and inclined to love our King and Queen and Princes and all the people of Spain, and that they might be eager to search for and gather and give to us what they abound in and we greatly need.

They do not practise idolatry; on the contrary, they believe that all strength, all power, in short, all blessings, are from Heaven, and that I have come down from there with these ships and sailors; and in this spirit was I received everywhere, after they had got over their fear. They are neither lazy nor awkward, but, on the contrary, are of an excellent and acute understanding. Those who have sailed these seas give excellent accounts of everything; but they have never seen men wearing clothes, or ships like ours.

As soon as I had come into this sea, I took by force some Indians from the first island, in order that they might learn from us, and at the same time tell us what they knew about affairs in these regions. This succeeded admirably; for in a short time we understood them and they us both by gesture and signs and words, and they were of great service to us. They are coming now with me, and have always believed that I have come from heaven, notwithstanding the long time they have been, and still remain, with us. They were the first who told this wherever we went, one calling to another, with a loud voice, "Come, come, you will see men from heaven." Whereupon both women and men, children and adults, young and old, laying aside the fear they had felt a little before, flocked eagerly to see us, a great crowd thronging about our steps, some bringing food, and others drink, with greatest love and incredible good will.

In each island are many boats made of solid wood; though narrow, yet in length and shape similar to our two-bankers, but swifter in motion, and managed by oars only. Some of them are large, some small, and some of medium size; but most are larger than a two-banker rowed by eighteen oars. With these they sail to all the islands, which are innumerable, engaging in traffic and commerce with each other. I saw some of these biremes, or boats, which carried seventy or eighty rowers. In all these islands there is no difference in the appearance of the inhabitants, and none in their customs and language, so that all understand one another. This is a circumstance most favorable for what I believe our most serene

King especially desires, that is, their conversion to the holy faith of Christ; for which, indeed, so far as I could understand they are very ready and prone.

I have told already how I sailed in a straight course along the island of Johana from west to east 322 miles. From this voyage and the extent of my journeyings I can say that this Johana is larger than England and Scotland together. For beyond the aforesaid 322 miles, in that portion which looks toward the west, there are two more provinces, which I did not visit. One of them the Indians called Anan, and its inhabitants are born with tails. These provinces extend 180 miles, as I learned from the Indians, whom I am bringing with me, and who are well acquainted with all these islands.

The distance around Hispana is greater than all Spain from Colonia to Fontarabia; as is readily proved, because its fourth side, which I myself traversed in a straight course from west to east, stretches 540 miles. This island is to be coveted, and not to be despised when acquired. As I have already taken possession of all the others, as I have said, for our most invincible King, and the rule over them is entirely committed to the said King, so in this one I have taken special possession of a certain large town, in a most convenient spot, well suited for all profit and commerce, to which I have given the name of the Nativity of our Lord; and there I ordered a fort to be built forthwith, which ought to be finished now. In it I left as many men as seemed necessary, with all kinds of arms, and provisions sufficient for more than a year; also a caravel and men to build others, skilled not only in this trade, but in others. I secured for them good will and remarkable friendship of the king of the island; for these people are very affectionate and kind, so much so that the aforesaid king took a pride in my being called his brother. Although they should change their minds, and wish to harm those who have remained in the fort, they cannot, because they are without arms, go naked, and are too timid; so that, in truth, those who hold the aforesaid fort can lay waste the whole of that island, without any danger to themselves, provided they do not violate the rules and instructions I have given them.

In all these islands, as I understand, every man is satisfied with only one wife, except the princes or kings, who are permitted to have 20. The women appear to work more than the men, but I could not well understand whether they have private property or not; for I saw that what every one had was shared with the others, especially meals, provisions, and such things. I found among them no monsters, as very many expected, but men of great deference and kind; nor are they black like the Ethiopians, but they have long, straight hair. They do not dwell where the rays of the sun have most power, although the sun's heat is very great there, as this region is twenty-six degrees distant from the equinoctial line. From the summits of the mountains there comes great cold, but the Indians mitigate it by being inured to the weather, and by the help of very hot food, which they consume frequently and in immoderate quantities.

I saw no monsters, neither did I hear accounts of any such except in an island called Charis, the second as one crosses over from Spain to India, which is inhabited by a certain race regarded by their neighbors as very ferocious. They eat human flesh, and make use of several kinds of boats by which they cross over to all the Indian islands, and plunder and carry off whatever they can. But they differ in no respect from the others except in wearing their hair long after the fashion of women. They make use of bows and arrows made of reeds, having pointed shafts fastened to the thicker portion, as we have before described. For this reason they are considered to be ferocious, and the other Indians consequently are terribly afraid of them; but I consider them of no more account than the others. They have intercourse with certain women who dwell alone upon the island of Mateurin, the first as one crosses from Spain to India. These women follow none of the usual occupations of their sex; but they use bows and arrows like those of their husbands, which I have described, and protect themselves with plates of copper, which is found in the greatest abundance among them.

I was informed that there is another island larger than the aforesaid Hispana, whose inhabitants have no hair; and that there is a greater abundance of gold in it than in any of the others. Some of the inhabitants of these islands and of the others I have seen I am bringing over with me to bear testimony to what I have reported. Finally, to sum up in a few words the chief results and advantages of our departure and speedy return, I make this promise to our most invincible Sovereigns, that, if I am supported by some little assistance from them, I will give them as much gold as they have need of, and in addition spices, cotton, and mastic, which is found only in Chios, and as much aloes-wood, and as many heathen slaves as their Majesties may choose to demand; besides these, rhubarb and other kinds of drugs, which I think the men I left in the fort before alluded to have already discovered, or will do so; as I have myself delayed nowhere longer than the winds compelled me, except while I was providing for the construction of a fort in the city of Nativity, and for making all things safe.

Although these matters are very wonderful and unheard of, they would have been much more so if ships to a reasonable amount had been furnished me. But what has been accomplished is great and wonderful, and not at all proportionate to my deserts, but to the sacred Christian faith, and to the piety and religion of our Sovereigns. For what the mind of man could not compass, the spirit of God has granted to mortals. For God is wont to listen to his servants who love his precepts, even in impossibilities, as has happened to me in the present instance, who have accomplished what human strength has hitherto never attained. For, if any one has written or told anything about these islands, all have done so either obscurely or by guesswork, so that it has almost seemed to be fabulous.

Therefore let King and Queen and Princes, and their most fortunate realms, and all other Christian provinces, let us all return thanks to our Lord and Saviour Jesus Christ, who has bestowed so great a victory and reward upon us; let there be processions and solemn sacrifices prepared; let the churches be decked with festal boughs; let Christ rejoice upon earth as he rejoices in heaven, as he foresees that so many souls of so many people heretofore lost are to be saved; and let us be glad not only for the exaltation of our faith, but also for the increase of temporal prosperity, in which not only Spain, but all Christendom is about to share.

As these things have been accomplished, so have they been briefly narrated. Farewell.

CHRISTOPHER COLOM,
Admiral of the Ocean Fleet.

Lisbon, March 14th [1493].

Niccolò Machiavelli

Niccolò Machiavelli (1469–1527) was a Florentine statesman and one of the outstanding writers on the theory of the state in early modern times. Keenly anxious to see Italy united, he opposed the papal claims to temporal power and advocated the doctrine of secular absolutism, of which his Prince was the personification. He differed with those who asserted that the state's principal objective was a moral one, and insisted that ethics must be divorced from politics. He advocated rather the doctrine that the ruler is justified in following any course which will serve the state. Machiavelli has been widely criticized for his views, and his name has become synonymous with political duplicity. In fairness to the man, however, his writings should be analyzed in terms of the political and social conditions of his age, and not by those of the present day. In reading the selections from The Prince note (1) the sources from which Machiavelli derived his knowledge, (2) the manner in which he addressed the Prince, (3) the method he advocated for ruling a conquered people who have been accustomed to governing themselves, (4) how the power of the state is to be measured, (5) the duties of a ruler concerning the study of warfare, (6) his discussion of the utility of cruelty, (7) the views on the keeping of good faith by the prince, (8) the problem of free will vs. chance, and his advice to the Prince on the issue, and (9) his views on the barbarians and their influence on his writings.

From: THE PRINCE

Niccolò Machiavelli
to
Lorenzo the Magnificent
Son of Piero Di Medici

It is customary for those who wish to gain the favour of a prince to endeavour to do so by offering him gifts of those things which they hold most precious, or in which they know him to take especial delight. In this way princes are often presented with horses, arms, cloth of gold, gems, and such-like ornaments worthy of their grandeur. In my desire, however, to offer to Your Highness some humble testimony of my devotion, I have been unable to find among my possessions anything which I hold so dear or esteem so highly as that knowledge of the deeds of great men which I have acquired

As translated by Luigi Ricci, revised by E. R. P. Vincent in Niccolò Machiavelli, *The Prince*, The World's Classics, Oxford University Press, London, 1935, 20–21; 47–49; 65–67; 73–80; 111–119. Courtesy of the Oxford University Press.

through a long experience of modern events and a constant study of the past.

With the utmost diligence I have long pondered and scrutinised the actions of the great, and now I offer the results to Your Highness within the compass of a small volume: and although I deem this work unworthy of Your Highness's acceptance, yet my confidence in your humanity assures me that you will receive it with favour, knowing that it is not in my power to offer you a greater gift than that of enabling you to understand in a very short time all those things which I have learnt at the cost of privation and danger in the course of many years. I have not sought to adorn my work with long phrases or high-sounding words or any of those superficial attractions and ornaments with which many writers seek to embellish their material, as I desire no honour for my work but such as the novelty and gravity of its subject may justly deserve. Nor will it, I trust, be deemed presumptuous on the part of a man of humble and obscure condition to attempt to discuss and direct the government of princes; for in the same way that landscape painters station themselves in the valleys in order to draw mountains or high ground, and ascend an eminence in order to get a good view of the plains, so it is necessary to be a prince to know thoroughly the nature of the people, and one of the populace to know the nature of princes.

May I trust, therefore, that Your Highness will accept this little gift in the spirit in which it is offered; and if Your Highness will deign to peruse it, you will recognise in it my ardent desire that you may attain to that grandeur which fortune and your own merits presage for you.

And should Your Highness gaze down from the summit of your lofty position towards this humble spot, you will recognise the great and unmerited sufferings inflicted on me by a cruel fate. . . .

THE WAY TO GOVERN CITIES OR DOMINIONS THAT, PREVIOUS TO BEING OCCUPIED, LIVED UNDER THEIR OWN LAWS

When those states which have been acquired are accustomed to live at liberty under their own laws, there are three ways of holding them. The first is to despoil them; the second is to go and live there in person; the third is to allow them to live under their own laws, taking tribute of them, and creating within the country a government composed of a few who will keep it friendly to you. Because this government, being created by the prince, knows that it cannot exist without his friendship and protection, and will do all it can to keep them. What is more, a city used to liberty can be more easily held by means of its citizens than in any other way, if you wish to preserve it.

There is the example of the Spartans and the Romans. The Spartans held Athens and Thebes by creating within them a government of a few; nevertheless they lost them. The Romans, in order to hold Capua, Carthage, and Numantia, ravaged them, but did not lose them. They wanted to hold Greece in almost the same way as the Spartans held it, leaving it free and under its own laws, but they did not succeed; so that they were compelled to lay waste many cities in that province in order to keep it, because in truth there is no sure method of holding them except by despoiling them. And whoever becomes the ruler of a free city and does not destroy it, can expect to be destroyed by it, for it can always find a motive for rebellion in the name of liberty and of its ancient usages, which are forgotten neither by lapse of time nor by benefits received; and whatever one does or provides, so long as the inhabitants are not separated or dispersed, they do not forget that name and those usages, but appeal to them at once in every emergency, as did Pisa after being so many years held in servitude by the Florentines. But when cities or provinces have been accustomed to live under a prince, and the family of that prince is extinguished, being on the one hand used to obey, and on the other not having their old prince, they cannot unite in choosing one from among themselves, and they do not know how to live in freedom, so that they are slower to take arms, and a prince can win them over with greater facility and establish himself securely. But in republics there is greater life, greater hatred, and more desire for vengeance; they do not and cannot cast aside the memory of their ancient liberty, so that the surest way is either to lay them waste or reside in them. . . .

HOW THE STRENGTH OF ALL STATES SHOULD BE MEASURED

In examining the character of these principalities it is necessary to consider another point, namely, whether the prince has such a position as to be able in case of need to maintain himself alone, or whether he has always need of the protection of others. The better to explain this I would say, that I consider those capable of maintaining themselves alone who can, through abundance of men or money, put together a sufficient army, and hold the field against any one who assails them; and I consider to have need of others, those who cannot take the field against their enemies, but are obliged to take refuge within their walls and stand on the defensive. We have already discussed the former case and will speak of it in future as occasion arises. In the second case there is nothing to be said except to encourage such a prince to provision and fortify his own town, and not to trouble about the surrounding country. And whoever has strongly fortified his town and, as regards the government of his subjects, has proceeded as we have already described and will further relate, will be attacked with great reluctance, for men are always averse to enterprises in which they foresee difficulties, and it can never appear easy to attack one who has his town stoutly defended and is not hated by the people.

The cities of Germany are absolutely free, have little surrounding country, and obey the emperor when they choose, and they do not fear him or any other potentate that they have about them. They are fortified in such a manner that every one thinks that to reduce them would be tedious and difficult, for they all have the necessary moats and bastions, sufficient artillery, and always keep food, drink, and fuel for one year in the public storehouses. Beyond which, to keep the lower classes satisfied, and without loss to the commonwealth, they have always enough means to give them work for one year in these employments which form the nerve and life of the town, and in the industries by which the lower classes live. Military exercises are still held in high reputation, and many regulations are in force for maintaining them.

A prince, therefore, who possesses a strong city and does not make himself hated, cannot be assaulted; and if he were to be so, the assailant would be obliged to retire shamefully; for so many things change, that it is almost impossible for any one to maintain a siege for a year with his armies idle. And to those who urge that the people, having their possessions outside and seeing them burnt, will not have patience, and the long siege and self-interest will make them forget their prince, I reply that a powerful and courageous prince will always overcome those difficulties by now raising the hopes of his subjects that the evils will not last long, now impressing them with fear of the enemy's cruelty, now by dextrously assuring himself of those who appear too bold. Besides which, the enemy would naturally burn and ravage the country on first arriving and at the time when men's minds are still hot and eager to defend themselves, and therefore the prince has still less to fear, for after some time, when people have cooled down, the damage is done, the evil has been suffered, and there is no remedy, so that they are the more ready to unite with their prince, as it appears that he is under an obligation to them, their houses having been burnt and their possessions ruined in his defence.

It is the nature of men to be as much bound by the benefits that they confer as by those they receive. From which it follows that, everything considered, a prudent prince will not find it difficult to uphold the courage of his subjects both at the commencement and during a state of siege, if he possesses provisions and means to defend himself. . . .

THE DUTIES OF A PRINCE WITH REGARD TO THE MILITIA

A prince should therefore have no other aim or thought, nor take up any other thing for his study, but war and its organisation and discipline, for that is the only art that is necessary to one who commands, and it is of such virtue that it not only maintains those who are born princes, but often enables men of private fortune to attain to that rank. And one sees, on the other hand, that when princes think more of luxury than of arms, they lose their state. The chief cause of the loss of states is the contempt of this art, and the way to acquire them is to be well versed in the same.

Francesco Sforza, through being well armed, became, from private status, Duke of Milan; his sons, through wishing to avoid the fatigue and hardship of war, from dukes became private persons. For among other evils caused by being disarmed, it renders you contemptible; which is one of those disgraceful things which a prince must guard against, as will be explained later. Because there is no comparison whatever between an armed and a disarmed man; it is not reasonable to suppose that one who is armed will obey willingly one who is unarmed; or that any unarmed man will remain safe among armed servants. For one being disdainful and the other suspicious, it is not possible for them to act well together. And therefore a prince who is ignorant of military matters, besides the other misfortunes already mentioned, cannot be esteemed by his soldiers, nor have confidence in them.

He ought, therefore, never to let his thoughts stray from the exercise of war; and in peace he ought to practise it more than in war, which he can do in two ways: by action and by study. As to action, he must, besides keeping his men well disciplined and exercised, engage continually in hunting, and thus accustom his body to hardships; and meanwhile learn the nature of the land, how steep the mountains are, how the valleys debouch, where the plains lie, and understand the nature of rivers and swamps. To all this he should devote great attention. This knowledge is useful in two ways. In the first place, one learns to know one's country, and can the better see how to defend it. Then by means of the knowledge and experience gained in one locality, one can easily understand any other that it may be necessary to observe; for the hills and valleys, plains and rivers of Tuscany, for instance, have a certain resemblance to those of other provinces, so that from a knowledge of the country in one province one can easily arrive at a knowledge of others. And that prince who is lacking in this skill is wanting in the first essentials of a leader; for it is this which teaches how to find the enemy, take up quarters, lead armies, plan battles and lay siege to towns with advantage.

Philopoemen, prince of the Achaei, among other praises bestowed on him by writers, is lauded because in times of peace he thought of nothing but the methods of warfare, and when he was in the country with his friends, he often stopped and asked them: If the enemy were on that hill and we found ourselves here with our army, which of us would have the advantage? How could we safely approach him maintaining our order? If we wished to retire, what ought we to do? If they retired, how should we follow them? And he put before them as they went along all the contingencies that might happen to an army, heard their opinion, gave his own, fortifying it by argument; so that thanks to these constant reflections there could never happen any incident when actually leading his armies for which he was not prepared.

But as to exercise for the mind, the prince ought to read history and study the actions of eminent men, see how they acted in warfare, examine the causes of their victories and defeats in order to imitate the former and to avoid the latter, and above all, do as some men have done in the past, who have imitated some one, who has been much praised and glorified, and have always kept his deeds and actions before them, as they say Alexander the Great imitated Achilles, Caesar Alexander, and Scipio Cyrus. And whoever reads the life of Cyrus written by Xenophon, will perceive in the life of Scipio how gloriously he imitated the former, and how, in chastity, affability, humanity, and liberality Scipio conformed to those qualities of Cyrus as described by Xenophon.

A wise prince should follow similar methods and never remain idle in peaceful times, but industriously make good use of them, so that when fortune changes she may find him prepared to resist her blows, and to prevail in adversity. . . .

OF CRUELTY AND CLEMENCY, AND WHETHER IT IS BETTER TO BE LOVED OR FEARED

Proceeding to the other qualities before named, I say that every prince must desire to be considered merciful and not cruel. He must, however, take care not to misuse this mercifulness. Cesare Borgia was considered cruel, but his cruelty had brought order to the Romagna, united it, and reduced it to peace and fealty. If this is considered well, it will be seen that he was really much more merciful than the Florentine people, who, to avoid the name of cruelty, allowed Pistoia to be destroyed. A prince, therefore, must not mind incurring the charge of cruelty for the purpose of keeping his subjects united and faithful; for, with a very few examples, he will be more merciful than those who, from excess of tenderness, allow disorders to arise, from whence spring bloodshed and rapine; for these as a rule injure the whole community, while the executions carried out by the prince injure only individuals. And of all princes, it is impossible for a new prince to escape the reputation of cruelty, new states being always full of dangers. Wherefore Virgil through the mouth of Dido says:

Res dura, et regni novitas me talia cogunt
Moliri, et late fines custode tueri.

Nevertheless, he must be cautious in believing and acting, and must not be afraid of his own shadow, and must proceed in a temperate manner with prudence and humanity, so that too much confidence does not render him incautious, and too much diffidence does not render him intolerant.

From this arises the question whether it is better to be loved more than feared, or feared more than loved. The reply is, that one ought to be both feared and loved, but as it is difficult for the two to go together, it is much safer to be feared than loved, if one of the two has to be wanting. For it may be said of men in general that they are ungrateful, voluble, dissemblers, anxious to avoid danger, and covetous of gain; as long as you benefit them, they are entirely yours; they offer you their blood, their goods, their life, and their children, as I have before said, when the necessity is remote; but when it approaches, they revolt. And the prince who has relied solely on their words, without making other preparations, is ruined; for the friendship which is gained by purchase and not through grandeur and nobility of spirit is bought but not secured, and at a pinch is not to be expended in your service. And men have less scruple in offending one who makes himself loved than one who makes himself feared;

for love is held by a chain of obligation which, men being selfish, is broken whenever it serves their purpose; but fear is maintained by a dread of punishment which never fails.

Still, a prince should make himself feared in such a way that if he does not gain love, he at any rate avoids hatred; for fear and the absence of hatred may well go together, and will be always attained by one who abstains from interfering with the property of his citizens and subjects or with their women. And when he is obliged to take the life of any one, let him do so when there is a proper justification and manifest reason for it; but above all he must abstain from taking the property of others, for men forget more easily the death of their father than the loss of their patrimony. Then also pretexts for seizing property are never wanting, and one who begins to live by rapine will always find some reason for taking the goods of others, whereas causes for taking life are rarer and more fleeting.

But when the prince is with his army and has a large number of soldiers under his control, then it is extremely necessary that he should not mind being thought cruel; for without this reputation he could not keep an army united or disposed to any duty. Among the noteworthy actions of Hannibal is numbered this, that although he had an enormous army, composed of men of all nations and fighting in foreign countries, there never arose any dissension either among them or against the prince, either in good fortune or in bad. This could not be due to anything but his inhuman cruelty, which together with his infinite other virtues, made him always venerated and terrible in the sight of his soldiers, and without it his other virtues would not have sufficed to produce that effect. Thoughtless writers admire on the one hand his actions, and on the other blame the principal cause of them.

And that it is true that his other virtues would not have sufficed may be seen from the case of Scipio (famous not only in regard to his own times, but all times of which memory remains), whose armies rebelled against him in Spain, which arose from nothing but his excessive kindness, which allowed more licence to the soldiers than was consonant with military discipline. He was reproached with this in the senate by Fabius Maximus, who called him a corrupter of the Roman militia. Locri having been destroyed by one of Scipio's officers was not revenged by him, nor was the insolence of that officer punished, simply by reason of his easy nature; so much so, that some one wishing to excuse him in the senate, said that there were many men who knew rather how not to err, than how to correct the errors of others. This disposition would in time have tarnished the fame and glory of Scipio had he persevered in it under the empire, but living under the rule of the senate this harmful quality was not only concealed but became a glory to him.

I conclude, therefore, with regard to being feared and loved, that men love at their own free will, but fear at the will of the prince, and that a wise prince must rely on what is in his power and not on what is in the power of others, and he must only contrive to avoid incurring hatred, as has been explained.

IN WHAT WAY PRINCES MUST KEEP FAITH

How laudable it is for a prince to keep good faith and live with integrity, and not with astuteness, every one knows. Still the experience of our times shows those princes to have done great things who have had little regard for good faith, and have been able by astuteness to confuse men's brains, and who have ultimately overcome those who have made loyalty their foundation.

You must know, then, that there are two methods of fighting, the one by law, the other by force: the first method is that of men, the second of beasts; but as the first method is often insufficient, one must have recourse to the second. It is therefore necessary for a prince to know well how to use both the beast and the man. This was covertly taught to rulers by ancient writers, who relate how Achilles and many others of those ancient princes were given to Chiron the centaur to be brought up and educated under his discipline. The parable of this semi-animal, semi-human teacher is meant to indicate that a prince must know how to use both natures, and that the one without the other is not durable.

A prince being thus obliged to know well

how to act as a beast must imitate the fox and the lion, for the lion cannot protect himself from traps, and the fox cannot defend himself from wolves. One must therefore be a fox to recognise traps, and a lion to frighten wolves. Those that wish to be only lions do not understand this. Therefore, a prudent ruler ought not to keep faith when by so doing it would be against his interest, and when the reasons which made him bind himself no longer exist. If men were all good, this precept would not be a good one; but as they are bad, and would not observe their faith with you, so you are not bound to keep faith with them. Nor have legitimate grounds ever failed a prince who wished to show colourable excuse for the non-fulfilment of his promise. Of this one could furnish an infinite number of modern examples, and show how many times peace has been broken, and how many promises rendered worthless, by the faithlessness of princes, and those that have been best able to imitate the fox have succeeded best. But it is necessary to be able to disguise this character well, and to be a great feigner and dissembler; and men are so simple and so ready to obey present necessities, that one who deceives will always find those who allow themselves to be deceived.

I will only mention one modern instance. Alexander VI did nothing else but deceive men, he thought of nothing else, and found the occasion for it; no man was ever more able to give assurances, or affirmed things with stronger oaths, and no man observed them less; however, he always succeeded in his deceptions, as he well knew this aspect of things.

It is not, therefore, necessary for a prince to have all the above-named qualities, but it is very necessary to seem to have them. I would even be bold to say that to possess them and always to observe them is dangerous, but to appear to possess them is useful. Thus it is well to seem merciful, faithful, humane, sincere, religious, and also to be so; but you must have the mind so disposed that when it is needful to be otherwise you may be able to change to the opposite qualities. And it must be understood that a prince, and especially a new prince, cannot observe all those things which are considered good in men, being often obliged, in order to maintain the state, to act against faith, against charity, against humanity, and against religion. And, therefore, he must have a mind disposed to adapt itself according to the wind, and as the variations of fortune dictate, and, as I said before, not deviate from what is good, if possible, but be able to do evil if constrained.

A prince must take great care that nothing goes out of his mouth which is not full of the above-named five qualities, and, to see and hear him, he should seem to be all mercy, faith, integrity, humanity, and religion. And nothing is more necessary than to seem to have this last quality, for men in general judge more by the eyes than by the hands, for every one can see, but very few have to feel. Everybody sees what you appear to be, few feel what you are, and those few will not dare to oppose themselves to the many, who have the majesty of the state to defend them; and in the actions of men, and especially of princes, from which there is no appeal, the end justifies the means. Let a prince therefore aim at conquering and maintaining the state, and the means will always be judged houourable and praised by every one, for the vulgar is always taken by appearances and the issue of the event; and the world consists only of the vulgar, and the few who are not vulgar are isolated when the many have a rallying point in the prince. A certain prince of the present time, whom it is well not to name, never does anything but preach peace and good faith, but he is really a great enemy to both, and either of them, had he observed them, would have lost him state or reputation on many occasions. . . .

HOW MUCH FORTUNE CAN DO IN HUMAN AFFAIRS AND HOW IT MAY BE OPPOSED

It is not unknown to me how many have been and are of opinion that worldly events are so governed by fortune and by God, that men cannot by their prudence change them, and that on the contrary there is no remedy whatever, and for this they may judge it to be useless to toil much about them, but let things be ruled by chance. This opinion has been more held in our day, from the great changes that have been seen, and are daily seen, be-yond every human conjecture. When I think about them, at times I am partly inclined to share this opinion. Nevertheless, that our free-will may not be altogether extinguished, I think it may be true that fortune is the ruler of half our actions, but that she allows the other half or thereabouts to be governed by us. I would compare her to an impetuous river that, when turbulent, inundates the plains, casts down trees and buildings, removes earth from this side and places it on the other; every one flees before it, and everything yields to its fury without being able to oppose it; and yet though it is of such a kind, still when it is quiet, men can make provision against it by dykes and banks, so that when it rises it will either go into a canal or its rush will not be so wild and dangerous. So it is with fortune, which shows her power where no measures have been taken to resist her, and directs her fury where she knows that no dykes or barriers have been made to hold her. And if you regard Italy, which has been the seat of these changes, and who has given the impulse to them, you will see her to be a country without dykes or banks of any kind. If she had been protected by proper measures, like Germany, Spain, and France, this inundation would not have caused the great changes that it has, or would not have happened at all.

This must suffice as regards opposition to fortune in general. But limiting myself more to particular cases, I would point out how one sees a certain prince to-day fortunate and to-morrow ruined, without seeing that he has changed in character or otherwise. I believe this arises in the first place from the causes that we have already discussed at length; that is to say, because the prince who bases himself entirely on fortune is ruined when fortune changes. I also believe that he is happy whose mode of procedure accords with the needs of the times, and similarly he is unfortunate whose mode of procedure is opposed to the times. For one sees that men in those things which lead them to the aim that each one has in view, namely, glory and riches, proceed in various ways; one with circumspection, an-other with impetuosity, one by violence, an-other by cunning, one with patience, another with the reverse; and each by these diverse ways may arrive at his aim. One sees also two cautious men, one of whom succeeds in his designs, and the other not, and in the same way two men succeed equally by different methods, one being cautious, the other impetuous, which arises only from the nature of the times, which does or does not conform to their method of procedure. From this it results, as I have said, that two men, acting differently, attain the same effect, and of two others acting in the same way, one attains his goal and not the other. On this depend also the changes in prosperity, for if it happens that time and circumstances are favourable to one who acts with caution and prudence he will be successful, but if time and circumstances change he will be ruined, because he does not change his mode of procedure. No man is found so prudent as to be able to adapt himself to this, either because he cannot deviate from that to which his nature disposes him, or else because having always prospered by walking in one path, he cannot persuade himself that it is well to leave it; and therefore the cautious man, when it is time to act suddenly, does not know how to do so and is consequently ruined; for if one could change one's nature with time and circumstances, fortune would never change.

Pope Julius II acted impetuously in everything he did and found the times and conditions so in conformity with that mode of procedure, that he always obtained a good result. Consider the first war that he made against Bologna while Messer Giovanni Bentivogli was still living. The Venetians were not pleased with it, neither was the King of Spain, France was conferring with him over the enterprise, notwithstanding which, owing to his fierce and impetuous disposition, he engaged personally in the expedition. This move caused both Spain and the Venetians to halt and hesitate, the latter through fear, the former through the desire to recover the entire kingdom of Naples. On the other hand, he engaged with him the King of France, because seeing him make this move and desiring his friendship in order to put down the Venetians, that king judged that he could not refuse him his troops without manifest injury. Thus Julius by his impetuous move achieved what no other pontiff with the utmost human prudence would

have succeeded in doing, because, if he had waited till all arrangements had been made and everything settled before leaving Rome, as any other pontiff would have done, it would never have succeeded. For the King of France would have found a thousand excuses, and the others would have inspired him with a thousand fears. I will omit his other actions, which were all of this kind and which all succeeded well, and the shortness of his life did not suffer him to experience the contrary, for had times followed in which it was necessary to act with caution, his ruin would have resulted, for he would never have deviated from these methods to which his nature disposed him.

I conclude then that fortune varying and men remaining fixed in their ways, they are successful so long as these ways conform to circumstances, but when they are opposed then they are unsuccessful. I certainly think that it is better to be impetuous than cautious, for fortune is a woman, and it is necessary, if you wish to master her, to conquer her by force; and it can be seen that she lets herself be overcome by the bold rather than by those who proceed coldly. And therefore, like a woman, she is always a friend to the young, because they are less cautious, fiercer, and master her with greater audacity.

EXHORTATION TO LIBERATE ITALY FROM THE BARBARIANS

Having now considered all the things we have spoken of, and thought within myself whether at present the time was not propitious in Italy for a new prince, and if there was not a state of things which offered an opportunity to a prudent and capable man to introduce a new system that would do honour to himself and good to the mass of the people, it seems to me that so many things concur to favour a new ruler that I do not know of any time more fitting for such an enterprise. And if, as I said, it was necessary in order that the power of Moses should be displayed that the people of Israel should be slaves in Egypt, and to give scope for the greatness and courage of Cyrus that the Persians should be oppressed by the Medes, and to illustrate the pre-eminence of Theseus that the Athenians should be dispersed, so at the present time, in order that the might of an Italian genius might be recognised, it was necessary that Italy should be reduced to her present condition, and that she should be more enslaved than the Hebrews, more oppressed than the Persians, and more scattered than the Athenians; without a head, without order, beaten, despoiled, lacerated, and overrun, and that she should have suffered ruin of every kind.

And although before now a gleam of hope has appeared which gave hope that some individual might be appointed by God for her redemption, yet at the highest summit of his career he was thrown aside by fortune, so that now, almost lifeless, she awaits one who may heal her wounds and put a stop to the pillaging of Lombardy, to the rapacity and extortion in the Kingdom of Naples and in Tuscany, and cure her of those sores which have long been festering. Behold how she prays God to send some one to redeem her from this barbarous cruelty and insolence. Behold her ready and willing to follow any standard if only there be some one to raise it. There is nothing now she can hope for but that your illustrious house may place itself at the head of this redemption, being by its power and fortune so exalted, and being favoured by God and the Church, of which it is now the ruler. Nor will this be very difficult, if you call to mind the actions and lives of the men I have named. And although those men were rare and marvellous, they were none the less men, and each of them had less opportunity than the present, for their enterprise was not juster than this, nor easier, nor was God more their friend than He is yours. Here is a just cause; *"iustum enim est bellum quibus necessarium, et pia arma ubi nulla nisi in armis spes est."* Here is the greatest willingness, nor can there be great difficulty where there is great willingness, provided that the measures are adopted of those whom I have set before you as examples. Besides this, unexampled wonders have been seen here performed by God, the sea has been opened, a cloud has shown you the road, the rock has given forth water, manna has rained, and everything has contributed to your greatness, the remainder must be done by you. God will not do everything, in order not to deprive us of free-will and the portion of the glory that falls to our lot.

It is no marvel that none of the before-mentioned Italians have done that which it is to be hoped your illustrious house may do; and if in so many revolutions in Italy and so many warlike operations, it always seems as if military capacity were extinct, this is because the ancient methods were not good, and no one has arisen who knew how to discover new ones. Nothing does so much honour to a newly-risen man than the new laws and measures which he introduces. These things, when they are well based and have greatness in them, render him revered and admired, and there is not lacking scope in Italy for the introduction of every kind of new organisation. Here there is great virtue in the members, if it were not wanting in the heads. Look how in duels and in contests of a few the Italians are superior in strength, dexterity, and intelligence. But when it comes to armies they make a poor show; which proceeds entirely from the weakness of the leaders, for those that know are not obeyed, and every one thinks that he knows, there being hitherto nobody who has raised himself so high both by valour and fortune as to make the others yield. Hence it comes about that for so long a time, in all the wars waged during the last twenty years, whenever there has been an entirely Italian army it has always been a failure, as witness first Taro, then Alexandria, Capua, Genoa, Vailà, Bologna, and Mestri.

If your illustrious house, therefore, wishes to follow those great men who redeemed their countries, it is before all things necessary, as the true foundation of every undertaking, to provide yourself with your own forces, for you cannot have more faithful, or truer and better soldiers. And although each one of them may be good, they will united become even better when they see themselves commanded by their prince, and honoured and favoured by him. It is therefore necessary to prepare such forces in order to be able with Italian prowess to defend the country from foreigners. And although both the Swiss and Spanish infantry are deemed terrible, none the less they each have their defects, so that a third method of array might not only oppose them, but be confident of overcoming them. For the Spaniards cannot sustain the attack of cavalry, and the Swiss have to fear infantry which meets them with resolution equal to their own. From which it has resulted, as will be seen by experience, that the Spaniards cannot sustain the attack of French cavalry, and the Swiss are overthrown by Spanish infantry. And although a complete example of the latter has not been seen, yet an instance was furnished in the battle of Ravenna, where the Spanish infantry attacked the German battalions, which are organised in the same way as the Swiss. The Spaniards, through their bodily agility and aided by their bucklers, had entered between and under their pikes and were in a position to attack them safely without the Germans being able to defend themselves; and if the cavalry had not charged them they would have utterly destroyed them. Knowing therefore the defects of both these kinds of infantry, a third kind can be created which can resist cavalry and need not fear infantry, and this will be done by the choice of arms and a new organisation. And these are the things which, when newly introduced, give reputation and grandeur to a new prince.

This opportunity must not, therefore, be allowed to pass, so that Italy may at length find her liberator. I cannot express the love with which he would be received in all those provinces which have suffered under these foreign invasions, with what thirst for vengeance, with what steadfast faith, with what love, with what grateful tears. What doors would be closed against him? What people would refuse him obedience? What envy could oppose him? What Italian would withhold allegiance? This barbarous domination stinks in the nostrils of every one. May your illustrious house therefore assume this task with that courage and those hopes which are inspired by a just cause, so that under its banner our fatherland may be raised up, and under its auspices be verified that saying of Petrarch:

Valour against fell wrath
Will take up arms; and be the combat quickly sped!
For, sure, the ancient worth,
That in Italians stirs the heart, is not yet dead.

Benvenuto Cellini

Benvenuto Cellini (1500–1571), the Florentine goldsmith, was in many ways typical of the Renaissance. He lived life to the fullest extent, and was above all else a child of will rather than a man of reason. Crimes, pranks, love, and art all blended together in his life to form a rich pattern of emotional existence. Thus his Autobiography serves as an invaluable document of the characteristics of his age. In reading the selections from it note (1) his motives in writing this work, (2) the discussion of his ancestry, (3) the nature of his craftsmanship in Rome, (4) the classes of people who patronized him, (5) his estimate of himself, (6) his relations with the papacy, (7) the commissions he performed for the French king, and (8) the description of the casting of the statue of Perseus.

From: THE AUTOBIOGRAPHY OF BENVENUTO CELLINI

All men of whatsoever quality they be, who have done anything of excellence, or which may properly resemble excellence, ought, if they are persons of truth and honesty, to describe their life with their own hand; but they ought not to attempt so fine an enterprise till

As translated by John Addington Symonds in *Autobiography of Benvenuto Cellini*, 2nd ed., London, 1888, 1–4; 34–51; 114–116; 310–320; 416–427.

they have passed the age of forty. This duty occurs to my own mind, now that I am travelling beyond the term of fifty-eight years, and am in Florence, the city of my birth. Many untoward things can I remember, such as happen to all who live upon our earth; and from those adversities I am now more free than at any previous period of my career—nay, it seems to me that I enjoy greater content of soul and health of body than ever I did in bygone years. I can also bring to mind some pleasant goods and some inestimable evils, which, when I turn my thoughts backward, strike terror in me, and astonishment that I should have reached this age of fifty-eight, wherein, thanks be to God, I am still travelling prosperously forward.

It is true that men who have laboured with some show of excellence, have already given knowledge of themselves to the world; and this alone ought to suffice them; I mean the fact that they have proved their manhood and achieved renown. Yet one must needs live like others; and so in a work like this there will always be found occasion for natural bragging, which is of divers kinds, and the first is that a man should let others know he draws his lineage from persons of worth and most ancient origin.

I am called Benvenuto Cellini, son of Maestro Giovanni, son of Andrea, son of Cristofano Cellini; my mother was Madonna Elisabetta, daughter to Stefano Granacci; both parents citizens of Florence. It is found written in chronicles made by our ancestors of Florence, men of old time and of credibility, even as Giovanni Villani writes, that the city of Florence was evidently built in imitation of the fair city of Rome; and certain remnants of the Colosseum and the Baths can yet be traced. These things are near Santa Croce. The Capitol was where is now the Old Market. The Rotunda is entire, which was made for the temple of Mars, and is now dedicated to our Saint John. That thus it was, can very well be seen, and cannot be denied; but the said buildings are much smaller than those of Rome. He who caused them to be built, they say, was Julius Caesar, in concert with some noble Romans, who, when Fiesole had been stormed and taken, raised a city in this place, and each of them took in hand to erect one of these notable edifices.

Julius Caesar had among his captains a man of highest rank and valour, who was called Fiorino of Cellino, which is a village about two miles distant from Monte Fiascone. Now this Fiorino took up his quarters under the hill of Fiesole, on the ground where Florence now stands, in order to be near the river Arno, and for the convenience of the troops. All those soldiers and others who had to do with the said captain used then to say: "Let us go to Fiorenze"; as well because the said captain was called Fiorino, as also because the place he had chosen for his quarters was by nature very rich in flowers. Upon the foundation of the city, therefore, since this name struck Julius Caesar as being fair and apt, and given by circumstance, and seeing furthermore that flowers themselves bring good augury, he appointed the name of Florence for the town. He wished besides to pay his valiant captain this compliment; and he loved him all the more for having drawn him from a very humble place, and for the reason that so excellent a man was a creature of his own. The name that learned inventors and investigators of such etymologies adduce, as that Florence is flowing at the Arno, cannot hold; seeing that Rome is flowing at the Tiber, Ferrara is flowing at the Po, Lyons is flowing at the Saone, Paris is flowing at the Seine, and yet the names of all these towns are different, and have come to them by other ways.

Thus then we find; and thus we believe that we are descended from a man of worth. Furthermore, we find that there are Cellinis of our stock in Ravenna, that most ancient town of Italy, where too are plenty of gentle folk. In Pisa also there are some, and I have discovered them in many parts of Christendom; and in this state also the breed exists, men devoted to the profession of arms; for not many years ago a young man, called Luca Cellini, a beardless youth, fought with a soldier of experience and a most valorous man, named Francesco da Vicorati, who had frequently fought before in single combat. This Luca, by his own valour, with sword in hand, overcame and slew him, with such bravery and stoutness that he moved the folk to wonder, who were expecting quite the contrary issue; so that I glory in tracing my descent from men of valour.

As for the trifling honours which I have gained for my house, under the well-known conditions of our present ways of living, and by means of my art, albeit the same are matters of no great moment, I will relate these in their proper time and place, taking much more pride in having been born humble and having laid some honourable foundation for my family, than if I had been born of great lineage and had stained or overclouded that by my base qualities. So then I will make a beginning by saying how it pleased God I should be born. . . .

At Siena I waited for the mail to Rome which I afterwards joined; and when we passed the Paglia, we met a courier carrying news of the new Pope, Clement VII. Upon my arrival in Rome, I went to work in the shop of the master-goldsmith Santi. He was dead; but a son of his carried on the business. He did not work himself, but entrusted all his commissions to a young man named Lucagnolo from Iesi, a country fellow, who while yet a child had come into Santi's service. This man was short but well proportioned, and was a more skilful craftsman than any one whom I had met with up to that time; remarkable for facility and excellent in design. He executed large plate only; that is to say, vases of the utmost beauty, basins, and such pieces. Having put myself to work there, I began to make some candelabra for the Bishop of Salamanca, a Spaniard. They were richly chased so far as that sort of work admits. A pupil of Raffaello da Urbino called Gian Francesco, and commonly known as Il Fattore, was a painter of great ability; and being on terms of friendship with the Bishop, he introduced me to his favour, so that I obtained many commissions from that prelate, and earned considerable sums of money.

During that time I went to draw, sometimes in Michel Agnolo's chapel, and sometimes in the house of Agostino Chigi of Siena, which contained many incomparable paintings by the hand of that great master Raffaello. This I did on feast-days, because the house was then inhabited by Messer Gismondo, Agostino's

brother. They plumed themselves exceedingly when they saw young men of my sort coming to study in their palaces. Gismondo's wife, noticing my frequent presence in that house— she was a lady as courteous as could be, and of surpassing beauty—came up to me one day, looked at my drawings, and asked me if I was a sculptor or a painter; to whom I said I was a goldsmith. She remarked that I drew too well for a goldsmith; and having made one of her waiting-maids bring a lily of the finest diamonds set in gold, she showed it to me, and bade me value it. I valued it at 800 crowns. Then she said I had very nearly hit the mark, and asked me whether I felt capable of setting the stones really well. I said that I should much like to do so, and began before her eyes to make a little sketch for it, working all the better because of the pleasure I took in conversing with so lovely and agreeable a gentlewoman. When the sketch was finished, another Roman lady of great beauty joined us; she had been above, and now descending to the ground-floor, asked Madonna Porzia what she was doing there. She answered with a smile: "I was amusing myself by watching this worthy young man at his drawing; he is as good as he is handsome." I had by this time acquired a trifle of assurance, mixed, however, with some honest bashfulness; so I blushed and said: "Such as I am, lady, I shall ever be most ready to serve you." The gentlewoman, also slightly blushing, said: "You know well that I want you to serve me"; and reaching me the lily, told me to take it away; and gave me besides twenty golden crowns which she had in her bag, and added: "Set me the jewel after the fashion you have sketched, and keep for me the old gold in which it is now set." On this the Roman lady observed: "If I were in that young man's body, I should go off without asking leave." Madonna Porzia replied that virtues rarely are at home with vices, and that if I did such a thing, I should strongly belie my good looks of an honest man. Then turning round, she took the Roman lady's hand, and with a pleasant smile said: "Farewell, Benvenuto." I stayed on a short while at the drawing I was making, which was a copy of a Jove by Raffaello. When I had finished it and left the house, I set myself to making a little model of wax, in order to show how the jewel would look when it was completed. This I took to Madonna Porzia, whom I found with the same Roman lady. Both of them were highly satisfied with my work, and treated me so kindly that, being somewhat emboldened, I promised the jewel should be twice as good as the model. Accordingly I set hand to it, and in twelve days I finished it in the form of a fleur-de-lys, as I have said above, ornamenting it with little masks, children, and animals, exquisitely enamelled, whereby the diamonds which formed the lily were more than doubled in effect.

While I was working at this piece, Lucagnolo, of whose ability I have before spoken, showed considerable discontent, telling me over and over again that I might acquire far more profit and honour by helping him to execute large plate, as I had done at first. I made him answer that, whenever I chose, I should always be capable of working at great silver pieces; but that things like that on which I was now engaged were not commissioned every day; and beside their bringing no less honour than large silver plate, there was also more profit to be made by them. He laughed me in the face, and said: "Wait and see, Benvenuto; for by the time that you have finished that work of yours, I will make haste to have finished this vase, which I took in hand when you did the jewel; and then experience shall teach you what profit I shall get from my vase, and what you will get from your ornament." I answered that I was very glad indeed to enter into such a competition with so good a craftsman as he was, because the end would show which of us was mistaken. Accordingly both the one and the other of us, with a scornful smile upon our lips, bent our heads in grim earnest to the work, which both were now desirous of accomplishing; so that after about ten days, each had finished his undertaking with great delicacy and artistic skill.

Lucagnolo's was a huge silver piece, used at the table of Pope Clement, into which he flung away bits of bone and the rind of divers fruits, while eating; an object of ostentation rather than necessity. The vase was adorned with two fine handles, together with many masks, both small and great, and masses of

lovely foliage, in as exquisite a style of elegance as could be imagined; on seeing which I said it was the most beautiful vase that ever I set eyes on. Thinking he had convinced me, Lucagnolo replied: "Your work seems to me no less beautiful, but we shall soon perceive the difference between the two." So he took his vase and carried it to the Pope, who was very well pleased with it, and ordered at once that he should be paid at the ordinary rate of such large plate. Meanwhile I carried mine to Madonna Porzia, who looked at it with astonishment, and told me I had far surpassed my promise. Then she bade me ask for my reward whatever I liked; for it seemed to her my desert was so great that if I craved a castle she could hardly recompense me; but since that was not in her hands to bestow, she added laughing that I must beg what lay within her power. I answered that the greatest reward I could desire for my labour was to have satisfied her ladyship. Then smiling in my turn, and bowing to her, I took my leave, saying I wanted no reward but that. She turned to the Roman lady and said: "You see that the qualities we discerned in him are companied by virtues, and not vices." They both expressed their admiration, and then Madonna Porzia continued: "Friend Benvenuto, have you never heard it said that when the poor give to the rich, the devil laughs?" I replied: "Quite true! and yet, in the midst of all his troubles, I should like this time to see him laugh"; and as I took my leave, she said that this time she had no will to bestow on him that favour.

When I came back to the shop, Lucagnolo had the money for his vase in a paper packet; and on my arrival he cried out: "Come and compare the price of your jewel with the price of my plate." I said that he must leave things as they were till the next day, because I hoped that even as my work in its kind was not less excellent than his, so I should be able to show him quite an equal price for it.

On the day following, Madonna Porzia sent a major-domo of hers to my shop, who called me out, and putting into my hands a paper packet full of money from his lady, told me that she did not choose the devil should have his whole laugh out: by which she hinted that the money sent me was not the entire payment merited by my industry, and other messages were added worthy of so courteous a lady. Lucagnolo, who was burning to compare his packet with mine, burst into the shop; then in the presence of twelve journeymen and some neighbours, eager to behold the result of this competition, he seized his packet, scornfully exclaiming "Ou! ou!" three or four times, while he poured his money on the counter with a great noise. They were twenty-five crowns in giulios; and he fancied that mine would be four or five crowns *di moneta*. I for my part, stunned and stifled by his cries, and by the looks and smiles of the bystanders, first peeped into my packet; then, after seeing that it contained nothing but gold, I retired to one end of the counter, and, keeping my eyes lowered and making no noise at all, I lifted it with both hands suddenly above my head, and emptied it like a mill hopper. My coin was twice as much as his; which caused the onlookers, who had fixed their eyes on me with some derision, to turn round suddenly to him and say: "Lucagnolo, Benvenuto's pieces, being all of gold and twice as many as yours, make a far finer effect." I thought for certain that, what with jealousy and what with shame, Lucagnolo would have fallen dead upon the spot; and though he took the third part of my gain, since I was a journeyman (for such is the custom of the trade, two-thirds fall to the workman and one-third to the masters of the shop), yet inconsiderate envy had more power in him than avarice: it ought indeed to have worked quite the other way, he being a peasant's son from Iesi. He cursed his art and those who taught it him, vowing that thenceforth he would never work at large plate, but give his whole attention to those whoreson gewgaws, since they were so well paid. Equally enraged on my side, I answered that every bird sang its own note; that he talked after the fashion of the hovels he came from; but that I dared to swear that I should succeed with ease in making his lubberly lumber, while he would never be successful in my whoreson gewgaws. Thus I flung off in a passion, telling him that I would soon show him that I spoke truth. The bystanders openly declared against him, holding him for a lout, as indeed he was, and me for a man, as I had proved myself.

Next day, I went to thank Madonna Porzia, and told her that her ladyship had done the opposite of what she said she would; for that while I wanted to make the devil laugh, she had made him once more deny God. We both laughed pleasantly at this, and she gave me other commissions for fine and substantial work.

Meanwhile, I contrived, by means of a pupil of Raffaello de Urbino, to get an order from the Bishop of Salamanca for one of those great water-vessels called *acquereccia*, which are used for ornaments to place on sideboards. He wanted a pair made of equal size; and one of them he intrusted to Lucagnolo, the other to me. Giovan Francesco, the painter I have mentioned, gave us the design. Accordingly I set hand with marvellous good-will to this piece of plate, and was accommodated with a part of his workshop by a Milanese named Maestro Giovan Piero della Tacca. Having made my preparations, I calculated how much money I should need for certain affairs of my own, and sent all the rest to assist my poor father.

It so happened that just when this was being paid to him in Florence, he stumbled upon one of those Radicals who were in the Eight at the time when I got into that little trouble there. It was the very man who had abused him so rudely, and who swore that I should certainly be sent into the country with the lances. Now this fellow had some sons of very bad morals and repute; wherefore my father said to him: "Misfortunes can happen to anybody, especially to men of choleric humour when they are in the right, even as it happened to my son; but let the rest of his life bear witness how virtuously I have brought him up. Would God, for your well-being, that your sons may act neither worse nor better toward you than mine do to me. God rendered me able to bring them up as I have done; and where my own power could not reach, 'twas He who rescued them, against your expectation, out of your violent hands." On leaving the man, he wrote me all this story, begging me for God's sake to practise music at times, in order that I might not lose the fine accomplishment which he had taught me with such trouble. The letter so overflowed with expressions of the tenderest fatherly affection, that I was moved to tears of filial piety, resolving, before he died, to gratify him amply with regard to music. Thus God grants us those lawful blessings which we ask in prayer, nothing doubting.

While I was pushing forward Salamanca's vase, I had one little boy as help, whom I had taken at the entreaty of friends, and half against my own will, to be my workman. He was about fourteen years of age, bore the name of Paulino, and was son to a Roman burgess, who lived upon the income of his property. Paulino was the best-mannered, the most honest, and the most beautiful boy I ever saw in my whole life. His modest ways and actions, together with his superlative beauty and his devotion to myself, bred in me as great an affection for him as a man's breast can hold. This passionate love led me oftentimes to delight the lad with music; for I observed that his marvellous features, which by complexion wore a tone of modest melancholy, brightened up, and when I took my cornet, broke into a smile so lovely and so sweet, that I do not marvel at the silly stories which the Greeks have written about the deities of heaven. Indeed, if my boy had lived in those times, he would probably have turned their heads still more. He had a sister named Faustina, more beautiful, I verily believe, than that Faustina about whom the old books gossip so. Sometimes he took me to their vineyard, and, so far as I could judge, it struck me that Paulino's good father would have welcomed me as a son-in-law. This affair led me to play more than I was used to do.

It happened at that time that one Giangiacomo of Cesena, musician in the Pope's band, and a very excellent performer, sent word through Lorenzo, the trumpeter of Lucca, who is now in our Duke's service, to inquire whether I was inclined to help them at the Pope's Ferragosto, playing soprano with my cornet in some motets of great beauty selected by them for that occasion. Although I had the greatest desire to finish the vase I had begun, yet since music has a wondrous charm of its own, and also because I wished to please my old father, I consented to join them. During eight days be-

fore the festival we practised two hours a day together; then on the first of August we went to the Belvedere, and while Pope Clement was at table, we played those carefully studied motets so well that his Holiness protested he had never heard music more sweetly executed or with better harmony of parts. He sent for Giangiacomo, and asked him where and how he had procured so excellent a cornet for soprano, and inquired particularly who I was. Giangiacomo told him my name in full. Whereupon the Pope said: "So, then, he is the son of Maestro Giovanni?" On being assured I was, the Pope expressed his wish to have me in his service with the other bandsmen. Giangiacomo replied: "Most blessed Father, I cannot pretend for certain that you will get him, for his profession, to which he devotes himself assiduously, is that of a goldsmith, and he works in it miraculously well, and earns by it far more than he could by playing." To this the Pope added: "I am the better inclined to him now that I find him possessor of a talent more than I expected. See that he obtains the same salary as the rest of you; and tell him from me to join my service, and that I will find work enough by the day for him to do in his other trade." Then stretching out his hand, he gave him a hundred golden crowns of the Camera in a handkerchief, and said: "Divide these so that he may take his share."

When Giangiacomo left the Pope, he came to us, and related in detail all that the Pope had said; and after dividing the money between the eight of us, and giving me my share, he said to me: "Now I am going to have you inscribed among our company." I replied: "Let the day pass; tomorrow I will give my answer." When I left them, I went meditating whether I ought to accept the invitation, inasmuch as I could not but suffer if I abandoned the noble studies of my art. The following night my father appeared to me in a dream, and begged me with tears of tenderest affection, for God's love and his, to enter upon this engagement. Methought I answered that nothing would induce me to do so. In an instant he assumed so horrible an aspect as to frighten me out of my wits, and cried: "If you do not, you will have a father's curse; but if you do, may you be ever blessed by me!" When I woke, I ran, for very fright, to have myself inscribed. Then I wrote to my old father, telling him the news, which so affected him with extreme joy that a sudden fit of illness took him, and well-nigh brought him to death's door. In his answer to my letter, he told me that he too had dreamed nearly the same as I had.

Knowing now that I had gratified my father's honest wish, I began to think that everything would prosper with me to a glorious and honourable end. Accordingly, I set myself with indefatigable industry to the completion of the vase I had begun for Salamanca. That prelate was a very extraordinary man, extremely rich, but difficult to please. He sent daily to learn what I was doing; and when his messenger did not find me at home, he broke into fury, saying that he would take the work out of my hands and give it to others to finish. This came of my slavery to that accursed music. Still I laboured diligently night and day, until, when I had brought my work to a point when it could be exhibited, I submitted it to the inspection of the Bishop. This so increased his desire to see it finished, that I was sorry I had shown it. At the end of three months I had it ready, with little animals and foliage and masks, as beautiful as one could hope to see. No sooner was it done than I sent it by the hand of my workman, Paulino, to show that able artist Lucagnolo, of whom I have spoken above. Paulino, with the grace and beauty which belonged to him, spoke as follows: "Messer Lucagnolo, Benvenuto bids me say that he has sent to show you his promises and your lumber, expecting in return to see from you his gewgaws." This message given, Lucagnolo took up the vase, and carefully examined it; then he said to Paulino: "Fair boy, tell your master that he is a great and able artist, and that I beg him to be willing to have me for a friend, and not to engage in aught else." The mission of that virtuous and marvellous lad caused me the greatest joy; and then the vase was carried to Salamanca, who ordered it to be valued. Lucagnolo took part in the valuation, estimating and praising it far above my own opinion. Salamanca, lifting up the vase, cried like a true Spaniard: "I swear by God that I will take as long in paying him as he has lagged in making it." When I heard

this, I was exceedingly put out, and fell to cursing all Spain and every one who wished well to it.

Amongst other beautiful ornaments, this vase had a handle, made all of one piece, with most delicate mechanism, which, when a spring was touched, stood upright above the mouth of it. While the prelate was one day ostentatiously exhibiting my vase to certain Spanish gentlemen of his suite, it chanced that one of them, upon Monsignor's quitting the room, began roughly to work the handle, and as the gentle spring which moved it could not bear his loutish violence it broke in his hand. Aware what mischief he had done, he begged the butler who had charge of the Bishop's plate to take it to the master who had made it, for him to mend it, and promised to pay what price he asked, provided it was set to rights at once. So the vase came once more into my hands, and I promised to put it forthwith in order, which indeed I did. It was brought to me before dinner; and at twenty-two o'clock the man who brought it returned, all in a sweat, for he had run the whole way, Monsignor having again asked for it to show to certain other gentlemen. The butler, then, without giving me time to utter a word, cried: "Quick, quick, bring the vase." I, who wanted to act at leisure and not to give it up to him, said that I did not mean to be so quick. The serving-man got into such a rage that he made as though he would put one hand to his sword, while with the other he threatened to break the shop open. To this I put a stop at once with my own weapon, using therewith spirited language, and saying: "I am not going to give it to you! Go and tell Monsignor, your master, that I want the money for my work before I let it leave this shop." When the fellow saw he could not obtain it by swaggering, he fell to praying me, as one prays to the Cross, declaring that if I would only give it up, he would take care I should be paid. These words did not make me swerve from my purpose; but I kept on saying the same thing. At last, despairing of success, he swore to come with Spaniards enough to cut me in pieces. Then he took to his heels; while I, who inclined to believe partly in their murderous attack, resolved that I would defend myself with courage. So I got an admirable little gun ready, which I used for shooting game, and muttered to myself: "He who robs me of my property and labour may take my life too, and welcome." While I was carrying on this debate in my own mind, a crowd of Spaniards arrived, led by their major-domo, who, with the headstrong rashness of his race, bade them go in and take the vase and give me a good beating. Hearing these words, I showed them the muzzle of my gun, and prepared to fire, and cried in a loud voice: "Renegade Jews, traitors, is it thus that one breaks into houses and shops in our city of Rome? Come as many of you thieves as like, an inch nearer to this wicket, and I'll blow all their brains out with my gun." Then I turned the muzzle toward their major-domo, and making as though I would discharge it, called out: "And you big thief, who are egging them on, I mean to kill you first." He clapped spurs to the jennet he was riding, and took flight headlong. The commotion we were making stirred up all the neighbours, who came crowding round, together with some Roman gentlemen who chanced to pass, and cried: "Do but kill the renegades, and we will stand by you." These words had the effect of frightening the Spaniards in good earnest. They withdrew, and were compelled by the circumstances to relate the whole affair to Monsignor. Being a man of inordinate haughtiness, he rated the members of his household, both because they had engaged in such an act of violence, and also because, having begun, they had not gone through with it. At this juncture the painter, who had been concerned in the whole matter, came in, and the Bishop bade him go and tell me that if I did not bring the vase at once, he would make mince-meat of me; but if I brought it, he would pay its price down. These threats were so far from terrifying me, that I sent him word I was going immediately to lay my case before the Pope.

In the meantime, his anger and my fear subsided; whereupon, being guaranteed by some Roman noblemen of high degree that the prelate would not harm me, and having assurance that I should be paid, I armed myself with a large poniard and my good coat of mail, and betook myself to his palace, where he had drawn up all his household. I entered, and

Paulino followed with the silver vase. It was just like passing through the Zodiac, neither more nor less; for one of them had the face of the lion, another of the scorpion, a third of the crab. However, we passed onward to the presence of the rascally priest, who spouted out a torrent of such language as only priests and Spaniards have at their command. In return I never raised my eyes to look at him, nor answered word for word. That seemed to augment the fury of his anger; and causing paper to be put before me, he commanded me to write an acknowledgment to the effect that I had been amply satisfied and paid in full. Then I raised my head, and said I should be very glad to do so when I had received the money. The Bishop's rage continued to rise; threats and recriminations were flung about; but at last the money was paid, and I wrote the receipt. Then I departed, glad at heart and in high spirits.

When Pope Clement heard the story—he had seen the vase before, but it was not shown him as my work—he expressed much pleasure and spoke warmly in my praise, publicly saying that he felt very favourably toward me. This caused Monsignor Salamanca to repent that he had hectored over me; and in order to make up our quarrel, he sent the same painter to inform me that he meant to give me large commissions. I replied that I was willing to undertake them, but that I should require to be paid in advance. This speech too came to Pope Clement's ears, and made him laugh heartily. Cardinal Cibo was in the presence, and the Pope narrated to him the whole history of my dispute with the Bishop. Then he turned to one of his people, and ordered him to go on supplying me with work for the palace. Cardinal Cibo sent for me, and after some time spent in agreeable conversation, gave me the order for a large vase, bigger than Salamanca's. I likewise obtained commissions from Cardinal Cornaro, and many others of the Holy College, especially Ridolfi and Salviati; they all kept me well employed, so that I earned plenty of money.

Madonna Porzia now advised me to open a shop of my own. This I did; and I never stopped working for that excellent and gentle lady, who paid me exceedingly well, and by whose means perhaps it was that I came to make a figure in the world.

I contracted close friendship with Signor Gabriello Ceserino, at that time Gonfalonier of Rome, and executed many pieces for him. One, among the rest, is worthy of mention. It was a large golden medal to wear in the hat. I engraved upon it Leda with her swan; and being very well pleased with the workmanship, he said he should like to have it valued, in order that I might be properly paid. Now, since the medal was executed with consummate skill, the valuers of the trade set a far higher price on it than he had thought of. I therefore kept the medal, and got nothing for my pains. The same sort of adventures happened in this case as in that of Salamanca's vase. But I shall pass such matters briefly by, lest they hinder me from telling things of greater importance.

Since I am writing my life, I must from time to time diverge from my profession in order to describe with brevity, if not in detail, some incidents which have no bearing on my career as artist. On the morning of St. John's Day I happened to be dining with several men of our nation, painters, sculptors, goldsmiths, amongst the most notable of whom was Rosso and Gianfrancesco, the pupil of Raffaello. I had invited them without restraint or ceremony to the place of our meeting; and they were all laughing and joking, as is natural when a crowd of men come together to make merry on so great a festival. It chanced that a light-brained swaggering young fellow passed by; he was a soldier of Rienzo da Ceri, who, when he heard the noise that we were making, gave vent to a string of opprobrious sarcasms upon the folk of Florence. I, who was the host of those great artists and men of worth, taking the insult to myself, slipped out quietly without being observed, and went up to him. I ought to say that he had a punk of his there, and was going on with his stupid ribaldries to amuse her. When I met him, I asked if he was the rash fellow who was speaking evil of the Florentines. He answered at once: "I am that man." On this I raised my hand, struck him in the face, and said: "And I am *this* man." Then we each of us drew our sword with spirit; but the fray had

hardly begun when a crowd of persons intervened, who rather took my part than not, hearing and seeing that I was in the right.

On the following day a challenge to fight with him was brought me, which I accepted very gladly, saying that I expected to complete this job far quicker than those of the other art I practised. So I went at once to confer with a fine old man called Bevilacqua, who was reputed to have been the first sword of Italy, because he had fought more than twenty serious duels and had always come off with honour. This excellent man was a great friend of mine; he knew me as an artist, and had also been concerned as intermediary in certain ugly quarrels between me and others. Accordingly, when he had learned my business, he answered with a smile: "My Benvenuto, if you had an affair with Mars, I am sure you would come out with honour, because through all the years that I have known you, I have never seen you wrongfully take up a quarrel." So he consented to be my second, and we repaired with sword in hand to the appointed place; but no blood was shed, for my opponent made the matter up, and I came with much credit out of the affair. I will not add further particulars; for though they would be very interesting in their own way, I wish to keep both space and words for my art, which has been my chief inducement to write as I am doing, and about which I shall have only too much to say.

The spirit of honourable rivalry impelled me to attempt some other masterpiece, which should equal, or even surpass, the productions of that able craftsman, Lucagnolo, whom I have mentioned. Still I did not on this account neglect my own fine art of jewellery; and so both the one and the other wrought me much profit and more credit and in both of them I continued to produce things of marked originality. There was at that time in Rome a very able artist of Perugia named Lautizio, who worked only in one department, where he was sole and unrivalled throughout the world. You must know that at Rome every cardinal has a seal, upon which his title is engraved, and these seals are made just as large as a child's hand of about twelve years of age; and, as I have already said, the cardinal's title is engraved upon the seal together with a great many ornamental figures. A well-made article of the kind fetches a hundred, or more than a hundred crowns. This excellent workman, like Lucagnolo, roused in me some honest rivalry, although the art he practised is far remote from the other branches of goldsmithery, and consequently Lautizio was not skilled in making anything but seals. I gave my mind to acquiring his craft also, although I found it very difficult; and, unrepelled by the trouble which it gave me, I went on zealously upon the path of profit and improvement.

There was in Rome another most excellent craftsman of ability, who was a Milanese named Messer Caradosso. He dealt in nothing but chiselled medals, made of plates of metal, and such-like things. I have seen of his some paxes in half relief, and some Christs a palm in length wrought of the thinnest golden plates, so exquisitely done that I esteemed him the greatest master in that kind I had ever seen, and envied him more than all the rest together. There were also other masters who worked at medals carved in steel, which may be called the models and true guides for those who aim at striking coins in the most perfect style. All these divers arts I set myself with unflagging industry to learn.

I must not omit the exquisite art of enamelling, in which I have never known any one excel save a Florentine, our countryman, called Amerigo. I did not know him, but was well acquainted with his incomparable masterpieces. Nothing in any part of the world or by any craftsman that I have seen, approached the divine beauty of their workmanship. To this branch too I devoted myself with all my strength, although it is extremely difficult, chiefly because of the fire, which, after long time and trouble spent in other processes, has to be applied at last, and not infrequently brings the whole to ruin. In spite of its great difficulties, it gave me so much pleasure that I looked upon them as recreation; and this came from the special gift which the God of nature bestowed on me, that is to say, a temperament so happy and of such excellent parts that I was freely able to accomplish whatever it pleased me to take in hand. The various departments of art which I have described are very different one from the other, so that a man who excels in one of them, if he undertakes the others, hardly ever achieves the same success; whereas I strove with all my power to become equally versed in all of them: and in the proper place I shall demonstrate that I attained my object. . . .

I went on applying myself with the utmost diligence upon the gold-work for Pope Clement's button. He was very eager to have it, and used to send for me two or three times a week, in order to inspect it; and his delight in the work was always increased. Often would he rebuke and scold me, as it were, for the great grief in which my brother's loss had plunged me; and one day, observing me more downcast and out of trim than was proper, he cried aloud: "Benvenuto, oh! I did not know that you were mad. Have you only just learned that there is no remedy against death? One would think that you were trying to run after him." When I left the presence, I continued working at the jewel and the dies for the Mint; but I also took to watching the arquebusier who shot my brother, as though he had been a girl I was in love with. The man had formerly been in the light cavalry, but afterwards had joined the arquebusiers as one of the Bargello's corporals; and what increased my rage was that he had used these boastful words: "If it had not been for me, who killed that brave young man, the least trifle of delay would have resulted in his putting us all to flight with great disaster." When I saw that the fever caused by always seeing him about was depriving me of sleep and appetite, and was bringing me by degrees to sorry plight, I overcame my repugnance to so low and not quite praiseworthy an enterprise, and made my mind up one evening to rid myself of the torment. The fellow lived in a house near a place called Torre Sanguigua, next door to the lodging of one of the most fashionable courtesans in Rome, named Signora Antea. It had just struck twenty-four, and he was standing at the house-door, with his sword in hand, having risen from supper. With great address I stole up to him, holding a large Pistojan dagger, and dealt him a back-handed stroke, with which I meant to cut his head clean off; but as he turned round very suddenly, the blow fell upon the point of his left shoulder and broke the the bone. He sprang up, dropped his sword, half-stunned with the great pain, and took to flight. I followed after, and in four steps caught him up, when I lifted my dagger above his head, which he was holding very low, and hit him in the back exactly at the juncture of the nape-bone and the neck. The poniard entered this point so deep into the bone, that, though I used all my strength to pull it out, I was not able. For just at that moment four soldiers with drawn swords sprang out from Antea's lodging, and obliged me to set hand to my own sword to defend my life. Leaving the poniard then, I made off, and fearing I might be recognised took refuge in the palace of Duke Alessandro, which was between Piazza Navona and the Rotunda. On my arrival, I asked to see the Duke; who told me that, if I was alone, I need only keep quiet and have no further anxiety, but go on working at the jewel which the Pope had set his heart on, and stay eight days indoors. He gave this advice the more securely, because the soldiers had now arrived who interrupted the completion of my deed; they held the dagger in their hand, and were relating how the matter happened, and the great trouble they had to pull the weapon from the neck and head-bone of the man, whose name they did not know. Just then Giovan Bandini came up, and said to them: "That poniard is mine, and I lent it to Benvenuto, who was bent on revenging his brother." The soldiers were profuse in their expressions of regret at having interrupted me, although my vengeance had been amply satisfied.

More than eight days elapsed, and the Pope did not send for me according to his custom. Afterwards he summoned me through his chamberlain, the Bolognese nobleman I have already mentioned, who let me, in his own modest manner, understand that his Holiness knew all, but was very well inclined toward me, and that I had only to mind my work and keep quiet. When we reached the presence, the Pope cast so menacing a glance towards me, that the mere look of his eyes made me tremble. Afterwards, upon examining my work, his countenance cleared, and he began to praise me beyond measure, saying that I had done a vast amount in a short time. Then,

looking me straight in the face, he added: "Now that you are cured, Benvenuto, take heed how you live." I, who understood his meaning, promised that I would. Immediately upon this, I opened a very fine shop in the Banchi, opposite Raffaello, and there I finished the jewel after the lapse of a few months. . . .

On our way to the lodgings of the King [Francis I of France] we passed before those of the Cardinal of Ferrara. Standing at his door, he called to me and said: "Our most Christian monarch has of his own accord assigned you the same appointments which his Majesty allowed the painter Lionardo da Vinci, that is, a salary of seven hundred crowns; in addition, he will pay you for all the works you do for him; also for your journey hither he gives you five hundred golden crowns, which will be paid you before you quit this place." At the end of this announcement, I replied that those were offers worthy of the great King he was. The messenger, not knowing anything about me, and hearing what splendid offers had been made me by the King, begged my pardon over and over again. Pagolo and Ascanio exclaimed: "It is God who has helped us to get back into so honoured a go-cart!"

On the day following I went to thank the King, who ordered me to make the models of twelve silver statues, which were to stand as candelabra round his table. He wanted them to represent six gods and six goddesses, and to have exactly the same height as his Majesty, which was a trifle under four cubits. Having dictated this commission, he turned to his treasurer, and asked whether he had paid me the five hundred crowns. The official said that he had received no orders to that effect. The King took this very ill, for he had requested the Cardinal to speak to him about it. Furthermore, he told me to go to Paris and seek out a place to live in, fitted for the execution of such works; he would see that I obtained it.

I got the five hundred crowns of gold, and took up my quarters at Paris in a house of the Cardinal of Ferrara. There I began, in God's name, to work, and fashioned four little waxen models, about two-thirds of a cubit each in height. They were Jupiter, Juno, Apollo, and Vulcan. In this while the King returned to

Paris; whereupon I went to him at once, taking my models with me, and my two prentices, Ascanio and Pagolo. On perceiving that the King was pleased with my work, and being commissioned to execute the Jupiter in silver of the height above described, I introduced the two young men, and said that I had brought them with me out of Italy to serve his Majesty; for inasmuch as they had been brought up by me, I could at the beginning get more help from them than from the Paris workmen. To this the King replied that I might name a salary which I thought sufficient for their maintenance. I said that a hundred crowns of gold apiece would be quite proper, and that I would make them earn their wages well. This agreement was concluded. Then I said that I had found a place which seemed to me exactly suited to my industry; it was his Majesty's own property, and called the Little Nello. The Provost of Paris was then in possession of it from his Majesty; but since the Provost made no use of the castle, his Majesty perhaps might grant it me to employ in his service. He replied upon the instant: "That place is my own house, and I know well that the man I gave it to does not inhabit it or use it. So you shall have it for the work you have to do." He then told his lieutenants to install me in the Nello. This officer made some resistance, pleading that he could not carry out the order. The King answered in anger that he meant to bestow his property on whom he pleased, and on a man who would serve him, seeing that he got nothing from the other; therefore he would hear no more about it. The lieutenant then submitted that some small force would have to be employed in order to effect an entrance. To which the King answered: "Go, then, and if a small force is not enough, use a great one."

The officer took me immediately to the castle, and there put me in possession, not, however, without violence; after that he warned me to take very good care that I was not murdered. I installed myself, enrolled serving-men, and bought a quantity of pikes and partisans; but I remained for several days exposed to grievous annoyances, for the Provost was a great nobleman of Paris, and all the other gentlefolk took part against me; they attacked me with such insults that I could hardly hold my own against them. I must not omit to mention that I entered the service of his Majesty in the year 1540, which was exactly the year in which I reached the age of forty.

The affronts and insults I received made me have recourse to the King, begging his Majesty to establish me in some other place. He answered: "Who are you, and what is your name?" I remained in great confusion, and could not comprehend what he meant. Holding my tongue thus, the King repeated the same words a second time angrily. Then I said my name was Benvenuto. "If, then, you are the Benvenuto of whom I have heard," replied the King, "act according to your wont, for you have my full leave to do so." I told his Majesty that all I wanted was to keep his favour; for the rest, I knew of nothing that could harm me. He gave a little laugh, and said: "Go your ways, then; you shall never want my favour." Upon this he told his first secretary, Monsignor di Villerois, to see me provided and accommodated with all I needed.

This Villerois was an intimate friend of the Provost, to whom the castle had been given. It was built in a triangle, right up against the city walls, and was of some antiquity, but had no garrison. The building was of considerable size. Monsignor di Villerois counselled me to look about for something else, and by all means to leave this place alone, seeing that its owner was a man of vast power, who would most assuredly have me killed. I answered that I had come from Italy to France only in order to serve that illustrious King; and as for dying, I knew for certain that die I must; a little earlier or a little later was a matter of supreme indifference to me.

Now Villerois was a man of the highest talent, exceptionally distinguished in all points, and possessed of vast wealth. There was nothing he would not gladly have done to harm me, but he made no open demonstration of his mind. He was grave, and of a noble presence, and spoke slowly, at his ease. To another gentleman, Monsignor di Marmagna, the treasurer of Languedoc, he left the duty of molesting me. The first thing which this man did was to look out the best apartments in the castle, and have them fitted up for himself. I told him that the King had given me the place to serve him in, and that I did not choose it should be occupied by any but myself and my attendants. The fellow, who was haughty, bold, and spirited, replied that he meant to do just what he liked; that I should run my head against a wall if I presumed to oppose him, and that Villerois had given him authority to do what he was doing. I told him that, by the King's authority given to me, neither he nor Villerois could do it. When I said that he gave vent to offensive language in French, whereat I retorted in my own tongue that he lied. Stung with rage, he clapped his hand upon a little dagger which he had; then I set my hand also to a large dirk which I always wore for my defence, and cried out: "If you dare to draw, I'll kill you on the spot." He had two servants to back him, and I had my two lads. For a moment or two Marmagna stood in doubt, not knowing exactly what to do, but rather inclined to mischief, and muttering: "I will never put up with such insults." Seeing then that the affair was taking a bad turn, I took a sudden resolution, and cried to Pagolo and Ascanio: "When you see me draw my dirk, throw yourselves upon those servingmen, and kill them if you can; I mean to kill this fellow at the first stroke, and then we will decamp together, with God's grace." Marmagna, when he understood my purpose, was glad enough to get alive out of the castle.

All these things, toning them down a trifle, I wrote to the Cardinal of Ferrara, who related them at once to the King. The King, deeply irritated, committed me to the care of another officer of his bodyguard who was named Monsignor lo Iscontro d'Orbech. By him I was accommodated with all that I required in the most gracious way imaginable.

After fitting up my own lodgings in the castle and the workshop with all conveniences for carrying on my business, and putting my household upon a most respectable footing, I began at once to construct three models exactly of the size which the silver statues were to be. These were Jupiter, Vulcan, and Mars. I moulded them in clay, and set them well up on irons; then I went to the King, who disbursed three hundred pounds weight of silver, if I remember rightly, for the commencement of the undertaking. While I was getting these things ready, we brought the little vase and oval basin to completion, which had been several months in hand. Then I had them richly gilt, and they showed like the finest piece of plate which had been seen in France.

Afterwards I took them to the Cardinal, who thanked me greatly; and, without requesting my attendance, carried and presented them to the King. He was delighted with the gift, and praised me as no artist was ever praised before. In return, he bestowed upon the Cardinal an abbey worth seven thousand crowns a year, and expressed his intention of rewarding me too. The Cardinal, however, prevented him, telling his Majesty that he was going ahead too fast, since I had as yet produced nothing for him. The King, who was exceedingly generous, replied: "For that very reason will I put heart and hope into him." The Cardinal, ashamed at his own meanness, said: "Sire, I beg you to leave that to me; I will allow him a pension of at least three hundred crowns when I have taken possession of the abbey." He never gave me anything; and it would be tedious to relate all the knavish tricks of this prelate. I prefer to dwell on matters of greater moment.

When I returned to Paris, the great favour shown me by the King made me a mark for all men's admiration. I received the silver and began my statue of Jupiter. Many journeymen were now in my employ; and the work went onward briskly day and night; so that, by the time I had finished the clay models of Jupiter, Vulcan, and Mars, and had begun to get the silver statue forward, my workshop made already a grand show.

The King now came to Paris, and I went to pay him my respects. No sooner had his Majesty set eyes upon me than he called me cheerfully, and asked if I had something fine to exhibit at my lodging, for he would come to inspect it. I related all I had been doing; upon which he was seized with a strong desire to come. Accordingly, after his dinner, he set off with Madame de Tampes, the Cardinal of Lorraine, and some other of his greatest nobles, among whom were the King of Navarre, his cousin, and the Queen, his sister; the Dauphin and Dauphiness also attended him; so that upon that day the very flower of the French court came to visit me. I had been some time at home, and was hard at work. When the King arrived at the door of the castle, and heard our hammers going, he bade his company keep silence. Everybody in my house was busily employed, so that the unexpected entrance of his Majesty took me by surprise. The first thing he saw on coming into the great hall was myself with a huge plate of silver in my hand, which I was beating for the body of my Jupiter; one of my men was finishing the head, another the legs; and it is easy to imagine what a din we made between us. It happened that a little French lad was working at my side, who had just been guilty of some trifling blunder. I gave the lad a kick, and, as my good luck would have it, caught him with my foot exactly in the fork between his legs, and sent him spinning several yards, so that he came stumbling up against the King precisely at the moment when his Majesty arrived. The King was vastly amused, but I felt covered with confusion. He began to ask me what I was engaged upon, and told me to go on working; then he said that he would much rather have me not employ my strength on manual labour, but take as many men as I wanted, and make them do the rough work; he should like me to keep myself in health, in order that he might enjoy my services through many years to come. I replied to his Majesty that the moment I left off working I should fall ill; also that my art itself would suffer, and not attain the mark I aimed at for his Majesty. Thinking that I spoke thus only to brag, and not because it was the truth, he made the Cardinal of Lorraine repeat what he had said; but I explained my reasons so fully and clearly, that the Cardinal perceived my drift; he then advised the King to let me labour as much or little as I liked.

Being very well satisfied with what he had seen, the King returned to his palace, after bestowing on me too many marks of favour to be here recorded. On the following day he sent for me at his dinner-hour. The Cardinal of Ferrara was there at meat with him. When I arrived, the King had reached his second course; he began at once to speak to me, saying, with a pleasant cheer, that having now so fine a basin and jug of my workmanship, he wanted an equally handsome salt-cellar to match them; and begged me to make a design, and to lose no time about it. I replied: "Your Majesty shall see a model of the sort even sooner than you have commanded; for while I was making the basin, I thought there ought to be a salt-cellar to match it; therefore I have already designed one, and if it is your pleasure, I will at once exhibit my conception." The King turned with a lively movement of surprise and pleasure to the lords in his company —they were the King of Navarre, the Cardinal of Lorraine, and the Cardinal of Ferrara—exclaiming as he did so: "Upon my word, this is a man to be loved and cherished by every one who knows him." Then he told me that he would very gladly see my model.

I set off, and returned in a few minutes; for I had only to cross the river, that is, the Seine. I carried with me the wax model which I had made in Rome at the Cardinal of Ferrara's request. When I appeared again before the King and uncovered my piece, he cried out in astonishment: "This is a hundred times more divine a thing than I had ever dreamed of. What a miracle of a man! He ought never to stop working." Then he turned to me with a beaming countenance, and told me that he greatly liked the piece, and wished me to execute it in gold. The Cardinal of Ferrara looked me in the face, and let me understand that he recognised the model as the same which I had made for him in Rome. I replied that I had already told him I should carry it out for one who was worthy of it. The Cardinal, remembering my words, and nettled by the revenge he thought that I was taking on him, remarked to the King: "Sire, this is an enormous undertaking; I am only afraid that we shall never see it finished. These able artists who have great conceptions in their brain are ready enough to put the same in execution without duly considering when they are to be accomplished. I therefore, if I gave commission for things of such magnitude, should like to know when I was likely to get them." The King replied that if a man was so scrupulous about the termination of a work, he would never begin anything at all; these words he uttered with a certain look, which implied that such enterprises were not for folk of little spirit. I then began to say my say: "Princes who put heart and courage in their servants, as your Majesty does by deed and word, render undertakings of the greatest magnitude quite easy. Now that God has sent me so magnificent a patron, I hope to perform for him a multitude of great and splendid masterpieces." "I believe it," said the King, and rose from table. Then he called me into his chamber, and asked how much gold was wanted for the salt-cellar. "A thousand crowns," I answered. He called his treasurer at once, who was the Viscount of Orbec, and ordered him that very day to disburse to me a thousand crowns of good weight and old gold.

When I left his Majesty, I went for the two notaries who had helped me in procuring silver for the Jupiter and many other things. Crossing the Seine, I then took a small hand-basket, which one of my cousins, a nun, had given me on my journey through Florence. It made for my good fortune that I took this basket and not a bag. So then, thinking I could do the business by daylight, for it was still early, and not caring to interrupt my workmen, and being indisposed to take a servant with me, I set off alone. When I reached the house of the treasurer, I found that he had the money laid out before him, and was selecting the best pieces as the King had ordered. It seemed to me, however, that that thief of a treasurer was doing all he could to postpone the payment of the money; nor were the pieces counted out until three hours after nightfall.

I meanwhile was not wanting in despatch, for I sent word to several of my journeymen that they should come and attend me, since the matter was one of serious importance. When I found that they did not arrive, I asked the messenger if he had done my errand. The rascal of a groom whom I had sent replied that he had done so, but that they had answered that they could not come; he, however, would gladly carry the money for me. I answered that I meant to carry the money myself. By this time the contract was drawn up and signed. On the money being counted, I put it all into my little basket, and then thrust my arm through the two handles. Since I did this with some difficulty, the gold was well shut in, and

I carried it more conveniently than if the vehicle had been a bag. I was well armed with shirt and sleeves of mail, and having my sword and dagger at my side, made off along the street as quick as my two legs would carry me.

Just as I left the house, I observed some servants whispering among themselves, who also went off at a round pace in another direction from the one I took. Walking with all haste, I passed the bridge of the Exchange, and went up along a wall beside the river which led to my lodging in the castle. I had just come to the Augustines—now this was a very perilous passage, and though it was only five hundred paces distant from my dwelling, yet the lodging in the castle being quite as far removed inside, no one could have heard my voice if I had shouted—when I saw four men with four swords in their hands advancing to attack me. My resolution was taken in an instant. I covered the basket with my cape, drew my sword, and seeing that they were pushing hotly forward, cried aloud: "With soldiers there is only the cape and sword to gain; and these, before I give them up, I hope you'll get not much to your advantage." Then crossing my sword boldly with them, I more than once spread out my arms, in order that, if the ruffians were put on by the servants who had seen me take my money, they might be led to judge I was not carrying it. The encounter was soon over; for they retired step by step, saying among themselves in their own language: "This is a brave Italian, and certainly not the man we are after; or if he be the man, he cannot be carrying anything." I spoke Italian, and kept harrying them with thrust and slash so hotly that I narrowly missed killing one or the other. My skill in using the sword made them think I was a soldier rather than a fellow of some other calling. They drew together and began to fall back, muttering all the while beneath their breath in their own tongue. I meanwhile continued always calling out, but not too loudly, that those who wanted my cape and blade would have to get them with some trouble. Then I quickened pace, while they still followed slowly at my heels; this augmented my fear, for I thought I might be falling into an ambuscade, which would have cut me off in front as well as rear. Accordingly, when I was at the distance of a hundred paces from my home, I ran with all my might, and shouted at the top of my voice: "To arms, to arms! out with you, out with you! I am being murdered." In a moment four of my young men came running, with four pikes in their hands. They wanted to pursue the ruffians, who could still be seen; but I stopped them, calling back so as to let the villains hear: "Those cowards yonder, four against one man alone, had not pluck enough to capture a thousand golden crowns in metal, which have almost broken this arm of mine. Let us haste inside and put the money away; then I will take my big two-handed sword, and go with you whithersoever you like." We went inside to secure the gold; and my lads, while expressing deep concern for the peril I had run, gently chided me, and said: "You risk yourself too much alone; the time will come when you will make us all bemoan your loss." A thousand words and exclamations were exchanged between us; my adversaries took to flight; and we all sat down and supped together with mirth and gladness, laughing over those great blows which fortune strikes, for good as well as evil, and which, what time they do not hit the mark, are just the same as though they had not happened. It is very true that one says to oneself: "You will have had a lesson for next time." But that is not the case; for fortune always comes upon us in new ways, quite unforeseen by our imagination. . . .

Having succeeded so well with the cast of the Medusa, I had great hope of bringing my Perseus through; for I had laid the wax on, and felt confident that it would come out in bronze as perfectly as the Medusa. The waxen model produced so fine an effect, that when the Duke saw it and was struck with its beauty— whether somebody had persuaded him it could not be carried out with the same finish in metal, or whether he thought so for himself— he came to visit me more frequently than usual, and on one occasion said: "Benvenuto, this figure cannot succeed in bronze; the laws of art do not admit of it." These words of

his Excellency stung me so sharply that I answered: "My lord, I know how very little confidence you have in me; and I believe the reason of this is that your most illustrious Excellency lends too ready an ear to my calumniators, or else indeed that you do not understand my art." He hardly let me close the sentence when he broke in: "I profess myself a connoisseur, and understand it very well indeed." I replied: "Yes, like a prince, not like an artist; for if your Excellency understood my trade as well as you imagine, you would trust me on the proofs I have already given. These are, first, the colossal bronze bust of your Excellency, which is now in Elba; secondly, the restoration of the Ganymede in marble, which offered so many difficulties and cost me so much trouble, that I would rather have made the whole statue new from the beginning; thirdly, the Medusa, cast by me in bronze, here now before your Excellency's eyes, the execution of which was a greater triumph of strength and skill than any of my predecessors in this fiendish art have yet achieved. Look you, my lord! I constructed that furnace anew on principles quite different from those of other founders; in addition to many technical improvements and ingenious devices, I supplied it with two issues for the metal, because this difficult and twisted figure could not otherwise have come out perfect. It is only owing to my intelligent insight into means and appliances that the statue turned out as it did; a triumph judged impossible by all the practitioners of this art. I should like you furthermore to be aware, my lord, for certain, that the sole reason why I succeeded with all those great and arduous works in France under his most admirable Majesty King Francis, was the high courage which that good monarch put into my heart by the liberal allowances he made me, and the multitude of work-people he left at my disposal. I could have as many as I asked for, and employed at times above forty, all chosen by myself. These were the causes of my having there produced so many masterpieces in so short a space of time. Now then, my lord, put trust in me; supply me with the aid I need. I am confident of being able to complete a work which will delight your soul. But if your Excellency goes on disheartening me, and does not advance me the assistance which is absolutely required, neither I nor any man alive upon this earth can hope to achieve the slightest thing of value."

It was as much as the Duke could do to stand by and listen to my pleadings. He kept turning first this way and then that; while I, in despair, poor wretched I, was calling up remembrance of the noble state I held in France, to the great sorrow of my soul. All at once he cried: "Come, tell me, Benvenuto, how is it possible that yonder splendid head of Medusa, so high up there in the grasp of Perseus, should ever come out perfect?" I replied upon the instant: "Look you now, my lord! If your Excellency possessed that knowledge of the craft which you affirm you have, you would not fear one moment for the splendid head you speak of. There is good reason, on the other hand, to feel uneasy about this right foot, so far below and at a distance from the rest." When he heard these words, the Duke turned, half in anger, to some gentlemen in waiting, and exclaimed: "I verily believe that this Benvenuto prides himself on contradicting everything one says." Then he faced round to me with a touch of mockery, upon which his attendants did the like, and began to speak as follows: "I will listen patiently to any argument you can possibly produce in explanation of your statement, which may convince me of its probability." I said in answer: "I will adduce so sound an argument that your Excellency shall perceive the full force of it." So I began: "You must know, my lord, that the nature of fire is to ascend, and therefore I promise you that Medusa's head will come out famously; but since it is not in nature of fire to descend, and I must force it downwards six cubits by artificial means, I assure your Excellency upon this most convincing ground of proof that the foot cannot possibly come out. It will, however, be quite easy for me to restore it." "Why, then," said the Duke, "did you not devise it so that the foot should come out as well as you affirm the head will?" I answered: "I must have made a much larger furnace, with a conduit as thick as my leg; and so I might have forced the molten metal by its own

weight to descend so far. Now, my pipe, which runs six cubits to the statue's foot, as I have said, is not thicker than two fingers. However, it was not worth the trouble and expense to make a larger; for I shall easily be able to mend what is lacking. But when my mould is more than half full, as I expect, from this middle point upwards, the fire ascending by its natural property, then the heads of Perseus and Medusa will come out admirably; you may be quite sure of it." After I had thus expounded these convincing arguments, together with many more of the same kind, which it would be tedious to set down here, the Duke shook his head and departed without further ceremony.

Abandoned thus to my own resources, I took new courage, and banished the sad thoughts which kept recurring to my mind, making me often weep bitter tears of repentance for having left France; for though I did so only to revisit Florence, my sweet birthplace, in order that I might charitably succour my six nieces, this good action, as I well perceived, had been the beginning of my great misfortune. Nevertheless, I felt convinced that when my Perseus was accomplished, all these trials would be turned to high felicity and glorious well-being.

Accordingly I strengthened my heart, and with all the forces of my body and my purse, employing what little money still remained to me, I set to work. First I provided myself with several loads of pinewood from the forests of Serristori, in the neighbourhood of Montelupo. While these were on their way, I clothed my Perseus with the clay which I had prepared many months beforehand, in order that it might be duly seasoned. After making its clay tunic (for that is the term used in this art) and properly arming it and fencing it with iron girders, I began to draw the wax out by means of a slow fire. This melted and issued through numerous air-vents I had made; for the more there are of these, the better will the mould fill. When I had finished drawing off the wax, I constructed a funnel-shaped furnace all round the model of my Perseus. It was built of bricks, so interlaced, the one above the other, that numerous apertures were left for the fire to exhale at. Then I began to lay on wood by degrees, and kept it burning two whole days and nights. At length, when all the wax was gone, and the mould was well baked, I set to work at digging the pit in which to sink it. This I performed with scrupulous regard to all the rules of art. When I had finished that part of my work, I raised the mould by windlasses and stout ropes to a perpendicular position, and suspending it with the greatest care one cubit above the level of the furnace, so that it hung exactly above the middle of the pit, I next lowered it gently down into the very bottom of the furnace, and had it firmly placed with every possible precaution for its safety. When this delicate operation was accomplished, I began to bank it up with the earth I had excavated; and, ever as the earth grew higher, I introduced its proper air-vents, which were little tubes of earthenware, such as folk use for drains and such-like purposes. At length, I felt sure that it was admirably fixed, and that the filling-in of the pit and the placing of the air-vents had been properly performed. I also could see that my work-people understood my method, which differed very considerably from that of all the other masters in the trade. Feeling confident, then, that I could rely upon them, I next turned to my furnace, which I had filled with numerous pigs of copper and other bronze stuff. The pieces were piled according to the laws of art, that is to say, so resting one upon the other that the flames could play freely through them, in order that the metal might heat and liquefy the sooner. At last I called out heartily to set the furnace going. The logs of pine were heaped in, and, what with the unctuous resin of the wood and the good draught I had given, my furnace worked so well that I was obliged to rush from side to side to keep it going. The labour was more than I could stand; yet I forced myself to strain every nerve and muscle. To increase my anxieties, the workshop took fire, and we were afraid lest the roof should fall upon our heads; while, from the garden, such a storm of wind and rain kept blowing in, that it perceptibly cooled the furnace.

Battling thus with all these untoward circumstances for several hours, and exerting myself beyond even the measure of my powerful constitution, I could at last bear up no longer, and a sudden fever, of the utmost possible intensity, attacked me. I felt absolutely obliged to go and fling myself upon my bed. Sorely against my will having to drag myself away from the spot, I turned to my assistants, about ten or more in all, what with master-founders, hand-workers, country-fellows, and my own special journeymen, among whom was Bernardino Mannellini of Mugello, my apprentice through several years. To him in particular I spoke: "Look, my dear Bernardino, that you observe the rules which I have taught you; do your best with all despatch, for the metal will soon be fused. You cannot go wrong; these honest men will get the channels ready; you will easily be able to drive back the two plugs with this pair of iron crooks; and I am sure that my mould will fill miraculously. I feel more ill than I ever did in all my life, and verily believe that it will kill me before a few hours are over." Thus, with despair at heart, I left them, and betook myself to bed.

No sooner had I got to bed, than I ordered my serving-maids to carry food and wine for all the men into the workshop; at the same time I cried: "I shall not be alive to-morrow." They tried to encourage me, arguing that my illness would pass over, since it came from excessive fatigue. In this way I spent two hours battling with the fever, which steadily increased, and calling out continually, "I feel that I am dying." My housekeeper, who was named Mona Fiore de Castel del Rio, a very notable manager and no less warm-hearted, kept chiding me for my discouragement; but, on the other hand, she paid me every kind attention which was possible. However, the sight of my physical pain and moral dejection so affected her, that, in spite of that brave heart of hers, she could not refrain from shedding tears; and yet, so far as she was able, she took good care I should not see them. While I was thus terribly afflicted, I beheld the figure of a man enter my chamber, twisted in his body into the form of a capital S. He raised a lamentable, doleful voice, like one who announces their last hour to men condemned to die upon the scaffold, and spoke these words: "O Benvenuto! your statue is spoiled, and there is no hope whatever of saving it." No sooner had I heard the shriek of that wretch than I gave a howl which might have been heard from the sphere of flame. Jumping from my bed, I seized my clothes and began to dress. The maids, and my lad, and every one who came around to help me, got kicks or blows of the fist, while I kept crying out in lamentation "Ah, traitors! enviers! This is an act of treason, done by malice prepense! But I swear by God that I will sift it to the bottom, and before I die will leave such witness to the world of what I can do as shall make a score of mortals marvel."

When I had got my clothes on, I strode with soul bent on mischief toward the workshop; there I beheld the men, whom I had left erewhile in such high spirits, standing stupefied and downcast. I began at once and spoke: "Up with you! Attend to me! Since you have not been able or willing to obey the directions I gave you, obey me now that I am with you to conduct my work in person. Let no one contradict me, for in cases like this we need the aid of hand and hearing, not of advice." When I had uttered these words, a certain Maestro Alessandro Lastricati broke silence and said: "Look you, Benvenuto, you are going to attempt an enterprise which the laws of art do not sanction, and which cannot succeed." I turned upon him with such fury and so full of mischief, that he and all the rest of them exclaimed with one voice: "On then! Give orders! We will obey your least commands, so long as life is left in us." I believe they spoke thus feelingly because they thought I must fall shortly dead upon the ground. I went immediately to inspect the furnace, and found that the metal was all curdled; an accident which we express by "being caked." I told two of the hands to cross the road, and fetch from the house of the butcher Capretta, a load of young oak-wood, which had lain dry for above a year; this wood had been previously offered me by Madame Ginevra, wife of the said Capretta. So soon as the first armfuls arrived, I began to fill the grate beneath the furnace. Now oakwood of that kind heats more powerfully than any other sort of tree; and for this reason, where a slow fire is wanted, as in the case of gun-foundry, alder or pine is preferred. Accordingly, when the logs took fire, oh! how the cake began to stir beneath that awful heat, to glow and sparkle in a blaze! At the same time I kept stirring up the channels, and sent men upon the roof to stop the conflagration, which had gathered force from the increased combustion in the furnace; also I caused boards, carpets, and other hangings to be set up against the garden, in order to protect us from the violence of the rain.

When I had thus provided against these several disasters, I roared out first to one man and then to another; "Bring this thing here! Take that thing there!" At this crisis, when the whole gang saw the cake was on the point of melting, they did my bidding, each fellow working with the strength of three. I then ordered half a pig of pewter to be brought, which weighed about sixty pounds, and flung it into the middle of the cake inside the furnace. By this means, and by piling on wood and stirring now with pokers and now with iron rods, the curdled mass rapidly began to liquefy. Then, knowing I had brought the dead to life again, against the firm opinion of those ignoramuses, I felt such vigour fill my veins, that all those pains of fever, all those fears of death, were quite forgotten.

All of a sudden an explosion took place, attended by a tremendous flash of flame, as though a thunderbolt had formed and been discharged amongst us. Unwonted and appalling terror astonied every one, and me more even than the rest. When the din was over and the dazzling light extinguished, we began to look each other in the face. Then I discovered that the cap of the furnace had blown up, and the bronze was bubbling over from its source beneath. So I had the mouths of my mould immediately opened, and at the same time drove in the two plugs which kept back the molten metal. But I noticed that it did not flow as rapidly as usual, the reason being probably that the fierce heat of the fire we kindled had consumed its base alloy. Accordingly I sent for all my pewter platters, porringers, and dishes, to the number of some two hundred pieces, and had a portion of them cast, one by one, into the channels, the rest into the furnace. This expedient succeeded, and every one could now perceive that my bronze was in most perfect liquefaction, and my mould was filling;

whereupon they all with heartiness and happy cheer assisted and obeyed by bidding, while I, now here, now there, gave orders, helped with my own hands, and cried aloud: "O God! Thou that by Thy immeasurable power didst rise from the dead, and in Thy glory didst ascent to heaven!". . . even thus in a moment my mould was filled; and seeing my work finished, I fell upon my knees, and with all my heart gave thanks to God.

After all was over, I turned to a plate of salad on a bench there, and ate with hearty appetite, and drank together with the whole crew. Afterwards I retired to bed, healthy and happy, for it was now two hours before morning, and slept as sweetly as though I had never felt a touch of illness. My good housekeeper, without my giving any orders, had prepared a fat capon for my repast. So that, when I rose, about the hour for breaking fast, she presented herself with a smiling countenance, and said: "Oh! is that the man who felt that he was dying? Upon my word, I think the blows and kicks you dealt us last night, when you were so enraged, and had that demon in your body as it seemed, must have frightened away your mortal fever! The fever feared that it might catch it too, as we did!" All my poor household, relieved in like measure from anxiety and overwhelming labour, went at once to buy earthen vessels in order to replace the pewter I had cast away. Then we dined together joyfully; nay, I cannot remember a day in my whole life when I dined with greater gladness or a better appetite.

After our meal I received visits from the several men who had assisted me. They exchanged congratulations, and thanked God for our success, saying they had learned and seen things done which other masters judged impossible. I too grew somewhat glorious; and deeming I had shown myself a man of talent, indulged a boastful humour. So I thrust my hand into my purse, and paid them all to their full satisfaction.

That evil fellow, my mortal foe, Messer Pier Francesco Ricci, major-domo of the Duke, took great pains to find out how the affair had gone. In answer to his questions, the two men whom I suspected of having caked my metal for me, said I was no man, but of a certainty some powerful devil, since I had accomplished what no craft of the art could do; indeed they did not believe a mere ordinary fiend could work such miracles as I in other ways had shown. They exaggerated the whole affair so much, possibly in order to excuse their own part in it, that the major-domo wrote an account to the Duke, who was then in Pisa, far more marvellous and full of thrilling incidents than what they had narrated.

After I had let my statue cool for two whole days, I began to uncover it by slow degrees. The first thing I found was that the head of Medusa had come out most admirably, thanks to the air-vents; for, as I had told the Duke, it is the nature of fire to ascend. Upon advancing farther, I discovered that the other head, that, namely, of Perseus, had succeeded no less admirably; and this astonished me far more, because it is at a considerably lower level than that of the Medusa. Now the mouths of the mould were placed above the head of Perseus and behind his shoulders; and I found that all the bronze my furnace contained had been exhausted in the head of this figure. It was a miracle to observe that not one fragment remained in the orifice of the channel, and that nothing was wanting to the statue. In my great astonishment I seemed to see in this the hand of God arranging and controlling all.

I went on uncovering the statue with success, and ascertained that everything had come out in perfect order, until I reached the foot of the right leg on which the statue rests. There the heel itself was formed, and going farther, I found the foot apparently complete. This gave me great joy on the one side, but was half unwelcome to me on the other, merely because I had told the Duke that it could not come out. However, when I reached the end, it appeared that the toes and a little piece above them were unfinished, so that about half the foot was wanting. Although I knew that this would add a trifle to my labour, I was very well pleased, because I could now prove to the Duke how well I understood my business. It is true that far more of the foot than I expected had been perfectly formed; the reason of this was that, from causes I have recently described, the bronze was hotter than our rules of art prescribe; also that I had been obliged to supplement the alloy with my pewter cups and platters, which no one else, I think, had ever done before.

Having now ascertained how successfully my work had been accomplished, I lost no time in hurrying to Pisa, where I found the Duke. He gave me a most gracious reception, as did also the Duchess; and although the major-domo had informed them of the whole proceedings, their Excellencies deemed my performance far more stupendous and astonishing when they heard the tale from my own mouth.

When I arrived at the foot of Perseus, and said it had not come out perfect, just as I previously warned his Excellency, I saw an expression of wonder pass over his face, while he related to the Duchess how I had predicted this beforehand. Observing the princes to be so well disposed towards me, I begged leave from the Duke to go to Rome. He granted it in most obliging terms, and bade me return as soon as possible to complete his Perseus; giving me letters of recommendation meanwhile to his ambassador, Averardo Serristori. We were then in the first years of Pope Giulio de Monti. . . .

Giorgio Vasari

Giorgio Vasari (1511–1571) was an Italian artist of the Late Renaissance who studied under Michelangelo. He is best known, however, for his classic work on the history of Italian painting, The Lives of the Painters. In this study he sought to trace the renaissance of his country's art, following the long decline which he considered had set in during the time of the Caesars. His method was to describe the life and work of the various Italian artists beginning with Cimabue, whom he considered to be the originator of the new method of design and painting. The following selection is Vasari's life of the artist, Leonardo da Vinci (1452–1519), perhaps the most famous name of the Italian Renaissance. In reading it note (1) Leonardo's personal qualities, (2) the fields of interest to which he turned his talents, (3) the comparison made between the creations of his mind and those of his hands, (4) his relationship with Andrea del Verrocchio, (5) the various technical skills he developed in painting, (6) the incidents connected with the production of the "Last Supper," (7) his contributions to the advance of science, (8) the description of the "Mona Lisa," (9) the relationship between Leonardo and Michelangelo, and (10) Vasari's estimate of Leonardo.

From: THE LIVES OF THE PAINTERS

The heavens often rain down the richest gifts on human beings, naturally, but sometimes with lavish abundance bestow upon a single individual beauty, grace and ability, so that, whatever he does, every action is so divine that he distances all other men, and clearly displays how his genius is the gift of God and not an acquirement of human art.

As translated by A. B. Hinds in Giorgio Vasari, *The Lives of the Painters, Sculptors and Architects,* Everyman's Library, 4 vols., J. M. Dent and Sons, Ltd., London, and E. P. Dutton and Company, New York, 1927, II, 156–168. Courtesy of E. P. Dutton and Company, Inc.

Men saw this in Lionardo da Vinci, whose personal beauty could not be exaggerated, whose every movement was grace itself and whose abilities were so extraordinary that he could readily solve every difficulty. He possessed great personal strength, combined with dexterity, and a spirit and courage invariably royal and magnanimous, and the fame of his name so spread abroad that, not only was he valued in his own day, but his renown has greatly increased since his death.

This marvellous and divine Lionardo was the son of Piero da Vinci. He would have made great profit in learning had he not been so capricious and fickle, for he began to learn many things and then gave them up. Thus in arithmetic, during the few months that he studied it, he made such progress that he frequently confounded his master by continually raising doubts and difficulties. He devoted some time to music, and soon learned to play the lyre, and, being filled with a lofty and delicate spirit, he could sing and improvise divinely with it. Yet though he studied so many different things, he never neglected design and working in relief, those being the things which appealed to his fancy more than any other. When Ser Piero perceived this, and knowing the boy's soaring spirit, he one day took some of his drawings to Andrea del Verrocchio, who was his close friend, and asked his opinion whether Lionardo would do anything by studying design. Andrea was so amazed at these early efforts that he advised Ser Piero to have the boy taught. So it was decided that Lionardo should go to Andrea's workshop. The boy was greatly delighted, and not only practised his profession, but all those in which design has a part. Possessed of a divine and marvellous intellect, and being an excellent geometrician, he not only worked in sculpture, doing some heads of women smiling, which were casts, and children's heads also, executed like a master, but also prepared many architectural plans and elevations, and he was the first, though so young, to propose to canalise the Arno from Pisa to Florence. He made designs for mills, fulling machines, and other engines to go by water, and as painting was to be his profession he studied drawing from life. He would make clay models of figures, draping

them with soft rags dipped in plaster, and would then draw them patiently on thin sheets of cambric or linen, in black and white, with the point of the brush. He did these admirably, as may be seen by specimens in my book of designs. He also drew upon paper so carefully and well that no one has ever equalled him. I have a head in grisaille which is divine. The grace of God so possessed his mind, his memory and intellect formed such a mighty union, and he could so clearly express his ideas in discourse, that he was able to confound the boldest opponents. Every day he made models and designs for the removal of mountains with ease and to pierce them to pass from one place to another, and by means of levers, cranes and winches to raise and draw heavy weights; he devised a method for cleansing ports, and to raise water from great depths, schemes which his brain never ceased to evolve. Many designs for these notions are scattered about, and I have seen numbers of them. He spent much time in making a regular design of a series of knots so that the cord may be traced from one end to the other, the whole filling a round space. There is a fine engraving of this most difficult design, and in the middle are the words: *Leonardus Vinci Academia.* Among these models and designs there was one which he several times showed to many able citizens who then ruled Florence, of a method of raising the church of S. Giovanni and putting steps under it without it falling down. He argued with so much eloquence that it was not until after his departure that they recognised the impossibility of such a feat.

His charming conversation won all hearts, and although he possessed nothing and worked little, he kept servants and horses of which he was very fond, and indeed he loved all animals, and trained them with great kindness and patience. Often, when passing places where birds were sold, he would let them out of their cages and pay the vendor the price asked. Nature had favoured him so greatly that in whatever his brain or mind took up he displayed unrivalled divinity, vigour, vivacity, excellence, beauty and grace. His knowledge of art, indeed, prevented him from finishing many things which he had begun, for he felt that his hand would be unable to realise the perfect creations of his imagination, as his mind formed such difficult, subtle and marvellous conceptions that his hands, skilful as they were, could never have expressed them. His interests were so numerous that his inquiries into natural phenomena led him to study the properties of herbs and to observe the movements of the heavens, the moon's orbit and the progress of the sun.

Lionardo was placed, as I have said, with Andrea del Verrocchio in his childhood by Ser Piero, and his master happened to be painting a picture of St. John baptising Christ. For this Lionardo did an angel holding some clothes, and, although quite young, he made it far better than the figures of Andrea. The latter would never afterwards touch colours, chagrined that a child should know more than he. Lionardo was next employed to draw a cartoon of the Fall [of Man] for a portière in tapestry, to be made in Flanders of gold and silk, to send to the King of Portugal. Here he did a meadow in grisaille, with the lights in white lead, containing much vegetation and some animals, unsurpassable for finish and naturalness. There is a fig-tree, the leaves and branches beautifully foreshortened and executed with such care that the mind is amazed at the amount of patience displayed. There is also a palm-tree, the rotundity of the dates being executed with great and marvellous art, due to the patience and ingenuity of Lionardo. This work was not carried farther, and the cartoon is now in Florence in the fortunate house of Ottaviano de' Medici the Magnificent, to whom it was given not long ago by Lionardo's uncle.

It is said that when Ser Piero was at his country-seat he was requested by a peasant of his estate to get a round piece of wood painted for him at Florence, which he had cut from a fig-tree on his farm. Piero readily consented, as the man was very skilful in catching birds and fishing, and was very useful to him in such matters. Accordingly Piero brought the wood to Florence and asked Lionardo to paint something upon it, without telling him its history. Lionardo, on taking it up to examine it one day, found it warped, badly prepared and rude, but with the help of fire he made it straight, and giving it to a turner, had it rendered soft

and smooth instead of being rough and rude. Then, after preparing the surface in his own way, he began to cast about what he should paint on it, and resolved to do the Medusa head to terrify all beholders. To a room, to which he alone had access, Lionardo took lizards, newts, maggots, snakes, butterflies, locusts, bats, and other animals of the kind, out of which he composed a horrible and terrible monster, of poisonous breath, issuing from a dark and broken rock, belching poison from its open throat, fire from its eyes, and smoke from its nostrils, of truly terrible and horrible aspect. He was so engrossed with the work that he did not notice the terrible stench of the dead animals, being absorbed in his love for art. His father and the peasant no longer asked for the work, and when it was finished Lionardo told his father to send for it when he pleased, as he had done his part. Accordingly Ser Piero went to his rooms one morning to fetch it. When he knocked at the door Lionardo opened it and told him to wait a little, and, returning to his room, put the round panel in the light on his easel, and having arranged the window to make the light dim, he called his father in. Ser Piero, taken unaware, started back, not thinking of the round piece of wood, or that the face which he saw was painted, and was beating a retreat when Lionardo detained him and said, "This work has served its purpose; take it away, then, as it has produced the effect intended." Ser Piero indeed thought it more than miraculous, and he warmly praised Lionardo's idea. He then quietly went and bought another round wheel with a heart transfixed by a dart painted upon it, and gave it to the peasant, who was grateful to Piero all his life. Piero took Lionardo's work secretly to Florence and sold it to some merchants for 100 ducats, and in a short time it came into the hands of the Duke of Milan, who bought it of them for 300 ducats.

Lionardo next did a very excellent Madonna, which afterwards belonged to Pope Clement VII. Among other things it contained a bowl of water with some marvellous flowers, the dew upon them seeming actually to be there, so that they looked more real than reality itself. For his good friend Antonio Segni he drew a Neptune on paper, with so much design and care that he seemed alive. The sea is troubled and his car is drawn by sea-horses, with the sprites, monsters, and south winds and other fine marine creatures. The drawing was given by Antonio's son Fabio to M. Giovanni Gaddi with this epigram:

Pinxit Virgilius Neptunum, pinxit Homerus;
Dum maris undisoni per vada flectit equos
Mente quidem vates illum conspexit uterque
Vincius ast oculis; jureque vincit eos.

Lionardo then had the fancy to paint a picture of the Medusa's head in oils with a garland of snakes about it, the most extraordinary idea imaginable, but as the work required time, it remained unfinished, the fate of nearly all his projects. This is among the treasures in the palace of Duke Cosimo, together with the head of an angel, who is raising an arm in the air, this arm being foreshortened from the shoulder to the elbow, while the other rests on its breast. So marvellous was Lionardo's mind that, desiring to throw his things into greater relief, he endeavoured to obtain greater depths of shadow, and sought the deepest blacks in order to render the lights clearer by contrast. He succeeded so well that his scenes looked rather like representations of the night, there being no bright light, than of the lightness of day, though all was done with the idea of throwing things into greater relief and to find the end and perfection of art.

Lionardo was so delighted when he saw curious heads, whether bearded or hairy, that he would follow about anyone who had thus attracted his attention for a whole day, acquiring such a clear idea of him that when he went home he would draw the head as well as if the man had been present. In this way many heads of men and women came to be drawn, and I have several such pen-and-ink drawings in my book, so often referred to. Among them is the head of Amerigo Vespucci, a fine old man, drawn in carbon, and that of Scaramuccia, the gipsy captain, which afterwards belonged to M. Donato Valdambrini of Arezzo, canon of S. Lorenzo, left to him by Giambullari. He began a picture of the Adoration of the Magi, containing many beautiful things, especially heads, which was in the house of Amerigo Benci, opposite the loggia of the Peruzzi, but

which was left unfinished like his other things.

On the death of Giovan. Galeazzo, Duke of Milan, and the accession of Ludovico Sforza in the same year, 1493, Lionardo was invited to Milan with great ceremony by the duke to play the lyre, in which that prince greatly delighted. Lionardo took his own instrument, made by himself in silver, and shaped like a horse's head, a curious and novel idea to render the harmonies more loud and sonorous, so that he surpassed all the musicians who had assembled there. Besides this he was the best reciter of improvised rhymes of his time. The duke, captivated by Lionardo's conversation and genius, conceived an extraordinary affection for him. He begged him to paint an altar-picture of the Nativity, which was sent by the duke to the emperor. Lionardo then did a Last Supper for the Dominicans at S. Maria delle Grazie in Milan, endowing the heads of the Apostles with such majesty and beauty that he left that of Christ unfinished, feeling that he could not give it that celestial divinity which it demanded. This work left in such a condition has always been held in the greatest veneration by the Milanese and by other foreigners, as Lionardo has seized the moment when the Apostles are anxious to discover who would betray their Master. All their faces are expressive of love, fear, wrath or grief at not being able to grasp the meaning of Christ, in contrast to the obstinacy, hatred and treason of Judas, while the whole work, down to the smallest details displays incredible diligence, even the texture of the tablecloth being clearly visible so that actual cambric would not look more real. It is said that the prior incessantly importuned Lionardo to finish the work, thinking it strange that the artist should pass half a day at a time lost in thought. He would have desired him never to lay down the brush, as if he were digging a garden. Seeing that his importunity produced no effect, he had recourse to the duke, who felt compelled to send for Lionardo to inquire about the work, showing tactfully that he was driven to act by the importunity of the prior. Lionardo, aware of the acuteness and discretion of the duke, talked with him fully about the picture, a thing which he had never done with the prior. He spoke freely of his art, and explained how men of genius really are doing most when they work least, as they are thinking out ideas and perfecting the conceptions, which they subsequently carry out with their hands. He added that there were still two heads to be done, that of Christ, which he would not look for on the earth, and felt unable to conceive the beauty of the celestial grace that must have been incarnate in the divinity. The other head was that of Judas, which also caused him thought, as he did not think he could express the face of a man who could resolve to betray his Master, the Creator of the world, after having received so many benefits. But he was willing in this case to seek no farther, and for lack of a better he would do the head of the importunate and tactless prior. The duke was wonderfully amused, and laughingly declared that he was quite right. Then the poor prior, covered with confusion, went back to his garden and left Lionardo in peace, while the artist indeed finished his Judas, making him a veritable likeness of treason and cruelty. The head of Christ was left unfinished, as I have said. The nobility of this painting, in its composition and the care with which it was finished, induced the King of France to wish to take it home with him. Accordingly he employed architects to frame it in wood and iron, so that it might be transported in safety, without any regard for the cost, so great was his desire. But the king was thwarted by its being done on the wall, and it remained with the Milanese.

While engaged upon the Last Supper, Lionardo painted the portrait of Duke Ludovico, with Maximilian, his eldest son, at the top of this same refectory, where there is a Passion in the old style. At the other end he did the Duchess Beatrice with Francesco, her other son, both of whom afterwards became Dukes of Milan, the portraits being marvellous. While thus employed, Lionardo suggested that the duke should set up a bronze horse of colossal size with the duke upon it in memory of himself. But he began it on such a scale that it could never be done. Such is the malice of man when stirred by envy that there are some who believe that Lionardo, as with so many of his things, began this with no intention of completing it, because its size was so great that extraordinary difficulties might be foreseen in

having it cast all in one piece. And it is probable that many have formed this opinion from the result, since so many of his things have been left unfinished. However, we can readily believe that his great and extraordinary talents suffered a check from being too venturesome, and that the real cause was his endeavour to go on from excellence to excellence and from perfection to perfection. *"Talche l'Opera fusse ritardata dal desio,"* as our Petrarca says. In truth, those who have seen Lionardo's large clay model aver that they never beheld anything finer or more superb. It was preserved until the French came to Milan with King Louis of France, and broke it all to pieces. Thus a small wax model, considered perfect, was lost, as well as a book of the anatomy of horses, done by him. He afterwards devoted even greater care to the study of the anatomy of men, aiding and being aided by M. Marcantonio della Torre, a profound philosopher, who then professed at Padua and wrote upon the subject. I have heard it said that he was one of the first who began to illustrate the science of medicine, by the learning of Galen, and to throw true light upon anatomy, up to that time involved in the thick darkness of ignorance. In this he was marvellously served by the genius, work and hands of Lionardo, who made a book about it with red crayon drawings, outlined with the pen, in which he foreshortened and portrayed with the utmost diligence. He did the skeleton, adding all the nerves and muscles, the first attached to the bone, the others keeping it firm and the third moving, and in the various parts he wrote notes in curious characters, using his left hand, and writing from right to left, so that it cannot be read without practice, and only at a mirror. A great part of the sheets of this anatomy is in the hands of M. Francesco de Melzo, a nobleman of Milan, who was a lovely child in Lionardo's time, who was very fond of him, and being now a handsome and courteous old man, he treasures up these drawings with a portrait of Lionardo. Whoever succeeds in reading these notes of Lionardo will be amazed to find how well that divine spirit has reasoned of the arts, the muscles, the nerves and veins, with the greatest diligence in all things. N. N., a painter of Milan, also possesses some writings of Lionardo, written in the same way, which treat of painting and of the methods of design and colour. Not long ago he came to Florence to see me, wishing to have the work printed. He afterwards went to Rome to put it in hand, but I do not know with what result.

To return to Lionardo's works. When Lionardo was at Milan the King of France came there and desired him to do something curious; accordingly he made a lion whose chest opened after he had walked a few steps, discovering himself to be full of lilies. At Milan Lionardo took Salai of that city as his pupil. This was a graceful and beautiful youth with fine curly hair, in which Lionardo greatly delighted. He taught him many things in art, and some works which are attributed in Milan to Salai were retouched by Lionardo. He returned to Florence, where he found that the Servite friars had allotted to Filippino the picture of the high altar of the Nunziata. At this Lionardo declared that he should like to have done a similar thing. Filippino heard this, and being very courteous, he withdrew. The friars, wishing Lionardo to paint it, brought him to their house, paying all his expenses and those of his household. He kept them like this for a long time, but never began anything. At length he drew a cartoon of the Virgin and St. Anne with a Christ, which not only filled every artist with wonder, but, when it was finished and set up in the room, men and women, young and old, flocked to see it for two days, as if it had been a festival, and they marvelled exceedingly. The face of the Virgin displays all the simplicity and beauty which can shed grace on the Mother of God, showing the modesty and humility of a Virgin contentedly happy, in seeing the beauty of her Son, whom she tenderly holds in her lap. As she regards it the little St. John at her feet is caressing a lamb, while St. Anne smiles in her great joy at seeing her earthly progeny become divine, a conception worthy of the great intellect and genius of Lionardo. This cartoon, as will be said below, afterwards went to France. He drew Ginevra, the wife of Amerigo Benci, a beautiful portrait, and then abandoned the work of the friars, who recalled Filippino, though he was prevented from finishing it by death.

For Francesco del Giocondo Lionardo undertook the portrait of Mona Lisa, his wife, and left it incomplete after working at it for four years. This work is now in the possession of Francis, King of France, at Fontainebleau. This head is an extraordinary example of how art can imitate Nature, because here we have all the details painted with great subtlety. The eyes possess that moist lustre which is constantly seen in life, and about them are those livid reds and hair which cannot be rendered without the utmost delicacy. The lids could not be more natural, for the way in which the hairs issue from the skin, here thick and there scanty, and following the pores of the skin. The nose possesses the fine delicate reddish apertures seen in life. The opening of the mouth, with its red ends, and the scarlet cheeks seem not colour but living flesh. To look closely at her throat you might imagine that the pulse was beating. Indeed, we may say that this was painted in a manner to cause the boldest artists to despair. Mona Lisa was very beautiful, and while Lionardo was drawing her portrait he engaged people to play and sing, and jesters to keep her merry, and remove that melancholy which painting usually gives to portraits. This figure of Lionardo's has such a pleasant smile that it seemed rather divine than human, and was considered marvellous, an exact copy of Nature.

The fame of this divine artist grew to such a pitch by the excellence of his works that all who delighted in the arts and the whole city wished him to leave some memorial, and they endeavoured to think of some noteworthy decorative work through which the state might be adorned and honoured by the genius, grace and judgment characteristic of his work. The great hall of the council was being rebuilt under the direction of Giuliano da S. Gallo, Simone Pollajuolo called Cronaca, Michelagnolo Buonarroti and Baccio d'Agnolo, by the judgment and advice of the gonfaloniere and leading citizens, as will be related at greater length in another place, and being finished with great speed, it was ordained by public decree that Lionardo should be employed to paint some fine work. Thus the hall was allotted to him by Piero Soderini, then gonfaloniere of justice. Lionardo began by drawing a cartoon at the hall of the Pope, a place in S. Maria Novella, containing the story of Niccolo Piccinino, captain of Duke Filippo of Milan. Here he designed a group of horsemen fighting for a standard, a masterly work on account of his treatment of the fight, displaying the wrath, anger and vindictiveness of men and horses; two of the latter, with their front legs involved, are waging war with their teeth no less fiercely than their riders are fighting for the standard. One soldier, putting his horse to the gallop, has turned round and, grasping the staff of the standard, is endeavouring by main force to wrench it from the hands of four others, while two are defending it, trying to cut the staff with their swords; an old soldier in a red cap has a hand on the staff, as he cries out, and holds a scimitar in the other and threatens to cut off both hands of the two, who are grinding their teeth and making every effort to defend their banner. On the ground, between the legs of the horses, are two foreshortened figures who are fighting together, while a soldier lying prone has another over him who is raising his arm as high as he can to run his dagger with his utmost strength into his adversary's throat; the latter, whose legs and arms are helpless, does what he can to escape death. The manifold designs Lionardo made for the costumes of his soldiers defy description, not to speak of the scimitars and other ornaments, and his incredible mastery of form and line in dealing with horses, which he made better than any other master, with their powerful muscles and graceful beauty. It is said that for designing the cartoon he made an ingenious scaffolding which rose higher when pressed together and broadened out when lowered. Thinking that he could paint on the wall in oils, he made a composition so thick for laying on the wall that when he continued his painting it began to run and spoil what had been begun, so that in a short time he was forced to abandon it.

Lionardo had a high spirit and was most generous in every action. It is said that when he went to the bank for the monthly provision that he used to receive from Piero Soderini, the cashier wanted to give him some rolls of farthings, but he would not take them, saying that he was not a painter for farthings. Learning that Piero Soderini accused him of deceiving him and that murmurs rose against him,

Lionardo with the help of his friends collected the money and took it back, but Piero would not accept it. He went to Rome with Duke Giuliano de' Medici on the election of Leo X., who studied philosophy and especially alchemy. On the way he made a paste with wax and constructed hollow animals which flew in the air when blown up, but fell when the wind ceased. On a curious lizard found by the vine-dresser of Belvedere he fastened scales taken from other lizards, dipped in quicksilver, which trembled as it moved, and after giving it eyes, a horn and a beard, he tamed it and kept it in a box. All the friends to whom he showed it ran away terrified. He would often dry and purge the guts of a wether and make them so small that they might be held in the palm of the hand. In another room he kept a pair of smith's bellows, and with these he would blow out one of the guts until it filled the room, which was a large one, forcing anyone there to take refuge in a corner. The fact that it had occupied such a little space at first only added to the wonder. He perpetrated many such follies, studied mirrors and made curious experiments to find oil for painting and varnish to preserve the work done. At this time he did a small picture for M. Baldassare Turini of Pescia, the datary of Leo, of the Virgin and Child, with infinite diligence and art. But to-day it is much spoiled either by neglect or because of his numerous fanciful mixtures and the colouring. In another picture he represented a little child, marvellously beautiful and graceful, both works being now at Pescia in the possession of M. Giulio Turini. It is said that, on being commissioned by the Pope to do a work, he straightway began to distil oils and herbs to make the varnish, which induced Pope Leo to say: "This man will never do anything, for he begins to think of the end before the beginning!"

There was no love lost between him and Michelagnolo Buonarroti, so that the latter left Florence owing to their rivalry, Duke Giuliano excusing him by saying that he was summoned by the Pope to do the façade of S. Lorenzo. When Lionardo heard this, he left for France, where the king had heard of his works and wanted him to do a cartoon of St. Anne in colours. But Lionardo, as was his wont, gave him nothing but words for a long time. At length, having become old, he lay sick for many months, and seeing himself near death, he desired to occupy himself with the truths of the Catholic Faith and the holy Christian religion. Then, having confessed and shown his penitence with much lamentation, he devoutly took the Sacrament out of his bed, supported by his friends and servants, as he could not stand. The king arriving, for he would often pay him friendly visits, he sat up in bed from respect, and related the circumstances of his sickness, showing how greatly he had offended God and man in not having worked in his art as he ought. He was then seized with a paroxysm, the harbinger of death, so that the king rose and took his head to assist him and show him favour as well as to alleviate the pain. Lionardo's divine spirit, then recognising that he could not enjoy a greater honour, expired in the king's arms, at the age of seventy-five. The loss of Lionardo caused exceptional grief to those who had known him, because there never was a man who did so much honour to painting. By the splendour of his magnificent mien he comforted every sad soul, and his eloquence could turn men to either side of a question. His personal strength was prodigious, and with his right hand he could bend the clapper of a knocker or a horseshoe as if they had been of lead. His liberality warmed the hearts of all his friends, both rich and poor, if they possessed talent and ability. His presence adorned and honoured the most wretched and bare apartment. Thus Florence received a great gift in the birth of Lionardo, and its loss

in his death was immeasurable. To the art of painting he added a type of darkness to the style of colouring in oils whereby the moderns have imparted great vigour and relief to their figures. He proved his powers in statuary in three figures in bronze over the door of S. Giovanni on the north side. They were executed by Gio. Francesco Rustici, but under Lionardo's direction, and are the finest casts for design and general perfection that have as yet been seen. To Lionardo we owe a greater perfection in the anatomy of horses and men. Thus, by his many surpassing gifts, even though he talked much more about his works than he actually achieved, his name and fame will never be extinguished. Therefore M. Gio. Battista Strozzi wrote thus in his praise:

> *Vince costui pur solo*
> *Tutti altri, e vince Fidia e vince Apelle,*
> *E tutto il lor vittorioso stuolo.*

Gio. Antonio Boltraffio of Milan was a pupil of Lionardo, and a very skilful and intelligent man, who in 1500 painted a panel in oils in the church of the Misericordia, outside Bologna, with the Virgin and Child, St. John the Baptist, and a nude St. Sebastian, including a portrait of the donor kneeling. To this fine work he signed his name, adding that he was a pupil of Lionardo. He did other works at Milan and elsewhere, but the one I have just referred to is the best. Marco Uggioni, another pupil, painted the Death of the Virgin and the Marriage of Cana in Galilee in S. Maria della Pace.

François Rabelais

François Rabelais (1490–1553), a contemporary of Cellini, was a Frenchman who gave expression to an aspect of the Renaissance which was particularly characteristic of the movement in the north. Although he studied for the priesthood, he gave up a career in the church in order to gain the intellectual and personal freedom he so passionately desired. While still a clergyman he had displayed a deep interest in classical writings, particularly those of the Greeks, and this humanistic interest may have been the determining factor in his decision to return to secular life.

He bitterly resented both the asceticism of the Catholic clergy and the puritanism of the Calvinists, for he wanted to live life fully, with the body as well as with the mind. He used his ability as a writer to satirize some of the things he disliked in the world about him. Gargantua and Pantagruel were members of an imaginary dynasty of giant kings, and around these characters Rabelais has woven his story of satire. In reading this selection note (1) the type of personnel admitted to the abbey, (2) the description of the edifice, (3) the inscription on the great gate, (4) the activities pursued by the inmates, (5) the apparel of the nuns, (6) the rule of the order, (7) the discussion of the effects of restraint, and (8) the relationship between the training in the abbey and life in the secular world.

From: GARGANTUA AND PANTAGRUEL

HOW GARGANTUA CAUSED TO BE BUILT FOR THE MONK THE ABBEY OF THELEME

There was left only the monk to provide for, whom Gargantua would have made Abbot of Sevillé, but he refused it. He would have given him the Abbey of Bourgueil, or of Sanct Florent which was better, or both, if it pleased him; but the monk gave him a very peremptory answer, that he would never take upon him the charge nor government of monks. For how shall I be able, said he, to rule over others, that have not full power and command over myself? If you think I have done you, or may hereafter do any acceptable service, give me leave to found an abbey after my own mind and fancy. The notion pleased Gargantua very well, who thereupon offered him all the country of Theleme by the river of Loire till within two leagues of the great forest of Port-Huaulx. The monk then requested Gargantua to institute his religious order contrary to all others. First, then, said Gargantua, you must not build a wall about your convent, for all other abbeys are strongly walled and mured about. See, said the monk, and not without cause (seeing wall and mur signify but one and the same thing); where there is mur before and mur behind, there is store of murmur, envy, and mutual conspiracy. Moreover, seeing there are certain convents in the world whereof the custom is, if any woman come in, I mean chaste and honest women, they immediately sweep the ground which they have trod upon; therefore was it ordained, that if any man or woman entered into religious orders should by chance come within this new abbey, all the rooms should be thoroughly washed and cleansed through which they had passed. And because in all other monasteries and nunneries all is compassed, limited and regulated by hours, it was decreed that in this new structure there should be neither clock nor dial, but that according to the opportunities and incident occasions, all their hours should be disposed of; for, said Gargantua, the greatest loss of time that I know is to count the hours. What good comes of it? Nor can there be any greater dotage in the world than for one to guide and direct his courses by the sound of a bell, and not by his own judgment and discretion.

Item, Because at that time they put no women into nunneries but such as were either purblind, blinkards, lame, crooked, ill-favoured, misshapen, fools, senseless, spoiled, or corrupt; nor encloistered any men but those that were either sickly, subject to defluxions, ill-bred louts, simple sots, or peevish trouble-houses. But to the purpose, said the monk. A woman that is neither fair nor good, to what use serves she? To make a nun of, said Gar-

François Rabelais, *Gargantua and Pantagruel*, edited by Donald Douglas, The Modern Library, New York, 1928, 131–147. Courtesy of Random House, Inc.

gantua. Yea, said the monk, and to make shirts and smocks. Therefore was it ordained that into this religious order should be admitted no women that were not fair, well-featured, and of a sweet disposition; nor men that were not comely, personable, and well conditioned.

Item, Because in the convents of women, men come not but underhand, privily, and by stealth, it was therefore enacted that in this house there shall be no women in case there be not men, nor men in case there be not women.

Item, Because both men and women that are received into religious orders after the expiring of their noviciate or probation year were constrained and forced perpetually to stay there all the days of their life, it was therefore ordered that all whatever, men or women, admitted within this abbey, should have full leave to depart with peace and contentment whensoever it should seem good to them so to do.

Item, For that the religious men and women did ordinarily make three vows, to wit, those of chastity, poverty and obedience, it was therefore constituted and appointed that in this convent they might be honourably married, that they might be rich, and live at liberty. In regard of the legitimate time of the persons to be initiated, and years under and above which they were not capable of reception, the women were to be admitted from ten till fifteen, and the men from twelve till eighteen.

HOW THE ABBEY
OF THE THELEMITES
WAS BUILT AND ENDOWED

For the fabric and furniture of the abbey Gargantua caused to be delivered out in ready money seven and twenty hundred thousand, eight hundred and one and thirty of those golden rams of Berry which have a sheep stamped on the one side and a flowered cross on the other; and for every year, until the whole work was completed, he allotted three score nine thousand crowns of the sun, and as many of the seven stars, to be charged all upon the receipt of the custom. For the foundation and maintenance thereof for ever, he settled a perpetual free-farm-rent of three and twenty hundred, three score and nine thousand, five hundred and fourteen rose nobles, exempted from all homage, fealty, service, or burden whatsoever, and payable every year at the gate of the abbey; and of this by letters patent passed a very good grant. The architecture was in a figure hexagonal, and in such a fashion that in every one of the six corners there was built a great round tower of threescore foot in diameter, and were all of a like form and bigness. Upon the north side ran along the river of Loire, on the bank whereof was situated the tower called Arctic. Going towards the east, there was another called Calaer,—the next following Anatole,—the next Mesembrine, —the next Hesperia, and the last Criere. Every tower was distant from other the space of three hundred and twelve paces. The whole edifice was everywhere six storeys high, reckoning the cellars underground for one. The second was arched after the fashion of a basket-handle; the rest were ceiled with pure wainscot, flourished with Flanders fretwork, in the form of the foot of a lamp, and covered above with fine slates, with an endorsement of lead, carrying the antique figures of little puppets and animals of all sorts, notably well suited to one another, and gilt, together with the gutters, which, jutting without the walls from betwixt the crossbars in a diagonal figure, painted with gold and azure, reached to the very ground, where they ended into great conduit-pipes, which carried all away into the river from under the house.

This same building was a hundred times more sumptuous and magnificent than ever was Bonnivet, Chambourg, or Chantilly; for there were in it nine thousand, three hundred and two and thirty chambers, every one whereof had a withdrawing room, a handsome closet, a wardrobe, an oratory, and neat passage, leading into a great and spacious hall. Between every tower in the midst of the said body of building there was a pair of winding, such as we now call lantern, stairs, whereof the steps were part of porphyry, which is a dark red marble spotted with white, part of Numidian stone, which is a kind of yellowishly-streaked marble upon various colours and part of serpentine marble, with light spots on a dark green ground, each of those steps being two and twenty foot in length and three fingers thick, and the just number of twelve betwixt every rest, or, as we now term it, landing-place. In every resting-place were two fair antique arches where the light came in: and by those they went into a cabinet, made even with and of the breadth of the said winding, and the reascending above the roofs of the house ended conically in a pavilion. By that vise or winding they entered on every side into a great hall, and from the halls into the chambers. From the Arctic tower unto the Criere were the fair great libraries in Greek, Latin, Hebrew, French, Italian, and Spanish, respectively distributed in their several cantons, according to the diversity of these languages. In the midst there was a wonderful scalier or winding-stair, the entry whereof was without the house, in a vault or arch six fathom broad. It was made in such symmetry and largeness that six men-at-arms with their lances in their rests might together in a breast ride all up to the very top of all the palace. From the tower Anatole to the Mesembrine were fair spacious galleries, all coloured over and painted with the ancient prowesses, histories, and descriptions of the world. In the midst thereof there was likewise such another ascent and gate as we said there was on the river-side. Upon that gate was written in great antique letters that which followeth.

THE INSCRIPTION SET UPON THE GREAT GATE OF THELEME

Here enter not vile bigots, hypocrites,
Externally devoted apes, base snites,
Puffed-up, wry-necked beasts, worse than the
    Huns,
Or Ostrogoths, forerunners of baboons:
Cursed snakes, dissembled varlets, seeming
    sancts,
Slipshod cafards, beggars pretending wants,
Fat chuffcats, smell-feast knockers, doltish
    gulls,
Out-strouting cluster-fists, contentious bulls,
Fomenters of divisions and debates,
Elsewhere, not here, make sale of your deceits.
        Your filthy trumperies
        Stuffed with pernicious lies
            (Not worth a bubble),
            Would do but trouble

            Our earthly paradise,
            Your filthy trumperies.
Here enter not attorneys, barristers,
Nor bridle-champing law practitioners:
Clerks, commissaries, scribes, nor pharisees,
Wilful disturbers of the people's ease:
Judges, destroyers, with an unjust breath,
Of honest men, like dogs, even unto death.
Your salary is at the gibbet-foot:
Go drink there! for we do not here fly out
On those excessive courses, which may draw
A waiting on your courts by suits in law.
        Lawsuits, debates, and wrangling
        Hence are exiled, and jangling.
            Here we are very
            Frolic and merry,
        And free from all entangling,
        Lawsuits, debates, and wrangling.
Here enter not base pinching usurers,
Pelf-lickers, everlasting gatherers,
Gold-graspers, coin-gripers, gulpers of mists,
Niggish deformed sots, who, though your
    chests
Vast sums of money should to you afford,
Would ne'ertheless add more unto that hoard,
And yet not be content,—you clunchfist das-
    tards,
Insatiable fiends, and Pluto's bastards,
Greedy devourers, chichy sneakbill rogues,
Hell-mastiffs gnaw your bones, you ravenous
    dogs.
        You beastly-looking fellows,
        Reason doth plainly tell us
            That we should not
            To you allot
        Room here, but at the gallows,
        You beastly-looking fellows.
Here enter not fond makers of demurs
In love adventures, peevish, jealous curs,
Sad pensive dotards, raisers of garboils,
Hags, goblins, ghosts, firebrands of household
    broils,
Nor drunkards, liars, cowards, cheaters, clowns,
Thieves, cannibals, faces o'ercast with frowns,
Nor lazy slugs, envious, covetous,
Nor blockish, cruel, nor too credulous,—
Here mangy, pocky folks shall have no place,
No ugly lusks, nor persons of disgrace.
        Grace, honour, praise, delight,
        Here sojourn day and night.
            Sound bodies lined
            With a good mind,

Do here pursue with might
Grace, honour, praise, delight.
Here enter you and welcome from our hearts,
All noble sparks endowed with gallant parts.
This is the glorious place which bravely shall
Afford wherewith to entertain you all.
Were you a thousand, here you shall not
    want
For anything; for what you'll ask we'll grant.
Stay here you lively, jovial, handsome, brisk,
Gay, witty, frolic, cheerful, merry, frisk,
Spruce, jocund, courteous, furtherers of trades,
And in a word, all worthy, gentle blades.

    Blades of heroic breasts
    Shall taste here of the feasts,
        Both privily
        And civilly
    Of the celestial guests,
    Blades of heroic breasts.

Here enter you, pure, honest, faithful, true
Expounders of the Scriptures old and new.
Whose glosses do not blind our reason, but
Make it to see the clearer, and who shut
Its passages from hatred, avarice,
Pride, factions, covenants, and all sort of vice.
Come, settle here a charitable faith,
Which neighbourly affection nourisheth.
And whose light chaseth all corrupters hence,
Of the blest word, from the aforesaid sense.

    The holy sacred Word,
    May it always afford
        T' us all in common,
        Both man and woman,
    A spiritual shield and sword,
    The holy sacred Word.

Here enter you all ladies of high birth,
Delicious, stately, charming, full of mirth,
Ingenious, lovely, miniard, proper, fair,
Magnetic, graceful, splendid, pleasant, rare,
Obliging, sprightly, virtuous, young, salacious,
Kind, neat, quick, feat, bright, compt, ripe,
    choice, dear, precious,
Alluring, courtly, comely, fine, complete,
Wise, personable, ravishing and sweet,
Come joys enjoy. The Lord celestial
Hath given enough wherewith to please us all.

    Gold give us, God forgive us,
    And from all woes relieve us;
        That we the treasure
        May reap of pleasure,
    And shun whate'er is grievous,
    Gold give us, God forgive us.

WHAT MANNER OF DWELLING THE THELEMITES HAD

In the middle of the lower court there was a stately fountain of fair alabaster. Upon the top thereof stood the three graces, with their cornucopias, or horns of abundance, and did jet out the water at their breasts, mouth, ears, eyes, and other open passages of the body. The inside of the buildings in this lower court stood upon great pillars of chalcedony stone, and porphyry marble, made archways after a goodly antique fashion. Within those were spacious galleries, long and large, adorned with curious pictures, the horns of bucks and unicorns: with rhinoceroses, water horses called hippopotamus, the teeth and tusks of elephants, and other things well worth the beholding. The lodging of the ladies, for so we may call those gallant women, took up all from the tower Arctic unto the gate Mesembrine. The men possessed the rest. Before the said lodging of the ladies, that they might have their recreation, between the first two towers, on the outside, were placed the tilt-yard, the barriers of lists for tournaments, the hippodrome or riding-court, the theatre or public playhouse, and natatory or place to swim in, with most admirable baths in three stages, situated above one another, well furnished with all necessary accommodation, and store of myrtle-water. By the riverside was the fair garden of pleasure, and in the midst of that the glorious labyrinth. Between the two other towers were the courts for the tennis and the balloon. Towards the tower Criere stood the orchard, full of all fruit-trees, set and ranged in a quincuncial order. At the end of that was the great park, abounding with all sorts of venison. Betwixt the third couple of towers were the butts and marks for shooting with a snap-work gun, an ordinary bow for common archery, or with a crossbow. The office-houses were without the tower Hesperia, of one storey high. The stables were beyond the offices, and before them stood the falconry, managed by ostrich-keepers and falconers very expert in the art, and it was yearly supplied and furnished by the Canadians, Venetians, Sarmates, now called Muscoviters, with all sorts of most excellent hawks, eagles, gerfalcons, goshawks, sacres, laniers, falcons, sparrowhawks, marlins, and all other kinds of them, so gentle and perfectly well manned, that, flying of themselves sometimes from the castle for their own disport, they would not fail to catch whatever they encountered. The venery, where the beagles and hounds were kept, was a little farther off, drawing towards the park.

All the halls, chambers and closets or cabinets were richly hung with tapestry and hangings of divers sorts, according to the variety of the seasons of the year. All the pavements and floors were covered with green cloth. The beds were all embroidered. In every back-chamber or withdrawing room there was a looking-glass of pure crystal set in a frame of fine gold, garnished all about with pearls, and was of such greatness that it would represent to the full the whole lineaments and proportion of the person that stood before it. At the going out of the halls which belong to the ladies' lodgings were the perfumers and trimmers through whose hands the gallants passed when they were to visit the ladies. Those sweet artificers did every morning furnish the ladies' chambers with the spirit of roses, orange-flower water, and angelica; and to each of them gave a little precious casket, vapouring forth the most odoriferous exhalations of the choicest aromatical scents.

HOW THE MEN AND WOMEN OF THE RELIGIOUS ORDER OF THELEME WERE APPARELLED

The ladies at the foundation of this order were apparelled after their own pleasure and liking; but, since that of their own accord and freewill they have reformed themselves, their accoutrements were in manner as followeth. They wore stockings of scarlet crimson, or ingrained purple dye, which reached just three inches above the knee, having a list beautified with exquisite embroideries and rare incisions of the cutter's art. The garters were of the colour of their bracelets, and circled the knee a little, both over and under. Their shoes, pumps and slippers, were either of red, violet, or crimson-velvet, pinked and jagged like lobster's wattles.

Next to their smock they put on the pretty kirtle or vasquin of pure silk camblet: above that went the taffety or tabby farthingale, of white, red, tawny, grey, or of any other colour. Above this taffety petticoat they had another of cloth of tissue or brocade, embroidered with fine gold and interlaced with needlework, or as they thought good, and according to the temperature and disposition of the weather, had their upper coats of satin, damask or velvet, and these either orange, tawny, green, ash-coloured, blue, yellow, bright-red, crimson or white, and so forth; or had them a cloth of gold, cloth of silver, or some other choice stuff, enriched with purple, or embroidered according to the dignity of the festival days and times wherein they wore them.

Their gowns being still correspondent to the season, were either of cloth of gold frizzled with a silver raised work; of red satin covered with gold purple; of tabby, or taffety, white, blue, black, tawny, &c., of silk serge, silk camblet, velvet, cloth of silver, silver tissue, cloth of gold, gold wire, figured velvet, or figured satin, tinselled and overcast with golden threads, in divers variously purfled draughts.

In summer, some days, instead of gowns, they wore light handsome mantles, made either of the stuff of the aforesaid attire, or like Moresco rugs, of violet velvet frizzled, with a raised work of gold upon silver purl, or with a knotted cord-work of gold embroidery, everywhere garnished with little Indian pearls. They always carried a fair pannache, or plume of feathers, of the colour of their muff, bravely adorned and tricked out with glistening spangles of gold. In the winter time they had their taffety gowns of all colours, as above-named, and those lined with rich furrings of hind-wolves, or speckled-lynxes, black-spotted weasels, martlet skins of Calabria, sables and other costly furs of an inestimable value. Their beads, rings, bracelets, collars, carcanets, and neck-chains were all of precious stones, such as carbuncles, rubies, baleus, diamonds, sapphires, emeralds, turquoises, garnets, agates, beryls, and excellent margarites. Their head-dressing also varied with the season of the year, according to which they decked themselves. In winter, it was of the French fashion; in the spring, of the Spanish; in summer, of the fashion of Tuscany, except only upon the holy days and Sundays, at which times they were accoutred in the French mode, because they accounted it more honourable and better befitting the garb of a matronal pudicity.

The men were apparelled after their fashion. Their stockings were of tamine or of cloth serge, of white, black, scarlet, or some other ingrained colour. Their breeches were of velvet, of the same colour with their stockings, or very near, embroidered and cut according to their fancy. Their doublet was of cloth of gold, of cloth of silver, of velvet, satin, damask, taffeties, &c., of the same colours, cut, embroidered, and suitably trimmed up in perfection. The points were of silk of the same colours; the tags were of gold well enamelled. Their coats and jerkins were of cloth of gold, cloth of silver, gold tissue or velvet embroidered, as they thought fit. Their gowns were every whit as costly as those of the ladies. Their girdles were of silk, of the colour of their doublets. Every one had a gallant sword by his side, the hilt and the handle whereof were gilt, and the scabbard of velvet, of the colour of his breeches, with a chape of gold, and pure goldsmith's work. The dagger was of the same. Their caps or bonnets were of black velvet, adorned with jewels and buttons of gold. Upon that they wore a white plume, most prettily and minion-like parted by so many rows of gold spangles, at the end whereof hung dangling in a more sparkling resplendency, fair rubies, emeralds, diamonds, &c., but there was such a sympathy betwixt the gallants and the ladies, that every day they were apparelled in the same livery. And that they might not miss, there were certain gentlemen appointed to tell the youths every morning what vestments the ladies would on that day wear: for all was done according to the pleasure of the ladies. In these so handsome clothes, and habiliments so rich, think not that either one or other of either sex did waste any time at all; for the masters of the wardrobes had all their raiments and apparel so ready for every morning, and the chamber-ladies so well skilled, that in a trice they would be dressed, and completely in their clothes from head to foot. And to have those accoutrements with the more conveniency, there was about the wood of Theleme, a row of houses of the extent of half a league, very neat and cleanly, wherein dwelt the gold-smiths, lapidaries, jewellers, embroiderers, tailors, gold-drawers, velvet-weavers, tapestry-makers and upholsterers, who wrought there every one in his own trade, and all for the aforesaid jolly friars and nuns of the new stamp. They were furnished with matter and stuff from the hands of the Lord Nausiclete, who every year brought them seven ships from the Perlas and Cannibal Islands, laden with ingots of gold, with raw silk, with pearls and precious stones. And if any margarites, called unions, began to grow old and lose somewhat of their natural whiteness and lustre, those with their art they did renew, by tendering them to eat to some pretty cocks, as they use to give casting unto hawks.

HOW THE THELEMITES WERE GOVERNED, AND OF THEIR MANNER OF LIVING

All their life was spent not in laws, statutes, or rules, but according to their own free will and pleasure. They rose out of their beds when they thought good; they did eat, drink, labour, sleep, when they had a mind to it, and were disposed for it. None did awake them, none did offer to constrain them to eat, drink, nor to do any other thing; for so had Gargantua established it. In all their rule and strictest tie of their order there was but this one clause to be observed,

DO WHAT THOU WILT.

Because men that are free, well-born, well-bred, and conversant in honest companies, have naturally an instinct and spur that prompteth them unto virtuous actions, and withdraws them from vice, which is called honour. Those same men, when by base subjection and constraint, they are brought under and kept down, turn aside from that noble disposition by which they formerly were inclined to virtue, to shake off and break that bond of servitude wherein they are so tyrannously enslaved; for it is agreeable with the nature of man to long after things forbidden and to desire what is denied us.

By this liberty they entered into a very laudable emulation to do all of them what they saw did please one. If any of the gallants or ladies should say, Let us drink, they would all drink. If any one of them said, Let us play, they all played. If one said, Let us go a-walking into the fields, they went all. If it were to go a-hawking or a-hunting, the ladies mounted upon dainty well-paced nags, seated in a stately palfrey saddle, carried on their lovely fists, miniardly begloved every one of them, either a sparrowhawk or a laneret or a marlin, and the young gallants carried the other kinds of hawks. So nobly were they taught, that there was neither he nor she amongst them but could read, write, sing, play upon several musical instruments, speak five or six several languages, and compose in them all very quaintly, both in verse and prose. Never were seen so valiant knights, so noble and worthy, so dextrous and skilful both on foot and ahorseback, more brisk and lively, more nimble and quick, or better handling all manner of weapons than were there. Never were seen ladies so proper and handsome, so miniard and dainty, less forward or more ready with their hand and with their needle in every honest and free action belonging to that sex, than were there. For this reason, when the time came that any man of the said abbey, either at the request of his parents, or for some other cause, had a mind to go out of it, he carried along with him one of the ladies, namely, her whom he had before that chosen for his mistress, and [they] were married together. And if they had formerly in Theleme lived in good devotion and amity, and did continue therein and increase it to a greater height in their state of matrimony; and did entertain that mutual love till the very last day of their life, in no less vigour and fervency than at the very day of their wedding.

Desiderius Erasmus

Desiderius Erasmus (1466–1536), a Dutch scholar with a vital interest in the Greek classics, represented the more intellectual phases of the Renaissance and the break from medieval scholaticism. Being a sincere Catholic priest, deeply interested in theology, he translated and edited, in true humanist tradition, the New Testament from the Greek, thereby developing further his erudite theological background. Using the knowledge acquired from his critical study of the early Christian record, he found much to condemn in the fruitless writings of the theologians and in the artificial ritualism of institutionalized Christianity. He considered that both of these developments had corrupted the simple teachings of Jesus and in his writings sought to expose the errors into which he considered the Church had fallen. In Praise of Folly is a delightfully straightforward satire in which Erasmus used a feminine personality, Folly, to expose many of the weaknesses and contradictions in the lives of the men of his time. In reading the selections note (1) the discussion of the efficacy of saints, (2) the observations on indulgences and the character of those who purchased them, (3) the part played by priests in popularizing saints and indulgences, (4) the value of the disputations carried on by the scholastic theologians, and (5) the activity of monks in relation to the teachings of Christ.

James Harvey Robinson, *Readings in European History*. . . ., 2 vols., Ginn and Company, Boston, 1906, II, 41–46. Courtesy of Ginn and Company.

From: IN PRAISE OF FOLLY

To this same class of fools belong those who beguile themselves with the silly but pleasing notion that if they look upon a picture or image of St. Christopher,—that huge Polyphemus,—they will not die that day; or that he who salutes an image of St. Barbara with the proper form of address will come back from battle safe; or that one who approaches St. Erasmus on certain days with wax candles and prayers will soon be rich. They have found a new Hercules in St. George,—a sort of second Hippolytus. They seem to adore even his horse, which is scrupulously decked out with gorgeous trappings, and additional offerings are constantly being made in the hope of gaining new favors. His bronze helmet one would think half divine, the way people swear by it.

And what shall I say of those who comfortably delude themselves with imaginary pardons for their sins, and who measure the time in purgatory with an hour glass into years, months, days, hours, with all the precision of a mathematical table? There are plenty, too, who, relying upon certain magical little certificates and prayers,—which some pious imposter devised either in fun or for the benefit of his pocket,—believe that they may procure riches, honor, future happiness, health, perpetual prosperity, long life, a lusty old age,—nay, in the end, a seat at the right hand of Christ in heaven; but as for this last, it matters not how long it be deferred: they will content themselves with the joys of heaven only when they must finally surrender the pleasures of this world, to which they lovingly cling.

The trader, the soldier, and the judge think that they can clean up the Augean stable of a lifetime, once for all, by sacrificing a single coin from their ill-gotten gains. They flatter themselves that all sorts of perjury, debauchery, drunkenness, quarrels, bloodshed, imposture, perfidy, and treason can be compounded for by contract and so adjusted that, having paid off their arrears, they can begin a new score.

How foolish, or rather how happy, are those who promise themselves more than supernal happiness if they repeat the verses of the seven holy psalms! Those magical lines are supposed to have been taught to St. Bernard by a demon, who seems to have been a wag; but he was not very clever, and, poor fellow, was frustrated in his attempt to deceive the saint. These silly things which even I, Folly, am almost ashamed of, are approved not only by the common herd but even by the teachers of religion.

How foolish, too, for religious bodies each to give preference to its particular guardian saint! Nay, each saint has his particular office allotted him, and is addressed each in his special way: this one is called upon to alleviate toothache; that, to aid in childbirth; others, to restore a stolen article, bring rescue to the shipwrecked, or protect cattle,—and so on with the rest, who are much too numerous to mention. A few indeed among the saints are good in more than one emergency, especially the Holy Virgin, to whom the common man now attributes almost more than to her Son.

And for what, after all, do men petition the saints except for foolish things? Look at the votive offerings which cover the walls of certain churches and with which you see even the ceiling filled; do you find any one who expresses his gratitude that he has escaped Folly or because he has become a whit wiser? One perhaps was saved from drowning, another recovered when he had been run through by his enemy; another, while his fellows were fighting, ran away with expedition and success; another, on the point of being hanged, escaped, through the aid of some saintly friend of thieves, and lived to relieve a few more of those whom he believed to be overburdened with their wealth. . . .

These various forms of foolishness so pervade the whole life of Christians that even the priests themselves find no objection to admitting, not to say fostering, them, since they do not fail to perceive how many tidy little sums accrue to them from such sources. But what if some odious philosopher should chime in and say, as is quite true: "You will not die badly if you live well. You are redeeming your sins when you add to the sum that you contribute a hearty detestation of evil doers: then you may spare yourself tears, vigils, invocations, fasts, and all that kind of life. You may rely upon any saint to aid you when once you begin to imitate his life."

As for the theologians, perhaps the less said the better on this gloomy and dangerous theme, since they are a style of man who show themselves exceeding supercilious and irritable unless they can heap up six hundred conclusions about you and force you to recant; and if you refuse, they promptly brand you as a heretic,— for it is their custom to terrify by their thunderings those whom they dislike. It must be confessed that no other group of fools are so reluctant to acknowledge Folly's benefits toward them, although I have many titles to their gratitude, for I make them so in love with themselves that they seem to be happily exalted to the third heaven, whence they look down with something like pity upon all other mortals, wandering about on the earth like mere cattle.

Then they hedge themselves about with such an array of magisterial definitions, conclusions, corollaries, propositions explicate and implicate, and do so abound in subterfuges, that chains forged by Vulcan himself could not hold them so firm but that they could escape by one of those distinctions which enable them to cut all knots as easily as with a two-edged ax, so readily do they think up and rattle out new and prodigious terms and expressions.

Finally, the theologians are at their best when they are explaining (in their own opinion) such deep mysteries as: How was the world founded and brought into order? How is original sin transmitted to posterity? . . . How can the accidents subsist in the eucharist without their substance? Nay, these are trite and easy questions. The great and illustrious theologians, as they dub themselves, will only awaken when something like the following is proposed: Does supernatural generation require time for its accomplishment? Has Christ a double relation of sonship? Is the proposition possible, "God the Father hates the Son"? Might God have chosen to assume the form of a woman, a devil, an ass, a gourd, or a stone? . . .

St. Paul, they admit, was distinguished for his faith, but nevertheless when he said, "Faith is the substance of things hoped for, the evidence of things not seen," he defined it but inaccurately. He may have excelled in charity, yet he fails to limit and define it with dialectic precision in his first letter to the Corinthians, Chapter XIII. The disciples administered the eucharist reverently, and yet had they been asked about the *terminus a quo* and the *terminus ad quem* of transubstantiation; as to how a body can be in two places at the same time; of the differences which exist between Christ's body in heaven, on the cross, and in the holy wafer; or at what point does transsubstantiation occur, since the prayer through which it is effected is, as a *quantitas discreta,* in a state of flux,—asked of these matters the apostles would not have replied with the acuteness with which the followers of Scotus distinguish and define these subtleties.

The apostles knew the mother of Jesus, but who of them could philosophically prove how she was preserved from the sin of Eve, as do our divines? Peter received the keys, and from one who would not commit them to unworthy hands, but whether or not he knew how one could have the key of knowledge without knowledge itself, he certainly never discussed the matter. The apostles baptized, but never taught the formal, material, efficient, or final cause of baptism, nor do they mention delible or indelible characters. . . . The apostles inculcated grace, but never distinguished between *gratia gratis data* and *gratia gratificans.* They exhorted to good works, but did not perceive the distinction between *opus operans* and *opus operatum.* They frequently urge charity upon us without dividing "infused" from "acquired," or explaining whether charity be an accident or a substance, a created or an uncreated thing.

Next to the theologians in their self-satisfaction may be ranked those who are commonly called the religious and the monks, both terms quite wide of the truth, since a good part of them are a long ways from religion, and as for the monks (whose name suggests solitude), they are to be met in every byway. I do not see who could be more miserable than they unless Folly came to their aid in many ways. Although every one so execrates that stripe of man that even a casual meeting with them is regarded as ominous, yet they have a magnificent idea of their own virtues. First they deem it the most exalted piety to have let learning so completely alone that they cannot even read. Then when they bray out the psalms —which they cannot understand—in the churches, they flatter themselves that they are delighting the ears of the saints with their sweet harmonies. Some of them laud their beggary and filth as great virtues and loudly clamor for bread from door to door. They beset the inns, coaches, and ships, not a little to the prejudice of other beggars. . . .

The greater part of the monks exhibit such confidence in ceremonies and trivial human traditions that one would think a single heaven would scarce suffice as a worthy reward for their merits. They little think that Christ will put them off with a "Who hath required these things at your hands?" and will call them to account only for the stewardship of his legacy of love. One will confidently call attention to his paunch, filled with all kinds of fish; another will pour out a hundred bushels of psalms; a third will enumerate his myriad fastings and will tell how a single meal nearly killed him; a fourth will produce as many ceremonies as would fill seven merchant ships; a fifth will plead that for threescore years he never so much as touched money except he fingered it through double thick gloves; a sixth will bring along his hood so old and nasty that no sailor would venture to protect himself with it. . . . But Christ shall interrupt their boastings: "Woe unto you, scribes and Pharisees! I left you one great precept, but of that alone I hear nothing from you. I told you plainly in my gospel, with no disguising parables, that my Father's kingdom was promised, not for cowls, petitions, and fastings, but for deeds of love. I know them not who rely on their own merits."

When the monks and friars shall hear these things and shall see simple sailors and carters preferred to them, how shall their faces fall as they look at one another!

John Tetzel

John Tetzel (1460–1519) was a Dominican monk who in 1517 was selling indulgences in Germany under the direction of the Archbishop of Mainz. The selection below is from a sermon preached by him in an effort to stimulate their sale. In reading it note (1) his definition of an indulgence, (2) the emotions to which he appealed, (3) the comparisons he made with monetary facilities, and (4) the extent and scope of the pardon described.

From: A SERMON ON INDULGENCES

Venerable Sir, I pray you that in your utterances you may be pleased to make use of such words as shall serve to open the eyes of the mind and cause your hearers to consider how great a grace and gift they have had and now have at their very doors. Blessed eyes indeed, which see what they see, because already they possess letters of safe conduct by which they are able to lead their souls through that valley of tears, through that sea of the mad world, where storms and tempests and dangers lie in wait, to the blessed land of Paradise. Know that the life of man upon earth is a constant struggle. We have to fight against the flesh, the world and the devil, who are always seeking to destroy the soul. In sin we are conceived,—alas! what bonds of sin encompass us, and how difficult and almost impossible it is to attain to the gate of salvation without divine aid; since He causes us to be saved, not

James Harvey Robinson and Merrick Whitcomb, eds., *Translations and Reprints from the Original Sources of European History*, vol. II, no. 6, *Period of the Early Reformation in Germany*, University of Pennsylvania Press, Philadelphia, n.d., 9–10. Courtesy of the University of Pennsylvania Press.

by virtue of the good works which we accomplish, but through His divine mercy; it is necessary then to put on the armor of God.

You may obtain letters of safe conduct from the vicar of our Lord Jesus Christ, by means of which you are able to liberate your soul from the hands of the enemy, and convey it by means of contrition and confession, safe and secure from all pains of Purgatory, into the happy kingdom. For we know that in these letters are stamped and engraven all the merits of Christ's passion there laid bare. Consider, that for each and every mortal sin it is necessary to undergo seven years of penitence after confession and contrition, either in this life or in Purgatory.

How many mortal sins are committed in a day, how many in a week, how many in a month, how many in a year, how many in the whole course of life! They are well-nigh numberless, and those that commit them must needs suffer endless punishment in the burning pains of Purgatory.

But with these confessional letters you will be able at any time in life to obtain full indulgence for all penalties imposed upon you, in all cases except the four reserved to the Apostolic See. Therefore throughout your whole life, whenever you wish to make confession, you many receive the same remission, except in cases reserved to the Pope, and afterwards, at the hour of death, a full indulgence as to all penalties and sins, and your share of all spiritual blessings that exist in the church militant and all its members.

Do you not know that when it is necessary for anyone to go to Rome, or undertake any other dangerous journey, he takes his money to a broker and gives a certain per cent—five or six or ten—in order that at Rome or else-where he may receive again his funds intact, by means of the letter of this same broker? Are you not willing, then, for the fourth part of a florin, to obtain these letters, by virtue of which you may bring, not your money, but your divine and immortal soul safe and sound into the land of Paradise?

Wherefore I counsel, order, and by virtue of my authority as shepherd, I command that they shall receive together with me and other priests, this precious treasure, especially those who were not confessed at the time of the holy Jubilee, that they may be able to obtain the same forever. For the time may come when you may desire, but yet be unable to obtain the least portion of the grace.

Also on the part of SS. D. N. the Pope and of the most Holy Apostolic See and of the most reverend sir, my legate, to each and every one who shall have profited by the sacred Jubilee and made confession, and to all who may profit by this present brief opportunity, and who shall have lent a helping hand to the construction of the aforesaid house of the Prince of the Apostles, they shall all be participants and sharers in all prayers, suffrages, alms, fasts, supplications, masses, canonical hours, disciplines, pilgrimages, papal stations, benedictions, and all other spiritual goods which now exist or may exist forever in the church militant, and in all of these, not only they themselves, but their relatives, kindred, and benefactors who have passed away; and as they were moved by charity, so God, and SS. Peter and Paul, and all the saints whose bodies rest in Rome, shall guard them in peace in this vale, and conduct them through it to the heavenly kingdom. Give everlasting thanks in the aforesaid names and in mine to the reverend secular priests and prelates, etc.

Martin Luther

Martin Luther (1483–1546) was a German religious leader who played an important role in the revolt which, during the sixteenth century, brought about a permanent division in the Christian community. On November 1, 1517 he posted ninety-five articles on the door of the castle church in Wittenberg. They were not a statement of doc-

trine but merely a list of topic questions which had been provoked in his thinking by Tetzel's method of selling indulgences and which Luther wanted to debate on an academic level. These articles were read extensively and soon became the basis for a widespread religious movement leading away from the authority of the Roman Church. In reading them note (1) the relationship indicated between Christian living and penitence, (2) the implied limitation Luther placed on the papal power of remitting penalties, (3) the nature of the authority he cited for his ideas, (4) the error he suggested that the preachers of indulgences made, (5) the implied motive behind the sale of indulgences, (6) the potential danger to a true Christian in the purchase of pardons, and (7) Luther's criticism of those Christians who failed to follow Christ.

THE NINETY-FIVE THESES

In the desire and with the purpose of elucidating the truth, a disputation will be held on the underwritten propositions at Wittenberg, under the presidency of the Reverend Father Martin Luther, Monk of the Order of St. Augustine, Master of Arts and of Sacred Theology, and ordinary Reader of the same in that place. He therefore asks those who cannot be present and discuss the subject with us orally, to do so by letter in their absence. In the name of our Lord Jesus Christ. Amen.

1. Our Lord and Master Jesus Christ in saying, "Repent ye" (*poenitentiam agite*), etc., intended that the whole life of believers should be penitence (*poenitentia*).

2. This word cannot be understood as sacramental penance (*poenitentia*), that is, of the confession and satisfaction which are performed under the ministry of priests.

3. It does not, however, refer solely to inward penitence (*poenitentia*); nay, such inward penitence is naught, unless it outwardly produces various mortifications of the flesh.

4. The penalty (*poena*) thus continues as long as the hatred of self (that is, true inward penitence); namely, till our entrance into the kingdom of heaven.

5. The Pope has neither the will nor the power to remit any penalties except those

which he has imposed by his own authority, or by that of the canons.

6. The Pope has no power to remit any guilt, except by declaring and warranting it to have been remitted by God; or at most by remitting cases reserved for himself; in which cases, if his power were despised, guilt would certainly remain.

7. Certainly God remits no man's guilt without at the same time subjecting him, humbled in all things, to the authority of his representative the priest.

8. The penitential canons are imposed only on the living, and no burden ought to be imposed on the dying, according to them.

9. Hence, the Holy Spirit acting in the Pope does well for us in that, in his decrees, he always makes exception of the article of death and of necessity.

10. Those priests act unlearnedly and wrongly who, in the case of the dying, reserve the canonical penances for Purgatory.

11. Those tares about changing the canonical penalty into the penalty of Purgatory seem surely to have been sown while the bishops were asleep.

12. Formerly the canonical penalties were imposed not after but before absolution, as tests of true contrition.

13. The dying pay all penalties by death,

James Harvey Robinson and Merrick Whitcomb, eds., *Translations and Reprints from the Original Sources of European History*, vol. II, no. 6, *Period of the Early Reformation in Germany*, University of Pennsylvania Press, Philadelphia, n.d., 11–18. Courtesy of the University of Pennsylvania Press.

and are already dead to the canon laws, and are by right relieved from them.

14. The imperfect vigor or love of a dying person necessarily brings with it great fear, and the less it is, the greater the fear it brings.

15. This fear and horror is sufficient by itself, to say nothing of other things, to constitute the pains of Purgatory, since it is very near to the horror of despair.

16. Hell, Purgatory, and Heaven appear to differ as despair, almost despair, and peace of mind differ.

17. With souls in Purgatory it seems that it must needs be that as horror diminishes so love increases.

18. Nor does it seem to be proved by any reasoning or any Scriptures, that they are outside of the state of merit or of the increase of love.

19. Nor does this appear to be proved, that they are sure and confident of their own blessedness, at least all of them, though we may be very sure of it.

20. Therefore the Pope, when he speaks of the plenary remission of all penalties, does not mean really of all, but only of those imposed by himself.

21. Thus those preachers of indulgences are in error who say that by the indulgences of the Pope a man is freed and saved from all punishment.

22. For in fact he remits to souls in Purgatory no penalty which they would have had to pay in this life according to the canons.

23. If any entire remission of all penalties can be granted to any one it is certain that it is granted to none but the most perfect, that is to very few.

24. Hence, the greater part of the people must needs be deceived by this indiscriminate and high-sounding promise of release from penalties.

25. Such power over Purgatory as the Pope has in general, such has every bishop in his own diocese, and every parish priest in his own parish, in particular.

26. The Pope acts most rightly in granting remission to souls not by the power of the keys (which is of no avail in this case), but by the way of intercession.

27. They preach man who say that the soul flies out of Purgatory as soon as the money thrown into the chest rattles.

28. It is certain that, when the money rattles in the chest, avarice and gain may be increased, but the effect of the intercession of the Church depends on the will of God alone.

29. Who knows whether all the souls in Purgatory desire to be redeemed from it—witness the story told of Saints Severinus and Paschal?

30. No man is sure of the reality of his own contrition, much less of the attainment of plenary remission.

31. Rare as is a true penitent, so rare is one who truly buys indulgences—that is to say, most rare.

32. Those who believe that, through letters of pardon, they are made sure of their own salvation will be eternally damned along with their teachers.

33. We must especially beware of those who say that these pardons from the Pope are that inestimable gift of God by which man is reconciled to God.

34. For the grace conveyed by these pardons has respect only to the penalties of sacramental satisfaction, which are of human appointment.

35. They preach no Christian doctrine who teach that contrition is not necessary for those who buy souls [out of Purgatory] or buy confessional licenses.

36. Every Christian who feels true compunction has of right plenary remission of punishment and guilt even without letters of pardon.

37. Every true Christian, whether living or dead, has a share in all the benefits of Christ and of the Church, given by God, even without letters of pardon.

38. The remission, however, imparted by the Pope is by no means to be despised, since it is, as I have said, a declaration of the divine remission.

39. It is a most difficult thing, even for the most learned theologians, to exalt at the same time in the eyes of the people the ample effect of pardons and the necessity of true contrition.

40. True contrition seeks and loves punishment; while the ampleness of pardons relaxes

it, and causes men to hate it, or at least gives occasion for them to do so.

41. Apostolic pardons ought to be proclaimed with caution, lest the people should falsely suppose that they are placed before other good works of charity.

42. Christians should be taught that it is not the wish of the Pope that the buying of pardons should be in any way compared to works of mercy.

43. Christians should be taught that he who gives to a poor man, or lends to a needy man, does better than if he bought pardons.

44. Because by works of charity, charity increases, and the man becomes better; while by means of pardons, he does not become better, but only freer from punishment.

45. Christians should be taught that he who sees any one in need, and, passing him by, gives money for pardons, is not purchasing for himself the indulgences of the Pope but the anger of God.

46. Christians should be taught that, unless they have superfluous wealth, they are bound to keep what is necessary for the use of their own households, and by no means to lavish it on pardons.

47. Christians should be taught that while they are free to buy pardons they are not commanded to do so.

48. Christians should be taught that the Pope, in granting pardons, has both more need and more desire that devout prayer should be made for him than that money should be readily paid.

49. Christians should be taught that the Pope's pardons are useful if they do not put their trust in them, but most hurtful if through them they lose the fear of God.

50. Christians should be taught that, if the Pope were acquainted with the exactions of the Preachers of pardons, he would prefer that the Basilica of St. Peter should be burnt to ashes rather than that it should be built up with the skin, flesh, and bones of his sheep.

51. Christians should be taught that as it would be the duty so it would be the wish of the Pope even to sell, if necessary, the Basilica of St. Peter, and to give of his own money to very many of those from whom the preachers of pardons extract money.

52. Vain is the hope of salvation through letters of pardon, even if a commissary—nay, the Pope himself—were to pledge his own soul for them.

53. They were enemies of Christ and of the Pope who, in order that pardons may be preached, condemn the Word of God to utter silence in other churches.

54. Wrong is done to the Word of God when, in the same sermon, an equal or longer time is spent on pardons than on it.

55. The mind of the Pope necessarily is that, if pardons, which are a very small matter, are celebrated with single bells, single processions, and single ceremonies, the Gospel, which is a very great matter, should be preached with a hundred bells, a hundred processions, and a hundred ceremonies.

56. The treasures of the Church, whence the Pope grants indulgences, are neither sufficiently named nor known among the people of Christ.

57. It is clear that they are at least not temporal treasures, for these are not so readily lavished, but only accumulated, by means of the preachers.

58. Nor are they the merits of Christ and of the saints, for these, independently of the Pope, are always working grace to the inner man, and the cross, death, and hell to the outer man.

59. St. Lawrence said that the treasures of the Church are the poor of the Church, but he spoke according to the use of the term in his time.

60. We are not speaking rashly when we say that the keys of the Church, bestowed through the merits of Christ, are that treasure.

61. For it is clear that the power of the Pope is sufficient of itself for the remission of [canonical] penalties and of [reserved] cases.

62. The true treasure of the Church is the Holy Gospel of the glory and grace of God.

63. This treasure, however, is deservedly most hateful, because it makes the first to be last.

64. While the treasure of indulgences is deservedly most acceptable, because it makes the last to be first.

65. Hence the treasures of the Gospel are

nets, wherewith of old they fished for the men of riches.

66. The treasures of indulgences are nets, wherewith they now fish for the riches of men.

67. Those indulgences, which the preachers loudly proclaim to be the greatest graces, are seen to be truly such as regards the promotion of gain.

68. Yet they are in reality most insignificant when compared to the grace of God and the piety of the cross.

69. Bishops and parish priests are bound to receive the commissaries of apostolical pardons with all reverence.

70. But they are still more bound to see to it with all their eyes, and take heed with all their ears, that these men do not preach their own dreams in place of the Pope's commission.

71. He who speaks against the truth of apostolical pardons, let him be anathema and accursed.

72. But he, on the other hand, who exerts himself against the wantonness and license of speech of the preachers of pardons, let him be blessed.

73. As the Pope justly thunders against those who use any kind of contrivance to the injury of the traffic in pardons,

74. Much more is it his intention to thunder against those who, under the pretext of pardons, use contrivances to the injury of holy charity and of truth.

75. To think that the Papal pardons have such power that they could absolve a man even if—by an impossibility—he had violated the Mother of God, is madness.

76. We affirm on the contrary that Papal pardons cannot take away even the least of venial sins, as regards its guilt.

77. The saying that, even if St. Peter were now Pope, he could grant no greater graces, is blasphemy against St. Peter and the Pope.

78. We affirm on the contrary that both he and any other Pope has greater graces to grant, namely, the Gospel, powers, gifts of healing, etc. (I Cor. XII).

79. To say that the cross set up among the insignia of the Papal arms is of equal power with the cross of Christ, is blasphemy.

80. Those bishops, priests and theologians who allow such discourses to have currency among the people will have to render an account.

81. This license in the preaching of pardons makes it no easy thing, even for learned men, to protect the reverence due to the Pope against the calumnies, or at all events, the keen questioning of the laity.

82. As for instance: Why does not the Pope empty Purgatory for the sake of most holy charity and of the supreme necessity of souls— this being the most just of all reasons—if he redeems an infinite number of souls for the sake of that most fatal thing, money, to be spent on building a basilica—this being a very slight reason?

83. Again; why do funeral masses and anniversary masses for the deceased continue, and why does not the Pope return, or permit the withdrawal of, the funds bequeathed for this purpose, since it is a wrong to pray for those who are already redeemed?

84. Again; what is this new kindness of God and the Pope, in that, for money's sake, they permit an impious man and an enemy of God to redeem a pious soul which loves God, and yet do not redeem that same pious and beloved soul out of free charity on account of its own need?

85. Again; why is it that the penitential canons, long since abrogated and dead in themselves, in very fact and not only by usage, are yet still redeemed with money, through the granting of indulgences, as if they were full of life?

86. Again; why does not the Pope, whose riches are at this day more ample than those of the wealthiest of the wealthy, build the single Basilica of St. Peter with his own money rather than with that of poor believers?

87. Again; what does the Pope remit or impart to those who through perfect contrition have a right to plenary remission and participation?

88. Again; what greater good could the Church receive than if the Pope, instead of once, as he does now, were to bestow these remissions and participations a hundred times a day on any one of the faithful?

89. Since it is the salvation of souls, rather than money, that the Pope seeks by his pardons, why does he suspend the letters and

pardons granted long ago, since they are equally efficacious?

90. To repress these scruples and arguments of the laity by force alone, and not to resolve them by giving reasons, is to expose the Church and the Pope to the ridicule of their enemies, and to make Christian men unhappy.

91. If then pardons were preached according to the spirit and mind of the Pope, all these questions would be resolved with ease; nay, would not exist.

92. Away then with all those prophets who say to the people of Christ: "Peace, peace," and there is no peace.

93. Blessed be all those prophets who say to the people of Christ: "The cross, the cross," and there is no cross.

94. Christians should be exhorted to strive to follow Christ their head through pains, deaths, and hells.

95. And thus trust to enter heaven through many tribulations, rather than in the security of peace.

MDXVII

John Calvin

John Calvin (1509–1564) was a Protestant leader who was born in France but was forced by persecution to flee to Switzerland where he took a prominent position in the reform movement. He had been trained for the law and it was inevitable, perhaps, that he should become concerned with matters of religious doctrine. In his Institutes of the Christian Religion Calvin developed the most logical presentation of Protestant theology ever written, and it became a guide both for study and discussion. The entire work was based upon Calvin's belief and faith in the infallible authority of the Bible literally interpreted. In reading the selections taken from this work note (1) Calvin's discussion of the relative authority of the Scriptures and the Church, (2) the evidences he gave to establish the authorship of the Scriptures, (3) the role of God as creator and governor of the world and of mankind, (4) the answer Calvin gave to those who claimed that man could not be held responsible for his evil actions, (5) his description of Christian liberty, (6) his exposition and justification of the doctrine of predestination, (7) Calvin's concept of the Church, (8) the two types of people who may be found in every congregation, (9) the reasons Calvin advanced for attendance at divine services, (10) the number and true nature of the sacraments according to the Bible, and (11) the limits he placed on a Christian's duty to obey civil rulers.

From: THE INSTITUTES OF THE CHRISTIAN RELIGION

Before I proceed any further, it is proper to introduce some remarks on the authority of the Scripture, not only to prepare the mind to regard it with due reverence, but also to remove every doubt. For, when it is admitted to be a declaration of the word of God, no man

As translated by John Allen in John Calvin, *Institutes of the Christian Religion*, 7th American edition, 2 vols., Presbyterian Board of Christian Education, Philadelphia, 1936, I, 85–86; 88–92; 217–218; 225–226; 236–239; 270–271; 273–274; II, 76–77; 280–281; 295–296; 730–732. Used by permission.

can be so deplorably presumptuous, unless he be also destitute of common sense and of the common feelings of men, as to dare to derogate from the credit due to the speaker. But since we are not favoured with daily oracles from heaven, and since it is only in the Scriptures that the Lord hath been pleased to preserve his truth in perpetual remembrance, it obtains the same complete credit and authority with believers, when they are satisfied of its divine origin, as if they heard the very words pronounced by God himself. The subject, indeed, merits a diffuse discussion, and a most accurate examination. But the reader will pardon me, if I attend rather to what the design of this work admits, than to what the extensive nature of the present subject requires. But there has very generally prevailed a most pernicious error, that the Scriptures have only so much weight as is conceded to them by the suffrages of the Church; as though the eternal and inviolable truth of God depended on the arbitrary will of men. For thus, with great contempt of the Holy Spirit, they inquire, Who can assure us that God is the author of them? Who can with certainty affirm, that they have been preserved safe and uncorrupted to the present age? Who can persuade us that this book ought to be received with reverence, and that expunged from the sacred number, unless all these things were regulated by the decisions of the Church? It depends, therefore, (say they) on the determination of the Church, to decide both what reverence is due to the Scripture, and what books are to be comprised in its canon. Thus sacrilegious men, while they wish to introduce an unlimited tyranny, under the name of the Church, are totally unconcerned with what absurdities they embarrass themselves and others, provided they can extort from the ignorant this one admission, that the Church can do every thing. But, if this be true, what will be the condition of those wretched consciences, which are seeking a solid assurance of eternal life, if all the promises extant concerning it rest only on the judgment of men? Will the reception of such an answer cause their fluctuations to subside, and their terrors to vanish? Again, how will the impious ridicule our faith, and all men call it in question, if it be understood to possess only a precarious authority depending on the favour of men! . . .

It must be maintained, as I have before asserted, that we are not established in the belief of the doctrine till we are indubitably persuaded that God is its Author. The principal proof, therefore, of the Scriptures is every where derived from the character of the Divine Speaker. The prophets and apostles boast not of their own genius, or any of those talents which conciliate the faith of the hearers; nor do they insist on arguments from reason; but bring forward the sacred name of God, to compel the submission of the whole world. We must now see how it appears, not from probable supposition, but from clear demonstration, that this use of the Divine name is neither rash nor fallacious. Now, if we wish to consult the true interest of our consciences; that they may not be unstable and wavering, the subjects of perpetual doubt; that they may not hesitate at the smallest scruples,—this persuasion must be sought from a higher source than human reasons, or judgments, or conjectures—even from the secret testimony of the Spirit. It is true that, if we were inclined to argue the point, many things might be adduced which certainly evince, if there be any God in heaven, that he is the Author of the Law, and the Prophecies, and the Gospel. Even though men of learning and deep judgment rise up in opposition, and exert and display all the powers of their minds in this dispute, yet, unless they are wholly lost to all sense of shame, this confession will be extorted from them, that the Scripture exhibits the plainest evidences that it is God who speaks in it, which manifests its doctrine to be Divine. And we shall soon see, that all the books of the sacred Scripture very far excel all other writings. If we read it with pure eyes and sound minds, we shall immediately perceive the majesty of God, which will subdue our audacious contradictions, and compel us to obey him. Yet it is acting a preposterous part, to endeavour to produce sound faith in the Scripture by disputations. Though, indeed, I am far from excelling in peculiar dexterity or eloquence, yet, if I were to contend with the most subtle despisers of God, who are ambitious to display their wit and their skill in weakening the authority of Scripture, I trust I should be able, without difficulty, to silence their obstreperous clamour. And, if it were of any use to attempt a refutation of their cavils, I would easily demolish the boasts which they mutter in secret corners. But though any one vindicates the sacred word of God from the aspersions of men, yet this will not fix in their hearts that assurance which is essential to true piety. Religion appearing, to profane men, to consist wholly in opinion, in order that they may not believe any thing on foolish or slight grounds, they wish and expect it to be proved by rational arguments, that Moses and the prophets spake by Divine inspiration. But I reply, that the testimony of the Spirit is superior to all reason. For as God alone is a sufficient witness of himself in his own word, so also the word will never gain credit in the hearts of men, till it be confirmed by the internal testimony of the Spirit. It is necessary, therefore, that the same Spirit, who spake by the mouths of the prophets, should penetrate into our hearts, to convince us that they faithfully delivered the oracles which were divinely instrusted to them. And this connection is very suitably expressed in these words: "My Spirit that is upon thee, and my word which I have put in thy mouth, shall not depart out of thy mouth, nor out of the mouth of thy seed, nor out of the mouth of thy seed's seed, for ever." Some good men are troubled that they are not always prepared with clear proof to oppose the impious, when they murmur with impunity against the divine word; as though the Spirit were not therefore denominated a "seal," and "an earnest," for the confirmation of the faith of the pious; because, till he illuminate their minds, they are perpetually fluctuating amidst a multitude of doubts.

Let it be considered, then, as an undeniable truth, that they who have been inwardly taught by the Spirit, feel an entire acquiescence in the Scripture, and that it is self-authenticated, carrying with it its own evidence, and ought not to be made the subject of demonstration and arguments from reason; but it obtains the credit which it deserves with us by the testimony of the Spirit. For though it conciliate our reverence by its internal majesty, it never seriously affects us till it is confirmed by the Spirit in our hearts. Therefore, being illuminated by him, we now believe the Divine original of the Scripture, not from our own judgment or that of others, but we esteem the certainty, that we have received it from God's own mouth by the ministry of men, to be superior to that of any human judgment, and equal to that of an intuitive perception of God himself in it. We seek not arguments or probabilities to support our judgment, but submit our judgments and understandings as to a thing concerning which it is impossible for us to judge; and that not like some persons, who are in the habit of hastily embracing what they do not understand, which displeases them as soon as they examine it, but because we feel the firmest conviction that we hold an invincible truth; nor like those unhappy men who surrender their minds captives to superstitions, but because we perceive in it the undoubted energies of the Divine power, by which we are attracted and inflamed to an understanding and voluntary obedience, but with a vigour and efficacy superior to the power of any human will or knowledge. With the greatest justice, therefore, God exclaims by Isaiah, that the prophets and all the people were his witnesses; because, being taught by prophecies, they were certain that God had spoken without the least fallacy or ambiguity. It is such a persuasion, therefore, as requires no reasons; such a knowledge as is supported by the highest reason, in which, indeed, the mind rests with greater security and constancy than in any reasons; it is, finally, such a sentiment as cannot be produced but by a revelation from heaven. I speak of nothing but what every believer experiences in his heart, except that my language falls far short of a just explication of the subject. I pass over many things at present, because this subject will present itself for discussion again in another place. Only let it be known here, that that alone is true faith which the Spirit of God seals in our hearts. And with this one reason every reader of modesty and docility will be satisfied: Isaiah predicts that "all the children" of the renovated Church "shall be taught of God." Herein God deigns to confer a singular privilege on his elect, whom he distinguishes from the rest of mankind. For what is the beginning of true learning but a prompt alacrity to hear the voice of God? By the mouth of Moses he demands our attention in these terms: "Say not in thine heart, Who shall ascend into heaven? or, Who shall descend into the deep? The word is even in thy mouth." If God hath determined that this treasury of wisdom shall be reserved for his children, it is neither surprising nor absurd, that we see so much ignorance and stupidity among the vulgar herd of mankind. By this appellation I designate even those of the greatest talents and highest rank, till they are incorporated into the Church. Moreover, Isaiah, observing that the prophetical doctrine would be incredible, not only to aliens, but also to the Jews, who wished to be esteemed members of the family, adds, at the same time, the reason —Because the arm of the Lord will not be revealed to all. Whenever, therefore, we are disturbed at the paucity of believers, let us, on the other hand, remember that none, but those to whom it was given, have any apprehension of the mysteries of God. . . .

To represent God as a Creator only for a moment, who entirely finished all his work at once, were frigid and jejune; and in this it behoves us especially to differ from the heathen, that the presence of the Divine power may appear to us no less in the perpetual state of the world than in its first origin. For although the minds even of impious men, by the mere contemplation of earth and heaven, are constrained to rise to the Creator, yet faith has a way peculiar to itself to assign to God the whole praise of creation. To which purpose is that assertion of an Apostle before cited, that it is only "through faith that we understand the worlds were framed by the word of God"; because, unless we proceed to his providence, we have no correct conception of the meaning of this article, "that God is the Creator"; however we may appear to comprehend it in our minds, and to confess it with our tongues. The carnal sense, when it has once viewed the power of God in the creation, stops there; and when it proceeds the furthest, it only examines and considers the wisdom, and power, and goodness, of the Author in producing such a work, which spontaneously present themselves to the view even of those who are unwilling to ob-

serve them. In the next place, it conceives of some general operation of God in preserving and governing it, on which the power of motion depends. Lastly, it supposes that the vigour originally infused by God into all things is sufficient for their sustentation. But faith ought to penetrate further. When it has learned that he is the Creator of all things, it should immediately conclude that he is also their perpetual governor and preserver; and that not by a certain universal motion, actuating the whole machine of the world, and all its respective parts, but by a particular providence sustaining, nourishing, and providing for every thing which he has made. . . .

But as we know that the world was made chiefly for the sake of mankind, we must also observe this end in the government of it. The Prophet Jeremiah exclaims, "I know that the way of man is not in himself: it is not in man that walketh to direct his steps." And Solomon: "Man's goings are of the Lord: how can a man then understand his own way?" Now, let them say that man is actuated by God according to the bias of his nature, but that he directs that influence according to his own pleasure. If this could be asserted with truth, man would have the free choice of his own ways. That, perhaps, they will deny, because he can do nothing independently of the power of God. But since it is evident that both the Prophet and Solomon ascribe to God choice and appointment, as well as power, this by no means extricates them from the difficulty. But Solomon, in another place, beautifully reproves this temerity of men, who predetermine on an end for themselves, without regard to God, as though they were not led by his hand: "The preparation of the heart in man," says he, "and the answer of the tongue, is from the Lord." It is, indeed, a ridiculous madness for miserable men to resolve on undertaking any work independently of God, whilst they cannot even speak a word but what he chooses. Moreover, the Scripture, more fully to express that nothing is transacted in the world but according to his destination, shows that those things are subject to him which appear most fortuitous. For what would you be more ready to attribute to chance, than when a limb broken off from a tree kills a passing traveller? But very different is the decision of the Lord, who acknowledges that he has delivered him into the hand of the slayer. Who, likewise, does not leave lots to the blindness of fortune? Yet the Lord leaves them not, but claims the disposal of them himself. He teaches us that it is not by any power of their own that lots are cast into the lap and drawn out; but the only thing which could be ascribed to chance, he declares to belong to himself. To the same purpose is another passage from Solomon: "The poor and the deceitful man meet together: the Lord enlighteneth the eyes of them both." For although the poor and the rich are blended together in the world, yet, as their respective conditions are assigned to them by Divine appointment, he suggests that God, who enlightens all, is not blind, and thus exhorts the poor to patience; because those who are discontented with their lot, are endeavouring to shake off the burden imposed on them by God. Thus also another Prophet rebukes profane persons, who attribute it to human industry, or to fortune, that some men remain in obscurity, and others rise to honours: "Promotion cometh neither from the east, nor from the west, nor from the south. But God is the Judge; he putteth down one, and setteth up another." Since God cannot divest himself of the office of a judge, hence he reasons, that it is from the secret counsel of God, that some rise to promotion, and others remain in contempt. . . .

Those who have learned this modesty, will neither murmur against God on account of past adversities, nor charge him with the guilt of their crimes, like Agamemnon, in Homer, who says, "The blame belongs not to me, but to Jupiter and Fate." Nor will they, as if hurried away by the Fates, under the influence of despair, put an end to their own lives, like the young man whom Plautus introduces as saying, "The condition of our affairs is inconstant; men are governed by the caprice of the Fates; I will betake myself to a precipice, and there destroy my life and every thing at once." Nor will they excuse their flagitious actions by ascribing them to God, after the example of another young man introduced by the same poet, who says, "God was the cause: I believe it was the

Divine will. For had it not been so, I know it would not have happened." But they will rather search the Scripture, to learn what is pleasing to God, that by the guidance of the Spirit they may strive to attain it; and at the same time, being prepared to follow God whithersoever he calls them, they will exhibit proofs in their conduct that nothing is more useful than a knowledge of this doctrine. Some profane men foolishly raise such a tumult with their absurdities, as almost, according to a common expression, to confound heaven and earth together. They argue in this manner: If God has fixed the moment of our death, we cannot avoid it; therefore all caution against it will be but lost labour. One man dares not venture himself in a way which he hears is dangerous, lest he should be assassinated by robbers; another sends for physicians, and wearies himself with medicines, to preserve his life; another abstains from the grosser kinds of food, lest he should injure his valetudinary constitution; another dreads to inhabit a ruinous house; and men in general exert all their faculties in devising and executing methods by which they may attain the object of their desires. Now, either all these things are vain remedies employed to correct the will of God, or life and death, health and disease, peace and war, and other things which, according to their desires or aversions, men industriously study to obtain or to avoid, are not determined by his certain decree. Moreover they conclude, that the prayers of the faithful are not only superfluous, but perverse, which contain petitions that the Lord will provide for those things which he has already decreed from eternity. In short, they supersede all deliberations respecting futurity, as opposed to the providence of God, who, without consulting men, has decreed whatever he pleased. And what has already happened they impute to the Divine providence in such a manner as to overlook the person, who is known to have committed any particular act. Has an assassin murdered a worthy citizen? they say he has executed the counsel of God. Has any one been guilty of theft or fornication? because he has done what was foreseen and ordained by the Lord, he is the minister of his providence. Has a son, neglecting all remedies, carelessly waited the death of his father? it was impossible for him to resist God, who had decreed this event from eternity. Thus by these persons all crimes are denominated virtues, because they are subservient to the ordination of God. . . .

The same persons inconsiderably and erroneously ascribe all past events to the absolute providence of God. For since all things which come to pass are dependent upon it, therefore, say they, neither thefts, nor adulteries, nor homicides, are perpetrated without the intervention of the Divine will. Why, therefore, they ask, shall a thief be punished for having pillaged him whom it has pleased the Lord to chastise with proverty? Why shall a homicide be punished for having slain him whose life the Lord had terminated? If all such characters are subservient to the Divine will, why shall they be punished? But I deny that they serve the will of God. For we cannot say, that he who is influenced by a wicked heart, acts in obedience to the commands of God, while he is only gratifying his own malignant passions. That man obeys God, who, being instructed in his will, hastens whither God calls him. Where can we learn his will, but in his word? Therefore in our actions we ought to regard the will of God, which is declared in his word. God only requires of us conformity to his precepts. If we do any thing contrary to them, it is not obedience, but contumacy and transgression. But it is said, if he would not permit it, we should not do it. This I grant. But do we perform evil actions with the design of pleasing him? He gives us no such command. We precipitate ourselves into them, not considering what is his will, but inflamed with the violence of our passions, so that we deliberately strive to oppose him. In this manner even by criminal actions we subserve his righteous ordination; because, in the infinite greatness of his wisdom, he well knows how to use evil instruments for the accomplishment of good purposes. . . .

Nor, to enable us to understand this subject, have we any need to enter on that tedious dispute, with which the fathers were not a little perplexed, whether the soul of a son proceeds by derivation or transmission from the soul of the father, because the soul is the principal

seat of the pollution. We ought to be satisfied with this, that the Lord deposited with Adam the endowments he chose to confer on the human nature; and therefore that when he lost the favours he had received, he lost them not only for himself, but for us all. Who will be solicitous about a transmission of the soul, when he hears that Adam received the ornaments that he lost, no less for us than for himself? that they were given, not to one man only, but to the whole human nature? There is nothing absurd therefore, if, in consequence of his being spoiled of his dignities, that nature be destitute and poor; if, in consequence of his being polluted with sin, the whole nature be infected with the contagion. From a putrefied root, therefore, have sprung putrid branches, which have transmitted their putrescence to remoter ramifications. For the children were so vitiated in their parent, that they became contagious to their descendants: there was in Adam such a spring of corruption, that it transfused from parents to children in a perpetual stream. But the cause of the contagion is not in the substance of the body or of the soul; but because it was ordained by God, that the gifts which he conferred on the first man should by him be preserved or lost both for himself and for all his posterity. . . .

We have now to treat of Christian liberty, an explanation of which ought not to be omitted in a treatise which is designed to comprehend a compendious summary of evangelical doctrine. For it is a subject of the first importance, and unless it be well understood, our consciences scarcely venture to undertake any thing without doubting, experience in many things hesitation and reluctance, and are always subject to fluctuations and fears. But especially it is an appendix to justification, and affords no small assistance towards the knowledge of its influence. Hence they who sincerely fear God will experience the incomparable advantage of that doctrine, which impious scoffers pursue with their railleries; because in the spiritual intoxication with which they are seized, they allow themselves the most unbounded impudence. Wherefore this is the proper time to introduce the subject; and though we have slightly touched upon it on some former occasions, yet it was useful to defer the full discussion of it to this place; because, as soon as any mention is made of Christian liberty, then either inordinate passions rage, or violent emotions arise, unless timely opposition be made to those wanton spirits, who must nefariously corrupt things which are otherwise the best. For some, under the pretext of this liberty, cast off all obedience to God, and precipitate themselves into the most unbridled licentiousness; and some despise it, supposing it to be subversive of all moderation, order, and moral distinctions. What can we do in this case, surrounded by such difficulties? Shall we entirely discard Christian liberty, and so preclude the occasion of such dangers? But, as we have observed, unless this be understood, there can be no right knowledge of Christ, or of evangelical truth, or of internal peace of mind. We should rather exert ourselves to prevent the suppression of such a necessary branch of doctrine, and at the same time to obviate those absurd objections which are frequently deduced from it.

Christian liberty, according to my judgment, consists of three parts. The first part is, that the consciences of believers, when seeking an assurance of their justification before God, should raise themselves above the law, and forget all the righteousness of the law. For since the law, as we have elsewhere demonstrated, leaves no man righteous, either we must be excluded from all hope of justification, or it is necessary for us to be delivered from it, and that so completely as not to have any dependence on works. For he who imagines, that in order to obtain righteousness he must produce any works, however small, can fix no limit or boundary, but renders himself a debtor to the whole law. Avoiding, therefore, all mention of the law, and dismissing all thought of our own works, in reference to justification, we must embrace the Divine mercy alone, and turning our eyes from ourselves, fix them solely on Christ. For the question is, not how we can be righteous, but how, though unrighteous and unworthy, we can be considered as righteous. And the conscience that desires to attain any certainty respecting this, must give no admission to the law. Nor will this authorize any one to conclude, that the law is of no use to believers, whom it still continues to instruct and exhort, and stimulate to duty, although it has no place in their consciences before the tribunal of God. For these two things, being very different, require to be properly and carefully distinguished by us. The whole life of Christians ought to be an exercise of piety, since they are called to sanctification. . . .

The second part of Christian liberty, which is dependent on the first, is, that their consciences do not observe the law, as being under any legal obligation; but that, being liberated from the yoke of the law, they yield a voluntary obedience to the will of God. For being possessed with perpetual terrors, as long as they remain under the dominion of the law, they will never engage with alacrity and promptitude in the service of God, unless they have previously received this liberty. . . .

The third part of Christian liberty teaches us, that we are bound by no obligation before God respecting external things, which in themselves are indifferent; but that we may indifferently sometimes use, and at other times omit them. And the knowledge of this liberty also is very necessary for us; for without it we shall have no tranquillity of conscience, nor will there be any end of superstitions. Many in the present age think it a folly to raise any dispute concerning the free use of meats, of days, and of habits, and similar subjects, considering these things as frivolous and nugatory; but they are of greater importance than is generally believed. For when the conscience has once fallen into the snare, it enters a long and inextricable labyrinth, from which it is afterwards difficult to escape; if a man begin to doubt the lawfulness of using flax in sheets, shirts, handkerchiefs, napkins, and table cloths, neither will he be certain respecting hemp, and at last he will doubt of the lawfulness of using tow; for he will consider with himself whether he cannot eat without table cloths or napkins, whether he cannot do without handkerchiefs. If any one imagine delicate food to be unlawful, he will ere long have no tranquillity before God in eating brown bread and common viands, while he remembers that he might support his body with meat of a quality still inferior. If he hesitate respecting good wine, he will afterwards be unable with any peace of conscience to drink the most vapid; and at last he will not presume even to touch purer and sweeter water than others. In short, he will come to think it criminal to step over a twig that lies across his path. For this is the commencement of no trivial controversy; but the dispute is whether the use of certain things be agreeable to God, whose will ought to guide all our resolutions and all our actions. The necessary consequence is, that some are hurried by despair into a vortex of confusion, from which they see no way of escape; and some, despising God, and casting off all fear of him, make a way of ruin for themselves. For all, who are involved in such doubts, which way soever they turn their views, behold something offensive to their consciences presenting itself on every side. . . .

The covenant of life not being equally preached to all, and among those to whom it is preached not always finding the same reception, this diversity discovers the wonderful depth of the Divine judgment. Nor is it to be doubted that this variety also follows, subject to the decision of God's eternal election. If it be evidently the result of the Divine will, that salvation is freely offered to some, and others are prevented from attaining it,—this immediately gives rise to important and difficult questions, which are incapable of any other explication, than by the establishment of pious minds in what ought to be received concerning election and predestination—a question, in the opinion of many, full of perplexity; for they consider nothing more unreasonable, than that, of the common mass of mankind, some should be predestined to salvation, and others to destruction. But how unreasonably they perplex themselves will afterwards appear from the sequel of our discourse. Besides, the very obscurity which excites such dread, not only displays the utility of this doctrine, but shows it to be productive of the most delightful benefit. We shall never be clearly convinced as we ought to be, that our salvation flows from the fountain of God's free mercy, till we are acquainted with his eternal election, which illus-trates the grace of God by this comparison, that he adopts not all promiscuously to the hope of salvation, but gives to some what he refuses to others. Ignorance of this principle evidently detracts from the Divine glory, and diminishes real humility. But according to Paul, what is so necessary to be known, never can be known, unless God, without any regard to works, chooses those whom he has decreed. "At this present time also, there is a remnant according to the election of grace. And if by grace, then it is no more of works; otherwise, grace is no more grace. But if it be of works, then it is no more grace; otherwise, work is no more work." If we need to be recalled to the origin of election, to prove that we obtain salvation from no other source than the mere goodness of God, they who desire to extinguish this principle, do all they can to obscure what ought to be magnificently and loudly celebrated, and to pluck up humility by the roots. In ascribing the salvation of the remnant of the people to the election of grace, Paul clearly testifies, that it is then only known that God saves whom he will of his mere good pleasure, and does not dispense a reward to which there can be no claim. They who shut the gates to prevent any one from presuming to approach and taste this doctrine, do no less injury to man than to God; for nothing else will be sufficient to produce in us suitable humility, or to impress us with a due sense of our great obligations to God. Nor is there any other basis for solid confidence, even according to the authority of Christ, who, to deliver us from all fear, and render us invincible amidst so many dangers, snares, and deadly conflicts, promises to preserve in safety all whom the Father has committed to his care. Whence we infer, that they who know not themselves to be God's peculiar people will be tortured with continual anxiety; and therefore, that the interest of all believers, as well as their own, is very badly consulted by those who, blind to the three advantages we have remarked, would wholly remove the foundation of our salvation. And hence the Church rises to our view, which otherwise, as Bernard justly observes, could neither be discovered nor recognized among creatures, being in two respects wonderfully concealed in the bosom of a blessed predestination, and in the mass of a miserable damnation. But before I enter on the subject itself, I must address some preliminary observations to two sorts of persons. The discussion of predestination—a subject of itself rather intricate—is made very perplexed, and therefore dangerous, by human curiosity, which no barriers can restrain from wandering into forbidden labyrinths, and soaring beyond its sphere, as if determined to leave none of the Divine secrets unscrutinized or unexplored. As we see multitudes every where guilty of this arrogance and presumption, and among them some who are not censurable in other respects, it is proper to admonish them of the bounds of their duty on this subject. First, then, let them remember that when they inquire into predestination, they penetrate the inmost recesses of Divine wisdom, where the careless and confident intruder will obtain not satisfaction to his curiosity, but will enter a labyrinth from which he will find no way to depart. For it is unreasonable that man should scrutinize with impunity those things which the Lord has determined to be hidden in himself; and investigate, even from eternity, that sublimity of wisdom which God would have us to adore and not comprehend, to promote our admiration of his glory. The secrets of his will which he determined to reveal to us, he discovers in his word; and these are all that he foresaw would concern us or conduce to our advantage. . . .

Predestination, by which God adopts some to the hope of life, and adjudges others to eternal death, no one, desirous of the credit of piety, dares absolutely to deny. But it is involved in many cavils, especially by those who make foreknowledge the cause of it. We maintain, that both belong to God; but it is preposterous to represent one as dependent on the other. When we attribute foreknowledge to God, we mean that all things have ever been, and perpetually remain, before his eyes, so that to his knowledge nothing is future or past, but all things are present; and present in such a manner, that he does not merely conceive of them from ideas formed in his mind, as things remembered by us appear present to our minds, but really beholds and sees them as if actually placed before him. And this foreknowledge extends to the whole world, and to all the creatures. Predestination we call the eternal decree of God, by which he has determined in himself, what he would have to become of every individual of mankind. For they are not all created with a similar destiny; but eternal life is foreordained for some, and eternal damnation for others. Every man, therefore, being created for one or the other of these ends, we say, he is predestinated either to life or to death. This God has not only testified in particular persons, but has given a specimen of it in the whole posterity of Abraham, which should evidently show the future condition of every nation to depend upon his decision. . . .

From what has been said, I conceive it must now be evident what judgment we ought to form respecting the Church, which is visible to our eyes, and falls under our knowledge. For we have remarked that the word *Church* is used in the sacred Scriptures in two senses. Sometimes, when they mention the Church, they intend that which is really such in the sight of God, into which none are received but those who by adoption and grace are the children of God, and by the sanctification of the Spirit are the true members of Christ. And then it comprehends not only the saints at any one time resident on earth, but all the elect who have lived from the beginning of the world. But the word *Church* is frequently used in the Scriptures to designate the whole multitude, dispersed all over the world, who profess to worship one God and Jesus Christ, who are initiated into his faith by baptism, who testify their unity in true doctrine and charity by a participation of the sacred supper, who consent to the word of the Lord, and preserve the ministry which Christ has instituted for the purpose of preaching it. In this Church are included many hypocrites, who have nothing of Christ but the name and appearance; many persons ambitious, avaricious, envious, slanderous, and dissolute in their lives, who are tolerated for a time, either because they cannot be convicted by a legitimate process, or because discipline is not always maintained with sufficient vigour. As it is necessary, therefore, to believe that Church, which is invisible to us, and known to God alone, so this Church, which is visible to men, we are commanded to honour, and to maintain communion with it.

As far, therefore, as was important for us to know it, the Lord has described it by certain marks and characters. It is the peculiar prerogative of God himself to "know them that are his," as we have already stated from Paul. And to guard against human presumption ever going to such an extreme, the experience of every day teaches us how very far his secret judgments transcend all our apprehensions. For those who seemed the most abandoned, and were generally considered past all hope, are recalled by his goodness into the right way; while some, who seemed to stand better than others, fall into perdition. "According to the secret predestination of God," therefore as Augustine observes, "there are many sheep without the pale of the Church, and many wolves within." For he knows and seals those who know not either him or themselves. Of those who externally bear his seal, his eyes alone can discern who are unfeignedly holy, and will persevere to the end; which is the completion of salvation. On the other hand, as he saw it to be in some measure requisite that we should know who ought to be considered as his children, he has in this respect accommodated himself to our capacity. And as it was not necessary that on this point we should have an assurance of faith, he has substituted in its place a judgment of charity, according to which we ought to acknowledge as members of the Church all those who by a confession of faith, an exemplary life, and a participation of the sacraments, profess the same God and Christ with ourselves. But the knowledge of the body itself being more necessary to our salvation, he has distinguished it by more clear and certain characters. . . .

Here are three things, therefore, worthy of our observation. First, that whatever holiness may distinguish the children of God, yet such is their condition as long as they inhabit a mortal body, that they cannot stand before God without remission of sins. Secondly, that this benefit belongs to the Church; so that we cannot enjoy it unless we continue in its communion. Thirdly, that it is dispensed to us by the ministers and pastors of the Church, either in the preaching of the gospel, or in the administration of the sacraments; and that this is the principal exercise of the power of the keys, which the Lord has conferred on the society of believers. Let every one of us, therefore, consider it as his duty, not to seek remission of sins any where but where the Lord has placed it. Of public reconciliation, which is a branch of discipline, we shall speak in its proper place. . . .

The readers may now see, collected into a brief summary, almost every thing that I have thought important to be known respecting these two sacraments; the use of which has been enjoined on the Christian Church from the commencement of the New Testament until the end of time; that is to say, baptism, to be a kind of entrance into the Church, and an initiatory profession of faith; and the Lord's supper, to be a continual nourishment, with which Christ spiritually feeds his family of believers. Wherefore, as there is but "one God, one Christ, one Faith," one Church, the body of Christ, so there is only "one baptism" and that is never repeated; but the supper is frequently distributed, that those who have once been admitted into the Church, may understand that they are continually nourished by Christ. Beside these two, as no other sacrament has been instituted by God, so no other ought to be acknowledged by the Church of believers. For that it is not left to the will of man to institute new sacraments, will be easily understood if we remember what has already been very plainly stated—that sacraments are appointed by God for the purpose of instructing us respecting some promise of his, and assuring us of his good-will towards us; and if we also consider, that no one has been the counsellor of God, capable of affording us any certainty respecting his will, or furnishing us any assurance of his disposition towards us, what he chooses to give or to deny us. Hence it follows, that no one can institute a sign to be a testimony respecting any determination or promise of his; he alone can furnish us a testimony respecting himself by giving a sign. I will express myself in terms more concise, and perhaps more homely, but more explicit—that there can be no sacrament unaccompanied with a promise of salvation. All mankind, collected in one assembly, can promise us nothing respecting our salvation. Therefore they can never institute or establish a sacrament.

Let the Christian Church, therefore, be content with these two, and not only neither admit nor acknowledge any other at present, but neither desire nor expect any other to the end of the world. For as the Jews, beside the ordinary sacraments given to them, had also several others, differing according to the varying circumstances of different periods, such as the manna, the water issuing from the rock, the brazen serpent, and the like, they were admonished by this variation not to rest in such figures, which were of short duration, but to expect from God something better, which should undergo no change and come to no end. But our case is very different: to us Christ has been revealed, "in whom are hid all the treasures of wisdom and knowledge," in such abundance and profusion, that to hope or desire any new accession to these treasures would really be to displease God, and provoke his wrath against us. We must hunger after Christ, we must seek, contemplate, and learn him alone, till the dawning of that great day, when our Lord will fully manifest the glory of his kingdom, and reveal himself to us, so that "we shall see him as he is." And for this reason, the dispensation under which we live is designated in the Scriptures as "the last time," "these last times," "the last days," that no one may deceive himself with a vain expectation of any new doctrine or revelation. For "God, who at sundry times and in divers manners spake in time past unto the fathers by the prophets, hath, in these last days, spoken unto us by his Son," who alone is able to "reveal the Father," and who, indeed, "hath declared him" fully, as far as is necessary for our happiness, while "now we see" him "through a glass darkly." As men are not left at liberty to institute new

sacraments in the Church of God, so it were to be wished that as little as possible of human invention should be mixed with those which have been instituted by God. For as wine is diluted and lost by an infusion of water, and as a whole mass of meal contracts acidity from a sprinkling of leaven, so the purity of Divine mysteries is only polluted when man makes any addition of his own. And yet we see, as the sacraments are observed in the present day, how very far they have degenerated from their original purity. There is every where an excess of pageantries, ceremonies, and gesticulations; but no consideration or mention of the word of God, without which even the sacraments themselves cease to be sacraments. And the very ceremonies which have been instituted by God are not to be discerned among such a multitude of others, by which they are overwhelmed. In baptism, how little is seen of that which ought to be the only conspicuous object—I mean baptism itself? And the Lord's supper has been completely buried since it has been transformed into the mass; except that it is exhibited once a year, but in a partial and mutilated form. . . .

But in the obedience which we have shown to be due to the authority of governors, it is always necessary to make one exception, and that is entitled to our first attention,—that it do not seduce us from obedience to him, to whose will the desires of all kings ought to be subject, to whose decrees all their commands ought to yield, to whose majesty all their sceptres ought to submit. And, indeed, how preposterous it would be for us, with a view to satisfy men, to incur the displeasure of him on whose account we yield obedience to men! The Lord, therefore, is the King of kings; who, when he has opened his sacred mouth, is to be heard alone, above all, for all, and before all; in the next place, we are subject to those men who preside over us; but no otherwise than in him. If they command any thing against him, it ought not to have the least attention; nor, in this case, ought we to pay any regard to all that dignity attached to magistrates; to which no injury is done when it is subjected to the unrivalled and supreme power of God.

Convocation of the Clergy

The Thirty-nine Articles of the Church of England were adopted in the early years of Queen Elizabeth's reign (1558–1603). They constitute the essential doctrine of the English Established Church and reflect the compromise reached in the English Reformation between the extremes of the Protestant revolt on the one hand and the traditional Roman Catholic position on the other. In reading them note (1) the relationship between God, the Son, and the Holy Ghost, (2) the authority placed in Holy Scripture, (3) the position taken on the historic Christian creeds, (4) the definition of original sin, (5) the relative importance of good works and faith in the justification of man before God, (6) the consideration of predestination and election, (7) the position taken on Christian universalism, (8) the "Romish" doctrines and practices which are condemned, (9) the number and nature of the sacraments, (10) the relationship between civil authority and the clergy, and (11) the attitude expressed concerning property and charity.

From: *THE THIRTY-NINE ARTICLES*

ARTICLES OF RELIGION

Article I. *Of Faith in the Holy Trinity.*

There is but one living and true God, everlasting, without body, parts, or passions; of infinite power, wisdom, and goodness; the Maker, and Preserver of all things both visible and invisible. And in unity of this Godhead there be three Persons, of one substance, power, and eternity; the Father, the Son, and the Holy Ghost.

Art. II. *Of the Word or Son of God, which was made very Man.*

The Son, which is the Word of the Father, begotten from everlasting of the Father, the very and eternal God, and of one substance with the Father, took Man's nature in the womb of the blessed Virgin, of her substance: so that two whole and perfect Natures, that is to say, the Godhead and Manhood, were joined together in one Person, never to be divided, whereof is one Christ, very God, and very Man; who truly suffered, was crucified, dead, and buried, to reconcile his Father to us, and to be a sacrifice, not only for original guilt, but also for all actual sins of men.

Art. III. *Of the going down of Christ into Hell.*

As Christ died for us, and was buried, so also is it to be believed, that he went down into Hell.

Art. IV. *Of the Resurrection of Christ.*

Christ did truly rise again from death, and took again his body, with flesh, bones, and all things appertaining to the perfection of Man's nature; wherewith he ascended into Heaven, and there sitteth, until he return to judge all Men at the last day.

Art. V. *Of the Holy Ghost.*

The Holy Ghost, proceeding from the Father and the Son, is of one substance, majesty, and glory, with the Father and the Son, very and eternal God.

The Book of Common Prayer, London, n.d., 621–633.

Art. VI. *Of the Sufficiency of the Holy Scriptures for Salvation.*

Holy Scripture containeth all things necessary to salvation: so that whatsoever is not read therein, nor may be proved thereby, is not to be required of any man, that it should be believed as an article of the Faith, or be thought requisite or necessary to salvation. In the name of the Holy Scripture we do understand those canonical Books of the Old and New Testament, of whose authority was never any doubt in the Church. . . .

Art. VII. *Of the Old Testament.*

The Old Testament is not contrary to the New: for both in the Old and New Testament everlasting life is offered to Mankind by Christ, who is the only Mediator between God and Man, being both God and Man. Wherefore they are not to be heard, which feign that the old Fathers did look only for transitory promises. Although the Law given from God by Moses, as touching Ceremonies and Rites, do not bind Christian men, nor the Civil precepts thereof ought of necessity to be received in any commonwealth; yet notwithstanding, no Christian man whatsoever is free from the obedience of the Commandments which are called Moral.

Art. VIII. *Of the Three Creeds.*

The Three Creeds, *Nicene* Creed, *Athanasius's* Creed, and that which is commonly called the *Apostles'* Creed, ought thoroughly to be received and believed: for they may be proved by most certain warrants of Holy Scripture.

Art. IX. *Of Original or Birth-Sin.*

Original Sin standeth not in the following of *Adam* (as the *Pelagians* do vainly talk); but it is the fault and corruption of the Nature of every man, that naturally is engendered of the offspring of *Adam;* whereby man is very far gone from original righteousness, and is of his own nature inclined to evil, so that the flesh lusteth always contrary to the spirit; and therefore in every person born into this world, it deserveth God's wrath and damnation. And this infection of nature doth remain, yea in them that are regenerated; whereby the lust of the flesh, called in Greek, *phronema sarkos,* which some do expound the wisdom, some sensuality, some the affection, some the desire, of the flesh, is not subject to the Law of God. And although there is no condemnation for them that believe and are baptized; yet the Apostle doth confess, that concupiscence and lust hath of itself the nature of sin.

Art. X. *Of Free-Will.*

The condition of Man after the fall of *Adam* is such, that he cannot turn and prepare himself, by his own natural strength and good works, to faith, and calling upon God: Wherefore we have no power to do good works pleasant and acceptable to God, without the grace of God by Christ preventing us, that we may have a good will, and working with us, when we have that good will.

Art. XI. *Of the Justification of Man.*

We are accounted righteous before God, only for the merit of our Lord and Saviour Jesus Christ by Faith, and not for our own works or deservings. Wherefore, that we are justified by Faith only, is a most wholesome Doctrine, and very full of comfort, as more largely is expressed in the Homily of Justification.

Art. XII. *Of Good Works.*

Albeit that Good Works, which are the fruits of Faith, and follow after Justification, cannot put away our sins, and endure the severity of God's Judgment; yet are they pleasing and acceptable to God in Christ, and do spring out necessarily of a true and lively Faith; insomuch that by them a lively Faith may be as evidently known as a tree discerned by the fruit.

Art. XIII. *Of Works before Justification.*

Works done before the grace of Christ, and the Inspiration of his Spirit, are not pleasant to God, forasmuch as they spring not of faith in Jesus Christ, neither do they make men meet to receive grace, or (as the School-authors say) deserve grace of congruity: yea rather, for that they are not done as God hath willed and commanded them to be done, we doubt not but they have the nature of sin.

Art. XIV. *Of Works of Supererogation.*

Voluntary Works besides, over and above, God's Commandments, which they call Works of Supererogation, cannot be taught without arrogancy and impiety: for by them men do declare, that they do not only render unto God as much as they are bound to do, but that they do more for his sake, than of bounden duty is required: whereas Christ saith plainly, When ye have done all that are commanded to you, say, We are unprofitable servants.

Art. XV. *Of Christ alone without Sin.*

Christ in the truth of our nature was made like unto us in all things, sin only except, from which he was clearly void, both in his flesh, and in his spirit. He came to be the Lamb without spot, who, by sacrifice of himself once made, should take away the sins of the world, and sin, as Saint *John* saith, was not in him. But all we the rest, although baptized, and born again in Christ, yet offend in many things; and if we say we have no sin, we deceive ourselves, and the truth is not in us.

Art. XVI. *Of Sin after Baptism.*

Not every deadly sin willingly committed after Baptism is sin against the Holy Ghost, and unpardonable. Wherefore the grant of repentance is not to be denied to such as fall into sin after Baptism. After we have received the Holy Ghost, we may depart from grace given, and fall into sin, and by the grace of God we may arise again, and amend our lives. And therefore they are to be condemned, which say, they can no more sin as long as they live here, or deny the place of forgiveness to such as truly repent.

Art. XVII. *Of Predestination and Election.*

Predestination to Life is the everlasting purpose of God, whereby (before the foundations of the world were laid) he hath constantly decreed by his counsel secret to us, to deliver from curse and damnation those whom he hath chosen in Christ out of mankind, and to bring them by Christ to everlasting salvation, as vessels made to honour. Wherefore, they which be endued with so excellent a benefit of God, be called according to God's purpose by his Spirit working in due season: they through Grace obey the calling: they be justified freely: they be made sons of God by adoption: they be made like the image of his only-begotten Son Jesus Christ: they walk religiously in good works, and at length, by God's mercy, they attain to everlasting felicity.

As the godly consideration of Predestination, and our Election in Christ, is full of sweet, pleasant, and unspeakable comfort to godly persons, and such as feel in themselves the working of the Spirit of Christ, mortifying the works of the flesh, and their earthly members, and drawing up their mind to high and heavenly things, as well because it doth greatly establish and confirm their faith of eternal Salvation to be enjoyed through Christ, as because it doth fervently kindle their love towards God: So, for curious and carnal persons, lacking the Spirit of Christ, to have continually before their eyes the sentence of God's Predestination, is a most dangerous downfall, whereby the Devil doth thrust them either into desperation, or into wretchlessness of most unclean living, no less perilous than desperation.

Furthermore, we must receive God's promises in such wise, as they be generally set forth to us in Holy Scripture: and, in our doings, that Will of God is to be followed, which we have expressly declared unto us in the Word of God.

Art. XVIII. *Of Obtaining Eternal Salvation only by the Name of Christ.*

They also are to be had accursed that presume to say, That every man shall be saved by the Law or Sect which he professeth, so that he be diligent to frame his life according to that Law, and the light of Nature. For Holy Scripture doth set out unto us only the Name of Jesus Christ, whereby men must be saved.

Art. XIX. *Of the Church.*

The visible Church of Christ is a congregation of faithful men, in the which the pure Word of God is preached, and the Sacraments be duly ministered according to Christ's ordinance, in all those things that of necessity are requisite to the same.

As the Church of *Jerusalem, Alexandria,* and *Antioch,* have erred; so also the Church of

Rome hath erred, not only in their living and manner of Ceremonies, but also in matters of Faith.

Art. XX. *Of the Authority of the Church.*

The Church hath power to decree Rites or Ceremonies, and authority in Controversies of Faith: and yet it is not lawful for the Church to ordain any thing that is contrary to God's Word written, neither may it so expound one place of Scripture, that it be repugnant to another. Wherefore, although the Church be a witness and a keeper of Holy Writ, yet, as it ought not to decree any thing against the same, so besides the same ought it not to enforce any thing to be believed for necessity of Salvation.

Art. XXI. *Of the Authority of General Councils.*

General Councils may not be gathered together without the commandment and will of Princes. And when they be gathered together (forasmuch as they be an assembly of men, whereof all be not governed with the Spirit and Word of God), they may err, and sometimes have erred, even in things pertaining unto God. Wherefore things ordained by them as necessary to salvation have neither strength nor authority, unless it may be declared that they be taken out of Holy Scripture.

Art. XXII. *Of Purgatory.*

The Romish Doctrine concerning Purgatory, Pardons, Worshipping and Adoration, as well of Images as of Reliques, and also Invocation of Saints, is a fond thing, vainly invented, and grounded upon no warranty of Scripture, but rather repugnant to the Word of God.

Art. XXIII. *Of Ministering in the Congregation.*

It is not lawful for any man to take upon him the office of publick preaching, or ministering the Sacraments in the Congregation, before he be lawfully called, and sent to execute the same. And those we ought to judge lawfully called and sent, which be chosen and called to this work by men who have publick authority given unto them in the Congregation, to call and send Ministers into the Lord's vineyard.

Art. XXIV. *Of Speaking in the Congregation in such a Tongue as the People Understandeth.*

It is a thing plainly repugnant to the Word of God, and the custom of the Primitive Church, to have publick Prayer in the Church, or to minister the Sacraments, in a tongue not understood of the people.

Art. XXV. *Of the Sacraments.*

Sacraments ordained of Christ be not only badges or tokens of Christian men's profession, but rather they be certain sure witnesses, and effectual signs of grace, and God's good will towards us, by the which he doth work invisibly in us, and doth not only quicken, but also strengthen and confirm our Faith in him.

There are two Sacraments ordained of Christ our Lord in the Gospel, that is to say, Baptism, and the Supper of the Lord.

Those five commonly called Sacraments, that is to say, Confirmation, Penance, Orders, Matrimony, and Extreme Unction, are not to be counted for Sacraments of the Gospel, being such as have grown partly of the corrupt following of the Apostles, partly are states of life allowed in the Scriptures; but yet have not like nature of Sacraments with Baptism, and the Lord's Supper, for that they have not any visible sign or ceremony ordained of God.

The Sacraments were not ordained of Christ to be gazed upon, or to be carried about, but that we should duly use them. And in such only as worthily receive the same they have a wholesome effect or operation: but they that receive them unworthily, purchase to themselves damnation, as Saint *Paul* saith.

Art. XXVI. *Of the Unworthiness of the Ministers, which Hinders not the Effect of the Sacraments.*

Although in the visible Church the evil be ever mingled with the good, and sometimes the evil have chief authority in the Ministration of the Word and Sacraments, yet forasmuch as they do not the same in their own name, but in Christ's, and do minister by his commission and authority, we may use their Ministry, both in hearing the Word of God, and in the receiving of the Sacraments. Neither is the effect of Christ's ordinance taken away by their wickedness, nor the grace of God's gifts diminished from such as by faith and rightly, do receive the Sacraments ministered unto them; which be effectual, because of Christ's institution and promise, although they be ministered by evil men.

Nevertheless, it appertaineth to the discipline of the Church, that enquiry be made of evil Ministers, and that they be accused by those that have knowledge of their offences; and finally, being found guilty, by just judgment be deposed.

Art. XXVII. *Of Baptism.*

Baptism is not only a sign of profession, and mark of difference, whereby Christian men are discerned from others that be not christened, but it is also a sign of Regeneration or new-birth, whereby, as by an instrument, they that receive Baptism rightly are grafted into the Church; the promises of the forgiveness of sin, and of our adoption to be the sons of God by the Holy Ghost, are visibly signed and sealed; Faith is confirmed, and Grace increased by virtue of prayer unto God.

The Baptism of young Children is in any wise to be retained in the Church, as most agreeable with the institution of Christ.

Art. XXVIII. *Of the Lord's Supper.*

The Supper of the Lord is not only a sign of love that Christians ought to have among themselves one to another; but rather it is a Sacrament of our Redemption by Christ's death: insomuch that to such as rightly, worthily, and with faith, receive the same, the Bread which we break is a partaking of the Body of Christ; and likewise the Cup of Blessing is a partaking of the Blood of Christ.

Transubstantiation (or the change of the substance of Bread and Wine) in the Supper of the Lord, cannot be proved by Holy Writ; but is repugnant to the plain words of Scripture, overthroweth the nature of a Sacrament, and hath given occasion to many superstitions.

The Body of Christ is given, taken, and eaten, in the Supper, only after an heavenly and spiritual manner. And the mean whereby the Body of Christ is received and eaten in the Supper, is Faith.

The Sacrament of the Lord's Supper was not by Christ's ordinance reserved, carried about, lifted up, or worshipped.

Art. XXIX. *Of the Wicked which eat not the Body of Christ in the Use of the Lord's Supper.*

The Wicked, and such as be void of a lively faith, although they do carnally and visibly press with their teeth (as Saint *Augustine* saith) the Sacrament of the Body and Blood of Christ; yet in no wise are they partakers of Christ: but rather, to their condemnation, do eat and drink the sign or Sacrament of so great a thing.

Art. XXX. *Of Both Kinds.*

The Cup of the Lord is not to be denied to the Lay-people: for both the parts of the Lord's Sacrament, by Christ's ordinance and commandment, ought to be ministered to all Christian men alike.

Art. XXXI. *Of the One Oblation of Christ Finished upon the Cross.*

The Offering of Christ once made is that perfect redemption, propitiation, and satisfaction, for all the sins of the whole world, both original and actual; and there is none other satisfaction for sin, but that alone. Wherefore the sacrifices of Masses, in the which it was commonly said, that the Priest did offer Christ for the quick and the dead, to have remission of pain or guilt, were blasphemous fables, and dangerous deceits.

Art. XXXII. *Of the Marriage of Priests.*

Bishops, Priests, and Deacons, are not commanded by God's Law, either to vow the estate of single life, or to abstain from marriage: therefore it is lawful also for them, as for all other Christian men, to marry at their own discretion, as they shall judge the same to serve better to godliness.

Art. XXXIII. *Of Excommunicate Persons, how They are to be Avoided.*

That person which by open denunciation of the Church is rightly cut off from the unity of the Church, and excommunicated, ought to be taken of the whole multitude of the faithful, as an Heathen and Publican, until he be openly reconciled by penance, and received into the Church by a Judge that hath authority thereunto.

Art. XXXIV. *Of the Traditions of the Church.*

It is not necessary that traditions and ceremonies be in all places one, or utterly like; for at all times they have been divers, and may be changed according to the diversities of countries, times, and men's manners, so that nothing be ordained against God's Word. Whosoever, through his private judgment, willingly and purposely, doth openly break the Traditions and Ceremonies of the Church, which be not repugnant to the Word of God, and be ordained and approved by common authority, ought to be rebuked openly (that others may fear to do the like), as he that offendeth against the common order of the Church, and hurteth the authority of the Magistrate, and woundeth the consciences of the weak brethren.

Every particular or national Church hath authority to ordain, change, and abolish, ceremonies or rites of the Church ordained only by man's authority, so that all things be done to edifying.

Art. XXXV. *Of Homilies.*

The Second Book of Homilies, the several titles whereof we have joined under this Article, doth contain a godly and wholesome Doctrine, and necessary for these times, as doth the former Book of Homilies, which were set forth in the time of *Edward* the Sixth; and therefore we judge them to be read in Churches by the Ministers, diligently and distinctly, that they may be understood of the people.

Art. XXXVI. *Of Consecration of Bishops and Ministers.*

The Book of Consecration of Archbishops and Bishops, and Ordering of Priests and Deacons, lately set forth in the time of *Edward* the Sixth, and confirmed at the same time by authority of Parliament, doth contain all things necessary to such Consecration and Ordering: neither hath it anything, that of itself is superstitious and ungodly. And therefore whosoever are consecrated or ordered according to the Rites of that Book, since the second year of the forenamed King *Edward* unto this time, or hereafter shall be consecrated or ordered according to the same Rites; we decree all such to be rightly, orderly, and lawfully consecrated and ordered.

Art. XXXVII. *Of the Civil Magistrates.*

The King's Majesty hath the chief power in this Realm of *England,* and other his Dominions, unto whom the chief Government of all Estates of this Realm, whether they be Ecclesiastical or Civil, in all causes doth appertain, and is not, nor ought to be, subject to any foreign Jurisdiction.

Where we attribute to the King's Majesty the chief government, by which Titles we understand the minds of some slanderous folks to be offended; we give not to our Princes the ministering either of God's Word, or of the Sacraments, the which thing the Injunctions also lately set forth by *Elizabeth* our Queen do most plainly testify; but that only prerogative, which we see to have been given always to all godly Princes in Holy Scriptures by God himself; that is, that they should rule all estates and degrees committed to their charge by God, whether they be Ecclesiastical or Temporal, and restrain with the civil sword the stubborn and evil-doers.

The Bishop of *Rome* hath no jurisdiction in this Realm of *England.*

The Laws of the Realm may punish Christian men with death, for heinous and grievous offences.

It is lawful for Christian men, at the commandment of the Magistrate, to wear weapons, and serve in the wars.

Art. XXXVIII. *Of Christian Men's Goods, which are not Common.*

The Riches and Goods of Christians are not common, as touching the right, title, and possession of the same, as certain Anabaptists do falsely boast. Notwithstanding, every man ought, of such things as he possesseth, liberally to give alms to the poor, according to his ability.

Art. XXXIX. *Of a Christian Man's Oath.*

As we confess that vain and rash Swearing is forbidden Christian men by our Lord Jesus Christ, and *James* his Apostle, so we judge, that Christian Religion doth not prohibit, but that a man may swear when the Magistrate requireth, in a cause of faith and charity, so it be done according to the Prophet's teaching, in justice, judgment, and truth.

Council of Trent

Between 1545 and 1564 the Catholic Church held a general council in the city of Trent. During that time a total of 25 sessions were called and important decisions reached about the vital religious issues of the Reformation period. The procedure followed was to discuss problems at some length, then to set forth the accepted view of the Church in a series of chapters, and finally to draw up a list of canons anathematizing those who held contrary views. In reading the selected chapters and canons note (1) the purposes for which the council was called, (2) the decree concerning the edition of the Bible to be considered authentic and who was to interpret it, (3) the position taken on original sin, (4) the admonition concerning predestination, (5) the canons treating with the number and character of the sacraments, (6) the attitude taken on the doctrine of transubstantiation, (7) the measures adopted affecting the lives and habits of the clergy, (8) the description of the character and ranks of the clergy, (9) the decision concerning the place of relics, saints, and images in religious practices, and (10) the position taken on the controversial issue of indulgences.

From: THE DECREES OF THE COUNCIL OF TRENT

DECREE TOUCHING THE OPENING OF THE COUNCIL

Doth it please you,—unto the praise and glory of the holy and undivided Trinity, Father, and Son, and Holy Ghost; for the increase and exaltation of the Christian faith and religion; for the extirpation of heresies; for the peace and union of the Church; for the reformation of the Clergy and Christian people; for the depression and extinction of the enemies of the Christian name,—to decree and declare that the sacred and general council of Trent do begin, and hath begun?

They answered: It pleaseth us.

DECREE CONCERNING THE EDITION, AND THE USE, OF THE SACRED BOOKS

Moreover, the same sacred and holy Synod, —considering that no small utility may accrue to the Church of God, if it be made known which out of all the Latin editions, now in circulation, of the sacred books, is to be held as authentic,—ordains and declares, that the said old and vulgate edition, which, by the lengthened usage of so many ages, has been approved of in the Church, be, in public lectures, disputations, sermons and expositions, held as authentic; and that no one is to dare, or presume to reject it under any pretext whatever.

Furthermore, in order to restrain petulant spirits, It decrees, that no one, relying on his own skill, shall,—in matters of faith, and of morals pertaining to the edification of Christian doctrine,—wrestling the sacred Scripture to his own senses, presume to interpret the said sacred Scripture contrary to that sense which holy mother Church,—whose it is to judge of the true sense and interpretation of the holy Scriptures,—hath held and doth hold; or even contrary to the unanimous consent of the Fathers; even though such interpretations were

As translated by J. Waterworth in *The Canons and Decrees of the Sacred and Œcumenical Council of Trent.* . . . London, 1848, 12; 19–23; 39–40; 54–55; 78; 82–84; 116–117; 158–159; 162–163; 173–174; 233–235; 270–271; 277–278.

never (intended) to be at any time published. Contraveners shall be made known by their Ordinaries, and be punished with the penalties by law established.

DECREE CONCERNING ORIGINAL SIN

That our Catholic *faith, without which it is impossible to please God,* may, errors being purged away, continue in its own perfect and spotless integrity, and that the Christian people may not *be carried about with every wind of doctrine;* whereas that old serpent, the perpetual enemy of mankind, amongst the very many evils with which the Church of God is in these our times troubled, has also stirred up not only new, but even old, dissensions touching original sin, and the remedy thereof; the sacred and holy, oecumenical and general Synod of Trent,—lawfully assembled in the Holy Ghost, the three same legates of the Apostolic See presiding therein,—wishing now to come to the reclaiming of the erring, and the confirming of the wavering,—following the testimonies of the sacred Scriptures, of the holy Fathers, of the most approved councils, and the judgment and consent of the Church itself, ordains, confesses, and declares these things touching the said original sin:

1. If any one does not confess that the first man, Adam, when he had transgressed the commandment of God in Paradise, immediately lost the holiness and justice wherein he had been constituted; and that he incurred, through the offence of that prevarication, the wrath and indignation of God, and consequently death, with which God had previously threatened him, and, together with death, captivity under his power who thenceforth *had the empire of death, that is to say, the devil,* and that the entire Adam, through that offence of prevarication, was changed, in body and soul, for the worse; let him be anathema.

2. If any one asserts, that the prevarication of Adam injured himself alone, and not his posterity; and that the holiness and justice, received of God, which he lost, he lost for himself alone, and not for us also; or that he, being defiled by the sin of disobedience, has only transfused death, and pains of the body, into the whole human race, but not sin also, which is the death of the soul; let him be anathema:—whereas he contradicts the apostle who says: *By one man sin entered into the world, and by sin death, and so death passed upon all men, in whom all have sinned.*

3. If any one asserts, that this sin of Adam,—which in its origin is one, and being transfused into all by propagation, not by imitation, is in each one as his own,—is taken away either by the powers of human nature, or by any other remedy than the merit of the *one mediator, our Lord Jesus Christ, who hath reconciled us to God in his own blood, made unto us justice, sanctification, and redemption;* or if he denies that the said merit of Jesus Christ is applied, both to adults and to infants, by the sacrament of baptism rightly administered in the form of the Church; let him be anathema: *For there is no other name under heaven given to men, whereby we must be saved.* Whence that voice: *Behold the lamb of God, behold him who taketh away the sins of the world;* and that other: *As many as have been baptized, have put on Christ.*

DECREE ON JUSTIFICATION

. . . No one, moreover, so long as he is in this mortal life, ought so far to presume as regards the secret mystery of divine predestination, as to determine for certain that he is assuredly in the number of the predestinate; as if it were true, that he that is justified, either cannot sin any more, or, if he do sin, that he ought to promise himself an assured repentance; for except by special revelation, it cannot be known whom God hath chosen unto Himself. . . .

DECREE ON THE SACRAMENTS IN GENERAL

Canon I.—If any one saith, that the sacraments of the New Law were not all instituted by Jesus Christ, our Lord; or, that they are more, or less, than seven, to wit, Baptism, Confirmation, the Eucharist, Penance, Extreme Unction, Order, and Matrimony; or even that any one of these seven is not truly and properly a sacrament; let him be anathema.

Canon IV.—If any one saith, that the sacraments of the New Law are not necessary unto salvation, but superfluous; and that, without them, or without the desire thereof, men obtain of God, through faith alone, the grace of justification;—though all (the sacraments) are not indeed necessary for every individual; let him be anathema.

Canon V.—If any one saith, that these sacraments were instituted for the sake of nourishing faith alone; let him be anathema.

Canon VI.—If any one saith, that the sacraments of the New Law do not contain the grace which they signify; or, that they do not confer that grace on those who do not place an obstacle thereunto; as though they were merely outward signs of grace or justice received through faith, and certain marks of the Christian profession, whereby believers are distinguished amongst men from unbelievers; let him be anathema.

Canon VII.—If any one saith, that grace, as far as God's part is concerned, is not given through the said sacraments, always, and to all men, even though they receive them rightly, but (only) sometimes, and to some persons; let him be anathema.

Canon VIII.—If any one saith, that by the said sacraments of the New Law grace is not conferred through the act performed, but that faith alone in the divine promise suffices for the obtaining of grace; let him be anathema.

Canon IX.—If any one saith, that, in the three sacraments, Baptism, to wit, Confirmation, and Order, there is not imprinted in the soul a character, that is, a certain spiritual and indelible sign, on account of which they cannot be repeated; let him be anathema.

Canon X.—If any one saith, that all Christians have power to administer the word, and all the sacraments; let him be anathema.

Canon XI.—If any one saith, that, in ministers, when they effect, and confer the sacraments, there is not required the intention at least of doing what the Church does; let him be anathema.

Canon XII.—If any one saith, that a minister, being in mortal sin,—if so be that he observe all the essentials which belong to the effecting, or conferring of, the sacrament,—neither effects, nor confers the sacrament; let him be anathema. . . .

DECREE CONCERNING THE MOST HOLY SACRAMENT OF THE EUCHARIST

. . . And because that Christ, our Redeemer, declared that which He offered under the species of bread to be truly His own body, therefore has it ever been a firm belief in the Church of God, and this holy Synod doth now declare it anew, that, by the consecration of the bread and of the wine, a conversion is made of the whole substance of the bread into the substance of the body of Christ our Lord, and of the whole substance of the wine into the substance of His blood; which conversion is, by the holy Catholic Church, suitably and properly called Transubstantiation.

ON THE MOST HOLY SACRAMENT OF THE EUCHARIST

Canon I.—If any one denieth, that, in the sacrament of the most holy Eucharist, are contained truly, really, and substantially, the body and blood together with the soul and divinity of our Lord Jesus Christ, and consequently the whole Christ; but saith that He is only therein as in a sign, or in figure, or virtue; let him be anathema.

Canon II.—If any one saith, that, in the sacred and holy sacrament of the Eucharist, the substance of the bread and wine remains conjointly with the body and blood of our Lord Jesus Christ, and denieth that wonderful and singular conversion of the whole substance of the bread into the Body, and of the whole substance of the wine into the Blood—the species only of the bread and wine remaining—which conversion indeed the Catholic Church most aptly calls Transubstantiation; let him be anathema.

Canon III.—If any one denieth, that, in the venerable sacrament of the Eucharist, the whole Christ is contained under each species, and under every part of each species, when separated; let him be anathema.

Canon IV.—If any one saith, that, after the consecration is completed, the body and blood of our Lord Jesus Christ are not in the admirable sacrament of the Eucharist, but (are there) only during the use, whilst it is being taken, and not either before or after; and that, in the hosts, or consecrated particles, which are reserved or which remain after communion, the true Body of the Lord remaineth not; let him be anathema.

Canon V.—If any one saith, either that the principal fruit of the most holy Eucharist is the remission of sins, or, that other effects do not result therefrom; let him be anathema.

Canon VI.—If any one saith, that, in the holy sacrament of the Eucharist, Christ, the only-begotten Son of God, is not to be adored with the worship, even external of latria; and is, consequently, neither to be venerated with a special festive solemnity, nor to be solemnly borne about in processions, according to the laudable and universal rite and custom of holy church; or, is not to be proposed publicly to the people to be adored, and that the adorers thereof are idolators; let him be anathema.

Canon VII.—If any one saith, that it is not lawful for the sacred Eucharist to be reserved in the *sacrarium,* but that, immediately after consecration, it must necessarily be distributed amongst those present; or, that it is not lawful that it be carried with honour to the sick; let him be anathema.

Canon VIII.—If any one saith, that Christ, given in the Eucharist, is eaten spiritually only, and not also sacramentally and really; let him be anathema.

Canon IX.—If any one denieth, that all and each of Christ's faithful of both sexes are bound, when they have attained to years of discretion, to communicate every year, at least at Easter, in accordance with the precept of holy Mother Church; let him be anathema.

Canon X.—If any one saith, that it is not lawful for the celebrating priest to communicate himself; let him be anathema.

Canon XI.—If any one saith, that faith alone is a sufficient preparation for receiving the sacrament of the most holy Eucharist; let him be anathema. And for fear lest so great a sacrament may be received unworthily, and so unto death and condemnation, this holy Synod ordains and declares, that sacramental confession, when a confessor may be had, is of necessity to be made beforehand, by those whose conscience is burthened with mortal sin, how contrite even soever they may think themselves. But if any one shall presume to teach, preach,

or obstinately to assert, or even in public disputation to defend the contrary, he shall be thereupon excommunicated.

DECREE ON REFORMATION

. . . And forasmuch as, though the habit does not make the monk, it is nevertheless needful that clerics always wear a dress suitable to their proper order, that by the decency of their outward apparel they may show forth the inward correctness of their morals; but to such a pitch, in these days, have the contempt of religion and the rashness of some grown, as that, making but little account of their own dignity, and of the clerical honour, they even wear in public the dress of laymen—setting their feet in different paths, one of God, the other of the flesh;—for this cause, all ecclesiastical persons, howsoever exempted, who are either in sacred orders or in possession of any manner of dignities, personates, or other offices, or benefices ecclesiastical; if, after having been admonished by their own bishop, even by a public edict, they shall not wear a becoming clerical dress, suitable to their order and dignity, and in conformity with the ordinance and mandate of the said bishop, they may, and ought to be, compelled thereunto, by suspension from their orders, office, benefice, and from the fruits, revenues, and proceeds of the said benefices; and also, if, after having been once rebuked, they offend again herein (they are to be coerced) even by deprivation of the said offices and benefices. . . .

Whereas too, *he who has killed his neighbour on set purpose and by lying in wait for him, is to be taken away from the altar,* because he has voluntarily committed a homicide; even though that crime have neither been proved by ordinary process of law, nor be otherwise public, but is secret, such an one can never be promoted to sacred orders; nor shall it be lawful to confer upon him any ecclesiastical benefices, even though they have no cure of souls; but he shall be for ever excluded from every ecclesiastical order, benefice, and office. . . .

ON THE SACRIFICE OF THE MASS

. . . Canon I.—If any one saith, that in the mass a true and proper sacrifice is not offered to God; or, that to be offered is nothing else but that Christ is given us to eat; let him be anathema.

Canon II.—If any one saith, that by those words, *Do this for the commemoration of me, . . .* Christ did not institute the apostles priests; or, did not ordain that they, and other priests should offer His own body and blood; let him be anathema.

Canon III.—If any one saith, that the sacrifice of the mass is only a sacrifice of praise and of thanksgiving; or, that it is a bare commemoration of the sacrifice consummated on the cross, but not a propitiatory sacrifice; or, that it profits him only who receives; and that it ought not to be offered for the living and the dead for sins, pains, satisfactions, and other necessities; let him be anathema.

DECREE ON REFORMATION

. . . There is nothing that continually *instructs others unto piety*, and the service of God, more than the life and example of those who have dedicated themselves to the divine ministry. For as they are seen to be raised to a higher position, above the things of this world, others fix their eyes upon them as upon a mirror, and derive from them what they are to imitate. Wherefore clerics called to have the Lord for their portion, ought by all means so to regulate their whole life and conversation, as that in their dress, comportment, gait, discourse, and all things else, nothing appear but what is grave, regulated, and replete with religiousness; avoiding even slight faults, which in them would be most grievous; that so their actions may impress all with veneration. Whereas, therefore, the more useful and decorous these things are for the Church of God, the more carefully also are they to be attended to; the holy Synod ordains, that those things which have been heretofore copiously and wholesomely enacted by sovereign pontiffs and sacred councils,—relative to the life, propriety of conduct, dress, and learning of clerics, and also touching the luxuriousness, feastings, dances, gambling, sports, and all sorts of crime whatever, as also the secular employments, to be by them shunned,—the same shall be henceforth observed, under the same penalties, or

greater, to be imposed at the discretion of the Ordinary; nor shall any appeal suspend the execution hereof, as relating to the correction of manners. But if anything of the above shall be found to have fallen into desuetude, they shall make it their care that it be brought again into use as soon as possible, and be accurately observed by all; any customs to the contrary notwithstanding; lest they themselves may have, God being the avenger, to pay the penalty deserved by their neglect of the correction of those subject to them. . . .

ON THE SACRAMENT OF ORDER

Canon I.—If any one saith, that there is not in the New Testament a visible and external priesthood; or that there is not any power of consecrating and offering the true body and blood of the Lord, and of forgiving and retaining sins; but only an office and bare ministry of preaching the Gospel; or, that those who do not preach are not priests at all; let him be anathema.

Canon II.—If any one saith, that, besides the priesthood, there are not in the Catholic Church other orders, both greater and minor, by which, as by certain steps, advance is made unto the priesthood; let him be anathema.

Canon III.—If any one saith, that order, or sacred ordination, is not truly and properly a sacrament instituted by Christ the Lord; or, that it is a kind of human figment devised by men unskilled in ecclesiastical matters; or, that it is only a kind of rite for choosing ministers of the word of God and of the sacraments; let him be anathema.

Canon IV.—If any one saith, that, by sacred ordination, the Holy Ghost is not given; and that vainly therefore do the bishops say, *Receive ye the Holy Ghost;* or, that a character is not imprinted by that ordination; or, that he who has once been a priest, can again become a layman; let him be anathema.

Canon V.—If any one saith, that the sacred unction which the Church uses in holy ordination, is not only not required, but is to be despised and is pernicious, as likewise are the other ceremonies of Order; let him be anathema.

Canon VI.—If any one saith, that, in the

Catholic Church there is not a hierarchy by divine ordination instituted, consisting of bishops, priests, and ministers; let him be anathema.

Canon VII.—If any one saith, that bishops are not superior to priests; or, that they have not the power of confirming and ordaining; or, that the power which they possess is common to them and to priests; or, that orders, conferred by them, without the consent, or vocation of the people, or of the secular power, are invalid; or, that those who have neither been rightly ordained, nor sent, by ecclesiastical and canonical power, but come from elsewhere, are lawful ministers of the word and of the sacraments; let him be anathema.

Canon VIII.—If any one saith, that the bishops, who are assumed by authority of the Roman Pontiff, are not legitimate and true bishops, but are a human figment; let him be anathema.

ON THE SACRAMENT OF MATRIMONY

Canon IX.—If any one saith, that clerics constituted in sacred orders, or Regulars, who have solemnly professed chastity, are able to contract marriage, and that being contracted it is valid, notwithstanding the ecclesiastical law, or vow; and that the contrary is nothing else than to condemn marriage; and, that all who do not feel that they have the gift of chastity, even though they have made a vow thereof, may contract marriage; let him be anathema: seeing that God refuses not that gift to those who ask for it rightly, neither does *He suffer us to be tempted above that which we are able.*

ON THE INVOCATION, VENERATION, AND RELICS, OF SAINTS, AND ON SACRED IMAGES

The holy Synod enjoins on all bishops, and others who sustain the office and charge of teaching, that, agreeably to the usage of the Catholic and Apostolic Church, received from the primitive times of the Christian religion, and agreeably to the consent of the holy Fathers, and to the decrees of sacred Councils, they especially instruct the faithful diligently concerning the intercession and invocation of saints; the honour (paid) to relics; and the legitimate use of images: teaching them, that the saints, who reign together with Christ, offer up their own prayers to God for men; that it is good and useful suppliantly to invoke them, and to have recourse to their prayers, aid, (and) help for obtaining benefits from God, through His Son, Jesus Christ our Lord, who is our alone Redeemer and Saviour; but that they think impiously, who deny that the saints, who enjoy eternal happiness in heaven, are to be invocated; or who assert either that they do not pray for men; or, that the invocation of them to pray for each of us even in particular, is idolatry; or, that it is repugnant to the word of God; and is opposed to the honour of the *one mediator of God and men, Christ Jesus;* or, that it is foolish to supplicate, vocally, or mentally, those who reign in heaven. Also, that the holy bodies of holy martyrs, and of others now living with Christ,—which bodies were the living members of Christ, and *the temple of the Holy Ghost,* and which are by Him to be raised unto eternal life, and to be glorified, —are to be venerated by the faithful; through which (bodies) many benefits are bestowed by God on men; so that they who affirm that veneration and honour are not due to the relics of saints; or, that these, and other sacred monuments, are uselessly honoured by the faithful; and that the places dedicated to the memories of the saints are in vain visited with the view of obtaining their aid; are wholly to be condemned, as the Church has already long since condemned, and now also condemns them.

Moreover, that the images of Christ, of the Virgin Mother of God, and of the other saints, are to be had and retained particularly in temples, and that due honour and veneration are to be given them; not that any divinity, or virtue, is believed to be in them, on account of which they are to be worshipped; or that anything is to be asked of them; or, that trust is to be reposed in images, as was of old done by the Gentiles who placed their hope in idols; but because the honour which is shown them is referred to the prototypes which those images represent; in such wise that by the images which we kiss, and before which we uncover the head, and prostrate ourselves, we adore Christ; and we venerate the saints, whose similitude they bear: as, by the decrees of Councils, and especially of the second Synod of Nicaea, has been defined against the opponents of images. . . .

ON REFORMATION

. . . How shameful a thing, and how unworthy it is of the name of clerics who have devoted themselves to the service of God, to live in the filth of impurity, and unclean bondage, the thing itself doth testify, in the common scandal of all the faithful, and the extreme disgrace entailed on the clerical order. To the end, therefore, that the ministers of the Church may be recalled to that continency and integrity of life which becomes them; and that the people may hence learn to reverence them the more, that they know them to be more pure of life: the holy Synod forbids all clerics whatsoever to dare to keep concubines, or any other woman of whom any suspicion can exist, either in their own houses, or elsewhere, or to presume to have any intercourse with them: otherwise they shall be punished with the penalties imposed by the sacred canons, or by the statutes of the (several) churches. But if, after being admonished by their superiors, they shall not abstain from these women, they shall be *ipso facto* deprived of the third part of the fruits, rents, and proceeds of all their benefices whatsoever, and pensions; which third part shall be applied to the fabric of the church, or to some other pious place, at the discretion of the bishop. If, however, persisting in the same crime, with the same or some other woman, they shall not even yet have obeyed upon a second admonition, not only shall they thereupon forfeit all the fruits and proceeds of their benefices and pensions, which shall be applied to the places aforesaid, but they shall also be suspended from the administration of the benefices themselves, for as long a period as shall seem fit to the Ordinary, even as the delegate of the Apostolic See. And if, having been thus suspended, they nevertheless shall not put away those women, or, even if they shall have intercourse with them, then shall they be for ever deprived of their ecclesiastical benefices,

portions, offices, and pensions of whatsoever kind, and be rendered thenceforth incapable and unworthy of any manner of honours, dignities, benefices and offices, until, after a manifest amendment of life, it shall seem good to their superiors, for a cause, to grant them a dispensation. But if, after having once put them away, they shall have dared to renew the interrupted connexion, or to take to themselves other scandalous women of this sort, they shall, in addition to the penalties aforesaid, be smitten with the sword of excommunication. Nor shall any appeal, or exemption, hinder or suspend the execution of the aforesaid; and the cognizance of all the matters above-named shall not belong to archdeacons, or deans, or other inferiors, but to the bishops themselves, who may proceed without the noise and the formalities of justice, and by the sole investigation of the truth of the fact. . . .

DECREE CONCERNING INDULGENCES

Whereas the power of conferring indulgences was granted by Christ to the Church; and she has, even in the most ancient times, used the said power, delivered unto her of God; the sacred holy Synod teaches, and enjoins, that the use of Indulgences, for the Christian people most salutary, and approved of by the authority of sacred Councils, is to be retained in the Church; and It condemns with anathema those who either assert, that they are useless; or who deny that there is in the Church the power of granting them. In granting them, however, It desires that, in accordance with the ancient and approved custom in the Church, moderation be observed; lest, by excessive facility, ecclesiastical discipline be enervated. And being desirous that the abuses which have crept therein, and by occasion of which this honourable name of Indulgences is blasphemed by heretics, be amended and corrected, It ordains generally by this decree, that all evil gains for the obtaining thereof,— whence a most prolific cause of abuses amongst the Christian people has been derived,—be wholly abolished. But as regards the other abuses which have proceeded from superstition, ignorance, irreverence, or from whatever other source, since, by reason of the manifold corruptions in the places and provinces where the said abuses are committed, they cannot conveniently be specially prohibited; It commands all bishops, diligently to collect, each in his own church, all abuses of this nature, and to report them in the first provincial Synod; that, after having been reviewed by the opinions of the other bishops also, they may forthwith be referred to the Sovereign Roman Pontiff, by whose authority and prudence that which may be expedient for the universal Church will be ordained; that thus the gift of holy Indulgences may be dispensed to all the faithful, piously, holily, and incorruptly. . . .

Amen.

Civilization in the Seventeenth and Eighteenth Centuries

By 1600, overseas economic and colonial expansion had given new wealth to the monarchs of Europe, and they were finding it increasingly possible to establish their independence from both the feudal nobility and the Christian hierarchy. As the power of the sovereigns and their states grew, political theorists wrote of new doctrines to justify their absolutism. When this control of authority was in turn challenged by the new mercantile classes, produced by the expansion of trade, other writers sought to justify parliamentary and even democratic control of the state. Culturally, these centuries were marked by a variety of trends, some of them reflecting the influence of the dynastic court life, and others the remarkable advances made in the realm of science. The stimulus to investigation and observation of nature which had come with the Renaissance continued to influence men, and with the epoch-making work of Isaac Newton a new era of science was initiated. In the eighteenth century, reason and the study of nature penetrated into nearly all phases of culture resulting in the Age of the Enlightenment, of which Voltaire was a leading exponent.

Jacques Bénigne Bossuet

Jacques Bénigne Bossuet (1627–1704) was a Frenchman in the age of Louis XIV. He became a distinguished cleric and scholar and was selected in 1670 to be the tutor of the young dauphin, the only child of Louis XIV. While serving in this capacity, Bossuet wrote his Political Economy Drawn from Holy Scripture. He undertook this work as part of his task of instructing the royal heir. In it he set forth one of the best-known statements of the divine right of kings to govern. He drew his conclusions from Holy Scripture in an age when the leaders of the Protestant revolt were emphasizing the importance of the Bible in religious matters. Thus he hoped to strengthen both the political and the religious unity of France by meeting the Protestants on their own ground. Throughout the book Bossuet sought to rationalize the absolutism of Louis XIV. In reading the translation from this work note (1) the sources to which Bossuet referred his young charge, (2) the characteristics of royal authority, (3) the relationship between monarchs and God, (4) the origins of kingship, (5) the nature of the royal person, (6) the responsibility of subjects to their rulers, and (7) the limitations placed upon royal authority.

From: POLITICAL ECONOMY DRAWN FROM HOLY SCRIPTURE

Monseigneur le Dauphin: God is the king of kings; it belongs to Him to instruct and direct them as His ministers. Heed then, Monseigneur, the lessons which He gives them in his Scriptures, and learn from Him the rules and the examples on which they ought to form their conduct.

In addition to the other advantages of the Scriptures, they have also this, that they trace the history of the world from its beginnings and reveal to us by this means, better than all other histories, the basic principles which have formed empires. No history better reveals what is good and what is evil in the human heart, what sustains and what overthrows kingdoms, what religion can do to establish them, what impiety can do toward destroying them. . . .

THIRD BOOK: THE NATURE OF ROYAL AUTHORITY

First Article: The essential characteristics. SINGLE PROPOSITION: There are four essential characteristics or qualities to royal authority: (1) royal authority is sacred; (2) it is paternal; (3) it is absolute; (4) it is subject to reason.

Second Article: Royal authority is sacred. FIRST PROPOSITION: God established kings as His ministers, and reigns through them over the peoples.—We have already seen that all power comes from God. The prince, adds Saint Paul, "is a minister of God to thee for good. But if thou do that which is evil, be afraid; for he beareth not the sword in vain; for he is a minister of God, an avenger for wrath to him that doeth evil."

The princes act therefore as ministers of God and as His lieutenants on earth. It is by them that He exercises His sway. "And now ye think to withstand the kingdom of Jehovah in the hand of the sons of David?"

For such a reason the royal throne is not the throne of a man, but the throne of God Himself. "God hath chosen Solomon my son to sit upon the throne of the kingdom of Jehovah over Israel." And further, "Then Solomon sat on the throne of Jehovah as king."

And in order that no one should think this

Reprinted from History 11, *History of Western Civilization, A Syllabus*, Stanford University Press, Stanford University, 1940, 34–35, with the permission of the author and of the publishers, Stanford University Press.

peculiar to the Israelites to have kings established by God, here is what the Book of Ecclesiastes says: "God gives to each people its governor; and Israel is manifestly reserved to Him." He therefore governs all peoples and gives them all their kings, although He governs Israel in a more special and declared manner

SECOND PROPOSITION: The person of kings is sacred.—It follows from all this that the person of kings is sacred, and that any attack on them is a sacrilege. God causes them to be anointed by his prophets with a sacred ointment, just as he causes the pontiffs and his altars to be anointed.

But even without the external application of this ointment, they are sacred by their charge, as being representatives of the divine majesty, deputed by His providence for the execution of His designs. "Thus saith Jehovah to his anointed, to Cyrus, whose right hand I have holden, to subdue nations before him."

The title of Christ is given to kings; one sees them everywhere called christs, or the anointed of the Lord. Under this venerable name, even the prophets revered them, and looked upon them as associated with the sovereign sway of God, for whom they exercise authority over the people. . . .

One must guard kings as sacred things; and he who neglects to guard them is worthy of death. "As Jehovah liveth," said David to the captains of Saul, "ye are worthy to die, because ye have not kept watch over your Lord, Jehovah's anointed.". . .

THIRD PROPOSITION: One should obey the prince on grounds of religion and of conscience. Saint Paul, after having said that the prince is the minister of God, concluded thus: "Wherefore ye must needs be in subjection, not only because of the wrath, but also for conscience's sake."

That is why it is necessary "to be obedient unto them that according to the flesh are your masters, with fear and trembling, in singleness of your heart, as unto Christ; not in the way of eyeservice, as men-pleasers; but as servants of Christ, doing the will of God from the heart.". . .

That is why Saint Peter said, "Be subject to every ordinance of man for the Lord's sake: whether to the king, as supreme; or unto governors, as sent by him for vengeance on evildoers and for praise to them that do well.". . .

FOURTH BOOK: FURTHER CONCERNING THE CHARACTER OF ROYALTY

First Article: Royal authority is absolute. FIRST PROPOSITION: The prince owes an explanation to no one for what he orders. "Keep the king's command, and that in regard of the oath of God. Be not hasty to go out of his presence; persist not in an evil thing: for he doeth whatsoever pleaseth him. For the king's word hath power; and who may say unto him, What doest thou? Whoso keepeth the commandment shall know no evil thing."

SECOND PROPOSITION: When the prince has judged, there is no other judgment—Sovereign judgments are attributed to God himself. When Jehosaphat established judges to judge the people he said, "Consider what ye do: for ye judge not for man, but for Jehovah: and he is with you in the judgment."

It is necessary to obey princes as justice itself, without which there is neither order nor an end to affairs. They are gods [that is, princes and rulers are gods] and participate in some manner in the divine independence. "I said, ye are gods, and all of you sons of the Most High. . . ."

Thomas Hobbes

Thomas Hobbes (1588–1679) was one of the earliest political philosophers to write in support of the modern sovereign state. He lived most of his life in an England at war, either foreign or civil, and inevitably he came to long for the peace and security of a strong government. To him absolute monarchy seemed to offer the best assurance *of a stable society. He also had a deep interest in mathematics and its application to the forces of nature, an interest which he developed while traveling on the continent where he came into contact with the theories of Galileo and Descartes. Following the execution of Charles I in 1649, advocacy of absolute monarchy needed a stronger support than an appeal to divine right. The natural order and natural law, soon to be used with great effectiveness by Newton and others, offered possibilities to Hobbes and other writers to whom divine right appeared as a shaky and faltering buttress. In The Leviathan (1651) Hobbes brought together his theories of government and his study of natural law and formulated a justification for absolutism. His basic thesis in this work was the assumption that the first law of man's nature was to seek peace. In the following selections from The Leviathan note (1) the discussion of human nature and its theoretical results, (2) the forces influencing mankind to seek peace, (3) the principal cause for the formation of commonwealths, (4) the method by which the commonwealth was contracted, (5) the responsibility of the contracting groups toward the sovereignty thereby established, (6) the authority and responsibility of the sovereignty, (7) the three types of sovereignty that may be established over the commonwealth, and (8) the advantages listed for absolute monarchy.*

From: THE LEVIATHAN

OF THE NATURAL CONDITION OF MANKIND AS CONCERNING THEIR FELICITY AND MISERY

Nature hath made men so equal, in the faculties of the body and mind; as that though there be found one man sometimes manifestly stronger in body, or of quicker mind than another, yet when all is reckoned together, the difference between man and man, is not so considerable, as that one man can thereupon claim to himself any benefit, to which another may not pretend, as well as he. For as to the strength of body, the weakest has strength enough to kill the strongest, either by secret machination, or by confederacy with others, that are in the same danger with himself.

And as to the faculties of the mind, setting aside the arts grounded upon words, and especially that skill of proceeding upon general and infallible rules, called science; which very few have, and but in few things; as being not a native faculty, born with us; nor attained, as prudence, while we look after somewhat else, I find yet a greater equality amongst men than that of strength. For prudence is but experience; which equal time, equally bestows on all men, in those things they equally apply themselves unto. That which may perhaps make such equality incredible, is but a vain conceit of one's own wisdom, which almost all men think they have in a greater degree than the vulgar; that is, than all men but themselves, and a few others, whom by fame or for concurring with themselves, they approve. For such is the nature of men, that howsoever they may acknowledge many others to be more witty, or more eloquent, or more learned; yet they will hardly believe there be many so wise as themselves; for they see their own wit at

Thomas Hobbes, *The Leviathan, or the Matter, Form and Power of a Commonwealth, Ecclesiastical and Civil*, London, n.d., 63–65; 82–88.

hand, and other men's at a distance. But this proveth rather that men are in that point equal, than unequal. For there is not ordinarily a greater sign of the equal distribution of anything, than that every man is contented with his share.

From this equality of ability, ariseth equality of hope in the attaining of our ends. And therefore if any two men desire the same thing, which nevertheless they cannot both enjoy, they become enemies; and in the way to their end, which is principally their own conservation, and sometimes their delectation only, endeavour to destroy or subdue one another. And from hence it comes to pass, that where an invader hath no more to fear than another man's single power; if one plant, sow, build, or possess a convenient seat, others may probably be expected to come prepared with forces united, to dispossess and deprive him, not only of the fruit of his labour, but also of his life or liberty. And the invader again is in the like danger of another.

And from this diffidence of one another, there is no way for any man to secure himself, so reasonable, as anticipation; that is, by force, or wiles, to master the persons of all men he can, so long, till he see no other power great enough to endanger him: and this is no more than his own conservation requireth, and is generally allowed. Also because there be some, that taking pleasure in contemplating their own power in the acts of conquest, which they pursue farther than their security requires; if others, that otherwise would be glad to be at ease within modest bounds, should not by invasion increase their power, they would not be able, long time, by standing only on their defence, to subsist. And by consequence, such augmentation of dominion over men being necessary to a man's conservation, it ought to be allowed him.

Again, men have no pleasure, but on the contrary a great deal of grief, in keeping company, where there is no power able to overawe them all. For every man looketh that his companion should value him, at the same rate he sets upon himself: and upon all signs of contempt, or undervaluing, naturally endeavours, as far as he dares (which amongst them that have no common power to keep them in quiet,

is far enough to make them destroy each other), to extort a greater value from his contemners, by damage; and from others, by the example.

So that in the nature of man, we find three principal causes of quarrel. First, competition; secondly, diffidence; thirdly, glory.

The first, maketh men invade for gain; the second, for safety; and the third, for reputation. The first use violence, to make themselves masters of other men's persons, wives, children, and cattle; the second, to defend them; the third, for trifles, as a word, a smile, a different opinion, and any other sign of undervalue, either direct in their persons, or by reflection in their kindred, their friends, their nation, their profession, or their name.

Hereby it is manifest, that during the time men live without a common power to keep them all in awe, they are in that condition which is called war; and such a war, as is of every man, against every man. For "war" consisteth not in battle only, or the act of fighting; but in a tract of time, wherein the will to contend by battle is sufficiently known: and therefore the notion of "time" is to be considered in the nature of war, as it is in the nature of weather. For as the nature of foul weather lieth not in a shower or two of rain, but in an inclination thereto of many days together; so the nature of war consisteth not in actual fighting, but in the known disposition thereto during all the time there is no assurance to the contrary. All other time is "peace."

Whatsoever therefore is consequent to a time of war, where every man is enemy to every man, the same is consequent to the time wherein men live without other security than what their own strength and their own invention shall furnish them withal. In such condition there is no place for industry, because the fruit thereof is uncertain, and consequently no culture of the earth; no navigation, nor use of the commodities that may be imported by sea; no commodious building; no instruments of moving and removing such things as require much force; no knowledge of the face of the earth; no account of time; no arts; no letters; no society; and, which is worst of all, continual fear and danger of violent death; and the life of man, solitary, poor, nasty, brutish, and short.

It may seem strange to some man, that has not well weighed these things, that Nature should thus dissociate, and render men apt to invade and destroy one another; and he may therefore, not trusting to this inference made from the passions, desire perhaps to have the same confirmed by experience. Let him therefore consider with himself, when taking a journey, he arms himself, and seeks to go well accompanied; when going to sleep, he locks his doors; when even in his house, he locks his chests; and this when he knows there be laws, and public officers, armed, to revenge all injuries shall be done him; what opinion he has of his fellow-subjects, when he rides armed; of his fellow-citizens, when he locks his doors; and of his children and servants, when he locks his chests. Does he not there as much accuse mankind by his actions as I do by my words? But neither of us accuse man's nature in it. The desires and other passions of man are in themselves no sin. No more are the actions that proceed from those passions, till they know a law that forbids them; which till laws be made they cannot know, nor can any law be made till they have agreed upon the person that shall make it.

It may peradventure be thought there was never such a time nor condition of war as this; and I believe it was never generally so, over all the world, but there are many places where they live so now. For the savage people in many places of America, except the government of small families, the concord whereof dependeth on natural lust, have no government at all, and live at this day in that brutish manner, as I said before. Howsoever, it may be perceived what manner of life there would be, where there were no common power to fear, by the manner of life which men that have formerly lived under a peaceful government, use to degenerate into a civil war.

But though there had never been any time, wherein particular men were in a condition of war one against another; yet in all times, kings, and persons of sovereign authority, because of their independency, are in continual jealousies, and in the state and posture of gladiators; having their weapons pointing, and their eyes fixed on one another; that is, their forts, garrisons, and guns upon the frontiers of their king-doms; and continual spies upon their neighbours; which is a posture of war. But because they uphold thereby the industry of their subjects; there does not follow from it that misery which accompanies the liberty of particular men.

To this war of every man, against every man, this also is consequent; that nothing can be unjust. The notions of right and wrong, justice and injustice, have there no place. Where there is no common power, there is no law: where no law, no injustice. Force and fraud, are in war the two cardinal virtues. Justice and injustice are none of the faculties neither of the body nor mind. If they were, they might be in a man that were alone in the world, as well as his senses, and passions. They are qualities that relate to men in society, not in solitude. It is consequent also to the same condition, that there be no propriety, no dominion, no "mine" and "thine" distinct; but only that to be every man's, that he can get; and for so long, as he can keep it. And thus much for the ill condition, which man by mere nature is actually placed in; though with a possibility to come out of it, consisting partly in the passions, partly in his reason.

The passions that incline men to peace, are fear of death; desire of such things as are necessary to commodious living; and a hope by their industry to obtain them. And reason suggesteth convenient articles of peace, upon which men may be drawn to agreement. These articles are they which otherwise are called the Laws of Nature. . . .

OF THE CAUSES, AND DEFINITION OF A COMMONWEALTH

The final cause, end, or design of men, who naturally love liberty, and dominion over others, in the introduction of that restraint upon themselves, in which we see them live in commonwealths, is the foresight of their own preservation, and of a more contented life thereby; that is to say, of getting themselves out from that miserable condition of war, which is necessarily consequent, as hath been shown [above] . . . to the natural passions of men, when there is no visible power to keep them in awe, and tie them by fear of punishment to the performance of their covenants, and observation of those laws of Nature. . . .

For the laws of Nature, as "justice," "equity," "modesty," "mercy," and, in sum, "doing to others, as we would be done to," of themselves, without the terror of some power, to cause them to be observed, are contrary to our natural passions, that carry us to partiality, pride, revenge, and the like. And covenants, without the sword, are but words, and of no strength to secure a man at all. Therefore notwithstanding the laws of Nature, which every one hath then kept, when he has the will to keep them, when he can do it safely, if there be no power erected, or not great enough for our security; every man will, and may lawfully rely on his own strength and art, for caution against all other men. And in all places, where men have lived by small families, to rob and spoil one another, has been a trade, and so far from being reputed against the law of Nature, that the greater spoils they gained, the greater was their honour; and men observed no other laws therein, but the laws of honour; that is, to abstain from cruelty, leaving to men their lives, and instruments of husbandry. And as small families did then; so now do cities and kingdoms, which are but greater families, for their own security, enlarge their dominions, upon all pretences of danger, and fear of invasion, or assistance that may be given to invaders, and endeavour as much as they can, to subdue, or weaken their neighbours, by open force and secret arts, for want of other caution, justly; and are remembered for it in after ages with honour.

Nor is it the joining together of a small number of men, that gives them this security; because in small numbers, small additions on the one side or the other, make the advantage of strength so great, as is sufficient to carry the victory; and therefore gives encouragement to an invasion. The multitude sufficient to confide in for our security, is not determined by any certain number, but by comparison with the enemy we fear; and is then sufficient, when the odds of the enemy is not of so visible and conspicuous moment, to determine the event of war, as to move him to attempt.

And be there never so great a multitude; yet if their actions be directed according to their particular judgments and particular appetites, they can expect thereby no defence, nor protection, neither against a common enemy, nor against the injuries of one another. For being distracted in opinions concerning the best use and application of their strength, they do not help but hinder one another; and reduce their strength by mutual opposition to nothing: whereby they are easily, not only subdued by a very few that agree together; but also when there is no common enemy, they make war upon each other, for their particular interests. For if we could suppose a great multitude of men to consent in the observation of justice, and other laws of Nature, without a common power to keep them all in awe; we might as well suppose all mankind to do the same; and then there neither would be, nor need to be any civil government or commonwealth at all; because there would be peace without subjection.

Nor is it enough for the security, which men desire should last all the time of their life, that they be governed and directed by one judgment, for a limited time: as in one battle, or one war. For though they obtain a victory by their unanimous endeavour against a foreign enemy; yet afterwards, when either they have no common enemy, or he that by one part is held for an enemy, is by another part held for a friend, they must needs by the difference of their interests dissolve, and fall again into a war amongst themselves.

It is true that certain living creatures, as bees and ants, live sociably one with another, which are therefore by Aristotle numbered amongst political creatures; and yet have no other direction, than their particular judgments and appetites; nor speech, whereby one of them can signify to another, what he thinks expedient for the common benefit: and therefore some man may perhaps desire to know, why mankind cannot do the same. To which I answer,

First, that men are continually in competition for honour and dignity, which these creatures are not; and consequently amongst men there ariseth on that ground, envy and hatred, and finally war; but amongst these not so.

Secondly, that amongst these creatures, the common good differeth not from the private;

and being by nature inclined to their private, they procure thereby the common benefit. But man, whose joy consisteth in comparing himself with other men, can relish nothing but what is eminent.

Thirdly, that these creatures, having not, as man, the use of reason, do not see, nor think they see any fault, in the administration of their common business; whereas amongst men, there are very many that think themselves wiser, and abler to govern the public, better than the rest; and these strive to reform and innovate, one this way, another that way; and thereby bring it into distraction and civil war.

Fourthly, that these creatures, though they have some use of voice, in making known to one another their desires and other affections; yet they want that art of words, by which some men can represent to others that which is good in the likeness of evil; and evil in the likeness of good; and augment or diminish the apparent greatness of good and evil; discontenting men, and troubling their peace at their pleasure.

Fifthly, irrational creatures cannot distinguish between "injury" and "damage;" and therefore as long as they be at ease, they are not offended with their fellows: whereas man is then most troublesome, when he is most at ease; for then it is that he loves to show his wisdom, and control the actions of them that govern the commonwealth.

Lastly, the agreement of these creatures is natural; that of men is by covenant only, which is artificial: and therefore it is no wonder if there be somewhat else required, besides covenant, to make their agreement constant and lasting; which is a common power, to keep them in awe, and to direct their actions to the common benefit.

The only way to erect such a common power, as may be able to defend them from the invasion of foreigners, and the injuries of one another, and thereby to secure them in such sort, as that by their own industry, and by the fruits of the earth, they may nourish themselves and live contentedly, is, to confer all their power and strength upon one man, or upon one assembly of men, that may reduce all their wills, by plurality of voices, unto one will: which is as much as to say, to appoint one man, or assembly of men, to bear their person; and

every one to own, and acknowledge himself to be author of whatsoever he that so beareth their person, shall act, or cause to be acted, in those things which concern the common peace and safety; and therein to submit their wills, every one to his will, and their judgments, to his judgment. This is more than consent, or concord; it is a real unity of them all, in one and the same person, made by covenant of every man with every man, in such manner, as if every man should say to every man, "I authorize and give up my right of governing myself, to this man, or to this assembly of men, on this condition, that thou give up thy right to him, and authorize all his actions in like manner." This done, the multitude so united in one person is called a "commonwealth," in Latin *civitas*. This is the generation of that great "leviathan," or rather, to speak more reverently, of that "mortal god," to which we owe under the "immortal God," our peace and defence. For by this authority, given him by every particular man in the commonwealth, he hath the use of so much power and strength conferred on him, that by terror thereof, he is enabled to perform the wills of them all, to peace at home, and mutual aid against their enemies abroad. And in him consisteth the essence of the commonwealth; which, to define it, is "one person, of whose acts a great multitude, by mutual covenants one with another, have made themselves every one the author, to the end he may use the strength and means of them all, as he shall think expedient, for their peace and common defence."

And he that carrieth this person is called "sovereign," and said to have "sovereign power"; and every one besides, his "subject."

The attaining to this sovereign power is by two ways. One, by natural force; as when a man maketh his children to submit themselves, and their children, to his government, as being able to destroy them if they refuse; or by war subdueth his enemies to his will, giving them their lives on that condition. The other is, when men agree amongst themselves to submit to some man, or assembly of men, voluntarily, on confidence to be protected by him against all others. This latter may be called a political commonwealth, or commonwealth by "institution"; and the former, a commonwealth by "acquisition." And first, I shall speak of a commonwealth by institution.

OF THE RIGHTS OF SOVEREIGNS BY INSTITUTION

A "COMMONWEALTH" is said to be "instituted," when a "multitude" of men do agree, and "covenant, every one, with every one," that to whatsoever "man," or "assembly of men," shall be given by the major part, the "right" to "present" the person of them all, that is to say, to be their "representative"; every one, as well he that "voted for it," as he that "voted against it," shall "authorize" all the actions and judgments, of that man, or assembly of men, in the same manner, as if they were his own, to the end, to live peaceably amongst themselves, and be protected against other men.

From this institution of a commonwealth are derived all the "rights" and "faculties" of him, or them, on whom sovereign power is conferred by the consent of the people assembled.

First, because they covenant, it is to be understood, they are not obliged by former covenant to anything repugnant hereunto. And consequently they that have already instituted a commonwealth, being thereby bound by covenant, to own the actions and judgments of one, cannot lawfully make a new covenant, amongst themselves, to be obedient to any other, in anything whatsoever, without his permission. And therefore, they that are subjects to a monarch, cannot without his leave cast off monarchy, and return to the confusion of a disunited multitude; nor transfer their person from him that beareth it, to another man, or other assembly of men: for they are bound, every man to every man, to own, and be reputed author of all, that he that already is their sovereign, shall do, and judge fit to be done: so that one man dissenting, all the rest should break their covenant made to that man, which is injustice: and they have also every man given the sovereignty to him that beareth their person; and therefore if they depose him, they take from him that which is his own, and so again it is injustice. Besides, if he that attempteth to depose his sovereign, be killed, or punished by him for such attempt, he is author

of his own punishment, as being by the institution, author of all his sovereign shall do: and because it is injustice for a man to do anything for which he may be punished by his own authority, he is also upon that title unjust. And whereas some men have pretended for their disobedience to their sovereign, a new covenant, made not with men, but with God; this also is unjust: for there is no covenant with God but by mediation of somebody that representeth God's person; which none doth but God's lieutenant, who hath the sovereignty under God. But this pretence of covenant with God, is so evident a lie, even in the pretenders' own consciences, that it is not only an act of an unjust, but also of a vile and unmanly disposition.

Secondly, because the right of bearing the person of them all, is given to him they make sovereign, by covenant only of one to another, and not of him to any of them; there can happen no breach of covenant on the part of the sovereign: and consequently none of his subjects, by any pretence of forfeiture, can be freed from his subjection. That he which is made sovereign maketh no covenant with his subjects beforehand, is manifest; because either he must make it with the whole multitude, as one party to the covenant; or he must make a several covenant with every man. With the whole, as one party, it is impossible; because as yet they are not one person; and if he make so many several covenants as there be men, those covenants after he hath the sovereignty are void; because what act soever can be pretended by any one of them for breach thereof, is the act both of himself and of all the rest, because done in the person and by the right of every one of them in particular. Besides, if any one or more of them, pretend a breach of the covenant made by the sovereign at his institution; and others, or one other of his subjects, or himself alone, pretend there was no such breach, there is in this case no judge to decide the controversy; it returns therefore to the sword again; and every man recovereth the right of protecting himself by his own strength, contrary to the design they had in the institution. It is therefore in vain to grant sovereignty by way of precedent covenant. The opinion that any monarch receiveth his power by covenant, that is to say, on condition, proceedeth from want of understanding this easy truth, that covenants being but words and breath, have no force to oblige, contain, constrain, or protect any man, but what it has from the public sword; that is, from the united hands of that man, or assembly of men that hath the sovereignty, and whose actions are avouched by them all, and performed by the strength of them all, in him united. But when an assembly of men is made sovereign; then no man imagineth any such covenant to have passed in the institution; for no man is so dull as to say, for example, the people of Rome made a covenant with the Romans, to hold the sovereignty on such or such conditions; which not performed, the Romans might lawfully depose the Roman people. That men see not the reason to be alike in a monarchy, and in a popular government, proceedeth from the ambition of some, that are kinder to the government of an assembly, whereof they may hope to participate, than of monarchy, which they despair to enjoy.

Thirdly, because the major part hath by consenting voices declared a sovereign; he that dissented must now consent with the rest; that is, be contented to avow all the actions he shall do, or else justly be destroyed by the rest. For if he voluntarily entered into the congregation of them that were assembled, he sufficiently declared thereby his will, and therefore tacitly covenanted to stand to what the major part should ordain: and therefore if he refuse to stand thereto, or make protestation against any of their decrees, he does contrary to his covenant, and therefore unjustly. And whether he be of the congregation or not; and whether his consent be asked or not, he must either submit to their decrees, or be left in the condition of war he was in before; wherein he might without injustice be destroyed by any man whatsoever.

Fourthly, because every subject is by this institution author of all the actions and judgments of the sovereign instituted, it follows, that whatsoever he doth it can be no injury to any of his subjects, nor ought he to be by any of them accused of injustice. For he that doth anything by authority from another doth therein no injury to him by whose authority he acteth: but by this institution of a commonwealth every particular man is author of all the sovereign doth; and consequently, he that complaineth of injury from his sovereign complaineth of that whereof he himself is author, and therefore ought not to accuse any man but himself; no, nor himself of injury; because to do injury to one's self is impossible. It is true that they that have sovereign power may commit iniquity, but not injustice or injury in the proper signification.

Fifthly, and consequently to that which was said last, no man that hath sovereign power can justly be put to death, or otherwise in any manner by his subjects punished. For seeing every subject is author of the actions of his sovereign, he punisheth another for the actions committed by himself.

And because the end of this institution is the peace and defence of them all; and whosoever has right to the end has right to the means; it belongeth of right to whatsoever man or assembly that hath the sovereignty to be judge both of the means of peace and defence, and also of the hindrances and disturbances of the same, and to do whatsoever he shall think necessary to be done, both beforehand, for the preserving of peace and security, by prevention of discord at home and hostility from abroad; and, when peace and security are lost, for the recovery of the same. And therefore,

Sixthly, it is annexed to the sovereignty to be judge of what opinions and doctrines are averse and what conducing to peace; and consequently, on what occasions, how far, and what men are to be trusted withal, in speaking to multitudes of people, and who shall examine the doctrines of all books before they be published. For the actions of men proceed from their opinions, and in the well-governing of opinions consisteth the well-governing of men's actions, in order to their peace and concord. And though in matter of doctrine nothing ought to be regarded but the truth; yet this is not repugnant to regulating the same by peace. For doctrine repugnant to peace can be no more true than peace and concord can be against the law of Nature. It is true that in a commonwealth, where, by the negligence or unskilfulness of governors and teachers, false doctrines are by time generally received; the contrary truths may be generally offensive. Yet the most sudden and rough bursting in of a new truth that can be, does never break the peace, but only sometimes awakes the war. For those men that are so remissly governed, that they dare take up arms to defend or introduce an opinion, are still in war; and their condition not peace, but only a cessation of arms for fear of one another; and they live, as it were, in the precincts of battle continually. It belongeth therefore to him that hath the sovereign power to be judge, or constitute all judges of opinions and doctrines, as a thing necessary to peace, thereby to prevent discord and civil war.

Seventhly, is annexed to the sovereignty, the whole power of prescribing the rules, whereby every man may know what goods he may enjoy, and what actions he may do, without being molested by any of his fellow subjects; and this is it men call "propriety." For before constitution of sovereign power, as hath already been shown, all men had right to all things, which necessarily causeth war: and therefore this propriety, being necessary to peace, and depending on sovereign power, is the act of that power, in order to the public peace. These rules of propriety, or *meum* and *tuum*, and of "good," "evil," "lawful," and "unlawful" in the actions of subjects, are the civil laws; that is to say, the laws of each commonwealth in particular; though the name of civil law be now restrained to the ancient civil laws of the city of Rome, which being the head of a great part of the world, her laws at that time were in these parts the civil law.

Eighthly, is annexed to the sovereignty, the right of judicature; that is to say, of hearing and deciding all controversies, which may arise concerning law, either civil or natural, or concerning fact. For without the decision of controversies, there is no protection of one subject against the injuries of another; the laws concerning *meum* and *tuum* are in vain, and to every man remaineth, from the natural and necessary appetite of his own conservation, the right of protecting himself by his private strength, which is the condition of war, and contrary to the end for which every commonwealth is instituted.

Ninthly, is annexed to the sovereignty, the right of making war and peace with other nations and commonwealths; that is to say, of judging when it is for the public good, and how great forces are to be assembled, armed, and paid for that end; and to levy money upon the subjects to defray the expenses thereof. For the power by which the people are to be defended consisteth in their armies, and the strength of an army, in the union of their strength under one command, which command the sovereign instituted, therefore hath; because the command of the "militia," without other institution, maketh him that hath it sovereign. And therefore whosoever is made general of an army, he that hath the sovereign power is always generalissimo.

Tenthly, is annexed to the sovereignty, the choosing of all counsellors, ministers, magistrates, and officers, both in peace and war. For seeing the sovereign is charged with the end, which is the common peace and defence, he is understood to have power to use such means as he shall think most fit for his discharge.

Eleventhly, to the sovereign is committed the power of rewarding with riches or honour, and of punishing with corporal or pecuniary punishment, or with ignominy, every subject according to the law he hath formerly made; or if there be no law made, according as he shall judge most to conduce to the encouraging of men to serve the commonwealth, or deterring of them from doing disservice to the same.

Lastly, considering what value men are naturally apt to set upon themselves; what respect they look for from others; and how little they value other men; from whence continually arise amongst them, emulation, quarrels, factions, and at last war, to the destroying of one another, and diminution of their strength against a common enemy; it is necessary that there be laws of honour, and a public rate of the worth of such men as have deserved, or are able to deserve well of the commonwealth; and that there be force in the hands of some or other, to put those laws in execution. But it hath already been shown, that not only the whole "militia," or forces of the commonwealth; but also the judicature of all controversies, is annexed to the sovereignty. To the sovereign therefore it belongeth also to give titles of honour; and to appoint what order of place and dignity each man shall hold; and what signs of respect, in public or private meetings, they shall give to one another. . . .

OF THE SEVERAL KINDS OF COMMONWEALTH BY INSTITUTION, AND OF SUCCESSION TO THE SOVEREIGN POWER

The difference of commonwealths consisteth in the difference of the sovereign, or the person representative of all and every one of the multitude. And because the sovereignty is either in one man, or in an assembly of more than one; and into that assembly either every man hath right to enter, or not every one, but certain men distinguished from the rest; it is manifest, there can be but three kinds of commonwealth. For the representative must needs be one man, or more: and if more, then it is the assembly of all, or but of a part. When the representative is one man, then is the commonwealth a "monarchy": when an assembly of all that will come together, then it is a "democracy," or popular commonwealth: when an assembly of a part only, then it is called an "aristocracy." Other kind of commonwealth there can be none: for either one or more, or all, must have the sovereign power, which I have shown to be indivisible, entire.

There be other names of government in the histories and books of policy, as "tyranny," and "oligarchy": but they are not the names of other forms of government, but of the same forms misliked. For they that are discontented under "monarchy," call it "tyranny"; and they that are displeased with "aristocracy," call it "oligarchy": so also they which find themselves grieved under a "democracy," call it "anarchy," which signifies want of government; and yet I think no man believes that want of government is any new kind of government: nor by the same reason ought they to believe that the government is of one kind when they like it, and another when they dislike it, or are oppressed by the governors.

It is manifest, that men who are in absolute liberty may, if they please, give authority to one man to represent them every one; as well as give such authority to any assembly of men whatsoever; and consequently may subject themselves, if they think good, to a monarch as absolutely as to any other representative. Therefore, where there is already erected a sovereign power, there can be no other representative of the same people, but only to certain particular ends, by the sovereign limited. For that were to erect two sovereigns; and every man to have his person represented by two actors, that by opposing one another, must needs divide that power, which, if men will live in peace, is indivisible, and thereby reduce the multitude into the condition of war, contrary to the end for which all sovereignty is instituted. And therefore as it is absurd to think that a sovereign assembly, inviting the people of their dominion to send up their deputies, with power to make known their advice, or desires, should therefore hold such deputies rather than themselves, for the absolute representatives of the people: so it is absurd also to think the same in a monarchy. And I know not how this so manifest a truth should of late be so little observed; that in a monarchy, he that had the sovereignty from a descent of six hundred years, was alone called sovereign, had the title of Majesty from every one of his subjects, and was unquestionably taken by them for their king, was notwithstanding never considered as their representative; the name without contradiction passing for the title of those men, which at his command were sent up by the people to carry their petitions, and give him, if he permitted it, their advice. Which may serve as an admonition, for those that are the true and absolute representative of a people, to instruct men in the nature of that office, and to take heed how they admit of any other general representation upon any occasion whatsoever, if they mean to discharge the trust committed to them.

The difference between these three kinds of commonwealth, consisteth not in the difference of power; but in the difference of convenience, or aptitude to produce the peace and security of the people; for which end they were instituted. And to compare monarchy with the other two, we may observe; first, that whosoever beareth the person of the people, or is one of that assembly that bears it, beareth also his own natural person. And though he be careful in his politic person to procure the common interest; yet he is more or no less careful to procure the private good of himself, his family, kindred, and friends; and for the most part, if the public interest chance to cross the private, he prefers the private: for the passions of men are commonly more potent than their reason. From whence it follows, that where the public and private interest are most closely united, there is the public most advanced. Now in monarchy, the private interest is the same with the public. The riches, power, and honour of a monarch, arise only from the riches, strength, and reputation of his subjects. For no king can be rich, nor glorious, nor secure, whose subjects are either poor, or contemptible, or too weak through want or dissension, to maintain a war against their enemies: whereas in a democracy, or aristocracy, the public prosperity confers not so much to the private fortune of one that is corrupt, or ambitious, as doth many times a perfidious advice, a treacherous action, or a civil war.

Secondly, that a monarch receiveth counsel of whom, when, and where he pleaseth; and consequently may hear the opinion of men versed in the matter about which he deliberates, of what rank or quality soever, and as long before the time of action, and with as much secrecy, as he will. But when a sovereign assembly has need of counsel, none are admitted but such as have a right thereto from the beginning; which for the most part are of those who have been versed more in the acquisition of wealth than of knowledge; and are to give their advice in long discourses, which may and do commonly excite men to action, but not govern them in it. For the "understanding" is by the flame of the passions, never enlightened, but dazzled. Nor is there any place, or time, wherein an assembly can receive counsel with secrecy, because of their own multitude.

Thirdly, that the resolutions of a monarch, are subject to no other inconstancy, than that of human nature; but in assemblies, besides that of Nature, there ariseth an inconstancy from the number. For the absence of a few, that would have the resolution once taken, continue firm, which may happen by security, negligence, or private impediments, or the diligent appearance of a few of the contrary opinion, undoes to-day all that was concluded yesterday.

Fourthly, that a monarch cannot disagree with himself, out of envy or interest; but an assembly may; and that to such a height, as may produce a civil war.

Fifthly, that in monarchy there is this inconvenience; that any subject, by the power of one man, for the enriching of a favourite or flatterer, may be deprived of all he possesseth; which I confess is a great and inevitable inconvenience.

But the same may as well happen, where the sovereign power is an assembly: for their power is the same; and they are as subject to evil counsel, and to be seduced by orators, as a monarch by flatterers; and becoming one another's flatterers, serve one another's covetousness and ambition by turns. And whereas the favourites of monarchs are few, and they have none else to advance but their own kindred; the favourites of an assembly are many; and the kindred much more numerous than of any monarch. Besides there is no favourite of a monarch, which cannot as well succour his friends as hurt his enemies; but orators, that is to say, favourites of sovereign assemblies, though they have great power to hurt, have little to save. For to accuse, requires less eloquence, such is man's nature, than to excuse; and condemnation, than absolution more resembles justice. . . .

John Locke

The great English scholar, John Locke (1632–1704), was born less than 50 years after Hobbes, but during that time England had undergone a rapid political development. In 1689, by the so-called Glorious Revolution, the English destroyed the principle of royal absolutism and established parliamentary supremacy. In the Second Treatise of Government, which appeared in 1690, Locke used Hobbes' contract theory to justify this political upheaval, although Hobbes, in The Leviathan, had specifically condemned revolution. Locke stressed the necessity of limiting power as well as of distributing power among different branches of government. In reading the Second Treatise of Government note (1) Locke's description of the formation of the state by a social compact, (2) the ends society expected to achieve by forming a commonwealth, (3) the significance of the separation of powers, (4) the principal obligation of government to its citizens, (5) Locke's definition of tyranny, (6) the distinction he made between the dissolution of society and the dissolution of government, (7) the final umpire as to whether or not the king or the legislature have exceeded their trust, and (8) the method advocated for handling such situations.

From: THE SECOND TREATISE ON GOVERNMENT

OF THE STATE OF NATURE

To understand political power aright, and derive it from its original, we must consider what estate all men are naturally in, and that is, a *state of perfect freedom* to order their actions, and dispose of their possessions and persons as they think fit, within the bounds of the law of nature, without asking leave or depending upon the will of any other man.

A *state* also *of equality,* wherein all the power and jurisdiction is reciprocal, no one having more than another, there being nothing more evident than that creatures of the same species and rank, promiscuously born to all the same advantages of nature, and the use of the same faculties, should also be equal one amongst another without subordination or subjection, unless the lord and master of them all should, by any manifest declaration of his will, set one above another, and confer on him, by an evident and clear appointment, an undoubted right to dominion and sovereignty. . . .

But though this be *a state of liberty,* yet *it is not a state of license;* though man in that state have an uncontrollable liberty to dispose of his person or possessions, yet he has not liberty to destroy himself, or so much as any creature in his possession, but where some nobler use than its bare preservation calls for it. The *state of nature* has a law of nature to govern it, which obliges every one, and reason, which is that law, teaches all mankind who will but consult it, that being all *equal and independent,* no one ought to harm another in his life, health, liberty or possessions: for men being all the workmanship of one omnipotent and infinitely wise Maker; all the servants of one sovereign Master, sent into the world by His order and about His business; they are His property, whose workmanship they are made to last during His, not one another's pleasure. And, being furnished with like faculties, sharing all in one community of nature, there cannot be supposed any such *subordination* among us that may authorize us to destroy one another, as if we were made for one another's uses, as the inferior ranks of creatures are for ours. Every one as he is *bound to preserve himself,* and not to quit his station wilfully, so by the like reason, when his own preservation comes not in competition, ought he as much as he can, to *preserve the rest of mankind,* and not unless it be to do justice on an offender, take away, or impair the life, or

John Locke, *The Second Treatise on Government,* in *Selections from John Locke's Second Treatise of Government, 1690, Old South Leaflets,* no. 208. Courtesy of the Old South Asociation.

what tends to the preservation of the life, the liberty, health, limb, or goods of another. . . .

OF SLAVERY

The *natural liberty* of man is to be free from any superior power on earth, and not to be under the will or legislative authority of man, but to have only the law of nature for his rule. The *liberty of man in society* is to be under no other legislative power but that established by consent in the commonwealth; nor under the dominion of any will, or restraint of any law, but what that legislative shall enact according to the trust put in it. Freedom, then, is not what Sir Robert Filmer tells us: "A liberty for every one to do what he lists, to live as he pleases, and not to be tied by any laws"; but *freedom of men under government* is to have a *standing rule* to live by, common to every one of that society, and made by the *legislative power* erected in it; a liberty to follow my own will in all things where that rule prescribes not, not to be subject to the inconstant, uncertain, unknown, arbitrary will of another man. . . .

OF THE BEGINNING OF POLITICAL SOCIETIES

Men being, as has been said, by nature all free, equal, and independent, no one can be put out of this estate and subjected to the political power of another without his own consent. The only way whereby anyone divests himself of his natural liberty and puts on the bonds of civil society, is by agreeing with other men, to join and unite into a community for their comfortable, safe and peaceable living one amongst another, in a secure enjoyment of their properties, and a greater security against any that are not of it. This any number of men may do, because it injures not the freedom of the rest; they are left, as they were, in the liberty of the state of nature. When any number of men have so *consented to make one community or government,* they are thereby presently incorporated, and make *one body politic,* wherein the *majority* have a right to act and conclude the rest. . . .

And thus every man, by consenting with others to make one body politic under one government, puts himself under an obligation to every one of that society to submit to the determination of the *majority,* and to be concluded by it; or else this *original compact,* whereby he with others incorporates into *one society,* would signify nothing. . . .

For if *the consent of the majority* shall not, in reason, be received as *the act of the whole,* and conclude every individual; nothing but the consent of every individual can make anything to be the act of the whole; but such a consent it is next to impossible ever to be had. . . .

OF THE ENDS OF POLITICAL SOCIETY AND GOVERNMENT

If man in the state of nature be so free as has been said, if he be absolute lord of his own person and possessions, equal to the greatest and subject to nobody, why will he part with his freedom? Why will he give up this empire, and subject himself to the dominion and control of any other power? To which it is obvious to answer, that though in the state of nature he hath such a right, yet the enjoyment of it is very uncertain and constantly exposed to the invasion of others; for all being kings as much as he, every man his equal, and the greater part no strict observers of equity and justice, the enjoyment of the property he has in this state is very unsafe, very insecure. This makes him willing to quit this condition which, however free, is full of fears and continual dangers; and it is not without reason that he seeks out and is willing to join in society with others who are already united, or have a mind to unite *for the mutual preservation of their lives, liberties and estates,* which I call by the general name—*property.*

The great and *chief end,* therefore, of men uniting into commonwealths, and putting themselves under government, *is the preservation of their property;* to which in the state of nature there are many things wanting.

First. There wants an *established,* settled, known *law,* received and allowed by common consent to be the standard of right and wrong, and the common measure to decide all controversies between them. For though the law of nature be plain and intelligible to all rational creatures, yet men, being biased by their interest, as well as ignorant for want of study of it, are not apt to allow of it as a law binding to them in the application of it to their particular cases.

Secondly. In the state of nature there wants a *known and indifferent judge,* with authority to determine all differences according to the established law. For every one in that state being both judge and executioner of the law of nature, men being partial to themselves, passion and revenge is very apt to carry them too far, and with too much heat in their own cases, as well as negligence and unconcernedness, make them too remiss in other men's.

Thirdly. In the state of nature there often wants *power* to back and support the sentence when right, and to *give* it due *execution.* They who by any injustice offended will seldom fail where they are able by force to make good their injustice. Such resistance many times makes the punishment dangerous, and frequently destructive to those who attempt it.

Thus mankind, notwithstanding all the privileges of the state of nature, being but in an ill condition while they remain in it, are quickly driven into society. Hence it comes to pass, that we seldom find any number of men live any time together in this state. The inconveniencies that they are therein exposed to by the irregular and uncertain exercise of the power every man has of punishing the transgressions of others, make them take sanctuary under the established laws of government, and therein seek *the preservation of their property.* It is this makes them so willingly give up every one his single power of punishing to be exercised by such alone as shall be appointed to it amongst them, and by such rules as the community, or those authorized by them to that purpose, shall agree on. And in this we have the original *right and rise of both the legislative and executive power* as well as of the governments and societies themselves.

For in the state of nature . . . a man has two powers. The first is to do whatsoever he thinks fit for the preservation of himself and others within the permission of the *law* of nature. . . . The other is the *power to punish the crimes* committed against that law. Both these he gives up when he joins in a private, if I may so call it, or particular political society, and incorporates into any commonwealth separate from the rest of mankind.

The first *power*—viz., *of doing whatsoever he thought fit for the preservation of himself* and the rest of mankind, *he gives up* to be regulated by laws made by the society, so far forth as the preservation of himself and the rest of that society shall require; which laws of the society in many things confine the liberty he had by the law of nature.

Secondly. The *power of punishing he wholly gives up,* and engages his natural force (which he might before employ in the execution of the law of nature, by his own single authority, as he thought fit), to assist the executive power of the society as the law thereof shall require. For being now in a new state, wherein he is to enjoy many conveniences from the labor, assistance, and society of others in the same community, as well as protection from its whole strength, he is to part also with as much of his natural liberty, in providing for himself, as the good, prosperity, and safety of the society shall require, which is not only necessary but just, since the other members of the society do the like.

But though men when they enter into society give up the equality, liberty, and executive power they had in the state of nature into the hands of the society, to be so far disposed of by the legislative as the good of the society shall require, yet it being only with an intention in every one the better to preserve himself, his liberty and property (for no rational creature can be supposed to change his condition with an intention to be worse), the power of the society or *legislative* constituted by them can *never be supposed to extend farther than the common good,* but is obliged to secure every one's property by providing against those three defects above mentioned that made the state of nature so unsafe and uneasy. And so, whoever has the legislative or supreme power of any commonwealth, is bound to govern by established *standing laws,* promulgated and known to the people, and not by extemporary decrees; by *indifferent* and upright *judges,* who are to decide controversies by those laws; and to employ the force of the community at home *only in the execution of such laws,* or abroad to prevent or redress foreign injuries and secure the community from inroads and invasion. And all this to be directed to no other *end* but the *peace, safety,* and *public good* of the people.

OF THE FORMS OF
A COMMONWEALTH

The majority having, as has been showed, upon men's first uniting into society, the whole power of the community naturally in them, may employ all that power in making laws for the community from time to time, and executing those laws by officers of their own appointing, and then the *form* of the government is a perfect *democracy:* or else may put the power of making laws into the hands of a few select men, and their heirs or successors, and then it is an *oligarchy;* or else into the hands of one man, and then it is a *monarchy;* if to him and his heirs, it is a *hereditary monarchy;* if to him only for life, but upon his death the power only of nominating a successor, to return to them, an *elective monarchy.* And so accordingly of these make compounded and mixed forms of government, as they think good. And if the legislative power be at first given by the majority to one or more persons only for their lives, or any limited time, and then the supreme power to revert to them again, when it is so reverted the community may dispose of it again anew into what hands they please, and so constitute a new form of government: for the *form of government depending upon the placing the supreme power,* which is the *legislative,* it being impossible to conceive that an inferior power should prescribe to a superior, or any but the supreme make laws, according as the power of making laws is placed, such is the *form of the commonwealth.*

By *commonwealth* I must be understood all along to mean not a democracy, or any *form* of government, but *any independent community,* which the Latins signified by the word *civitas,* to which the word which best answers in our language is *commonwealth.*

OF THE EXTENT OF
THE LEGISLATIVE POWER

The great end of men's entering into society being the enjoyment of their properties in peace and safety, and the great instrument and means of that being the laws established in that society, the *first and fundamental positive law* of all commonwealths is the *establishing of the legislative power.* . . . This *legislative* is not only the *supreme power* of the commonwealth, but sacred and unalterable in the hands where the community have once placed it. Nor can any edict of anybody else, in what form soever conceived, or by what power soever backed, have the force and obligation of a *law* which has not its *sanction* from that legislative which the public has chosen and appointed. . . . Nor can any oaths to any foreign power whatsoever, or any domestic subordinate power, discharge any member of the society from his *obedience to the legislative,* acting pursuant to their trust, nor oblige him to any obedience contrary to the laws so enacted or farther than they do allow, it being ridiculous to imagine one can be tied ultimately to *obey* any *power* in the society which is not the *supreme.*

Though the legislative . . . be the *supreme* power in every commonwealth; yet,

First, it is *not,* nor can possibly be, absolutely *arbitrary* over the lives and fortunes of the people. . . . For nobody can transfer to another more power than he has in himself, and nobody has an absolute arbitrary power over himself, or over any other, to destroy his own life, or take away the life or property of another. A man, as has been proved, cannot subject himself to the arbitrary power of another; and having, in the state of nature, no arbitrary power over the life, liberty, or possession of another, but only so much as the law of nature gave him for the preservation of himself and the rest of mankind, this is all he doth, or can give up to the commonwealth, and by it to the legislative power; so that the legislative can have no more than this. Their power in the utmost bounds of it is *limited to the public good of the society.* It is a power that hath no other end but preservation, and therefore can never have a right to destroy, enslave, or designedly to impoverish the subjects. The obligations of the law of nature cease not in society, but only in many cases are drawn closer, and have, by human laws, known penalties annexed to them to enforce their observation. Thus the law of nature stands as an eternal rule to all men, *legislators* as well as others. The rules that they make for other men's actions must, as well as their own and other men's actions, be conformable to the law of nature—*i.e.,* to the will of God, of which that is a declaration, and the fundamental law of nature being the preservation of mankind, no human sanction can be good or valid against it.

Secondly, the *legislative* or supreme authority cannot assume to itself a power to rule by extemporary arbitrary decrees, but *is bound to dispense justice* and decide the rights of the subject by *promulgated standing laws, and known authorized judges.* For the law of nature being unwritten, and so nowhere to be found but in the minds of men, they who, through passion or interest, shall miscite or misapply it, cannot so easily be convinced of their mistake where there is no established judge. To avoid these inconveniences which disorder men's properties in the state of nature, men unite into societies that they may have the united strength of the whole society to secure and defend their properties, and may have *standing rules* to bound it by which every one may know what is his. To this end it is that men give up all their natural power to the society they enter into, and the community put the legislative power into such hands as they think fit, with this trust, that they shall be governed by *declared laws,* or else their peace, quiet, and property will still be at the same uncertainty as it was in the state of nature.

Absolute arbitrary power, or governing without *settled standing laws,* can neither of them consist with the ends of society and government. . . . It cannot be supposed that [men] should intend, had they a power so to do, to give any one or more an *absolute arbitrary power* over their persons and estates, and put a force into the magistrate's hand to execute his unlimited will arbitrarily upon them;

this were to put themselves into a worse condition than the state of nature, wherein they had a liberty to defend their right against the injuries of others, and were upon equal terms of force to maintain it, whether invaded by a single man or many in combination. Whereas by supposing they have given up themselves to the absolute arbitrary power and will of a legislator, they have disarmed themselves, and armed him to make a prey of them when he pleases; he being in a much worse condition that is exposed to the arbitrary power of one man who has the command of a hundred thousand than he that is exposed to the arbitrary power of a hundred thousand single men. . . . And, therefore, whatever form the commonwealth is under, the ruling power ought to govern by *declared* and *received* laws, and not by extemporary dictates and undetermined resolutions. . . . For all the power the government has, being only for the good of the society, as it ought not to be *arbitrary* and at pleasure, so it ought to be exercised by *established and promulgated laws,* that both the people may know their duty, and be safe and secure within the limits of the law, and the rulers, too, kept within their due bounds, and not be tempted by the power they have in their hands to employ it to purposes, and by such measures as they would not have known, and own not willingly.

Thirdly, the supreme power cannot take from any man any part of his *property* without his own consent. For the preservation of property being the end of government, and that for which men enter into society, it necessarily supposes and requires that the people should *have property,* without which they must be supposed to lose that by entering into society, which was the end for which they entered into it; too gross an absurdity for any man to own. Men, therefore, in society having property, they have such a right to the goods, which by the law of the community are theirs, that nobody hath a right to take them, or any part of them, from them without their own consent; without this they have no *property* at all. For I have truly no property in that which another can by right take from me when he pleases against my consent. Hence it is a mistake to think that the *supreme or legislative power* of any commonwealth can do what it will, and dispose of the estates of the subject arbitrarily, or take any part of them at pleasure. This is not much to be feared in governments where the legislative consists wholly or in part in assemblies which are variable, whose members upon the dissolution of the assembly are subjects under the common laws of their country, equally with the rest. But in governments where the legislative is in one lasting assembly, always in being or in one man as in absolute monarchies, there is danger still, that they will think themselves to have a distinct interest from the rest of the community, and so will be apt to increase their own riches and power by taking what they think fit from the people. For a man's *property* is not at all secure, though there be good and equitable laws to set the bounds of it between him and his fellow-subjects, if he who commands those subjects have power to take from any private man what part he pleases of his *property,* and use and dispose of it as he thinks good.

But government into whosesoever hands it is put, being as I have before showed, entrusted with this condition, and *for this end,* that men might have and secure their properties, the prince or senate, however it may have power to make laws for the *regulating of property* between the subjects one amongst another, yet can never have a power to take to themselves the whole, or any part of the subjects' *property,* without their own consent; for this would be in effect to leave them no property at all. And to let us see that even absolute power, where it is necessary, is not arbitrary by being absolute, but is still limited by that reason, and confined to those ends which required it in some cases to be absolute, we need look no farther than the common practice of martial discipline. For the preservation of the army, and in it of the whole commonwealth, requires an absolute obedience to the command of every superior officer, and it is justly death to disobey or dispute the most dangerous or unreasonable of them; but yet we see that neither the sergeant that could command a soldier to march up to the mouth of a cannon, or stand in a breach where he is almost sure to perish, can command that soldier to give him one penny of his money; nor the general that can condemn him to death for deserting his post, or not obeying the most desperate orders, cannot yet with all his absolute power of life and death dispose of one farthing of that soldier's estate, or seize one jot of his goods; whom yet he can command anything, and hang for the least disobedience. Because such a blind obedience is necessary to that end for which the commander has his power—viz., the preservation of the rest, but the disposing of his goods has nothing to do with it.

It is true governments cannot be supported without great charge, and it is fit every one who enjoys his share of the protection should pay out of his estate his proportion for the maintenance of it. But still it must be with his own consent—*i.e.,* the consent of the majority, giving it either by themselves or their representatives chosen by them; for if any one shall claim a *power to lay and levy taxes* on the people by his *own authority,* and without such consent of the people, he thereby invades the *fundamental law of property,* and subverts the end of government. For what property have I in that which another may by right take when he pleases to himself?

Fourthly. The legislative *cannot transfer the power of making laws* to any other hands, for it being but a delegated power from the people, they who have it cannot pass it over to others. The people alone can appoint the form of the commonwealth, which is by constituting the legislative, and appointing in whose hands that shall be. And when the people have said, "We will submit, and be governed by *laws* made by such men, and in such forms," nobody else can say other men shall make laws for them; nor can they be bound by any laws but such as are enacted by those whom they have chosen and authorized to make laws for them. . . .

These are the bounds which the trust that is put in them by the society and the law of God and nature have *set to the legislative power* of every commonwealth, in all forms of government.

First: They are to govern by *promulgated established laws,* not to be varied in particular cases, but to have one rule for rich and poor, for the favorite at court, and the countryman at plough.

Secondly: These laws also ought to be designed for no other end ultimately but the *good of the people.*

Thirdly: They must not raise taxes on the property of the people *without the consent of the people* given by themselves or their deputies. . . .

Fourthly: The legislative neither must nor can *transfer the power of making laws* to anybody else, or place it anywhere but where the people have.

OF THE LEGISLATIVE, EXECUTIVE, AND FEDERATIVE POWER OF THE COMMONWEALTH

The *legislative* power is that which has a right *to direct how the force of the commonwealth* shall be employed for preserving the community and the members of it. Because those laws which are constantly to be executed, and whose force is always to continue, may be made in a little time; therefore there is no need that the *legislative* should be always in being, not having always business to do. And because it may be too great temptation to human frailty, apt to grasp at power, for the same persons who have the power of making laws to have also in their hands the power to execute them; . . . therefore in well-ordered commonwealths . . . the *legislative* power is put into the hands of divers persons who, duly assembled, have by themselves, or jointly with others, a power to make laws, which when they have done, being separated again, they are themselves subject to the laws they have made; which is a new and near tie upon them to take care that they make them for the public good.

But because the laws that are at once, and in a short time made, have a constant and lasting force, and need a *perpetual execution,* or an attendance thereunto, therefore it is necessary there should be a *power always in being* which should see to the *execution* of the laws that are made, and remain in force. And thus the *legislative* and *executive power* come often to be *separated.* . . .

OF THE SUBORDINATION OF THE POWERS OF THE COMMONWEALTH

Though in a constituted commonwealth . . . there can be but *one supreme power,* which is the legislative, to which all the rest are and must be subordinate, yet the legislative being only a fiduciary power to act for certain ends, there remains still *in the people a supreme power to remove or alter the legislative,* when they find the legislative act contrary to the trust reposed in them. For all *power given with trust* for the attaining an *end* being limited by that end; whenever that end is manifestly neglected or opposed, the *trust* must necessarily be *forfeited,* and the power devolve into the hands of those that gave it, who may place it anew where they shall think best for their safety and security. And thus the *community* perpetually *retains a supreme power* of saving themselves from the attempts and designs of anybody, even of their legislators, whenever they shall be so foolish or so wicked as to lay and carry on designs against the liberties and properties of the subject. For no man or society of men having a power to deliver up their preservation, or consequently the means of it, to the absolute will and arbitrary dominion of another, whenever any one shall go about to bring them into such a slavish condition, they will always have a right to preserve what they have not a power to part with, and to rid thmeselves of those who invade this fundamental, sacred, and unalterable law of *self-preservation* for which they entered into society. And thus the *community* may be said in this respect to be *always the supreme power,* but not as considered under any form of government, because this power of the people can never take place till the government be dissolved.

In all cases *whilst the government subsists, the legislative is the supreme power.* For what can give laws to another must needs be superior to him. . . .

It may be demanded here, what if the executive power, being possessed of the force of the commonwealth, shall make use of that force to hinder the *meeting* and *acting of the legislative,* when the original constitution or the public exigencies require it? I say, using force upon the people, without authority, and contrary to the trust put in him that does so, is a state of war with the people, who have a right to *reinstate* their *legislative in the exercise of* their power. . . . In all states and conditions the true remedy of *force* without authority is to oppose *force* to it. The use of force without authority always puts him that uses it into a *state of war* as the aggressor, and renders him liable to be treated accordingly. . . .

OF TYRANNY

As usurpation is the exercise of power which another hath a right to, so *tyranny is the exercise of power beyond right,* which nobody can have a right to; and this is making use of the power any one has in his hands, not for the good of those who are under it, but for his own private, separate advantage. When the governor, however entitled, makes not the law, but his will, the rule, and his commands and actions are not directed to the preservation of the properties of his people, but the satisfaction of his own ambition, revenge, covetousness, or any other irregular passion. . . .

It is a mistake to think this fault is proper only to monarchies. Other forms of government are liable to it as well as that; for wherever the power that is put in any hands for the government of the people and the preservation of their properties is applied to other ends, and made use of to impoverish, harass, or subdue them to the arbitrary and irregular commands of those that have it, there it presently becomes tyranny, whether those that thus use it are one or many. Thus we read of the thirty tyrants at *Athens,* as well as one at *Syracuse;* and the intolerable dominion of the *Decemviri* at *Rome* was nothing better.

Wherever law ends, tyranny begins, if the law be transgressed to another's harm; and whosoever in authority exceeds the power given him by the law, and makes use of the force he has under his command to compass that upon the subject which the law allows not, ceases in that to be a magistrate, and acting without authority may be opposed, as any other man who by force invades the right of another. This is acknowledged in subordinate magistrates. He that hath authority to seize my person in the street may be opposed as a thief and a robber if he endeavors to break into my house to execute a writ, notwithstanding that I know he has such a warrant and such a legal authority as will empower him to arrest me abroad. And why this should not hold in the highest, as well as in the most inferior magistrate, I would gladly be informed. Is it

reasonable that the eldest brother, because he has the greatest part of his father's estate, should thereby have a right to take away any of his younger brothers' portions? Or, that a rich man, who possessed a whole country, should from thence have a right to seize, when he pleased, the cottage and garden of his poor neighbor? The being rightfully possessed of great power and riches, exceedingly beyond the greatest part of the sons of Adam, is so far from being an excuse, much less a reason for rapine and oppression, which the endamaging another without authority is, that it is a great aggravation of it. For the exceeding the bounds of authority is no more a right in a great than a petty officer, no more justifiable in a king than a constable. . . .

May the *commands,* then, *of a prince be opposed?* May he be resisted, as often as anyone shall find himself aggrieved, and but imagine he has not right done him? This will unhinge and overturn all polities, and instead of government and order, leave nothing but anarchy and confusion.

To this I answer: That *force* is to be opposed to nothing but to *unjust and unlawful force.* Whoever makes any opposition in any other case draws on himself a just condemnation, both from God and man; and so no such danger or confusion will follow, as is often suggested. . . .

OF THE DISSOLUTION OF GOVERNMENTS

He that will, with any clearness, speak of the *dissolution of government,* ought in the first place to distinguish between the dissolution of the *society* and the dissolution of the *government.* That which makes the community, and brings men out of the loose state of nature into *one politic society,* is the agreement which every one has with the rest to incorporate and act as one body, and so be one distinct commonwealth. The usual, and almost only way whereby *this union is dissolved,* is the inroad of foreign force making a conquest upon them. . . . The world is too well instructed in, and too forward to allow of this way of dissolving of governments, to need any more to be said of it. . . .

There is, therefore, secondly, another way

whereby *governments are dissolved,* and that is, when the legislative, or the prince, either of them act contrary to their trust.

First: the *legislative acts against the trust* reposed in them when they endeavor to invade the property of the subject, and to make themselves, or any part of the community, masters or arbitrary disposers of the lives, liberties, or fortunes of the people.

. . . Whensoever, therefore, the legislative shall transgress this fundamental rule of society, and either by ambition, fear, folly, or corruption, *endeavor to grasp themselves,* or *put into the hands of any other, an absolute power* over the lives, liberties, and estates of the people; by this breach of trust they *forfeit the power* the people had put into their hands for quite contrary ends; and it devolves to the people, who have a right to resume their original liberty, and by the establishment of a new legislative (such as they shall think fit), provide for their own safety and security, which is the end for which they are in society. What I have said here concerning the legislative in general holds true also concerning the supreme executor, who having a double trust put in him, both to have a part in the legislative and the supreme execution of the law, acts against both, when he goes about to set up his own arbitrary will as the law of the society. He acts also *contrary to his trust* when he employs the force, treasure, and offices of the society to *corrupt the representatives,* and gain them to his purposes, when he openly pre-engages the electors, and pre-scribes, to their choice, such whom he has, by solicitation, threats, promises, or otherwise, won to his designs, and employs them to bring in such who have promised beforehand what to vote and what to enact. Thus to regulate candidates and electors, and new model the ways of election, what is it but to cut up the government by the roots, and poison the very fountain of public security? . . .

To this, perhaps, it will be said that the people being ignorant and always discontented, to lay the foundation of government in the unsteady opinion and uncertain humor of the people, is to expose it to certain ruin; and *no government will be able long to subsist* if the people may set up a new legislative whenever they take offence at the old one. To this I answer, quite the contrary. People are not so easily got out of their old forms as some are apt to suggest. They are hardly to be prevailed with to amend the acknowledged faults in the frame they have been accustomed to. And if there be any original defects, or adventitious ones introduced by time or corruption, it is not an easy thing to get them changed, even when all the world sees there is an opportunity for it. This slowness and aversion in the people to quit their old constitutions has in the many revolutions that have been seen in this kingdom, in this and former ages, still kept us (or after some interval of fruitless attempts, still brought us back again) to our old legislative of kings, lords and commons; and whatever provocations have made the crown be taken from some of our princes' heads, they never carried the people so far as to place it in another line.

But it will be said this *hypothesis* lays a *ferment* for frequent *rebellion.* To which I answer:

First: no more than any other hypothesis. For when the people are made miserable, and find themselves *exposed to the ill usage or arbitrary power,* cry up their governors as much as you will for sons of Jupiter, let them be sacred and divine, descended or authorized from Heaven; give them out for whom or what you please, the same will happen. *The people generally ill treated,* and contrary to right, will be ready upon any occasion to ease themselves of a burden that sits heavy upon them. They will wish and seek for the opportunity, which in the change, weakness, and accidents of human affairs, seldom delays long to offer itself. He must have lived but a little while in the world, who has not seen examples of this in his time; and he must have read very little who cannot produce examples of it in all sorts of governments in the world.

Secondly: I answer, such *revolutions happen* not upon every little mismanagement in public affairs. *Great mistakes* in the ruling part, many wrong and inconvenient laws, and all the slips of human frailty will be *borne by the people* without mutiny or murmur. But if a *long train of abuses,* prevarications, and artifices, all tending the same way, make the design visible to the people, and they cannot but feel what they lie under, and see whither they are going, it is not to be wondered that they should then rouse themselves, and endeavor to put the rule into such hands which may secure to them the ends for which government was at first erected, and without which, ancient names and specious forms are so far from being better, that they are much worse than the state of nature or pure anarchy; the inconveniences being all as great and as near, but the remedy farther off and more difficult.

Thirdly: I answer, that this . . . power in the people of providing for their safety anew by a new legislative when their legislators have acted contrary to their trust by invading their property, is the *best fence against rebellion,* and the probablest means to hinder it. For rebellion being an opposition, not to persons, but authority, which is founded only in the constitutions and laws of the government; those, whoever they be, who by force break through, and by force justify their violation of them, are truly and properly *rebels.* For when men, by entering into society and civil government, have excluded force, and introduced laws for the preservation of property, peace, and unity amongst themselves, those who set up force again in opposition to the laws, do *rebellare*— that is, bring back again the state of war, and are properly rebels, which they who are in power (by the pretence they have to authority, the temptation of force they have in their hands, and the flattery of those about them), being likeliest to do, the properest way to prevent the evil is to show them the danger and injustice of it who are under the greatest temptation to run into it. . . .

But if they who say *it lays a foundation for rebellion* mean that it may occasion civil wars or intestine broils to tell the people they are absolved from obedience when illegal attempts are made upon their liberties or properties, and may oppose the unlawful violence of those who were their magistrates when they invade their properties, contrary to the trust put in them, and that, therefore, this doctrine is not to be allowed, being so destructive to the peace of the world; they may as well say, upon the same ground, that honest men may not oppose robbers or pirates, because this may occasion disorder or bloodshed. If any mischief come in such cases, it is not to be charged upon him who defends his own right, but on *him that invades his neighbor's.* If the innocent honest

man must quietly quit all he has for peace's sake to him who will lay violent hands upon it, I desire it may be considered what a kind of peace there will be in the world which consists only in violence and rapine, and which is to be maintained only for the benefit of robbers and oppressors. Who would not think it an admirable peace betwixt the mighty and the mean, when the lamb, without resistance, yielded his throat to be torn by the imperious wolf? *Polyphemus's* den gives us a perfect pattern of such a peace. Such a government wherein *Ulysses* and his companions had nothing to do but quietly to suffer themselves to be devoured. And no doubt *Ulysses,* who was a prudent man, preached up *passive obedience,* and exhorted them to a quiet submission by representing to them of what concernment peace was to mankind, and by showing the inconveniences [that] might happen if they should offer to resist *Polyphemus,* who had now the power over them.

The end of government is the good of mankind; and which is *best for mankind,* that the people should be always exposed to the boundless will of tyranny, or that the rulers should be sometimes liable to be opposed when they grow exorbitant in the use of their power, and employ it for the destruction, and not the preservation, of the properties of their people?

Nor let any one say that mischief can arise from hence as often as it shall please a busy head or turbulent spirit to desire the alteration of the government. It is true such men may stir whenever they please, but it will be only to their own just ruin and perdition. For till the mischief be grown general, and the ill designs of the rulers become visible, or their attempts sensible to the greater part, the people, who are more disposed to suffer than right themselves by resistance, are not apt to stir. The examples of particular injustice or oppression of here and there an unfortunate man moves them not. But if they universally have a persuasion grounded upon manifest evidence that designs are carrying on against their liberties, and the general course and tendency of things cannot but give them strong suspicions of the evil intention of their governors, who is to be blamed for it? Who can help it if they, who might avoid it, bring themselves into this suspicion? Are the people to be blamed if they have the sense of rational creatures, and can think of things no otherwise than as they find and feel them? And is it not rather *their fault* who put things in such a posture that they would not have them thought as they are? I grant that the pride, ambition, and turbulency of private men have sometimes caused great disorders in commonwealths, and factions have been fatal to states and kingdoms. But whether the mischief hath oftener begun in the *people's wantoness,* and a desire to cast off the lawful authority of their rulers, or in the *rulers' insolence* and endeavors to get and exercise an arbitrary power over their people, whether oppression or disobedience gave the first rise to the disorder, I leave it to impartial history to determine. This I am sure, whoever, either ruler or subject, by force goes about to invade the rights of either prince or people, and lays the foundation for *overturning* the constitution and frame of any *just government,* he is guilty of the greatest crime I think a man is capable of, being to answer for all those mischiefs of blood, rapine, and desolation, which the breaking to pieces of governments bring on a country; and he who does it is justly to be esteemed the common enemy and pest of mankind, and is to be treated accordingly. . . .

Here, it is like, the common question will be made, *Who shall be judge* whether the prince or legislative act contrary to their trust? . . . To this I reply, *The people shall be judge;* for who shall be *judge* whether his trustee or deputy acts well and according to the trust reposed in him, but he who deputes him and must, by having deputed him, have still a power to discard him when he fails in his trust? If this be reasonable in particular cases of private men, why should it be otherwise in that of the greatest moment, where the welfare of millions is concerned and also where the evil, if not prevented, is greater, and the redress very difficult, dear, and dangerous? . . .

If a controversy arise betwixt a prince and some of the people in a matter where the law is silent or doubtful, and the thing be of great consequence, I should think the proper *umpire* in such a case should be the *body of the people.* For in cases where the prince hath a trust reposed in him, and is dispensed from the common, ordinary rules of the law, there, if any men find themselves aggrieved, and think the prince acts contrary to, or beyond that trust, who so proper to *judge* as the *body of the people* (who at first lodged that trust in him) how far they meant it should extend? But if the prince, or whoever they be in the administration, decline that way of determination, the appeal then lies nowhere but to Heaven. Force between either persons who have no known superior on earth, or which permits no appeal to a judge on earth, being properly a state of war, wherein the appeal lies only to Heaven; and in that state the injured party must judge for himself when he will think fit to make use of that appeal and put himself upon it.

To conclude: The *power that every individual gave the society* when he entered into it can never revert to the individuals again, as long as the society lasts, but will always remain in the community; because without this there can be no community—no commonwealth, which is contrary to the original agreement; so also when the society hath placed the legislative in any assembly of men, to continue in them and their successors, with direction and authority for providing such successors, *the legislative can never revert to the people whilst that government lasts;* because, having provided a legislative with power to continue for ever, they have given up their political power to the legislative, and cannot resume it. But if they have set limits to the duration of their legislative, and made this supreme power in any person or assembly only temporary; or else, when, by the miscarriages of those in authority, it is forfeited; upon the forfeiture of their rulers, or at the determination of the time set, *it reverts to the society,* and the people have a right to act as supreme, and continue the legislative in themselves or place it in a new form, or new hands, as they think good.

Jean-Jacques Rousseau ·

Jean-Jacques Rousseau (1712–1778), a French intellectual of the Enlightenment, adapted the theory of the social contract to the growing concept of popular sovereignty. Influenced by his age, with its emphasis upon natural law and the idea of progress, he conceived of a society which, if it followed its natural capacity for development, could achieve the ultimate in human freedom. To him the social contract was between all the individuals composing the state but did not include the government. The latter existed only to carry out the expressed will of the people. For Rousseau the ultimate human freedom consisted of the voluntary submission by the individual to the general will. Thus in his writings there existed the seeds both of revolution against constituted government whenever it ceased to perform its functions dutifully, and of the present-day concept of complete democratic sovereignty with the will of the majority becoming the will of all. In reading the following selections from Rousseau's great book, The Social Contract, note (1) Rousseau's justification for undertaking this work, (2) the discussion of "right" and "might" and their relationship to the exercise of authority in government, (3) the fundamental human problem that the social contract solved, (4) the identity of interest between the sovereign and its subjects, (5) the distinction made between the individual will and the general will, (6) the need for force in making an individual free, (7) the balance sheet of gains and losses in forming the social contract, (8) how the general will may be corrupted, (9) how the sovereign power is limited, and (10) the methods by which government may be prevented from usurping power.

From: THE SOCIAL CONTRACT

I propose to inquire if, in the civil order, there can be any certain and legitimate administration, men being what they are and the laws what they might be. In this investigation I shall always try to combine right sanctions with what interest prescribes, so that justice and utility in no case may be divided.

I begin my task without proving the importance of the subject. I shall be asked if I am a ruler or a legislator, to write about politics. I answer that I am neither, and that is why I write. If I were a ruler or a legislator, I should not waste time saying what needs doing; I should do it, or keep quiet.

As I was born a citizen of a free State, and a member of the Sovereign, I feel that, however weak my influence on public affairs, the right of voting makes it my duty to study them; and I am happy, when I reflect upon governments, to discover that my inquiries always provide me with new reasons for loving that of my own country.

As translated by the editors from Jean-Jacques Rousseau, *Du Contrat Social*, Paris, 1903, 105–107; 113–114; 125–137; 150–162; 271–274.

SUBJECT OF THE FIRST BOOK

Man is born free; and everywhere he is in chains. One believes himself the master of others, yet remains a greater slave than they. How did this change occur? I do not know. What can render it legitimate? I think I can answer that question.

If I considered only force, and the effects derived therefrom, I should say: "As long as a people is forced to obey, and it obeys, it does well; as soon as it can shake off the yoke, and it shakes it off, it does still better; for, in recovering its liberty by the same right by which it was removed, either it is justified in regaining it, or there was no justification for those who took it away." But the social order is a sacred right which is the basis of all the others. Nevertheless, this right does not come from nature; it is founded on conventions. . . .

THE RIGHT OF THE STRONGEST

The strongest is never strong enough always to be the master, if he fails to transform strength into right, and obedience into duty. Hence the right of the strongest, which right, though to all appearances meant ironically, is really established as a principle. But are we never to have an explanation of this phrase? Might is physical power; I cannot see what moral effects it can have. To yield to might is an act of necessity, not of will; at the most, it is an act of prudence. In what sense can it be a duty?

Suppose for a moment the existence of this so-called right. I say that the only result is inexplicable nonsense; for, if might makes right, the effect changes with the cause; every force that is greater than the first succeeds to its right. As soon as it is possible to disobey with impunity, one does so legitimately; and, the strongest always being in the right, needs only to act so as to become the strongest. But what kind of right is that which perishes when might fails? If we must obey by force, there is no need to obey because we ought; and if we are not forced to obey, we are not obliged to do so. Clearly, the word *right* adds nothing to force; here, it means absolutely nothing.

Obey the powers that be. If this means: yield to force, the precept is good, but superflous; I reply that it will never be violated. All power comes from God, I admit; so does all sickness. Does that mean that we are forbidden to call the doctor? A robber surprises me at the edge of a forest: must I not merely give up my purse on compulsion; but, even if I could keep it, am I in conscience obliged to give it up? Certainly the pistol he holds is also a power.

Let us then admit that might does not create right, and that we are only obliged to obey legitimate powers. In that case, my original question recurs. . . .

THE SOCIAL COMPACT

I suppose men to have reached that point where the obstacles to their preservation in the state of nature reveal their resistance to be greater than the resources available to each individual for his maintenance in that state. Then that primitive condition can subsist no longer; and the human race would perish unless it changed its way of being.

But, as men cannot engender new forces, but only unite and direct existing ones, they have no other means of preserving themselves, save the formation, by aggregation, of a sum of forces great enough to overcome the resistance; these they must initiate by means of a single motive power, and cause to act in concert.

This sum of forces can arise only when several persons come together; but, since the force and the liberty of each man constitute the principal instruments of his self-preservation, how can he pledge them without hurting his own interests and neglecting the care which he owes himself? This difficulty, in its bearing on my subject, may be stated in these terms:

"Find a form of association which defends and protects with the whole force of the community the person and the goods of each associate, and in which each, while uniting with all, may still obey himself alone, and remain as free as before." This is the fundamental problem of which the *Social Contract* offers the solution.

The clauses of this contract are so determined by the nature of the act, that the slightest modification would render them vain and of no effect; so that, although they have perhaps never been formally announced, they are always the same and everywhere tacitly admitted and recognized, and, when the social compact is violated, each regains his original rights and regains his natural liberty while losing the conventional liberty for which he renounced it.

These clauses, properly understood, may be reduced to a single one—the total alienation of each associate with all his rights to the whole community; for, in the first place, as each gives himself entirely, the conditions are equal for all, and, the condition being equal for all, no one has an interest in making them burdensome to the others.

Moreover, the alienation being without reserve, the union is as perfect as it can be, and no associate has anything to demand: for, if the individuals retained certain rights in particular, as there would be no common superior to decide between them and the public, each, being on one point his own judge, would ask to be so on all; the state of nature would continue, and the association would necessarily become tyrannical or useless.

Finally, each in giving himself to all, gives himself to no one; and as there is no associate over whom he does not gain the same right as he grants to others over himself, he gains the equivalent for all that he loses, and a greater force for the conservation of what he has.

If then we discard from the social compact what is not of its essence, we shall find that it reduces itself to the following terms:

"Each of us puts his person and all his power in common under the supreme direction of the general will, and as in a body, we receive each member as an indivisible part of the whole."

At once, in place of the individual personality of each contracting party, this act of association produces a moral and collective body, composed of as many members as the assembly contains votes, and which receives from this same act its unity, its common identity, its life and its will. This public person, so formed by the union of all the others, formerly took the name of *city,* and now takes that of *Republic,* or *body politic.* It is called by its members,

State, when it is passive; *Sovereign,* when it is active; and *Power,* when compared with others like itself. Respecting the associates, they take collectively the name of *people,* and are called *citizens,* as participating in the sovereign power, and *subjects,* as being under the laws of the State. But these terms are often confused and taken the one for the other; it is sufficient to know how to distinguish them when they are used with precision. . . .

THE SOVEREIGN

We see by this formula that the act of association comprises a reciprocal undertaking between the public and individuals, and that each individual, contracting as it were, with himself, is bound in a double capacity: as a member of the Sovereign he is bound to the individuals, and as a member of the State, to the Sovereign. But we do not apply here the maxim of civil right that no one is bound by undertakings made to himself; for there is a great difference between undertaking an obligation to one's self and incurring one to a whole of which one is a part.

It is further necessary to call attention to the fact that public deliberation, while able to bind all the subjects to the Sovereign, because of the two different capacities in which each of them may be regarded, cannot, for the opposite reason, bind the Sovereign to itself; and that consequently it is against the nature of the body politic for the Sovereign to impose on itself a law which it cannot infringe. Being able to consider itself in only one capacity, it is in the position of an individual contracting with himself; thus one sees that there neither is nor can be a kind of fundamental law binding the body of the people—not even the social contract itself. This does not mean that the body politic cannot enter into undertakings with others, provided there is no infringement of the terms of the contract; for regarding what is external to it, it becomes a simple being, an individual.

But the body politic or the Sovereign, drawing its being only from the sanctity of the contract, can never bind itself, even to an outsider, to do anything derogatory to the original act, that is, to alienate any part of itself, or to submit to another Sovereign. Violation of the act by which it exists would be self-annihilation; and that which is itself nothing, can create nothing.

As soon as this multitude is thus united in one body, it cannot offend one of the members without attacking the whole, and still more to offend against the body without the members resenting it. Thus duty and interest equally oblige the two contracting parties mutually to aid each other; and the same men should seek to combine, in their double capacity, all the advantages dependent upon that capacity.

Again, the Sovereign, being formed entirely of the individuals comprising it, neither has nor can have any interest contrary to theirs; consequently the sovereign power need give no guarantee to its subjects, because it is impossible for the body to will to injure all its members. And we shall also see later on that it cannot hurt any in particular. The Sovereign, because of what it is, is always what it should be.

But this is not the case with the relation of the subjects to the Sovereign, which, in spite of the common interest, lacks a guarantee of fulfilment of their undertakings, unless it found means to assure itself of their fidelity.

In fact, each individual, as a man, may have a particular will contrary or dissimilar to the general will which he possesses as a citizen. His particular interest may speak to him quite differently from that of the common interest; his sole existence and natural independence, may make him look upon that which he owes to the common cause as a free contribution, the loss of which will do less harm to the others than the payment of it is onerous to himself; and concerning the moral person which constitutes the State as an imaginary being, because not a man, he may wish to enjoy the rights of citizenship without being willing to fulfil the duties of a subject. The continuance of such an injustice could not but prove the ruin of the body politic.

So that the social compact may not be an empty formula, it tacitly includes that undertaking, which alone can give force to the others, that whoever refuses to obey the general will shall be forced to do so by the whole body. This means nothing less than that he will be compelled to be free; for this is the condition which, by giving each citizen to his country, it guarantees him against all personal dependence. This condition permits the smooth operation of the political machine, and this alone renders civil undertakings legitimate, which, without it, would be absurd, tyrannical, and subject to the most enormous abuses.

THE CIVIL STATE

The passage from the state of nature to the civil state produces in man a very remarkable change, by substituting in his conduct justice for instinct, and giving his actions the morality they had formerly lacked. It is then only that the voice of duty supplants physical impulses and the right of appetite, and man, who so far had regarded himself only, finds that he is compelled to act on different principles, and to consult his reason before listening to his inclinations. Being in this state, he deprives himself of several advantages which he held from nature, but in return he receives others so great, his faculties are so stimulated and developed, his ideas so extended, his feelings so ennobled, and his whole soul so elevated, that, did not the abuses of this new condition often degrade him below that which he left, he must bless continually the happy hour which took him from it forever, and which, instead of a stupid and unimaginative animal, made him an intelligent being and a man.

Let us balance the whole in easily commensurable terms. That which man loses by the social contract is his natural liberty and an unlimited right to everything he attempts to get and succeeds in getting; that which he gains is civil liberty and the proprietorship of all he possesses. To avoid error in evaluating one against the other, we must clearly distinguish natural liberty, which is limited only by the strength of the individual, from civil liberty, which is limited by the general will; and possession, which is merely the effect of might or the right of the first occupant, from property, which can be founded only on a positive title.

We might, moreover, add moral liberty to what man acquires in the civil state, which alone renders him truly master of himself; for the mere impulse of appetite is slavery, while obedience to a law which we prescribe for ourselves is liberty. But I have already said too much about this, and the philosophical sense of the word *liberty* does not here concern me. . . .

WHETHER THE GENERAL WILL IS FALLIBLE

It follows from what has been said that the general will is always right and always tends to the public advantage; but it does not follow that the deliberations of the people are always equally right. Our will is always for our good, but we do not always recognize what that is; the people is never corrupted, but often deceived, and only on such occasions does it seem to will that which is bad.

There is often considerable difference between the will of all and the general will; the latter only regards the common interest, while the former considers private interest, and is only a sum of particular wills; but take away from these same wills the pluses and minuses that cancel one another, and the sum of the differences constitutes the general will.

If, when the people, having sufficient information, deliberate, the citizens lacked communication one with another, the grand total of the small differences would always represent the general will, and the decision would always be good. But when factions arise, and partial associations are formed at the expense of the great association, the will of each of these associations becomes general in relation to its members, and particular in relation to the State; one may then say that there are no longer as many votes as men, but only as many as there are associations. The differences become less numerous and give a less general result. Finally, when one of these associations is so great as to prevail over all the rest, you no longer have a sum of small differences, but a single difference; then there is no longer a general will, and the opinion which prevails is a purely particular opinion.

It is therefore essential, if the general will is to express itself, that there should be no partial society within the State, and that each citizen should think only his own thoughts; such

was indeed the unique and sublime system instituted by the great Lycurgus. But if there are partial societies, it is best to multiply the number and to prevent them from being unequal, as was done by Solon, Numa, and Servius. These precautions are the only guarantees that the general will shall always be enlightened, and that the people shall not deceive itself.

THE LIMITS OF THE SOVEREIGN POWER

If the State or the City is only a moral person whose life consists in the union of its members, and if the most important of its concerns is the care for its proper preservation, it must have a universal and compulsive force to move and dispose each part to the greatest advantage for the whole. As nature gives each man absolute power over all his members, so the social compact gives to the body politic absolute power over all its members; and it is this power which, under the direction of the general will, bears, as I have said, the name of Sovereignty.

But, besides the public person, we have to consider the private persons who compose it, and whose life and liberty are naturally independent of it. We must then clearly distinguish between the respective rights of the citizens and of the Sovereign, and between the duties the former are to fulfil as subjects, and the natural rights which they should enjoy in their capacity as men.

By the social compact each man alienates such part of his powers, goods, and liberty as it is important for the community to control; but it must be granted also that the Sovereign is alone judge of what is important.

All of the services that a citizen can render the State, he ought to render as soon as the Sovereign demands them; but the Sovereign, for its part, cannot impose upon its subjects any fetters that are useless to the community: nor can it even wish to do so; for, under the law of reason, nothing occurs without a cause, no more than under the law of nature.

The undertakings binding us to the social body are obligatory only because they are mutual; and their nature is such that in fulfilling them we cannot work for others without working for ourselves. Why is it that the general will is always right, and why does it seek continually to will the happiness of each one, unless it is because there is no man who does not think of *each* as meaning him, and who considers himself in voting for all? This proves that equality of rights and the notion of justice which such equality produces derives from the preference each man gives to himself, and consequently in the very nature of man. [It proves] that the general will, to be truly such, must be [general] in its object as well as in its essence; that it must proceed from all as well as apply to all; and that it loses its natural rectitude when it tends to some particular and determinate object, because in such a case we judge of something foreign to us, and we have no true principle of equity to guide us.

In effect, as soon as a question of fact or of a particular right arises on a point not regulated previously by a general convention, the matter becomes contentious. It is a process where the interested individuals are one party, and the public the other, but where I can see neither the law that ought to be followed nor the judge who ought to render the decision. It would be ridiculous to wish in that case to refer it to an express decision of the general will, which could only be the conclusion of one of the parties, and which consequently for the other party, would be only an external and particular will, inclined on this occasion to injustice and subject to error. Thus, just as a particular will cannot represent the general will, the general will, in turn, changes its nature, having a particular object, and cannot, as general, pronounce on a man or a fact. When, for example, the people of Athens nominated or displaced its rulers, decreed honors to one, and imposed penalties on another, and, by a multitude of particular decrees, exercised indiscriminately all the functions of government, it no longer had in such cases a general will properly speaking; it was acting no longer as Sovereign, but as magistrate. This will seem contrary to common views; but I must be given time to expound my own.

One can see from the foregoing that what makes the will general is less the number of voters than the common interest which unites them; for, under this institution, each neces-

sarily submits to the conditions he imposes on the others: this admirable agreement between interest and justice, gives to the common deliberations an equitable character which at once vanishes in the discussion of any particular question, in the absence of a common interest which unites and identifies the ruling of the judge with that of the party.

From whatever side we approach our principle, we arrive at the same conclusion; that the social compact establishes among the citizens such an equality, that they all bind themselves to observe the same conditions and should all enjoy the same rights. Thus, from the very nature of the compact, every act of Sovereignty, that is to say every authentic act of the general will, binds or favours equally all the citizens; so that the Sovereign recognizes only the body of the nation, and draws no distinctions between those of whom it is composed. What, then, properly speaking is an act of Sovereignty? It is not a convention between a superior and an inferior, but a convention between the body with each of its members: a legitimate convention, because it is based on the social contract; equitable, because common to all; useful, because it can have no other object than the general good; and stable, because guaranteed by the public force and the supreme power. So long as the subjects have to submit only to conventions of this sort, they obey no one, but only their own will; and to ask how far the respective rights of the Sovereign and the citizens extend, is to ask to what point the latter can contract with themselves, each with all, and all with each.

We see from this that the sovereign power, entirely absolute, wholly sacred and inviolable as it is, does not and cannot exceed the limits of general conventions, and that every man may fully dispose of such goods and liberty as these conventions leave him; so that the Sovereign never has a right to charge one subject more than another, because, in that case, the issue becomes particular, and ceases to be within its competency.

When one once admits these distinctions, it is seen to be so untrue that there is, in the social contract, any genuine renunciation on the part of the individuals; so that their position, as a result of the contract, is truly preferable to that in which they were before. Instead of an alienation they have made an advantageous exchange; instead of an uncertain and precarious manner of living, they have one that is better and more secure; instead of natural independence, they have liberty; instead of the power to harm others, security for themselves; and instead of their might, which others might overcome, a right which social union makes invincible. Their very life, which they have devoted to the State, is by it constantly protected; and when they risk it in its defence, what more are they doing than giving back what they have received from it? What are they doing that they would not do more often and with greater danger in the state of nature, in which they would fight inevitable battles at the peril of their lives, to preserve the means of their preservation? All have indeed to fight when their country needs them; but then no one has ever to fight for himself. Do we not gain something by running, for that which gives us our security, only some of the risks we should have to run for ourselves, as soon as we lost it?

THE MEANS OF PREVENTING THE USURPATIONS OF GOVERNMENT

What we have just said . . . makes it clear that the institution of government is not a contract, but a law; that the repositories of the executive power are not the people's masters, but its officers; that it can set them up and pull them down when it pleases; that for them there is no question of contract, but of obedience; and that in undertaking the functions the State imposes on them, they are merely fulfilling their duty as citizens, without having the remotest right to dispute about the conditions.

When therefore the people establish a hereditary government, whether it be monarchical within one family, or aristocratic of one class of citizens, it is not an undertaking that it enters: a provisional form is given the administration, until the people choose to order it otherwise.

It is true that these changes are always dangerous, and that the established government should never be touched except when it becomes incompatible with the public good; but this circumspection is a maxim of policy, and not a rule of right; and the State is no more bound to leave civil authority to its rulers than military authority to its generals.

It is also true that it is impossible, in such cases to observe, with too much care, all the formalities required to distinguish a regular and legitimate act from a seditious tumult, and the will of a whole people from the clamour of a faction. It is here, above all, that no further concession should be made to the untoward possibility that cannot, strictly speaking, be refused it. And it is also from this obligation that the prince derives a great advantage in preserving his power despite the people, without it being possible to say that he has usurped it; for, appearing to avail himself only of his rights, he finds it very easy to extend them, and to prevent, under the pretext of keeping the peace, assemblies that are destined to re-establish good order; with the result that he takes advantage of a silence he does not permit to be broken, or of irregularities he causes to be committed, to assume that he has the support of those whom fear prevents from speaking, and to punish those who dare to speak. Thus it was that the Decemvirs, having been elected for one year and then kept on in office for another year, tried to retain their power in perpetuity by forbidding the Comitia to assemble; and by this easy method every government in the world, once clothed with the public power, sooner or later usurps the sovereign authority.

The periodical assemblies of which I have spoken are designed especially to prevent or postpone this evil, above all when they need no formal convocation; for then, the prince cannot stop them without openly declaring himself a breaker of the laws and an enemy of the State.

The opening of these assemblies, whose only object is the maintenance of the social treaty, should always take the form of making two propositions that may never be suppressed, which should be voted on separately by the voters.

First: "Does it please the Sovereign to preserve the present form of government?"

Second: "Does it please the people to leave its administration in the hands of those actually in charge of it?"

I assume here what I believe I have demonstrated, namely, that there is in the State no fundamental law that cannot be revoked, not excluding the social compact itself; for if all the citizens assembled of one accord to break the compact, one cannot doubt that it would be very legitimately broken. Grotius even thinks that each man can renounce the State of which he is a member and recover his natural liberty and his goods on leaving the country.

It would truly be absurd if all the citizens together could not do what each can do by himself.

Thomas Mun

Thomas Mun (1571–1641), a director of the British East India Company, sought to broaden prevailing English ideas concerning mercantilism away from the narrow tenets of bullionism and toward a greater emphasis upon trade. Before he died he incorporated his economic views into a volume which he called England's Treasure by Forraign Trade, but it was not published until 23 years after his death. One of the principles which Mun presented in this well-known work was the theory of the balance of trade. In reading the following selections from Mun's volume note (1) the methods he advocated for increasing England's wealth, (2) suggested ways of augmenting exports and diminishing imports, (3) the circumstances under which he considered the export of bullion could be justified, (4) his discussion of invisible items in international trade, and (5) his estimate of foreign trade as an aspect of national strength.

From: ENGLAND'S TREASURE BY FORRAIGN TRADE

THE MEANS TO ENRICH THE KINGDOM, AND TO ENCREASE OUR TREASURE

Although a Kingdom may be enriched by gifts received, or by purchase taken from some other Nations, yet these are things uncertain and of small consideration when they happen. The ordinary means therefore to encrease our wealth and treasure is by *Forraign Trade,* wherein we must ever observe this rule: to sell more to strangers yearly than we consume of theirs in value. For suppose that when this Kingdom is plentifully served with the Cloth, Lead, Tinn, Iron, Fish and other native commodities, we doe yearly export the overplus to forraign Countries to the value of twenty two hundred thousand pounds; by which means we are enabled beyond the Seas to buy and bring in forraign wares for our use and Consumptions, to the value of twenty hundred thousand pounds; By this order duly kept in our trading, we may rest assured that the Kingdom shall be enriched yearly two hundred thousand pounds, which must be brought to us in so much Treasure; because that part of our stock which is not returned to us in wares must necessarily be brought home in treasure.

For in this case it cometh to pass in the stock of a Kingdom, as in the estate of a private man; who is supposed to have one thousand pounds yearly revenue and two thousand pounds of ready money in his Chest: If such a man through excess shall spend one thousand

Thomas Mun, *England's Treasure by Forraign Trade,* Macmillan and Company, New York and London, 1895, 7–27; 113–119. Courtesy of The Macmillan Company.

five hundred pounds *per annum*, all his ready money will be gone in four years; and in the like time his said money will be doubled if he take a Frugal course to spend but five hundred pounds *per annum;* which rule never faileth likewise in the Commonwealth, but in some cases (of no great moment) which I will hereafter declare, when I shall shew by whom and in what manner this ballance of the Kingdom's account ought to be drawn up yearly, or so often as it shall please the State to discover how much we gain or lose by trade with forraign Nations. But first I will say something concerning those ways and means which will encrease our exportations and diminish our importations of wares; which being done, I will then set down some other arguments both affirmative and negative to strengthen that which is here declared, and thereby to shew that all the other means which are commonly supposed to enrich the Kingdom with Treasure are altogether insufficient and meer fallacies.

THE PARTICULAR WAYS AND MEANS TO ENCREASE THE EXPORTATION OF OUR COMMODITIES, AND TO DECREASE OUR CONSUMPTION OF FORRAIGN WARES

The revenue or stock of a Kingdom by which it is provided of forraign wares is either *Natural* or *Artificial*. The Natural wealth is so much only as can be spared from our own use and necessities to be exported unto strangers. The Artificial consists in our manufactures and industrious trading with forraign commodities, concerning which I will set down such particulars as may serve for the cause we have in hand.

1. First, although this Realm be already exceeding rich by nature, yet might it be much encreased by laying the waste grounds (which are infinite) into such employments as should no way hinder the present revenues of other manured lands, but hereby to supply our selves and prevent the importations of Hemp, Flax, Cordage, Tobacco, and divers other things which now we fetch from strangers to our great impoverishing.

2. We may likewise diminish our importa-

tions, if we would soberly refrain from excessive consumption of forraign wares in our diet and rayment, with such often change of fashions as is used, so much the more to encrease the waste and charge; which vices at this present are more notorious amongst us than in former ages. Yet might they easily be amended by enforcing the observation of such good laws as are strictly practised in other Countries against the said excesses; where likewise by commanding their own manufactures to be used, they prevent the coming in of others, without prohibition, or offence to strangers in their mutual commerce.

3. In our exportations we must not only regard our own superfluities, but also we must consider our neighbours necessities, that so upon the wares which they cannot want, nor yet be furnished thereof elsewhere, we may (besides the vent of the Materials) gain so much of manifacture as we can, and also endeavour to sell them dear, so far forth as the high price cause not a less vent in the quantity. But the superfluity of our commodities which strangers use, and may also have the same from other Nations, or may abate their vent by the use of some such like wares from other places, and with little inconvenience; we must in this case strive to sell as cheap as possible we can, rather than to lose the utterance of such wares. For we have found of late years by good experience, that being able to sell our Cloth cheap in Turkey, we have greatly encreased the vent thereof, and the *Venetians* have lost as much in the utterance of theirs in those Countreys, because it is dearer. And on the other side a few years past, when by the excessive price of Wools our Cloth was exceeding dear, we lost at the least half our clothing for forraign parts, which since is no otherwise (well neer) recovered again than by the great fall of price for Wools and Cloth. We find that twenty five in the Hundred less in the price of these and some other wares, to the loss of private mens revenues, may raise above fifty upon the hundred in the quantity vented to the benefit of the publique. For when Cloth is dear, other Nations doe presently practise clothing, and we know they want neither art nor materials to this performance. But when by cheapness we drive them from this employment, and so

in time obtain our dear price again, then do they also use their former remedy. So that by these alterations we learn, that it is in vain to expect a greater revenue of our wares than their condition will afford, but rather it concerns us to apply our endeavours to the times with care and diligence to help our selves the best we may, by making our cloth and other manufactures without deceit, which will encrease their estimation and use.

4. The value of our exportations likewise may be much advanced when we perform it ourselves in our own Ships, for then we get only not the price of our wares as they are worth here, but also the Merchants gains, the charges of ensurance, and fraight to carry them beyond the seas. As for example, if the *Italian* Merchants should come hither in their own shipping to fetch our Corn, our red Herrings or the like, in this case the Kingdom should have ordinarily but 25.*s.* for a quarter of Wheat, and 20.*s.* for a barrel of red herrings, whereas if we carry these wares ourselves into *Italy* upon the said rates, it is likely that wee shall obtain fifty shillings for the first, and forty shillings for the last, which is a great difference in the utterance or vent of the Kingdoms stock. And although it is true that the commerce ought to be free to strangers to bring in and carry out at their pleasure, yet nevertheless in many places the exportation of victuals and munition are either prohibited, or at least limited to be done onely by the people and Shipping of those places where they abound.

5. The frugal expending likewise of our own natural wealth might advance much yearly to be exported unto strangers; and if in our rayment we will be prodigal, yet let this be done with our own materials and manufactures, as Cloth, Lace, Imbroderies, Cutworks and the like, where the excess of the rich may be the employment of the poor, whose labours notwithstanding of this kind, would be more profitable for the Commonwealth, if they were done to the use of Strangers.

6. The Fishing in his Majesties seas of *England*, *Scotland*, and *Ireland* is our natural wealth, and would cost nothing but labour, which the *Dutch* bestow willingly and thereby draw yearly a very great profit to themselves by serving many places of Christendom with our Fish, for which they return and supply their wants both of forraign Wares and Mony, besides the multitudes of Mariners and Shipping, which hereby are maintain'd, whereof a long discourse might be made to shew the particular manage of this important business. Our Fishing plantation likewise in *New-England*, *Virginia*, *Groenland*, the *Summer Islands* and the *New-found-land*, are of the like nature, affording much wealth and employments to maintain a great number of poor, and to encrease our decaying trade.

7. A Staple or Magazin for forraign Corn, Indico, Spices, Raw-silks, Cotton wool or any other commodity whatsoever, to be imported will encrease Shipping, Trade, Treasure, and the Kings customes, by exporting them again where need shall require, which course of Trading hath been the chief means to raise *Venice*, *Genoa*, the *low-Countreys*, with some others; and for such a purpose *England* stands most commodiously, wanting nothing to this performance but our own diligence and endeavour.

8. Also wee ought to esteem and cherish those trades which we have in remote or far Countreys, for besides the encrease of Shipping and Mariners thereby, the wares also sent thither and receiv'd from thence are far more profitable unto the kingdom than by our trades neer at hand; As for example; suppose Pepper to be worth here two Shillings the pound constantly, if then it be brought from the *Dutch* at *Amsterdam*, the Merchant may give there twenty pence the pound, and gain well by the bargain, but if he fetch this Pepper from the East-indies, he must not give above three pence the pound at the most, which is a mighty advantage, not only in that part which serveth for our own use, but also for the great quantity which (from hence) we transport yearly unto divers other Nations to be sold at a higher price: whereby it is plain, that we make a far greater stock by gain upon these *Indian* Commodities, than those Nations doe where they grow, and to whom they properly appertain, being the natural wealth of their Countries. But for the better understanding of this particular, we must ever distinguish between the gain of the Kingdom, and the profit of the Mer-

chant; for although the Kingdom payeth no more for this Pepper than is before supposed, nor for any other commodity bought in forraign parts more than the Stranger receiveth from us for the same, yet the Merchant payeth not only that price, but also the fraight, ensurance, customes and other charges which are exceeding great in these long voyages; but yet all these in the Kingdoms accompt are but commutations among our selves, and no privation of the Kingdoms stock, which being duly considered, together with the support also of our other trades in our best Shipping to *Italy, France, Turkey,* the *East Countreys* and other places, by transporting and venting the wares which we bring yearly from the *East Indies.* It may well stir up our utmost endeavours to maintain and enlarge this great and noble business, so much importing the Publique wealth, Strength, and Happiness. Neither is there less honour and judgment by growing rich (in this manner) upon the stock of other Nations, than by an industrious encrease of our own means, especially when this later is advanced by the benefit of the former, as we have found in the *East Indies* by sale of much of our Tin, Cloth, Lead and other Commodities, the vent whereof doth daily encrease in those Countreys which formerly had no use of our wares.

9. It would be very beneficial to export money as well as wares, being done in trade only, it would encrease our Treasure; but of this I write more largely in the next Chapter to prove it plainly.

10. It were policie and profit for the State to suffer manufactures made of forraign Materials to be exposed custome-free, as Velvets and all other wrought Silks, Fustians, thrown Silks and the like, it would employ very many poor people, and much encrease the value of our stock yearly issued into other Countreys, and it would (for this purpose) cause the more forraign Materials to be brought in, to the improvement of His Majesties Customes. I will here remember a notable increase in our manufacture of winding and twisting only of forraign raw Silk, which within 35. years to my knowledge did not employ more than 300. people in the City and suburbs of London, where at this present time it doth set on work above fourteen thousand souls, as upon diligent enquiry hath been credibly reported unto His Majesties Commissioners for Trade. And it is certain, that if the said forraign Commodities might be exported from hence, free of custome, this manufacture would yet encrease very much, and decrease as fast in *Italy* and the *Netherlands.* But if any man allege the *Dutch* proverb, *Live and let others live;* I answer, that the Dutchmen notwithstanding their own Proverb, doe not onely in these Kingdoms, encroach upon our livings, but also in other forraign parts of our trade (where they have power) they do hinder and destroy us in our lawful course of living, hereby taking the bread out of our mouth, which we shall never prevent by plucking the pot from their nose, as of late years too many of us do practise to the great hurt and dishonour of this famous Nation; We ought rather to imitate former times in taking sober and worthy courses more pleasing to God and suitable to our ancient reputation.

11. It is needful also not to charge the native commodities with too great customes, lest by indearing them to the strangers use, it hinder their vent. And especially forraign wares brought in to be transported again should be favoured, for otherwise that manner of trading (so much importing the good of the Common wealth) cannot prosper nor subsist. But the Consumption of such forraign wares in the Realm may be the more charged, which will turn to the profit of the Kingdom in the *Ballance of the Trade,* and thereby also enable the King to lay up the more Treasure out of his yearly incomes, as of this particular I intend to write more fully in his proper place, where I shall shew how much money a Prince may conveniently lay up without the hurt of his subjects.

12. Lastly, in all things we must endeavour to make the most we can of our own, whether it be *Natural* or *Artificial;* And forasmuch as the people which live by the Arts are far more in number than they who are masters of the fruits, we ought the more carefully to maintain those endeavours of the multitude, in whom doth consist the greatest strength and riches both of King and Kingdom: for where the people are many, and the arts good, there the traffique must be great, and the Countrey rich. The *Italians* employ a greater number of peo-

ple, and get more money by their industry and manufactures of the raw Silks of the Kingdom of *Cicilia,* than the King of *Spain* and his Subjects have by the revenue of this rich commodity. But what need we fetch the example so far, when we know that our own natural wares doe not yield us so much profit as our industry? For Iron oar in the Mines is of no great worth, when it is compared with the employment and advantage it yields being digged, tried, transported, bought, sold, cast into Ordnance, Muskets, and many other instruments of war for offence and defence, wrought into Anchors, bolts, spikes, nayles and the like, for the use of Ships, Houses, Carts, Coaches, Ploughs, and other instruments for Tillage. Compare our Fleece-wools with our Cloth, which requires shearing, washing, carding, spinning, Weaving, fulling, dying, dressing and other trimmings, and we shall find these Arts more profitable than the natural wealth, whereof I might instance other examples, but I will not be more tedious, for if I would amplify upon this and the other particulars before written, I might find matter sufficient to make a large volume, but my desire in all is only to prove what I propound with brevity and plainness.

THE EXPORTATION OF OUR MONEYS IN TRADE OF MERCHANDIZE IS A MEANS TO ENCREASE OUR TREASURE

This Position is so contrary to the common opinion, that it will require many and strong arguments to prove it before it can be accepted of the Multitude, who bitterly exclaim when they see any monies carried out of the Realm; affirming thereupon that we have absolutely lost so much Treasure, and that this is an act directly against the long continued laws made and confirmed by the wisdom of this Kingdom in the High Court of Parliament, and that many places, nay *Spain* it self which is the Fountain of Mony, forbids the exportation thereof, some cases only excepted. To all which I might answer that *Venice, Florence, Genoa,* the *Low Countreys* and divers other places permit it, their people applaud it, and find great benefit by it; but all this makes a noise and proves nothing, we must therefore come to those reasons which concern the business in question.

First, I will take that for granted which no man of judgment will deny, that we have no other means to get Treasure but by forraign trade, for Mines wee have none which do afford it, and how this mony is gotten in the managing of our said Trade I have already shewed, that it is done by making our commodities which are exported yearly to over ballance in value the forraign wares which we consume; so that it resteth only to shew how our monyes may be added to our commodities, and being jointly exported may so much the more encrease our Treasure.

Wee have already supposed our yearly consumptions of forraign wares to be for the value of twenty hundred thousand pounds, and our exportations to exceed that two hundred thousand pounds, which sum wee have thereupon affirmed is brought to us in treasure to ballance the accompt. But now if we add three hundred thousand pounds more in ready mony unto our former exportations in wares, what profit can we have (will some men say) although by this means we should bring in so much ready mony more than wee did before, seeing that we have carried out the like value.

To this the answer is, that when wee have prepared our exportations of wares, and sent out as much of everything as wee can spare or vent abroad: It is not therefore said that then we should add our money thereunto to fetch in the more mony immediately, but rather first to enlarge our trade by enabling us to bring in more forraign wares, which being sent out again will in due time much encrease our Treasure.

For although in this manner wee do yearly multiply our importations to the maintenance of more Shipping and Mariners, improvement of His Majesties Customs and other benefits: yet our consumption of those forraign wares is no more than it was before; so that all the said encrease of commodities brought in by the means of our ready mony sent out as it afore written, doth in the end become an exportation unto us of far greater value than our said moneys were, which is proved by three several examples following.

1. For I suppose that 100000. £. being sent in our Shipping to the East Countreyes, will buy there one hundred thousand quarters of wheat cleer abroad the Ships, which after being brought into *England* and housed, to export the same at the best time for vent thereof in *Spain* or *Italy*, it cannot yield less in those parts than two hundred thousand pounds to make the Merchant but a saver, yet by this reckning we see the Kingdom hath doubled that Treasure.

2. Again this profit will be far greater when wee trade thus in remote Countreys, as for example, if wee send one hundred thousand pounds into the *East-Indies* to buy Pepper there, and bring it hither, and from hence send it for *Italy* or *Turkey*, it must yield seven hundred thousand pounds at least in those places, in regard of the excessive charge which the Merchant disburseth in those long voyages in Shipping, Wages, Victuals, Insurance, Interest, Customes, Imposts, and the like, all which notwithstanding the King and the Kingdom gets.

3. But where the voyages are short & the wares rich, which therefore will not employ much Shipping, the profit will be far less. As when another hundred thousand pounds shall be employed in *Turkey* in raw Silks, and brought hither to be after transported from hence into *France*, the *Low Countreys*, or *Germany*, the Merchant shall have good gain, although he sell it there but for one hundred and fifty thousand pounds: and thus take the voyages altogether in their *Medium*, the moneys exported will be returned unto us more than Trebled. But if any man will yet object, that these returns come to us in wares, and not really in mony as they were issued out,

The answer is (keeping our first ground) that if our consumption of forraign wares be no more yearly than is already supposed, and that our exportations be so mightily encreased by this manner of Trading with ready money as is before declared: it is not then possible but that all the over-ballance or difference should return either in mony or in such wares as we must export again, which, as is already plainly shewed will be still a greater means to encrease our Treasure.

For it is in the stock of the Kingdom as in the estates of private men, who having store of wares, doe not therefore say that they will not venture out or trade with their mony (for this were ridiculous) but do also turn that into wares, whereby they multiply their Mony, and so by a continual and orderly change of one into the other grow rich, and when they please turn all their estates into Treasure; for they that have Wares cannot want money.

Neither is it said that Mony is the Life of Trade, as if it could not subsist without the same; for we know that there was great trading by way of commutation or barter when there was little mony stirring in the world. The *Italians* and some other Nations have such remedies against this want, that it can neither decay nor hinder their trade, for they transfer bills of debt, and have Banks both publick and private, wherein they do assign their credits from one to another daily for very great sums with ease and satisfaction by writings only, whilst in the mean time the Mass of Treasure which gave foundation to these credits is employed in Forraign Trade as a Merchandize, and by the said means they have little other use of money in those countreys more than for their ordinary expences. It is not therefore the keeping of our mony in the Kingdom, but the necessity and use of our wares in forraign Countries, and our want of their commodities that causeth the vent and consumption on all sides, which makes a quick and ample Trade. If wee were once poor, and now having gained some store of mony by trade with resolution to keep it still in the Realm; shall this cause other Nations to spend more of our commodities than formerly they have done, whereby we might say that our trade is Quickned and Enlarged? no verily it will produce no such good effect: but rather according to the alteration of times by their true causes wee may expect the contrary; for all men do consent that plenty of mony in a Kingdom doth make the native commodities dearer, which as it is to the profit of some private men in their revenues, so is it directly against the benefit of the Publique in the quantity of the trade; for as plenty of mony makes wares dearer, so dear wares decline their use and consumption, as hath been already plainly shewed in the last Chapter upon that particular of our cloth; And although this is a very hard lesson for some great landed men to learn, yet I am sure it is a true lesson for all the land to observe, lest when wee have gained some store of mony by trade, wee lose it again by not trading with our mony. I knew a Prince in *Italy* (of famous memory) *Ferdinando the first*, great Duke of *Tuscanie*, who being very rich in Treasure, endevoured therewith to enlarge his trade by issuing out to his Merchants great sums of money for very small profit; I my self had forty thousand crowns of him *gratis* for a whole year, although he knew that I would presently send it away in *Specie* for the parts of *Turkey* to be employed in wares for his Countries, he being well assured that in this course of trade it would return again (according to the old saying) with a Duck in the mouth. This noble and industrious Prince by his care and diligence to countenance and favour Merchants in their affairs, did so encrease the practice thereof, that there is scarce a Nobleman or Gentleman in all his dominions that doth not Merchandize either by himself or in partnership with others, whereby within these thirty years the trade to his port of *Leghorn* is so much encreased, that of a poor little town (as I my self knew it) it is now become a fair and strong City, being one of the most famous places for trade in all Christendom. And yet it is worthy our observation, that the multitude of Ships and wares which come hither from *England*, the *Low Countreys*, and other places, have little or no means to make their returns from thence but only in ready mony, which they may and do carry away freely at all times, to the incredible advantage of the said great Duke of *Tuscanie* and his subjects, who are much enriched by the continual great concourse of Merchants from all the States of the neighbour Princes, bringing them plenty of mony daily to supply their wants of the said wares. And thus we see that the current of Merchandize which carries away their Treasure, becomes a flowing stream to fill them again in a greater measure with mony.

There is yet an objection or two as weak as all the rest: that is, if wee trade with our Mony wee shall issue out the less wares; as if a man should say, those Countreys which heretofore had occasion to consume our Cloth, Lead, Tin, Iron, Fish, and the like, shall now make use of our monies in the place of these necessaries,

which were most absurd to affirm, or that the Merchant had not rather carry out wares by which there is ever some gains expected, than to export mony which is still but the same without any encrease.

But on the contrary there are many Countreys which may yield us very profitable trade for our mony, which otherwise afford us no trade at all, because they have no use of our wares, as namely the *East-Indies* for one in the first beginning thereof, although since by industry in our commerce with those Nations we have brought them into the use of much of our Lead, Cloth, Tin, and other things, which is a good addition to the former vent of our commodities.

Again, some men have alleged that those Countries which permit mony to be carried out, do it because they have few or no wares to trade withall: but wee have great store of commodities, and therefore their action ought not to be our example.

To this the answer is briefly, that if we have such a quantity of wares as doth fully provide us of all things needful from beyond the seas: why should we then doubt that our monys sent out in trade, must not necessarily come back again in treasure; together with the great gains which it may procure in such manner as is before set down? And on the other side, if those Nations which send out their monies do it because they have but few wares of their own, how come they then to have so much Treasure as we ever see in those places which suffer it freely to be exported at all times and by whomsoever? I answer, *Even by trading with their Moneys;* for by what other means can they get it, having no Mines of Gold or Silver?

Thus may we plainly see, that when this weighty business is duly considered in his end, as all our humane actions ought well to be weighed, it is found much contrary to that which most men esteem thereof, because they search no further than the beginning of the work, which mis-informs their judgments, and leads them into error: For if we only behold the actions of the husbandman in the feed-time when he casteth away much good corn into the ground, we will rather accompt him a mad man than a husbandman: but when we consider his labours in the harvest which is the end of his endeavours, we find the worth and plentiful encrease of his actions. . . .

THE ORDER AND MEANS WHEREBY WE MAY DRAW UP THE BALANCE OF OUR FORRAIGN TRADE

Now, that we have sufficiently proved the Ballance of our Forraign Trade to be the true rule of our Treasure; It resteth that we shew by whom and in what manenr the said ballance may be drawn up at all times, when it shall please the State to discover how we prosper or decline in this great and weighty business, wherein the Officers of his Majesties Customes are the onely Agents to be employed, because they have the accounts of all the wares which are issued out or brought into the Kingdome; and although (it is true) they cannot exactly set down the cost and charges of other men's goods bought here or beyond the seas; yet nevertheless, if they ground themselves upon the book of Rates, they shall be able to make such an estimate as may well satisfie this enquiry: for it is not expected that such an account can possibly be drawn up to a just ballance, it will suffice onely that the difference be not over great.

First therefore, concerning our Exportations, when we have valued their first cost, we must add twenty-five *per cent.* thereunto for the charges here, for fraight of Ships, ensurance of the *Adventure,* and the *Merchants* Gains; and for our Fishing Trades, which pay no Custome to his Majesty, the value of such Exportations may be easily esteem'd by good observations which have been made, and may continually be made, according to the increase or decrease of those affairs, the present state of this commodity being valued at one hundred and forty thousand pounds issued yearly. Also we must add to our Exportations all the moneys which are carried out in Trade by license from his Majesty.

Secondly, for our Importations of Forraign Wares, the Custome-books serve onely to direct us concerning the quantity, for we must not value them as they are rated here, but as they cost us with all charges laden into our Ships beyond the Seas, in the respective places where they are bought: for the Merchants gain, the charges of Insurance, Fraight of Ships, Customes, Imposts, and other Duties here, which doe greatly indear them unto our use and consumption, are notwithstanding but Commutations amongst our selves, for the Stranger hath no part thereof: wherefore our said Importations ought to be valued at twenty-five *per cent.* less than they are rated to be worth here. And although this may seem to be too great allowance upon many rich Commodities, which come but from the *Low Countryes* and other places neer hand, yet will it be found reasonable, when we consider it in gross Commodities, and upon Wares laden in remote Countreys, as our Pepper, which cost us, with charges, but four pence the pound in the *East Indies,* and it is here rated at twenty pence the pound: so that when all is brought into a *medium,* the valuation ought to be made as afore-written. And therefore, the order which hath been used to multiply the full rates upon wares inwards by twenty, would produce a very great errour in the Ballance, for in this manner the ten thousand bags of Pepper, which this year we have brought hither from the *East Indies,* should be valued at very near two hundred and fifty thousand pounds, whereas all this Pepper in the Kingdomes accompt, cost not above fifty thousand pounds, because the Indians have had no more of us, although we paid them extraordinary dear prices for the same. All the other charges (as I have said before) is but a change of effects amongst our selves, and from the Subject to the King, which cannot impoverish the Commonwealth. But it is true, that whereas nine thousand bags of the said Pepper are already shipped out for divers forraign parts; These and all other Wares, forraign or domestick, which are thus transported Outwards, ought to be cast up by the rates of his Majesties Custome-money, multiplyed by twenty, or rather by twenty-five (as I conceive) which will come neerer the reckoning, when we consider all our Trades to bring them into a *medium.*

Thirdly, we must remember, that all Wares exported or imported by Strangers (in their shipping) be esteemed by themselves, for what they carry out, the Kingdom hath only the first cost and the custom: And what they bring in, we must rate it as it is worth here, the Custom, Impost, and petty charges only deducted.

Lastly, there must be good notice taken of all the great losses which we receive at Sea in our Shipping either outward or homeward bound: for the value of the one is to be deducted from our Exportations, and the value of the other is to be added to our Importations: for to lose and to consume doth produce one and the same reckoning. Likewise if it happen that His Majesty doth make over any great sums of mony by Exchange to maintain a forraign war, where we do not feed and clothe the Souldiers, and Provide the armies, we must deduct all this charge out of our Exportations or add it to our Importations; for this expence doth either carry out or hinder the coming in of so much Treasure. And here we must remember the great collections of mony which are supposed to be made throughout the Realm yearly from our Recusants by Priests and Jesuits, who secretly convey the same unto their Colleges, Cloysters and Nunneries beyond the Seas, from whence it never returns to us again in any kind; therefore if this mischief cannot be prevented, yet it must be esteemed and set down as a cleer loss to the Kingdome, except (to ballance this) we will imagine that as great a value may perhaps come in from forraign Princes to their Pensioners here for Favours or Intelligence, which some States account good Policy, to purchase with great Liberality; the receipt whereof notwithstanding is plain Treachery.

There are yet some other petty things which seem to have reference to this Ballance, of which the said Officers of His Majesties Customs can take no notice, to bring them into the accompt. As namely, the expences of travailers, the gifts to Ambassadors and Strangers, the fraud of some rich goods not entred into the Custom-house, the gain which is made here by Strangers by change and re-change, Interest of mony, ensurance upon English mens goods and their lives: which can be little when the charges of their living here is deducted; besides that the very like advantages are as amply ministred unto the English in forraign Countreys, which doth counterpoize all these things, and therefore they are not considerable in the drawing up of the said Ballance.

THE CONCLUSION
UPON ALL THAT HATH BEEN SAID, CONCERNING THE EXPORTATION OR IMPORTATION OF TREASURE

The sum of all that hath been spoken, concerning the enriching of the Kingdom, and th' encrease of our treasure by commerce with strangers, is briefly thus. That it is a certain rule in our forraign trade, in those places where our commodities exported are overballanced in value by forraign wares brought into this Realm, there our mony is undervalued in exchange; and where the contrary of this is performed, there our mony is overvalued. But let the Merchants exchange be at a high rate, or at a low rate, or at the *Par pro pari,* or put down altogether; Let Forraign Princes enhance their Coins, or debase their Standards, and let His Majesty do the like, or keep them constant as they now stand; Let forraign Coins pass current here in all payments at higher rates than they are worth at the Mint; Let the Statutes for employments by Strangers stand in force or be repealed; Let the meer Exchanger do his worst; Let Princes oppress, Lawyers extort, Usurers bite, Prodigals wast, and lastly let Merchants carry out what mony they shall have occasion to use in traffique. Yet all these actions can work no other effects in the course of trade than is declared in this discourse. For so much Treasure only will be brought in or carried out of a Commonwealth, as the Forraign Trade doth over or under ballance in value. And this must come to pass by a Necessity beyond all resistance. So that all other courses (which tend not to this end) howsoever they may seem to force mony into a Kingdom for a time, yet are they (in the end) not only fruitless but also hurtful: they are like to violent flouds which bear down their banks, and suddenly remain dry again for want of waters.

Behold then the true form and worth of forraign Trade, which is, *The great Revenue of the King, The honour of the Kingdom, The Noble profession of the Merchant, The School of our Arts, The supply of our wants, The employment of our poor, The improvement of our Lands, The Nurcery of our Mariners, The walls of the Kingdoms, The means of our Treasure,*

The Sinnews of our wars, The terror of our Enemies. For all which great and weighty reasons, do so many well governed States highly countenance the profession, and carefully cherish the action, not only with Policy to encrease it, but also with power to protect it from all forraign injuries: because they know it is a Principal in Reason of State to maintain and defend that which doth Support them and their estates.

Daniel Defoe

Daniel Defoe (about 1659–1731) was an outstanding English literary figure during the last decades of the Stuart dynasty and the first years of the Hanoverian. In many ways he personified the rising commercial middle class which, in these decades, was achieving both social and political prestige alongside the cavalier society of the period. He was born into a nonconformist family of some means, and for a time he followed a commercial career which included participation in the import trade. The wide variety of topics on which he wrote made of his works an excellent reflection of the historical trends of the time. Thus the rise of parliament was reflected in The Original Power of the Collective Body of the People of England Examined and Asserted; the religious conflict was revealed in Shortest Way with Dissenters; the interest in discovery and exploration in Robinson Crusoe and A New Voyage Around the World; and the rise of commercial capitalism in The Complete English Tradesman, which appeared in 1726. In the following selections from the latter work note (1) the evidences of national pride, (2) the social position of tradesmen, (3) the services this class rendered to the nation, (4) the comparison he made between the gentry and tradesmen, (5) his explanation for England's greatness, and (6) the significance of trade to America.

From: THE COMPLETE ENGLISH TRADESMAN

Of the dignity of trade in England, more than in other countries. That England is the greatest trading country in the world; that our climate is the best to live in; that our men are the stoutest and best; that the tradesmen in England are not of the meanest of the people; that the wealth of the nation lies chiefly among them; that trade is a continual fund for supplying the decays in the rank of gentry; that an ordinary trader can spend more than a gentleman of 500£. a year; that an estate is a pond, but trade a spring; that the descendants of tradesmen here, for gallantry of spirit and greatness of soul, are not inferior to the descendants of the best families. Further hints to the ladies whose pride will not let them stoop to marry a tradesman. To trade, and not to conquest, is owing the present grandeur of the English nation. How much the landed interest owes to trade.

Daniel Defoe, *The Complete English Tradesman,* vols. 17–18 of *The Novels and Miscellaneous Works of Daniel De Foe.* . . . Oxford, 1840–1841, chapter 25.

The instances which we have given in the last chapter, abundantly make for the honour of the British traders; and we may venture to say, at the same time, are very far from doing dishonour to the nobility who have from time to time entered into alliance with them; for it is very well known, that besides the benefit which we reap by being a trading nation, which is our principal glory, trade is a very different thing in England than it is in many other countries, and is carried on by persons who, both in their education and descent, are far from being the dregs of the people.

King Charles II, who was perhaps the prince of all the kings that ever reigned in England, who best understood the country and the people he governed, used to say, that the tradesmen were the only gentry in England. His majesty spoke it merrily, but it had a happy signification in it, such as was peculiar to the bright genius of that prince, who, though he was not the best governor, was the best acquainted with the world of all the princes of his age, if not of all the men in it; and I make no scruple to advance these three points in honour of our country; viz.—

1. That we are the greatest trading country in the world, because we have the greatest exportation of the growth and product of our land, and of the manufacture and labour of our people; and the greatest importation and consumption of the growth, product, and manufactures of other countries from abroad, of any nation in the world.

2. That our climate is the best and most agreeable to live in, because a man can be more out of doors in England than in other countries.

3. That our men are the stoutest and best, because, strip them naked from the waist upwards, and give them no weapons at all but their hands and heels, and turn them into a room or stage, and lock them in with the like number of other men of any nation, man for man, and they shall beat the best men you shall find in the world.

And so many of our noble and wealthy families, as we have shown, are raised by and derived from trade, so it is true, and indeed it cannot well be otherwise, that many of the younger branches of our gentry, and even of the nobility itself, have descended again into the spring from whence they flowed, and have become tradesmen; and thence it is that, as I said above, our tradesmen in England are not, as it generally is in other countries, always of the meanest of our people. Nor is trade itself in England, as it generally is in other countries, the meanest thing that men can turn their hand to; but, on the contrary, trade is the readiest way for men to raise their fortunes and families; and therefore it is a field for men of figure and of good families to enter upon.

N. B. By trade we must be understood to include navigation and foreign discoveries; because they are, generally speaking, all promoted and carried on by trade, and even by tradesmen, as well as merchants; and the tradesmen, as owners, are at this time as much concerned in shipping as the merchants, only the latter may be said to be the chief employers of the shipping.

Having thus done a particular piece of justice to ourselves, in the value we put upon trade and tradesmen in England, it reflects very much upon the understandings of those refined heads who pretend to depreciate that part of the nation which is so infinitely superior in wealth to the families who call themselves gentry, and so infinitely more numerous.

As to the wealth of the nation, that undoubtedly lies chiefly among the trading part of the people; and though there are a great many families raised within few years, in the late war, by great employments and by great actions abroad, to the honour of the English gentry, yet how many more families among the tradesmen have been raised to immense estates, even during the same time, by the attending circumstances of the war; such as the clothing, the paying, the victualling and furnishing, &c., both army and navy. And by whom have the prodigious taxes been paid, the loans supplied, and money advanced upon all occasions? By whom are the banks and companies carried on, and on whom are the customs and excises levied? Have not the trade and tradesmen borne the burden of the war? And do they not still pay four millions a year interest for the public debts. On whom are the funds levied, and by whom the public credit supported? Is not trade the inexhausted fund of all funds, and upon which all the rest depend?

As is the trade, so in proportion are the tradesmen; and how wealthy are tradesmen in almost all the several parts of England, as well as in London? How common is it to see a tradesman go off the stage, even but from mere shopkeeping, with from ten to forty thousand pounds' estate to divide among his family! when, on the contrary, take the gentry in England, from one end to the other, except a few here and there, what with excessive high living, which is of late grown so much into a disease, and the other ordinary circumstances of families, we find few families of the lower gentry, that is to say from six or seven hundred a year downwards, but they are in debt, and in necessitous circumstances, and a great many of greater estates also.

On the other hand, let any one who is acquainted with England, look but abroad into the several counties, especially near London, or within fifty miles of it; how are the ancient families worn out by time and family misfortunes, and the estates possessed by a new race of tradesmen, grown up into families of gentry, and established by the immense wealth gained, as I may say, behind the counter; that is, in the shop, the warehouse, and the counting-house.

How many noble seats, superior to the palaces of sovereign princes, in some countries, do we see erected within few miles of this city by tradesmen, or the sons of tradesmen, while the seats and castles of the ancient gentry, like their families, look worn out and fallen into decay! witness the noble house of sir John Eyles, himself a merchant, at Giddyhall, near Romford; sir Gregory Page, on Blackheath, the son of a brewer; sir Nathanael Mead, near Weal-green, his father a linen draper, with many others, too long to repeat; and, to crown all, the lord Castlemain's, now earl of Tilney, at Wanstead, his father, sir Josiah Child, originally a tradesman.

Again; in how superior a port or figure (as we now call it) do our tradesmen live, to what the middling gentry either do or can support! An ordinary tradesman now, not in the city only, but in the country, shall spend more money by the year, than a gentleman of four or five hundred pounds a year can do, and shall increase and lay up every year too; whereas the gentleman shall at the best stand stock still just where he began, nay, perhaps, decline: and as for the lower gentry, from a hundred pounds a year to three hundred, or thereabouts, though they are often as proud and high in their appearance as the other; as to them, I say, a shoemaker in London shall keep a better house, spend more money, clothe his family better, and yet grow rich too. It is evident where the difference lies; an estate's a pond, but trade's a spring: the first, if it keeps full, and the water wholesome, by the ordinary supplies and drains from the neighbouring grounds, it is well, and it is all that is expected; but the other is an inexhausted current, which not only fills the pond, and keeps it full, but is continually running over, and fills all the lower ponds and places about it.

This being the case in England, and our trade being so vastly great, it is no wonder that the tradesmen in England fill the lists of our nobility and gentry; no wonder that the gentlemen of the best families marry tradesmen's daughters, and put their younger sons apprentices to tradesmen; and how often do these younger sons come to buy the elder sons' estates, and restore the family, when the elder and head of the house, proving rakish and extravagant, has wasted his patrimony, and is obliged to make out the blessing of Israel's family, where the younger son bought the birthright, and the elder was doomed to serve him!

Trade is so far here from being inconsistent with a gentleman, that, in short, trade in England makes gentlemen, and has peopled this nation with gentlemen; for, after a generation or two, the tradesman's children, or at least their grandchildren, come to be as good gentlemen, statesmen, parliamentmen, privy-counsellors, judges, bishops, and noblemen, as those of the highest birth and the most ancient families; as we have shown. Nor do we find any defect either in the genius or capacities of the posterity of tradesmen, arising from any remains of mechanic blood, which, it is pretended, should influence them; but all the gallantry of spirit, greatness of soul, and all the generous principles that can be found in any of the ancient families, whose blood is the most untainted, as they call it, with the low mixtures of a mechanic race, are found in these; and, as is said before, they generally go beyond them in knowledge of the world, which is the best education.

We see the tradesmen of England, as they grow wealthy, coming every day to the herald's office to search for the coats of arms of their ancestors, in order to paint them upon their coaches, and engrave them upon their plate, embroider them upon their furniture, or carve them upon the pediments of their new houses; and how often do we see them trace the registers of their families up to the prime nobility, or the most ancient gentry of the kingdom!

In this search we find them often qualified to raise new families, if they do not descend from old; as was said of a certain tradesman of London, that if he could not find the ancient race of gentlemen, from which he came, he would begin a new race, who should be as good gentlemen as any that went before him.

Thus, in the late wars between England and France, how was our army full of excellent officers, who went from the shop, and behind the counter, into the camp, and who distinguished themselves there by their merits and gallant behaviour! And several such came to command regiments, and even to be general officers, and to gain as much reputation in the service as any; as colonel Pierce, Wood, Richards, and several others that may be named.

All this confirms what I have said before, viz., that trade in England neither is or ought to be levelled with what it is in other countries; or the tradesmen depreciated as they are abroad, and as some of our gentry would pretend to do in England; but that as many of our best families rose from trade, so many branches of the best families in England, under the nobility, have stooped so low as to be put apprentices to tradesmen in London, and to set up and follow those trades when they have come out of their times, and have thought it no dishonour to their blood.

To bring this once more home to the ladies, who are scandalized at that mean step, which they call it, of marrying a tradesman, it may be told them, for their humiliation, that, however they think fit to act, sometimes those trades-

men come of better families than their own; and oftentimes, when they have refused them to their loss, those very tradesmen have married ladies of superior fortune to them, and have raised families of their own, who, in one generation, have been superior to those nice ladies both in dignity and estate; and have, to their great mortification, been ranked above them upon all public occasions.

The word "tradesmen," in England, does not sound so harsh as it does in other countries; and to say a gentleman-tradesman, is not so much nonsense as some people would persuade us to reckon it; and, indeed, the very name of an English tradesman, will and does already obtain in the world; and as our soldiers, by the late war, gained the reputation of being some of the best troops in the world; and our seamen are at this day, and very justly too, esteemed the best sailors in the world; so the English tradesman may be allowed to rank with the best gentlemen in Europe. . . .

And hence it is natural to ask, whence comes all this to be so? How is it produced? War has not done it; no, nor so much as helped or assisted to it; it is not by any martial exploits; we have made no conquests abroad, added no new kingdoms to the British empire, reduced no neighbouring nations, or extended the possession of our monarchs into the properties of others; we have gained nothing by war and encroachment; we are butted and bounded just where we were in queen Elizabeth's time; the Dutch, the Flemings, the French, are in view of us, just as they were then; we have subjected no new provinces or people to our government; and, with few or no exceptions, we are almost, for dominion, where king Edward I. left us: nay, we have lost all the dominions which our ancient kings for some hundreds of years held in France; such as the rich and powerful provinces of Normandy, Poictou, Gascoigne, Bretagne, and Aquitaine; and, instead of being enriched by war and victory, on the contrary, we have been torn in pieces by civil wars and rebellions, as well in Ireland as in England, and that several times, to the ruin of our richest families, and the slaughter of our nobility and gentry; nay, to the destruction even of monarchy itself, as in the long bloody wars between the houses of Lancaster and

York, the many rebellions of the Irish, as well in queen Elizabeth's time, as in king Charles I time; and the fatal massacre, and almost extirpation of the English name in that kingdom; and, at last, the late rebellion in England, in which the monarch fell a sacrifice to the fury of the people, and monarchy itself gave way to tyranny and usurpation, for almost twenty years.

These things prove abundantly that the greatness of the British nation is not owing to war and conquests, to enlarging its dominions by the sword, or subjecting the people of other countries to our power; but it is all owing to trade, to the increase of our commerce at home, and the extending it abroad.

It is owing to trade, that new discoveries have been made in lands unknown, and new settlements and plantations made, new colonies planted, and new governments formed, in the uninhabited islands, and the uncultivated continent of America; and those plantings and settlements have again enlarged and increased the trade, and thereby the wealth and power of the nation by whom they were discovered and planted; we have not increased our power,

or the number of our subjects, by subduing the nations which possess those countries, and incorporating them into our own; but have entirely planted our colonies, and peopled the countries with our own subjects, natives of this island; and, excepting the negroes, which we transport from Africa to America, as slaves to work in the sugar and tobacco plantations, all our colonies, as well in the islands, as on the continent of America, are entirely peopled from Great Britain and Ireland, and chiefly the former; the natives having either removed further up into the country, or, by their own folly and treachery raising war against us, been destroyed and cut off.

As trade has thus extended our colonies abroad [Defoe here refers primarily to the colonies in the New World], so it has (except those colonies) kept our people at home, where they are multiplied to that prodigious degree, and do still continue to multiply in such a manner, that, if it goes on so, time may come that all the lands in England will do little more than serve for gardens for them and to feed their cows, and their corn and cattle be supplied from Scotland and Ireland. . . .

Jeremy Taylor

Jeremy Taylor (1613–1667), an English clergyman and author, was closely associated with Charles I. During the civil wars he suffered as a royalist, and after the restoration Charles II appointed Taylor to an Irish bishopric. In harmony with absolutist tendencies of the age, Taylor sought to enlist religion in support of authoritarianism, and in his writings he stressed the importance of piety and obedience to all legally constituted authority, whether civil or temporal. His Rule and Exercises of Holy Living and Dying was designed as an exhaustive guide for the life of a devout Christian, complete with prayers, definitions, and admonitions. In reading the selections from this work note (1) the teaching of Holy Scripture on obedience to civil and ecclesiastical rulers, (2) a Christian's duty in the observance of law, (3) the distinction he made between punishment by the law of man and the will of God, (4) his instructions concerning reverence to the person of the king, (5) the source of all authority, (6) the sin which God punishes with the most severity, and (7) the divine effect of obedience upon the human soul.

Jeremy Taylor, *Holy Living and Dying: With Prayers Containing the Whole Duty of a Christian*, London, 1888, 129–135.

From: THE RULE AND EXERCISES OF HOLY LIVING

OF OBEDIENCE TO OUR SUPERIORS

Our superiors are set over us in affairs of the world, or the affairs of the soul and things pertaining to religion, and are called accordingly ecclesiastical or civil. Towards whom our duty is thus generally described in the New Testament. For temporal or civil governors the commands are these: "Render to Caesar the things that are Caesar's;" and, "Let every soul be subject to the higher powers: for there is no power but of God; the powers that be are ordained of God: whosoever, therefore, resisteth the power resisteth the ordinance of God; and they that resist shall receive to themselves damnation:" and, "Put them in mind to be subject to principalities and powers, and to obey magistrates:" and, "Submit yourselves to every ordinance of man, for the Lord's sake: whether it be to the king, as supreme; or unto governors, as unto them that are sent by him for the punishment of evil-doers, and the praise of them that do well."

For spiritual or ecclesiastical governors, thus we are commanded: "Obey them that have the rule over you, and submit yourselves; for they watch for your souls, as they that must give an account:" and, "Hold such in reputation:" and, "To this end did I write, that I might know the proof of you, whether ye be obedient in all things," said St. Paul to the church of Corinth. Our duty is reducible to practice by the following rules.

ACTS AND DUTIES OF OBEDIENCE TO ALL OUR SUPERIORS

1. We must obey all human laws appointed and constituted by lawful authority, that is, of the supreme power, according to the constitution of the place in which we live; all laws, I mean, which are not against the law of God.

2. In obedience to human laws, we must observe the letter of the law where we can, without doing violence to the reason of the law and the intention of the lawgiver; but where they cross each other the charity of the law is to be preferred before its discipline, and the reason of it before the letter.

3. If the general reason of the law ceases in our particular, and a contrary reason rises upon us, we are to procure dispensation, or leave to omit the observation of it in such circumstances, if there be any persons or office appointed for granting it; but if there be none, or if it is not easily to be had, or not without an inconvenience greater than the good of the observation of the law in our particular, we are dispensed withal in the nature of the thing, without further process or trouble.

4. As long as the law is obligatory, so long our obedience is due; and he that begins a contrary custom without reason, sins: but he that breaks the law, when the custom is entered and fixed, is excused; because it is supposed the legislative power consents, when, by not punishing, it suffers disobedience to grow to a custom.

5. Obedience to human laws must be for conscience' sake; that is, because in such obedience public order, and charity, and benefit, are concerned, and because the law of God commands us; therefore we must make a conscience in keeping the just laws of superiors: and, although the matter before the making of the law was indifferent, yet now the obedience is not indifferent; but, next to the laws of God, we are to obey the laws of all our superiors, who, the more public they are, the first they are to be in the order of obedience.

6. Submit to the punishment and censure of the laws, and seek not to reverse their judgment by opposing, but by submitting, or flying, or silence, to pass through it or by it, as we can; and although from inferior judges we may appeal where the law permits us, yet we must sit down and rest in the judgment of the supreme; and if we be wronged, let us complain to God of the injury, not of the persons; and He will deliver thy soul from unrighteous judges.

7. Do not believe thou hast kept the law, when thou hast suffered the punishment. For although patiently to submit to the power of the sword be a part of obedience, yet this is such a part as supposes another left undone; and the law punishes, not because she is as well pleased in taking vengeance as in being obeyed; but, because she is pleased, she uses

punishment as a means to secure obedience for the future, or in others. Therefore, although in such cases the law is satisfied, and the injury and the injustice are paid for, yet the sins of irreligion, and scandal, and disobedience to God, must still be so accounted for, as to crave pardon and be washed off by repentance.

8. Human laws are not to be broken with scandal, nor at all without reason; for he that does it causelessly is a despiser of the law, and undervalues the authority. For human laws differ from Divine laws principally in this: 1. That the positive commands of a man may be broken upon smaller and more reasons than the positive commands of God; we may, upon a smaller reason, omit to keep any of the fasting-days of the church than omit to give alms to the poor: only this, the reason must bear weight according to the gravity and concernment of the law; a law, in a small matter, may be omitted for a small reason; in a great matter, not without a greater reason. And, 2. The negative precepts of men may cease by many instruments, by contrary customs, by public disrelish, by long omission: but the negative precepts of God never can cease, but when they are expressly abrogated by the same authority. But what those reasons are that can dispense with the command of a man, a man may be his own judge, and sometimes take his proportions from his own judge, and sometimes take his proportions from his own reason and necessity, sometimes from public fame, and the practice of pious and severe persons, and from popular customs; in which a man shall walk most safely when he does not walk alone, but a spiritual man takes him by the hand.

9. We must not be too forward in procuring dispensations, nor use them any longer than the reason continues for which we first procured them: for to be dispensed withal is an argument of natural infirmity, if it be necessary; but if it be not, it signifies an undisciplined and unmortified spirit.

10. We must not be too busy in examining the prudence and unreasonableness of human laws: for, although we are not bound to believe them all to be the wisest, yet if, by inquiring into the lawfulness of them, or by any other instrument, we find them to fail of that wisdom with which some others are ordained, yet we must never make use of it to disparage the person of the lawgiver, or to countenance any man's disobedience, much less our own.

11. Pay that reverence to the person of thy prince, of his ministers, of thy parents and spiritual guides, which, by the customs of the place thou livest in, are usually paid to such persons in their several degrees: that is, that the highest reverence be paid to the highest person, and so still in proportion; and that this reverence be expressed in all the circumstances and manners of the city and nation.

12. Lift not up thy hand against thy prince or parent, upon what pretence soever; but bear all personal affronts and inconveniences at their hands, and seek no remedy but by patience and piety, yielding and praying, or absenting thyself.

13. Speak not evil of the ruler of thy people, neither curse thy father or mother, nor revile thy spiritual guides, nor discover and lay naked their infirmities; but treat them with reverence and religion, and preserve their authority sacred by esteeming their persons venerable.

14. Pay tribute and customs to princes according to the laws, and maintenance to thy parents according to their necessity, and honourable support to the clergy according to the dignity of the work, and the customs of the place.

15. Remember always, that duty to our superiors is not an act of commutative justice, but of distributive; that is, although kings and parents and spiritual guides are to pay a great duty to their inferiors, the duty of their several charges and government, yet the good government of a king and of parents are actions of religion, as they relate to God, and of piety, as they relate to their people and families. And, although we usually call them just princes who administer their laws exactly to the people, because the actions are in the manner of justice, yet, in propriety of speech, they are rather to be called pious and religious. For as he is not called a just father that educates his children well, but pious; so that prince who defends and well rules his people is religious, and does that duty for which alone he is answerable to God. The consequence of which is this, so far as concerns our duty: if the prince

or parent fail of their duty, we must not fail of ours; for we are answerable to them and to God too, as being accountable to all our superiors, and so are they to theirs: they are above us, and God is above them.

REMEDIES AGAINST DISOBEDIENCE, AND MEANS TO ENDEAR OUR OBEDIENCE; BY WAY OF CONSIDERATION

1. Consider, that all authority descends from God, and our superiors bear the image of the Divine power, which God imprints on them as on an image of clay, or a coin upon a less perfect metal, which whoso defaces shall not be answerable for the loss or spoil of the materials, but the defacing the king's image; and in the same measure will God require it at our hands, if we despise His authority, upon whomsoever He hath imprinted it. "He that despiseth you, despiseth me." And Dathan and Abiram were said to be "gathered together against the Lord." And this was St. Paul's argument for our obedience: "The powers that be are ordained of God."

2. There is very great peace and immunity from sin in resigning our wills up to the command of others: for, provided that our duty to God be secured, their commands are warrants to us in all things else; and the case of conscience is determined, if the command be evident and pressing: and it is certain, the action that is but indifferent and without reward, if done only upon our own choice, is an action of duty and of religion, and rewardable by the grace and favour of God, if done in obedience to the command of our superiors. For, since naturally we desire what is forbidden us, (and sometimes there is no other evil in the thing but that it is forbidden us,) God hath in grace enjoined and proportionably accepts obedience, as being directly opposed to the former irregularity; and it is acceptable, although there be no other good in the thing that is commanded us but that it is commanded.

3. By obedience we are made a society and a republic, and distinguished from herds of beasts, and heaps of flies, who do what they list, and are incapable of laws, and obey none: and therefore are killed and destroyed, though never punished, and they never can have a reward.

4. By obedience we are rendered capable of all the blessings of government, signified by St. Paul in these words: "He is the minister of God to thee for good;" and by St. Peter in these, "Governors are sent by Him for the punishment of evil-doers, and for the praise of them that do well." And he that ever felt, or saw, or can understand, the miseries of confusion in public affairs, or amazement in a heap of sad, tumultuous, and indefinite thoughts, may from thence judge of the admirable effects of order, and the beauty of government. What health is to the body, and peace is to the spirit, that is government to the societies of men; the greatest blessing which they can receive in that temporal capacity.

5. No man shall ever be fit to govern others that knows not first how to obey. For if the spirit of a subject be rebellious, in a prince it will be tyrannical and intolerable; and of so ill example, that, as it will encourage the disobedience of others, so it will render it unreasonable for him to exact of others what in the like case he refused to pay.

6. There is no sin in the world which God hath punished with so great severity and high detestation as this of disobedience. For the crime of idolatry God sent the sword amongst His people; but it was never heard that the earth opened and swallowed up any but rebels against their prince.

7. Obedience is better than the particular actions of religion; and he serves God better that follows his prince in lawful services than he that refuses his command upon pretence he must go say his prayers. But rebellion is compared to that sin which of all sin seems the most unnatural and damned impiety,—"Rebellion is as the sin of witchcraft."

8. Obedience is a complicated act of virtue, and many graces are exercised in one act of obedience. It is an act of humility, of mortification and self-denial, of charity to God, of care of the public, of order and charity to ourselves and all our society, and a great instance of a victory over the most refractory and unruly passions.

9. To be a subject is a greater temporal felicity than to be a king: for all eminent gov-

ernments, according to their height, have a great burden, huge care, infinite business, little rest, innumerable fears; and all that he enjoys above another is, that he does enjoy the things of the world with other circumstances and a bigger noise; and if others go at his single command, it is also certain he must suffer inconvenience at the needs and disturbances of all his people: and the evils of one man and of one family are not enough for him to bear, unless also he be almost crushed with the evils of mankind. He, therefore, is an ungrateful person that will press the scales down with a voluntary load, and, by disobedience, put more thorns into the crown or mitre of his superior. Much better is the advice of St. Paul; "Obey them that have the rule over you, as they that must give an account for your souls; that they may do it with joy and not with grief: for (besides that it is unpleasant to them) it is unprofitable for you."

10. The angels are ministering spirits, and perpetually execute the will and commandment of God: and all the wise men and all the good men of the world are obedient to their governors; and the eternal Son of God esteemed it His "meat and drink to do the will of His Father," and for His obedience alone obtained the greatest glory: and no man ever came to perfection but by obedience; and thousands of saints have chosen such institutions and manners of living, in which they might not choose their own work, nor follow their own will, nor please themselves but be accountable to others, and subject to discipline, and obedient to command; as knowing this to be the highway of the cross, the way that the King of sufferings and humility did choose, and so became the King of glory.

11. No man ever perished who followed first the will of God, and then the will of his superiors: but thousands have been damned merely for following their own will, and relying upon their own judgments, and choosing their own work, and doing their own fancies. For if we begin with ourselves, whatsoever seems good in our eyes is most commonly displeasing in the eyes of God.

12. The sin of rebellion, though it be a spiritual sin, and imitable by devils, yet it is of that disorder, unreasonableness, and impossibility, amongst intelligent spirits, that they never murmured or mutinied in their lower stations against their superiors. Nay, the good angels of an inferior order durst not revile a devil of a higher order. . . .

John Milton

John Milton (1608–1674) was a great English poet who lived during the arbitrary rule of the Stuart dynasty. He originally studied for the ministry, but the religious absolutism of Archbishop Laud turned him away from the profession, and eventually he left the Established Church to become a nonconformist. As a consequence of this change, he devoted his life to scholarship and literary efforts. He took part in the religious controversy between the high-church Anglicans and the Puritans who desired to destroy the episcopacy. As might be expected, Milton used his pen in support of the reform movement. In the civil wars he defended the parliamentary party and Cromwell's army. When the Commonwealth was established, he held a political office in which he made use of his literary talents. For some unaccountable reason he was not executed after the Restoration in 1660, although he had been one of the most ardent supporters of Cromwell. For both political and personal reasons Milton spent the remaining years of his life in semi-retirement and devoted himself to his literary work.

It was during this period, while totally blind, that he dictated his two great poems, Paradise Lost and its sequel, Paradise Regained. Despite their deeply religious character, Milton himself never attended any church in his later years, although he was sympathetic with the Society of Friends. In the following excerpts from Paradise Lost note (1) Milton's purpose in composing Paradise Lost, (2) God's purpose in allowing evil to exist, (3) Satan's attitude toward power, and his human characteristics, (4) Milton's concept of God and of man's place in the universe as compared with that of Calvin, 100 years earlier, (5) the passage describing his blindness, (6) God's discussion with His Son on the future fall of man, (7) Jesus' attitude toward the Fall of Man, (8) evidences of predestination and election, (9) the clever manner in which Jesus made His offer to God (10) the beautiful and familiar passages, and (11) any baroque characteristics in Milton's theme and style.

From: *PARADISE LOST*

Of man's first disobedience, and the fruit
Of that forbidden tree, whose mortal taste
Brought death into the world, and all our woe,
With loss of Eden, till one greater Man
Restore us, and regain the blissful seat,
Sing, heavenly Muse, . . .

              What in me is dark,
Illumine; what is low raise and support;
That to the height of this great argument
I may assert Eternal Providence,
And justify the ways of God to men.

    Say first—for Heaven hides nothing from
        thy view,
Nor the deep tract of Hell—say first, what
        cause
Moved our grand parents, in that happy state,
Favoured of Heaven so highly, to fall off
From their Creator, and transgress His will
For one restraint, lords of the world besides?
Who first seduced them to that foul revolt?
The infernal Serpent; he it was, whose guile,
Stirred up with envy and revenge, deceived
The mother of mankind; what time his pride
Had cast him out from Heaven, with all his
        host
Of rebel Angels; by whose aid, aspiring
To set himself in glory above his peers,
He trusted to have equalled the Most High,

If he opposed; and, with ambitious aim,
Against the throne and monarchy of God,
Raised impious war in Heaven, and battle
        proud,
With vain attempt. Him the Almighty Power
Hurled headlong flaming from the ethereal sky,
With hideous ruin and combustion, down
To bottomless perdition; there to dwell
In adamantine chains and penal fire,
Who durst defy the Omnipotent to arms.
Nine times the space that measures day and
        night
To mortal men, he with his horrid crew
Lay vanquished rolling in the fiery gulf,
Confounded, though immortal.

              [Satan speaks]
    Fallen cherub! to be weak is miserable,
Doing or suffering: but of this be sure,
To do aught good never will be our task,
But ever to do ill our sole delight,
As being contrary to His high will
Whom we resist. If then His providence
Out of our evil seek to bring forth good,
Our labour must be to pervert that end,
And out of good still to find means of evil;
Which oft-times may succeed, so as perhaps
Shall grieve him, if I fail not, and disturb
His inmost counsels from their destined aim.

John Milton, *Paradise Lost*, 2 vols., London, 1774, I, 1–3; 7–8; 11–12; 54–55; 83–92.

But see! the angry Victor hath recalled
His ministers of vengeance and pursuit
Back to the gates of Heaven. The sulphurous
     hail,
Shot after us in storm, o'erblown, hath laid
The fiery surge, that from the precipice
Of Heaven received us falling, and the thunder,
Winged with red lightning and impetuous rage,
Perhaps hath spent his shafts, and ceases now
To bellow through the vast and boundless
     Deep.

     Is this the region, this the soil, the clime,
Said then the lost archangel, this the seat
That we must change for Heaven; this mourn-
     ful gloom
For that celestial light? Be it so! Since He,
Who now is Sovran, can dispose and bid
What shall be right: furthest from him is best,
Whom reason hath equalled, force hath made
     supreme
Above His equals. Farewell, happy fields,
Where joy for ever dwells! Hail, horrors! hail,
Infernal world! And thou, profoundest Hell,
Receive thy new possessor! One who brings
A mind not to be changed by place or time.
The mind is its own place, and in itself
Can make a Heaven of Hell, a Hell of Heaven.
What matters where, if I be still the same;
And what I should be, all but less than He
Whom thunder hath made greater? Here at
     least
We shall be free; the Almighty hath not built
Here for his envy; will not drive us hence.
Here we may reign secure, and, in my choice,
To reign is worth ambition, though in Hell.
Better to reign in Hell than serve in Heaven.
But wherefore let we then our faithful friends,
The associates and copartners of our loss,
Lie thus astonished on the oblivious pool,
And call them not to share with us their part
In this unhappy mansion; or once more
With rallied arms to try what may be yet
Regained in Heaven, or what more lost in Hell?

                    [Beelzebub speaks]
                         There is a place—
If ancient and prophetic fame in heaven
Err not,—another world, the happy seat
Of some new race, called Man, about this time
To be created like to us, though less

In power and excellence, but favoured more
Of him who rules above. So was his will
Pronounced among the gods, and by an oath,
That shook Heaven's whole circumference,
     confirmed.
Thither let us bend all our thoughts, to learn
What creatures there inhabit, of what mould
Or substance, how endued, and what their
     power,
And where their weakness, how attempted best,
By force or subtlety. Though heaven be shut,
And heaven's high Arbitrator sit secure
In his own strength, this place may lie ex-
     posed,
The utmost border of his kingdom, left
To their defence who hold it. Here perhaps
Some advantageous act may be achieved
By sudden onset, either with hell-fire
To waste his whole creation, or possess
All as our own, and drive, as we were driven,
The puny habitants. Or, if not drive,
Seduce them to our party, that their God
May prove their foe, and with repenting hand
Abolish his own works. This would surpass
Common revenge, and interrupt his joy
In our confusion, and our joy upraise
In his disturbance; when his darling sons,
Hurled headlong to partake with us, shall
     curse
Their frail original, and faded bliss,
Faded so soon. Advise, if this be worth
Attempting, or to sit in darkness here
Hatching vain empires.—Thus Beelzebub
Pleaded his devilish counsel, first devised
By Satan, and in part proposed. For whence,
But from the author of all ill, could spring
So deep a malice, to confound the race
Of mankind in one root, and earth with hell
To mingle and involve, done all to spite
The great Creator? But their spite still serves
His glory to augment. The bold design
Pleased highly those infernal states, and joy
Sparkled in all their eyes. With full assent
They vote.

Hail, holy Light! offspring of Heaven first born!
Or of the eternal co-eternal beam,
May I express the unblamed? since God is light,
And never but in unapproached light
Dwelt from eternity, dwelt then in thee,
Bright effluence of bright essence increate.

Or hear'st thou rather, pure ethereal stream,
Whose fountain who shall tell? Before the sun,
Before the heavens thou wert, and at the voice
Of god, as with a mantle, didst invest
The rising world of waters dark and deep,
Won from the void and formless infinite.
Thee I revisit now with bolder wing,
Escaped the Stygian pool, though long de-
    tained
In that obscure sojourn, while in my flight
Through utter and through middle darkness
    borne,
With other notes than to the Orphean lyre,
I sung of Chaos and eternal Night;
Taught by the heavenly muse to venture down
The dark descent, and up to reascend,
Though hard and rare;—thee I revisit safe,
And feel thy sovereign vital lamp; but thou
Revisit'st not these eyes, that roll in vain
To find thy piercing ray, and find no dawn;
So thick a drop serene hath quenched their
    orbs,
Or dim suffusion veiled.

    Now had the Almighty Father from above,
From the pure Empyrean where he sits
High throned above all height, bent down his
    eye,
His own works, and their works at once to
    view:
About him all the sanctities of heaven
Stood thick as stars, and from his sight received
Beatitude past utterance; on his right
The radiant image of his glory sat,
His only Son. On earth he first beheld
Our two first parents, yet the only two
Of mankind, in the happy garden placed,
Reaping immortal fruits of joy and love,
Uninterrupted joy, unrivalled love,
In blissful solitude. He then surveyed
Hell and the gulf between, and Satan there
Coasting the wall of heaven on this side Night
In the dun air sublime, and ready now
To stoop with wearied wings, and willing feet,
On the bare outside of this world, that seemed
Firm land imbosomed, without firmament,
Uncertain which, in ocean or in air.
Him God beholding from his prospect high,
Wherein past, present, future, he beholds,
Thus to his only Son foreseeing spake:
    Only-begotten Son, seest thou what rage

Transports our adversary? whom no bounds
Prescribed, no bars of Hell, nor all the chains
Heaped on him there, nor yet the main abyss
Wide interrupt, can hold; so bent he seems
On desperate revenge, that shall redound
Upon his own rebellious head. And now,
Through all restraint broke loose, he wings his
    way
Not far off heaven, in the precincts of light,
Directly towards the new-created world,
And men there placed, with purpose to essay
If him by force he can destroy, or, worse,
By some false guile pervert; and shall pervert;
For man will harken to his glozing lies,
And easily transgress the sole command,
Sole pledge of his obedience. So will fall
He and his faithless progeny. Whose fault?
Whose but his own? Ingrate, he had of me
All he could have. I made him just and right,
Sufficient to have stood, though free to fall.
Such I created all the ethereal powers
And spirits, both them who stood, and fell and
    fell.
Not free, what proof could they have given
    sincere
Of true allegiance, constant faith, or love,
Where only what they needs must do appeared,
Not what they would? What praise could they
    receive?
What pleasure I from such obedience paid?
When will and reason—reason also is choice—
Useless and vain, of freedom both despoiled,
Made passive both, and served necessity,
Not me? They therefore, as to right belonged,
So were created, nor can justly accuse
Their maker, or their making, or their fate,
As if predestination overruled
Their will, disposed by absolute decree
Or high foreknowledge. They themselves de-
    creed
Their own revolt, not I. If I foreknew,
Foreknowledge had no influence on their fault,
Which had no less proved certain unforeknown.
So without least impulse or shadow of fate,
Or aught by me immutably forseen,
They trespass, authors to themselves in all
Both what they judge, and what they choose;
    for so
I formed them free: and free they must remain,
Till they enthrall themselves; I else must
    change

Their nature, and revoke the high decree
Unchangeable, eternal, which ordained
Their freedom; they themselves ordained their
   fall.
The first sort by their own suggestion fell,
Self-tempted, self-depraved: Man falls, de-
   ceived
By the other first: Man therefore shall find
   grace,
The other none. In mercy and justice both,
Through heaven and earth, so shall my glory
   excel;
But mercy first and last shall brightest shine.
   Thus while God spake, ambrosial fragrance
   filled
All heaven, and in the blessed spirits elect
Sense of new joy ineffable diffused.
Beyond compare the Son of God was seen
Most glorious: in him all his Father shone
Substantially expressed; and in his face
Divine compassion visibly appeared,
Love without end, and without measure grace,
Which uttering, thus he to his Father spake:
   O Father, gracious was that word which
   closed
Thy sovereign sentence, that man should find
   grace;
For which both heaven and earth shall high
   extol
Thy praises, with the innumerable sound
Of hymns and sacred songs, wherewith thy
   throne
Encompassed shall resound thee ever blessed.
For should Man finally be lost, should Man,
Thy creature late so loved, thy youngest son,
Fall circumvented thus by fraud, though joined
With his own folly? That be from thee far,
That far be from thee, Father, who art judge
Of all things made, and judgest only right.
Or shall the Adversary thus obtain
His end, and frustrate thine? Shall he fulfill
His malice, and thy goodness bring to nought;
Or proud return, though to his heavier doom,
Yet with revenge accomplished, and to Hell
Draw after him the whole race of mankind,
By him corrupted? Or wilt thou thyself
Abolish thy creation, and unmake,
For him, what for thy glory thou hast made?
So should thy goodness and thy greatness both
Be questioned and blasphemed without de-
   fence.

To whom the great Creator thus replied:
O Son, in whom my soul hath chief delight,
Son of my bosom, Son who art alone
My word, my wisdom, and effectual might,
All hast thou spoken as my thoughts are, all
As my eternal purpose hath decreed.
Man shall not quite be lost, but saved who will;
Yet not of will in him, but grace in me
Freely vouchsafed. Once more I will renew
His lapsed powers, though forfeit, and en-
   thralled
By sin to foul exorbitant desires;
Upheld by me, yet once more he shall stand
On even ground against his mortal foe;
By me upheld, that he may know how frail
His fallen condition is, and to me owe
All his deliverance, and to none but me.
Some I have chosen of peculiar grace,
Elect above the rest; so is my will:
The rest shall hear me call, and oft be warned
Their sinful state, and to appease betimes
The incensed Deity, while offered grace
Invites; for I will clear their senses dark
What may suffice, and soften stony hearts
To pray, repent, and bring obedience due,
To prayer, repentance, and obedience due,
Though but endeavoured with sincere intent,
Mine ear shall not be slow, mine eye not shut.
And I will place within them as a guide
My umpire, Conscience; whom if they will
   hear,
Light after light, well used, they shall attain,
And to the end persisting, safe arrive.
This my long sufferance, and my day of grace,
They who neglect and scorn, shall never taste;
But hard be hardened, blind be blinded more,
That they may stumble on, and deeper fall;
And none but such from mercy I exclude.
But yet all is not done; man disobeying,
Disloyal, breaks his fealty, and sins
Against the high supremacy of heaven,
Affecting God head, and, so losing all,
To expiate his treason hath nought left,
But to destruction sacred and devote,
He, with his whole posterity, must die.
Die he or Justice must; unless for him
Some other able, and as willing, pay
The rigid satisfaction, death for death.
Say, heavenly Powers, where shall we find such
   love?
Which of ye will be mortal, to redeem

Man's mortal crime, and just the unjust to save?
Dwells in all Heaven charity so dear?
   He asked, but all the heavenly quire stood
     mute,
And silence was in Heaven. On man's behalf
Patron or intercessor none appeared,
Much less than durst upon his own head draw
The deadly forfeiture, and ransom set.
And now without redemption all mankind
Must have been lost, adjudged to Death and
     Hell
By doom severe, had not the Son of God,
In whom the fulness dwells of love divine,
His dearest mediation thus renewed:
   Father, thy word is passed, man shall find
     grace;
And shall not grace not find means, that finds
     her way
The speediest of thy winged messengers,
To visit all thy creatures, and to all
Comes unprevented, unimplored, unsought?
Happy for Man, so coming; he her aid
Can never seek, once dead in sins, and lost;
Atonement for himself, or offering meet,
Indebted and undone, hath none to bring.
Behold me, then; me for him, life for life
I offer; on me let thine anger fall;
Account me Man: I for his sake will leave
Thy bosom, and this glory next to Thee
Freely put off, and for him lastly die

Well pleased; on me let Death wreak all his
     rage;
Under his gloomy power I shall not long
Lie vanquished. Thou hast given me to possess
Life in myself for ever; by thee I live,
Though now to Death I yield, and am his due,
All that of me can die. Yet, that debt paid,
Thou wilt not leave me in the loathsome grave,
His prey, nor suffer my unspotted soul
For ever with corruption there to dwell:
But I shall rise victorious, and subdue
My vanquisher, spoiled of his vaunted spoil;
Death his death's wound shall then receive,
     and stoop
Inglorious, of his mortal sting disarmed.
I, through the ample air, in triumph high
Shall lead Hell captive, maugre Hell, and show
The powers of darkness bound. Thou, at the
     sight
Pleased, out of Heaven shalt look down and
     smile,
While, by thee raised, I ruin all my foes,
Death last, and with his carcass glut the grave;
Then, with the multitude of my redeemed,
Shall enter heaven, long absent, and return,
Father, to see thy face, wherein no cloud
Of anger shall remain, but peace assured
And reconcilement; wrath shall be no more
Thenceforth, but in thy presence joy entire.

Pierre Corneille

Pierre Corneille (1606–1684) was one of the great dramatists of seventeenth-century France. In his writings he reflected the civilization which flourished in that country during the absolutism of Louis XIV. In his dramas he made use of the so-called unities of time, space, and action, thereby harmonizing his plays with the insistence of the age on reason. In Cinna, which perhaps was his greatest work, he told the story of the reign of Augustus. Writing in a century when absolutism was supreme in his native land, it was perhaps natural that he should stress the stability of absolutism and the evils of popular government. In reading this selection from the second act of Cinna note (1) the proposition which Augustus has just made to his friends, Cinna and Maximus, (2) Cinna's reply in which he analyzed the value of liberty to Rome, (3) his comments on rule by the people, (4) his estimate of Rome under the rule *of Augustus, (5) the influence he thought Augustus could have on the unity of Rome, (6) the decision which Augustus made, and (7) the significant rewards he gave to his faithful friends for their counsel.*

From: CINNA

SCENE ONE

Augustus, Cinna, Maximus,
Group of courtiers.

Augustus

Let everyone retire; let no one enter;
Only you, Cinna and Maximus, remain.

All retire, except Augustus, Cinna, and Maximus

This empire o'er the land and o'er the sea,
This sovereign power that's mine o'er all the world
This grandeur without bounds, illustrious rank,
Which cost so much of pain, so much of blood,
In short, all that's admired in my high fortune
By importunate courtiers in this flattering court,
Is only a beauty whose surface brilliance dazzles,
Which loses its attraction, once enjoyed.
Ambition cools when it has had its way
And some contrary passion takes its place,
And, as our spirit toward some fond desire
Forever pushing to the peak of strife,
Recoils, without another way to turn,
Having reached this peak, would fain descend.
I longed for empire; now the empire's mine;
But while I wished I knew not what it was.
Now, having it, I find in it no charms,
But only heavy cares, eternal fear,
A thousand secret fears, death everywhere,
No pleasure without trouble, no repose.
Sulla preceded me in this high rank;
Great Julius, my Father, had it, too.
But with what different eyes these two regarded it!
One gave it up, the other would have stayed;
One, cruel, barbarous, died in peace, belovèd,
Like some good citizen within his town;

The other, good, upon the Senate floor
Saw his days cut off by the assassins' daggers.
Examples that might sufficiently instruct me,
If by example only one might learn:
For the one I'd follow; the other inspires fear.
But example's only a deceptive mirror,
And the plan of fate that so disturbs our thoughts
Is written not, nor clearly, in things past.
Sometimes one man is broken, one preserved;
What crushes one, another often saves.

Behold, my dearest friends, what troubles me.
You, who for me are Agrippa and Maecenas,
To resolve this problem I with them debated,
Take, o'er my spirit, the power they have had.
Consider not this grandeur that is mine,
Hateful to Romans, weighing on myself;
Treat me as friend, and not as sovereign.
Rome, the State—all is in your hands.
Europe, Asia, Africa, you shall place
Beneath the laws of monarch or republic;
Your counsel is my law, by this device
Emperor I become—or simple citizen.

Cinna

Despite surprise and insufficiency,
I shall obey you, Sire, against my will,
Suppress the reverence that might forbid me
To oppose this plan toward which you seem inclined.
Indulge a spirit jealous for your glory,
That you will darken with a blot too deep
By opening your soul to these impressions
Which dare condemn your every imperial action.
One does not renounce one's rightful grandeur.
One justly holds what one acquired by right;
The nobler, grander be the prize surrendered,

Reprinted from Maxwell H. Savelle, editor, History 11, *History of Western Civilization, A Syllabus*, Stanford University Press, Stanford University, 1942, 31–33, with the permission of the editor and of the publishers, Stanford University Press.

The more he who abandons seems to deem it
Badly won. Mark not with this impression
Those virtues rare by which you won your
  crown;
Your title's just; for without the stain of crime
You changed the framework of the Roman
  State.
Rome obeys your laws by the right of war
That brought the world beneath the laws of
  Rome.
Your arms have conquered Rome, and con-
  querors,
Though called usurpers, tyrants never are.
When under their arms they've brought the
  provinces,
Governing justly, they become just princes:
Thus did Caesar; we today must do
As Caesar did, or condemn his memory.
If Augustus repudiates the sovereign power,
Caesar was tyrant, his execution just,
And to the gods you stand accountable
For all the blood with which you avenged him
To climb to his exalted imperial station.
Fear not, my Lord, an unhappy end;
A spirit far more powerful guards your years.
Ten times vain men have sought to end your
  life:
Who would destroy has only strengthened you.
Many attempt, but no one e'er succeeds;
Many assassins are there, but no Brutus;
In short, if regicide we must expect,
How great to die master of the universe!
These are the few small words I dare to speak,
Believing Maximus agrees with me.

Maximus

Yes, I agree, Augustus has the right
To rule the empire his own virtue's won;
That at the price of his own blood, and peril
Of his head, his conquest of the state
Is just; without disgrace he cannot drop
The burden that his hand grows tired of carry-
  ing.
That he by that accuses Caesar of tyranny,
Or approves great Caesar's death, that I deny.
  Rome is yours, my Lord, the empire yours
And freely one disposes of his own:
Freely he retains, or puts away.
Can you alone not do what common men
So freely do? Have you who conquered all
Become the slave of the grandeur you have
  won?

Possess it, Sire, let it not possess you;
Far from enslaving you, make it obey;
Bring men at last highly to know that you
Can rise above the power of rank and glory.
'Twas Rome, in years gone by, that gave you
  birth;
Now you'd return to Rome your sovereign
  power.
And Cinna imputes to you as mortal crime
Your generous impulse toward your native
  land!
He calls remorse your love of fatherland!
By highest virtue glory now is withered,
Become an object meriting our scorn,
Since glory's highest act is known as infamy!
No! I would say a gesture great as this
Would give to Rome more than you hold from
  her;
Does one commit a crime beyond our pardon
When restitution's richer than the gift?
Hear, hear, my Lord, the heaven who inspires
  you;
Your glory doubles when you renounce the
  empire,
And men will know your fame through all
  posterity,
Less for conquest than for renunciation.
Happy fate may lead to supreme power,
But to renounce it calls for purest virtue,
Few are so generous, nobly to disdain,
Once the scepter's won, the joys of sovereignty.
Consider, besides, that you are ruling Rome,
Where, whatever be the fashion of your nam-
  ing,
Men hate all monarchy; and the name of em-
  peror,
Concealing that of king, is no less horrible.
They take for tyrant who makes himself their
  master,
Who serves him for a slave, who loves him,
  traitor;
Who endures him has a craven heart, soft,
  cowardly;
And all that's done for freedom is thought
  virtuous.
Of that, my Lord, the proof is all too sure:
Ten times against you hands were raised in
  vain;
Mayhap the eleventh is ready to burst upon
  you;
Mayhap this foreboding mood that darkly
  moves you

Is but the secret warning sent from heaven,
Who, for your salvation, has no other way.
Expose yourself no more to evil fortune;
'Tis good to die a ruler of the universe,
But the sweetest death but saddens the memory
Of one who might have lived to greater glory.

Cinna

If love of country should determine us,
'Tis the country's good alone you should desire;
This liberty which Rome esteems so dear
Is nothing, Sire, but an imagined good,
More troublesome than useful, in no wise rivalling
The benefit a good prince brings the state.
    With order and reason he dispenses honors;
Evenly he punishes and rewards;
Of everything disposes as possessor,
Nor is he hurried by fear of his successor.
When the people rule, all action is by tumult,
The voice of reason never can be heard,
Honors are sold for a price to the ambitious,
Authority to traitors to the state.
These petty sovereigns, their one year given power,
Seeing by time so short their power bounded,
To abortive fruitage rush their dark designs,
For fear that those who follow them might reap.
As they have little stake in what they govern
They harvest richly in the public field,
Assured each one of easy public pardon,
Since every citizen desires the same himself.
Of all state forms the popular state is worst.

Augustus

And yet the only kind that Rome will have.
This hate of kings that these five hundred years
Rome's children suckle with their mother's milk,
Cannot now be uprooted from their hearts.

Maximus

In this dear vice Rome, Sire, is obstinate;
Her people, who enjoy it, flee its cure;
Her custom rules her, not dictate of reason;
And this old error that Cinna would erase,
She worships as the happiest of errors,
By which the world entire, beneath her sway,

Has seen her tread upon a thousand thrones,
Her treasury grow rich upon their spoil.
What more could the best of princes give to Rome?
    I dare, my Lord, to say that every clime
May not enjoy all systems of the state:
To each people its own, according to its nature,
A form not altered without injury:
Such is the law of heaven, whose wise justice
Sows in the world this wise diversity.
The Macedonians love their monarchy,
The rest of Greece prefers its liberty;
The Parthians and the Persians keep their despots;
The consulate alone is meet for Rome.

Cinna

'Tis true, indeed, that heaven's infinite wisdom,
Assigns each people a genius of its own;
Yet no less true that under heaven's guidance
This order changes according to place and time.
From kings Rome had her walls and her beginnings,
She holds from consuls all her growth to power,
And now receives from your imperial bounty
The highest reaches of prosperity.
The state's no longer victim of its armies,
The gates of Janus by your hands are closed,
Which under the consuls never once was true,
Nor in the ages since Rome's second king.

Maximus

The changes in the state that are of heaven
Come not at cost of blood, nor bring they ill.

Cinna

It is a rule of heaven, never broken,
That the blessings sold to men are dearly bought:
E'en Tarquin's exile bathed our land in blood,
And our first consuls cost us many wars.

Maximus

Thus your grandfather, Pompey, resisted heaven
When he was struggling for our liberty!

Cinna

Had heaven wished that Rome might lose her freedom,
By the hands of Pompey Rome had been defended;

Nay, by his death heaven chose to mark more
    worthily,
With a sign eternal, this eternal change;
Heaven owed this glory to the shade of such
    a man,
That it carry with it the liberty of Rome.
For long, Rome's name serves but the world
    to dazzle;
Its very grandeur works against enjoyment.
Since Rome herself made mistress of the world,
Since wealth mounts high within the Roman
    walls,
And since her breast, fruitful of great deeds,
Rears citizens more powerful than kings,
The great, to fix their power, buy votes of
    citizens,
And pompously hold their masters in their pay,
Who meekly with gilded iron accept enchain-
    ment,
To receive from them the laws they thought to
    give.
Envious men, they govern by intrigue
That their ambition turns to bloody plots.
Thus Marius stirred the jealousy of Sulla;
My grandfather, that of Caesar, you of An-
    thony;
Thus liberty no longer use retains,
Except to stir the fires of civil war,
When, amid disorder fatal to the universe,
One wants no master, another wants no peer.
  Rome, my Lord, to be saved, must be united
In the rule of some good chief whom all obey.
If you still wish to serve her well and truly,
Take from her the means for further strife.
Sulla, quitting the place he had usurped,
Opened the field to Caesar and to Pompey,
Which the evil of the time had hid from us,
Had he but fixed his power in his family.
What did the cruel murder of great Caesar
But raise against you Anthony and Lepidus,
Who never had destroyed Rome by the Romans
Had Caesar left the empire in your hands?
Again you'll plunge her, quitting the empire
    thus,
Into those ills from which she suffers still,
And of that little blood that yet remains,
New civil war will drain her to her death.
  Let love of country, let sweet pity, touch
    you,

On bended knee Rome prays to you through
    me.
Consider well the price that you have cost
    her—
Nor that she thinks you were too dearly
    bought:
For the ills that she has suffered, she's repaid;
But one just fear now holds her terrified.
If, jealous of her good, and tired of govern-
    ing,
You return to her a power she cannot keep,
At this price another she must buy,
If you prefer your welfare to her good,
This fatal gift must bring her to despair;
I dare not tell here what I dare forsee.
Sire, save yourself, a master under whom
Rome's happiness begins to be reborn;
And, the better to assure the common good,
Name a successor who will be worthy of you.

Augustus

Let's speak no more; pity has won the day.
Repose to me is dear, but Rome is stronger,
And, whatever evil fate await me now,
I am resigned, if so I may save Rome.
In vain my heart sighs for tranquility;
For by your counsel, Cinna, I retain
The empire; yet I keep it but to share
The rule with you. I see full well that your
Two hearts wear no disguise for me, or guile,
And each of you, in the counsel that he gives,
Thinks only of the state and my best good:
It is your love makes this conflict of counsel,
And both of you shall have a fit reward.
You, Maximus, be governor of Sicily.
Go, give my laws to this good and fertile land;
Remember 'tis for me that you are governing;
I'll be responsible for what you do.
On you, Cinna, Amelia I bestow
For wife. You know she holds the place of Julia,
And that, if grim necessity, now past,
Forced me to treat her father with severity,
My generous bounty, opened in her favor,
Has sought to assuage the bitterness of that
    loss.
See her for me; go, and try to win her,
You're not the sort of man she might disdain;
By the offer of your troth she will be charmed.
Adieu. I go to bear the news to Livia.

Isaac Newton

Isaac Newton (1642–1727) was an English intellectual who contributed much to the rise of science and to the era of modern rationalism. When only 23 years of age he worked out the fundamentals of calculus; but this represented only the beginning of his contribution to knowledge. Newton achieved his greatest fame in the field of astrophysics when he worked out the principles of gravitation. Relying upon the work of his predecessors as well as upon his own labors, Newton brought together the laws of planetary motion as developed by Kepler and Galileo's laws of falling bodies into a synthesis that at once related occurrences among the heavenly bodies with action upon the surface of the Earth. The Mathematical Principles of Natural Philosophy, embodying this universal synthesis, became the guiding light of scientists for more than two centuries and brought to Newton the reputation of the lawgiver for the natural universe. The following selection is from one of the prefaces which Newton wrote for his Principles, and in reading it note (1) the degree of complexity which the philosopher should attribute to nature, (2) how Newton extended the law of cause and effect, (3) the importance of the senses in the work of the philosopher, (4) the method by which the character of the heavenly bodies might be determined, (5) how he arrived at his conclusion that the principle of mutual gravitation applied to all heavenly bodies, and (6) the warning he gave to those who would inject hypotheses into experimental philosophy.

From: THE MATHEMATICAL PRINCIPLES OF NATURAL PHILOSOPHY

NEWTON'S RULES OF REASONING IN PHILOSOPHY

RULE I

We are to admit no more causes of natural things than such as are both true and sufficient to explain their appearances.

To this purpose the philosophers say that Nature does nothing in vain, and more is in vain when less will serve; for Nature is pleased with simplicity, and affects not the pomp of superfluous causes.

RULE II

Therefore to the same natural effects we must, as far as possible, assign the same causes.

As to respiration in a man and in a beast; the descent of stones in Europe and in America; the light of our culinary fire and of the sun; the reflection of light on the earth, and in the planets.

RULE III

The qualities of bodies, which admit neither intension nor remission of degrees, and which are found to belong to all bodies within the reach of our experiments, are to be esteemed the universal qualities of all bodies whatsoever.

For since the qualities of bodies are only known to us by experiments, we are to hold for universal all such as universally agree with experiments and such as are not liable to

Isaac Newton, *The Mathematical Principles of Natural Philosophy*, 2 vols., London, 1803, II, 160–162.

diminution can never be quite taken away. We are certainly not to relinquish the evidence of experiments for the sake of dreams and vain fictions of our own devising; nor are we to recede from the analogy of Nature, which uses to be simple, and always consonant to itself. We no other way know the extension of bodies than by our senses, nor do these reach it in all bodies; but because we perceive extension in all that are sensible, therefore we ascribe it universally to all others also. That abundance of bodies are hard, we learn by experience; and because the hardness of the whole arises from the hardness of the parts, we therefore justly infer the hardness of the undivided particles not only of the bodies we feel but of all others. That all bodies are impenetrable, we gather not from reason, but from sensation. The bodies which we handle we find impenetrable, and thence conclude impenetrability to be an universal property of all bodies whatsoever. That all bodies are moveable, and endowed with certain powers (which we call the *vires inertiae*) of persevering in their motion, or in their rest, we only infer the like properties observed in the bodies which we have seen. The extension, hardness, impenetrability, mobility, and *vis inertiae* of the whole, result from the extension, hardness, impenetrability, mobility, and *vires inertiae* of the parts; and thence we conclude the least particles of all bodies to be also all extended, and hard, and impenetrable, and moveable, and endowed with their proper *vires inertiae*. And this is the foundation of all philosophy. Moreover, that the divided but contiguous particles of bodies may be separated from one another, is matter of observation; and, in the particles that remain undivided, our minds are able to distinguish yet lesser parts, as is mathematically demonstated. But whether the parts so distinguished, and not yet divided, may, by the powers of Nature, be actually divided and separated from one

another, we cannot certainly determine. Yet, had we the proof of but one experiment that any undivided particle, in breaking a hard and solid body, suffered a division, we might by virtue of this rule conclude that the undivided as well as the divided particles may be divided and actually separated to infinity.

Lastly, if it universally appears, by experiments and astronomical observations, that all bodies about the earth gravitate towards the earth, and that in proportion to the quantity of matter which they severally contain; that the moon likewise, according to the quantity of its matter, gravitates towards the earth; that, on the other hand, our sea gravitates towards the moon; and all the planets mutually one towards another; and the comets in like manner towards the sun; we must, in consequence of this rule, universally allow that all bodies whatsoever are endowed with a principle of mutual gravitation. For the argument from the appearances concludes with more force for the universal gravitation of all bodies than for their impenetrability; of which, among those in the celestial regions, we have no experiments, nor any manner of observation. Not that I affirm gravity to be essential to bodies: by their *vis infita* I mean nothing but their *vis inertiae*. This is immutable. Their gravity is diminished as they recede from the earth.

RULE IV

In experimental philosophy we are to look upon propositions collected by general induction from phaenomena as accurately or very nearly true, notwithstanding any contrary hypotheses that may be imagined, till such time as other phaenomena occur, by which they may either be made more accurate, or liable to exceptions.

This rule must follow, that the argument of induction may not be evaded by hypotheses.

John Locke

J ohn Locke is well known for his ideas on political theory (see p. 420), but his greatest work was done in the field of philosophy. In 1690 he published An Essay Concerning Human Understanding, *in which he made a definitive study of the entire problem of knowledge. In keeping with the scientific and rational spirit of the seventeenth century, Locke rejected Plato's theory of innate ideas and insisted that the mind at birth was a tabula rasa, and that all knowledge was acquired empirically. In reading the following selections from this great work note (1) the product which thinking produced in the mind, (2) the two sources of all ideas which the mind possessed, (3) how knowledge is formed from these ideas, (4) the character of intuitive knowledge, (5) the additional process required in demonstrative knowledge, (6) the situations to which Locke applied the term "sensitive" knowledge, and (7) why clear ideas did not always result in comparably clear knowledge.*

From: AN ESSAY CONCERNING HUMAN UNDERSTANDING

OF IDEAS IN GENERAL, AND THEIR ORIGINAL

1. *Idea is the object of thinking.* —Every man being conscious to himself, that he thinks, and that which his mind is applied about, whilst thinking, being the ideas that are there, it is past doubt that men have in their mind several ideas, such as are those expressed by the words, "whiteness, hardness, sweetness, thinking, motion, man, elephant, army, drunkenness," and others. It is in the first place then to be inquired, How he comes by them? I know it is a received doctrine, that men have native ideas and original characters stamped upon their minds in their very first being. This opinion I have at large examined already; and, I suppose, what I have said in the foregoing book will be much more easily admitted, when I have shown whence the understanding may get all the ideas it has, and by what ways and degrees they may come into the mind; for which I shall appeal to every one's own observation and experience.

2. *All ideas come from sensation or reflection.* —Let us then suppose the mind to be, as we say, white paper, void of all characters, without any ideas; how comes it to be furnished? Whence comes it by that vast store, which the busy and boundless fancy of man has painted on it with an almost endless variety? Whence has it all the materials of reason and knowledge? To this I answer, in one word, From experience: in that all our knowledge is founded, and from that it ultimately derives itself. Our observation, employed either about external sensible objects, or about the internal operations of our minds, perceived and reflected on by ourselves, is that which supplies our understandings with all the materials of thinking. These two are the fountains of knowledge, from whence all the ideas we have, or can naturally have, do spring.

3. *The object of sensation one source of ideas.* —First. Our senses, conversant about particular sensible objects, do convey into the mind several distinct perceptions of things, according to those various ways wherein those objects do affect them; and thus we come by those ideas we have of yellow, white, heat, cold, soft, hard, bitter, sweet, and all those which we call sensible qualities; which when I say the senses convey into the mind, I mean, they from external objects convey into the mind what produces there those perceptions. This great source of most of the ideas we have, depending wholly upon our senses, and derived by them to the understanding, I call "sensation."

4. *The operations of our minds the other source of them.* —Secondly. The other fountain, from which experience furnisheth the understanding with ideas, is the perception of the operations of our own minds within us, as it is employed about the ideas it has got; which operations, when the soul comes to reflect on

John Locke, *An Essay Concerning the Human Understanding*, London, 1881, 59–61; 424; 433–434; 438–439.

and consider, do furnish the understanding with another set of ideas which could not be had from things without; and such are perception, thinking, doubting, believing, reasoning, knowing, willing, and all the different actings of our own minds; which we, being conscious of, and observing in ourselves, do from these receive into our understanding as distinct ideas, as we do from bodies affecting our senses. This source of ideas every man has wholly in himself; and though it be not sense as having nothing to do with external objects, yet it is very like it, and might properly enough be called "internal sense." But as I call the other "sensation," so I call this "reflection," the ideas it affords being such only as the mind gets by reflecting on its own operations within itself. By reflection, then, in the following part of this discourse, I would be understood to mean that notice which the mind takes of its own operations, and the manner of them, by reason whereof there come to be ideas of these operations in the understanding. These two, I say, viz., external material things as the objects of sensation, and the operations of our own minds within as the objects of reflection, are, to me, the only originals from whence all our ideas take their beginnings. The term "operations" here, I use in a large sense, as comprehending not barely the actions of the mind about its ideas, but some sort of passions arising sometimes from them, such as is the satisfaction or uneasiness arising from any thought.

5. *All our ideas are of the one or the other of these.* —The understanding seems to me not to have the least glimmering of any ideas which it doth not receive from one of these two. External objects furnish the mind with the ideas of sensible qualities, which are all those different perceptions they produce in us; and the mind furnishes the understanding with ideas of its own operations.

These, when we have taken a full survey of them, and their several modes, combinations, and relations, we shall find to contain all our whole stock of ideas; and that we have nothing in our minds which did not come in one of these two ways. Let any one examine his own thoughts, and thoroughly search into his understanding, and then let him tell me, whether all the original ideas he has there, are any

other than of the objects of his senses, or of the operations of his mind considered as objects of his reflection; and how great a mass of knowledge soever he imagines to be lodged there, he will, upon taking a strict view, see that he has not any idea in his mind but what one of these two hath imprinted, though perhaps with infinite variety compounded and enlarged by the understanding, as we shall see hereafter. . . .

OF KNOWLEDGE IN GENERAL

1. *Our knowledge conversant about our ideas.* —Since the mind, in all its thoughts and reasonings, hath no other immediate object but its own ideas, which it alone does or can contemplate, it is evident that our knowledge is only conversant about them.

2. *Knowledge is the perception of the agreement or disagreement of two ideas.* —Knowledge then seems to me to be nothing but the perception of the connection and agreement, or disagreement and repugnancy, of any of our ideas. In this alone it consists. Where this perception is, there is knowledge; and where it is not, there, though we may fancy, guess, or believe, yet we always come short of knowledge. For, when we know that white is not black, what do we else but perceive that these two ideas do not agree? When we possess ourselves with the utmost security of the demonstration that the three angles of a triangle are equal to two right ones, what do we more but perceive, that equality to two right ones does necessarily agree to, and is inseparable from the three angles of a triangle?

3. *This agreement fourfold.* —But, to understand a little more distinctly, wherein this agreement or disagreement consists, I think we may reduce it all to these four sorts: (1.) Identity, or diversity. (2.) Relation. (3.) Coexistence, or necessary connection. (4.) Real existence. . . .

OF THE DEGREES
OF OUR KNOWLEDGE

1. *Intuitive.* —All our knowledge consisting, as I have said, in the view the mind has of its own ideas, which is the utmost light and great-

est certainty we, with our faculties and in our way of knowledge, are capable of, it may not be amiss to consider a little the degrees of its evidence. The different clearness of our knowledge seems to me to lie in the different way of perception the mind has of the agreement or disagreement of any of its ideas. For if we will reflect on our own ways of thinking, we shall find that sometimes the mind perceives the agreement or disagreement of two ideas immediately by themselves, without the intervention of any other: and this, I think, we may call "intuitive knowledge." For in this the mind is at no pains of proving or examining, but perceives the truth, as the eye doth light, only by being directed towards it. Thus the mind perceives that white is not black, that a circle is not a triangle, that three are more than two, and equal to one and two. Such kind of truths the mind perceives at the first sight of the ideas together, by bare intuition, without the intervention of any other idea; and this kind of knowledge is the clearest and most certain that human frailty is capable of. This part of knowledge is irresistible, and, like bright sunshine, forces itself immediately to be perceived as soon as ever the mind turns its view that way; and leaves no room for hesitation, doubt, or examination, but the mind is presently filled with the clear light of it. It is on this intuition that depends all the certainty and evidence of all our knowledge, which certainty every one finds to be so great that he cannot imagine, and therefore not require, a greater: for a man cannot conceive himself capable of a greater certainty, than to know that any idea in his mind is such as he perceives it to be; and that two ideas, wherein he perceives a difference, are different, and not precisely the same. He that demands a greater certainty than this demands he knows not what, and shows only that he has a mind to be a sceptic without being able to be so. Certainty depends so wholly on this intuition, that in the next degree of knowledge, which I call "demonstrative," this intuition is necessary in all the connexions of the intermediate ideas, without which we cannot attain knowledge and certainty.

2. *Demonstrative.* —The next degree of knowledge is, where the mind perceives the agreement or disagreement of any ideas, but not immediately. Though wherever the mind perceives the agreement or disagreement of any of its ideas, there be certain knowledge; yet it does not always happen that the mind sees that agreement or disagreement which there is between them, even where it is discoverable; and in that case remains in ignorance, and at most gets no farther than a probable conjecture. The reason why the mind cannot always perceive presently the agreement or disagreement of two ideas, is, because those ideas concerning whose agreement or disagreement the inquiry is made, cannot by the mind be so put together as to show it. In this case then, when the mind cannot so bring its ideas together as, by their immediate comparison and, as it were, juxtaposition or application one to another, to perceive their agreement or disagreement, it is fain, by the intervention of other ideas (one or more, as it happens), to discover the agreement or disagreement which it searches; and this is that which we call "reasoning." Thus the mind, being willing to know the agreement or disagreement in bigness between the three angles of a triangle and two right ones, cannot, by an immediate view and comparing them, do it: because the three angles of a triangle cannot be brought at once, and be compared with any one or two angles; and so of this the mind has no immediate, no intuitive knowledge. In this case the mind is fain to find out some other angles, to which the three angles of a triangle have an equality; and finding those equal to two right ones, comes to know their equality to two right ones.

3. *Depends on proofs.* —Those intervening ideas which serve to show the agreement of any two others, are called "proofs"; and where the agreement or disagreement is by this means plainly and clearly perceived, it is called "demonstration," it being shown to the understanding, and the mind made to see that it is so. A quickness in the mind to find out these intermediate ideas (that shall discover the agreement or disagreement of any other), and to apply them right, is, I suppose, that which is called "sagacity."

4. *But not so easy.*—This knowledge by intervening proofs, though it be certain, yet the

evidence of it is not altogether so clear and bright, nor the assent so ready, as in intuitive knowledge. For though in demonstration the mind does at last perceive the agreement or disagreement of the ideas it considers, yet it is not without pains and attention; there must be more than one transient view to find it. . . .

14. *Sensitive knowledge of particular existence.* —These two, viz., intuition and demonstration, are the degrees of our knowledge; whatever comes short of one of these, with what assurance soever embraced, is but faith or opinion, but not knowledge, at least in all general truths. There is, indeed, another perception of the mind employed about the particular existence of finite beings without us; which going beyond bare probability, and yet not reaching perfectly to either of the foregoing degrees of certainty, passes under the name of "knowledge." There can be nothing more certain, than that the idea we receive from an external object is in our minds; this is intuitive knowledge. But whether there be any thing more than barely that idea in our minds, whether we can hence certainly infer the existence of any thing without us which corresponds to that idea, is that whereof some men think there may be a question made; because men may have such ideas in their minds when no such thing exists, no such object affects their senses. But yet here, I think, we are provided with an evidence that puts us past doubting; for I ask any one, whether he be not invincibly conscious to himself of a different perception when he looks on the sun by day, and thinks on it by night; when he actually tastes wormwood, or smells a rose, or only thinks on that savour or odour? We as plainly find the difference there is between any idea revived in our minds by our own memory, and actually coming into our minds by our senses, as we do between any two distinct ideas. If any one say, "A dream may do the same thing, and all these ideas may be produced in us without any external objects;" he may please to dream that I make him this answer: (1.) That it is no great matter whether I remove his scruple or no: where all is but dream, reasoning and arguments are of no use, truth and knowledge nothing. (2.) That I believe he will allow a very manifest difference between dreaming of being in the fire, and being actually in it. But yet if he be resolved to appear so sceptical as to maintain, that what I call "being actually in the fire" is nothing but a dream; and that we cannot thereby certainly know that any such thing as fire actually exists without us; I answer, that we certainly find that pleasure or pain follows upon the application of certain objects to us, whose existence we perceive, or dream that we perceive, by our senses: this certainty is as great as our happiness or misery, beyond which we have no concernment to know or to be. So that, I think, we may add to the two former sorts of knowledge this also, of the existence of particular external objects by that perception and consciousness we have of the actual entrance of ideas from them, and allow these three degrees of knowledge, viz., intuitive, demonstrative, and sensitive: in each of which there are different degrees and ways of evidence and certainty.

15. *Knowledge not always clear, where the ideas are so.* —But since our knowledge is founded on and employed about our ideas only, will it not follow from thence that it is conformable to our ideas; and that where our ideas are clear and distinct, or obscure and confused, our knowledge will be so too? To which I answer, No; for our knowledge consisting in the perception of the agreement or disagreement of any two ideas, its clearness or obscurity consists in the clearness or obscurity of that perception, and not in the clearness or obscurity of the ideas themselves; v. g., a man that has as clear ideas of the angles of a triangle, and of equality to two right ones, as any mathematician in the world, may yet have but a very obscure perception of their agreement, and so have but a very obscure knowledge of it. But ideas which by reason of their obscurity or otherwise are confused, cannot produce any clear or distinct knowledge; because as far as any ideas are confused, so far the mind cannot perceive clearly whether they agree or disagree. Or, to express the same thing in a way less apt to be misunderstood, he that hath not determined the ideas to the words he uses cannot make propositions of them, of whose truth he can be certain.

Alexander Pope

Alexander Pope (1688–1744) was born of a good family in London, where his father was a substantial merchant. Never physically strong, he early devoted himself to literature as a principal interest. At the age of twenty he published his Essay on Criticism and four years later he brought out his Rape of the Lock. Many more poems and essays poured from his prolific pen. In 1729 he turned to a moral and philosophical subject which resulted in An Essay on Man, from which the following selection is taken. In this poem Pope gave popular expression to the glowing faith displayed by the Age of Reason in the simple harmony of nature revealed by Newton. Pope had sung:

> Nature and Nature's laws lay hid in night:
> God said, Let Newton be! and all was Light.

In addition to voicing the veneration of nature and of Newton, Pope phrased into familiar maxims (universal laws) the moral and intellectual convictions of his day. His style likewise reflected his age, for he evidenced a strong dependence upon nature, reason, common sense, and classicism. In reading this passage note (1) Pope's stated objective in writing the essay, (2) the sources of our information about man, (3) man's relationship to the rest of nature, (4) upon what man's happiness depends, (5) the causes of man's unhappiness, (6) the results of pride in man, (7) the unreasonableness of man's complaints against providence, (8) the ranking of man's attributes and the place of reason in this scale, (9) the interrelationships sustained by man with nature, (10) the character of the universe as a whole and Pope's worship of the perfection of nature, and (11) the natural rhythm in which he cast his verses.

From: AN ESSAY ON MAN

Epistle I

Awake, my St. John! leave all meaner things
To low ambition and the pride of kings,
Let us (since life can little more supply
Than just to look about us and to die)
Expatiate free o'er all this scene of Man;
A mighty maze! but not without a plan;
A wild, where weeds and flowers promiscuous
    shoot;
Or garden, tempting with forbidden fruit.
Together let us beat this ample field,

Try what the open, what the covert yield;
The latent tracts, the giddy heights, explore,
Of all who blindly creep, or sightless soar;
Eye Nature's walks, shoot Folly as it flies,
And catch the Manners living as they rise;
Laugh where we must, be candid where we
    can;
But vindicate the ways of God to Man.

I.

Say first of God above or Man below,
What can we reason but from what we know?

Alexander Pope, *An Essay on Man*, London, 1815, 43–57.

Of man, what see we but his station here,
From which to reason, or to which refer?
Through worlds unnumber'd tho' the God be
    known,
'Tis ours to trace him only in our own.
He, who through vast immensity can pierce,
See worlds on worlds compose one universe,
Observe how system into system runs,
What other planets circle other suns,
What vary'd being peoples every star,
May tell why heaven has made us as we are.
But of this frame, the bearings, and the ties,
The strong connections, nice dependencies,
Gradations just; has thy pervading soul
Look'd through? or can a part contain the
    whole?
Is the great chain, that draws all to agree,
And drawn supports, upheld by God, or thee?

II.

Presumptuous man! the reason wouldst thou
    find,
Why form'd so weak, so little and so blind?
First, if thou canst, the harder reason guess,
Why form'd no weaker, blinder, and no less.
Ask of thy mother earth, why oaks are made
Taller or stronger than the weeds they shade?
Or ask of yonder argent fields above,
Why Jove's satellites are less than Jove?
    Of systems possible, if 'tis confest
That wisdom infinite must form the best,
Where all must fall or not coherent be,
And all that rises, rise in due degree;
Then, in the scale of reas'ning life, 'tis plain,
There must be, somewhere, such a rank as
    man:
And all the question (wrangle e'er so long)
Is only this, if God has plac'd him wrong?
    Respecting man, whatever wrong we call,
Nay, must be right, as relative to all.
In human works, tho' labour'd on with pain,
A thousand movements scarce one purpose
    gain;
In God's one single can its end produce;
Yet serves to second too some other use.
So man, who here seems principal alone,
Perhaps acts second to some sphere unknown;
Touches some wheel, or verges to some goal;
'Tis but a part we see, and not the whole.
    When the proud steed shall know why man
    retains

His fiery course, or drives him o'er the plains;
When the dull ox, why now he breaks the
    clod,
Is now a victim, and now Ægypt's God:
Then shall man's pride and dulness compre-
    hend
His actions', passions', being's, use and end;
Why doing, suff'ring, check'd, impell'd; and
    why
This hour a slave, the next a deity.
    Then say not man's imperfect, Heaven in
    fault;
Say rather man's as perfect as he ought;
His knowledge measur'd to his state and place;
His time a moment, and a point his space.
If to be perfect in a certain sphere,
What matter, soon or late, or here or there?
The blest to-day is as completely so,
As who began a thousand years ago.

III.

Heaven from all creatures hides the book of
    fate,
All but the page prescrib'd, their present state:
From brutes what men, from men what spirits
    know;
Or who could suffer being here below?
The lamb thy riot dooms to bleed to-day,
Had he thy reason, would he skip and play?
Pleas'd to the last he crops the flow'ry food,
And licks the hand just rais'd to shed his blood.
O blindness to the future! kindly given,
That each may fill the circle mark'd by heaven!
Who sees with equal eye, as God of all,
A hero perish, or a sparrow fall;
Atoms or systems into ruin hurl'd,
And now a bubble burst, and now a world.
    Hope humbly then; with trembling pinions
    soar;
Wait the great teacher Death; and God adore.
What future bliss, he gives not thee to know,
But gives that hope to be thy blessing now.
Hope springs eternal in the human breast;
Man never is, but always *to be* blest:
The soul, uneasy and confin'd from home,
Rests and expatiates in a life to come.
    Lo, the poor Indian! whose untutor'd mind
Sees God in clouds, or hears him in the wind;
His soul, proud science never taught to stray,
Far as the solar walk or milky way;
Yet simple Nature to his hope has giv'n

Behind the cloud-top hill, an humbler heav'n;
Some safer world in depth of woods embrac'd,
Some happier island in the wat'ry waste,
Where slaves once more their native land be-
　　hold,
No fiends torment, no Christians thirst for gold.
To be content's his natural desire,
He asks no angel's wing, no seraph's fire;
But thinks admitted to that equal sky,
His faithful dog shall bear him company.

IV.

Go, wiser thou! and, in thy scale of sense,
Weigh thy opinions against providence;
Call imperfection what thou fancy'st such,
Say here he gives too little, there too much;
Destroy all creatures for thy sport or gust,
Yet cry, if man's unhappy, God's unjust;
If man alone engross not Heaven's high care,
Alone made perfect here, immortal there:
Snatch from his hand the balance and the rod,
Re-judge his justice, be the God of God.
In pride, in reas'ning pride, our error lies;
All quit their sphere and rush into the skies.
Pride still is aiming at the blest abodes,
Men would be angels, angels would be gods.
Aspiring to be gods, if angels fell,
Aspiring to be angels, men rebel:
And who but wishes to invert the laws
Of Order, sins against the eternal cause.

V.

Ask for what end the heavenly bodies shine,
Earth for whose use? Pride answers, " 'Tis for
　　mine.
For me kind nature wakes her genial power,
Suckles every herb, and spreads out ev'ry
　　flower;
Annual for me, the grape, the rose renew
The juice nectareous, and the balmy dew;
For me, the mine a thousand treasures brings;
For me, health gushes from a thousand springs;
Seas roll to waft me, suns to light me rise;
My footstool earth, my canopy the skies."
But errs not Nature from this gracious end,
From burning suns when livid deaths descend,
When earthquakes swallow, or when tempests
　　sweep
Towns to one grave, whole nations to the deep?
"No ('tis reply'd,) the first Almighty Cause

Acts not by partial, but by gen'ral laws;
The exceptions few; some change since all be-
　　gan;
And what created perfect?"—Why then man?
If the great end be human happiness,
Then Nature deviates; and can man do less?
As much that end a constant course requires,
Of showers and sunshine, as of man's desires:
As much eternal springs and cloudless skies,
As men for ever temperate, calm, and wise.
If plagues or earthquakes break not heaven's
　　design,
Why then a Borgia or a Cataline?
Who knows but he whose hand the lightning
　　forms,
Who heaves old ocean, and wings the storms;
Pours fierce ambition in a Caesar's mind,
Or turns young Ammon loose to scourge man-
　　kind?
From pride, from pride, our very reas'ning
　　springs;
Account for moral, as for natural things:
Why charge we heaven in those, in these ac-
　　quit?
In both, to reason right is to submit.
Better for us, perhaps, it might appear,
Were there all harmony, all virtue here;
That never air or ocean felt the wind;
That never passion discompos'd the mind.
But ALL subsists by elemental strife;
And passions are the elements of life.
The gen'ral ORDER since the whole began,
Is kept in nature, and is kept in man.

VI.

What would this man? now upward will he
　　soar,
And little less than angel, would be more;
Now looking downwards, just as griev'd ap-
　　pears
To want the strength of bulls, the fur of bears.
Made for his use, all creatures, if he call,
Say what their use, had he the powers of all?
Nature to these, without profusion kind,
The proper organs proper powers assign'd;
Each seeming want compensated of course,
Here with degrees of swiftness, there of force:
All in exact proportion to the state;
Nothing to add, and nothing to abate.
Each beast, each insect, happy in its own;

Is heaven unkind to man, and man alone?
Shall he alone, whom rational we call,
Be pleas'd with nothing, if not pleas'd with all?
    The bliss of man (could pride that blessing
      find)
Is not to act or think beyond mankind;
No powers of body or of soul to share,
But what his nature and his state can bear.
Why has not man a microscopic eye?
For this plain reason, man is not a fly.
Say what the use, were finer optics given,
T' inspect a mite, not comprehend the heaven?
Or touch, if tremblingly alive all o'er,
To smart and agonize at every pore?
Or quick effluvia darting through the brain,
Die of a rose in aromatic pain?
If Nature thunder'd in his op'ning ears,
And stunn'd him with the music of the spheres,
How would he wish that heaven had left him
    still
The whisp'ring zephyr and the purling rill?
Who finds not Providence all good and wise,
Alike in what it gives, and what denies?

VII.

    Far as creation's ample range extends,
The scale of sensual, mental power ascends:
Mark how it mounts, to man's imperial race,
From the green myriads in the peopled grass:
What modes of sight betwixt each wide ex-
    treme,
The mole's dim curtain, and the lynx's beam!
Of smell, the headlong lioness between,
And hound sagacious on the tainted green!
Of hearing, from the life that fills the flood,
To that which warbles through the vernal
    wood!
The spider's touch, how exquisitely fine!
Feels at each thread, and lives along the line:
In the nice bee, what sense so subtilely true,
From pois'nous herbs extracts the healing dew!
How instinct varies in the grov'ling swine,
Compar'd, half reas'ning elephant, with thine!
'Twixt that and reason, what a nice barrier!
For ever separate, yet for ever near!
Remembrance and reflection how ally'd!
What thin partitions sense from thought di-
    vide!
And middle natures, how they long to join,
Yet never pass the insuperable line!

Without this just gradation could they be
Subjected, these to those, or all to thee?
The powers of all subdu'd by thee alone,
Is not thy reason all these powers in one?

VIII.

    See through this air, this ocean, and this
    earth,
All matter quick, and bursting into birth.
Above, how high, progressive life may go!
Around how wide! how deep extend below!
Vast chain of being! which from God began,
Natures aethereal, human, angel, man,
Beast, bird, fish, insect, what no eye can see,
No glass can reach; from infinite to thee;
From thee to nothing. On superior powers
Were we to press, inferior might on our's:
Or in the full creation leave a void,
Where, one step broken, the great scale's de-
    stroy'd:
From Nature's chain, whatever link you strike,
Tenth, or ten thousandth, breaks the chain
    alike.
    And, if each system in gradation roll
Alike essential to th' amazing whole,
The least confusion but in one, not all
That system only, but the whole must fall.
Let earth, unbalanc'd from her orbit fly,
Planets and suns run lawless through the sky;
Let ruling angels from their spheres be hurl'd,
Being on being wreck'd, and world on world;
Heaven's whole foundations to their centre
    nod,
And Nature tremble to the throne of God.
All this dread Order break—for whom? for
    thee?
Vile worm! ah madness! pride! impiety!

IX.

    What if the foot, ordain'd the dust to tread,
Or hand, to toil, aspir'd to be the head?
What if the head, the eye, or ear repin'd
To serve mere engines to the ruling mind?
Just as absurd for any part to claim
To be another, in this gen'ral frame:
Just as absurd to mourn the tasks or pains
The great directing Mind of All ordains.
    All are but parts of one stupendous whole,
Whose body Nature is, and God the soul:
That chang'd through all, and yet in all the
    same:

Great in the earth, as in th' aethereal frame;
Warms in the sun, refreshes in the breeze,
Glows in the stars, and blossoms in the trees;
Lives through all life, extends through all extent,
Spreads undivided, operates unspent;
Breathes in our soul, informs our mortal part,
As full, as perfect, in a hair as heart;
As full, as perfect, in vile man that mourns,
As the rapt seraph that adores and burns:
To him no high, no low, no great, no small;
He fills, he bounds, connects, and equals all.

X.

Cease then, nor Order imperfection name;
Our proper bliss depends on what we blame.

Know thy own point: this kind, this due degree
Of blindness, weakness, Heaven bestows on thee.
Submit. In this, or any other sphere,
Secure to be as blest as thou canst bear:
Safe in the hand of one disposing Power,
Or in the natal, or the mortal hour.
All nature is but art, unknown to thee;
All chance, direction, which thou canst not see;
All discord, harmony not understood;
All partial evil, universal good:
And, spite of Pride, in erring Reason's spite,
One truth is clear, WHATEVER IS, IS RIGHT.

Voltaire

François Marie Arouet de Voltaire (1694–1778) was a French writer and philosopher who personified the rationalism of the eighteenth-century Enlightenment. Living in a France still dominated by Bourbon absolutism, he nevertheless daringly espoused the cause of tolerance, progress, and cosmopolitanism while at the same time attacking orthodoxy, both political and religious. In 1759, he wrote Candide, taking only three days to write this famous satire. Four years earlier the city of Lisbon, Portugal, had been badly damaged by one of the great forces of nature, an earthquake. Voltaire used this incident in Candide as one of the means of ridiculing the excessive and complacent optimism which had been reflected by some of the intellectuals of his day. He directed his satire particularly at the German philosopher, Leibnitz (1646–1716). Voltaire also used Candide to uphold some of the ideals of the Enlightenment. In reading the following passage [Part One] from this great work, note (1) evidence of Voltaire's attitude toward the belief in the perfection of nature, (2) his position regarding the extreme emphasis which the Enlightenment placed on reason, (3) the fun he poked at those who try to express everything in terms of mathematics, (4) his position in regard to nationalism and war, (5) the attitude he expressed toward the clergy and organized Christianity, (6) the opposition he displayed toward tyrannical government, (7) evidences of Voltaire's belief in social equality, and (8) how he believed morality could best be obtained.

Voltaire, *Candide*, The Modern Library, New York, 1930, 3–149. Courtesy of Random House, Inc.

From: *CANDIDE*

HOW CANDIDE WAS BROUGHT UP IN A NOBLE CASTLE AND HOW HE WAS EXPELLED FROM THE SAME

In the castle of Baron Thunder-ten-tronckh in Westphalia there lived a youth, endowed by Nature with the most gentle character. His face was the expression of his soul. His judgment was quite honest and he was extremely simple-minded; and this was the reason, I think, that he was named Candide. Old servants in the house suspected that he was the son of the Baron's sister and a decent honest gentleman of the neighbourhood, whom this young lady would never marry because he could only prove seventy-one quarterings, and the rest of his genealogical tree was lost, owing to the injuries of time. The Baron was one of the most powerful lords in Westphalia, for his castle possessed a door and windows. His Great Hall was even decorated with a piece of tapestry. The dogs in his stable-yards formed a pack of hounds when necessary; his grooms were his huntsmen; the village curate was his Grand Almoner. They all called him "My Lord," and laughed heartily at his stories. The Baroness weighed about three hundred and fifty pounds, was therefore greatly respected, and did the honours of the house with a dignity which rendered her still more respectable. Her daughter Cunegonde, aged seventeen, was rosy-cheeked, fresh, plump and tempting. The Baron's son appeared in every respect worthy of his father. The tutor Pangloss was the oracle of the house, and little Candide followed his lessons with all the candour of his age and character. Pangloss taught metaphysico-theologo-cosmolonigology. He proved admirably that there is no effect without a cause and that in this best of all possible worlds, My Lord the Baron's castle was the best of castles and his wife the best of all possible Baronesses. " 'Tis demonstrated," said he, "that things cannot be otherwise; for, since everything is made for an end, everything is necessarily for the best end. Observe that noses were made to wear spectacles; and so we have spectacles. Legs were visibly instituted to be breeched, and we have breeches. Stones were formed to be quarried and to build castles; and My Lord has a very noble castle; the greatest Baron in the province should have the best house; and as pigs were made to be eaten, we eat pork all the year round; consequently, those who have asserted that all is well talk nonsense; they ought to have said that all is for the best." Candide listened attentively and believed innocently; for he thought Mademoiselle Cunegonde extremely beautiful, although he was never bold enough to tell her so. He decided that after the happiness of being born Baron of Thunder-ten-tronckh, the second degree of happiness was to be Mademoiselle Cunegonde; the third, to see her every day; and the fourth, to listen to Doctor Pangloss, the greatest philosopher of the province and therefore of the whole world. One day when Cunegonde was walking near the castle, in a little wood which was called The Park, she observed Doctor Pangloss in the bushes, giving a lesson in experimental physics to her mother's waiting-maid, a very pretty and docile brunette. Mademoiselle Cunegonde had a great inclination for science and watched breathlessly the reiterated experiments she witnessed; she observed clearly the Doctor's sufficient reason, the effects and the causes, and returned home very much excited, pensive, filled with the desire of learning, reflecting that she might be the sufficient reason of young Candide and that he might be hers. On her way back to the castle she met Candide and blushed; Candide also blushed. She bade him good-morning in a hesitating voice; Candide replied without knowing what he was saying. Next day, when they left the table after dinner, Cunegonde and Candide found themselves behind a screen; Cunegonde dropped her handkerchief, Candide picked it up; she innocently held his hand; the young man innocently kissed the young lady's hand with remarkable vivacity, tenderness and grace; their lips met, their eyes sparkled, their knees trembled, their hands wandered. Baron Thunder-ten-tronckh passed near the screen, and, observing this cause and effect, expelled Candide from the castle by kicking him in the backside frequently and hard. Cunegonde swooned; when she recovered her senses, the Baroness slapped her in the face; and all was in consternation in the noblest and most agreeable of all possible castles.

WHAT HAPPENED TO CANDIDE AMONG THE BULGARIANS

Candide, expelled from the earthly paradise, wandered for a long time without knowing where he was going, turning up his eyes to Heaven, gazing back frequently at the noblest of castles which held the most beautiful of young Baronesses; he lay down to sleep supperless between two furrows in the open fields; it snowed heavily in large flakes. The next morning the shivering Candide, penniless, dying of cold and exhaustion, dragged himself towards the neighbouring town, which was called Waldberghoff-trarbk-dikdorff. He halted sadly at the door of an inn. Two men dressed in blue noticed him. "Comrade," said one, "there's a well-built young man of the right height." They went up to Candide and very civilly invited him to dinner. "Gentlemen," said Candide with charming modesty, "you do me a great honour, but I have no money to pay my share." "Ah, sir," said one of the men in blue, "persons of your figure and merit never pay anything; are you not five feet five tall?" "Yes, gentlemen," said he, bowing, "that is my height." "Ah, sir, come to table; we will not only pay your expenses, we will never allow a man like you to be short of money; men were only made to help each other." "You are in the right," said Candide, "that is what Doctor Pangloss was always telling me, and I see that everything is for the best." They begged him to accept a few crowns, he took them and wished to give them an IOU; they refused to take it and all sat down to table. "Do you not love tenderly . . ." "Oh, yes," said he. "I love Mademoiselle Cunegonde tenderly." "No," said one of the gentlemen. "We were asking if you do not tenderly love the King of the Bulgarians." "Not a bit," said he, "for I have never seen him." "What! He is the most charming of Kings, and you must drink his health." "Oh, gladly, gentlemen." And he drank. "That is

sufficient," he was told. "You are now the support, the aid, the defender, the hero of the Bulgarians; your fortune is made and your glory assured." They immediately put irons on his legs and took him to a regiment. He was made to turn to the right and left, to raise the ramrod and return the ramrod, to take aim, to fire, to double up, and he was given thirty strokes with a stick; the next day he drilled not quite so badly, and received only twenty strokes; the day after, he only had ten and was looked on as a prodigy by his comrades. Candide was completely mystified and could not make out how he was a hero. One fine spring day he thought he would take a walk, going straight ahead, in the belief that to use his legs as he pleased was a privilege of the human species as well as of animals. He had not gone two leagues when four other heroes, each six feet tall, fell upon him, bound him and dragged him back to a cell. He was asked by his judges whether he would rather be thrashed thirty-six times by the whole regiment or receive a dozen lead bullets at once in his brain. Although he protested that men's wills are free and that he wanted neither one nor the other, he had to make a choice; by virtue of that gift of God which is called *liberty*, he determined to run the gauntlet thirty-six times and actually did so twice. There were two thousand men in the regiment. That made four thousand strokes which laid bare the muscles and nerves from his neck to his backside. As they were about to proceed to a third turn, Candide, utterly exhausted, begged as a favour that they would be so kind as to smash his head; he obtained this favour; they bound his eyes and he was made to kneel down. At that moment the King of the Bulgarians came by and inquired the victim's crime; and as this King was possessed of a vast genius, he perceived from what he learned about Candide that he was a young metaphysician very ignorant in worldly matters, and therefore pardoned him with a clemency which will be praised in all newspapers and all ages. An honest surgeon healed Candide in three weeks with the ointments recommended by Dioscorides. He had already regained a little skin and could walk when the King of the Bulgarians went to war with the King of the Abares.

HOW CANDIDE ESCAPED
FROM THE BULGARIANS
AND WHAT BECAME OF HIM

Nothing could be smarter, more splendid, more brilliant, better drawn up than the two armies. Trumpets, fifes, hautboys, drums, cannons, formed a harmony such as has never been heard even in hell. The cannons first of all laid flat about six thousand men on each side; then the musketry removed from the best of worlds some nine or ten thousand blackguards who infested its surface. The bayonet also was the sufficient reason for the death of some thousands of men. The whole might amount to thirty thousand souls. Candide, who trembled like a philosopher, hid himself as well as he could during this heroic butchery. At last, while the two Kings each commanded a Te Deum in his camp, Candide decided to go elsewhere to reason about effects and causes. He clambered over heaps of dead and dying men and reached a neighbouring village, which was in ashes; it was an Abare village which the Bulgarians had burned in accordance with international law. Here, old men dazed with blows watched the dying agonies of their murdered wives who clutched their children to their bleeding breasts; there, disembowelled girls who had been made to satisfy the natural appetites of heroes gasped their last sighs; others, half-burned, begged to be put to death. Brains were scattered on the ground among dismembered arms and legs. Candide fled to another village as fast as he could; it belonged to the Bulgarians, and Abarian heroes had treated it in the same way. Candide, stumbling over quivering limbs or across ruins, at last escaped from the theatre of war, carrying a little food in his knapsack, and never forgetting Mademoiselle Cunegonde. His provisions were all gone when he reached Holland; but, having heard that everyone in that country was rich and a Christian, he had no doubt at all but that he would be as well treated as he had been in the Baron's castle before he had been expelled on account of Mademoiselle Cunegonde's pretty eyes. He asked an alms of several grave persons, who all replied that if he continued in that way he would be shut up in a house of correction to teach him how to live. He then addressed himself to a man who had been discoursing on charity in a large assembly for an hour on end. This orator, glancing at him askance, said: "What are you doing here? Are you for the good cause?" "There is no effect without a cause," said Candide modestly. "Everything is necessarily linked up and arranged for the best. It was necessary that I should be expelled from the company of Mademoiselle Cunegonde, that I ran the gauntlet, and that I beg my bread until I can earn it; all this could not have happened differently." "My friend," said the orator, "do you believe that the Pope is Anti-Christ?" "I had never heard so before," said Candide, "but whether he is or isn't, I am starving." "You don't deserve to eat," said the other. "Hence, rascal; hence, you wretch; and never come near me again." The orator's wife thrust her head out of the window and seeing a man who did not believe that the Pope was Anti-Christ, she poured on his head a full . . . O Heavens! To what excess religious zeal is carried by ladies! A man who had not been baptized, an honest Anabaptist named Jacques, saw the cruel and ignominious treatment of one of his brothers, a featherless two-legged creature with a soul; he took him home, cleaned him up, gave him bread and beer, presented him with two florins, and even offered to teach him to work at the manufacture of Persian stuffs which are made in Holland. Candide threw himself at the man's feet, exclaiming: "Doctor Pangloss was right in telling me that all is for the best in this world, for I am vastly more touched by your extreme generosity than by the harshness of the gentleman in the black cloak and his good lady." The next day when he walked out he met a beggar covered with sores, dull-eyed, with the end of his nose fallen away, his mouth awry, his teeth black, who talked huskily, was tormented with a violent cough and spat out a tooth at every cough.

HOW CANDIDE MET
HIS OLD MASTER IN PHILOSOPHY,
DOCTOR PANGLOSS,
AND WHAT HAPPENED

Candide, moved even more by compassion than by horror, gave this horrible beggar the two florins he had received from the honest Anabaptist, Jacques. The phantom gazed fixedly at him, shed tears and threw its arms round his neck. Candide recoiled in terror. "Alas!" said the wretch to the other wretch, "don't you recognise your dear Pangloss?" "What do I hear? You, my dear master! You, in this horrible state! What misfortune has happened to you? Why are you no longer in the noblest of castles? What has become of Mademoiselle Cunegonde, the pearl of young ladies, the masterpiece of Nature?" "I am exhausted," said Pangloss. Candide immediately took him to the Anabaptist's stable where he gave him a little bread to eat; and when Pangloss had recovered: "Well!" said he, "Cunegonde?" "Dead," replied the other. At this word Candide swooned; his friend restored him to his senses with a little bad vinegar which happened to be in the stable. Candide opened his eyes. "Cunegonde dead! Ah! best of worlds, where are you? But what illness did she die of? Was it because she saw me kicked out of her father's noble castle?" "No," said Pangloss. "She was disembowelled by Bulgarian soldiers, after having been raped to the limit of possibility; they broke the Baron's head when he tried to defend her; the Baroness was cut to pieces; my poor pupil was treated exactly like his sister; and as to the castle, there is not one stone standing on another, not a barn, not a sheep, not a duck, not a tree; but we were well avenged, for the Abares did exactly the same to a neighbouring barony which belonged to a Bulgarian Lord." At this, Candide swooned again; but, having recovered and having said all that he ought to say, he inquired the cause and effect, the sufficient reason which had reduced Pangloss to so piteous a state. "Alas!" said Pangloss, " 'tis love; love, the consoler of the human race, the preserver of the universe, the soul of all tender creatures, gentle love." "Alas!" said Candide, "I am acquainted with this love, this sovereign of hearts, this soul of our soul; it has never brought me anything but one kiss and twenty kicks in the backside. How could this beautiful cause produce in you so abominable an effect?" Pangloss replied as follows: "My dear Candide! You remember Paquette, the maid-servant of our august Baroness; in her arms I enjoyed the delights of Paradise which have produced the tortures of Hell by which you see I am devoured; she was infected and perhaps is dead. Paquette received this present from a most learned monk, who had it from the source; for he received it from an old countess, who had it from a cavalry captain, who owed it to a marchioness, who derived it from a page, who had received it from a Jesuit, who, when a novice, had it in a direct line from one of the companions of Christopher Columbus. For my part, I shall not give it to anyone, for I am dying." "O Pangloss!" exclaimed Candide, "this is a strange genealogy! Wasn't the devil at the root of it?" "Not at all," replied that great man. "It was something indispensable in this best of worlds, a necessary ingredient; for, if Columbus in an island of America had not caught this disease, which poisons the source of generation, and often indeed prevents generation, we should not have chocolate and cochineal; it must also be noticed that hitherto in our continent this disease is peculiar to us, like theological disputes. The Turks, the Indians, the Persians, the Chinese, the Siamese and the Japanese are not yet familiar with it; but there is a sufficient reason why they in their turn should become familiar with it in a few centuries. Meanwhile, it has made marvellous progress among us, and especially in those large armies composed of honest, well-bred stipendiaries who decide the destiny of States; it may be asserted that when thirty thousand men fight a pitched battle against an equal number of troops, there are about twenty thousand with the pox on either side." "Admirable!" said Candide. "But you must get cured." "How can I?" said Pangloss. "I haven't a sou, my friend, and in the whole extent of this globe, you cannot be bled or receive an enema without paying or without someone paying for you." This last speech determined Candide; he went and threw himself at the feet of his charitable Anabaptist, Jacques, and drew so touching a picture of the state to which his friend was reduced that the good easy man did not hesitate to succour Pangloss; he had him cured at his own expense. In this cure Pangloss only lost one eye and one ear. He could write well and knew arithmetic perfectly. The Anabaptist made him his book-keeper. At the end of two months he was compelled to go to Lisbon on business and took his two philosophers on the boat with him. Pangloss explained to him how everything was for the best. Jacques was not of this opinion. "Men," said he, "must have corrupted nature a little, for they were not born wolves, and they have become wolves. God did not give them twenty-four-pounder cannons or bayonets, and they have made bayonets and cannons to destroy each other. I might bring bankruptcies into the account and Justice which seizes the goods of bankrupts in order to deprive the creditors of them." "It was all indispensable," replied the one-eyed doctor," and private misfortunes make the public good, so that the more private misfortunes there are, the more everything is well." While he was reasoning, the air grew dark, the winds blew from the four quarters of the globe and the ship was attacked by the most horrible tempest in sight of the port of Lisbon.

STORM, SHIPWRECK, EARTHQUAKE, AND WHAT HAPPENED TO DR. PANGLOSS, TO CANDIDE AND THE ANABAPTIST JACQUES

Half the enfeebled passengers, suffering from that inconceivable anguish which the rolling of a ship causes in the nerves and in all the humours of bodies shaken in contrary directions, did not retain strength enough even to trouble about the danger. The other half screamed and prayed; the sails were torn, the masts broken, the vessel leaking. Those worked who could, no one co-operated, no one commanded. The Anabaptist tried to help the crew a little; he was on the main-deck; a furious sailor struck him violently and stretched him on the deck; but the blow he delivered gave him so violent a shock that he fell head-first out of the ship. He remained hanging and clinging to part of the broken mast. The good Jacques ran to his aid, helped him to climb back, and from the effort he made was flung into the sea in full view of the sailor, who allowed him to drown without condescending even to look at him. Candide came up, saw his benefactor reappear for a moment and then be engulfed for ever. He tried to throw himself after him into the sea; he was prevented by the philosopher Pangloss, who proved to him that the Lisbon roads had been expressly created for the Anabaptist to be drowned in them. While he was proving this *a priori*, the vessel sank, and every one perished except Pangloss, Candide and the brutal sailor who had drowned the virtuous Anabaptist; the blackguard swam successfully to the shore and Pangloss and Candide were carried there on a plank. When they had recovered a little, they walked toward Lisbon; they had a little money by the help of which they hoped to be saved from hunger after having escaped the storm. Weeping the death of their benefactor, they had scarcely set foot in the town when they felt the earth tremble under their feet; the sea rose in foaming masses in the port and smashed the ships which rode at anchor. Whirlwinds of flame and ashes covered the streets and squares; the houses collapsed, the roofs were thrown upon the foundations, and the foundations were scattered; thirty thousand inhabitants of every age and both sexes were crushed under the ruins. Whistling and swearing, the sailor said: "There'll be something to pick up here." "What can be the sufficient reason for this phenomenon?" said Pangloss. "It is the last day!" cried Candide. The sailor immediately ran among the debris, dared death to find money, found it, seized it, got drunk, and having slept off his wine, purchased the favours of the first woman of goodwill he met on the ruins of the houses and among the dead and dying. Pangloss, however, pulled him by the sleeve. "My friend," said he, "this is not well, you are disregarding universal reason, you choose the wrong time." "Blood and 'ounds!" he retorted, "I am a sailor and I was born in Batavia; four times have I stamped on the crucifix during four voyages to Japan; you have found the right man for your universal reason!" Candide had been hurt by some falling stones; he lay in the street covered with debris. He said to Pangloss: "Alas! Get me a little wine and oil; I am dying." "This earthquake is not a new thing," replied Pangloss. "The town of Lima felt the same shocks in America last year; similar causes produce similar effects; there must certainly be a train of sulphur underground from Lima to Lisbon." "Nothing is more probable," replied Candide; "but, for God's sake, a little oil and wine."

"What do you mean, probable?" replied the philosopher; "I maintain that it is proved." Candide lost consciousness, and Pangloss brought him a little water from a neighbouring fountain. Next day they found a little food as they wandered among the ruins and regained a little strength. Afterwards they worked like others to help the inhabitants who had escaped death. Some citizens they had assisted gave them as good a dinner as could be expected in such a disaster; true, it was a dreary meal; the hosts watered their bread with their tears, but Pangloss consoled them by assuring them that things could not be otherwise. "For," said he, "all this is for the best; for, if there is a volcano at Lisbon, it cannot be anywhere else; for it is impossible that things should not be where they are; for all is well." A little, dark man, a familiar of the Inquisition, who sat beside him, politely took up the conversation, and said: "Apparently, you do not believe in original sin; for, if everything is for the best, there was neither fall nor punishment." "I most humbly beg your excellency's pardon," replied Pangloss still more politely, "for the fall of man and the curse necessarily entered into the best of all possible worlds." "Then you do not believe in free-will?" said the familiar. "Your excellency will pardon me," said Pangloss; "free-will can exist with absolute necessity; for it was necessary that we should be free; for in short, limited will . . ." Pangloss was in the middle of his phrase when the familiar nodded to his armed attendant who was pouring out port or Oporto wine for him.

HOW A SPLENDID AUTO-DA-FÉ WAS HELD TO PREVENT EARTHQUAKES, AND HOW CANDIDE WAS FLOGGED

After the earthquake which destroyed three-quarters of Lisbon, the wise men of that country could discover no more efficacious way of preventing a total ruin than by giving the people a splendid *auto-da-fé*. It was decided by the university of Coimbre that the sight of several persons being slowly burned in great ceremony is an infallible secret for preventing earthquakes. Consequently they had arrested a Biscayan convicted of having married his fellow-godmother, and two Portuguese who,

when eating a chicken, had thrown away the bacon; after dinner they came and bound Dr. Pangloss and his disciple Candide, one because he had spoken and the other because he had listened with an air of approbation; they were both carried separately to extremely cool apartments, where there was never any discomfort from the sun; a week afterwards each was dressed in a sanbenito and their heads were ornamented with paper mitres; Candide's mitre and sanbenito were painted with flames upside down and with devils who had neither tails nor claws; but Pangloss's devils had claws and tails, and his flames were upright. Dressed in this manner they marched in procession and listened to a most pathetic sermon, followed by lovely plain-song music. Candide was flogged in time to the music, while the singing went on; the Biscayan and the two men who had not wanted to eat bacon were burned, and Pangloss was hanged, although this is not the custom. The very same day, the earth shook again with a terrible clamour. Candide, terrified, dumbfounded, bewildered, covered with blood, quivering from head to foot, said to himself: "If this is the best of all possible worlds, what are the others? Let it pass that I was flogged, for I was flogged by the Bulgarians, but, O my dear Pangloss! The greatest of philosophers! Must I see you hanged without knowing why! O my dear Anabaptist! The best of men! Was it necessary that you should be drowned in port! O Mademoiselle Cunegonde! The pearl of women! Was it necessary that your belly should be slit!" He was returning, scarcely able to support himself, preached at, flogged, absolved and blessed, when an old woman accosted him and said: "Courage, my son, follow me."

HOW AN OLD WOMAN TOOK CARE OF CANDIDE AND HOW HE REGAINED THAT WHICH HE LOVED

Candide did not take courage, but he followed the old woman to a hovel; she gave him a pot of ointment to rub on, and left him food and drink; she pointed out a fairly clean bed; near the bed there was a suit of clothes. "Eat, drink, sleep," said she, "and may our Lady of Atocha, my Lord Saint Anthony of Padua and my Lord Saint James of Compostella take care of you; I shall come back tomorrow." Candide, still amazed by all he had seen, by all he had suffered, and still more by the old woman's charity, tried to kiss her hand. " 'Tis not my hand you should kiss," said the old woman, "I shall come back to-morrow. Rub on the ointment, eat and sleep." In spite of all his misfortune, Candide ate and went to sleep. Next day the old woman brought him breakfast, examined his back and smeared him with another ointment; later she brought him dinner, and returned in the evening with supper. The next day she went through the same ceremony. "Who are you?" Candide kept asking her. "Who has inspired you with so much kindness? How can I thank you?" The good woman never made any reply; she returned in the evening without any supper. "Come with me," said she, "and do not speak a word." She took him by the arm and walked into the country with him for about a quarter of a mile; they came to an isolated house, surrounded with gardens and canals. The old woman knocked at a little door. It was opened; she led Candide up a back stairway into a gilded apartment, left him on a brocaded sofa, shut the door and went away. Candide thought he was dreaming, and felt that his whole life was a bad dream and the present moment an agreeable dream. The old woman soon reappeared; she was supporting with some difficulty a trembling woman of majestic stature, glittering with precious stones and covered with a veil. "Remove the veil," said the old woman to Candide. The young man advanced and lifted the veil with a timid hand. What a moment! What a surprise! He thought he saw Mademoiselle Cunegonde, in fact he was looking at her, it was she herself. His strength failed him, he could not utter a word and fell at her feet. Cunegonde fell on the sofa. The old woman dosed them with distilled waters; they recovered their senses and began to speak: at first they uttered only broken words, questions and answers at cross purposes, sighs, tears, exclamations. The old woman advised them to make less noise and left them alone. "What! Is it you?" said Candide. "You are alive, and I find you here in Portugal! Then you were not raped? Your belly was not slit, as the philosopher Pangloss assured me?" "Yes, indeed," said the fair Cune-

gonde; "but those two accidents are not always fatal." "But your father and mother were killed?", " 'Tis only too true," said Cunegonde, weeping. "And your brother?" "My brother was killed too." "And why are you in Portugal? And how did you know I was here? And by what strange adventure have you brought me to this house?" "I will tell you everything," replied the lady, "but first of all you must tell me everything that has happened to you since the innocent kiss you gave me and the kicks you received." Candide obeyed with profound respect; and, although he was bewildered, although his voice was weak and trembling, although his back was still a little painful, he related in the most natural manner all he had endured since the moment of their separation. Cunegonde raised her eyes to heaven; she shed tears at the death of the good Anabaptist and Pangloss, after which she spoke as follows to Candide, who did not miss a word and devoured her with his eyes.

CUNEGONDE'S STORY

I was fast asleep in bed when it pleased Heaven to send the Bulgarians to our noble castle of Thunder-ten-tronckh; they murdered my father and brother and cut my mother to pieces. A large Bulgarian six feet tall, seeing that I had swooned at the spectacle, began to rape me; this brought me to, I recovered my senses, I screamed, I struggled, I bit, I scratched, I tried to tear out the big Bulgarian's eyes, not knowing that what was happening in my father's castle was a matter of custom; the brute stabbed me with a knife in the left side where I still have the scar." "Alas! I hope I shall see it," said the naïf Candide. "You shall see it," said Cunegonde, "but let me go on." "Go on," said Candide. She took up the thread of her story as follows: "A Bulgarian captain came in, saw me covered with blood, and the soldier did not disturb himself. The captain was angry at the brute's lack of respect to him, and killed him on my body. Afterwards, he had me bandaged and took me to his billet as a prisoner of war. I washed the few shirts he had and did the cooking; I must admit he thought me very pretty; and I will not deny that he was very well built and that his skin was white and soft; otherwise he had little wit and little philosophy; it was plain that he had not been brought up by Dr. Pangloss. At the end of three months he lost all his money and got tired of me; he sold me to a Jew named Don Issachar, who traded in Holland and Portugal and had a passion for women. This Jew devoted himself to my person but he could not triumph over it; I resisted him better than the Bulgarian soldier; a lady of honour may be raped once, but it strengthens her virtue. In order to subdue me, the Jew brought me to this country house. Up till then I believed that there was nothing on earth so splendid as the castle of Thunder-ten-tronckh; I was undeceived. One day the Grand Inquisitor noticed me at Mass; he ogled me continually and sent a message that he wished to speak to me on secret affairs. I was taken to his palace; I informed him of my birth; he pointed out how much it was beneath my rank to belong to an Israelite. A proposition was made on his behalf to Don Issachar to give me up to His Lordship. Don Issachar, who is the court banker and a man of influence, would not agree. The Inquisitor threatened him with an *auto-da-fé*. At last the Jew was frightened and made a bargain whereby the house and I belong to both in common. The Jew has Mondays, Wednesdays and the Sabbath day, and the Inquisitor has the other days of the week. This arrangement has lasted for six months. It has not been without quarrels; for it has often been debated whether the night between Saturday and Sunday belonged to the old law or the new. For my part, I have hitherto resisted them both; and I think that is the reason why they still love me. At last My Lord the Inquisitor was pleased to arrange an *auto-da-fé* to remove the scourge of earthquakes and to intimidate Don Issachar. He honoured me with an invitation. I had an excellent seat; and refreshments were served to the ladies between the Mass and the execution. I was indeed horror-stricken when I saw the burning of the two Jews and the honest Biscayan who had married his fellow-godmother; but what was my surprise, my terror, my anguish, when I saw in a sanbenito and under a mitre a face which resembled Pangloss's! I rubbed my eyes, I looked carefully, I saw him hanged; and I fainted. I had scarcely recovered my senses when I saw you stripped naked; that was the height of horror, of consternation, of grief and despair. I will frankly tell you that your skin is even whiter and of a more perfect tint than that of my Bulgarian captain. This spectacle redoubled all the feelings which crushed and devoured me. I exclaimed, I tried to say: 'Stop, Barbarians!' but my voice failed and my cries would have been useless. When you had been well flogged, I said to myself: 'How does it happen that the charming Candide and the wise Pangloss are in Lisbon, the one to receive a hundred lashes, and the other to be hanged, by order of My Lord the Inquisitor, whose darling I am? Pangloss deceived me cruelly when he said that all is for the best in the world.' I was agitated, distracted, sometimes beside myself and sometimes ready to die of faintness, and my head was filled with the massacre of my father, of my mother, of my brother, the insolence of my horrid Bulgarian soldier, the gash he gave me, my slavery, my life as a kitchen-wench, my Bulgarian captain, my horrid Don Issachar, my abominable Inquisitor, the hanging of Dr. Pangloss, that long plain-song *miserere* during which you were flogged, and above all the kiss I gave you behind the screen that day when I saw you for the last time. I praised God for bringing you back to me through so many trials, I ordered my old woman to take care of you and to bring you here as soon as she could. She has carried out my commission very well; I have enjoyed the inexpressible pleasure of seeing you again, of listening to you, and of speaking to you. You must be very hungry; I have a good appetite; let us begin by having supper." Both sat down to supper; and after supper they returned to the handsome sofa we have already mentioned; they were still there when Signor Don Issachar, one of the masters of the house, arrived. It was the day of the Sabbath. He came to enjoy his rights and to express his tender love.

WHAT HAPPENED TO CUNEGONDE, TO CANDIDE, TO THE GRAND INQUISITOR AND TO A JEW

This Issachar was the most choleric Hebrew who had been seen in Israel since the Babylonian captivity. "What!" said he. "Bitch of a Galilean, isn't it enough to have the Inquisitor? Must this scoundrel share with me too? So saying, he drew a long dagger which he always carried and, thinking that his adversary was unarmed, threw himself upon Candide; but our good Westphalian had received an excellent sword from the old woman along with his suit of clothes. He drew his sword, and although he had a most gentle character, laid the Israelite stone-dead on the floor at the feet of the fair Cunegonde. "Holy Virgin!" she exclaimed, "what will become of us? A man killed in my house! If the police come we are lost." "If Pangloss had not been hanged," said Candide, "he would have given us good advice in this extremity, for he was a great philosopher. In default of him, let us consult the old woman." She was extremely prudent and was beginning to give her advice when another little door opened. It was an hour after midnight, and Sunday was beginning. This day belonged to My Lord the Inquisitor. He came in and saw the flogged Candide sword in hand, a corpse lying on the ground, Cunegonde in terror, and the old woman giving advice. At this moment, here is what happened in Candide's soul and the manner of his reasoning: "If this holy man calls for help, he will infallibly have me burned; he might do as much to Cunegonde; he had me pitilessly lashed; he is my rival; I am in the mood to kill, there is no room for hesitation." His reasoning was clear and swift; and, without giving the Inquisitor time to recover from his surprise, he pierced him through and through and cast him beside the Jew. "Here's another," said Cunegonde, "there is no chance of mercy; we are excommunicated, our last hour has come. How does it happen that you, who were born so mild, should kill a Jew and a prelate in two minutes?" "My dear young lady," replied Candide, "when a man is in love, jealous, and has been flogged by the Inquisition, he is beside himself." The old woman then spoke up and said: "In the stable are three Andalusian horses, with their saddles and bridles; let the brave Candide prepare them; mademoiselle has moidores and diamonds; let us mount quickly, although I can only sit on one buttock, and go to Cadiz; the weather is beautifully fine, and it is most pleas-

ant to travel in the coolness of the night." Candide immediately saddled the three horses. Cunegonde, the old woman and he rode thirty miles without stopping. While they were riding away, the Holy Hermandad arrived at the house; My Lord was buried in a splendid church and Issachar was thrown into a sewer. Candide, Cunegonde and the old woman had already reached the little town of Avacena in the midst of the mountains of the Sierra Morena; and they talked in their inn as follows.

HOW CANDIDE, CUNEGONDE AND THE OLD WOMAN ARRIVED AT CADIZ IN GREAT DISTRESS, AND HOW THEY EMBARKED

"Who can have stolen my pistoles and my diamonds?" said Cunegonde, weeping. "How shall we live? What shall we do? Where shall we find Inquisitors and Jews to give me others?" "Alas!" said the old woman, "I strongly suspect a reverend Franciscan father who slept in the same inn at Badajoz with us; Heaven forbid that I should judge rashly! But he twice came into our room and left long before we did." "Alas!" said Candide, "the good Pangloss often proved to me that this world's goods are common to all men and that every one has an equal right to them. According to these principles the monk should have left us enough to continue our journey. Have you nothing left then, my fair Cunegonde?" "Not a maravedi," said she. "What are we to do?" said Candide. "Sell one of the horses," said the old woman. "I will ride postillion behind Mademoiselle Cunegonde, although I can only sit on one buttock, and we will get to Cadiz." In the same hotel there was a Benedictine friar. He bought the horse very cheap. Candide, Cunegonde and the old woman passed through Lucena, Chillas, Lebrixa, and at last reached Cadiz. A fleet was there being equipped and troops were being raised to bring to reason the reverend Jesuit fathers of Paraguay, who were accused of causing the revolt of one of their tribes against the kings of Spain and Portugal near the town of Sacramento. Candide, having served with the Bulgarians, went through the Bulgarian drill before the general of the little army with so much grace, celerity, skill, pride and agility, that he was given the command of an infantry company. He was now a captain; he embarked with Mademoiselle Cunegonde, the old woman, two servants, and the two Andalusian horses which had belonged to the Grand Inquisitor of Portugal. During the voyage they had many discussions about the philosophy of poor Pangloss. "We are going to a new world," said Candide, "and no doubt it is there that everything is for the best; for it must be admitted that one might lament a little over the physical and moral happenings in our own world." "I love you with all my heart," said Cunegonde, "but my soul is still shocked by what I have seen and undergone." "All will be well," replied Candide; "the sea in this new world already is better than the seas of our Europe; it is calmer and the winds are more constant. It is certainly the new world which is the best of all possible worlds." "God grant it!" said Cunegonde, "but I have been so horribly unhappy in mine that my heart is nearly closed to hope." "You complain," said the old woman to them. "Alas! you have not endured such misfortunes as mine." Cunegonde almost laughed and thought it most amusing of the old woman to assert that she was more unfortunate. "Alas! my dear," said she, "unless you have been raped by two Bulgarians, stabbed twice in the belly, have had two castles destroyed, two fathers and mothers murdered before your eyes, and have seen two of your lovers flogged in an *auto-da-fé*, I do not see how you can surpass me; moreover, I was born a Baroness with seventy-two quarterings and I have been a kitchen wench." "You do not know my birth," said the old woman, "and if I showed you my backside you would not talk as you do and you would suspend your judgment." This speech aroused intense curiosity in the minds of Cunegonde and Candide. And the old woman spoke as follows.

THE OLD WOMAN'S STORY

"My eyes were not always bloodshot and red-rimmed; my nose did not always touch my chin and I was not always a servant. I am the daughter of Pope Urban X and the Princess of Palestrina. Until I was fourteen I was brought up in a palace to which all the castles of your German Barons would not have served as stables; and one of my dresses cost more than all the magnificence of Westphalia. I increased in beauty, in grace, in talents, among pleasures, respect and hopes; already I inspired love, my breasts were forming; and what breasts! White, firm, carved like those of the Venus de' Medici. And what eyes! What eyelids! What black eyebrows! What fire shone from my two eye-balls, and dimmed the glitter of the stars, as the local poets pointed out to me. The women who dressed and undressed me fell into ecstasy when they beheld me in front and behind; and all the men would have liked to be in their place. I was betrothed to a ruling prince of Massa-Carrara. What a prince! As beautiful as I was, formed of gentleness and charms, brilliantly witty and burning with love; I loved him with a first love, idolatrously and extravagantly. The marriage ceremonies were arranged with unheard-of pomp and magnificence; there were continual fêtes, revels and comic operas; all Italy wrote sonnets for me and not a good one among them. I touched the moment of my happiness when an old marchioness who had been my prince's mistress invited him to take chocolate with her; less than two hours afterwards he died in horrible convulsions; but that is only a trifle. My mother was in despair, though less distressed than I, and wished to absent herself for a time from a place so disastrous. She had a most beautiful estate near Gaeta; we embarked on a galley, gilded like the altar of St. Peter's at Rome. A Salle pirate swooped down and boarded us; our soldiers defended us like soldiers of the Pope; they threw down their arms, fell on their knees and asked the pirates for absolution *in articulo mortis*. They were immediately stripped as naked as monkeys and my mother, our ladies of honour and myself as well. The diligence with which these gentlemen strip people is truly admirable; but I was still more surprised by their inserting a finger in a place belonging to all of us where we women usually only allow the end of a syringe. This appeared to me a very strange ceremony; but that is how we judge everything when we leave our own country. I soon learned that it was to find out if we had hidden any diamonds there; 'tis a custom established from time immemorial among the civilized nations who roam the seas. I have learned that the religious Knights of Malta never fail in it when they capture Turks and Turkish women; this is an international law which has never been broken. I will not tell you how hard it is for a young princess to be taken with her mother as a slave to Morocco; you will also guess all we had to endure in the pirates' ship. My mother was still very beautiful; our ladies of honour, even our waiting-maids possessed more charms than could be found in all Africa; and I was ravishing, I was beauty, grace itself, and I was a virgin; I did not remain so long; the flower which had been reserved for the handsome prince of Massa Carrara was ravished from me by a pirate captain; he was an abominable negro who thought he was doing me a great honour. The Princess of Palestrina and I must indeed have been strong to bear up against all we endured before our arrival in Morocco! But let that pass; these things are so common that they are not worth mentioning. Morocco was swimming in blood when we arrived. The fifty sons of the Emperor Muley Ismael had each a faction; and this produced fifty civil wars, of blacks against blacks, browns against browns, mulattoes against mulattoes. There was continual carnage throughout the whole extent of the empire. Scarcely had we landed when the blacks of a party hostile to that of my pirate arrived with the purpose of depriving him of his booty. After the diamonds and the gold, we were the most valuable possessions. I witnessed a fight such as is never seen in your European climates. The blood of the northern peoples is not sufficiently ardent; their madness for women does not reach the point which is common in Africa. The Europeans seem to have milk in their veins; but vitriol and fire flow in the veins of the inhabitants of Mount Atlas and the neighbouring countries. They fought with the fury of the lions, tigers and serpents of the country to determine who should have us. A Moor grasped my mother by the right arm, my captain's lieutenant held her by the left arm; a Moorish soldier held one leg and one of our pirates seized the other. In a moment nearly all our women were seized in the same way by four soldiers. My captain kept me hidden behind him; he had a scimitar in his hand and killed everybody who opposed his fury. I saw my mother and all our Italian women torn in pieces, gashed, massacred by the monsters who disputed them. The prisoners, my companions, those who had captured them, soldiers, sailors, blacks, browns, whites, mulattoes and finally my captain were all killed and I remained expiring on a heap of corpses. As every one knows, such scenes go on in an area of more than three hundred square leagues and yet no one ever fails to recite the five daily prayers ordered by Mahomet. With great difficulty I extricated myself from the bloody heaps of corpses and dragged myself to the foot of a large orange-tree on the bank of a stream; there I fell down with terror, weariness, horror, despair and hunger. Soon afterwards, my exhausted senses fell into a sleep which was more like a swoon than repose. I was in this state of weakness and insensibility between life and death when I felt myself oppressed by something which moved on my body. I opened my eyes and saw a white man of good appearance who was sighing and muttering between his teeth: O che sciagura d'essere senza coglioni!

CONTINUATION OF THE OLD WOMAN'S MISFORTUNES

"Amazed and delighted to hear my native language, and not less surprised at the words spoken by this man, I replied that there were greater misfortunes than that of which he complained. In a few words I informed him of the horrors I had undergone and then swooned again. He carried me to a neighbouring house, had me put to bed, gave me food, waited on me, consoled me, flattered me, told me he had never seen anyone so beautiful as I, and that he had never so much regretted that which no one could give back to him. 'I was born at Naples,' he said, 'and every year they make two or three thousand children there into capons; some die of it, others acquire voices more beautiful than women's, and others become the governors of States. This operation was performed upon me with very great success and I was a musician in the chapel of the Princess of Palestrina!' 'Of my mother,' I exclaimed. 'Of your mother!' cried he, weeping.

'What! Are you that young princess I brought up to the age of six and who even then gave promise of being as beautiful as you are?' 'I am! my mother is four hundred yards from here, cut into quarters under a heap of corpses. . . .' I related all that had happened to me; he also told me his adventures and informed me how he had been sent to the King of Morocco by a Christian power to make a treaty with that monarch whereby he was supplied with powder, cannons and ships to help to exterminate the commerce of other Christians. 'My mission is accomplished,' said this honest eunuch, 'I am about to embark at Ceuta and I will take you back to Italy. Ma che sciagura d'essere senza coglioni!' I thanked him with tears of gratitude; and instead of taking me back to Italy he conducted me to Algiers and sold me to the Dey. I had scarcely been sold when the plague which had gone through Africa, Asia and Europe, broke out furiously in Algiers. You have seen earthquakes; but have you ever seen the plague?" "Never," replied the Baroness. "If you had," replied the old woman, "you would admit that it is much worse than an earthquake. It is very common in Africa; I caught it. Imagine the situation of a Pope's daughter aged fifteen, who in three months had undergone poverty and slavery, had been raped nearly every day, had seen her mother cut into four pieces, had undergone hunger and war, and was now dying of the plague in Algiers. However, I did not die; but my eunuch and the Dey and almost all the seraglio of Algiers perished. When the first ravages of this frightful plague were over, the Dey's slaves were sold. A merchant bought me and carried me to Tunis; he sold me to another merchant who re-sold me at Tripoli; from Tripoli I was re-sold to Alexandria, from Alexandria re-sold to Smyrna, from Smyrna to Constantinople. I was finally bought by an Aga of the Janizaries, who was soon ordered to defend Azov against the Russians who were besieging it. The Aga, who was a man of great gallantry, took his whole seraglio with him, and lodged us in a little fort on the Islands of Palus-Maeotis, guarded by two black eunuchs and twenty soldiers. He killed a prodigious number of Russians but they returned the compliment as well. Azov was given up to fire

and blood, neither sex nor age was pardoned; only our little fort remained; and the enemy tried to reduce it by starving us. The twenty Janizaries had sworn never to surrender us. The extremities of hunger to which they were reduced forced them to eat our two eunuchs for fear of breaking their oath. Some days later they resolved to eat the women. We had with us a most pious and compassionate Imam who delivered a fine sermon to them by which he persuaded them not to kill us altogether. 'Cut,' said he, 'only one buttock from each of these ladies and you will make very good cheer; if you have to return, there will still be as much left in a few days; Heaven will be pleased at so charitable an action and you will be saved.' He was very eloquent and persuaded them. This horrible operation was performed upon us; the Imam anointed us with the same balm that is used for children who have just been circumcised; we were all at the point of death. Scarcely had the Janizaries finished the meal we had supplied when the Russians arrived in flat-bottomed boats; not a Janizary escaped. The Russians paid no attention to the state we were in. There are French doctors everywhere; one of them, who was very skilful, took care of us; he healed us and I shall remember all my life that, when my wounds were cured, he made propositions to me. For the rest, he told us all to cheer up; he told us that the same thing had happened in several sieges and that it was a law of war. As soon as my companions could walk they were sent to Moscow. I fell to the lot of a Boyar who made me his gardener and gave me twenty lashes a day. But at the end of two years this lord was broken on the wheel with thirty other Boyars owing to some court disturbance, and I profited by this adventure; I fled; I crossed all Russia; for a long time I was servant in an inn at Riga, then at Rostock, at Wismar, at Leipzig, at Cassel, at Utrecht, at Leyden, at the Hague, at Rotterdam; I have grown old in misery and in shame, with only half a backside, always remembering that I was the daughter of a Pope; a hundred times I wanted to kill myself, but I still loved life. This ridiculous weakness is perhaps the most disastrous of our inclinations; for is there anything sillier than to desire to bear continually a burden one always wishes to throw on the ground; to look upon oneself with horror and yet to cling to oneself; in short, to caress the serpent which devours us until he has eaten our heart? In the countries it has been my fate to traverse and in the inns where I have served I have seen a prodigious number of people who hated their lives; but I have only seen twelve who voluntarily put an end to their misery: three negroes, four Englishmen, four Genevans and a German professor named Robeck. I ended up as servant to the Jew, Don Issachar; he placed me in your service, my fair young lady; I attached myself to your fate and have been more occupied with your adventures than with my own. I should never even have spoken of my misfortunes, if you had not piqued me a little and if it had not been the custom on board ship to tell stories to pass the time. In short, Mademoiselle, I have had experience, I know the world; provide yourself with an entertainment, make each passenger tell you his story; and if there is one who has not often cursed his life, who has not often said to himself that he was the most unfortunate of men, throw me head-first into the sea."

HOW CANDIDE WAS OBLIGED TO SEPARATE FROM THE FAIR CUNEGONDE AND THE OLD WOMAN

The fair Cunegonde, having heard the old woman's story, treated her with all the politeness due to a person of her rank and merit. She accepted the proposition and persuaded all the passengers one after the other to tell her their adventures. She and Candide admitted that the old woman was right. "It was most unfortunate," said Candide, "that the wise Pangloss was hanged contrary to custom at an *auto-de-fé;* he would have said admirable things about the physical and moral evils which cover the earth and the sea, and I should feel myself strong enough to urge a few objections with all due respect." While each of the passengers was telling his story the ship proceeded on its way. They arrived at Buenos Ayres. Cunegonde, Captain Candide and the old woman went to call on the governor, Don Fernando d'Ibaraa y Figueora y Mascarenes y Lampourdos y Souza. This gentleman had the pride befitting a man

who owned so many names. He talked to men with a most noble disdain, turning his nose up so far, raising his voice so pitilessly, assuming so imposing a tone, affecting so lofty a carriage, that all who addressed him were tempted to give him a thrashing. He had a furious passion for women. Cunegonde seemed to him the most beautiful woman he had ever seen. The first thing he did was to ask if she were the Captain's wife. The air with which he asked this question alarmed Candide; he did not dare say that she was his wife, because as a matter of fact she was not; he dared not say she was his sister, because she was not that either; and though this official lie was formerly extremely fashionable among the ancients, and might be useful to the moderns, his soul was too pure to depart from truth. "Mademoiselle Cunegonde," said he, "is about to do me the honour of marrying me, and we beg your excellency to be present at the wedding." Don Fernando d'Ibaraa y Figueora y Mascarenes y Lampourdos y Souza twisted his moustache, smiled bitterly and ordered Captain Candide to go and inspect his company. Candide obeyed; the governor remained with Mademoiselle Cunegonde. He declared his passion, vowed that the next day he would marry her publicly, or otherwise, as it might please her charms. Cunegonde asked for a quarter of an hour to collect herself, to consult the old woman and to make up her mind. The old woman said to Cunegonde: "You have seventy-two quarterings and you haven't a shilling; it is in your power to be the wife of the greatest Lord in South America, who has an exceedingly fine moustache; is it for you to pride yourself on a rigid fidelity? You have been raped by Bulgarians, a Jew and an Inquisitor have enjoyed your good graces; misfortunes confer certain rights. If I were in your place, I confess I should not have the least scruple in marrying the governor and making Captain Candide's fortune." While the old woman was speaking with all that prudence which comes from age and experience, they saw a small ship come into the harbour; an Alcayde and some Alguazils were on board, and this is what had happened. The old woman had guessed correctly that it was a long-sleeved monk who stole Cunegonde's money and jewels at Badajoz, when she was flying in all haste with Candide. The monk tried to sell some of the gems to a jeweller. The merchant recognised them as the property of the Grand Inquisitor. Before the monk was hanged he confessed that he had stolen them; he described the persons and the direction they were taking. The flight of Cunegonde and Candide was already known. They were followed to Cadiz; without any waste of time a vessel was sent in pursuit of them. The vessel was already in the harbour at Buenos Ayres. The rumour spread that an Alcayde was about to land and that he was in pursuit of the murderers of His Lordship the Grand Inquisitor. The prudent old woman saw in a moment what was to be done. "You cannot escape," she said to Cunegonde, "and you have nothing to fear; you did not kill His Lordship; moreover, the governor is in love with you and will not allow you to be maltreated; stay here." She ran to Candide at once. "Fly," said she, "or in an hour's time you will be burned." There was not a moment to lose; but how could he leave Cunegonde and where could he take refuge?

The Revolutionary Era and the Conservative Reaction

Beginning in the seventeenth century the English made a notable contribution to the expansion of European civilization when they established a colonial empire in North America. Gradually these British subjects, living in a new environment and exploiting their extensive natural resources, developed political and social points of view and economic interests that not only differed from those of the mother country but actually conflicted with them. Independence became the inevitable result of of this deviation, and in the eighteenth century the leaders of the thirteen colonies turned to the principles of the Enlightenment to justify the revolution they were embarking upon. Shortly thereafter, France, laboring under the political and social encumbrances of the Old Regime, followed a similar trend toward revolution in order to obtain more enlightened government. On both sides of the Atlantic the initial liberal impulse of the revolution was eventually diverted into more conservative channels. In the new world this reaction found expression in the constitutional convention of 1787 and the federal union, while in the old it came about through the career of Napoleon. Political conservatism found its literary exponents who sought to justify it on such grounds as the value of historical experience and the concept of the organic growth of the State. This trend in political thought was paralleled in literature and the arts by the romantic movement. Poets and authors wrote in strongly emotional terms of man and his feelings of love, romance, sentiment, and passion. Painters gave expression to their feelings by painting romantic scenes from the past in warm colors and with much movement and linear contrast.

Michel-Guillaume Jean de Crèvecoeur

Michel-Guillaume Jean de Crèvecoeur (1735–1813) was a Frenchman who migrated to Canada, where he fought under Montcalm at Quebec and later explored in the Great Lakes region. In 1759 he went south to the English colonies, and, following the pattern set by other immigrants, became naturalized, married an American, and became a successful farmer. In 1782 he published a series of essays under the title of Letters From an American Farmer. This work, written as it was by a recent arrival who saw America as a new land and Americans as a new race, is a valuable social document illustrating the transit of European society and civilization across the Atlantic. In reading the letter "What Is an American" from Crèvecoeur's writings note (1) what he had to say about class distinctions in American society, (2) the extent of American resources, (3) the general description of the countryside, (4) the effect of the American environment upon the downtrodden of Europe, (5) the emergence of the American, (6) the influence environment had had on Americans in different parts of the country, (7) the description of the crudeness of life on the frontier, (8) the foreign group he found most successful and his explanation for it, and (9) the note of gratitude on which he concluded the essay.

From: LETTERS FROM AN AMERICAN FARMER

I wish I could be acquainted with the feelings and thoughts which must agitate the heart and present themselves to the mind of an enlightened Englishman, when he first lands on this continent. He must greatly rejoice, that he lived at a time to see this fair country discovered and settled; he must necessarily feel a share of national pride, when he views the chain of settlements which embellishes these extended shores. When he says to himself, this is the work of my countrymen, who, when convulsed by factions, afflicted by a variety of miseries and wants, restless and impatient, took refuge here. They brought along with them their national genius, to which they principally owe what liberty they enjoy, and what substance they possess. Here he sees the industry of his native country, displayed in a new manner, and traces in their works the embrios of all the arts, sciences, and ingenuity which flourish in Europe. Here he beholds fair cities, substantial villages, extensive fields, an immense country filled with decent houses, good roads, orchards, meadows, and bridges, where an hundred years ago all was wild, woody, and uncultivated!

What a train of pleasing ideas this fair spectacle must suggest! it is a prospect which must inspire a good citizen with the most heartfelt pleasure. The difficulty consists in the manner of viewing so extensive a scene. He is arrived on a new continent; a modern society offers itself to his contemplation, different from what he had hitherto seen. It is not composed, as in Europe, of great lords who possess every thing, and of a herd of people who have nothing. Here are no aristocratical families, no courts, no kings, no bishops, no ecclesiastical dominion, no invisible power giving to a few a very visible one; no great manufactures employing thousands, no great refinements of luxury. The rich and the poor are not so far removed from each other as they are in Europe.

Some few towns excepted, we are all tillers

J. Hector St. John, A Farmer in Pennsylvania, *Letters from an American Farmer . . .* , London, 1782, 45–87.

of the earth, from Nova Scotia to West Florida. We are a people of cultivators, scattered over an immense territory, communicating with each other by means of good roads and navigable rivers, united by the silken bands of mild government, all respecting the laws without dreading their power, because they are equitable. We are all animated with the spirit of industry, which is unfettered, and unrestrained, because each person works for himself. If he travels through our rural districts, he views not the hostile castle, and the haughty mansion, contrasted with the clay-built hut and miserable cabbin, where cattle and men help to keep each other warm, and dwell in meanness, smoke and indigence. A pleasing uniformity of decent competence appears throughout our habitations. The meanest of our log-houses is a dry and comfortable habitation. Lawyer or merchant are the fairest titles our towns afford; that of a farmer is the only appellation of the rural inhabitants of our country. It must take some time ere he can reconcile himself to our dictionary, which is but short in words of dignity, and names of honour. There, on a Sunday, he sees a congregation of respectable farmers and their wives, all clad in neat homespun, well mounted, or riding in their own humble waggons. There is not among them an esquire, saving the unlettered magistrate. There he sees a parson as simple as his flock, a farmer who does not riot on the labour of others. We have no princes, for whom we toil, starve, and bleed: we are the most perfect society now existing in the world. Here man is free as he ought to be; nor is this pleasing equality so transitory as many others are. Many ages will not see the shores of our great lakes replenished with inland nations, nor the unknown bounds of North America entirely peopled. Who can tell how far it extends? Who can tell the millions of men whom it will feed and contain? for no European foot has as yet travelled half the extent of this mighty continent!

The next wish of this traveller will be to know whence came all these people? they are a mixture of English, Scotch, Irish, French, Dutch, Germans, and Swedes. From this promiscuous breed, that race now called Americans have arisen. The eastern provinces must indeed be excepted, as being the unmixed descendants of Englishmen. I have heard many wish they had been more intermixed also: for my part, I am no wisher; and think it much better as it has happened. They exhibit a most conspicuous figure in this great and variegated picture; they too enter for a great share in the pleasing perspective displayed in these thirteen provinces. I know it is fashionable to reflect on them; but I respect them for what they have done; for the accuracy and wisdom with which they have settled their territory; for the decency of their manners; for their early love of letters; their ancient college, the first in this hemisphere; for their industry, which to me, who am but a farmer, is the criterion of every thing. There never was a people, situated as they are, who, with so ungrateful a soil, have done more in so short a time. Do you think that the monarchial ingredients which are more prevalent in other governments, have purged them from all foul stains? Their histories assert the contrary.

In this great American asylum, the poor of Europe have by some means met together, and in consequence of various causes; to what purpose should they ask one another, what countrymen they are? Alas, two thirds of them had no country. Can a wretch who wanders about, who works and starves, whose life is a continual scene of sore affliction or pinching penury; can that man call England or any other kingdom his country? A country that had no bread for him, whose fields procured him no harvest, who met with nothing but the frowns of the rich, the severity of the laws, with jails and punishments; who owned not a single foot of the extensive surface of this planet? No! urged by a variety of motives, here they came. Every thing has tended to regenerate them; new laws, a new mode of living, a new social system; here they are become men: in Europe they were as so many useless plants, wanting vegetative mould, and refreshing showers; they withered, and were mowed down by want, hunger, and war: but now, by the power of transplantation, like all other plants, they have taken root and flourished! Formerly they were not numbered in any civil list of their country, except in those of the poor; here they rank as citizens. By what invisible power has this surprizing metamorphosis been performed? By that of the laws and that of their industry. The laws, the indulgent laws, protect them as they arrive, stamping on them the symbol of adoption; they receive ample rewards for their labours; these accumulated rewards procure them lands; those lands confer on them the title of freemen; and to that title every benefit is affixed which men can possibly require. This is the great operation daily performed by our laws. From whence proceed these laws? From our government. Whence that government? It is derived from the original genius and strong desire of the people, ratified and confirmed by government. This is the great chain which links us all, this is the picture which every province exhibits, Nova Scotia excepted. There the crown has done all; either there were no people who had genius, or it was not much attended to: the consequence is, that the province is very thinly inhabited indeed; the power of the crown, in conjunction with the musketos, has prevented men from settling there. Yet some part of it flourished once, and it contained a mild harmless set of people. But for the fault of a few leaders the whole were banished. The greatest political error the crown ever committed in America, was to cut off men from a country which wanted nothing but men.

What attachment can a poor European emigrant have for a country where he had nothing? The knowledge of the language, the love of a few kindred as poor as himself, were the only cords that tied him: his country is now that which gives him land, bread, protection, and consequence: *Ubi panis ibi patria*, is the motto of all emigrants. What then is the American, this new man? He is either an European, or the descendant of an European; hence that strange mixture of blood, which you will find in no other country. I could point out to you a man, whose grandfather was an Englishman, whose wife was Dutch, whose son married a French woman, and whose present four sons have now four wives of different nations. *He* is an American, who, leaving behind him all his ancient prejudices and manners, receives new ones from the new mode of life he has embraced, the new government he obeys, and the new rank he holds. He becomes an American by being received in the broad lap of our great *Alma Mater*.

Here individuals of all nations are melted into a new race of men, whose labours and posterity will one day cause great change in the world. Americans are the western pilgrims, who are carrying along with them that great mass of arts, sciences, vigour, and industry, which began long since in the east; they will finish the great circle. The Americans were once scattered all over Europe; here they are incorporated into one of the finest systems of population which has ever appeared, and which will hereafter become distinct by the power of the different climates they inhabit. The American ought, therefore, to love this country much better than that wherein either he or his forefathers were born. Here the rewards of his industry follow with equal steps the progress of his labour; his labour is founded on the basis of nature, *self-interest;* can it want a stronger allurement? Wives and children, who before in vain demanded of him a morsel of bread, now, fat and frolicsome, gladly help their father to clear those fields whence exuberant crops are to arise to feed and to clothe them all; without any part being claimed, either by a despotic prince, a rich abbot, or a mighty lord. Here religion demands but little of him; a small voluntary salary to the minister, and gratitude to God; can he refuse these? The American is a new man, who acts upon new principles; he must therefore entertain new ideas, and form new opinions. From involuntary idleness, servile dependance, penury, and useless labour, he has passed to toils of a very different nature, rewarded by ample subsistence.—This is an American.

North America is divided into many provinces, forming a large association, scattered along a coast 1,500 miles extent and about 200 wide. This society I would fain examine, at least such as it appears in the middle provinces; if it does not afford that variety of tinges and gradations which may be observed in Europe, we have colours peculiar to ourselves. For instance, it is natural to conceive that those who live near the sea, must be very different from those who live in the woods; the intermediate space will afford a separate and distinct class.

Men are like plants; the goodness and flavour of the fruit proceed from the peculiar soil and exposition in which they grow. We are nothing but what we derive from the air we breathe, the climate we inhabit, the government we obey, the system of religion we profess, and the nature of our employment. Here you will find but few crimes; these have acquired as yet no root among us. I wish I were able to trace all my ideas; if my ignorance prevents me from describing them properly, I hope I shall be able to delineate a few of the outlines, which are all I propose.

Those who live near the sea, feed more on fish than on flesh, and often encounter that boisterous element. This renders them more bold and enterprising; this leads them to neglect the confined occupations of the land. They see and converse with a variety of people; their intercourse with mankind becomes extensive. The sea inspires them with a love of traffic, a desire of transporting produce from one place to another; leads them to a variety of resources, which supply the place of labour. Those who inhabit the middle settlements, by far the most numerous, must be very different; the simple cultivation of the earth purifies them; but the indulgences of the government, the soft remonstrances of religion, the rank of independent freeholders, must necessarily inspire them with sentiments, very little known in Europe among people of the same class. What do I say? Europe has no such class of man; the early knowledge they acquire, the early bargains they make, give them a great degree of sagacity. As freemen, they will be litigious; pride and obstinacy are often the cause of law suits; the nature of our laws and governments may be another. As citizens, it is easy to imagine, that they will carefully read the newspapers, enter into every political disquisition, freely blame or censure governors and others. As farmers, they will be careful and anxious to get as much as they can, because what they get is their own. As northern men, they will love the cheerful cup. As christians, religion curbs them not in their opinions; the general indulgence leaves every one to think for himself in spiritual matters; the laws inspect our actions; our thoughts are left to God. Industry, good living, selfishness, litigiousness, country politics, the pride of freemen, religious indifference, are their characteristics. If you recede

still farther from the sea, you will come into more modern settlements; they exhibit the same strong lineaments, in a ruder appearance. Religion seems to have still less influence, and their manners are less improved.

Now we arrive near the great woods, near the last inhabited districts; there men seem to be placed still farther beyond the reach of government, which in some measure leaves them to themselves. How can it pervade every corner? as they were driven there by misfortunes, necessity of beginnings, desire of acquiring large tracts of land, idleness, frequent want of economy, ancient debts; the reunion of such people does not afford a very pleasing spectacle. When discord, want of unity and friendship—when either drunkenness or idleness prevail in such remote districts—contention, inactivity, and wretchedness must ensue. There are not the same remedies to these evils as in a long established community. The few magistrates they have are in general little better than the rest; they are often in a perfect state of war; that of man against man, sometimes decided by blows, sometimes by means of the law; that of man against every wild inhabitant of these venerable woods, of which they are come to dispossess them. There men appear to be no better than carnivorous animals of a superior rank, living on the flesh of wild animals when they can catch them; and when they are not able, they subsist on the grain.

He who would wish to see America in its proper light, and have a true idea of its feeble beginnings and barbarous rudiments, must visit our extended line of frontiers where the last settlers dwell, and where he may see the first labours of settlement, the mode of clearing the earth, in all their different appearances; where men are wholly left dependent on their native tempers, and on the spur of uncertain industry, which often fails, when not sanctified by the efficacy of a few moral rules. There, remote from the power of example, and check of shame, many families exhibit the most hideous parts of our society. They are a kind of forlorn hope, preceding by ten or twelve years the most respectable army of veterans which come after them. In that space, prosperity will polish some, vice and the law will drive off the rest, who uniting again with others like themselves will recede still farther; making room for more industrious people, who will finish their improvements, convert the log-house into a convenient habitation, and rejoicing that the first heavy labours are finished, will change in a few years that hitherto barbarous country into a fine, fertile, well regulated district.

Such is our progress, such is the march of the Europeans toward the interior parts of this continent. In all societies there are off-casts; this impure part serves as our precursors or pioneers; my father himself was one of that class; but he came upon honest principles, and was therefore one of the few who held fast; by good conduct and temperance, he transmitted to me his fair inheritance, when not above one in fourteen of his contemporaries had the same good fortune.

Forty years ago, this smiling country was thus inhabited; it is now purged, a general decency of manners prevails throughout; and such has been the fate of our best countries.

Exclusive of those general characteristics, each province has its own, founded on the government, climate, mode of husbandry, customs, and peculiarity of circumstances. Europeans submit insensibly to these great powers, and become in the course of a few generations, not only Americans in general, but either Pennsylvanians, Virginians, or provincials under some other name. Whoever traverses the continent, must easily observe those strong differences, which will grow more evident in time. The inhabitants of Canada, Massachusetts, the middle provinces, the southern ones will be as different as their climates; their only points of unity will be those of religion and language. . . . Europe contains hardly any other distinctions but lords and tenants; this fair country alone is settled by freeholders, the possessors of the soil they cultivate, members of the government they obey, and the framers of their own laws, by means of their representatives. This is a thought which you have taught me to cherish; our distance from Europe, far from diminishing, rather adds to our usefulness and consequence as men and subjects. Had our forefathers remained there, they would only have crouded it, and perhaps prolonged those convulsions which had shook it so long. Every industrious European who transports

himself here, may be compared to a sprout growing at the foot of a great tree; it enjoys and draws but a little portion of sap; wrench it from the parent roots, transplant it, and it will become a tree bearing fruit also. Colonists are therefore intitled to the consideration due to the most useful subjects; a hundred families, barely existing in some parts of Scotland, will here in six years, cause an annual exportation of 10,000 bushels of wheat: 100 bushels being but a common quantity for an industrious family to sell, if they cultivate good land. It is here, then, that the idle may be employed, the useless become useful, and the poor become rich: but by riches I do not mean gold and silver; we have but little of those metals; I mean a better sort of wealth, cleared lands, cattle, good houses, good clothes, and an increase of people to enjoy them.

There is no wonder that this country has so many charms, and presents to Europeans so many temptations to remain in it. A traveller in Europe becomes a stranger as soon as he quits his own kingdom; but it is otherwise here. We know, properly speaking, no strangers; this is every person's country; the variety of our soils, situations, climates, governments, and produce, hath something which must please every body. No sooner does an European arrive, no matter of what condition, than his eyes are opened upon the fair prospects; he hears his language spoke, he retraces many of his own country manners, he perpetually hears the names of families and towns with which he is acquainted; he sees happiness and prosperity in all places disseminated; he meets with hospitality, kindness, and plenty every where: he beholds hardly any poor, he seldom hears of punishments and executions; and he wonders at the elegance of our towns, those miracles of industry and freedom. He cannot admire enough our rural districts, our convenient roads, good taverns, and our many accommodations; he involuntarily loves a country where every thing is so lovely. When in England, he was a mere Englishman; here he stands on a larger portion of the globe, not less than its fourth part, and may see the productions of the north, in iron and naval stores; the provisions of Ireland, the grain of Egypt, the indigo, the rice of China. He does not find, as in Europe, a crouded society, where every place is over-stocked; he does not feel that perpetual collision of parties, that difficulty of beginning, that contention which oversets so many.

There is room for every body in America: has he any particular talent, or industry? he exerts it in order to procure a livelihood, and it succeeds. Is he a merchant? the avenues of trade are infinite; is he eminent in any respect? he will be employed and respected. Does he love a country life? pleasant farms present themselves; he may purchase what he wants, and thereby become an American farmer. Is he a labourer, sober and industrious; he need not go many miles, nor receive many informations before he will be hired, well fed at the table of his employer, and paid four or five times more than he can get in Europe. Does he want uncultivated lands? thousands of acres present themselves, which he may purchase cheap. Whatever be his talents or inclinations, if they are moderate, he may satisfy them. I do not mean, that every one who comes will grow rich in a little time; no, but he may procure an easy, decent maintenance, by his industry. Instead of starving, he will be fed; instead of being idle, he will have employment; and these are riches enough for such men as come over here. The rich stay in Europe; it is only the middling and poor that emigrate. Would you wish to travel in independent idleness, from north to south, you will find easy access, and the most chearful reception at every house; society without ostentation, good cheer without pride, and every decent diversion which the country affords, with little expense. It is no wonder that the European who has lived here a few years is desirous to remain; Europe, with all its pomp, is not to be compared to this continent, for men of middle stations or labourers.

An European, when he first arrives, seems limited in his intentions, as well as in his views; but he very suddenly alters his scale; two hundred miles formerly appeared a very great distance; it is now but a trifle; he no sooner breathes our air than he forms schemes, and embarks in designs he never would have thought of in his own country. There the plentitude of society confines many useful ideas, and often extinguishes the most laudable schemes which here ripen into maturity. Thus Europeans become Americans.

But how is this accomplished in that croud of low, indigent people, who flock here every year from all parts of Europe? I will tell you; they no sooner arrive than they immediately feel the good effects of that plenty of provisions we possess: they fare on our best food, and are kindly entertained; their talents, character, and peculiar industry are immediately enquired into; they find countrymen every where disseminated, let them come from whatever part of Europe.

Let me select one as an epitome of the rest; he is hired, he goes to work, and works moderately; instead of being employed by a haughty person, he finds himself with his equal, placed at the substantial table of the farmer, or else at an inferior one as good; his wages are high, his bed is not like that bed of sorrow on which he used to lie: if he behaves with propriety, and is faithful, he is caressed, and becomes, as it were, a member of the family. He begins to feel the effects of a sort of resurrection; hitherto he had not lived, but simply vegetated; he now feels himself a man, because he is treated as such; the laws of his own country had overlooked him in his insignificancy; the laws of this cover him with their mantle. Judge what an alteration there must arise in the mind and thoughts of this man; he begins to forget his former servitude and dependence; his heart involuntarily swells and glows; this first swell inspires him with those new thoughts which constitute an American. What love can he entertain for a country where his existence was a burden to him! if he is a generous good man, the love of his new adoptive parent, will sink deep into his heart. He looks around, and sees many a prosperous person, who but a few years before was as poor as himself. This encourages him much; he begins to form some little scheme, the first, alas, he ever formed in his life. If he is wise, he thus spends two or three years, in which time he acquires knowledge, the use of tools, the modes of working the lands, felling trees, &c. This prepares the foundation of a good name, the most useful acquisition he can make. He is encouraged; he has gained friends; he is advised and directed; he feels bold; he purchases some land; he gives all the money he has brought over, as well as what he has earned, and trusts to the God of harvests for the discharge of the rest. His good name procures him credit; he is now possessed of the deed, conveying to him and his posterity the fee simple, and absolute property of two hundred acres of land, situated on such a river. What an epocha in this man's life! He is become a freeholder, from perhaps a German boor—he is now an American, a Pennsylvanian. He is naturalized; his name is enrolled with those of the other citizens of the province. Instead of being a vagrant, he has a place of residence; he is called the inhabitant of such a county, or of such a district, and for the first time in his life counts for something; for hitherto he had been a cypher. I only repeat what I have heard many say, and no wonder their hearts should glow, and be agitated with a multitude of feelings, not easy to describe. From nothing to start into being; from a servant to the rank of master; from being the slave of some despotic prince, to become a free man, invested with lands, to which every municipal blessing is annexed! What a change indeed! It is in consequence of that change, that he becomes an American.

This great metamorphosis has a double effect; it extinguishes all his European prejudices; he forgets that mechanism of subordination, that servility of disposition which poverty had taught him; and sometimes he is apt to forget it too much, often passing from one extreme to the other. If he is a good man, he forms schemes of future prosperity; he proposes to educate his children better than he has been educated himself; he thinks of future modes of conduct, feels an ardour to labour he never felt before. Pride steps in, and leads him to every thing that the laws do not forbid: he respects them; with a heart-felt gratitude he looks toward that government from whose wisdom all his new felicity is derived, and under whose wings and protection he now lives. These reflexions constitute him the good man and the good subject.

Ye poor Europeans, ye, who sweat and work for the great—ye, who are obliged to give so many sheaves to the church, so many to your lords, so many to your government, and have hardly any left for yourselves—ye, who are held in less estimation than favourite hunters or useless lap-dogs—ye, who only breathe the air of nature, because it cannot be withheld from you; it is here that ye can conceive the possibility of those feelings I have been describing; it is here the laws of naturalization invite every one to partake of our great labours and felicity, to till unrented, untaxed lands!

Many, corrupted beyond the power of amendment, have brought with them all their vices, and, disregarding the advantages held out to them, have gone on in their former career of iniquity, until they have been overtaken and punished by our laws. It is not every emigrant who succeeds; no, it is only the sober, the honest, and industrious: happy those, to whom this transition has served as a powerful spur to labour, to prosperity, and to the good establishment of children, born in the days of their poverty: and who had no other portion to expect, but the rags of their parents, had it not been for their happy emigration. Others again, have been led astray by this enchanting scene; their new pride, instead of leading them to the fields, has kept them in idleness; the idea of possessing lands is all that satisfies them—though surrounded with fertility, they have mouldered away their time in inactivity, misinformed husbandry, and ineffectual endeavours. How much wiser, in general, the honest Germans than almost all other Europeans; they hire themselves to some of their wealthy landsmen, and in that apprenticeship learn every thing that is necessary. They attentively consider the prosperous industry of others, which imprints on their minds a strong desire of possessing the same advantages. This forcible idea never quits them; they launch forth, and by dint of sobriety, rigid parsimony, and the most persevering industry, they commonly succeed. Their astonishment at their first arrival from Germany is very great; it is to them a dream; the contrast must be very powerful indeed; they observe their countrymen flourishing in every place; they travel through whole counties where not a word of English is spoken; and in the names and the language of the people they retrace Germany. They have been an useful acquisition to this continent, and to Pennsylvania in particular; to them it owes some share of its prosperity; to their mechanical knowledge and patience, it owes the finest mills in all America, the best teams of horses, and many other advantages. The recollection of their former poverty and slavery never quits them as long as they live.

The Scotch and the Irish might have lived in their own country perhaps as poor; but enjoying more civil advantages, the effects of their new situation do not strike them so forcibly, nor has it so lasting an effect. From whence the difference arises, I know not; but out of twelve families of emigrants of each country, generally seven Scotch will succeed, nine German, and four Irish. The Scotch are frugal and laborious; but their wives cannot work so hard as the German women, who, on the contrary, vie with their husbands, and often share with them the most severe toils of the field, which they understand better. They have therefore nothing to struggle against, but the common casualties of nature. The Irish do not prosper so well; they love to drink and to quarrel; they are litigious, and soon take to the gun, which is the ruin of every thing; they seem, beside, to labour under a greater degree of ignorance in husbandry than the others; perhaps it is that their industry had less scope, and was less exercised at home. I have heard many relate, how the land was parcelled out in that kingdom; their ancient conquest has been a great detriment to them, by over-setting their landed property. The lands, possessed by a few, are leased down *ad infinitum;* and the occupiers often pay five guineas an acre. The poor are worse lodged there than any where else in Europe; their potatoes, which are easily raised, are perhaps an inducement to laziness: their wages are too low, and their whiskey too cheap.

There is no tracing observations of this kind, without making at the same time very great allowances; as there are everywhere to be found a great many exceptions. The Irish themselves, from different parts of that kingdom are very different. It is difficult to account for this surprising locality; one would think on so small an island all Irishmen must be alike; yet it is not so; they are different in their aptitude to, and in their love of labour.

The Scotch, on the contrary, are all industrious and saving; they want nothing more than a field to exert themselves in; and they are commonly sure of succeeding. The only difficulty they labour under is, that technical American knowledge, which requires some time to obtain; it is not easy for those who seldom saw a tree, to conceive how it is to be felled, cut up, and split into rails and posts.

. . . After a foreigner from any part of Europe is arrived, and become a citizen; let him devoutly listen to the voice of our great parent, which says to him, "Welcome to my shores, distressed European; bless the hour in which thou didst see my verdant fields, my fair navigable rivers, and my green mountains!— If thou wilt work, I have bread for thee; if thou wilt be honest, sober and industrious, I have greater rewards to confer on thee—ease and independence. I will give thee fields to feed and clothe thee; a comfortable fire-side to sit by, and tell thy children by what means thou hast prospered; and a decent bed to repose on. I shall endow thee, beside, with the immunities of a freeman. If thou wilt carefully educate thy children, teach them gratitude to God, and reverence to that government, that philanthropic government, which has collected here so many men and made them happy, I will also provide for thy progeny: and to every good man this ought to be the most holy, the most powerful, the most earnest wish he can possibly form, as well as the most consolatory prospect when he dies.

"Go thou, and work and till; thou shalt prosper, provided thou be just, grateful and industrious."

Benjamin Franklin

Benjamin Franklin (1706–1790) is remembered by most Americans as a statesman, scientist, and philanthropist, but it should also be noted that he was a true son of the Enlightenment and practiced nearly all the ideals of that age. He endeavored to use reason at all times; he had a passion for progress; his humanitarian deeds were legion; and he was as cosmopolitan as any figure of his century, equally at home in Philadelphia, London, and Paris. For superstition and tradition he had little sympathy, while on the other hand, he was an ardent supporter of experimentation and change. In 1771, Franklin began his famous Autobiography as a helpful guide to his son, but he did not complete it until many years later, and then only shortly before his death in 1790. This work is not only considered to be one of the best of all autobiographies, but it is also highly regarded as an excellent personal documentation of the American version of the Age of the Enlightenment. In reading the following selections from Franklin's Autobiography note (1) the clear and readable style with which he wrote, (2) the discourse on his ancestry, (3) the great works which he read as a boy, (4) men of the Enlightenment who influenced him, (5) the nature of his early religious training and subsequent religious beliefs, (6) his numerous efforts to improve society, (7) the method Franklin used to achieve his own moral perfection, (8) the devices he used to instruct society, (9) his humanitarian interests, (10) his use of the scientific method and the contributions he made to the advance of scientific knowledge, and (11) evidences of Franklin's cosmopolitanism.

From: THE AUTOBIOGRAPHY

TWYFORD, at the Bishop of St. Asaph's, 1771.

DEAR SON: I have ever had pleasure in obtaining any little anecdotes of my ancestors. You may remember the inquiries I made among the remains of my relations when you were with me in England, and the journey I undertook for that purpose. Imagining it may be equally agreeable to you to know the circumstances of my life, many of which you are yet unacquainted with, and expecting the enjoyment of a week's uninterrupted leisure in my present country retirement, I sit down to write them for you. To which I have besides some other inducements. Having emerged from the poverty and obscurity in which I was born and bred, to a state of affluence and some degree of reputation in the world, and having gone so far through life with a considerable share of felicity, the conducing means I made use of, which with the blessing of God so well succeeded, my posterity may like to know, as they may find some of them suitable to their own situations, and therefore fit to be imitated.

That felicity, when I reflected on it, has induced me sometimes to say, that were it offered to my choice, I should have no objection to a

Adapted from Benjamin Franklin, *Memoirs of Benjamin Franklin*, 2 vols., Philadelphia, 1840, I, 1–3; 5; 7; 23–24; 26–28; 32–39; 41–44; 46–48; 50–51; 62–63.

repetition of the same life from its beginning, only asking the advantages authors have in a second edition to correct some faults of the first. So I might, besides correcting the faults, change some sinister accidents and events of it for others more favourable. But though this were denied, I should still accept the offer. Since such a repetition is not to be expected, the next thing most like living one's life over again seems to be a recollection of that life, and to make that recollection as durable as possible by putting it down in writing.

Hereby, too, I shall indulge the inclination so natural in old men, to be talking of themselves and their own past actions; and I shall indulge it without being tiresome to others, who, through respect to age, might conceive themselves obliged to give a hearing, since this may be read or not as any one pleases. And, lastly (I may as well confess it, since my denial of it will be believed by nobody), perhaps I shall a good deal gratify my own *vanity*. Indeed, I scarce ever heard or saw the introductory words, "*Without vanity I may say,*" etc., but some vain thing immediately followed. Most people dislike vanity in others, whatever share they have of it themselves; but I give it fair quarter wherever I meet with it, being persuaded that it is often productive of good to the possessor, and to others that are within his sphere of action; and therefore, in many cases, it would not be altogether absurd if a man were to thank God for his vanity among the other comforts of life.

And now I speak of thanking God, I desire with all humility to acknowledge that I owe the mentioned happiness of my past life to His kind providence, which lead me to the means I used and gave them success. My belief of this induces me to *hope*, though I must not *presume*, that the same goodness will still be exercised toward me, in continuing that happiness, or enabling me to bear a fatal reverse, which I may experience as others have done; the complexion of my future fortune being known to Him only in whose power it is to bless to us even our afflictions.

The notes one of my uncles (who had the same kind of curiosity in collecting family anecdotes) once put into my hands, furnished me with several particulars relating to our ances-tors. From these notes I learned that the family had lived in the same village, Ecton, in Northamptonshire, for three hundred years, and how much longer he knew not (perhaps from the time when the name of Franklin, that before was the name of an order of people, was assumed by them as a surname when others took surnames all over the kingdom), on a free-hold of about thirty acres, aided by the smith's business, which had continued in the family till his time, the eldest son being always bred to that business; a custom which he and my father followed as to their eldest sons. When I searched the registers at Ecton, I found an account of their births, marriages and burials from the year 1555 only, there being no registers kept in that parish at any time preceding. By that register I perceived that I was the youngest son of the youngest son for five generations back. My grandfather Thomas, who was born in 1598, lived at Ecton till he grew too old to follow business longer, when he went to live with his son John, a dyer at Banbury, in Oxfordshire, with whom my father served an apprenticeship. There my grandfather died and lies buried. We saw his gravestone in 1758. His eldest son Thomas lived in the house at Ecton, and left it with the land to his only child, a daughter, who, with her husband, one Fisher, of Wellingborough, sold it to Mr. Isted, now lord of the manor there. My grandfather had four sons that grew up, viz.: Thomas, John, Benjamin, and Josiah. . . .

Josiah, my father, married young, and carried his wife with three children into New England, about 1682. The conventicles having been forbidden by law, and frequently disturbed, induced some considerable men of his acquaintance to remove to that country, and he was prevailed with to accompany them thither, where they expected to enjoy their mode of religion with freedom. By the same wife he had four children more born there, and by a second wife ten more, in all seventeen; of which I remember thirteen sitting at one time at his table, who all grew up to be men and women, and married; I was the youngest son, and the youngest child but two, and was born in Boston, New England. My mother, the second wife, was Abiah Folger, daughter of Peter

Folger, one of the first settlers of New England, of whom honourable mention is made by Cotton Mather, in his church history of that country, entitled *Magnalia Christi Americana*, as "A godly, learned Englishman," if I remember the words rightly. I have heard that he wrote sundry small occasional pieces, but only one of them was printed, which I saw now many years since. It was written in 1675, in the home-spun verse of that time and people, and addressed to those then concerned in the government there. It was in favor of liberty of conscience, and in behalf of the Baptists, Quakers, and other sectaries that had been under persecution, ascribing the Indian wars, and other distresses that had befallen the country, to that persecution, as so many judgments of God to punish so heinous an offense, and exhorting a repeal of those uncharitable laws. The whole appeared to me as written with a good deal of decent plainness and manly freedom. The six concluding lines I remember, though I have forgotten the two first of the stanza; but the purport of them was, that his censures proceeded from good-will, and, therefore, he would be known to be the author.

"Because to be a libeller (says he)
    I hate it with my heart;
From Sherburne town, where now I dwell
    My name I do put here;
Without offense your real friend,
    It is Peter Folgier."

. . . .

From a child I was fond of reading, and all the little money that came into my hands was ever laid out in books. Pleased with the *Pilgrim's Progress*, my first collection was of John Bunyan's works in separate little volumes. I afterward sold them to enable me to buy R. Burton's *Historical Collections;* they were small chapmen's books, and cheap, 40 or 50 in all. My father's little library consisted chiefly of books in polemic divinity, most of which I read, and have since often regretted that, at a time when I had such a thirst for knowledge, more proper books had not fallen in my way, since it was now resolved I should not be a clergyman. Plutarch's *Lives* there was in which I read abundantly, and I still think that time spent to great advantage. There was also a

book of De Foe's, called an *Essay on Projects,* and another of Dr. Mather's called *Essays to do Good,* which perhaps gave me a turn of thinking that had an influence on some of the principal future events of my life. . . .

And now it was that, being on some occasion made asham'd of my ignorance in figures, which I had twice failed in learning when at school, I took Cocker's book of Arthimetick, and went through the whole by myself with great ease. I also read Seller's and Shermy's books of Navigation, and became acquainted with the little geometry they contain; but never proceeded far in that science. And I read about this time Locke *On Human Understanding,* and the *Art of Thinking,* by Messrs. du Port Royal.

While I was intent on improving my language, I met with an English grammar (I think it was Greenwood's), at the end of which there were two little sketches of the arts of rhetoric and logic, the latter finishing with a specimen of a dispute in the Socratic method; and soon after I procur'd Xenophon's *Memorable Things of Socrates,* wherein there are many instances of the same method. I was charm'd with it, adopted it, dropt my abrupt contradiction and positive argumentation, and put on the humble inquirer and doubter. And being then, from reading Shaftesbury and Collins, become a real doubter in many points of our religious doctrine, I found this method safest for myself and very embarrassing to those against whom I used it; therefore I took a delight in it, practis'd it continually, and grew very artful and expert in drawing people, even of superior knowledge, into concessions, the consequences of which they did not foresee, entangling them in difficulties out of which they could not extricate themselves, and so obtaining victories that neither myself nor my cause always deserved. I continu'd this method some few years, but gradually left it, retaining only the habit of expressing myself in terms of modest diffidence; never using, when I advanced anything that may possibly be disputed, the words *certainly, undoubtedly,* or any others that gave the air of positiveness to an opinion; but rather say, I conceive or apprehend a thing to be so and so; it appears to me, or I *should think it so or so,* for such and such reasons; or *I imagine it to be so,* or *it is so, if I am not mistaken.* This habit, I believe, has been of great advantage to me when I have had occasion to inculcate my opinions, and persuade men into measures that I have been from time to time engag'd in promoting; and, as the chief ends of conversation are to *inform* or to be *informed,* to *please* or to *persuade,* I wish well-meaning, sensible men would not lessen their power of doing good by a positive, assuming manner, that seldom fails to disgust, tends to create opposition, and to defeat everyone of those purposes for which speech was given to us, to wit, giving or receiving information or pleasure. For, if you would inform, a positive and dogmatical manner in advancing your sentiments may provoke contradiction and prevent a candid attention. If you wish information and improvement from the knowledge of others, and yet at the same time express yourself as firmly fix'd in your present opinions, modest, sensible men, who do not love disputation, will probably leave you undisturbed in the possession of your error. And by such a manner, you can seldom hope to recommend yourself in *pleasing* your hearers, or to persuade those whose concurrence you desire. . . .

Before I enter upon my public appearance in business, it may be well to let you know the then state of my mind with regard to my principles and morals, that you may see how far those influenc'd the future events of my life. My parents had early given me religious impressions, and brought me through my childhood piously in the Dissenting way. But I was scarce fifteen, when, after doubting by turns of several points, as I found them disputed in the different books I read, I began to doubt of Revelation itself. Some books against Deism fell into my hands; they were said to be the substance of sermons preached at Boyle's Lectures. It happened that they wrought an effect on me quite contrary to what was intended by them; for the arguments of the Deists, which were quoted to be refuted, appeared to me much stronger than the refutations; in short, I soon became a thorough Deist. My arguments perverted some others, particularly Collins and Ralph; but, each of them having

afterwards wrong'd me greatly without the least compunction, and recollecting Keith's conduct towards me (who was another free-thinker), and my own towards Vernon and Miss Read, which at times gave me great trouble, I began to suspect that this doctrine, tho' it might be true, was not very useful. My London pamphlet, which had for its motto these lines of Dryden:

"Whatever is is right. Though purblind man
See but a part o' the chain, the nearest link:
His eyes not carrying to the equal beam,
That poises all above;"

and from the attributes of God, his infinite wisdom, goodness and power, concluded that nothing could possibly be wrong in the world, and that vice and virtue were empty distinctions, no such things existing, appear'd now not so clever a performance as I once thought it; and I doubted whether some error had not insinuated itself unperceiv'd into my argument, so as to infect all that follow'd, as is common in metaphysical reasonings.

I grew convinc'd that *truth, sincerity* and *integrity* in dealings between man and man were of the utmost importance to the felicity of life; and I form'd written resolutions, which still remain in my journal book, to practice them ever while I lived. Revelation had indeed no weight with me, as such; but I entertain'd an opinion that, though certain actions might not be bad *because* they were forbidden by it, or good *because* it commanded them, yet probably these actions might be forbidden *because* they were bad for us, or commanded *because* they were beneficial to us, in their own natures, all the circumstances of things considered. And this persuasion, with the kind hand of Providence, or some guardian angel, or accidental favorable circumstances and situations, or all together, preserved me, thro' this dangerous time of youth, and the hazardous situations I was sometimes in among strangers, remote from the eye and advice of my father, without any willful gross immorality or injustice, that might have been expected from my want of religion. I say willful, because the instances I have mentioned had something of *necessity* in them, from my youth, inexperience, and the knavery of others. I had therefore a tolerable character to begin the world with; I value it properly, and determin'd to preserve it. . . .

About this time [1729] there was a cry among the people for more paper money, only fifteen thousand pounds being extant in the province, and that soon to be sunk. The wealthy inhabitants oppos'd any addition, being against all paper currency, from an apprehension that it would depreciate, as it had done in New England, to the prejudice of all creditors. We had discuss'd this point in our Junto, where I was on the side of an addition, being persuaded that the first small sum struck in 1723 had done much good by increasing the trade, employment, and number of inhabitants in the province, since I now saw all the old houses inhabited, and many new ones building: whereas I remembered well, that when I first walk'd about the streets of Philadelphia, eating my roll, I saw most of the houses in Walnut Street, between Second and Front streets, with bills on their doors, "To be let"; and many likewise in Chestnut Street and other streets, which made me then think the inhabitants of the city were deserting it one after another.

Our debates possess'd me so fully of the subject, that I wrote and printed an anonymous pamphlet on it, entitled *"The Nature and Necessity of a Paper Currency."* It was well receiv'd by the common people in general; but the rich men dislik'd it, for it increas'd and strengthen'd the clamour for more money, and they happening to have no writers among them that were able to answer it, their opposition slacken'd, and the point was carried by a majority in the House. My friends there, who conceiv'd I had been of some service, thought fit to reward me by employing me in printing the money; a very profitable jobb and a great help to me. This was another advantage gain'd by my being able to write.

The utility of this currency became by time and experience so evident as never afterwards to be much disputed; so that it grew soon to fifty-five thousand pounds, and in 1739 to eighty thousand pounds, since which it arose during war to upwards of three hundred and fifty thousand pounds, trade, building, and inhabitants all the while increasing, tho' I now think there are limits beyond which the quantity may be hurtful.

I soon after obtain'd, thro' my friend Hamilton, the printing of the Newcastle paper money, another profitable jobb as I then thought it; small things appearing great to those in small circumstances; and these, to me, were really great advantages, as they were great encouragements. He procured for me, also, the printing of the laws and notes of that government, which continu'd in my hands as long as I follow'd the business.

I now open'd a little stationer's shop. I had in it blanks of all sorts, the correctest that ever appear'd among us, being assisted in that by my friend Breintnal. I had also paper, parchment, chapmen's books, etc. One Whitemash, a compositor I had known in London, an excellent workman, now came to me, and work'd with me constantly and diligently; and I took an apprentice, the son of Aquila Rose.

I began now gradually to pay off the debt I was under for the printing-house. In order to secure my credit and character as a tradesman, I took care not only to be in *reality* industrious and frugal, but to avoid all appearances to the contrary. I drest plainly; I was seen at no places of idle diversion. I never went out a fishing or shooting; a book, indeed, sometimes debauch'd me from my work, but that was seldom, snug, and gave no scandal; and, to show that I was not above my business, I sometimes brought home the paper I purchas'd at the stores thro' the streets on a wheelbarrow. Thus being esteem'd an industrious, thriving young man, and paying duly for what I bought, the merchants who imported stationery solicited my custom; others proposed supplying me with books, and I went on swimmingly. In the mean time, Keimer's credit and business declining daily, he was at last forc'd to sell his printing-house to satisfy his creditors. He went to Barbadoes, and there lived some years in very poor circumstances. . . .

I had hitherto continu'd to board with Godfrey, who lived in part of my house with his wife and children, and had one side of the shop for his glazier's business, tho' he worked little, being always absorbed in his mathematics. Mrs. Godfrey projected a match for me with a relation's daughter, took opportunities of bringing us often together, till a serious courtship on my part ensu'd, the girl being in herself very deserving. The old folks encourag'd me by continual invitations to supper, and by leaving us together, till at length it was time to explain. Mrs. Godfrey manag'd our little treaty. I let her know that I expected as much money with their daughter as would pay off my remaining debt for the printing-house, which I believe was not then above a hundred pounds. She brought me word they had no such sum to spare; I said they might mortgage their house in the loan-office. The answer to this, after some days, was, that they did not approve the match; that, on inquiry of Bradford, they had been informed the printing business was not a profitable one; the types would soon be worn out, and more wanted; that S. Keimer and D. Harry had failed one after the other, and I should probably soon follow them; and, therefore, I was forbidden the house, and the daughter shut up.

Whether this was a real change of sentiment or only artifice, on a supposition of our being too far engaged in affection to retract, and therefore that we should steal a marriage, which would leave them at liberty to give or withhold what they pleas'd, I know not; but I suspected the latter, resented it, and went no more. Mrs. Godfrey brought me afterward some more favorable accounts of their disposition, and would have drawn me on again; but I declared absolutely my resolution to have nothing more to do with that family. This was resented by the Godfrey's; we differ'd, and they removed, leaving me the whole house, and I resolved to take no more inmates.

But this affair having turned my thoughts to marriage, I look'd around me and made overtures of acquaintance in other places; but soon found that, the business of a printer being generally thought a poor one, I was not to expect money with a wife, unless with such a one as I should not otherwise think agreeable. In the meantime, that hard-to-be-governed passion of youth hurried me frequently into intrigues with low women that fell in my way, which were attended with some expense and great inconvenience, besides a continual risque to my health by a distemper which of all things

I dreaded, though by great good luck I escaped it. A friendly correspondence as neighbors and old acquaintances had continued between me and Mrs. Read's family, who all had a regard for me from the time of my first lodging in their house. I was often invited there and consulted in their affairs, wherein I sometimes was of service. I piti'd poor Miss Read's unfortunate situation, who was generally dejected, seldom cheerful, and avoided company. I considered my giddiness and inconstancy when in London as in a great degree the cause of her unhappiness, tho' the mother was good enough to think the fault more her own than mine, as she had prevented our marrying before I went thither, and persuaded the other match in my absence. Our mutual affection was revived, but there were now great objections to our union. The match was indeed looked upon as invalid, a preceding wife being said to be living in England; but this could not easily be prov'd, because of the distance; and, tho' there was a report of his death, it was not certain. Then, tho' it should be true, he had left many debts, which his successor might be call'd upon to pay. We ventured, however, over all these difficulties, and I took her to wife, September 1st, 1730. None of the inconveniences happened that we had apprehended; she proved a good and faithful helpmate, assisted me much by attending the shop; we throve together, and have ever mutually endeavor'd to make each other happy. Thus I corrected that great *erratum* as well as I could.

About this time, our club meeting, not at a tavern, but in a little room of Mr. Grace's, set apart for that purpose, a proposition was made by me, that, since our books were often referr'd to in our disquisitions upon the queries, it might be convenient to us to have them altogether where we met, that upon occasion they might be consulted; and by thus clubbing our books to a common library, we should, while we lik'd to keep them together, have each of us the advantage of using the books of all the other members, which would be nearly as beneficial as if each owned the whole.

It was lik'd and agreed to, and we fill'd one end of the room with such books as we could best spare. The number was not so great as we expected; and tho' they had been of great use, yet some inconveniences occurring for want of due care of them, the collection, after about a year, was separated, and each took his books home again.

And now I set on foot my first project of a public nature, that for a subscription library. I drew up the proposals, got them put into form by our great scrivener, Brockden, and, by the help of my friends in the Junto, procured fifty subscribers of forty shillings each to begin with, and ten shillings a year for fifty years, the term our company was to continue. We afterwards obtain'd a charter, the company being increased to one hundred: this was the mother of all the North American subscription libraries, now so numerous. It is become a great thing itself, and continually increasing. These libraries have improved the general conversation of the Americans, made the common tradesmen and farmers as intelligent as most gentlemen from other countries, and perhaps have contributed in some degree to the stand so generally made throughout the colonies in defence of their privileges. . . .

This library afforded me the means of improvement by constant study, for which I set apart an hour or two each day, and thus repair'd in some degree the loss of the learned education my father once intended for me. Reading was the only amusement I allow'd myself. I spent no time in taverns, games, or frolicks of any kind; and my industry in my business continu'd as indefatigable as it was necessary. I was indebted for my printing-house; I had a young family coming on to be educated, and I had to contend with for business two printers, who were established in the place before me. My circumstances, however, grew daily easier. My original habits of frugality continuing, and my father having, among his instructions to me when a boy, frequently repeated a proverb of Solomon, "Seest thou a man diligent in his calling, he shall stand before kings, he shall not stand before mean men," I from thence considered industry as a means of obtaining wealth and distinction, which encourag'd me, tho' I did not think that I should ever literally *stand before kings*, which, however, has since happened; for I have stood before *five*, and even had the hon-

our of sitting down with one, the King of Denmark, to dinner.

We have an English proverb that says, *"He that would thrive, must ask his wife."* It was lucky for me that I had one as much dispos'd to industry and frugality as myself. She assisted me cheerfully in my business, folding and stitching pamphlets, tending shop, purchasing old linen rags for the paper-makers, etc., etc. We kept no idle servants, our table was plain and simple, our furniture of the cheapest. For instance, my breakfast was a long time bread and milk (no tea), and I ate it out of a twopenny earthen porringer, with a pewter spoon. But mark how luxury will enter families, and make a progress, in spite of principle: being call'd one morning to breakfast, I found it in a China bowl, with a spoon of silver! They had been bought for me without my knowledge by my wife, and had cost her the enormous sum of three-and-twenty shillings, for which she had no other excuse or apology to make, but that she thought *her* husband deserv'd a silver spoon and China bowl as well as any of his neighbors. This was the first appearance of plate and China in our house, which afterward, in a course of years, as our wealth increas'd, augmented gradually to several hundred pounds in value.

I had been religiously educated as a Presbyterian; and tho' some of the dogmas of that persuasion, such as *the eternal decrees of God, election, reprobation, etc.*, appeared to me unintelligible, others doubtful, and I early absented myself from the public assemblies of the sect, Sunday being my studying day, I never was without some religious principles. I never doubted, for instance, the existence of the Deity; that he made the world, and govern'd it by his Providence; that the most acceptable service of God was the doing good to man; that our souls are immortal; and that all crime will be punished, and virtue rewarded, either here or hereafter. These I esteem'd the essentials of every religion; and, being to be found in all the religions we had in our country, I respected them all, tho' with different degrees of respect, as I found them more or less mix'd with other articles, which, without any tendency to inspire, promote, or confirm morality, serv'd principally to divide us, and make us unfriendly to one another. This respect to all, with an opinion that the worst had some good effects, induc'd me to avoid all discourse that might tend to lessen the good opinion another might have of his own religion; and as our province increas'd in people, and new places of worship were continually wanted, and generally erected by voluntary contribution, my mite for such purpose, whatever might be the sect, was never refused.

Tho' I seldom attended any public worship, I had still an opinion of its propriety, and of its utility when rightly conducted, and I regularly paid my annual subscription for the support of the only Presbyterian minister or meeting we had in Philadelphia. He us'd to visit me sometimes as a friend, and admonish me to attend his administrations, and I was now and then prevail'd on to do so, once for five Sundays successively. Had he been in my opinion a good preacher, perhaps I might have continued, notwithstanding the occasion I had for the Sunday's leisure in my course of study; but his discourses were chiefly either polemic arguments, or explications of the peculiar doctrines of our sect, and were all to me very dry, uninteresting, and unedifying, since not a single moral principle was inculcated or enforc'd, their aim seeming to be rather to make us Presbyterians than good citizens.

At length he took for his text that verse of the fourth chapter of Philippians, *"Finally, brethren, whatsoever things are true, honest, just, pure, lovely, or of good report, if there be any virtue, or any praise, think on these things."* And I imagin'd, in a sermon on such a text, we could not miss of having some morality. But he confin'd himself to five points only, as meant by the apostle, viz.: 1. Keeping holy the Sabbath day. 2. Being diligent in reading the holy Scriptures. 3. Attending duly the publick worship. 4. Partaking of the Sacrament. 5. Paying a due respect to God's ministers. These might be all good things; but, as they were not the kind of good things that I expected from that text, I despaired of ever meeting with them from any other, was disgusted and attended his preaching no more. I had some years before compos'd a little Liturgy, or form of prayer, for my own private use (viz., in 1728), entitled, *Articles of Belief and Acts of Religion.* I re-

turn'd to the use of this, and went no more to the public assemblies. My conduct might be blameable, but I leave it, without attempting further to excuse it; my present purpose being to relate facts, and not to make apologies for them.

It was about this time I conceiv'd the bold and arduous project of arriving at moral perfection. I wish'd to live without committing any fault at any time; I would conquer all that either natural inclination, custom, or company might lead me into. As I knew, or thought I knew, what was right and wrong, I did not see why I might not always do the one and avoid the other. But I soon found I had undertaken a task of more difficulty than I had imagined. While my care was employ'd in guarding against one fault, I was often surprised by another; habit took the advantage of inattention; inclination was sometimes too strong for reason. I concluded, at length, that the mere speculative conviction that it was our interest to be completely virtuous, was not sufficient to prevent our slipping; and that the contrary habits must be broken, and good ones acquired and established, before we can have any dependence on a steady, uniform rectitude of conduct. For this purpose I therefore contrived the following method.

In the various enumerations of the moral virtues I had met with in my reading, I found the catalogue more or less numerous, as different writers included more or fewer ideas under the same name. Temperance, for example, was by some confined to eating and drinking, while by others it was extended to mean the moderating every other pleasure, appetite, inclination, or passion, bodily or mental, even to our avarice and ambition. I propos'd to myself, for the sake of clearness, to use rather more names, with fewer ideas annex'd to each, than a few names with more ideas; and I included under thirteen names of virtues all that at that time occurr'd to me as necessary or desirable, and annexed to each a short precept, which fully express'd the extent I gave to its meaning. These names of virtues, with their precepts, were:

1. TEMPERANCE.
Eat not to dulness; drink not to elevation.

2. SILENCE.

Speak not but what may benefit others or yourself; avoid trifling conversation.

3. ORDER.

Let all your things have their places; let each part of your business have its time.

4. RESOLUTION.

Resolve to perform what you ought; perform without fail what you resolve.

5. FRUGALITY.

Make no expense but to do good to others or yourself; *i.e.*, waste nothing.

6. INDUSTRY.

Lose no time; be always employ'd in something useful; cut off all unnecessary actions.

7. SINCERITY.

Use no hurtful deceit; think innocently and justly, and, if you speak, speak accordingly.

8. JUSTICE.

Wrong none by doing injuries, or omitting the benefits that are your duty.

9. MODERATION.

Avoid extreams; forbear resenting injuries so much as you think they deserve.

10. CLEANLINESS.

Tolerate no uncleanliness in body, cloaths, or habitation.

11. TRANQUILLITY.

Be not disturbed at trifles, or at accidents common or unavoidable.

12. CHASTITY.

Rarely use venery but for health or offspring, never to dulness, weakness, or the injury of your own or another's peace or reputation.

13. HUMILITY.

Imitate Jesus and Socrates.

My intention being to acquire the *habitude* of all these virtues, I judg'd it would be well not to distract my attention by attempting the whole at once, but to fix it on one of them at a time; and, when I should be master of that, then to proceed to another, and so on, till I should have gone thro' the thirteen; and, as the previous acquisition of some might facili-

tate the acquisition of certain others, I arrang'd them with that view, as they stand above. *Temperance* first, as it tends to procure that coolness and clearness of head, which is so necessary where constant vigilance was to be kept up, and guard maintained against the unremitting attraction of ancient habits, and the force of perpetual temptations. This being acquir'd and establish'd, *Silence* would be more easy; and my desire being to gain knowledge at the same time that I improv'd in virtue, and considering that in conversation it was obtain'd rather by the use of the ears than of the tongue, and therefore wishing to break a habit I was getting into of prattling, punning, and joking, which only made me acceptable to trifling company, I gave *Silence* the second place. This and the next, *Order,* I expected would allow me more time for attending to my project and my studies. *Resolution,* once become habitual, would keep me firm in my endeavors to obtain all the subsequent virtues; *Frugality* and *Industry* freeing me from my remaining debt, and producing affluence and independence, would make more easy the practice of *Sincerity* and *Justice,* etc., etc. Conceiving then, that, agreeably to the advice of Pythagoras in his Golden Verses, daily examination would be necessary, I contrived the following method for conducting that examination.

Form of the pages.

	TEMPERANCE						
	EAT NOT TO DULNESS; DRINK NOT TO ELEVATION.						
	S.	M.	T.	W.	T.	F.	S.
T.							
S.	*	*		*		*	
O.	**	*	*		*	*	*
R.			*			*	
F.		*			*		
I.			*				
S.							
J.							
M.							
C.							
T.							
C.							
H.							

I made a little book, in which I allotted a page for each of the virtues. I ruled each page with red ink, so as to have seven columns, one for each day of the week, marking each column with a letter for the day. I cross'd these columns with thirteen red lines, marking the beginning of each line with the first letter of one of the virtues, on which line, and in its proper column, I might mark, by a little black spot, every fault I found upon examination to have been committed respecting that virtue upon that day.

I determined to give a week's strict attention to each of the virtues successively. Thus, in the first week, my great guard was to avoid ever the least offence against *Temperance,* leaving the other virtues to their ordinary chance, only marking every evening the faults of the day. Thus, if in the first week I could keep my first line, marked T, clear of spots, I suppos'd the habit of that virtue so much strengthen'd, and its opposite weaken'd, that I might venture extending my attention to include the next, and for the following week keep both lines clear of spots. Proceeding thus to the last, I could go thro' a course compleat in thirteen weeks, and four courses in a year. And like him, who, having a garden to weed, does not attempt to eradicate all the bad herbs at once, which would exceed his reach and his strength, but works on one of the beds at a time, and, having accomplish'd the first, proceeds to a second, so I should have, I hoped, the encouraging pleasure of seeing on my pages the progress I made in virtue, by clearing successively my lines of their spots, till in the end, by a number of courses, I should be happy in viewing a clean book, after a thirteen weeks' daily examination.

This my little book had for its motto these lines from Addison's *Cato:*

"Here will I hold. If there's a power above us
(And that there is, all nature cries aloud
Thro' all her works), He must delight in virtue;
And that which he delights in must be happy."

Another from Cicero,

"O vitae Philosophia dux! O virtutum indagatrix expultrixque vitiorum! Unus dies, bene et ex praeceptis tuis actus, peccanti immortalitati est anteponendus."

Another from the Proverbs of Solomon, speaking of wisdom or virtue:

"Length of days is in her right hand, and in her left hand riches and honour. Her ways are ways of pleasantness, and all her paths are peace." III. 16, 17.

And conceiving God to be the fountain of wisdom, I thought it right and necessary to solicit his assistance for obtaining it; to this end I formed the following little prayer, which was prefix'd to my tables of examination, for daily use.

"*O Powerful Goodness! bountiful Father! merciful Guide! Increase in me that wisdom which discovers my truest interest. Strengthen my resolutions to perform what that wisdom dictates. Accept my kind offices to thy other children as the only return in my power for thy continual favours to me.*"

I used also sometimes a little prayer which I took from Thomson's Poems, viz.:

"Father of light and life, thou Good Supreme!
O teach me what is good; teach me Thyself!
Save me from folly, vanity, and vice,
From every low pursuit; and fill my soul
With knowledge, conscious peace, and virtue
    pure;
Sacred, substantial, never-fading bliss!"

The precept of *Order* requiring that *every part of my business should have its allotted time,* one page in my little book contain'd the following scheme of employment for the twenty-four hours of a natural day.

THE MORNING. *Question.* What good shall I do this day?	5 6 7	Rise, wash and address *Powerful Goodness!* Contrive day's business, and take the resolution of the day; prosecute the present study, and breakfast.
	8 9 10 11	Work.

NOON.	$\left\{\begin{array}{c}12\\1\end{array}\right.$	Read, or overlook my accounts, and dine.
	$\left.\begin{array}{c}2\\3\\4\\5\end{array}\right\}$	Work.
EVENING. *Question.* What good have I done to-day?	$\left.\begin{array}{c}6\\7\\8\\9\end{array}\right\}$	Put things in their places. Supper. Music or diversion, or conversation. Examination of the day.
NIGHT.	$\left\{\begin{array}{c}10\\11\\12\\1\\2\\3\\4\end{array}\right.$	Sleep.

I enter'd upon the execution of this plan for self-examination, and continu'd it with occasional intermissions for some time. I was surpris'd to find myself so much fuller of faults than I had imagined; but I had the satisfaction of seeing them diminish. To avoid the trouble of renewing now and then my little book, which, by scraping out the marks on the paper of old faults to make room for new ones in a new course, became full of holes, I transferr'd my tables and precepts to the ivory leaves of a memorandum book, on which the lines were drawn with red ink, that made a durable stain, and on those lines I mark'd my faults with a black-lead pencil, which marks I could easily wipe out with a wet sponge. After a while I went thro' one course only in a year, and afterward only one in several years, till at length I omitted them entirely, being employ'd in voyages and business abroad, with a multiplicity of affairs that interfered; but I always carried my little book with me.

My scheme of ORDER gave me the most trouble; and I found that, tho' it might be practicable where a man's business was such as to leave him the disposition of his time, that of a journeyman printer, for instance, it was not possible to be exactly observed by a master, who must mix with the world, and often receivé people of business at their own hours. *Order,* too, with regard to places for things, papers, etc., I found extreamly difficult to acquire. I had not been early accustomed to it, and, having an exceeding good memory, I was not so sensible of the inconvenience attending want of method. This article, therefore, cost me so much painful attention, and my faults in it vexed me so much, and I made so little progress in amendment, and had such frequent relapses, that I was almost ready to give up the attempt, and content myself with a faulty character in that respect, like the man who, in buying an ax of a smith, my neighbour, desired to have the whole of its surface as bright as the edge. The smith consented to grind it bright for him if he would turn the wheel; he turn'd, while the smith press'd the broad face of the ax hard and heavily on the stone, which made the turning of it very fatiguing. The man came every now and then from the wheel to see how the work went on, and at length would take his ax as it was, without farther grinding. "No," said the smith, "turn on, turn on; we shall have it bright by-and-by; as yet, it is only speckled." "Yes," says the man, *"but I think I like a speckled ax best."* And I believe this may have been the case with many, who, having, for want of some such means as I employ'd, found the difficulty of obtaining good and breaking bad habits in other points of vice and virtue, have given up the struggle, and concluded that *"a speckled ax was best";* for something, that pretended to be reason, was every now and then suggesting to me that such extream nicety as I exacted of myself might be a kind of foppery in morals, which, if it were known, would make me ridiculous; that a perfect character might be attended with the inconvenience of being envied and hated; and that a benevolent man should allow a few faults in himself, to keep his friends in countenance.

In truth, I found myself incorrigible with respect to *Order;* and now I am grown old, and my memory bad, I feel very sensibly the want of it. But, on the whole, tho' I never arrived at the perfection I had been so ambitious of obtaining, but fell far short of it, yet I was, by the endeavour, a better and a happier man than I otherwise should have been if I had not attempted it; as those who aim at perfect writing by imitating the engraved copies, tho' they never reach the wish'd-for excellence of those copies, their hand is mended by the endeavour, and is tolerable while it continues fair and legible.

It may be well my posterity should be informed that to this little artifice, with the blessing of God, their ancestor ow'd the constant felicity of his life, down to his 79th year, in which this is written. What reverses may attend the remainder is in the hand of Providence; but, if they arrive, the reflection on past happiness enjoy'd ought to help his bearing them with more resignation. To Temperance he ascribes his long-continued health, and what is still left to him of a good constitution; to Industry and Frugality, the early easiness of his circumstances and acquisition of his fortune, with all that knowledge that enabled him to be a useful citizen, and obtained for him some degree of reputation among the learned; to Sincerity and Justice, the confidence of his country, and the honorable employs it conferred upon him; and to the joint influence of the whole mass of the virtues, even in the imperfect state he was able to acquire them, all that evenness of temper, and that cheerfulness in conversation, which makes his company still sought for, and agreeable even to his younger acquaintance. I hope, therefore, that some of my descendants may follow the example and reap the benefit.

It will be remark'd that, tho' my scheme was not wholly without religion, there was in it no mark of any of the distinguishing tenets of any particular sect. I had purposely avoided them; for, being fully persuaded of the utility and excellency of my method, and that it might be serviceable to people in all religions, and intending some time or other to publish it, I would not have anything in it that should prejudice any one, of any sect, against it. I purposed writing a little comment on each virtue, in which I would have shown the advantages of possessing it, and the mischiefs attending its opposite vice; and I should have called my book THE ART OF VIRTUE, because it would have shown the means and manner of obtaining virtue, which would have distinguished it from the mere exhortation to be good, that does not instruct and indicate the means, but is like the apostle's man of verbal charity, who only without showing to the naked and hungry how or where they might get clothes or victuals, exhorted them to be fed and clothed.—James II. 15, 16.

But it so happened that my intention of writing and publishing this comment was never fulfilled. I did, indeed, from time to time, put down short hints of the sentiments, reasonings, etc., to be made use of in it, some of which I have still by me; but the necessary close attention to private business in the earlier part of my life, and public business since, have occasioned my postponing it; for, it being connected in my mind with *a great and extensive project*, that required the whole man to execute, and which an unforeseen succession of employs prevented my attending to, it has hitherto remain'd unfinish'd.

In this piece it was my design to explain and enforce this doctrine, that vicious actions are not hurtful because they are forbidden, but forbidden because they are hurtful, the nature of man alone considered; that it was, therefore, every one's interest to be virtuous who wish'd to be happy even in this world; and I should, from this circumstance (there being always in the world a number of rich merchants, nobility, states, and princes, who have need of honest instruments for the management of their affairs, and such being so rare), have endeavored to convince young persons that no qualities were so likely to make a poor man's fortune as those of probity and integrity.

My list of virtues contain'd at first but twelve; but a Quaker friend having kindly informed me that I was generally thought proud; that my pride show'd itself frequently in conversation; that I was not content with being in the right when discussing any point, but was overbearing, and rather insolent, of which he convinc'd me by mentioning several instances; I determined endeavouring to cure myself, if I could, of this vice or folly among the rest, and I added *Humility* to my list, giving an extensive meaning to the word. . . .

In reality, there is, perhaps, no one of our national passions so hard to subdue as pride. Disguise it, struggle with it, beat it down, stifle it, mortify it as much as one pleases, it is still alive, and will every now and then peep out and show itself; you will see it, perhaps, often in this history; for, even if I could conceive that I had compleatly overcome it, I should probably be proud of my humility.

HAVING mentioned *a great and extensive project* which I had conceiv'd, it seems proper that some account should be here given of that project and its object. Its first rise in my mind appears in the following little paper, accidentally preserv'd, viz:

Observations on my reading history, in Library, May 19th, 1731.

"That the great affairs of the world, the wars, revolutions, etc., are carried on and affected by parties.

"That the view of these parties is their present general interest, or what they take to be such.

"That the different views of these different parties occasion all confusion.

"That while a party is carrying on a general design, each man has his particular private interest in view.

"That as soon as a party has gain'd its general point, each member becomes intent upon his particular interest; which, thwarting others, breaks that party into divisions, and occasions more confusion.

"That few in public affairs act from a meer view of the good of their country, whatever they may pretend; and, tho' their actings bring real good to their country, yet men primarily considered that their own and their country's interest was united, and did not act from a principle of benevolence.

"That fewer still, in public affairs, act with a view to the good of mankind.

"There seems to me at present to be great occasion for raising a United Party for Virtue, by forming the virtuous and good men of all nations into a regular body, to be govern'd by suitable good and wise rules, which good and wise men may probably be more unanimous in their obedience to, than common people are to common laws.

"I at present think that whoever attempts this aright, and is well qualified, can not fail of pleasing God, and of meeting with success.

B. F."

Resolving this project in my mind, as to be undertaken hereafter, when my circumstances should afford me the necessary leisure, I put down from time to time, on pieces of paper, such thoughts as occurr'd to me respecting it. Most of these are lost; but I find one purporting to be the substance of an intended creed, containing, as I thought, the essentials of every known religion, and being free of every thing that might shock the professor of any religion. It is express'd in these words, viz.:

"That there is one God, who made all things.

"That he governs the world by his providence.

"That he ought to be worshiped by adoration, prayer, and thanksgiving.

"But that the most acceptable service of God is doing good to man.

"That the soul is immortal.

"And that God will certainly reward virtue and punish vice, either here or hereafter."

My ideas at that time were, that the sect should be begun and spread at first among young and single men only; that each person to be initiated should not only declare his assent to such creed, but should have exercised himself with the thirteen weeks' examination and practice of the virtues, as in the before-mention'd model; that the existence of such a society should be kept a secret, till it was become considerable, to prevent solicitations for the admission of improper persons, but that the members should each of them search among his acquaintance for ingenuous, well-disposed youths, to whom, with prudent caution, the scheme should be gradually communicated; that the members should engage to afford their advice, assistance, and support to each other in promoting one another's interests, business, and advancement in life; that, for distinction, we should be call'd *The Society of the Free and Easy:* free, as being, by the general practice and habit of the virtues, free from the dominion of vice; and particularly by the practice of industry and frugality, free from debt, which exposes a man to confinement, and a species of slavery to his creditors.

This is as much as I can now recollect of the project, except that I communicated it in part to two young men, who adopted it with some enthusiasm; but my then narrow circumstances, and the necessity I was under of sticking close to my business, occasion'd my postponing the further prosecution of it at that time; and my multifarious occupations, public and private, induc'd me to continue postponing, so that it has been omitted till I have no longer strength or activity left sufficient for such an enterprise; tho' I am still of opinion that it was a practicable scheme, and might have been very useful, by forming a great number of good citizens; and I was not discourag'd by the seeming magnitude of the undertaking, as I have always thought that one man of tolerable abilities may work great changes, and accomplish great affairs among mankind, if he first forms a good plan, and, cutting off all amusements or other employments that would divert his attention, makes the execution of that same plan his sole study and business.

In 1732 I first publish'd my Almanack, under the name of *Richard Saunders;* it was continu'd by me about twenty-five years, commonly call'd *Poor Richard's Almanack.* I endeavor'd to make it both entertaining and useful, and it accordingly came to be in such demand, that I reap'd considerable profit from it, vending annually near ten thousand. And observing that it was generally read, scarce any neighborhood in the province being without it, I consider'd it as a proper vehicle for conveying instruction among the common people, who bought scarcely any other books; I therefore filled all the little spaces that occurr'd between the remarkable days in the calandar with proverbial sentences, chiefly such as inculcated industry and frugality, as the means of procuring wealth, and thereby securing virtue; it being more difficult for a man in want, to act always honestly, as, to use here one of those proverbs, *it is hard for an empty sack to stand upright.*

These proverbs, which contained the wisdom of many ages and nations, I assembled and form'd into a connected discourse prefix'd to the Almanack of 1757, as the harangue of a wise old man to the people attending an auction. The bringing all these scatter'd counsels thus into a focus enabled them to make greater impression. The piece, being universally approved, was copied in all the newspapers of the Continent; reprinted in Britain on a broad side, to be stuck up in houses; two translations were made of it in French, and great numbers bought by the clergy and gentry, to distribute gratis among their poor parishioners and tenants. In Pennsylvania, as it discouraged useless expense in foreign superfluities, some thought it had its share of influence in producing that growing plenty of money which was observable for several years after its publication.

I considered my newspaper, also, as another means of communicating instruction, and in that view frequently reprinted in it extracts from the Spectator, and other moral writers; and sometimes publish'd little pieces of my own, which had been first compos'd for reading in our Junto. Of these are a Socratic dialogue, tending to prove that, whatever might be his parts and abilities, a vicious man could not properly be called a man of sense; and a discourse on self-denial, showing that virtue was not secure till its practice became a habitude, and was free from the opposition of contrary inclinations. These may be found in the papers about the beginning of 1735.

In the conduct of my newspaper, I carefully excluded all libelling and personal abuse, which is of late years become so disgraceful to our country. Whenever I was solicited to insert any thing of that kind, and the writers pleaded, as they generally did, the liberty of the press, and that a newspaper was like a stage-coach, in which any one who would pay had a right to a place, my answer was, that I would print the piece separately if desired, and the author might have as many copies as he pleased to distribute himself, but that I would not take upon me to spread his detraction; and that, having contracted with my subscribers to furnish them with what might be either useful or entertaining, I could not fill their papers with private altercation, in which they had no concern, without doing them manifest injustice. Now, many of our printers make no scruple of gratifying the malice of individuals by false accusations of the fairest characters among ourselves, augmenting animosity even to the producing of duels; and are, moreover, so indiscreet as to print scurrilous reflections on the government of neighboring states, and even on the conduct of our best national allies, which may be attended with the most pernicious consequences. These things I mention as a caution to young printers, and that they may be encouraged not to pollute their presses and disgrace their profession by such infamous practices, but refuse steadily, as they may see by my example that such a course of conduct will not, on the whole, be injurious to their interests.

I began now to turn my thoughts a little to public affairs, beginning, however, with small matters. The city watch was one of the first things that I conceiv'd to want regulation. It was managed by the constables of the respective wards in turn; the constable warned a number of housekeepers to attend him for the night. Those who chose never to attend, paid him six shillings a year to be excus'd, which was suppos'd to be for hiring substitutes, but was, in reality, much more than was necessary for that purpose, and made the constableship a place of profit; and the constable, for a little drink, often got such ragamuffins about him as a watch, that respectable housekeepers did not choose to mix with. Walking the rounds, too, was often neglected, and most of the nights spent in tippling. I thereupon wrote a paper to be read in Junto, representing these irregularities, but insisting more particularly on the inequality of this six-shilling tax of the constables, respecting the circumstances of those who paid it, since a poor widow housekeeper, all whose property to be guarded by the watch did not perhaps exceed the value of fifty pounds, paid as much as the wealthiest merchant, who had thousands of pounds' worth of goods in his stores.

On the whole, I proposed as a more effectual watch, the hiring of proper men to serve constantly in that business; and as a more equitable way of supporting the charge, the levying a tax that should be proportion'd to the property. This idea, being approv'd by the Junto, was communicated to the other clubs, but as arising in each of them; and though the plan was not immediately carried into execution, yet, by preparing the minds of people for the change, it paved the way for the law obtained a few years after, when the members of our clubs were grown into more influence.

About this time I wrote a paper (first to be read in Junto, but it was afterward publish'd) on the different accidents and carelessnesses by which houses were set on fire, with cautions against them, and means proposed of avoiding them. This was much spoken of as a useful piece, and gave rise to a project, which soon followed it, of forming a company for the more ready extinguishing of fires, and mutual assistance in removing and securing of goods when in danger. Associates in this scheme were presently found, amounting to thirty. Our articles of agreement oblig'd every member to keep always in good order, and fit for use, a certain number of leather buckets, with strong bags and baskets (for packing and transporting of goods), which were to be brought to every fire; and we agreed to meet once a month to spend a social evening together, in discoursing and communicating such ideas as occurred to us upon the subject of fires, as might be useful in our conduct on such occasions.

The utility of this institution soon appeared, and many more desiring to be admitted than we thought convenient for one company, they were advised to form another, which was accordingly done; and this went on, one new company being formed after another, till they became so numerous as to include most of the inhabitants who were men of property; and now, at the time of my writing this, tho' upward of fifty years since its establishment, that which I first formed, called the Union Fire Company, still subsists and flourishes, tho' the first members are all deceas'd but myself and one, who is older by a year than I am. The small fines that have been paid by members for absence at the monthly meetings have been apply'd to the purchase of fire-engines, ladders, fire-hooks, and other useful implements for each company, so that I question whether there is a city in the world better provided with the means of putting a stop to beginning conflagrations; and, in fact, since these institutions, the city has never lost by fire more than one or two houses at a time, and the flames have often been extinguished before the house in which they began has been half consumed.

In 1739 arrived among us from Ireland the Reverend Mr. Whitefield, who had made himself remarkable there as an itinerant preacher. He was at first permitted to preach in some of our churches; but the clergy, taking a dislike to him, soon refus'd him their pulpits, and he was oblig'd to preach in the fields. The multitudes of all sects and denominations that attended his sermons were enormous, and it was matter of speculation to me, who was one of the number, to observe the extraordinary influence of his oratory on his hearers, and how much they admir'd and respected him, notwithstanding his common abuse of them, by assuring them they were naturally *half beasts and half devils*. It was wonderful to see the change soon made in the manners of our inhabitants. From being thoughtless or indifferent about religion, it seem'd as if all the world were growing religious, so that one could not walk thro' the town in an evening without hearing psalms sung in different families of every street.

And it being found inconvenient to assemble in the open air, subject to its inclemencies, the building of a house to meet in was no sooner propos'd, and persons appointed to receive contributions, but sufficient sums were soon received to procure the ground and erect the building, which was one hundred feet long and seventy broad, about the size of Westminster Hall; and the work was carried on with such spirit as to be finished in a much shorter time than could have been expected. Both house and ground were vested in trustees, expressly for the use of any preacher of any religious persuasion who might desire to say something to the people at Philadelphia; the design in building not being to accommodate any particular sect, but the inhabitants in general; so that even if the Mufti of Constantinople were to send a missionary to preach Mohammedanism to us, he would find a pulpit at his service.

Mr. Whitefield, in leaving us, went preaching all the way thro' the colonies to Georgia. The settlement of that province had lately been begun, but, instead of being made with hardy, industrious husbandmen, accustomed to labor, the only people fit for such an enterprise, it was with families of broken shop-keepers and other insolvent debtors, many of indolent and idle habits, taken out of the jails, who, being set down in the woods, unqualified for clearing land, and unable to endure the hardships of a new settlement, perished in numbers, leaving many helpless children unprovided for. The sight of their miserable situation inspir'd the benevolent heart of Mr. Whitefield with the idea of building an Orphan House there, in which they might be supported and educated. Returning northward, he preach'd up this char-

ity, and made large collections, for his eloquence had a wonderful power over the hearts and purses of his hearers, of which I myself was an instance.

I did not disapprove of the design, but, as Georgia was then destitute of materials and workmen, and it was proposed to send them from Philadelphia at a great expense, I thought it would have been better to have built the house there, and brought the children to it. This I advis'd; but he was resolute in his first project, rejected my counsel, and I therefor refus'd to contribute. I happened soon after to attend one of his sermons, in the course of which I perceived he intended to finish with a collection, and I silently resolved he should get nothing from me. I had in my pocket a handful of copper money, three or four silver dollars, and five pistoles in gold. As he proceeded I began to soften, and concluded to give the coppers. Another stroke of his oratory made me asham'd of that, and determin'd me to give the silver; and he finish'd so admirably, that I empty'd my pocket wholly into the collector's dish, gold and all. At this sermon there was also one of our club, who, being of my sentiments respecting the building in Georgia, and suspecting a collection might be intended, had, by precaution, emptied his pockets before he came from home. Towards the conclusion of the discourse, however, he felt a strong desire to give, and apply'd to a neighbour, who stood near him, to borrow some money for the purpose. The application was unfortunately [made] to perhaps the only man in the company who had the firmness not to be affected by the preacher. His answer was, "*At any other time, Friend Hopkinson, I would lend to thee freely; but not now, for thee seems to be out of thy right senses.*"

Some of Mr. Whitefield's enemies affected to suppose that he would apply these collections to his own private emolument; but I, who was intimately acquainted with him (being employed in printing his Sermons and Journals, etc.), never had the least suspicion of his integrity, but am to this day decidedly of opinion that he was in all his conduct a perfectly *honest man*; and methinks my testimony in his favour ought to have the more weight, as we had no religious connection. He us'd, indeed, sometimes to pray for my conversion, but never had the satisfaction of believing that his prayers were heard. Ours was a mere civil friendship, sincere on both sides, and lasted to his death. . . .

I had, on the whole, abundant reason to be satisfied with my being established in Pennsylvania. There were, however, two things that I regretted, there being no provision for defense, nor for a compleat education of youth; no militia, nor any college. I therefore, in 1743, drew up a proposal for establishing an academy; and at that time, thinking the Reverend Mr. Peters, who was out of employ, a fit person to superintend such an institution, I communicated the project to him; but he, having more profitable views in the service of the proprietaries, which succeeded, declin'd the undertaking; and, not knowing another at that time suitable for such a trust, I let the scheme lie a while dormant. I succeeded better the next year, 1744, in proposing and establishing a Philosophical Society. The paper I wrote for that purpose will be found among my writings, when collected.

With respect to defense, Spain having been several years at war against Great Britain, and being at length join'd by France, which brought us into great danger; and the laboured and long-continued endeavour of our governor, Thomas, to prevail with our Quaker Assembly to pass a militia law, and make other provisions for the security of the province, having proved abortive, I determined to try what might be done by a voluntary association of the people. To promote this, I first wrote and published a pamphlet, entitled PLAIN TRUTH, in which I stated our defenceless situation in strong lights, with the necessity of union and discipline for our defense, and promis'd to propose in a few days an association, to be generally signed for that purpose. The pamphlet had a sudden and surprising effect. I was call'd upon for the instrument of association, and having settled the draft of it with a few friends, I appointed a meeting of the citizens in the large building before mentioned. The house was pretty full; I had prepared a number of printed copies, and provided pens and ink dispers'd all over the room. I harangued them a little on the subject, read the paper, and explained it, and then distributed the copies, which were eagerly signed, not the least objection being made. . . .

My being many years in the Assembly, the majority of which were constantly Quakers, gave me frequent opportunities of seeing the embarrassment given them by their principle against war, whenever application was made to them, by order of the crown, to grant aids for military purposes. They were unwilling to offend government, on the one hand, by a direct refusal; and their friends, the body of the Quakers, on the other, by a compliance contrary to their principles; hence a variety of evasions to avoid complying, and modes of disguising the compliance when it became unavoidable. The common mode at last was, to grant money under the phrase of its being "*for the king's use*," and never to inquire how it was applied.

But, if the demand was not directly from the crown, that phrase was found not so proper, and some other was to be invented. As, when powder was wanting (I think it was for the garrison at Louisburg), and the government of New England solicited a grant of some from Pennsylvania, which was much urg'd on the House by Governor Thomas, they could not grant money to buy powder, because that was an ingredient of war; but they voted an aid to New England of three thousand pounds, to be put into the hands of the governor, and appropriated it for the purchasing of bread, flour, wheat, or *other grain*. Some of the council, desirous of giving the House still further embarrassment, advis'd the governor not to accept provision, as not being the thing he had demanded; but he reply'd, "I shall take the money, for I understand very well their meaning; other grain is gunpowder," which he accordingly bought, and they never objected to it. . . .

In order of time, I should have mentioned before, that having, in 1742, invented an open stove for the better warming of rooms, and at the same time saving fuel, as the fresh air admitted was warmed in entering, I made a present of the model to Mr. Robert Grace, one of my early friends, who, having an iron-furnace, found the casting of the plates for these stoves a profitable thing, as they were growing in demand. To promote that demand, I wrote and published a pamphlet, entitled *"An Account of the new-invented Pennsylvania Fireplaces; wherein their Construction and Manner of Operation is particularly explained; their Advantages above every other Method of warming Rooms demonstrated; and all Objections that have been raised against the Use of them answered and obviated,"* etc. This pamphlet had a good effect. Gov'r. Thomas was so pleas'd with the construction of this stove, as described in it, that he offered to give me a patent for the sole vending of them for a term of years; but I declin'd it from a principle which has ever weighed with me on such occasions, viz., *That, as we enjoy great advantages from the inventions of others, we should be glad of an opportunity to serve others by any invention of ours; and this we should do freely and generously. . . .*

Peace being concluded, and the association business therefore at an end, I turn'd my thoughts again to the affair of establishing an academy. The first step I took was to associate in the design a number of active friends, of whom the Junto furnished a good part; the next was to write and publish a pamphlet, entitled *Proposals Relating to the Education of Youth in Pennsylvania.* This I distributed among the principal inhabitants gratis; and as soon as I could suppose their minds a little prepared by the perusal of it, I set on foot a subscription for opening and supporting an academy; it was to be paid in quotas yearly for five years; by so dividing it, I judg'd the subscription might be larger, and I believed it was so, amounting to no less, if I remember right, than five thousand pounds. . . .

The trustees of the academy, after a while, were incorporated by a charter from the governor; their funds were increas'd by contributions in Britain and grants of land from the proprietaries, to which the Assembly has since made considerable addition; and thus was established the present University of Philadelphia. I have been continued one of its trustees from the beginning, now near forty years, and have had the very great pleasure of seeing a number of

the youth who have receiv'd their education in it, distinguish'd by their improv'd abilities, serviceable in public stations, and ornaments to their country. . . .

After some time I drew a bill for paving the city, and brought it into the Assembly. It was just before I went to England, in 1757, and did not pass till I was gone, and then with an alteration in the mode of assessment, which I thought for the better, but with an additional provision for lighting as well as paving the streets, which was a great improvement. It was by a private person, the late Mr. John Clifton, his giving a sample of the utility of lamps, by placing one at his door, that the people were first impress'd with the idea of enlighting all the city. The honour of this public benefit has also been ascrib'd to me, but it belongs truly to that gentleman. I did but follow his example, and have only some merit to claim respecting the form of our lamps, as differing from the globe lamps we were at first supply'd with from London. Those we found inconvenient in these respects: they admitted no air below; the smoke, therefore, did not readily go out above, but circulated in the globe, lodg'd on its inside, and soon obstructed the light they were intended to afford; giving, besides the daily trouble of wiping them clean; and an accidental stroke on one of them would demolish it, and render it totally useless. I therefore suggested the composing them of four flat panes, with a long funnel above to draw up the smoke, and crevices admitting air below, to facilitate the ascent of the smoke; by this means they were kept clean, and did not grow dark in a few hours, as the London lamps do, but continu'd bright till morning, and an accidental stroke would generally break but a single pane, easily repaired. . . .

It may not be amiss here to give some account of the rise and progress of my philosophical reputation.

In 1746, being in Boston, I met there with a Dr. Spence, who was lately arrived from Scotland, and show'd me some electric experiments. They were imperfectly perform'd, as he was not very expert; but, being on a subject quite new to me, they equally surpris'd and pleased me.

Soon after my return to Philadelphia, our library company receiv'd from Mr. P. Collinson, Fellow of the Royal Society of London, a present of a glass tube, with some account of the use of it in making such experiments. I eagerly seized the opportunity of repeating what I had seen at Boston; and, by much practice, acquir'd great readiness in performing those, also, which we had an account of from England, adding a number of new ones. I say much practice, for my house was continually full, for some time, with people who came to see these new wonders.

To divide a little this incumbrance among my friends, I caused a number of similar tubes to be blown at our glass-house, with which they furnish'd themselves, so that we had at length several performers. Among these, the principal was Mr. Kinnersley, an ingenious neighbor, who, being out of business, I encouraged to undertake showing the experiments for money, and drew up for him two lectures, in which the experiments were rang'd in such order, and accompanied with such explanations in such method, as that the foregoing should assist in comprehending the following. He procur'd an elegant apparatus for the purpose, in which all the little machines that I had roughly made for myself were nicely form'd by instrument-makers. His lectures were well attended, and gave great satisfaction; and after some time he went thro' the colonies, exhibiting them in every capital town, and pick'd up some money. In the West India islands, indeed, it was with difficulty the experiments could be made, from the general moisture of the air.

Oblig'd as we were to Mr. Collinson for his present of the tube, etc., I thought it right he should be inform'd of our success in using it, and wrote him several letters containing accounts of our experiments. He got them read in the Royal Society, where they were not at first thought worth so much notice as to be printed in their Transactions. One paper, which I wrote for Mr. Kinnersley, on the sameness of lightning with electricity, I sent to Dr. Mitchel, an acquaintance of mine, and one of the members also of that society, who wrote me word that it had been read, but was laughed at by the connoisseurs. The papers, however, being shown to Dr. Fothergill, he thought them of too much value to be stifled, and advis'd the printing of them. Mr. Collinson then gave them to *Cave* for publication in his Gentleman's Magazine; but he chose to print them separately in a pamphlet, and Dr. Fothergill wrote the preface. Cave, it seems, judged rightly for his profit, for by the additions that arrived afterward they swell'd, to a quarto volume, which has had five editions, and cost him nothing for copy-money.

It was, however, some time before those papers were much taken notice of in England. A copy of them happening to fall into the hands of the Count de Buffon, a philosopher deservedly of great reputation in France, and, indeed, all over Europe, he prevailed with M. Dalibard to translate them into French, and they were printed at Paris. The publication offended the Abbé Nollet, preceptor in Natural Philosophy to the royal family, and an able experimenter, who had form'd and publish'd a theory of electricity, which then had the general vogue. He could not at first believe that such a work came from America, and said it must have been fabricated by his enemies at Paris, to decry his system. Afterwards, having been assur'd that there really existed such a person as Franklin at Philadelphia, which he had doubted, he wrote and published a volume of Letters, chiefly address'd to me, defending his theory, and denying the verity of my experiments, and of the positions deduc'd from them.

I once purpos'd answering the abbé, and actually began the answer; but, on consideration that my writings contain'd a description of experiments which any one might repeat and verify, and if not to be verifi'd, could not be defended; or of observations offer'd as conjectures, and not delivered dogmatically, therefore not laying me under any obligation to defend them; and reflecting that a dispute between two persons, writing in different languages, might be lengthened greatly by mistranslations, and thence misconceptions of one another's meaning, much of one of the abbé's letters being founded on an error in the translation, I concluded to let my papers shift for themselves, believing it was better to spend what time I could spare from public business in making new experiments, than in disputing about those already made. I therefore never answered M. Nollet, and the event gave me no cause to repent my silence; for my friend M. le Roy, of the Royal Academy of Sciences, took up my cause and refuted him; my book was translated into the Italian, German, and Latin languages; and the doctrine it contain'd was by degrees universally adopted by the philosophers of Europe, in preference to that of the abbé; so that he lived to see himself the last of his sect, except Monsieur B——, of Paris, his *élève* and immediate disciple.

What gave my book the more sudden and general celebrity, was the success of one of its proposed experiments, made by Messrs. Dalibard and De Lor at Marly, for drawing lightning from the clouds. This engag'd the public attention every where. M. de Lor, who had an apparatus for experimental philosophy, and lectur'd in that branch of sicence, undertook to repeat what he called the *Philadelphia Experiments;* and, after they were performed before the king and court, all the curious of Paris flocked to see them. I will not swell this narrative with an account of that capital experiment, nor of the infinite pleasure I received in the success of a similar one I made soon after with a kite at Philadelphia, as both are to be found in the histories of electricity.

Dr. Wright, an English physician, when at Paris, wrote to a friend, who was of the Royal Society, an account of the high esteem my experiments were in among the learned abroad, and of their wonder that my writings had been so little noticed in England. The society, on this, resum'd the consideration of the letters that had been read to them; and the celebrated Dr. Watson drew up a summary account of them, and of all I had afterwards sent to England on the subject, which he accompanied with some praise of the writer. This summary was then printed in their Transactions; and some members of the society in London, particularly the very ingenious Mr. Canton, having verified the experiment of procuring lightning from the clouds by a pointed rod, and acquainting them with the success, they soon made me more than amends for the slight with which they had before treated me. Without my having made any application for that honor, they chose me a member, and voted that I should be excus'd the customary payments, which would have amounted to twenty-five guineas; and ever since have given me their Transactions gratis. They also presented me with the gold medal of Sir Godfrey Copley for the year 1753, the delivery of which was accompanied by a very handsome speech of the president, Lord Macclesfield, wherein I was highly honoured.

Second Continental Congress

The Declaration of American Independence was written to justify a resolution of independence adopted by the Second Continental Congress on July 2, 1776. It was largely the work of Thomas Jefferson, an American who was representative of the Enlightenment. As a consequence, this famous document naturally reflected certain political theories which had already been expressed by others and widely accepted. John Locke, in particular, should be noted in this regard. In reading the Declaration note (1) the appeal in the preamble to the laws of nature and of nature's God, (2) the secular purposes for which governments were formed, (3) evidences of the social contract, (4) the appeal to the "right" of revolution, (5) the branch of the English government against which the principal charges were made, (6) the political abuses cited, (7) the evidences of economic discontent contained in the charges,

(8) the references to tyranny in a neighboring province, (9) the charge that the Indians were being incited to destroy civilized communities, (10) evidences that the writers already looked upon themselves as a people independent of the English, and (11) the conclusion reached.

THE DECLARATION OF AMERICAN INDEPENDENCE

In Congress, July 4, 1776
The Unanimous Declaration of the Thirteen
United States of America

When, in the course of human events, it becomes necessary for one people to dissolve the political bands which have connected them with another, and to assume among the powers of the earth the separate and equal station to which the laws of nature and of nature's God entitle them, a decent respect to the opinions of mankind requires that they should declare the causes which impel them to the separation.

We hold these truths to be self-evident: That all men are created equal; that they are endowed by their Creator with certain unalienable rights; that among these are life, liberty, and the pursuit of happiness; that, to secure these rights, governments are instituted among men, deriving their just powers from the consent of the governed; that whenever any form of government becomes destructive of these ends, it is the right of the people to alter or to abolish it and to institute a new government, laying its foundation on such principles, and organizing its powers in such form, as to them shall seem most likely to effect their safety and happiness. Prudence, indeed, will dictate that governments long established should not be changed for light and transient causes; and, accordingly, all experience hath shown that mankind are more disposed to suffer while evils are sufferable, than to right themselves by abolishing the forms to which they are accustomed. But when a long train of abuses and usurpations, pursuing invariably the same object, evinces a design to reduce them under absolute despotism, it is their right, it is their duty, to throw off such government and to provide new guards for their future security. Such

has been the patient sufferance of these colonies; and such is now the necessity which constrains them to alter their former systems of government.

The history of the present King of Great Britain is a history of repeated injuries and usurpations, all having in direct object the establishment of an absolute tyranny over these States. To prove this, let facts be submitted to a candid world:

He has refused his assent to laws, the most wholesome and necessary for the public good.

He has forbidden his Governors to pass laws of immediate and pressing importance, unless suspended in their operation till his assent should be obtained; and, when so suspended, he has utterly neglected to attend to them.

He has refused to pass other laws for the accommodation of large districts of people, unless those people would relinquish the right of representation in the Legislature, a right inestimable to them and formidable to tyrants only.

He has called together legislative bodies at places unusual, uncomfortable, and distant from the depository of their public records, for the sole purpose of fatiguing them into compliance with his measures.

He has dissolved representative Houses repeatedly for opposing with manly firmness his invasions on the rights of the people.

He has refused for a long time after such dissolutions to cause others to be elected; whereby the legislative powers, incapable of annihilation, have returned to the people at large for their exercise; the State remaining, in the meantime, exposed to all the dangers of invasions from without and convulsions within.

He has endeavored to prevent the population of these States; for that purpose obstruct-

Adapted from a photograph of the original document now in the Library of Congress.

ing the laws for naturalization of foreigners, refusing to pass others to encourage their migration hither, and raising the conditions of new appropriations of lands.

He has obstructed the administration of justice by refusing his assent to laws for establishing judiciary powers.

He has made judges dependent on his will alone for the tenure of their offices and the amount and payment of their salaries.

He has erected a multitude of new offices, and sent hither swarms of officers to harass our people and eat out their substance.

He has kept among us, in times of peace, standing armies, without the consent of our Legislatures.

He has affected to render the military independent of, and superior to, the civil power.

He has combined with others to subject us to a jurisdiction foreign to our Constitution and unacknowledged by our laws, giving his assent to their acts of pretended legislation:

For quartering large bodies of armed troops among us;

For protecting them, by a mock trial, from punishment for any murders which they should commit on the inhabitants of these States;

For cutting off our trade with all parts of the world;

For imposing taxes on us without our consent;

For depriving us, in many cases, of the benefits of trial by jury;

For transporting us beyond seas to be tried for pretended offenses;

For abolishing the free system of English laws in a neighboring province, establishing therein an arbitrary government, and enlarging its boundaries so as to render it at once an example and fit instrument for introducing the same absolute rule into these colonies;

For taking away our charters, abolishing our most valuable laws, and altering fundamentally the forms of our governments;

For suspending our own Legislatures, and declaring themselves invested with power to legislate for us in all cases whatsoever.

He has abdicated government here by declaring us out of his protection and waging war against us.

He has plundered our seas, ravaged our coasts, burnt our towns, and destroyed the lives of our people.

He is at this time transporting large armies of foreign mercenaries to complete the works of death, desolation, and tyranny, already begun with circumstances of cruelty and perfidy scarcely paralleled in the most barbarous ages, and totally unworthy the head of a civilized nation.

He has constrained our fellow citizens, taken captive on the high seas, to bear arms against their country, to become the executioners of their friends and brethren, or to fall themselves by their hands.

He has excited domestic insurrections amongst us, and has endeavored to bring on the inhabitants of our frontiers the merciless Indian savages, whose known rule of warfare is an undistinguished destruction of all ages, sexes, and conditions.

In every stage of these oppressions we have petitioned for redress in the most humble terms: our repeated petitions have been answered only by repeated injury. A prince, whose character is thus marked by every act which may define a tyrant, is unfit to be the ruler of a free people.

Nor have we been wanting in attentions to our British brethren. We have warned them from time to time of attempts by their Legislature to extend an unwarrantable jurisdiction over us. We have reminded them of the circumstances of our emigration and settlement here. We have appealed to their native justice and magnanimity, and we have conjured them by the ties of our common kindred to disavow these usurpations which would inevitably interrupt our connections and correspondence. They, too, have been deaf to the voice of justice and of consanguinity. We must, therefore, acquiesce in the necessity which denounces our separation, and hold them, as we hold the rest of mankind, enemies in war; in peace, friends.

WE, THEREFORE, THE REPRESENTATIVES OF THE UNITED STATES OF AMERICA, in General Congress assembled, appealing to the Supreme

Judge of the world for the rectitude of our intentions, do, in the name and by the authority of the good people of these colonies, solemnly publish and declare that these United Colonies are, and of right ought to be, FREE AND INDEPENDENT STATES; that they are absolved from all allegiance to the British Crown, and that all political connection between them and the State of Great Britain is, and ought to be, totally dissolved; and that as free and independent states they have full power to levy war, conclude peace, contract alliances, establish commerce, and to do all other acts and things which independent States may of right do. And for the support of this declaration, with a firm reliance on the protection of Divine Providence, we mutually pledge to each other our lives, our fortunes, and our sacred honor.

James Madison

James Madison (1751–1836) was born in the tidewater section of Virginia. He graduated from the College of New Jersey (Princeton) in 1771, studied law, then entered upon a long career in the service of his country. In 1787 Madison associated himself with Alexander Hamilton and John Jay in writing a series of letters to the New York press during the debate over the ratification of the Constitution of the United States in an effort to influence opinion in support of the Federal Constitution. Its framers aimed to place effective checks upon democratic government in America, and they achieved signal success in the document submitted to the states for ratification in 1787. Madison approached the problem of government in a coldly realistic and non-romantic fashion and defended the new instrument of government on the grounds that it would protect not only the majority against a minority, but also would protect a minority against the majority. The following was the tenth in the series of papers written in 1787 to the people of the state of New York. In reading it note (1) what Madison regarded as one of the major vices confronting popular governments, (2) his definition of faction, (3) available remedies for curing the evils of faction, (4) where Madison found the latent causes of faction, (5) what he saw as the most common source of factions, (6) what he conceived the principal tasks of government to be, (7) how he arrived at the conclusion that relief from faction could only be sought in controlling its effects, (8) the bases for his argument that a republic promises the best cure for the effects of faction, (9) his differentiation between democracy and a republic, and (10) his reasons for defending a republic as against a democracy.

THE FEDERALIST, NO. 10

Among the numerous advantages promised by a well-constructed union, none deserves to be more accurately developed than its tendency to break and control the violence of faction. The friend of popular governments never finds himself so much alarmed for their charac-

Adapted from Alexander Hamilton, Jay and Madison, *The Federalist* . . . , Philadelphia, 1892, 104–112.

ter and fate as when he contemplates their propensity to this dangerous vice. He will not fail, therefore, to set a due value on any plan which, without violating the principles to which he is attached, provides a proper cure for it. The instability, injustice, and confusion introduced into the public councils have, in truth, been the mortal diseases under which popular governments have everywhere perished; as they continue to be the favorite and fruitful topics from which the adversaries to liberty derive their most specious declamations. The valuable improvements made by the American constitutions on the popular models, both ancient and modern, cannot certainly be too much admired; but it would be an unwarrantable partiality, to contend that they have as effectually obviated the danger on this side as was wished and expected. Complaints are everywhere heard from our most considerate and virtuous citizens, equally the friends of public and private faith and of public and personal liberty, that our governments are too unstable; that the public good is disregarded in the conflicts of rival parties; and that measures are too often decided, not according to the rules of justice, and the rights of the minor party, but by the superior force of an interested and overbearing majority. However anxiously we may wish that these complaints had no foundation, the evidence of known facts will not permit us to deny that they are in some degree true. It will be found, indeed, on a candid review of our situation, that some of the distresses under which we labor have been erroneously charged on the operation of our governments; but it will be found, at the same time, that other causes will not alone account for many of our heaviest misfortunes; and, particularly, for that prevailing and increasing distrust of public engagements, and alarm for private rights, which are echoed from one end of the continent to the other. These must be chiefly, if not wholly, effects of the unsteadiness and injustice with which a factious spirit has tainted our public administrations.

By a faction, I understand a number of citizens, whether amounting to a majority or minority of the whole, who are united and actuated by some common impulse of passion, or of interest, adverse to the rights of other citizens or to the permanent and aggregate interests of the community.

There are two methods of curing the mischiefs of faction: the one, by removing its causes; the other, by controlling its effects.

There are again two methods of removing the causes of faction: the one, by destroying the liberty which is essential to its existence; the other, by giving to every citizen the same opinions, the same passions, and the same interests.

It could never be more truly said than of the first remedy, that it was worse than the disease. Liberty is to faction what air is to fire, an ailment without which it instantly expires. But it could not be less folly to abolish liberty, which is essential to political life, because it nourishes faction, than it would be to wish the annihilation of air, which is essential to animal life, because it imparts to fire its destructive agency.

The second expedient is as impracticable as the first would be unwise. As long as the reason of man continues fallible, and he is at liberty to exercise it, different opinions will be formed. As long as the connection subsists between his reason and his self-love, his opinions and his passions will have a reciprocal influence on each other; and the former will be objects to which the latter will attach themselves. The diversity in the faculties of men, from which the rights of property originate, is not less an insuperable obstacle to a uniformity of interests. The protection of these faculties is the first object of government. From the protection of different and unequal faculties of acquiring property, the possession of different degrees and kinds of property immediately results; and from the influence of these on the sentiments and views of the respective proprietors ensues a division of the society into different interests and parties.

The latent causes of faction are thus sown in the nature of man; and we see them everywhere brought into different degrees of activity, according to the different circumstances of civil society. A zeal for different opinions concerning religion, concerning government and many other points, as well as speculation as of practice; an attachment to different leaders ambitiously contending for pre-eminence and power, or to persons of other descriptions whose fortunes have been interesting to the human passions, have, in turn, divided mankind into parties, inflamed them with mutual animosity, and rendered them much more disposed to vex and oppress each other, than to co-operate for their common good. So strong is this propensity of mankind to fall into mutual animosities, that where no substantial occasion presents itself, the most frivolous and fanciful distinctions have been sufficient to kindle their unfriendly passions and excite their most violent conflicts. But the most common and durable source of factions has been the various and unequal distribution of property. Those who hold and those who are without property have ever formed distinct interests in society. Those who are creditors and those who are debtors fall under a like discrimination. A landed interest, a manufacturing interest, a mercantile interest, a moneyed interest, with many lesser interests, grow up of necessity in civilized nations, and divide them into different classes, actuated by different sentiments and views. The regulation of these various and interfering interests forms the principal task of modern legislation, and involves the spirit of party and faction in the necessary and ordinary operations of the government.

No man is allowed to be a judge in his own cause; because his interest would certainly bias his judgment and, not improbably, corrupt his integrity. With equal, nay, with greater reason, a body of men are unfit to be both judges and parties at the same time; yet what are many of the most important acts of legislation, but so many judicial determinations, not indeed concerning the rights of single persons, but concerning the rights of large bodies of citizens? and what are the different classes of legislators, but advocates and parties to the causes which they determine? Is a law proposed concerning private debts?—it is a question to which the creditors are parties on one side, and the debtors on the other. Justice ought to hold the balance between them. Yet the parties are, and must be, themselves the judges; and the most numerous party, or, in other words, the most powerful faction, must be expected to prevail. Shall domestic manufactures be encouraged, and in what degree by restrictions on foreign manufactures? are questions which would be differently decided by the landed and the manufacturing classes, and probably by neither with a sole regard to justice and the public good. The apportionment of taxes on the various descriptions of property is an act which seems to require the most exact impartiality; yet there is, perhaps, no legislative act in which greater opportunity and temptation are given to a predominant party, to trample on the rules of justice. Every shilling with which they overburden the inferior number is a shilling saved to their own pockets.

It is in vain to say that enlightened statesmen will be able to adjust these clashing interests and render them all subservient to the public good. Enlightened statesmen will not always be at the helm; nor, in many cases, can such an adjustment be made at all, without taking into view indirect and remote considerations, which will rarely prevail over the immediate interest which one party may find in disregarding the rights of another or the good of the whole.

The inference to which we are brought is that the causes of faction cannot be removed, and that relief is only to be sought in the means of controlling its effects.

If a faction consists of less than a majority, relief is supplied by the republican principle, which enables the majority to defeat its sinister views by regular vote. It may clog the administration, it may convulse the society; but it will be unable to execute and mask its violence under the forms of the Constitution. When a majority is included in a faction, the form of popular government, on the other hand, enables it to sacrifice to its ruling passion or interest both the public good and the rights of other citizens. To secure the public good, and private rights, against the danger of such a faction, and at the same time to preserve the spirit and the form of popular government, is then the great object to which our inquiries are directed. Let me add that it is the great *desideratum,* by which alone this form of government can be rescued from the opprobrium under which it has so long labored, and be recommended to the esteem and adoption of mankind.

By what means is this object attainable?

Evidently by one of two only. Either the existence of the same passion or interest in a majority, at the same time, must be prevented; or the majority, having such coexistent passion or interest, must be rendered, by their number and local situation, unable to concert and carry into effect schemes of oppression. If the impulse and the opportunity be suffered to coincide, we well know that neither moral nor religious motives can be relied on as an adequate control. They are not found to be such on the injustice and violence of individuals, and lose their efficacy in proportion to the number combined together; that is, in proportion as their efficacy becomes needful.

From this view of the subject it may be concluded that a pure democracy, by which I mean a society consisting of a small number of citizens, who assemble and administer the government in person, can admit of no cure for the mischiefs of faction. A common passion or interest will, in almost every case, be felt by a majority of the whole; a communication and concert results from the form of government itself; and there is nothing to check the inducements to sacrifice the weaker party or an obnoxious individual. Hence it is that such democracies have ever been spectacles of turbulence and contention; have ever been found incompatible with personal security, or the rights of property, and have in general been as short in their lives as they have been violent in their deaths. Theoretic politicians, who have patronized this species of government, have erroneously supposed that by reducing mankind to a perfect equality in their political rights, they would at the same time be perfectly equalized and assimilated in their possessions, their opinions, and their passions.

A republic, by which I mean a government in which the scheme of representation takes place, opens a different prospect, and promises the cure for which we are seeking. Let us examine the points in which it varies from pure democracy, and we shall comprehend both the nature of the cure and the efficacy which it must derive from the union.

The two great points of difference between a democracy and a republic are: First, the delegation of the government, in the latter, to a small number of citizens elected by the rest; secondly, the greater number of citizens, and greater sphere of country, over which the latter may be extended.

The effect of the first difference is, on the one hand, to refine and enlarge the public views, by passing them through the medium of a chosen body of citizens, whose wisdom may best discern the true interest of their country, and whose patriotism and love of justice will be least likely to sacrifice it to temporary or partial considerations. Under such a regulation, it may well happen that the public voice, pronounced by the representatives of the people, will be more consonant to the public good than if pronounced by the people themselves, convened for the purpose. On the other hand, the effect may be inverted. Men of factious tempers, of local prejudices, or of sinister designs, may by intrigue, by corruption, or by other means, first obtain the suffrages, and then betray the interests of the people. The question resulting is, whether small or extensive republics are most favorable to the election of proper guardians of the public weal; and it is clearly decided in favor of the latter by two obvious considerations.

In the first place, it is to be remarked that, however small the republic may be, the representatives must be raised to a certain number, in order to guard against the cabals of a few; and that, however large it may be, they must be limited to a certain number, in order to guard against the confusion of a multitude. Hence, the number of representatives in the two cases not being in proportion to that of the constituents, and being proportionally greatest in the small republic, it follows that if the proportion of fit characters be not less in the large than in the small republic, the former will present a greater option, and consequently a greater probability of a fit choice.

In the next place, as each representative will be chosen by a greater number of citizens in the large than in the small republic, it will be more difficult for unworthy candidates to practise with success the vicious arts, by which elections are too often carried; and the suffrages of the people, being more free, will be more likely to centre in men who possess the most attractive merit and the most diffusive and established characters.

It must be confessed that in this as in most other cases, there is a mean, on both sides of which inconveniences will be found to lie. By enlarging too much the number of electors, you render the representative too little acquainted with all their local circumstances and lesser interests; as by reducing it too much, you render him unduly attached to these, and too little fit to comprehend and pursue great and national objects. The federal Constitution forms a happy combination in this respect; the great and aggregate interests being referred to the national, the local and particular to the State, legislatures.

The other point of difference is, the greater number of citizens and extent of territory which may be brought within the compass of republican than of democratic government; and it is this circumstance principally which renders factious combinations less to be dreaded in the former, than in the latter. The smaller the society, the fewer probably will be the distinct parties and interests composing it; the fewer the distinct parties and interests, the more frequently will a majority be found of the same party; and the smaller the number of individuals composing a majority, and the smaller the compass within which they are placed, the more easily will they concert and execute their plans of oppression. Extend the sphere, and you take in a greater variety of parties and interests; you make it less probable that a majority of the whole will have a common motive to invade the rights of other citizens; or if such a common motive exists, it will be more difficult for all who feel it to discover their own strength, and to act in unison with each other. Besides other impediments, it may be remarked that where there is a consciousness of unjust or dishonorable purposes, communication is always checked by distrust, in proportion to the number whose concurrence is necessary.

Hence it clearly appears that the same advantage which a republic has over a democracy, in controlling the effects of faction, is enjoyed by a large over a small republic—is enjoyed by the Union over the States composing it. Does the advantage consist in the substitution of representatives, whose enlightened views and virtuous sentiments render them superior to local prejudices, and to schemes of injustice? It will not be denied that the representation of the Union will be most likely to possess these requisite endowments. Does it consist in the greater security afforded by a greater variety of parties, against the event of any one party being able to outnumber and oppress the rest? In an equal degree does the increased variety of parties, comprised within the Union, increase this security. Does it, in fine, consist in the greater obstacles opposed to the concert and accomplishment of the secret wishes of an unjust and interested majority? Here, again, the extent of the Union gives it the most palpable advantage.

The influence of factious leaders may kindle a flame within their particular States, but will be unable to spread a general conflagration through the other States. A religious sect may degenerate into a political faction in a part of the confederacy; but the variety of sects dispersed over the entire face of it must secure the national councils against any danger from that source. A rage for paper money, for an abolition of debts, for an equal division of property, or for any other improper and wicked project will be less apt to pervade the whole body of the union than a particular member of it; in the same proportion as such a malady is more likely to taint a particular county or district than an entire State.

In the extent and proper structure of the Union, therefore, we behold a republican remedy for the diseases most incident to republican government. And according to the degree of pleasure and pride we feel in being republicans, ought to be our zeal in cherishing the spirit and supporting the character of federalists.

PUBLIUS [Madison]

French National Assembly

In 1789 the Bourbon dynasty in France faced a financial crisis growing out of the excesses of the Old Regime. In a last desperate effort to raise money Louis XVI convened the almost forgotten Estates General, and its meeting provided an opportunity for those leaders bent on reforming the French government. The members of the Third Estate quickly formed a national assembly and began writing a constitution for France. Following the example set by the English in 1689, and by the Americans in 1787, they drew up, as the first part of the new instrument of government, a bill of rights which is known as The Declaration of the Rights of Man and Citizen. It reflected the essentially middle-class character of the revolution in its early stages in that it stressed laissez-faire principles and property rights. In addition to its influence on the French reform movement, The Declaration of the Rights of Man served as a pattern for liberal constitutions drawn up in other European countries during the nineteenth century. In reading this famous document note (1) the motives directing the actions of the Declaration's authors, (2) the stated primary aim of all political institutions, (3) the ideas of Rousseau which were incorporated, (4) the freedom claimed for every citizen, (5) the abuses of the Old Regime which it condemned, (6) the stress placed upon specific laws for each power of the government, and (7) the particular emphasis given to property rights.

DECLARATION OF THE RIGHTS OF MAN AND CITIZEN

The representatives of the French people, organized in National Assembly, considering that ignorance, forgetfulness or contempt of the rights of man are the sole causes of the public miseries and of the corruption of governments, have resolved to set forth in a solemn declaration the natural, inalienable, and sacred rights of man, in order that this declaration, being ever present to all the members of the social body, may unceasingly remind them of their rights and their duties: in order that the acts of the legislative power and those of the executive power may be each moment compared with the aim of every political institution and thereby may be more respected; and in order that the demands of the citizens, grounded henceforth upon simple and incontestable principles, may always take the direction of maintaining the constitution and the welfare of all.

In consequence, the National Assembly recognizes and declares, in the presence and under the auspices of the Supreme Being, the following rights of man and citizen.

1. Men are born and remain free and equal in rights. Social distinctions can be based only upon public utility.

2. The aim of every political association is the preservation of the natural and imprescriptible rights of man. These rights are liberty, property, security, and resistance to oppression.

3. The source of all sovereignty is essen-

Frank Maloy Anderson, *The Constitutions and other Select Documents Illustrative of the History of France 1789–1901,* Minneapolis, 1904, 58–60. Courtesy of Frank Maloy Anderson.

tially in the nation; no body, no individual can exercise authority that does not proceed from it in plain terms.

4. Liberty consists in the power to do anything that does not injure others; accordingly, the exercise of the natural rights of each man has for its only limits those that secure to the other members of society the enjoyment of these same rights. These limits can be determined only by law.

5. The law has the right to forbid only such actions as are injurious to society. Nothing can be forbidden that is not interdicted by the law and no one can be constrained to do that which it does not order.

6. Law is the expression of the general will. All citizens have the right to take part personally or by their representatives in its formation. It must be the same for all, whether it protects or punishes. All citizens being equal in its eyes, are equally eligible to all public dignities, places, and employments, according to their capacities, and without other distinction than that of their virtues and their talents.

7. No man can be accused, arrested, or detained except in the cases determined by the law and according to the forms that it has prescribed. Those who procure, expedite, execute, or cause to be executed arbitrary orders ought to be punished: but every citizen summoned or seized in virtue of the law ought to render instant obedience; he makes himself guilty by resistance.

8. The law ought to establish only penalties that are strictly and obviously necessary and no one can be punished except in virtue of a law established and promulgated prior to the offence and legally applied.

9. Every man being presumed innocent until he has been pronounced guilty, if it is thought indispensable to arrest him, all severity that may not be necessary to secure his person ought to be strictly suppressed by law.

10. No one ought to be disturbed on account of his opinions, even religious, provided their manifestation does not derange the public order established by law.

11. The free communication of ideas and opinions is one of the most precious of the rights of man; every citizen then can freely speak, write, and print, subject to responsibility for the abuse of this freedom in the cases determined by law.

12. The guarantee of the rights of man and citizen requires a public force; this force then is instituted for the advantage of all and not for the personal benefit of those to whom it is entrusted.

13. For the maintenance of the public force and for the expenses of administration a general tax is indispensable; it ought to be equally apportioned among all the citizens according to their means.

14. All the citizens have the right to ascertain, by themselves or by their representatives, the necessity of the public tax, to consent to it freely, to follow the employment of it, and to determine the quota, the assessment, the collection, and the duration of it.

15. Society has the right to call for an account from every public agent of its administration.

16. Any society in which the guarantee of the rights is not secured or the separation of powers not determined has no constitution at all.

17. Property being a sacred and inviolable right, no one can be deprived of it unless a legally established public necessity evidently demands it, under the condition of a just and prior indemnity.

Maximilien Robespierre

In 1792 the French Revolution entered a second and more radical stage. The lower classes rather than the bourgeoisie came to dominate the government, and a republic replaced the limited monarchy. Violence became the order of the day, and the lives of those who opposed radicalism were in constant danger. A national convention was elected to draft a new constitution for France. This body com-

*pleted its task, but the results were never put into opera-
tion because of the disorder and violence. Maximilien
Robespierre (1758–1794) was a leader of the radical movement and a member of the convention. In 1793 he presented a draft of the Proposed Declaration of Rights for
the republican constitution. It was not adopted, but its
clauses revealed some of the rational ideals held by its author, and which he put into effect as president of the national convention. In reading Robespierre's Proposed Declaration of Rights note (1) the terminology of the preamble which is suggestive of the precepts of the Enlightenment, (2) the title he gave to God, (3) the purpose he
ascribed to all governments, (4) his definition of property
and the restrictions he would place on its owners, (5) evidences of social security and social justice permeating
Robespierre's ideas, (6) his views on taxation, (7) the influence of Rousseau on Robespierre, (8) his position regarding insurrection and revolution, and (9) Robespierre's
attitude toward the peoples and rulers of other nations.*

PROPOSED DECLARATION OF RIGHTS

The representatives of the French people, met in National Convention, recognizing that human laws which do not flow from the eternal laws of justice and reason are only the outrages of ignorance and despotism upon humanity; convinced that neglect and contempt of the natural rights of man are the sole causes of the crimes and misfortunes of the world; have resolved to set forth in a solemn declaration these sacred and inalienable rights, in order that all citizens, being enabled to compare constantly the acts of the government with the purpose of every social institution, may never permit themselves to be oppressed and disgraced by tyranny; and in order that the people may always have before their eyes the foundations of their liberty and their welfare; the magistrate, the rule of his duties; the legislator, the purpose of his mission.

In consequence, the National Convention proclaims in the face of the world and under the eyes of the Immortal Legislator the following declaration of the rights of man and citizen.

1. The purpose of every political association is the maintenance of the natural and imprescriptible rights of man and the development of all his faculties.

2. The principal rights of man are those of providing for the preservation of his existence and his liberty.

3. These rights belong equally to all men, whatever may be the difference of their physical and mental powers.

4. Equality of rights is established by nature: society, far from impairing it, exists only to guarantee it against the abuse of power which renders it illusory.

5. Liberty is the power which belongs to man to exercise at his will all his faculties; it has justice for rule, the rights of others for limits, nature for principle, and the law for safeguard.

6. The right to assemble peaceably, the right to express one's opinions, either by means of the press or in any other manner, are such necessary consequences of the principle of the liberty of man, that the necessity to enunciate them supposes either the presence or the fresh recollection of despotism.

7. The law can forbid only that which is injurious to society; it can order only that which is useful.

8. Every law which violates the imprescriptible rights of man is essentially unjust and tyrannical; it is not a law.

Frank Maloy Anderson, *The Constitutions and other Select Documents Illustrative of the History of France 1789–1901*, Minneapolis, 1904, 160–164. Courtesy of Frank Maloy Anderson.

9. Property is the right which each citizen has, to enjoy and dispose of the portion of goods which the law guarantees to him.

10. The right of property is restricted, as are all the others, by the obligation to respect the possessions of others.

11. It cannot prejudice the security, nor the liberty, nor the existence, nor the property of our fellow creatures.

12. All traffic which violates this principle is essentially illicit and immoral.

13. Society is under obligation to provide for the support of all its members either by procuring work for them or by assuring the means of existence to those who are not in condition to work.

14. The relief indispensable for those who lack the necessities of life is a debt of those who possess a superfluity; it belongs to the law to determine the manner in which this debt must be discharged.

15. The citizens whose incomes do not exceed what is necessary for their subsistence are exempted from contributing to the public expenses; the others shall support them progressively, according to the extent of their fortunes.

16. Society ought to favor with all its power the progress of public reason and to put instruction at the door of all the citizens.

17. Law is the free and solemn expression of the will of the people.

18. The people are the sovereign, the government is their creation, the public functionaries are their agents; the people can, when they please, change their government and recall their mandatories.

19. No portion of the people can exercise the power of the entire people; but the opinion which it expresses shall be respected as the opinion of a portion of the people who ought to participate in the formation of the general will. Each section of the assembled sovereign ought to enjoy the right to express its will with entire liberty; it is essentially independent of all the constituted authorities and is capable of regulating its police and its deliberations.

20. The law ought to be equal for all.

21. All citizens are admissible to all public offices, without any other distinctions than those of their virtues and talents and without any other title than the confidence of the people.

22. All citizens have an equal right to participate in the selection of the mandatories of the people and in the formation of the law.

23. In order that these rights may not be illusory and the equality chimerical, society ought to give salaries to the public functionaries and to provide so that all the citizens who live by their labor can be present in the public assemblies to which the law calls them, without compromising their existence or that of their families.

24. Every citizen ought to obey religiously the magistrates and the agents of the government, when they are the organs or the executors of the law.

25. But every act against the liberty, security, or property of a man, committed by anyone whomsoever, even in the name of the law outside of the cases determined by it and the forms which it prescribes, is arbitrary and void; respect for the law even forbids submission to it; and if an attempt is made to execute it by violence, it is permissible to repel it by force.

26. The right to present petitions to the depositories of the public authority belongs to every person. Those to whom they are addressed ought to pass upon the points which are the object thereof; but they can never interdict, nor restrain, nor condemn their use.

27. Resistance to oppression is a consequence of the other rights of man and citizen.

28. There is oppression against the social body when one of its members is oppressed. There is oppression against each member of the social body when the social body shall be oppressed.

29. When the government violates the rights of the people, insurrection is for the people and for each portion of the people the most sacred of rights and the most indispensable of duties.

30. When the social guarantee is lacking to a citizen he re-enters into the natural right to defend all his rights himself.

31. In either case, to tie down to legal forms resistance to oppression is the last refinement of tyranny. In every free State the law ought especially to defend public and personal liberty against the abuse of the authority of those who govern: every institution which is not based upon the assumption that the people

are good and the magistrate is corruptible is vicious.

32. The public offices cannot be considered as distinctions, nor as rewards, but only as duties.

33. The offences of the mandatories of the people ought to be severely and quickly punished. No one has the right to claim for himself more inviolability than other citizens. The people have the right to know all the transactions of their mandatories: these ought to render to them a faithful account of their own administration and to submit to their judgment with respect.

34. Men of all countries are brothers and the different peoples ought to aid one another, according to their power, as if citizens of the same State.

35. The one who oppresses a single nation declares himself the enemy of all.

36. Those who make war on a people in order to arrest the progress of liberty and to destroy the rights of man ought to be pursued by all, not as ordinary enemies, but as assassins and rebellious brigands.

37. Kings, aristocrats, and tyrants, whoever they may be, are slaves in rebellion against the sovereign of the earth, which is mankind, and against the legislator of the universe, which is nature.

Napoleon Bonaparte

In 1795 the French Revolution entered a reactionary third phase, during which a small group known as the Directory largely controlled the government. Its rule was characterized by four years of corruption and greed, and a general neglect of the reforms enacted in the earlier stages. The masses suffered untold hardships, and everywhere there was despair and disillusion. Meanwhile, Napoleon Bonaparte (1769–1821) had been leading French troops to victory over the coalitions formed by the monarchs of Europe to check the revolution. To most Frenchmen Napoleon seemed to be the only person who could restore order at home and win victory abroad. Only the extreme Jacobin radicals remained unfriendly, but their opposition was not sufficient to prevent him from staging a coup d'état at St. Cloud in November, 1799. The two councils (Elders and Five Hundred) quickly granted the executive power to Napoleon and two others, and the revolution was over. On the following day Napoleon issued a proclamation, explaining his part in the affair. It was typical of the arguments generally advanced by dictators and should be read in order to understand (1) the situation Napoleon found when he returned to France, (2) the reason why he guarded the Council of Elders, (3) the acts he performed in the Council of Elders and the Council of Five Hundred, (4) the position he claimed for himself in regard to the law and the councils, (5) his characterization of those who used force to outlaw him, and (6) his closing profession of zeal for liberty and the republic.

James Harvey Robinson and Charles A. Beard, *Readings in Modern European History* . . . , 2 vols., Ginn and Company, Boston, 1908, I, 322–323. Courtesy of Ginn and Company.

PROCLAMATION 19TH BRUMAIRE

PROCLAMATION

19th Brumaire, 11 o'clock P.M.

To the People:

Frenchmen, on my return to France I found division reigning among all the authorities. They agreed only on this single point, that the constitution was half destroyed and was unable to protect liberty.

Each party in turn came to me, confided to me their designs, imparted their secrets, and requested my support. But I refused to be the man of any party.

The Council of Elders appealed to me. I answered their appeal. A plan of general restoration had been conspired at by men whom the nation has been accustomed to regard as the defenders of liberty, equality, and property. This plan required calm deliberation, free from all influence and all fear. The Elders therefore resolved upon the removal of the legislative bodies to St. Cloud. They placed at my disposal the force necessary to secure their independence. I was bound, in duty to my fellow-citizens, to the soldiers perishing in our armies, and to the national glory acquired at the cost of so much blood, to accept the command.

The Council assembled at St. Cloud. Republican troops guaranteed their safety from without, but assassins created terror within. Many deputies in the Council of Five Hundred, armed with stilettos and pistols, spread the menace of death around them.

The plans which ought to have been developed were withheld. The majority of the Council was disorganized, the boldest orators were disconcerted, and the futility of submitting any salutary proposition was quite evident.

I proceeded, filled with indignation and chagrin, to the Council of the Elders. I besought them to carry their noble designs into execution. I directed their attention to the evils of the nation, which were their motives for conceiving those designs. They concurred in giving me new proofs of their unanimous good will.

I presented myself before the Council of the Five Hundred alone, unarmed, my head uncovered, just as the Elders had received and applauded me. My object was to restore to the majority the expression of its will and to secure to it its power.

The stilettos which had menaced the deputies were instantly raised against their deliverer. Twenty assassins rushed upon me and aimed at my breast. The grenadiers of the legislative body, whom I had left at the door of the hall, ran forward and placed themselves between me and the assassins. One of these brave grenadiers had his clothes pierced by a stiletto. They bore me out.

At the same moment cries of "Outlaw him!" were raised against the defender of the law. It was the horrid cry of assassins against the power destined to repress them. They crowded around the president, uttering threats. With arms in their hands, they commanded him to declare me outlawed. I was informed of this. I ordered him to be rescued from their fury, and six grenadiers of the legislative body brought him out. Immediately afterwards some grenadiers of the legislative body charged the hall and cleared it.

The seditious, thus intimidated, dispersed and fled. The majority, freed from their assailants, returned freely and peaceably into the hall, listened to the propositions for the public safety, deliberated, and drew up the salutary resolution which will become the new and provisional law of the republic.

Frenchmen, you will doubtless recognize in this conduct the zeal of a soldier of liberty, of a citizen devoted to the republic. Conservative, judicial, and liberal ideas resumed their sway upon the dispersion of those seditious persons who had domineered in the councils and who proved themselves the most odious and contemptible of men.

BONAPARTE

Edmund Burke

Edmund Burke (1729–1797) was an English intellectual and politician who was deeply concerned with some of the political theories produced by the Age of the Enlightenment. He did not adhere to the view that reason could construct a new and better society, nor did he accept Rousseau's view of popular sovereignty. He also looked with apprehension upon Locke's social contract with its implication that society could form governments and destroy them. Burke maintained that society was an organic whole, experiencing gradual growth, and that sudden, violent change was detrimental and might even destroy it. Thus Burke was reverting back to the medieval Christian concept of society and was attempting to conserve for England those ideals of government and of liberty which had been the product of historical growth. To him the French Revolution was a catastrophe from which he wished to spare England. He wrote his Reflections on the French Revolution in 1790 as a warning to his countrymen, some of whom were expressing sympathy with the events occurring across the channel. He approached the problem on the philosophical level, and his calm, clear analysis not only accomplished Burke's immediate purpose, but it has persisted as one of the best defenses of conservatism ever written. The Reflections were written in the form of a correspondence to a resident of Paris, a fact which helps to explain the terminology. In reading the following excerpts from this work note (1) the immediate incident motivating Burke to write this essay, (2) his answer to the assertion that the English king was chosen by the people, (3) the appeal to history to illustrate the evolution of the English constitution, (4) the reasons he gave why governments could not be constructed à priori, (5) the colorful passage in which he ridiculed the extreme emphasis of the reformers on the use of reason and the rights of man, (6) the criticism of the French intellectuals and politicians who condemned all that was old and admired anything new, (7) his answer to the French assertion that they were following the English example, (8) the attitude he recommended for all reformers when considering the defects of government, and (9) Burke's interpretation of society as a contract.

From: REFLECTIONS ON THE FRENCH REVOLUTION

On the forenoon of the 4th of November last, Doctor Richard Price, a non-conforming minister of eminence, preached at the dissenting meeting-house of the Old Jewry, to his club or society, a very extraordinary miscellaneous sermon, in which there are some good

Edmund Burke, *Reflections on the Revolution in France*, 3 vols., New York, 1836, I, 459–461; 469–470; 482; 493–494.

moral and religious sentiments, and not ill expressed, mixed up in a sort of porridge of various political opinions and reflections; but the Revolution in France is the grand ingredient in the cauldron. I consider the address transmitted by the Revolution Society to the National Assembly, through Earl Stanhope, as originating in the principles of the sermon, and as a corollary from them. It was moved by the preacher of that discourse. It was passed by those who came reeking from the effect of the sermon, without any censure or qualification, expressed or implied. If, however, any of the gentlemen concerned shall wish to separate the sermon from the resolution, they know how to acknowledge the one, and to disavow the other. They may do it: I cannot.

For my part, I looked on that sermon as the public declaration of a man much connected with literary caballers, and intriguing philosophers; with political theologians, and theological politicians, both at home and abroad. I know they set him up as a sort of oracle; because, with the best intentions in the world, he naturally *philippizes,* and chants his prophetic song in exact unison with their designs. . . .

He tells the Revolution Society in this political sermon, that his Majesty "is almost the *only* lawful king in the world, because the *only* one who owes his crown to the *choice of his people.*" As to the kings of *the world,* all of whom (except one) this archpontiff of the *rights of men,* with all the plenitude, and with more than the boldness, of the papal deposing power in its meridian fervour of the twelfth century, puts into one sweeping clause of ban and anathema, and proclaims usurpers by circles of longitude and latitude, over the whole globe, it behoves them to consider how they admit into their territories these apostolic missionaries, who are to tell their subjects they are not lawful kings. That is their concern. It is ours, as a domestic interest of some moment, seriously to consider the solidity of the *only* principle upon which these gentlemen acknowledge a king of Great Britain to be entitled to their allegiance.

This doctrine, as applied to the prince now on the British throne, either is nonsense, and therefore neither true nor false, or it affirms a most unfounded, dangerous, illegal, and unconstitutional position. According to this spiritual doctor of politics, if his Majesty does not owe his crown to the choice of his people, he is no *lawful king.* Now nothing can be more untrue than that the crown of this kingdom is so held by his Majesty. Therefore if you follow their rule, the king of Great Britain, who most certainly does not owe his high office to any form of popular election, is in no respect better than the rest of the gang of usurpers, who reign, or rather rob, all over the face of this our miserable world, without any sort of right or title to the allegiance of their people. The policy of this general doctrine, so qualified, is evident enough. The propagators of this political gospel are in hopes that their abstract principle (their principle that a popular choice is necessary to the legal existence of the sovereign magistracy) would be overlooked, whilst the king of Great Britain was not affected by it. In the mean time the ears of their congregations would be gradually habituated to it, as if it were a first principle admitted without dispute. For the present it would only operate as a theory, pickled in the preserving juices of pulpit eloquence, and laid by for future use. *Condo et compono quae mox depromere possim.* By this policy, whilst our government is soothed with a reservation in its favour, to which it has no claim, the security, which it has in common with all governments, so far as opinion is security, is taken away.

Thus these politicians proceed, whilst little notice is taken of their doctrines; but when they come to be examined upon the plain meaning of their words, and the direct tendency of their doctrines, then equivocations and slippery constructions come into play. When they say the king owes his crown to the choice of his people, and is therefore the only lawful sovereign in the world, they will perhaps tell us they mean to say no more than that some of the king's predecessors have been called to the throne by some sort of choice; and therefore he owes his crown to the choice of his people. Thus, by a miserable subterfuge, they hope to render their proposition safe, by rendering it nugatory. They are welcome to the asylum they seek for their offence, since they take refuge in their folly. For, if you admit this interpretation, how does their idea of election differ from our idea of inheritance? And how does the settlement of the crown in the Brunswick line derived from James the First come to legalize our monarchy, rather than that of any of the neighbouring countries? At some time or other, to be sure, all the beginners of dynasties were chosen by those who called them to govern. There is ground enough for the opinion that all the kingdoms of Europe were, at a remote period, elective, with more or fewer limitations in the objects of choice. But whatever kings might have been here, or elsewhere, a thousand years ago, or in whatever manner the ruling dynasties of England or France may have begun, the king of Great Britain is, at this day, king by a fixed rule of succession, according to the laws of his country; and whilst the legal conditions of the compact of sovereignty are performed by him (as they are performed), he holds his crown in contempt of the choice of the Revolution Society, who have not a single vote for a king amongst them, either individually or collectively; though I make no doubt they would soon erect themselves into an electoral college, if things were ripe to give effect to their claim. His Majesty's heirs and successors, each in his time and order, will come to the crown with the same contempt of their choice with which his Majesty has succeeded to that he wears. . . .

You will observe, that from Magna Charta to the Declaration of Right, it has been the uniform policy of our constitution to claim and assert our liberties, as an *entailed inheritance* derived to us from our forefathers, and to be transmitted to our posterity; as an estate specially belonging to the people of this kingdom, without any reference whatever to any other more general or prior right. By this means our constitution preserves a unity in so great a diversity of its parts. We have an inheritable crown; an inheritable peerage; and a House of Commons and a people inheriting privileges, franchises, and liberties, from a long line of ancestors.

This policy appears to me to be the result of profound reflection; or rather the happy effect of following nature, which is wisdom without reflection, and above it. A spirit of innovation is generally the result of a selfish temper and confined views. People will not look forward to posterity, who never look backward to their ancestors. Besides, the people of England well know, that the idea of inheritance furnishes a sure principle of conservation and a sure principle of transmission; without at all excluding a principle of improvement. It leaves acquisition free; but it secures what it acquires. Whatever advantages are obtained by a state proceeding on these maxims, are locked fast as in a sort of family settlement; grasped as in a kind of mortmain for ever. By a constitutional policy, working after the pattern of nature, we receive, we hold, we transmit our government and our privileges, in the same manner in which we enjoy and transmit our property and our lives. The institutions of policy, the goods of fortune, the gifts of providence, are handed down to us, and from us, in the same course and order. Our political system is placed in a just correspondence and symmetry with the order of the world, and with the mode of existence decreed to a permanent body composed of transitory parts; wherein, by the disposition of a stupendous wisdom, moulding together the great mysterious incorporation of the human race, the whole, at one time, is never old, or middle-aged, or young, but, in a condition of unchangeable constancy, moves on through the varied tenor of perpetual decay, fall, renovation, and progression. Thus, by preserving the method of nature in the conduct of the state, in what we improve, we are never wholly new; in what we retain, we are never wholly obsolete. By adhering in this manner and on those principles to our forefathers, we are guided not by the superstition of antiquarians, but by the spirit of philosophic analogy. In this choice of inheritance we have given to our frame of polity the image of a relation in blood; binding up the constitution of our country with our dearest domestic ties; adopting our fundamental laws into the bosom of our family affections; keeping inseparable, and cherishing with the warmth of all their combined and mutually reflected charities, our state, our hearths, our sepulchres, and our altars. . . .

The science of constructing a commonwealth, or renovating it, or reforming it, is, like every other experimental science, not to be taught *à priori*. Nor is it a short experience that can instruct us in that practical science; because the real effects of moral causes are not always immediate; but that which in the first instance is prejudicial may be excellent in its remoter operation; and its excellence may arise even from the ill effects it produces in the beginning. The reverse also happens: and very plausible schemes, with very pleasing commencements, have often shameful and lamentable conclusions. In states there are often some obscure and almost latent causes, things which appear at first view of little moment, on which a very great part of its prosperity or adversity may most essentially depend. The science of government being therefore so practical in itself, and intended for such practical purposes, a matter which requires experience, and even more experience than any person can gain in his whole life, however sagacious and observing he may be, it is with infinite caution that any man ought to venture upon pulling down an edifice, which has answered in any tolerable degree for ages the common purposes of society, or on building it up again, without having models and patterns of approved utility before his eyes. . . .

Thanks to our sullen resistance to innovation, thanks to the cold sluggishness of our national character, we still bear the stamp of our forefathers. We have not (as I conceive) lost the generosity and dignity of thinking of the fourteenth century; nor as yet have we subtilized ourselves into savages. We are not the converts of Rousseau; we are not the disciples of Voltaire; Helvetius has made no progress amongst us. Atheists are not our preachers; madmen are not our lawgivers. We know that *we* have made no discoveries, and we think that no discoveries are to be made, in morality; nor many in the great principles of government, nor in the ideas of liberty, which were understood long before we were born, altogether as well as they will be after the grave has heaped its mould upon our presumption, and the silent tomb shall have imposed its law on our pert loquacity. In England we have not yet been completely embowelled of our natural entrails; we still feel within us, and we cherish and cultivate, those inbred sentiments which are the faithful guardians, the active monitors of our duty, the true supporters of all liberal and manly morals. We have not been drawn and trussed, in order that

we may be filled, like stuffed birds in a museum, with chaff and rags and paltry blurred shreds of paper about the rights of man. We preserve the whole of our feelings still native and entire, unsophisticated by pedantry and infidelity. We have real hearts of flesh and blood beating in our bosoms. We fear God; we look up with awe to kings; with affection to parliaments; with duty to magistrates; with reverence to priests; with respect to nobility. Why? Because when such ideas are brought before our minds, it is *natural* to be so affected; because all other feelings are false and spurious, and tend to corrupt our minds, to vitiate our primary morals, to render us unfit for rational liberty; and by teaching us a servile, licentious, and abandoned insolence, to be our low sport for a few holidays, to make us perfectly fit for, and justly deserving of, slavery, through the whole course of our lives.

You see, Sir, that in this enlightened age I am bold enough to confess, that we are generally men of untaught feelings; that instead of casting away all our old prejudices, we cherish them to a very considerable degree, and, to take more shame to ourselves, we cherish them because they are prejudices; and the longer they have lasted, and the more generally they have prevailed, the more we cherish them. We are afraid to put men to live and trade each on his own private stock of reason; because we suspect that this stock in each man is small, and that the individuals would do better to avail themselves of the general bank and capital of nations and of ages. Many of our men of speculation, instead of exploding general prejudices, employ their sagacity to discover the latent wisdom which prevails in them. If they find what they seek, and they seldom fail, they think it more wise to continue the prejudice, with the reason involved, than to cast away the coat of prejudice, and to leave nothing but the naked reason; because prejudice, with its reason, has a motive to give action to that reason, and an affection which will give it permanence. Prejudice is of ready application in the emergency; it previously engages the mind in a steady course of wisdom and virtue, and does not leave the man hesitating in the moment of decision, sceptical, puzzled, and unresolved. Prejudice renders a man's virtue his habit; and not a series of unconnected acts. Through just prejudice, his duty becomes a part of his nature.

Your literary men, and your politicians, and so do the whole clan of the enlightened among us, essentially differ in these points. They have no respect for the wisdom of others; but they pay it off by a very full measure of confidence in their own. With them it is a sufficient motive to destroy an old scheme of things, because it is an old one. As to the new, they are in no sort of fear with regard to the duration of a building run up in haste; because duration is no object to those who think little or nothing has been done before their time, and who place all their hopes in discovery. They conceive, very systematically, that all things which give perpetuity are mischievous, and therefore they are at inexpiable war with all establishments. They think that government may vary like modes of dress, and with as little ill effect: that there needs no principle of attachment, except a sense of present conveniency, to any constitution of the state. They always speak as if they were of opinion that there is a singular species of compact between them and their magistrates, which binds the magistrate, but which has nothing reciprocal in it, but that the majesty of the people has a right to dissolve it without any reason, but its will. Their attachment to their country itself is only so far as it agrees with some of their fleeting projects; it begins and ends with that scheme of polity which falls in with their momentary opinion.

These doctrines, or rather sentiments, seem prevalent with your new statesmen. But they are wholly different from those on which we have always acted in this country.

I hear it is sometimes given out in France, that what is doing among you is after the example of England. I beg leave to affirm, that scarcely anything done with you has originated from the practice or the prevalent opinions of this people, either in the act or in the spirit of the proceeding. Let me add, that we are as unwilling to learn these lessons from France, as we are sure that we never taught them to that nation. The cabals here, who take a sort of share in your transactions, as yet consist of but a handful of people. If unfortunately by their intrigues, their sermons, their publica-

tions, and by a confidence derived from an expected union with the counsels and forces of the French nation, they should draw considerable numbers into their faction, and in consequence should seriously attempt anything here in imitation of what has been done with you, the event, I dare venture to prophesy, will be, that, with some trouble to their country, they will soon accomplish their own destruction. This people refused to change their law in remote ages from respect to the infallibility of popes; and they will not now alter it from a pious implicit faith in the dogmatism of philosophers; though the former was armed with the anathema and crusade, and though the latter should act with the libel and the lamp-iron.

Formerly your affairs were your own concern only. We felt for them as men; but we kept aloof from them, because we were not citizens of France. But when we see the model held up to ourselves, we must feel as Englishmen, and feeling, we must provide as Englishmen. Your affairs, in spite of us, are made a part of our interest; so far at least as to keep at a distance your panacea, or your plague. If it be a panacea, we do not want it. We know the consequences of unnecessary physic. If it be a plague, it is such a plague that the precautions of the most severe quarantine ought to be established against it. . . .

To avoid therefore the evils of inconstancy and versatility, ten thousand times worse than those of obstinacy and the blindest prejudice, we have consecrated the state, that no man should approach to look into its defects or corruptions but with due caution; that he should never dream of beginning its reformation by its subversion; that he should approach to the faults of the state as to the wounds of a father, with pious awe and trembling solicitude. By this wise prejudice we are taught to look with horror on those children of their country, who are prompt rashly to hack that aged parent in pieces, and put him into the kettle of magicians, in hopes that by their poisonous weeds, and wild incantations, they may regenerate the paternal constitution, and renovate their father's life.

Society is indeed a contract. Subordinate contracts for objects of mere occasional interest may be dissolved at pleasure—but the state ought not to be considered as nothing better than a partnership agreement in a trade of pepper and coffee, calico or tobacco, or some other such low concern, to be taken up for a little temporary interest, and to be dissolved by the fancy of the parties. It is to be looked on with other reverence; because it is not a partnership in things subservient only to the gross animal existence of a temporary and perishable nature. It is a partnership in all science; a partnership in all art; a partnership in every virtue, and in all perfection. As the ends of such a partnership cannot be obtained in many generations, it becomes a partnership not only between those who are living, but between those who are living, those who are dead, and those who are to be born. Each contract of each particular state is but a clause in the great primaeval contract of eternal society, linking the lower with the higher natures, connecting the visible and invisible world, according to a fixed compact sanctioned by the inviolable oath which holds all physical and all moral natures, each in their appointed place. This law is not subject to the will of those, who by an obligation above them, and infinitely superior, are bound to submit their will to that law. The municipal corporations of that universal kingdom are not morally at liberty at their pleasure, and on their speculations of a contingent improvement, wholly to separate and tear asunder the bands of their subordinate community, and to dissolve it into an unsocial, uncivil, unconnected chaos of elementary principles. It is the first and supreme necessity only, a necessity that is not chosen, but chooses, a necessity paramount to deliberation, that admits no discussion, and demands no evidence, which alone can justify a resort to anarchy. This necessity is no exception to the rule; because this necessity itself is a part too of that moral and physical disposition of things, to which man must be obedient by consent or force: but if that which is only submission to necessity should be made the object of choice, the law is broken, nature is disobeyed, and the rebellious are outlawed, cast forth, and exiled, from this world of reason, and order, and peace, and virtue, and fruitful penitence, into the antagonist world of madness, discord, vice, confusion, and unavailing sorrow. . . .

William Wordsworth

Wiliam Wordsworth (1770–1850) was an English poet who lived his early years in a world shaken by the French Revolution, and reached maturity during the conservative reaction to that epoch-making event. In the realm of culture he was familiar as a young man with the last period of the Enlightenment and its emphasis on nature and natural law; but he wrote some of his best known works in the decades when the romantic movement was emerging as a protest against the extremes of the Age of Reason. In his poetry he reflected some of the interest of the leaders of the Enlightenment in nature, but to Wordsworth nature was more than a source of law—it was a manifestation of the all-pervading spirit which unites all mankind. Thus by communing with the beauties of the natural world one could become aware of the universal brotherhood of man and the true meaning of life. It was this mystical idealization of nature that gave to Wordsworth's poetry its romantic character. The two following selections were written by him in 1798. "The Tables Turned" reflected his interest in nature as a source of inspiration for the guidance of men, while in "We Are Seven" he has

*given us in the form of the maiden's devotion to her family
an indication of the unity of all life. In reading the first
selection note (1) Wordsworth's attitude toward the study
of books, (2) the role he assigned to nature, (3) his comparison of the relative value of impulses and the teaching
of the learned, (4) the effect intellect has on the beauties
of nature, and (5) the part played by the heart in understanding nature. In "We Are Seven" note (1) the description of the child, (2) her simple response to the writer's
query, (3) the argument that developed between them,
(4) the child's devotion to the two in the church-yard,
(5) the spiritual unity of her family, and (6) the beautiful
simplicity of Wordsworth's lines.*

THE TABLES TURNED and WE ARE SEVEN

THE TABLES TURNED

An Evening Scene . . . [Alfoxden, 1798?].

Up, up! my Friend, and quit your books;
Or surely you'll grow double:
Up, up! my Friend, and clear your looks;
Why all this toil and trouble?

The sun, above the mountain's head,
A freshening lustre mellow
Through all the long green fields has spread,
His first sweet evening yellow.

Books! 'tis a dull and endless strife:
Come, hear the woodland linnet,
How sweet his music! on my life,
There's more of wisdom in it.

And hark! how blithe the throstle sings!
He, too, is no mean preacher:
Come forth into the light of things,
Let Nature be your teacher.

She has a world of ready wealth,
Our minds and hearts to bless—
Spontaneous wisdom breathed by health,
Truth breathed by cheerfulness.

One impulse from a vernal wood
May teach you more of man,
Of moral evil and of good,
Than all the sages can.

Sweet is the lore which Nature brings;
Our meddling intellect
Mis-shapes the beauteous forms of things:—
We murder to dissect.

Enough of Science and of Art;
Close up those barren leaves;
Come forth, and bring with you a heart
That watches and receives.

WE ARE SEVEN

—A simple Child,
That lightly draws its breath,
And feels its life in every limb,
What should it know of death?

I met a little cottage Girl:
She was eight years old, she said;
Her hair was thick with many a curl
That clustered round her head.

She had a rustic, woodland air,
And she was wildly clad:
Her eyes were fair, and very fair;
—Her beauty made me glad.

"Sisters and brothers, little Maid,
How many may you be?"
"How many? Seven in all," she said,
And wondering looked at me.

Ernest Rhys, ed., *The Lyric Poems of William Wordsworth*, London, n.d., 119–120; 126–129.

"And where are they? I pray you tell."
She answered, "Seven are we;
And two of us at Conway dwell,
And two are gone to sea.

"Two of us in the church-yard lie,
My sister and my brother;
And, in the church-yard cottage, I
Dwell near them with my mother."

"You say that two at Conway dwell,
And two are gone to sea,
Yet ye are seven!—I pray you tell,
Sweet Maid, how this may be."

Then did the little Maid reply,
"Seven boys and girls are we;
Two of us in the church-yard lie,
Beneath the church-yard tree."

"You run about, my little Maid,
Your limbs they are alive;
If two are in the church-yard laid,
Then ye are only five."

"Their graves are green, they may be seen,"
The little Maid replied,
"Twelve steps or more from my mother's door,
And they are side by side.

"My stockings there I often knit,
My kerchief there I hem;

And there upon the ground I sit,
And sing a song to them.

"And often after sunset, Sir,
When it is light and fair,
I take my little porringer,
And eat my supper there.

"The first that died was sister Jane;
In bed she moaning lay,
Till God released her of her pain;
And then she went away.

"So in the church-yard she was laid;
And, when the grass was dry,
Together round her grave we played,
My brother John and I.

"And when the ground was white with snow,
And I could run and slide,
My brother John was forced to go,
And he lies by her side."

"How many are you, then," said I,
"If they two are in heaven?"
Quick was the little Maid's reply,
"O Master! we are seven."

"But they are dead; those two are dead!
Their spirits are in heaven!"
'Twas throwing words away; for still
The little Maid would have her will,
And said, "Nay, we are seven!"

Thomas Malthus

homas Robert Malthus (1766–1834) was a clergyman
and professor of history and political economy at Hai-
leybury College, near London. He became interested in the
doctrine of human perfectibility through his reading of
William Godwin and J. A. N. Condorcet. Malthus, who
lived his mature life during the period of the romantic reaction against the Age of Reason, rejected the belief in
man's ability indefinitely to extend the world's food supply
and refused to abandon a morality that would operate to
control population growth. As a counter to the easy optimistic notion of human perfectibility, Malthus proposed
the idea that man endured the conflict with evil and that
this conflict enobled the race. He first published his study
in 1798, later republishing it several times. The selection
given here is chapter one taken from the first edition. In it

*Malthus presented a succinct account of his leading princi-
ples. In reading it note (1) Malthus's statement of the
great issue confronting men, (2) his description of the position of the two advocates in the contest and the limitations under which each suffered, (3) the two postulates he
advanced, (4) his treatment of the argument of the opposition, (5) the ratios of increase of population and food supply, (6) the new problem involved in the inequality of the
two powers, (7) the implication for population control,
(8) his description of the law of nature respecting population and production, and of its consequences, and (9) his
conclusions.*

From: AN ESSAY ON POPULATION

OUTLINE OF THE PRINCIPAL ARGU-
MENT OF THE ESSAY

The great and unlooked for discoveries that
have taken place of late years in natural philosophy; the increasing diffusion of general
knowledge from the extension of the art of
printing; the ardent and unshackled spirit of
inquiry that prevails throughout the lettered,
and even unlettered, world; the new and extraordinary lights that have been thrown on
political subjects, which dazzle and astonish
the understanding; and particularly that tremendous phenomenon in the political horizon,
the French Revolution, which, like a blazing
comet, seems destined either to inspire with
fresh life and vigour, or to scorch up and destroy the thinking inhabitants of the earth, have
all concurred to lead able men into the opinion,
that we are touching upon a period big with
the most important changes, changes that
would in some measure be decisive of the future fate of mankind.

It has been said, that the great question is
now at issue, whether man shall henceforth
start forwards with accelerated velocity towards illimitable, and hitherto unconceived improvement; or be condemned to a perpetual
oscillation between happiness and misery, and
after every effort remain still at an immeasurable distance from the wished-for goal.

Yet, anxiously as every friend of mankind
must look forwards to the termination of this
painful suspense; and, eagerly as the inquiring
mind would hail every ray of light that might
assist its view into futurity, it is much to be
lamented, that the writers on each side of this
momentous question still keep far aloof from
each other. Their mutual arguments do not
meet with a candid examination. The question
is not brought to rest on fewer points; and
even in theory scarcely seems to be approaching to a decision.

The advocate for the present order of things,
is apt to treat the sect of speculative philosophers, either as a set of artful and designing
knaves, who preach up ardent benevolence,
and draw captivating pictures of a happier
state of society, only the better to enable them
to destroy the present establishments, and to
forward their own deep-laid schemes of ambition: or, as wild and mad-headed enthusiasts,
whose silly speculations, and absurd paradoxes,
are not worthy the attention of any reasonable
man.

The advocate for the perfectibility of man,
and of society, retorts on the defender of establishments a more than equal contempt. He
brands him as the slave of the most miserable
and narrow prejudices; or, as the defender of
the abuses of civil society, only because he
profits by them. He paints him either as a character who prostitutes his understanding to his
interest; or as one whose powers of mind are
not of a size to grasp anything great and noble;
who cannot see above five yards before him;

Thomas Robert Malthus, *An Essay on the Principles of Population as it Affects the Future Improvement of Society
. . .* , London, 1798, chapter 1.

the way to perfectibility of society. All other arguments are of slight and subordinate consideration in comparison of this. I see no way by which man can escape from the weight of this law which pervades all animated nature. No fancied equality, no agrarian regulations in their utmost extent, could remove the pressure of it even for a single century. And it appears, therefore, to be decisive against the possible existence of a society, all the members of which should live in ease, happiness, and comparative leisure; and feel no anxiety about providing the means of subsistence for themselves and families.

Consequently, if the premises are just, the argument is conclusive against the perfectibility of the mass of mankind.

I have thus sketched the general outline of the argument; but I will examine it more particularly; and I think it will be found that experience, the true source and foundation of all knowledge, invariably confirms its truth.

Johann Wolfgang von Goethe

Johann Wolfgang von Goethe (1749–1832) was one of the outstanding German literary figures who, in the late eighteenth and early nineteenth centuries, endeavored to free German culture from its artificial imitation of foreign, and particularly French, patterns. He and his contemporaries, Gottfried Lessing and Friedrich Schiller, used both legend and history as the subject matter for romantic novels, plays, and poems in order to stir the latent spirit of the German people. Goethe's greatest work was the drama, Faust, the first part of which he completed in 1808, and the second in 1831. Based upon a sixteenth-century German legend, it tells the story of the scholarly Faust who, restless for knowledge about the supernatural, bargained with the Devil (Mephistopheles), and risked his soul as the possible cost. In the character of Faust, Goethe personified the romantic individualism of the nineteenth century, the emotional restlessness and striving so characteristic of the romantic reaction to the rationalism of the Enlightenment. Thus this drama, one of the great literary masterpieces of all time, not only symbolized the stirring of German national feeling, but it stands as one of the signposts marking the end of the culture of the Enlightenment. In reading the prologue, Faust's opening soliloquy, and the scene between Faust and Mephistopheles note (1) the fluent and glowing description of the universe made by the three archangels, (2) the contrasting humor and sarcasm in the words of Mephistopheles, (3) his implied criticism of the extremes to which man had carried reason, (4) the Lord's query about earthly conditions, (5) their discussion of Faust and the Devil's description of the Faust spirit, (6) the agreement which they made concerning Faust's soul, (7) the romantic gratitude expressed by the Devil for God's conversation with him, (8) Faust's restless lamentation over the futility of learning, and his willingness to resort to the mystical to find that which he was seeking and could not find through study, (9) Faust's moving description of the longing in his breast, (10) Mephistopheles' offer to guide Faust, (11) Faust's insistence on establishing the terms of the agreement, and the manner in which Mephistopheles wanted the contract sealed, and (12) Mephistopheles' triumphant musing over his victim.

From: FAUST

PROLOGUE IN HEAVEN

The Lord.   The Heavenly Hosts.   *Afterwards*
Mephistopheles
(*The* Three Archangels *come forward.*)

Raphael

The sun-orb sings, in emulation,
'Mid brother-spheres, his ancient round:
His path predestined through Creation
He ends with step of thunder-sound.
The angels from his visage splendid
Draw power, whose measure none can say;
The lofty works, uncomprehended,
Are bright as on the earliest day.

Gabriel

And swift, and swift beyond conceiving,
The splendor of the world goes round,
Day's Edenbrightness still relieving
The awful Night's intense profound:
The ocean-tides in foam are breaking,
Against the rocks' deep bases hurled,
And both, the spheric race partaking,
Eternal, swift, are onward whirled!

Michael

And rival storms abroad are surging
From sea to land, from land to sea.
A chain of deepest action forging
Round all, in wrathful energy.
There flames a desolation, blazing
Before the Thunder's crashing way:
Yet, Lord, Thy messengers are praising
The gentle movement of Thy Day.

The Three

Though still by them uncomprehended,
From these the angels draw their power,
And all Thy works, sublime and splendid,
Are bright as in Creation's hour.

Mephistopheles

Since Thou, O Lord, deign'st to approach again
And ask us how we do, in manner kindest,
And heretofore to meet myself wert fain,
Among Thy menials, now, my face Thou findest.
Pardon, this troop I cannot follow after
With lofty speech, though by them scorned
   and spurned,
My pathos certainly would move Thy laughter,
If Thou hadst not all merriment unlearned.
Of suns and worlds I've nothing to be quoted;
How men torment themselves, is all I've noted.
The little god o' the world sticks to the same
   old way,
And is as whimsical as on Creation's day.
Life somewhat better might content him,
But for the gleam of heavenly light which
   Thou hast lent him:
He calls it Reason—thence his power's in-
   creased,
To be far beastlier than any beast.
Saving Thy Gracious Presence, he to me
A long-legged grasshopper appears to be,
That springing flies, and flying springs,
And in the grass the same old ditty sings.
Would he still lay among the grass he grows in!
Each bit of dung he seeks, to stick his nose in.

The Lord

Hast thou, then, nothing more to mention?
Com'st ever, thus, with ill intention?
Find'st nothing right on earth, eternally?

Mephistopheles

No, Lord! I find things, there, still bad as they
   can be.

As translated by Bayard Taylor in Johann Wolfgang von Goethe, *Faust, A Tragedy*, Boston, 1871, 13–24; 85–103.

Man's misery even to pity moves my nature;
I've scarce the heart to plague the wretched
creature.

The Lord

Know'st Faust?

Mephistopheles

The Doctor Faust?

The Lord

My servant, he!

Mephistopheles

Forsooth! He serves you after strange devices:
No earthly meat or drink the fool suffices:
His spirit's ferment far aspireth;
Half conscious of his frenzied, crazed unrest,
The fairest stars from Heaven he requireth,
From Earth the highest raptures and the best,
And all the Near and Far that he desireth
Fails to subdue the tumult of his breast.

The Lord

Though still confused his service unto Me,
I soon shall lead him to a clearer morning.
Sees not the gardener, even while buds his
tree,
Both flower and fruit the future years adorn-
ing?

Mephistopheles

What will you bet? There's still a chance to
gain him,
If unto me full leave you give,
Gently upon *my* road to train him!

The Lord

As long as he on earth shall live,
So long I make no prohibition.
While Man's desires and aspirations stir,
He cannot choose but err.

Mephistopheles

My thanks! I find the dead no acquisition,
And never cared to have them in my keeping.
I much prefer the cheeks where ruddy blood
is leaping,
And when a corpse approaches, close my
house:
It goes with me, as with the cat the mouse.

The Lord

Enough! What thou hast asked is granted.
Turn off this spirit from his fountain-head;
To trap him, let thy snares be planted,
And him, with thee, be downward led;
Then stand abashed, when thou art forced to
say:
A good man, through obscurest aspiration,
Has still an instinct of the one true way.

Mephistopheles

Agreed! But 't is a short probation.
About my bet I feel no trepidation.
If I fulfil my expectation,
You'll let me triumph with a swelling breast:
Dust shall he eat, and with a zest,
As did a certain snake, my near relation.

The Lord

Therein thou 'rt free, according to thy merits;
The like of thee have never moved My hate.
Of all the bold, denying Spirits,
The waggish knave least trouble doth create.
Man's active nature, flagging, seeks too soon
the level;
Unqualified repose he learns to crave;
Whence, willingly, the comrade him I gave,
Who works, excites, and must create, as Devil.
But ye, God's sons in love and duty,
Enjoy the rich, the ever-living Beauty!
Creative Power, that works eternal schemes,
Clasp you in bonds of love, relaxing never,
And what in wavering apparition gleams
Fix in its place with thoughts that stand for-
ever!

(*Heaven closes: the* Archangels *separate.*)

Mephistopheles (solus)

I like, at times, to hear The Ancient's word,
And have a care to be most civil:
It's really kind of such a noble Lord
So humanly to gossip with the Devil!

FIRST PART OF THE TRAGEDY

I

Night

(*A lofty-arched, narrow, Gothic chamber.*
Faust, *in a chair at his desk, restless.*)

Faust

I've studied now Philosophy
And jurisprudence, Medicine,—

And even, alas! Theology,—
From end to end, with labor keen;
And here, poor fool! with all my lore
I stand, no wiser than before:
I'm Magister—yea, Doctor—hight,
And straight or cross-wise, wrong or right,
These ten years long, with many woes,
I've led my scholars by the nose,—
And see, that nothing can be known!
That knowledge cuts me to the bone.
I'm cleverer, true, than those fops of teachers,
Doctors and Magisters, Scribes and Preach-
   ers;
Neither scruples nor doubts come now to
   smite me,
Nor Hell nor Devil can longer affright me.
For this, all pleasure am I foregoing;
I do not pretend to aught worth knowing,
I do not pretend I could be a teacher
To help or convert a fellow-creature.
Then, too, I've neither lands nor gold,
Nor the world's least pomp or honor hold—
No dog would endure such a curst existence!
Wherefore, from Magic I seek assistance,
That many a secret perchance I reach
Through spirit-power and spirit-speech,
And thus the bitter task forego
Of saying the things I do not know,—
That I may detect the inmost force
Which binds the world, and guides its course;
Its germs, productive powers explore,
And rummage in empty words no more!

O full and splendid Moon, whom I
Have, from this desk, seen climb the sky
So many a midnight,—would thy glow
For the last time beheld my woe!
Ever thine eye, most mournful friend,
O'er books and papers saw me bend;
But would that I, on mountains grand,
Amid thy blessed light could stand,
With spirits through mountain-caverns hover,
Float in thy twilight the meadows over,
And, freed from the fumes of lore that swathe
   me,
To health in thy dewy fountains bathe me!

Ah, me! this dungeon still I see,
This drear, accursed masonry,
Where even the welcome daylight strains
But duskly through the painted panes.

Hemmed in by many a toppling heap
Of books worm-eaten, gray with dust,
Which to the vaulted ceiling creep,
Against the smoky papers thrust,—
With glasses, boxes, round me stacked,
And instruments together hurled,
Ancestral lumber, stuffed and packed—
Such is my world: and what a world!

And do I ask, wherefore my heart
Falters, oppressed with unknown needs?
Why some inexplicable smart
All movement of my life impedes?
Alas! in living Nature's stead,
Where God His human creature set,
In smoke and mould the fleshless dead
And bones of beasts surround me yet!

Fly! Up, and seek the broad, free land!
And this one Book of Mystery
From Nostradamus' very hand,
Is 't not sufficient company?
When I the starry courses know,
And Nature's wise instruction seek,
With light of power my soul shall glow,
As when to spirits spirits speak.
'T is vain, this empty brooding here,
Though guessed the holy symbols be:
Ye, Spirits, come—ye hover near—
Oh, if you hear me, answer me! . . .

IV

THE STUDY

Faust. Mephistopheles.

Faust

A knock? Come in! Again my quiet broken?

Mephistopheles

'T is I!

Faust

Come in!

Mephistopheles

Thrice must the words be spoken.

Faust

Come in, then!

Mephistopheles

Thus thou pleasest me.
I hope we'll suit each other well;

For now, thy vapors to dispel,
I come, a squire of high degree,
In scarlet coat, with golden trimming,
A cloak in silken lustre swimming,
A tall cock's-feather in my hat,
A long, sharp sword for show or quarrel,—
And I advise thee, brief and flat,
To don the self-same gay apparel,
That, from this den released, and free,
Life be at last revealed to thee!

Faust

This life of earth, whatever my attire,
Would pain me in its wonted fashion.
Too old am I to play with passion;
Too young, to be without desire.
What from the world have I to gain?
Thou shalt abstain—renounce—refrain!
Such is the everlasting song
That in the ears of all men rings,—
That unrelieved, our whole life long,
Each hour, in passing, hoarsely sings.
In very terror I at morn awake,
Upon the verge of bitter weeping,
To see the day of disappointment break,
To no one hope of mine—not one—its promise
     keeping:—
That even each joy's presentiment
With wilful cavil would diminish,
With grinning masks of life prevent
My mind its fairest work to finish!
Then, too, when night descends, how anxiously
Upon my couch of sleep I lay me:
There, also, comes no rest to me,
But some wild dream is sent to fray me.
The God that in my breast is owned
Can deeply stir the inner sources;
The God, above my powers enthroned,
He cannot change external forces.
So, by the burden of my days oppressed,
Death is desired, and Life a thing unblest!

Mephistopheles

And yet is never Death a wholly welcome
     guest.

Faust

O fortunate, for whom, when victory glances,
The bloody laurels on the brow he bindeth!
Whom, after rapid, maddening dances,
In clasping maiden-arms he findeth!

O would that I, before that spirit-power,
Ravished and rapt from life, had sunken!

Mephistopheles

And yet, by some one, in that nightly hour,
A certain liquid was not drunken.

Faust

Eavesdropping, ha! thy pleasure seems to be.

Mephistopheles

Omniscient am I not; yet much is known to me.

Faust

Though some familiar tone, retrieving
My thoughts from torment, led me on,
And sweet, clear echoes came, deceiving
A faith bequeathed from Childhood's dawn,
Yet now I curse whate'er entices
And snares the soul with visions vain;
With dazzling cheats and dear devices
Confines it in this cave of pain!
Cursed be, at once, the high ambition
Wherewith the mind itself deludes!
Cursed be the glare of apparition
That on the finer sense intrudes!
Cursed be the lying dream's impression
Of name, and fame, and laurelled brow!
Cursed, all that flatters as possession,
As wife and child, as knave and plow!
Cursed Mammon be, when he with treasures
To restless action spurs our fate!
Cursed when, for soft, indulgent leisures,
He lays for us the pillows straight!
Cursed be the vine's transcendent nectar,—
The highest favor Love lets fall!
Cursed, also, Hope!—cursed Faith, the spec-
     tre!
And cursed be Patience most of all!

Chorus of Spirits (invisible)

Woe! woe!
Thou hast it destroyed,
The beautiful world,
With powerful fist:
In ruin 't is hurled,
By the blow of a demigod shattered!
The scattered
Fragments into the Void we carry,
Deploring
The beauty perished beyond restoring.

Mightier
For the children of men,
Brightlier
Build it again,
In thine own bosom build it anew!
Bid the new career
Commence,
With clearer sense,
And the new songs of cheer
Be sung thereto!

Mephistopheles

These are the small dependants
Who give me attendance.
Hear them, to deeds and passion
Counsel in shrewd old-fashion!
Into the world of strife,
Out of this lonely life,
That of senses and sap has betrayed thee,
They would persuade thee.
This nursing of the pain forego thee,
That, like a vulture, feeds upon thy breast!
The worst society thou find'st will show thee
Thou art a man among the rest.
But 't is not meant to thrust
Thee into the mob thou hatest!
I am not one of the greatest,
Yet, wilt thou to me entrust
Thy steps through life, I'll guide thee,—
Will willingly walk beside thee,—
Will serve thee at once and forever
With best endeavor,
And, if thou art satisfied,
Will as servant, slave, with thee abide.

Faust

And what shall be my counter-service therefor?

Mephistopheles

The time is long: thou need'st not now insist.

Faust

No—no! The Devil is an egotist,
And is not apt, without a why or wherefore,
"For God's sake," others to assist.
Speak thy conditions plain and clear!
With such a servant danger comes, I fear.

Mephistopheles

Here, an unwearied slave, I'll wear thy tether,
And to thine every nod obedient be:

When *There* again we come together,
Then shalt thou do the same for me.

Faust

The *There* my scruples naught increases.
When thou hast dashed this world to pieces,
The other, then, its place may fill.
Here, on this earth, my pleasures have their
sources;
Yon sun beholds my sorrows in his courses;
And when from these my life itself divorces,
Let happen all that can or will!
I'll hear no more: 't is vain to ponder
If there we cherish love or hate,
Or, in the spheres we dream of yonder,
A High and Low our souls await.

Mephistopheles

In this sense, even, canst thou venture.
Come, bind thyself by prompt indenture,
And thou mine arts with joy shalt see:
What no man ever saw, I'll give to thee.

Faust

Canst thou, poor Devil, give me whatsoever?
When was a human soul, in its supreme en-
deavor,
E'er understood by such as thou?
Yet, hast thou food which never satiates,
now,—
The restless, ruddy gold hast thou,
That runs, quicksilver-like, one's fingers
through,—
A game whose winnings no man ever knew,—
A maid, that, even from my breast,
Beckons my neighbor with her wanton glances,
And Honor's godlike zest,
The meteor that a moment dances,—
Show me the fruits that, ere they're gathered,
rot,
And trees that daily with new leafage clothe
them!

Mephistopheles

Such a demand alarms me not:
Such treasures have I, and can show them.
But still the time may reach us, good my friend,
When peace we crave and more luxurious diet.

Faust

When on an idler's bed I stretch myself in
quiet,

There let, at once, my record end!
Canst thou with lying flattery rule me,
Until, self-pleased, myself I see,—
Canst thou with rich enjoyment fool me,
Let that day be the last for me!
The bet I offer.

Mephistopheles

Done!

Faust

And heartily!
When thus I hail the Moment flying:
"Ah, still delay—thou art so fair!"
Then bind me in thy bonds undying,
My final ruin then declare!
Then let the death-bell chime the token,
Then art thou from thy service free!
The clock may stop, the hand be broken,
Then Time be finished unto me!

Mephistopheles

Consider well: my memory good is rated.

Faust

Thou hast a perfect right thereto.
My powers I have not rashly estimated:
A slave am I, whate'er I do—
If thine, or whose? 'tis needless to debate it.

Mephistopheles

Then at the Doctors'-banquet I, to-day,
Will as a servant wait behind thee.
But one thing more! Beyond all risk to bind
    thee,
Give me a line or two, I pray.

Faust

Demand'st thou, Pedant, too, a document?
Hast never known a man, nor proved his word's
    intent?
Is 't not enough, that what I speak to-day
Shall stand, with all my future days agreeing?
In all its tides sweeps not the world away,
And shall a promise bind my being?
Yet this delusion in our hearts we bear:
Who would himself therefrom deliver?
Blest he, whose bosom Truth makes pure and
    fair!
No sacrifice shall he repent of ever.
Nathless a parchment, writ and stamped with
    care,

A spectre is, which all to shun endeavor.
The word, alas! dies even in the pen,
And wax and leather keep the lordship then.
What wilt from me, Base Spirit, say?—
Brass, marble, parchment, paper, clay?
The terms with graver, quill, or chisel, stated?
I freely leave the choice to thee.

Mephistopheles

Why heat thyself, thus instantly,
With eloquence exaggerated?
Each leaf for such a pact is good;
And to subscribe thy name thou 'lt take a drop
    of blood.

Faust

If thou therewith art fully satisfied,
So let us by the farce abide.

Mephistopheles

Blood is a juice of rarest quality.

Faust

Fear not that I this pact shall seek to sever!
The promise that I make to thee
Is just the sum of my endeavor.
I have myself inflated all too high;
My proper place is thy estate:
The Mighty Spirit deigns me no reply,
And Nature shuts on me her gate.
The thread of Thought at last is broken,
And knowledge brings disgust unspoken.
Let us the sensual deeps explore,
To quench the fervors of glowing passion!
Let every marvel take form and fashion
Through the impervious veil it wore!
Plunge we in Time's tumultuous dance,
In the rush and roll of Circumstance!
Then may delight and distress,
And worry and success,
Alternately follow, as best they can:
Restless activity proves the man!

Mephistopheles

For you no bound, no term is set.
Whether you everywhere be trying,
Or snatch a rapid bliss in flying,
May it agree with you, what you get!
Only fall to, and show no timid balking.

Faust

But thou hast heard, 't is not of joy we're talk-
    ing.

I take the wildering whirl, enjoyment's keenest
    pain,
Enamored hate, exhilarant disdain.
My bosom, of its thirst for knowledge sated,
Shall not, henceforth, from any pang be
    wrested,
And all of life for all mankind created
Shall be within mine inmost being tested:
The highest, lowest forms my soul shall bor-
    row,
Shall heap upon itself their bliss and sorrow,
And thus, my own sole self to all their selves
    expanded
I too, at last, shall with them all be stranded!

Mephistopheles

Believe me, who for many a thousand year
The same tough meat have chewed and tested,
That from the cradle to the bier
No man the ancient leaven has digested!
Trust one of us, this Whole supernal
Is made but for a God's delight!
He dwells in splendor single and eternal,
But *us* he thrusts in darkness, out of sight,
And *you* he dowers with Day and Night.

Faust

Nay, but I will!

Mephistopheles

    A good reply!
One only fear still needs repeating:
The art is long, the time is fleeting.
Then let thyself be taught, say I!
Go, league thyself with a poet,
Give the rein to his imagination,
Then wear the crown, and show it,
Of the qualities of his creation,—
The courage of the lion's breed.
The wild stag's speed,
The Italian's fiery blood,
The North's firm fortitude!
Let him find for thee the secret tether
That binds the Noble and Mean together,
And teach thy pulses of youth and pleasure
To love by rule, and hate by measure!
I'd like, myself, such a one to see:
Sir Microcosm his name should be.

Faust

What am I, then, if 't is denied my part
The crown of all humanity to win me,
Whereto yearns every sense within me?

Mephistopheles

Why, on the whole, thou 'rt—what thou art.
Set wigs of million curls upon thy head, to
    raise thee,
Wear shoes an ell in height,—the truth betrays
    thee,
And thou remainest—what thou art.

Faust

I feel, indeed, that I have made the treasure
Of human thought and knowledge mine, in
    vain;
And if I now sit down in restful leisure,
No fount of newer strength is in my brain:
I am no hair's-breadth more in height,
Nor nearer to the Infinite.

Mephistopheles

Good Sir, you see the facts precisely
As they are seen by each and all.
We must arrange them now, more wisely,
Before the joys of life shall pall.
Why, Zounds! Both hands and feet are, truly—
And head and virile forces—thine:
Yet all that I indulge in newly,
Is 't thence less wholly mine?
If I've six stallions in my stall,
Are not their forces also lent me?
I speed along, completest man of all,
As though my legs were four-and-twenty.
Take hold, then! let reflection rest,
And plunge into the world with zest!
I say to thee, a speculative wight
Is like a beast on moorlands lean,
That round and round some fiend misleads to
    evil plight,
While all about lie pastures fresh and green.

Faust

Then how shall we begin?

Mephistopheles

    We'll try a wider sphere.
What place of martyrdom is here!
Is 't life, I ask, is 't even prudence,
To bore thyself and bore the students?
Let Neighbor Paunch to that attend!
Why plague thyself with threshing straw for-
    ever?
The best thou learnest, in the end
Thou dar'st not tell the youngsters—never!
I hear one's footsteps, hither steering.

Faust

To see him now I have no heart.

Mephistopheles

So long the poor boy waits a hearing,
He must not unconsoled depart.
Thy cap and mantle straightway lend me!
I'll play the comedy with art.

      (*He disguises himself.*)

My wits, be certain, will befriend me.
But fifteen minutes' time is all I need;
For our fine trip, meanwhile, prepare thyself
   with speed!

        [*Exit* Faust

Mephistopheles

    (*In* Faust's *long mantle.*)

Reason and Knowledge only thou despise,
The highest strength in man that lies!
Let but the Lying Spirit bind thee

With magic works and shows that blind thee,
And I shall have thee fast and sure!
Fate such a bold, untrammelled spirit gave
   him,
As forwards, onwards, ever must endure;
Whose over-hasty impulse drave him
Past earthly joys he might secure.
Dragged through the wildest life, will I enslave
   him,
Through flat and stale indifference;
With struggling, chilling, checking, so deprave
   him
That, to his hot, insatiate sense,
The dream of drink shall mock, but never lave
   him:
Refreshment shall his lips in vain implore—
Had he not made himself the Devil's, naught
   could save him,
Still were he lost forevermore! . . .

Clemens Metternich

The Austrian statesman, Clemens Metternich (1773–1859) dominated the European political scene from the Congress of Vienna in 1815 to the liberal revolutions of 1848. He led the conservative reaction which swept over Europe following the close of the revolutionary and Napoleonic eras. In an effort to restore Austria to its former strategic position he espoused the principles of restoration, legitimacy, and absolutism, and sought in every possible way to beat down the rising tide of liberalism and nationalism. The Confession of Faith which follows was written by him in 1820, and in it he summarized his political and social philosophy. In reading it note (1) the events which prompted Metternich to write his Confession, (2) the evil which he believed threatened to destroy civilization, (3) the cause for this evil, (4) his attitude toward secret societies, (5) his characterization of the great mass of the people, (6) the class from which the discontented were largely drawn, (7) his attitude toward the past, and (8) the various proposals he offered to monarchs to correct the evil.

CONFESSION OF FAITH

SECRET MEMORANDUM TO THE EMPEROR ALEXANDER

"*L'Europe*," a celebrated writer has recently said, "*fait aujourd'hui pitié à l'homme d'esprit et horreur à l'homme vertueux.*"

It would be difficult to comprise in a few words a more exact picture of the situation at the time we are writing these lines!

Kings have to calculate the chances of their very existence in the immediate future; passions are let loose, and league together to over-

As translated by Mrs. Alexander Napier in *Memoirs of Prince Metternich,* edited by Prince Richard Metternich, 5 vols., London, 1880–1882, III, 454–476.

throw everything which society respects as the basis of its existence; religion, public morality, laws, customs, rights, and duties, all are attacked, confounded, overthrown, or called in question. The great mass of the people are tranquil spectators of these attacks and revolutions, and of the absolute want of all means of defence. A few are carried off by the torrent, but the wishes of the immense majority are to maintain a repose which exists no longer, and of which even the first elements seem to be lost.

What is the cause of all these evils? By what methods has this evil established itself, and how is it that it penetrates into every vein of the social body?

Do remedies still exist to arrest the progress of this evil, and what are they?

These are doubtless questions worthy of the solicitude of every good man who is a true friend to order and public peace—two elements inseparable in principle, and which are at once the first needs and the first blessings of humanity.

Has there never been offered to the world an institution really worthy of the name? Has truth been always confounded with error ever since society has believed itself able to distinguish one from the other? Have the experiences bought at the price of so many sacrifices, and repeated at intervals, and in so many different places, been all in error? Will a flood of light be shed upon society at one stroke? Will knowledge come by inspiration? If one could believe in such phenomena it would not be the less necessary, first of all, to assure oneself of their reality. Of all things, nothing is so fatal as error; and it is neither our wish nor our intention ever to give ourselves up to it. Let us examine the matter!

THE SOURCE OF THE EVIL

Man's nature is immutable. The first needs of society are and remain the same, and the differences which they seem to offer find their explanation in the diversity of influences, acting on the different races by natural causes, such as the diversity of climate, barrenness or richness of soil, insular or continental position, &c. &c. These local differences no doubt produce effects which extend far beyond purely physical necessities; they create and determine particular needs in a more elevated sphere; finally, they determine the laws, and exercise an influence even on religions.

It is, on the other hand, with institutions as with everything else. Vague in their origin, they pass through periods of development and perfection, to arrive in time at their decadence; and, conforming to the laws of man's nature, they have, like him, their infancy, their youth, their age of strength and reason, and their age of decay.

Two elements alone remain in all their strength, and never cease to exercise their indestructible influence with equal power. These are the precepts of morality, religious as well as social, and the necessities created by locality. From the time that men attempt to swerve from these bases, to become rebels against these sovereign arbiters of their destinies, society suffers from a *malaise* which sooner or later will lead to a state of convulsion. The history of every country, in relating the consequences of such errors, contains many pages stained with blood; but we dare to say, without fear of contradiction, one seeks in vain for an epoch when an evil of this nature has extended its ravages over such a vast area as it has done at the present time. The causes are natural.

History embraces but a very limited space of time. It did not begin to deserve the name of history until long after the fall of great empires. There, where it seems to conduct us to the cradle of civilisation, it really conducts us to ruins. We see republics arise and prosper, struggle, and then submit to the rule of one fortunate soldier. We see one of these republics pass through all the phases common to society, and end in an almost universal monarchy—that is to say, subjugating the scattered portions of the then civilised world. We see this monarchy suffer the fate of all political bodies: we see its first springs become enfeebled, and finally decay.

Centuries of darkness followed the irruption of the barbarians. The world, however, could not return to barbarism. The Christian religion had appeared; imperishable in its essence, its very existence was sufficient to disperse the darkness and establish civilisation on new foundations, applicable to all times and all places, satisfying all needs, and establishing the most important of all on the basis of a pure and eternal law! To the formation of new Christian States succeeded the Crusades, a curious mixture of good and evil.

A decisive influence was shortly exercised on the progress of civilisation by three discoveries —the invention of printing, that of gunpowder, and the discovery of the New World. Still later came the Reformation—another event which had incalculable effects, on account of its influence on the moral world. From that time the face of the world was changed.

The facilitation of the communication of thoughts by printing; the total change in the means of attack and defence brought about by the invention of gunpowder; the difference suddenly produced in the value of property by the quantity of metals which the discovery of America put in circulation; the spirit of adventure provoked by the chances of fortune opened in a new hemisphere; the modifications in the relations of society caused by so many and such important changes, all became more developed, and were in some sort crowned by the revolution which the Reformation worked in the moral world.

The progress of the human mind has been extremely rapid in the course of the last three centuries. This progress having been accelerated more rapidly than the growth of wisdom (the only counterpoise to passions and to error); a revolution prepared by the false systems, the fatal errors into which many of the most illustrious sovereigns of the last half of the eighteenth century fell, has at last broken out in a country advanced in knowledge, and enervated by pleasure, in a country inhabited by a people whom one can only regard as frivolous, from the facility with which they comprehend and the difficulty they experience in judging calmly.

Having now thrown a rapid glance over the first causes of the present state of society, it is necessary to point out in a more particular manner the evil which threatens to deprive it, at one blow, of the real blessings, the fruits of genuine civilisation, and to disturb it in the midst of its enjoyments. This evil may be described in one word—presumption; the natural effect of the rapid progression of the human mind towards the perfecting of so many things. This it is which at the present day leads so many individuals astray, for it has become an almost universal sentiment.

Religion, morality, legislation, economy, politics, administration, all have become common and accessible to everyone. Knowledge seems to come by inspiration; experience has no value for the presumptuous man; faith is nothing to him; he substitutes for it a pretended individual conviction, and to arrive at this conviction dispenses with all inquiry and with all study; for these means appear too trivial to a mind which believes itself strong enough to embrace at one glance all questions and all facts. Laws have no value for him, because he has not contributed to make them, and it would be beneath a man of his parts to recognise the limits traced by rude and ignorant generations. Power resides in himself; why should he submit himself to that which was only useful for the man deprived of light and knowledge? That which, according to him, was required in an age of weakness cannot be suitable in an age of reason and vigour, amounting to universal perfection, which the German innovators designate by the idea, absurd in itself, of the Emancipation of the People! Morality itself he does not attack openly, for without it he could not be sure for a single instant of his own existence; but he interprets its essence after his own fashion, and allows every other person to do so likewise, provided that other person neither kills nor robs him.

In thus tracing the character of the presumptuous man, we believe we have traced that of the society of the day, composed of like elements, if the denomination of society is applicable to an order of things which only tends in principle towards individualising all the elements of which society is composed. Presumption makes every man the guide of his own belief, the arbiter of laws according to which he is pleased to govern himself, or to allow some one else to govern him and his neighbours; it makes him, in short, the sole judge of his own faith, his own actions, and the principles according to which he guides them.

Is it necessary to give a proof of this last fact? We think we have furnished it in remarking that one of the sentiments most natural to man, that of nationality, is erased from the Liberal catechism, and that where the word is still employed, it is used by the heads of the party as a pretext to enchain Governments, or as a lever to bring about destruction. The real aim of the idealists of the party is religious and political fusion, and this being analysed is nothing else but creating in favour of each individual an existence entirely independent of all authority, or of any other will than his own, an idea absurd and contrary to the nature of man, and incompatible with the needs of human society.

THE COURSE WHICH THE EVIL HAS FOLLOWED AND STILL FOLLOWS

The causes of the deplorable intensity with which this evil weighs on society appear to us to be of two kinds. The first are so connected with the nature of things that no human foresight could have prevented them. The second should be subdivided into two classes, however similar they may appear in their effects.

Of these causes, the first are negative, the others positive. We will place among the first the feebleness and the inertia of Governments.

It is sufficient to cast a glance on the course which the Governments followed during the eighteenth century, to be convinced that not one among them was ignorant of the evil or of the crisis towards which the social body was tending. There were, however, some men, unhappily endowed with great talents, who felt their own strength, and were not slow to appraise the progressive course of their influence, taking into account the weakness or the inertia of their adversaries; and who had the art to prepare and conduct men's minds to the triumph of their detestable enterprise—an enterprise all the more odious as it was pursued without regard to results, simply abandoning themselves to the one feeling of hatred of God and of His immutable moral laws.

France had the misfortune to produce the greatest number of these men. It is in her midst that religion and all that she holds sacred, that morality and authority, and all connected with them, have been attacked with a steady and systematic animosity, and it is

there that the weapon of ridicule has been used with the most ease and success.

Drag through the mud the name of God and the powers instituted by His divine decrees, and the revolution will be prepared! Speak of a social contract, and the revolution is accomplished! The revolution was already completed in the palaces of Kings, in the drawing-rooms and boudoirs of certain cities, while among the great mass of the people it was still only in a state of preparation.

It would be difficult not to pause here to consider the influence which the example of England had for a long time exercised on France. England is herself placed in such a peculiar situation that we believe we may safely say that not one of the forms possible to that State, not one of its customs or institutions, would suit any Continental State, and that where we might wish to take them for models, we should only obtain inconvenience and danger, without securing a single one of the advantages which accompany them.

According to the bent of minds in France, at the time of the convocation of the *notables,* and in consequence of the direction which public opinion had received for more than fifty years—a direction which, latterly, had been strengthened and in some sort adapted to France by the imprudent help which her Government had given to the American revolution —all reform in France touching the very foundations of the monarchy was soon transformed into a revolution. What might have been foreseen, and what had been foretold by everybody, the Government alone excepted, was realised but too soon. The French Revolution broke out, and has gone through a complete revolutionary cycle in a very short period, which could only have appeared long to its victims and to its contemporaries.

The scenes of horror which accompanied the first phases of the French Revolution prevented the rapid propagation of its subversive principles beyond the frontiers of France, and the wars of conquest which succeeded them gave to the public mind a direction little favourable to revolutionary principles. Thus the Jacobin propaganda failed entirely to realise criminal hopes.

Nevertheless the revolutionary seed had penetrated into every country and spread more or less. It was greatly developed under the *régime* of the military despotism of Bonaparte. His conquests displaced a number of laws, institutions, and customs; broke through bonds sacred among all nations, strong enough to resist time itself; which is more than can be said of certain benefits conferred by these innovators. From these perturbations it followed that the revolutionary spirit could in Germany, Italy, and later on in Spain, easily hide itself under the veil of patriotism.

Prussia committed a grave fault in calling to her aid such dangerous weapons as secret associations always will be: a fault which could not be justified even by the deplorable situation in which that Power then found itself. This it was that first gave a strong impulse to the revolutionary spirit in her States, and this spirit made rapid progress, supported as it was in the rest of Germany by the system of foreign despotism which since 1806 has been there developed. Many Princes of the Rhenish Confederation were secretly auxiliaries and accomplices of this system, to which they sacrificed the institutions which in their country from time immemorial had served as a protection against despotism and democracy.

The war of the Allies, by putting bounds to the predominance of France, was vigorously supported in Germany by the same men whose hatred of France was in reality nothing but hatred of the military despotism of Bonaparte, and also of the legitimate power of their own masters. With wisdom in the Governments and firmness in principles, the end of the war in 1814 might nevertheless have insured to the world the most peaceful and happy future. Great experiences had been gained and great lessons, which might have been usefully applied. But fate had decided otherwise.

The return of the usurped to France, and the completely false steps taken by the French Government from 1815 to 1820, accumulated a mass of new dangers and great calamities for the whole civilised world. It is to the first of these misfortunes that is partly due the critical state in which France and the whole social body is placed. Bonaparte destroyed in a hundred days the work of the fourteen years during which he had exercised his authority. He set free the revolution which he came to France to subdue; he brought back men's minds, not to the epoch of the 18th Brumaire, but to the principles which the National Assembly had adopted in its deplorable blindness.

What Bonaparte had thus done to the detriment of France and Europe, the grave errors which the French Government have since committed, and to which other Governments have yielded—all these unhappy influences weigh heavily on the world of to-day; they threaten with total ruin the work of restoration, the fruit of so many glorious efforts, and of a harmony between the greatest monarchs unparalleled in the records of history, and they give rise to fears of indescribable calamities to society.

In this memoir we have not yet touched on one of the most active and at the same time most dangerous instruments used by the revolutionists of all countries, with a success which is no longer doubtful. I refer to the secret societies, a real power, all the more dangerous as it works in the dark, undermining all parts of the social body, and depositing everywhere the seeds of a moral gangrene which is not slow to develop and increase. This plague is one of the worst which those Governments who are lovers of peace and of their people have to watch and fight against.

DO REMEDIES FOR THIS EVIL EXIST, AND WHAT ARE THEY?

We look upon it as a fundamental truth, that for every disease there is a remedy, and that the knowledge of the real nature of the one should lead to the discovery of the other. Few men, however, stop thoroughly to examine a disease which they intend to combat. There are hardly any who are not subject to the influence of passion, or held under the yoke of prejudice; there are a great many who err in a way more perilous still, on account of its flattering and often brilliant appearance: we speak of *l'esprit de système;* that spirit always false, but indefatigable, audacious and irrepressible, is satisfactory to men imbued with it (for they live in and govern a world created by themselves), but it is so much the more dangerous for the inhabitants of the real world, so different from that created by *l'esprit de système.*

There is another class of men who, judging of a disease by its outward appearance, confound the accessory manifestations with the root of the disease, and, instead of directing their efforts to the source of the evil, content themselves with subduing some passing symptoms.

It is our duty to try and avoid both of these dangers.

The evil exists and it is enormous. We do not think we can better define it and its cause at all times and in all places than we have already done by the word "presumption" [that inseparable companion of the half-educated, that spring of an unmeasured ambition, and yet easy to satisfy in times of trouble and confusion].

It is principally the middle classes of society which this moral gangrene has affected, and it is only among them that the real heads of the party are found.

For the great mass of the people it has no attraction and can have none. The labours to which this class—the real people—are obliged to devote themselves, are too continuous and too positive to allow them to throw themselves into vague abstractions and ambitions. The people know what is the happiest thing for them: namely, to be able to count on the morrow, for it is the morrow which will repay them for the cares and sorrows of to-day. The laws which afford a just protection to individuals, to families, and to property, are quite simple in their essence. The people dread any movement which injures industry and brings new burdens in its train.

Men in the higher classes of society who join the revolution are either falsely ambitious men or, in the widest acceptation of the word, lost spirits. Their career, moreover, is generally short! They are the first victims of political reforms, and the part played by the small number among them who survive is mostly that of courtiers despised by upstarts, their inferiors, promoted to the first dignities of the State; and of this France, Germany, Italy, and Spain furnish a number of living examples.

We do not believe that fresh disorders with a directly revolutionary end—not even revolutions in the palace and the highest places in the Government—are to be feared at present in France, because of the decided aversion of the people to anything which might disturb the peace they are now enjoying after so many troubles and disasters.

In Germany, as in Spain and Italy, the people ask only for peace and quiet.

In all four countries the agitated classes are principally composed of wealthy men—real cosmopolitans, securing their personal advantage at the expense of any order of things whatever—paid State officials, men of letters, lawyers, and the individuals charged with the public education.

To these classes may be added that of the falsely ambitious, whose number is never considerable among the lower orders, but is larger in the higher ranks of society.

There is besides scarcely any epoch which does not offer a rallying cry to some particular faction. This cry, since 1815, has been *Constitution*. But do not let us deceive ourselves: this word, susceptible of great latitude of interpretation, would be but imperfectly understood if we supposed that the factions attached quite the same meaning to it under the different *régimes*. Such is certainly not the case. In pure monarchies it is qualified by the name of "national representation." In countries which have lately been brought under the representative *régime* it is called "development," and promises charters and fundamental laws. In the only State which possesses an ancient national representation it takes "reform" as its object. Everywhere it means change and trouble.

In pure monarchies it may be paraphrased thus:—"The level of equality shall pass over your heads; your fortunes shall pass into other hands; your ambitions, which have been satisfied for centuries, shall now give place to our ambitions, which have been hitherto repressed."

In the States under a new *régime* they say:—"The ambitions satisfied yesterday must give place to those of the morrow, and this is the morrow for us."

Lastly, in England, the only place in the third class, the rallying cry—that of Reform—combines the two meanings.

Europe thus presents itself to the impartial observer under an aspect at the same time deplorable and peculiar. We find everywhere the people praying for the maintenance of peace and tranquillity, faithful to God and their Princes, remaining proof against the efforts and seductions of the factions who call themselves friends of the people and wish to lead them to an agitation which the people themselves do not desire!

The Governments, having lost their balance, are frightened, intimidated, and thrown into confusion by the cries of the intermediary class of society, which, placed between the Kings and their subjects, breaks the sceptre of the monarch, and usurps the cry of the people— that class so often disowned by the people, and nevertheless too much listened to, caressed and feared by those who could with one word reduce it again to nothingness.

We see this intermediary class abandon itself with a blind fury and animosity which proves much more its own fears than any confidence in the success of its enterprises, to all the means which seem proper to assuage its thirst for power, applying itself to the task of persuading Kings that their rights are confined to sitting upon a throne, while those of the people are to govern, and to attack all that centuries have bequeathed as holy and worthy of man's respect—denying, in fact, the value of the past, and declaring themselves the masters of the future. We see this class take all sorts of disguises, uniting and subdividing as occasion offers, helping each other in the hour of danger, and the next day depriving each other of all their conquests. It takes possession of the press, and employs it to promote impiety, disobedience to the laws of religion and the State, and goes so far as to preach murder as a duty for those who desire what is good.

One of its leaders in Germany defined public opinion as "the will of the strong man in the spirit of the party"—a maxim too often put in practice, and too seldom understood by those whose right and duty it is to save society from its own errors, its own weaknesses, and the crimes which the factious commit while pretending to act in its interests.

The evil is plain; the means used by the faction which causes these disorders are so blameable in principle, so criminal in their application, and expose the faction itself to so many dangers, that what men of narrow views

(whose head and heart are broken by circumstances stronger than their calculations or their courage) regard as the end of society may become the first step towards a better order of things. These weak men would be right unless men stronger than they are come forward to close their ranks and determine the victory.

We are convinced that society can no longer be saved without strong and vigorous resolutions on the part of the Governments still free in their opinions and actions.

We are also convinced that this may yet be, if the Governments face the truth, if they free themselves from all illusion, if they join their ranks and take their stand on a line of correct, unambiguous, and frankly announced principles.

By this course the monarchs will fulfil the duties imposed upon them by Him who, by entrusting them with power, has charged them to watch over the maintenance of justice, and the rights of all, to avoid the paths of error, and tread firmly in the way of truth. Placed beyond the passions which agitate society, it is in days of trial chiefly that they are called upon to despoil realities of their false appearances, and to show themselves as they are, fathers invested with the authority belonging by right to the heads of families, to prove that, in days of mourning, they know how to be just, wise, and therefore strong, and that they will not abandon the people whom they ought to govern to be the sport of factions, to error and its consequences, which must involve the loss of society. The moment in which we are putting our thoughts on paper is one of these critical moments. The crisis is great; it will be decisive according to the part we take or do not take.

There is a rule of conduct common to individuals and to States, established by the experience of centuries as by that of everyday life. This rule declares "that one must not dream of reformation while agitated by passion; wisdom directs that at such moments we should limit ourselves to maintaining."

Let the monarchs vigorously adopt this principle; let all their resolutions bear the impression of it. Let their actions, their measures, and even their words announce and prove to the world this determination—they will find allies everywhere. The Governments, in establishing the principle of *stability,* will in no wise exclude the development of what is good, for stability is not immobility. But it is for those who are burdened with the heavy task of government to augment the well-being of their people! It is for Governments to regulate it according to necessity and to suit the times. It is not by concessions, which the factions strive to force from legitimate power, and which they have neither the right to claim nor the faculty of keeping within just bounds, that wise reforms can be carried out. That all the good possible should be done is our most ardent wish; but that which is not good must never be confounded with that which is, and even real good should be done only by those who unite to the right of authority the means of enforcing it. Such should be also the sincere wish of the people, who know by sad experience the value of certain phrases and the nature of certain caresses.

Respect for all that is; liberty for every Government to watch over the well-being of its own people; a league between all Governments against factions in all States; contempt for the meaningless words which have become the rallying cry of the factions; respect for the progressive development of institutions in lawful ways; refusal on the part of every monarch to aid or succour partisans under any mask whatever—such are happily the ideas of the great monarchs: the world will be saved if they bring them into action—it is lost if they do not.

Union between the monarchs is the basis of the policy which must now be followed to save society from total ruin.

What is the particular object towards which this policy should be directed? The more important this question is, the more necessary it is to solve it. A principle is something, but it acquires real value only in its application.

The first sources of the evil which is crushing the world have been indicated by us in a paper which has no pretension to be anything more than a mere sketch. Its further causes have also there been pointed out, if, with respect to individuals, it may be defined by the word *presumption,* in applying it to society,

taken as a whole, we believe we can best describe the existing evil as the *confusion of ideas,* to which too much generalisation constantly leads. This is what now troubles society. Everything which up to this time has been considered as fixed in principle is attacked and overthrown.

In religious matters criticism and inquiry are to take the place of faith, Christian morality is to replace the Law of Christ as it is interpreted by Christian authorities.

In the Catholic Church, the Jansenists and a number of isolated sectarians, who wish for a religion without a Church, have devoted themselves to this enterprise with ardent zeal: among the Protestant sects, the Methodists, sub-divided into almost as many sects as there are individuals; then the enlightened promoters of the Bible Societies and the Unitarians—the promoters of the fusion of Lutherans and Calvinists in one Evangelical community—all pursue the same end.

The object which these men have in common, to whatever religion they may ostensibly belong, is simply to overthrow all authority. Put on moral grounds, they wish *to enfranchise souls* in the same way as some of the political revolutionists who were not actuated by motives of personal ambition wished to *enfranchise the people.*

If the same elements of destruction which are now throwing society into convulsion have existed in all ages—for every age has seen immoral and ambitious men, hypocrites, men of heated imaginations, wrong motives, and wild projects—yet ours, by the single fact of the liberty of the press, possesses more than any preceding age the means of contact, seduction, and attraction whereby to act on these different classes of men.

We are certainly not alone in questioning if society can exist with the liberty of the press, a scourge unknown to the world before the latter half of the seventeenth century, and restrained until the end of the eighteenth, with scarcely any exceptions but England—a part of Europe separated from the continent by the sea, as well as by her language and by her peculiar manners.

The first principle to be followed by the

monarchs, united as they are by the coincidence of their desires and opinions, should be that of maintaining the stability of political institutions against the disorganised excitement which has taken possession of men's minds; the immutability of principles against the madness of their interpretation; and respect for laws actually in force against a desire for their destruction.

The hostile faction is divided into two very distinct parties. One is that of the Levellers; the other, that of the Doctrinaires. United in times of confusion, these men are divided in times of inaction. It is for the Governments to understand and estimate them at their just value.

In the class of Levellers there are found men of strong will and determination. The Doctrinaires can count none such among their ranks. If the first are more to be feared in action, the second are more dangerous in that time of deceitful calm which precedes it; as with physical storms, so with those of social order. Given up to abstract ideas inapplicable to real wants, and generally in contradiction to those very wants, men of this class unceasingly agitate the people by their imaginary or simulated fears, and disturb Governments in order to make them deviate from the right path. The world desires to be governed by facts and according to justice, not by phrases and theories; the first need of society is to be maintained by strong authority (no authority without real strength deserves the name) and not to govern itself. In comparing the number of contests between parties in mixed Governments, and that of just complaints caused by aberrations of power in a Christian State, the comparison would not be in favour of the new doctrines. The first and greatest concern for the immense majority of every nation is the stability of the laws, and their uninterrupted action—never their change. Therefore let the Governments govern, let them maintain the groundwork of their institutions, both ancient and modern; for if it is at all times dangerous to touch them, it certainly would not now, in the general confusion, be wise to do so.

Let them announce this determination to their people, and demonstrate it by facts. Let them reduce the Doctrinaires to silence within their States, and show their contempt for them abroad. Let them not encourage by their attitude or actions the suspicion of being favourable or indifferent to error: let them not allow it to be believed that experience has lost all its rights to make way for experiments which at the least are dangerous. Let them be precise and clear in all their words, and not seek by concessions to gain over those parties who aim at the destruction of all power but their own, whom concessions will never gain over, but only further embolden in their pretensions to power.

Let them in these troublous times be more than usually cautious in attempting real ameliorations, not imperatively claimed by the needs of the moment, to the end that good itself may not turn against them—which is the case whenever a Government measure seems to be inspired by fear.

Let them not confound concessions made to parties with the good they ought to do for their people, in modifying, according to their recognised needs, such branches of the administration as require it.

Let them give minute attention to the financial state of their kingdoms, so that their people may enjoy, by the reduction of public burdens, the real, not imaginary, benefits of a state of peace.

Let them be just, but strong; beneficent, but strict.

Let them maintain religious principles in all their purity, and not allow the faith to be attacked and morality interpreted according to the *social contract* or the visions of foolish sectarians.

Let them suppress Secret Societies, that gangrene of society.

In short, let the great monarchs strengthen their union, and prove to the world that if it exists, it is beneficent, and ensures the political peace of Europe: that it is powerful only for the maintenance of tranquillity at a time when so many attacks are directed against it; that the principles which they profess are paternal and protective, menacing only the disturbers of public tranquillity.

The Governments of the second order will

see in such a union the anchor of their salvation, and they will be anxious to connect themselves with it. The people will take confidence and courage, and the most profound and salutary peace which the history of any time can show will have been effected. This peace will first act on countries still in a good state, but will not be without a very decided influence on the fate of those threatened with destruction, and even assist the restoration of those which have already passed under the scourge of revolution.

To every great State determined to survive the storm there still remain many chances of salvation, and a strong union between the States on the principles we have announced will overcome the storm itself.

Industrialism, Liberalism, and Democracy in the Nineteenth Century

Beginning in the late eighteenth century and continuing through the nineteenth, a series of important developments occurred in the production system of Western Europe and the United States. These changes have been given the name Industrial Revolution, and in the sense that they profoundly altered the economic and social phases of Western Civilization, this is an accurate term. The introduction of machinery in production and its concentration in factories located in cities induced large sections of the population to adopt a new way of life. Factory workers found themselves victims of poor working and living conditions, and efforts to improve their condition were frowned upon as contrary to the liberal principles of the period. Economic liberalism stressed the importance of free enterprise and free trade together with a laissez-faire attitude on the part of government, while political liberalism looked with favor upon the least government possible. As the nineteenth century advanced, however, a new political phenomenon began to emerge in the form of democracy. It developed most rapidly in the United States where the frontier environment helped to foster it, but Europeans, too, were attracted by its principles; some came to the United States to observe democracy in action. Gradually, its principles began to take root in Europe, and a new force was thus developing through which the social and economic evils of industrialism could be attacked.

Parliamentary Committee

During the latter part of the eighteenth century Western Civilization experienced the beginnings of a tremendous change in its method of producing goods. The various events associated with this important development are known as the Industrial Revolution. For a variety of reasons, some economic and social, others political and geographic, Great Britain was the first country to experience these advances. Two of the products of the Industrial Revolution, the factory system and the mill towns, presented England with some unfortunate social results. The laissez-faire doctrine, exalting free enterprise and frowning upon mercantilism and state control, dominated the political thought of the era, thereby intensifying these evils. In the decade of the 1830's a group of reformers, which included Michael Sadler, began agitating for some governmental controls, and in 1832 a Parliamentary committee was appointed, with Sadler as chairman, to investigate the abuses of child labor in English factories. As a consequence of this investigation, Parliament passed the Factory Act of 1833. This measure marked the end of unrestricted laissez faire in England. The following selections are from the evidence presented before the committee. In reading them note (1) the working and health conditions the witnesses described, (2) the length of hours children worked, (3) the reasons given for working, (4) why the workers did not quit their jobs as a protest, (5) the amount of pay given for overtime work, (6) evidence of pressure brought to bear upon mill workers to prevent them from testifying, (7) why workers did not join unions, (8) the comparison made with slave labor in the West Indies, and (9) the humanitarianism expressed by the doctor.

From: THE SADLER REPORT

MINUTES OF EVIDENCE

Jovis, 12° *die Aprilis,* 1832
Michael Thomas Sadler, Esquire, in the Chair.
William Cooper called in; and Examined.

What is your business? —I follow the cloth-dressing at present.

What is your age? —I was eight-and-twenty last February.

When did you first begin to work in mills or factories? —When I was about 10 years of age.

With whom did you first work? —At Mr. Benyon's flax mills, in Meadow's-lane, Leeds.

What were your usual hours of working? —We began at five, and gave over at nine; at five o'clock in the morning.

And you gave over at nine o'clock? —At nine at night.

At what distance might you have lived from the mill? —About a mile and a half.

At what time had you to get up in the morning to attend to your labour? —I had to be up soon after four o'clock.

Every morning? —Every morning.

What intermissions had you for meals? —When we began at five in the morning, we went on until noon, and then we had 40 minutes for dinner.

Great Britain, *Sessional Papers,* 1833, vol. 123, cd. 706, pp. 5–11; 158–164; 428–430; 598–602.

Had you no time for breakfast? —No, we got it as we could, while we were working.

Had you any time for an afternoon refreshment, or what is called in Yorkshire your "drinking"? —No; when we began at noon, we went on till night; there was only one stoppage, the 40 minutes for dinner.

Then as you had to get your breakfast, and what is called "drinking" in that manner, you had to put it on one side? —Yes, we had to put it on one side; and when we got our frames doffed, we ate two or three mouthfuls, and then put it by again.

Is there not considerable dust in a flax mill? —A flax mill is very dusty indeed.

Was not your food therefore frequently spoiled? —Yes, at times with the dust; sometimes we could not eat it, when it had got a lot of dust on.

What were you when you were ten years old? —What is called a bobbin-doffer; when the frames are quite full, we have to doff them.

Then as you lived so far from home, you took your dinner to the mill? —We took all our meals with us, living so far off.

During the 40 minutes which you were allowed for dinner, had you ever to employ that time in your turn in cleaning the machinery? —At times we had to stop to clean the machinery, and then we got our dinner as well as we could; they paid us for that.

At these times you had no resting at all? —No.

How much had you for cleaning the machinery? —I cannot exactly say what they gave us, as I never took any notice of it.

Did you ever work even later than the time you have mentioned? —I cannot say that I worked later there. I had a sister who worked upstairs, and she worked till 11 at night, in what they call the card-room.

At what time in the morning did she begin to work? —At the same time as myself.

And they kept her there till 11 at night? —Till 11 at night.

You say that your sister was in the card-room? —Yes.

Is not that a very dusty department? —Yes, very dusty indeed.

She had to be at the mill at five, and was kept at work till eleven at night? —Yes.

During the whole time she was there? —During the whole time; there was only 40 minutes allowed at dinner out of that.

To keep you at your work for such a length of time, and especially towards the termination of such a day's labour as that, what means were taken to keep you awake and attentive? —They strapped us at times, when we were not quite ready to be doffing the frame when it was full.

Were you frequently strapped? —At times we were frequently strapped.

What sort of strap was it? —About this length [describing it].

What was it made of? —Of leather.

Were you occasionally very considerably hurt with the strap? —Sometimes it hurt us very much, and sometimes they did not lay on so hard as they did at others.

Were the girls strapped in that sort of way? —They did not strap what they called the grown-up women.

Were any of the female children strapped? —Yes; they were strapped in the same way as the lesser boys.

What were your wages at 10 years old at Mr. Benyon's? —I think it was 4 s. a week.

When you left Mr. Benyon, to what mill did you then go? —To Mr. Clayton's; that was a flax mill.

What age were you when you went there? —I was at Mr. Benyon's nearly a year and a half.

Then you were eleven years and a half old? —Yes.

What were your hours of work at Mr. Clayton's? —We started at five in the morning, and worked till ten minutes past eight at night.

That is 15 hours and 10 minutes? —Yes; and we had only 40 minutes out of that for dinner.

You assembled at five in the morning? —From five in the morning until ten minutes past eight at night.

Had you any time allowed for breakfast or drinking at that mill? —No, it was just the same as the other, with only 40 minutes for dinner.

So that, in point of fact, you had to be attending to your work on your legs for that length of time, with the short intermission of

40 minutes? —Yes, we had to get our meals as we could get them, all but our dinner.

Were your punishments the same in that mill as in the other? —Yes, they used the strap the same there.

How long did you work in that mill? —Five years.

And how did it agree with your health? —I was sometimes well, and sometimes not very well.

Did it affect your breathing at all? —Yes; sometimes we were stuffed.

When your hours were so long, you had not any time to attend to a day-school? —We had no time to go to a day-school, only to a Sunday-school; and then with working such long hours we wanted to have a bit of rest, so that I slept till the afternoon, sometimes till dinner, and sometimes after.

Did you attend a place of worship? —I should have gone to a place of worship many times, but I was in the habit of falling asleep, and that kept me away; I did not like to go for fear of being asleep.

Do you mean that you could not prevent yourself from falling asleep, in consequence of the fatigue of the preceding week? —Yes.

Did you work in any other flax mill? —In no other flax mill.

Did you afterwards work in a woollen mill? —I worked in what they call a cloth-dressing mill.

In whose mill did you next work? —I went to Mr. Pearson's.

What were your hours there? —I think it was from six to eight.

What time was allowed there for meals? —Half an hour for breakfast, an hour at dinner, and half an hour at drinking.

That was 12 hours at the woollen mill? —Yes.

When you left that mill, where did you go to next? —I went to Mr. Wilks's, in Meadow's-lane; that is a cloth mill.

Were your hours the same there? —No; there were short hours there.

Did you find the short hours working suit your health better? —It did a great deal better with me.

Where did you go to then? —To Mr. Giles, in Bowman-lane; that is a cloth mill.

What hours did you work there? —From six to eight, and from six to nine.

With the same intermissions? —Yes, with the same intermissions.

What was the next mill you worked at? —Then I went to Mr. Chorley's.

Were your hours the same there? —Not quite so long there; they were from six to seven.

With the same intervals for meals? —Yes.

You have already stated that your health was better when the labour was shorter? —It was a deal better when only working these hours.

Where did you go then? —To Mr. James Brown's.

What were you at Mr. James Brown's? —I was a gigger and a boiler.

When did you go there? —I should think I must be about 20 years of age when I went there.

Were you a gigger and a boiler when you first went to Mr. Brown's? —I was a gigger when I went to Mr. Brown's; I was a boiler a good while after.

State what was your usual work when you were only a gigger. —When I was only a gigger I went at five o'clock on a Monday morning, and had half an hour at breakfast and an hour at dinner, and half an hour at drinking; then went on till nine on Monday evening, and stopped half an hour; then went on to twelve at midnight, and stopped an hour; then went on to half-past four on Tuesday morning, and stopped half an hour; then went on again from five to eight, and stopped half an hour; then went on till twelve, and stopped an hour; then went on again from one to five, and stopped half an hour; then went on again to nine o'clock at night, when we went home.

What did you do on the Wednesday? —Went again at five o'clock in the morning.

What time did you close at night? —At nine.

What did you do on the Thursday? —Went again on Thursday morning at five, and returned at nine at night. On Friday morning we went at five; worked all Friday, Friday night, and till Saturday evening at five, with the same time for meals as before.

When you became a boiler, will you state the number of hours you had to labour at the same mill? —When I was a boiler, I began work at one o'clock on the Monday morning;

went on till five, and stopped half an hour; then went on to eight, and stopped half an hour; then went on to twelve, and stopped an hour; then went on to five, and stopped half an hour; then went on to nine, and stopped half an hour; then went on to twelve, and stopped an hour; then began again, and went on to half-past four on Tuesday morning, and stopped half an hour; then went on to eight, and stopped half an hour; then went on to twelve, and stopped an hour; then went on to five, and stopped half an hour; then went on to nine, and then gave over on the Tuesday night. On Wednesday morning we went at five, and stopped half an hour at breakfast; then went on to twelve, and stopped an hour; then went on to five, and stopped half an hour; then went on to nine, and then gave over. Thursday was the same as Wednesday. On Friday morning we went at five, and stopped half an hour at breakfast; then we went on to twelve, and stopped an hour; then we went on to five, and stopped half an hour; then we went on to nine, and stopped half an hour; then we went on to twelve at midnight, and stopped an hour; then we went on to half-past four, and stopped half an hour; then we went on to eight, and stopped half an hour; then we went on to twelve, and stopped an hour; then we went on to five o'clock on Saturday night, and gave over.

Then in the whole week you had only four nights' rest, exclusive of Sunday night? —No.

And that rest was after nine o'clock, and before five? —Yes.

As I calculate, you laboured as a boiler 44 hours running, from Monday morning till Tuesday night, having 10 intervals, amounting altogether to only six hours and a half, and never going to bed? —You cannot go to bed.

And 36 hours of labour from Friday morning till you were let loose on Saturday evening, including five hours and an half for meals? —Yes.

On Wednesday and Thursday you had, from five till nine, 16 hours of labour, including meals? —Yes.

Then on Monday and Friday nights you had no rest? —No rest.

What was the effect of this excessive labour upon you? —We all felt unwell, and were stiff, and could not make proper use of our limbs till we had worked a little, when it went off.

Had this a serious effect on your health? —Yes, it had a great deal of effect on our health.

But as to yourself personally? —Yes.

After working at a mill to this excess, how did you find your health at last? —I found it very bad indeed; I found illness coming on me a long time before I fell down.

Did you at length become so ill as to be unable to pursue your work? —I was obliged to give it up entirely.

How long were you ill? —For six months.

Who attended? —Mr. Metcalf and Mr. Freeman.

What were you told by your medical attendants was the reason of your illness? —Nothing but hard labour, and working long hours; and they gave me up, and said no good could be done for me, that I must go into the country.

Did this excessive labour not only weaken you, but destroy your appetite? —It destroyed the appetite, and I became so feeble, that I could not cross the floor unless I had a stick to go with; I was in great pain, and could find ease in no posture.

You could drink in the meantime, if you could not eat? —Yes, I could drink.

But you found that [did] not improve your health? —No.

Has it been remarked that your excessive labour from early life has greatly diminished your growth? —A number of persons have said that such was the case, and that I was the same as if I had been made of iron or stone.

What height are you? —About five feet. It is that that has hindered me of my growth.

When you were somewhat recovered, did you apply for labour? —I applied for my work again, but the overlooker said I was not fit to work; he was sure of that, and he would not let me have it. I was then obliged to throw myself on the parish.

Have you subsisted on the parish ever since? —Yes.

Have you been always willing and anxious to work? —I was always willing and anxious to work from my infancy.

Have you been on the parish since your severe illness? —Yes.

How long is that ago? —Six months. When I was ill I got something from the Society; they relieved me then, but when I became better I received no benefit from it.

Yours is not what is called a Friendly Society? —No, it is what we call Odd Fellows.

And they do not extend relief after a certain period? —Not after you get better.

What age were you when you became burthensome to the parish, in consequence of your being too weak to follow your employment? —I have never troubled the parish till within this last six months.

What age were you when you first applied to the parish? —It is about six months ago, and I was twenty-eight the 4th of last February.

Had you any assistance from your employer? —No assistance from my employer.

Merely from the Odd Fellows? —Merely from the Odd Fellows.

How long were you attended by these two medical gentlemen? —I was attended for six months.

And Dr. Freemen informed you, on his last attendance, that it was from over-work? —He said it was from over-work.

During the time that you were so over-worked, it is almost superfluous to ask you how you felt? —I was always very tired and weary, and did not know what to do with myself; there were times when I could not eat, and it was not likely I could keep up my strength if I did not eat.

How did you spend your Sundays? —I never liked to go to a place of worship, for I was in the habit of falling asleep; I always kept away from such places, and either stopped at home or took a walk to get some fresh air.

Did you go to the public-house? —Sometimes I got a pint or a gill.

Is it your impression that your growth has been very much stunted, your health injured, and your constitution thus early destroyed by excessive labour? —Yes, it is.

When you first went into a flax-mill, were you put in by your parents? —My parents were not able to keep us, and they sent us to work at such places.

What did your parents work at themselves? —My father was a shoemaker, but he is not now living.

You say that your sister worked in the same mill? —Yes.

And till 11 at night? —Yes.

Do you know what wages she received? —It is so long since that I do not know whether she received 5 *s.* and over-hours, or not; but I think it was 5 *s.* a week.

Did she receive extra wages for over-hours? —Yes.

Was she also put in the mill by her parents? —Yes.

If she had refused to work over-hours, would she have been kept any longer at the mill? —If she had not chosen to work long hours she might have gone about her business.

Might she have remained in the mill if she had refused to work any longer than you, or must she have worked the extra hours? —If she had not chosen to work the extra hours she might have gone about her business; somebody else would have done so.

You say that you were strapped when at the mill? —When the frames wanted doffing they strapped us to keep us up to it.

Was it when you went to sleep that you were strapped? —If we were getting our meals when any of the frames were full, and did not go just at the moment, they would fall on us and strap us.

Was it to keep you awake, or to make you work? —To make us work; if we slept or sat down for two or three minutes, they would strap us to it; sometimes we got two or three minutes to sit down, and then we dropped asleep.

You say that you had no time to go to school during the week, but that you went on Sunday? —I went on Sunday; I had no time to go to a day-school.

Can you read or write? —I can read, but I cannot write.

When you were at school, was there any sort of punishment when you did not attend to your lessons? —They used to give us a clout on the side of the head if we did not attend to our lessons.

Did they use any strap in the school? —They used a stick in the school I went to.

Did it not hurt you nearly as much as the strap in the factory? —Yes.

But you never went to a schoolmaster who

paid such attention to your learning, as to keep you forty-four hours to your book? —No; I have many times fallen asleep at the Sunday-school, instead of looking at my book.

You went to this mill, where you were a gigger and boiler, when you were 20? —Yes.

Were your parents then dead? —No.

Did you engage in the mill of your own accord, voluntarily? —Yes; I engaged of my own accord.

You knew what sort of work you were going to have? —Yes; I knew what time they worked, but it would not do for me to be travelling the streets doing nothing.

What wages did you receive? —Fourteen shillings a week when I first went to Mr. Brown's.

When you became a boiler, as well as a gigger, did you get additional wages? —When I became a boiler I got more; I then had 18 s.

Is that more wages than common labourers get in your part of the country? —No, some get more; some gigger men get 22 s. a week, and are paid for over-time.

What do you consider the regular time? —They reckon from six to seven and eight.

That is the regular time? —Yes; what is done before six in the morning, and after seven at night, is called over-time, and is paid for.

Does the 14 s. a week include the over-work, or not? —They gave us 14 s. a week, and over-work besides.

How much did you ever get for over-work in the course of the week? —I cannot reckon it up.

How much was it an hour? —I believe it was 3 d. an hour.

If you had refused to work over-hours, would they have turned you off altogether? —Yes, they would have turned us off. If one will not do it, another will.

At this particular period, when you were thus over-worked, were there not a great number of able-bodied individuals in Leeds totally out of employment? —A great number. A few individuals have it all, and the rest, of course, are obliged to apply to the parish.

If you had refused to work the over-work, there were plenty of others willing to undertake it? —That is very true.

And they were people able to perform the sort of work you were engaged in? —They were.

You of course know your trade? —Yes.

Were those people out of work persons who could have undertaken your situation? —They were out of work.

At the time that you were working these over-hours were there a great many out of work in Leeds? —Yes.

And were they capable of doing your work? —Yes, capable of doing the same work.

Do you work anywhere now? —I have not worked anywhere for rather more than a year. I have been constantly out to seek for employment since I have been better.

How are you supported? —By the town.

Do you mean by the parish?— Yes.

Of what place? —Leeds.

What sort of health were you in when you went into this mill of Mr. Brown's? —In middling health. I was pretty well sometimes, and sometimes I was a little poorly.

You felt yourself strong enough to undertake this very severe labour? —Yes, I thought I was strong enough then.

Had you been out of work for any length of time before you went to Mr. Brown's? —No.

You went straight from some other place to that? —From Mr. Chorley's mill to Mr. Brown's.

What you had done before you went to Mr. Brown's mill had not injured you much? —No; it was going to Mr. Brown's, where I worked such long hours.

Do you recollect what sort of health you were in when you left the spinning-mills and went to the cloth-mills? —The cloth-mills agreed better with me than the spinning-mills.

When you had moderate labour your health was always better? —Yes; when I had only moderate labour I was a deal better.

The shortest hours that you worked in the cloth-mills were twelve hours a day, were they not? —Yes.

How old were you when you first hired yourself? —I did not go on hire; I went for weekly wages. I was not hired.

You said your parents hired you? —They did not hire me; they sent me to work.

Were the wages paid to your parents? —No; we received them ourselves.

When did you first begin to receive wages yourself? —Ever since I began to work; I gave them to my parents.

How old were you then? —Ten years.

How soon did you begin to work on your own account and make your own bargain with your master for wages? —I always bargained for my wages ever since I began to work for wages; always; my parents never bargained for me. I always bargained for myself.

Not when you were 10 years old? —Yes.

Do you know anything, of your own knowledge, of the hours of working at present in Mr. Benyon's and Mr. Clayton's flax-mills? —Mr. Clayton's flax-mill is not going; Mr. Benyon's is going; but I do not know what hours they are working now.

Is not trade rather slack in that part of the country just now? —It is very slack at present.

While you were with Mr. Pearson, Mr. Giles and Mr. Chorley, you were in a better state of health? —Yes.

How old were you when you became a boiler in Mr. Brown's mill? —I believe I was about 20 years of age when I went to Mr. Brown.

You said you were a gigger at first? —That is, what I mean, when I became a boiler, I was somewhere about between 25 and 26.

You received 18 *s.* a week wages? —Yes.

Was that the regular wages without the extra hours, or did you receive more than 18 *s.* a week when you worked all these extra hours? —Yes.

How much did you ever receive? —I received 18 *s.* and over-hours; about 26 *s.* or 27 *s.* and sometimes 28 *s.*

At a regular charge of 3 *d.* an hour? —No, at 18 *s.* a week; it is 3½ *d.* for all the hours over.

If you had not worked these over-hours, you would not have been kept in your employment? —No, I should not have been kept in employ if I had not worked them.

Did not you and others choose to undergo this excessive labor, rather than incur the disgrace of throwing yourselves on the parish? —Yes.

You attended at the mill at five in the morning; was that both winter and summer? —It has been, for two years back, winter and summer, working at Mr. Brown's.

Were you able to be punctual in your attendance at five o'clock? —I was always there at five o'clock; if we were too late they took us off what we call bating; if we were a quarter of an hour too late in the morning they took off a penny.

Are they ever turned away for being too late? —If they are what is called "bad comers," they turn them off and get fresh ones.

Are they ever strapped for being too late? —They did not strap them at the room that I was in.

How did you contrive to be awake so soon in the morning? —My father always used to call me up.

Did he get up so early as that for his own business? —He got up on purpose to call me.

How many hours did he work in a day at his own business? —Sometimes from five in the morning till eight at night.

You say he was a shoemaker? —Yes.

Then, according to this, he worked more hours than you did? —I think not so long.

Did your father take his regular intervals for his meals? —I should think so.

And walked about to market for his family; had he not many pauses in his labour? —He worked at home, and therefore could do as he pleased.

After you worked a month at these long hours, could you not get back into lighter employment? —I do not know whether you could get back or not.

You said that you were about 17 when you first went from the flax-spinning mills into the cloth-mills? —Yes.

Was that before the Act of Parliament made to regulate the hours? —I know nothing about that.

How often did these extra hours come about? —Very often.

Describe to us a period in which you have worked the greatest possible number of hours; how many weeks running have you worked? —I have gone on for a year round.

Working all the Monday night and Friday night? —Yes; always working long hours.

Is your sister older or younger than yourself? —There is a year and a half between us; I am the elder.

Has your health improved since you left off working long hours? —I am a deal better than

I was; but I believe that if I could have got work, and have had something to support me, I should have recruited my health better. I have been very poorly kept for these last six months, having been out of work. I have only half a crown a week allowed from the parish for my wife and myself.

When you were working the long hours, were there any people in the same employment, when you were a gigger, for instance, who were working the short hours? —Yes; some mills were working short hours in the same line; there were none in the same room that worked less hours than I did.

[*Joseph Hebergam examined.*] What particular department of the mill had you to attend to? —I attended what are called the throstle machines.

How long did you continue in that mill? —I attended the throstles two years and a half, and then I went to the steam looms for half a year.

Were there many children in that mill? —Yes, I believe there were about fifty, of about the same age that I was.

State to the Committee how this excessive labour agreed with the health of these children so employed? —They were often sick and poorly; there were always, perhaps, half a dozen regularly that were ill.

From excessive labour? —Yes.

Did you consider the work to be hard work? —It was not very hard, but having to work so very many hours made it worse; it was rather hard of itself, but it would have been better if we had not had so long to stand.

Did you not become very drowsy and sleepy towards the end of the day, and feel much fatigued? —Yes; that began about 3 o'clock, and grew worse and worse, and it came to be very bad towards 6 and 7.

And still you had to labour on? —Yes.

What means were taken to keep you at your work so long? —There were three overlookers; there was a head overlooker, and then there was one man kept to grease the machines, and then there was one kept on purpose to strap.

Was the main business of one of the overlookers that of strapping the children up to this excessive labour? —Yes, the same as strapping an old restive horse that has fallen down and will not get up.

Was that the constant practice? —Yes, day by day.

Were there straps regularly provided for that purpose? —Yes, he is continually walking up and down with it in his hand.

And his office is to strap you on to your labour? —Yes.

Do you think the children could be kept so long to labour as you have stated, if they were not so treated? —No, they could not; they are obliged to do it.

Was it not reckoned by the children to be very bad usage, and did they not conceive themselves to be very unfortunate in being subject to such a course of labour as this? —Yes; and towards the end of the day the flies of the machines would burst their knuckles.

Did you meet with frequent accidents? —Yes.

So that you were not capable of performing the labour that was exacted from you without this perpetual cruelty? —No.

Had you any brothers or sisters similarly occupied? —I had at that time a brother and a sister; they called him John, and my sister Charlotte.

What ages were they when they began working at the mills? —I cannot say how old my sister Charlotte was, but my brother John was 7.

How did it suit their health? —It did not suit it at all; they were often sick.

Where is your brother John working now? —He died three years ago.

What age was he when he died? —Sixteen years and eight months.

To what was his death attributed by your mother and the medical attendants? —It was attributed to this, that he died from working such long hours, and that it had been brought on by the factory. They have to stop the flies with their knees, because they go so swift they cannot stop them with their hands; he got a bruise on the shin by a spindle-board, and it went on to that degree that it burst; the surgeon cured that, then he was better; then he went to work again; but when he had worked about two months more his spine became affected, and he died.

Did his medical attendants state that that spinal affection was owing to his having been so over-laboured at the mill? —Yes.

He died in consequence? —Yes.

What effect had this labour upon your own health? —It had a great deal; I have had to drop it several times in the year.

How long was it before the labour took effect on your health? —Half a year.

And did it at length begin to affect your limbs? —When I had worked about half a year, a weakness fell into my knees and ankles; it continued, and it has got worse and worse.

Was that weakness attended with very great pain, and the sense of extreme fatigue? —Yes.

Had you to work as often as you could under these circumstances? —Yes.

Otherwise no allowance would have been made to you by the occupier of the mill? —No.

How far did you live from the mill? —A good mile.

Was it very painful for you to move? —Yes, in the morning I could scarcely walk, and my brother and sister used out of kindness to take me under each arm, and run with me to the mill, and my legs dragged on the ground in consequence of the pain; I could not walk.

Were you sometimes too late? —Yes; and if we were five minutes too late, the overlooker would take a strap, and beat us till we were black and blue.

The overlooker nevertheless knew the occasion of your being a little too late? —Yes.

Did you state to him the reason? —Yes, he never minded that; and he used to watch us out of the windows.

Did the pain and weakness in your legs increase? —Yes.

Just show the Committee the situation in which your limbs are now? —

[*The Witness accordingly stood up, and showed his limbs.*]

Were you originally a straight and healthy boy? —Yes, I was straight and healthful as any one when I was 7 years and a quarter old.

Were there other children at the mill that were also made ill by this labour, and who became deformed in like manner? —Yes, there were some very often sick, and some were deformed; but the parents who were able to support their children took them away, in con-

sequence of seeing that they would be deformed if they did not take them away.

Your mother being a widow and having but little, could not afford to take you away? —No.

Would the parish have relieved you if your mother had taken you away? —No, she has oftentimes been to them, but she was no better for it.

Was your poor mother made very unhappy by seeing that you were getting crooked and deformed? —I have seen her weep oftentimes, and I have asked her why she was weeping, but she would not tell me then, but she has told me since.

What did she tell you affected her? —Seeing my limbs giving way by working such long hours.

The overlooker, you say, was employed to strap you? —Yes.

You were cruelly beaten if you happened to be a little too late? —Yes.

And you were constantly strapped up to your work at the latter part of the day? —Not only me, but many others.

The overlookers under whom you have worked hitherto have been in the habit of thus strapping and cruelly beating the children? —Yes, one of them professed to be very religious, and he beat us sadly.

What were the faults for which you were generally beaten? —Very little faults; for being late in the morning, and for letting the ends run down.

Should you have been beat for speaking to each other? —Yes, cruelly.

Is one part of the discipline of these mills profound silence? —Yes, they will not allow them to speak; if they chance to see two speaking, they are beaten with the strap.

Are they beaten, both of them? —Yes.

If they are working adjacent to each other? —Yes.

Suppose any of these children talked to each other, is it customary for the overlooker to come and beat them with the strap? —Yes.

Do you think that the masters are aware that the overlookers treat the children in that manner? —Yes; and they encourage them to do it.

Are you sure of that from your own observations? —I have seen them when the master has been standing at one end of the room, and two of the overlookers speaking to him, and if he has chanced to see two girls speaking to each other, he has said, "Look yonder, at those two girls talking;" and he has run and beat them the same as they beat soldiers in the barrack-yard for deserting.

When was the strapping principally going on? —In the morning from 5 to half-past 6; for if there were twenty that were too late, he would beat them all.

And at the after part of the day also? —Yes, it began about 3 o'clock, and continued then till the time that they dropped their work; very cruel strapping.

In consequence of the increasing fatigue, the cruelty increased? —If they had not strapped them they would have fallen asleep.

You stated you had thirty minutes allowed to you for your dinner? —Yes, and we had to clean the spindles out of that thirty minutes.

How much of that time do you think was occupied in cleaning the spindles? —Five minutes at the least; sometimes ten.

Do you give over earlier of a Saturday night? —Six o'clock, and we used to be made to fettle the machines then, which took an hour and a half.

So that though you professed to give over earlier for your convenience on a Saturday evening than on the other days of the week, yet in fact you were kept nearly as long, from having to clean your machinery that day? —Yes.

Do you believe that there were frequent errors in the clock by which your labour was regulated? —Sometimes during the time I worked at that place, it was a quarter of an hour too soon in the meal-time; we had just done fettling, and we had but half got our dinners, and he put the clock forward to 1, and he rang the bell, and we were obliged to run back to our work.

That was not an uncommon practice? —No.

You spoke as to a number of the children being poorly with whom you worked at this mill; can you state whether any of them died during the two years and a half you worked there? —There were about a dozen died during that time.

Did the owner or the manager of the mill send after these children to inquire about them, or to relieve them when they were disabled by their long-continued labour? —No, nobody looked after them; they lived sometimes for two or three months after they left.

So that if anybody had had the curiosity to have taken an account of the deaths at the mill, the deaths of those children would not have been included in that statement? —No, they did not die in the mill; but I know one boy who died when he had been out of the mill only two days; he was stuffed up by the dust.

Is there not considerable dust in that employment? —Yes.

Does it not injure your food very much? —Yes, you cannot take the food out of your basket or handkerchief but what it is covered with dust directly.

And is it not then the more necessary that you should have a little time to get your breakfast, and what is called your drinking, which are brought to you? —We should have; but they will allow us no time, and we have to bite our food as we can; it is laid up on the board; sometimes the flew gets into it, so that we cannot eat it.

Do not your meals frequently make you sick, having to eat so much of this dirt and dust with your meat? —Yes, and at times they can pull the hair which hangs from the mouth when they put their bread in.

Now if they were to allow you a little time to get your breakfast and drinking in, of course you would get your food clean and comfortable? —Yes, because we could then go out of doors, and get the meat clean and comfortable, and the dust would not get into it.

They never allowed you that opportunity? —No.

Did you eat your dinner at the mill, or did you go home? —We ate it on the boiler-house thatch, or anywhere, as we could not go home; I lived a good mile off.

Do you eat it out of doors in the winter? —Yes, we sometimes do, and sometimes remain in the mill.

What did you afterwards go to in the mill? —Bobbin-winding at the steam-looms.

Was the labour continued for an equal length of time? —Yes, the same hours, from 5 in the morning till 8 at night.

Did you ever work later than 8? —When trade was brisk, I have worked from 5 in the morning to 9 at night.

In that department were you also strapped? —Yes.

When you have worked an hour additional, did you get any more wages? —We worked two summers, and during that time my master had a strong order, and we worked for six months, all the summer, beginning at the spring and ending in August, and we had only 10½ *d.* a piece, big and little, for the whole time.

For what hours? —From 5 in the morning till 9 at night.

And for this additional hour for six months you had only 10½ *d.*? —Only 10½ *d.*

A week? —No, for the whole time.

Need you have worked that additional hour without you chose? —Yes, we were forced to work it.

Should you not have been discharged if you had refused to work that extra hour? —Yes.

Were you still chastised in that department of the mill? —When we worked at the bobbin work, we were not used so cruelly.

Was it when you were a bobbin-winder that you worked all those hours, and received only 10½ *d.*? —No, it was when I worked at the throstles.

What was your chastisement at the bobbin-winding? —There was no strap; only the over-looker was a very savage man, and he used to strike them under the ribs, till it took their wind away, and they fell on the floor, and perhaps lay there for two minutes.

That was not the same man you spoke of before? —No, not the same.

Are all the overlookers in the habit of treating children with this severity? —Yes.

And does the master know of it? —Yes, they put them up to it, because they could not get the quantity of work done they wanted, unless they were to beat them.

When you left that mill, to what place did you go? —I went to Mr. Brooks's woollen manufactory, Upper Mill, Huddersfield.

What were your usual hours of labour there? —Our regular hours were 12 hours a day. We worked from 6 in the morning till 8 at night; we had half an hour to breakfast, an hour at noon, and half an hour at drinking time.

Making altogether twelve hours of actual labour? —Yes.

Was that too much for you? —Yes, we could not stand it.

What age were you at that time? —I was 10 when I went there first.

How long did you stay there? —Nearly four years.

What department of the business was it you worked at? —At the Lewis machine, in the dressing department.

You have stated the regular hours of working; mention to the Committee how long you were required to work when trade was particularly brisk? —I was obliged to work from 5 in the morning till half-past 10, sometimes till 11, and once all night, for four months together.

What was your additional wages for that extra labour? —I had 5 *s.* a week, and they gave us a shilling for over-hours.

And again you had no option; you must either have worked those over-hours or have left your place? —Yes; and if we had left it, it was the same in other places when trade was good. If we had left and gone to another place, we should perhaps, in the course of a fortnight, have had to work till 10 at night there.

Was it easy to get a new place in those times? —No, it was not easy to get a place, because there are so many boys; there is always somebody out of work.

You found that labour to be very distressing to you? —Yes.

And did it increase the pain in your limbs? —Very much.

Did it also increase the deformity which came upon you? —Yes, and I have had to drop it several times for a fortnight together.

Were you beaten up to that degree of labour in that mill? —Yes; they used not to strap them; they used to strike them with their fist, and kick them with their foot. During the time I worked there I wished many times they would have sent me for a West India slave.

You had heard the condition of the slaves in the West Indies described to you? —Yes, I had.

Did you feel yourself very much overworked, with insufficient rest, and very much injured by that length of labour? —Yes.

Did that render you very miserable in your mind? —Yes, it did; and I thought there could be nothing worse, and that there could not be worse slaves than those who worked in factories.

To what department were you then removed? —To the Davis's machines.

What were your hours there? —I have worked the same hours, from 5 in the morning till 10 at night, and half-past 10.

Did you ever work all Friday, Friday night, and Saturday, when you were working at the Davis's machines? —Yes, one night I worked all night at the Davis's machines.

Did you leave that situation? —Yes; one morning I was between ten minutes and a quarter of an hour too late, and the overlooker met me, and he gave me a knock on the head and sent my head against a step, and caused a great bump to rise; he said he would turn me off, "a young devil, for being too late;" he followed me up the steps, but he could not catch me; I ran round the steps to get away from him, and I left that place.

How old were you then? —Near 14.

So that he beat you and kicked you to that degree for being too late? —Yes.

Do they stop your wages also for being too late? —Yes, they do sometimes; they would bate a man 6 d. for being a quarter of an hour too late; but I do not think they did that at Mr. Brooks's.

Did they stop the children's wages also? —Yes, 1 d., and 2 d. at another mill; but it was not a regular rule there.

Does the Committee understand you to state that to be a regular thing at the other mills? —Yes.

State the scale of forfeiture you have known at any mill? —I left that mill, and I went to Mr. William Firth's, Greenhead, Huddersfield, and they began this rule,—they bated the boys 1½ d. for six minutes, and a man 3 d.; and when it got to sixteen minutes they doubled it, 6 d. for a man and 3 d. for a boy, and it was dou-

bled again when it got up to thirty-one minutes.

What was the forfeiture for thirty-one minutes for a boy? —Four-pence halfpenny.

And what was a boy's daily wages? —Ten-pence, a shilling, and so on.

Who took the fines, the master or the overlooker? —I do not know whether the overlooker kept the fines or not; he used to take them when he paid the wages.

Were you beaten for being too late, as well as fined? —Yes.

Was it a general system in that mill to beat the children as well as stop their wages? —They did not beat them so cruelly; but at times they would beat them, not with straps, but with their fists.

Do you think the regulation of stopping their wages for being too late prevented so much beating as you had at other mills? —Yes, it prevents beating.

Does it not entirely do it away? —No, it does not do it away; but they were beat the more where they did not pay the fines.

How many hours did you work at Mr. Firth's? —The longest hours I worked there were from 5 in the morning till 9 at night.

What intervals had you for refreshment? —Two hours.

So that you had fourteen hours of actual labours? —Yes.

Why did you leave that employment? —I left it because I could stand it no longer; the weakness was so bad in my knees and ankles, I was obliged totally to give up work.

Had your health been very much injured also? —I believe I should have died if I had not given up; the doctors have nearly cured me.

Under whose medical treatment did your mother place you? —Dr. Walker's, of the Huddersfield Infirmary.

Was you an in-patient or an out-patient? —An out-patient.

Why did they not take you into the house? —They could only take in twenty at once, because there are not subscribers enough to enable them to take more, and there are so many accidents that they are obliged to take in; they would have taken me in if they could; they have twenty-two in sometimes, but twenty is the regular rule.

So that there was no room for you, on account of the accidents from the factories, to which they must pay instant attention? —Yes.

Has that been established long? —No, it is a new place.

Who sent you to the Infirmary? —My mother got a recommendation from Mr. Bradley Clay.

Did you leave your work to go to the Infirmary? —Yes; it is near eleven weeks since I dropped work.

Where did you go to when you left the Huddersfield Infirmary? —Mr. Oastler got me into Leeds Infirmary, as an in-patient.

Under whose care? —Mr. Hey.

Did Mr. Hey examine you? —He did; and he said it was come on with the factory system. He said, he thought he could have done me good if he had had me a few years ago; there would have been means of bringing me straight; he said it was all from the factory system, working so long, and standing so many hours.

Did he give you any hopes of recovering your limbs? —No; he said there were poor hopes of me. Dr. Walker says I never shall be right any more.

Have you got worse since you were 14 years of age? —It was continuing on all along, but I have got rather worse since.

Are you capable of walking? —I cannot walk above thirty yards before my legs begin aching very bad, and then I cannot walk at all.

Had you any opportunity of learning to read and write while you went to the factory? —No; only a little bit on the Sabbath-day.

Are you learning to write a little now? —Yes, I have tried within this last ten or eleven weeks.

You could not previously write? —No; I did not know how to hold my pen.

What proportion of the children in the factories in which you have worked can write? —I do not think there is above one in a hundred that can write.

You said you were an in-patient of the Leeds Infirmary; are there any cases similar to yours there, that have been brought on by this excess labour in the factories? —Yes, there is one boy; he is weak in the knees, the same as I am, but not quite so far gone; he is under Mr. Smith, I think, a surgeon; and there is another boy in the same ward as I am, he was struck by a slubber with a billy-roller on his hip; there is another boy who was kicked by an overlooker with his foot, and his body is the same as if it was taken off and set on behind him; his body is twisted, and he goes upon crutches.

How long have you been in the Leeds Infirmary? —A week last Saturday night; if I had been this week at Leeds I should have been a fortnight next Saturday.

Have any cases of accidents in mills or factories been brought into the Infirmary since you were there? —Yes, last Tuesday but one there was a boy brought in about 5 or 6 o'clock in the evening from a mill; he had got catched with the shaft, and he had both his thighs broke, and from his knee to his hip the flesh was ripped up the same as if it had been cut by a knife, his head was bruised, his eyes were nearly torn out, and his arms broken. His sister, who ran to pull him off, got both her arms broke and her head bruised, and she is bruised all over her body. The boy died last Thursday night but one, about 8 o'clock; I do not know whether the girl is dead, but she was not expected to live.

Did that accident occur in consequence of the shaft not being sheathed? —Yes.

Do not you happen to know that the shafts of mills could be sheathed at comparatively very small expense? —Yes, all could be boxed off for a very little expense. In the mill I worked at last I do not think it would take above 10 s. to box them all off; and a man has had his two fingers cut off for want of its being done.

Something has been said about the fear of giving evidence regarding this factory question; do you know whether any threats have ever been used on that account? —Yes; Dr. Walker ordered me to wear irons from the ankle to the thigh; my mother was not able to get them, and he said he would write a note, and she might go to some gentlemen in the town, and give them that note, and see if they would not give her something towards them;

and so she did, and I have got the bare irons made; and I was coming into the yard where I live; and there was a man who worked at the same place that I did, asked me to let him look at them; I told him I could not get money to line them with, and he said, "I will tell you where there is a gentleman who will give you the money;" he told me of Mr. Oastler, and he said, "I will go and see if he is at home, that you may not lose your trouble." Mr. Oastler was at home, and said I was to be there at 8 o'clock in the morning, because he wanted to go off on a journey; I got there about half-past 8. Mr. Wood of Bradford gave me a sovereign, and Mr. Oastler gave me 3 s. 6 d., and so I had them made. He asked me questions what my lameness came on with, and I told him, and he happened to mention it at the County Meeting at York; my master saw it in the newspaper; I think it was in Mr. Baines's newspaper, of Leeds; he is an enemy to the Ten Hours' Bill, and he happened to see it in the paper, and he sent the foreman on to our house where I lived; he had not patience to read it, and he said to my mother, "I suppose it is owing to our place that your Joseph got the use of his limbs taken away?" and my mother said he was informed wrong, that he had it before he went to that factory; but he said, "If he has said anything about our factory, we shall certainly turn him off, and both his brothers." I have two little brothers working at the same place.

Did the foreman say this to you? —To my mother and me; he said he did not know exactly how it was, but he would go back and see the paper himself, and if he found out that we said anything about the factory system, that we should be turned off.

Have you been turned off? —I have not, but my master will not speak to me or look at me: I do not know whether he will let me start again or not.

You have been unwell? —Yes.

Have your brothers been turned off? —No.

You are able to work now? —I cannot work, because I have not strength in my legs.

When you left the mill, could that machine at which you worked be worked without you? —No, they have another boy working in the place.

Then the machine could not go on without another boy being put in your place? —No; there is often a boy kept in case any one falls poorly.

You never met with any accident in your limbs? —Yes, I have got one of my arms broken.

Are you sure the injury you suffered was entirely owing to working in factories? —Yes, and standing so many hours.

When did you begin to feel the weakness in your limbs? —When I had worked about half a year.

Did you not say that at 14 you ran away from the over-looker? —I said he turned me away; it is generally their way to beat them out of the place; so I got up the stairs before him, and ran round the machine, and he could not catch me.

Then your limbs were not much injured then? —I had just been lying up at home a fortnight, a little before.

Does it hurt you to walk now? —Yes, a great deal.

Did you not state that you met with an accident in the mill? —Yes, I had one of my arms broke.

What were you doing when that occurred? —I was working at what is called a brushing mill; there is a pin they put into the roller to make it run round, and the pin catched my sleeve, and twisted my arm round and broke it, and another boy has had his arm broken in the same way.

Is there any way of avoiding such accidents? —Yes; at Mr. Brooks's mill they cannot break their arms by that part of the machine, owing to a different arrangement. There was a boy who, to fettle the machine, was kneeling down, and a strap catched him about his ankles, and carried him round the wheel, and dashed his brains out on the floor.

Do you think these accidents usually happen at the latter end of the day, when the children get tired? —Yes, that boy got killed at a quarter past 7 at night.

Do you think it is possible for the children to be so active and nimble as to avoid the danger of the machinery when they are so overworked and fatigued? —No, because they are sleepy.

It appears you have worked, in all, ten years in these mills? —Yes.

Have you found that in all those mills you have been required to labour longer than your strength could bear? —Yes, I have.

And have you found that, on the whole, you have been rendered ill, deformed and miserable, by the factory system, as at present pursued? —Yes; oh! if I had a thousand pounds, I would give them to have the use of my limbs again.

Would not you and the rest of the children be very happy to avail yourselves of an opportunity of learning the rudiments of a decent education, if leisure were afforded you after your day's toil? —I have tried to read after I have come home at 9 o'clock, but I have fallen asleep directly, with my book open.

When you were so long worked, you could not avail yourselves of the Sunday-school very profitably, on account of the fatigue you endured? —No; when we worked so long, I could not get to school at all on the Sabbath-day.

Though you have been required to work so long at a particular period of the year, have there not been other parts of the year in which you had not full employment? —We have worked during the summer all those hours at Brooks's mill; and in winter, perhaps, we have not had four days' work in the week.

You stated that you found it your duty to go to those mills, in order to maintain your mother, who is a widow, and very poor? —Yes.

Veneris, 6° die Julii, 1832

Michael Thomas Sadler, Esquire, in the Chair.
William Longston, called in; and Examined

Where do you reside? —At Stockport.

What is your age? —Between 40 and 41.

Have you had considerable experience in the spinning of cotton, and in other operations connected with that trade? —Some little in the spinning, but more in the previous preperations.

Have you known the operatives in the manufacture of cotton from your youth up? —Not without intervals; for about six years in my youth, and in maturer years as a manager.

Is it a subject, on the whole, to which you have paid much and serious attention,—the management of the cotton factories of this country? —Yes, my attention has been very frequently called to it in disputed and difficult matters.

Are the hours of labour more now than they were when you were a boy? —I should think they are fully as short now as then.

Have the laws, then, already enacted, diminished the hours of labour, or have they had a tendency to do so? —I should think, in the general struggle of competition, if it had not been for the enactment of some restrictive law, that the hours must have been now longer.

But, in point of fact, in consequence of such restrictive laws, they have somewhat abated? —I think not abated, but I think they may have had this tendency, that occasional convictions for working young persons too long hours may have operated as a salutary check, and have prevented them from working as long as they otherwise would have done. In country places they work even longer than they do at Stockport; and in Manchester the hours are not so long as they are usually at Stockport and the country places; not being under the eyes of those who might be likely to inform, they take liberties and work longer hours; and from this I infer that those checks have a good tendency in preventing the owners from working so long as they otherwise would.

So that at all events, it is your impression, that legislative interference has been beneficial, though not to the extent that it is desirable it should be carried? —Yes, that is my opinion.

You have already stated that, in country places, the law is evaded to a considerable extent; I would ask whether you think that any legal provisions can be so constructed as to become effectual? —Yes, I think they might, in case the penalties were made adequate to the offence and the restriction; if they were made such that a large capitalist would regard them; at present I think them insignificant; and if they can be evaded 500 times, one penalty may be considered trifling, in comparison with the profit which might arise from transgressing the law.

Is it your opinion, that personal punishment ought to await those who habitually and intentionally evade the law made to protect the infant and rising generation; I am meaning now to allude to the incarceration of offenders? —The question is indeed a delicate one to be answered, but in conscience I should think that masters who set to their workmen the example of transgressing the law, and so diminish that respect that ought to be maintained in them for the laws, I think, and must say, that their criminality is augmented by that circumstance, and that (as you term it) personal punishment, and (as you explained it) incarceration, I really think would be a punishment not more than adequate to the criminality.

Do the operatives connive at the violations of laws which have been enacted for their own express protection? —Yes, almost universally.

State why and how they do so? —If they do not connive, they must be brought forward as witnesses against the masters; but, being brought forward as a witness against the master, if the person be a voluntary witness, it is ten to one if they can obtain employment anywhere in the district where they are known, and where their name could be sent, so that their persons could be in anywise identified; I think this explanation will show and prove that employment would be exceedingly improbable for them anywhere, as employers would never deem themselves safe where they had in employ one who had been a voluntary witness against them.

So that the operatives themselves, in such cases, are obliged to become parties to a breach of the law enacted for their own protection? —There are other reasons; for instance, in the case of a spinner; a spinner has piecers; they (the piecers) are universally persons who are under the age limited by the law for protection; in case the piecers are taken away from the spinner, he finds then a difficulty in turning off the quantity which is required; and even were it not so, a wish to do as much as they can, causes them to keep the piecers more than the law prescribes; the spinners in general (though some of them are well-meaning people), I think deserve, at the very least, censure for their eagerness to keep those little piecers in the factory so many hours.

You mean by that, to keep them in longer than the law allows? —To keep them in at work as long as they are kept in in general.

You spoke as to the difficulty of finding employment, in case any operative employed in a mill or factory should be a party to asking redress by legal means, for a breach of that law which has been enacted for his protection; is that difficulty so general as to operate upon the minds of the working people in mills and factories, so as to deter them from seeking redress by such legal means? —It may be thought that there have not occurred instances sufficiently numerous to justify the assertion which I have made; but, for example, there was an arbitration law enacted, amended and extended in 1824, and made applicable to persons of all trades or employments; and yet, since the enactment of that law, none of the operatives of Stockport have dared to avail themselves of it, when their wages have been arbitrarily abated. I allude to fines; the law is this, that if the parties complaining do not wish the matter in dispute to go before a magistrate, it is legal to refer it to persons who understand it, and their decision is legally binding upon the parties complaining and those complained of.

So that you think that, in a case in which the operative has either to inform against his employer, or to be a principal witness to sustain some other information for breaches of an Act passed for his protection, that in those cases the interference of any such operative would be very highly to his disadvantage, and that he would find it difficult to obtain his employment there, or anywhere else? —Yes, and I saw an instance of it, perhaps four or five months ago; a manufacturer in the town of Stockport was brought before the magistrates for overworking children, and the decision was in the manufacturer's favour; curiosity caused me to go, and I do not think he was guilty; I think it was one of the cases wherein the manufacturer really was wronged; the decision, however, was in his favour; but the persons who came as witnesses against him I saw in the streets afterwards, and they told me that they could not get employment.

Neither with their actual master nor with any other person? —Nowhere; they told me they had applied at various places, but that their having become witnesses, occasioned them to be refused employment wherever they applied.

Then you presume that there is a combination among the masters, to exclude from work those individuals who give information upon the infraction of the law? —I am not aware that there is any combination, I have judged it rather to be a tacit consent, or a general practice, than a combination.

Perhaps you have known of instances, since you speak so fully upon this subject, in which employers have dictated terms of the employed, which interfere with their rights as workmen? —Yes, I have known a great many instances of that kind; but one or two I remember which seemed extraordinary.

Will you state them? —There was a contention between the employers and the employed at Stockport, in the beginning of 1829, about wages; and of this contest a strike was the consequence; and the masters of Hyde thought proper to interfere, and that interference it may be necessary to give in their own words, as published and placarded. They say—

"We, the undersigned Spinners and Power-loom Manufacturers of Hyde, Staley, Bridge, Dukenfield, and the neighbourhood,

Having observed with regret the self-inflicted and continuing distress of the operatives of Stockport, instigated by evil-designing persons to turn out against their masters, and being informed that this distress is prolonged by assistance being rendered by our work-people to the turn-outs in that town, do hereby agree to abate ten per cent, every fortnight from the wages of such of our piece-work hands who shall refuse to sign a declaration, that they will not remain or become members of any combination, interfering with the free exercise of individual labour; or directly or indirectly contribute to the support of any turn-outs, on pain of forfeiting a fortnight's wages, should they be found so doing."

Were any other steps taken to prevent the free-agency of the work-people on that occasion? —It appears that there had been a combination; for immediately afterwards, as is seen by that placard on the walls of Stockport, a written requirement, called an agreement, was offered by the masters for the operatives to sign, which was a *sine quâ non* of employment; the operatives were to sign the following words, or not be employed; and thousands of them did so, and were obliged to do so.

[*The following Document was then put in, and read:*]

"We, the undersigned, agree with Messrs. ———, that we will work for them on the following terms:

"We declare that we do not belong to the society called the 'Union,' or any other society for the support of turn-outs, or which has for its object any interference with the rules laid down for the government of mills or manufactories.

"We agree with our said masters, that we will not become members of, or be connected with, any such society, while we remain in our present employ.

"That we will not, directly or indirectly, subscribe or contribute to any such society, or to any turn-out hands whatsoever.

"That we will give a fortnight's notice previous to leaving our employ; and we will observe all the other rules of this mill, and all special agreements that we may enter into with our masters.

"And if we are discovered to act contrary to the above agreement, each of us so offending will forfeit a sum equal to a fortnight's wages; and our masters shall have power to deduct the same from our wages, or discharge us from their employ without any notice, at their own option."

I may observe, that by the wording of this document, they say they would not directly or indirectly support any turn-out hands whatsoever; that they were liable to the penalty here announced, in case they supported a son, or even gave anything, directly or indirectly, to a starving daughter or other relative.

Do not the operatives of that town and neighbourhood consider themselves not only exceedingly interfered with in their lawful rights, but entirely degraded by conditions of that sort being imposed upon them when they were entering into employment, or were already in it? —They did consider themselves exceedingly degraded; and a Member of Parliament, in the presence of several operatives, said that any person of spirit would rather be reduced to the necessity of eating cabbage-stalks than sign such a document. That is the same document which Mr. Edward Davenport so strongly reprobated upon presenting a petition to the House of Commons, of which I hold a copy in my hand.

Do not those facts impress you more strongly with the conviction of the necessity of the legislative interference in regard to the labour of the children and young persons in the employ of the owners of mills and factories? —Yes, those and other facts convince me that the legislative protection is necessary; that the operatives are perfectly powerless in fixing the hours of their own labour; that it is a mistake in legislators to think that they are such free agents as the hand-loom weavers who work at home, or tailors or others who are employed in domestic employment, and who certainly can fix the hours of their own labour; but an instance of those employed in a cotton-mill fixing the hours of their own labour never was known, and therefore I consider that legislative protection is as necessary for them as it is for persons liable to be overwrought abroad.

Did you not say that the hours of labour now are about the same as when you were a boy? —I think they are.

Is the intensity of application and of labour altered, either against or in favour of the operative and of the children employed in mills and factories? —I was a great number of years out of any factory, but those who were my acquaintances during my boyhood have often conversed with me, and they very frequently say that it cannot be less than double in intensity and exertion of physical application. . . .

Martis, 7° die Augusti, 1832

Michael Thomas Sadler, Esquire, in the Chair.
John Richard Farre, Esq., M.D., called in;
and Examined

What is your profession? —That of a physician.

Have you had considerable experience in this city in attending to the diseases of the poor, whether in hospitals or in private practice? —The whole period of my medical study and experience in all the branches of the profession, for the purposes of a consulting physician, has extended to forty-two years.

Do you not regard it as an established principle in your profession, that moderate exercise, with due intervals for rest and for meals, are necessary for the preservation of health? —So essential that without it medical treatment is unavailing.

It is found, on the contrary, that excessive labour, exertion or employment, so as to produce weariness of body and mind, and without due intervals for meals and refreshment, must in ordinary cases be extremely prejudicial to the human constitution? —Man can do no more than he is allowed or permitted to do by nature, and in attempting to transgress the bounds Providence has pointed out for him, he abridges his life in the exact proportion in which he transgresses the laws of nature and the Divine command.

You would think that one of those violations of the laws of nature is excessive labour, excessive both as to its length and the fatigue which it induces, and that it is more prejudicial to young persons than to those advanced to full maturity? —In exact proportion to their feebleness.

Do you conceive that the ordinary limits of a day's labour, as already settled by universal custom, whether in agriculture or mechanical pursuits, namely, about twelve hours a day, with due intermission, is, generally speaking, as much as the human constitution is capable of sustaining without injury? —It depends upon the kind and degree of exertion, for the human being is the creature of a day, and it is possible for the most athletic man under the highest conflicts of body or mind, and especially of both, to exhaust in one hour the whole of his nervous energy provided for that day, so as to be reduced, even in that short space of time, to a state of extreme torpor, confounded with apoplexy, resembling and sometimes terminating in death.

Would labour, too long continued, of a less strenuous nature, but becoming very wearisome both to body and mind, be prejudicial if persevered in? —The injury is in proportion to the exhaustion of the sensorial power. Let me take the life of a day to make myself clearly understood. It consists of alternate action and repose, and repose is not sufficient without sleep. The alternation of the day and the night is a beautiful provision in the order of Providence for the healing of man, so that the night repairs the waste of the day; and he is thereby fitted for the labour of the ensuing day. If he attempt to live two days in one, or to give only one night and two days' labour, he abridges his life in the same, or rather in a greater proportion, for as his days are, so will his years be.

Upon the whole, then, recurring to the question, should not you think that a day's labour, consisting of twelve hours, pursued for a continuance, would, in ordinary cases, be as much as a human being could endure with impunity? —I think that twelve hours' labour is too much for a very large majority of human beings. If I am to state the precise quantity, in my experience, as tending to give the longest and the most vigorous life, I should take it, even in the adult, at eight hours' active exertion, eight hours' sleep, and eight hours allowed for recreation and meals. Those are the divisions of the day which would procure the happiest and the most vigorous life, and which would, I think, yield the greatest sum of labour; but the child requires a greater proportion of sleep than the adult; for sleep is not simply repose, but it is a restorative process.

You are aware that a much greater duration of labour is required than that to which you have alluded, as the most consistent with health; have you seen the effect of forced labour upon the human body? —In the course of my medical life I have seen it extensively; the first part of my medical education was conducted in the West Indies, where I had an opportunity of observing the effects of slavery, and the diseases produced by slavery.

Were you engaged in medical practice as well as medical studies in the West Indies? —I was.

Will you state to this Committee whether, when human beings are regarded as mere property, it is not found necessary, with a view to

the preservation of that property, to limit the duration of their labour, and more particularly the labour of young persons? —It has been found necessary to diminish that labour, especially in regard to the young, insomuch that the young are never accounted fit for labour; their employment is always of the lightest kind.

Until what age? —The exact time for employing them in the field varies with their growth. In the West Indies, human life is often precocious: in the island in which my observations were made, namely, the island of Barbadoes, the oldest established colony, a colony in which there is the hardest work, for it is a hill country, and the whole production of that island is the effect of manual labour, as it is a rocky, and often an artificial soil, through the greater part of the island: it affords therefore a fair specimen of the effect of the fullest labour on the human constitution, and the returns of the increase in the slave population in that island would be a fair criterion to enable the Committee to judge of the effect of that labour, and whether proper provisions were used to render it less injurious. I have reason to believe, it would be found that the population has been for a great many years considerably on the increase, notwithstanding that labour.

Have the regulations recommended by medical authorities in that island been adopted with a view to the preservation of the youth of that colony; and if so, what is their nature? —Each plantation has its regular medical superintendent; but there is a number of highly educated gentlemen in that island; and to my knowledge, an agricultural society was established about a quarter of a century ago, for the express purpose of improving the condition of the slaves, without reference at all to the proceedings on that subject which have occurred in this country. Medical gentlemen, I say, of the highest education were members of that society, and to my certain knowledge, took the two main questions of labour and feeding into their consideration, and communicated papers to that society for their guidance respecting the management of the slaves, both old and young, as to labour and as to food, and as to the proper labour and rest; and I know that extraordinary care was taken, both in regard to regulating the labour of the young and in feeding them, to make them a vigorous race and fit for the work.

What were the regulations in respect of the labour of the children and young persons? —As far as I am acquainted with them, they consisted in not employing them in field labour, in digging or in carrying manure, but in exercising them in gathering the green crops for the stock. The plan of working them lightly in the open air and feeding them, not trusting to the food provided by the parents' care, but by the care of the master, had the most beneficial effect in improving their condition. When I contributed to superintend the negro population, I never knew the young over-worked. I observed that their diseases were more frequently the effect of improper feeding.

Supposing that the employment of children in the factories of this country is spread over twelve or fourteen hours a day, and often with but very short intervals for the taking of their meals; is there any thing equal to that sort of labour imposed upon the children of the slaves in that island? —Nothing of the kind; even the adult, in the most vigorous condition of body, is not subjected to labour of that duration.

Do you happen to know whether the owners of those slaves, alluding to the children, attempt to make a profit by their labour before they arrive at that period of life when they are capable of rendering it? —Never; I have always, as a medical observer, considered that their employment was used only as a training for health and for future occupation.

So that you consider that the limitation of the length and degree of the labour of the children and young persons in Barbadoes is eminently advantageous to the planter himself, with a view merely to his own interest and future advantage? —Certainly; it is necessary. In English factories, every thing which is valuable in manhood is sacrificed to an inferior advantage in childhood. You purchase your advantage at the price of infanticide; the profit thus gained is death to the child. Looking at its effects, I should suppose it was a system directly intended to diminish population.

What have been the provisions to guard against the ill effects of excessive labour? —The provisions consist in the proper management of the youth, in not sacrificing them, and in exercising them in the open air.

Do you consider that labour in the open air, at a given high temperature, is less pernicious than labour performed in a confined atmosphere artificially heated to the same degree of temperature? —There is only a certain portion of labour which any human being can bear in a day, but that labour is better accomplished in a pure atmosphere than in a confined and impure one, because air is vital food, and the relative value of a pure air to the blood is to the grosser aliments which supply blood, as one minute to fourteen days; and it admits of this demonstration, that if a human being, by malformation, disease, or the accidents of life, be deprived of the grosser aliments of bread, flesh and water, he dies in a period of from eleven to nineteen days, and the ordinary period may be taken at fourteen; if he be *completely* deprived of air, he dies in one minute. The relative value therefore of food through the organs of supply, to sanguinification effected in the lungs by pure atmospheric air, is as the value of one minute to fourteen days, according to my estimate. And the deterioration of the atmosphere in which human beings are working produces a deleterious effect in proportion to that deterioration. Supposing that in a place where human beings are congregated, and the air, for want of ventilation and from having been breathed, is impaired, the blood is immediately deteriorated; it passes from its red or vital state to black blood, and the vitality of the being is lowered; it gives a pallid or livid expression, according to its degree; it destroys the appetite, diminishes the action of the heart and arteries, lowers gradually the whole vigour of the system, and produces premature death. This is the inevitable effect of continued labour in a confined, heated and foul atmosphere.

Are the children in the West Indies ever employed in night-work? —I never knew an instance of that.

None are employed in night-work but those who are called the strong gang? —It is only a privileged and higher class, often the most valuable persons on the property, who are employed during a part of the night in the manufacture of sugar in Barbadoes, as far as I recollect.

None but persons in the full enjoyment of strength are employed in night-work? —None but a select class of adults.

Should you conceive any child under 9 years of age ought to be made habitually to labour in a mill or a factory; and do you think that before that period, a considerable number of hours of labour can be endured in such a situation with impunity? —I think that, to insure a vigorous manhood, the period of 9 years of age is too early to commence labour.

Should you conceive that between that period and the time when the system has arrived at its growth and maturity, namely, about 18 years of age, more than ten hours a day of labour could be imposed upon those children and young persons, without producing, generally speaking, mischievous effects? —In considering the order of the human growth, the first seven years of the child properly constitute its infancy, which is closed by the change of teeth, in order to its future sustentation; the second seven years terminate in the development of the generic system, by which the being is to continue the species, and to prevent its deterioration. Now it is manifest, that if the child be deprived of its red blood and muscular fibre during these important periods of its growth, it cannot have a vigorous generic system; but at 14 the changes are so delicate in relation to the provision for the future being, that if forced labour be carried to excess, even between 14 and 21, the value of manhood will be considerably diminished. I call the British system a forcing system, which departs from the truth of Nature, and from the revealed will of God. I have no hesitation in affirming, that there is not a due regard to the preservation of life, either in the British system of education or of labour generally, both as regards the child and the adult; and what I say of the adult, applies still more strongly to the child.

Too great exertion is imposed on both mind and body? —Yes, certainly.

In what manner does this forcing system of too long continued exertion impair health, and occasion premature death? —The first effect of forced labour, is to injure the organs of supply, commonly called the organs of digestion. The absorbent system is divided into two branches, one employed on the alimentary canal, to live on things without us; the other employed on the whole of the animal body; and there is a balance between these two functions, so that if the lacteal absorption be impaired by over-labour, the lymphatic system immediately begins to absorb the body; and this will explain why the body becomes not only pale, but thin. If the labour be pressed, the absorption of fluids is succeeded by the absorption of solids, the fibre is taken up, and thus the muscular fibre is diminished. If the labour be still further pressed, the earthy matter is absorbed, and the bones bend. Thus by premature labour, the child is robbed of its blood, of its muscle, and of its bone; it is crippled for life, and, both in the male and in the female, the species is deteriorated.

It appears, from an official document presented to this Committee, that a greater proportion of mortality exists wherever this system of long and irksome labour is allowed; would you be prepared for such results from the principles you have stated? —I think that the result is so inevitable, that I view it as a species of infanticide, and a very cruel, because lingering species of infanticide, resulting from the over-extension of a principle in itself good, the principle of cheap production demanding over-labour; and that the only safeguard to the state consists in opposing this principle of political economy by the medical voice, whenever it trenches on vital economy.

You think that political economy, supposing it were made manifest that the system would produce national wealth, ought not to be suffered to interfere with vital economy? —It ought not to be suffered to trench on vital economy, because if it does, it is guilty of homicide. I have no hesitation in affirming that the voice of the profession would maintain this truth, and never assent to life being balanced against wealth. That the life is more than the meat, is a divine maxim which we are bound to obey.

So that it is your settled conviction, that what you have denominated, very properly, the forcing system, injures the present generation, and threatens the most injurious effects regarding the future? —The vigour of the animal life depends upon the perfection of the blood, and the balance preserved between the pulmonary and aortic circulation; but in the aortic circulation there is also a balance between the arterial and the venous systems, and the heart is the regulating organ of the whole. Now if the arterial circulation be too much exhausted, an accumulation necessarily takes place on the venous side, and the blood is deteriorated, and organic diseases, which abridge life, are produced. It would carry me too far to investigate this point; I only state the fact which can be demonstrated; but there is another and a higher effect; for man is to be considered as something vastly better than an animal; and the effect of diminishing the power of the heart and arteries by over-labour in a confined atmosphere is to deteriorate the blood, and to excite, in the *animal* part of the mind, gloomy and discontented trains of thought, which disturb and destroy human happiness, and lead to habits of over-stimulation. The reflecting or spiritual mind gradually becomes debased; and unless education interpose to meet the difficulties of the case, the being is necessarily ruined, both for present and for future life.

Are there any countervailing means which suggest themselves to your mind, which would render this continued labour less injurious to present health and happiness, and more conducive to the prosperity of future life? —Ventilation, exercise and diminished exertion, are the most obvious means of meeting the difficulties of the case, joined to the change of ideas resulting from an education adapted to the spiritual nature of man.

So that you think it would be eminently beneficial if the hours of labour were somewhat abated during the day, so as to afford an opportunity for the change of mental exertion, and to direct that exertion to the purposes of education? —It would be a positive gain to the child, which not only mercy, but justice demands; and I think, also, it would be beneficial to the state.

It appears in evidence before this Committee, that the labour in mills and factories undergone by children and young persons of both sexes, is rarely less than fourteen hours a day, including the time allowed for meals; and that in many instances it greatly exceeds that term, and extends sometimes to eighteen or twenty hours, or upwards; during your residence in the West Indies, was there any system of labour imposed upon any of the children and young persons at all equal to that? —Never in the slightest degree approaching to it.

It is in evidence, that the children and young persons employed in factories have often to be roused from their lethargy induced by exertions too long continued, and to be stimulated to their labour (their strength being exhausted) by constant whippings, beatings, or other means of a like nature; are the children of the slaves in the West Indies more hardly worked or more cruelly treated than this state of things implies? —In the colony of which I have spoken, I never saw nor heard of such inhumanity.

Assuming that the children of this country are not free agents, can you have any doubt whatever, the slightest hesitation upon your mind, that they demand protection equally with the child of the West Indian slave? —I think the word "demand" is a very proper mode of putting the question; for I myself consider that the nation is responsible for it, and, as a medical man, I assert that if you deem it a part of your duty to make laws against murder, I consider that legislation is equally necessary for the prevention of death in any mode in which it can be prematurely inflicted; and certainly this must be viewed as a most cruel mode of inflicting it.

You have no hesitation then, in saying that whether considered as a medical, or a political question, a remission of the hours of labour imposed upon the children and young persons of this country would be essentially beneficial? —I view it not only as a benefit, but as a duty; and I would say, not only as a physician, a Christian, and a parent, but also from the common sympathies of a man, that you are bound to afford it.

Herman Melville

Herman Melville (1819–1892) was an American humanitarian and writer, best known for his novel Moby Dick. One of the outstanding features of his style was a remarkable ability of incorporating personal experiences into his accounts. His love for his country as well as his humanitarian feeling led him to fear the development of industrialism in America. To Melville the introduction of machines and factories meant the extension of American slavery in a new form. He was convinced, too, that America would cease to be a land of opportunity if she succumbed to the disintegrating influence of industrial warfare. He wrote The Tartarus of Maids in 1855, as a protest against the evils of the factory system, and in it he made full use of all his literary talents. In reading it note (1) the psychological impression given by Melville in describing his entrance into the Devil's Dungeon, (2) the contrast he drew between this visit and the one he made to the "Paradise of Bachelors" in London (Melville had previously described the luxurious student life of young lawyers in training at the Inns of Court in London), (3) the appearances of the girl operatives, (4) the description of the great machine, (5) the reason for his use of the phrase, "Tartarus of Maids," and (6) the vivid character of Melville's style.

THE TARTARUS OF MAIDS

It lies not far from Woedolor Mountain in New England. Turning to the east, right out from among bright farms and sunny meadows, nodding in early June with odorous grasses, you enter ascendingly among bleak hills. These gradually close in upon a dusky pass, which, from the violent Gulf Stream of air unceasingly driving between its cloven walls of haggard rock, as well as from the tradition of a crazy spinster's hut having long ago stood somewhere hereabouts, is called the Mad Maid's Bellows'-pipe.

Winding along at the bottom of the gorge is a dangerously narrow wheel-road, occupying the bed of a former torrent. Following this road to its highest point, you stand as within a Dantean gateway. From the steepness of the walls here, their strangely ebon hue, and the sudden contraction of the gorge, this particular point is called the Black Notch. The ravine now expandingly descends into a great, purple, hopper-shaped hollow, far sunk among many Plutonian, shaggy-wooded mountains. By the country people this hollow is called the Devil's Dungeon. Sounds of torrents fall on all sides upon the ear. These rapid waters unite at last in one turbid brick-coloured stream, boiling through a flume among enormous boulders. They call this strange-coloured torrent Blood River. Gaining a dark precipice it wheels suddenly to the west, and makes one maniac spring of sixty feet into the arms of a stunted wood of gray-haired pines, between which it thence eddies on its further way down to the invisible lowlands.

Conspicuously crowning a rocky bluff high to one side, at the cataract's verge, is the ruin of an old saw-mill, built in those primitive times when vast pines and hemlocks superabounded throughout the neighbouring region.

Herman Melville, "The Tartarus of Maids," in Harper's New Monthly Magazine, X (April, 1855), 673–678.

The black-mossed bulk of those immense, rough-hewn, and spike-knotted logs, here and there tumbled all together, in long abandonment and decay, or left in solitary, perilous projection over the cataract's gloomy brink, impart to this rude wooden ruin not only much of the aspect of one of rough-quarried stone, but also a sort of feudal, Rhineland and Thurmberg look, derived from the pinnacled wildness of the neighbouring scenery.

Not far from the bottom of the Dungeon stands a large whitewashed building, relieved, like some great white sepulchre, against the sullen background of mountainside firs, and other hardy evergreens, inaccessibly rising in grim terraces for some two thousand feet.

The building is a paper-mill.

Having embarked on a large scale in the seedman's business (so extensively and broadcast, indeed, that at length my seeds were distributed through all the Eastern and Northern States, and even fell into the far soil of Missouri and the Carolinas), the demand for paper at my place became so great, that the expenditure soon amounted to a most important item in the general account. It need hardly be hinted how paper comes into use with seedsmen, as envelopes. These are mostly made of yellowish paper, folded square; and when filled, are all but flat, and being stamped, and superscribed with the nature of the seeds contained, assume not a little the appearance of business letters ready for the mail. Of these small envelopes I used an incredible quantity—several hundreds of thousands in a year. For a time I had purchased my paper from the wholesale dealers in a neighbouring town. For economy's sake, and partly for the adventure of the trip, I now resolved to cross the mountains, some sixty miles, and order my future paper at the Devil's Dungeon paper-mill.

The sleighing being uncommonly fine toward the end of January, and promising to hold so for no small period, in spite of the bitter cold I started one gray Friday noon in my pung, well fitted with buffalo and wolf robes; and, spending one night on the road, next noon came in sight of Woedolor Mountain.

The far summit fairly smoked with frost; white vapours curled up from its white-wooded top, as from a chimney. The intense congelation made the whole country look like one petrifaction. The steel shoes of my pung craunched and gritted over the vitreous, chippy snow, as if it had been broken glass. The forests here and there skirting the route, feeling the same all-stiffening influence, their inmost fibres penetrated with the cold, strangely groaned—not in the swaying branches merely, but likewise in the vertical trunk—as the fitful gusts remorselessly swept through them. Brittle with excessive frost, many colossal tough-grained maples, snapped in twain like pipe-stems, cumbered the unfeeling earth.

Flaked all over with frozen sweat, white as a milky ram, his nostrils at each breath sending forth two horn-shaped shoots of heated respiration, Black, my good horse, but six years old, started at a sudden turn, where, right across the track—not ten minutes fallen—an old distorted hemlock lay, darkly undulatory as an anaconda.

Gaining the Bellows'-pipe, the violent blast, dead from behind, all but shoved my high-backed pung uphill. The gust shrieked through the shivered pass, as if laden with lost spirits bound to the unhappy world. Ere gaining the summit, Black, my horse, as if exasperated by the cutting wind, slung out with his strong hind-legs, tore the light pung straight uphill, and sweeping grazingly through the narrow notch, sped downward madly past the ruined sawmill. Into the Devil's Dungeon horse and cataract rushed together.

With might and main, quitting my seat and robes, and standing backward, with one foot braced against the dashboard, I rasped and churned the bit, and stopped him just in time to avoid collision, at a turn, with the bleak nozzle of a rock, couchant like a lion in the way—a roadside rock.

At first I could not discover the paper-mill.

The whole hollow gleamed with the white, except, here and there, where a pinnacle of granite showed one windswept angle bare. The mountains stood pinned in shrouds—a pass of Alpine corpses. Where stands the mill? Suddenly a whirling, humming sound broke upon my ear. I looked, and there, like an arrested avalanche, lay the large white-washed factory. It was subordinately surrounded by a cluster of other and smaller buildings, some of which, from their cheap, blank air, great length, gregarious windows, and comfortless expression, no doubt were boarding-houses of the operatives. A snow-white hamlet amidst the snows. Various rude, irregular squares and courts resulted from the somewhat picturesque clusterings of these buildings, owing to the broken, rocky nature of the ground, which forbade all method in their relative arrangement. Several narrow lanes and alleys, too, partly blocked with snow fallen from the roof, cut up the hamlet in all directions.

When, turning from the travelled highway, jingling with bells of numerous farmers—who, availing themselves of the fine sleighing, were dragging their wood to market—and frequently diversified with swift cutters dashing from inn to inn of the scattered villages—when, I say, turning from that bustling main-road, I by degrees wound into the Mad Maid's Bellows'-pipe, and saw the grim Black Notch beyond, then something latent, as well as something obvious in the time and scene, strangely brought back to my mind my first sight of dark and grimy Temple Bar. And when Black, my horse, went darting through the Notch, perilously grazing its rocky wall, I remembered being in a runaway London omnibus, which in much the same sort of style, though by no means at an equal rate, dashed through the ancient arch of Wren. Though the two objects did by no means completely correspond, yet this partial inadequacy but served to tinge the similitude not less with the vividness than the disorder of a dream. So that, when upon reining up at the protruding rock I at last caught sight of the quaint groupings of the factory-buildings, and with the travelled highway and the Notch behind, found myself all alone, silently and privily stealing through deep-cloven passages into this sequestered spot, and saw the long, high-gabled main factory edifice, with a rude tower—for hoisting heavy boxes—at one end, standing among its crowded outbuildings and boarding-houses, as the Temple Church amidst the surrounding offices and dormitories, and when the marvellous retirement of this mysterious mountain nook fastened its whole spell upon me, then, what memory lacked, all tributary imagination furnished, and I said to myself, "This is the very counterpart of the Paradise of Bachelors, but snowed upon, and frost-painted to a sepulchre."

Dismounting, and warily picking my way down the dangerous declivity—horse and man both sliding now and then upon the icy ledges—at length I drove, or the blast drove me, into the largest square, before one side of the main edifice. Piercingly and shrilly the shotted blast blew by the corner; and redly and demoniacally boiled Blood River at one side. A long wood-pile, of many scores of cords, all glittering in mail of crusted ice, stood crosswise in the square. A row of horse-posts, their north sides plastered with adhesive snow, flanked the factory wall. The bleak frost packed and paved the square as with some ringing metal.

The inverted similitude recurred—"The sweet, tranquil Temple garden, with the Thames bordering its green beds," strangely meditated I.

But where are the gay bachelors?

Then, as I and my horse stood shivering in the windspray, a girl ran from a neighbouring dormitory door, and throwing her thin apron over her bare head, made for the opposite building.

"One moment, my girl; is there no shed hereabouts which I may drive into?"

Pausing, she turned upon me a face pale with work, and blue with cold; an eye supernatural with unrelated misery.

"Nay," faltered I, "I mistook you. Go on; I want nothing."

Leading my horse close to the door from which she had come, I knocked. Another pale, blue girl appeared, shivering in the doorway as, to prevent the blast, she jealously held the door ajar.

"Nay, I mistake again. In God's name shut the door. But hold, is there no man about?"

That moment a dark-complexioned, well-wrapped personage passed, making for the factory door, and spying him coming, the girl rapidly closed the other one.

"Is there no horse-shed here, sir?"

"Yonder, the wood-shed," he replied, and disappeared inside the factory.

With much ado I managed to wedge in horse and pung between the scattered piles of wood all sawn and split. Then, blanketing my horse, and piling my buffalo on the blanket's top, and tucking in its edges well around the breast-band and breeching, so that the wind might not strip him bare, I tied him fast, and ran lamely for the factory door, stiff with frost, and cumbered with my driver's dreadnaught.

Immediately I found myself standing in a spacious place, intolerably lighted by long rows of windows, focusing inward the snowy scene without.

At rows of blank-looking counters sat rows of blank-looking girls, with blank, white folders in their blank hands, all blankly folding blank paper.

In one corner stood some huge frame of ponderous iron, with a vertical thing like a piston periodically rising and falling upon a heavy wooden block. Before it—its tame minister—stood a tall girl, feeding the iron animal with half-quires of rose-hued note-paper, which, at every downward dab of the piston-like machine, received in the corner the impress of a wreath of roses. I looked from the rosy paper to the pallid cheek, but said nothing.

Seated before a long apparatus, strung with long, slender strings like any harp, another girl was weeding it with foolscap sheets, which, so soon as they curiously travelled from her on the cords, were withdrawn at the opposite end of the machine by a second girl. They came to the first girl blank; they went to the second girl ruled.

I looked upon the first girl's brow, and saw it was young and fair; I looked upon the second girl's brow, and saw it was ruled and wrinkled. Then, as I still looked, the two—for some small variety to the monotony—changed places; and where had stood the young, fair brow, now stood the ruled and wrinkled one.

Perched high upon a narrow platform, and still higher upon a high stool crowning it, sat another figure serving some other iron animal; while below the platform sat her mate in some sort of reciprocal attendance.

Not a syllable was breathed. Nothing was heard but the low, steady, overruling hum of the iron animals. The human voice was banished from the spot. Machinery—that vaunted slave of humanity—here stood menially served by human beings, who served mutely and cringingly as the slave serves the Sultan. The girls did not so much seem accessory wheels to the general machinery as mere cogs to the wheels.

All this scene around me was instantaneously taken in at one sweeping glance—even before I had proceeded to unwind the heavy fur tippet from around my neck. But as soon as this fell from me the dark-complexioned man, standing close by, raised a sudden cry, and seizing my arm, dragged me out into the open air, and without pausing for a word instantly caught up some congealed snow and began rubbing both my cheeks.

"Two white spots like the whites of your eyes," he said; "man, your cheeks are frozen."

"That may well be," muttered I; "'tis some wonder the frost of the Devil's Dungeon strikes in no deeper. Rub away."

Soon a horrible, tearing pain caught at my reviving cheeks. Two gaunt blood-hounds, one on each side, seemed mumbling them. I seemed Actaeon.

Presently, when all was over, I re-entered the factory, made known my business, concluded it satisfactorily, and then begged to be conducted throughout the place to view it.

"Cupid is the boy for that," said the dark-complexioned man. "Cupid!" and by this odd fancy-name calling a dimpled, red-cheeked, spirited-looking, forward little fellow, who was rather impudently, I thought, gliding about among the passive-looking girls—like a goldfish through hueless waves—yet doing nothing in particular that I could see, the man bade him lead the stranger through the edifice.

"Come first and see the water-wheel," said this lively lad, with the air of boyishly-brisk importance.

Quitting the folding-room, we crossed some damp, cold boards, and stood beneath a great wet shed, incessantly showering with foam, like the green barnacled bow of some East India-man in a gale. Round and round here went the enormous revolutions of the dark colossal water-wheel, grim with its one immutable purpose.

"This sets our whole machinery a-going, sir; in every part of all these buildings; where the girls work and all."

I looked, and saw that the turbid waters of

Blood River had not changed their hue by coming under the use of man.

"You make only blank paper; no printing of any sort, I suppose? All blank paper, don't you?"

"Certainly; what else should a paper-factory make?"

The lad here looked at me as if suspicious of my common-sense.

"Oh, to be sure!" said I, confused and stammering; "it only struck me as so strange that red waters should turn out pale chee— paper, I mean."

He took me up a wet and rickety stair to a great light room, furnished with no visible thing but rude, manger-like receptacles running all round its sides; and up to these mangers, like so many mares haltered to the rack, stood rows of girls. Before each was vertically thrust up a long, glittering scythe, immovably fixed at bottom to the manger-edge. The curve of the scythe, and its having no snath to it, made it look exactly like a sword. To and fro, across the sharp edge, the girls forever dragged long strips of rags, washed white, picked from baskets at one side; thus ripping asunder every seam, and converting the tatters almost into lint. The air swam with the fine, poisonous particles, which from all sides darted, subtilely, as motes in sunbeams, into the lungs.

"This is the rag-room," coughed the boy.

"You find it rather stifling here," coughed I, in answer; "but the girls don't cough."

"Oh, they are used to it."

"Where do you get such hosts of rags?" picking up a handful from a basket.

"Some from the country round about; some from far over sea—Leghorn and London."

" 'Tis not unlikely, then," murmured I, "that among these heaps of rags there may be some old shirts, gathered from the dormitories of the Paradise of Bachelors. But the buttons are all dropped off. Pray, my lad, do you ever find any bachelor's buttons hereabouts?"

"None grow in this part of the country. The Devil's Dungeon is no place for flowers."

"Oh! you mean the *flowers* so called—the Bachelor's Buttons?"

"And was not that what you asked about? Or did you mean the gold bosom-buttons of our boss, Old Bach, as our whispering girls all call him?"

"The man, then, I saw below is a bachelor, is he?"

"Oh yes, he's a Bach."

"The edges of those swords, they are turned outward from the girls, if I see right; but their rags and fingers fly so, I cannot distinctly see."

"Turned outward."

Yes, murmured I to myself; I see it now; turned outward; and each erected sword is so borne, edge outward, before each girl. If my reading fails me not, just so, of old, condemned state-prisoners went from the hall of judgment to their doom: an officer before, bearing a sword, its edge turned outward, in significance of their fatal sentence. So, through consumptive pallors of this blank, raggy life, go these white girls to death.

"Those scythes look very sharp," again turning toward the boy.

"Yes; they have to keep them so. Look!"

That moment two of the girls, dropping their rags, plied each a whetstone up and down the sword-blade. My unaccustomed blood curdled at the sharp shriek of the tormented steel.

Their own executioners; themselves whetting the very swords that slay them, meditated I.

"What makes those girls so sheet-white, my lad?"

"Why"—with a roguish twinkle, pure ignorant drollery, not-knowing heartlessness—"I suppose the handling of such white bits of sheets all the time makes them so sheety."

"Let us leave the rag-room now, my lad."

More tragical and more inscrutably mysterious than any mystic sight, human or machine, throughout the factory, was the strange innocence of cruel-heartedness in this usage-hardened boy.

"And now," said he, cheerily, "I suppose you want to see our great machine, which cost us twelve thousand dollars only last autumn. That's the machine that makes the paper, too. This way, sir."

Following him, I crossed a large, bespattered place, with two great round vats in it, full of a white, wet, woolly-looking stuff, not unlike the albuminous part of an egg, soft-boiled.

"There," said Cupid, tapping the vats carelessly, "these are the first beginnings of the paper; this white pulp you see. Look how it swims bubbling round and round, moved by the paddle here. From hence it pours from both vats into that one common channel yonder; and so goes, mixed up and leisurely, to the great machine. And now for that."

He led me into a room, stifling with a strange, blood-like, abdominal heat, as if here, true enough, were being finally developed the germinous particles lately seen.

Before me, rolled out like some long Eastern manuscript, lay stretched one continuous length of iron framework—multitudinous and mystical, with all sorts of rollers, wheels, and cylinders, in slowly-measured and unceasing motion.

"Here first comes the pulp now," said Cupid, pointing to the nighest end of the machine. "See; first it pours out and spreads itself upon this wide, sloping board; and then—look—slides, thin and quivering, beneath the first roller there. Follow on now, and see it as it slides from under that to the next cylinder. There; see how it has become just a very little less pulpy now. One step more, and it grows still more to some slight consistence. Still another cylinder, and it is so knitted—though as yet mere dragon-fly wing—that it forms an air-bridge here, like a suspended cobweb, between two more separated rollers; and flowing over the last one, and under again, and doubling about there out of sight for a minute among all those mixed cylinders you indistinctly see, it reappears here, looking now at last a little less like pulp and more like paper, but still quite delicate and defective yet awhile. But—a little further onward, sir, if you please—here now, at this further point, it puts on something of a real look, as if it might turn out to be something you might possibly handle in the end. But it's not yet done, sir. Good way to travel yet, and plenty more of cylinders must roll it."

"Bless my soul!" said I, amazed at the elongation, interminable convolutions, and deliberate slowness of the machine; "it must take a long time for the pulp to pass from end to end, and come out paper."

"Oh, not so long," smiled the precocious lad, with a superior and patronising air; "only nine minutes. But look; you may try it for yourself.

Have you a bit of paper? Ah! here's a bit on the floor. Now mark that with any word you please, and let me dab it on here, and we'll see how long before it comes out at the other end."

"Well, let me see," said I, taking out my pencil; "come, I'll mark it with your name."

Bidding me take out my watch, Cupid adroitly dropped the inscribed slip on an exposed part of the incipient mass.

Instantly my eye marked the second-hand on my dial-plate.

Slowly I followed the slip, inch by inch; sometimes pausing for full half a minute as it disappeared beneath inscrutable groups of the lower cylinders, but only gradually to emerge again; and so, on, and on, and on—inch by inch; now in open sight, sliding along like a freckle on the quivering sheet; and then again wholly vanished; and so, on, and on, and on—inch by inch; all the time the main sheet growing more and more to final firmness—when, suddenly, I saw a sort of paper-fall, not wholly unlike a water-fall; a scissory sound smote my ear, as of some cord being snapped; and down dropped an unfolded sheet of perfect foolscap, with my "Cupid" half faded out of it, and still moist and warm.

My travels were at an end, for here was the end of the machine.

"Well, how long was it?" said Cupid.

"Nine minutes to a second," replied I, watch in hand.

"I told you so."

For a moment a curious emotion filled me, not wholly unlike that which one might experience at the fulfilment of some mysterious prophecy. But how absurd, thought I again; the thing is a mere machine, the essence of which is unvarying punctuality and precision.

Previously absorbed by the wheels and cylinders, my attention was now directed to a sad-looking woman standing by.

"That is rather an elderly person so silently tending the machine-end here. She would not seem wholly used to it either."

"Oh," knowingly whispered Cupid, through the din, "she only came last week. She was a nurse formerly. But the business is poor in these parts, and she's left it. But look at the paper she is piling there."

"Ay, foolscap," handling the piles of moist,

warm sheets, which continually were being delivered into the woman's waiting hands. "Don't you turn out anything but foolscap at this machine?"

"Oh, sometimes, but not often, we turn out finer work—cream-laid and royal sheets, we call them. But foolscap being in chief demand, we turn out foolscap most."

It was very curious. Looking at that blank paper continually dropping, dropping, dropping, my mind ran on in wonderings of those strange uses to which those thousand sheets eventually would be put. All sorts of writings would be writ on those now vacant things— sermons, lawyers' briefs, physicians' prescriptions, love-letters, marriage certificates, bills of divorce, registers of births, death-warrants, and so on, without end. Then, recurring back to them as they here lay all blank, I could not but bethink me of that celebrated comparison of John Locke, who, in demonstration of his theory that man had no innate ideas, compared the human mind at birth to a sheet of blank paper; something destined to be scribbled on, but what sort of characters no soul might tell.

Pacing slowly to and fro along the involved machine, still humming with its play, I was struck as well by the inevitability as the evolvement-power in all its motions.

"Does that thin cobweb there," said I, pointing to the sheet in its more imperfect stage, "does that never tear or break? It is marvellous fragile, and yet this machine it passes through is so mighty."

"It never is known to tear a hair's point."

"Does it never stop—get clogged?"

"No. It *must* go. The machinery makes it go just *so;* just that very way, and at that very pace you there plainly *see* it go. The pulp can't help going."

Something of awe now stole over me, as I gazed upon this inflexible iron animal. Always, more or less, machinery of this ponderous, elaborate sort strikes, in some moods, strange dread into the human heart, as some living, panting Behemoth might. But what made the thing I saw so specially terrible to me was the metallic necessity, the unbudging fatality which governed it. Though, here and there, I could not follow the thin, gauzy veil of pulp in the course of its more mysterious or entirely invisible advance, yet it was indubitable that, at those points where it eluded me, it still marched on in unvarying docility to the autocratic cunning of the machine. A fascination fastened on me. I stood spellbound and wandering in my soul. Before my eyes—there, passing in slow procession along the wheeling cylinders, I seemed to see, glued to the pallid incipience of the pulp, the yet more pallid faces of all the pallid girls I had eyed that heavy day. Slowly, mournfully, beseechingly, yet unresistingly, they gleamed along, their agony dimly outlined on the imperfect paper, like the print of the tormented face on the handkerchief of Saint Veronica.

"Halloa! the heat of the room is too much for you," cried Cupid, staring at me.

"No—I am rather chill, if anything."

"Come out, sir—out—out," and, with the protecting air of a careful father, the precocious lad hurried me outside.

In a few moments, feeling revived a little, I went into the folding-room—the first room I had entered, and where the desk for transacting business stood, surrounded by the blank counters and blank girls engaged at them.

"Cupid here has led me a strange tour," said I to the dark-complexioned man before mentioned, whom I had ere this discovered not only to be an old bachelor, but also the principal proprietor. "Yours is a most wonderful factory. Your great machine is a miracle of inscrutable intricacy."

"Yes, all our visitors think it so. But we don't have many. We are in a very out-of-the-way corner here. Few inhabitants, too. Most of our girls come from far-off villages."

"The girls," echoed I, glancing round at their silent forms. "Why is it, sir, that in most factories, female operatives, of whatever age, are indiscriminately called girls, never women?"

"Oh! as to that—why, I suppose, the fact of their being generally unmarried—that's the reason, I should think. But it never struck me before. For our factory here, we will not have married women; they are apt to be off-and-on too much. We want none but steady workers: twelve hours to the day, day after day, through the three hundred and sixty-five days, excepting Sundays, Thanksgiving, and Fast-days. That's our rule. And so, having no married women, what females we have are rightly enough called girls."

"Then these are all maids," said I, while some pained homage to their pale virginity made me involuntarily bow.

"All maids."

Again the strange emotion filled me.

"Your cheeks look whitish yet, sir," said the man, gazing at me narrowly. "You must be careful going home. Do they pain you at all now? It's a bad sign, if they do."

"No doubt, sir," answered I, "when once I have got out of the Devil's Dungeon, I shall feel them mending."

"Ah, yes; the winter air in valleys, or gorges, or any sunken place, is far colder and more bitter than elsewhere. You would hardly be-lieve it now, but it is colder here than at the top of Woedolor Mountain."

"I dare say it is, sir. But time presses me; I must depart."

With that, remuffling myself in dreadnaught and tippet, thrusting my hands into my huge sealskin mittens, I sallied out into the nipping air, and found poor Black, my horse, all cringing and doubled up with the cold.

Soon, wrapped in furs and meditations, I ascended from the Devil's Dungeon.

At the Black Notch I paused, and once more bethought me of Temple Bar. Then, shooting through the pass, all alone with inscrutable nature, I exclaimed—Oh! Paradise of Bachelors! and oh! Tartarus of Maids!

Adam Smith

Adam Smith (1723–1790) was an English educator and economist who deeply affected the thinking of the nineteenth century. He himself lived in the Age of Enlightenment and was strongly influenced by the emphasis which some of his contemporaries placed upon natural law and the advantage of achieving the natural order unrestricted by man-made regulations. It was this phase of his thinking that appealed to the economic liberals of the nineteenth century and which was used by them to support their doctrine of laissez faire. Like the mercantilists of an earlier day, Smith was interested in increasing the prosperity of the nation, but unlike them he found the answer, not in a favorable trade balance, but in the production of goods which would have the greatest exchange value in the world's markets. This advantage could be achieved, according to Smith, by permitting each individual the freedom to follow his natural self-interest in both production and trade. Thus, the state should remove restrictions on all economic pursuits. In 1776, Smith published his great work, An Inquiry into the Nature and Causes of the Wealth of Nations, in which he summarized his theories. In reading the following selections from it note (1) the importance which Smith attached to labor in the production of wealth, (2) the advantages of division of labor, (3) the three factors contributing to increased output through division of labor, (4) the natural human quality to which Smith attributed the division of labor, (5) his implied estimate of human nature, (6) the importance of the size of the market to the division of labor, (7) the effect of import duties upon the division of labor, (8) the relative ability of the individual and the lawgiver to determine what was to the individual's self-interest, (9) his analysis of the infant-industry argument, (10) the cases in which protective duties might be advantageous, (11) the problem of retaliatory duties, (12) his consideration of humanitarianism in removing duties, and (13) the vested interests and political lobbies resulting from protection.

From: AN INQUIRY INTO THE NATURE AND CAUSES OF THE WEALTH OF NATIONS

INTRODUCTION

The annual labour of every nation is the fund which originally supplies it with all the necessaries and conveniences of life which it annually consumes, and which consist always either in the immediate produce of that labour, or in what is purchased with that produce from other nations.

According, therefore, as this produce, or what is purchased with it, bears a greater or smaller proportion to the number of those who are to consume it, the nation will be better or worse supplied with all the necessaries and conveniences for which it has occasion.

But this proportion must in every nation be regulated by two different circumstances: first, by the skill, dexterity, and judgment with which its labour is generally aplied; and, secondly, by the proportion between the number of those who are employed in useful labour, and that of those who are not so employed. Whatever be the soil, climate, or extent of territory of any particular nation, the abundance or scantiness of its annual supply must, in that particular situation, depend upon those two circumstances.

The abundance or scantiness of this supply, too, seems to depend more upon the former of those two circumstances than upon the latter. Among the savage nations of hunters and fishers, every individual who is able to work is more or less employed in useful labour, and endeavours to provide, as well as he can, the necessaries and conveniences of life, for himself, and such of his family or tribe as are either too old, or too young, or too infirm, to go a-hunting and fishing. Such nations, however, are so miserably poor, that, from mere want, they are frequently reduced, or at least think themselves reduced, to the necessity sometimes of directly destroying, and sometimes of abandoning, their infants, their old people, and those afflicted with lingering diseases, to perish with hunger, or to be devoured by wild beasts. Among civilised and thriving nations, on the contrary, though a great number of people do not labour at all, many of whom consume the produce of ten times, frequently of a hundred times, more labour than the greater part of those who work; yet the produce of the whole labour of the society is so great, that all are often abundantly supplied; and a workman, even of the lowest and poorest order, if he is frugal and industrious, may enjoy a greater share of the necessaries and conveniences of life than it is possible for any savage to acquire.

The causes of this improvement in the productive powers of labour, and the order according to which its produce is naturally distributed among the different ranks and conditions of men in the society, make the subject of the first book of this Inquiry. . . .

The greatest improvements in the productive powers of labour, and the greater part of the skill, dexterity, and judgment, with which it is anywhere directed, or applied, seem to have been the effects of the division of labour.

The effects of the division of labour, in the general business of society, will be more easily understood, by considering in what manner it operates in some particular manufactures. It is commonly supposed to be carried furthest in some very trifling ones; not perhaps that it

Adam Smith, *An Inquiry into the Nature and Causes of the Wealth of Nations*, London, 1870, 1; 3–8; 183–191.

really is carried further in them than in others of more importance: but in those trifling manufactures which are destined to supply the small wants of but a small number of people, the whole number of workmen must necessarily be small; and those employed in every different branch of the work can often be collected into the same workhouse, and placed at once under the view of the spectator. In those great manufactures, on the contrary, which are destined to supply the great wants of the great body of the people, every different branch of the work employs so great a number of workmen, that it is impossible to collect them all into the same workhouse. We can seldom see more, at one time, than those employed in one single branch. Though in such manufactures, therefore, the work may really be divided into a much greater number of parts, than in those of a more trifling nature, the division is not near so obvious, and has accordingly been much less observed.

To take an example, therefore, from a very trifling manufacture, but one in which the division of labour has been very often taken notice of, the trade of a pinmaker: a workman not educated to this business (which the division of labour has rendered a distinct trade), nor acquainted with the use of the machinery employed in it (to the invention of which the same division of labour has probably given occasion), could scarce, perhaps, with his utmost industry, make one pin in a day, and certainly could not make twenty. But in the way in which this business is now carried on, not only the whole work is a peculiar trade, but it is divided into a number of branches, of which the greater part are likewise peculiar trades. One man draws out the wire; another straights it; a third cuts it; a fourth points it; a fifth grinds it at the top for receiving the head; to make the head requires two or three distinct operations; to put it on is a peculiar business; to whiten the pins is another, it is even a trade by itself to put them into the paper; and the important business of making a pin is, in this manner, divided into about eighteen distinct operations, which, in some manufactories, are all performed by distinct hands, though in others the same man will sometimes perform two or three of them. I have seen a small manufactory of this kind, where ten men only were employed, and where some of them consequently performed two or three distinct operations. But though they were very poor, and therefore but indifferently accommodated with the necessary machinery, they could, when they exerted themselves, make among them about twelve pounds of pins in a day. There are in a pound upwards of four thousand pins of a middling size. Those ten persons, therefore, could make among them upwards of forty-eight thousand pins in a day. Each person, therefore, making a tenth part of forty-eight thousand pins, might be considered as making four thousand eight hundred pins in a day. But if they had all wrought separately and independently, and without any of them having been educated to this peculiar business, they certainly could not each of them have made twenty, perhaps not one pin in a day; that is, certainly, not the two hundred and fortieth, perhaps not the four thousand eight hundredth, part of what they are at present capable of performing, in consequence of a proper division and combination of their different operations.

In every other art and manufacture, the effects of the division of labour are similar to what they are in this very trifling one, though, in many of them, the labour can neither be so much subdivided, nor reduced to so great a simplicity of operation. The division of labour, however, so far as it can be introduced, occasions, in every art, a proportionable increase of the productive powers of labour. The separation of different trades and employments from one another, seems to have taken place in consequence of this advantage. This separation, too, is generally carried furthest in those countries which enjoy the highest degree of industry and improvement; what is the work of one man, in a rude state of society, being generally that of several in an improved one. In every improved society, the farmer is generally nothing but a farmer; the manufacturer, nothing but a manufacturer. The labour, too, which is necessary to produce any one complete manufacture, is almost always divided among a great number of hands. How many different trades are employed in each branch of the linen and woollen manufactures, from the growers of the flax and the wool, to the bleachers and smoothers of the linen, or to the dyers and dressers of the cloth! The nature of agriculture, indeed, does not admit of so many subdivisions of labour, nor of so complete a separation of one business from another, as manufactures. It is impossible to separate so entirely the business of the grazier from that of the corn-farmer, as the trade of the carpenter is commonly separated from that of the smith. The spinner is almost always a distinct person from the weaver; but the ploughman, the harrower, the sower of the seed, and the reaper of the corn, are often the same. The occasions for those different sorts of labour returning with the different seasons of the year, it is impossible that one man should be constantly employed in any one of them. This impossibility of making so complete and entire a separation of all the different branches of labour employed in agriculture, is perhaps the reason why the improvement of the productive powers of labour, in this art, does not always keep pace with their improvement in manufactures. The most opulent nations, indeed, generally excel all their neighbours in agriculture as well as in manufactures; but they are commonly more distinguished by their superiority in the latter than in the former. . . .

This great increase in the quantity of work, which, in consequence of the division of labour, the same number of people are capable of performing, is owing to three different circumstances; first, to the increase of dexterity in every particular workman; secondly, to the saving of the time which is commonly lost in passing from one species of work to another; and, lastly, to the invention of a great number of machines which facilitate and abridge labour, and enable one man to do the work of many. . . .

It is the great multiplication of the productions of all the different arts, in consequence of the division of labour, which occasions, in a well-governed society, that universal opulence which extends itself to the lowest ranks of the people. Every workman has a great quantity of his own work to dispose of beyond what he himself has occasion for; and every

other workman being exactly in the same situation, he is enabled to exchange a great quantity of his own goods for a great quantity, or, what comes to the same thing, for the price of a great quantity of theirs. He supplies them abundantly with what they have occasion for, and they accommodate him as amply with what he has occasion for, and a general plenty diffuses itself through all the different ranks of the society.

Observe the accommodation of the most common artificer or day-labourer in a civilised and thriving country, and you will perceive that the number of people, of whose industry a part, though but a small part, has been employed in procuring him this accommodation, exceeds all computation. The woollen coat, for example, which covers the day-labourer, as coarse and rough as it may appear, is the produce of the joint labour of a great multitude of workmen. The shepherd, the sorter of the wool, the wool-comber or carder, the dyer, the scribbler, the spinner, the weaver, the fuller, the dresser, with many others, must all join their different arts in order to complete even this homely production. How many merchants and carriers, besides, must have been employed in transporting the materials from some of those workmen to others who often live in a very distant part of the country? How much commerce and navigation in particular, how many ship-builders, sailors, sail-makers, ropemakers, must have been employed in order to bring together the different drugs made use of by the dyer, which often come from the remotest corners of the world? . . .

. . . If we examine, I say, all these things, and consider what a variety of labour is employed about each of them, we shall be sensible that, without the assistance and co-operation of many thousands, the very meanest person in a civilised country could not be provided, even according to, what we very falsely imagine, the easy and simple manner in which he is commonly accommodated. Compared, indeed, with the more extravagant luxury of the great, his accommodation must no doubt appear extremely simple and easy; and yet it may be true, perhaps, that the accommodation of an European prince does not always so much exceed that of an industrious and frugal peasant, as the accommodation of the latter exceeds that of many an African king, the absolute masters of the lives and liberties of ten thousand naked savages.

OF THE PRINCIPLE WHICH GIVES OCCASION TO THE DIVISION OF LABOUR

This division of labour, from which so many advantages are derived, is not originally the effect of any human wisdom, which foresees and intends that general opulence to which it gives occasion. It is the necessary, though very slow and gradual, consequence of a certain propensity in human nature, which has in view no such extensive utility; the propensity to truck, barter, and exchange one thing for another.

Whether this propensity be one of those original principles in human nature, of which no further account can be given, or whether, as seems more probable, it be the necessary consequence of the faculties of reason and speech, it belongs not to our present subject to inquire. It is common to all men, and to be found in no other race of animals, which seem to know neither this nor any other species of contracts. Two greyhounds, in running down the same hare, have sometimes the appearance of acting in some sort of concert. Each turns her towards his companion, or endeavours to intercept her when his companion turns her toward himself. This, however, is not the effect of any contract, but of the accidental concurrence of their passions in the same object at that particular time. Nobody ever saw a dog make a fair and deliberate exchange of one bone for another with another dog. Nobody ever saw one animal, by its gestures and natural cries, signify to another, this is mine, that yours; I am willing to give this for that. When an animal wants to obtain something either of a man, or of another animal, it has no other means of persuasion, but to gain the favour of those whose service it requires. A puppy fawns upon its dam, and a spaniel endeavours, by a thousand attractions, to engage the attention of its master who is at dinner, when it wants to be fed by

him. Man sometimes uses the same arts with his brethren, and when he has no other means of engaging them to act according to his inclinations, endeavours by every servile and fawning attention to obtain their good will. He has not time, however, to do this upon every occasion. In civilised society he stands at all times in need of the co-operation and assistance of great multitudes, while his whole life is scarce sufficient to gain the friendship of a few persons. In almost every other race of animals, each individual, when it is grown up to maturity, is entirely independent, and in its natural state has occasion for the assistance of no other living creature. But man has almost constant occasion for the help of his brethren, and it is in vain for him to expect it from their benevolence only. He will be more likely to prevail if he can interest their self-love in his favour, and show them that it is for their own advantage to do for him what he requires of them. Whoever offers to another a bargain of any kind, proposes to do this. Give me that which I want, and you shall have this which you want, is the meaning of every such offer; and it is in this manner that we obtain from one another the far greater part of those good offices which we stand in need of. It is not from the benevolence of the butcher, the brewer, or the baker, that we expect our dinner, but from their regard to their own interest. We address ourselves, not to their humanity, but to their self-love, and never talk to them of our own necessities, but of their advantages. Nobody but a beggar chooses to depend chiefly upon the benevolence of his fellow-citizens. Even a beggar does not depend upon it entirely. The charity of well-disposed people, indeed, supplies him with the whole fund of his subsistence. But though this principle ultimately provides him with all the necessaries of life which he has occasion for, it neither does nor can provide him with them as he has occasion for them. The greater part of his occasional wants are supplied in the same manner as those of other people, by treaty, by barter, and by purchase. With the money which one man gives him he purchases food. The old clothes which another bestows upon him he exchanges for other clothes which suit him better, or for lodging, or for food, or for money, with which he can buy either food, clothes, or lodging, as he has occasion.

As it is by treaty, by barter, and by purchase, that we obtain from one another the greater part of those mutual good offices which we stand in need of, so it is this same trucking disposition which originally gives occasion to the division of labour. In a tribe of hunters or shepherds, a particular person makes bows and arrows, for example, with more readiness and dexterity than any other. He frequently exchanges them for cattle or for venison, with his companions; and he finds at last that he can, in this manner, get more cattle and venison, than if he himself went to the field to catch them. From a regard to his own interest, therefore, the making of bows and arrows grows to be his chief business, and he becomes a sort of armourer. Another excels in making the frames and covers of their little huts or moveable houses. He is accustomed to be of use in this way to his neighbours, who reward him in the same manner with cattle and with venison, till at last he finds it his interest to dedicate himself entirely to this employment, and to become a sort of house-carpenter. In the same manner a third becomes a smith or a brazier; a fourth, a tanner or dresser of hides or skins, the principal part of the clothing of savages. And thus the certainty of being able to exchange all that surplus part of the produce of his own labour, which is over and above his own consumption, for such parts of the produce of other men's labour as he may have occasion for, encourages every man to apply himself to a particular occupation, and to cultivate and bring to perfection whatever talent of genius he may possess for that particular species of business.

The difference of natural talents in different men, is, in reality, much less than we are aware of; and the very different genius which appears to distinguish men of different professions, when grown up to maturity, is not upon many occasions so much the cause, as the effect of the division of labour. The difference between the most dissimilar characters, between a philosopher and a common street porter, for example, seems to arise not so much from nature, as from habit, custom, and education. When they came into the world, and for the first six or eight years of their existence, they were, perhaps, very much alike, and neither their parents nor playfellows could perceive any remarkable difference. About that age, or soon after, they come to be employed in very different occupations. The difference of talents comes then to be taken notice of, and widens by degrees till at last the vanity of the philosopher is willing to acknowledge scarce any resemblance. But without the disposition to truck, barter, and exchange, every man must have procured to himself every necessary and conveniency of life which he wanted. All must have had the same duties to perform, and the same work to do, and there could have been no such difference of employment as could alone give occasion to any great difference of talents.

As it is this disposition which forms that difference of talents, so remarkable among men of different professions, so it is this same disposition which renders that difference useful. Many tribes of animals, acknowledged to be all of the same species, derive from nature a much more remarkable distinction of genius, than what, antecedent to custom and education, appears to take place among men. By nature a philosopher is not in genius and disposition half so different from a street porter, as a mastiff is from a greyhound, or a greyhound from a spaniel, or this last from a shepherd's dog. Those different tribes of animals, however, though all of the same species, are of scarce any use to one another. The strength of the mastiff is not in the least supported either by the swiftness of the greyhound, or by the sagacity of the spaniel, or by the docility of the shepherd's dog. The effects of those different geniuses and talents, for want of the power or disposition to barter and exchange, cannot be brought into a common stock, and do not in the least contribute to the better accommodation and conveniency of the species. Each animal is still obliged to support and defend itself, separately and independently, and derives no sort of advantage from that variety of talents with which nature has distinguished its fellows. Among men, on the contrary, the most dissimilar geniuses are of use to one another; the different produces of their respective talents, by the general disposition to truck, barter, and exchange, being brought, as it were, into a common stock, where every man may purchase whatever part of the produce of other men's talent he has occasion for.

THAT THE DIVISION OF LABOUR IS LIMITED BY THE EXTENT OF THE MARKET

As it is the power of exchanging that gives occasion to the division of labour, so the extent of this division must always be limited by the extent of the market. When the market is very small, no person can have any encouragement to dedicate himself entirely to one employment, for want of the power to exchange all that surplus part of the produce of his own labour, which is over and above his own consumption, for such parts of the produce of other men's labour as he has occasion for.

There are some sorts of industry, even of the lowest kind, which can be carried on nowhere but in a great town. A porter, for example, can find employment and subsistence in no other place. A village is by much too narrow a sphere for him; even an ordinary market-town is scarce large enough to afford him constant occupation. In the lone houses and very small villages which are scattered about in so desert a country as the highlands of Scotland, every farmer must be butcher, baker, and brewer, for his own family. In such situations we can scarce expect to find even a smith, a carpenter, or a mason, within less than twenty miles of another of the same trade. The scattered families that live at eight or ten miles distance from the nearest of them, must learn to perform themselves a great number of little pieces of work, for which, in more populous countries, they would call in the assistance of those workmen. Country workmen are almost everywhere obliged to apply themselves to all the different branches of industry that have so much affinity to one another as to be employed about the same sort of materials. A country carpenter deals in every sort of work that is made of wood; a country smith in every sort of work that is made of iron. The former is not only a

carpenter, but a joiner, a cabinet-maker, and even a carver in wood, as well as a wheelwright, a plough-wright, a cart and waggon-maker. The employments of the latter are still more various. It is impossible that there should be such a trade as even that of a nailer in the remote and inland parts of the highlands of Scotland. Such a workman at the rate of a thousand nails a-day, and three hundred working days in the year, will make three hundred thousand nails in the year. But in such a situation it would be impossible to dispose of one thousand, that is, of one day's work in the year.

As by means of water-carriage, a more expensive market is opened to every sort of industry than what land-carriage alone can afford it, so it is upon the seacoast, and along the banks of navigable rivers, that industry of every kind naturally begins to subdivide and improve itself, and it is frequently not till a long time after that those improvements extend themselves to the inland parts of the country. A broad-wheeled waggon, attended by two men, and drawn by eight horses, in about six weeks' time, carries and brings back between London and Edinburgh near four ton weight of goods. In about the same time a ship navigated by six or eight men, and sailing between the ports of London and Leith, frequently carries and brings back two hundred ton weight of goods. Six or eight men, therefore, by the help of water-carriage, can carry and bring back, in the same time, the same quantity of goods between London and Edinburgh as fifty broad-wheeled waggons, attended by a hundred men, and drawn by four hundred horses. Upon two hundred tons of goods, therefore, carried by the cheapest land-carriage from London to Edinburgh, there must be charged the maintenance of a hundred men for three weeks, and both the maintenance and what is nearly equal to maintenance the wear and tear of four hundred horses, as well as of fifty great waggons. Whereas, upon the same quantity of goods carried by water, there is to be charged only the maintenance of six or eight men, and the wear and tear of a ship of two hundred tons burthen, together with the value of the superior risk, or the difference of the insurance between land and water-carriage. Were there no other communication between those two places, therefore, but by land-carriage, as no goods could be transported from the one to the other, except such whose price was very considerable in proportion to their weight, they could carry on but a small part of that commerce which at present subsists between them, and consequently could give but a small part of that encouragement which they at present mutually afford to each other's industry. There could be little or no commerce of any kind between the distant parts of the world. What goods could bear the expense of land-carriage between London and Calcutta? Or if there were any so precious as to be able to support this expense, with what safety could they be transported through the territories of so many barbarous nations? Those two cities, however, at present carry on a very considerable commerce with each other, and by mutually affording a market, give a good deal of encouragement to each other's industry. . . .

OF RESTRAINTS UPON IMPORTATION FROM FOREIGN COUNTRIES OF SUCH GOODS AS CAN BE PRODUCED AT HOME

By restraining, either by high duties, or by absolute prohibitions, the importations of such goods from foreign countries as can be produced at home, the monopoly of the home market is more or less secured to the domestic industry employed in producing them. Thus the prohibition of importing either live cattle or salt provisions from foreign countries, secures to the graziers of Great Britain the monopoly of the home market for butcher's meat. The high duties upon the importation of corn, which in times of moderate plenty, amount to a prohibition, give a like advantage to the growers of that commodity. The prohibition of the importation of foreign woollens is equally favourable to the woollen manufacturers. The silk manufacture, though altogether employed upon foreign materials, has lately obtained the same advantage. The linen manufacture has not yet obtained it, but is making great strides towards it. Many other sorts of manufactures have, in the same manner obtained in Great Britain, either altogether, or very nearly, a monopoly against their countrymen. The va-

riety of goods, of which the importation into Great Britain is prohibited, either absolutely, or under certain circumstances, greatly exceeds what can easily be suspected by those who are not well acquainted with the laws of the customs.

That this monopoly of the home market frequently gives great encouragement to that particular species of industry which enjoys it, and frequently turns towards that employment a greater share of both the labour and stock of the society than would otherwise have gone to it, cannot be doubted. But whether it tends either to increase the general industry or the society, or to give it the most advantageous direction, is not, perhaps, altogether so evident.

The general industry of the society can never exceed what the capital of the society can employ. As the number of workmen that can be kept in employment by any particular person must bear a certain proportion to his capital, so the number of those that can be continually employed by all the members of a great society must bear a certain proportion to the whole capital of the society, and never can exceed that proportion. No regulation of commerce can increase the quantity of industry in any society beyond what its capital can maintain. It can only divert a part of it into a direction into which it might not otherwise have gone; and it is by no means certain that this artificial direction is likely to be more advantageous to the society than that into which it would have gone of its own accord.

Every individual is continually exerting himself to find out the most advantageous employment for whatever capital he can command. It is his own advantage, indeed, and not that of the society, which he has in view. But the study of his own advantage naturally, or rather necessarily, leads him to prefer that employment which is most advantageous to the society. . . .

The produce of industry is what it adds to the subject or materials upon which it is employed. In proportion as the value of this produce is great or small, so will likewise be the profits of the employer. But it is only for the sake of profit that any man employs a capital in the support of industry; and he will always, therefore, endeavour to employ it in the support of that industry of which the produce is likely to be of the greatest value, or to exchange for the greatest quantity either of money or of other goods.

But the annual revenue of every society is always precisely equal to the exchangeable value of the whole annual produce of its industry, or rather is precisely the same thing with that exchangeable value. As every individual, therefore, endeavours as much as he can, both to employ his capital in the support of domestic industry, and so to direct that industry that its produce may be of the greatest value, every individual necessarily labours to render the annual revenue of the society as great as he can. He generally, indeed, neither intends to promote the public interest, nor knows how much he is promoting it. By preferring the support of domestic to that of foreign industry, he intends only his own security; and by directing that industry in such a manner as its produce may be of the greatest value, he intends only his own gain; and he is in this, as in many other cases, led by an invisible hand to promote an end which was no part of his intention. Nor is it always the worse for the society that it was no part of it. By pursuing his own interest, he frequently promotes that of the society more effectually than when he really intends to promote it. I have never known much good done by those who affected to trade for the public good. It is an affectation, indeed, not very common among merchants, and very few words need be employed in dissuading them from it.

What is the species of domestic industry which his capital can employ, and of which the produce is likely to be of the greatest value, every individual, it is evident, can in his local situation judge much better than any statesman or lawgiver can do for him. The statesman, who should attempt to direct private people in what manner they ought to employ their capitals, would not only load himself with a most unnecessary attention, but assume an authority which could safely be trusted, not only to no single person, but to no council or senate whatever, and which would nowhere be so dangerous as in the hands of a man who had folly and presumption enough to fancy himself fit to exercise it.

To give the monopoly of the home market to the produce of domestic industry, in any particular art or manufacture, is in some measure to direct private people in what manner they ought to employ their capitals, and must in almost all cases be either a useless or a hurtful regulation. If the produce of domestic can be brought there as cheap as that of foreign industry, the regulation is evidently useless. If it cannot, it must generally be hurtful. It is the maxim of every prudent master of a family, never to attempt to make at home what it will cost him more to make than to buy. The tailor does not attempt to make his own shoes, but buys them of the shoemaker. The shoemaker does not attempt to make his own clothes, but employs a tailor. The farmer attempts to make neither the one nor the other, but employs those different artificers. All of them find it for their interest to employ their whole industry in a way in which they have some advantage over their neighbours, and to purchase with a part of its produce, or, what is the same thing, with the price of a part of it, whatever else they have occasion for.

What is prudence in the conduct of every private family, can scarcely be folly in that of a great kingdom. If a foreign country can supply us with a commodity cheaper than we ourselves can make it, better buy it of them with some part of the produce of our own industry, employed in a way in which we have some advantage. The general industry of the country being always in proportion to the capital which employs it, will not thereby be diminished, no more than that of the above-mentioned artificers; but only left to find out the way in which it can be employed with the greatest advantage. It is certainly not employed to the greatest advantage, when it is thus directed towards an object which it can buy cheaper than it can make. The value of its annual produce is certainly more or less diminished, when it is thus turned away from producing commodities evidently of more value than the commodity which it is directed to produce. According to the supposition, that commodity could be purchased from foreign countries cheaper than it can be made at home; it could therefore have been purchased with a part only of the commodities, or, what is the same thing, with a part only of the price of the commodities, which the industry employed by an equal capital would have produced at home, had it been left to follow its natural course. The industry of the country, therefore, is thus turned away from a more to a less advantageous employment; and the exchangeable value of its annual produce, instead of being increased, according to the intention of the lawgiver, must necessarily be diminished by every such regulation.

By means of such regulations, indeed, a particular manufacture may sometimes be acquired sooner than it could have been otherwise, and after a certain time may be made at home as cheap, or cheaper, than in the foreign country. But though the industry of the society may be thus carried with advantage into a particular channel sooner than it could have been otherwise, it will by no means follow that the sum total, either of its industry, or of its revenue, can ever be augmented by any such regulation. The industry of the society can augment only in proportion as its capital augments, and its capital can augment only in proportion to what can be gradually saved out of its revenue. But the immediate effect of every such regulation is to diminish its revenue; and what diminishes its revenue is certainly not very likely to augment its capital faster than it would have augmented of its own accord, had both capital and industry been left to find out their natural employments.

Though, for want of such regulations, the society should never acquire the proposed manufacture, it would not upon that account necessarily be the poorer in any one period of its duration. In every period of its duration its whole capital and industry might still have been employed, though upon different objects, in the manner that was most advantageous at the time. In every period its revenue might have been the greatest which its capital could afford, and both capital and revenue might have been augmented with the greatest possible rapidity.

The natural advantages which one country has over another, in producing particular commodities, are sometimes so great, that it is acknowledged by all the world to be in vain to struggle with them. By means of glasses, hot-beds, and hot-walls, very good grapes can be raised in Scotland, and very good wine, too, can be made of them, at about thirty times the expense for which at least equally good can be brought from foreign countries. Would it be a reasonable law to prohibit the importation of all foreign wines, merely to encourage the making of claret and Burgundy in Scotland? But if there would be a manifest absurdity in turning towards any employment thirty times more of the capital and industry of the country than would be necessary to purchase from foreign countries an equal quantity of the commodities wanted, there must be an absurdity, though not altogether so glaring, yet exactly of the same kind, in turning towards any such employment a thirtieth, or even a three hundredth part more of either. Whether the advantages which one country has over another be natural or acquired, is in this respect of no consequence. As long as the one country has those advantages, and the other wants them, it will always be more advantageous for the latter rather to buy of the former than to make. It is an acquired advantage only, which one artificer has over his neighbour, who exercises another trade; and yet they both find it more advantageous to buy of one another, than to make what does not belong to their particular trades. . . .

There seem, however, to be two cases, in which it will generally be advantageous to lay some burden upon foreign, for the encouragement of domestic industry.

The first is, when some particular sort of industry is necessary for the defence of the country. The defence of Great Britain, for example, depends very much upon the number of its sailors and shipping. The act of navigation, therefore, very properly endeavours to give the sailors and shipping of Great Britain the monopoly of the trade of their own country, in some cases, by absolute prohibitions, and in others, by heavy burdens upon the shipping of foreign countries. . . .

The second case, in which it will generally be advantageous to lay some burden upon foreign for the encouragement of domestic industry, is when some tax is imposed at home upon the produce of the latter. In this case, it seems reasonable that an equal tax should be imposed upon the like produce of the former. This would not give the monopoly of the home market to domestic industry, nor turn towards a particular employment a greater share of the stock and labour of the country, than what would naturally go to it. It would only hinder any part of what would naturally go to it from being turned away by the tax into a less natural direction, and would leave the competition between foreign and domestic industry, after the tax, as nearly as possible upon the same footing as before it. In Great Britain, when any such tax is laid upon the produce of domestic industry, it is usual, at the same time, in order to stop the clamorous complaints of our merchants and manufacturers, that they will be undersold at home, to lay a much heavier duty upon the importation of all foreign goods of the same kind. . . .

As there are two cases in which it will generally be advantageous to lay some burden upon foreign for the encouragement of domestic industry, so there are two others in which it may sometimes be a matter of deliberation, in the one, how far it is proper to continue the free importation of certain foreign goods; and, in the other, how far, or in what manner, it may be proper to restore that free importation, after it has been for some time interrupted.

The case in which it may sometimes be a matter of deliberation how far it is proper to continue the free importation of certain foreign goods, is when some foreign nation restrains, by high duties or prohibitions, the importation of some of our manufactures into their country. Revenge, in this case, naturally dictates retaliation, and that we should impose the like duties and prohibitions upon the importation of some or all of their manufactures into ours. Nations, accordingly, seldom fail to retaliate in this manner. The French have been particularly forward to favour their own manufactures, by restraining the importation of such foreign goods as could come into competition with them. . . .

There may be good policy in retaliations of this kind when there is a probability that they will procure the repeal of the high duties or prohibitions complained of. The recovery of a great foreign market will generally more than compensate the transitory inconveniency of paying dearer during a short time for some sorts of goods. To judge whether such retaliations are likely to produce such an effect, does not, perhaps, belong so much to the science of a legislator, whose deliberations ought to be governed by general principles, which are always the same, as to the skill of that insidious and crafty animal vulgarly called a statesman or politician, whose councils are directed by the momentary fluctuations of affairs. When there is no probability that any such repeal can be procured, it seems a bad method of compensating the injury done to certain classes of our people, to do another injury ourselves, not only to those classes, but to almost all the other classes of them. When our neighbours prohibit some manufacture of ours, we generally prohibit, not only the same, for that alone would seldom affect them considerably, but some other manufacture of theirs. This may, no doubt, give encouragement to some particular class of workmen among ourselves, and, by excluding some of their rivals, may enable them to raise their price in the home market. Those workmen, however, who suffered by our neighbours prohibition, will not be benefited by ours. On the contrary, they, and almost all the other classes of our citizens, will thereby be obliged to pay dearer than before for certain goods. Every such law, therefore, imposes a real tax upon the whole country, not in favour of that particular class of workmen who were injured by our neighbours' prohibitions, but of some other class.

The case in which it may sometimes be a matter of deliberation, how far, or in what manner, it is proper to restore the free importation of foreign goods, after it has been for some time interrupted, is when particular manufactures, by means of high duties or prohibitions upon all foreign goods which can come into competition with them, have been so far extended as to employ a great multitude of hands. Humanity may in this case require that the freedom of trade should be restored only by slow gradations, and with a good deal of reserve and circumspection. Were those high duties and prohibitions taken away all at once, cheaper foreign goods of the same kind might be poured so fast into the home market, as to deprive all at once many thousands of our people of their ordinary employment and means of subsistence. The disorder which this would occasion might no doubt be very considerable. . . .

To expect, indeed, that the freedom of trade should ever be entirely restored in Great Britain, is as absurd as to expect that an Oceana or Utopia should ever be established in it. Not only the prejudices of the public, but, what is much more unconquerable, the private interests of many individuals, irresistibly oppose it. Were the officers of the army to oppose, with the same zeal and unanimity, any reduction in the number of forces, with which master manufacturers set themselves against every law that is likely to increase the number of their rivals in the home market; were the former to animate the soldiers, in the same manner as the latter inflame their workmen, to attack with violence and outrage the proposers of any such regulation; to attempt to reduce the army would be as dangerous as it has now become to attempt to diminish, in any respect, the monopoly which our manufacturers have obtained against us. This monopoly has so much increased the number of some particular tribes of them, that like an overgrown standing army, they have become formidable to the government, and, upon many occasions, intimidate the legislature. The member of parliament who supports every proposal for strengthening this monopoly, is sure to acquire not only the reputation of understanding trade, but great popularity and influence with an order of men whose numbers and wealth render them of great importance. If he opposes them, on the contrary, and still more, if he has authority enough to be able to thwart them, neither the most acknowledged probity, nor the highest rank, nor the greatest public services, can protect him from the most infamous abuse and detraction, from personal insults, nor sometimes from real danger, arising from the insolent outrage of furious and disappointed monopolists.

The undertaker of a great manufacture, who, by the home markets being suddenly laid open to the competition of foreigners, should be obliged to abandon his trade, would no doubt suffer very considerably. That part of his capital which had usually been employed in purchasing materials, and in paying his workmen, might, without much difficulty, perhaps, find another employment; but that part of it which was fixed in workhouses, and in the instruments of trade, could scarce be disposed of without considerable loss. The equitable regard, therefore, to his interest, requires that changes of this kind should never be introduced suddenly, but slowly, gradually, and after a very long warning. The legislature, were it possible that its deliberations could be always directed, not by the clamorous importunity of partial interests, but by an extensive view of the general good, ought, upon this very account, perhaps, to be particularly careful, neither to establish any new monopolies of this kind, nor to extend further those which are already established. Every such regulation introduces some degree of real disorder into the constitution of the state, which it will be difficult afterwards to cure without occasioning another disorder.

Thomas Jefferson

Thomas Jefferson (1743–1826), third president of the United States, was the first occupant of that office to hold distinctly liberal political views in the nineteenth-century meaning of the term. He was an apostle of the Enlightenment in America, and like many intellectuals of his time, believed in the worth of the individual, and in certain natural rights from which he should not be alienated. The aim of government, therefore, should be to assure the liberty or freedom of the individual to enjoy these rights, and leave him otherwise unmolested. Political liberalism meant, therefore, a minimum of governmental functions. The administrations of George Washington and John Adams had been characterized by conservatism and a paternalistic attitude toward the citizenry, but with Jefferson's election the entire tone of American political life changed. A forecast of what was to come was given by him in his "First Inaugural Address," delivered March 4, 1801. In reading it note (1) his attitude toward the majority and the minority, (2) the advantages which Americans as a people had, (3) his description of what good government was, (4) the goal which he hoped to achieve for all, and (5) Jefferson's illustrations of the ideals of the Enlightenment.

JEFFERSON'S FIRST INAUGURAL ADDRESS

Friends and Fellow-Citizens:

Called upon to undertake the duties of the first executive office of our country, I avail myself of the presence of that portion of my fellow-citizens which is here assembled to express my grateful thanks for the favor with which they have been pleased to look toward me, to declare a sincere consciousness that the task is above my talents, and that I approach it with those anxious and awful presentiments which the greatness of the charge and the weakness of my powers so justly inspire. A rising nation, spread over a wide and fruitful land, traversing all the seas with the rich productions of their industry, engaged in commerce with nations who feel power and forget right, advancing rapidly to destinies beyond the reach of mortal eye—when I contemplate these transcendent objects, and see the honor, the happiness, and the hopes of this beloved country committed to the issue and the auspices of this day, I shrink from the contemplation, and humble myself before the magnitude of the undertaking. Utterly, indeed, should I despair did not the presence of many whom I here see remind me that in the other high authorities provided by our Constitution I shall find resources of wisdom, of virtue, and of zeal on which to rely under all difficulties. To you, then, gentlemen, who are charged with the sovereign functions of legislation, and to those associated with you, I look with encouragement for that guidance and support which

may enable us to steer with safety the vessel in which we are all embarked amidst the conflicting elements of a troubled world.

During the contest of opinion through which we have passed the animation of discussions and of exertions has sometimes worn an aspect which might impose on strangers unused to think freely and to speak and to write what they think; but this being now decided by the voice of the nation, announced according to the rules of the Constitution, all will, of course, arrange themselves under the will of the law, and unite in common efforts for the common good. All, too, will bear in mind this sacred principle, that though the will of the majority is in all cases to prevail, that will to be rightful must be reasonable; that the minority possess their equal rights, which equal law must protect, and to violate would be oppression. Let us, then, fellow-citizens, unite with one heart and one mind. Let us restore to social intercourse that harmony and affection without which liberty and even life itself are but dreary things. And let us reflect that, having banished from our land that religious intolerance under which mankind so long bled and suffered, we have yet gained little if we countenance a political intolerance as despotic, as wicked, and capable of as bitter and bloody persecutions. During the throes and convulsions of the ancient world, during the agonizing spasms of infuriated man, seeking through blood and slaughter his long-lost liberty, it was not won-

Thomas Jefferson, "Inaugural Address," in United States, *Journal of the Executive Proceedings of the Senate of the United States of America. . . . ,* Washington, 1828, I, 392–395.

derful that the agitation of the billows should reach even this distant and peaceful shore; that this should be more felt and feared by some and less by others, and should divide opinions as to measures of safety. But every difference of opinion is not a difference of principle. We have called by different names brethren of the same principle. We are all Republicans, we are all Federalists. If there be any among us who would wish to dissolve this Union or to change its republican form, let them stand undisturbed as monuments of the safety with which error of opinion may be tolerated where reason is left free to combat it. I know, indeed, that some honest men fear that a republican government cannot be strong, that this Government is not strong enough; but would the honest patriot, in the full tide of successful experiment, abandon a government which has so far kept us free and firm on the theoretic and visionary fear that this Government, the world's best hope, may by possibility want energy to preserve itself? I trust not. I believe this, on the contrary, the strongest Government on earth. I believe it the only one where every man, at the call of the law, would fly to the standard of the law, and would meet invasions of the public order as his own personal concern. Sometimes it is said that man cannot be trusted with the government of himself. Can he, then, be trusted with the government of others? Or have we found angels in the forms of kings to govern him? Let history answer this question.

Let us, then, with courage and confidence pursue our own Federal and Republican principles, our attachment to union and representative government. Kindly separated by nature and a wide ocean from the exterminating havoc of one quarter of the globe; too high-minded to endure the degradations of the others; possessing a chosen country, with room enough for our descendants to the thousandth and thousandth generation; entertaining a due sense of our equal right to the use of our own faculties, to the acquisitions of our own industry, to honor and confidence from our fellow-citizens, resulting not from birth, but from our actions and their sense of them; enlightened by a benign religion, professed, indeed, and practiced in various forms, yet all of them inculcating honesty, truth, temperance, gratitude, and the love of man; acknowledging and adoring an overruling Providence, which by all its dispensations proves that it delights in the happiness of man here and his greater happiness hereafter—with all these blessings, what more is necessary to make us a happy and a prosperous people? Still one thing more, fellow-citizens—a wise and frugal Government, which shall restrain men from injuring one another, shall leave them otherwise free to regulate their own pursuits of industry and improvement, and shall not take from the mouth of labor the bread it has earned. This is the sum of good government, and this is necessary to close the circle of our felicities.

About to enter, fellow-citizens, on the exercise of duties which comprehend everything dear and valuable to you, it is proper you should understand what I deem the essential principles of our Government, and consequently those which ought to shape its Administration. I will compress them within the narrowest compass they will bear, stating the general principle, but not all its limitations. Equal and exact justice to all men, of whatever state or persuasion, religious or political; peace, commerce, and honest friendship with all nations, entangling alliances with none; the support of the State governments in all their rights, as the most competent administrations for our domestic concerns and the surest bulwarks against antirepublican tendencies; the preservation of the General Government in its whole constitutional vigor, as the sheet anchor of our peace at home and safety abroad; a jealous care of the right of election by the people—a mild and safe corrective of abuses which are lopped by the sword of revolution where peaceable remedies are unprovided; absolute acquiescence in the decisions of the majority, the vital principle of republics, from which is no appeal but to force, the vital principle and immediate parent of despotism; a well-disciplined militia, our best reliance in peace and for the first moments of war, till regulars may relieve them; the supremacy of the civil over the military authority; economy in the public expense, that labor may be lightly burthened; the honest payment of our debts and sacred preservation of the public faith;

encouragement of agriculture, and of commerce as its handmaid; the diffusion of information and arraignment of all abuses at the bar of the public reason; freedom of religion; freedom of the press, and freedom of person under the protection of the habeas corpus, and trial by juries impartially selected. These principles form the bright constellation which has gone before us and guided our steps through an age of revolution and reformation. The wisdom of our sages and blood of our heroes have been devoted to their attainment. They should be the creed of our political faith, the text of civic instruction, the touchstone by which to try the services of those we trust; and should we wander from them in moments of error or of alarm, let us hasten to retrace our steps and to regain the road which alone leads to peace, liberty, and safety.

I repair, then, fellow-citizens, to the post you have assigned me. With experience enough in subordinate offices to have seen the difficulties of this the greatest of all, I have learnt to expect that it will rarely fall to the lot of imperfect man to retire from this station with the reputation and the favor which bring him into it. Without pretensions to that high confidence you reposed in our first and greatest revolutionary character, whose preëminent services had entitled him to the first place in his country's love and destined for him the fairest page in the volume of faithful history, I ask so much confidence only as may give firmness and effect to the legal administration of your affairs. I shall often go wrong through defect of judgment. When right, I shall often be thought wrong by those whose positions will not command a view of the whole ground. I ask your indulgence for my own errors, which will never be intentional, and your support against the errors of others, who may condemn what they would not if seen in all its parts. The approbation implied by your suffrage is a great consolation to me for the past, and my future solicitude will be to retain the good opinion of those who have bestowed it in advance, to conciliate that of others by doing them all the good in my power, and to be instrumental to the happiness and freedom of all.

Relying, then, on the patronage of your good will, I advance with obedience to the work, ready to retire from it whenever you become sensible how much better choice it is in your power to make. And may that Infinite Power which rules the destinies of the universe lead our councils to what is best, and give them a favorable issue for your peace and prosperity.

John Stuart Mill

John Stuart Mill (1806–1873), English economist, philosopher, and political figure, was the son of James Mill, the famous utilitarian. Educated in the classical tradition by his father, it was only natural that the younger Mill should accept some of the elder's principles, particularly in philosophy. In politics he was a Liberal and sat in Parliament as a member of the Liberal Party. He did not agree with some of his colleagues in regard to the extreme laissez-faire policy, however, and he was one of the first to advocate some governmental regulation in the interest of individual freedom, a cause for which he fought unceasingly. In 1859 he wrote his great essay, On Liberty, selections from which follow. In reading them note (1) his discussion of the tyranny of the majority, (2) the one principle that should determine society's interference with an individual's actions, (3) the evil involved in suppressing freedom of expression, (4) the utilitarian value of freedom of individual action, (5) the relationship between individual develop-

ment and the Will of God, (6) where the limits of society's control over the individual should be set, (7) the only pressure society might use against an individual when his acts injure only himself, (8) the examples he cited to illustrate his principles, and (9) Mill's typically Liberal objections to governmental action even when it did not involve the liberty of its citizens.

From: ON LIBERTY

The subject of this Essay is not the so-called Liberty of the Will, so unfortunately opposed to the misnamed doctrine of Philosophical Necessity; but Civil, or Social Liberty: the nature and limits of the power which can be legitimately exercised by society over the individual: a question seldom stated, and hardly ever discussed, in general terms, but which profoundly influences the practical controversies of the age by its latent presence and is likely soon to make itself recognized as the vital question of the future. It is so far from being new, that, in a certain sense, it has divided mankind almost from the remotest ages; but in the stage of progress into which the more civilised portions of the species have now entered, it presents itself under new conditions, and requires a different and more fundamental treatment.

The struggle between Liberty and Authority is the most conspicuous feature in the portions of history with which we are earliest familiar, particularly in that of Greece, Rome, and England. But in old times this contest was between subjects, or some classes of subjects, and the Government. By liberty, was meant protection against the tyranny of the political rulers. The rulers were conceived (except in some of the popular governments of Greece) as in a necessarily antagonistic position to the people whom they ruled. They consisted of a governing One, or a governing tribe or caste, who derived their authority from inheritance or conquest, who, at all events, did not hold it at the pleasure of the governed, and whose supremacy men did not venture, perhaps did not desire, to contest, whatever precautions might be taken against its oppressive exercise. Their power was regarded as necessary, but

also as highly dangerous; as a weapon which they would attempt to use against their subjects, no less than against external enemies. To prevent the weaker members of the community from being preyed upon by innumerable vultures, it was needful that there should be an animal of prey stronger than the rest, commissioned to keep them down. But as the king of the vultures would be no less bent upon preying on the flock than any of the minor harpies, it was indispensable to be in a perpetual attitude of defence against his beak and claws. The aim, therefore, of patriots was to set limits to the power which the ruler should be suffered to exercise over the community; and this limitation was what they meant by liberty. It was attempted in two ways. First, by obtaining a recognition of certain immunities, called political liberties or rights, which it was to be regarded as a breach of duty in the ruler to infringe, and which if he did infringe, specific resistance, or general rebellion, was held to be justifiable. A second, and generally a later expedient, was the establishment of constitutional checks, by which the consent of the community, or of a body of some sort, supposed to represent its interests, was made a necessary condition to some of the more important acts of the governing power. To the first of these modes of limitation, the ruling power, in most European countries, was compelled, more or less, to submit. It was not so with the second; and, to attain this or, when already in some degree possessed, to attain it more completely, became everywhere the principal object of the lovers of liberty. And so long as mankind were content to combat one enemy by another, and to be ruled by a master, on condition of being guaranteed more or

John Stuart Mill, *On Liberty*, London, 1870, 1–6; 9–10; 30–37; 44–46; 64–68.

less efficaciously against his tyranny, they did not carry their aspirations beyond this point.

A time, however, came, in the progress of human affairs, when men ceased to think it a necessity of nature that their governors should be an independent power, opposed in interest to themselves. It appeared to them much better that the various magistrates of the State should be their tenants or delegates, revocable at their pleasure. In that way alone, it seemed, could they have complete security that the powers of government would never be abused to their disadvantage. By degrees this new demand for elective and temporary rulers became the prominent object of the exertions of the popular party, wherever any such party existed; and superseded, to a considerable extent, the previous efforts to limit the power of rulers. As the struggle proceeded for making the ruling power emanate from the periodical choice of the ruled, some persons began to think that too much importance had been attached to the limitation of the power itself. *That* (it might seem) was a resource against rulers whose interests were habitually opposed to those of the people. What was now wanted was, that the rulers should be identified with the people; that their interest and will should be the interest and will of the nation. The nation did not need to be protected against its own will. There was no fear of its tyrannising over itself. Let the rulers be effectually responsible to it, promptly removable by it, and it could afford to trust them with power of which it could itself dictate the use to be made. Their power was but the nation's own power, concentrated, and in a form convenient for exercise. This mode of thought, or rather perhaps of feeling, was common among the last generation of European liberalism, in the Continental section of which it still apparently predominates. Those who admit any limit to what a government may do, except in the case of such governments as they think ought not to exist, stand out as brilliant exceptions among the political thinkers of the Continent. A similar tone of sentiment might by this time have been prevalent in our own country, if the circumstances which for a time encouraged it, had continued unaltered.

But in political and philosophical theories, as well as in persons, success discloses faults and infirmities which failure might have concealed from observation. The notion that the people have no need to limit their power over themselves might seem axiomatic, when popular government was a thing only dreamed about, or read of as having existed at some distant period of the past. Neither was that notion necessarily disturbed by such temporary aberrations as those of the French Revolution, the worst of which were the work of a usurping few, and which, in any case, belonged, not to the permanent working of popular institutions, but to a sudden and convulsive outbreak against monarchical and aristocratic despotism. In time, however, a democratic republic came to occupy a large portion of the earth's surface, and made itself felt as one of the most powerful members of the community of nations; and elective and responsible government became subject to the observations and criticisms which wait upon a great existing fact. It was now perceived that such phrases as "self-government," and "the power of the people over themselves," do not express the true state of the case. "The people" who exercise the power are not always the same people with those over whom it is exercised; and the "self-government" spoken of is not the government of each by himself, but of each by all the rest. The will of the people, moreover, practically means the will of the most numerous or the most active *part* of the people—the majority, or those who succeed in making themselves accepted as the majority; the people, consequently, *may* desire to oppress a part of their number; and precautions are as much needed against this as against any other abuse of power. The limitation, therefore, of the power of government over individuals loses none of its importance when the holders of power are regularly accountable to the community; that is, to the strongest party therein. This view of things, recommending itself equally to the intelligence of thinkers and to the inclination of those important classes in European society to whose real or supposed interests democracy is adverse, has had no difficulty in establishing itself; and in political speculations, "the tyranny of the majority" is now generally included among the evils against which society requires to be on its guard.

Like other tyrannies, the tyranny of the majority was at first, and is still vulgarly, held in dread, chiefly as operating through the acts of the public authorities. But reflecting persons perceived that when society is itself the tyrant —society collectively over the separate individuals who compose it—its means of tyrannising are not restricted to the acts which it may do by the hands of its political functionaries. Society can and does execute its own mandates; and if it issues wrong mandates instead of right, or any mandates at all in things with which it ought not to meddle, it practises a social tyranny more formidable than many kinds of political oppression; since, though not usually upheld by such extreme penalties, it leaves fewer means of escape, penetrating much more deeply into the details of life, and enslaving the soul itself. Protection, therefore, against the tyranny of the magistrate is not enough: there needs protection also against the tyranny of the prevailing opinion and feeling; against the tendency of society to impose, by other means than civil penalties, its own ideas and practises as rules of conduct on those who dissent from them; to fetter the development, and, if possible, prevent the formation, of any individuality not in harmony with its ways, and compels all characters to fashion themselves upon the model of its own. There is a limit to the legitimate interference of collective opinion with individual independence: and to find that limit, and maintain it against encroachment, is as indispensable to a good condition of human affairs, as protection against political despotism.

But though this proposition is not likely to be contested in general terms, the practical question, where to place the limit,—how to make the fitting adjustment between individual independence and social control,—is a subject on which nearly everything remains to be done. All that makes existence valuable to anyone depends on the enforcement of restraints upon the actions of other people. Some rules of conduct, therefore, must be imposed, by law in the first place, and by opinion on many things which are not fit subjects for the operation of law. What these rules should be is the principal question in human affairs; but if we except a few of the most obvious cases, it is one of those which least progress has been made in resolving. No two ages, and scarcely any two countries, have decided it alike; and the decision of one age or country is a wonder to another. Yet the people of any given age and country no more suspect any difficulty in it, than if it were a subject on which mankind had always been agreed. The rules which obtain among themselves appear to them self-evident and self-justifying. This all but universal illusion is one of the examples of the magical influence of custom, which is not only, as the proverb says, a second nature, but is continually mistaken for the first. The effect of custom, in preventing any misgiving respecting the rules of conduct which mankind impose on one another, is all the more complete because the subject is one on which it is not generally considered necessary that reasons should be given, either by one person to others or by each to himself. People are accustomed to believe, and have been encouraged in the belief by some who aspire to the character of philosophers, that their feelings, on subjects of this nature, are better than reasons, and render reasons unnecessary. The practical principle which guides them to their opinions on the regulation of human conduct is the feeling in each person's mind that everybody should be required to act as he, and those with whom he sympathises, would like them to act. No one, indeed, acknowledges to himself that his standard of judgment is his own liking; but an opinion on a point of conduct, not supported by reasons, can only count as one person's preference; and if the reasons, when given, are a mere appeal to a similar preference felt by other people, it is still only many people's liking instead of one. To an ordinary man, however, his own preference, thus supported, is not only a perfectly satisfactory reason, but the only one he generally has for any of his notions of morality, taste, or propriety, which are not expressly written in his religious creed; and his chief guide in the interpretation even of that. Men's opinions, accordingly, on what is laudable or blamable, are affected by all the multifarious causes which influence their wishes in regard to the conduct of others, and which are as numerous as those which determine their wishes on any other subject. Sometimes their reason—at other times their prejudices or superstitions: often their social affections, not seldom their antisocial ones, their envy or jealousy, their arrogance or contemptuousness: but most commonly their desires or fears for themselves—their legitimate or illegitimate self-interest. Wherever there is an ascendant class, a large portion of the morality of the country emanates from its class interests, and its feelings of class superiority. The morality between Spartans and Helots, between planters and negroes, between princes and subjects, between nobles and roturiers, between men and women, has been for the most part the creation of these class interests and feelings: and the sentiments thus generated react in turn upon the moral feelings of the members of the ascendant class, in their relations among themselves. Where, on the other hand, a class, formerly ascendant, has lost its ascendancy, or where its ascendancy is unpopular, the prevailing moral sentiments frequently bear the impress of an impatient dislike of superiority. Another grand determining principle of the rules of conduct, both in act and forbearance, which have been enforced by law or opinion, has been the servility of mankind towards the supposed preferences or aversions of their temporal masters or of their gods. This servility, though essentially selfish, is not hypocrisy: it gives rise to perfectly genuine sentiments of abhorrence; it made men burn magicians and heretics. Among so many baser influences, the general and obvious interests of society have of course had a share, and a large one, in the direction of the moral sentiments: less, however, as a matter of reason and on their own account, than as a consequence of the sympathies and antipathies which grew out of them: and sympathies and antipathies which had little or nothing to do with the interests of society have made themselves felt in the establishment of moralities with quite as great force.

The likings and dislikings of society, or of some powerful portion of it, are thus the main thing which has practically determined the rules laid down for general observance, under the penalties of law or opinion. And, in general, those who have been in advance of society in thought and feeling have left this condition of things unassailed in principle, however they may have come into conflict with it in some of its details. They have occupied themselves rather in inquiring what things society ought to like or dislike, than in questioning whether its likings or dislikings should be a law to individuals. They preferred endeavouring to alter the feelings of mankind on the particular points on which they were themselves heretical, rather than make common cause, in defence of freedom, with heretics generally. The only case in which the higher ground has been taken on principle and maintained with consistency, by any but an individual here and there, is that of religious belief: a case instructive in many ways, and not least so as forming a most striking instance of the fallibility of what is called the moral sense: for the *odium theologicum*, in a sincere bigot, is one of the most unequivocal cases of moral feeling. Those who first broke the yoke of what called itself the Universal Church were, in general, as little willing to permit difference of religious opinion as that church itself. But when the heat of the conflict was over, without giving a complete victory to any party, and each church or sect was reduced to limit its hopes to retaining possession of the ground it already occupied, minorities—seeing that they had no chance of becoming majorities—were under the necessity of pleading to those whom they could not convert for permission to differ. It is accordingly on this battlefield, almost solely, that the rights of the individual against society have been asserted on broad grounds of principle, and the claim of society to exercise authority over dissentients openly controverted. The great writers to whom the world owes what religious liberty it possesses, have mostly asserted freedom of conscience as an indefeasible right, and denied absolutely that a human being is accountable to others for his religious belief. Yet so natural to mankind is intolerance in whatever they really care about, that religious freedom has hardly anywhere been practically realised, except where religious indifference, which dislikes to have its peace disturbed by theological quarrels, has added its weight to the scale. In the minds of almost all religious persons, even in the most tolerant countries, the duty of toleration is admitted with tacit reserves. One person will bear with dissent in matters of church government, but not of dogma; another can tolerate everybody, short of a Papist or a Unitarian; another everyone who believes in revealed religion; a few extend their charity a little further, but stop at the belief in a God and in a future state. Wherever the sentiment of the majority is still genuine and intense, it is found to have abated little of its claim to be obeyed.

In England, from the peculiar circumstances of our political history, though the yoke of opinion is perhaps heavier, that of law is lighter than in most other countries of Europe; and there is considerable jealousy of direct interference, by the legislative or the executive power, with private conduct; not so much from any just regard for the independence of the individual, as from the still subsisting habit of looking on the government as representing an opposite interest to the public. The majority have not yet learnt to feel the power of the government their power, or its opinions their opinions. When they do so, individual liberty will probably be as much exposed to invasion from the government, as it already is from public opinion. But, as yet, there is a considerable amount of feeling ready to be called forth against any attempt of the law to control individuals in things in which they have not hitherto been accustomed to be controlled by it; and this with very little discrimination as to whether the matter is, or is not, within the legitimate sphere of legal control; insomuch that the feeling, highly salutary on the whole, is perhaps quite as often misplaced as well grounded in the particular instances of its application. There is, in fact, no recognised principle by which the propriety or impropriety of government interference is customarily tested. People decide according to their personal preferences. Some, whenever they see any good to be done, or evil to be remedied, would willingly instigate the government to undertake the business; while others prefer to bear almost any amount of social evil rather than add one to the departments of human interests amenable to governmental control. And men range themselves on one or the other side in any particular case according to this general direction of their sentiments; or according to the degree of interest which they feel in the particular thing which it is proposed that the government should do; or according to the belief they entertain that the government would, or would not, do it in the manner they prefer; but very rarely on account of any opinion to which they consistently adhere, as to what things are fit to be done by a government. And it seems to me that, in consequence of this absence of rule or principle, one side is at present as often wrong as the other; the interference of government is, with about equal frequency, improperly invoked and improperly condemned.

The object of this Essay is to assert one very simple principle, as entitled to govern absolutely the dealings of society with the individual in the way of compulsion and control, whether the means used be physical force in the form of legal penalties, or the moral coercion of public opinion. That principle is, that the sole end for which mankind are warranted, individually or collectively, in interfering with the liberty of action of any of their number, is self-protection. That the only purpose for which power can be rightfully exercised over any member of a civilised community, against his will, is to prevent harm to others. His own good, either physical or moral, is not a sufficient warrant. He cannot rightfully be compelled to do or to forbear because it will be better for him to do so, because it will make him happier, because, in the opinions of others, to do so would be wise, or even right. These are good reasons for remonstrating with him, or reasoning with him, or persuading him, or entreating him, but not for compelling him, or visiting him with any evil in case he do otherwise. To justify that, the conduct from which it is desired to deter him must be calculated to produce evil to someone else. The only part of the conduct of anyone, for which he is amenable to society, is that which concerns others.

In the part which merely concerns himself, his independence is, of right, absolute. Over himself, over his own body and mind, the individual is sovereign. . . .

OF THE LIBERTY OF THOUGHT AND DISCUSSION

The time, it is to be hoped, is gone by, when any defence would be necessary of the "liberty of the press" as one of the securities against corrupt or tyrannical government. No argument, we may suppose, can now be needed, against permitting a legislature or an executive, not identified in interest with the people, to prescribe opinions to them and determine what doctrines or what arguments they shall be allowed to hear. This aspect of the question, besides, has been so often and so triumphantly enforced by preceding writers, that it needs not be specially insisted on in this place. Though the law of England, on the subject of the press, is as servile to this day as it was in the time of the Tudors, there is little danger of its being actually put in force against political discussion, except during some temporary panic, when fear of insurrection drives ministers and judges from their propriety; and, speaking generally, it is not, in constitutional countries, to be apprehended, that the government, whether completely responsible to the people or not, will often attempt to control the expression of opinion, except when in doing so it makes itself the organ of the general intolerance of the public. Let us suppose, therefore, that the government is entirely at one with the people, and never thinks of exerting any power of coercion unless in agreement with what it conceives to be their voice. But I deny the right of the people to exercise such coercion, either by themselves or by their government. The power itself is illegitimate. The best government has no more title to it than the worst. It is as noxious, or more noxious, when exerted in accordance with public opinion, than when in opposition to it. If all mankind minus one were of one opinion, and only one person were of the contrary opinion, mankind would be no more justified in silencing that one person, than he, if he had the power, would be justified in silencing mankind. Were an opinion a personal possession of no value except to the owner; if to be obstructed in the enjoyment of it were simply a private injury, it would make some difference whether the injury was inflicted only on a few persons or on many. But the peculiar evil of silencing the expression of an opinion is, that it is robbing the human race: posterity as well as the existing generation; those who dissent from the opinion still more than those who hold it. If the opinion is right, they are deprived of the opportunity of exchanging error for truth; if wrong, they lose, what is almost as great a benefit, the clearer perception and livelier impression of truth, produced by its collision with error. . . .

We have now recognised the necessity to the mental well-being of mankind (on which all their other well-being depends) of freedom of opinion, and freedom of the expression of opinion, on four distinct grounds; which we will now briefly recapitulate.

First, if any opinion is compelled to silence, that opinion may, for aught we can certainly know, be true. To deny this is to assume our own infallibility.

Secondly, though the silenced opinion be an error, it may, and very commonly does, contain a portion of truth; and since the general or prevailing opinion on any subject is rarely or never the whole truth, it is only by the collision of adverse opinions that the remainder of the truth has any chance of being supplied.

Thirdly, even if the received opinion be not only true, but the whole truth; unless it is suffered to be, and actually is, vigorously and earnestly contested, it will, by most of those who receive it, be held in the manner of a prejudice, with little comprehension or feeling of its rational grounds. And not only this, but, fourthly, the meaning of the doctrine itself will be in danger of being lost, or enfeebled, and deprived of its vital effect on the character and conduct: the dogma becoming a mere formal profession, inefficacious for good, but cumbering the ground, and preventing the growth of any real and heartfelt conviction, from reason or personal experience.

Before quitting the subject of freedom of opinion, it is fit to take some notice of those who say that the free expression of all opinions should be permitted, on condition that the manner be temperate, and do not pass the bounds of fair discussion. Much might be said on the impossibility of fixing where these supposed bounds are to be placed; for if the test be offence to those whose opinions are attacked, I think experience testifies that this offence is given whenever the attack is telling and powerful, and that every opponent who pushes them hard, and whom they find it difficult to answer, appears to them, if he shows any strong feeling on the subject, an intemperate opponent. But this, though an important consideration in a practical point of view, merges in a more fundamental objection. Undoubtedly the manner of asserting an opinion, even though it be a true one, may be very objectionable, and may justly incur severe censure. But the principal offences of the kind are such as it is mostly impossible, unless by accidental self-betrayal, to bring home to conviction. The gravest of them is, to argue sophistically, to suppress facts or arguments, to misstate the elements of the case, or misrepresent the opposite opinion. But all this, even to the most aggravated degree, is so continually done in perfect good faith, by persons who are not considered, and in many other respects may not deserve to be considered, ignorant or incompetent, that it is rarely possible, on adequate grounds, conscientiously to stamp the misrepresentation as morally culpable; and still less could law presume to interfere with this kind of controversial misconduct. With regard to what is commonly meant by intemperate discussion, namely invective, sarcasm, personality, and the like, the denunciation of these weapons would deserve more sympathy if it were ever proposed to interdict them equally to both sides; but it is only desired to restrain the employment of them against the prevailing opinion: against the unprevailing they may not only be used without general disapproval, but will be likely to obtain for him who uses them the praise of honest zeal and righteous indignation. Yet whatever mischief arises from their use is greatest when they are employed against the comparatively defenceless; and whatever unfair advantage can be derived by any opinion from this mode of asserting it, accrues almost exclusively to received opinions. The worst offence of this kind which can be committed by a polemic is to stigmatise those who hold the contrary opinion as bad and immoral men. To calumny of this sort, those who hold any unpopular opinion are peculiarly exposed, because they are in general few and uninfluential, and nobody but themselves feels much interested in seeing justice done them; but this weapon is, from the nature of the case, denied to those who attack a prevailing opinion: they can neither use it with safety to themselves, nor, if they could, would it do anything but recoil on their own cause. In general, opinions contrary to those commonly received can only obtain a hearing by studied moderation of language, and the most cautious avoidance of unnecessary offence, from which they hardly ever deviate even in a slight degree without losing ground: while unmeasured vituperation employed on the side of the prevailing opinion really does deter people from professing contrary opinions, and from listening to those who profess them. For the interest, therefore, of truth and justice, it is far more important to restrain this employment of vituperative language than the other; and, for example, if it were necessary to choose, there would be much more need to discourage offensive attacks on infidelity than on religion. It is, however, obvious that law and authority have no business with restraining either, while opinion ought, in every instance, to determine its verdict by the circumstances of the individual case; condemning everyone, on whichever side of the argument he places himself, in whose mode of advocacy either want of candour, or malignity, bigotry, or intolerance of feeling manifest themselves; but not inferring these vices from the side which a person takes, though it be the contrary side of the question to our own; and giving merited honour to everyone, whatever opinion he may hold, who has calmness to see and honesty to state what his opponents and their opinions really are, exaggerating nothing to their discredit, keeping nothing back which tells, or can be supposed to tell, in their favour. This is the real morality of public discussion; and if often violated, I am happy to think that there are many controversialists who to a great extent observe it, and a still greater number who conscientiously strive towards it.

OF INDIVIDUALITY, AS ONE OF THE ELEMENTS OF WELL-BEING

Such being the reasons which make it imperative that human beings should be free to form opinions, and to express their opinions without reserve; and such the baneful consequences to the intellectual and, through that, to the moral nature of man, unless this liberty is either conceded, or asserted in spite of prohibition, let us next examine whether the same reasons do not require that men should be free to act upon their opinions—to carry these out in their lives, without hindrance, either physical or moral, from their fellow men, so long as it is at their own risk and peril. This last proviso is of course indispensable. No one pretends that actions should be as free as opinions. On the contrary even opinions lose their immunity when the circumstances in which they are expressed are such as to constitute their expression a positive instigation to some mischievous act. An opinion that corn-dealers are starvers of the poor, or that private property is robbery, ought to be unmolested when simply circulated through the press, but may justly incur punishment when delivered orally to an excited mob assembled before the house of a corn-dealer, or when handed about among the same mob in the form of a placard. Acts, of whatever kind, which, without justifiable cause, do harm to others, may be, and in the more important cases absolutely require to be, controlled by the unfavourable sentiments, and, when needful, by the active interference, of mankind. The liberty of the individual must be thus far limited: he must not make himself a nuisance to other people. But if he refrains from molesting others in what concerns them, and merely acts according to his own inclination and judgment in things which concern himself, the same reasons which show that opinion should be free prove also that he should be allowed, without molestation, to carry his opinions into practise at his own cost. That mankind are not infallible; that their truths, for the most part, are only half-truths; that unity of opinion, unless resulting from the fullest and freest comparison of opposite opinions, is not desirable, and diversity not an evil, but a good, until mankind are much more capable than at present of recognising all sides of the truth, are principles applicable to men's modes of action, not less than to their opinions. As it is useful that while mankind are imperfect there should be different opinions, so it is that there should be different experiments of living; that free scope should be given to varieties of character, short of injury to others; and that the worth of different modes of life should be proved practically, when anyone thinks fit to try them. It is desirable, in short, that in things which do not primarily concern others, individuality should assert itself. Where, not the person's own character, but the traditions or customs of other people, are the rule of conduct, there is wanting one of the principal ingredients of human happiness, and quite the chief ingredient of individual and social progress.

In maintaining this principle, the greatest difficulty to be encountered does not lie in the appreciation of means towards an acknowledged end, but in the indifference of persons in general to the end itself. If it were felt that the free development of individuality is one of the leading essentials of well-being; that it is not only a coördinate element with all that is designated by the terms civilisation, instruction, education, culture, but is itself a necessary part and condition of all those things, there would be no danger that liberty should be undervalued, and the adjustment of the boundaries between it and social control would present no extraordinary difficulty. But the evil is, that individual spontaneity is hardly recognised by the common modes of thinking as having any intrinsic worth, or deserving any regard on its own account. The majority, being satisfied with the ways of mankind as they now are (for it is they who make them what they are), cannot comprehend why those ways should not be good enough for everybody; and, what is more, spontaneity forms no part of the ideal of the majority of moral and social reformers, but is rather looked on with jealousy, as a troublesome and perhaps rebellious obstruction to the general acceptance of what these reformers, in their own judgment, think would be best for mankind. Few persons, out of Germany, even comprehend the meaning of the doctrine which Wilhelm von Humboldt, so eminent both as a *savant* and as a politician, made the text of a treatise—that "the end of man, or that which is prescribed by the eternal or immutable dictates of reason, and not suggested by vague and transient desires, is the highest and most harmonious development of his powers to a complete and consistent whole"; that, therefore, the object "towards which every human being must ceaselessly direct his efforts, and on which especially those who design to influence their fellow men must ever keep their eyes, is the individuality of power and development"; that for this there are two requisites, "freedom, and variety of situations"; and that from the union of these arise "individual vigour and manifold diversity," which combine themselves in "originality."

Little, however, as people are accustomed to a doctrine like that of von Humboldt, and surprising as it may be to them to find so high a value attached to individuality, the question, one must nevertheless think, can only be one of degree. No one's idea of excellence in conduct is that people should do absolutely nothing but copy one another. No one would assert that people ought not to put into their mode of life, and into the conduct of their concerns, any impress whatever of their own judgment, or of their own individual character. On the other hand, it would be absurd to pretend that people ought to live as if nothing whatever had been known in the world before they came into it; as if experience had as yet done nothing towards showing that one mode of existence, or of conduct, is preferable to another. Nobody denies that people should be so taught and trained in youth as to know and benefit by the ascertained results of human experience. But it is the privilege and proper condition of a human being, arrived at the maturity of his faculties, to use and interpret experience in his own way. It is for him to find out what part of recorded experience is properly applicable to his own circumstances and character. The traditions and customs of other people are, to a certain extent, evidence of what their experience has taught *them*—presumptive evidence, and as such, have a claim to his deference: but, in the first place, their experience may be too narrow, or they may not have interpreted it rightly. Secondly, their interpretation of experience may be correct, but unsuitable to him. Customs are made for customary circumstances and customary characters; and his circumstances or his character may be uncustomary. Thirdly, though the customs be both good as customs, and suitable to him, yet to conform to custom, merely *as* custom, does not educate or develop in him any of the qualities which are the distinctive endowment of a human being. The human faculties of perception, judgment, discriminative feeling, mental activity, and even moral preference, are exercised only in making a choice. He who does anything because it is the custom makes no choice. He gains no practise either in discerning or in desiring what is best. The mental and moral, like the muscular powers, are improved only by being used. The faculties are called into no exercise by doing a thing merely because others do it, no more than by believing a thing only because others believe it. If the grounds of an opinion are not conclusive to the person's own reason, his reason cannot be strengthened, but is likely to be weakened, by his adopting it: and if the inducements to an act are not such as are consentaneous to his own feelings and character (where affection, or the rights of others, are not concerned), it is so much done towards rendering his feelings and character inert and torpid, instead of active and energetic.

He who lets the world, or his own portion of it, choose his plan of life for him, has no need of any other faculty than the ape-like one of imitation. He who chooses his plan for himself, employs all his faculties. He must use observation to see, reasoning and judgment to foresee, activity to gather materials for decision, discrimination to decide, and, when he has decided, firmness and self-control to hold to his deliberate decision. And these qualities he requires and exercises exactly in proportion as the part of his conduct which he determines according to his own judgment and feelings is a large one. It is possible that he might be guided in some good path, and kept out of harm's way, without any of these things. But what will be his comparative worth as a human being? It really is of importance, not only what men do, but also what manner of men they are that do it. Among the works of man, which human life is rightly employed in perfecting and beautifying, the first in importance surely is man himself. Supposing it were possible to get houses built, corn grown, battles fought, causes tried, and even churches erected and prayers said, by machinery,—by automatons in human form,—it would be a considerable loss to exchange for these automatons even the men and women who at present inhabit the more civilised parts of the world, and who assuredly are but starved specimens of what nature can and will produce. Human nature is not a machine to be built after a model, and set to do exactly the work prescribed for it, but a tree, which requires to grow and develop itself on all sides, according to the tendency of the inward forces which make it a living thing.

It will probably be conceded that it is desirable people should exercise their understandings, and that an intelligent following of custom, or even occasionally an intelligent deviation from custom, is better than a blind and simply mechanical adhesion to it. To a certain extent it is admitted that our understanding should be our own: but there is not the same willingness to admit that our desires and impulses should be our own likewise; or that to possess impulses of our own, and of any strength, is anything but a peril and a snare. Yet desires and impulses are as much a part of a perfect human being as beliefs and restraints; and strong impulses are only perilous when not properly balanced; when one set of aims and inclinations is developed into strength, while others, which ought to co-exist with them, remain weak and inactive. It is not because men's desires are strong that they act ill; it is because their consciences are weak. There is no natural connection between strong impulses and a weak conscience. The natural connection is the other way. To say that one person's desires and feelings are

stronger and more various than those of another, is merely to say that he has more of the raw material of human nature, and is therefore capable, perhaps, of more evil, but certainly of more good. Strong impulses are but another name for energy. Energy may be turned to bad uses; but more good may always be made of an energetic nature, than of an indolent and impassive one. Those who have most natural feeling are always those whose cultivated feelings may be made the strongest. The same strong susceptibilities which make the personal impulses vivid and powerful, are also the source from whence are generated the most passionate love of virtue, and the sternest self-control. It is through the cultivation of these that society both does its duty and protects its interests: not by rejecting the stuff of which heroes are made, because it knows not how to make them. A person whose desires and impulses are his own—are the expression of his own nature, as it has been developed and modified by his own culture—is said to have a character. One whose desires and impulses are not his own has no character, no more than a steam-engine has a character. If, in addition to being his own, his impulses are strong, and are under the government of a strong will, he has an energetic character. Whoever thinks that individuality of desires and impulses should not be encouraged to unfold itself must maintain that society has no need of strong natures—is not the better for containing many persons who have much character—and that a high general average of energy is not desirable.

In some early states of society, these forces might be, and were, too much ahead of the power which society then possessed of disciplining and controlling them. There has been a time when the element of spontaneity and individuality was in excess, and the social principle had a hard struggle with it. The difficulty then was to induce men of strong bodies or minds to pay obedience to any rules which required them to control their impulses. To overcome this difficulty, law and discipline, like the Popes struggling against the Emperors, asserted a power over the whole man, claiming to control all his life in order to control his character—which society had not found any other sufficient means of binding. But society has now fairly got the better of individuality; and the danger which threatens human nature is not the excess, but the deficiency, of personal impulses and preferences. Things are vastly changed since the passions of those who were strong by station or by personal endowment were in a state of habitual rebellion against laws and ordinances, and required to be rigorously chained up to enable the persons within their reach to enjoy any particle of security. In our times, from the highest class of society down to the lowest, everyone lives as under the eye of a hostile and dreaded censorship. Not only in what concerns others, but in what concerns only themselves, the individual or the family do not ask themselves—what do I prefer? or, what would suit my character and disposition? or, what would allow the best and highest in me to have fair play, and enable it to grow and thrive? They ask themselves, what is suitable to my position? what is usually done by persons of my station and pecuniary circumstances? or (worse still) what is usually done by persons of a station and circumstances superior to mine? I do not mean that they choose what is customary in preference to what suits their own inclination. It does not occur to them to have any inclination, except for what is customary. Thus the mind itself is bowed to the yoke: even in what people do for pleasure, conformity is the first thing thought of; they like in crowds; they exercise choice only among things commonly done: peculiarity of taste, eccentricity of conduct, are shunned equally with crimes: until, by dint of not following their own nature, they have no nature to follow; their human capacities are withered and starved; they become incapable of any strong wishes or native pleasures, and are generally without either opinions or feelings of home growth, or properly their own. Now is this, or is it not, the desirable condition of human nature?

It is so, on the Calvinistic theory. According to that, the one great offence of man is self-will. All the good of which humanity is capable is comprised in obedience. You have no choice; thus you must do, and no otherwise; "whatever is not a duty, is a sin." Human nature being radically corrupt, there is no redemption for anyone until human nature is killed within him. To one holding this theory of life, crushing out any of the human faculties, capacities, and susceptibilities, is no evil: man needs no capacity but that of surrendering himself to the will of God: and if he uses any of his faculties for any other purpose but to do that supposed will more effectually, he is better without them. This is the theory of Calvinism; and it is held, in a mitigated form, by many who do not consider themselves Calvinists; the mitigation consisting in giving a less ascetic interpretation to the alleged will of God; asserting it to be his will that mankind should gratify some of their inclinations; of course, not in the manner they themselves prefer, but in the way of obedience, that is, in a way prescribed to them by authority; and, therefore, by the necessary condition of the case, the same for all.

In some such insidious form there is at present a strong tendency to this narrow theory of life, and to the pinched and hidebound type of human character which it patronises. Many persons, no doubt, sincerely think that human beings thus cramped and dwarfed are as their Maker designed them to be; just as many have thought that trees are a much finer thing when clipped into pollards, or cut out into figures of animals, than as nature made them. But if it be any part of religion to believe that man was made by a good Being, it is more consistent with that faith to believe that this Being gave all human faculties that they might be cultivated and unfolded, not rooted out and consumed, and that he takes delight in every nearer approach made by his creatures to the ideal conception embodied in them, every increase in any of their capabilities of comprehension, of action, or of enjoyment. There is a different type of human excellence from the Calvinistic: a conception of humanity as having its nature bestowed on it for other purposes than merely to be abnegated. "Pagan self-assertion" is one of the elements of human worth, as well as "Christian self-denial." There is a Greek ideal of self-development, which the Platonic and Christian ideal of self-government blends with, but does not supersede. It may be better to be a John Knox than an Alcibiades, but it is better to be a Pericles than either; nor would a Pericles, if we had one in these days, be without anything good which belonged to John Knox.

It is not by wearing down unto uniformity all that is individual in themselves, but by cultivating it, and calling it forth, within the limits imposed by the rights and interests of others, that human beings become a noble and beautiful object of contemplation; and as the works partake the character of those who do them, by the same process human life also becomes rich, diversified, and animating, furnishing more abundant aliment to high thoughts and elevating feelings, and strengthening the tie which binds every individual to the race, by making the race infinitely better worth belonging to. In proportion to the development of his individuality, each person becomes more valuable to himself, and is therefore capable of being more valuable to others. There is a greater fulness of life about his own existence, and when there is more life in the units there is more in the mass which is composed of them. As much compression as is necessary to prevent the stronger specimens of human nature from encroaching on the rights of others cannot be dispensed with; but for this there is ample compensation, even in the point of view of human development. The means of development which the individual loses by being prevented from gratifying his inclinations to the injury of others, are chiefly obtained at the expense of the development of other people. And even to himself there is a full equivalent in the better development of the social part of his nature, rendered possible by the restraint put upon the selfish part. To be held to rigid rules of justice for the sake of others develops the feelings and capacities which have the good of others for their object. But to be restrained in things not affecting their good, by their mere displeasure, develops nothing valuable, except such force of character as may unfold itself in resisting the restraint. If acquiesced in, it dulls and blunts the whole nature. To give any fair play to the nature of each, it is essential that different persons should be allowed to lead different lives. In proportion as this latitude has been exercised in any age, has that age been noteworthy

to posterity. Even despotism does not produce its worst effects so long as individuality exists under it; and whatever crushes individuality is despotism, by whatever name it may be called, and whether it professes to be enforcing the will of God or the injunctions of men. . . .

OF THE LIMITS TO THE AUTHORITY OF SOCIETY OVER THE INDIVIDUAL

What, then, is the rightful limit to the sovereignty of the individual over himself? Where does the authority of society begin? How much of human life should be assigned to individuality, and how much to society?

Each will receive its proper share, if each has that which more particularly concerns it. To individuality should belong the part of life in which it is chiefly the individual that is interested; to society, the part which chiefly interests society.

Though society is not founded on a contract, and though no good purpose is answered by inventing a contract in order to deduce social obligations from it, everyone who receives the protection of society owes a return for the benefit, and the fact of living in society renders it indispensable that each should be bound to observe a certain line of conduct towards the rest. This conduct consists, first, in not injuring the interests of one another; or rather certain interests, which, either by express legal provision or by tacit understanding, ought to be considered as rights; and secondly, in each person's bearing his share (to be fixed on some equitable principle) of the labours and sacrifices incurred for defending the society or its members from injury and molestation. These conditions society is justified in enforcing, at all costs to those who endeavour to withhold fulfilment. Nor is this all that society may do. The acts of an individual may be hurtful to others, or wanting in due consideration for their welfare, without going to the length of violating any of their constituted rights. The offender may then be justly punished by opinion, though not by law. As soon as any part of a person's conduct affects prejudicially the interests of others, society has jurisdiction over it, and the question whether the general welfare will or will not be promoted by interfering with it becomes open to discussion. But there is no room for entertaining any such question when a person's conduct affects the interests of no persons beside himself, or needs not affect them unless they like (all the persons concerned being of full age, and the ordinary amount of understanding). In all such cases, there should be perfect freedom, legal and social, to do the action and stand the consequences.

It would be a great misunderstanding of this doctrine to suppose that it is one of selfish indifference, which pretends that human beings have no business with each other's conduct in life, and that they should not concern themselves about the well-doing or well-being of one another, unless their own interest is involved. Instead of any diminution, there is need of a great increase of disinterested exertion to promote the good of others. But disinterested benevolence can find other instruments to persuade people to their good than whips and scourges, either of the literal or the metaphorical sort. I am the last person to undervalue the self-regarding virtues; they are only second in importance, if even second, to the social. It is equally the business of education to cultivate both. But even education works by conviction and persuasion as well as by compulsion, and it is by the former only that, when the period of education is passed, the self-regarding virtues should be inculcated. Human beings owe to each other help to distinguish the better from the worse, and encouragement to choose the former and avoid the latter. They should be for ever stimulating each other to increased exercise of their higher faculties, and increased direction of their feelings and aims towards wise instead of foolish, elevating instead of degrading, objects and contemplations. But neither one person, nor any number of persons, is warranted in saying to another human creature of ripe years, that he shall not do with his life for his own benefit what he chooses to do with it. He is the person most interested in his own well-being: the interest which any other person, except in cases of strong personal attachment, can have in it, is trifling, compared with that which he himself has; the interest which society has in him individually (except as to his conduct to others) is fractional, and altogether indirect; while

with respect to his own feelings and circumstances, the most ordinary man or woman has means of knowledge immeasurably surpassing those that can be possessed by anyone else. The interference of society to overrule his judgment and purposes in what only regards himself must be grounded on general presumptions, which may be altogether wrong, and, even if right, are as likely as not to be misapplied to individual cases, by persons no better acquainted with the circumstances of such cases than those are who look at them merely from without. In this department, therefore, of human affairs, Individuality has its proper field of action. In the conduct of human beings towards one another it is necessary that general rules should for the most part be observed, in order that people may know what they have to expect: but in each person's own concerns his individual spontaneity is entitled to free exercise. Considerations to aid his judgment, exhortations to strengthen his will, may be offered to him, even obtruded on him, by others; but he himself is the final judge. All errors which he is likely to commit against advice and warning are far outweighed by the evil of allowing others to constrain him to what they deem his good.

I do not mean that the feelings with which a person is regarded by others ought not to be in any way affected by his self-regarding qualities or deficiencies. This is neither possible nor desirable. If he is eminent in any of the qualities which conduce to his own good, he is, so far, a proper object of admiration. He is so much the nearer to the ideal perfection of human nature. If he is grossly deficient in those qualities, a sentiment the opposite of admiration will follow. There is a degree of folly, and a degree of what may be called (though the phrase is not unobjectionable) lowness or depravation of taste, which, though it cannot justify doing harm to the person who manifests it, renders him necessarily and properly a subject of distaste, or, in extreme cases, even of contempt; a person could not have the opposite qualities in due strength without entertaining these feelings. Though doing no wrong to anyone, a person may so act as to compel us to judge him, and feel to him, as a fool, or as a being of an inferior order: and since this judgment and feeling are a fact which he would prefer to avoid, it is doing him a service to warn him of it beforehand, as of any other disagreeable consequence to which he exposes himself. It would be well, indeed, if this good office were much more freely rendered than the common notions of politeness at present permit, and if one person could honestly point out to another that he thinks him in fault, without being considered unmannerly or presuming. We have a right, also, in various ways, to act upon our unfavourable opinion of anyone, not to the oppression of his individuality, but in the exercise of ours. We are not bound, for example, to seek his society; we have a right to avoid it (though not to parade the avoidance), for we have a right to choose the society most acceptable to us. We have a right, and it may be our duty, to caution others against him, if we think his example or conversation likely to have a pernicious effect on those with whom he associates. We may give others a preference over him in optional good offices, except those which tend to his improvement. In these various modes a person may suffer very severe penalties at the hands of others for faults which directly concern only himself; but he suffers these penalties only in so far as they are the natural and, as it were, the spontaneous consequences of the faults themselves, not because they are purposely inflicted on him for the sake of punishment. A person who shows rashness, obstinacy, self-conceit—who cannot live within moderate means—who cannot restrain himself from hurtful indulgences—who pursues animal pleasures at the expense of those of feeling and intellect—must expect to be lowered in the opinion of others, and to have a less share of their favourable sentiments; but of this he has no right to complain, unless he has merited their favour by special excellence in his social relations, and has thus established a title to their good offices, which is not affected by his demerits toward himself.

What I contend for is, that the inconveniences which are strictly inseparable from the unfavourable judgment of others are the only ones to which a person should ever be subjected for that portion of his conduct and character which concerns his own good, but which does not affect the interest of others in their relations with him. Acts injurious to others require a totally different treatment. Encroachment on their rights; infliction on them of any loss or damage not justified by his own rights; falsehood or duplicity in dealing with them; unfair or ungenerous use of advantages over them; even selfish abstinence from defending them against injury—these are fit objects of moral reprobation, and, in grave cases, of moral retribution and punishment. And not only these acts, but the dispositions which lead to them are properly immoral, and fit subjects of disapprobation which may rise to abhorrence. Cruelty of disposition; malice and ill-nature; that most anti-social and odious of all passions, envy; dissimulation and insincerity; irascibility on insufficient cause, and resentment disproportioned to the provocation; the love of domineering over others; the desire to engross more than one's share of advantages . . . ; the pride which derives gratification from the abasement of others; the egotism which thinks self and its concerns more important than everything else, and decides all doubtful questions in its own favour—these are moral vices, and constitute a bad and odious moral character; unlike the self-regarding faults previously mentioned, which are not properly immoralities, and, to whatever pitch they may be carried, do not constitute wickedness. They may be proofs of any amount of folly, or want of personal dignity and self-respect; but they are only a subject of moral reprobation when they involve a breach of duty to others, for whose sake the individual is bound to have care for himself. What are called duties to ourselves are not socially obligatory, unless circumstances render them at the same time duties to others. The term duty to oneself, when it means anything more than prudence, means self-respect or self-development, and for none of these is anyone accountable to his fellow-creatures, because for none of them is it for the good of mankind that he be held accountable to them. . . .

APPLICATIONS

The principles asserted in these pages must be more generally admitted as the basis for discussion of details, before a consistent application of them to all the various departments of government and morals can be attempted with any prospect of advantage. The few observations I propose to make on questions of detail are designed to illustrate the principles, rather than to follow them out to their consequences. I offer, not so much applications, as specimens of application; which may serve to bring into greater clearness the meaning and limits of the two maxims which together form the entire doctrine of this Essay, and to assist the judgment in holding the balance between them, in the cases where it appears doubtful which of them is applicable to the case.

The maxims are, first, that the individual is not accountable to society for his actions, in so far as these concern the interests of no person but himself. Advice, instruction, persuasion, and avoidance by other people, if thought necessary by them for their own good, are the only measures by which society can justifiably express its dislike or disapprobation of his conduct. Secondly, that for such actions as are prejudicial to the interests of others, the individual is accountable, and may be subjected either to social or to legal punishment, if society is of opinion that the one or the other is requisite for its protection.

In the first place, it must by no means be supposed, because damage, or probability of damage, to the interests of others, can alone justify the interference of society, that therefore it always does justify such interference. In many cases, an individual, in pursuing a legitimate object, necessarily and therefore legitimately causes pain or loss to others, or intercepts a good which they had a reasonable hope of obtaining. Such oppositions of interest between individuals often arise from bad social institutions, but are unavoidable while those institutions last; and some would be unavoidable under any institutions. Whoever succeeds in an overcrowded profession, or in a competitive examination; whoever is preferred to another in any contest for an object which both desire, reaps benefit from the loss of others, from their wasted exertion and their disappointment. But it is, by common admission, better for the general interest of mankind, that persons should pursue their objects undeterred by this sort of consequences. In other words, society admits no right, either legal or moral, in the disappointed competitors to immunity from this kind of suffering; and feels called on to interfere, only when means of success have been employed which it is contrary to the general interest to permit—namely, fraud or treachery, and force.

Again, trade is a social act. Whoever undertakes to sell any description of goods to the public does what affects the interest of other persons, and of society in general; and thus his conduct, in principle, comes within the jurisdiction of society: accordingly, it was once held to be the duty of governments, in all cases which were considered of importance, to fix prices, and regulate the processes of manufacture. But it is now recognised, though not till after a long struggle, that both the cheapness and the good quality of commodities are most effectually provided for by leaving the producers and sellers perfectly free, under the sole check of equal freedom to the buyers for supplying themselves elsewhere. This is the so-called doctrine of Free Trade, which rests on grounds different from, though equally solid with, the principle of individual liberty asserted in this Essay. Restrictions on trade, or on production for purposes of trade, are indeed restraints; and all restraint, *quâ* restraint, is an evil: but the restraints in question affect only that part of conduct which society is competent to restrain, and are wrong solely because they do not really produce the results which it is desired to produce by them. As the principle of individual liberty is not involved in the doctrine of Free Trade, so neither is it in most of the questions which arise respecting the limits of that doctrine; as, for example, what amount of public control is admissible for the prevention of fraud by adulteration; how far sanitary precautions, or arrangements to protect workpeople employed in dangerous occupations, should be enforced on employers. Such questions involve considerations of liberty, only in so far as leaving people to themselves is always better, *caeteris paribus*, than controlling them: but that they may be legitimately controlled for these ends is in principle undeniable. On the other hand, there are questions relating to interference with trade which are essentially questions of liberty; such as the Maine Law [prohibition of liquor], already touched upon; the prohibition of the importation of opium into China; the restriction of the sale of poisons; all cases, in short, where the object of the interference is to make it impossible or difficult to obtain a particular commodity. These interferences are objectionable, not as infringements on the liberty of the producer or seller, but on that of the buyer.

One of these examples, that of the sale of poisons, opens a new question: the proper limits of what may be called the functions of police; how far liberty may legitimately be invaded for the prevention of crime, or of accident. It is one of the undisputed functions of government to take precautions against crime before it has been committed, as well as to detect and punish it afterwards. The preventive function of government, however, is far more liable to be abused, to the prejudice of liberty, than the punitory function; for there is hardly any part of the legitimate freedom of action of a human being which would not admit of being represented, and fairly too, as increasing the facilities for some form or other of delinquency. Nevertheless, if a public authority, or even a private person, sees anyone evidently preparing to commit a crime, they are not bound to look on inactive until the crime is committed, but may interfere to prevent it. If poisons were never bought or used for any purpose except the commission of murder, it would be right to prohibit their manufacture and sale. They may, however, be wanted not only for innocent but for useful purposes, and restrictions cannot be imposed in the one case without operating in the other. Again, it is a proper office of public authority to guard against accidents. If either a public officer or anyone else saw a person attempting to cross a bridge which had been ascertained to be unsafe, and there were no time to warn him of his danger, they might seize him and turn him back, without any real infringement of his liberty; for liberty consists in doing what one desires, and he does not desire to fall into the river. Nevertheless, when there is not a certainty, but only a danger of mischief, no one but the person himself can judge of the sufficiency of the motive which may prompt him to incur the risk: in this case, therefore (unless he is a child, or delirious, or in some state of excitement or absorption incompatible with the full use of the reflecting faculty), he ought, I conceive, to be only warned of the danger; not forcibly prevented from exposing himself to it. Similar considerations, applied to such a question as the sale of poisons, may enable us to decide which among the possible modes of regulation are or are not contrary to principle. Such a precaution, for example, as that of labelling the drug with some word expressive of its dangerous character, may be enforced without violation of liberty: the buyer cannot wish not to know that the thing he possesses has poisonous qualities. But to require in all cases the certificate of a medical practitioner would make it sometimes impossible, always expensive, to obtain the article for legitimate uses. The only mode apparent to me in which difficulties may be thrown in the way of crime committed through this means, without any infringement worth taking into account upon the liberty of those who desire the poisonous substance for other purposes, consists in providing what, in the apt language of Bentham, is called "preappointed evidence." This provision is familiar to everyone in the case of contracts. It is usual and right that the law, when a contract is entered into, should require as the condition of its enforcing performance, that certain formalities should be observed, such as signatures, attestation of witnesses, and the like, in order that in case of subsequent dispute there may be evidence to prove that the contract was really entered into, and that there was nothing in the circumstances to render it legally invalid; the effect being to throw great obstacles in the way of fictitious contracts, or contracts made in circumstances which, if known, would destroy their validity. Precautions of a similar nature might be enforced in the sale of articles adapted to be instruments of crime. The seller, for example, might be required to enter in a register the exact time of the transaction, the name and address of the buyer, the precise quality and quantity sold; to ask the purpose for which it was wanted, and record the answer he received. When there was no medical prescription, the presence of some third person might be required, to bring home the fact to the purchaser, in case there should afterwards be reason to believe that the article had been applied to criminal purposes. Such regulations would in general be no material impediment to obtaining the article, but a very considerable one to making an improper use of it without detection.

The right, inherent in society, to ward off crimes against itself by antecedent precautions, suggests the obvious limitations to the maxim that purely self-regarding misconduct cannot properly be meddled with in the way of prevention or punishment. Drunkenness, for example, in ordinary cases, is not a fit subject for legislative interference; but I should deem it perfectly legitimate that a person, who had once been convicted of any act of violence to others under the influence of drink, should be placed under a special legal restriction, personal to himself; that if he were afterwards found drunk, he should be liable to a penalty; and that if, when in that state, he committed another offence, the punishment to which he would be liable for that other offence should be increased in severity. The making himself drunk, in a person whom drunkenness excites to do harm to others, is a crime against others. So, again, idleness, except in a person receiving support from the public, or except when it constitutes a breach of contract, cannot without tyranny be made a subject of legal punishment; but if, either from idleness or from any other avoidable cause, a man fails to perform his legal duties to others, as for instance to support his children, it is no tyranny to force him to fulfil that obligation, by compulsory labour, if no other means are available.

Again, there are many acts which, being directly injurious only to the agents themselves, ought not to be legally interdicted, but which, if done publicly, are a violation of good manners and, coming thus within the category of offences against others, may rightly be prohibited. Of this kind are offences against decency; on which it is unnecessary to dwell, the rather as they are connected only indirectly with our subject, the objection to publicity being equally strong in the case of many actions not in themselves condemnable, nor supposed to be so. . . .

I have reserved for the last place a large class of questions respecting the limits of government interference, which, though closely connected with the subject of this Essay, do not, in strictness, belong to it. These are cases in which the reasons against interference do not turn upon the principle of liberty: the question is not about restraining the actions of individuals, but about helping them; it is asked whether the government should do, or cause to be done, something for their benefit, instead of leaving it to be done by themselves, individually or in voluntary combination.

The objections to government interference, when it is not such as to involve infringement of liberty, may be of three kinds.

The first is, when the thing to be done is likely to be better done by individuals than by the government. Speaking generally, there is no one so fit to conduct any business, or to determine how or by whom it shall be conducted, as those who are personally interested in it. This principle condemns the interferences, once so common, of the legislature, or the officers of government, with the ordinary processes of industry. But this part of the subject has been sufficiently enlarged upon by political economists, and is not particularly related to the principles of this Essay.

The second objection is more nearly allied to our subject. In many cases, though individuals may not do the particular thing so well, on the average, as the officers of government, it is nevertheless desirable that it should be done by them, rather than by the government, as a means to their own mental education—a mode of strengthening their active faculties, exercising their judgment, and giving them a familiar knowledge of the subjects with which they are thus left to deal. This is a principal, though not the sole, recommendation of jury trial (in cases not political); of free and popular local and municipal institutions; of the conduct of industrial and philanthropic enterprises by voluntary associations. These are not questions of liberty, and are connected with that subject only by remote tendencies; but they are questions of development. It belongs to a different occasion from the present to dwell on these things as parts of national education; as being, in truth, the peculiar training of a citizen, the practical part of the political education of a free people, taking them out of the narrow circle of personal and family selfishness, and accustoming them to the comprehension of joint interests, the management of joint concerns—habituating them to act from public or semi-public motives, and guide their conduct by aims which unite instead of isolating them from one another. Without these habits and powers, a free constitution can neither be worked nor preserved; as is exemplified by the too-often transitory nature of political freedom in countries where it does not rest upon a sufficient basis of local liberties. The management of purely local business by the localities, and of the great enterprises of industry by the union of those who voluntarily supply the pecuniary means, is further recommended by all the advantages which have been set forth in this Essay as belonging to individuality of development, and diversity of modes of action. Government operations tend to be everywhere alike. With individuals and voluntary associations, on the contrary, there are varied experiments, and endless diversity of experience. What the State can usefully do is to make itself a central depository, and active circulator and diffuser, of the experience resulting from many trials. Its business is to enable each experimentalist to benefit by the experiments of others, instead of tolerating no experiments but its own.

The third and most cogent reason for restricting the interference of government is the great evil of adding unnecessarily to its power. Every function superadded to those already exercised by the government causes its influence over hopes and fears to be more widely diffused, and converts, more and more, the active and ambitious part of the public into hangers-on of the government, or of some party which aims at becoming the government. If the roads, the railways, the banks, the insurance offices, the great joint-stock companies, the universities, and the public charities, were all of them branches of the government; if, in addition, the municipal corporations and local boards, with all that now devolves on them, became departments of the central administration; if the employees of all these different enterprises were appointed and paid by the government, and looked to the government for

every rise in life; not all the freedom of the press and popular constitution of the legislature would make this or any other country free otherwise than in name. And the evil would be greater, the more efficiently and scientifically the administrative machinery was constructed —the more skilful the arrangements for obtaining the best qualified hands and heads with which to work it.

In England it has of late been proposed that all the members of the civil service of government should be selected by competitive examination, to obtain for these employments the most intelligent and instructed persons procurable; and much has been said and written for and against this proposal. One of the arguments most insisted on by its opponents is that the occupation of a permanent official servant of the State does not hold out sufficient prospects of emolument and importance to attract the highest talents, which will always be able to find a more inviting career in the professions, or in the service of companies and other public bodies. One would not have been surprised if this argument had been used by the friends of the proposition, as an answer to its principal difficulty. Coming from the opponents it is strange enough. What is urged as an objection is the safety-valve of the proposed system. If indeed all the high talent of the country *could* be drawn into the service of the government, a proposal tending to bring about that result might well inspire uneasiness. If every part of the business of society which required organised concert, or large and comprehensive views, were in the hands of the government, and if government offices were universally filled by the ablest men, all the enlarged culture and practised intelligence in the country, except the purely speculative, would be concentrated in a numerous bureaucracy, to whom alone the rest of the community would look for all things: the multitude for direction and dictation in all they had to do; the able and aspiring for personal advancement. To be admitted into the ranks of this bureaucracy, and when admitted, to rise therein, would be the sole objects of ambition. Under this *régime,* not only is the outside public ill qualified, for want of practical experience, to criticise or check the mode of operation of the bureaucracy, but even if the accidents of despotic or the natural working of popular institutions occasionally raise to the summit a ruler or rulers of reforming inclinations, no reform can be effected which is contrary to the interest of the bureaucracy. Such is the melancholy condition of the Russian empire, as shown in the accounts of those who have had sufficient opportunity of observation. The Czar himself is powerless against the bureaucratic body; he can send any one of them to Siberia, but he cannot govern without them, or against their will. On every decree of his they have a tacit veto, by merely refraining from carrying it into effect. In countries of more advanced civilisation and of a more insurrectionary spirit, the public, accustomed to expect everything to be done for them by the State, or at least to do nothing for themselves without asking from the State not only leave to do it, but even how it is to be done, naturally hold the State responsible for all evil which befalls them; and when the evil exceeds their amount of patience, they rise against the government, and make what is called a revolution; whereupon somebody else, with or without legitimate authority from the nation, vaults into the seat, issues his orders to the bureaucracy, and everything goes on much as it did before, the bureaucracy being unchanged, and nobody else being capable of taking their place.

A very different spectacle is exhibited among a people accustomed to transact their own business. In France, a large part of the people having been engaged in military service, many of whom have held at least the rank of non-commissioned officers, there are in every popular insurrection several persons competent to take the lead, and improvise some tolerable plan of action. What the French are in military affairs, the Americans are in every kind of civil business: let them be left without a government, every body of Americans is able to improvise one, and to carry on that or any other public business with a sufficient amount of intelligence, order, and decision. This is what every free people ought to be: and a people capable of this is certain to be free; it will never let itself be enslaved by any man or body of men because these are able to seize and pull the

reins of the central administration. No bureaucracy can hope to make such a people as this do or undergo anything that they do not like. But where everything is done through the bureaucracy, nothing to which the bureaucracy is really adverse can be done at all. The constitution of such countries is an organisation of the experience and practical ability of the nation into a disciplined body for the purpose of governing the rest; and the more perfect that organisation is in itself, the more successful in drawing to itself and educating for itself the persons of greatest capacity from all ranks of the community, the more complete is the bondage of all, the members of the bureaucracy included. For the governors are as much the slaves of their organisation and discipline as the governed are of the governors. A Chinese mandarin is as much the tool and creature of a despotism as the humblest cultivator. An individual Jesuit is to the utmost degree of abasement the slave of his order, though the order itself exists for the collective power and importance of its members.

It is not, also, to be forgotten, that the absorption of all the principal ability of the country into the governing body is fatal, sooner or later, to the mental activity and progressiveness of the body itself. Banded together as they are, —working a system which, like all systems, necessarily proceeds in a great measure by fixed rules—the official body are under the constant temptation of sinking into indolent routine; or, if they now and then desert that mill-horse round, of rushing into some half-examined crudity which has struck the fancy of some leading member of the corps; and the sole check to these closely allied, though seemingly opposite, tendencies, the only stimulus which can keep the ability of the body itself up to a high standard, is liability to the watchful criticism of equal ability outside the body. It is indispensable, therefore, that the means should exist, independently of the government, of forming such ability, and furnishing it with the opportunities and experience necessary for a correct judgment of great practical affairs. If we would possess permanently a skilful and efficient body of functionaries—above all, a body able to originate and willing to adopt improvements; if we would not have our bureaucracy degenerate into a pedantocracy, this body must not engross all the occupations which form and cultivate the faculties required for the government of mankind.

To determine the point at which evils, so formidable to human freedom and advancement, begin, or rather at which they begin to predominate over the benefits attending the collective application of the force of society, under its recognised chiefs, for the removal of the obstacles which stand in the way of its well-being; to secure as much of the advantages of centralised power and intelligence as can be had without turning into governmental channels too great a proportion of the general activity—is one of the most difficult and complicated questions in the art of government. It is, in a great measure, a question of detail, in which many and various considerations must be kept in view, and no absolute rule can be laid down. But I believe that the practical principle in which safety resides, the ideal to be kept in view, the standard by which to test all arrangements intended for overcoming the difficulty, may be conveyed in these words: the greatest dissemination of power consistent with efficiency; but the greatest possible centralisation of information, and diffusion of it from the centre. Thus, in municipal administration, there would be, as in the New England States, a very minute division among separate officers, chosen by the localities, of all business which is not better left to the persons directly interested; but besides this, there would be, in each department of local affairs, a central superintendence, forming a branch of the general government. The organ of this superintendence would concentrate, as in a focus, the variety of information and experience derived from the conduct of that branch of public business in all the localities, from everything analogous which is done in foreign countries, and from the general principles of political science. This central organ should have a right to know all that is done, and its special duty should be that of making the knowledge acquired in one place available for others. Emancipated from the petty prejudices and narrow views of a locality by its elevated position and comprehensive sphere of observation, its advice would naturally carry much authority; but its actual power, as a permanent institution, should, I conceive, be limited to compelling the local officers to obey the laws laid down for their guidance. In all things not provided for by general rules, those officers should be left to their own judgment, under responsibility to their constituents. For the violation of rules, they should be responsible to law, and the rules themselves should be laid down by the legislature; the central administrative authority only watching over their execution, and, if they were not properly carried into effect, appealing, according to the nature of the case, to the tribunals to enforce the law, or to the constituencies to dismiss the functionaries who had not executed it according to its spirit. Such, in its general conception, is the central superintendence which the Poor Law Board is intended to exercise over the administrators of the Poor Rate throughout the country. Whatever powers the Board exercises beyond this limit were right and necessary in that peculiar case, for the cure of rooted habits of maladministration in matters deeply affecting not the localities merely, but the whole community; since no locality has a moral right to make itself by mismanagement a nest of pauperism, necessarily overflowing into other localities, and impairing the moral and physical condition of the whole labouring community. The powers of administrative coercion and subordinate legislation possessed by the Poor Law Board (but which, owing to the state of opinion on the subject, are very scantily exercised by them), though perfectly justifiable in a case of first-rate national interest, would be wholly out of place in the superintendence of interests purely local. But a central organ of information and instruction for all the localities would be equally valuable in all departments of administration. A government cannot have too much of the kind of activity which does not impede, but aids and stimulates, individual exertion and development. The mischief begins when, instead of calling forth the activity and powers of individuals and bodies, it substitutes its own activity for theirs; when, instead of informing, advising, and, upon occasion, denouncing, it makes them work in fetters, or bids them stand aside and does their work instead of them.

The worth of a State, in the long run, is the worth of the individuals composing it; and a State which postpones the interests of *their* mental expansion and elevation to a little more of administrative skill, or of that semblance of it which practice gives, in the details of business; a State which dwarfs its men, in order that they may be more docile instruments in its hands even for beneficial purposes, will find that with small men no great thing can really be accomplished; and that the perfection of machinery to which it has sacrificed everything will in the end avail it nothing, for want of the vital power which, in order that the machine might work more smoothly, it has preferred to banish.

Alexis de Tocqueville

Alexis de Tocqueville (1805–1859) was a French aristocrat who became deeply concerned with the problem of liberty. He was trained for the magistracy and served for a time in that capacity. Subsequently he entered the French Chamber of Deputies and, after the Liberal revolution of 1848, served in the government as minister of foreign affairs. In 1830 he came to the United States ostensibly to study the American penal system, but in reality to study American life generally. He returned to Europe deeply impressed with what he had seen of democracy in action. He was particularly concerned about the future of individual liberty under this form of government. In 1835 he published his Democracy in America, which was the first comprehensive analysis written on the American political experiment. The book received widespread attention throughout Europe and helped to inspire the democratic movement on the continent. Thus de Tocqueville was a force in the backward flow of Western Civilization from America to Europe. In reading the following selections from this work note (1) the similar situation in Europe and the United States which influenced de Tocqueville to write Democracy in America, (2) the extent to which popular sovereignty had developed in America, (3) why he thought the people there truly governed, (4) the pragmatic character of American philosophy, (5) the tendency for popular opinion to supersede thought, (6) the effect of equalitarianism on American concepts of human perfectibility, (7) the effect of democracy upon the arts, (8) de Tocqueville's discussion of freedom and equality and which of these democratic communities preferred, (9) the methods by which Americans successfully combatted the dangers of equality, (10) the possibility of democratic America producing an industrial autocracy, (11) the threat of despotic government emerging over a people socially equal, and (12) the means by which he believed democratic nations could preserve personal freedom.

As translated by Henry Reeves in Alexis de Tocqueville, *The Republic of the United States of America, and its Political Institutions, Reviewed and Examined*, 2 vols. in 1, New York, 1856, I, 1; 57; 59; 184–185; II, 1–3; 9–11; 33–34; 49–53; 99–103; 110–113; 169–172; 343–344; 346; 347–351.

From: DEMOCRACY IN AMERICA

Among the novel objects that attracted my attention during my stay in the United States, nothing struck me more forcibly than the general equality of conditions. I readily discovered the prodigious influence which this primary fact exercises on the whole course of society, by giving a certain direction to public opinion, and a certain tenor to the laws; by imparting new maxims to the governing powers, and peculiar habits to the governed.

I speedily perceived that the influence of this fact extends far beyond the political character and the laws of the country, and that it has no less empire over civil society than over the government; it creates opinions, engenders sentiments, suggests the ordinary practices of life, and modifies whatever it does not produce.

The more I advanced in the study of American society, the more I perceived that the equality of conditions is the fundamental fact from which all others seem to be derived, and the central point at which all my observations constantly terminated.

I then turned my thoughts to our own hemisphere, where I imagined that I discerned something analogous to the spectacle which the New World presented to me. I observed that the equality of conditions is daily advancing toward those extreme limits which it seems to have reached in the United States; and that the democracy which governs the American communities, appears to be rapidly rising into power in Europe.

I hence conceived the idea of the book which is now before the reader. . . .

THE PRINCIPLE OF THE SOVEREIGNTY OF THE PEOPLE IN AMERICA

Whenever the political laws of the United States are to be discussed, it is with the doctrine of the sovereignty of the people that we must begin.

The principle of the sovereignty of the people, which is to be found, more or less, at the bottom of almost all human institutions, generally remains concealed from view. It is obeyed without being recognised, or if for a moment it be brought to light, it is hastily cast back into the gloom of the sanctuary.

"The will of the nation" is one of those expressions which have been most profusely abused by the wily and the despotic of every age. To the eyes of some it has been represented by the venal suffrages of a few of the satellites of power; to others, by the votes of a timid or an interested minority; and some have even discovered it in the silence of a people, on the supposition that the fact of submission established the right of command.

In America, the principle of the sovereignty of the people is not either barren or concealed, as it is with some other nations; it is recognised by the customs and proclaimed by the laws; it spreads freely, and arrives without impediment at its most remote consequences. If there be a country in the world where the doctrine of the sovereignty of the people can be fairly appreciated, where it can be studied in its application to the affairs of society, and where its dangers and its advantages may be foreseen, that country is assuredly America. . . .

At the present day the principle of the sovereignty of the people has acquired, in the United States, all the practical development which the imagination can conceive. It is unencumbered by those fictions which have been thrown over it in other countries, and it appears in every possible form according to the exigency of the occasion. Sometimes the laws are made by the people in a body, as at Athens; and sometimes its representatives, chosen by universal suffrage, transact business in its name, and almost under its immediate control.

In some countries a power exists which, though it is in a degree foreign to the social body, directs it, and forces it to pursue a certain track. In others the ruling force is divided, being partly within and partly without the ranks of the people. But nothing of the kind is to be seen in the United States; there society governs itself for itself. All power centres in its bosom; and scarcely an individual is to be met with who would venture to conceive, or, still more, to express, the idea of seeking it elsewhere. The nation participates in the making of its laws by the choice of its legislators, and in the execution of them by the choice of the agents of the executive government; it may almost be said to govern itself, so feeble and so restricted is the share left to the administration, so little do the authorities forget their popular origin and the power from which they emanate. . . .

WHY THE PEOPLE MAY STRICTLY BE SAID TO GOVERN IN THE UNITED STATES

In America the people appoints the legislative and the executive power, and furnishes the jurors who punish all offences against the laws. The American institutions are democratic, not only in their principle but in all their consequences; and the people elects its representatives *directly*, and for the most part *annually*, in order to ensure their dependance. The people is therefore the real directing power; and although the form of government is representative, it is evident that the opinions, the prejudices, the interests, and even the passions of the community are hindered by no durable obstacles from exercising a perpetual influence on society. In the United States the majority governs in the name of the people, as is the case in all the countries in which the people is supreme. This majority is principally composed of peaceable citizens, who, either by inclination or by interest, are sincerely desirous of the welfare of their country. But they are surrounded by the incessant agitation of parties, which attempt to gain their co-operation and to avail themselves of their support. . . .

PHILOSOPHICAL METHOD AMONG THE AMERICANS

I think that in no country in the civilized world is less attention paid to philosophy than in the United States. The Americans have no philosophical school of their own; and they care but little for all the schools into which Europe is divided, the very names of which are scarcely known to them.

Nevertheless it is easy to perceive that almost all the inhabitants of the United States conduct their understanding in the same manner, and govern it by the same rules; that is to say, that without ever having taken the trouble to define the rules of a philosophical method, they are in possession of one, common to the whole people.

To evade the bondage of system and habit, of family-maxims, class-opinions, and, in some degree, of national prejudices; to accept tradition only as a means of information, and existing facts only as a lesson used in doing otherwise and doing better; to seek the reason of things for oneself, and in oneself alone; to tend to results without being bound to means, and to aim at the substance through the form;— such are the principal characteristics of what I shall call the philosophical method of the Americans.

But if I go further, and if I seek among these characteristics that which predominates over and includes almost all the rest, I discover, that in most of the operations of the mind, each American appeals to the individual exercise of his own understanding alone.

America is therefore one of the countries in the world where philosophy is least studied, and where the precepts of Descartes are best applied. Nor is this surprising. The Americans do not read the works of Descartes, because their social condition deters them from speculative studies; but they follow his maxims, because this very social condition naturally disposes their understanding to adopt them.

In the midst of the continual movement which agitates a democratic community, the tie which unites one generation to another is relaxed or broken; every man readily loses the trace of the ideas of his forefathers or takes no care about them.

Nor can men living in this state of society derive their belief from the opinions of the class to which they belong; for, so to speak, there are no longer any classes, or those which still exist are composed of such mobile elements, that their body can never exercise a real control over its members.

As to the influence which the intelligence of one man has on that of another, it must necessarily be very limited in a country where the citizens, placed on the footing of a general similitude, are all closely seen by each other;

and where, as no signs of incontestable greatness or superiority are perceived in any one of them, they are constantly brought back to their own reason as the most obvious and proximate source of truth. It is not only confidence in this or that man which is then destroyed, but the taste for trusting the *ipse dixit* of any man whatsoever. Every one shuts himself up in his own breast, and affects from that point to judge the world.

The practice which obtains among the Americans of fixing the standard of their judgement in themselves alone, leads them to other habits of mind. As they perceive that they succeed in resolving without assistance all the little difficulties which their practical life presents, they readily conclude that every thing in the world may be explained, and that nothing in it transcends the limits of the understanding. Thus they fall to denying what they cannot comprehend; which leaves them but little faith for whatever is extraordinary, and an almost insurmountable distaste for whatever is supernatural. As it is on their own testimony that they are accustomed to rely, they like to discern the object which engages their attention with extreme clearness; they therefore strip off as much as possible all that covers it, they rid themselves of whatever separates them from it, they remove whatever conceals it from sight, in order to view it more closely and in the broad light of day. This disposition of the mind soon leads them to contemn forms, which they regard as useless and inconvenient veils placed between them and the truth.

The Americans then have not required to extract their philosophical method from books; they have found it in themselves. The same thing may be remarked in what has taken place in Europe.

This same method has only been established and made popular in Europe in proportion as the condition of society has become more equal, and men have grown more like each other. . . .

OF THE PRINCIPAL SOURCE OF BELIEF AMONG DEMOCRATIC NATIONS

. . . When the ranks of society are unequal, and men unlike each other in condition, there are some individuals invested with all the power of superior intelligence, learning, and enlightenment, while the multitude is sunk in ignorance and prejudice. Men living at these aristocratic periods are therefore naturally induced to shape their opinions by the superior standard of a person or a class of persons, while they are averse to recognise the infallibility of the mass of the people.

The contrary takes place in ages of equality. The nearer the citizens are drawn to the common level of an equal and similar condition, the less prone does each man become to place implicit faith in a certain man or a certain class of men. But his readiness to believe the multitude increases, and opinion is more than ever mistress of the world. Not only is common opinion the only guide which private judgement retains among a democratic people, but among such a people it possesses a power infinitely beyond what it has elsewhere. At periods of equality men have no faith in one another, by reason of their common resemblance; but this very resemblance gives them almost unbounded confidence in the judgement of the public; for it would not seem probable, as they are all endowed with equal means of judging, but that the greater truth should go with the greater number.

When the inhabitant of a democratic country compares himself individually with all those about him, he feels with pride that he is the equal of any one of them; but when he comes to survey the totality of his fellows, and to place himself in contrast to so huge a body, he is instantly overwhelmed by the sense of his own insignificance and weakness.

The same equality which renders him independent of each of his fellow-citizens, taken severally, exposes him alone and unprotected to the influence of the greater number.

The public has therefore among a democratic people a singular power, of which aristocratic nations could never so much as conceive an idea; for it does not persuade to certain opinions, but it enforces them, and infuses them into the faculties by a sort of enormous pressure of the minds of all upon the reason of each.

In the United States the majority undertakes to supply a multitude of ready-made opinions for the use of individuals, who are thus relieved from the necessity of forming opinions of their own. Everybody there adopts great numbers of theories on philosophy, morals, and politics, without inquiry, upon public trust; and if we look to it very narrowly, it will be perceived that religion herself holds her sway there, much less as a doctrine of revelation than as a commonly received opinion.

The fact that the political laws of the Americans are such that the majority rules the community with sovereign sway, materially increases the power which that majority naturally exercises over the mind. For nothing is more customary in man than to recognise superior wisdom in the person of his oppressor. This political omnipotence of the majority in the United States doubtless augments the influence which public opinion would obtain without it over the mind of each member of the community; but the foundations of that influence do not rest upon it. They must be sought for in the principle of equality itself, not in the more or less popular institutions which men living under that condition may give themselves. The intellectual dominion of the greater number would probably be less absolute among a democratic people governed by a king than in the sphere of a pure democracy, but it will always be extremely absolute; and by whatever political laws men are governed in the ages of equality, it may be foreseen that faith in public opinion will become a species of religion there, and the majority its ministering prophet.

Thus intellectual authority will be different, but it will not be diminished; and far from thinking that it will disappear, I augur that it may readily acquire too much preponderance, and confine the action of private judgement within narrower limits than are suited either to the greatness or the happiness of the human race. In the principle of equality I very clearly discern two tendencies; the one leading the mind of every man to untried thoughts, the other inclined to prohibit him from thinking at all. And I perceive how, under the dominion of certain laws, democracy would extinguish that liberty of the mind to which a democratic social condition is favorable; so that, after having broken all the bondage once imposed on it by ranks or by men, the human mind would

be closely fettered to the general will of the greatest number.

If the absolute power of a majority were to be substituted by democratic nations, for all the different powers which checked or retarded overmuch the energy of individual minds, the evil would only have changed its symptoms. Men would not have found the means of independent life; they would simply have invented (no easy task) a new dress for servitude. There is—and I cannot repeat it too often—there is in this matter for profound reflection for those who look on freedom as a holy thing, and who hate not only the despot, but despotism. For myself, when I feel the hand of power lie heavy on my brow, I care but little to know who oppresses me; and I am not the more disposed to pass beneath the yoke, because it is held out to me by the arms of a million men. . . .

THE PRINCIPLE OF EQUALITY SUGGESTS TO THE AMERICANS THE IDEA OF THE INDEFINITE PERFECTIBILITY OF MAN

Equality suggests to the human mind several ideas which would not have originated from any other source, and it modifies almost all those previously entertained. I take as an example the idea of human perfectibility, because it is one of the principal notions that the intellect can conceive, and because it constitutes of itself a great philosophical theory, which is every instant to be traced by its consequences in the practice of human affairs.

Although man has many points of resemblance with the brute creation, one characteristic is peculiar to himself—he improves; they are incapable of improvement. Mankind could not fail to discover this difference from its earliest period. The idea of perfectibility is therefore as old as the world: equality did not give birth to it, although it has imparted to it a novel character.

When the citizens of a community are classed according to their rank, their profession or their birth, and when all men are constrained to follow the career which happens to open before them, every one thinks that the utmost limits of human power are to be discerned in proximity to himself, and none seeks any longer to resist the inevitable law of his destiny. Not indeed that an aristocratic people absolutely contests man's faculty of self-improvement, but they do not hold it to be indefinite; amelioration they conceive, but not change: they imagine that the future condition of society may be better, but not essentially different; and while they admit that mankind has made vast strides in improvement, and may still have some to make, they assign to it beforehand certain impassable limits.

Thus they do not presume that they have arrived at the supreme good or at absolute truth (what people or what man was ever wild enough to imagine it?), but they cherish a persuasion that they have pretty nearly reached that degree of greatness and knowledge which our imperfect nature admits of; and, as nothing moves about them, they are willing to fancy that every thing is in its fit place. Then it is that the legislator affects to lay down eternal laws; that kings and nations will raise none but imperishable monuments; and that the present generation undertakes to spare generations to come the care of regulating their destinies.

In proportion as castes disappear and the classes of society approximate—as manners, customs and laws vary, from the tumultuous intercourse of men—as new facts arise—as new truths are brought to light—as ancient opinions are dissipated and others take their place—the image of an ideal perfection, for ever on the wing, presents itself to the human mind. Continual changes are then every instant occurring under the observation of every man: the position of some is rendered worse; and he learns but too well, that no people and no individual, how enlightened soever they may be, can lay claim to infallibility;—the condition of others is improved; whence he infers that man is endowed with an indefinite faculty of improvement. His reverses teach him that none may hope to have discovered absolute good—his success stimulates him to the never-ending pursuit of it. Thus, for ever seeking—for ever falling, to rise again—often disappointed, but not discouraged—he tends unceasingly toward that unmeasured greatness so indistinctly visible at the end of the long track which humanity has yet to tread.

It can hardly be believed how many facts naturally flow from the philosophical theory of the indefinite perfectibility of man, or how strong an influence it exercises even on men who, living entirely for the purposes of action and not of thought, seem to conform their actions to it, without knowing anything about it.

I accost an American sailor, and I inquire why the ships of his country are built so as to last but for a short time; he answers without hesitation that the art of navigation is every day making such rapid progress, that the finest vessel would become almost useless if it lasted beyond a certain number of years. In these words, which fell accidentally and on a particular subject from a man of rude attainments, I recognise the general and systematic idea upon which a great people directs all its concerns.

Aristocratic nations are naturally too apt to narrow the scope of human perfectibility; democratic nations to expand it beyond compass. . . .

CONCERNING THE SPIRIT IN WHICH THE AMERICANS CULTIVATE THE ARTS

It would be to waste the time of my readers and my own, if I strove to demonstrate how the general mediocrity of fortunes, the absence of superfluous wealth, the universal desire of comfort, and the constant efforts by which every one attempts to procure it, make the taste for the useful predominate over the love of the beautiful in the heart of man. Democratic nations, among which all these things exist, will therefore cultivate the arts which serve to render life easy, in preference to those whose object is to adorn it. They will habitually prefer the useful to the beautiful, and they will require that the beautiful should be useful.

But I propose to go further; and after having pointed out this first feature, to sketch several others.

It commonly happens that in the ages of privilege the practice of almost all the arts becomes a privilege; and that every profession is a separate walk upon which it is not allowable for every one to enter. Even when productive industry is free, the fixed character which belongs to aristocratic nations gradually segregates all the persons who practise the same art, till they form a distinct class, always composed of the same families, whose members are all known to each other, and among whom a public opinion of their own, and a species of corporate pride soon spring up. In a class or guild of this kind, each artisan has not only his fortune to make, but his reputation to preserve. He is not exclusively swayed by his own interest, or even by that of his customer, but by that of the body to which he belongs; and the interest of that body is, that each artisan should produce the best possible workmanship. In aristocratic ages, the object of the arts is therefore to manufacture as well as possible—not with the greatest dispatch, or at the lowest rate.

When, on the contrary, every profession is open to all—when a multitude of persons are constantly embracing and abandoning it—and when its several members are strangers to each other, indifferent and from their numbers hardly seen among themselves; the social tie is destroyed, and each workman, standing alone, endeavours simply to gain the greatest possible quantity of money at the least possible cost. The will of the customer is then his only limit. But at the same time a corresponding revolution takes place in the customer also. In countries in which riches as well as power are concentrated and retained in the hands of the few, the use of the greater part of this world's goods belongs to a small number of individuals, who are always the same. Necessity, public opinion, or moderate desires exclude all others from the enjoyment of them. As this aristocratic class remains fixed at the pinnacle of greatness on which it stands, without diminution or increase, it is always acted upon by the same wants and affected by them in the same manner. The men of whom it is composed naturally derive from their superior and hereditary position a taste for what is extremely well-made and lasting. This affects the general way of thinking of the nation in relation to the arts. It often occurs, among such a people, that even the peasant will rather go without the objects he covets, than procure them in a state of imperfection. In aristocracies, then, the handicraftsmen work for only a limited number of very fastidious customers: the profit they hope to make depends principally on the perfection of their workmanship.

Such is no longer the case when, all privileges being abolished, ranks are intermingled, and men are for ever rising or sinking upon the ladder of society. Among a democratic people a number of citizens always exist whose patrimony is divided and decreasing. They have contracted, under more prosperous circumstances, certain wants, which remain after the means of satisfying such wants are gone; and they are anxiously looking out for some surreptitious method of providing for them. On the other hand, there are always in democracies a large number of men whose fortune is upon the increase, but whose desires grow much faster than their fortunes; and who gloat upon the gifts of wealth in anticipation, long before they have means to command them. Such men are eager to find some short cut to these gratifications, already almost within their reach. From the combination of these two causes the result is, that in democracies there are always a multitude of individuals whose wants are above their means, and who are very willing to take up with imperfect satisfaction, rather than abandon the object of their desires.

The artisan readily understands these passions, for he himself partakes in them: in an aristocracy he would seek to sell his workmanship at a high price to the few; he now conceives that the more expeditious way of getting rich is to sell them at a low price to all. But there are only two ways of lowering the price of commodities. The first is to discover some better, shorter, and more ingenious method of producing them: the second is to manufacture a larger quantity of goods, nearly similar, but of less value. Among a democratic population, all the intellectual faculties of the workman are directed to these two objects: he strives to invent methods which may enable him not only to work better, but quicker and cheaper; or, if he cannot succeed in that, to diminish the intrinsic qualities of the thing he makes, without rendering it wholly unfit for the use for which it is intended. When none but the wealthy had watches, they were almost all very good ones: few are now made which are worth much, but every body has one in his pocket. Thus the democratic principle not only tends to direct the human mind to the useful arts, but it induces the artisan to produce with great rapidity a quantity of imperfect commodities, and the consumer to content himself with these commodities.

Not that in democracies the arts are incapable of producing very commendable works, if such be required. This may occasionally be the case, if customers appear who are ready to pay for time and trouble. In this rivalry of every kind of industry—in the midst of this immense competition and these countless experiments, some excellent workmen are formed who reach the utmost limits of their craft. But they have rarely an opportunity of displaying what they can do; they are scrupulously sparing of their powers; they remain in a state of accomplished mediocrity, which condemns itself, and, though it be very well able to shoot beyond the mark before it, aims only at what it hits. In aristocracies, on the contrary, workmen always do all they can; and when they stop, it is because they have reached the limit of their attainments.

When I arrive in a country where I find some of the finest productions of the arts, I learn from this fact nothing of the social condition or of the political constitution of the country. But if I perceive that the productions of the arts are generally of an inferior quality, very abundant and very cheap, I am convinced that, among the people where this occurs, privilege is on the decline, and that ranks are beginning to intermingle and will soon be confounded together.

The handicraftsmen of democratic ages endeavour not only to bring their useful productions within the reach of the whole community, but they strive to give to all their commodities attractive qualities which they do not in reality possess. In the confusion of all ranks every one hopes to appear what he is not, and makes great exertions to succeed in this object. This sentiment indeed, which is but too natural to the heart of man, does not originate in the democratic principle; but that principle applies it to material objects. To mimic virtue is of every age; but the hypocrisy of luxury belongs more particularly to the ages of democracy.

To satisfy these new cravings of human vanity, the arts have recourse to every species of imposture: and these devices sometimes go so far as to defeat their own purpose. Imitation

diamonds are now made which may be easily mistaken for real ones; as soon as the art of fabricating false diamonds shall have reached so high a degree of perfection that they cannot be distinguished from real ones, it is probable that both one and the other will be abandoned, and become mere pebbles again.

This leads me to speak of those arts which are called the fine arts, by way of distinction. I do not believe that it is a necessary effect of a democratic social condition and of democratic institutions to diminish the number of men who cultivate the fine arts; but these causes exert a very powerful influence on the manner in which these arts are cultivated. Many of those who had already contracted a taste for the fine arts are impoverished; on the other hand, many of those who are not yet rich begin to conceive that taste, at least by imitation; and the number of consumers increases, but opulent and fastidious consumers become more scarce. Something analogous to what I have already pointed out in the useful arts then takes place in the fine arts; the productions of artists are more numerous, but the merit of each production is diminished. No longer able to soar to what is great, they cultivate what is pretty and elegant; and appearance is more attended to than reality.

In aristocracies a few great pictures are produced; in democratic countries, a vast number of insignificant ones. In the former, statues are raised of bronze; in the latter, they are modelled in plaster.

When I arrived for the first time at New York, by that part of the Atlantic Ocean which is called the Narrows, I was surprised to perceive along the shore, at some distance from the city, a considerable number of little palaces of white marble, several of which were built after the models of ancient architecture. When I went the next day to inspect more closely the buildings which had particularly attracted my notice, I found that its walls were of whitewashed brick, and its columns of painted wood. All the edifices which I had admired the night before were of the same kind.

The social condition and the institutions of democracy impart, moreover, certain peculiar tendencies to all the imitative arts which it is easy to point out. They frequently withdraw them from the delineation of the soul to fix them exclusively on that of the body: and they substitute the representation of motion and sensation for that of sentiment and thought: in a word, they put the Real in the place of the Ideal. . . .

WHY DEMOCRATIC NATIONS SHOW A MORE ARDENT AND ENDURING LOVE OF EQUALITY THAN OF LIBERTY

The first and most intense passion which is engendered by the equality of conditions is, I need hardly say, the love of that same equality. My readers will therefore not be surprised that I speak of it before all others.

Everybody has remarked, that in our time, and especially in France, this passion for equality is every day gaining ground in the human heart. It has been said a hundred times that our contemporaries are far more ardently and tenaciously attached to equality than to freedom; but, as I do not find that the causes of the fact have been sufficiently analyzed, I shall endeavour to point them out.

It is possible to imagine an extreme point at which freedom and equality would meet and be confounded together. Let us suppose that all the members of the community take a part in the government, and that each one of them has an equal right to take a part in it. As none is different from his fellows, none can exercise a tyrannical power: men will be perfectly free, because they will all be entirely equal; and they will all be perfectly equal, because they will be entirely free. To this ideal state democratic nations tend. Such is the completest form that equality can assume upon earth; but there are a thousand others which, without being equally perfect, are not less cherished by those nations.

The principle of equality may be established in civil society, without prevailing in the political world. Equal rights may exist of indulging in the same pleasures, of entering the same professions, of frequenting the same places—in a word, of living in the same manner and seeking wealth by the same means, although all men do not take an equal share in the government.

A kind of equality may even be established in the political world, though there should be no political freedom there. A man may be the equal of all his countrymen save one, who is the master of all without distinction, and who selects equally from among them all the agents of his power.

Several other combinations might be easily imagined, by which very great equality would be united to institutions more or less free, or even to institutions wholly without freedom.

Although men cannot become absolutely equal unless they be entirely free, and consequently equality, pushed to its furthest extent, may be confounded with freedom, yet there is good reason for distinguishing the one from the other. The taste which men have for liberty, and that which they feel for equality, are, in fact, two different things; and I am not afraid to add, that, among democratic nations, they are two unequal things.

Upon close inspection, it will be seen that there is in every age some peculiar and preponderating fact with which all others are connected; this fact almost always gives birth to some pregnant idea or some ruling passion, which attracts to itself, and bears away in its course, all the feelings and opinions of the time: it is like a great stream, toward which each of the surrounding rivulets seem to flow.

Freedom has appeared in the world at different times and under various forms; it has not been exclusively bound to any social condition, and it is not confined to democracies. Freedom cannot, therefore, form the distinguishing characteristic of democratic ages. The peculiar and preponderating fact which marks those ages as its own is the equality of conditions; the ruling passion of men in those periods is the love of this equality. Ask not what singular charm the men of democratic ages find in being equal, or what special reasons they may have for clinging so tenaciously to equality rather than to the other advantages which society holds out to them: equality is the distinguishing characteristic of the age they live in; that, of itself, is enough to explain that they prefer it to all the rest.

But independently of this reason there are several others, which will at all times habitually lead men to prefer equality to freedom.

If a people could ever succeed in destroying, or even in diminishing, the equality which prevails in its own body, this could only be accomplished by long and laborious efforts. Its social condition must be modified, its laws abolished, its opinions superseded, its habits changed, its manners corrupted. But political liberty is more easily lost; to neglect to hold it fast, is to allow it to escape.

Men therefore not only cling to equality because it is dear to them; they also adhere to it because they think it will last for ever.

That political freedom may compromise in its excesses the tranquillity, the property, the lives of individuals, is obvious to the narrowest and most unthinking minds. But, on the contrary, none but attentive and clear-sighted men perceive the perils with which equality threatens us, and they commonly avoid pointing them out. They know that the calamities they apprehend are remote, and flatter themselves that they will only fall upon future generations, for which the present generation takes but little thought. The evils which freedom sometimes brings with it are immediate; they are apparent to all, and all are more or less affected by them. The evils which extreme equality may produce are slowly disclosed; they creep gradually into the social frame; they are only seen at intervals, and at the moment at which they become most violent, habit already causes them to be no longer felt.

The advantages which freedom brings are only shown by length of time; and it is always easy to mistake the cause in which they originate. The advantages of equality are instantaneous, and they may constantly be traced from their source.

Political liberty bestows exalted pleasures, from time to time, upon a certain number of citizens. Equality every day confers a number of small enjoyments on every man. The charms of equality are every instant felt, and are within the reach of all: the noblest hearts are not insensible to them, and the most vulgar souls exult in them. The passion which equality engenders must therefore be at once strong and general. Men cannot enjoy political liberty unpurchased by some sacrifices, and they never obtain it without great exertions. But the pleasures of equality are self-proffered: each of the petty incidents of life seems to occasion them, and in order to taste them nothing is required but to live.

Democratic nations are at all times fond of equality, but there are certain epochs at which the passion they entertain for it swells to the height of fury. This occurs at the moment when the old social system, long menaced, completes its own destruction after a last intestine struggle, and when the barriers of rank are at length thrown down. At such times men pounce upon equality as their booty, and they cling to it as to some precious treasure which they fear to lose. The passion for equality penetrates on every side into men's hearts, expands there, and fills them entirely. Tell them not that by this blind surrender of themselves to an exclusive passion, they risk their dearest interests: they are deaf. Show them not freedom escaping from their grasp, while they are looking another way: they are blind—or rather, they can discern but one sole object to be desired in the universe.

What I have said is applicable to all democratic nations: what I am about to say concerns the French alone. Among most modern nations, and especially among all those of the continent of Europe, the taste and the idea of freedom only began to exist and to extend itself at the time when social conditions were tending to equality, and as a consequence of that very equality. Absolute kings were the most efficient levellers of ranks among their subjects. Among these nations equality preceded freedom: equality was therefore a fact of some standing, when freedom was still a novelty: the one had already created customs, opinions, and laws belonging to it, when the other, alone and for the first time, came into actual existence. Thus the latter was still only an affair of opinion and of taste, while the former had already crept into the habits of the people, possessed itself of their manners, and given a particular turn to the smallest actions in their lives. Can it be wondered that the men of our own time prefer the one to the other?

I think that democratic communities have a natural taste for freedom: left to themselves, they will seek it, cherish it, and view any privation of it with regret. But for equality, their passion is ardent, insatiable, incessant, invincible: they call for equality in freedom; if they cannot obtain that, they still call for equality in slavery. They will endure poverty, servitude, barbarism—but they will not endure aristocracy.

This is true at all times, and especially true in our own. All men and all powers seeking to cope with this irresistible passion, will be overthrown and destroyed by it. In our age, freedom cannot be established without it, and despotism itself cannot reign without its support. . . .

THAT THE AMERICANS COMBAT THE EFFECTS OF INDIVIDUALISM BY FREE INSTITUTIONS

. . . The Americans have combated by free institutions the tendency of equality to keep men asunder, and they have subdued it. The legislators of America did not suppose that a general representation of the whole nation would suffice to ward off a disorder at once so natural to the frame of democratic society, and so fatal: they also thought that it would be well to infuse political life into each portion of the territory, in order to multiply to an infinite extent opportunities of acting in concert, for all the members of the community, and to make them constantly feel their mutual dependance on each other. The plan was a wise one. The general affairs of a country only engage the attention of leading politicians, who assemble from time to time in the same places; and as they often lose sight of each other afterward, no lasting ties are established between them. But if the object be to have the local affairs of a district conducted by the men who reside there, the same persons are always in contact, and they are, in a manner, forced to be acquainted, and to adapt themselves to one another.

It is difficult to draw a man out of his own circle to interest him in the destiny of the state, because he does not clearly undestand what influence the destiny of the state can have upon his own lot. But if it be proposed to make a road cross the end of his estate, he will see at a glance that there is a connexion between this small public affair and his greatest private affairs; and he will discover, without its being shown to him, the close tie which unites private to general interest. Thus, far more may be done by entrusting to the citizens the administration of minor affairs than by surrendering to them the control of important ones, toward interesting them in the public welfare, and convincing them that they constantly stand in need one of the other in order to provide for it. A brilliant achievement may win for you the favour of a people at one stroke; but to earn the love and respect of the population which surrounds you, a long succession of little services rendered and of obscure good deeds—a constant habit of kindness, and an established reputation for disinterestedness—will be required. Local freedom, then, which leads a great number of citizens to value the affection of their neighbours and of their kindred, perpetually brings men together, and forces them to help one another, in spite of the propensities which sever them.

In the United States the more opulent citizens take great care not to stand aloof from the people; on the contrary, they constantly keep on easy terms with the lower classes: they listen to them, they speak to them every day. They know that the rich in democracies always stand in need of the poor; and that in democratic ages you attach a poor man to you more by your manner than by benefits conferred. The magnitude of such benefits, which sets off the difference of conditions, causes a secret irritation to those who reap advantage from them; but the charm of simplicity of manners is almost irresistible: their affability carries men away, and even their want of polish is not always displeasing. This truth does not take root at once in the minds of the rich. They generally resist it as long as the democratic revolution lasts, and they do not acknowledge it immediately after that revolution is accomplished. They are very ready to do good to the people, but they still choose to keep them at arm's length; they think that is sufficient, but they are mistaken. They might spend fortunes thus without warming the hearts of the population around them;—that population does not ask them for the sacrifice of their money, but of their pride.

It would seem as if every imagination in the United States were upon the stretch to invent means of increasing the wealth and satisfying the wants of the public. The best informed inhabitants of each district constantly use their information to discover new truths which may augment the general prosperity; and, if they have made any such discoveries, they eagerly surrender them to the mass of the people.

When the vices and weaknesses, frequently exhibited by those who govern in America, are closely examined, the prosperity of the people occasions—but improperly occasions—surprise. Elected magistrates do not make the American democracy flourish; it flourishes because the magistrates are elective.

It would be unjust to suppose that the patriotism and the zeal which every American displays for the welfare of his fellow-citizens are wholly insincere. Although private interest directs the greater part of human actions in the United States, as well as elsewhere, it does not regulate them all. I must say that I have often seen Americans make great and real sacrifices to the public welfare; and I have remarked a hundred instances in which they hardly ever failed to lend faithful support to each other. The free institutions which the inhabitants of the United States possess, and the political rights of which they make so much use, remind every citizen, and in a thousand ways, that he lives in society. They every instant impress upon his mind the notion that it is the duty as well as the interest of men to make themselves useful to their fellow-creatures; and as he sees no particular ground of animosity to them, since he is never either their master or their slave, his heart readily leans to the side of kindness. Men attend to the interests of the public, first by necessity, afterward, by choice: what was intentional becomes an instinct; and by dint of working for the good of one's fellow-citizens, the habit and the taste for serving them is at length acquired.

Many people in France consider equality of conditions as one evil, and political freedom as a second. When they are obliged to yield to the former, they strive at least to escape from the latter. But I contend, that in order to combat the evils which equality may produce, there is only one effectual remedy—namely, political freedom. . . .

THAT ARISTOCRACY MAY BE ENGENDERED BY MANUFACTURES

I have shown that democracy is favourable to the growth of manufactures, and that it increases without limit the numbers of the manufacturing classes: we shall now see by what side-road manufactures may possibly in their turn bring men back to aristocracy.

It is acknowledged, that when a workman is engaged every day upon the same detail, the whole commodity is produced with greater ease, promptitude, and economy. It is likewise acknowledged, that the cost of the production of manufactured goods is diminished by the extent of the establishment in which they are made, and by the amount of capital employed or of credit. These truths had long been imperfectly discerned, but in our time they have been demonstrated. They have been already applied to many very important kinds of manufactures, and the humblest will gradually be governed by them. I know of nothing in politics which deserves to fix the attention of the legislator more closely than these two new axioms of the science of manufactures.

When a workman is unceasingly and exclusively engaged in the fabrication of one thing, he ultimately does his work with singular dexterity; but at the same time he loses the general faculty of applying his mind to the direction of the work. He every day becomes more adroit and less industrious; so that it may be said of him, that in proportion as the workman improves the man is degraded. What can be expected of a man who has spent twenty years of his life in making heads for pins? and to what can that mighty human intelligence, which has so often stirred the world, be applied to him, except it be to investigate the best method of making pins' heads? When a workman has spent a considerable portion of his existence in this manner, his thoughts are for ever set upon the object of his daily toil: his body has contracted certain fixed habits, which it can never shake off: in a word, he no longer belongs to himself, but to the calling which he has chosen. It is in vain that laws and manners have been at the pains to level all barriers round such a man, and to open to him on every side a thousand different paths to fortune; a theory of manufactures more powerful than manners and laws binds him to a craft, and frequently to a spot, which he cannot leave: it assigns to him a certain place in society, beyond which he cannot go: in the midst of universal movement, it has rendered him stationary.

In proportion as the principle of the division of labour is more extensively applied, the workman becomes more weak, more narrow-minded and more dependant. The art advances, the artisan recedes. On the other hand, in proportion as it becomes more manifest that the productions of manufactures are by so much the cheaper and better as the manufacture is larger and the amount of capital employed more considerable, wealthy and educated men come forward to embark in manufactures which were heretofore abandoned to poor or ignorant handicraftsmen. The magnitude of the efforts required, and the importance of the results to be obtained, attract them. Thus, at the very time at which the science of manufactures lowers the class of workmen, it raises the class of masters.

Whereas the workman concentrates his faculties more and more upon the study of a single detail, the master surveys a more extensive whole, and the mind of the latter is enlarged in proportion as that of the former is narrowed. In a short time the one will require nothing but physical strength without intelligence; the other stands in need of science, and almost of genius, to ensure success. This man resembles more and more the administrator of a vast empire—that man, a brute.

The master and the workman have then here no similarity, and their differences increase every day. They are only connected as the two rings at the extremities of a long chain. Each of them fills the station which is made for him, and out of which he does not get: the one is continually, closely, and necessarily dependant upon the other, and seems as much born to obey as that other is to command. What is this but aristocracy?

As the conditions of men constituting the nation become more and more equal, the demand for manufactured commodities becomes more general and more extensive; and the cheapness which places these objects within the reach of slender fortunes becomes a great element of success. Hence there are every day more men of great opulence and education who devote their wealth and knowledge to manufactures; and who seek, by opening large establishments, and by a strict division of labour, to meet the fresh demands which are made on all sides. Thus, in proportion as the mass of the nation turns to democracy, that particular class which is engaged in manufactures becomes more aristocratic. Men grow more alike in the one—more different in the other; and inequality increases in the less numerous class, in the same ratio in which it decreases in the community.

Hence it would appear, on searching to the bottom, that aristocracy should naturally spring out of the bosom of democracy.

But this kind of aristocracy by no means resembles those kinds which preceded it. It will be observed at once, that, as it applies exclusively to manufactures and to some manufacturing callings, it is a monstrous exception in the general aspect of society. The small aristocratic societies which are formed by some manufacturers in the midst of the immense democracy of our age, contain, like the great aristocratic societies of former ages, some men who are very opulent, and a multitude who are wretchedly poor. The poor have few means of escaping from their condition and becoming rich; but the rich are constantly becoming poor, or they give up business when they have realized a fortune. Thus the elements of which the class of the poor is composed are fixed; but the elements of which the class of the rich is composed are not so. To say the truth, though there are rich men, the class of rich men does not exist; for these rich individuals have no feelings or purposes in common, no mutual traditions or mutual hopes: there are therefore members, but no body.

Not only are the rich not compactly united among themselves, but there is no real bond between them and the poor. Their relative position is not a permanent one; they are constantly drawn together or separated by their interests. The workman is generally dependant on the master, but not on any particular master; these two men meet in the factory, but know not each other elsewhere; and while they come into contact on one point, they stand very wide apart on all others. The manufacturer asks nothing of the workman but his labour; the workman expects nothing from him but his wages. The one contracts no obligation to protect, nor the other to defend; and they are not permanently connected either by habit or by duty.

The aristocracy created by business rarely settles in the midst of the manufacturing population which it directs: the object is not to govern that population, but to use it. An aristocracy thus constituted can have no great hold upon those whom it employs; and even if it succeed in retaining them at one moment, they escape the next: it knows not how to will, and it cannot act.

The territorial aristocracy of former ages was either bound by law, or thought itself bound by usage, to come to the relief of its serving-men, and to succour their distresses. But the manufacturing aristocracy of our age first impoverishes and debases the men who serve it, and then abandons them to be supported by the charity of the public. This is a natural consequence of what has been said before. Between the workman and the master there are frequent relations, but in no real partnership.

I am of opinion, upon the whole, that the manufacturing aristocracy which is growing up under our eyes, is one of the harshest which ever existed in the world; but at the same time it is one of the most confined and least dangerous. Nevertheless the friends of democracy should keep their eyes anxiously fixed in this direction; for if ever a permanent inequality of conditions and aristocracy again penetrate into the world, it may be predicted that this is the channel by which they will enter. . . .

DESPOTISM IN A SOCIETY PRACTICING EQUALITY

I believe that it is easier to establish an absolute and despotic government among a people in which the conditions of society are equal, than among any other; and I think that if such a government were once established among such a people, it would not only oppress men, but would eventually strip each of them of several of the highest qualities of humanity. Despotism therefore appears to me peculiarly to be dreaded in democratic ages. I should have loved freedom, I believe, at all times, but in the time in which we live I am ready to worship it.

On the other hand, I am persuaded that all who shall attempt, in the ages upon which we are entering, to base freedom upon aristocratic privilege, will fail;—that all who shall attempt to draw and to retain authority within a single class, will fail. At the present day no ruler is skilful or strong enough to found a despotism, by re-establishing permanent distinctions of rank among his subjects: no legislator is wise or powerful enough to preserve free institutions, if he does not take equality for his first principle and his watchword. All those of our contemporaries who would establish or secure the independence and the dignity of their fellowmen, must show themselves the friends of equality; and the only worthy means of showing themselves as such, is to be so: upon this depends the success of their holy enterprise. Thus the question is not how to reconstruct aristocratic society, but how to make liberty proceed out of that democratic state of society in which God has placed us.

These two truths appear to me simple, clear, and fertile in consequences; and they naturally lead me to consider what kind of free government can be established among a people in which social conditions are equal.

It results from the very constitution of democratic nations and from their necessities, that the power of government among them must be more uniform, more centralized, more extensive, more searching, and more efficient than in other countries. Society at large is naturally stronger and more active, individuals more subordinate and weak; the former does more, the latter less; and this is inevitably the case.

It is not therefore to be expected that the range of private independence will ever be as extensive in democratic as in aristocratic countries—nor is this to be desired; for, among aristocratic nations, the mass is often sacrificed to the individual, and the prosperity of the greater number to the greatness of the few. It is both necessary and desirable that the government of a democratic people should be active and powerful: and our object should not be to render it weak or indolent, but solely to prevent it from abusing its aptitude and its strength. . . .

I think that men living in aristocracies may, strictly speaking, do without the liberty of the press: but such is not the case with those who live in democratic countries. To protect their personal independence I trust not to great political assemblies, to parliamentary privilege, nor to the assertion of popular sovereignty. All these things may, to a certain extent, be reconciled with personal servitude—but that servitude cannot be complete if the press is free: the press is the chiefest democratic instrument of freedom.

Something analogous may be said of the judicial power. It is a part of the essence of judicial power to attend to private interests, and to fix itself with predilection on minute objects submitted to its observation: another essential quality of judicial power is never to volunteer its assistance to the oppressed, but always to be at the disposal of the humblest of those who solicit it; their complaint, however feeble they may themselves be, will force itself upon the ear of justice and claim redress, for this is inherent in the very constitution of the courts of justice.

A power of this kind is therefore peculiarly adapted to the wants of freedom, at a time when the eye and finger of the government are constantly intruding into the minutest details of human actions, and when private persons are at once too weak to protect themselves, and too much isolated for them to reckon upon the assistance of their fellows. The strength of the courts of law has ever been the greatest security which can be offered to personal independence; but this is more especially the case in democratic ages: private rights and interests are in constant danger, if the judicial power does not grow more extensive and more strong to keep pace with the growing equality of conditions. . . .

Another tendency, which is extremely natural to democratic nations and extremely dangerous, is that which leads them to despise and undervalue the rights of private persons. The attachment which men feel to a right, and the respect which they display for it, is generally proportioned to its importance, or to the length of time during which they have enjoyed it. The rights of private persons among democratic nations are commonly of small importance, of recent growth, and extremely precarious—the consequence is that they are often sacrificed without regret, and almost always violated without remorse.

But it happens that at the same period and among the same nations in which men conceive a natural contempt for the rights of private persons, the rights of society at large are naturally extended and consolidated: in other words, men become less attached to private rights at the very time at which it would be most necessary to retain and to defend what little remains of them. It is therefore most especially in the present democratic ages, that the true friends of the liberty and the greatness of man ought constantly to be on the alert to prevent the power of government from lightly sacrificing the private rights of individuals to the general execution of its designs. At such times no citizen is so obscure that it is not very dangerous to allow him to be oppressed—no private rights are so unimportant that they can be surrendered with impunity to the caprices of a government. The reason is plain:—if the private right of an individual is violated at a time when the human mind is fully impressed with the importance and the sanctity of such rights, the injury is confined to the individual whose right is infringed; but to violate such a right, at the present day, is deeply to corrupt the manners of the nation and to put the whole community in jeopardy, because the very notion of this kind of right constantly tends among us to be impaired and lost. . . .

I shall conclude by one general idea, which comprises not only all the particular ideas which have been expressed in the present chapter, but also most of those which it is the object of this book to treat of. In the ages of aristocracy which preceded our own, there were private persons of great power, and a social authority of extreme weakness. The outline of society itself was not easily discernible, and constantly confounded with the different powers by which the community was ruled. The principal efforts of the men of those times were required to strengthen, aggrandize, and secure the supreme power; and on the other hand, to circumscribe individual independence within narrower limits, and to subject private interests to the interests of the public. Other perils and other cares await the men of our age. Among the greater part of modern nations, the government, whatever may be its origin, its constitution, or its name, has become almost omnipotent, and private persons are falling, more and more, into the lowest stage of weakness and dependance.

In olden society everything was different: unity and uniformity were nowhere to be met with. In modern society everything threatens to become so much alike, that the peculiar characteristics of each individual will soon be entirely lost in the general aspect of the world. Our forefathers were ever prone to make an improper use of the notion that private rights ought to be respected; and we are naturally prone on the other hand to exaggerate the idea that the interest of a private individual ought always to bend to the interest of the many.

The political world is metamorphosed: new remedies must henceforth be sought for new disorders. To lay down extensive, but distinct and settled limits, to the action of the government; to confer certain rights on private persons, and to secure to them the undisputed enjoyment of those rights; to enable individual man to maintain whatever independence, strength, and original power he still possesses; to raise him by the side of society at large, and uphold him in that position—these appear to me the main objects of legislators in the ages upon which we are now entering.

It would seem as if the rulers of our time sought only to use men in order to make things great; I wish that they would try a little more to make great men; that they would set less value on the work, and more upon the workman; that they would never forget that a nation cannot long remain strong when every man belonging to it is individually weak, and that no form or combination of social polity has yet been devised, to make an energetic people out of a community of pusillanimous and enfeebled citizens.

I trace among our contemporaries two contrary notions which are equally injurious. One set of men can perceive nothing in the principle of equality but the anarchical tendencies which it engenders: they dread their own free agency—they fear themselves. Other thinkers, less numerous but more enlightened, take a different view: beside that track which starts from the principle of equality to terminate in anarchy, they have at last discovered the road which seems to lead men to inevitable servitude. They shape their souls beforehand to this necessary condition; and, despairing of remaining free, they already do obeisance in their hearts to the master who is soon to appear. The former abandon freedom, because they think it dangerous; the latter, because they hold it to be impossible.

If I had entertained the latter conviction, I should not have written this book, but I should have confined myself to deploring in secret the destiny of mankind. I have sought to point out the dangers to which the principle of equality exposes the independence of man, because I firmly believe that these dangers are the most formidable, as well as the least foreseen, of all those which futurity holds in store; but I do not think that they are insurmountable.

The men who live in the democratic ages upon which we are entering have naturally a taste for independence: they are naturally impatient of regulation, and they are wearied by the permanence even of the condition they themselves prefer. They are fond of power; but they are prone to despise and hate those who wield it, and they easily elude its grasp by their own mobility and insignificance.

These propensities will always manifest themselves, because they originate in the groundwork of society, which will undergo no change: for a long time they will prevent the establishment of any despotism, and they will furnish fresh weapons to each succeeding generation which shall struggle in favour of the liberty of mankind. Let us then look forward to the future with that salutary fear which makes men keep watch and ward for freedom, not with that faint and idle terror which depresses and enervates the heart.

Social and Cultural Trends in the Nineteenth Century

The social evils resulting from the Industrial Revolution became an object of concern to many groups, and during the nineteenth century numerous programs of social reform were advanced. Prominent among these was socialism, which assumed a variety of forms including revolutionary socialism at one extreme and moderate Fabian socialism at the other. In the United States the trend was generally in the direction of collective bargaining for better working conditions with labor organized into unions for this purpose. Others, including leaders in the Catholic Church, stressed the teachings of Christ as the solution for the social ills of the modern world. Germany, after it achieved unification, favored state socialism, a policy of paternalism on the part of the State toward its subjects. Culturally the nineteenth century produced a variety of trends, but the principal influence stemmed from the new scientific theory of evolution. This idea modified scientific principles generally, but it also made an impact upon literature and philosophy as well. Inevitably, there were reactions away from the dominant mood, and in some instances these took the form of highly individualized literary expression, while in others it resulted in distorted applications of the theory of evolution. Generally, however, nineteenth-century culture strongly reflected the scientific and social changes of the time, while realism characterized both the method of producing it and the results attained.

Karl Marx and Friedrich Engels

Karl Marx (1818–1883) was a German intellectual who came under the influence of the Hegelian philosophy while a student at the University of Berlin. He had intended to enter the teaching profession, but was unable to do so because of his unorthodox political views. For a time he worked on the staff of a radical newspaper, first as a writer and then as editor. In 1843 he went to Paris, at that time the center for intellectuals interested in socialism and working-class movements. There he met another German, Friedrich Engels (1820–1895), and the two became active associates in the Communist League. In 1848 they wrote the Communist Manifesto, which appeared shortly before the revolutions of that year. In this work they traced the history of the working-class movement, which they interpreted as a series of class struggles. In developing this thesis Marx reflected both the early training he had received in Hegelian idealism and the nineteenth-century concept of evolutionary growth resulting from struggle and survival. In place of Hegel's concept of the evolutionary development of society out of the conflict of ideas, however, Marx substituted a materialistic conflict of classes centering around the mode of economic production and exchange of goods prevailing in each historical epoch. The survival of the proletariat in the last of these struggles was the inevitable conclusion of Marx's historical materialism. The worldwide popularity which the Communist Manifesto has achieved among certain groups of intellectuals and of the working class is largely the result of the way in which it placed communism in the stream of history and made its final triumph seem inevitable. In reading the selections from this work note (1) why the Manifesto was written, (2) the authors' description of how classes have been formed by the various historical systems of production, (3) the explanation as to how the bourgeoisie rose to power, (4) how the authors distinguished the bourgeois epoch from all earlier ones, (5) the influences they saw of bourgeois capitalism on imperialism and urban development, (6) their description of the weapons which the bourgeoisie have forged and which will destroy them, (7) the analysis of the growing degradation of the proletariat, (8) the process by which the proletariat constantly gained recruits, (9) how the authors integrated the proletarian movement into the stream of history, both past and future, (10) the relationship between the Communists and the other members of the working class, (11) the writers' clarification of the communist stand on the abolition of property, (12) their analysis of capital, (13) the authors' answers to the various objections raised against communism, (14) how the relationship of ideas to the system of material production was analyzed, (15) the steps they described for the revolution, including the use of the state by the workers as a *means of gaining their ends, (16) the destruction of classes by destroying the basis on which they exist, (17) the decline of the state as a political force when its reason for existence is thus destroyed, and (18) any points made by the authors that have not been realized in the course of history since their time.*

From: THE COMMUNIST MANIFESTO

A spectre is haunting Europe—the spectre of Communism. All the powers of old Europe have entered into a holy alliance to exorcise this spectre: Pope and Czar, Metternich and Guizot, French Radicals and German police-spies.

Where is the party in opposition that has not been decried as communistic by its opponents in power? Where the Opposition that has not hurled back the branding reproach of Communism, against the more advanced opposition parties, as well as against its reactionary adversaries?

Two things result from this fact:

I. Communism is already acknowledged by all European powers to be itself a power.

II. It is high time that Communists should openly, in the face of the whole world, publish their views, their aims, their tendencies, and meet this nursery tale of the spectre of Communism with a manifesto of the party itself.

To this end, Communists of various nationalities have assembled in London, and sketched the following manifesto, to be published in the English, French, German, Italian, Flemish, and Danish languages.

BOURGEOIS AND PROLETARIANS

The history of all hitherto existing society is the history of class struggles.

Freeman and slave, patrician and plebeian, lord and serf, guild-master and journeyman, in a word, oppressor and oppressed, stood in constant opposition to one another, carried on an uninterrupted, now hidden, now open fight, a fight that each time ended, either in a revolutionary reconstitution of society at large, or in the common ruin of the contending classes.

In the earlier epochs of history, we find almost everywhere a complicated arrangement of society into various orders, a manifold gradation of social rank. In ancient Rome we have patricians, knights, plebeians, slaves; in the Middle Ages, feudal lords, vassals, guild-masters, journeymen, apprentices, serfs; in almost all of these classes, again, subordinate gradations.

The modern bourgeois society that has sprouted from the ruins of feudal society, has not done away with class antagonisms. It has but established new classes, new conditions of oppression, new forms of struggle in place of the old ones.

Our epoch, the epoch of the bourgeoisie, possesses, however, this distinctive feature: It has simplified the class antagonisms. Society as a whole is more and more splitting up into two great hostile camps, into two great classes directly facing each other—bourgeoisie and proletariat.

From the serfs of the Middle Ages sprang the chartered burghers of the earliest towns. From these burgesses the first elements of the bourgeoisie were developed.

The discovery of America, the rounding of the Cape, opened up fresh ground for the rising bourgeoisie. The East-Indian and Chinese markets, the colonisation of America, trade with the colonies, the increase in the means of exchange and in commodities generally, gave to commerce, to navigation, to industry, an impulse never before known, and thereby, to the revolutionary element in the tottering feudal society, a rapid development.

The feudal system of industry, in which industrial production was monopolised by closed guilds, now no longer sufficed for the growing

Karl Marx and Friedrich Engels, *Manifesto of the Communist Party*, International Publishers, New York, 1932, 3–31. Courtesy of International Publishers.

wants of the new markets. The manufacturing system took its place. The guild-masters were pushed aside by the manufacturing middle class; division of labour between the different corporate guilds vanished in the face of division of labour in each single workshop.

Meantime the markets kept ever growing, the demand ever rising. Even manufacture no longer sufficed. Thereupon, steam and machinery revolutionised industrial production. The place of manufacture was taken by the giant, modern industry, the place of the industrial middle class, by industrial millionaires— the leaders of whole industrial armies, the modern bourgeois.

Modern industry has established the world market, for which the discovery of America paved the way. This market has given an immense development to commerce, to navigation, to communication by land. This development has, in its turn, reacted on the extension of industry; and in proportion as industry, commerce, navigation, railways extended, in the same proportion the bourgeoisie developed, increased its capital, and pushed into the background every class handed down from the Middle Ages.

We see, therefore, how the modern bourgeoisie is itself the product of a long course of development, of a series of revolutions in the modes of production and of exchange.

Each step in the development of the bourgeoisie was accompanied by a corresponding political advance of that class. An oppressed class under the sway of the feudal nobility, it became an armed and self-governing association in the mediaeval commune; here independent urban republic (as in Italy and Germany), there taxable "third estate" of the monarchy (as in France); afterwards, in the period of manufacture proper, serving either the semi-feudal or the absolute monarchy as a counterpoise against the nobility, and, in fact, corner-stone of the great monarchies in general —the bourgeoisie has at last, since the establishment of modern industry and of the world market, conquered for itself, in the modern representative state, exclusive political sway. The executive of the modern state is but a committee for managing the common affairs of the whole bourgeoisie.

The bourgeoisie has played a most revolutionary rôle in history.

The bourgeoisie, wherever it has got the upper hand, has put an end to all feudal, patriarchal, idyllic relations. It has pitilessly torn asunder the motley feudal ties that bound man to his "natural superiors," and has left no other bond between man and man than naked self-interest, than callous "cash payment." It has drowned the most heavenly ecstasies of religious fervour, of chivalrous enthusiasm, of philistine sentimentalism, in the icy water of egotistical calculation. It has resolved personal worth into exchange value, and in place of the numberless indefeasible chartered freedoms, has set up that single, unconscionable freedom —Free Trade. In one word, for exploitation, veiled by religious and political illusions, it has substituted naked, shameless, direct, brutal exploitation.

The bourgeoisie has stripped of its halo every occupation hitherto honoured and looked up to with reverent awe. It has converted the physician, the lawyer, the priest, the poet, the man of science, into its paid wage-labourers.

The bourgeoisie has torn away from the family its sentimental veil, and has reduced the family relation to a mere money relation.

The bourgeoisie has disclosed how it came to pass that the brutal display of vigour in the Middle Ages, which reactionaries so much admire, found its fitting complement in the most slothful indolence. It has been the first to show what man's activity can bring about. It has accomplished wonders far surpassing Egyptian pyramids, Roman aqueducts, and Gothic cathedrals; it has conducted expeditions that put in the shade all former migrations of nations and crusades.

The bourgeoisie cannot exist without constantly revolutionising the instruments of production, and thereby the relations of production, and with them the whole relations of society. Conservation of the old modes of production in unaltered form, was, on the contrary, the first condition of existence for all earlier industrial classes. Constant revolutionising of production, uninterrupted disturbance of all social conditions, everlasting uncertainty and agitation distinguish the bourgeois epoch from all earlier ones. All fixed, fast-frozen relations, with their train of ancient and venerable prejudices and opinions, are swept away, all new-formed ones become antiquated before they can ossify. All that is solid melts into air, all that is holy is profaned, and man is at last compelled to face with sober senses his real conditions of life and his relations with his kind.

The need of a constantly expanding market for its products chases the bourgeoisie over the whole surface of the globe. It must nestle everywhere, settle everywhere, establish connections everywhere.

The bourgeoisie has through its exploitation of the world market given a cosmopolitan character to production and consumption in every country. To the great chagrin of reactionaries, it has drawn from under the feet of industry the national ground on which it stood. All old-established national industries have been destroyed or are daily being destroyed. They are dislodged by new industries, whose introduction becomes a life and death question for all civilised nations, by industries that no longer work up indigenous raw material, but raw material drawn from the remotest zones; industries whose products are consumed, not only at home, but in every quarter of the globe. In place of the old wants, satisfied by the production of the country, we find new wants, requiring for their satisfaction the products of distant lands and climes. In place of the old local and national seclusion and self-sufficiency, we have intercourse in every direction, universal inter-dependence of nations. And as in material, so also in intellectual production. The intellectual creations of individual nations become common property. National one-sidedness and narrow-mindedness become more and more impossible, and from the numerous national and local literatures there arises a world literature.

The bourgeoisie, by the rapid improvement of all instruments of production, by the immensely facilitated means of communication, draws all nations, even the most barbarian, into civilisation. The cheap prices of its commodities are the heavy artillery with which it batters down all Chinese walls, with which it forces the barbarians' intensely obstinate hatred of foreigners to capitulate. It compels all nations, on pain of extinction, to adopt the bourgeois mode of production; it compels them to introduce what it calls civilisation into their midst, i.e., to become bourgeois themselves. In a word, it creates a world after its own image.

The bourgeoisie has subjected the country to the rule of the towns. It has created enormous cities, has greatly increased the urban population as compared with the rural, and has thus rescued a considerable part of the population from the idiocy of rural life. Just as it has made the country dependent on the towns, so it has made barbarian and semi-barbarian countries dependent on the civilised ones, nations of peasants on nations of bourgeois, the East on the West.

More and more the bourgeoisie keeps doing away with the scattered state of the population, of the means of production, and of property. It has agglomerated population, centralised means of production, and has concentrated property in a few hands. The necessary consequence of this was political centralisation. Independent, or but loosely connected provinces, with separate interests, laws, governments and systems of taxation, became lumped together into one nation, with one government, one code of laws, one national class interest, one frontier and one customs tariff.

The bourgeoisie, during its rule of scarce one hundred years, has created more massive and more colossal productive forces than have all preceding generations together. Subjection of nature's forces to man, machinery, application of chemistry to industry and agriculture, steam-navigation, railways, electric telegraphs, clearing of whole continents for cultivation, canalisation of rivers, whole populations conjured out of the ground—what earlier century had even a presentiment that such productive forces slumbered in the lap of social labour?

We see then that the means of production and of exchange, which served as the foundation for the growth of the bourgeoisie, were generated in feudal society. At a certain stage in the development of these means of production and of exchange, the conditions under which feudal society produced and exchanged, the feudal organisation of agriculture and manufacturing industry, in a word, the feudal relations of property became no longer compatible with the already developed productive forces; they became so many fetters. They had to be burst asunder; they were burst asunder.

Into their place stepped free competition, accompanied by a social and political constitution adapted to it, and by the economic and political sway of the bourgeois class.

A similar movement is going on before our own eyes. Modern bourgeois society with its relations of production, of exchange and of property, a society that has conjured up such gigantic means of production and of exchange, is like the sorcerer who is no longer able to control the powers of the nether world whom he has called up by his spells. For many a decade past, the history of industry and commerce is but the history of the revolt of modern productive forces against modern conditions of production, against the property relations that are the conditions for the existence of the bourgeoisie and of its rule. It is enough to mention the commercial crisis that by their periodical return put the existence of the entire bourgeois society on trial, each time more threateningly. In these crises a great part not only of the existing products, but also of the previously created productive forces, are periodically destroyed. In these crises there breaks out an epidemic that, in all earlier epochs, would have seemed an absurdity—the epidemic of over-production. Society suddenly finds itself put back into a state of momentary barbarism; it appears as if a famine, a universal war of devastation had cut off the supply of every means of subsistence; industry and commerce seem to be destroyed. And why? Because there is too much civilisation, too much means of subsistence, too much industry, too much commerce. The productive forces at the disposal of society no longer tend to further the development of the conditions of bourgeois property; on the contrary, they have become too powerful for these conditions, by which they are fettered, and no sooner do they overcome these fetters than they bring disorder into the whole of bourgeois society, endanger the existence of bourgeois property. The conditions of bourgeois society are too narrow to comprise the wealth created by them. And how does the bourgeoisie get over these crises? On the one hand by enforced de-

struction of a mass of productive forces; on the other, by the conquest of new markets, and by the more thorough exploitation of the old ones. That is to say, by paving the way for more extensive and more destructive crises, and by diminishing the means whereby crises are prevented.

The weapons with which the bourgeoisie felled feudalism to the ground are now turned against the bourgeoisie itself.

But not only has the bourgeoisie forged the weapons that bring death to itself; it has also called into existence the men who are to wield those weapons—the modern working class—the proletarians.

In proportion as the bourgeoisie, i.e., capital, is developed, in the same proportion is the proletariat, the modern working class, developed—a class of labourers, who live only so long as they find work, and who find work only so long as their labour increases capital. These labourers, who must sell themselves piecemeal, are a commodity, like every other article of commerce, and are consequently exposed to all the vicissitudes of competition, to all the fluctuations of the market.

Owing to the extensive use of machinery and to division of labour, the work of the proletarians has lost all individual character, and, consequently, all charm for the workman. He becomes an appendage of the machine, and it is only the most simple, most monotonous, and most easily acquired knack, that is required of him. Hence, the cost of production of a workman is restricted, almost entirely, to the means of subsistence that he requires for his maintenance, and for the propagation of his race. But the price of a commodity, and therefore also of labour, is equal to its cost of production. In proportion, therefore, as the repulsiveness of the work increases, the wage decreases. Nay more, in proportion as the use of machinery and division of labour increases, in the same proportion the burden of toil also increases, whether by prolongation of the working hours, by increase of the work exacted in a given time, or by increased speed of the machinery, etc.

Modern industry has converted the little workshop of the patriarchal master into the great factory of the industrial capitalist. Masses of labourers, crowded into the factory, are organised like soldiers. As privates of the industrial army they are placed under the command of a perfect hierarchy of officers and sergeants. Not only are they slaves of the bourgeois class, and of the bourgeois state; they are daily and hourly enslaved by the machine, by the overlooker, and, above all, by the individual bourgeois manufacturer himself. The more openly this despotism proclaims gain to be its end and aim, the more petty, the more hateful and the more embittering it is.

The less the skill and exertion of strength implied in manual labour, in other words, the more modern industry develops, the more is the labour of men superseded by that of women. Differences of age and sex have no longer any distinctive social validity for the working class. All are instruments of labour, more or less expensive to use, according to their age and sex.

No sooner has the labourer received his wages in cash, for the moment escaping exploitation by the manufacturer, than he is set upon by the other portions of the bourgeoisie, the landlord, the shopkeeper, the pawnbroker, etc.

The lower strata of the middle class—the small tradespeople, shopkeepers, and retired tradesmen generally, the handicraftsmen and peasants—all these sink gradually into the proletariat, partly because their diminutive capital does not suffice for the scale on which modern industry is carried on, and is swamped in the competition with the large capitalists, partly because their specialised skill is rendered worthless by new methods of production. Thus the proletariat is recruited from all classes of the population.

The proletariat goes through various stages of development. With its birth begins its struggle with the bourgeoisie. At first the contest is carried on by individual labourers, then by the work people of a factory, then by the operatives of one trade, in one locality, against the individual bourgeois who directly exploits them. They direct their attacks not against the bourgeois conditions of production, but against the instruments of production themselves; they destroy imported wares that compete with their labour, they smash machinery to pieces, they set factories ablaze, they seek to restore by force the vanished status of the workman of the Middle Ages.

At this stage the labourers still form an incoherent mass scattered over the whole country, and broken up by their mutual competition. If anywhere they unite to form more compact bodies, this is not yet the consequence of their own active union, but of the union of the bourgeoisie, which class, in order to attain its own political ends, is compelled to set the whole proletariat in motion, and is moreover still able to do so for a time. At this stage, therefore, the proletarians do not fight their enemies, but the enemies of their enemies, the remnants of absolute monarchy, the landowners, the nonindustrial bourgeois, the petty bourgeoisie. Thus the whole historical movement is concentrated in the hands of the bourgeoisie; every victory so obtained is a victory for the bourgeoisie.

But with the development of industry the proletariat not only increases in number; it becomes concentrated in greater masses, its strength grows, and it feels that strength more. The various interests and conditions of life within the ranks of the proletariat are more and more equalised, in proportion as machinery obliterates all distinctions of labour and nearly everywhere reduces wages to the same low level. The growing competition among the bourgeois, and the resulting commercial crises, make the wages of the workers ever more fluctuating. The unceasing improvement of machinery, ever more rapidly developing, makes their livelihood more and more precarious; the collisions between individual workmen and individual bourgeois take more and more the character of collisions between two classes. Thereupon the workers begin to form combinations (trade unions) against the bourgeoisie; they club together in order to keep up the rate of wages; they found permanent associations in order to make provision beforehand for these occasional revolts. Here and there the contest breaks out into riots.

Now and then the workers are victorious, but only for a time. The real fruit of their battles lies, not in the immediate result, but in the ever expanding union of the workers. This union is furthered by the improved means of communication which are created by modern industry, and which place the workers of different localities in contact with one another. It was just this contact that was needed to centralise the numerous local struggles, all of the same character, into one national struggle between classes. But every class struggle is a political struggle. And that union, to attain which the burghers of the Middle Ages, with their miserable highways, required centuries, the modern proletarians, thanks to railways, achieve in a few years.

This organisation of the proletarians into a class, and consequently into a political party, is continually being upset again by the competition between the workers themselves. But it ever rises up again, stronger, firmer, mightier. It compels legislative recognition of particular interests of the workers, by taking advantage of the divisions among the bourgeoisie itself. Thus the ten-hour bill in England was carried.

Altogether, collisions between the classes of the old society further the course of development of the proletariat in many ways. The bourgeoisie finds itself involved in a constant battle. At first with the aristocracy; later on, with those portions of the bourgeoisie itself whose interests have become antagonistic to the progress of industry; at all times with the bourgeoisie of foreign countries. In all these battles it sees itself compelled to appeal to the proletariat, to ask for its help, and thus, to drag it into the political arena. The bourgeoisie itself, therefore, supplies the proletariat with its own elements of political and general education, in other words, it furnishes the proletariat with weapons for fighting the bourgeoisie.

Further, as we have already seen, entire sections of the ruling classes are, by the advance of industry, precipitated into the proletariat, or are at least threatened in their conditions of existence. These also supply the proletariat with fresh elements of enlightenment and progress.

Finally, in times when the class struggle nears the decisive hour, the process of dissolution going on within the ruling class, in fact within the whole range of old society, assumes such a violent, glaring character, that a small section of the ruling class cuts itself adrift, and joins the revolutionary class, the class that holds the future in its hands. Just as, therefore, at an earlier period, a section of the nobility went over to the bourgeoisie, so now a portion of the bourgeoisie goes over to the proletariat, and in particular, a portion of the bourgeois ideologists, who have raised themselves to the level of comprehending theoretically the historical movement as a whole.

Of all the classes that stand face to face with the bourgeoisie today, the proletariat alone is a really revolutionary class. The other classes decay and finally disappear in the face of modern industry; the proletariat is its special and essential product.

The lower middle class, the small manufacturer, the shopkeeper, the artisan, the peasant, all these fight against the bourgeoisie, to save from extinction their existence as fractions of the middle class. They are therefore not revolutionary, but conservative. Nay more, they are reactionary, for they try to roll back the wheel of history. If by chance they are revolutionary, they are so only in view of their impending transfer into the proletariat; they thus defend not their present, but their future interests; they desert their own standpoint to adopt that of the proletariat.

The "dangerous class," the social scum (*Lumpenproletariat*), that passively rotting mass thrown off by the lowest layers of old society, may, here and there, be swept into the movement by a proletarian revolution; its conditions of life, however, prepare it far more for the part of a bribed tool of reactionary intrigue.

The social conditions of the old society no longer exist for the proletariat. The proletarian is without property; his relation to his wife and children has no longer anything in common with bourgeois family relations; modern industrial labour, modern subjection to capital, the same in England as in France, in America as in Germany, has stripped him of every trace of national character. Law, morality, religion, are to him so many bourgeois prejudices, behind which lurk in ambush just as many bourgeois interests.

All the preceding classes that got the upper hand, sought to fortify their already acquired status by subjecting society at large to their conditions of appropriation. The proletarians cannot become masters of the productive forces of society, except by abolishing their own previous mode of appropriation, and thereby also every other previous mode of appropriation. They have nothing of their own to secure and to fortify; their mission is to destroy all previous securities for, and insurances of, individual property.

All previous historical movements were movements of minorities, or in the interest of minorities. The proletarian movement is the self-conscious, independent movement of the immense majority, in the interest of the immense majority. The proletariat, the lowest stratum of our present society, cannot stir, cannot raise itself up, without the whole super-incumbent strata of official society being sprung into the air.

Though not in substance, yet in form, the struggle of the proletariat with the bourgeoisie is at first a national struggle. The proletariat of each country must, of course, first of all settle matters with its own bourgeoisie.

In depicting the most general phases of the development of the proletariat, we traced the more or less veiled civil war, raging within existing society, up to the point where that war breaks out into open revolution, and where the violent overthrow of the bourgeoisie lays the foundation for the sway of the proletariat.

Hitherto, every form of society has been based, as we have already seen, on the antagonism of oppressing and oppressed classes. But in order to oppress a class, certain conditions must be assured to it under which it can, at least, continue its slavish existence. The serf, in the period of serfdom, raised himself to membership in the commune, just as the petty bourgeois, under the yoke of feudal absolutism, managed to develop into a bourgeois. The modern labourer, on the contrary, instead of rising with the progress of industry, sinks deeper and deeper below the conditions of existence of his own class. He becomes a pauper, and pauperism develops more rapidly than population and wealth. And here it becomes evident, that the bourgeoisie is unfit any longer to be the ruling class in society, and to impose

its conditions of existence upon society as an over-riding law. It is unfit to rule because it is incompetent to assure an existence to its slave within his slavery, because it cannot help letting him sink into such a state, that it has to feed him, instead of being fed by him. Society can no longer live under this bourgeoisie, in other words, its existence is no longer compatible with society.

The essential condition for the existence and sway of the bourgeois class, is the formation and augmentation of capital; the condition for capital is wage-labour. Wage-labour rests exclusively on competition between the labourers. The advance of industry, whose involuntary promoter is the bourgeoisie, replaces the isolation of the labourers, due to competition, by their revolutionary combination, due to association. The development of modern industry, therefore, cuts from under its feet the very foundation on which the bourgeoisie produces and appropriates products. What the bourgeoisie therefore produces, above all, are its own grave-diggers. Its fall and the victory of the proletariat are equally inevitable.

PROLETARIANS AND COMMUNISTS

In what relation do the Communists stand to the proletarians as a whole?

The Communists do not form a separate party opposed to other working class parties.

They have no interests separate and apart from those of the proletariat as a whole.

They do not set up any sectarian principles of their own, by which to shape and mould the proletarian movement.

The Communists are distinguished from the other working class parties by this only: 1. In the national struggles of the proletarians of the different countries, they point out and bring to the front the common interests of the entire proletariat, independently of all nationality. 2. In the various stages of development which the struggle of the working class against the bourgeoisie has to pass through, they always and everywhere represent the interests of the movement as a whole.

The Communists, therefore, are on the one hand, practically, the most advanced and resolute section of the working class parties of every country, that section which pushes forward all others; on the other hand, theoretically, they have over the great mass of the proletariat the advantage of clearly understanding the line of march, the conditions, and the ultimate general results of the proletarian movement.

The immediate aim of the Communists is the same as that of all the other proletarian parties: formation of the proletariat into a class, overthrow of bourgeois supremacy, conquest of political power by the proletariat.

The theoretical conclusions of the Communists are in no way based on ideas or principles that have been invented, or discovered, by this or that would-be universal reformer.

They merely express, in general terms, actual relations springing from an existing class struggle, from a historical movement going on under our very eyes. The abolition of existing property relations is not at all a distinctive feature of Communism.

All property relations in the past have continually been subject to historical change consequent upon the change in historical conditions.

The French Revolution, for example, abolished feudal property in favour of bourgeois property.

The distinguishing feature of Communism is not the abolition of property generally, but the abolition of bourgeois property. But modern bourgeois private property is the final and most complete expression of the system of producing and appropriating products that is based on class antagonisms, on the exploitation of the many by the few.

In this sense, the theory of the Communists may be summed up in the single sentence: Abolition of private property.

We Communists have been reproached with the desire of abolishing the right of personally acquiring property as the fruit of a man's own labour, which property is alleged to be the groundwork of all personal freedom, activity, and independence.

Hard-won, self-acquired, self-earned property! Do you mean the property of the petty artisan and of the small peasant, a form of property that preceded the bourgeois form? There is no need to abolish that; the development of industry has to a great extent already destroyed it, and is still destroying it daily.

Or do you mean modern bourgeois private property?

But does wage-labour create any property for the labourer? Not a bit. It creates capital, i.e., that kind of property which exploits wage-labour, and which cannot increase except upon condition of begetting a new supply of wage-labour for fresh exploitation. Property, in its present form, is based on the antagonism of capital and wage-labour. Let us examine both sides of this antagonism.

To be a capitalist, is to have not only a purely personal, but a social *status* in production. Capital is a collective product, and only by the united action of many members, nay, in the last resort, only by the united action of all members of society, can it be set in motion.

Capital is therefore not a personal, it is a social, power.

When, therefore, capital is converted into common property, into the property of all members of society, personal property is not thereby transformed into social property. It is only the social character of the property that is changed. It loses its class character.

Let us now take wage-labour.

The average price of wage-labour is the minimum wage, i.e., that quantum of the means of subsistence which is absolutely requisite to keep the labourer in bare existence as a labourer. What, therefore, the wage-labourer appropriates by means of his labour, merely suffices to prolong and reproduce a bare existence. We by no means intend to abolish this personal appropriation of the products of labour, an appropriation that is made for the maintenance and reproduction of human life, and that leaves no surplus wherewith to command the labour of others. All that we want to do away with is the miserable character of this appropriation, under which the labourer lives merely to increase capital, and is allowed to live only insofar as the interest of the ruling class requires it.

In bourgeois society, living labour is but a

means to increase accumulated labour. In Communist society, accumulated labour is but a means to widen, to enrich, to promote the existence of the labourer.

In bourgeois society, therefore, the past dominates the present; in Communist society, the present dominates the past. In bourgeois society capital is independent and has individuality, while the living person is dependent and has no individuality.

And the abolition of this state of things is called by the bourgeois, abolition of individuality and freedom! And rightly so. The abolition of bourgeois individuality, bourgeois independence, and bourgeois freedom is undoubtedly aimed at.

By freedom is meant, under the present bourgeois conditions of production, free trade, free selling and buying.

But if selling and buying disappears, free selling and buying disappears also. This talk about free selling and buying, and all the other "brave words" of our bourgeoisie about freedom in general, have a meaning, if any, only in contrast with restricted selling and buying, with the fettered traders of the Middle Ages, but have no meaning when opposed to the Communist abolition of buying and selling, of the bourgeois conditions of production, and of the bourgeoisie itself.

You are horrified at our intending to do away with private property. But in your existing society, private property is already done away with for nine-tenths of the population; its existence for the few is solely due to its non-existence in the hands of those nine-tenths. You reproach us, therefore, with intending to do away with a form of property, the necessary condition for whose existence is the non-existence of any property for the immense majority of society.

In a word, you reproach us with intending to do away with your property. Precisely so; that is just what we intend.

From the moment when labour can no longer be converted into capital, money, or rent, into a social power capable of being monopolised, i.e., from the moment when individual property can no longer be transformed into bourgeois property, into capital, from that moment, you say, individuality vanishes.

You must, therefore, confess that by "individual" you mean no other person than the bourgeois, than the middle-class owner of property. This person must, indeed, be swept out of the way, and made impossible.

Communism deprives no man of the power to appropriate the products of society; all that it does is to deprive him of the power to subjugate the labour of others by means of such appropriation.

It has been objected, that upon the abolition of private property all work will cease, and universal laziness will overtake us.

According to this, bourgeois society ought long ago to have gone to the dogs through sheer idleness; for those of its members who work, acquire nothing, and those who acquire anything, do not work. The whole of this objection is but another expression of the tautology: There can no longer be any wage-labour when there is no longer any capital.

All objections urged against the Communist mode of producing and appropriating material products, have, in the same way, been urged against the Communist modes of producing and appropriating intellectual products. Just as, to the bourgeois, the disappearance of class property is the disappearance of production itself, so the disappearance of class culture is to him identical with the disappearance of all culture.

That culture, the loss of which he laments, is, for the enormous majority, a mere training to act as a machine.

But don't wrangle with us so long as you apply, to our intended abolition of bourgeois property, the standard of your bourgeois notions of freedom, culture, law, etc. Your very ideas are but the outgrowth of the conditions of your bourgeois production and bourgeois property, just as your jurisprudence is but the will of your class made into a law for all, a will whose essential character and direction are determined by the economic conditions of existence of your class.

The selfish misconception that induces you to transform into eternal laws of nature and of reason, the social forms springing from your present mode of production and form of property—historical relations that rise and disappear in the progress of production—this misconception you share with every ruling class that has preceded you. What you see clearly in the case of ancient property, what you admit in the case of feudal property, you are of course forbidden to admit in the case of your own bourgeois form of property.

Abolition of the family! Even the most radical flare up at this infamous proposal of the Communists.

On what foundation is the present family, the bourgeois family, based? On capital, on private gain. In its completely developed form this family exists only among the bourgeoisie. But this state of things finds its complement in the practical absence of the family among the proletarians, and in public prostitution.

The bourgeois family will vanish as a matter of course when its complement vanishes, and both will vanish with the vanishing of capital.

Do you charge us with wanting to stop the exploitation of children by their parents? To this crime we plead guilty.

But, you will say, we destroy the most hallowed of relations, when we replace home education by social.

And your education! Is not that also social, and determined by the social conditions under which you educate, by the intervention of society, direct or indirect, by means of schools, etc.? The Communists have not invented the intervention of society in education; they do but seek to alter the character of that intervention, and to rescue education from the influence of the ruling class.

The bourgeois claptrap about the family and education, about the hallowed co-relation of parent and child, becomes all the more disgusting, the more, by the action of modern industry, all family ties among the proletarians are torn asunder, and their children transformed into simple articles of commerce and instruments of labour.

But you Communists would introduce community of women, screams the whole bourgeoisie in chorus.

The bourgeois sees in his wife a mere instrument of production. He hears that the instruments of production are to be exploited in common, and, naturally, can come to no other conclusion than that the lot of being common to all will likewise fall to the women.

He has not even a suspicion that the real point aimed at is to do away with the status of women as mere instruments of production.

For the rest, nothing is more ridiculous than the virtuous indignation of our bourgeois at the community of women which, they pretend, is to be openly and officially established by the Communists. The Communists have no need to introduce community of women; it has existed almost from time immemorial.

Our bourgeois, not content with having the wives and daughters of their proletarians at their disposal, not to speak of common prostitutes, take the greatest pleasure in seducing each other's wives.

Bourgeois marriage is in reality a system of wives in common and thus, at the most, what the Communists might possibly be reproached with is that they desire to introduce, in substitution for a hypocritically concealed, an openly legalised community of women. For the rest, it is self-evident, that the abolition of the present system of production must bring with it the abolition of the community of women springing from that system, i.e., of prostitution both public and private.

The Communists are further reproached with desiring to abolish countries and nationality.

The workingmen have no country. We cannot take from them what they have not got. Since the proletariat must first of all acquire political supremacy, must rise to be the leading class of the nation, must constitute itself *the* nation, it is, so far, itself national, though not in the bourgeois sense of the word.

National differences and antagonisms between peoples are vanishing gradually from day to day, owing to the development of the bourgeoisie, to freedom of commerce, to the world market, to uniformity in the mode of production and in the conditions of life corresponding thereto.

The supremacy of the proletariat will cause them to vanish still faster. United action, of the leading civilised countries at least, is one of the first conditions for the emancipation of the proletariat.

In proportion as the exploitation of one individual by another is put an end to, the exploitation of one nation by another will also be put an end to. In proportion as the antagonism between classes within the nation vanishes, the hostility of one nation to another will come to an end.

The charges against Communism made from a religious, a philosophical, and, generally, from an ideological standpoint, are not deserving of serious examination.

Does it require deep intuition to comprehend that man's ideas, views, and conceptions, in one word, man's consciousness, changes with every change in the conditions of his material existence, in his social relations, and in his social life?

What else does the history of ideas prove, than that intellectual production changes its character in proportion as material production is changed? The ruling ideas of each age have ever been the ideas of its ruling class.

When people speak of ideas that revolutionise society, they do but express the fact that within the old society the elements of a new one have been created, and that the dissolution of the old ideas keeps even pace with the dissolution of the old conditions of existence.

When the ancient world was in its last throes, the ancient religions were overcome by Christianity. When Christian ideas succumbed in the 18th century to rationalist ideas, feudal society fought its death-battle with the then revolutionary bourgeoisie. The ideas of religious liberty and freedom of conscience, merely gave expression to the sway of free competition within the domain of knowledge.

"Undoubtedly," it will be said, "religion, moral, philosophical and juridical ideas have been modified in the course of historical development. But religion, morality, philosophy, political science, and law, constantly survived this change.

"There are, besides, eternal truths, such as Freedom, Justice, etc., that are common to all states of society. But Communism abolishes eternal truths, it abolishes all religion, and all morality, instead of constituting them on a new basis; it therefore acts in contradiction to all past historical experience."

What does this accusation reduce itself to? The history of all past society has consisted in the development of class antagonisms, antagonisms that assumed different forms at different epochs.

But whatever form they may have taken, one fact is common to all past ages, viz., the exploitation of one part of society by the other. No wonder, then, that the social consciousness of past ages, despite all the multiplicity and variety it displays, moves within certain common forms, or general ideas, which cannot completely vanish except with the total disappearance of class antagonisms.

The Communist revolution is the most radical rupture with traditional property relations; no wonder that its development involves the most radical rupture with traditional ideas.

But let us have done with the bourgeois objections to Communism.

We have seen above, that the first step in the revolution by the working class, is to raise the proletariat to the position of ruling class, to establish democracy.

The proletariat will use its political supremacy to wrest, by degrees, all capital from the bourgeoisie, to centralise all instruments of production in the hands of the state, i.e., of the proletariat organised as the ruling class; and to increase the total of productive forces as rapidly as possible.

Of course, in the beginning, this cannot be effected except by means of despotic inroads on the rights of property, and on the conditions of bourgeois production; by means of measures, therefore, which appear economically insufficient and untenable, but which, in the course of the movement, outstrip themselves, necessitate further inroads upon the old social order, and are unavoidable as a means of entirely revolutionising the mode of production.

These measures will of course be different in different countries.

Nevertheless in the most advanced countries, the following will be pretty generally applicable.

1. Abolition of property in land and application of all rents of land to public purposes.
2. A heavy progressive or graduated income tax.
3. Abolition of all right of inheritance.

4. Confiscation of the property of all emigrants and rebels.

5. Centralisation of credit in the hands of the state, by means of a national bank with state capital and an exclusive monopoly.

6. Centralisation of the means of communication and transport in the hands of the state.

7. Extension of factories and instruments of production owned by the state; the bringing into cultivation of waste lands, and the improvement of the soil generally in accordance with a common plan.

8. Equal obligation of all to work. Establishment of industrial armies, especially for agriculture.

9. Combination of agriculture with manufacturing industries; gradual abolition of the distinction between town and country, by a more equable distribution of the population over the country.

10. Free education for all children in public schools. Abolition of child factory labour in its present form. Combination of education with industrial production, etc.

When, in the course of development, class distinctions have disappeared, and all production has been concentrated in the hands of a vast association of the whole nation, the public power will lose its political character. Political power, properly so called, is merely the organised power of one class for oppressing another. If the proletariat during its contest with the bourgeoisie is compelled, by the force of circumstances, to organise itself as a class; if, by means of a revolution, it makes itself the ruling class, and, as such, sweeps away by force the old conditions of production, then it will, along with these conditions, have swept away the conditions for the existence of class antagonisms, and of classes generally, and will thereby have abolished its own supremacy as a class.

In place of the old bourgeois society, with its classes and class antagonisms, we shall have an association, in which the free development of each is the condition for the free development of all. [The text concludes with a description of the types of socialism and their literature.]

Peter Kropotkin

Peter Kropotkin (1842–1921), a Russian prince who had been trained for the army, became a prominent figure in the proletarian movement of the nineteenth and early twentieth centuries. His first association with workers occurred in 1872 when he joined the International Workingmen's Association at Geneva. This group was not radical enough to fit in with Kropotkin's ideals, however, and he finally associated himself with the anarchist movement. Originally, this group had favored the immediate destruction of the state and the substitution for it of entirely free co-operation among individuals, groups, and areas. Under the influence of Marxian or "scientific socialism," however, anarchism moved gradually in the direction of a communistic society. It was with this trend that Kropotkin associated himself. He believed that a new society could be constructed on the ruins of the state—a society composed of the community voluntarily co-operating on a high moral level and for the common good of all. In 1896 he published his concepts in Anarchism, Its Philosophy and Ideal. In reading the following excerpts from this work note (1) the emphasis he placed on individual development under anarchism, (2) the widespread development of the principle of voluntary federation existing in Europe during the Middle Ages, (3) how these groups carried on voluntarily the functions of the state, (4) the groups who found mutual insurance in the state, (5) the relationship between the rise and fall of the moral level of society, and the rise and fall of governments, (6) his description of society under communism and how it will evolve from smaller into larger units, (7) how he harmonized communism and anarchism, and (8) the evils which governments have produced.

From: ANARCHISM, ITS PHILOSOPHY AND IDEAL

Under the name Anarchy, a new interpretation of the past and present life of society arises, giving at the same time a forecast as regards its future. . . . It seeks the most complete development of individuality combined with the highest development of voluntary association in all its aspects, in all possible degrees, for all imaginable aims; ever changing, ever modified associations which carry in themselves the elements of their durability and constantly assume new forms, which answer best to the multiple aspirations of all. . . .

This conception and ideal of society is certainly not new. On the contrary, when we analyse the history of popular institutions—the clan, the village community, the guild and even the urban commune of the Middle Ages in their first stages,—we find the same popular tendency to constitute a society according to this idea; a tendency, however, always trammelled by domineering minorities. . . .

It was only in the sixteenth century that a mortal blow was dealt to ideas of local independence, to free union and organisation, to federation of all degrees among sovereign groups, possessing all functions now seized upon by the State. It was only then that the alliance between Church and the nascent power of Royalty put an end to an organisation, based on the principle of federation, which had existed from the ninth to the fifteenth century, and which had produced in Europe the great period of free cities of the Middle Ages. . . .

It is now hardly thirty or forty years ago

that we began to reconquer by struggle, by revolt, the first steps of the right of association, that was freely practised by the artisans and the tillers of the soil through the whole of the Middle Ages.

And, already now, Europe is covered by thousands of voluntary associations for study and teaching, for industry, commerce, science, art, literature, exploitation, resistance to exploitation, amusement, serious work, gratification, and self-denial, for all that makes up the life of an active and thinking being. . . . These societies already begin to encroach everywhere on the functions of the State, and strive to substitute free action of volunteers for that of a centralised State. . . .

And when we mark the progress already accomplished in that direction, in spite of and against the State, which tries by all means to maintain its supremacy of recent origin; when we see how voluntary societies invade everything and are only impeded in their development by the State, we are forced to recognise a powerful *tendency*, a latent force in modern society. And we ask ourselves this question: If, five, ten, or twenty years hence—it matters little—the workers succeed by revolt in destroying the said mutual insurance society of landlords, bankers, priests, judges, and soldiers; if the people become masters of their destiny for a few months, and lay hands on the riches they have created, and which belong to them by right—will they really begin to reconstitute that blood-sucker, the State? Or will they not rather try to organise from the simple

Peter Kropotkin, *Anarchism, Its Philosophy and Ideal, Freedom Pamphlets*, no. 10, n.p., 1896.

to the complex, according to mutual agreement and to the infinitely varied, ever-changing needs of each locality, in order to secure the possession of those riches for themselves, to mutually guarantee one another's life, and to produce what will be found necessary for life?

Will they follow the dominant tendency of the century, towards decentralisation, home rule, and free agreement; or will they march contrary to this tendency and strive to reconstitute demolished authority? . . .

It is often said that Anarchists live in a world of dreams to come, and do not see the things which happen today. . . .

Far from living in a world of visions and imagining men better than they are, we see them as they are; and that is why we affirm that the best of men is made essentially bad by the exercise of authority. . . .

Oh, the beautiful utopia, the lovely Christmas dream we can make as soon as we admit that those who govern represent a superior caste, and have hardly any or no knowledge of simple mortals' weaknesses! . . . All the science of government, imagined by those who govern, is imbibed with these utopias. But we know men too well to dream such dreams. We have not two measures for the virtues of the governed and those of the governors; we know that we ourselves are not without faults and that the best of us would soon be corrupted by the exercise of power. We take men for what they are worth—and that is why we hate the government of man by man, and that we work with all our might—perhaps not strong enough—to put an end to it.

But it is not enough to destroy. We must also know how to build, and it is owing to not having thought about it that the masses have always been led astray in all their revolutions. After having demolished they abandoned the care of reconstruction to the middle-class people, who possessed a more or less precise conception of what they wished to realise, and who consequently reconstituted authority to their own advantage.

That is why Anarchy, when it works to destroy authority in all its aspects, when it demands that abrogation of laws and the abolition of the mechanism that serves to impose them, when it refuses all hierarchical organisation and preaches free agreement—at the same time strives to maintain and enlarge the precious kernel of social customs without which no human or animal society can exist. Only, instead of demanding that those social customs should be maintained through the authority of a few, it demands it from the continued action of all.

Communist customs and institutions are of absolute necessity for society, not only to solve economic difficulties, but also to maintain and develop social customs that bring men in contact with one another; they must be looked to for establishing such relations between men that the interest of each should be the interest of all; and this alone can unite men instead of dividing them. . . .

As to the impotence of repression—it is sufficiently demonstrated by the disorder of present society and by the necessity of a revolution that we all desire or feel inevitable. . . .

All that was an element of progress in the past or an instrument of moral and intellectual improvement of the human race is due *to the practice of mutual aid,* to the customs that recognised the equality of men and brought them to ally, to unite, to associate for the purpose of producing and consuming, to unite for purposes of defence, to federate and to recognise no other judges in fighting out their differences than the arbitrators they took from their own midst.

Each time these institutions, issued from popular genius, when it had reconquered its liberty for a moment,—each time these institutions developed in a new direction, the moral level of society, its material well-being, its liberty, its intellectual progress, and the affirmation of individual originality made a step in advance. And, on the contrary, each time that in the course of history, whether following upon a foreign conquest, or whether by developing authoritarian prejudices men become more and more divided into governors and governed, exploiters and exploited, the moral level fell, the well-being of the masses decreased in order to insure riches to a few, and the spirit of the age declined.

History teaches us this, and from this lesson

we have learned to have confidence in free Communist institutions to raise the moral level of societies, debased by the practice of authority.

Today we live side by side without knowing one another. We come together at meetings on an election day; we listen to the lying or fanciful professions of faith of a candidate, and we return home. The State has the care of all questions of public interest; the State alone has the function of seeing that we do not harm the interests of our neighbour, and, if it fails in this, of punishing us in order to repair the evil. . . .

In a Communist society such estrangement, such confidence in an outside force, could not exist. Communist organisation cannot be left to be constructed by legislative bodies called parliaments, municipal or communal councils. It must be the work of all, a natural growth, a product of the constructive genius of the great mass. Communism cannot be imposed from above; it could not live even for a few months if the constant and daily co-operation of all did not uphold it. It must be free.

It cannot exist without creating a continual contact between all for the thousands and thousands of common transactions; it cannot exist without creating local life, independent in the smallest unities—the block of houses, the street, the district, the commune. It would not answer its purpose if it did not cover society with a network of thousands of associations to satisfy its thousand needs: the necessaries of life, articles of luxury, of study, enjoyment, amusements. And such associations cannot remain narrow and local; they must necessarily tend (as is already the case with learned societies, cyclist clubs, humanitarian societies, and the like) to become international. . . .

This, then, is the form—sociable institution —of which we ask the development of the spirit of harmony that Church and State had undertaken to impose on us—with the sad result we know only too well. And these remarks contain our answer to those who affirm that Communism and Anarchy cannot go together. They are, you see, a necessary complement to one another. The most powerful development of individuality of individual

originality—as one of our comrades has so well said,—can be produced only when the first needs of food and shelter are satisfied; when the struggle for existence against the forces of nature has been simplified; when man's time is no longer taken up entirely by the meaner side of daily subsistence,—then, only, his intelligence, his artistic taste, his inventive spirit, his genius, can develop freely and ever strive to greater achievements.

Communism is the best basis for individual development and freedom; not that individualism which drives man to the war of each against all—this is the only one known up till now—but that which represents the full expansion of man's faculties, the superior development of what is original in him, the greatest fruitfulness of intelligence, feeling and will.

Such being our ideal, what does it matter to us that it cannot be realised at once! . . .

It is evident that so profound a revolution producing itself in people's minds cannot be confined to the domain of ideas without expanding to the sphere of action. . . . Consequently, the new ideas have provoked a multitude of acts of revolt in all countries, under all possible conditions: first, individual revolt against Capital and State; then collective revolt—strikes and working-class insurrections—both preparing, in men's minds as in actions, a revolt of the masses, a revolution. . . .

And, during this same period, massacres, wholesale and retail, organised by *governments*, follow their regular course. . . . What a terrible indictment the balance-sheet of the sufferings endured by workers and their friends, during this last quarter of a century, would be! What a multitude of horrible details that are unknown to the public at large! . . .

As long as society accepts the law of retaliation, as long as religion and law, the barrack and the law-courts, the prison and industrial penal servitude, the press and the school continue to teach supreme contempt for the life of the individual,—do not ask the rebels against that society to respect it. It would be exacting a degree of gentleness and magnanimity from them infinitely superior to that of the whole of society.

If you wish, like us, that the entire liberty of the individual and, consequently, his life be respected, you are necessarily brought to repudiate the government of man by man, whatever shape it assumes; you are forced to accept the principles of Anarchy that you have spurned so long. You must then search with us the forms of society that can best realise that ideal and put an end to all the violence that arouses your indignation.

George Bernard Shaw

In 1883 a group of English intellectuals who were interested in socialism founded the Fabian Society. They were not, however, sympathetic with the assertion of Marxian socialists that class conflict and violence were inevitable prerequisites to the triumph of socialism, but rather they believed that by parliamentary procedure and through evolutionary growth the transition from capitalism to socialism could be made. At the outset they sought to educate the public through lectures and pamphlets, but in the early part of the twentieth century they turned to the working classes for organized support. Thus, when the English Labour Party was formed in 1906, the Fabian Society became a constituent member. However, the Fabians never emphasized their program in terms of a class movement, and as a consequence the English Labour Party has been able to attract support from all classes in British society. In 1884 the British playright George Bernard Shaw (1856–1950) joined the society; he wrote the following report in 1896. In reading it note (1) the object of the Fabian Society, (2) the methods it advocated in achieving its objective, (3) its attitude toward those who expected a great historical crisis in the socialist movement, (4) what the Fabians meant by socialism, (5) their attitude toward individualism and individual enterprise, and (6) the ideas which Shaw specifically repudiated.

From: REPORT ON THE FABIAN POLICY

I. THE MISSION OF THE FABIANS

The object of the Fabian Society is to persuade the English people to make their political constitution thoroughly democratic and so to socialize their industries as to make the livelihood of the people entirely independent of private capitalism.

The Fabian Society endeavors to pursue its Socialist and Democratic objects with complete singleness of aim. For example:

It has no distinctive opinions on the Marriage Question, Religion, Art, abstract Economics, historic Evolution, Currency, or any other subject than its own special business of practical Democracy and Socialism.

It brings all the pressure and persuasion in its power to bear on existing forces, caring nothing by what name any party calls itself, or what principles, Socialist or other, it professes, but having regard solely to the tendency of its actions, supporting those which

Report on Fabian Policy and Resolutions Presented by the Fabian Society to the . . . [Second International], 1896, Fabian Tract no. 70 in The Fabian Society, *Fabian Tracts. . . .* London, n.d. (1900?).

make for Socialism and Democracy, and opposing those which are reactionary.

It does not propose that the practical steps towards Social-Democracy should be carried out by itself, or by any other specially organized society or party.

It does not ask the English people to join the Fabian Society.

II. FABIAN ELECTORAL TACTICS

The Fabian Society does not claim to be the people of England, or even the Socialist party, and therefore does not seek direct political representation by putting forward Fabian candidates at elections. But it loses no opportunity of influencing elections and inducing constituencies to select Socialists as their candidates. . . .

III. FABIAN TOLERATION

The Fabian Society, far from holding aloof from other bodies, urges its members to lose no opportunity of joining them and permeating them with Fabian ideas as far as possible. Almost all organizations and movements contain elements making for Socialism, no matter how remote the sympathies and intentions of their founders may be from those of the Socialists. On the other hand, unintentionally reactionary proposals are constantly being brought forward in Socialist bodies. Fabians are therefore encouraged to join all other organizations, Socialist or non-Socialist, in which Fabian work can be done.

IV. FABIAN CONSTITUTIONALISM

The Fabian Society is perfectly constitutional in its attitude; and its methods are those usual in political life in England.

The Fabian Society accepts the conditions imposed on it by human nature and by the national character and political circumstances of the English people. It sympathizes with the ordinary citizen's desire for gradual, peaceful changes, as against revolution, conflict with the army and police, and martyrdom. It recognizes the fact that Social-Democracy is not the whole of the working-class program, and that every separate measure towards the socialization of industry will have to compete for precedence with numbers of other reforms. It therefore does not believe that the moment will ever come when the whole of Socialism will be staked on the issue of a single General Election or a single Bill in the House of Commons, as between the proletariat on one side and the proprietariat on the other. Each installment of Social-Democracy will only be a measure among other measures, and will have to be kept to the front by an energetic Socialist section. The Fabian Society therefore begs those Socialists who are looking forward to a sensational historical crisis, to join some other Society.

V. FABIAN DEMOCRACY

Democracy, as understood by the Fabian Society, means simply the control of the administration by freely elected representatives of the people. The Fabian Society energetically repudiates all conceptions of Democracy as a system by which the technical work of government administration, and the appointment of public officials, shall be carried on by referendum or any other form of direct popular decision. Such arrangements may be practical in a village community, but not in the complicated industrial civilizations which are ripening for Social-Democracy. When the House of Commons is freed from the veto of the House of Lords and thrown open to candidates from all classes by an effective system of Payment of Representatives and a more rational method of election, the British parliamentary system will be, in the opinion of the Fabian Society, a first-rate practical instrument of democratic government.

Democracy, as understood by the Fabian Society, makes no political distinction between men and women.

VI. FABIAN COMPROMISE

The Fabian Society, having learnt from experience that Socialists cannot have their own way in everything any more than other people, recognizes that in a Democratic community Compromise is a necessary condition of political progress.

VII. FABIAN SOCIALISM

Socialism, as understood by the Fabian Society, means the organization and conduct of the necessary industries of the country, and the appropriation of all forms of economic rent of land and capital by the nation as a whole, through the most suitable public authorities, parochial, municipal, provincial, or central.

The Socialism advocated by the Fabian Society is State Socialism exclusively. The foreign friends of the Fabian Society must interpret this declaration in view of the fact that since England now possesses an elaborate democratic State machinery, graduated from the Parish Council or Vestry up to the central Parliament, and elected under a franchise which enables the working-class vote to overwhelm all others, the opposition which exists in the Continental monarchies between the State and the people does not hamper English Socialists. For example, the distinction made between State Socialism and Social-Democracy in Germany, where the municipalities and other local bodies are closed against the working classes, has no meaning in England. The difficulty in England is not to secure more political power for the people, but to persuade them to make any sensible use of the power they already have.

VIII. FABIAN INDIVIDUALISM

The Fabian Society does not suggest that the State should monopolize industry as against private enterprise or individual initiative further than may be necessary to make the livelihood of the people and their access to the sources of production completely independent of both. The freedom of individuals to test the social value of new inventions; to initiate improved methods of production; to anticipate and lead public enterprise in catering for new social wants; to practise all arts, crafts, and professions independently; in short, to complete the social organization by adding the resources of private activity and judgment to those of public routine, is, subject to the above conditions, as highly valued by the Fabian Society as Freedom of Speech, Freedom of the Press, or any other article in the charter of popular liberties.

IX. FABIAN FREEDOM OF THOUGHT

The Fabian Society strenuously maintains its freedom of thought and speech with regard to the errors of Socialist authors, economists, leaders, and parties, no less than to those of its opponents. For instance, it insists on the necessity of maintaining as critical an attitude towards Marx and Lassalle, some of whose views must by this time be discarded as erroneous or obsolete, as these eminent Socialists themselves maintained towards their predecessors, St. Simon and Robert Owen. . . .

XII. FABIAN NATURAL PHILOSOPHY

The Fabian Society endeavors to rouse social compunction by making the public conscious of the evil condition of society under the present system. This it does by the collection and publication of authentic and impartial statistical tracts, compiled, not from the works of Socialists, but from official sources. The first volume of Karl Marx's *Das Kapital*, which contains an immense mass of carefully verified facts concerning modern capitalistic civilization, and practically nothing about Socialism, is probably the most successful propagandist work ever published. The Fabian Society, in its endeavors to continue the work of Marx in this direction, has found that the guesses made by Socialists at the condition of the people almost invariably flatter the existing system instead of, as might be suspected, exaggerating its evils. The Fabian Society therefore concludes that in the natural philosophy of Socialism, light is a more important factor than heat.

XIII. FABIAN REPUDIATIONS

The Fabian Society discards such phrases as "the abolition of the wage system," which can only mislead the public as to the aims of Socialism. Socialism does not involve the abolition of wages, but the establishment of standard allowances for the maintenance of all workers by the community in its own service, as an alternative to wages fixed by the competition of destitute men and women for private employment, as well as to commercial profits, commissions, and all other speculative and competitive forms of remuneration. In short, the Fabian Society, far from desiring to abolish wages, wishes to secure them for everybody.

The Fabian Society resolutely opposes all pretensions to hamper the socialization of industry with equal wages, equal hours of labor, equal official status, or equal authority for everyone. Such conditions are not only impracticable, but incompatible with the equality of subordination to the common interest which is fundamental in modern Socialism.

The Fabian Society steadfastly discountenances all schemes for securing to any person, or any group of persons, "the entire product of their labor." It recognizes that wealth is social in its origin and must be social in its distribution, since the evolution of industry has made it impossible to distinguish the particular contribution that each person makes to the common product, or to ascertain its value.

The Fabian Society desires to offer to all projectors and founders of Utopian communities in South America, Africa, and other remote localities, its apologies for its impatience of such adventures. To such projectors, and all patrons of schemes for starting similar settlements and workshops at home, the Society announces emphatically that it does not believe in the establishment of Socialism by private enterprise.

XIV. FINALLY

The Fabian Society does not put Socialism forward as a panacea for the ills of human society, but only for those produced by defective organization of industry and by a radically bad distribution of wealth.

American Labor Leaders

Since medieval times employers throughout Europe had been successful in influencing the state to prohibit the organization of workers for collective action. Labor was forced to submit to these restrictions until the beginning of the nineteenth century, but with the tremendous increase in their numbers resulting from the Industrial Revolution, the workers gradually succeeded in having this handicap removed. The earliest combinations of laborers took the form of trade unions and were formed primarily for economic rather than for political aims. It was this pattern that was followed by labor in the United States where local trade unions were first formed in the early years of the last century. In 1850 American printers formed the first national trade union and their example was quickly followed by other trades. In the eighties these unions formed the American Federation of Labor which has consistently adhered to the original policy of trade unionism regarding political action. In reading the following selections from statements by prominent American labor leaders note (1) the attitude expressed toward capital, (2) the program which unions support, (3) Samuel Gompers' position on industrial as opposed to trade unions, (4) his warning to labor in its use of the sympathetic strike, (5) wherein the strength of labor lies, and (6) the issue of political partisanship within the American Federation of Labor.

Reprinted from David Harris and Easton Rothwell, eds., *Selected Documents of Social Reform and Revolution,* Stanford University Press, Stanford University, 1939, 21–25, with the permission of the editors and of the publishers.

STATEMENTS FROM AMERICAN LABOR LEADERS

THE PURPOSE OF UNIONS: SELECTIONS FROM JOHN MITCHELL, *ORGANIZED LABOR, ITS PROBLEMS, PURPOSES, AND IDEALS*, 1903

The average wage earner has made up his mind that he must remain a wage earner. He has given up the hope of a kingdom to come, where he himself will be a capitalist, and he asks that the reward for his work be given to him as a workingman. Singly, he has been too weak to enforce his just demands and he has sought strength in union and has associated himself into labor organizations.

Labor unions are *for* the workman, but *against* no one. They are not hostile to employers, not inimical to the interests of the general public. They are for a class, because that class exists and has class interests, but the unions did not create and do not perpetuate the class or its interests and do not seek to evoke a class conflict.

There is no necessary hostility between labor and capital. Neither can do without the other; each has evolved from the other. Capital is labor saved and materialized; the power to labor is in itself a form of capital. There is not even a necessary, fundamental antagonism between the laborer and the capitalist. Both are men, with the virtues and vices of men, and each wishes at times more than his fair share. Yet, broadly considered, the interest of the one is the interest of the other, and the prosperity of the one is the prosperity of the other. . . .

The trade unions stand for the principle of united action and for the policy of a living wage earned under fair living conditions. In union there is strength, justice, and moderation; in disunion, nothing but an alternating humility and insolence, a state of industrial despotism tempered by futile and passing revolutions. Unions stand for the right of association, self-government, and free speech, for the dignity and self-respect of the workman, for the mutual esteem of capitalist and wage earner, and for a wide, far-seeing, open-minded, democratic conduct of industry. . . .

PRESIDENT GOMPERS ON INDUSTRIAL UNIONISM, 1903

The attempt to force the trade unions into what has been termed industrial organization is perversive to the history of the labor movement, runs counter to the best conceptions of the toilers' interests now, and is sure to lead to the confusion which precedes dissolution and disruption. It is time for the American Federation of Labor solemnly to call a halt. . . .

The advocates of the so-called industrial system of labor organizations urge that an effective strike can be conducted only when all workmen, regardless of trade, calling, or occupation, are affected.

That this is not borne out by the history of strikes in the whole labor movement is easily demonstrable. Though here and there such strikes have been temporarily successful, in the main they have been fraught with injury to all. The so-called industrial system of organization implies sympathetic strikes, and these time and experience have demonstrated as a general proposition should be discarded, while strikes of particular trades or callings have had the largest number of successes and the minimum of defeats. Quite apart from these considerations, however, are the splendid advantages obtained by the trade unions without the necessity of strikes or the interruption of industry. No one will attempt to say that a sympathetic strike shall under no circumstances occur. Under certain conditions it may be not only justifiable but practical and successful, even if only as an emphatic protest against a great injustice or wrong; but generally and normally considered, such strikes cannot be of advantage.

One feature in connection with a system of industrial organization and its concomitant, the sympathetic strike, has been overlooked. By its methods any one of our international organizations could be financially drained and actually ruined in a very brief period in an effort to sustain the members involved; while, on the other hand, in a well-formulated trade union movement, a large number of men of different crafts, belonging to their own international trade unions, could be indefinitely sustained financially and victory achieved. At least the organizations could be maintained, not only to continue that battle, but to take up the cudgels in defense of their members elsewhere.

THE VALUE OF ECONOMIC ORGANIZATION: REPORT OF THE EXECUTIVE COUNCIL, AMERICAN FEDERATION OF LABOR PROCEEDINGS, 1914

The principle that has directed and controlled all policies of the A. F. of L. is that organization in industry is the key to the betterment of conditions for the workers. Organization for the purpose of making united effort to remedy wrongs that affect the work and the lives of all has been the instrumentality that has brought cheer and hope and betterment to the workers.

Economic organization gives power—power to protect the workers against industrial exploitation and injustice; power to secure for them opportunities for development; power to secure for them things that will make life sane, whole, and good; power to bring into their lives something of beauty and pleasure; power to secure political representation for their ideals and recognition of their demands in legislation. The influence of organization in industry and its infinite number of contacts with other organizations constitute an intricate force that is the most powerful single force in society. The power of Labor is commensurate with its unity, solidarity and federation.

Economic organization is that upon which we justly concentrate our thought and effort. When economic organization is achieved, every other good thing becomes possible for the workers. But because of the great power attaching to this agency, many other movements or forces seek to destroy or to use them. For this reason, the A. F. of L. early adopted the policy of avoiding entangling alliances. This policy has been consistently pursued during all these years. But with great success and increased growth come additional power. Many and tempting will be the avenues for activity and the associations open to the A. F. of L. Increasingly difficult will it be to distinguish the things which are most important and vital for the continuous development of the Federation—the things which make for life rather than mere power. Ever must be held up the policy, the organization—federation, that is the thing.

POLITICAL NON-PARTISANSHIP: FROM AN A. F. OF L. PAMPHLET, *FORTY YEARS OF ACTION*

The partisanship of Labor is a partisanship of principle. The American Federation of Labor is not partisan to a political party, it is partisan to a principle, the principle of equal rights and human freedom. We, therefore, repeat: Stand faithfully by our friends and *elect* them. Oppose our enemies and *defeat* them; whether they be candidates for President, for Congress, or for other offices; whether Executive, Legislative, or Judicial.

The experiences and results attained through the non-partisan political policy of the American Federation of Labor cover a generation. They indicate that through its application the workers of America have secured a much larger measure of fundamental legislation, establishing their rights, safeguarding their interests, protecting their welfare and opening the doors of opportunity than have been secured by the workers of any other country. . . .

In these nearly forty years of actively taking part in the making of the economic and political history of this nation our Federation has witnessed the birth, the struggle for life, and the passing away of all sorts of political movements designed to save the republic from varying degrees of destruction; it has been coddled and mauled, petted and cajoled by the cohorts of particular brands of Liberty; it has been assailed by isms and ologies without number; it has been baited with sugared doses for economic chills and political fevers; it has heard the dirge and attended the last sad rites over many a promising political corpse. It has been courted by all the allurements of the partisan politician; all of the thralling visions of the emotional enthusiast have been pictured for its enticement; all the arts of the crafty self-seeker have been practiced to tempt it. But, despite all these, the American Federation of Labor has never been swerved from its non-partisan political course. . . .

Pope Leo XIII

Pope Leo XIII (1810–1903) became the supreme head of the Roman Catholic Church in 1878, at a time when the problems created for labor by the Industrial Revolution were attracting the attention of the church and the state, as well as of men like Marx and Engels. In 1891 Leo issued his encyclical, Rerum Novarum, written to relate Catholic principles to the political and social problems of his day. The relatively liberal position taken by Leo XIII on these matters earned for him the title of the "workingmen's pope." In reading the following selections from this encyclical, note (1) the problem which Leo proposed to resolve, (2) the church's attitude toward private property, (3) the importance of private property to the family relationship, (4) the position taken on the issue of the class conflict and on the distribution of wealth, (5) the part the church played in remedying the problem, (6) the role the state should take in regulating economic problems, and (7) the authorities whom Leo cited.

From: RERUM NOVARUM

Once the passion for revolutionary change was aroused—a passion long disturbing governments—it was bound to follow sooner or later that eagerness for change would pass from the political sphere over into the related field of economics. In fact, new developments in industry, new techniques striking out on new paths, changed relations of employer and employee, abounding wealth among a very small number and destitution among the masses, increased self-reliance on the part of workers as well as a closer bond of union with one another, and, in addition to all this, a decline in morals have caused conflict to break forth.

The momentous nature of the questions involved in this conflict is evident from the fact that it keeps men's minds in anxious expectation, occupying the talents of the learned, the discussions of the wise and experienced, the assemblies of the people, the judgment of lawmakers, and the deliberations of rulers, so that now no topic more strongly holds men's interests.

Therefore, Venerable Brethren, with the cause of the Church and the common welfare before Us, We have thought it advisable, following Our custom on other occasions when We issued to you the Encyclicals *On Political Power, On Human Liberty, On the Christian Constitution of States,* and others of similar nature, which seemed opportune to refute erroneous opinions, that We ought to do the same now, and for the same reasons, *On the Condition of Workers.* We have on occasion touched more than once upon this subject. In this Encyclical, however, consciousness of Our Apostolic office admonishes Us to treat the entire question thoroughly, in order that the principles may stand out in clear light, and the conflict may thereby be brought to an end as required by truth and equity.

The problem is difficult to resolve and is not free from dangers. It is hard indeed to fix the boundaries of the rights and duties within which the rich and the proletariat—those who furnish material things and those who furnish work—ought to be restricted in relation to each other. The controversy is truly dangerous, for in various places it is being twisted by

Pope Leo XIII, *Rerum Novarum: Encyclical Letter on the Condition of Labor,* Washington, D. C., n.d., 5–7; 8–9; 10–15; 17–18; 21–27.

turbulent and crafty men to pervert judgment as to truth and seditiously to incite the masses.

In any event, We see clearly, and all are agreed that the poor must be speedily and fittingly cared for, since the great majority of them live undeservedly in miserable and wretched conditions.

After the old trade guilds had been destroyed in the last century, and no protection was substituted in their place, and when public institutions and legislation had cast off traditional religious teaching, it gradually came about that the present age handed over the workers, each alone and defenseless, to the inhumanity of employers and the unbridled greed of competitors. A devouring usury, although often condemned by the Church, but practiced nevertheless under another form by avaricious and grasping men, has increased the evil; and in addition the whole process of production as well as trade in every kind of goods has been brought almost entirely under the power of a few, so that a very few rich and exceedingly rich men have laid a yoke almost of slavery on the unnumbered masses of non-owning workers.

To cure this evil, the Socialists, exciting the envy of the poor toward the rich, contend that it is necessary to do away with private possession of goods and in its place to make the goods of individuals common to all, and that the men who preside over a municipality or who direct the entire State should act as administrators of these goods. They hold that, by such a transfer of private goods from private individuals to the community, they can cure the present evil through dividing wealth and benefits equally among the citizens.

But their program is so unsuited for terminating the conflict that it actually injures the workers themselves. Moreover, it is highly unjust, because it violates the rights of lawful owners, perverts the functions of the State, and throws governments into utter confusion.

Clearly the essential reason why those who engage in any gainful occupation undertake labor, and at the same time the end to which workers immediately look, is to procure property for themselves and to retain it by individual right as theirs and as their very own.

When the worker places his energy and his labor at the disposal of another, he does so for the purpose of getting the means necessary for livelihood. He seeks in return for the work done, accordingly, a true and full right not only to demand his wage but to dispose of it as he sees fit. Therefore, if he saves something by restricting expenditures and invests his savings in a piece of land in order to keep the fruit of his thrift more safe, a holding of this kind is certainly nothing else than his wage under a different form; and on this account land which the worker thus buys is necessarily under his full control as much as the wage which he earned by his labor. But, as is obvious, it is clearly in this that the ownership of movable and immovable goods consists. Therefore, inasmuch as the Socialists seek to transfer the goods of private persons to the community at large, they make the lot of all wage earners worse, because in abolishing the freedom to dispose of wages they take away from them by this very act the hope and the opportunity of increasing their property and of securing advantages for themselves.

But, what is of more vital concern, they propose a remedy openly in conflict with justice, inasmuch as nature confers on man the right to possess things privately as his own. . . .

The fact that God gave the whole human race the earth to use and enjoy cannot indeed in any manner serve as an objection against private possessions. For God is said to have given the earth to mankind in common, not because He intended indiscriminate ownership of it by all, but because He assigned no part to anyone in ownership, leaving the limits of private possessions to be fixed by the industry of men and the institutions of peoples. Yet, however the earth may be apportioned among private owners, it does not cease to serve the common interest of all, inasmuch as no living being is sustained except by what the fields bring forth. Those who lack resources supply labor, so that it can be truly affirmed that the entire scheme of securing a livelihood consists in the labor which a person expends either on his own land or in some working occupation, the compensation for which is drawn ultimately from no other source than from the varied products of the earth and is exchanged for them.

For this reason it also follows that private possessions are clearly in accord with nature. The earth indeed produces in great abundance the things to preserve and, especially, to perfect life, but of itself it could not produce them without human cultivation and care. Moreover, since man expends his mental energy and his bodily strength in procuring the goods of nature, by this very act he appropriates that part of physical nature to himself which he has cultivated. On it he leaves impressed, as it were, a kind of image of his person, so that it must be altogether just that he should possess that part as his very own and that no one in any way should be permitted to violate his right. . . .

It is a most sacred law of nature that the father of a family see that his offspring are provided with all the necessities of life, and nature even prompts him to desire to provide and to furnish his children, who, in fact reflect and in a sense continue his person, with the means of decently protecting themselves against harsh fortune in the uncertainties of life. He can do this surely in no other way than by owning fruitful goods to transmit by inheritance to his children. As already noted, the family like the State is by the same token a society in the strictest sense of the term, and it is governed by its own proper authority, namely, by that of the father. Wherefore, assuming, of course, that those limits be observed which are fixed by its immediate purpose, the family assuredly possesses rights, at least equal with those of civil society, in respect to choosing and employing the things necessary for its protection and its just liberty. We say "at least equal" because, inasmuch as domestic living together is prior both in thought and in fact to uniting into a polity, it follows that its rights and duties are also prior and more in conformity with nature. But if citizens, if families, after becoming participants in common life and society, were to experience injury in a commonwealth instead of help, impairment of their rights instead of protection, society would be something to be repudiated rather than to be sought for.

To desire, therefore, that the civil power should enter arbitrarily into the privacy of homes is a great and pernicious error. If a family perchance is in such extreme difficulty and is so completely without plans that it is entirely unable to help itself, it is right that the distress be remedied by public aid, for each individual family is a part of the community. Similarly, if anywhere there is a grave violation of mutual rights within the family walls, public authority shall restore to each his right: for this is not usurping the rights of citizens, but protecting and confirming them with just and due care. Those in charge of public affairs, however, must stop here: nature does not permit them to go beyond these limits. Paternal authority is such that it can be neither abolished nor absorbed by the State, because it has the same origin in common with that of man's own life. "Children are a part of their father," and, as it were, a kind of extension of the father's person; and, strictly speaking, not through themselves, but through the medium of the family society in which they are begotten, they enter into and participate in civil society. And for the very reason that children "are by nature part of their father . . . before they have the use of free will, they are kept under the care of their parents." Inasmuch as the Socialists, therefore, disregard care by parents and in its place introduce care by the State, they act *against natural justice* and dissolve the structure of the home.

And apart from the injustice involved, it is also only too evident what turmoil and disorder would obtain among all classes; and what a harsh and odious enslavement of citizens would result! The door would be open to mutual envy, detraction, and dissension. If incentives to ingenuity and skill in individual persons were to be abolished, the very fountains of wealth would necessarily dry up; and the equality conjured up by the Socialist imagination would, in reality, be nothing but uniform wretchedness and meanness for one and all, without distinction.

From all these considerations, it is perceived that the fundamental principle of Socialism which would make all possessions public property is to be utterly rejected because it injures the very ones whom it seeks to help, contravenes the natural rights of individual persons, and throws the functions of the State and public peace into confusion. Let it be regarded, therefore, as established that in seeking help for the masses this principle before all is to be considered as basic, namely, that private ownership must be preserved inviolate. . . .

It is a capital evil with respect to the question We are discussing to take for granted that the one class of society is of itself hostile to the other, as if nature had set rich and poor against each other to fight fiercely in implacable war. This is so abhorrent to reason and truth that the exact opposite is true; for just as in the human body the different members harmonize with one another, whence arises that disposition of parts and proportion in the human figure rightly called symmetry, so likewise nature has commanded in the case of the State that the two classes mentioned should agree harmoniously and should properly form equally balanced counterparts to each other. Each needs the other completely: neither capital can do without labor, nor labor without capital. Concord begets beauty and order in things. Conversely, from perpetual strife there must arise disorder accompanied by bestial cruelty. But for putting an end to conflict and for cutting away its very roots, there is wondrous and multiple power in Christian institutions.

And first and foremost, the entire body of religious teaching and practice, of which the Church is the interpreter and guardian, can pre-eminently bring together and unite the rich and the poor by recalling the two classes of society to their mutual duties, and in particular to those duties which derive from justice.

Among these duties the following concern the poor and the workers: To perform entirely and conscientiously whatever work has been voluntarily and equitably agreed upon; not in any way to injure the property or to harm the person of employers; in protecting their own interests, to refrain from violence and never to engage in rioting; not to associate with vicious men who craftily hold out exaggerated hopes and make huge promises, a course usually ending in vain regrets and in the destruction of wealth.

The following duties, on the other hand, concern rich men and employers: Workers are not to be treated as slaves; justice demands that the dignity of human personality be respected in them, ennobled as it has been through what we call the Christian character. If we hearken to natural reason and to Christian philosophy, gainful occupations are not a mark of shame to man, but rather of respect, as they provide him with an honorable means of supporting life. It is shameful and inhuman, however, to use men as things for gain and to put no more value on them than what they are worth in muscle and energy. Likewise it is enjoined that the religious interests and the spiritual well-being of the workers receive proper consideration. Wherefore, it is the duty of employers to see that the worker is free for adequate periods to attend to his religious obligations; not to expose anyone to corrupting influences or the enticements of sin, and in no way to alienate him from care for his family and the practice of thrift. Likewise, more work is not to be imposed than strength can endure, nor that kind of work which is unsuited to a worker's age or sex.

Among the most important duties of employers the principal one is to give every worker what is justly due him. Assuredly, to establish a rule of pay in accord with justice, many factors must be taken into account. But, in general, the rich and employers should remember that no laws, either human or divine, permit them for their own profit to oppress the needy and the wretched or to seek gain from another's want. To defraud anyone of the wage due him is a great crime that calls down avenging wrath from Heaven. "Behold, the wages of the laborers . . . which have been kept back by you unjustly, cry out: and their cry has entered into the ears of the Lord of Hosts." Finally, the rich must religiously avoid harming in any way the savings of the workers either by coercion, or by fraud, or by the arts of usury; and the more for this reason, that the workers are not sufficiently protected against injustices and violence, and their property, being so meagre, ought to be regarded as all the more sacred. Could not the observance alone of the foregoing laws remove the bitterness and the causes of conflict? . . .

Those who lack fortune's goods are taught by the Church that, before God as Judge, poverty is no disgrace, and that no one should be ashamed because he makes his living by toil. And Jesus Christ has confirmed this by fact and by deed, Who for the salvation of men, "being rich, became poor;" and although He was the Son of God and God Himself, yet He willed to seem and to be thought the son of a carpenter; nay, He even did not disdain to spend a great part of his life at the work of a carpenter. "Is not this the carpenter, the Son of Mary?" Those who contemplate this Divine example will more easily understand these truths: True dignity and excellence in men resides in moral living, that is, in virtue; virtue is the common inheritance of man, attainable equally by the humblest and the mightiest, by the rich and the poor; and the reward of eternal happiness will follow upon virtue and merit alone, regardless of the person in whom they may be found. Nay, rather the favor of God Himself seems to incline more toward the unfortunate as a class; for Jesus Christ calls the poor blessed, and He invites most lovingly all who are in labor or sorrow to come to Him for solace, embracing with special love the lowly and those harassed by injustice. At the realization of these things the proud spirit of the rich is easily brought down, and the downcast heart of the afflicted is lifted up; the former are moved toward kindness, the latter, toward reasonableness in their demands. Thus the distance between the classes which pride seeks is reduced, and it will easily be brought to pass that the two classes, with hands clasped in friendship, will be united in heart.

Yet, if they obey Christian teachings, not merely friendship but brotherly love also will bind them to each other. They will feel and understand that all men indeed have been created by God, their common Father; that all strive for the same object of good, which is God Himself, Who alone can communicate to both men and angels perfect and absolute happiness; that all equally have been redeemed by the grace of Jesus Christ and restored to the dignity of the sons of God, so that they are clearly united by the bonds of brotherhood not only with one another but also with Christ the Lord, "the firstborn among many brethren," and further, that the goods of nature and the gifts of divine grace belong in common and without distinction to all human kind, and that no one, unless he is unworthy, will be deprived of the inheritance of Heaven. "But if we are sons, we are also heirs: heirs indeed of God and joint heirs with Christ."

Such is the economy of duties and rights according to Christian philosophy. Would it not seem that all conflict would soon cease wherever this economy were to prevail in civil society?

Finally, the Church does not consider it enough to point out the way of finding the cure, but she administers the remedy herself. For she occupies herself fully in training and forming men according to discipline and doctrine; and through the agency of bishops and clergy, she causes the health-giving streams of this doctrine to be diffused as widely as possible. Furthermore, she strives to enter into men's minds and to bend their wills so that they may suffer themselves to be ruled and governed by the discipline of the divine precepts. And in this field, which is of first and greatest importance because in it the whole substance and matter of benefits consists, the Church indeed has a power that is especially unique. For the instruments which she uses to move souls were given her for this very purpose by Jesus Christ, and they have an efficacy implanted in them by God. Such instruments alone can properly penetrate the inner recesses of the heart and lead man to obedience to duty, to govern the activities of his self-seeking mind, to love God and his neighbors with a special and sovereign love, and to overcome courageously all things that impede the path of virtue. . . .

But it is now in order to inquire what portion of the remedy should be expected from the State. By State here We understand not the form of government which this or that people has, but rather that form which right reason in accordance with nature requires and the teachings of Divine wisdom approve, matters that We have explained specifically in Our Encyclical *On the Christian Constitution of States.*

Therefore those governing the State ought primarily to devote themselves to the service of individual groups and of the whole commonwealth, and through the entire scheme of laws and institutions to cause both public and individual well-being to develop spontaneously out of the very structure and administration of the State. For this is the duty of wise statesmanship and the essential office of those in charge of the State. Now, States are made prosperous especially by wholesome morality, properly ordered family life, protection of religion and justice, moderate imposition and equitable distribution of public burdens, progressive development of industry and trade, thriving agriculture, and by all other things of this nature, which the more actively they are promoted, the better and happier the life of the citizens is destined to be. Therefore, by virtue of these things, it is within the competence of the rulers of the State that, as they benefit other groups, they also improve in particular the condition of the workers. Furthermore, they do this with full right and without laying themselves open to any charge of unwarranted interference. For the State is bound by the very law of its office to serve the common interest. And the richer the benefits which come from this general providence on the part of the State, the less necessary it will be to experiment with other measures for the well-being of workers.

This ought to be considered, as it touches the question more deeply, namely, that the State has one basic purpose for existence, which embraces in common the highest and the lowest of its members. Non-owning workers are unquestionably citizens by nature in virtue of the same right as the rich, that is, true and vital parts whence, through the medium of families, the body of the State is constituted; and it hardly need be added that they are by far the greatest number in every urban area. Since it would be quite absurd to look out for one portion of the citizens and to neglect another, it follows that public authority ought to exercise due care in safeguarding the well-being and the interests of non-owning workers. Unless this is done, justice, which commands that everyone be given his own, will be violated. Wherefore St. Thomas says wisely: "Even as part and whole are in a certain way the same, so too that which pertains to the whole pertains in a certain way to the part also." Consequently, among the numerous and weighty duties of rulers who would serve their people well, this is first and foremost, namely, that they protect equitably each and every class of citizens, maintaining inviolate that justice especially which is called *distributive.*

Although all citizens, without exception, are obliged to contribute something to the sumtotal common goods, some share of which naturally goes back to each individual, yet all can by no means contribute the same amount and in equal degree. Whatever the vicissitudes that occur in the forms of government, there will always be those differences in the condition of citizens without which society could neither exist nor be conceived. It is altogether necessary that there be some who dedicate themselves to the service of the State, who make laws, who dispense justice, and finally, by whose counsel and authority civil and military affairs are administered. These men, as is clear, play the chief role in the State, and among every people are to be regarded as occupying first place, because they work for the common good most directly and preeminently. On the other hand, those engaged in some calling benefit the State, but not in the same way as the men just mentioned, nor by performing the same duties; yet they, too, in a high degree, although less directly, serve the public weal. Assuredly, since social good must be of such a character that men through its acquisition are made better, it must necessarily be founded chiefly on virtue.

Nevertheless, an abundance of corporeal and external goods is likewise a characteristic of a well constituted State, "the use of which goods is necessary for the practice of virtue." To produce these goods the labor of the workers, whether they expend their skill and strength on farms or in factories, is most efficacious and necessary. Nay, in this respect, their energy and effectiveness are so important that it is incontestable that the wealth of nations originates from no other source than from the labor of workers. Equity therefore commands that public authority show proper concern for the worker so that from what he contributes to the common good he may receive what will enable him, housed, clothed, and secure, to live his life without hardship. Whence, it follows that all those measures ought to be favored which seem in any way capable of benefiting the condition of workers. Such solicitude is so far from injuring anyone, that it is destined rather to benefit all, because it is of absolute interest to the State that those citizens should not be miserable in every respect from whom such necessary goods proceed.

It is not right, as We have said, for either the citizen or the family to be absorbed by the State; it is proper that the individual and the family should be permitted to retain their freedom of action, so far as this is possible without jeopardizing the common good and without injuring anyone. Nevertheless, those who govern must see to it that they protect the community and its constituent parts: the community, because nature has entrusted its safeguarding to the sovereign power in the State to such an extent that the protection of the public welfare is not only the supreme law, but is the entire cause and reason for sovereignty; and the constituent parts, because philosophy and Christian faith agree that the administration of the State has from nature as its purpose, not the benefit of those to whom it has been entrusted, but the benefit of those who have been entrusted to it. And since the power of governing comes from God and is a participation, as it were, in His supreme sovereignty, it ought to be administered according to the example of the Divine power, which looks with paternal care to the welfare of individual creatures as well as to that of all creation. If, therefore, any injury has been done to or threatens either the common good or the interests of individual groups, which injury cannot in any other way be repaired or prevented, it is necessary for public authority to intervene.

It is vitally important to public as well as to private welfare that there be peace and good order; likewise, that the whole regime of family life be directed according to the ordinances of God and the principles of nature, that religion be observed and cultivated, that sound morals flourish in private and public life, that justice be kept sacred and that no one be wronged with impunity by another, and that strong citizens grow up, capable of supporting, and, if necessary, of protecting the State. Wherefore, if at any time disorder should threaten because of strikes or concerted stoppages of work, if the natural bonds of family life should be relaxed among the poor, if religion among the workers should be outraged by failure to provide sufficient opportunity for performing religious duties, if in factories danger should assail the integrity of morals through the mixing of the sexes or other pernicious incitements to sin, or if the employer class should oppress the working class with unjust burdens or should degrade them with conditions inimical to human personality or to human dignity, if health should be injured by immoderate work and such as is not suited to sex or age—in all these cases, the power and authority of the law, but of course within certain limits, manifestly ought to be employed. And these limits are determined by the same reason which demands the aid of the law, that is, the law ought not undertake more, nor it go farther, than the remedy of evils or the removal of danger requires.

Rights indeed, by whomsoever possessed, must be religiously protected; and public authority, in warding off injuries and punishing wrongs, ought to see to it that individuals may have and hold what belongs to them. In protecting the rights of private individuals, however, special consideration must be given to the weak and the poor. For the nation, as it were, of the rich, is guarded by its own defences and is in less need of governmental protection, whereas the suffering multitude, without the means to protect itself, relies especially on the protection of the State. Wherefore, since wage workers are numbered among the great mass of the needy, the State must include them under its special care and foresight.

But it will be well to touch here expressly on certain matters of special importance. The capital point is this, that private property ought to be safeguarded by the sovereign power of the State and through the bulwark of its laws. And especially, in view of such a great flaming up of passion at the present time, the masses ought to be kept within the bounds of their moral obligations. For while justice does not oppose our striving for better things, on the other hand, it does forbid anyone to take from another what is his and, in the name of a certain absurd equality, to seize forcibly the property of others; nor does the interest of the common good itself permit this. Certainly, the great majority of working people prefer to secure better conditions by honest toil, without doing wrong to anyone. Nevertheless, not a few individuals are found who, imbued with evil ideas and eager for revolution, use every means to stir up disorder and incite to violence. The authority of the State, therefore, should intervene and, by putting restraint upon such disturbers, protect the morals of workers from their corrupting arts and lawful owners from the danger of spoliation.

Labor which is too long and too hard and the belief that pay is inadequate not infrequently give workers cause to strike and become voluntarily idle. This evil, which is frequent and serious, ought to be remedied by public authority, because such interruption of work inflicts damage not only upon employers and upon the workers themselves, but also injures trade and commerce and the general interests of the State; and, since it is usually not far removed from violence and rioting, it very frequently jeopardizes public peace. In this matter it is more effective and salutary that the authority of the law anticipate and completely prevent the evil from breaking out by removing early the causes from which it would seem that conflict between employers and workers is bound to arise.

And in like manner, in the case of the worker, there are many things which the power of the State should protect; and, first of all, the goods of his soul. For however good and desirable mortal life be, yet it is not the ultimate goal for which we are born, but a road

only and a means for perfecting, through knowledge of truth and love of good, the life of the soul. The soul bears the express image and likeness of God, and there resides in it that sovereignty through the medium of which man has been bidden to rule all created nature below him and to make all lands and all seas serve his interests. "Fill the earth and subdue it, and rule over the fishes of the sea and the fowls of the air and all living creatures that move upon the earth." In this respect all men are equal, and there is no difference between rich and poor, between masters and servants, between rulers and subjects: "For there is the same Lord of all." No one may with impunity outrage the dignity of man, which God Himself treats with great reverence, nor impede his course to that level of perfection which accords with eternal life in heaven. Nay, more, in this connection a man cannot even by his own free choice allow himself to be treated in a way inconsistent with his nature, and suffer his soul to be enslaved; for there is no question here of rights belonging to man, but of duties owed to God, which are to be religiously observed.

Hence follows necessary cessation from toil and work on Sundays and Holy Days of Obligation. Let no one, however, understand this in the sense of greater indulgence of idle leisure, and much less in the sense of that kind of cessation from work, such as many desire, which encourages vice and promotes wasteful spending of money, but solely in the sense of a repose from labor made sacred by religion. Rest combined with religion calls man away from toil and the business of daily life to admonish him to ponder on heavenly goods and to pay his just and due homage to the Eternal Deity. This is especially the nature, and this the cause, of the rest to be taken on Sundays and Holy Days of Obligation, and God has sanctioned the same in the Old Testament by a special law: "Remember thou keep holy the Sabbath Day," and He Himself taught it by His own action: namely the mystical rest taken immediately after He had created man: "He rested on the seventh day from all His work which He had done."

Now as concerns the protection of corporeal and physical goods, the oppressed workers, above all, ought to be liberated from the savagery of greedy men, who inordinately use human beings as things of gain. Assuredly, neither justice nor humanity can countenance the exaction of so much work that the spirit is dulled from excessive toil and that along with it the body sinks crushed from exhaustion. The working energy of a man, like his entire nature, is circumscribed by definite limits beyond which it cannot go. It is developed indeed by exercise and use, but only on condition that a man cease from work at regular intervals and rest. With respect to daily work, therefore, care ought to be taken not to extend it beyond the hours that human strength warrants. The length of rest intervals ought to be decided on the basis of the varying nature of the work, of the circumstances of time and place, and of the physical condition of the workers themselves. Since the labor of those who quarry stone from the earth, or who mine iron, copper, and other underground materials, is much more severe and harmful to health, the working period for such men ought to be correspondingly shortened. The seasons of the year also must be taken into account; for often a given kind of work is easy to endure in one season but cannot be endured at all in another, or not without the greatest difficulty.

Finally, it is not right to demand of a woman or a child what a strong adult man is capable of doing or would be willing to do. Nay, as regards children, special care ought to be taken that the factory does not get hold of them before age has sufficiently matured their physical, intellectual, and moral powers. For budding strength in childhood, like greening verdure in spring, is crushed by premature harsh treatment; and under such circumstances all education of the child must needs be foregone. Certain occupations likewise are less fitted for women, who are intended by nature for work of the home—work indeed which especially protects modesty in women and accords by nature with the education of children and the well-being of the family. Let it be the rule everywhere that workers be given as much leisure as will compensate for the energy consumed by toil, for rest from work is necessary to restore strength consumed by use. In every obligation which is mutually contracted between employers and workers, this condition, either written or tacit, is always present, that both kinds of rest be provided for; nor would it be equitable to make an agreement otherwise, because no one has the right to demand of, or to make an agreement with anyone to neglect those duties which bind a man to God or to himself. . . .

Otto von Bismarck

While Marx and Engels were still predicting the withering away of the state, and while the Fabians were only beginning to propagandize for democratic socialism through the state, Prince Otto von Bismarck (1815–1898), chancellor of Germany, was already using the state to improve the condition of the German working classes. As the leading political figure in the new German Empire, he sponsored various acts designed, not only to strengthen his country socially and economically, but also to halt the growth of Marxian socialism within her frontiers. Prussia, the largest state in the Empire, had a long tradition of royal paternalism, and it was only natural, therefore, that Germany should take the lead in the movement away from the laissez-faire policy of the mid-nineteenth century, and toward the goal of state socialism. The following excerpts are from various speeches made by Bismarck on the subject of state reform and state socialism. In reading them note

(1) Bismarck's attitude toward those groups who opposed state intervention, (2) his feeling for the poor, (3) his position on capital and capitalism, (4) the distinction he made between urban and rural landowners, (5) the program he advocated for social security, (6) the goal he hoped to achieve by such a program, (7) the responsibility of the state to provide work for its citizens, and (8) his reaction to the term "socialism."

From: THE SPEECHES OF CHANCELLOR BISMARCK

Herr Richter has called attention to the responsibility of the State for what it does. But it is my opinion that the State can also be responsible for what it does not do. I do not think that doctrines like those of *"Laissez-faire, laissez-aller,"* "Pure Manchesterdom in politics," *"Jeder sehe, wie er's treibe, Jeder sehe, wo er bleibe,"* "He who is not strong enough to stand must be knocked down, and trodden to the ground," "To him that hath shall be given, and from him that hath not shall be taken away even that which he hath" —that doctrines like these should be applied in the State, and especially in a monarchically, paternally governed State. On the other hand, I believe that those who profess horror at the intervention of the State for the protection of the weak lay themselves open to the suspicion that they are desirous of using their strength —be it that of capital, that of rhetoric, or whatever it be—for the benefit of a section, for the oppression of the rest, for the introduction of party domination, and that they will be chagrined as soon as this design is disturbed by any action of the government.

I ask you what right had I to close the way to the throne against these people? The kings of Prussia have never been by preference kings of the rich. Frederick the Great said when Crown Prince: *"Quand je serai roi, je serai un vrai roi des gueux."* He undertook to be the protector of the poor, and this principle has been followed by our later kings. At their throne suffering has always found a refuge and a hearing. . . .

Our kings have secured the emancipation of the serfs, they have created a thriving peasantry, and they may possibly be successful— the earnest endeavour exists, at any rate—in improving the condition of the working classes somewhat. To have refused access to the throne to the complaints of these operatives would not have been the right course to pursue, and it was, moreover, not my business to do it. The question would afterwards have been asked: "How rich must a deputation be in order to insure its reception by the King?". . . .

I am not antagonistic to the rightful claims of capital; I am far from wanting to flourish a hostile flag; but I am of opinion that the masses, too, have rights which should be considered.

I wish we could immediately create a few hundred millionaires. They would expend their money in the country, and this expenditure would act fruitfully on labour all round. They could not eat their money themselves; they would have to spend the interest on it. Be glad, then, when people become rich with us. The community at large, and not only the tax authority, is sure to benefit.

The large land-owner who lives in the country is not the worst evil; the worst is the large land-owner who lives in the town, be it Paris, Rome, or Berlin, and who only requires money from his estates and agents, who does not represent his estates in the Reichstag or Landtag, and does not even know how it fares with them. Therein lies the evil of large estates. Large estates whose owners live in the country are under certain circumstances a great blessing, and very useful. . . . I regard the large land-owners who are really farmers, and

William H. Dawson, *Bismarck and State Socialism: An Exposition of the Social and Economic Legislation of Germany Since 1870*, London, 1891, 29; 31–35; 53–64.

buy land from a predilection for this industry, as a blessing for our country, and especially for the provinces where I live. And if you succeed in destroying this race, you would see the result in the palsying of our entire economic and political life. . . . But so long as God is still minded to preserve the German Empire and the Kingdom of Prussia, this war of yours against landed proprietorship will not succeed, however many allies you may obtain.

Give the working-man the right to work as long as he is healthy; assure him care when he is sick; assure him maintenance when he is old. If you do that, and do not fear the sacrifice, or cry out at State Socialism directly the words "provision for old age" are uttered,—if the State will show a little more Christian solicitude for the working-man, then I believe that the gentlemen of the Wyden [Social-Democratic] programme will sound their bird-call in vain, and that the thronging to them will cease as soon as working-men see that the Government and legislative bodies are earnestly concerned for their welfare.

Yes, I acknowledge unconditionally a right to work, and I will stand up for it as long as I am in this place. But here I do not stand upon the ground of Socialism, which is said to have only begun with the Bismarck Ministry, but on that of the Prussian common law. . . . Was not the right to work openly proclaimed at the time of the publication of the common law? Is it not established in all our social arrangements that the man who comes before his fellow-citizens and says, "I am healthy, I desire to work, but can find no work," is entitled to say also, "Give me work," and that the State is bound to give him work?

I will further every endeavour which positively aims at improving the condition of the working classes. . . . As soon as a positive proposal came from the Socialists for fashioning the future in a sensible way, in order that the lot of the working-man might be improved, I would not at any rate refuse to examine it favourably, and I would not even shrink from the idea of State help for the people who would help themselves.

The establishment of the freedom of the peasantry was Socialistic; Socialistic, too, is every expropriation in favour of railways; Socialistic to the utmost extent is the aggregation of estates—the law exists in many provinces—taking from one and giving to another, simply because this other can cultivate the land more conveniently; Socialistic is expropriation under the Water Legislation, on account of irrigation, etc., where a man's land is taken away from him because another can farm it better; Socialistic is our entire poor relief, compulsory school attendance, compulsory construction of roads, so that I am bound to maintain a road upon my lands for travellers. That is all Socialistic, and I could extend the register further; but if you believe that you can frighten any one or call up spectres with the word "Socialism," you take a standpoint which I abandoned long ago, and the abandonment of which is absolutely necessary for our entire imperial legislation.

Ralph Waldo Emerson

Ralph Waldo Emerson (1803–1882) began his professional career as a clergyman but gave up his calling when he could no longer harmonize his convictions with the religious practices then current in New England. He became instead a scholar, a popular lecturer, and a writer, reflecting in his work some of the dominant philosophical and cultural trends of the nineteenth century. Prominent among these was his romantic idealization of nature and of man, which, with Emerson, bordered on a form of pantheism. He was vigorously optimistic about the future of man, and particularly of man in the unlimited natural environment of America. He was not blind, however, to cer-

tain disintegrating forces in American life, such as material-
ism and mediocrity, which might handicap its develop-
ment. He frequently lashed out at Americans for these
weaknesses and also for the tendency to stultify the develop-
ment of a national culture by following too closely the pat-
tern established by Europeans. In 1837 he delivered an
address of this nature to the Phi Beta Kappa Society of
Harvard College. He called it The American Scholar and
it still stands as a monument to his thought, his energy,
and his patriotic devotion to his native land. In reading
it note (1) Emerson's explanation, in the opening para-
graph, for the title of his address, (2) his development of
the concept of the ideal Man, (3) the importance he at-
tributed to nature in the education of the scholar, (4) the
danger as well as the advantage of books, (5) the import-
ance of experience to a scholar's development, (6) the du-
ties of a scholar, (7) his analysis of the advantage of living
in an age of revolution, (8) the importance of man in re-
lation to the world, (9) his admonition to American schol-
ars to launch out on their own, and (10) the strong em-
phasis on nature.

THE AMERICAN SCHOLAR

Mr. President and Gentlemen, I greet you on the recommencement of our literary year. Our anniversary is one of hope, and, perhaps, not enough of labor. We do not meet for games of strength or skill, for the recitation of histories, tragedies, and odes, like the ancient Greeks; for parliaments of love and poesy, like the Troubadours; nor for the advancement of science, like our contemporaries in the British and European capitals. Thus far, our holiday has been simply a friendly sign of the survival of the love of letters amongst a people too busy to give to letters any more. As such, it is precious as the sign of an indestructible instinct. Perhaps the time is already come when it ought to be, and will be, something else; when the sluggard intellect of this continent will look from under its iron lids, and fill the postponed expectation of the world with something better than the exertions of mechanical skill. Our day of dependence, our long apprenticeship to the learning of other lands, draws to a close. The millions that around us are rushing into life, cannot always be fed on the sere remains of foreign harvests. Events, actions arise, that must be sung, that will sing themselves. Who can doubt that poetry will revive and lead in a new age, as the star in the constellation Harp, which now flames in our zenith, astronomers announce, shall one day be the pole-star for a thousand years?

In this hope, I accept the topic which not only usage but the nature of our association seem to prescribe to this day,—the *American Scholar*. Year by year we come up hither to read one more chapter of his biography. Let us inquire what light new days and events have thrown on his character and his hopes.

It is one of those fables, which, out of an unknown antiquity, convey an unlooked-for wisdom, that the gods, in the beginning, divided Man into men, that he might be more helpful to himself; just as the hand was divided into fingers, the better to answer its end.

The old fable covers a doctrine ever new and sublime; that there is One Man,—present to all particular men only partially, or through one faculty; and that you must take the whole

Ralph Waldo Emerson, "The American Scholar," in Willard Thorp, Merle Curti, and Carlos Baker, *American Issues,* 2 vols., J. B. Lippincott Company, Philadelphia, 1941, II, 298–307. Courtesy of J. B. Lippincott Company.

society to find the whole man. Man is not a farmer, or a professor, or an engineer, but he is all. Man is priest, and scholar, and statesman, and producer, and soldier. In the *divided* or social state these functions are parcelled out to individuals, each of whom aims to do his stint of the joint work, whilst each other performs his. The fable implies that the individual, to possess himself, must sometimes return from his own labor to embrace all the other laborers. But, unfortunately, this original unit, this fountain of power, has been so distributed to multitudes, has been so minutely subdivided and peddled out, that it is spilled into drops, and cannot be gathered. The state of society is one in which the members have suffered amputation from the trunk, and strut about so many walking monsters,—a good finger, a neck, a stomach, an elbow, but never a man.

Man is thus metamorphosed into a thing, into many things. The planter, who is Man sent out into the field to gather food, is seldom cheered by any idea of the true dignity of his ministry. He sees his bushel and his cart, and nothing beyond, and sinks into the farmer, instead of Man on the farm. The tradesman scarcely ever gives an ideal worth to his work, but is ridden by the routine of his craft, and the soul is subject to dollars. The priest becomes a form; the attorney a statute-book; the mechanic a machine; the sailor a rope of the ship.

In this distribution of functions the scholar is the delegated intellect. In the right state, he is *Man Thinking*. In the degenerate state, when the victim of society, he tends to become a mere thinker, or, still worse, the parrot of other men's thinking.

In this view of him, as Man Thinking, the theory of his office is contained. Him Nature solicits with all her placid, all her monitory pictures; him the past instructs; him the future invites. Is not indeed every man a student, and do not all things exist for the student's behoof? And, finally, is not the true scholar the only true master? But the old oracle said, "All things have two handles: beware of the wrong one." In life, too often, the scholar errs with mankind and forfeits his privilege. Let us see him in his school, and consider him in reference to the main influences he receives.

I. The first in time and the first in importance of the influences upon the mind is that of nature. Every day, the sun; and, after the sunset, night and her stars. Ever the winds blow; ever the grass grows. Every day, men and women, conversing, beholding and beholden. The scholar is he of all men whom this spectacle most engages. He must settle its value in his mind. What is nature to him? There is never a beginning, there is never an end, to the inexplicable continuity of this web of God, but always circular power returning into itself. Therein it resembles his own spirit, whose beginning, whose ending, he never can find,—so entire, so boundless. Far too as her splendors shine, system on system shooting like rays, upward, downward, without centre, without circumference,—in the mass and in the particle, nature hastens to render account of herself to the mind. Classification begins. To the young mind, every thing is individual, stands by itself. By and by, it finds how to join two things, and see in them one nature; then three, then three thousand; and so, tyrannized over by its own unifying instinct, it goes on tying things together, diminishing anomalies, discovering roots running under ground whereby contrary and remote things cohere and flower out from one stem. It presently learns that since the dawn of history there has been a constant accumulation and classifying of facts. But what is classification but the perceiving that these objects are not chaotic, and are not foreign, but have a law which is also a law of the human mind? The astronomer discovers that geometry, a pure abstraction of the human mind, is the measure of planetary motion. The chemist finds proportions and intelligible method throughout matter; and science is nothing but the finding of analogy, identity, in the most remote parts. The ambitious soul sits down before each refractory fact: one after another, reduces all strange constitutions, all new powers, to their class and their law, and goes on forever to animate the last fibre of organization, the outskirts of nature, by insight.

Thus to him, to this school-boy under the bending dome of day, is suggested that he and it proceed from one root; one is leaf and one is flower; relation, sympathy, stirring in every vein. And what is that root? Is not that the soul of his soul? A thought too bold; a dream too wild. Yet when this spiritual light shall have revealed the law of more earthy natures,— when he has learned to worship the soul, and to see that the natural philosophy that now is, is only the first gropings of its gigantic hand, he shall look forward to an ever expanding knowledge as to a becoming creator. He shall see that nature is the opposite of the soul, answering to it part for part. One is seal, and one is print. Its beauty is the beauty of his own mind. Its laws are the laws of his own mind. Nature then becomes to him the measure of his attainments. So much of nature as he is ignorant of, so much of his own mind does he not yet possess. And, in fine, the ancient precept, "Know thyself," and the modern precept, "Study nature," become at last one maxim.

II. The next great influence into the spirit of the scholar is the mind of the Past,—in whatever form, whether of literature, of art, of institutions, that mind is inscribed. Books are the best type of the influence of the past, and perhaps we shall get at the truth,—learn the amount of this influence more conveniently,— by considering their value alone.

The theory of books is noble. The scholar of the first age received into him the world around; brooded thereon; gave it the new arrangement of his own mind, and uttered it again. It came into him life; it went out from him truth. It came to him short-lived actions; it went out from him immortal thoughts. It came to him business; it went from him poetry. It was dead fact; now, it is quick thought. It can stand, and it can go. It now endures, it now flies, it now inspires. Precisely in proportion to the depth of mind from which it issued, so high does it soar, so long does it sing.

Or, I might say, it depends on how far the process had gone, of transmuting life into truth. In proportion to the completeness of the distillation, so will the purity and imperishableness of the product be. But none is quite perfect. As no air-pump can by any means make a perfect vacuum, so neither can any artist entirely exclude the conventional, the local, the perishable from his book, or write a book of pure thought, that shall be as efficient, in all respects, to a remote posterity, as to contemporaries, or rather to the second age. Each age, it is found, must write its own books; or rather, each generation for the next succeeding. The books of an older period will not fit this.

Yet hence arises a grave mischief. The sacredness which attaches to the act of creation, the act of thought, is transferred to the record. The poet chanting was felt to be a divine man: henceforth the chant is divine also. The writer was a just and wise spirit: henceforward it is settled, the book is perfect; as love of the hero corrupts into worship of his statue. Instantly, the book becomes noxious; the guide is a tyrant. The sluggish and perverted mind of the multitude, slow to open to the incursions of Reason, having once so opened, having once received this book, stands upon it, and makes an outcry if it is disparaged. Colleges are built on it. Books are written on it by thinkers, not by Man Thinking; by men of talent, that is, who start wrong, who set out from accepted dogmas, not from their own sight of principles. Meek young men grow up in libraries, believing it their duty to accept the views which Cicero, which Locke, which Bacon, have given; forgetful that Cicero, Locke, and Bacon were only young men in libraries when they wrote these books.

Hence, instead of Man Thinking we have the bookworm. Hence the book-learned class, who value books, as such; not as related to nature and the human constitution, but as making a sort of Third Estate with the world and the soul. Hence, the restorers of readings, the emendators, the bibliomaniacs of all degrees.

Books are the best of things, well used; abused, among the worst. What is the right use? What is the one end which all means go to effect? They are for nothing but to inspire. I had better never see a book than to be warped by its attraction clean out of my own orbit, and made a satellite instead of a system. The one thing in the world, of value, is the active soul. This every man is entitled to; this every man contains within him, although in almost all men obstructed, and as yet unborn. The soul active sees absolute truth; and utters truth, or creates. In this action it is genius; not the privilege of here and there a favorite, but the sound estate of every man. In its essence it is progressive. The book, the college, the school of art, the institution of any kind, stop with some past utterance of genius. This is good, say they,—let us hold by this. They pin me down. They look backward and not forward. But genius looks forward; the eyes of man are set in his forehead, not in his hindhead; man hopes; genius creates. Whatever talents may be, if the man create not, the pure efflux of the Deity is not his; cinders and smoke there may be, but not yet flame. There are creative manners, there are creative actions, and creative words; manners, actions, words, that is, indicative of no custom or authority, but springing spontaneous from the mind's own sense of good and fair.

On the other part, instead of being its own seer, let it receive from another mind its truth, though it were in torrents of light, without periods of solitude, inquest, and self-recovery, and a fatal disservice is done. Genius is always sufficiently the enemy of genius by over-influence. The literature of every nation bears me witness. The English dramatic poets have Shakspearized now for two hundred years.

Undoubtedly there is a right way of reading, so it be sternly subordinated. Man Thinking must not be subdued by his instruments. Books are for the scholar's idle times. When he can read God directly, the hour is too precious to be wasted in other men's transcripts of their readings. But when the intervals of darkness come, as come they must,—when the sun is hid and the stars withdraw their shining,—we repair to the lamps which were kindled by their ray, to guide our steps to the East again, where the dawn is. We hear, that we may speak. The Arabian proverb says, "A fig tree, looking on a fig tree, becometh fruitful."

It is remarkable, the character of the pleasure we derive from the best books. They impress us with the conviction that one nature wrote and the same reads. We read the verses of one of the great English poets, of Chaucer, of Marvell, of Dryden, with the most modern joy,—with a pleasure, I mean, which is in great part caused by the abstraction of all *time* from their verses. There is some awe mixed with the joy of our surprise, when this poet, who lived in some past world, two or three hundred years ago, says that which lies close to my own soul, that which I also had well-nigh thought and

said. But for the evidence thence afforded to the philosophical doctrine of the identity of all minds, we should suppose some pre-established harmony, some foresight of souls that were to be, and some preparation of stores for their future wants, like the fact observed in insects, who lay up food before death for the young grub they shall never see.

I would not be hurried by any love of system, by any exaggeration of instincts, to underrate the Book. We all know, that as the human body can be nourished on any food, though it were boiled grass and the broth of shoes, so the human mind can be fed by any knowledge. And great and heroic men have existed who had almost no other information than by the printed page. I only would say that it needs a strong head to bear that diet. One must be an inventor to read well. As the proverb says, "He that would bring home the wealth of the Indies, must carry out the wealth of the Indies." There is then creative reading as well as creative writing. When the mind is braced by labor and invention, the page of whatever book we read becomes luminous with manifold allusion. Every sentence is doubly significant, and the sense of our author is as broad as the world. We then see, what is always true, that as the seer's hour of vision is short and rare among heavy days and months, so is its record, perchance, the least part of his volume. The discerning will read, in his Plato or Shakspeare, only that least part,—only the authentic utterances of the oracle;—all the rest he rejects, were it never so many times Plato's and Shakspeare's.

Of course there is a portion of reading quite indispensable to a wise man. History and exact science he must learn by laborious reading. Colleges, in like manner, have their indispensable office,—to teach elements. But they can only highly serve us when they aim not to drill, but to create; when they gather from far every ray of various genius to their hospitable halls, and, by the concentrated fires, set the hearts of their youth on flame. Thought and knowledge are natures in which apparatus and pretension avail nothing. Gowns, and pecuniary foundations, though of towns of gold, can never countervail the least sentence or syllable of wit. Forget this, and our American colleges will recede in their public importance, whilst they grow richer every year.

III. There goes in the world a notion that the scholar should be a recluse, a valetudinarian,—as unfit for any handiwork or public labor as a pen-knife for an axe. The so-called "practical men" sneer at speculative men, as if, because they speculate or *see*, they could do nothing. I have heard it said that the clergy,—who are always, more universally than any other class, the scholars of their day,—are addressed as women; that the rough, spontaneous conversation of men they do not hear, but only a mincing and diluted speech. They are often virtually disfranchised; and, indeed, there are advocates for their celibacy. As far as this is true of the studious classes, it is not just and wise. Action is with the scholar subordinate, but it is essential. Without it, he is not yet man. Without it, thought can never ripen into truth. Whilst the world hangs before the eye as a cloud of beauty, we cannot even see its beauty. Inaction is cowardice, but there can be no scholar without the heroic mind. The preamble of thought, the transition through which it passes from the unconscious to the conscious, is action. Only so much do I know, as I have lived. Instantly we know whose words are loaded with life, and whose not.

The world,—this shadow of the soul, or *other me*,—lies wide around. Its attractions are the keys which unlock my thoughts and make me acquainted with myself. I run eagerly into this resounding tumult. I grasp the hands of those next me, and take my place in the ring to suffer and to work, taught by an instinct that so shall the dumb abyss be vocal with speech. I pierce its order; I dissipate its fear; I dispose of it within the circuit of my expanding life. So much only of life as I know by experience, so much of the wilderness have I vanquished and planted, or so far have I extended my being, my dominion. I do not see how any man can afford, for the sake of his nerves and his nap, to spare any action in which he can partake. It is pearls and rubies to his discourse. Drudgery, calamity, exasperation, want, are instructors in eloquence and wisdom. The true scholar grudges every opportunity of action past by, as a loss of power. It is the raw material out of which the intellect moulds her splendid products. A strange process too, this, by which experience is converted into thought, as a mulberry leaf is converted into satin. The manufacture goes forward at all hours.

The actions and events of our childhood and youth are now matters of calmest observation. They lie like fair pictures in the air. Not so with our recent actions,—with the business which we now have in hand. On this we are quite unable to speculate. Our affections as yet circulate through it. We no more feel or know it than we feel the feet, or the hand, or the brain of our body. The new deed is yet a part of life,—remains for a time immersed in our unconscious life. In some contemplative hour it detaches itself from the life like a ripe fruit, to become a thought of the mind. Instantly it is raised, transfigured; the corruptible has put on incorruption. Henceforth it is an object of beauty, however base its origin and neighborhood. Observe, too, the impossibility of antedating this act. In its grub state, it cannot fly, it cannot shine, it is a dull grub. But suddenly, without observation, the selfsame thing unfurls beautiful wings, and is an angel of wisdom. So is there no fact, no event, in our private history, which shall not, sooner or later, lose its adhesive, inert form, and astonish us by soaring from our body into the empyrean. Cradle and infancy, school and playground, the fear of boys, and dogs, and ferules, the love of little maids and berries, and many another fact that once filled the whole sky, are gone already; friend and relative, profession and party, town and country, nation and world, must also soar and sing.

Of course, he who has put forth his total strength in fit actions has the richest return of wisdom. I will not shut myself out of this globe of action, and transplant an oak into a flowerpot, there to hunger and pine; nor trust the revenue of some single faculty, and exhaust one vein of thought, much like those Savoyards, who, getting their livelihood by carving shepherds, shepherdesses, and smoking Dutchmen, for all Europe, went out one day to the mountain to find stock, and discovered that they had whittled up the last of their pinetrees. Authors we have, in numbers, who have written out their vein, and who, moved by a commendable prudence, sail for Greece or Palestine, follow the trapper into the prairie, or ramble round Algiers, to replenish their merchantable stock.

If it were only for a vocabulary, the scholar would be covetous of action. Life is our dictionary. Years are well spent in country labors; in town; in the insight into trades and manufactures; in frank intercourse with many men and women; in science; in art; to the one end of mastering in all their facts a language by which to illustrate and embody our perceptions. I learn immediately from any speaker how much he has already lived, through the poverty or the splendor of his speech. Life lies behind us as the quarry from whence we get tiles and copestones for the masonry of to-day. This is the way to learn grammar. Colleges and books only copy the language which the field and the work-yard made.

But the final value of action, like that of books, and better than books, is that it is a resource. That great principle of Undulation in nature, that shows itself in the inspiring and expiring of the breath; in desire and satiety; in the ebb and flow of the sea; in day and night; in heat and cold; and, as yet more deeply ingrained in every atom and every fluid, is known to us under the name of Polarity,—these "fits of easy transmission and reflection," as Newton called them, are the law of nature because they are the law of spirit.

The mind now thinks; now acts; and each fit reproduces the other. When the artist has exhausted his materials, when the fancy no longer paints, when thoughts are no longer apprehended, and books are a weariness,—he has always the resource *to live*. Character is higher than intellect. Thinking is the function. Living is the functionary. The stream retreats to its source. A great soul will be strong to live, as well as strong to think. Does he lack organ or medium to impart his truths? He can still fall back on this elemental force of living them. This is a total act. Thinking is a partial act. Let the grandeur of justice shine in his affairs. Let the beauty of affection cheer his lowly roof. Those "far from fame," who dwell and act with him, will feel the force of his constitution in the doings and passages of the day better than it can be measured by any public and designed display. Time shall teach him that the scholar loses no hour which the man lives. Herein he unfolds the sacred germ of his instinct, screened from influence. What is lost in seemliness is gained in strength. Not out of those on whom systems of education have exhausted their culture, comes the helpful giant to destroy the old or to build the new, but out of unhandselled savage nature; out of terrible Druids and Berserkers come at last Alfred and Shakspeare.

I hear therefore with joy whatever is beginning to be said of the dignity and necessity of labor to every citizen. There is virtue yet in the hoe and the spade, for learned as well as for unlearned hands. And labor is everywhere welcome; always we are invited to work; only be this limitation observed, that a man shall not for the sake of wider activity sacrifice any opinion to the popular judgments and modes of action.

I have now spoken of the education of the scholar by nature, by books, and by action. It remains to say somewhat of his duties.

They are such as become Man Thinking. They may all be comprised in self-trust. The office of the scholar is to cheer, to raise, and to guide men by showing them facts amidst appearances. He plies the slow, unhonored, and unpaid task of observation. Flamsteed and Herschel, in their glazed observatories, may catalogue the stars with the praise of all men, and, the results being splendid and useful, honor is sure. But he, in his private observatory, cataloguing obscure and nebulous stars of the human mind, which as yet no man has thought of as such,—watching days and months sometimes for a few facts; correcting still his old records,—must relinquish display and immediate fame. In the long period of his preparation he must betray often an ignorance and shiftlessness in popular arts, incurring the disdain of the able who shoulder him aside. Long he must stammer in his speech; often forego the living for the dead. Worse yet, he must accept —how often!—poverty and solitude. For the ease and pleasure of treading the old road, accepting the fashions, the education, the religion of society, he takes the cross of making his own, and, of course, the self-accusation, the faint heart, the frequent uncertainty and loss of time, which are the nettles and tangling vines in the way of the self-relying and self-directed;

and the state of virtual hostility in which he seems to stand to society, and especially to educated society. For all this loss and scorn, what offset? He is to find consolation in exercising the highest functions of human nature. He is one who raises himself from private considerations, and breathes and lives on public and illustrious thoughts. He is the world's eye. He is the world's heart. He is to resist the vulgar prosperity that retrogrades ever to barbarism, by preserving and communicating heroic sentiments, noble biographies, melodious verse, and the conclusions of history. Whatsoever oracles the human heart, in all emergencies, in all solemn hours, has uttered as its commentary on the world of actions,—these he shall receive and impart. And whatsoever new verdict Reason from her inviolable seat pronounces on the passing men and events of to-day,—this he shall hear and promulgate.

These being his functions, it becomes him to feel all confidence in himself, and to defer never to the popular cry. He and he only knows the world. The world of any moment is the merest appearance. Some great decorum, some fetish of a government, some ephemeral trade, or war, or man, is cried up by half mankind and cried down by the other half, as if all depended on this particular up or down. The odds are that the whole question is not worth the poorest thought which the scholar has lost in listening to the controversy. Let him not quit his belief that a popgun is a popgun, though the ancient and honorable of the earth affirm it to be the crack of doom. In silence, in steadiness, in severe abstraction, let him hold by himself; add observation to observation, patient of neglect, patient of reproach, and bide his own time,—happy enough if he can satisfy himself alone that this day he has seen something truly. Success treads on every right step. For the instinct is sure, that prompts him to tell his brother what he thinks. He then learns that in going down into the secrets of his own mind he has descended into the secrets of all minds. He learns that he who has mastered any law in his private thoughts, is master to that extent of all men whose language he speaks, and of all into whose language his own can be translated. The poet, in utter solitude remembering his spontaneous thoughts and recording them, is found to have recorded that which men in crowded cities find true for them also. The orator distrusts at first the fitness of his frank confessions, his want of knowledge of the person he addresses, until he finds that he is the complement of his hearers; that they drink his words because he fulfils for them their own nature; the deeper he dives into his privatest, secretest presentiment, to his wonder he finds this is the most acceptable, most public, and universally true. The people delight in it; the better part of every man feels, This is my music; this is myself.

In self-trust all the virtues are comprehended. Free should the scholar be,—free and brave. Free even to the definition of freedom, "without any hindrance that does not arise out of his own constitution." Brave; for fear is a thing which a scholar by his very function puts behind him. Fear always springs from ignorance. It is a shame to him if his tranquillity, amid dangerous times, arise from the presumption that, like children and women, his is a protected class; or if he seek a temporary peace by the diversion of his thoughts from politics or vexed questions, hiding his head like an ostrich in the flowering bushes, peeping into microscopes, and turning rhymes, as a boy whistles to keep his courage up. So is the danger a danger still; so is the fear worse. Manlike let him turn and face it. Let him look into its eye and search its nature, inspect its origin,—see the whelping of this lion,—which lies no great way back; he will then find in himself a perfect comprehension of its nature and extent; he will have made his hands meet on the other side, and can henceforth defy it, and pass on superior. The world is his who can see through its pretension. What deafness, what stone-blind custom, what overgrown error you behold is there only by sufferance,—by your sufferance. See it to be a lie, and you have already dealt it its mortal blow.

Yes, we are the cowed,—we the trustless. It is a mischievous notion that we are come late into nature; that the world was finished a long time ago. As the world was plastic and fluid in the hands of God, so it is ever to so much of his attributes as we bring to it. To ignorance and sin, it is flint. They adapt themselves to it as they may; but in proportion as a man has any thing in him divine, the firmament flows before him and takes his signet and form. Not he is great who can alter matter, but he who can alter my state of mind. They are the kings of the world who give the color of their present thought to all nature and all art, and persuade men by the cheerful serenity of their carrying the matter, that this thing which they do is the apple which the ages have desired to pluck, now at last ripe, and inviting nations to the harvest. The great man makes the great thing. Wherever Macdonald sits, there is the head of the table. Linnaeus makes botany the most alluring of studies, and wins it from the farmer and the herb-woman; Davy, chemistry; and Cuvier, fossils. The day is always his who works in it with serenity and great aims. The unstable estimates of men crowd to him whose mind is filled with a truth, as the heaped waves of the Atlantic follow the moon.

For this self-trust, the reason is deeper than can be fathomed,—darker than can be enlightened. I might not carry with me the feeling of my audience in stating my own belief. But I have already shown the ground of my hope, in adverting to the doctrine that man is one. I believe man has been wronged; he has wronged himself. He has almost lost the light that can lead him back to his prerogatives. Men are become of no account. Men in history, men in the world of to-day are bugs, are spawn, and are called "the mass" and "the herd." In a century, in a millennium, one or two men; that is to say, one or two approximations to the right state of every man. All the rest behold in the hero or the poet their own green and crude being,—ripened; yes, and are content to be less, so *that* may attain to its full stature. What a testimony, full of grandeur, full of pity, is borne to the demands of his own nature, by the poor clansman, the poor partisan, who rejoices in the glory of his chief. The poor and the low find some amends to their immense moral capacity, for their acquiescence in a political and social inferiority. They are content to be brushed like flies from the path of a great person, so that justice shall be done by him to that common nature which it is the dearest desire of all to see enlarged and glorified. They sun themselves in the great man's light, and feel it to be their own element. They

cast the dignity of man from their downtrod selves upon the shoulders of a hero, and will perish to add one drop of blood to make that great heart beat, those giant sinews combat and conquer. He lives for us, and we live in him.

Men such as they are, very naturally seek money or power; and power because it is as good as money,—the "spoils," so called, "of office." And why not? for they aspire to the highest, and this, in their sleep-walking, they dream is highest. Wake them, and they shall quit the false good, and leap to the true, and leave governments to clerks and desks. This revolution is to be wrought by the gradual domestication of the idea of Culture. The main enterprise of the world for splendor, for extent, is the upbuilding of a man. Here are the materials strewn along the ground. The private life of one man shall be a more illustrious monarchy, more formidable to its enemy, more sweet and serene in its influence to its friend, than any kingdom in history. For a man, rightly viewed, comprehendeth the particular natures of all men. Each philosopher, each bard, each actor has only done for me, as by a delegate, what one day I can do for myself. The books which once we valued more than the apple of the eye, we have quite exhausted. What is that but saying that we have come up with the point of view which the universal mind took through the eyes of one scribe; we have been that man, and have passed on. First, one; then another; we drain all cisterns, and, waxing greater by all these supplies, we crave a better and more abundant food. The man has never lived that can feed us ever. The human mind cannot be enshrined in a person who shall set a barrier on any one side to this unbounded, unboundable empire. It is one central fire, which, flaming now out of the lips of Etna, lightens the capes of Sicily, and now out of the throat of Vesuvius, illuminates the towers and vineyards of Naples. It is one light which beams out of a thousand stars. It is one soul which animates all men.

But I have dwelt perhaps tediously upon this abstraction of the Scholar. I ought not to delay longer to add what I have to say of nearer reference to the time and to this country.

Historically, there is thought to be a difference in the ideas which predominate over successive epochs, and there are data for marking the genius of the Classic, of the Romantic, and now of the Reflective or Philosophical age. With the views I have intimated of the oneness or the identity of the mind through all individuals, I do not much dwell on these differences. In fact, I believe each individual passes through all three. The boy is a Greek; the youth, romantic; the adult reflective. I deny not, however, that a revolution in the leading idea may be distinctly enough traced.

Our age is bewailed as the age of Introversion. Must that needs be evil? We, it seems, are critical; we are embarrassed with second thoughts; we cannot enjoy any thing for hankering to know whereof the pleasure consists; we are lined with eyes; we see with our feet; the time is infected with Hamlet's unhappiness,—

"Sicklied o'er with the pale cast of thought."

It is so bad then? Sight is the last thing to be pitied. Would we be blind? Do we fear lest we should outsee nature and God, and drink truth dry? I look upon the discontent of the literary class as a mere announcement of the fact that they find themselves not in the state of mind of their fathers, and regret the coming state as untried; as a boy dreads the water before he has learned that he can swim. If there is any period one would desire to be born in, is it not the age of Revolution; when the old and the new stand side by side and admit of being compared; when the energies of all men are searched by fear and by hope; when the historic glories of the old can be compensated by the rich possibilities of the new era? This time, like all times, is a very good one, if we but know what to do with it.

I read with some joy of the auspicious signs of the coming days, as they glimmer already through poetry and art, through philosophy and science, through church and state.

One of these signs is the fact that the same movement which effected the elevation of what was called the lowest class in the state, assumed in literature a very marked and as benign an aspect. Instead of the sublime and beautiful, the near, the low, the common, was explored and poetized. That which had been negligently trodden under foot by those who were harnessing and provisioning themselves for long journeys into far countries, is suddenly found to be richer than all foreign parts. The literature of the poor, the feelings of the child, the philosophy of the street, the meaning of household life, are the topics of the time. It is a great stride. It is a sign—is it not?—of new vigor when the extremities are made active, when currents of warm life run into the hands and the feet. I ask not for the great, the remote, the romantic; what is doing in Italy or Arabia; what is Greek art, or Provençal minstrelsy; I embrace the common, I explore and sit at the feet of the familiar, the low. Give me insight into to-day, and you may have the antique and future worlds. What would we really know the meaning of? The meal in the firkin; the milk in the pan; the ballad in the street; the news of the boat; the glance of the eye; the form and the gait of the body;—show me the ultimate reason of these matters; show me the sublime presence of the highest spiritual cause lurking, as always it does lurk, in these suburbs and extremities of nature; let me see every trifle bristling with the polarity that ranges it instantly on an eternal law; and the shop, the plough, and the ledger referred to the like cause by which light undulates and poets sing; —and the world lies no longer a dull miscellany and lumber-room, but has form and order; there is no trifle, there is no puzzle, but one design unites and animates the farthest pinnacle and the lowest trench.

This idea has inspired the genius of Goldsmith, Burns, Cowper, and, in a newer time, of Goethe, Wordsworth, and Carlyle. This idea they have differently followed and with various success. In contrast with their writing, the style of Pope, of Johnson, of Gibbon, looks cold and pedantic. This writing is blood-warm. Man is surprised to find that things near are not less beautiful and wondrous than things remote. The near explains the far. The drop is a small ocean. A man is related to all nature. This perception of the worth of the vulgar is fruitful in discoveries. Goethe, in this very thing the most modern of the moderns, has shown us, as none ever did, the genius of the ancients.

There is one man of genius who has done

much for this philosophy of life, whose literary value has never yet been rightly estimated;— I mean Emanuel Swedenborg. The most imaginative of men, yet writing with the precision of a mathematician, he endeavored to engraft a purely philosophical Ethics on the popular Christianity of his time. Such an attempt of course must have difficulty which no genius could surmount. But he saw and showed the connection between nature and the affections of the soul. He pierced the emblematic or spiritual character of the visible, audible, tangible world. Especially did his shade-loving muse hover over and interpret the lower parts of nature; he showed the mysterious bond that allies moral evil to the foul material forms, and has given in epical parables a theory of insanity, of beasts, of unclean and fearful things.

Another sign of our times, also marked by an analogous political movement, is the new importance given to the single person. Every thing that tends to insulate the individual,—to surround him with barriers of natural respect, so that each man shall feel the world is his, and man shall treat with man as a sovereign state with a sovereign state,—tends to true union as well as greatness. "I learned," said the melancholy Pestalozzi, "that no man in God's wide earth is either willing or able to help any other man." Help must come from the bosom alone. The scholar is that man who must take up into himself all the ability of the time, all the contributions of the past, all the hopes of the future. He must be an university of knowledges. If there be one lesson more than another which should pierce his ear, it is: The world is nothing, the man is all; in yourself is the law of all nature, and you know not yet how a globule of sap ascends; in yourself slumbers the whole of Reason; it is for you to know all; it is for you to dare all.

Mr. President and Gentlemen, this confidence in the unsearched might of man belongs, by all motives, by all prophecy, by all preparation, to the American Scholar. We have listened too long to the courtly muses of Europe.

The spirit of the American freeman is already suspected to be timid, imitative, tame. Public and private avarice make the air we breathe thick and fat. The scholar is decent, indolent, complaisant. See already the tragic consequence. The mind of this country, taught to aim at low objects, eats upon itself. There is no work for any but the decorous and the complaisant. Young men of the fairest promise, who begin life upon our shores, inflated by the mountain winds, shined upon by all the stars of God, find the earth below not in unison with these, but are hindered from action by the disgust which the principles on which business is managed inspire, and turn drudges, or die of disgust, some of them suicides. What is the remedy? They did not yet see, and thousands of young men as hopeful now crowding to the barriers for the career do not yet see, that if the single man plant himself indomitably on his instincts, and there abide, the huge world will come round to him. Patience,—patience; with the shades of all the good and great for company; and for solace the perspective of your own infinite life; and for work the study and the communication of principles, the making those instincts prevalent, the conversion of the world. Is it not the chief disgrace in the world, not to be an unit;—not to be reckoned one character;—not to yield that peculiar fruit which each man was created to bear, but to be reckoned in the gross, in the hundred, or the thousand, of the party, the section, to which we belong; and our opinion predicted geographically, as the north, or the south? Not so, brothers and friends,—please God, ours shall not be so. We will walk on our own feet; we will work with our own hands; we will speak with our own minds. The study of letters shall be no longer a name for pity, for doubt, and for sensual indulgence. The dread of man and the love of man shall be a wall of defence and a wreath of joy around all. A nation of men will for the first time exist, because each believes himself inspired by the Divine Soul which also inspires all men.

Walt Whitman

Walt Whitman (1819–1892), American poet, lived most of his life in and near his beloved Manhattan. An office boy, printer's devil, country school teacher, editor of newspapers, war nurse, traveler, and observer of and prophet for American democracy, Whitman celebrated in his writings the common man and everyday things. He sang a mystic internationalism based upon universal brotherhood and at the same time expressed a fervent love for the whole of America. He believed his native land to be the natural home of the ordinary man and looked for the emergence of a new race fashioned from the many people seeking asylum upon the American continent. In reading the selections from Song of Myself note (1) Whitman's emphasis upon the universal character of all life and spirit, (2) his expression of the brotherhood of all men, (3) his identification of himself with individual men, women, and children as well as with all mankind, and (4) the freedom from conventionality in the subject matter as well as the form of his poetry.

From: SONG OF MYSELF

1

I celebrate myself, and sing myself,
And what I assume you shall assume,
For every atom belonging to me as good belongs to you.

I loafe and invite my soul,
I lean and loafe at my ease observing a spear of summer grass.

My tongue, every atom of my blood, form'd from this soil, this air,
Born here of parents born here from parents the same, and their parents the same,
I, now thirty-seven years old in perfect health begin,
Hoping to cease not till death.

Creeds and schools in abeyance,
Retiring back a while sufficed at what they are, but never forgotten,
I harbor for good or bad, I permit to speak at every hazard,
Nature without check with original energy.

. . . .

3

I have heard what the talkers were talking, the talk of the beginning and the end,
But I do not talk of the beginning or the end.

Walt Whitman, *Leaves of Grass*, Philadelphia, 1883, 29–33; 34–43; 48–50; 55–61.

There was never any more inception than there is now,
Nor any more youth or age than there is now,
And will never be any more perfection than there is now,
Nor any more heaven or hell than there is now.

Urge and urge and urge,
Always the procreant urge of the world.
Out of the dimness opposite equals advance, always substance and increase, always sex,
Always a knit of identity, always distinction, always a breed of life.

To elaborate is no avail, learn'd and unlearn'd feel that it is so.
Sure as the most certain sure, plumb in the uprights, well entretied, braced in the beams,
Stout as a horse, affectionate, haughty, electrical,
I and this mystery here we stand.

Clear and sweet is my soul, and clear and sweet is all that is not my soul.

Lack one lacks both, and the unseen is proved by the seen,
Till that becomes unseen and receives proof in its turn.

Showing the best and dividing it from the worst age vexes age,
Knowing the perfect fitness and equanimity of things, while they discuss I am silent, and go
    bathe and admire myself.

Welcome is every organ and attribute of me, and of any man hearty and clean,
Not an inch nor a particle of an inch is vile, and none shall be less familiar than the rest.

I am satisfied—I see, dance, laugh, sing;
As the hugging and loving bed-fellow sleeps at my side through the night, and withdraws at
    the peep of the day with stealthy tread,
Leaving me baskets cover'd with white towels swelling the house with their plenty.
Shall I postpone my acceptation and realization and scream at my eyes,
That they turn from gazing after and down the road,
And forthwith cipher and show me to a cent,
Exactly the value of one and exactly the value of two, and which is ahead?

. . . .

5

I believe in you my soul, the other I am must not abase itself to you,
And you must not be abased to the other.

Loafe with me on the grass, loose the stop from your throat,
Not words, not music or rhyme I want, not custom or lecture, not even the best,
Only the lull I like, the hum of your valvèd voice.

I mind how once we lay such a transparent summer morning,
How you settled your head athwart my hips and gently turn'd over upon me,
And parted the shirt from my bosom-bone, and plunged your tongue to my bare-stript heart,
And reach'd till you felt my beard, and reach'd till you held my feet.

Swiftly arose and spread around me the peace and knowledge that pass all the argument of
    the earth,
And I know that the hand of God is the promise of my own,
And I know that the spirit of God is the brother of my own,
And that all the men ever born are also my brothers, and the women my sisters and lovers,
And that a kelson of the creation is love,
And limitless are leaves stiff or drooping in the fields,
And brown ants in the little wells beneath them,
And mossy scabs of the worm fence, heap'd stones, elder, mullein and poke-weed.

. . . .

7

Has any one supposed it lucky to be born?
I hasten to inform him or her it is just as lucky to die, and I know it.

I pass death with the dying and birth with the new-wash'd babe, and am not contain'd between
    my hat and boots,
And peruse manifold objects, no two alike and every one good,
The earth good and the stars good, and their adjuncts all good.

I am not an earth nor an adjunct of an earth,
I am the mate and companion of people, all just as immortal and fathomless as myself,
(They do not know how immortal, but I know.)

Every kind for itself and its own, for me mine male and female,
For me those that have been boys and that love women,
For me the man that is proud and feels how it stings to be slighted,
For me the sweet-heart and the old maid, for me mothers and mothers of mothers,
For me lips that have smiled, eyes that have shed tears,
For me children and the begetters of children.
Undrape! you are not guilty to me, nor stale nor discarded,
I see through the broadcloth and gingham whether or no,
And am around, tenacious, acquisitive, tireless, and cannot be shaken away.

8

The little one sleeps in its cradle,
I lift the gauze and look a long time, and silently brush away flies with my hand.
The youngster and the red-faced girl turn aside up the bushy hill,
I peeringly view them from the top.
The suicide sprawls on the bloody floor of the bedroom,
I witness the corpse with its dabbled hair, I note where the pistol has fallen.

The blab of the pave, tires of carts, sluff of boot-soles, talk of the promenaders,
The heavy omnibus, the driver with his interrogating thumb, the clank of the shod horses on
    the granite floor,
The snow-sleighs, clinking, shouted jokes, pelts of snow-balls,
The hurrahs for popular favorites, the fury of rous'd mobs,

The flap of the curtain'd litter, a sick man inside borne to the hospital,
The meeting of enemies, the sudden oath, the blows and fall,
The excited crowd, the policeman with his star quickly working his passage to the centre of the
    crowd,
The impassive stones that receive and return so many echoes,
What groans of over-fed or half-starv'd who fall sunstruck or in fits,
What exclamations of women taken suddenly who hurry home and give birth to babes,
What living and buried speech is always vibrating here, what howls restrain'd by decorum,
Arrests of criminals, slights, adulterous offers made, acceptances, rejections with convex lips,
I mind them or the show or resonance of them—I come and I depart.

9

The big doors of the country barn stand open and ready,
The dried grass of the harvest-time loads the slow-drawn wagon,
The clear light plays on the brown gray and green intertinged,
The armfuls are pack'd to the sagging mow.

I am there, I help, I came stretch'd atop of the load,
I felt its soft jolts, one leg reclined on the other,
I jump from the cross-beams and seize the clover and timothy,
And roll head over heels and tangle my hair full of wisps.

10

Alone far in the wilds and mountains I hunt,
Wandering amazed at my own lightness and glee,
In the late afternoon choosing a safe spot to pass the night,
Kindling a fire and broiling the fresh-kill'd game,
Falling asleep on the gather'd leaves with my dog and gun by my side.

The Yankee clipper is under her sky-sails, she cuts the sparkle and scud,
My eyes settle the land, I bend at her prow or shout joyously from the deck.

The boatmen and clam-diggers arose early and stopt for me,
I tuck'd my trowser-ends in my boots and went and had a good time;
You should have been with us that day round the chowder-kettle.

I saw the marriage of the trapper in the open air in the far west, the bride was a red girl,
Her father and his friends sat near cross-legged and dumbly smoking, they had moccasins to
    their feet and large thick blankets hanging from their shoulders,
On a bank lounged the trapper, he was drest mostly in skins, his luxuriant beard and curls
    protected his neck, he held his bride by the hand,
She had long eyelashes, her head was bare, her coarse straight locks descended upon her vo-
    luptuous limbs and reach'd to her feet.
The runaway slave came to my house and stopt outside,
I heard his motions crackling the twigs of the woodpile,
Through the swung half-door of the kitchen I saw him limpsy and weak,
And went where he sat on a log and led him in and assured him,

And brought water and fill'd a tub for his sweated body and bruis'd feet,
And gave him a room that enter'd from my own, and gave him some coarse clean clothes,
And remember perfectly well his revolving eyes and his awkwardness,
And remember putting plasters on the galls of his neck and ankles;
He staid with me a week before he was recuperated and pass'd north,
I had him sit next me at table, my fire-lock lean'd in the corner.

11

Twenty-eight young men bathe by the shore,
Twenty-eight young men and all so friendly;
Twenty-eight years of womanly life and all so lonesome.

She owns the fine house by the rise of the bank,
She hides handsome and richly drest aft the blinds of the window.

Which of the young men does she like the best?
Ah the homeliest of them is beautiful to her.

Where are you off to, lady? for I see you,
You splash in the water there, yet stay stock still in your room.

Dancing and laughing along the beach came the twenty-ninth bather,
The rest did not see her, but she saw them and loved them.
The beards of the young men glisten'd with wet, it ran from their long hair,
Little streams pass'd all over their bodies.

An unseen hand also pass'd over their bodies,
It descended tremblingly from their temples and ribs.

The young men float on their backs, their white bellies bulge to the sun, they do not ask who
    seizes fast to them,
They do not know who puffs and declines with pendant and bending arch,
They do not think whom they souse with spray.

12

The butcher-boy puts off his killing-clothes, or sharpens his knife at the stall in the market,
I loiter enjoying his repartee and his shuffle and break-down.

Blacksmiths with grimed and hairy chests environ the anvil,
Each has his main-sledge, they are all out, there is a great heat in the fire.

From the cinder-strew'd threshold I follow their movements,
The lithe sheer of their waists plays even with their massive arms,
Overhand the hammers swing, overhand so slow, overhand so sure,
They do not hasten, each man hits in his place.

13

The negro holds firmly the reins of his four horses, the block swags underneath on its tied-over chain,
The negro that drives the long dray of the stone-yard, steady and tall he stands pois'd on one leg on the string-piece,
His blue shirt exposes his ample neck and breast and loosens over his hip-band,
His glance is calm and commanding, he tosses the slouch of his hat away from his forehead,
The sun falls on his crispy hair and mustache, falls on the black of his polish'd and perfect limbs.

I behold the picturesque giant and love him, and I do not stop there,
I go with the team also.

In me the caresser of life wherever moving, backward as well as forward sluing,
To niches aside and junior bending, not a person or object missing,
Absorbing all to myself and for this song.

Oxen that rattle the yoke and chain or halt in the leafy shade, what is that you express in your eyes?
It seems to me more than all the print I have read in my life.

My tread scares the wood-drake and wood-duck on my distant and day-long ramble,
They rise together, they slowly circle around.

I believe in those wing'd purposes,
And acknowledge red, yellow, white, playing within me,
And consider green and violet and the tufted crown intentional,
And do not call the tortoise unworthy because she is not something else,
And the jay in the woods never studied the gamut, yet trills pretty well to me,
And the look of the bay mare shames silliness out of me.

14

The wild gander leads his flock through the cool night,
Ya-honk he says, and sounds it down to me like an invitation,
The pert may suppose it meaningless, but I listening close,
Find its purpose and place up there toward the wintry sky.

The sharp-hoof'd moose of the north, the cat on the house-sill, the chickadee, the prairie-dog,
The litter of the grunting sow as they tug at her teats,
The brood of the turkey-hen and she with her half-spread wings,
I see in them and myself the same old law.

The press of my foot to the earth springs a hundred affections,
They scorn the best I can do to relate them.

I am enamour'd of growing out-doors,
Of men that live among cattle or taste of the ocean or woods,
Of the builders and steerers of ships and the wielders of axes and mauls, and the drivers of horses,
I can eat and sleep with them week in and week out.

What is commonest, cheapest, nearest, easiest, is Me,
Me going in for my chances, spending for vast returns,
Adorning myself to bestow myself on the first that will take me,
Not asking the sky to come down to my good will,
Scattering it freely forever.

15

The pure contralto sings in the organ loft,
The carpenter dresses his plank, the tongue of his foreplane whistles its wild ascending lisp,
The married and unmarried children ride home to their Thanksgiving dinner,
The pilot seizes the king-pin, he heaves down with a strong arm,
The mate stands braced in the whale-boat, lance and harpoon are ready,
The duck-shooter walks by silent and cautious stretches,
The deacons are ordain'd with cross'd hands at the altar,
The spinning-girl retreats and advances to the hum of the big wheel,
The farmer stops by the bars as he walks on a First-day loafe and looks at the oats and rye,
The lunatic is carried at last to the asylum a confirm'd case,
(He will never sleep any more as he did in the cot in his mother's bed-room;)
The jour printer with gray head and gaunt jaws works at his case,
He turns his quid of tobacco while his eyes blurr with the manuscript;
The malform'd limbs are tied to the surgeon's table,
What is removed drops horribly in a pail;
The quadroon girl is sold at the auction-stand, the drunkard nods by the bar-room stove,
The machinist rolls up his sleeves, the policeman travels his beat, the gate-keeper marks who pass,
The young fellow drives the express-wagon, (I love him, though I do not know him;)
The half-breed straps on his light boots to compete in the race,
The western turkey-shooting draws old and young, some lean on their rifles, some sit on logs,
Out from the crowd steps the marksman, takes his position, levels his piece;
The groups of newly-come immigrants cover the wharf or levee,
As the woolly-pates hoe in the sugar-field, the overseer views them from his saddle,
The bugle calls in the ball-room, the gentlemen run for their partners, the dancers bow to each
    other,
The youth lies awake in the cedar-roof'd garret and harks to the musical rain,
The Wolverine sets traps on the creek that helps fill the Huron,
The squaw wrapt in her yellow-hemm'd cloth is offering moccasins and bead-bags for sale,
The connoisseur peers along the exhibition-gallery with half-shut eyes bent sideways,
As the deck-hands make fast the steamboat the plank is thrown for the shore-going passengers,
The young sister holds out the skein while the elder sister winds it off in a ball, and stops now
    and then for the knots,
The one-year wife is recovering and happy having a week ago borne her first child,
The clean-hair'd Yankee girl works with her sewing-machine or in the factory or mill,
The paving-man leans on his two-handed rammer, the reporter's lead flies swiftly over the note-
    book, the sign-painter is lettering with blue and gold,
The canal boy trots on the tow-path, the bookkeeper counts at his desk, the shoemaker waxes
    his thread,
The conductor beats time for the band and all the performers follow him,
The child is baptized, the convert is making his first professions,
The regatta is spread on the bay, the race is begun, (how the white sails sparkle!)
The drover watching his drove sings out to them that would stray,

The pedler sweats with his pack on his back, (the purchaser higgling about the odd cent;)
The bride unrumples her white dress, the minute-hand of the clock moves slowly,
The opium-eater reclines with rigid head and just-open'd lips,
The prostitute draggles her shawl, her bonnet bobs on her tipsy and pimpled neck,
The crowd laugh at her blackguard oaths, the men jeer and wink to each other,
(Miserable! I do not laugh at your oaths nor jeer you;)
The President holding a cabinet council is surrounded by the great Secretaries,
On the piazza walk three matrons stately and friendly with twined arms,
The crew of the fish-smack pack repeated layers of halibut in the hold,
The Missourian crosses the plains toting his wares and his cattle,
As the fare-collector goes through the train he gives notice by the jingling of loose change,
The floor-men are laying the floor, the tinners are tinning the roof, the masons are calling for
    mortar,
In single file each shouldering his hod pass onward the laborers;
Seasons pursuing each other the indescribable crowd is gather'd, it is the fourth of Seventh-
    month, (what salutes of cannon and small arms!)
Seasons pursuing each other the plougher ploughs, the mower mows, and the winter-grain falls
    in the ground;
Off on the lakes the pike-fisher watches and waits by the hole in the frozen surface,
The stumps stand thick round the clearing, the squatter strikes deep with his axe,
Flatboatmen make fast towards dusk near the cotton-wood or pecan-trees,
Coon-seekers go through the regions of the Red river or through those drain'd by the Tennessee,
    or through those of the Arkansas,
Torches shine in the dark that hangs on the Chattahooche or Altamahaw,
Patriarchs sit at supper with sons and grandsons and great-grandsons around them,
In walls of adobie, in canvas tents, rest hunters and trappers after their day's sport,
The city sleeps and the country sleeps,
The living sleep for their time, the dead sleep for their time,
The old husband sleeps by his wife and the young husband sleeps by his wife;
And these tend inward to me, and I tend outward to them,
And such as it is to be of these more or less I am,
And of these one and all I weave the song of myself.

16

I am of old and young, of the foolish as much as the wise,
Regardless of others, ever regardful of others,
Maternal as well as paternal, a child as well as a man,
Stuff'd with the stuff that is coarse and stuff'd with the stuff that is fine,
One of the Nation of many nations, the smallest the same and the largest the same,
A Southerner soon as a Northerner, a planter nonchalant and hospitable down by the Oconee I
    live,
A Yankee bound my own way ready for trade, my joints the limberest joints on earth and the
    sternest joints on earth,
A Kentuckian walking the vale of the Elkhorn in my deer-skin leggings, a Louisianian or
    Georgian,
A boatman over lakes or bays or along coasts, a Hoosier, Badger, Buckeye;
At home on Kanadian snow-shoes or up in the bush, or with fishermen off Newfoundland,
At home in the fleet of ice-boats, sailing with the rest and tacking,
At home on the hills of Vermont or in the woods of Maine, or the Texan ranch,

Comrade of Californians, comrade of free North Westerners, (loving their big proportions,)
Comrade of raftsmen and coalmen, comrade of all who shake hands and welcome to drink and
      meat,
A learner with the simplest, a teacher of the thoughtfullest,
A novice beginning yet experient of myriads of seasons,
Of every hue and caste am I, of every rank and religion,
A farmer, mechanic, artist, gentleman, sailor, quaker,
Prisoner, fancy-man, rowdy, lawyer, physician, priest.

I resist any thing better than my own diversity,
Breathe the air but leave plenty after me,
And am not stuck up, and am in my place.

(The moth and the fish-eggs are in their place,
The bright suns I see and the dark suns I cannot see are in their place,
The palpable is in its place and the impalpable is in its place.)

17

These are really the thoughts of all men in all ages and lands, they are not original with me,
If they are not yours as much as mine they are nothing, or next to nothing,
If they are not the riddle and the untying of the riddle they are nothing,
If they are not just as close as they are distant they are nothing.

This is the grass that grows wherever the land is and the water is,
This the common air that bathes the globe.

. . . .

24

Walt Whitman, a kosmos, of Manhattan the son,
Turbulent, fleshy, sensual, eating, drinking and breeding,
No sentimentalist, no stander above men and women or apart from them,
No more modest than immodest.

Unscrew the locks from the doors!
Unscrew the doors themselves from their jambs!

Whoever degrades another degrades me,
And whatever is done or said returns at last to me.

Through me the afflatus surging and surging, through me the current and index.

I speak the pass-word primeval, I give the sign of democracy,
By God! I will accept nothing which all cannot have their counterpart of on the same terms.

Through me many long dumb voices,
Voices of the interminable generations of prisoners and slaves,

Voices of the diseas'd and despairing and of thieves and dwarfs,
Voices of cycles of preparation and accretion,
And of the threads that connect the stars, and of wombs and of the father-stuff,

And of the rights of them the others are down upon,
Of the deform'd, trivial, flat, foolish, despised,
Fog in the air, beetles rolling balls of dung.

Through me forbidden voices,
Voices of sexes and lusts, voices veil'd and I remove the veil,
Voices indecent by me clarified and transfigur'd.
I do not press my fingers across my mouth,
I keep as delicate around the bowels as around the head and heart,
Copulation is no more rank to me than death is.

I believe in the flesh and the appetites,
Seeing, hearing, feeling, are miracles, and each part and tag of me is a miracle.
Divine am I inside and out, and I make holy whatever I touch or am touch'd from,
The scent of these arm-pits aroma finer than prayer,
This head more than churches, bibles, and all the creeds.

If I worship one thing more than another it shall be the spread of my own body, or any part of it,
Translucent mould of me it shall be you!
Shaded ledges and rests it shall be you!
Firm masculine colter it shall be you!
Whatever goes to the tilth of me it shall be you!
You my rich blood! your milky stream pale strippings of my life!
Breast that presses against other breasts it shall be you!
My brain it shall be your occult convolutions!
Root of wash'd sweet flag! timorous pond-snipe! nest of guarded duplicate eggs! it shall be you!
Mix'd tussled hay of head, beard, brawn, it shall be you!
Trickling sap of maple, fibre of manly wheat, it shall be you!
Sun so generous it shall be you!
Vapors lighting and shading my face it shall be you!
You sweaty brooks and dews it shall be you!
Winds whose soft-tickling genitals rub against me it shall be you!
Broad muscular fields, branches of live oak, loving lounger in my winding paths, it shall be you!
Hands I have taken, face I have kiss'd, mortal I have ever touch'd, it shall be you.

I dote on myself, there is that lot of me and all so luscious,
Each moment and whatever happens thrills me with joy,
I cannot tell how my ankles bend, nor whence the cause of my faintest wish,
Nor the cause of the friendship I emit, nor the cause of the friendship I take again.

That I walk up my stoop, I pause to consider if it really be,
A morning-glory at my window satisfies me more than the metaphysics of books.

To behold the day-break!
The little light fades the immense and diaphanous shadows,
The air tastes good to my palate.
Hefts of the moving world at innocent gambols silently rising, freshly exuding,
Scooting obliquely high and low.

Something I cannot see puts upward libidinous prongs,
Seas of bright juice suffuse heaven.
The earth by the sky staid with, the daily close of their junction,
The heav'd challenge from the east that moment over my head,
The mocking taunt, See then whether you shall be master!

. . . .

33

Space and Time! now I see it is true, what I guess'd at,
What I guess'd when I loaf'd on the grass,
What I guess'd while I lay alone in my bed,
And again as I walk'd the beach under the paling stars of the morning.
My ties and ballasts leave me, my elbows rest in sea-gaps,
I skirt sierras, my palms cover continents,
I am afoot with my vision.

. . . .

I ascend to the foretruck,
I take my place late at night in the crow's-nest,
We sail the arctic sea, it is plenty light enough,
Through the clear atmosphere I stretch around on the wonderful beauty,
The enormous masses of ice pass me and I pass them, the scenery is plain in all directions,
The white-topt mountains show in the distance, I fling out my fancies toward them,
We are approaching some great battle-field in which we are soon to be engaged,
We pass the colossal outposts of the encampment, we pass with still feet and caution,
Or we are entering by the suburbs some vast and ruin'd city,
The blocks and fallen architecture more than all the living cities of the globe.

I am a free companion, I bivouac by invading watchfires,
I turn the bridegroom out of bed and stay with the bride myself,
I tighten her all night to my thighs and lips.

My voice is the wife's voice, the screech by the rail of the stairs,
They fetch my man's body up dripping and drown'd.

I understand the large hearts of heroes,
The courage of present times and all times,
How the skipper saw the crowded and rudderless wreck of the steam-ship, and Death chasing it
    up and down the storm,
How he knuckled tight and gave not back an inch, and was faithful of days and faithful of
    nights,
And chalk'd in large letters on a board, *Be of good cheer, we will not desert you;*
How he follow'd with them and tack'd with them three days and would not give it up,
How he saved the drifting company at last,
How the lank loose-gown'd women look'd when boated from the side of their prepared graves,
How the silent old-faced infants and the lifted sick, and the sharp-lipp'd unshaven men;
All this I swallow, it tastes good, I like it well, it becomes mine,
I am the man, I suffer'd, I was there.

The disdain and calmness of martyrs,
The mother of old, condemn'd for a witch, burnt with dry wood, her children gazing on,
The hounded slave that flags in the race, leans by the fence, blowing, cover'd with sweat.
The twinges that sting like needles his legs and neck, the murderous buckshot and the bullets
All these I feel or am.

I am the hounded slave, I wince at the bite of the dogs,
Hell and despair are upon me, crack and again crack the marksmen,
I clutch the rails of the fence, my gore drips, thinn'd with the ooze of my skin,
I fall on the weeds and stones,
The riders spur their unwilling horses, haul close,
Taunt my dizzy ears and beat me violently over the head with whip-stocks.

Agonies are one of my changes of garments,
I do not ask the wounded person how he feels, I myself become the wounded person,
My hurts turn livid upon me as I lean on a cane and observe.

I am the mash'd fireman with breast-bone broken,
Tumbling walls buried me in their debris,
Heat and smoke I inspired, I heard the yelling shouts of my comrades,
I heard the distant click of their picks and shovels,
They have clear'd the beams away, they tenderly lift me forth.
I lie in the night air in my red shirt, the pervading hush is for my sake,
Painless after all I lie exhausted but not so unhappy,
White and beautiful are the faces around me, the heads are bared of their fire-caps,
The kneeling crowd fades with the light of the torches.

Distant and dead resuscitate,
They show as the dial or move as the hands of me, I am the clock myself.

I am an old artillerist, I tell of my fort's bombardment,
I am there again.

Again the long roll of the drummers,
Again the attacking cannon, mortars,
Again to my listening ears the cannon responsive.
I take part, I see and hear the whole,
The cries, curses, roar, the plaudits for well-aim'd shots,
The ambulanza slowly passing trailing its red drip,
Workmen searching after damages, making indispensable repairs,
The fall of grenades through the rent roof, the fan-shaped explosion,
The whizz of limbs, heads, stone, wood, iron, high in the air.
Again gurgles the mouth of my dying general, he furiously waves with his hand,
He gasps through the clot *Mind not me—mind—the entrenchments.*

· · · ·

Charles Darwin

Charles Darwin (1809–1882) was a member of an English family noted for its intellectual accomplishments. From an early age he displayed a remarkable interest in nature and its ramifications. In 1831 Darwin left Cambridge University to serve as naturalist on a scientific surveying expedition aboard the Beagle to South America and the southern hemisphere. The voyage lasted five years and gave him the opportunity of observing in great detail the immense variation in, and distribution of, the organic beings in South America, as well as the geological relations of the existing to the past inhabitants of that continent. In 1832 he read the thought-provoking essay by Malthus on population with its emphasis on the struggle for existence, and this essay helped to confirm Darwin's theory of the survival of those variants possessing characteristics favorable to life in their particular environment. In 1859 he published The Origin of Species, in which he summarized his views of organic evolution by means of variation, natural selection, and survival of the fittest. The following selection is from the recapitulation and conclusion of this momentous work. In reading it note (1) Darwin's summary of his theory, (2) his reply to those who objected to his views on religious grounds, (3) what he considered the chief cause of men's unwillingness to accept his theory, (4) his argument for refuting the idea of special creations for each species, (5) the evidence he presented to substantiate the idea that all animals and plants are descended from one prototype, (6) the possibility of using organic change as a measure of time, (7) Darwin's argument that organic evolution is an enobling act on the part of the Creator, and (8) his illustration, in the final paragraph of the selection, of the various phases of his theory.

From: THE ORIGIN OF SPECIES

I have now recapitulated the facts and considerations which have thoroughly convinced me that species have been modified, during a long course of descent. This has been effected chiefly through the natural selection of numerous successive, slight, favourable variations; aided in an important manner by the inherited effects of the use and disuse of parts; and in an unimportant manner, that is in relation to adaptive structures, whether past or present, by the direct action of external conditions, and by variations which seem to us in our ignorance to arise spontaneously. It appears that I formerly underrated the frequency and value of these latter forms of variation, as leading to permanent modifications of structure independently of natural selection. But as my conclusions have lately been much misrepresented, and it has been stated that I attribute the modification of species exclusively to natural selec-

Charles Darwin, The Origin of Species by Means of Natural Selection or the Preservation of Favored Races in the Struggle for Life, 6th ed., New York, n.d., 465–474.

tion, I may be permitted to remark that in the first edition of this work, and subsequently, I placed in a most conspicuous position—namely, at the close of the Introduction—the following words: "I am convinced that natural selection has been the main but not the exclusive means of modification." This has been of no avail. Great is the power of steady misrepresentation; but the history of science shows that fortunately this power does not long endure.

It can hardly be supposed that a false theory would explain, in so satisfactory a manner as does the theory of natural selection, the several large classes of facts above specified. It has recently been objected that this is an unsafe method of arguing; but it is a method used in judging of the common events of life, and has often been used by the greatest natural philosophers. The undulatory theory of light has thus been arrived at; and the belief in the revolution of the earth on its axis was until lately supported by hardly any direct evidence. It is no valid objection that science as yet throws no light on the far higher problem of the essence or origin of life. Who can explain what is the essence of the attraction of gravity? No one now objects to following out the results consequent on this unknown element of attraction; notwithstanding that Leibnitz formerly accused Newton of introducing "occult qualities and miracles into philosophy."

I see no good reason why the views given in this volume should shock the religious feelings of any one. It is satisfactory, as showing how transient such impressions are, to remember that the greatest discovery ever made by man, namely, the law of the attraction of gravity, was also attacked by Leibnitz, "as subversive of natural, and inferentially of revealed, religion." A celebrated author and divine has written to me that "he has gradually learnt to see that it is just as noble a conception of the Deity to believe that He created a few original forms capable of self-development into other and needful forms, as to believe that He required a fresh act of creation to supply the voids caused by the action of His laws."

Why, it may be asked, until recently did nearly all the most eminent living naturalists and geologists disbelieve in the mutability of species. It cannot be asserted that organic beings in a state of nature are subject to no variation; it cannot be proved that the amount of variation in the course of long ages is a limited quantity; no clear distinction has been, or can be, drawn between species and well-marked varieties. It cannot be maintained that species when intercrossed are invariably sterile, and varieties invariably fertile; or that sterility is a special endowment and sign of creation. The belief that species were immutable productions was almost unavoidable as long as the history of the world was thought to be of short duration; and now that we have acquired some idea of the lapse of time, we are too apt to assume, without proof, that the geological record is so perfect that it would have afforded us plain evidence of the mutation of species, if they had undergone mutation.

But the chief cause of our natural unwillingness to admit that one species has given birth to other and distinct species, is that we are always slow in admitting great changes of which we do not see the steps. The difficulty is the same as that felt by so many geologists, when Lyell first insisted that long lines of inland cliffs had been formed, and great valleys excavated, by the agencies which we see still at work. The mind cannot possibly grasp the full meaning of the term of even a million years; it cannot add up and perceive the full effects of many slight variations, accumulated during an almost infinite number of generations.

Although I am fully convinced of the truth of the views given in this volume under the form of an abstract, I by no means expect to convince experienced naturalists whose minds are stocked with a multitude of facts all viewed, during a long course of years, from a point of view directly opposite to mine. It is so easy to hide our ignorance under such expressions as the "plan of creation," "unity of design," etc., and to think that we give an explanation when we only restate a fact. Any one whose disposition leads him to attach more weight to unexplained difficulties than to the explanation of a certain number of facts will certainly reject the theory. A few naturalists, endowed with much flexibility of mind, and who have already begun to doubt the immutability of species, may be influenced by this volume; but I look with confidence to the future, to young and rising naturalists, who will be able to view both sides of the question with impartiality. Whoever is led to believe that species are mutable will do good service by conscientiously expressing his conviction; for thus only can the load of prejudice by which this subject is overwhelmed be removed.

Several eminent naturalists have of late published their belief that a multitude of reputed species in each genus are not real species; but that other species are real, that is, have been independently created. This seems to me a strange conclusion to arrive at. They admit that a multitude of forms, which till lately they themselves thought were special creations, and which are still thus looked at by the majority of naturalists, and which consequently have all the external characteristic features of true species,—they admit that these have been produced by variation, but they refuse to extend the same view to other and slightly different forms. Nevertheless they do not pretend that they can define, or even conjecture, which are the created forms of life, and which are those produced by secondary laws. They admit variation as a *vera causa* in one case, they arbitrarily reject it in another, without assigning any distinction in the two cases. The day will come when this will be given as a curious illustration of the blindness of preconceived opinion. These authors seem no more startled at a miraculous act of creation than at an ordinary birth. But do they really believe that at innumerable periods in the earth's history certain elemental atoms have been commanded suddenly to flash into living tissues? Do they believe that at each supposed act of creation one individual or many were produced? Were all the infinitely numerous kinds of animals and plants created as egg or seed, or as full grown? and in the case of mammals, were they created bearing the false marks of nourishment from the mother's womb? Undoubtedly some of these same questions cannot be answered by those who believe in the appearance or creation of only a few forms of life, or of some one form alone. It has been maintained by several authors that it is as easy to believe in the creation of a million beings as of one; but Maupertuis'

philosophical axiom "of least action" leads the mind more willingly to admit the smaller number; and certainly we ought not to believe that innumerable beings within each great class have been created with plain, but deceptive, marks of descent from a single parent.

As a record of a former state of things, I have retained in the foregoing paragraphs, and elsewhere, several sentences which imply that naturalists believe in the separate creation of each species; and I have been much censured for having thus expressed myself. But undoubtedly this was the general belief when the first edition of the present work appeared. I formerly spoke to very many naturalists on the subject of evolution, and never once met with any sympathetic agreement. It is probable that some did then believe in evolution, but they were either silent, or expressed themselves so ambiguously that it was not easy to understand their meaning. Now, things are wholly changed, and almost every naturalist admits the great principle of evolution. There are, however, some who still think that species have suddenly given birth, through quite unexplained means, to new and totally different forms: but, as I have attempted to show, weighty evidence can be opposed to the admission of great and abrupt modifications. Under a scientific point of view, and as leading to further investigation, but little advantage is gained by believing that new forms are suddenly developed in an inexplicable manner from old and widely different forms, over the old belief in the creation of species from the dust of the earth.

It may be asked how far I extend the doctrine of the modification of species. The question is difficult to answer, because the more distinct the forms are which we consider, by so much the arguments in favour of community of descent become fewer in number and less in force. But some arguments of the greatest weight extend very far. All the members of whole classes are connected together by a chain of affinities, and all can be classed on the same principle, in groups subordinate to groups. Fossil remains sometimes tend to fill up very wide intervals between existing orders.

Organs in a rudimentary condition plainly show that an early progenitor had the organ in a fully developed condition; and this in some cases implies an enormous amount of modification in the descendants. Throughout whole classes various structures are formed on the same pattern, and at a very early age the embryos closely resemble each other. Therefore I cannot doubt that the theory of descent with modification embraces all the members of the same great class or kingdom. I believe that animals are descended from at most only four or five progenitors, and plants from an equal or lesser number.

Analogy would lead me one step farther, namely, to the belief that all animals and plants are descended from some one prototype. But analogy may be a deceitful guide. Nevertheless all living things have much in common, in their chemical composition, their cellular structure, their laws of growth, and their liability to injurious influences. We see this even in so trifling a fact as that the same poison often similarly affects plants and animals; or that the poison secreted by the gallfly produces monstrous growths on the wild rose or oak tree. With all organic beings, excepting perhaps some of the very lowest, sexual reproduction seems to be essentially similar. With all, as far as is at present known, the germinal vesicle is the same; so that all organisms start from a common origin. If we look even to the two main divisions—namely, to the animal and vegetable kingdoms—certain low forms are so far intermediate in character that naturalists have disputed to which kingdom they should be referred. As Professor Asa Gray has remarked, "the spores and other reproductive bodies of many of the lower algae may claim to have first a characteristically animal, and then an unequivocal vegetable, existence." Therefore, on the principle of natural selection with divergence of character, it does not seem incredible that, from some such low and intermediate form, both animals and plants may have been developed; and, if we admit this, we must likewise admit that all the organic beings which have ever lived on this earth may be descended from some one primordial form. But this inference is chiefly grounded on analogy, and it is immaterial whether or not it be accepted. No doubt it is possible, as Mr. G. H. Lewes has urged, that at the first commencement of

life many different forms were evolved; but if so, we may conclude that only a very few have left modified descendants. For, as I have recently remarked in regard to the members of each great kingdom, such as the Vertebrata, Articulata, etc., we have distinct evidence in their embryological, homologous, and rudimentary structures, that within each kingdom all the members are descended from a single progenitor.

When the views advanced by me in this volume, and by Mr. Wallace, or when analogous views on the origin of species are generally admitted, we can dimly forsee that there will be a considerable revolution in natural history. Systematists will be able to pursue their labours as at present; but they will not be incessantly haunted by the shadowy doubt whether this or that form be a true species. This, I feel sure and I speak after experience, will be no slight relief. The endless disputes whether or not some fifty species of British brambles are good species will cease. Systematists will have only to decide (not that this will be easy) whether any form be sufficiently constant and distinct from other forms, to be capable of definition; and if definable, whether the differences be sufficiently important to deserve a specific name. This latter point will become a far more essential consideration than it is at present; for differences, however slight, between any two forms, if not blended by intermediate gradations, are looked at by most naturalists as sufficient to raise both forms to the rank of species.

Hereafter we shall be compelled to acknowledge that the only distinction between species and well-marked varieties is, that the latter are known, or believed, to be connected at the present day by intermediate gradations whereas species were formerly thus connected. Hence, without rejecting the consideration of the present existence of intermediate gradations between any two forms, we shall be led to weigh more carefully and to value higher the actual amount of difference between them. It is quite possible that forms now generally acknowledged to be merely varieties may hereafter be thought worthy of specific names; and in this case scientific and common language will come into accordance. In short, we shall have to treat species in the same manner as those naturalists treat genera, who admit that genera are merely artificial combinations made for convenience. This may not be a cheering prospect; but we shall at least be freed from the vain search for the undiscovered and undiscoverable essence of the term species.

The other and more general departments of natural history will rise greatly in interest. The terms used by naturalists, of affinity, relationship, community of type, paternity, morphology, adaptive characters, rudimentary and aborted organs, etc., will cease to be metaphorical, and will have a plain signification. When we no longer look at an organic being as a savage looks at a ship, as something wholly beyond his comprehension; when we regard every production of nature as one which has had a long history; when we contemplate every complex structure and instinct as the summing up of many contrivances, each useful to the possessor, in the same way as any great mechanical invention is the summing up of the labour, the experience, the reason, and even the blunders of numerous workmen; when we thus view each organic being, how far more interesting—I speak from experience—does the study of natural history become!

A grand and almost untrodden field of inquiry will be opened, on the causes and laws of variation, on correlation, on the effects of use and disuse, on the direct action of external conditions, and so forth. The study of domestic productions will rise immensely in value. A new variety raised by man will be a more important and interesting subject for study than one more species added to the infinitude of already recorded species. Our classifications will come to be, as far as they can be so made, genealogies; and will then truly give what may be called the plan of creation. The rules for classifying will no doubt become simpler when we have a definite object in view. We possess no pedigrees or amorial bearings; and we have to discover and trace the many diverging lines of descent in our natural genealogies, by characters of any kind which have long been inherited. Rudimentary organs will speak infallibly with respect to the nature of long-lost structures. Species and groups of species which are called aberrant, and which may fancifully

be called living fossils, will aid us in forming a picture of the ancient forms of life. Embryology will often reveal to us the structure, in some degree obscured, of the prototypes of each great class.

When we can feel assured that all the individuals of the same species, and all the closely allied species of most genera, have, within a not very remote period descended from one parent, and have migrated from some one birth-place; and when we better know the many means of migration, then, by the light which geology now throws, and will continue to throw, on former changes of climate and of the level of the land, we shall surely be enabled to trace in an admirable manner the former migrations of the inhabitants of the whole world. Even at present, by comparing the differences between the inhabitants of the sea on the opposites sides of a continent, and the nature of the various inhabitants on that continent in relation to their apparent means of immigration, some light can be thrown on ancient geography.

The noble science of Geology loses glory from the extreme imperfection of the record. The crust of the earth with its imbedded remains must not be looked at as a well-filled museum, but as a poor collection made at hazard and at rare intervals. The accumulation of each great fossiliferous formation will be recognised as having depended on an unusual concurrence of favourable circumstances, and the blank intervals between the successive stages as having been of vast duration. But we shall be able to gauge with some security the duration of these intervals by a comparison of the preceding and succeeding organic forms. We must be cautious in attempting to correlate as strictly contemporaneous two formations, which do not include many identical species, by the general succession of the forms of life. As species are produced and exterminated by slowly acting and still existing causes, and not by miraculous acts of creation; and as the most important of all cause of organic change is one which is almost independent of altered and perhaps suddenly altered physical conditions, namely, the mutual relation of organism to organism,—the improvement of one organism entailing the improvement or the extermination of others; it follows, that the amount of organic change in the fossils of consecutive formations probably serves as a fair measure of the relative, though not actual lapse of time. A number of species, however, keeping in a body might remain for a long period unchanged, whilst within the same period, several of these species by migrating into new countries and coming into competition with foreign associates, might become modified; so that we must not overrate the accuracy of organic change as a measure of time.

In the future I see open fields for far more important researches. Psychology will be securely based on the foundation already well laid by Mr. Herbert Spencer, that of the necessary acquirement of each mental power and capacity by gradation. Much light will be thrown on the origin of man and his history.

Authors of the highest eminence seem to be fully satisfied with the view that each species has been independently created. To my mind it accords better with what we know of the laws impressed on matter by the Creator, that the production and extinction of the past and present inhabitants of the world should have been due to secondary causes, like those determining the birth and death of the individual. When I view all beings not as special creations, but as the lineal descendants of some few beings which lived long before the first bed of the Cambrian system was deposited, they seem to me to become ennobled. Judging from the past, we may safely infer that not one living species will transmit its unaltered likeness to a distant futurity. And of the species now living very few will transmit progeny of any kind to a far distant futurity; for the manner in which all organic beings are grouped, shows that the greater number of species in each genus, and all the species in many genera, have left no descendants, but have become utterly extinct.

We can so far take a prophetic glance into futurity as to foretell that it will be the common and widely spread species, belonging to the larger and dominant groups within each class, which will ultimately prevail and procreate new and dominant species. As all the living forms of life are the lineal descendants of those which lived long before the Cambrian epoch, we may feel certain that the ordinary succession by generation has never once been broken, and that no cataclysm has desolated the whole world. Hence we may look with some confidence to a secure future of great length. And as natural selection works solely by and for the good of each being, all corporeal and mental endowments will tend to progress towards perfection.

It is interesting to contemplate a tangled bank, clothed with many plants of many kinds, with birds singing on the bushes, with various insects flitting about, and with worms crawling through the damp earth, and to reflect that these elaborately constructed forms, so different from each other, and dependent upon each other in so complex a manner, have all been produced by laws acting around us. These laws, taken in the largest sense, being Growth with Reproduction; Inheritance which is almost implied by reproduction; Variability from the indirect and direct action of the conditions of life, and from use and disuse: a Ratio of Increase so high as to lead to a Struggle for Life, and as a consequence to Natural Selection, entailing Divergence of Character and the Extinction of less improved forms. Thus, from the war of nature, from famine and death, the most exalted object which we are capable of conceiving, namely, the production of the higher animals, directly follows. There is grandeur in this view of life, with its several powers, having been originally breathed by the Creator into a few forms or into one; and that, whilst this planet has gone cycling on according to the fixed law of gravity, from so simple a beginning endless forms most beautiful and most wonderful have been, and are being, evolved.

John Stuart Mill

J ohn Stuart Mill (1806–1873), in addition to his interest in the nature and scope of governmental authority (see p. 608), was vitally concerned with the whole problem of human knowledge and morality. His philosophic position, similar to that of Jeremy Bentham, was known as utilitarianism. In 1863 he published an essay on Utilitarianism, selections from which follow. In reading them note (1) the two opinions regarding moral standards described by Mill, (2) the one he upheld in this essay, (3) his definition of utilitarianism, (4) how moral standards were determined by this philosophy, (5) his discussion of happiness and how it differed from "animal" pleasure, (6) the forces impelling man to chose the "higher" rather than the "lower" pleasures, (7) the social consciousness implicit in the utilitarian concept of happiness, (8) the external and internal sanctions which generally enforce moral standards, and (9) the extent to which these were effective in the utilitarian concept of morality.

From: UTILITARIANISM

GENERAL REMARKS

There are few circumstances among those which make up the present condition of human knowledge, more unlike what might have been expected, or more significant of the backward state in which speculation on the most important subjects still lingers, than the little progress which has been made in the decision of the controversy respecting the criterion of right and wrong. From the dawn of philosophy, the question concerning the *summum bonum,* or, what is the same thing, concerning the foundation of morality, has been accounted the main problem in speculative thought, has occupied the most gifted intellects, and divided them into sects and schools, carrying on a vigorous warfare against one another. And after more than two thousand years the same discussions continue, philosophers are still ranged under the same contending banners, and neither thinkers nor mankind at large seem nearer to being unanimous on the subject, than when the youth Socrates listened to the old Protagoras, and asserted (if Plato's dialogue be grounded on a real conversation) the theory of utilitarianism against the popular morality of the so-called sophist.

It is true that similar confusion and uncertainty, and in some cases similar discordance, exist respecting the first principles of all the sciences, not excepting that which is deemed the most certain of them, mathematics; without much impairing, generally indeed without impairing at all, the trustworthiness of the conclusions of those sciences. An apparent anomaly, the explanation of which is, that the detailed doctrines of a science are not usually deduced from, nor depend for their evidence upon, what are called its first principles. Were it not so, there would be no science more precarious, or whose conclusions were more insufficiently made out, than algebra; which derives none of its certainty from what are commonly taught to learners as its elements, since these, as laid down by some of its most eminent teachers, are as full of fictions as English law, and of mysteries as theology. The truths which are ultimately accepted as the first principles of a science, are really the last results of metaphysical analysis, practised on the elementary notions with which the science is conversant; and their relation to the science is not that of foundations to an edifice, but of roots to a tree, which may perform their office equally well though they be never dug down to and exposed to light. But though in science the particular truths precede the general theory, the contrary might be expected to be the case with a practical art, such as morals or legislation. All action is for the sake of some end, and rules of action, it seems natural to suppose, must take their whole character and colour from the end to which they are subservient. When we engage in a pursuit, a clear and precise conception of what we are pursuing would seem to be the first thing we need, instead of the last we are to look forward to. A test of right and wrong must be the means, one would think, of ascertaining what is right or wrong, and not a consequence of having already ascertained it.

The difficulty is not avoided by having recourse to the popular theory of a natural faculty, a sense or instinct, informing us of right and wrong. For—besides that the existence of such a moral instinct is itself one of the matters in dispute—those believers in it who have any pretensions to philosophy, have been obliged to abandon the idea that it discerns what is right or wrong in the particular case in hand, as our other senses discern the sight or sound actually present. Our moral faculty, according to all those of its interpreters who are entitled to the name of thinkers, supplies us only with the general principles of moral judgments; it is a branch of our reason, not of our sensitive faculty; and must be looked to for the abstract doctrines of morality, not for perception of it in the concrete. The intuitive, no less than what may be termed the inductive, school of ethics, insists on the necessity of general laws. They both agree that the morality of an individual action is not a question of direct perception, but of the application of a law to an individual case. They recognise also, to a great extent, the same moral laws; but differ as to their evidence, and the source from which they derive their authority. According to the one opinion, the principles of morals are evident à priori, requiring nothing to command assent, except that the meaning of the terms be understood. According to the other doctrine, right and wrong, as well as truth and falsehood, are questions of observation and experience. But both hold equally that morality must be deduced from principles; and the intuitive school affirm as strongly as the inductive, that there is a science of morals. Yet they seldom attempt to make out a list of the à priori principles which are to serve as the premises of the science; still more rarely do they make any effort to reduce those various principles to one first principle, or common ground of obligation. They either assume the ordinary precepts of morals as of à priori authority, or they lay down as the common groundwork of those maxims, some generality much less obviously authoritative than the maxims themselves, and which has never succeeded in gaining popular acceptance. Yet to support their pretensions there ought either to be some one fundamental principle or law, at the root of all morality, or if there be several, there would be a determinate order of precedence among them; and the one principle, or the rule for deciding between the various principles when they conflict, ought to be self-evident.

To inquire how far the bad effects of this deficiency have been mitigated in practice, or to what extent the moral beliefs of mankind have been vitiated or made uncertain by the absence of any distinct recognition of an ultimate standard, would imply a complete survey and criticism of past and present ethical doctrine. It would, however, be easy to show that whatever steadiness or consistency these moral beliefs have attained, has been mainly due to the tacit influence of a standard not recognised. Although the non-existence of an acknowledged first principle has made ethics not so much a guide as a consecration of men's actual sentiments, still, as men's sentiments, both of favour and of aversion, are greatly influenced by what they suppose to be the effects of things upon their happiness, the principle of utility, or as Bentham latterly called it, the greatest happiness principle, has had a large share in forming the moral doctrines even of those who most scornfully reject its authority. Nor is there any school of thought which refuses to admit that the influence of actions on happiness is a most material and even predominant consideration in many of the details of morals, however unwilling to acknowledge it as the fundamental principle of morality, and the source of moral obligation. I might go much further, and say that to all those *à priori* moralists who deem it necessary to argue at all, utilitarian arguments are indispensable. It is not my present purpose to criticise these thinkers; but I cannot help referring, for illustration, to a systematic treatise by one of the most illustrious of them, the *Metaphysics of Ethics* by Kant. This remarkable man, whose system of thought will long remain one of the landmarks in the history of philosophical speculation, does, in the treatise in question, lay down a universal first principle as the origin and ground of moral obligation; it is this:—"So act, that the rule on which thou actest would admit of being adopted as a law by all rational beings." But when he begins to deduce from this precept any of the actual duties of morality, he fails, almost grotesquely, to show that there would be any contradiction, any logical (not to say physical) impossibility, in the adoption by all rational beings of the most outrageously immoral rules of conduct. All he shows is that the *consequences* of their universal adoption would be such as no one would choose to incur.

On the present occasion, I shall, without further discussion of the other theories, attempt to contribute something towards the understanding and appreciation of the Utilitarian or Happiness theory, and towards such proof as it is susceptible of. It is evident that this cannot be proof in the ordinary and popular meaning of the term. Questions of ultimate ends are not amenable to direct proof. Whatever can be proved to be good, must be so by being shown to be a means to something admitted to be good without proof. The medical art is proved to be good by its conducing to health; but how is it possible to prove that health is good? The art of music is good, for the reason, among others, that it produces pleasure; but what proof is it possible to give that pleasure is good? If, then, it is asserted that there is a comprehensive formula, including all things which are in themselves good, and whatever else is good,

is not so as an end, but as a mean, the formula may be accepted or rejected, but is not a subject of what is commonly understood by proof. We are not, however, to infer that its acceptance or rejection must depend on blind impulse, or arbitrary choice. There is a larger meaning of the word proof, in which this question is as amenable to it as any other of the disputed questions of philosophy. The subject is within the cognisance of the rational faculty; and neither does that faculty deal with it solely in the way of intuition. Considerations may be presented capable of determining the intellect either to give or withhold its assent to the doctrine; and this is equivalent to proof.

We shall examine presently of what nature are these considerations; in what manner they apply to the case, and what rational grounds, therefore, can be given for accepting or rejecting the utilitarian formula. But it is a preliminary condition of rational acceptance or rejection, that the formula should be correctly understood. I believe that the very imperfect notion ordinarily formed of its meaning, is the chief obstacle which impedes its reception; and that could it be cleared, even from only the grosser misconceptions, the question would be greatly simplified, and a large proportion of its difficulties removed. Before, therefore, I attempt to enter into the philosophical grounds which can be given for assenting to the utilitarian standard, I shall offer some illustrations of the doctrine itself; with the view of showing more clearly what it is, distinguishing it from what it is not, and disposing of such of the practical objections to it as either originate in, or are closely connected with, mistaken interpretations of its meaning. Having thus prepared the ground, I shall afterwards endeavour to throw such light as I can upon the question, considered as one of philosophical theory.

WHAT UTILITARIANISM IS

A passing remark is all that needs be given to the ignorant blunder of supposing that those who stand up for utility as the test of right and wrong, use the term in that restricted and merely colloquial sense in which utility is opposed to pleasure. An apology is due to the philosophical opponents of utilitarianism, for even the momentary appearance of confounding them with any one capable of so absurd a misconception; which is the more extraordinary, inasmuch as the contrary accusation, of referring everything to pleasure, and that too in its grossest form, is another of the common charges against utilitarianism: and, as has been pointedly remarked by an able writer, the same sort of persons, and often the very same persons, denounce the theory "as impracticably dry when the word utility precedes the word pleasure, and as too practicably voluptuous when the word pleasure precedes the word utility." Those who know anything about the matter are aware that every writer, from Epicurus to Bentham, who maintained the theory of utility, meant by it, not something to be contradistinguished from pleasure, but pleasure itself, together with exemption from pain; and instead of opposing the useful to the agreeable or the ornamental, have always declared that the useful means these, among other things. Yet the common herd, including the herd of writers, not only in newspapers and periodicals, but in books of weight and pretension, are perpetually falling into this shallow mistake. Having caught up the word utilitarian, while knowing nothing whatever about it but its sound, they habitually express by it the rejection, or the neglect, of pleasure in some of its forms; of beauty, of ornament, or of amusement. Nor is the term thus ignorantly misapplied solely in disparagement, but occasionally in compliment; as though it implied superiority to frivolity and the mere pleasures of the moment. And this perverted use is the only one in which the word is popularly known, and the one from which the new generation are acquiring their sole notion of its meaning. Those who introduced the word, but who had for many years discontinued it as a distinctive appellation, may well feel themselves called upon to resume it, if by doing so they can hope to contribute anything towards rescuing it from this utter degradation.

The creed which accepts as the foundation of morals, Utility, or the Greatest Happiness Principle, holds that actions are right in proportion as they tend to promote happiness, wrong as they tend to produce the reverse of happiness. By happiness is intended pleasure, and the absence of pain; by unhappiness, pain, and the privation of pleasure. To give a clear view of the moral standard set up by the theory, much more requires to be said; in particular, what things it includes in the ideas of pain and pleasure; and to what extent this is left an open question. But these supplementary explanations do not affect the theory of life on which this theory of morality is grounded—namely, that pleasure, and freedom from pain, are the only things desirable as ends; and that all desirable things (which are as numerous in the utilitarian as in any other scheme) are desirable either for the pleasure inherent in themselves, or as means to the promotion of pleasure and the prevention of pain.

Now, such a theory of life excites in many minds, and among them in some of the most estimable in feeling and purpose, inveterate dislike. To suppose that life has (as they express it) no higher end than pleasure—no better and nobler object of desire and pursuit—they designate as utterly mean and grovelling; as a doctrine worthy only of swine, to whom the followers of Epicurus were, at a very early period, contemptuously likened; and modern holders of the doctrine are occasionally made the subject of equally polite comparisons by its German, French, and English assailants.

When thus attacked, the Epicureans have always answered, that it is not they, but their accusers, who represent human nature in a degrading light; since the accusation supposes human beings to be capable of no pleasures except those of which swine are capable. If this supposition were true, the charge could not be gainsaid, but would then be no longer an imputation; for if the sources of pleasure were precisely the same to human beings and to swine, the rule of life which is good enough for the one would be good enough for the other. The comparison of the Epicurean life to that of beasts is felt as degrading, precisely because a beast's pleasures do not satisfy a human being's conceptions of happiness. Human beings have faculties more elevated than the animal appetites, and when once made conscious of them, do not regard anything as happiness which does not include their gratification. I do not, indeed, consider the Epicureans to have been by any means faultless in drawing out their scheme of consequences from the utilitarian principle. To do this in any sufficient manner, many Stoic, as well as Christian elements require to be included. But there is no known Epicurean theory of life which does not assign to the pleasures of the intellect, of the feelings and imagination, and of the moral sentiments, a much higher value as pleasures than to those of mere sensation. It must be admitted, however, that utilitarian writers in general have placed the superiority of mental over bodily pleasures chiefly in the greater permanency, safety, uncostliness, etc., of the former—that is, in their circumstantial advantages rather than in their intrinsic nature. And on all these points utilitarians have fully proved their case; but they might have taken the other, and, as it may be called, higher ground, with entire consistency. It is quite compatible with the principle of utility to recognise the fact, that some *kinds* of pleasure are more desirable and more valuable than others. It would be absurd that while, in estimating all other things, quality is considered as well as quantity, the estimation of pleasures should be supposed to depend on quantity alone.

If I am asked, what I mean by difference of quality in pleasures, or what makes one pleasure more valuable than another, merely as a pleasure, except its being greater in amount, there is but one possible answer. Of two pleasures, if there be one to which all or almost all who have experience of both give a decided preference, irrespective of any feeling of moral obligation to prefer it, that is the more desirable pleasure. If one of the two is, by those who are competently acquainted with both, placed so far above the other that they prefer it, even though knowing it to be attended with a greater amount of discontent, and would not resign it for any quantity of the other pleasure which their nature is capable of, we are justified in ascribing to the preferred enjoyment a superiority in quality, so far out-weighing quantity as to render it, in comparison, of small account.

Now it is an unquestionable fact that those who are equally acquainted with, and equally capable of appreciating and enjoying, both, do give a most marked preference to the manner of existence which employs their higher faculties. Few human creatures would consent to be changed into any of the lower animals, for a promise of the fullest allowance of a beast's pleasures; no intelligent human being would consent to be a fool, no instructed person would be an ignoramus, no person of feeling and conscience would be selfish and base, even though they should be persuaded that the fool, the dunce, or the rascal is better satisfied with his lot than they are with theirs. They would not resign what they possess more than he for the most complete satisfaction of all the desires which they have in common with him. If they ever fancy they would, it is only in cases of unhappiness so extreme, that to escape from it they would exchange their lot for almost any other, however undesirable in their own eyes. A being of higher faculties requires more to make him happy, is capable probably of more acute suffering, and certainly accessible to it at more points, than one of an inferior type; but in spite of these liabilities, he can never really wish to sink into what he feels to be a lower grade of existence. We may give what explanation we please of this unwillingness; we may attribute it to pride, a name which is given indiscriminately to some of the most and to some of the least estimable feelings of which mankind are capable: we may refer it to the love of liberty and personal independence, an appeal to which was with the Stoics one of the most effective means for the inculcation of it; to the love of power, or to the love of excitement, both of which do really enter into and contribute to it: but its most appropriate appellation is a sense of dignity, which all human beings possess in one form or other, and in some, though by no means in exact, proportion to their higher faculties, and which is so essential a part of the happiness of those in whom it is strong, that nothing which conflicts with it could be, otherwise than momentarily, an object of desire to them. Whoever supposes that this preference takes place at a sacrifice of happiness—that the superior being, in anything like equal circumstances, is not happier than the inferior—confounds the two very different ideas, of happiness, and content. It is indisputable that the being whose capacities of enjoyment are low, has the greatest chance of having them fully satisfied; and a highly endowed being will always feel that any happiness which he can look for, as the world is constituted, is imperfect. But he can learn to bear its imperfections, if they are at all bearable; and they will not make him envy the being who is indeed unconscious of the imperfections, but only because he feels not at all the good which those imperfections qualify. It is better to be a human being dissatisfied than a pig satisfied; better to be Socrates dissatisfied than a fool satisfied. And if the fool, or the pig, are of a different opinion, it is because they only know their own side of the question. The other party to the comparison knows both sides.

It may be objected, that many who are capable of the higher pleasures, occasionally, under the influence of temptation, postpone them to the lower. But this is quite compatible with a full appreciation of the intrinsic superiority of the higher. Men often, from infirmity of character, make their election for the nearer good, though they know it to be the less valuable; and this no less when the choice is between two bodily pleasures, than when it is between bodily and mental. They pursue sensual indulgences to the injury of health, though perfectly aware that health is the greater good. It may be further objected, that many who begin with youthful enthusiasm for everything noble, as they advance in years sink into indolence and selfishness. But I do not believe that those who undergo this very common change, voluntarily choose the lower description of pleasures in preference to the higher. I believe that before they devote themselves exclusively to the one, they have already become incapable of the other. Capacity for the nobler feelings is in most natures a very tender plant, easily killed, not only by hostile influences, but by mere want of sustenance; and in the majority of young persons it speedily dies away if the occupations to which their position in life has devoted them, and the society into which it has thrown them, are not favourable to keeping that higher capacity in exercise. Men lose their high aspirations as they lose their intellectual tastes, because they have not time or opportunity for indulging them; and they addict themselves to inferior pleasures, not because they deliberately prefer them, but because they are either the only ones to which

they have access, or the only ones which they are any longer capable of enjoying. It may be questioned whether any one who has remained equally susceptible to both classes of pleasures, ever knowingly and calmly preferred the lower; though many, in all ages, have broken down in an ineffectual attempt to combine both.

From this verdict of the only competent judges, I apprehend there can be no appeal. On a question which is the best worth having of two pleasures, or which of two modes of existence is the most grateful to the feelings, apart from its moral attributes and from its consequences, the judgment of those who are qualified by knowledge of both, or, if they differ, that of the majority among them, must be admitted as final. And there needs be the less hesitation to accept this judgment respecting the quality of pleasures, since there is no other tribunal to be referred to even on the question of quantity. What means are there of determining which is the acutest of two pains, or the intensest of two pleasurable sensations, except the general suffrage of those who are familiar with both? Neither pains nor pleasures are homogeneous, and pain is always heterogeneous with pleasure. What is there to decide whether a particular pleasure is worth purchasing at the cost of a particular pain, except the feelings and judgment of the experienced? When, therefore, those feelings and judgment declare the pleasures derived from the higher faculties to be preferable *in kind,* apart from the question of intensity, to those of which the animal nature, disjoined from the higher faculties, is susceptible, they are entitled on this subject to the same regard.

I have dwelt on this point, as being a necessary part of a perfectly just conception of Utility or Happiness, considered as the directive rule of human conduct. But it is by no means an indispensable condition to the acceptance of the utilitarian standard; for that standard is not the agent's own greatest happiness, but the greatest amount of happiness altogether; and if it may possibly be doubted whether a noble character is always the happier for its nobleness, there can be no doubt that it makes other people happier, and that the world in general is immensely a gainer by it. Utilitarianism, therefore, could only attain its end by the general cultivation of nobleness of character, even if each individual were only benefited by the nobleness of others, and his own, so far as happiness is concerned, were a sheer deduction from the benefit. But the bare enunciation of such an absurdity as this last, renders refutation superfluous. . . .

OF THE ULTIMATE SANCTION OF THE PRINCIPLE OF UTILITY

The question is often asked, and properly so, in regard to any supposed moral standard—What is its sanction? what are the motives to obey it? or more specifically, what is the source of its obligation? whence does it derive its binding force? It is a necessary part of moral philosophy to provide the answer to this question; which, though frequently assuming the shape of an objection to the utilitarian morality, as if it had some special applicability to that above others, really arises in regard to all standards. It arises, in fact, whenever a person is called on to *adopt* a standard, or refer morality to any basis on which he has not been accustomed to rest it. For the customary morality, that which education and opinion have consecrated, is the only one which presents itself to the mind with the feeling of being *in itself* obligatory; and when a person is asked to believe that this morality *derives* its obligation from some general principle round which custom has not thrown the same halo, the assertion is to him a paradox; the supposed corollaries seem to have a more binding force than the original theorem; the super-structure seems to stand better without, than with, what is represented as its foundation. He says to himself, I feel that I am bound not to rob or murder, betray or deceive; but why am I bound to promote the general happiness? If my own happiness lies in something else, why may I not give that the preference?

If the view adopted by the utilitarian philosophy of the nature of the moral sense be correct, this difficulty will always present itself, until the influences which form moral character have taken the same hold of the principle which they have taken of some of the consequences—until, by the improvement of education, the feeling of unity with our fellow-crea-

tures shall be (what it cannot be denied that Christ intended it to be) as deeply rooted in our character, and to our own consciousness as completely a part of our nature, as the horror of crime is in an ordinarily well brought up young person. In the meantime, however, the difficulty has no peculiar application to the doctrine of utility, but is inherent in every attempt to analyse morality and reduce it to principles; which, unless the principle is already in men's minds invested with as much sacredness as any of its applications, always seems to divest them of a part of their sanctity.

The principle of utility either has, or there is no reason why it might not have, all the sanctions which belong to any other system of morals. Those sanctions are either external or internal. Of the external sanctions it is not necessary to speak at any length. They are, the hope of favour and the fear of displeasure, from our fellow-creatures or from the Ruler of the Universe, along with whatever we may have of sympathy or affection for them, or of love and awe of Him, inclining us to do his will independently of selfish consquences. There is evidently no reason why all these motives for observance should not attach themselves to the utilitarian morality, as completely and as powerfully as to any other. Indeed, those of them which refer to our fellow-creatures are sure to do so, in proportion to the amount of general intelligence; for whether there be any other ground of moral obligation than the general happiness or not, men do desire happiness; and however imperfect may be their own practice, they desire and commend all conduct in others towards themselves, by which they think their happiness is promoted. With regard to the religious motive, if men believe, as most profess to do, in the goodness of God, those who think that conduciveness to the general happiness is the essence, or even only the criterion of good, must necessarily believe that it is also that which God approves. The whole force therefore of external reward and punishment, whether physical or moral, and whether proceeding from God or from our fellow men, together with all that the capacities of human nature admit of disinterested devotion to either, become available to enforce the utilitarian morality, in proportion as that morality is recognised; and the more powerfully, the more the appliances of education and general cultivation are bent to the purpose.

So far as to external sanctions. The internal sanction of duty, whatever our standard of duty may be, is one and the same—a feeling in our own mind; a pain, more or less intense, attendant on violation of duty, which in properly cultivated moral natures rises, in the more serious cases, into shrinking from it as an impossibility. This feeling, when disinterested, and connecting itself with the pure idea of duty, and not with some particular form of it, or with any of the merely accessory circumstances, is the essence of Conscience; though in that complex phenomenon as it actually exists, the simple fact is in general all encrusted over with collateral associations, derived from sympathy, from love, and still more from fear; from all the forms of religious feeling; from the recollections of childhood and of all our past life; from self-esteem, desire of the esteem of others, and occasionally even self-abasement. This extreme complication is, I apprehend, the origin of the sort of mystical character, which, by a tendency of the human mind of which there are many other examples, is apt to be attributed to the idea of moral obligation, and which leads people to believe that the idea cannot possibly attach itself to any other objects than those which, by a supposed mysterious law, are found in our present experience to excite it. Its binding force, however, consists in the existence of a mass of feeling which must be broken through in order to do what violates our standard of right, and which, if we do nevertheless violate that standard, will probably have to be encountered afterwards in the form of remorse. Whatever theory we have of the nature or origin of conscience, this is what essentially constitutes it.

The ultimate sanction, therefore, of all morality (external motives apart) being a subjective feeling in our own minds, I see nothing embarrassing to those whose standard is utility, in the question, what is the sanction of that particular standard? We may answer, the same as of all other moral standards—the conscientious feelings of mankind. Undoubtedly this sanction has no binding efficacy on those who do not possess the feelings it appeals to; but neither will these persons be more obedient to any other moral principle than to the utilitarian one. On them morality of any kind has no hold but through the external sanctions. Meanwhile the feelings exist, a fact in human nature, the reality of which, and the great power with which they are capable of acting on those in whom they have been duly cultivated, are proved by experience. No reason has ever been shown why they may not be cultivated to as great intensity in connection with the utilitarian, as with any other rule of morals.

There is, I am aware, a disposition to believe that a person who sees in moral obligation a transcendental fact, an objective reality belonging to the province of "Things in themselves," is likely to be more obedient to it than one who believes it to be entirely subjective, having its seat in human consciousness only. But whatever a person's opinion may be on this point of Ontology, the force he is really urged by is his own subjective feeling, and is exactly measured by its strength. No one's belief that duty is an objective reality is stronger than the belief that God is so; yet the belief in God, apart from the expectation of actual reward and punishment, only operates on conduct through, and in proportion to, the subjective religious feeling. The sanction, so far as it is disinterested, is always in the mind itself; and the notion therefore of the transcendental moralists must be, that this sanction will not exist *in* the mind unless it is believed to have its root out of the mind; and that if a person is able to say to himself, This which is restraining me, and which is called my conscience, is only a feeling in my own mind, he may possibly draw the conclusion that when the feeling ceases the obligation ceases, and that if he find the feeling inconvenient, he may disregard it, and endeavour to get rid of it. But is this danger confined to the utilitarian morality? Does the belief that moral obligation has its seat outside the mind make the feeling of it too strong to be got rid of? The fact is so far otherwise, that all moralists admit and lament the ease with which, in the generality of minds, conscience can be silenced or stifled. The question, Need I obey my conscience? is quite as often put to themselves by persons who never heard of the principle of utility, as by its adherents. Those whose conscientious feelings are so weak as to allow of their asking this question, if they answer it affirmatively, will not do so because they believe in the transcendental theory, but because of the external sanctions.

It is not necessary, for the present purpose, to decide whether the feeling of duty is innate or implanted. Assuming it to be innate, it is an open question to what objects it naturally attaches itself; for the philosophic supporters of that theory are now agreed that the intuitive perception is of principles of morality and not of the details. If there be anything innate in the matter, I see no reason why the feeling which is innate should not be that of regard to the pleasures and pains of others. If there is any principle of morals which is intuitively obligatory, I should say it must be that. If so, the intuitive ethics would coincide with the utilitarian, and there would be no further quarrel between them. Even as it is, the intuitive moralists, though they believe that there are other intuitive moral obligations, do already believe this to be one; for they unanimously hold that a large *portion* of morality turns upon the consideration due to the interests of our fellow-creatures. Therefore, if the belief in the transcendental origin of moral obligation gives any additional efficacy to the internal sanction, it appears to me that the utilitarian principle has already the benefit of it.

On the other hand, if, as is my own belief, the moral feelings are not innate, but acquired, they are not for that reason the less natural. It is natural to man to speak, to reason, to build cities, to cultivate the ground, though these are acquired faculties. The moral feelings are not indeed a part of our nature, in the sense of being in any perceptible degree present in all of us; but this, unhappily, is a fact admitted by those who believe the most strenuously in their transcendental origin. Like the other acquired capacities above referred to, the moral faculty, if not a part of our nature, is a natural outgrowth from it; capable, like them, in a certain small degree, of springing up spontaneously; and susceptible of being brought by cultivation to a high degree of development. Unhappily it is also susceptible, by a sufficient use of the external sanctions and of the force of early impressions, of being cultivated in almost any direction: so that there is hardly anything so absurd

or so mischievous that it may not, by means of these influences, be made to act on the human mind with all the authority of conscience. To doubt that the same potency might be given by the same means to the principle of utility, even if it had no foundation in human nature, would be flying in the face of all experience.

But moral associations which are wholly of artificial creation, when intellectual culture goes on, yield by degrees to the dissolving force of analysis: and if the feeling of duty, when associated with utility, would appear equally arbitrary; if there were no leading department of our nature, no powerful class of sentiments, with which that association would harmonise, which would make us feel it congenial, and incline us not only to foster it in others (for which we have abundant interested motives), but also to cherish it in ourselves; if there were not, in short, a natural basis of sentiment for utilitarian morality, it might well happen that this association also, even after it had been implanted by education, might be analysed away.

But there *is* this basis of powerful natural sentiment; and this it is which, when once the general happiness is recognised as the ethical standard, will constitute the strength of the utilitarian morality. This firm foundation is that of the social feelings of mankind; the desire to be in unity with our fellow creatures, which is already a powerful principle in human nature, and happily one of those which tend to become stronger, even without express inculcation, from the influences of advancing civilisation. The social state is at once so natural, so necessary, and so habitual to man, that, except in some unusual circumstances or by an effort of voluntary abstraction, he never conceives himself otherwise than as a member of a body; and this association is riveted more and more, as mankind are further removed from the state of savage independence. Any condition, therefore, which is essential to a state of society, becomes more and more an inseparable part of every person's conception of the state of things which he is born into, and which is the destiny of a human being. Now, society between human beings, except in the relation of master and slave, is manifestly impossible on any other footing than that the interests of all are to be consulted. Society between equals can only exist on the understanding that the interests of all are to be regarded equally. And since in all states of civilisation, every person, except an absolute monarch, has equals, every one is obliged to live on these terms with somebody; and in every age some advance is made towards a state in which it will be impossible to live permanently on other terms with anybody. In this way people grow up unable to conceive as possible to them a state of total disregard of other people's interests. They are under a necessity of conceiving themselves as at least abstaining from all the grosser injuries, and (if only for their own protection) living in a state of constant protest against them. They are also familiar with the fact of co-operating with others and proposing to themselves a collective, not an individual interest as the aim (at least for the time being) of their actions. So long as they are co-operating, their ends are identified with those of others; there is at least a temporary feeling that the interests of others are their own interests. Not only does all strengthening of social ties, and all healthy growth of society, give to each individual a stronger personal interest in practically consulting the welfare of others; it also leads him to identify his *feelings* more and more with their good, or at least with an even greater degree of practical consideration for it. He comes, as though instinctively, to be conscious of himself as a being who *of course* pays regard to others. The good of others becomes to him a thing naturally and necessarily to be attended to, like any of the physical conditions of our existence. Now, whatever amount of this feeling a person has, he is urged by the strongest motives both of interest and of sympathy to demonstrate it, and to the utmost of his power encourage it in others; and even if he has none of it himself, he is as greatly interested as any one else that others should have it. Consequently the smallest germs of the feeling are laid hold of and nourished by the contagion of sympathy and the influences of education; and a complete web of corroborative association is woven round it, by the powerful agency of the external sanctions. This mode of conceiving ourselves and human life, as civilisation goes on, is felt to be more and more natural. Every

step in political improvement renders it more so, by removing the sources of opposition of interest, and levelling those inequalities of legal privilege between individuals or classes, owing to which there are large portions of mankind whose happiness it is still practicable to disregard. In an improving state of the human mind, the influences are constantly on the increase, which tend to generate in each individual a feeling of unity with all the rest; which, if perfect, would make him never think of, or desire, any beneficial condition for himself, in the benefits of which they are not included. If we now suppose this feeling of unity to be taught as a religion, and the whole force of education, of institutions, and of opinion, directed, as it once was in the case of religion, to make every person grow up from infancy surrounded on all sides both by the profession and the practice of it, I think that no one, who can realise this conception, will feel any misgiving about the sufficiency of the ultimate sanction for the Happiness morality. To any ethical student who finds the realisation difficult, I recommend, as a means of facilitating it, the second of M. Comte's two principal works, the *Traité de Politique Positive*. I entertain the strongest objections to the system of politics and morals set forth in that treatise; but I think it has superabundantly shown the possibility of giving to the service of humanity, even without the aid of belief in a Providence, both the psychological power and the social efficacy of a religion; making it take hold of human life, and colour all thought, feeling, and action, in a manner of which the greatest ascendancy ever exercised by any religion may be but a type and foretaste; and of which the danger is, not that it should be insufficient, but that it should be so excessive as to interfere unduly with human freedom and individuality.

Neither is it necessary to the feeling which constitutes the binding force of the utilitarian morality on those who recognise it, to wait for those social influences which would make its obligation felt by mankind at large. In the comparatively early state of human advancement in which we now live, a person cannot indeed feel that entireness of sympathy with all others, which would make any real discordance in the general direction of their conduct in life impossible; but already a person in whom the social feeling is at all developed, cannot bring himself to think of the rest of his fellow-creatures as struggling rivals with him for the means of happiness, whom he must desire to see defeated in their object in order that he may succeed in his. The deeply rooted conception which every individual even now has of himself as a social being, tends to make him feel it one of his natural wants that there should be harmony between his feelings and aims and those of his fellow-creatures. If differences of opinion and of mental culture make it impossible for him to share many of their actual feelings—perhaps make him denounce and defy those feelings—he still needs to be conscious that his real aim and theirs do not conflict; that he is not opposing himself to what they really wish for, namely their own good, but is, on the contrary, promoting it. This feeling in most individuals is much inferior in strength to their selfish feelings, and is often wanting altogether. But to those who have it, it possesses all the characters of a natural feeling. It does not present itself to their minds as a superstition of education, or a law despotically imposed by the power of society, but as an attribute which it would not be well for them to be without. This conviction is the ultimate sanction of the greatest happiness morality. This it is which makes any mind, of well-developed feelings, work with, and not against, the outward motives to care for others, afforded by what I have called the external sanctions; and when those sanctions are wanting, or act in an opposite direction, constitutes in itself a powerful internal binding force, in proportion to the sensitiveness and thoughtfulness of the character; since few but those whose mind is a moral blank, could bear to lay out their course of life on the plan of paying no regard to others except so far as their own private interest compels. . . .

Friedrich Nietzsche

Friedrich Nietzsche (1844–1900), a German educator and philosopher, reacted rather violently to some of the prevailing intellectual trends of the nineteenth century. In his later years he developed a mental and emotional instability that finally resulted in complete insanity. This tragic climax to his life undoubtedly helped to explain the character of Nietzsche's thought. He studied the Darwinian theory and became convinced that natural selection, as applied to human reproduction, was being circumvented by the Christian ethical insistence on protection of the weak. Thus he advocated a new and "nobler" morality for those with the will to achieve power, and through them a super-race would evolve. He also rejected the democratic notion of equality, a concept he regarded as contrary to natural reality. The fateful importance of Nietzsche's emphasis upon the decadence of Christianity and democracy, upon the Will to Power, and upon the emergence of the Super-man is only too apparent in the recent history of his unhappy native land. In 1886 he wrote Beyond Good and Evil, which is characteristic of his rambling style and which presents the essence of his ethics. In reading the following selections from this work note (1) the importance of slavery in the advance of the type "man," (2) the attitude a "good" aristocracy should assume toward the suppressed classes, (3) Nietzsche's definition of life and its relationship to the Will to Power, (4) his rejection of Marxian doctrine concerning exploitation, (5) the dual morality that he described, (6) the subjective character of the master-morality, (7) the utilitarian nature of the slave-morality, (8) his attitude toward the Christian Church, (9) the position of women in his thinking, (10) his interpretation of the struggle for existence and the part mediocrity plays in it, and (11) Nietzsche's emphasis upon rank.

From: BEYOND GOOD AND EVIL

WHAT IS NOBLE?

Every elevation of the type "man," has hitherto been the work of an aristocratic society —and so will it always be—a society believing in a long scale of gradations of rank and differences of worth among human beings, and requiring slavery in some form or other. Without the *pathos of distance,* such as grows out of the incarnated difference of classes, out of the constant outlooking and downlooking of the ruling caste on subordinates and instruments, and out of their equally constant practice of obeying and commanding, of keeping down and keeping at a distance—that other more mysterious pathos could never have arisen, the longing for an ever new widening of distance within the soul itself, the formation of ever higher, rarer, further, more extended, more comprehensive states, in short, just the elevation of the type "man," the continued "self-surmounting of man," to use a moral formula in a supermoral sense. To be sure, one must not resign oneself to any humanitarian illusions about the history of the origin of an aristocratic society (that is to say, of the preliminary condition for the elevation of the type "man"): the truth is hard. Let us acknowledge unprejudicedly how every higher civilisation hitherto has *originated!* Men with a still natural nature, barbarians in every terrible sense of the word, men of prey, still in possession of unbroken strength of will and desire for power, threw themselves upon weaker, more moral, more peaceful races (perhaps trading or cattle-rearing communities), or upon old mellow civilisations in which the final vital force was flickering out in brilliant fireworks of wit and depravity. At the commencement, the noble caste was always the barbarian caste: their superiority did not consist first of all in their physical, but in their psychical power— they were more *complete* men (which at every point also implies the same as "more complete beasts").

Corruption—as the indication that anarchy threatens to break out among the instincts, and that the foundation of the emotions, called "life," is convulsed—is something radically different according to the organisation in which it manifests itself. When, for instance, an aristocracy like that of France at the beginning of the Revolution, flung away its privileges with sublime disgust and sacrificed itself to an excess of its moral sentiments, it was corruption: —it was really only the closing act of the corruption which had existed for centuries, by virtue of which that aristocracy had abdicated step by step its lordly prerogatives and lowered itself to a *function* of royalty (in the end even to its decoration and parade-dress). The essential thing, however, in a good and healthy aristocracy is that it should *not* regard itself as a function either of the kingship or the commonwealth, but as the *significance* and highest justification thereof—that it should therefore accept with a good conscience the sacrifice of a legion of individuals, who, *for its sake,* must be suppressed and reduced to imperfect men, to slaves and instruments. Its fundamental belief must be precisely that society is *not* allowed to exist for its own sake, but only as a foundation and scaffolding, by means of which a select class of beings may be able to elevate themselves to their higher duties, and in general to a higher *existence:* like those sun-seeking climbing plants in Java—they are called

As translated by Helen Zimmern in Friedrich Nietzsche, *Beyond Good and Evil, Prelude to a Philosophy of the Future,* T. N. Foulis, Edinburgh, 1911, 223–239. Courtesy of Peter Davies, Ltd.

Sipo Matador,—which encircle an oak so long and so often with their arms, until at last, high above it, but supported by it, they can unfold their tops in the open light, and exhibit their happiness.

To refrain mutually from injury, from violence, from exploitation, and put one's will on a par with that of others: this may result in a certain rough sense in good conduct among individuals when the necessary conditions are given (namely, the actual similarity of the individuals in amount of force and degree of worth, and their co-relation within one organisation). As soon, however, as one wished to take this principle more generally, and if possible even as *the fundamental principle of society,* it would immediately disclose what it really is— namely, a Will to the *denial* of life, a principle of dissolution and decay. Here one must think profoundly to the very basis and resist all sentimental weakness: life itself is *essentially* appropriation, injury, conquest of the strange and weak, suppression, severity, obtrusion of peculiar forms, incorporation, and at the least, putting it mildest, exploitation;—but why should one for ever use precisely these words on which for ages a disparaging purpose has been stamped? Even the organisation within which, as was previously supposed, the individuals treat each other as equal—it takes place in every healthy aristocracy—must itself, if it be a living and not a dying organisation, do all that towards other bodies, which the individuals within it refrain from doing to each other: it will have to be the incarnated Will to Power, it will endeavour to grow, to gain ground, attract to itself and acquire ascendency—not owing to any morality or immorality, but because it *lives,* and because life *is* precisely Will to Power. On no point, however, is the ordinary consciousness of Europeans more unwilling to be corrected than on this matter; people now rave everywhere, even under the guise of science, about coming conditions of society in which "the exploiting character" is to be absent:—that sounds to my ears as if they promised to invent a mode of life which should refrain from all organic functions. "Exploitation" does not belong to a depraved, or imperfect and primitive society; it belongs to the *nature* of the living being as a primary organic func-

tion; it is a consequence of the intrinsic Will to Power, which is precisely the Will to Life. —Granting that as a theory this is a novelty— as a reality it is the *fundamental fact* of all history: let us be so far honest towards ourselves!

In a tour through the many finer and coarser moralities which have hitherto prevailed or still prevail on the earth, I found certain traits recurring regularly together, and connected with one another, until finally two primary types revealed themselves to me, and a radical distinction was brought to light. There is *master-morality* and *slave-morality;* —I would at once add, however, that in all higher and mixed civilisations, there are also attempts at the reconciliation of the two moralities; but one finds still oftener the confusion and mutual misunderstanding of them, indeed, sometimes their close juxtaposition—even in the same man, within one soul. The distinctions of moral values have either originated in a ruling caste, pleasantly conscious of being different from the ruled—or among the ruled class, the slaves and dependents of all sorts. In the first case, when it is the rulers who determine the conception "good," it is the exalted, proud disposition which is regarded as the distinguishing feature, and that which determines the order of rank. The noble type of man separates from himself the beings in whom the opposite of this exalted, proud disposition displays itself: he despises them. Let it at once be noted that in this first kind of morality the antithesis "good" and "bad" means practically the same as "noble" and "despicable";—the antithesis "good" and "*evil*" is of a different origin. The cowardly, the timid, the insignificant, and those thinking merely of narrow utility are despised; moreover, also, the distrustful, with their constrained glances, the self-abasing, the dog-like kind of men who let themselves be abused, the mendicant flatterers, and above all the liars:—it is a fundamental belief of all aristocrats that the common people are untruthful. "We truthful ones"—the nobility in ancient Greece called themselves. It is obvious that everywhere the designations of moral value were at first applied to *men,* and were only derivatively and at a later period applied to *actions;* it is a gross mistake, therefore, when historians of morals start with questions like, "Why have sympathetic actions been praised?" The noble type of man regards *himself* as a determiner of values; he does not require to be approved of; he passes the judgment: "What is injurious to me is injurious in itself"; he knows that it is he himself only who confers honour on things; he is a *creator of values*. He honours whatever he recognises in himself: such morality is self-glorification. In the foreground there is the feeling of plenitude, of power, which seeks to overflow, the happiness of high tension, the consciousness of a wealth which would fain give and bestow:—the noble man also helps the unfortunate, but not—or scarcely—out of pity, but rather from an impulse generated by the superabundance of power. The noble man honours in himself the powerful one, him also who has power over himself, who knows how to speak and how to keep silence, who takes pleasure in subjecting himself to severity and hardness, and has reverence for all that is severe and hard. "Wotan placed a hard heart in my breast," says an old Scandinavian Saga: it is thus rightly expressed from the soul of a proud Viking. Such a type of man is even proud of *not* being made for sympathy; the hero of the Saga therefore adds warningly: "He who has not a hard heart when young, will never have one." The noble and brave who think thus are the furthest removed from the morality which sees precisely in sympathy, or in acting for the good of others, or in *désintéressement,* the characteristic of the moral; faith in oneself, pride in oneself, a radical enmity and irony towards "selflessness," belong as definitely to noble morality, as do a careless scorn and precaution in presence of sympathy and the "warm heart." —It is the powerful who *know* how to honour, it is their art, their domain for invention. The profound reverence for age and for tradition—all law rests on this double reverence,—the belief and prejudice in favour of ancestors and unfavourable to newcomers, is typical in the morality of the powerful; and if, reversely, men of "modern ideas" believe almost instinctively in "progress" and the "future," and are more and more lacking in respect for old age, the ignoble origin of these "ideas" has complacently betrayed itself thereby. A morality of the ruling class, however, is more especially foreign and irritating to present-day taste in the sternness of its principle that one has duties only to one's equals; that one may act towards beings of a lower rank, towards all that is foreign, just as seems good to one, or "as the heart desires," and in any case "beyond good and evil": it is here that sympathy and similar sentiments can have a place. The ability and obligation to exercise prolonged gratitude and prolonged revenge—both only within the circle of equals,—artfulness in retaliation, *raffinement* of the idea in friendship, a certain necessity to have enemies (as outlets for the emotions of envy, quarrelsomeness, arrogance—in fact, in order to be a good *friend*): all these are typical characteristics of the noble morality, which, as has been pointed out, is not the morality of "modern ideas," and is therefore at present difficult to realise, and also to unearth and disclose. —It is otherwise with the second type of morality, *slave-morality*. Supposing that the abused, the oppressed, the suffering, the unemancipated, the weary, and those uncertain of themselves, should moralise, what will be the common element in their moral estimates? Probably a pessimistic suspicion with regard to the entire situation of man will find expression, perhaps a condemnation of man, together with his situation. The slave has an unfavourable eye for the virtues of the powerful; he has a scepticism and distrust, a *refinement* of distrust of everything "good" that is there honoured—he would fain persuade himself that the very happiness there is not genuine. On the other hand, *those* qualities which serve to alleviate the existence of sufferers are brought into prominence and flooded with light; it is here that sympathy, the kind, helping hand, the warm heart, patience, diligence, humility, and friendliness attain to honour; for here these are the most useful qualities, and almost the only means of supporting the burden of existence. Slave-morality is essentially the morality of utility. Here is the seat of the origin of the famous antithesis "good" and "*evil*":—power and dangerousness are assumed to reside in the evil, a certain dreadfulness, subtlety, and strength, which do not admit of being despised. According to slave-morality, therefore, the "evil" man arouses fear; according to master-morality, it is precisely the "good" man who arouses fear and seeks to arouse it, while the bad man is regarded as the despicable being. The contrast attains its maximum when, in accordance with the logical consequences of slave-morality, a shade of depreciation—it may be slight and well-intentioned—at last attaches itself even to the "good" man of this morality; because, according to the servile mode of thought, the good man must in any case be the *safe* man: he is good-natured, easily deceived, perhaps a little stupid, *un bonhomme.* Everywhere that slave-morality gains the ascendency, language shows a tendency to approximate the significations of the words "good" and "stupid." —A last fundamental difference: the desire for *freedom,* the instinct for happiness and the refinements of the feeling of liberty belong as necessarily to slave-morals and morality, as artifice and enthusiasm in reverence and devotion are the regular symptoms of an aristocratic mode of thinking and estimating. —Hence we can understand without further detail why love *as a passion*—it is our European speciality—must absolutely be of noble origin; as is well known, its invention is due to the Provençal poet-cavaliers, those brilliant ingenious men of the *"gai saber,"* to whom Europe owes so much, and almost owes itself.

Vanity is one of the things which are perhaps most difficult for a noble man to understand: he will be tempted to deny it, where another kind of man thinks he sees it self-evidently. The problem for him is to represent to his mind beings who seek to arouse a good opinion of themselves which they themselves do not possess—and consequently also do not "deserve,"—and who yet *believe* in this good opinion afterwards. This seems to him on the one hand such bad taste and so self-disrespectful, and on the other hand so grotesquely unreasonable, that he would like to consider vanity an exception, and is doubtful about it in most cases when it is spoken of. He will say, for instance: "I may be mistaken about my value, and on the other hand may nevertheless demand that my value should be acknowledged by others precisely as I rate it:—that, however, is not vanity (but self-conceit, or, in most cases, that which is called 'humility,' and also 'modesty')." Or he will even say: "For

many reasons I can delight in the good opinion of others, perhaps because I love and honour them, and rejoice in all their joys, perhaps also because their good opinion endorses and strengthens my belief in my own good opinion, perhaps because the good opinion of others, even in cases where I do not share it, is useful to me, or gives promise of usefulness:—all this, however, is not vanity." The man of noble character must first bring it home forcibly to his mind, especially with the aid of history, that, from time immemorial, in all social strata in any way dependent, the ordinary man *was* only that which he *passed for:*—not being at all accustomed to fix values, he did not assign even to himself any other value than that which his master assigned to him (it is the peculiar *right of masters* to create values). It may be looked upon as the result of an extraordinary atavism, that the ordinary man, even at present, is still always *waiting* for an opinion about himself, and then instinctively submitting himself to it; yet by no means only to a "good" opinion, but also to a bad and unjust one (think, for instance, of the greater part of the self-appreciations and self-depreciations which believing women learn from their confessors, and which in general the believing Christian learns from his Church). In fact, conformably to the slow rise of the democratic social order (and its cause, the blending of the blood of masters and slaves), the originally noble and rare impulse of the masters to assign a value to themselves and to "think well" of themselves, will now be more and more encouraged and extended; but it has at all times an older, ampler, and more radically ingrained propensity opposed to it—and in the phenomenon of "vanity" this older propensity overmasters the younger. The vain person rejoices over *every* good opinion which he hears about himself (quite apart from the point of view of its usefulness, and equally regardless of its truth or falsehood), just as he suffers from every bad opinion: for he subjects himself to both, he *feels* himself subjected to both, by that oldest instinct of subjection which breaks forth in him. —It is "the slave" in the vain man's blood, the remains of the slave's craftiness—and how much of the "slave" is still left in woman, for instance!—which seeks to *se-*

duce to good opinions of itself; it is the slave, too, who immediately afterwards falls prostrate himself before these opinions, as though he had not called them forth. —And to repeat it again: vanity is an atavism.

A *species* originates, and a type becomes established and strong in the long struggle with essentially constant *unfavourable* conditions. On the other hand, it is known by the experience of breeders that species which receive superabundant nourishment, and in general a surplus of protection and care, immediately tend in the most marked way to develop variations, and are fertile in prodigies and monstrosities (also in monstrous vices). Now look at an aristocratic commonwealth, say an ancient Greek *polis,* or Venice, as a voluntary or involuntary contrivance for the purpose of *rearing* human beings; there are there men beside one another, thrown upon their own resources, who want to make their species prevail, chiefly because they *must* prevail, or else run the terrible danger of being exterminated. The favour, the superabundance, the protection are there lacking under which variations are fostered; the species needs itself as species, as something which, precisely by virtue of its hardness, its uniformity, and simplicity of structure, can in general prevail and make itself permanent in constant struggle with its neighbours, or with rebellious or rebellion-threatening vassals. The most varied experience teaches it what are the qualities to which it principally owes the fact that it still exists, in spite of all Gods and men, and has hitherto been victorious: these qualities it calls virtues, and these virtues alone it develops to maturity. It does so with severity, indeed it desires severity; every aristocratic morality is intolerant in the education of youth, in the control of women, in the marriage customs, in the relations of old and young, in the penal laws (which have an eye only for the degenerating): it counts intolerance itself among the virtues, under the name of "justice." A type with few, but very marked features, a species of severe, warlike, wisely silent, reserved and reticent men (and as such, with the most delicate sensibility for the charm and *nuances* of society) is thus established, unaffected by the vicissitudes of generations; the constant struggle with uni-

form *unfavourable* conditions is, as already remarked, the cause of a type becoming stable and hard. Finally, however, a happy state of things results, the enormous tension is relaxed; there are perhaps no more enemies among the neighbouring peoples, and the means of life, even of the enjoyment of life, are present in superabundance. With one stroke the bond and constraint of the old discipline severs: it is no longer regarded as necessary, as a condition of existence—if it would continue, it can only do so as a form of *luxury*, as an archaïsing *taste*. Variations, whether they be deviations (into the higher, finer, and rarer), or deteriorations and monstrosities, appear suddenly on the scene in the greatest exuberance and splendour; the individual dares to be individual and detach himself. At this turning-point of history there manifest themselves, side by side, and often mixed and entangled together, a magnificent, manifold, virgin-forest-like up-growth and up-striving, a kind of *tropical tempo* in the rivalry of growth, and an extraordinary decay and self-destruction, owing to the savagely opposing and seemingly exploding egoisms, which strive with one another "for sun and light," and can no longer assign any limit, restraint, or forbearance for themselves by means of the hitherto existing morality. It was this morality itself which piled up the strength so enormously, which bent the bow in so threatening a manner:—it is now "out of date," it is getting "out of date." The dangerous and disquieting point has been reached when the greater, more manifold, more comprehensive life *is lived beyond* the old morality; the "individual" stands out, and is obliged to have recourse to his own law-giving, his own arts and artifices for self-preservation, self-elevation, and self-deliverance. Nothing but new "Whys," nothing but new "Hows," no common formulas any longer, misunderstanding and disregard in league with each other, decay, deterioration, and the loftiest desires frightfully entangled, the genius of the race overflowing from all the cornucopias of good and bad, a portentous simultaneousness of Spring and Autumn, full of new charms and mysteries peculiar to the fresh, still inexhausted, still unwearied corruption. Danger is again present, the mother of morality, great danger; this time shifted into the individual, into the neighbour and friend, into the street, into their own child, into their own heart, into all the most personal and secret recesses of their desires and volitions. What will the moral philosophers who appear at this time have to preach? They discover, these sharp onlookers and loafers, that the end is quickly approaching, that everything around them decays and produces decay, that nothing will endure until the day after to-morrow, except one species of man, the incurably *mediocre.* The mediocre alone have a prospect of continuing and propagating themselves—they will be the men of the future, the sole survivors; "be like them! become mediocre!" is now the only morality which has still a significance, which still obtains a hearing. —But it is difficult to preach this morality of mediocrity! it can never avow what it is and what it desires! it has to talk of moderation and dignity and duty and brotherly love—it will have difficulty *in concealing its irony!*

There is an *instinct for rank,* which more than anything else is already the sign of a *high* rank; there is a *delight* in the *nuances* of reverence which leads one to infer noble origin and habits. The refinement, goodness, and loftiness of a soul are put to a perilous test when something passes by that is of the highest rank, but is not yet protected by the awe of authority from obtrusive touches and incivilities: something that goes its way like a living touchstone, undistinguished, undiscovered, and tentative, perhaps voluntarily veiled and disguised. He whose task and practice it is to investigate souls, will avail himself of many varieties of this very art to determine the ultimate value of a soul, the unalterable, innate order of rank to which it belongs: he will test it by its *in-stinct for reverence. Différence engendre haine:* the vulgarity of many a nature spurts up suddenly like dirty water, when any holy vessel, any jewel from closed shrines, any book bearing the marks of great destiny, is brought before it; while on the other hand, there is an involuntary silence, a hesitation of the eye, a cessation of all gestures, by which it is indicated that a soul *feels* the nearness of what is worthiest of respect. The way in which, on the whole, the reverence for the *Bible* has hitherto been maintained in Europe, is perhaps the best example of discipline and refinement of manners which Europe owes to Christianity: books of such profoundness and supreme significance require for their protection an external tyranny of authority, in order to acquire the *period* of thousands of years which is necessary to exhaust and unriddle them. Much has been achieved when the sentiment has been at last instilled into the masses (the shallow-pates and the boobies of every kind) that they are not allowed to touch everything, that there are holy experiences before which they must take off their shoes and keep away the unclean hand—it is almost their highest advance towards humanity.

On the contrary, in the so-called cultured classes, the believers in "modern ideas," nothing is perhaps so repulsive as their lack of shame, the easy insolence of eye and hand with which they touch, taste, and finger everything; and it is possible that even yet there is more *relative* nobility of taste, and more tact for reverence among the people, among the lower classes of the people, especially among peasants, than among the newspaper-reading *demimonde* of intellect, the cultured class. . . .

Nationalism, Imperialism, and the War of 1914-1918

During the nineteenth century, Western Civilization felt the impact of the growing spirit of nationalism which permeated various ethnic groups in Europe and elsewhere throughout the world. A variety of factors, some stemming from the French Revolution and others from recent industrial and economic changes, contributed to the growth of this emotional feeling. Prominent among the fruits of this development were the political unification of the German and Italian peoples, and the intensification of national pride in countries already unified. Another result was the growth of militarism as a guaranty of national security. In the last quarter of the century nationalism combined with the expanding industrial activity of the time to bring about another phenomenon of the nineteenth century—imperialism. Colonies were sought as sources of raw materials, as outlets for manufactured products, and as areas for profitable investment of surplus capital; there ensued an intensive race to appropriate the backward areas of the world. This imperial rivalry, together with the rising spirit of nationalism, resulted in frequent international incidents, and it became increasingly evident, as Western Civilization entered the twentieth century, that a major war was inevitable. It finally came in 1914, and four years of bitter combat followed, with each of the major belligerents insisting that it was fighting a defensive war with no idea of furthering its colonial holdings. Secret treaties entered into during the course of the war contradicted these professions of altruism. The war, with its heavy expenditure of blood and treasure, rudely shocked the civilized world, which had come to believe that progress in time would outmode such conflicts. It was in the hope that war, imperialism, and intrigue might be forever removed from society that the leading statesmen drew up a covenant for a league of nations in order to further international cooperation and to outlaw aggressive warfare.

Giuseppe Mazzini

Giuseppe Mazzini (1805–1872), Italian patriot and writer, helped to inspire the spirit of liberal nationalism that emerged among the various European groups suppressed by the Congress of Vienna in 1815. His ideals were largely determined by his education, which was concentrated in the fields of history and theology. From the former he derived his romanticism, his interest in republican governmental forms, and his intense feeling for the Italian nation, while from the latter he acquired his high idealism, a belief in human liberty, and his interest in Humanity and a united mankind. He urged his countrymen to liberate themselves from foreign domination by uniting politically, and to free themselves from domestic tyranny by replacing monarchies with a republic. Only when national groups were organized into liberal political units could they participate in a larger movement to unite Humanity, which, to Mazzini, was God's ultimate plan. He wrote The Duties of Man as a series of essays to be read by the Italian working class, and they were published between 1844 and 1858. In reading the following, entitled "Duties toward Your Company" note (1) Mazzini's concept of the first duty of Italians, (2) the means God gave them of accomplishing this duty, (3) those who have disfigured God's design, (4) his appeal to all the factors producing a national feeling, (5) his comparison of Humanity with an army and of the nation as a family, (6) his definition of a country, (7) the form of government essential to a true country, (8) the stress he placed on Italy's history as a unifying force in Europe, and (9) the emotional tone characterizing the entire essay.

From: THE DUTIES OF MAN

Your first Duties—first, at least, in importance—are, as I have told you, to Humanity. You are *men* before you are *citizens* or *fathers*. If you do not embrace the whole human family in your love, if you do not confess your faith in its unity—consequent on the unity of God—and in the brotherhood of the Peoples who are appointed to reduce that unity to fact—if wherever one of your fellowmen groans, wherever the dignity of human nature is violated by falsehood or tyranny, you are not prompt, being able, to succour that wretched one, or do not feel yourself called, being able, to fight for the purpose of relieving the deceived or oppressed—you disobey your law of life, or do not comprehend the religion which will bless the future.

But what can *each* of you, with his isolated powers, *do* for the moral improvement, for the progress of Humanity? You can, from time to time, give sterile expression to your belief; you may, on some rare occasion, perform an act of *charity* to a brother not belonging to your own land, no more. Now, *charity* is not the watchword of the future faith. The watchword of the future faith is *association*, fraternal co-opera-

As translated by Thomas Okey in *Essays by Joseph Mazzini*, London, 1894, and reprinted in Joseph Mazzini, *The Duties of Man and Other Essays*, Everyman's Library, J. M. Dent and Sons, Ltd., London and Toronto, E. P. Dutton and Company, New York, 1915, 51–59. Courtesy of E. P. Dutton and Company, Inc.

tion towards a common aim, and this is as much superior to *charity* as the work of many uniting to raise with one accord a building for the habitation of all together would be superior to that which you would accomplish by raising a separate hut each for himself, and only helping one another by exchanging stones and bricks and mortar. But divided as you are in language, tendencies, habits, and capacities, you cannot attempt this common work. The *individual* is too weak, and Humanity too vast. *My God,* prays the Breton mariner as he puts out to sea, *protect me, my ship is so little, and Thy ocean so great!* And this prayer sums up the condition of each of you, if no means is found of multiplying your forces and your powers of action indefinitely. But God gave you this means when he gave you a Country, when, like a wise overseer of labour, who distributes the different parts of the work according to the capacity of the workmen, he divided Humanity into distinct groups upon the face of our globe, and thus planted the seeds of nations. Bad governments have disfigured the design of God, which you may see clearly marked out, as far, at least, as regards Europe, by the courses of the great rivers, by the lines of the lofty mountains, and by other geographical conditions; they have disfigured it by conquest, by greed, by jealousy of the just sovereignty of others; disfigured it so much that to-day there is perhaps no nation except England and France whose confines correspond to this design. They did not, and they do not, recognise any country except their own families and dynasties, the egoism of caste. But the divine design will infallibly be fulfilled. Natural divisions, the innate spontaneous tendencies of the peoples will replace the arbitrary divisions sanctioned by bad governments. The map of Europe will be remade. The Countries of the People will rise, defined by the voice of the free, upon the ruins of the Countries of Kings and privileged castes. Between these Countries there will be harmony and brotherhood. And then the work of Humanity for the general amelioration, for the discovery and application of the real law of life, carried on in association and distributed according to local capacities, will be accomplished by peaceful and progressive development; then each of

you, strong in the affections and in the aid of many millions of men speaking the same language, endowed with the same tendencies, and educated by the same historic tradition, may hope by your personal effort to benefit the whole of Humanity.

To you, who have been born in Italy, God has allotted, as if favouring you specially, the best-defined country in Europe. In other lands, marked by more uncertain or more interrupted limits, questions may arise which the pacific vote of all will one day solve, but which have cost, and will yet perhaps cost, tears and blood; in yours, no. God has stretched round you sublime and indisputable boundaries; on one side the highest mountains of Europe, the Alps; on the other the sea, the immeasurable sea. Take a map of Europe and place one point of a pair of compasses in the north of Italy on Parma; point the other to the mouth of the Var, and describe a semicircle with it in the direction of the Alps; this point, which will fall, when the semicircle is completed, upon the mouth of the Isonzo, will have marked the frontier which God has given you. As far as this frontier your language is spoken and understood; beyond this you have no rights. Sicily, Sardinia, Corsica, and the smaller islands between them and the mainland of Italy belong undeniably to you. Brute force may for a little while contest these frontiers with you, but they have been recognised from of old by the tacit general consent of the peoples; and the day when, rising with one accord for the final trial, you plant your tricoloured flag upon that frontier, the whole of Europe will acclaim re-risen Italy, and receive her into the community of the nations. To this final trial all your efforts must be directed.

Without Country you have neither name, token, voice, nor rights, no admission as brothers into the fellowship of the Peoples. You are the bastards of Humanity. Soldiers without a banner, Israelites among the nations, you will find neither faith nor protection; none will be sureties for you. Do not beguile yourselves with the hope of emancipation from unjust social conditions if you do not first conquer a Country for yourselves; where there is no Country there is no common agreement to which you can appeal; the egoism of self-interest rules alone, and he who has the upper hand keeps it, since there is no common safeguard for the interests of all. Do not be led away by the idea of improving your material conditions without first solving the national question. You cannot do it. Your industrial associations and mutual help societies are useful as a means of educating and disciplining yourselves; as an economic fact they will remain barren until you have an Italy. The economic problem demands, first and foremost, an increase of capital and production; and while your Country is dismembered into separate fragments—while shut off by the barrier of customs and artificial difficulties of every sort, you have only restricted markets open to you —you cannot hope for this increase. To-day— do not delude yourselves—you are not the working-class of Italy; you are only fractions of that class; powerless, unequal to the great task which you propose to yourselves. Your emancipation can have no practical beginning until a National Government, understanding the signs of the times, shall, seated in Rome, formulate a Declaration of Principles to be the guide for Italian progress, and shall insert into it these words, *Labour is sacred, and is the source of the wealth of Italy*.

Do not be led astray, then, by hopes of material progress which in your present conditions can only be illusions. Your Country alone, the vast and rich Italian Country, which stretches from the Alps to the farthest limit of Sicily, can fulfil these hopes. You cannot obtain your *rights* except by obeying the commands of *Duty*. Be worthy of them, and you will have them. O my Brothers! love your Country. Our Country is our home, the home which God has given us, placing therein a numerous family which we love and are loved by, and with which we have a more intimate and quicker communion of feeling and thought than with others; a family which by its concentration upon a given spot, and by the homogeneous nature of its elements, is destined for a special kind of activity. Our Country is our field of labour; the products of our activity must go forth from it for the benefit of the whole earth; but the instruments of labour which we can use best and most effectively

exist in it, and we may not reject them without being unfaithful to God's purpose and diminishing our own strength. In labouring according to true principles for our Country we are labouring for Humanity; our Country is the fulcrum of the lever which we have to wield for the common good. If we give up this fulcrum we run the risk of becoming useless to our Country and to Humanity. Before *associating* ourselves with the Nations which compose Humanity we must exist as a Nation. There can be no association except among equals; and you have no recognised collective existence.

Humanity is a great army moving to the conquest of unknown lands, against powerful and wary enemies. The Peoples are the different corps and divisions of that army. Each has a post entrusted to it; each a special operation to perform; and the common victory depends on the exactness with which the different operations are carried out. Do not disturb the order of the battle. Do not abandon the banner which God has given you. Wherever you may be, into the midst of whatever people circumstances may have driven you, fight for the liberty of that people if the moment calls for it; but fight as Italians, so that the blood which you shed may win honour and love, not for you only, but for your Country. And may the constant thought of your soul be for Italy, may all the acts of your life be worthy of her, and may the standard beneath which you range yourselves to work for Humanity be Italy's. Do not say *I*; say *we*. Be every one of you an incarnation of your Country, and feel himself and make himself responsible for his fellow-countrymen; let each one of you learn to act in such a way that in him men shall respect and love his Country.

Your Country is one and indivisible. As the members of a family cannot rejoice at the common table if one of their number is far away, snatched from the affection of his brothers, so you should have no joy or repose as long as a portion of the territory upon which your language is spoken is separated from the Nation.

Your Country is the token of the mission which God has given you to fulfil in Humanity. The faculties, the strength of *all* its sons should be united for the accomplishment of this mission. A certain number of common duties and rights belong to every man who answers to the *Who are you?* of the other peoples, *I am an Italian.* Those duties and those rights cannot be represented except by one *single* authority resulting from your votes. A Country must have, then, a single government. The politicians who call themselves federalists, and who would make Italy into a brotherhood of different states, would dismember the Country, not understanding the idea of Unity. The States into which Italy is divided to-day are not the creation of our own people; they are the result of the ambitions and calculations of princes or of foreign conquerors, and serve no purpose but to flatter the vanity of local aristocracies for which a narrower sphere than a great Country is necessary. What you, the people, have created, beautified, and consecrated with your affections, with your joys, with your sorrows, and with your blood, is the City and the Commune, not the Province or the State. In the City, in the Commune, where your fathers sleep and where your children will live, where you exercise your faculties and your personal rights, you live out your lives as *individuals.* It is of your City that each of you can say what the Venetians say of theirs: "Venice is our own: we have made her." In your City you have need of *liberty* as in your Country you have need of *association.* The Liberty of the Commune and the Unity of the Country—let that, then, be your faith. Do not say Rome and Tuscany, Rome and Lombardy, Rome and Sicily; say Rome and Florence, Rome and Siena, Rome and Leghorn, and so through all the Communes of Italy. Rome for all that represents Italian life; your Commune for whatever represents the *individual* life. All the other divisions are artificial, and are not confirmed by your national tradition.

A Country is a fellowship of free and equal men bound together in a brotherly concord of labour towards a single end. You must make it and maintain it such. A Country is not an aggregation, it is an *association.* There is no true Country without a uniform right. There is no true Country where the uniformity of that right is violated by the existence of caste, privilege, and inequality—where the powers and faculties of a large number of individuals are sup-pressed or dormant—where there is no common principle accepted, recognised, and developed by all. In such a state of things there can be no Nation, no People, but only a multitude, a fortuitous agglomeration of men whom circumstances have brought together and different circumstances will separate. In the name of your love for your Country you must combat without truce the existence of every privilege, every inequality, upon the soil which has given you birth. One privilege only is lawful—the privilege of Genius when Genius reveals itself in brotherhood with Virtue; but it is a privilege conceded by God and not by men, and when you acknowledge it and follow its inspirations, you acknowledge it freely by the exercise of your own reason and your own choice. Whatever privilege claims your submission in virtue of force or heredity, or any right which is not a common right, is a usurpation and a tyranny, and you ought to combat it and annihilate it. Your Country should be your Temple. God at the summit, a People of equals at the base. Do not accept any other formula, any other moral law, if you do not want to dishonour your Country and yourselves. Let the secondary laws for the gradual regulation of your existence be the progressive application of this supreme law.

And in order that they should be so, it is necessary that *all* should contribute to the making of them. The laws made by one fraction of the citizens only can never by the nature of things and men do otherwise than reflect the thoughts and aspirations and desires of that fraction; they represent, not the whole country, but a third, a fourth part, a class, a zone of the country. The law must express the general aspiration, promote the good of all, respond to a beat of the nation's heart. The whole nation therefore should be, directly or indirectly, the legislator. By yielding this mission to a few men, you put the egoism of one class in the place of the Country, which is the union of *all* the classes.

A Country is not a mere territory; the particular territory is only its foundation. The Country is the idea which rises upon that foundation; it is the sentiment of love, the sense of fellowship which binds together all the sons of that territory. So long as a single one of your brothers is not represented by his own vote in the development of the national life—so long as a single one vegetates uneducated among the educated—so long as a single one able and willing to work languishes in poverty for want of work—you have not got a Country such as it ought to be, the Country of all and for all. *Votes, education, work* are the three main pillars of the nation; do not rest until your hands have solidly erected them.

And when they have been erected—when you have secured for every one of you food for both body and soul—when freely united, entwining your right hands like brothers round a beloved mother, you advance in beautiful and holy concord towards the development of your faculties and the fulfilment of the Italian mission—remember that that mission is the moral unity of Europe; remember the immense duties which it imposes upon you. Italy is the only land that has twice uttered the great word of unification to the disjoined nations. Twice Rome has been the metropolis, the temple, of the European world; the first time when our conquering eagles traversed the known world from end to end and prepared it for union by introducing civilised institutions; the second time when, after the Northern conquerors had themselves been subdued by the potency of Nature, of great memories and of religious inspiration, the genius of Italy incarnated itself in the Papacy and undertook the solemn mission—abandoned four centuries ago—of preaching the union of souls to the peoples of the Christian world. To-day a third mission is dawning for our Italy; as much vaster than those of old as the Italian People, the free and united Country which you are going to found, will be greater and more powerful than Caesars or Popes. The presentiment of this mission agitates Europe and keeps the eye and the thought of the nations chained to Italy.

Your duties to your Country are proportioned to the loftiness of this mission. You have to keep it pure from egoism, uncontaminated by falsehood and by the arts of that political Jesuitism which they call diplomacy.

The government of the country will be based through your labours upon the worship of principles, not upon the idolatrous worship of interests and of opportunity. There are countries in Europe where Liberty is sacred within, but is systematically violated without; peoples who say, *Truth is one thing, utility another: theory is one thing, practice another.* Those countries will have inevitably to expiate their guilt in long isolation, oppression, and anarchy. But you know the mission of our Country, and will pursue another path. Through you Italy will have, with one only God in the heavens, one only truth, one only faith, one only rule of political life upon earth. Upon the edifice, sublimer than Capitol or Vatican, which the people of Italy will raise, you will plant the banner of Liberty and of Association, so that it shines in the sight of all the nations, nor will you lower it ever for terror of despots or lust for the gains of a day. You will have boldness as you have faith. You will speak out aloud to the world, and to those who call themselves the lords of the world, the thought which thrills in the heart of Italy. You will never deny the sister nations. The life of the Country shall grow through you in beauty and in strength, free from servile fears and the hesitations of doubt, keeping as its *foundation* the people, as its *rule* the consequences of its principles logically deduced and energetically applied, as its *strength* the strength of all, as its *outcome* the amelioration of all, as its *end* the fulfilment of the mission which God has given it. And because you will be ready to die for Humanity, the life of your Country will be immortal.

Otto von Bismarck

Otto von Bismarck (1815–1898) played an important role in the unification of Germany, which was finally achieved after the Franco-Prussian war (1870–1871). Born in Brandenburg and a member of the land-holding gentry of Prussia, he was politically devoted to the King of Prussia, but he also realized the desirability of a powerful Germany which could take its rightful place among the great nations of the world. In 1857 he was appointed minister-president and foreign minister of Prussia, two influential positions which enabled him to work effectively for national unity among the German states. He was essentially a man of action rather than a political theorist, and thus while exceedingly loyal to the house of Hohenzollern, Bismarck was not adverse to using the king as a means to his goal. In this regard he recognized that Frederick William IV of Prussia would not of his own initiative be an active force in furthering German unification since he was bound by dynastic principles and adherence to them as far as his relations with the dynasties in the lesser German states were concerned. For this reason Bismarck never made a point of emphasizing his goal to the king, and it is therefore difficult to find any clear-cut statement of Bismarck's aims in his writings. The extent of Bismarck's reputed militarism may have been in part the result of expediency in achieving his aim rather than an inherent characteristic of the man himself. The student will be better able to decide this after reading the following selections from his Memoirs. The idea for this work was first conceived in 1877, but Bismarck did not begin serious work on it until 1890, after his dismissal from the chancellorship by the new Emperor, William II. It is rather clear that he originally undertook this task to justify his position in the quarrel with William II that had led to his discharge. Later, through the influence of his friends and editors, he enlarged the scope of the text so that it assumed more the character of an autobiography. The entire work was informally dictated to his friend Lothar Bucher, a member of the ministry of foreign affairs. This fact helps to explain the personal and vivid style of the contents, for he picked events at random from his sixty years of experience, and only later were they put in order and completed by Bucher and the chancellor's son, Herbert. It should be remembered, too, that Bismarck recalled these events when he was in his declining years, and therefore there may be discrepancies between what actually occurred and his memory of these events. In reading the following selections from the Memoirs of Bismarck, note (1) the youthful views of Bismarck, (2) his feelings toward the French, (3) his analysis of the Frankfurt parliament of 1848, (4) his reasons for believing that German unification could not have been achieved in 1848, (5) Bismarck's comments on his "blood and iron" speech of 1862, (6) the skill with which he handled the king in winning his support, (7) his analysis of the dynastic problem as it related to German unity, (8) his gradual realization of the incompatibility between Austria and Prussia in any unification program, (9) his conviction about the inevitability of a

Franco-Prussian war and his preparation for it, (10) the Machiavellian principles he expressed, (11) Bismarck's analysis of the Prussian constitution, (12) the French desire for a casus belli in 1870, (13) Bismarck's use of the Ems telegram and its effect, and (14) his vision and statesmanship in forcing the title of Emperor upon the Hohenzollerns rather than that of King of Germany.

From: REFLECTIONS AND MEMOIRS

I left school in 1832, at the conclusion of the normal course of state-sponsored education. I was at that time a pantheist, and, if not a republican, was at least convinced that a republic was the most reasonable form of government. I also held critical ideas concerning the causes which led millions of people to obey one ruler, while I constantly heard among adults bitter criticism of these rulers. In addition, I had picked up German national ideas in the Turnverein school which I attended from my sixth to my twelfth year. These ideas, however, remained only in the theoretical stage, and were not sufficiently strong to outweigh my Prussian monarchial sentiments. My historical preferences remained on the side of authority. . . . [I found that in studying history] every German prince who, prior to the Thirty Years' War had opposed the Emperor, aroused my anger. From the time of the Great Elector on, however, I found my Prussian partisanism leading me into an anti-imperial point of view, and I found it quite natural that the Seven Years' War [against the Austrian Habsburgs] should have occurred when it did. Yet my German national feeling remained strong enough to lead me to affiliate with the national student corps at the beginning of my university career. This organization had as its main purpose the cultivation of German nationalism. After coming to know the members personally, however, I disliked their refusal to accept challenges to duel, and their lack of self-discipline and social etiquette. Upon knowing them better, I also disliked their somewhat fantastic political views which were the result of a lack of training and knowledge of existing historical realities, which

I, during my seventeen years, had had more opportunity to observe than most of the students whose average age was older. I gained the impression that their views were a combination of utopian ideals and of ignorance. I nevertheless retained my national sentiment and the conviction that developments in the near future would lead us to German unity. In fact, I made a bet with my American friend, Coffin, that this goal would be reached within twenty years.

During my third semester the Frankfurt "Putsch" occurred, and also the celebration at Hambach, the festive songs of which remained in my memory. Events such as these I found distasteful because as a result of my Prussian training I disliked tumultuous interferences with orderly government. Thus I returned to Berlin with a less liberal attitude than when I had left the city, a reaction which was in turn somewhat mitigated after I had been in direct contact with the endless clock-like routine of government administration. Foreign policy was of little concern to the general public in those days, while my own views on the subject were colored by the spirit of the anti-Napoleonic wars of liberation as experienced by the average Prussian officer of the time. Thus, whenever I looked at the map, I was upset by the French domination of Strassburg; and their military visitation to Heidelberg, Speyer, and the Palatinate made me belligerent and thirsty for revenge. . . .

The Frankfurt parliament, caught in this same double error [of underestimating the power of the German dynasties and their states and overestimating the revolutionary forces which are conveniently symbolized by "barri-

Translated by Franz Thomas Geyling from Otto von Bismarck, *Erinnerung und Gedanke.* . . . Berlin, n.d. (1932?), 5–6; 43–45; 193–198; 201–202; 282–283; 287–288; 304–305; 307–310; 324–325.

cade"], treated dynastic questions as something obsolete, even when related to Prussia and Austria. Those delegates at Frankfurt who were asked to give an expert account of public opinion in the Prussian provinces and in the German parts of Austria were to some extent interested in suppressing the truth. The parliament, whether honestly or otherwise, fooled itself about the fact that in the event of a conflict between a decree from Frankfurt and an order from the Prussian king, the former would have less weight or none at all with seven-eighths of the Prussian people. Anyone who lived in the eastern provinces in those days will still remember that the Frankfurt discussions were not taken as seriously by the groups in whose hands lay the actual power, and who, in case of conflict, carried the weapons or had the command, as should have been warranted by the dignity of the scientific and parliamentarian celebrities who had assembled there. At that time not only in Prussia but also in the larger central states any order from the sovereign calling the fighting power of the masses to his aid would have been effective. This was not as true in all states as it was in Prussia, yet it was sufficiently so to guarantee the necessary policing power wherever the sovereign had the courage to appoint ministers who would firmly and openly carry through. Such a condition did not occur in Prussia in the summer of 1848; in November, however, when the king decided to appoint ministers who were ready to support the rights of the crown without consideration for parliamentary decrees, the entire spectre of revolution disappeared, and there was left merely the danger that the reaction, in turn, might exceed reasonable limits. In the other North German states events did not even approach a conflict like the one that the Prussian ministry had to fight out in several provincial towns. In Bavaria and Württemberg the royal houses ultimately turned out to be stronger than the revolution in spite of anti-royalist ministries.

On April 3, 1849, the king of Prussia refused to accept the imperial crown, but he interpreted the decree of the Frankfurt parliament as implying "his right" to the title, which right he valued highly. He refused the offer mainly because of its revolutionary or at least parliamentary origin and because of the absence of any legal mandate for the Frankfurt parliament from the dynasties. But even if all these handicaps had not existed, or for that matter had not existed in the king's opinion, the development of a strong Reich could not have been expected at that time to the extent which it later came to be realized under him when he did become Emperor William I. The wars which he had to fight could not have been avoided; however, they would have occurred after the establishment of the Empire and as a consequence of its creation, and not in advance, as it were, to prepare the way for building the Empire. I do not know whether Frederick William IV could have been made to fight these wars [under the first alternative] at the strategic moment. . . .

Although considering the state of affairs in Prussia during those days as too immature for its taking the leadership in Germany either during war or peace, I do not insist that my insight at that time was as clear as it is now in retrospect after forty years of subsequent experience. My satisfaction then over the king's refusal of the crown was not founded on the above view of his shortcomings, but rather on a strong interest in the prestige of the Prussian crown and its wearer, and even more on my instinctive distrust of the developments since the "barricades" of 1848 and their parliamentarian consequences. Together with my political friends I shared an impression in connection with these events that the leading men in parliament and in the press consciously, or to a greater extent even intuitively, sponsored and carried out a program of "turning everything upside down." The existing ministers were not the men either to get the movement under control or to block it. . . .

During the first days of October [1862] I went to meet the king at Jüterbog on his return from Baden-Baden where he had gone for his wife's birthday, the thirtieth of September. Sitting on a wheelbarrow, I waited in the still unfinished station which was filled with third-class travelers and artisans. I was thinking of a topic of conversation to use on his majesty in order to calm him down about a sensational statement which I had made on the thirtieth of September to the budget committee and which had not been taken down by stenographers, but nevertheless had been reported quite accurately in most newspapers.

For people who were not too much embittered and blinded by ambition, I had stated clearly enough what I was heading for. As a single glance at the map would show, we could not, with the long and narrow territory of Prussia, carry the armament by ourselves which was needed for the security of all of Germany. Such armament should be distributed uniformly over all of Germany—that had been the meaning of my speech. We could not approach this goal by orations, political assemblies, and majority decisions, but on the contrary, a serious struggle would be unavoidable, a struggle which could only be decided by blood and iron. To ensure our success in such a fight, the representatives would have to put the maximum weight of blood and iron into the hands of the King of Prussia, so that he in turn could throw it on either side of the balance according to his judgment. . . .

I had a little difficulty learning from the unfriendly conductors on the arriving train which first-class carriage the king was traveling in alone. Obviously, his majesty was in a low mood on account of the conversations he had recently had with his wife about my speech, and when I asked permission to present the events as they had actually occurred during his absence, he interrupted me with the words: "I can clearly see how all this will end. Right there on the Opera Square beneath my window they will chop off your head and shortly thereafter mine." I readily guessed, and this was later confirmed by witnesses, that during his eight-day stay in Baden he had been worked on with variations of the theme "Polignac, Strafford, and Louis XVI!" When he stopped talking, I answered with the short phrase, "*Et après,* sire?—" "Yes, *après,* then we will be dead!" answered the king. "Yes," I continued, "indeed we will be dead, but we will have to die sooner or later in any event, and is there a more honorable way of dying— I myself perishing in the struggle for my king, and his majesty vindicating his royal rights from the grace of God by his own blood? Whether you do this on the scaffold or on the battlefield it is still a glorious forfeiture of body and life for the rights given you by God. His majesty should not think of Louis XVI; he lived and died without strength of character, and did not leave a good impression in history. Charles I, however, will he not always remain a noble historical figure? To think how he drew the sword for his rights, and after he had lost the battle, still unbowed, vindicated his royal spirit with his blood! His majesty faces the necessity of fighting, you cannot capitulate, you must meet the challenge, even if it were to involve bodily danger."

The longer I talked in this manner, the more inspired the king became, and saw himself as an officer fighting for kingdom and fatherland. In the face of external and personal dangers he displayed extraordinary and perfectly natural fearlessness, as well on the battlefield as against possible assassination; his attitude toward any kind of danger was always moving and inspiring. He was the ideal type of Prussian officer who in the line of duty meets certain death with the simple word, "According to your command," unselfish and intrepid; but who, if he must act on his own responsibility, dreads the criticism of his superior or the world more than death and in such a manner that the energy and correctness of his decisions is hampered by the fear of reprimand and reproof. These characteristics were developed in him to a high degree. Until then all during his journey he had only asked himself if he could face the criticism of his wife and the public opinion in Prussia resulting from the policy that he, together with me, was embarking upon. In contrast to that, our conversation in that dark railway carriage had the effect of leading him to consider the situation from the point of view of an officer. He now felt himself called by his military honor and saw himself in a situation where he had to defend his position to the bitter end, even if he perished on such duty. Thus he was led into a trend of thought where he felt at home, and in a few minutes had regained his confidence and even his sense of humor which he had lost in Baden. To sacrifice his life for kingdom and fatherland was the duty of any Prussian officer and especially that of the king, he being the "First Officer of the Country.". . . The proof of the accuracy of my judgment of his change of disposition was demonstrated by the fact that the same king whom I had found meek, downcast, and discouraged in Jüterbog, even before our arrival in Berlin began to display a spirited, happy, and belligerent mood which was clearly recognized by the ministers and officials awaiting us in the station. . . .

Never had I any doubts, not even in Frankfurt [in 1848], that the key to German politics was to be found in the various sovereigns and their dynasties, and not in the publicity of parliaments and the press, nor in the "barricade." The declarations of public opinion as given by the educated in parliament and in the press could either encourage or discourage the decisions of the dynasties, but such declarations increased the opposition of the latter more often than they exerted a pressure in the national interest. The weaker dynasties looked for security by conforming with the national interest; rulers and houses who considered themselves capable of resistance distrusted the national movement because an increase of German unity would result in a reduction of their independence to the advantage of the central power or the popular representative assembly. The Prussian dynasty could anticipate that it would eventually attain the hegemony in the future German empire with due increase of prestige and power. It would probably profit from the decline of the other dynasties to the extent that this situation was not exploited by a national representative parliament.

Up to the meeting of the Old German Union at Frankfurt I had been accustomed to look at problems from the point of view of Austro-Prussian dualism; but from that time I realized that it was Prussia's primary concern to defend her position against attacks and intrigues coming through this praesidial organ. [Austria dominated this body.] I also gained the impression that the mutual assistance of Austria and Prussia had been a dream of my youth created by the after effects of the wars of liberation and of my schooling; thus I was convinced that the Austria which I had visualized did not exist for Prussia. I became convinced that on the basis of the existing authority in the Union, Prussia wouldn't even be able to regain a position comparable to the one she

had before the revolution of 1848, to say nothing of a reform of the constitution of the Union, by which the German people could have realized their claim for political existence as one of the major European nations. . . . The Gordian knot of the German situation could not be solved through dualistic accord, but only by military blows. It was necessary to win the king of Prussia and therewith the Prussian army for the service of national interests, regardless of whether the main objective from the Prussian point of view seemed to be Prussian leadership, or from the national point of view seemed to be the unification of Germany; actually both goals coincided. This was clear to me, and I indicated it when I made that much abused statement about blood and iron in the budget committee [30 September, 1862]. . . .

The prevalence of loyalty to a dynasty and the necessity of such a dynasty as a binding force holding together any particular part of the nation under the name of its house, is a specifically German characteristic of the Reich. The particular "nationalities" which have formed in our lands on the basis of dynastic family domains usually embrace heterogeneous people whose living together is based neither on ethnological equality nor on similarity of their historical past, but only on the acquisitions of the dynasty which are often questionable, depending either on the force of the stronger or on hereditary claims. Whatever the origin of these particularistic trends in Germany may be, their result remains the same, namely that the German is very readily disposed toward battling against his own German neighbor and kinsmen with fire and sword and to kill him personally if he receives the dynastic order for doing it, such order arising from conflicts which he himself doesn't even understand. It is not the concern of a German statesman to test the justification or rationality of this characteristic just so long as it shows itself strong enough to be a valid factor in political calculations. The difficulty of destroying or ignoring this characteristic, or of trying to promote theoretical unity without consideration of this practical handicap has often been disastrous for the pioneers of unity, especially during the last national movement from 1848 to 1850, which otherwise had such particularly favorable chances. . . .

Dynastic interests in Germany have a justification only in so far as they conform with the general national interests; they could very well go hand in hand with the latter, and a duke loyal to the Reich in the historical sense can sometimes be more useful to the general cause than a direct relationship of the emperor to the ducal followers. As soon, however, as these dynastic interests threaten us with further disunity and national weakness, they should be reduced to their proper proportion. The German people and their national life cannot be divided up as private property of the sovereigns. I have always been convinced that this consideration is applicable to the Brandenburg dynasty as it is also to the Bavarian and the Guelfian, and others. I wouldn't have had any weapons against the Brandenburg dynasty if I had been forced to put my German national feeling in action against them by an open break and by falling out. However, historical predestination was such that my talents at court sufficed to win the king and therewith ultimately his army for pan-German interests. My struggle against Prussian particularism has probably been more strenuous than those I had to fight against the other German states and dynasties, and my inherent relation to the Emperor William I served to increase the difficulties of this struggle. Nevertheless, I always succeeded in the end, in spite of his strong dynastic interests, by making use of his dynastically justified and, in decisive moments, his increasing nationalist tendencies, to win his approval for the pan-German aspects of our program, even if from other sides the major emphasis was placed on the dynastic and particularistic aspects. . . .

In Berlin [1866–1870] I was outwardly occupied with the relationship of Prussia to the newly acquired provinces and to the other North German states; inwardly I was concerned with the attitude of foreign powers and with speculations about their probable reactions. Our internal situation appeared to me, and perhaps to everybody else, to be in a provisional stage and quite immature. The repercussions from the expansion of Prussia and from the approaching conferences about the North German Union and its constitution made our internal development appear to be in a state of fluctuation, just as were our relations with the rest of Germany and with foreign countries on account of the European situation which prevailed when the war [1866] was broken off. I took it for certain that a war with France would have to be fought as a step in our national development which was turned toward internal goals as well as heading for extension across the Main River. I was also convinced that we had to keep an eye on this eventuality in all internal and external situations. Louis Napoleon not only disregarded the expansion of Prussia as such in North Germany as a danger to France, but even considered it an expedient against the unification and national development of Germany. He believed that as a consequence the non-Prussian states would lean toward French protection more than ever. He had memories of the Rhine Federation and thought to hinder development in the direction of a united Germany. He thought that this was possible because he did not know the national feeling of the time and judged the situation by his recollections of his schooling in southern Germany and by diplomatic reports based only on ministerial and sporadic dynastic opinions. I was convinced that such opinions would quickly lose their weight; my estimate was that a united Germany was only a question of time and that for the solution of this problem the North German Union represented the first step. . . .

I never doubted at all that a Franco-German war would have to be fought before the establishment of a united Germany could be realized. It was my chief concern to put this war off until our fighting power had been strengthened through universal application of the Prussian laws of military training, not only to Hanover, Hesse, and Holstein, but to the South German states as well. I considered a war with France a danger which I at that time overestimated, remembering the successes of the French in the Crimean war and in Italy. In so doing I had a maximum French military potential in mind, and their order, organization, and skill of leadership of a higher quality than it actually showed itself in 1870. The courage of the French troopers, and the height of their national feeling and of their wounded vanity have completely lived up to the standards that I expected to meet in case of a German invasion into France. I had always kept in mind the events of 1814, 1792, and, at the beginning of the 18th century, during the war of the Spanish succession when the intrusion by foreign armies inevitably produced effects similar to those created by stirring up an ant-hill. I never considered the French war as an easy venture, to say nothing of the allies which France could find in the Austrian thirst for revenge and in the Russian desire for balance of power. It was therefore quite natural that I desired to put off this war until the complete effect of our military training had been realized, in all the non-Prussian sections of the country; in 1867 during the Luxemburg incident this, my goal, had not nearly been approached. Every year of delaying the war strengthened our army by more than 100,000 trained soldiers. In issues like the question of indemnity which I had to fight out with the king and in constitutional questions to be discussed with parliament I had to take good care not to give any evidence to foreign countries of existing or anticipated handicaps in our internal situation but only to demonstrate our unified national spirit—this was all the more important since it could not be predicted what allies France would have in a war against us. The conferences and attempts at agreement between France and Austria at Salzburg and elsewhere soon after 1866 could be successful under the guidance of Herr von Beust. Even the appointment of this dissatisfied Saxon minister to direct Vienna politics led one to expect that Vienna would veer in the direction of revenge. . . .

Considering it necessary to use even the most revolutionary means in this struggle against a possible superior coalition, I did not hesitate to throw on to our side of the scale the then strongest liberal device, the right of manhood suffrage, provided for in the circular despatch of June 10, 1866. This was intended to make the monarchial foreign powers abstain from attempts "to stick their fingers into our national pie." I have never doubted that the Germans would be strong enough to free themselves from such an institution if they decided that it was detrimental. If they couldn't do that, then I was in error when I stated that they would be able "to ride as soon as they were placed in the saddle." The granting of the general right to vote was a weapon in the struggle against Austria and other foreign powers in the fight for German unity and simultaneously a last threat in the battle against superior coalition. In a struggle of that sort, being fought on a life and death basis, one does not examine the weapons being used and the values being destroyed by their use; the prime consideration for the time being is only the outcome of the struggle, the preservation of independence from foreign powers. The liquidation and repair of damages done by these means has to be carried out when peace has been restored. Besides, I even today consider the general right to vote not merely a theoretically but also a practically justified principle, if only its secrecy were abolished, which, incidentally, had a character that is incompatible with the nature of the German people. . . .

I do not consider absolutism as a form of government which in the long run could successfully exist in Germany. The Prussian constitution in its main principles is quite reasonable; it has three branches, the king and the two chambers, each of which can check an undue change of the *status quo* by its vote. Therein lies a just distribution of legislative power. If this group is freed from public criticism as voiced in the press and in parliamentary debates, there is a danger that it will not function properly. Absolutism of the crown is just as untenable as absolutism of parliamentarian majorities, and it is just to require the agreement of both for every change in the legal *status quo*. We therefore had no need to change any essentials of the Prussian constitution. . . .

[In 1870] France was looking for a cause of war against Prussia [now becoming the expedient of unification] which would be as devoid as possible of national German implications, and she thought to have found such a cause in dynastic issues when a member of the Hohenzollern family appeared as a pretender to the Spanish throne. By overestimating

French military superiority and underestimating German national sentiment, France failed to examine the validity of this reason for war with sufficient honesty and knowledge. German national sentiment which did rise in response to the French declaration of war was comparable to a stream that broke the dam and was a surprise to French politicians. Their lives, speculations, and actions were based on memories of the Rhine federation, these reminiscences being supported by the attitude of a few West German ministers and by ultramontane [papal] influences which hoped that French victories as a "gesture of God" would assist the Vatican in furthering its influence in Germany, while using Catholic Austria as an ally. . . .

I invited the generals, Roon and Moltke, for the 13th of July, 1870, to dine with me and at the table I told them about my views and intentions. . . . During our discussion it was announced to me that a coded telegram from Ems of about 200 words, signed by his majesty's secret adviser, Abeken, was just then being deciphered. After I was given the deciphered version which had been signed by Abeken, I read it to my two guests. . . . After scrutinizing the document several times, I abided by an authorization from his majesty for publicizing the contents partially or in their entirety. I asked Moltke several questions about his confidence in the extent of our military preparations, particularly about the time that these would still require in the face of this suddenly arising danger of war. He answered that he did not anticipate any advantage for us in a delay of military action if war were necessary. . . . All in all he considered an immediate outbreak as more advantageous than putting it off. . . .

I made use of the king's permission to publicize the contents of the telegram, partially or as a whole, and in the presence of my two guests I reduced the telegram by deletions, without adding or changing a word, to the following form: "After the news of the resignation of the Hohenzollern claimant had been conveyed by the royal Spanish government to the imperial French government, the French ambassador in Ems demanded from his majesty the king [of Prussia] to authorize him to wire Paris that his majesty promised never again to give his approval if the Hohenzollerns should resume their candidacy. His majesty the king had thereupon refused to receive the French ambassador again and informed him through the adjutant on duty that his majesty had nothing else to tell the French ambassador."

The difference in the effect between this abbreviated text of the Ems telegram as compared with the one that the original would have caused if it had been released, was not the result of stronger words but of its form which made the declaration appear as final whereas the original text would merely have appeared to be the fragment of a pending negotiation which was to be continued in Berlin. . . .

The acceptance of the title of emperor by the king upon the extension of the North German Union [after 1871] was a political necessity because it served as an element sponsoring unity and centralization by recalling the times when this title had more theoretical and less actual significance than today. I was convinced that the stabilizing pressure would be the more lasting upon the institutions of the Reich the more the Prussian wearer of the title avoided the dangerous inclination, which had its roots deep in German history, to demonstrate his own superiority to the other dynasties. Emperor William I was not free from this tendency and his dissatisfaction with the title was based partially on his very intention of gaining more recognition for the superior prestige of his traditional Prussian crown than for the imperial title. The position of emperor seemed to him to be an assigned office of modern times, the authority of which had been used to handicap the Great Elector and had been resisted by Frederick the Great. In our first conversation he said, "What should I do with that picturesque title?" Whereupon I answered: "Your majesty wouldn't like to remain a neuter, the praesidium? In this expression lies only an abstraction, the title however, carries great driving power."

Even from the crown prince during the first months of the [Franco-Prussian] war I did not always receive support for my intention to establish the imperial title. My motive was not based on Prussian dynastic vanity, but solely on my belief in its usefulness in sponsoring national unity. His royal highness had picked up the thought of one of the political dreamers with whom he was closely associated, that the heritage of Charlemagne's revived Roman Empire had been Germany's misfortune, a foreign institution which had been disadvantageous for the nation. As readily to be proved as this may have been on historical grounds, it did not justify the alternative title of king of Germany to avoid these historical dangers. In our present times there was no likelihood that the imperial title which only lived in the memories of people would tend to divert Germany's power from domestic interests and toward trans-Alpine goals in Italy. The crown prince's preference for the royal title which he expressed to me and which was based on these erroneous views seemed to my mind to be a serious and business-like matter with him and one which I was supposed to put through. My objection which referred to the co-existence of the kings of Bavaria, Saxony, and Württemberg along with the would-be king of Germany, led him, surprisingly enough, to conclude that the aforementioned dynasties would have to abandon the royal title and be reduced to a ducal standing. I was convinced that they would not in their good will agree to do this. However, should force be used against them, such an act would not be forgotten for centuries to come and would sow distrust and hatred. . . .

Joseph Chamberlain

Joseph Chamberlain (1836–1914), British industrialist and statesman, entered Parliament in 1876 as a representative of a Birmingham constituency. For a variety of reasons the countries of Europe were manifesting a new interest in colonial expansion during the last quarter of the nineteenth century, and Chamberlain rapidly developed into an outstanding exponent of British imperialism in Africa and elsewhere. In the eighties English and German business interests were penetrating into Uganda, and the British East Africa Company undertook the construction of a railroad from the coast into Uganda in order to gain control of its trade. In 1890, however, the two rivals reached an agreement whereby Uganda was placed in the British sphere of influence and Heligoland was ceded to the Germans. Shortly thereafter the company experienced financial difficulties and appealed to the British government for monetary aid. In 1893 the issue came before Parliament and a portion of the debate is reproduced below. Mr. Storey, as an anti-imperialist radical, spoke against the loan, while Chamberlain argued for it as an aid to imperialism. In reading the debate, note (1) the domestic social reform advocated by Mr. Storey, (2) Chamberlain's appeal to history as a justification for colonial expansion, (3) his references to the colonizing ability of the Anglo-Saxon race, (4) the discussion of the "white man's burden," (5) his description of the pax Britannica, (6) the moral obligation which he believed the government had in Uganda, (7) the economic motives mentioned for the development of Uganda, and (8) Chamberlain's humanitarian justification for the construction of the railroad.

From: A PARLIAMENTARY DEBATE ON UGANDA

MR. STOREY: He would ask right hon. Gentlemen on the Treasury Bench, and the Radicals who were in the last House of Commons, if the late Government had done this thing what would have been the attitude that they (the Radicals) would have assumed? They would have condemned such a thing as wrong, and they would have said, and with immense force, to the then Government, "You may wish to spend British money, and expend British lives in Uganda, but if you have got millions to spare, and time at your command, we would ask you to use those millions first for the good of our own country." As a Radical he should hold himself for ever disgraced if, on a matter like this—when he lived in a country which called itself Christian, but in which, at this time, millions of people were living under shameful and insanitary conditions, and which yet permitted hundreds of poor men and women to die in the workhouse wearing pauper garb—the Government should come and say they would expend these millions of money, annex a territory in Central Africa, where they were not wanted, separated by 700 miles of desert through which they would have to build a railway, he did not at once protest. If that Government came to him and proposed such a wild scheme as that, he would have said to them, "Your business is first at home, and if you have got millions to spare spend them here.". . .

MR. JOSEPH CHAMBERLAIN: He [Mr. Storey] is opposed to expansion of the Empire and to any expense, on the ground, as I understand, that we have enough to do at home. Now, suppose this view which he puts before the Committee, and which I suppose will not be accepted even to-day by the majority of the Committee, had been put 50 or 100 years ago, and suppose it had been accepted by the Parliament of that day, I ask myself what would now be the position of this country, what would be the position of persons in the slums for whom my hon. Friend has so much sympathy and feeling? Does my hon. Friend believe, if it were not for the gigantic foreign trade that has been created by the policy of expansion, that we could subsist in this country in any kind of way—I do not say in luxury, but in the condition in which at present a great part of our population live? Does he think that we could support 40,000,000 of people in these small islands? Is it not the fact that the great proportion of the 40,000,000 people of this country earns its livelihood by the trade brought to the country in consequence of the action of our ancestors 50 or 100 years ago who did not shrink from making sacrifices, and who were not ashamed—if I may borrow the expression which has been referred to more than once to-night—to peg our claims for posterity? We are the posterity who enjoy the result of that policy; and are we to be meaner and more selfish than those who preceded us? Are we to do nothing for those who come after us? Are we to sacrifice that which those who went before have gained for us? Why, if this idea of closing all the doors through which all new trade is to come to us is to be accepted by this House, we must adopt some means or other by which our population can be kept stationary. And I venture to say that when our ancestors pegged out claims for us, as they did in many parts of the world, they were not at the time more promising than the claims which are now under consideration. Well, what is it we are asked to do to-night? This is not a question of Uganda only; but we are asked to reverse the whole policy of this country—a policy undertaken, I believe, with the consent of the vast majority of the people of this country. We are asked to give up all the advantages which have been secured by the surrender of Heligoland, and by the Treaties and arrangements made with foreign Powers. My hon. Friend does not take into account any advantages. At any rate, we have made sacrifices. We gave up territory with the full consent of the majority of our people in the belief that we were getting a *quid pro quo*. Parliament is now asked to sacrifice the *quid*

Great Britain, *The Parliamentary Debates*, 4th series, 2nd Sess., 25th Parl., 57 Victoriae, X, 14 March–10 April 1893, cols. 559; 593–595; 597–599; 601–604.

pro quo which this country obtained. We are asked to give up all part and share in what has been called the partition of Africa. I am bound to do my hon. Friend this justice—to point out that he always speaks in the first person singular; therefore, I do not suppose that he claims to speak for more than himself. He will be in a minority in the House to-day. I believe he will be in a small minority in the House, and I believe that in the country he is in a still smaller minority. I believe that the people of this country have decided this matter in their minds, and have determined that they will take their full share in the disposition of these new lands and in the work of civilisation they have to carry out there. I think they are justified in that determination—justified by the spirit of the past, justified by that spirit which has shown that the spirit of travel and adventure and enterprise distinguishing the Anglo-Saxon race has made us peculiarly fit to carry out the work of colonisation. It is a curious fact, and one which I have never been able to explain, that of all the nations of the world we are the only one able to carry out this work without absolute cost to ourselves. Take, for instance, the case of France, which has been for a long time ruling in Algeria. Up to this moment, although French rule there has been beneficent, Algeria costs to the French Exchequer large sums every year. The same is the case with regard to Tunis, and the German possessions with regard to Italy in Abyssinia, and also with the foreign possessions of Portugal. There is no other country in the world except Spain, in the early days of America and Holland up to comparatively recent times, which has been able permanently to carry out a policy of colonisation without imposing burdens on its subjects. I say that all these facts should lead us to be hopeful in undertaking this new work of colonisation, which does not differ in any respect from the work we have carried out successfully in the past. If we are not going to give up this mission—to use a word I do not much like, but it has been previously employed—let us look the matter courageously in the face, and be prepared, if need be, for sacrifice of life and money, which, in the first instance, we may have to make in order to carry it out. We have come to the point at which we do not consider life so sacred that it may not be sacrificed to save life. For my own part, I hold that, both in matters of life and money, we may sacrifice both, if we see before us a prospect of good and a satisfaction for the sacrifice we may make. The people of this country, in my opinion, have by large majorities declared that it is our duty to take our share in the work of civilisation in Africa. I do not believe they are at all prepared to sympathise with my hon. Friend below me. They know that an omelette cannot be made without breaking eggs, and I do not believe that they are prepared to count the cost. They think that in the long run any expenditure they may have incurred will prove to have been well expended. . . .

What have we done there? By a Charter we gave to a Company certain powers. Not only was the Company entrusted with discretion, but distinct and definite pressure was put upon it to go forward and to prevent other countries from coming in and taking possession of territories which were within the sphere of British influence. Rightly or wrongly, the Company yielded to the pressure of public opinion; they went forward in Uganda; they broke up such government as there was in Uganda. I am told the hon. Member for Dumfries has said, in an excellent and powerful speech, which I had not the advantage of hearing, that the normal condition there was one of massacre. But, of course, there was a Government there—such a Government as you may expect in those countries. But after all, suppose we have no business there whatever, and no responsibility, and never intend to take any, we had better have left those people to work out their own salvation for themselves, be it by massacre or in any other way. However, as a matter of fact we did not do so. We broke up the authority of those who were held to be chiefs and rulers in Uganda. We came in at a cost which to my mind was trifling in comparison with the results achieved. We have secured for Uganda the *pax Britannica* which has been so beneficial in India. I heard the Prime Minister to-night—and I confess I was delighted to hear him—I heard him talk about the sad and deplorable occurrence in Uganda. I think he spoke of those occurrences as constituting massacre.

There was no massacre at all. What existed in Uganda at that time were anarchy and civil war of the worst kind. If we had not been there thousands and perhaps hundreds of thousands of people would have been cruelly massacred; and after the victory of one party or the other what remained of the minority would have been cruelly tortured to death. Captain Lugard was on the spot. Let me say in passing that I sometimes feel we do not do justice to our bravest and noblest citizens. Of Captain Lugard I know no more than any Member of the House may know—I know him only through reading his works. He was, I believe, an Indian officer who was sent to Uganda under the orders of the Company. He undertook a work of the highest responsibility and the greatest importance, and I say that anyone who reads his accounts impartially will agree with me to this extent, that he was, at all events, a man of extraordinary power and capacity, tact, discretion, and courage. Courage is a common virtue, but he has shown it in no common way, and he has exhibited a modesty which is beyond all praise. I say it is something for England, for the United Kingdom, to glory in that we can still boast such servants as these. I was saying that Captain Lugard was present in Uganda when this state of things arose. He took his measures, and as a matter of fact in all the confusion which followed, 400 lives at the outside—he himself puts the number at considerably less—were killed. It was deplorable, no doubt; but that sacrifice cheaply purchased the peace, the pacification, and temporary civilisation which followed; and at all events, long before now the people of that great country would have been at each other's throats but for the presence of the English. You have taken this responsibility through the Company to whom you gave a Charter; you have never disavowed them; and now you cannot leave that country whatever it cost you. Even if, as the hon. Member for Northampton said, it cost you another expedition, you are bound at all costs to fulfil the obligations of this country to maintain the faith of this country to the people to whom it is pledged. What would happen if you left? Would not the Protestants, Catholics, and Mahomedans be at one another's throats, and would there not be a

massacre almost unparalleled even in the history of Africa? And who would suffer most? Those who have been our allies. They are the people whom we have disarmed and who would now fall an easy prey to their enemies. I do not think my hon. Friend contemplated such an abandonment as that. I am quite ready to protest against any further extension of the Empire. But we are dealing now with what has taken place and cannot be recalled; and I say it would be a greater disgrace than ever befell England if you were to retire from a country whose prosperity and the lives of whose people depended absolutely upon your continuance of the hold you have upon them. . . .

As to the commerce of Uganda, the late Mr. Mackay, the missionary, who was universally respected, said that the climate of Uganda was excellent, that the country would produce almost anything, and that the only difficulty was the want of transport and of British enterprise, but that once those two things were secured there was no reason whatever why Uganda should not be a most prosperous, even a wealthy, country. Of course, Uganda, 600 miles from the coast, in such a position that everything brought there from the coast or taken to the coast from there costs £ 200 per ton in transport, is not likely to have a very brisk trade at present. But I would ask hon. Gentlemen what they would have said about the cost of carriage to the North-West of Canada 100 years ago? Until the Canadian Pacific Railway was constructed there was scarcely any trade in those great dominions of the British Crown. I say that the prospects of Uganda at this moment are quite equal to those of the North-West of Canada 50 years ago. This is what Lord Rosebery means by pegging out claims for prosperity. Lord Rosebery is sensible that our returns cannot be immediate, but, on the other hand, a return at some time or another is almost certain. . . .

I firmly believe that the railway will pay in the end, and will prove a good investment. If you spend this £ 1,500,000 or £ 3,000,000, the working classes of this country, and the people in the slums, for whom the hon. Member for Sunderland is so anxious, will benefit, for the whole of the work will, of course, be done in this country, and the line will be engineered by natives of this country. Even in the hon. Member's view, therefore, the money will not be wholly thrown away. I believe that the chances of this railway are every bit as good as the railways which this country made 30 years ago in the Peninsular of India, and which are now bringing in a good revenue. This railway will bring us into contact with 12,000,000 of people, as, besides the people of Uganda, there is the population of the countries conterminous with the Victoria Lake and the other great lakes to be considered, and whatever may be said of Uganda, nobody will deny that the neighbouring countries, like Unyoro and Usoga, are countries of enormous natural wealth. I believe that just as soon as you make porterage possible, we shall have a very large commerce. We shall get from this country gum and rubber, and perhaps even wheat, and in return we shall send out large quantities of our manufactures. One thing I must say in confirmation of this. I think it is a most remarkable fact that since we created this Company and this sphere of influence, the British and the general trade of Zanzibar has been increasing at a perfectly marvellous rate. In one year—the last year for which we have Returns—it nearly doubled, increasing from 72,000 to 131,000 tons. If that is done in the green tree, what will be done in the dry? I have no hesitation in saying, therefore, that the investment is one which a rich country can wisely undertake. The hon. Member for Sunderland says he does feel a certain amount of obligation in connection with the suppression of the Slave Trade, though to his mind it is inferior to the obligation we have to the inhabitants of the slums. Well, I say with regard to the Slave Trade, that the railway will do more to suppress that abominable traffic than can be accomplished by any other expenditure of the same sum. What is the Slave Trade, and what is the cause of it? People do not make slaves through love of cruelty or mischief, but they do so because they made their livelihood by it. Tribes are enslaved, are taken as slaves, in order to carry burdens to the coast, and when they have done that they are sold for what they will fetch. If you could give to the slave-raiding Arabs, who at the present moment are the most barbarous and brutal people on the face of the earth, peaceful means of making an honest livelihood, do you mean to say that they enjoy war so much that they will not accept these means? If you say so, I think all history and experience is against you. You have never found a case where it has been made profitable to a nation or tribe to keep the peace that they have not done so. Take an illustration. In the old days we had to fight with the Punjabees, and when we had conquered them they supplied us with our best soldiers in India. But now that we established peace, and the country is more prosperous than it ever was before, and people, who were once the most warlike race in India, are settling down, or I should say, rising up, into agriculturalists and peasants, and we cannot get from them an adequate number of recruits for our Army. We have to go farther afield. What happened in India will happen in Africa. Make it the interest of the Arab slave traders to give up the Slave Trade, and you will see the end of that traffic. It costs at present between £200 and £300 to carry a ton of merchandise to Uganda. Construct your railway, and increase the means of traffic, and you will take away three-fourths, almost the whole, of the temptation to carry on the Slave Trade. I ask the Committee, and I should like to put it to the country: Are they in earnest in this matter of the Slave Trade? Is the hereditary sentiment of the British people still existent amongst us? Do we hold it to be one of our prime duties, as Lord Rosebery said, and great glories, to take a prominent part in suppressing this trade? If we do, let us look boldly in the face the necessities of the situation and let us spend our money wisely and direct it to this purpose. We are spending £200,000 a year for a squadron on the East Coast, as I said just now, which I am afraid, has too often increased indirectly the horrors and sufferings in connection with the trade. . . .

Albert J. Beveridge

Albert J. Beveridge (1862–1927) was an American politician, lawyer, historian, and orator who served two terms (1899–1911) as a United States Senator from Indiana. He became associated toward the close of the century with a group of young men actively interested in American imperialism. In 1898 he favored the war against Spain, and in the congressional elections of that year, he warmly defended the peace terms demanded of Spain by the McKinley administration. In thus supporting the Republicans and opposing the free silver Democrats, Beveridge revealed himself as an ardent imperialist, advocating American expansion both in the Pacific and in the Caribbean area. At times his speeches had a decided jingoistic tinge, as, for example, "The March of the Flag" address given in Indianapolis during the campaign. In reading the following selections from this speech note (1) the references Beveridge made to Divine participation in American progress, (2) the size and nature of the issue before the voters, (3) what he considered to be the fruits of victory, (4) the manner in which he related the deeds of McKinley with those of earlier Americans, (5) his reply to those who opposed colonial expansion on grounds of democratic principles, (6) how he refuted the opposition's "contiguous territory" argument, (7) the economic arguments he advanced for the annexation of the new territories, (8) the importance of a sound financial system to a trading nation, (9) his emphasis upon America's manifest destiny, and (10) the similarities between his arguments and those of Joseph Chamberlain.

From: THE MARCH OF THE FLAG

Fellow-Citizens—It is a noble land that God has given us; a land that can feed and clothe the world: a land whose coast lines would inclose half the countries of Europe; a land set like a sentinel between the two imperial oceans of the globe; a greater England with a nobler destiny. It is a mighty people that He has planted on this soil; a people sprung from the most masterful blood of history; a people perpetually revitalized by the virile workingfolk of all the earth; a people imperial by virtue of their power, by right of their institutions, by authority of their heaven-directed purposes, the propagandists and not the misers of liberty. It is a glorious history our God has bestowed upon His chosen people; a history whose keynote was struck by Liberty Bell; a history heroic with faith in our mission and our future; a history of statesmen, who flung the boundaries of the Republic out into unexplored lands and savage wildernesses; a history of soldiers, who carried the flag across blazing deserts and through the ranks of hostile mountains, even to the gates of sunset: a history of a multiplying people, who overran a continent in half a century; a history divinely logical, in the process

Albert J. Beveridge, *The Meaning of the Times*, The Bobbs-Merrill Company, Inc., Indianapolis, 1908. Copyright 1908, 1936; used by special permission of the publisher, The Bobbs-Merrill Company, Inc.

of whose tremendous reasoning we find our-selves to-day.

Therefore, in this campaign the question is larger than a party question. It is an American question. It is a world question. Shall the American people continue their resistless march toward the commercial supremacy of the world? Shall free institutions broaden their blessed reign as the children of liberty wax in strength until the empire of our principles is established over the hearts of all mankind? Have we no mission to perform—no duty to discharge to our fellow-man? Has the Almighty Father endowed us with gifts beyond our de-serts, and marked us as the people of His peculiar favor, merely to rot in our own selfish-ness, as men and nations must who take cow-ardice for their companion and self for their deity—as China has, as India has, as Egypt has? Shall we be as the man who had one talent and hid it, or as he who had ten talents and used them until they grew to riches. And shall we reap the reward that waits on the discharge of our high duty as the sovereign power of earth; shall we occupy new markets for what our farmers raise, new markets for what our factories make, new markets for what our merchants sell,—aye, and please God, new markets for what our ships shall carry? Shall we avail ourselves of new sources of supply of what we do not raise or make, so that what are luxuries to-day shall be necessities to-morrow? Shall we conduct the mightiest commerce of history with the best money known to man or shall we use the pauper money of Mexico, China and the Chicago [Democratic Party] platform? Shall we be worthy of our mighty past of progress, brushing aside, as we have always done, the spider webs of technicality, and march ever onward upon the highway of development, to the doing of real deeds, the achievement of real things, and the winning of real victories?

In a sentence, shall the American people en-dorse at the polls the American administration of William McKinley, which, under the guid-ance of Divine Providence, has started the Re-public on its noblest career of prosperity, duty and glory; or shall the American people rebuke that administration, reverse the wheels of his-tory, halt the career of the flag and turn to that purposeless horde of criticism and carping that is assailing the government at Washing-ton? Shall it be McKinley, sound money and a world-conquering commerce, or Bryan, Bailey, Bland, and Blackburn, a bastard currency and a policy of commercial retreat? In the only foreign war that this Nation has had in two generations, will you, the voters of this Repub-lic and the guardians of its good repute, give the other nations of the world to understand that the American people do not approve and indorse the administration that conducted it? These are the questions that you must answer at the polls, and I well know how you will an-swer them. The thunder of American guns at Santiago and Manila will find its answer in the approval of the voters of the Republic. For the administration of William McKinley, in both peace and war, will receive the mightiest en-dorsement of a grateful people ever registered. In both peace and war, for we rely on the new birth of national prosperity as well as on the new birth of national glory. Think of both! Think of our country two years ago, and think of it to-day! . . .

For William McKinley is continuing the pol-icy that Jefferson began, Monroe continued, Seward advanced, Grant promoted, Harrison championed. Hawaii is ours; Porto Rico is to be ours; at the prayer of its people Cuba will finally be ours; in the islands of the East, even to the gates of Asia, coaling stations are to be ours; at the very least the flag of a liberal gov-ernment is to float over the Philippines, and it will be the stars and stripes of glory. And the burning question of this campaign is whether the American people will accept the gifts of events; whether they will rise, as lifts their soaring destiny; whether they will proceed along the lines of national development sur-veyed by the statesmen of our past; or whether, for the first time, the American people doubt their mission, question their fate, prove apos-tate to the spirit of their race, and halt the ceaseless march of free institutions?

The opposition tells us that we ought not to govern a people without their consent. I an-swer, the rule of liberty that all just govern-ment derives its authority from the consent of the governed, applies only to those who are capable of self-government. We govern the

Indians without their consent; we govern our Territories without their consent; we govern our children without their consent. I answer, would not the natives of the Philippines prefer the just, humane, civilizing government of this Republic to the savage, bloody rule of pillage and extortion from which we have rescued them? Do not the blazing fires of joy and the ringing bells of gladness in Porto Rico prove the welcome of our flag? And regardless of this formula of words made only for enlightened, self-governing peoples, do we owe no duty to the world? Shall we turn these peoples back to the reeking hands from which we have taken them? Shall we save them from those nations, to give them to a self-rule of tragedy? It would be like giving a razor to a babe and telling it to shave itself. It would be like giving a typewriter to an Esquimau and telling him to publish one of the great dailies of the world. . . .

Distance and oceans are no longer arguments. The fact that all the territory our fathers bought and seized is contiguous is no longer an argument. In 1819 Florida was further from New York than Porto Rico is from Chicago today; Texas further from Washington in 1845 than Hawaii is from Boston in 1898; California more inaccessible in 1847 than the Philippines are now. Gibraltar is further from London than Havana is from Washington; Melbourne is further from Liverpool than Manila is from San Francisco. The ocean does not separate us from the lands of our duty and desire—the ocean to join us, a river never to be dredged, a canal never to be repaired. Steam joins us; electricity joins us—the very elements are in league with our destiny. Cuba not contiguous! Porto Rico not contiguous! Hawaii and the Philippines not contiguous! Our navy will make them contiguous. Dewey and Sampson and Schley have made them contiguous and American speed, American guns, American heart and brain and nerve will keep them contiguous forever.

But there is a difference. We did not need the western Mississippi valley when we acquired it, nor Florida, nor Texas, nor California, nor the royal provinces of the far Northwest. We had no emigrants to people this vast wilderness, no money to develop it, even no

highways to cover it. No trade awaited us in its savage fastnesses. Our productions were not greater than our internal trade. There was not one reason for the land lust of our statesmen from Jefferson to Harrison other than the prophet and the Saxon within them. But today, we are raising more than we can consume. Today, we are making more than we can use. Therefore, we must find new markets for our produce, new occupation for our capital, new work for our labor. And so, while we did not need the territory taken during the past century at the time it was acquired, we do need what we have taken in 1898, and we need it now. Think of the thousands of Americans who will pour into Hawaii and Porto Rico when the Republic's laws cover those islands with justice and safety. Think of the tens of thousands of Americans who will invade the Philippines when a liberal government shall establish order and equity there. Think of the hundreds of thousands of Americans who will build a soap-and-water, common school civilization of energy and industry in Cuba, when a government of law replaces the double reign of anarchy and tyranny. Think of the prosperous millions that empress of islands will support when, obedient to the law of political gravitation, her people ask for the highest honor liberty can bestow—the sacred order of the stars and stripes, the citizenship of the great Republic!

What does all this mean for every one of us? First of all, it means opportunity for all the glorious young manhood of the Republic. It means that the resources and the commerce of those immensely rich dominions will be increased as much as American energy is greater than Spanish sloth; for Americans, henceforth, will monopolize those resources and that commerce. In Cuba, alone, there are 15,000,000 acres of forest unacquainted with the ax. There are exhaustless mines of iron. There are priceless deposits of manganese. There are millions of acres yet unexplored. The resources of Porto Rico have only been trifled with. The resources of the Philippines have hardly been touched by the finger tips of modern methods. And they produce what we cannot, and they consume what we produce—the very predestination of reciprocity. And William McKinley intends that their trade shall be ours. It means an opportunity for the rich man to do something with his money, besides hoarding it or lending it. It means occupation for every workingman in the country at wages which the development of new resources, the launching of new enterprises, the monopoly of new markets always brings. Cuba is as large as Pennsylvania, and is the richest spot on all the globe. Hawaii is as large as New Jersey; Porto Rico half as large as Hawaii; the Philippines larger than all New England, New York, New Jersey and Delaware. The trade of these islands, developed as we will develop it, will set every reaper in the Republic singing, every furnace spouting the flames of industry. . . .

Now on the threshold of our career as the first power of earth, is the time to permanently adjust our system of finance. The American people have the most tremendous tasks of history to perform. They have the mightiest commerce of the world to conduct. They cannot halt their progress of wealth and power to unsettle their money system at the command of ignorance. Think of Great Britain becoming the commercial monarch of the world with her financial system periodically assailed! Think of Holland or Germany or France yet sending their flag in every sea, with their money at the mercy of politicians seeking for an issue! Sixteen to one is passed in our career. Why go back to it, like the victim of opium to his deadly pipe? Now, when new rivers of gold are pouring through the fields of business, the foundation of all silver-standard argument that there is not enough gold, is swept away. Why mumble the meaningless phrases of a tale that is told when the golden future is before us, the world calls us, its wealth awaits us and God's command is on us? There are so many real things to be done—canals to be dug, railways to be laid, forests to be felled, cities to be builded, unviolated fields to be tilled, priceless markets to be won, ships to be launched, peoples to be saved, civilization to be proclaimed and the flag of liberty flung to the eager air of every sea. Is this an hour to waste upon triflers with Nature's laws? Is this a season to give our

destiny over to word mongers and prosperity wreckers? No! It is an hour to remember your duty to the home. It is a moment to realize the opportunities Fate has opened to this favored people and to you. It is a time to bethink you of your Nation and its sovereignty of the seas. It is a time to remember that the God of our fathers is our God and that the gifts and the duties He gave to them, enriched and multiplied, He renews to us, their children. It is a time to sustain that devoted man, servant of the people and of the most high God, who is guiding the Republic out into the ocean of infinite possibilities. It is a time to cheer the beloved President of God's chosen people, till the whole world is vocal with American loyalty to the American government and William McKinley, its head and chief.

Fellow-Americans, we are God's chosen people. Yonder at Bunker Hill and Yorktown His providence was above us. At New Orleans and on ensanguined seas His hand sustained us. Abraham Lincoln was His minister, and His was the altar of freedom the boys in blue set up on a hundred smoking battlefields. His power directed Dewey in the east, and He delivered the Spanish fleet into our hands on Liberty's natal day as He delivered the elder Armada into the hands of our English sires two centuries ago. His great purposes are revealed in the progress of the flag, which surpasses the intentions of Congresses and Cabinets, and leads us, like a holier pillar of cloud by day and pillar of fire by night, into situations unforeseen by finite wisdom and duties unexpected by the unprophetic heart of selfishness. The American people cannot use a dishonest medium of exchange; it is ours to set the world its example of right and honor. We cannot fly from our world duties; it is ours to execute the purposes of a fate that has driven us to be greater than our small intentions. We cannot retreat from any soil where Providence has unfurled our banner; it is ours to save that soil for liberty and civilization. For liberty and civilization and God's promises fulfilled, the flag must henceforth be the symbol and the sign to all mankind.

William II, Poincaré, Nicholas II, and Asquith

On June 28, 1914 the Archduke, Franz Ferdinand, was assassinated in the Bosnian capital of Sarajevo as the result of a Serbian nationalist plot. One month later, on July 28, the Austro-Hungarian government declared war on Serbia with the intention of punishing her for this fatal attack on the heir to the Habsburg throne and of removing the Serbian threat to the empire of the dual monarchy. Immediately, the system of alliances which had divided Europe into two hostile groups, began to function, and within a week five of the six major European powers were at war. In the first days of the struggle the governmental heads of the belligerent nations issued statements to their peoples to justify their action and to arouse popular feeling in support of the struggle ahead. In reading these statements compare them on such points as (1) which nations were waging defensive war, (2) the emphasis each placed on national honor, (3) the appeals to Divine assistance, (4) their concern for conquest, (5) the efforts made to preserve peace, and (6) the references made to obligations to support alliances.

STATEMENTS MADE AT THE OUTBREAK OF WORLD WAR I

GERMAN STATEMENTS

*Speech of Emperor William II
from the balcony of the Imperial Palace,
31 July 1914*

A momentous hour has struck for Germany. Envious rivals everywhere drive us to legitimate defense. The sword has been forced into our hand. I hope that, if my endeavors up to the very last moment should not succeed in bringing the adversaries to reason and in preserving peace, we may wield the sword, with God's help, so that we may sheathe it again with honor. War would demand enormous sacrifices from the German people, but we would show the enemy what it means to attack Germany. And so I commend you to God. Go now into the churches, kneel before God, and implore His help for our brave army.

*Emperor William's Speech from the Throne,
4 August 1914*

Honored gentlemen, at a time of such importance I have assembled the elected representatives of the German people about me. For nearly half a century we have been allowed to follow the ways of peace. The attempts to attribute to Germany warlike intentions and to hedge in her position in the world have often sorely tried the patience of my people. Undeterred, my Government has pursued the development of our moral, spiritual,

Speech of the Emperor William II, 31 July 1914, from Ralph Haswell Lutz, *Fall of the German Empire, 1914–1918*, Stanford University Press, Stanford University, 1932, I, 4; statement of the Emperor William II, 4 August 1914, from *ibid.*, I, 8–9. Courtesy of the Stanford University Press. Manifesto of Tsar Nicholas II, 2 August 1914, from Frank Alfred Golder, *Documents of Russian History, 1914–1917*, The Century Company, New York, 1927, 29–30. Courtesy of Appleton-Century-Crofts, Inc. Message, President Poincaré, Chamber of Deputies, 4 August 1914, translated by the editors from France, *Assemblée nationale, Annales de la Chambre des deputes, 1914*, sess. ord. et ext., II, 907–910. Prime Minister Asquith, House of Commons, 6 August 1914 from Great Britain, *The Parliamentary Debates*, 5th series, Commons, 1914, LXV, cols. 2078–2079.

and economic strength as its highest aim, with all frankness, even under provocative circumstances. The world has been witness that during the last years, under all pressure and confusion, we have stood in the first rank in saving the nations of Europe from a war between the great powers.

The most serious dangers to which the events in the Balkans had given rise seemed to have been overcome—then suddenly an abyss was opened through the murder of my friend the Archduke Franz Ferdinand. My lofty ally, the Emperor and King Franz Josef, was forced to take up arms to defend the security of his empire against dangerous machinations from a neighboring state. The Russian Empire stepped in to hinder the allied monarchy from following out her just interests. Not only does our duty as ally call us to the side of Austria-Hungary, but it is our great task to protect our own position and the old community of culture between the two Empires against the attack of hostile forces. . . .

The present situation is the result of an ill will which has been active for many years against the power and the prosperity of the German Empire.

No lust of conquest drives us on; we are inspired by the unalterable will to protect the place in which God has set us for ourselves and all coming generations. From the documents which have been submitted to you, you will see how my Government, and especially my Chancellor, have endeavored even to the last moment to stave off the inevitable. In a defensive war that has been forced upon us, with a clear conscience and a clean hand we take up the sword. . . .

FRENCH STATEMENT

Message of President Poincaré to the Chamber of Deputies, 4 August 1914

Gentlemen of the Chamber of Deputies, France has become the object of a brutal and premeditated aggression which is an insolent defiance of international law. Before a declaration of war was addressed to us, before even the German ambassador had asked for his passport, our territory was invaded. . . .

For more than forty years the French, in a sincere love of peace, have stifled the desire for legitimate reparation. They have given to the world the example of a great nation which, definitively resurrected from defeat by strength of will, by patience and work, has used its renewed and revived force only in the interest of progress and for the good of humanity.

Since the Austrian crisis opened up a situation threatening to the whole of Europe, France has set herself to follow and to recommend everywhere a policy of prudence, wisdom, and moderation. No one can charge her with an act, with a gesture, with a word which has not been peaceful and conciliating. In this hour of the first combats, she has the right to credit herself with the fact that she made supreme efforts up until the last moment to avoid this war which has just broken out and for which Germany will bear before history the crushing responsibility. . . .

In the war which has begun, France will have on her side that right whose eternal moral force no people, no individual can defy with impunity. She will be heroically defended by her sons whose sacred unity before the enemy nothing can break and who are today joined in the same indignation against the aggressor and in the same patriotic faith. She is faithfully seconded by Russia, her ally; she is supported by the loyal friendship of England.

Already from all parts of the civilized world come to her expressions of sympathy and good wishes. Because she represents again today before the universe liberty, justice, and reason.

Haut les coeurs et vive la France!

RUSSIAN STATEMENT

Manifesto of Tsar Nicholas II, 2 August 1914

By the Grace of God, We, Nicholas II, Emperor and Autocrat of all Russia, Tsar of Poland, Grand Duke of Finland, etc., etc., etc., proclaim to all Our loyal subjects:

Following her historical traditions, Russia, united in faith and blood with the Slav nations, has never regarded their fate with indifference. The unanimous fraternal sentiments of the Russian people for the Slavs have been aroused to special intensity in the past few days, when Austria-Hungary presented to Serbia demands which she foresaw would be unacceptable to a Sovereign State.

Having disregarded the conciliatory and peaceable reply of the Serbian Government, and having declined Russia's well-intentioned mediation, Austria hastened to launch an armed attack in a bombardment of unprotected Belgrad.

Compelled, by the force of circumstances thus created, to adopt the necessary measures of precaution, We commanded that the army and the navy be put on a war footing, but, at the same time, holding the blood and the treasure of Our subjects dear, We made every effort to obtain a peaceable issue of the negotiations that had been started.

In the midst of friendly communications, Austria's Ally, Germany, contrary to Our trust in century-old relations of neighborliness, and paying no heed to Our assurances that the measures We had adopted implied no hostile aims whatever, insisted upon their immediate abandonment, and, meeting with a rejection of this demand, suddenly declared war on Russia.

We have now to intercede not only for a related country, unjustly attacked, but also to safeguard the honor, dignity, and integrity of Russia, and her position among the Great Powers. We firmly believe that all Our loyal subjects will rally self-sacrificingly and with one accord to the defense of the Russian soil.

At this hour of threatening danger, let domestic strife be forgotten. Let the union between the Tsar and His people be stronger than ever, and let Russia, rising like one man, repel the insolent assault of the enemy.

With a profound faith in the justice of Our cause, and trusting humbly in Almighty Providence, We invoke prayerfully the Divine blessing for Holy Russia and Our valiant troops. . . .

BRITISH STATEMENT

Statement by Prime Minister Asquith in the House of Commons, 6 August 1914

. . . I am entitled to say, and I do so on behalf of this country—I speak not for a party, I speak for the country as a whole—that we made every effort any Government could possibly make for peace. But this war has been forced upon us. What is it we are fighting for? Everyone knows, and no one knows better than the Government, the terrible, incalculable suffering, economic, social, personal, and political, which war, and especially a war between the Great Powers of the world, must entail. There is no man amongst us sitting upon this bench in these trying days—more trying perhaps than any body of statesmen for a hundred years have had to pass through—there is not a man amongst us who has not, during the whole of that time, had clearly before his vision the almost unequalled suffering which war, even in a just cause, must bring about, not only to the peoples who are for the moment living in this country and in other countries of the world, but to posterity and to the whole prospects of European civilisation. Every step we took we took with that vision before our eyes, and with a sense of responsibility which it is impossible to describe. . . .

If I am asked what we are fighting for I reply in two sentences. In the first place, to fulfil a solemn international obligation, an obligation which, if it had been entered into between private persons in the ordinary concerns of life, would have been regarded as an obligation not only of law but of honour, which no self-respecting man could possibly have repudiated. I say, secondly, we are fighting to vindicate the principle which, in these days when force, material force, sometimes seems to be the dominant influence and factor in the development of mankind, we are fighting to vindicate the principle that small nationalities are not to be crushed, in defiance of international good faith, by the arbitrary will of a strong and overmastering Power.

I do not believe that any nation ever entered into a great controversy—and this is one of the greatest history will ever know—with a clearer conscience and a stronger conviction that it is fighting, not for aggression, not for the maintenance even of its own selfish interest, but that it is fighting in defence of principles the maintenance of which is vital to the civilisation of the world. With a full conviction, not only of the wisdom and justice, but of the obligations which lay upon us to challenge this great issue, we are entering into the struggle. . . .

Entente Diplomacy

For generations the Russian ambition to control Constantinople and the adjacent straits leading to the Mediterranean had been opposed by the British. On October 28, 1914, Turkey entered the war on the side of the Central Powers and the Czarist government was not slow in pressing its claims for Turkish territory upon Great Britain and France. Naturally, the British assent was given more reluctantly than that of the French, a fact which was revealed by the memorandums exchanged among the three powers in March, 1915. The British and French replies to the Russian demands are significant in that they prepared the way for the partition of the Turkish Empire among the members of the Entente. In reading them note (1) the description of the territory demanded by the Russian Minister of Foreign Affairs, (2) the importance attached to the demand by the British Embassy in Petrograd, (3) the statement by the British on how their assent fitted in with their traditional policy, (4) the British request for future concessions in the ceded area, (5) the reservations regarding Moslem holy places, (6) why the British wanted the understanding kept secret, and (7) the statement in the memorandum to the Russian ambassador in Paris of the political aspirations of England.

From: THE SECRET AGREEMENT OF MARCH, 1915

MEMORANDUM OF THE RUSSIAN FOREIGN OFFICE

On February 19 (March 4), 1915, the Minister of Foreign Affairs handed to the French and British Ambassadors a Memorandum which set forth the desire to add the following territories to Russia as the result of the present war:

The town of Constantinople, the western coast of the Bosphorus, the Sea of Marmora, and the Dardanelles; Southern Thrace, as far as the Enos-Media line; the coast of Asia Minor between the Bosphorus and the River Sakaria, and a point on the Gulf of Ismid to be defined later; the islands in the Sea of Marmora, and the Islands of Imbros and Tenedos. The special rights of France and England in the above territories were to remain inviolate.

MEMORANDUM OF THE BRITISH EMBASSY IN PETROGRAD, 12 MARCH 1915

. . . The claim made by the Imperial [Russian] Government in their Aide-Mémoire of February 19—March 4, 1915 considerably exceeds the desiderata which were foreshadowed by M. Sasonow as probable a few weeks ago. Before His Majesty's Government have had time to take into consideration what their own desiderata elsewhere would be in the final terms of peace, Russia is asking for a definite promise that her wishes shall be satisfied with

Memorandum of the Russian Foreign Office, March 1915, from F. Seymour Cocks, *The Secret Treaties and Understandings*, London, 1918, 19–24. Memorandum of the British Embassy in Petrograd, 12 March 1915, from Frank A Golder, *Documents of Russian History, 1914–1917*, The Century Company, New York, 1927, 60–62. Courtesy of Appleton-Century-Crofts, Inc. Russian Minister of Foreign Affairs to Russian Ambassador, Paris, 5/18 March 1915, from F. Seymour Cocks, *op. cit.*, 17–18.

regard to what is in fact the richest prize of the entire war. Sir Edward Grey accordingly hopes that M. Sasonow will realize that it is not in the power of His Majesty's Government to give a greater proof of friendship than that which is afforded by the terms of the above-mentioned Aide-Mémoire. That document involves a complete reversal of the traditional policy of His Majesty's Government and is in direct opposition to the opinions and sentiment at one time universally held in England and which have still by no means died out. Sir Edward Grey therefore trusts that the Imperial Government will recognize that the recent general assurances given to M. Sasonow have been most loyally and amply fulfilled. In presenting the Aide-Mémoire now, His Majesty's Government believe and hope that a lasting friendship between Russia and Great Britain will be assured as soon as the proposed settlement is realized.

From the British Aide-Mémoire it follows that the desiderata of His Majesty's Government, however important they may be to British interests in other parts of the world, will contain no condition which could impair Russia's control over the territories described in the Russian Aide-Mémoire of February 19—March 4, 1915.

In view of the fact that Constantinople will always remain a trade entrepôt for South-Eastern Europe and Asia Minor, His Majesty's Government will ask that Russia shall, when she comes in the possession of it, arrange for a free port for goods in transit to and from non-Russian territory. His Majesty's Government will also ask that there shall be commercial freedom for merchant ships passing through the Straits, as M. Sasonow has already promised. . . .

Sir E. Grey points out that it will obviously be necessary to take into consideration the whole question of the future interests of France and Great Britain in what is now Asiatic Turkey; and, in formulating the desiderata of His Majesty's Government with regard to the Ottoman Empire, he must consult the French as well as the Russian Government. As soon, however, as it becomes known that Russia is to have Constantinople at the conclusion of the war, Sir E. Grey will wish to state that,

throughout the negotiations, His Majesty's Government have stipulated that the Mussulman Holy Places and Arabia shall under all circumstances remain under independent Mussulman dominion.

Sir E. Grey is as yet unable to make any definitive proposal on any point of the British desiderata; but one of the points of the latter will be the revision of the Persian portion of the Anglo-Russian Agreement of 1907, so as to recognize the present neutral sphere as a British sphere.

Until the Allies are in a position to give to the Balkan States, and especially to Bulgaria and Rumania, some satisfactory assurance as to their prospects and general position with regard to the territories contiguous to their frontiers, to the possession of which they are known to aspire; and until a more advanced stage of the agreement as to the French and British desiderata in the final peace terms is reached, Sir E. Gray points out that it is most desirable that the understanding now arrived at between the Russian, French, and British Governments should remain secret.

THE RUSSIAN MINISTER OF FOREIGN AFFAIRS TO THE RUSSIAN AMBASSADOR IN PARIS, 5/18 MARCH 1915

On February 23 (March 8) the French Ambassador, on behalf of his Government, announced to me that France was prepared to take up a most favourable attitude in the matter of realisation of our desires as set out in my telegram to you, No. 937, in respect of the Straits and Constantinople, for which I charged you to tender Delcassé my gratitude.

In his conversations with you, Delcassé had previously more than once given his assurance that we could rely on the sympathy of France, and only referred to the need of elucidating the question of the attitude of England, from whom he feared some objections, before he could give us a more definite assurance in the above sense. Now the British Government has given its complete consent in writing to the annexation by Russia of the Straits and Constantinople within the limits indicated by us, and only demanded security for its economic interests and a similar benevolent attitude on our part towards the political aspirations of England in other parts.

For me, personally, filled as I am with most complete confidence in Delcassé, the assurance received from him is quite sufficient, but the Imperial Government would desire a more definite pronouncement of France's assent to the complete satisfaction of our desires, similar to that made by the British Government.

The Governments of France, Russia, Great Britain, and Italy

When the war broke out in August, 1914, Italy, despite her membership in the Triple Alliance, remained neutral. She claimed that Germany and Austria were waging an offensive war and that, therefore, the terms of their alliance, which were defensive in character, did not apply. In May, 1915, Italy joined the Entente against the Central Powers. Subsequently, it has been revealed that France, Russia, and Great Britain signed a secret treaty with Italy in London on April 26, 1915, the terms of which are given below. Undoubtedly, the agreement influenced Italy's decision to enter the war. Note, in reading (1) the obligation Russia assumed, (2) the extent of Italian military aid promised, (3) the naval agreement entered into by France and Great Britain, (4) the Austrian areas promised to Italy, (5) the terms reached regarding Albania, (6) the projected division of the Turkish Empire, and (7) evidences of Anglo-French imperialistic plans in Africa and elsewhere.

From: THE SECRET TREATY OF LONDON, 1915

Article 1. A military convention shall be immediately concluded between the General Staffs of France, Great Britain, Italy and Russia. This convention shall settle the minimum number of military forces to be employed by Russia against Austria-Hungary in order to prevent that Power from concentrating all its strength against Italy, in the event of Russia deciding to direct her principal effort against Germany.

This military convention shall settle the question of armistices, which necessarily comes within the scope of the Commanders-in-Chief of the Armies.

Article 2. On her part, Italy undertakes to use her entire resources for the purpose of waging war jointly with France, Great Britain and Russia against all their enemies.

Article 3. The French and British fleets shall

Great Britain, *Parliamentary Papers*, 1920, LI, Cmd. 671.

render active and permanent assistance to Italy until such time as the Austro-Hungarian fleet shall have been destroyed or until peace shall have been concluded.

A naval convention shall be immediately concluded to this effect between France, Great Britain and Italy.

Article 4. Under the Treaty of Peace, Italy shall obtain the Trentino, Cisalpine Tyrol with its geographical and natural frontier (the Brenner frontier), as well as Trieste, the counties of Gorizia and Gradisca, all Istria as far as the Quarnero and including Volosca and the Istrian islands of Cherso and Lussin, as well as the small islands. . . .

Article 5. Italy shall also be given the province of Dalmatia within its present administrative boundaries. . . .

Article 6. Italy shall receive full sovereignty

over Valona, the island of Saseno and surrounding territory of sufficient extent to assure defence of these points (from the Voïussa to the north and east, approximately to the northern boundary of the district of Chimara on the south).

Article 7. Should Italy obtain the Trentino and Istria in accordance with the provisions of Article 4, together with Dalmatia and the Adriatic islands within the limits specified in Article 5, and the Bay of Valona (Article 6), and if the central portion of Albania is reserved for the establishment of a small autonomous neutralised State, Italy shall not oppose the division of Northern and Southern Albania between Montenegro, Serbia and Greece, should France, Great Britain and Russia so desire. The coast from the southern boundary . . . of Valona . . . to Cape Stylos shall be neutralised.

Italy shall be charged with the representation of the State of Albania in its relations with foreign Powers. . . .

Article 8. Italy shall receive entire sovereignty over the Dodecanese Islands which she is at present occupying.

Article 9. Generally speaking, France, Great Britain and Russia recognise that Italy is interested in the maintenance of the balance of power in the Mediterranean and that, in the event of the total or partial partition of Turkey in Asia, she ought to obtain a just share of the Mediterranean region adjacent to the province of Adalia, where Italy has already acquired rights and interests which formed the subject of an Italo-British convention. The zone which shall eventually be allotted to Italy shall be delimited, at the proper time, due account being taken of the existing interests of France and Great Britain.

The interests of Italy shall also be taken into consideration in the event of the territorial integrity of the Turkish Empire being maintained and of alterations being made in the zones of interest of the Powers.

If France, Great Britain and Russia occupy any territories in Turkey in Asia during the course of the war, the Mediterranean region bordering on the Province of Adalia within the limits indicated above shall be reserved to Italy, who shall be entitled to occupy it.

Article 10. All rights and privileges in Libya at present belonging to the Sultan by virtue of the Treaty of Lausanne are transferred to Italy.

Article 11. Italy shall receive a share of any eventual war indemnity corresponding to her efforts and her sacrifices.

Article 12. Italy declares that she associates herself in the declaration made by France, Great Britain and Russia to the effect that Arabia and the Moslem Holy Places in Arabia shall be left under the authority of an independent Moslem Power.

Article 13. In the event of France and Great Britain increasing their colonial territories in Africa at the expense of Germany, those two Powers agree in principle that Italy may claim some equitable compensation, particularly as regards the settlement in her favour of the questions relative to the frontiers of the Italian colonies of Eritrea, Somaliland and Libya and the neighbouring colonies belonging to France and Great Britain.

Article 14. Great Britain undertakes to facilitate the immediate conclusion, under equitable conditions, of a loan of at least £50,000,000 to be issued on the London market.

Article 15. France, Great Britain and Russia shall support such opposition as Italy may make to any proposal in the direction of introducing a representative of the Holy See in any peace negotiations or negotiations for the settlement of questions raised by the present war.

Article 16. The present arrangement shall be held secret. The adherence of Italy to the Declaration of the 5th September, 1914, shall alone be made public, immediately upon declaration of war by or against Italy.

Woodrow Wilson

On several occasions during the course of the war the leading statesmen of the allied nations issued declarations of war aims. The best-known statement, and certainly the most influential in bringing about the end of hostilities, was that of President Woodrow Wilson given in an address to Congress on January 8, 1918. This statement came to be known as Wilson's "Fourteen Points," and was widely publicized both in allied countries and throughout Germany. Leaflets containing these points were scattered from planes over the German trenches and over enemy cities and towns. They had considerable influence on German morale and certainly helped to bring about the armistice on November 11, 1918. The British, French, and Italian leaders never accepted the fourteen points officially, however, although they never repudiated them. Thus, considerable misunderstanding and ill-will developed at the subsequent peace conference over the fulfillment of these points. In reading them note (1) Wilson's idealism in the introduction, (2) the clauses providing for greater harmony in future international relations, (3) the principle on which colonial claims were to be adjusted, (4) the attitude Wilson took toward the future of Russia, (5) the importance he attached to the restoration of Belgium, (6) the extent to which he applied the principle of "self-determination of peoples," (7) the program outlined for the Ottoman Empire, and (8) the significance of the fourteenth point.

From: THE FOURTEEN POINTS

. . . It will be our wish and purpose that the processes of peace, when they are begun, shall be absolutely open and that they shall involve and permit henceforth no secret understandings of any kind. The day of conquest and aggrandizement is gone by; so is also the day of secret covenants entered into in the interest of particular governments and likely at some unlooked-for moment to upset the peace of the world. It is this happy fact, now clear to the view of every public man whose thoughts do not still linger in an age that is dead and gone, which makes it possible for every nation whose purposes are consistent with justice and the peace of the world to avow now or at any other time the objects it has in view.

We entered this war because violations of right had occurred which touched us to the quick and made the life of our own poeple impossible unless they were corrected and the world secured once for all against their recurrence. What we demand in this war, therefore, is nothing peculiar to ourselves. It is that the world be made fit and safe to live in; and particularly that it be made safe for every peace-loving nation which, like our own, wishes to live its own life, determine its own institutions, be assured of justice and fair dealing by the other peoples of the world as against force and selfish aggression. All the peoples of the world are in effect partners in this interest, and for our own part we see very clearly that unless justice be done to others it will not be done to us. The programme of the world's peace, there-

United States, *Foreign Relations of the United States*, 1918, Supplement 1, vol. I, 12–17.

fore, is our programme; and that programme, the only possible programme, as we see it, is this:

I. Open covenants of peace, openly arrived at, after which there shall be no private international understandings of any kind, but diplomacy shall proceed always frankly and in the public view.

II. Absolute freedom of navigation upon the seas, outside territorial waters, alike in peace and in war, except as the seas may be closed in whole or in part by international action for the enforcement of international covenants.

III. The removal, so far as possible, of all economic barriers and the establishment of an equality of trade conditions among all the nations consenting to the peace and associating themselves for its maintenance.

IV. Adequate guarantees given and taken that national armaments will be reduced to the lowest point consistent with domestic safety.

V. A free, open-minded, and absolutely impartial adjustment of all colonial claims, based upon a strict observance of the principle that in determining all such questions of sovereignty the interests of the populations concerned must have equal weight with the equitable claims of the government whose title is to be determined.

VI. The evacuation of all Russian territory and such a settlement of all questions affecting Russia as will secure the best and freest cooperation of the other nations of the world in obtaining for her an unhampered and unembarrassed opportunity for the independent determination of her own political development and national policy and assure her of a sincere welcome into the society of free nations under institutions of her own choosing; and, more than a welcome, assistance also of every kind that she may need and may herself desire. The treatment accorded Russia by her sister nations in the months to come will be the acid test of their good will, of their comprehension of her needs as distinguished from their own interests, and of their intelligent and unselfish sympathy.

VII. Belgium, the whole world will agree, must be evacuated and restored, without any attempt to limit the sovereignty which she enjoys in common with all other free nations. No other single act will serve as this will serve to restore confidence among the nations in the

laws which they have themselves set and determined for the government of their relations with one another. Without this healing act the whole structure and validity of international law is forever impaired.

VIII. All French territory should be freed and the invaded portions restored, and the wrong done to France by Prussia in 1871 in the matter of Alsace-Lorraine, which has unsettled the peace of the world for nearly fifty years, should be righted, in order that peace may once more be made secure in the interest of all.

IX. A readjustment of the frontiers of Italy should be effected along clearly recognizable lines of nationality.

X. The peoples of Austria-Hungary, whose place among the nations we wish to see safeguarded and assured, should be accorded the freest opportunity of autonomous development.

XI. Rumania, Serbia, and Montenegro should be evacuated; occupied territories restored; Serbia accorded free and secure access to the sea; and the relations of the several Balkan states to one another determined by friendly counsel along historically established lines of allegiance and nationality; and international guarantees of the political and economic independence and territorial integrity of the several Balkan states should be entered into.

XII. The Turkish portions of the present Ottoman Empire should be assured a secure sovereignty, but the other nationalities which are now under Turkish rule should be assured an undoubted security of life and an absolutely unmolested opportunity of autonomous development, and the Dardanelles should be permanently opened as a free passage to the ships and commerce of all nations under international guarantees.

XIII. An independent Polish state should be erected which should include the territories inhabited by indisputably Polish populations, which should be assured a free and secure access to the sea, and whose political and economic independence and territorial integrity should be guaranteed by international covenant.

XIV. A general association of nations must be formed under specific covenants for the purpose of affording mutual guarantees of political independence and territorial integrity to great and small states alike.

In regard to these essential rectifications of wrong and assertions of right we feel ourselves to be intimate partners of all the governments and peoples associated together against the Imperialists. We cannot be separated in interest or divided in purpose. We stand together until the end. . . .

We have spoken now, surely, in terms too concrete to admit of any further doubt or question. An evident principle runs through the whole programme I have outlined. It is the principle of justice to all peoples and nationalities, and their right to live on equal terms of liberty and safety with one another, whether they be strong or weak. Unless this principle be made its foundation no part of the structure of international justice can stand. . . .

Versailles Peace Conference

For generations prior to the Versailles Conference of 1919, men had cherished the altruistic dream of a league which would bind the nations of the world together in the interests of co-operation and peace. Strangely enough, the framework for such an organization emerged from the most destructive of all wars then known, for in developing the machinery necessary for winning victory, the statesmen of the allied nations learned to work together. A few of these men, such as Jan Smuts of South Africa, Lord Robert Cecil of England, Leon Bourgeois of France, and Woodrow Wilson of the United States, had independently formulated preliminary plans for a league of nations. Wilson had included the idea in his "Fourteen Points," and he and the others who were interested were able to get the plenary session of the peace conference to make the covenant of the League of Nations an integral part of the peace treaty. Wilson was appointed chairman of a committee to draft the instrument, which the conference, in a revised form, finally adopted and included as Part I in the treaties signed with Germany, Austria, Bulgaria, and Hungary. In reading the covenant note (1) the purposes for which the League was formed, (2) how membership was obtained, (3) the nature of the League organization, (4) provisions for the reduction of armaments, (5) the methods provided for averting war, (6) the system of sanctions, (7) the articles dealing with treaties, (8) the description of the colonial possessions of late enemy countries, (9) the social activities to be undertaken, and (10) any other activities to be assumed by the League of Nations.

From: THE COVENANT OF THE LEAGUE OF NATIONS

THE PREAMBLE

The High Contracting Parties,
In order to promote international co-opera-

tion and to achieve international peace and security;

By the acceptance of obligations not to resort to war;

United States, Senate Documents, 348, 67th Cong., 4th sess., serial 8167, *Treaties, Conventions, etc., 1910–1923,* III, 3336–3345, Washington, 1923.

By the prescription of open, just, and honourable relations between nations;

By the firm establishment of the understandings of international law as the actual rule of conduct among Governments;

And by the maintenance of justice and a scrupulous respect for all treaty obligations in the dealings of organised peoples with one another;

Agree to this Covenant of the League of Nations.

THE COVENANT

Article 1 (Membership)

1. The original Members of the League of Nations shall be those of the Signatories which are named in the Annex to this Covenant and also such of those other States named in the Annex as shall accede without reservation to this Covenant. Such accession shall be effected by a Declaration deposited with the Secretariat within two months of the coming into force of the Covenant. Notice thereof shall be sent to all other Members of the League.

2. Any fully self-governing State, Dominion, or Colony not named in the Annex may become a Member of the League if its admission is agreed to by two-thirds of the Assembly, provided that it shall give effective guarantees of its sincere intention to observe its international obligations, and shall accept such regulations as may be prescribed by the League in regard to its military, naval, and air forces and armaments.

3. Any Member of the League may, after two years' notice of its intention so to do, withdraw from the League, provided that all its international obligations and all its obligations under this Covenant shall have been fulfilled at the time of its withdrawal.

Article 2 (Executive Machinery)

The action of the League under this Covenant shall be effected through the instrumentality of an Assembly and of a Council, with a permanent Secretariat.

Article 3 (Assembly)

1. The Assembly shall consist of Representatives of the Members of the League.

2. The Assembly shall meet at stated intervals and from time to time as occasion may require at the Seat of the League or at such other place as may be decided upon.

3. The Assembly may deal at its meetings with any matter within the sphere of action of the League or affecting the peace of the world.

4. At meetings of the Assembly each Member of the League shall have one vote, and may have not more than three Representatives.

Article 4 (Council)

1. The Council shall consist of Representatives of the Principal Allied and Associated Powers, together with Representatives of four other Members of the League. These four Members of the League shall be selected by the Assembly from time to time in its discretion. Until the appointment of the Representatives of the four Members of the League first selected by the Assembly, Representatives of Belgium, Brazil, Spain, and Greece shall be members of the Council.

2. With the approval of the majority of the Assembly, the Council may name additional Members of the League whose Representatives shall always be members of the Council; the Council with like approval may increase the number of Members of the League to be selected by the Assembly for representation on the Council.

3. The Council shall meet from time to time as occasion may require, and at least once a year, at the Seat of the League, or at such other place as may be decided upon.

4. The Council may deal at its meetings with any matter within the sphere of action of the League or affecting the peace of the world.

5. Any Member of the League not represented on the Council shall be invited to send a Representative to sit as a Member at any meeting of the Council during the consideration of matters specially affecting the interests of that Member of the League.

6. At meetings of the Council, each Member of the League represented on the Council shall have one vote, and may have not more than one Representative.

Article 5 (Voting and Procedure)

1. Except where otherwise expressly provided in this Covenant or by the terms of the

present Treaty, decisions at any meeting of the Assembly or of the Council shall require the agreement of all the Members of the League represented at the meeting.

2. All matters of procedure at meetings of the Assembly or of the Council, including the appointment of Committees to investigate particular matters, shall be regulated by the Assembly or by the Council and may be decided by a majority of the Members of the League represented at the meeting.

3. The first meeting of the Assembly and the first meeting of the Council shall be summoned by the President of the United States of America.

Article 6 (Secretariat)

1. The permanent Secretariat shall be established at the Seat of the League. The Secretariat shall comprise a Secretary-General and such secretaries and staff as may be required.

2. The first Secretary-General shall be the person named in the Annex; thereafter the Secretary-General shall be appointed by the Council with the approval of the majority of the Assembly.

3. The secretaries and staff of the Secretariat shall be appointed by the Secretary-General with the approval of the Council.

4. The Secretary-General shall act in that capacity at all meetings of the Assembly and of the Council.

Article 7 (Seat. Qualifications for Officials. Immunities)

1. The Seat of the League is established at Geneva.

2. The Council may at any time decide that the Seat of the League shall be established elsewhere.

3. All positions under or in connection with the League, including the Secretariat, shall be open equally to men and women.

4. Representatives of the Members of the League and officials of the League when engaged on the business of the League shall enjoy diplomatic privileges and immunities.

5. The buildings and other property occupied by the League or its officials or by Representatives attending its meetings shall be inviolable.

Article 8 (Reduction of Armaments)

1. The Members of the League recognise that the maintenance of peace requires the reduction of national armaments to the lowest point consistent with national safety and the enforcement by common action of international obligations.

2. The Council, taking account of the geographical situation and circumstances of each State, shall formulate plans for such reduction for the consideration and action of the several Governments.

3. Such plans shall be subject to reconsideration and revision at least every ten years.

4. After these plans shall have been adopted by the several Governments, the limits of armaments therein fixed shall not be exceeded without the concurrence of the Council.

5. The Members of the League agree that the manufacture by private enterprise of munitions and implements of war is open to grave objections. The Council shall advise how the evil effects attendant upon such manufacture can be prevented, due regard being had to the necessities of those Members of the League which are not able to manufacture the munitions and implements of war necessary for their safety.

6. The Members of the League undertake to interchange full and frank information as to the scale of their armaments, their military, naval, and air programmes and the condition of such of their industries as are adaptable to warlike purposes.

Article 9 (Permanent Military Commission)

A permanent Commission shall be constituted to advise the Council on the execution of the provisions of Arts. 1 and 8 and on military, naval, and air questions generally.

Article 10 (Guarantees Against Aggression)

The Members of the League undertake to respect and preserve as against external aggression the territorial integrity and existing political independence of all Members of the League. In case of any such aggression or in case of any threat or danger of such aggression the Council shall advise upon the means by which this obligation shall be fulfilled.

Article 11 (Action in Case of War or Danger of War)

1. Any war or threat of war, whether immediately affecting any of the Members of the League or not, is hereby declared a matter of concern to the whole League, and the League shall take any action that may be deemed wise and effectual to safeguard the peace of nations. In case any such emergency should arise the Secretary-General shall on the request of any Member of the League forthwith summon a meeting of the Council.

2. It is also declared to be the friendly right of each Member of the League to bring to the attention of the Assembly or of the Council any circumstance whatever affecting international relations which threatens to disturb international peace or the good understanding between nations upon which peace depends.

Article 12 (Disputes to be Submitted to Arbitration or Inquiry)

1. The Members of the League agree that, if there should arise between them any dispute likely to lead to a rupture, they will submit the matter either to arbitration or to inquiry by the Council and they agree in no case to resort to war until three months after the award by the arbitrators or the report by the Council.

2. In any case under this Article, the award of the arbitrators shall be made within a reasonable time, and the report of the Council shall be made within six months after the submission of the dispute.

Article 13 (Arbitration of Disputes)

1. The Members of the League agree that, whenever any dispute shall arise between them which they recognise to be suitable for submission to arbitration and which cannot be satisfactorily settled by diplomacy, they will submit the whole subject-matter to arbitration.

2. Disputes as to the interpretation of a treaty, as to any question of international law, as to the existence of any fact which, if established, would constitute a breach of any international obligation, or as to the extent and nature of the reparation to be made for any such breach, are declared to be among those which are generally suitable for submission to arbitration.

3. The Members of the League agree that they will carry out in full good faith any award that may be rendered, and that they will not resort to war against any Member of the League that complies therewith. In the event of any failure to carry out such an award the Council shall propose what steps should be taken to give effect thereto.

Article 14 (Permanent Court of International Justice)

The Council shall formulate and submit to the Members of the League for adoption plans for the establishment of a Permanent Court of International Justice. The Court shall be competent to hear and determine any dispute of an international character which the parties thereto submit to it. The Court may also give an advisory opinion upon any dispute or question referred to it by the Council or by the Assembly.

Article 15 (Disputes not Submitted to Arbitration)

1. If there should arise between Members of the League any dispute likely to lead to a rupture, which is not submitted to arbitration in accordance with Article 13, the Members of the League agree that they will submit the matter to the Council. Any party to the dispute may effect such submission by giving notice of the existence of the dispute to the Secretary-General, who will make all necessary arrangements for a full investigation and consideration thereof.

2. For this purpose the parties to the dispute will communicate to the Secretary-General, as promptly as possible, statements of their case, with all the relevant facts and papers, and the Council may forthwith direct the publication thereof.

3. The Council shall endeavour to affect a settlement of the dispute, and if such efforts are successful, a statement shall be made public giving such facts and explanations regarding the dispute and the terms of settlement thereof as the Council may deem appropriate.

4. If the dispute is not thus settled, the Council either unanimously or by a majority vote shall make and publish a report containing a statement of the facts of the dispute and

the recommendations which are deemed just and proper in regard thereto.

5. Any Member of the League represented on the Council may make public a statement of the facts of the dispute and of its conclusions regarding the same.

6. If a report by the Council is unanimously agreed to by the members thereof other than the Representatives of one or more of the parties to the dispute, the Members of the League agree that they will not go to war with any party to the dispute which complies with the recommendations of the report.

7. If the Council fails to reach a report which is unanimously agreed to by the members thereof, other than the Representatives of one or more of the parties to the dispute, the Members of the League reserve to themselves the right to take such action as they shall consider necessary for the maintenance of right and justice.

8. If the dispute between the parties is claimed by one of them, and is found by the Council to arise out of a matter which by international law is solely within the domestic jurisdiction of that party, the Council shall so report, and shall make no recommendation as to its settlement.

9. The Council may in any case under this Article refer the dispute to the Assembly. The dispute shall be so referred at the request of either party to the dispute, provided that such request be made within fourteen days after the submission of the dispute to the Council.

10. In any case referred to the Assembly, all the provisions of this Article and of Article 12 relating to the action and powers of the Council shall apply to the action and powers of the Assembly, provided that a report made by the Assembly, if concurred by the Representatives of those Members of the League represented on the Council and of a majority of the other Members of the League, exclusive in each case of the Representatives of the parties to the dispute, shall have the same force as a report by the Council concurred in by all the members thereof other than the Representatives of one or more of the parties to the dispute.

Article 16 ("Sanctions" of the League)

1. Should any Member of the League resort to war in disregard of its covenants under Article 12, 13, or 15, it shall *ipso facto* be deemed to have committed an act of war against all other Members of the League, which hereby undertake immediately to subject it to the severance of all trade or financial relations, the prohibition of all intercourse between their nationals and the nationals of the covenant-breaking State, and the prevention of all financial, commercial, or personal intercourse between the nationals of the covenant-breaking State and the nationals of any other State, whether a Member of the League or not.

2. It shall be the duty of the Council in such case to recommend to the several Governments concerned what effective military, naval, or air force the Members of the League shall severally contribute to the armed forces to be used to protect the covenants of the League.

3. The Members of the League agree, further, that they will mutually support one another in the financial and economic measures which are taken under this Article, in order to minimise the loss and inconvenience resulting from the above measures, and that they will mutually support one another in resisting any special measures aimed at one of their number by the covenant-breaking State, and that they will take the necessary steps to afford passage through their territory to the forces of any of the Members of the League which are co-operating to protect the covenants of the League.

4. Any Member of the League which has violated any covenant of the League may be declared to be no longer a Member of the League by a vote of the Council concurred in by the Representatives of all the other Members of the League represented thereon.

Article 17 (Disputes with Non-Members)

1. In the event of a dispute between a Member of the League and a State which is not a Member of the League, or between States not Members of the League, the State or States not Members of the League shall be invited to accept the obligations of Membership in the League for the purposes of such dispute, upon such conditions as the Council may deem just. If such invitation is accepted, the provision of Articles 12–16 inclusive shall be

applied with such modifications as may be deemed necessary by the Council.

2. Upon such invitation being given the Council shall immediately institute an inquiry into the circumstances of the dispute and recommend such action as may seem best and most effectual in the circumstances.

3. If a State so invited shall refuse to accept the obligations of membership in the League for the purposes of such dispute, and shall resort to war against a Member of the League, the provisions of Article 16 shall be applicable as against the State taking such action.

4. If both parties to the dispute when so invited refuse to accept the obligations of membership in the League for the purposes of such dispute, the Council may take such measures and make such recommendations as will prevent hostilities and will result in the settlement of the dispute.

Article 18 (Registration and Publication of all Future Treaties)

Every treaty or international engagement entered into hereafter by any Member of the League shall be forthwith registered with the Secretariat and shall as soon as possible be published by it. No such treaty or international engagement shall be binding until so registered.

Article 19 (Review of Treaties)

The Assembly may from time to time advise the reconsideration by Members of the League of treaties which have become inapplicable and the consideration of international conditions whose continuance might endanger the peace of the world.

Article 20 (Abrogation of Inconsistent Obligations)

1. The Members of the League severally agree that this Covenant is accepted as abrogating all obligations or understandings *inter se* which are inconsistent with the terms thereof, and solemnly undertake that they will not hereafter enter into any engagements inconsistent with the terms thereof.

2. In case any Member of the League shall, before becoming a Member of the League, have undertaken any obligations inconsistent with the terms of this Covenant, it shall be the duty of such Member to take immediate steps to procure its release from such obligations.

Article 21 (Engagements that Remain Valid)

Nothing in the Covenant shall be deemed to affect the validity of international engagements, such as treaties of arbitration or regional understandings like the Monroe doctrine, for securing the maintenance of peace.

Article 22 (Mandatories, Control of Colonies and Territories)

1. To those colonies and territories which as a consequence of the late war have ceased to be under the sovereignty of the States which formerly governed them and which are inhabited by peoples not yet able to stand by themselves under the strenuous conditions of the modern world, there should be applied the principle that the well-being and development of such peoples form a sacred trust of civilisation and that securities for the performance of this trust should be embodied in this Covenant.

2. The best method of giving practical effect to this principle is that the tutelage of such peoples should be entrusted to advanced nations who by reason of their resources, their experience, or their geographical position can best undertake this responsibility, and who are willing to accept it, and that this tutelage should be exercised by them as Mandatories on behalf of the League.

3. The character of the mandate must differ according to the stage of the development of the people, the geographical situation of the territory, its economic conditions, and other similar circumstances.

4. Certain communities formerly belonging to the Turkish Empire have reached a stage of development where their existence as independent nations can be provisionally recognised subject to the rendering of administrative advice and assistance by a Mandatory until such time as they are able to stand alone. The wishes of these communities must be a principal consideration in the selection of the Mandatory.

5. Other peoples, especially those of Central Africa, are at such a stage that the Mandatory must be responsible for the administration of the territory under conditions which will guarantee freedom of conscience and religion,

subject only to the maintenance of public order and morals, the prohibition of abuses such as the slave trade, the arms traffic and the liquor traffic, and the prevention of the establishment of fortifications or military and naval bases and of military training of the natives for other than police purposes and the defence of territory, and will also secure equal opportunities for the trade and commerce of other Members of the League.

6. There are territories, such as South-West Africa and certain of the South Pacific Islands, which, owing to the sparseness of their population, or their small size, or their remoteness from the centres of civilisation, or their geographical contiguity to the territory of the Mandatory, and other circumstances, can be best administered under the laws of the Mandatory as integral portions of its territory, subject to the safeguards above mentioned in the interests of the indigenous population.

7. In every case of mandate, the Mandatory shall render to the Council an annual report in reference to the territory committed to its charge.

8. The degree of authority, control, or administration to be exercised by the Mandatory shall, if not previously agreed upon by the Members of the League, be explicitly defined in each case by the Council.

9. A permanent Commission shall be constituted to receive and examine the annual reports of the Mandatories and to advise the Council on all matters relating to the observance of the mandates.

Article 23 (Social Activities)

Subject to and in accordance with the provisions of international conventions existing or hereafter to be agreed upon, the Members of the League:

(a) Will endeavour to secure and maintain fair and humane conditions of labour for men, women, and children, both in their own countries and in all countries to which their commercial and industrial relations extend, and for that purpose will establish and maintain the necessary international organisations;

(b) Undertake to secure just treatment of the native inhabitants of territories under their control;

(c) Will entrust the League with the general supervision over the execution of agreements with regard to the traffic in women and children, and the traffic in opium and other dangerous drugs;

(d) Will entrust the League with the general supervision of the trade in arms and ammunition with the countries in which the control of this traffic is necessary in the common interest;

(e) Will make provision to secure and maintain freedom of communications and of transit and equitable treatment for the commerce of all Members of the League. In this connection, the special necessities of the regions devastated during the war of 1914–1918 shall be borne in mind;

(f) Will endeavour to take steps in matters of international concern for the prevention and control of disease.

Article 24 (International Bureaux)

1. There shall be placed under the direction of the League all international bureaux already established by general treaties if the parties to such treaties consent. All such international bureaux and all commissions for the regulation of matters of international interest hereafter constituted shall be placed under the direction of the League.

2. In all matters of international interest which are regulated by general conventions but which are not placed under the control of international bureaux or commissions, the Secretariat of the League shall, subject to the consent of the Council and if desired by the parties, collect and distribute all relevant information and shall render any other assistance which may be necessary or desirable.

3. The Council may include as part of the expenses of the Secretariat the expenses of any bureau or commission which is placed under the direction of the League.

Article 25 (Promotion of Red Cross)

The Members of the League agree to encourage and promote the establishment and co-operation of duly authorised voluntary national Red Cross organisations having as purposes the improvement of health, the prevention of disease and the mitigation of suffering throughout the world.

Article 26 (Amendments)

1. Amendments to this Covenant will take effect when ratified by the Members of the League whose Representatives compose the Council and by a majority of the Members of the League whose Representatives compose the Assembly.

2. No such amendment shall bind any Member of the League which signifies its dissent therefrom, but in that case it shall cease to be a Member of the League.

Economic, Social, and Political Changes in the Twentieth Century

In the twentieth century steady progress has been made in improving the techniques of industrial production, thereby making it possible to manufacture an ever-growing volume of goods. Profits, too, have increased, giving rise to concentrations of wealth which have enabled small minorities to dominate the industrial and financial life of large areas. Industrialists have sponsored research which has produced new processes for saving labor, thus creating instabilities within the social order. Even before 1914, statesmen in the western democracies recognized the problem and began to lead their governments away from laissez-faire principles and toward the assumption by the states of greater responsibility for the welfare of their citizens. Governments were elected with popular mandates to impose regulations on the large corporations, while, with the other hand, extending various forms of social security to the workers. Following the 1914–1918 war and the great depression of 1929, the trend was accelerated on both sides of the Atlantic. Russia, after a revolution in 1917, which took her out of the war then raging, turned to communism as a means of improving the social and economic condition of the masses. Italy and Germany experienced serious economic maladjustment following the 1918 armistice, and in the postwar period attempted to build up national morale and to restore economic prosperity by accepting the totalitarian programs advocated by fascist groups. Thus, by 1939 the countries of Western Civilization were struggling to improve the lives of their citizens, but by methods so different as to make any peaceful understanding between them extremely difficult.

Economic, Social, and Political
Changes in the Twentieth
Century

Louis Brandeis

ouis D. Brandeis (1856–1941) was an American lawyer and jurist who served as counsel in many freight-rate, wage-hour, and public utility cases. His experiences in these investigations gave him an unparalleled insight into the financial and industrial developments which transformed American economic life in the early years of the twentieth century. He was particularly conversant with the methods used by financial interests to gain control of industrial production, the development which President Wilson considered to be the greatest problem of American democracy. In 1916 Wilson appointed Brandeis to the Supreme Court, but prior to that event, this eminent American jurist wrote Other People's Money, a chapter from which is given below. In reading "Big Men and Little Business" note (1) the relation between the great banking houses and the growth of American industry, (2) the method by which the large corporations had been created, (3) the number of activities in which J. P. Morgan & Co. had been a participant, (4) the extent to which the great banking houses had arrested the industrial development of America, (5) the concentration of wealth made possible by stock exchange transactions, (6) the practices of the General Electric Company carried on through subsidiaries, and (7) the recommendations made by Mr. Brandeis for checking these practices.

From: OTHER PEOPLE'S MONEY

J. P. Morgan & Co. declare, in their letter to the Pujo Committee, that "practically all the railroad and industrial development of this country has taken place initially through the medium of the great banking houses." That statement is entirely unfounded in fact. On the contrary, nearly every such contribution to our comfort and prosperity was "initiated" *without* their aid. The "great banking houses" came into relation with these enterprises, either after success had been attained, or upon "reorganization" after the possibility of success had been demonstrated, but the funds of the hardy pioneers, who had risked their all, were exhausted.

This is true of our early railroads, of our early street railways, and of the automobile; of the telegraph, the telephone and the wireless; of gas and oil; of harvesting machinery, and of our steel industry; of the textile, paper and shoe industries; and of nearly every other important branch of manufacture. The *initiation* of each of these enterprises may properly be characterized as "great transactions"; and the men who contributed the financial aid and business management necessary for their introduction are entitled to share, equally with inventors, in our gratitude for what has been accomplished. But the instances are extremely rare where the original financing of such enterprises was undertaken by investment bankers, great or small. It was usually done by some common business man, accustomed to taking risks; or by some well-to-do friend of the inventor or pioneer, who was influenced largely by considerations other than money-getting. Here and there you will find that banker-aid was given; but usually in those

Louis D. Brandeis, *Other People's Money and How the Bankers Use It*, new edition, Frederick A. Stokes Company, New York, 1932, 135–161. Courtesy of Mrs. Susan Brandeis Gilbert.

cases it was a small local banking concern, not a "great banking house" which helped to "initiate" the undertaking.

RAILROADS

We have come to associate the great bankers with railroads. But their part was not conspicuous in the early history of the Eastern railroads; and in the Middle West the experience was, to some extent, similar. The Boston & Maine Railroad owns and leases 2,215 miles of line; but it is a composite of about 166 separate railroad companies. The New Haven Railroad owns and leases 1,996 miles of line; but it is a composite of 112 separate railroad companies. The necessary capital to build these little roads was gathered together, partly through state, county or municipal aid; partly from business men or landholders who sought to advance their special interests; partly from investors; and partly from well-to-do public-spirited men, who wished to promote the welfare of their particular communities. About seventy-five years after the first of these railroads was built, J. P. Morgan & Co. became fiscal agent for all of them by creating the New Haven-Boston & Maine monopoly.

STEAMSHIPS

The history of our steamship lines is similar. In 1807, Robert Fulton, with the financial aid of Robert R. Livingston, a judge and statesman—not a banker—demonstrated with the *Claremont,* that it was practicable to propel boats by steam. In 1833 the three Cunard brothers of Halifax and 232 other persons—stockholders of the Quebec and Halifax Steam Navigation Company—joined in supplying about $80,000 to build the *Royal William*—the first steamer to cross the Atlantic. In 1902, many years after individual enterprises had developed practically all the great ocean lines, J. P. Morgan & Co. floated the International Mercantile Marine with its $52,744,000 of 4½ bonds, now selling at about 60, and $100,-000,000 of stock (preferred and common) on which no dividend has ever been paid. It was just sixty-two years after the first regular line

of transatlantic steamers—The Cunard—was founded that Mr. Morgan organized the Shipping Trust.

TELEGRAPH

The story of the telegraph is similar. The money for developing Morse's invention was supplied by his partner and co-worker, Alfred Vail. The initial line (from Washington to Baltimore) was built with an appropriation of $30,000 made by Congress in 1843. Sixty-six years later J. P. Morgan & Co. became bankers for the Western Union through financing its purchase by the American Telephone & Telegraph Company.

HARVESTING MACHINERY

Next to railroads and steamships, harvesting machinery has probably been the most potent factor in the development of America; and most important of the harvesting machines was Cyrus H. McCormick's reaper. That made it possible to increase the grain harvest twenty- or thirty-fold. No investment banker had any part in introducing this great businessman's invention.

McCormick was without means; but William Butler Ogden, a railroad builder, ex-Mayor and leading citizen of Chicago, supplied $25,-000 with which the first factory was built there in 1847. Fifty-five years later, J. P. Morgan & Co. performed the service of combining the five great harvester companies, and received a commission of $3,000,000. The concerns then consolidated as the International Harvester Company, with a capital stock of $120,000,-000, had, despite their huge assets and earning power, been previously capitalized, in the aggregate, at only $10,500,000—strong evidence that in all the preceding years no investment banker had financed them. Indeed, McCormick was as able in business as in mechanical invention. Two years after Ogden paid him $25,000 for a half interest in the business, McCormick bought it back for $50,-000; and thereafter, until his death in 1884, no one but members of the McCormick family had any interest in the business.

THE BANKER ERA

It may be urged that railroads and steamships, the telegraph and harvesting machinery were introduced before the accumulation of investment capital had developed the investment banker, and before America's "great banking houses" had been established; and that, consequently, it would be fairer to inquire what services bankers had rendered in connection with later industrial development. The firm of J. P. Morgan & Co. is fifty-five years old; Kuhn, Loeb & Co. fifty-six years old; Lee, Higginson & Co. over fifty years; and Kidder, Peabody & Co. forty-eight years; and yet the investment banker seems to have had almost as little part in "initiating" the great improvements of the last half century, as did bankers in the earlier period.

STEEL

The modern steel industry of America is forty-five years old. The "great bankers" had no part in initiating it. Andrew Carnegie, then already a man of large means, introduced the Bessemer process in 1868. In the next thirty years our steel and iron industry increased greatly. By 1898 we had far outstripped all competitors. America's production about equalled the aggregate of England and Germany. We had also reduced costs so much that Europe talked of the "American Peril." It was 1898, when J. P. Morgan & Co. took their first step in forming the Steel Trust, by organizing the Federal Steel Company. Then followed the combination of the tube mills into an $80,000,-000 corporation, J. P. Morgan & Co. taking for their syndicate services $20,000,000 of common stock. About the same time the consolidation of the bridge and structural works, the tin plate, the sheet steel, the hoop and other mills followed; and finally, in 1901, the Steel Trust was formed, with a capitalization of $1,402,-000,000. These combinations came thirty years after the steel industry had been "initiated."

THE TELEPHONE

The telephone industry is less than forty years old. It is probably America's greatest contribution to industrial development. The bankers had no part in "initiating" it. The glory belongs to a simple, enthusiastic, warm-hearted, business man of Haverhill, Massachusetts, who was willing to risk *his own* money. H. N. Casson tells of this, most interestingly, in his "History of the Telephone":

"The only man who had money and dared to stake it on the future of the telephone was Thomas Sanders, and he did this not mainly for business reasons. Both he and Hubbard were attached to Bell primarily by sentiment, as Bell had removed the blight of dumbness from Sanders' little son, and was soon to marry Hubbard's daughter. Also, Sanders had no expectation, at first, that so much money would be needed. He was not rich. His entire business, which was that of cutting out soles for shoe manufacturers, was not at any time worth more than thirty-five thousand dollars. Yet, from 1874 to 1878, he had advanced nine-tenths of the money that was spent on the telephone. The first five thousand telephones, and more, were made with his money. And so many long, expensive months dragged by before any relief came to Sanders, that he was compelled, much against his will and his business judgment, to stretch his credit within an inch of the breaking-point to help Bell and the telephone. Desperately he signed note after note until he faced a total of one hundred and ten thousand dollars. If the new 'scientific toy' succeeded, which he often doubted, he would be the richest citizen in Haverhill; and if it failed, which he sorely feared, he would be a bankrupt. Sanders and Hubbard were leasing telephones two by two, to business men who previously had been using the private lines of the Western Union Telegraph Company. This great corporation was at this time their natural and inevitable enemy. It had swallowed most of its competitors, and was reaching out to monopolize all methods of communication by wire. The rosiest hope that shone in front of Sanders and Hubbard was that the Western Union might conclude to buy the Bell patents, just as it had already bought many others. In one moment of discouragement they had offered the telephone to President Orton, of the Western Union, for $100,000; and Orton had refused it. 'What use,' he asked pleasantly, 'could this company make of an electrical toy?'

"But besides the operation of its own wires, the Western Union was supplying customers with various kinds of printing-telegraphs and dial-telegraphs, some of which could transmit sixty words a minute. These accurate instruments, it believed, could never be displaced by such a scientific oddity as the telephone, and it continued to believe this until one of its subsidiary companies—the Gold and Stock —reported that several of its machines had been superseded by telephones.

"At once the Western Union awoke from its indifference. Even this tiny nibbling at its business must be stopped. It took action quickly, and organized the 'American Speaking-Telephone Company,' and with $300,000 capital, and with three electrical inventors, Edison, Gray, and Dolbear, on its staff. With all the bulk of its great wealth and prestige, it swept down upon Bell and his little body-guard. It trampled upon Bell's patent with as little concern as an elephant can have when he tramples upon an ant's nest. To the complete bewilderment of Bell, it coolly announced that it had the only original telephone, and that it was ready to supply superior telephones with all the latest improvements made by the original inventors—Dolbear, Gray, and Edison.

"The result was strange and unexpected. The Bell group, instead of being driven from the field, were at once lifted to a higher level in the business world. And the Western Union, in the endeavor to protect its private lines, became involuntarily a 'bell-wether' to lead capitalists in the direction of the telephone."

Even then, when financial aid came to the Bell enterprise, it was from capitalists, not from bankers, and among these capitalists was William H. Forbes (son of the builder of the Burlington) who became the first President of the Bell Telephone Company. That was in 1878. More than twenty years later, after the telephone had spread over the world, the great house of Morgan came into financial control of the property. The American Telephone & Telegraph Company was formed. The process of combination became active. Since January, 1900, its stock has increased from $25,886,300 to $344,606,400. In six years (1906 to 1912),

the Morgan associates marketed about $300,-000,000 bonds of that company or its subsidiaries. In that period the volume of business done by the telephone companies had, of course, grown greatly, and the plant had to be constantly increased; but the proceeds of these huge security issues were used, to a large extent, in effecting combinations; that is, in buying out telephone competitors; in buying control of the Western Union Telegraph Company; and in buying up outstanding stock interests in semi-independent Bell companies. It is these combinations which have led to the investigation of the Telephone Company by the Department of Justice; and they are, in large part, responsible for the movement to have the government take over the telephone business.

ELECTRICAL MACHINERY

The business of manufacturing electrical machinery and apparatus is only a little over thirty years old. J. P. Morgan & Co. became interested early in one branch of it; but their dominance of the business today is due, not to their "initiating" it, but to their effecting a combination, and organizing the General Electric Company in 1892. There were then three large electrical companies, the Thomson-Houston, the Edison, and the Westinghouse, besides some small ones. The Thomson-Houston of Lynn, Massachusetts, was in many respects the leader, having been formed to introduce, among other things, important inventions of Prof. Elihu Thomson and Prof. Houston. Lynn is one of the principal shoe-manufacturing centers of America. It is within ten miles of State Street, Boston; but Thomson's early financial support came not from Boston bankers, but mainly from Lynn business men and investors; men active, energetic, and used to taking risks with *their own* money. Prominent among them was Charles A. Coffin, a shoe manufacturer, who became connected with the Thomson-Houston Company upon its organization and president of the General Electric when Mr. Morgan formed that company in 1892, by combining the Thomson-Houston and the Edison. To his continued service, supported by other Thomson-Houston men in high positions, the great prosperity of the company is, in large part, due. The two companies so combined controlled probably one-half of all electrical patents then existing in America; and certainly more than half of those which had any considerable value.

In 1896 the General Electric pooled its patents with the Westinghouse, and thus competition was further restricted. In 1903 the General Electric absorbed the Stanley Electric Company, its other large competitor; and became the largest manufacturer of electric apparatus and machinery in the world. In 1912 the resources of the Company were $131,942,-144. It billed sales to the amount of $89,182,-185. It employed directly over 60,000 persons, —more than a fourth as many as the Steel Trust. And it is protected against "undue" competition; for one of the Morgan partners has been a director, since 1909, in the Westinghouse—the only other large electrical machinery company in America.

THE AUTOMOBILE

The automobile industry is about twenty years old. It is now America's most prosperous business. When Henry B. Joy, President of the Packard Motor Car Company, was asked to what extent the bankers aided in "initiating" the automobile, he replied:

"It is the observable facts of history, it is also my experience of thirty years as a business man, banker, etc., that first the seer conceives an opportunity. He has faith in his almost second sight. He believes he can do something—develop a business—construct an industry—build a railroad—or Niagara Falls Power Company, —and make it pay!

"Now the human measure is not the actual physical construction, but the 'make it pay'!

"A man raised the money in the late '90s and built a beet sugar factory in Michigan. Wiseacres said it was nonsense. He gathered together the money from his friends who would take a chance with him. He not only built the sugar factory (and there was never any doubt of his ability to do that) but he made it pay. The next year two more sugar factories were built, and were financially successful. These were built by private individuals

of wealth, taking chances in the face of cries of doubting bankers and trust companies.

"Once demonstrated that the industry was a sound one financially and *then* bankers and trust companies would lend the new sugar companies which were speedily organized a large part of the necessary funds to construct and operate.

"The motor-car business was the same.

"When a few gentlemen followed me in my vision of the possibilities of the business, the banks and older business men (who in the main were the banks) said, 'fools and their money soon to be parted'—etc., etc.

"Private capital at first establishes an industry, backs it through its troubles, and, if possible, wins financial success when banks would not lend a dollar of aid.

"The business once having proved to be practicable and financially successful, then do the banks lend aid to its needs."

Such also was the experience of the greatest of the many financial successes in the automobile industry—the Ford Motor Company.

HOW BANKERS ARREST DEVELOPMENT

But "great banking houses" have not merely failed to initiate industrial development; they have definitely arrested development because to them the creation of the trusts is largely due. The recital in the Memorial addressed to the President by the Investors' Guild in November, 1911, is significant:

"It is a well-known fact that modern trade combinations tend strongly toward constancy of process and products, and by their very nature are opposed to new processes and new products originated by independent inventors, and hence tend to restrain competition in the development and sale of patents and patent rights; and consequently tend to discourage independent inventive thought, to the great detriment of the nation, and with injustice to inventors whom the Constitution especially intended to encourage and protect in their rights."

And more specific was the testimony of the *Engineering News:*

"We are today something like five years behind Germany in iron and steel metallurgy, and such innovations as are being introduced by our iron and steel manufacturers are most of them merely following the lead set by foreigners years ago.

"We do not believe this is because American engineers are any less ingenious or original than those of Europe, though they may indeed be deficient in training and scientific education compared with those of Germany. We believe the main cause is the wholesale consolidation which has taken place in American industry. A huge organization is too clumsy to take up the development of an original idea. With the market closely controlled and profits certain by following standard methods, those who control our trusts do not want the bother of developing anything new.

"We instance metallurgy only by way of illustration. There are plenty of other fields of industry where exactly the same condition exists. We are building the same machines and using the same methods as a dozen years ago, and the real advances in the art are being made by European inventors and manufacturers."

To which President Wilson's statement may be added:

"I am not saying that all invention had been stopped by the growth of trusts, but I think it is perfectly clear that invention in many fields has been discouraged, that inventors have been prevented from reaping the full fruits of their ingenuity and industry, and that mankind has been deprived of many comforts and conveniences, as well as the opportunity of buying at lower prices.

"Do you know, have you had occasion to learn, that there is no hospitality for invention, now-a-days?"

TRUSTS AND FINANCIAL CONCENTRATION

The fact that industrial monopolies arrest development is more serious even than the direct burden imposed through extortionate prices. But the most harm-bearing incident of the trusts is their promotion of financial concentration. Industrial trusts feed the money trust.

Practically every trust created has destroyed the financial independence of some communities and of many properties; for it has centered the financing of a large part of whole lines of business in New York, and this usually with one of a few banking houses. This is well illustrated by the Steel Trust, which is a trust of trusts; that is, the Steel Trust combines in one huge holding company the trusts previously formed in the different branches of the steel business. Thus the Tube Trust combined 17 tube mills, located in 16 different cities, scattered over 5 states and owned by 13 different companies. The wire trust combined 19 mills; the sheet steel trust 26; the bridge and structural trust 27; and the tin plate trust 36; all scattered similarly over many states. Finally these and other companies were formed into the United States Steel Corporation, combining 228 companies in all, located in 127 cities and towns, scattered over 18 states. Before the combinations were effected, nearly every one of these companies was owned largely by those who managed it, and had been financed, to a large extent, in the place, or in the state, in which it was located. When the Steel Trust was formed all these concerns came under one management. Thereafter, the financing of each of these 228 corporations (and some which were later acquired) had to be done through or with the consent of J. P. Morgan & Co. *That was the greatest step in financial concentration ever taken.*

STOCK EXCHANGE INCIDENTS

The organization of trusts has served in another way to increase the power of the Money Trust. Few of the independent concerns out of which the trusts have been formed, were listed on the New York Stock Exchange; and few of them had financial offices in New York. Promoters of large corporations, whose stock is to be held by the public, and also investors, desire to have their securities listed on the New York Stock Exchange. Under the rules of the Exchange, no security can be so listed unless the corporation has a transfer agent and registrar in New York City. Furthermore, banker-directorships have contributed largely to the establishment of the financial offices of the trusts in New York City. That alone would tend to financial concentration. But the listing of the stock enhances the power of the Money Trust in another way. An industrial stock, once listed, frequently becomes the subject of active speculation; and speculation feeds the Money Trust indirectly in many ways. It draws the money of the country to New York. The New York bankers handle the loans of other people's money on the Stock Exchange; and members of the Stock Exchange receive large amounts from commissions. For instance: There are 5,084,952 shares of United States Steel common stock outstanding. But in the five years ending December 31, 1912, speculation in that stock was so extensive that there were sold on the Exchange an average of 29,380,888 shares a year; or nearly six times as much as there is Steel common in existence. Except where the transactions are by or for the brokers, sales on the Exchange involve the payment of twenty-five cents in commission for each share of stock sold; that is, twelve and one-half cents by the seller and twelve and one-half cents by the buyer. Thus the commission from the Steel common alone afforded a revenue averaging many millions a year. The Steel preferred stock is also much traded in; and there are 138 other industrials, largely trusts, listed on the New York Stock Exchange.

TRUST RAMIFICATIONS

But the potency of trusts as a factor in financial concentration is manifested in still other ways; notably through their ramifying operations. This is illustrated forcibly by the General Electric Company's control of water-power companies which has now been disclosed in an able report of the United States Bureau of Corporations:

"The extent of the General Electric influence is not fully revealed by its consolidated balance sheet. A very large number of corporations are connected with it through its subsidiaries and through corporations controlled by these subsidiaries or affiliated with them. There is a still wider circle of influence due to the fact that officers and directors of the General Electric Company and its subsidiaries are also officers or directors of many other corporations,

some of whose securities are owned by the General Electric Company.

"The General Electric Company holds in the first place all the common stock in three security holding companies: the United Electric Securities Co., the Electrical Securities Corporation, and the Electric Bond and Share Co. Directly and through these corporations and their officers the General Electric controls a large part of the water power of the United States. . . .

"The water-power companies in the General Electric group are found in 18 States. These 18 States have 2,325,757 commercial horsepower developed or under construction, and of this total the General Electric group includes 939,115 h. p. or 40.4 per cent. The greatest amount of power controlled by the companies in the General Electric group in any State is found in Washington. This is followed by New York, Pennsylvania, California, Montana, Iowa, Oregon, and Colorado. In five of the States shown in the table the water-power companies included in the General Electric group control more than 50 per cent of the commercial power, developed and under construction. The percentage of power in the States included in the General Electric group ranges from a little less than 2 per cent in Michigan to nearly 80 per cent in Pennsylvania. In Colorado they control 72 per cent; in New Hampshire 61 per cent; in Oregon 58 per cent; and in Washington 55 per cent.

Besides the power developed and under construction water-power concerns included in the General Electric group own in the States shown in the table 641,600 h. p. undeveloped."

This water-power control enables the General Electric group to control other public service corporations:

"The water-power companies subject to General Electric influence control the street railways in at least 16 cities and towns; the electric-light plants in 78 cities and towns; gas plants in 19 cities and towns; and are affiliated with the electric light and gas plants in other towns. Though many of these communities, particularly those served with light only, are small, several of them are the most important in the States where these water-power companies operate. The water-power companies in the General Electric group own, control, or are closely affiliated with, the street railways in Portland and Salem, Ore.; Spokane, Wash.; Great Falls, Mont.; St. Louis, Mo.; Winona, Minn.; Milwaukee and Racine, Wis.; Elmira, N. Y.; Asheville and Raleigh, N. C., and other relatively less important towns. The towns in which the lighting plants (electric or gas) are owned or controlled include Portland, Salem, Astoria, and other towns in Oregon; Bellingham and other towns in Washington; Butte, Great Falls, Bozeman and other towns in Montana; Leadville and Colorado Springs in Colorado; St. Louis, Mo.; Milwaukee, Racine and several small towns in Wisconsin; Hudson and Rensselaer, N. Y.; Detroit, Mich.; Asheville and Raleigh, N. C.; and in fact one or more towns in practically every community where developed water power is controlled by this group. In addition to the public-service corporations thus controlled by the water-power companies subject to General Electric influence, there are numerous public-service corporations in other municipalities that purchase power from the hydroelectric developments controlled by or affiliated with the General Electric Co. This is true of Denver, Colo., which has already been discussed. In Baltimore, Md., a water-power concern in the General Electric group, namely, the Pennsylvania Water & Power Co., sells 20,-000 h. p. to the Consolidated Gas, Electric Light & Power Co., which controls the entire light and power business of that city. The power to operate all the electric street railway systems of Buffalo, N. Y., and vicinity, involving a trackage of approximately 375 miles, is supplied through a subsidiary of the Niagara Falls Power Co."

And the General Electric Company, through the financing of public service companies, exercises a like influence in communities where there is no water power:

"It, or its subsidiaries, has acquired control of or an interest in the public-service corporations of numerous cities where there is no water-power connection, and it is affiliated with still others by virtue of common directors. . . . This vast network of relationship between hydro-electric corporations through prominent officers and directors of the largest manufacturer of electrical machinery and supplies in the United States is highly significant. . . .

"It is possible that this relationship to such a large number of strong financial concerns, through common officers and directors, affords the General Electric Company an advantage that may place rivals at a corresponding disadvantage. Whether or not this great financial power has been used to the particular disadvantage of any rival water-power concern is not so important as the fact that such power exists and that it might be so used at any time."

THE SHERMAN LAW

The Money Trust cannot be broken, if we allow its power to be constantly augmented. To break the Money Trust, we must stop that power at its source. The industrial trusts are among its most effective feeders. Those which are illegal should be dissolved. The creation of new ones should be prevented. To this end the Sherman Law should be supplemented both by providing more efficient judicial machinery, and by creating a commission with administrative functions to aid in enforcing the law. When that is done, another step will have been taken toward securing the New Freedom. But restrictive legislation alone will not suffice. We should bear in mind the admonition with which the Commissioner of Corporations closes his review of our water-power development:

"There is . . . presented such a situation in water powers and other public utilities as might bring about at any time under a single management the control of a majority of the developed water power in the United States and similar control over the public utilities in a vast number of cities and towns, including some of the most important in the country."

We should conserve all rights which the Federal Government and the States now have in our natural resources, and there should be a complete separation of our industries from railroads and public utilities.

Sherwood Anderson

Sherwood Anderson (1876–1941) was an American industrialist who in his fortieth year left the business world and turned to writing. He quickly moved into a position of prominence among American literary figures, reflecting in his work the new emphasis on realism and insisting that the fundamental truths of human existence should be revealed. Like Theodore Dreiser and Eugene O'Neill, Anderson was in revolt against the great illusion built up in the mind of America that its civilization was the ultimate in man's progress. Quite naturally he drew upon his earlier experiences for his material and criticized in his novels and essays the technical progress which had transformed American production during the second and third industrial revolutions. To Anderson modern machinery was invading and destroying the pioneer American civilization built by earlier generations. In the short essay Lift Up Thine Eyes Anderson condemned the modern factory and its influence upon the workers. In reading it note (1) the importance of salesmanship in modern economic life, (2) the description and characterization of "the belt," (3) the element of competition employed in modern production, (4) how Anderson related the title of the essay to the process he was describing, and (5) how he used his literary style to enhance "the speed-up" theme he was describing.

LIFT UP THINE EYES

In verses twenty-three to twenty-seven of the third chapter of Deuteronomy, Moses speaks these words to his people in the wilderness:

And I besought the Lord at that time, saying, O Lord God, thou hast begun to shew thy servant thy greatness, and thy mighty hand: for what God is there in heaven or earth, that can do according to thy works, and according to thy might?

I pray thee, let me go over, and see the good land that is beyond Jordan, that goodly mountain, and Lebanon.

But the Lord was wroth with me for your sakes, and would not hear me: and the Lord said unto me, Let it suffice thee; speak no more unto me of this matter.

Get thee up into the top of Pisgah, and lift up thine eyes westward, and northward, and southward, and eastward, and behold it with thine eyes: for thou shalt not go over this Jordan.

It is a big assembling plant in a city of the Northwest. They assemble there the Bogel car. It is a car that sells in large numbers and at a low price. The parts are made in one great central plant and shipped to the places where they are to be assembled. There is little or no manufacturing done in the assembling plant itself. The parts come in. These great companies have learned to use the railroad cars for storage.

At the central plant everything is done on schedule. As soon as the parts are made they

Sherwood Anderson, "Lift Up Thine Eyes," in *The Nation*, 28 May 1930. Courtesy of *The Nation*.

go into railroad cars. They are on their way to the assembling plants scattered all over the United States and they arrive on schedule.

The assembling plant assembles cars for a certain territory. A careful survey has been made. This territory can afford to buy so and so many cars per day.

"But suppose the people do not want the cars?"

"What has that to do with it?"

People, American people, no longer buy cars. They do not buy newspapers, books, foods, pictures, clothes. Things are sold to people now. If a territory can take so and so many Bogel cars, find men who can make them take the cars. That is the way things are done now.

In the assembling plant everyone works "on the belt." This is a big steel conveyor, a kind of moving sidewalk, waist-high. It is a great river running down through the plant. Various tributary streams come into the main stream, the main belt. They bring tires, they bring headlights, horns, bumpers for cars. They flow into the main stream. The main stream has its source at the freight cars, where the parts are unloaded, and it flows out to the other end of the factory and into other freight cars.

The finished automobiles go into the freight cars at the delivery end of the belt. The assembly plant is a place of peculiar tension. You feel it when you go in. It never lets up. Men here work always on tension. There is no let-up to the tension. If you can't stand it get out.

It is the belt. The belt is boss. It moves always forward. Now the chassis goes on the belt. A hoist lifts it up and places it just so. There is a man at each corner. The chassis is deposited on the belt and it begins to move. Not too rapidly. There are things to be done.

How nicely everything is calculated. Scientific men have done this. They have watched men work. They have stood looking, watch in hand. There is care taken about everything. Look up. Lift up thine eyes. Hoists are bringing engines, bodies, wheels, fenders. These come out of side streams flowing into the main stream. They move at a pace very nicely calculated. They will arrive at the main stream at just a certain place at just a certain time.

In this shop there is no question of wages to be wrangled about. The men work but eight hours a day and are well paid. They are, almost without exception, young, strong men. It is, however, possible that eight hours a day in this place may be much longer than twelve or even sixteen hours in the old carelessly run plants.

They can get better pay here than at any other shop in town. Although I am a man wanting a good many minor comforts in life, I could live well enough on the wages made by the workers in this place. Sixty cents an hour to begin and then, after a probation period of sixty days, if I can stand the pace, seventy cents or more.

To stand the pace is the real test. Special skill is not required. It is all perfectly timed, perfectly calculated. If you are a body upholsterer, so many tacks driven per second. Not too many. If a man hurries too much too many tacks drop on the floor. If a man gets too hurried he is not efficient. Let an expert take a month, two months, to find out just how many tacks the average good man can drive per second.

There must be a certain standard maintained in the finished product. Remember that. It must pass inspection after inspection.

Do not crowd too hard.

Crowd all you can.

Keep crowding.

There are fifteen, twenty, thirty, perhaps fifty such assembling plants, all over the country, each serving its own section. Wires pass back and forth daily. The central office—from which all the parts come—at Jointville is the nerve center. Wires come in and go out of Jointville. In so and so many hours Williamsburg, with so and so many men, produced so and so many cars.

Now Burkesville is ahead. It stays ahead. What is up at Burkesville? An expert flies there.

The man at Burkesville was a major in the army. He is the manager there. He is a cold, rather severe, rather formal man. He has found out something. He is a real Bogel man, an ideal Bogel man. There is no foolishness about him. He watches the belt. He does not say foolishly to himself, "I am the boss here." He knows the belt is boss.

He says there is a lot of foolishness talked about the belt. The experts are too expert, he says. He has found out that the belt can be made to move just a little faster than the experts say. He has tried it. He knows. Go and look for yourself. There are the men out there on the belt, swarming along the belt, each in his place. They are all right, aren't they?

Can you see anything wrong?

Just a trifle more speed in every man. Shove the pace up just a little, not much. With the same number of men, in the same number of hours, six more cars a day.

That's the way a major gets to be a colonel, a colonel to a general. Watch that fellow at Burkesville, the man with the military stride, the cold steady voice. He'll go far.

Everything is nicely, perfectly calculated in all the Bogel assembling plants. There are white marks on the floor everywhere. Everything is immaculately clean. No one smokes, no one chews tobacco, no one spits. There are white banks on the cement floor along which the men walk. As they work, sweepers follow them. Tacks dropped on the floor are at once swept up. You can tell by the sweepings in a plant where there is too much waste, too much carelessness. Sweep everything carefully and frequently. Weigh the sweepings. Have an expert examine the sweepings. Report to Jointville.

Jointville says: "Too many upholsterers' tacks wasted in the plant at Port Smith. Belleville produced one hundred and eleven cars a day, with seven hundred and forty-nine men, wasting only nine hundred and six tacks."

It is a good thing to go through the plant now and then, select one man from all the others, give him a new and bigger job, just like that, offhand. If he doesn't make good, fire him.

It is a good thing to go through the plant occasionally, pick out some man, working apparently as the others are, fire him.

If he asks why, just say to him, "You know."

He'll know all right. He'll imagine why.

The thing is to build up Jointville. This country needs a religion. You have got to build up the sense of a mysterious central thing, a thing working outside your knowledge.

Let the notion grow and grow that there is something superhuman at the core of all this.

Lift up thine eyes, lift up thine eyes.

The central office reaches down into your secret thoughts. It knows, it knows.

Jointville knows.

Do not ask questions of Jointville. Keep up the pace.

Get the cars out.

Get the cars out.

Get the cars out.

The pace can be accelerated a little this year. The men have all got tuned into the old pace now.

Step it up a little, just a little.

They have got a special policeman in all the Bogel assembling plants. They have got a special doctor there. A man hurts his finger a little. It bleeds a little, a mere scratch. The doctor reaches down for him. The finger is fixed. Jointville wants no blood poisonings, no infections.

The doctor puts men who want jobs through a physical examination, as in the army. Try his nerve reactions. We want only the best men here, the youngest, the fastest.

Why not?

We pay the best wages, don't we?

The policeman in the plant has a special job. That's queer. It is like this. Now and then the big boss passes through. He selects a man off the belt.

"You're fired."

"Why?"

"You know."

Now and then a man goes off his nut. He goes fantoed. He howls and shouts. He grabs up a hammer.

A stream of crazy profanity comes from his lips.

There is Jointville. That is the central thing. That controls the belt.

The belt controls me.

It moves.

It moves.

It moves.

I've tried to keep up.

I tell you I have been keeping up.

Jointville is God.

Jointville controls the belt.

The belt is God.

God has rejected me.

You're fired.

Sometimes a man, fired like that, goes nutty. He gets dangerous. A strong policeman on hand knocks him down, takes him out.

You walk within certain definite white lines.

It is calculated that a man, rubbing automobile bodies with pumice, makes thirty thousand and twenty-one arm strokes per day. The difference between thirty thousand and twenty-one and twenty-eight thousand and four will tell a vital story of profits or loss at Jointville.

Do you think things are settled at Jointville, or at the assembling plants of the Bogel car scattered all over America? Do you think men know how fast the belt can be made to move, what the ultimate, the final pace will be, can be?

Certainly not.

There are experts studying the nerves of men, the movements of men. They are watching, watching. Calculations are always going on. The thing is to produce goods and more goods at less cost. Keep the standard up. Increase the pace a little.

Stop waste.

Calculate everything.

A man walking to and from his work between white lines saves steps. There is a tremendous science of lost motion not perfectly calculated yet.

More goods at less cost.

Increase the pace.

Keep up standards.

It is so you advance civilization.

In the Bogel assembling plants, as at Jointville itself, there isn't any laughter. No one stops work to play. No one fools around or throws things, as they used to do in the old factories. That is why Bogel is able to put the old-fashioned factories, one by one, out of business.

It is all a matter of calculation. You feel it when you go in. You feel rigid lines. You feel movement. You feel a strange tension in the air. There is a quiet terrible intensity.

The belt moves. It keeps moving. The day I was there a number of young boys had come in. They had been sent by a Bogel car dealer, away back somewhere in the country. They had driven in during the night and were to drive Bogel cars back over the country roads to some dealer. A good many Bogel cars go out to dealers from the assembling plants, driven out by boys like that.

Such boys, driving all night, fooling along the road, getting no sleep.

They have a place for them to wait for the cars in the Bogel assembling plants. You have been at dog shows and have seen how prize dogs are exhibited, each in his nice clean cage. They have nice clean cages like that for country boys who drive in to Bogel assembling plants to get cars.

The boys come in. There is a place to lie down in there. It is clean. After the boy goes into his cage a gate is closed. He is fastened in.

If a country boy, sleepy like that, waiting for his car, wandered about in a plant he might get hurt.

There might be damage suits, all sorts of things.

Better to calculate everything. Be careful. Be exact.

Jointville thought of that. Jointville thinks of everything. It is the center of power, the new mystery.

Every year in America Jointville comes nearer and nearer being the new center. Men nowadays do not look to Washington. They look to Jointville.

Lift up thine eyes, lift up thine eyes.

Stuart Chase

Stuart Chase (1888–) is an American writer trained as a public accountant. He has been associated with various government agencies for many years and has participated in numerous investigations of business and industrial practices. He is the author of a long series of books and

articles analyzing and criticizing the American economic
structure. In particular he has been concerned about machine production and its implications, both actual and
potential, for human labor. In 1930, Chase wrote an article
for Fortune entitled "Danger at the A. O. Smith Corporation," an analytical study of trends in industrial production.
In reading it note (1) Chase's reply to those who feared
industrial workers were becoming robots, (2) the innovation developed at the Smith plant, (3) what had become
the chief business of the company, (4) the vivid description of the "dragon," (5) the contrast between the old and
the new mills, (6) what Chase considered the danger at
the A. O. Smith Corporation to be, and (7) the ultimate
utopia which might emerge from this development.

DANGER AT THE A. O. SMITH CORPORATION

Jeremiahs of monumental profundity wring
their hands and tear their beards lamenting the
conversion of men into robots in the age of the
machine. They adduce no figures, but the impression given is a wholesale operation, affecting nearly all of us. Elsewhere I have sought to
verify, quantitively, the strength of this indictment. With the Census of Occupations as a
base, I found that of 42,000,000 Americans
gainfully employed, not more than 10,000,000
spent their working hours in close contact with
machinery. Further analysis discloses that only
about 5,000,000 can properly be called robots
at all in that they surrender their personalities
to the machine.

The other 5,000,000 either are handicraft
men and other helpers about factories who
have little to do with machinery, or—and this
is important—they themselves *dominate* the
mechanism, and thus let some of its energy into
their own veins. Air pilots are not robots by
any stretch of the imagination, and neither are
operators of motor cars, locomotive engineers,
or structural steel workers. Lastly, of those who
might be termed robots—some 12 per cent of
the gainfully employed—the number is actually declining, and for two reasons. Due to
technical improvements in output per man,
factory employees are growing fewer. Second,
the automatic function in industry is steadily
gaining around, displacing machine-feeders

and nut-screwers by skilled designers, inspec-
tors, dial-watchers. A large number of so-called
robots give way to a small number of workers
with reasonably intelligent and independent
jobs.

In order that the Jeremiahs may see exactly
what I mean, I take pleasure in presenting in
some detail the most advanced single exhibit
of the automatic function in the world. The
honor belongs beyond peradventure to the mill
which makes automobile frames practically by
itself on the premises of the A. O. Smith Corporation in the city of Milwaukee. And I take
pleasure in presenting one or two additional aspects of this extraordinary company which
ought to give the machine age philosophers,
both gloomy and cheerio, enough to reflect on
for quite a while to come. This plant not only
threatens to end the scourge of the robot; it
threatens to end industry itself—in the form
that we have hitherto known it. There is a mixture brewing here which if it explodes, will
make Milwaukee more famous than ever did its
beer.

The company was founded over half a century ago with the commendable purpose of
fabricating baby carriages. In due time, babies
were abandoned for bicycle riders. About
1900, Mr. A. O. Smith, the son of the founder,
gave the first recorded example of that policy
to which the company now dedicates itself. He

Stuart Chase, "Danger at the A. O. Smith Corporation," in *Fortune*, November, 1930. Courtesy of Stuart Chase and
of *Fortune*.

had been following the early flounderings of
the automobile. Bankers and other sensible
folk knew it for what it was—a crazy, impracticable contraption. Not so Mr. Smith. He was
convinced that the motor car had a future.
Some day it would be made in large quantities.
It would need a frame on which its engine
would rest. That frame might be made of
wood, iron, or pressed steel. He pondered over
these three alternatives as the one-lungers gur-
gled, back-fired, and frightened live stock out
of its wits. He concluded his ruminations in
favor of pressed steel. With a group of men
from the bicycle shop, he proceeded to design
and erect special machinery for making steel
frames, *a full year before there was any call for
them, or indeed any evidence that America
would take to making automobiles in a determined way at all!* He had thought out his problem, designed and set up his equipment in advance of the world's recognition that there was
a problem. This is the sort of thinking which is
coming out of Milwaukee to-day.

In 1902, the orders—more or less on schedule—began to arrive, the machines were put at
productive labor, and the first frames shipped
out. They came from the shop at the rate of ten
per day, and Mr. Smith offered a house and lot
to the foreman who could get out twelve.
(Now they are coming at 10,000 a day.) It
was hand and machine work, much of it robot
work, if you please. The business prospered.
The grandson of the founder Mr. L. R. Smith,
took the helm his father laid down. He looked
at the rows of men handling heavy steel side
bars, performing a single operation. "It's stupid," he thought, "and wasteful. It costs too
much; it's bad for the men. Men have too much
innate ability to be condemned to such work as
this." He turned to his engineers, a growing
corps and one upon which he came more and
more to depend. (He is himself an engineer.)
"Could we design a machine to do this whole
job automatically, a machine as big as a factory, to pick up the raw steel and throw these
things out at four or five thousand a day? I
know it is a crazy idea, but can we do it?" His
engineers had learned to expect anything from
this man. The T-squares spanked and the
drawing boards groaned. Ten times the plant

was built on paper, and the cost of the crazy
idea had mounted to $1,500,000.

Finally, after incredible labor and some of
the boldest mechanical thinking ever done on
this planet, a plan was evolved which looked
as though, by the grace of God, it might work.
Bankers were called in and their advice asked.
The rosy-gilled fraternity was petrified, and advised, whatever it was, not to do it. They were
thanked politely, and the metamorphosis of paper into concrete and steel promptly begun.
Fortunately, money in the home stocking was
still available.

Beyond the technical incredibility of the
project was the whole question of the potential
market. Suppose the plant could be built, who
was to buy frames in lots of 7,000 each and
every day; 2,000,000 frames a year? Competitors were in the field, and in 1916 only 1,500,-
000 motor cars were manufactured the country
over. The blueprints called for more frames
than there were engines to mount on them. But
even as his father had sensed the beginning of
an industry in 1900, the son sensed the postwar automotive boom. "We were aiming at
million-lot machinery, million-lot production,
and million-lot costs," and lo! the market came
to meet this million-lot expectancy. The plant
was built in 1920. Soon afterward the roaring
twenties, building 3,000,000, 4,000,000, 5,-
000,000 motor cars a year, were in full swing
and demanding Smith frames.

By the time the mill was built, $6,000,000
had been sunk in it, including the drawing paper. Would the damn thing work? The blueprints were optimistic, but how about Madame
Nature? Here were 552 separate operations to
be performed on every frame. If any one of
them went wrong, the whole gigantic mechanism might jam.

I will never forget that moment when it became
necessary for me or an associate to throw on the
power. Both of us were stalling, one waiting for the
other. Neither can remember clearly which one
threw the switch. But for an hour and fifty-seven
minutes, the unit functioned without a hitch. Then
it shut down for want of raw material!

The damn thing would work. It has been
working ever since. And, of course, for all the

palpitations when the first switch was thrown, Mr. Smith and his engineers *knew* it would work. Too much sound research had already gone in to permit of failure. It was no miracle nor are the subsequent achievements miracles, spectacular as they appear. It is the sort of thing to be expected when engineering takes the place of rule of thumb, and its possibilities developed *to the limit*. In due time production was stepped up from 7,000 frames a day to 10,000—and the end is not yet.

One goes through a guarded gate into the great enclosure upon which the company's property stands: a company which sells $60,-000,000 of tonnage products a year, moving out on 30,000 freight cars. The buildings are not huge but squat and grim, full of noise and full of power. There is an air of spaciousness and cleanliness, but no hint of lawns, flowers and the tra la la la school of mill design. Clean, muscled, and stripped to the waist is the dominant note. But stop a moment. What is this partly finished building of peculiar steel construction with black granite base and fluted aluminum creeping up over the stanchions? It is the new Research Building, equipped to house 1,000 engineers. It could have been built for $400,000 but is costing $1,500,000. And why, pray, the extra $1,000,000? It is expended to make as just and lovely a temple to the god of science as devoted hands have reared to other gods in other ages. Engineering research is the chief business of this company. Frames for motor cars, pipes for oil fields, pressure vessels—these are by-products.

We enter a door in one of the squat mills and are suddenly drowned in sound. We are in a room perhaps 300 feet long and 200 wide, with walls of glass. Its floor is one solid mass of glittering steel, a thousand shapes which rush and stop, rise and fall, advance and retreat, dancing to some gigantic rhythm, yet to a counterpoint which sets up no vibration. One quadrille offsets the other, leaving the building without a tremor. The multiplicity of moving shapes confuses us, but as we mount a platform, a sense of discipline, of patterned harmony, becomes apparent. Wide, clean aisles separate the moving groups. There are no towering mechanisms, no belts; the whole upper part of the building is clear. The largest single shape is near the door by which we entered. It is also the noisiest. With drum-shattering gasps it is solemnly picking up pieces of steel, fitting them to a pattern, dropping the unit down for some attention (the seat of the noise apparently), raising it up, placing it on a little carriage of delicate steel rods . . . carriage after carriage, which rush and stop, rush and stop, rush and stop, in our direction.

Comprehension dawns. Upon each carriage is obviously a motor car frame; the hissing mechanism has assembled the various side bars and cross bars which compose it, and the dropping motion—our guide assists us here—is the automatic insertion of 100 rivets into their waiting holes. The assembled frame moves toward us for the job of heading the rivets and so locking the parts finally together.

As the frames advance and stop, two batteries of steel dragons, with jaws like those of stone Aztec serpents, move forward upon them, one from either side. Their round metal eyes glitter, their jaws are distended to cavernous proportions, they nuzzle into their victim's vitals, select each a sought-for rivet, then slowly, relentlessly, even softly, the great jaws close. The final crunch of 40,000 pounds upon the rivet head is effortless. Gently the jaw opens; gently and solemnly both batteries retreat. The frame moves on to another group of monsters, where the process is repeated with a second set of rivets. One hundred rivets require about 100 dragons, and only about six can operate comfortably at one "station."

Sometimes, if you please, the beast opens its mouth to bite, thinks better of it, retires, rears up into a more ferocious position, and then comes dreadfully down. It is reported that Mr. Otto Kahn could not be budged from his entranced survey of this deliberate animal. "I have seen many ingenious machines," he said, "but this is the first that ever I saw which started to do a job, stopped, spit on its hands, hitched up its overalls, and then went to work!" This is a good story—but dragons, my dear Mr. Kahn, really, dragons do not spit on their hands.

There are nine units in the total process. In each unit are a number of stations—connecting a single operation. What I have described is but the operation of several stations on unit No. 6, the general assembly line. As we walk along our platform which runs the length of the building, each unit is identified between its dividing aisles, and its general function if not its bewildering detail, made plain. A little table tells the story.

Unit	Function
No. 1.—	Picks up the raw steel strips, examines them, throws out those which do not meet the required standards of length, breadth, and thickness.
No. 2.—	Douses the admitted strips into baths of pickle for cleaning.
No. 3.—	Fabricates the longer strips into right and left side bars—bending them, turning up their edges, punching holes for future rivets.
No. 4.—	Fabricates the shorter strips into cross bars.
No. 5.—	Assembles the various parts of the side bars.
No. 6.—	Assembles the whole frame, inserts and drives home the rivets—by virtue of monsters altogether fabulous, as we have seen.
No. 7.—	General inspection of the assembled frame, a partly human job.
No. 8.—	Automatic washing, painting, and drying.
No. 9.—	The snatching of the painted, dried, completed frame by the left hind leg, as it were, and bearing it, like a hog in a packing house, to a vast overhead storage space. There it hangs, in carload lots, until a man in a little underslung crane, which crawls like a busy beetle among these towering heights, drops it, kerplunk, into a waiting freight car.

One hour and a half from raw steel to suspension by the hind leg, and a minute or two more to freight car if there is any rush. Every eight seconds a completed frame goes swinging into storage, 420 an hour, 10,000 a day. Frames for Pontiac, Chrysler, Chevrolet, Buick. For each type of frame, the great dance

stops for a few hours. Skilled mechanics swarm out from the tool shop at the end of the building and reset the dragons' jaws and the other mechanisms to take care of the new size. Given an over-all length and width, any variety— past, present, or future—of frame can be made. About thirty different styles are now fabricated, but the total variety is virtually limitless. The goal of standardization with *flexibility* has been won. In nine years of operation no automobile maker has ever had to shut down his assembly line for lack of frames, this in spite of eleventh-hour increases in orders on the part of customers.

Are the Jeremiahs answered? Academically no. Practically yes, if this sort of thing is to expand. Mr. Smith admits his mill to be an engineering failure though a huge commercial success. He set out to build a machine that would make frames without men. He did not quite succeed. At one or two stations, men touch the frame with their hands, thus breaking 100 per cent performance, though this is still the goal. The Jeremiahs, I among them, find other objections in the thought of ex-robots walking the streets. As technological unemployment advances, a technological solution must be found. I was glad to hear Mr. Smith say that shorter hours offered one remedy from the long swing point of view.

But consider the tangible achievement. Not a stone's throw away is the old "hand" mill. I went through it, and the contrast was staggering. Here are 2,000 men in long assembly lines, drilling holes, driving bolts, twisting shapes, conveying the growing frame by hand from process to process. Yet work as they may, they can make no more frames a day than can the automatic mill with a scant 200 men, not more than fifty of whom actually touch the product. Two thousand dreary jobs against 200 amusing ones, for an identical output! Ponder this well, ye Jeremiahs. The cost of the automatic frame to the hand frames is as two to three (and rather less in total than a good pair of shoes), with a very large absorption of development overhead. Some day when this overhead cost is all absorbed, the automatic cost will fall into the subcellar. . . .

Few men ever voluntarily leave the automatic mill. There is a long waiting list. They appreciate it as "something different"; they appreciate the boldness of the boss in designing it, and their jobs are certainly far more independent and interesting than those in the hand mill. One man sits in a little tower, the control switches of a whole unit under his hand; another resets the gape of the dragon's jaws; another adjusts the "nailing machine," the automatic riveter which shoots by compressed air a hundred tiny bars of steel at once. (To skilled technicians this is the supreme mechanical achievement of the mill and the engine of which Mr. Smith is himself the proudest.) Skill varies; some jobs can be taught in a few days, others require months and months of intensive training, while in design, erection, and repair we have as skilled a group of crafts as this, or any other age, has ever glimpsed. The whole building is one vast integrated machine. Another major job remains, however, before the Jeremiahs are completely routed. There is, I believe, too much noise in that place for human ears to stand indefinitely without injury.

I asked Mr. Smith if the process were applicable to other industries. "Yes," he said, "almost everywhere when the demand is great enough to warrant 'million-lots.' Even automobiles could be assembled automatically if we were sure of their general style long enough to spend the time and money."

All the eggs of the A. O. Smith Corporation are not in one basket. Far from it. Frame-making is depressed at the present time due to the slump in motor cars (90 per cent of the frame makers retain their jobs at shorter hours), but the pipe business is roaring as never before. Nor is the demand for pressure vessels in the doldrums, due to its close association with the developing chemical industry. . . .

One last field observation before we move to general principles. In a rambling wing I found the very efficient safety department and the department of preventive medicine equipped for as complete a physical examination as the best hospital can give. This is said to be the most thorough-going medical study of *normal* persons ever conducted. As the records grow and the years go by, it will be profoundly helpful in telling the well person what he must do to keep well. . . . There are scientists of steel in this company and scientists of flesh and blood.

The Smith dynasty has a guiding star. It employs seven salesmen—I counted them—and not far from 600 engineers. Presently the new research building will house 1,000 engineers in quarters equipped with facilities beyond their wildest dreams. Their work is not primarily to keep the present output increasingly efficient, but to develop new varieties of output, and totally new processes for fabricating them. A program of industrial depth bombs, but geared to three basic principles:

I.—The product must lie in the field of mass production, with an established market, or one which the economic research staff knows can be established.

II.—A product to be made so much better and cheaper than anything else in the field that it will sell itself on its engineering merits alone, with no outlays for high pressure salesmanship or advertising.

III.—A product profitable enough to liquidate its fixed investment in not longer than a year or two. (The success of this principle hitherto is reflected in the company's luxuriant profit and loss accounts. I speak as a sometime C. P. A.)

The product having been determined according to these principles, it is put through three stages, or stations as Mr. Smith calls them. First comes the "pencil sketch" station. It may die there. But if the figures look sound, it goes to the "test tube" station, of laboratory analysis. If it survives this manhandling, it goes to the "pilot plant" station—a miniature factory where it is actually produced under normal operating conditions, and its performance, and particularly its costs per unit, accurately determined. The pilot plant answers the question: can it be made in the expected quantities at the calculated costs and how big must the real operating plant be? This delimits the design of the proposed plant and makes its construction practically automatic, with everything accounted for in advance. If the answer is in the negative, whatever the time and money spent upon the idea, it goes down the trap door. "I can get out of a business faster than anyone in the country," says Mr. Smith— an art which few executives have learned. . . .

Certain by-products of profound industrial significance arise from this program. The production of a given article under these principles of engineering research, automatic fabrication, low costs, tends to insure high quality. If the mill is not to jam, every incoming piece of raw material—as we saw in the frame plant —must pass rigid tests of inspection. The delicate controls demand an absolutely uniform product, without flaw or break. Engineering and its handmaiden, mathematics, are sciences to which the word "elegance" has been frequently applied. In full control of the job, other things being equal, the output will share that perfection and that elegance. Mr. Lewis Mumford, the distinguished architectural critic, has been hinting at this for a long time. I am glad to supply him with concrete evidence of the soundness of his stand.

A second philosophical by-product—and not so exclusively philosophical either—is the factor of obsolescence. The Smith policy is ruthlessly to scrap anything which is not a jump or two ahead of the rest of the world; to scrap indeed when it *is* ahead, if the research staff has developed a better process. Certain great corporations buy up, or develop, improvements and file them in their safes. Mr. Smith puts them to work instanter; ground for the new plant is broken before the signature of the patent office is dry. "I grant it is wasteful, I grant the overhead cost is enormous, but it is far more wasteful to burn up men and materials in the old way when a better way has been found."

It all boils down, of course, to the margin of economy in the new way. If the margin is demonstrably greater than the cost of installing the method, it is cheaper to the company and to society to scrap the old; aye, to throw uncounted millions of investment on the dump heap. The only trouble is in locating the marginal point. Aging boards of corporate directors have some difficulty in the premises, but to a stripped, flexible organization with every executive ready to go through hell and out again with Mr. Smith, and 1,000 engineers supplying the facts, the point is easier to determine. Nine times out of ten an organization like this will succeed, where the ordinary manufacturer, regarding engineers as so many expensive plumbers, will fail if he attempts to flirt with the ballistics of obsolescence. "How can you afford to spend so much for engineers?" these gentlemen ask our hero. "I can't afford not to," says a lean, brown man in the upper forties, with a face like a Yankee skipper's.

I regard Milwaukee as the most dangerous area in the U. S. It promises, in the persons of the Smith dynasty, to deal American industry a wallop beside which the late stock market crash was a chuck under the chin. Any determined adoption of its principles will turn the economic structure upside down and inside out, scrap billions of dollars of investment, shatter the nerves of untold bankers, and set the exalted profession of high-pressure salesmanship in a roadside ditch.

But when the hurricane is over, we may find a world where poverty has disappeared, where robots are unheard of, where working hours have been cut in two, where waste is at a minimum, and where the era of the salesman has given way to the era of the engineer.

Woodrow Wilson

Woodrow Wilson (1856–1924) forsook his chosen profession of education in order to enter public life as a defender of democratic principles against the growing power of monopolies. He was convinced that the freedom of the individual, which in Jefferson's day had to be protected from too much government power, could in the twentieth century only be preserved from the encroachment of big business by that same power of government. He campaigned for, and won, the presidency in 1912 on a platform designed to control corporations, to lower tariffs, and to levy income taxes to pay the cost of increased government functions. During his two terms in the White House, Wilson was largely successful in bringing about a silent revolution from the old liberalism of Jefferson's day to the "New Freedom" of his own. In 1913 he published The New Freedom, a book of speeches delivered during the 1912 presidential campaign. The first chapter is entitled "The Old Order Changeth"; in reading it note (1) what Wilson meant by the "old order," (2) the relationship of existing laws to the "new order," (3) why there existed a labor question, (4) how Americans were unintentionally victimized by corporations, (5) what had happened to freedom of economic enterprise, (6) what he considered the country needed above everything else, (7) where the treasured strength of America lay, (8) his analysis of Jefferson's ideal of government, (9) the duties the government must assume in the "new order," (10) the intolerable relationship existing between government and business, and (11) the nature and purpose of the revolution which Wilson believed was about to sweep America.

From: THE NEW FREEDOM

There is one great basic fact which underlies all the questions that are discussed on the political platform at the present moment. That singular fact is that nothing is done in this country as it was done twenty years ago.

We are in the presence of a new organization of society. Our life has broken away from the past. The life of America is not the life that it was twenty years ago. We have changed our economic conditions, absolutely, from top to bottom; and, with our economic society, the organization of our life. The old political formulas do not fit the present problems; they read now like documents taken out of a forgotten age. The older cries sound as if they belonged to a past age which men have almost forgotten. Things which used to be put into the party platforms of ten years ago would sound antiquated if put into a platform now. We are facing the necessity of fitting a new social organization, as we did once fit the old organization, to the happiness and prosperity of the great body of citizens; for we are conscious that the new order of society has not been made to fit and provide the convenience or prosperity of the average man. The life of the nation has grown infinitely varied. It does not centre now upon questions of governmental structure or of the distribution of governmental powers. It centres upon questions of the very structure and operation of society itself, of which government is only the instrument. Our development has run so fast and so far along the lines sketched in the earlier day of constitutional definition, has so crossed and interlaced those lines, has piled upon them such novel structures of trust and combination, has elaborated within them a life so manifold, so full of forces which transcend the boundaries of the country itself and fill the eyes of the world, that a new nation seems to have been created which the old formulas do not fit or afford a vital interpretation of.

We have come upon a very different age from any that preceded us. We have come upon an age when we do not do business in the way in which we used to do business,—when we do not carry on any of the operations of manufacture, sale, transportation, or communication as men used to carry them on. There is a sense in which in our day the individual has been submerged. In most parts of our country men work, not for themselves, not as partners in the old way in which they used to work, but generally as employees,—in a higher or lower grade,—of great corporations. There was a time when corporations played a very minor part in our business affairs, but now they play the chief part, and most men are the servants of corporations.

You know what happens when you are the servant of a corporation. You have in no instance access to the men who are really determining the policy of the corporation. If the corporation is doing the things that it ought not to do, you really have no voice in the matter and must obey the orders, and you have oftentimes with deep mortification to co-operate in the doing of things which you know are against the public interest. Your individuality is swallowed up in the individuality and purpose of a great organization.

It is true that, while most men are thus submerged in the corporation, a few, a very few, are exalted to a power which as individuals they could never have wielded. Through the great organizations of which they are the heads, a few are enabled to play a part unprecedented by anything in history in the control of the business operations of the country and in the determination of the happiness of great numbers of people.

Yesterday, and ever since history began, men were related to one another as individuals. To be sure there were the family, the Church, and the State, institutions which associated men in certain wide circles of relationship. But in the ordinary concerns of life, in the ordinary work, in the daily round, men dealt freely and directly with one another. To-day, the everyday relationships of men are largely with great impersonal concerns, with organizations, not with other individual men.

Now this is nothing short of a new social age, a new era of human relationships, a new stage-setting for the drama of life.

In this new age we find, for instance, that our laws with regard to the relations of employer and employee are in many respects wholly antiquated and impossible. They were framed for another age, which nobody now living remembers, which is, indeed, so remote from our life that it would be difficult for many of us to understand it if it were described to us. The employer is now generally a corporation or a huge company of some kind; the employee is one of hundreds or of thousands brought together, not by individual masters whom they know and with whom they have personal relations, but by agents of one sort or another. Workingmen are marshaled in great numbers for the performance of a multitude of particular tasks under a common discipline. They generally use dangerous and powerful machinery, over whose repair and renewal they have no control. New rules must be devised with regard to their obligations and their rights, their obligations to their employers and their responsibilities to one another. Rules must be devised for their protection, for their compensation when injured, for their support when disabled.

There is something very new and very big and very complex about these new relations of capital and labor. A new economic society has sprung up, and we must effect a new set of adjustments. We must not pit power against weakness. The employer is generally, in our day, as I have said, not an individual, but a powerful group; and yet the workingman when dealing with his employer is still, under our existing law, an individual.

Why is it that we have a labor question at all? It is for the simple and very sufficient reason that the laboring man and the employer are not intimate associates now as they used to be in time past. Most of our laws were formed in the age when employer and employees knew each other, knew each other's characters, were associates with each other, dealt with each other as man with man. That is no longer the case. You not only do not come into personal contact with the men who have the supreme command in those corporations, but it would be out of the question for you to do it. Our modern corporations employ thousands, and in some instances hundreds of thousands, of men. The only persons whom you see or deal with are local superintendents or local representatives of a vast organization, which is not like anything that the workingmen of the time in which our laws were framed knew anything about. A little group of workingmen, seeing their employer every day, dealing with him in a personal way, is one thing, and the modern body of labor engaged as employees of the huge enterprises that spread all over the country, dealing with men of whom they can form no personal conception, is another thing. A very different thing. You never saw a corporation, any more than you ever saw a government. Many a workingman to-day never saw the body of men who are conducting the industry in which he is employed. And they never saw him. What they know about him is written in ledgers and books and letters, in the correspondence of the office, in the reports of the superintendents. He is a long way off from them.

So what we have to discuss is, not wrongs which individuals intentionally do,—I do not believe there are a great many of those,—but the wrongs of a system. I want to record my protest against any discussion of this matter which would seem to indicate that there are bodies of our fellow-citizens who are trying to grind us down and do us injustice. There are some men of that sort. I don't know how they sleep o' nights, but there are men of that kind. Thank God, they are not numerous. The truth is, we are all caught in a great economic system which is heartless. The modern corporation is not engaged in business as an individual. When we deal with it, we deal with an impersonal element, an immaterial piece of society. A modern corporation is a means of co-operation in the conduct of an enterprise which is so big that no one man can conduct it, and which the resources of no one man are sufficient to finance. A company is formed; that company puts out a prospectus; the promoters expect to raise a certain fund as capital stock. Well, how are they going to raise it? They are going to raise it from the public in general, some of whom will buy their stock. The moment that begins, there is formed—what? A joint stock corporation. Men begin to pool their earnings, little piles, big piles. A certain number of men are elected by the stockholders to be directors, and these directors elect a president. This president is the head of the undertaking, and the directors are its managers.

Now, do the workingmen employed by that stock corporation deal with that president and those directors? Not at all. Does the public deal with that president and that board of directors? It does not. Can anybody bring them to account? It is next to impossible to do so. If you undertake it you will find it a game of hide and seek, with the objects of your search taking refuge now behind the tree of their individual personality, now behind that of their corporate irresponsibility.

And do our laws take note of this curious state of things? Do they even attempt to distinguish between a man's act as a corporation director and as an individual? They do not. Our laws still deal with us on the basis of the old system. The law is still living in the dead past which we have left behind. This is evident, for instance, with regard to the matter of employers' liability for workingmen's injuries. Suppose that a superintendent wants a workman to use a certain piece of machinery which it is not safe for him to use, and that the workman is injured by that piece of machinery. Some of our courts have held that the superintendent is a fellow-servant, or, as the law states it, a fellow-employee, and that, therefore, the man cannot recover damages for his injury. The superintendent who probably engaged the man is not his employer. Who is his employer? And whose negligence could conceivably come in there? The board of directors did not tell the employee to use that piece of machinery; and the president of the corporation did not tell him to use that piece of machinery. And so forth. Don't you see by that theory that a man never can get redress for negligence on the part of the employer? When I hear judges reason upon the analogy of the relationships that used to exist between workmen and their employers a generation ago, I wonder if they have not opened their eyes to the modern world. You know, we have a right to expect that judges will have their eyes open, even though the law which they administer hasn't awakened.

Yet that is but a single small detail illustrative of the difficulties we are in because we have not adjusted the law to the facts of the new order.

Since I entered politics, I have chiefly had

men's views confided to me privately. Some of the biggest men in the United States, in the field of commerce and manufacture, are afraid of somebody, are afraid of something. They know that there is a power somewhere so organized, so subtle, so watchful, so interlocked, so complete, so pervasive, that they had better not speak above their breath when they speak in condemnation of it.

They know that America is not a place of which it can be said, as it used to be, that a man may choose his own calling and pursue it just as far as his abilities enable him to pursue it; because to-day, if he enters certain fields, there are organizations which will use means against him that will prevent his building up a business which they do not want to have built up; organizations that will see to it that the ground is cut from under him and the markets shut against him. For if he begins to sell to certain retail dealers, to any retail dealers, the monopoly will refuse to sell to those dealers, and those dealers, afraid, will not buy the new man's wares.

And this is the country which has lifted to the admiration of the world its ideals of absolutely free opportunity, where no man is supposed to be under any limitation except the limitations of his character and of his mind; where there is supposed to be no distinction of class, no distinction of blood, no distinction of social status, but where men win or lose on their merits.

I lay it very close to my own conscience as a public man whether we can any longer stand at our doors and welcome all newcomers upon those terms. American industry is not free, as once it was free; American enterprise is not free; the man with only a little capital is finding it harder to get into the field, more and more impossible to compete with the big fellow. Why? Because the laws of this country do not prevent the strong from crushing the weak. That is the reason, and because the strong have crushed the weak, the strong dominate the industry and the economic life of this country. No man can deny that the lines of endeavor have more and more narrowed and stiffened; no man who knows anything about the development of industry in this country

can have failed to observe that the larger kinds of credit are more and more difficult to obtain, unless you obtain them upon the terms of uniting your efforts with those who already control the industries of the country; and nobody can fail to observe that any man who tries to set himself up in competition with any process of manufacture which has been taken under the control of large combinations of capital will presently find himself either squeezed out or obliged to sell and allow himself to be absorbed.

There is a great deal that needs reconstruction in the United States. I should like to take a census of the business men,—I mean the rank and file of the business men,—as to whether they think that business conditions in this country, or rather whether the organization of business in this country, is satisfactory or not. I know what they would say if they dared. If they could vote secretly they would vote overwhelmingly that the present organization of business was meant for the big fellows and was not meant for the little fellows; that it was meant for those who are at the top and was meant to exclude those who were at the bottom; that it was meant to shut out beginners, to prevent new entries in the race, to prevent the building up of competitive enterprises that would interfere with the monopolies which the great trusts have built up.

What this country needs above everything else is a body of laws which will look after the men who are on the make rather than the men who are already made. Because the men who are already made are not going to live indefinitely, and they are not always kind enough to leave sons as able and as honest as they are.

The originative part of America, the part of America that makes new enterprises, the part into which the ambitious and gifted workingman makes his way up, the class that saves, that plans, that organizes, that presently spreads its enterprises until they have a national scope and character,—that middle class is being more and more squeezed out by the processes which we have been taught to call processes of prosperity. Its members are sharing prosperity, no doubt; but what alarms me is that they are not *originating* prosperity. No country can afford to have its prosperity originated by a small controlling class. The treasury of America does not lie in the brains of the small body of men now in control of the great enterprises that have been concentrated under the direction of a very small number of persons. The treasury of America lies in those ambitions, those energies, that cannot be restricted to a special favored class. It depends upon the inventions of unknown men, upon the originations of unknown men, upon the ambitions of unknown men. Every country is renewed out of the ranks of the unknown, not out of the ranks of those already famous and powerful and in control.

There has come over the land that un-American set of conditions which enables a small number of men who control the government to get favors from the government; by those favors to exclude their fellows from equal business opportunity; by those favors to extend a network of control that will presently dominate every industry in the country, and so make men forget the ancient time when America lay in every hamlet, when America was to be seen in every fair valley, when America displayed her great forces on the broad prairies, ran her fine fires of enterprise up over the mountainsides and down into the bowels of the earth, and eager men were everywhere captains of industry, not employees; not looking to a distant city to find out what they might do, but looking about among their neighbors, finding credit according to their character, not according to their connections, finding credit in proportion to what was known to be in them and behind them, not in proportion to the securities they held that were approved where they were not known. In order to start an enterprise now, you have to be authenticated, in a perfectly impersonal way, not according to yourself, but according to what you own that somebody else approves of your owning. You cannot begin such an enterprise as those that have made America until you are so authenticated, until you have succeeded in obtaining the good-will of large allied capitalists. Is that freedom? That is dependence, not freedom.

We used to think in the old-fashioned days when life was very simple that all that government had to do was to put on a policeman's uniform, and say, "Now don't anybody hurt anybody else." We used to say that the ideal of government was for every man to be left alone and not interfered with, except when he interfered with somebody else; and that the best government was the government that did as little governing as possible. That was the idea that obtained in Jefferson's time. But we are coming now to realize that life is so complicated that we are not dealing with the old conditions, and that the law has to step in and create new conditions under which we may live, the conditions which will make it tolerable for us to live. . . .

One of the most alarming phenomena of the time,—or rather it would be alarming if the nation had not awakened to it and shown its determination to control it,—one of the most significant signs of the new social era is the degree to which government has become associated with business. I speak, for the moment, of the control over the government exercised by Big Business. Behind the whole subject, of course, is the truth that, in the new order, government and business must be associated closely. But that association is at present of a nature absolutely intolerable; the precedence is wrong, the association is upside down. Our government has been for the past few years under the control of heads of great allied corporations with special interests. It has not controlled these interests and assigned them a proper place in the whole system of business; it has submitted itself to their control. As a result, there have grown up vicious systems and schemes of governmental favoritism (the most obvious being the extravagant tariff), far-reaching in effect upon the whole fabric of life, touching to his injury every inhabitant of the land, laying unfair and impossible handicaps upon competitors, imposing taxes in every direction, stifling everywhere the free spirit of American enterprise.

Now this has come about naturally; as we go on we shall see how very naturally. It is no use denouncing anybody, or anything, except human nature. Nevertheless, it is an intolerable thing that the government of the republic should have got so far out of the hands of the people; should have been captured by interests which are special and not general. In the train of this capture follow the troops of scandals, wrongs, indecencies, with which our politics swarm.

There are cities in America of whose government we are ashamed. There are cities everywhere, in every part of the land, in which we feel that, not the interests of the public, but the interests of special privileges, of selfish men, are served; where contracts take precedence over public interest. Not only in big cities is this the case. Have you not noticed the growth of socialistic sentiment in the smaller towns? Not many months ago I stopped at a little town in Nebraska, and while my train lingered I met on the platform a very engaging young fellow dressed in overalls who introduced himself to me as the mayor of the town, and added that he was a Socialist. I said, "What does that mean? Does that mean that this town is socialistic?" "No, sir," he said; "I have not deceived myself; the vote by which I was elected was about 20 per cent socialistic and 80 per cent protest." It was protest against the treachery to the people of those who led both the other parties of that town.

All over the Union people are coming to feel that they have no control over the course of affairs. I live in one of the greatest States in the union, which was at one time in slavery. Until two years ago we had witnessed with increasing concern the growth in New Jersey of a spirit of almost cynical despair. Men said: "We vote; we are offered the platform we want; we elect the men who stand on that platform, and we get absolutely nothing." So they began to ask: "What is the use of voting? We know that the machines of both parties are subsidized by the same persons, and therefore it is useless to turn in either direction."

This is not confined to some of the state governments and those of some of the towns and cities. We know that something intervenes between the people of the United States and the control of their own affairs at Washington. It is not the people who have been ruling there of late.

Why are we in the presence, why are we at the threshold, of a revolution? Because we are profoundly disturbed by the influences which we see reigning in the determination of our public life and our public policy. There was a time when America was blithe with self-confidence. She boasted that she, and she alone, knew the processes of popular government; but now she sees her sky overcast; she sees that there are at work forces which she did not dream of in her hopeful youth.

Don't you know that some man with eloquent tongue, without conscience, who did not care for the nation, could put this whole country into a flame? Don't you know that this country from one end to the other believes that something is wrong? What an opportunity it would be for some man without conscience to spring up and say: "This is the way. Follow me!" —and lead in paths of destruction!

The old order changeth—changeth under our very eyes, not quietly and equably, but swiftly and with the noise and heat and tumult of reconstruction.

I suppose that all struggle for law has been conscious, that very little of it has been blind or merely instinctive. It is the fashion to say, as if with superior knowledge of affairs and of human weakness, that every age has been an age of transition, and that no age is more full of change than another; yet in very few ages of the world can the struggle for change have been so widespread, so deliberate, or upon so great a scale as in this in which we are taking part.

The transition we are witnessing is no equable transition of growth and normal alteration; no silent, unconscious unfolding of one age into another, its natural heir and successor. Society is looking itself over, in our day, from top to bottom; is making fresh and critical analysis of its very elements; is questioning its oldest practices as freely as its newest, scrutinizing every arrangement and motive of its life; and it stands ready to attempt nothing less than a radical reconstruction, which only frank and honest counsels and the forces of generous cooperation can hold back from becoming a revolution. We are in a temper to reconstruct economic society, as we were once in a temper to reconstruct political society, and political society may itself undergo a radical modification in the process. I doubt if any age was ever more conscious of its task or more unanimously desirous of radical and extended changes in its economic and political practice.

We stand in the presence of a revolution,—not a bloody revolution; America is not given to the spilling of blood,—but a silent revolution, whereby America will insist upon recovering in practice those ideals which she has always professed, upon securing a government devoted to the general interest and not to special interests.

We are upon the eve of a great reconstruction. It calls for creative statesmanship as no age has done since that great age in which we set up the government under which we live, that government which was the admiration of the world until it suffered wrongs to grow up under it which have made many of our own compatriots question the freedom of our institutions and preach revolution against them. I do not fear revolution. I have unshaken faith in the power of America to keep its self-possession. Revolution will come in peaceful guise, as it came when we put aside the crude government of the Confederation and created the great Federal Union which governs individuals, not States, and which has been these hundred and thirty years our vehicle of progress. Some radical changes we must make in our law and practice. Some reconstructions we must push forward, which a new age and new circumstances impose upon us. But we can do it all in calm and sober fashion, like statesmen and patriots.

I do not speak of these things in apprehension, because all is open and above-board. This is not a day in which great forces rally in secret. The whole stupendous program must be publicly planned and canvassed. Good temper, the wisdom that comes of sober counsel, the energy of thoughtful and unselfish men, the habit of cooperation and of compromise which has been bred in us by long years of free government, in which reason rather than passion has been made to prevail by the sheer virtue of candid and universal debate, will enable us to win through to still another great age without violence.

Philip Snowden

Philip Snowden (1864–1937), a British statesman and author, devoted most of his life to the Labor movement. In 1893 he joined the Independent Labor Party, and in 1906 won a parliamentary seat as a Laborite. He served as Chancellor of the Exchequer in the first and second Labor governments, directing his efforts to preserving free trade on the one hand, and to relieving the poor of their tax burden on the other. The extension of social democracy in the form of increased state activity in the social service field was also of primary interest to him. Snowden considered the war of 1914–1918 a crime against society which would deprive it of many of the gains it had made in recent years. To prevent future wars of equal or greater magnitude he advocated the extension of democracy into the field of diplomacy, insisting that the common people were as well qualified to control their foreign as their domestic interests. Thus his idea marked a further development of the democratic principle in an effort to solve social and economic problems on the international as well as on the domestic scene. Snowden wrote the essay Democracy and Publicity in Foreign Affairs in order to publicize his views, and selections from this work follow. In reading them note (1) Snowden's attitude toward secret diplomacy, (2) the two conclusions he reached from the diplomatic intrigues preceding the first world war, (3) the influence diplomats may have upon the course of democratic reform in the domestic sphere, (4) his answer to those who objected to the popular control of foreign affairs, (5) the reasons why he thought publicity in the conduct of foreign affairs would help to avert wars, (6) other advantages he cited which would result from greater publicity in diplomacy, and (7) evidences of Snowden's confidence in the people.

From: DEMOCRACY AND PUBLICITY IN FOREIGN AFFAIRS

The Great War will have been fought in vain if it has not taught the working classes of Europe the paramount necessity of publicity in foreign affairs. When the multi-coloured books containing such notes and dispatches as it has suited the several Governments to give to the world have been exhausted in the effort to apportion the responsibility for the war, the conviction must be left upon the mind of every impartial person that a system of diplomacy carried on in secret is an anachronism in an age when democratic government is, in every country in Europe, acknowledged, more or less, to be a sound principle for the control of domestic politics.

Unless it can be shown that there is something in the nature of foreign affairs which distinguishes them so radically from domestic politics that the accepted principles of national government are quite inapplicable to the control of foreign policy, then the present system of conducting foreign affairs stands condemned. But an examination of the arguments advanced against the popular control of foreign policy reveals the fact that they are precisely the same as those which have been invariably employed against every demand for the extension of political liberty and the enfranchisement of the people.

The case for the popular control of domestic policy can be stated in a simple but sufficient phrase. It is that every citizen of a State has a right to a voice in determining the extent of and the form in which the State shall interfere with his personal liberty. In these days the formula of democracy cannot be fully expressed in the old phrase, "Taxation without representation is tyranny." Every year the State interferes more and more with the life of the individual. It regulates his conditions of work, his business, his wages, his housing, his education, and disposes of an ever-increasing proportion of his personal property. Nobody publicly suggests nowadays that we should revert to the old political system under which the disposal and direction of the lives and liberties of the people was in the hands of a king or aristocracy. Because the acts of Government and Parliament affect the condition of the people it is an uncontroverted doctrine that the people should control the political affairs of the nation.

With the object-lesson of this war before the eyes of the nation the concern of the people in foreign affairs needs neither emphasis nor exposition. We see the lives of the people sacrificed by hundreds of thousands; taxation is being imposed upon all classes to an extent which seems likely to be a heavy, if not intolerable, burden upon them; we see, perhaps for our lifetime, the high hopes we had entertained of a great social reconstruction dissipated; we see the wealth and energy which should have been devoted to dealing with the problems of child life, of education, of public health, of unemployment, of housing, and with all those industrial and social evils in our land, devoted to the destruction of life and treasure on a scale so vast that the imagination reels before the spectacle. This surely is the concern of the masses of the people.

The war is the outcome of foreign policy. We are not concerned here to apportion the

Philip Snowden, "Democracy and Publicity in Foreign Affairs," in Charles Roden Buxton, ed., *Towards a Lasting Settlement*, George Allen and Unwin, Ltd., London, 1915, 179–200. Courtesy of George Allen and Unwin, Ltd.

blame or the responsibility. The war is the failure of diplomacy. It may be the fault of German, or French, or Russian, or Austrian, or British diplomacy, or of all in some measure. The system of secret diplomacy, the divorcement of democracy from the control of foreign affairs, is common to all European countries. The war is indisputable proof that this system of diplomacy has failed to maintain peace. It may, of course, be argued that any system of diplomacy or of the conduct of foreign affairs would not prevent war. But the first answer to that assertion is that this system has failed, and that the result of that failure is a calamity so colossal that no other system of diplomacy could be more disastrous.

Two conclusions, therefore, must be accepted—namely, that the results of foreign policy are of the most serious concern to the people of every country, and that whether it be possible or not to devise some system of foreign policy and of the conduct of foreign affairs which will prevent or lessen the disastrous results of international policy with which we are now painfully familiar, the present method is a failure. The failure of the present system of diplomacy justifies us in not only considering, but in demanding, some change in the control of foreign affairs.

The conduct of foreign affairs, in all European countries, has, up to the present, been in the hands of a small body of diplomatists, rulers, and ministers. Neither Parliament nor the people know what is going on in the secret chambers of diplomacy. The nations are committed to the most serious obligations without their knowledge. . . .

Such a method of conducting the foreign affairs of a country is pure autocracy. It places the destinies of a nation, the lives of the people, the hopes and welfare of the democracy entirely at the mercy of a small handful of persons. These persons have the power to thwart all the aims of the democracy in the sphere of domestic reform. So long as such a power is in the hands of a few persons democratic government is a mockery, and the working classes are the playthings of rulers and diplomatists. It is a monstrous thing that a score of European diplomatists and rulers should have the power to involve practically the whole of Europe in a devastating war. By such a system the nations of Europe are committed in secret to tremendous responsibilities, and when this system of diplomacy has brought the nations to the verge of war, the people are induced to support a war they have never wanted, and which they have not expected, by appeals to their fear, their party loyalty, and their national patriotism. Democratic government to be a reality must give to the people control over such matters as treaty obligations with foreign countries, and Parliament must be trusted with the final decision on such matters and with the supreme question of peace or war.

The objections which are brought against the demand for publicity in foreign affairs are precisely those which have done duty in every past campaign against the extension of the political franchise. It is said that the people do not understand foreign affairs; that it is essential that such matters must be conducted by men of special knowledge and training. But experience of democratic control of home affairs has falsified all the arguments and fears of the opponents of a popular franchise. It is not, of course, maintained that the democracy has risen to the full height of its responsibilities and opportunities. It has made many mistakes. It has often disappointed the hopes of ardent reformers. But with all its failings and weaknesses democratic control of home affairs has been a vast improvement, from the point of view of national welfare, on the former system of aristocratic government. The people are slowly learning to understand and to use their power, and every decade shows an advance in the intelligence of the democratic vote.

We are justified in feeling a very considerable amount of confidence that the system of democratic control which has for two generations been the method for conducting our national affairs would, if applied to the control of foreign affairs, be equally satisfactory. If the extension of the franchise has not altogether changed the character of parliamentary representation, it has changed the atmosphere and outlook of Parliament. In regard to home affairs the rights and wrongs of democracy have become the main subject-matter of political contention and of legislative effort. The point of view of the working classes receives a consideration in Parliament now which was not possible when the landed aristocracy shared with the plutocracy the control of national affairs.

But as the control of foreign affairs is still in the hands of the same class which formerly monopolized all political power, the conduct of foreign affairs and the personnel of the Diplomatic Service have remained unchanged, and are still the preserve of the landed and privileged classes. The natural result of that system is that these affairs have not been conducted in the democratic interests, but in the interests of the same class whose evil control of home affairs gave rise to the great popular demands for the democratic control of domestic politics. The popular control of home affairs has brought the democratic outlook and sympathy into legislation; and, in like manner, the popular control of foreign affairs would change the character of diplomacy. It would be recognized that the people were the controlling authority, and the administrators would naturally try to represent the people's point of view, instead of that of the financial and commercial interests. If it were known by our statesmen and diplomatists that the results of their diplomatic efforts were dependent for confirmation upon the approval of the popular representatives, they would strive to achieve such results as would be likely to secure that approval. In other words, diplomacy, knowing that democracy was its master, would endeavour to serve the interests of democracy. . . .

Though the instincts of the people are towards peace, it does not necessarily follow that, if there were publicity in the conduct of foreign affairs, there would be a greater likelihood of averting wars. But there are grounds for a reasonable supposition that such a result would ensue. Let us bear in mind the fact that secrecy in diplomacy has not prevented war. On the contrary, the policies which the rulers and diplomatists have pursued in recent years have brought about the Great War. If we agree with the popular view in this country that the Prussian militarists have for years been preparing for this war, it is certain that the great Social-Democratic party in Germany were ignorant of that movement. On the other hand,

if the people of Great Britain had been aware of the secret missions to foreign Courts for the purpose of furthering a policy for the isolation of Germany, it is probable that public opinion in this country would not have approved such a policy. That this diplomatic policy was being pursued behind the backs of Parliament and the people was well known in the inner circles of the European Courts. After the mischief has been done, these truths have been permitted to come to the light. For instance, the Belgian Minister in London (Count de Lalaing), in a dispatch to his Government dated May 24, 1907, said: "It is plain that official England is quietly pursuing a policy opposed to Germany and aimed at her isolation, and that King Edward has not hesitated to use his personal influence in the service of this scheme."

Such a policy as that was bound to eventuate in war. If these facts had been known to Parliament five years ago this war would never have taken place, for the danger of the policy of attempting to isolate Germany would have been realized, and before matters had developed to the point of hostilities the public opinion of Great Britain and Germany would have interfered. Similarly the secret mission of Lord Haldane to Berlin in 1912 failed because of its secrecy. The disclosures made by the German Chancellor and by Sir Edward Grey show that the margin of difference between the proposals of the two Governments was so small that if there had been an earnest desire on both sides to come to an agreement the difference could easily have been bridged. The secret knowledge and the suspicion in the minds of both parties—the knowledge of the German Chancellor of the secret intrigues which for years had been going on between England, France, Russia, and Spain for the isolation of Germany, and the knowledge in Sir Edward Grey's mind of the secret understanding between this country and France—made it impossible for a satisfactory agreement to be reached. But if the final differences could have been submitted to the respective Parliaments, if the people of Germany and England, both anxious for friendly relations, could have been consulted, if in an atmosphere of peace these matters could have been discussed with full knowledge, it is as certain as day follows night that some basis would have been found for a friendly settlement.

But even if that had not happened, the advantage of publicity would have been immense. If the negotiations had failed, plainly because Germany was determined to accept no agreement which would not give her a free hand against France and Russia, then the public in all European countries would have known the real facts. If war was seen to be inevitable, our Government would have been in a far stronger position. . . .

A great advantage which would come from publicity in foreign affairs would be in the parliamentary and public discussion which would arise. This public discussion would have a three times blessed result. It would have a restraining influence upon ministers and diplomats in the preliminary negotiations. The aloofness of foreign policy from parliamentary control and public discussion must have the effect of making foreign ministers and diplomatists rather contemptuous of Parliament and

people. It must subject them to a constant temptation to do things which they would not do if they knew that their action would come before a committee of Parliament and be subjected to criticism. It would put an end to the secret intrigues of financiers and armament interests to direct foreign policy. The second great benefit which publicity would confer would be that the discussion of questions of foreign relations would help to clear away mutual misunderstandings between nations, which are so often due to the suspicion which secrecy always encourages. This discussion would bring the peoples of the different nations more closely together, because no such discussion of international relations could take place without making plain the common interests of the workers. The third great benefit which would result would be the gradual education of the democracy in foreign politics, the expansion of their horizon, and the development of the international spirit and outlook. When the democracies have the international spirit there will be no more wars.

Lenin

Vladimir Ilich Lenin (1870–1924) was a Russian revolutionary who devoted his life to bringing about the destruction of the Czarist regime and the establishment of Marxian socialism in Russia. He participated in the abortive revolution of 1905, and then, of necessity, lived in exile, first in Germany and England, and later in Switzerland. He devoted his time to study, writing, and propagandist activities until 1917, when the Russian effort in the First World War collapsed and internal revolution broke out. With the help of the Germans, who sent him across Central Europe in a sealed car, Lenin returned to Russia to become a participant in the civil strife and later to be the first leader of Soviet Russia. Between the March and November revolutions of 1917, Lenin was forced into hiding because of the hostility of the provisional government toward him. During this period he wrote State and Revolution, largely as a reply to the revisionist socialists of Europe who, according to him, were distorting the teachings of Marx and Engels in regard to the "withering away of the state." His interpretation of Marx has provided one of the principal ideological supports for Russian Soviet Communism. In reading the following selections from this work note (1) Lenin's *method of dependence upon authority, (2) what he asserted the bourgeoisie were doing to Marxism, (3) Lenin's description of the Marxian characterization of the state, (4) his view of the essential power of the state, (5) the special privileges Lenin accorded to the police force, (6) what Marxism proposed the proletariat should do in regard to the state, (7) the author's explanation of what Marx meant by the state "withering away," (8) how, according to Lenin, this concept had been shorn of its revolutionary implications, (9) his analysis of the exact time when the state "becomes dormant," (10) what he meant by the evolutionary nature of the "withering away" process, (11) the "scientific" character of communism's evolution from capitalism, (12) Lenin's explanation of how the "dictatorship" of the proletariat fitted into the evolutionary development of communism, (13) Lenin's description of capitalist democracy, and (14) his characterization of the transitional "state."*

From: STATE AND REVOLUTION

What is now happening to Marx's doctrine has, in the course of history, often happened to the doctrines of other revolutionary thinkers and leaders of oppressed classes struggling for emancipation. During the lifetime of great revolutionaries, the oppressing classes have visited relentless persecution on them and received their teaching with the most savage hostility, the most furious hatred, the most ruthless campaign of lies and slanders. After their death, attempts are made to turn them into harmless icons, canonise them, and surround their *names* with a certain halo for the "consolation" of the oppressed classes and with the object of duping them, while at the same time emasculating and vulgarising the *real essence* of their revolutionary theories and blunting their revolutionary edge. At the present time, the bourgeoisie and the opportunists within the labour movement are co-operating in this work of adulterating Marxism. They omit, obliterate, and distort the revolutionary side of its teaching, its revolutionary soul. They push to the foreground and extol what is, or seems, acceptable to the bourgeoisie. All the social-chauvinists are now "Marxists"—joking aside! And more and more do German bourgeois professors,

erstwhile specialists in the demolition of Marx, speak now of the "national-German" Marx, who, they aver, has educated the labour unions which are so splendidly organised for conducting the present predatory war!

In such circumstances, the distortion of Marxism being so widespread, it is our first task to *resuscitate* the real teachings of Marx on the state. For this purpose it will be necessary to quote at length from the works of Marx and Engels themselves. . . .

Let us begin with the most popular of Engels' works, *Der Ursprung der Familie, des Privateigentums und des Staats,* the sixth edition of which was published in Stuttgart as far back as 1894. We must translate the quotations from the German originals, as the Russian translations, although very numerous, are for the most part either incomplete or very unsatisfactory.

Summarising his historical analysis Engels says:

The state is therefore by no means a power imposed on society from the outside; just as little is it "the reality of the moral idea," "the image and reality of reason," as Hegel asserted. Rather, it is a product of society at a certain stage of development; it is the admission that this society has be-

Vladimir Ilich Lenin, *State and Revolution,* International Publishers, New York, 1932, 7–10; 12–13; 15–17; 69–75. Courtesy of International Publishers.

come entangled in an insoluble contradiction with itself, that it is cleft into irreconcilable antagonisms which it is powerless to dispel. But in order that these antagonisms, classes with conflicting economic interests, may not consume themselves and society in sterile struggle, a power apparently standing above society becomes necessary, whose purpose is to moderate the conflict and keep it within the bounds of "order"; and this power arising out of society, but placing itself above it, and increasingly separating itself from it, is the state.

Here we have, expressed in all its clearness, the basic idea of Marxism on the question of the historical rôle and meaning of the state. The state is the product and the manifestation of the *irreconcilability* of class antagonisms. The state arises when, where, and to the extent that the class antagonisms *cannot* be objectively reconciled. And, conversely, the existence of the state proves that the class antagonisms *are* irreconcilable.

It is precisely on this most important and fundamental point that distortions of Marxism arise along two main lines.

On the one hand, the bourgeois, and particularly the petty-bourgeois, ideologists, compelled under the pressure of indisputable historical facts to admit that the state only exists where there are class antagonisms and the class struggle, "correct" Marx in such a way as to make it appear that the state is an organ for *reconciling* the classes. According to Marx, the state could neither arise nor maintain itself if a reconciliation of classes were possible. But with the petty-bourgeois and philistine professors and publicists, the state—and this frequently on the strength of benevolent references to Marx!—becomes a conciliator of the classes. According to Marx, the state is an organ of class *domination*, an organ of *oppression* of one class by another; its aim is the creation of "order" which legalises and perpetuates this oppression by moderating the collisions between the classes. But in the opinion of the petty-bourgeois politicians, order means reconciliation of the classes, and not oppression of one class by another; to moderate collisions does not mean, they say, to deprive the oppressed classes of certain definite means and methods of struggle for overthrowing the oppressors, but to practice reconciliation. . . .

Engels develops the conception of that "power" which is termed the state—a power arising from society, but placing itself above it and becoming more and more separated from it. What does this power mainly consist of? It consists of special bodies of armed men who have at their disposal prisons, etc.

We are justified in speaking of special bodies of armed men, because the public power peculiar to every state is not "absolutely identical" with the armed population, with its "self-acting armed organisation.". . .

For the maintenance of a special public force standing above society, taxes and state loans are needed.

Having at their disposal the public force and the right to exact taxes, the officials now stand as organs of society *above* society. The free, voluntary respect which was accorded to the organs of the gentilic form of government does not satisfy them, even if they could have it. . . .

Special laws are enacted regarding the sanctity and the inviolability of the officials. "The shabbiest police servant . . . has more authority" than the representative of the clan, but even the head of the military power of a civilised state "may well envy the least among the chiefs of the clan the unconstrained and uncontested respect which is paid to him.". . .

Engels' words regarding the "withering away" of the state enjoy such popularity, they are so often quoted, and they show so clearly the essence of the usual adulteration by means of which Marxism is made to look like opportunism, that we must dwell on them in detail. Let us quote the whole passage from which they are taken.

The proletariat seizes state power, and then transforms the means of production into state property. But in doing this, it puts an end to itself as the proletariat, it puts an end to all class differences and class antagonisms, it puts an end also to the state as the state. Former society, moving in class antagonisms, had need of the state, that is, an organisation of the exploiting class at each period for the maintenance of its external conditions of production; therefore, in particular, for the forcible holding down of the exploited class in the conditions of oppression (slavery, bondage or serfdom, wage-labour) determined by the existing mode of production. The state was the official representative of society as a whole, its embodiment in a visible corporate body; but it was this only in so far as it was the state of that class which itself, in its epoch, represented society as a whole: in ancient times, the state of the slave-owning citizens; in the Middle Ages, of the feudal nobility; in our epoch, of the bourgeoisie. When ultimately it becomes really representative of society as a whole, it makes itself superfluous. As soon as there is no longer any class of society to be held in subjection; as soon as, along with class domination and the struggle for individual existence based on the former anarchy of production, the collisions and excesses arising from these have also been abolished, there is nothing more to be repressed, and a special repressive force, a state, is no longer necessary. The first act in which the state really comes forward as the representative of society as a whole— the seizure of the means of production in the name of society—is at the same time its last independent act as a state. The interference of a state power in social relations becomes superfluous in one sphere after another, and then becomes dormant of itself. Government over persons is replaced by the administration of things and the direction of the processes of production. The state is not "abolished," *it withers away*. It is from this standpoint that we must appraise the phrase "people's free state"— both its justification at times for agitational purposes, and its ultimate scientific inadequacy—and also the demand of the so-called Anarchists that the state should be abolished overnight.

Without fear of committing an error, it may be said that of this argument by Engels so singularly rich in ideas, only one point has become an integral part of Socialist thought among modern Socialist parties, namely, that, unlike the Anarchist doctrine of the "abolition" of the state, according to Marx the state "withers away." To emasculate Marxism in such a manner is to reduce it to opportunism, for such an "interpretation" only leaves the hazy conception of a slow, even, gradual change, free from leaps and storms, free from revolution. The current popular conception, if one may say so, of the "withering away" of the state undoubtedly means a slurring over, if not a negation, of revolution.

Yet, such an "interpretation" is the crudest distortion of Marxism, which is advantageous only to the bourgeoisie; in point of theory, it is based on a disregard for the most important

circumstances and considerations pointed out in the very passage summarising Engels' ideas, which we have just quoted in full.

In the first place, Engels at the very outset of his argument says that, in assuming state power, the proletariat by that very act "puts an end to the state as the state." One is "not accustomed" to reflect on what this really means. Generally, it is either ignored altogether, or it is considered as a piece of "Hegelian weakness" on Engels' part. As a matter of fact, however, these words express succinctly the experience of one of the greatest proletarian revolutions—the Paris Commune of 1871, of which we shall speak in greater detail in its proper place. As a matter of fact, Engels speaks here of the destruction of the bourgeois state by the proletarian revolution, while the words about its withering away refer to the remains of *proletarian* statehood *after* the Socialist revolution. The bourgeois state does not "wither away," according to Engels, but is "put an end to" by the proletariat in the course of the revolution. What withers away after the revolution is the proletarian state or semi-state.

Secondly, the state is a "special repressive force." This splendid and extremely profound definition of Engels' is given by him here with complete lucidity. It follows from this that the "special repressive force" of the bourgeoisie for the suppression of the proletariat, of the millions of workers by a handful of the rich, must be replaced by a "special repressive force" of the proletariat for the suppression of the bourgeoisie (the dictatorship of the proletariat). It is just this that constitutes the destruction of "the state as the state." It is just this that constitutes the "act" of "the seizure of the means of production in the name of society." And it is obvious that such a substitution of one (proletarian) "special repressive force" for another (bourgeois) "special repressive force" can in no way take place in the form of a "withering away."

Thirdly, as to the "withering away" or, more expressively and colourfully, as to the state "becoming dormant," Engels refers quite clearly and definitely to the period *after* "the seizure of the means of production [by the state] in the name of society," that is *after* the Socialist revolution. We all know that the political form of the "state" at that time is complete democracy. But it never enters the head of any of the opportunists who shamelessly distort Marx that when Engels speaks here of the state "withering away," or "becoming dormant," he speaks of *democracy*. At first sight this seems very strange. But it is "unintelligible" only to one who has not reflected on the fact that democracy is *also* a state and that, consequently, democracy will *also* disappear when the state disappears. The bourgeois state can only be "put an end to" by a revolution. The state in general, *i.e.*, most complete democracy, can only "wither away.". . .

It is clear that there can be no question of defining the exact moment of the *future* withering away—the more so as it must obviously be a rather lengthy process. . . .

The whole theory of Marx is an application of the theory of evolution—in its most consistent, complete, well considered and fruitful form—to modern capitalism. It was natural for Marx to raise the question of applying this theory both to the *coming* collapse of capitalism and to the *future* evolution of *future* Communism.

On the basis of what *data* can the future evolution of future Communism be considered?

On the basis of the fact that *it has its origin* in capitalism, that it develops historically from capitalism, that it is the result of the action of a social force to which capitalism *has given birth*. There is no shadow of an attempt on Marx's part to conjure up a Utopia, to make idle guesses about that which cannot be known. Marx treats the question of Communism in the same way as a naturalist would treat the question of the evolution of, say, a new biological species, if he knew that such and such was its origin, and such and such the direction in which it changed. . . .

The first fact that has been established with complete exactness by the whole theory of evolution, by science as a whole—a fact which the Utopians forgot, and which is forgotten by the present-day opportunists who are afraid of the Socialist revolution—is that, historically, there

must undoubtedly be a special stage or epoch of *transition* from capitalism to Communism.

Between capitalist and Communist society—Marx continues—lies the period of the revolutionary transformation of the former into the latter. To this also corresponds a political transition period, in which the state can be no other than *the revolutionary dictatorship of the proletariat*.

This conclusion Marx bases on an analysis of the rôle played by the proletariat in modern capitalist society, on the data concerning the evolution of this society, and on the irreconcilability of the opposing interests of the proletariat and the bourgeoisie

Earlier the question was put thus: to attain its emancipation, the proletariat must overthrow the bourgeoisie, conquer political power and establish its own revolutionary dictatorship.

Now the question is put somewhat differently: the transition from capitalist society, developing towards Communism, towards a Communist society, is impossible without a "political transition period," and the state in this period can only be the revolutionary dictatorship of the proletariat.

What, then, is the relation of this dictatorship to democracy?

We have seen that the *Communist Manifesto* simply places side by side the two ideas: the "transformation of the proletariat into the ruling class" and the "establishment of democracy." On the basis of all that has been said above, one can define more exactly how democracy changes in the transition from capitalism to Communism.

In capitalist society, under the conditions most favourable to its development, we have more or less complete democracy in the democratic republic. But this democracy is always bound by the narrow framework of capitalist exploitation, and consequently always remains, in reality, a democracy for the minority, only for the possessing classes, only for the rich. Freedom in capitalist society always remains just about the same as it was in the ancient Greek republics: freedom for the slave-owners. The modern wage-slaves, owing to the conditions of capitalist exploitation, are so much crushed by want and poverty that "democracy is nothing to them," "politics is nothing to them"; that, in the ordinary peaceful course of events, the majority of the population is debarred from participating in social and political life.

The correctness of this statement is perhaps most clearly proved by Germany, just because in this state constitutional legality lasted and remained stable for a remarkably long time—for nearly half a century (1871–1914)—and because Social-Democracy in Germany during that time was able to achieve far more than in other countries in "utilising legality," and was able to organise into a political party a larger proportion of the working class than anywhere else in the world.

What, then, is this largest proportion of politically conscious and active wage-slaves that has so far been observed in capitalist society? One million members of the Social-Democratic Party—out of fifteen million wage-workers! Three million organised in trade unions—out of fifteen million!

Democracy for an insignificant minority, democracy for the rich—that is the democracy of capitalist society. If we look more closely into the mechanism of capitalist democracy, everywhere, both in the "petty"—so-called petty—details of the suffrage (residential qualification, exclusion of women, etc.), and in the technique of the representative institutions, in the actual obstacles to the right of assembly (public buildings are not for "beggars"!), in the purely capitalist organisation of the daily press, etc., etc.—on all sides we see restriction after restriction upon democracy. These restrictions, exceptions, exclusions, obstacles for the poor, seem slight, especially in the eyes of one who has himself never known want and has never been in close contact with the oppressed classes in their mass life (and nine-tenths, if not ninety-nine hundredths, of the bourgeois publicists and politicians are of this class), but in their sum total these restrictions exclude and squeeze out the poor from politics and from an active share in democracy.

Marx splendidly grasped this *essence* of capitalist democracy, when, in analysing the experience of the Commune, he said that the oppressed were allowed, once every few years, to decide which particular representatives of the oppressing class should be in parliament to represent and repress them!

But from this capitalist democracy—inevitably narrow, subtly rejecting the poor, and therefore hypocritical and false to the core—progress does not march onward, simply, smoothly and directly, to "greater and greater democracy," as the liberal professors and petty-bourgeois opportunists would have us believe. No, progress marches onward, *i.e.*, towards Communism, through the dictatorship of the proletariat; it cannot do otherwise, for there is no one else and no other way to *break the resistance* of the capitalist exploiters.

But the dictatorship of the proletariat—*i.e.*, the organisation of the vanguard of the oppressed as the ruling class for the purpose of crushing the oppressors—cannot produce merely an expansion of democracy. *Together* with an immense expansion of democracy which *for the first time* becomes democracy for the poor, democracy for the people, and not democracy for the rich folk, the dictatorship of the proletariat produces a series of restrictions of liberty in the case of the oppressors, the exploiters, the capitalists. We must crush them in order to free humanity from wage-slavery; their resistance must be broken by force; it is clear that where there is suppression there is also violence, there is no liberty, no democracy.

Engels expressed this splendidly in his letter to Bebel when he said, as the reader will remember, that "as long as the proletariat still *needs* the state, it needs it not in the interests of freedom, but for the purpose of crushing its antagonists; and as soon as it becomes possible to speak of freedom, then the state, as such, ceases to exist."

Democracy for the vast majority of the people, and suppression by force, *i.e.*, exclusion from democracy, of the exploiters and oppressors of the people—this is the modification of democracy during the *transition* from capitalism to Communism.

Only in Communist society, when the resistance of the capitalists has been completely broken, when the capitalists have disappeared, when there are no classes (*i.e.*, there is no difference between the members of society in their relation to the social means of production), *only then* "the state ceases to exist," and *"it becomes possible to speak of freedom."* Only then a really full democracy, a democracy without any exceptions, will be possible and will be realised. And only then will democracy itself begin to *wither away* due to the simple fact that, freed from capitalist slavery, from the untold horrors, savagery, absurdities and infamies of capitalist exploitation, people will gradually *become accustomed* to the observance of the elementary rules of social life that have been known for centuries and repeated for thousands of years in all school books; they will become accustomed to observing them without force, without compulsion, without subordination, without the *special apparatus* for compulsion which is called the state.

The expression "the state *withers away*," is very well chosen, for it indicates both the gradual and the elemental nature of the process. Only habit can, and undoubtedly will, have such an effect; for we see around us millions of times how readily people get accustomed to observe the necessary rules of life in common, if there is no exploitation, if there is nothing that causes indignation, that calls forth protest and revolt and has to be *suppressed.*

Thus, in capitalist society, we have a democracy that is curtailed, poor, false; a democracy only for the rich, for the minority. The dictatorship of the proletariat, the period of transition to Communism, will, for the first time, produce democracy for the people, for the majority, side by side with the necessary suppression of the minority—the exploiters. Communism alone is capable of giving a really complete democracy, and the more complete it is the more quickly will it become unnecessary and wither away of itself.

In other words: under capitalism we have a state in the proper sense of the word, that is, special machinery for the suppression of one class by another, and of the majority by the minority at that. Naturally, for the successful discharge of such a task as the systematic suppression by the exploiting minority of the exploited majority, the greatest ferocity and savagery of suppression are required, seas of blood are required, through which mankind is marching in slavery, serfdom, and wage-labour.

Again, during the *transition* from capitalism to Communism, suppression is *still* necessary; but it is the suppression of the minority of exploiters by the majority of exploited. A special apparatus, special machinery for suppression, the "state," is *still* necessary, but this is now a transitional state, no longer a state in the usual sense, for the suppression of the minority of exploiters, by the majority of the wage slaves *of yesterday,* is a matter comparatively so easy, simple and natural that it will cost far less bloodshed than the suppression of the risings of slaves, serfs or wage labourers, and will cost mankind far less. This is compatible with the diffusion of democracy among such an overwhelming majority of the population, that the need for *special machinery* of suppression will begin to disappear. The exploiters are, naturally, unable to suppress the people without a most complex machinery for performing this task; but *the people* can suppress the exploiters even with very simple "machinery," almost without any "machinery," without any special apparatus, by the simple *organisation of the armed masses* (such as the Soviets of Workers' and Soldiers' Deputies, we may remark, anticipating a little).

Finally, only Communism renders the state absolutely unnecessary, for there is *no one* to be suppressed—"no one" in the sense of a *class,* in the sense of a systematic struggle with a definite section of the population. We are not Utopians, and we do not in the least deny the possibility and inevitability of excesses on the part of *individual persons,* nor the need to suppress *such* excesses. But, in the first place, no special machinery, no special apparatus of repression is needed for this; this will be done by the armed people itself, as simply and as readily as any crowd of civilised people, even in modern society, parts a pair of combatants or does not allow a woman to be outraged. And, secondly, we know that the fundamental social cause of excesses which consist in violating the rules of social life is the exploitation of the masses, their want and their poverty. With the removal of this chief cause, excesses will inevitably begin to *"wither away."* We do not know how quickly and in what succession, but we know that they will wither away. With their withering away, the state will also *wither away.* . . .

Government of the Soviet Union

║n the Soviet constitutions of 1918 and 1924, distinct limitations were placed upon the political rights and liberties of those Russians who were considered to be unfriendly to communism. These instruments of government were designed to establish the "dictatorship of the proletariat" and specifically of industrial workers. This group was given marked advantages since it had been most oppressed by the old order and had the most enthusiasm for establishing the new. In 1936, as a result of the success of social planning, those in control of Russian affairs decided that sufficient progress had been made toward socialism and the classless society to warrant the adoption of a more liberal constitution. It was designed partially to ease internal discontent and partially to serve as a propaganda instrument abroad. It was made definitely flexible in character in order to serve the immediate purposes of the communist authorities. In reading the following selections from the Soviet Constitution of December 6, 1936, note (1) the social and economic foundations of the USSR, (2) the extent to which private economy and ownership was permitted, (3) the nature of the political organization of the USSR, (4) the "rights" included in the civil liberties of Russians, (5) the facilities provided to ensure these rights, (6) the provisions included which concern the Communist Party, (7) evidences of nationalism, (8) the provisions regarding voting and elections, and (9) the responsibilities of the elected deputy.

From: THE SOVIET CONSTITUTION OF 1936

SOCIAL ORGANIZATION

Article 1. The Union of Soviet Socialist Republics (USSR) is a socialist state of workers and peasants.

Article 2. The political foundation of the USSR is formed by the Soviets of toilers' deputies which have grown and become strong as a result of the overthrow of the power of the landlords and capitalists and the conquests of the dictatorship of the proletariat.

Article 3. All power in the USSR belongs to the toilers of the town and village in the form of Soviets of toilers' deputies.

Article 4. The economic foundation of the USSR consists in the socialist system of economy and socialist ownership of the implements and means of production, firmly established as a result of the liquidation of the capitalist system of economy, the abolition of private ownership of the implements and means of production and the abolition of exploitation of man by man.

Article 5. Socialist ownership in the USSR has either the form of state ownership (public property) or the form of co-operative and collective-farm ownership (property of individual collective farms, property of co-operative associations).

Article 6. The land, its deposits, waters, for-

Sir Bernard Pares, ed., "Text of the New Constitution of the U.S.S.R.," in *International Conciliation*, February, 1937, no. 327, Articles 1–13; 118–142. Courtesy of the Carnegie Endowment for International Peace.

ests, mills, factories, mines, railway, water and air transport, banks, means of communication, large agricultural enterprises organized by the state (state farms, machine-tractor stations, and so on), as well as communal enterprises and the essential part of housing in the cities and industrial centers, are state property, that is, public property.

Article 7. Public enterprises in collective farms and co-operative organizations, with their livestock and implements, products produced by the collective farms and co-operative organizations as well as their public buildings, constitute the public, socialist property of the collective farms and co-operative organizations.

Each collective farm household, in addition to the basic income from the socialized collective-farm economy, has for its own use a plot of land attached to the household and, as individual property, subsidiary establishments on the land attached to the household, a house, productive livestock and poultry, and minor agricultural implements—in accordance with the statutes of the agricultural *artel*.

Article 8. The land occupied by collective farms is secured to them for use without payment and time limit, that is, in perpetuity.

Article 9. Alongside the socialist system of economy, which is the dominant form of economy in the USSR, the law allows small private economy of individual peasants and handicraftsmen based on individual labor and excluding the exploitation of the labor of others.

Article 10. The right of personal ownership by citizens of their income from work and savings, home and auxiliary household economy, of objects of domestic and household economy, of objects of personal use and comfort, as well as the right of inheritance of the personal property of citizens—is protected by law.

Article 11. The economic life of the USSR is determined and directed by the national economic state plan for the purposes of increasing public wealth, of a steady rise in the material and cultural level of the toilers, of strengthening the independence of the USSR and its defense capacity.

Article 12. Work in the USSR is the obligation and matter of honor of each citizen capable of working, according to the principle: "He who does not work shall not eat." In the USSR the principle of socialism is being realized: "From each according to his ability, to each according to his work."

STATE ORGANIZATION

Article 13. The USSR is a federal state, formed on the basis of the voluntary association of the Soviet Socialist Republics with equal rights:

Russian Soviet Federated Socialist Republic
Ukrainian Soviet Socialist Republic
White-Russian Soviet Socialist Republic
Azerbaizhan Soviet Socialist Republic
Georgian Soviet Socialist Republic
Armenian Soviet Socialist Republic
Turkmenian Soviet Socialist Republic
Uzbek Soviet Socialist Republic
Tadzhik Soviet Socialist Republic
Kazakh Soviet Socialist Republic
Kirghiz Soviet Socialist Republic

BASIC RIGHTS AND OBLIGATIONS OF CITIZENS

Article 118. Citizens of the USSR have the right to work, that is the right to receive guaranteed work with payment for their work in accordance with its quantity and quality.

The right to work is ensured by the socialist organization of national economy, the steady growth of the productive forces of Soviet society, the absence of economic crises, and the abolition of unemployment.

Article 119. Citizens of the USSR have the right to rest.

The right to rest is ensured by the reduction of the working day to seven hours for the overwhelming majority of the workers, establishment of annual vacations with pay for workers and employees, and provision for a wide network of sanatoria, rest-homes and clubs for the accommodation of the toilers.

Article 120. Citizens of the USSR have the right to material security in old age as well as in the event of sickness and loss of capacity to work.

This right is ensured by the wide development of social insurance of workers and employees at the expense of the state, free medical aid, and the provision of a wide network of health resorts for the use of the toilers.

Article 121. Citizens of the USSR have the right to education.

This right is ensured by universal compulsory elementary education, free of charge, including higher education, by the system of state stipends for the overwhelming majority of students in higher schools, instruction in schools in the native language, and organization of free industrial, technical and agronomic education for the toilers at the factories, state farms, machine-tractor stations, and collective farms.

Article 122. Women in the USSR are accorded equal rights with men in all fields of economic, state, cultural, social, and political life.

The possibility of realizing these rights of women is ensured by affording women equally with men the right to work, payment for work, rest, social insurance and education, state protection of the interests of mother and child, granting pregnancy leave with pay, and the provision for a wide network of maternity homes, nurseries and kindergartens.

Article 123. The equality of the rights of citizens of the USSR, irrespective of their nationality or race, in all fields of economic, state, cultural, social and political life, is an irrevocable law.

Any direct or indirect restriction of these rights, or conversely, the establishment of direct or indirect privileges for citizens on account of the race or nationality to which they belong, as well as any propagation of racial or national exceptionalism or hatred and contempt, is punishable by law.

Article 124. To ensure to citizens freedom of conscience the church in the USSR is separated from the state and the school from the church. Freedom to perform religious rites and freedom of anti-religious propaganda is recognized for all citizens.

Article 125. In accordance with the interests of the toilers and for the purpose of strengthening the socialist system, the citizens of the USSR are guaranteed:

(a) Freedom of speech;

(b) Freedom of the press;

(c) Freedom of assembly and meetings;

(d) Freedom of street processions and demonstrations.

These rights of the citizens are ensured by placing at the disposal of the toilers and their organizations printing presses, supplies of paper, public buildings, streets, means of communication and other material conditions necessary for their realization.

Article 126. In accordance with the interests of the toilers and for the purpose of developing the organizational self-expression and political activity of the masses of the people, citizens of the USSR are ensured the right of combining in public organizations: trade unions, co-operative associations, youth organizations, sport and defense organizations, cultural, technical and scientific societies, and for the most active and conscientious citizens from the ranks of the working class and other strata of the toilers, of uniting in the All-Union Communist Party (of Bolsheviks), which is the vanguard of the toilers in their struggle for strengthening and developing the socialist system and which represents the leading nucleus of all organizations of the toilers, both public and state.

Article 127. The citizens of the USSR are ensured the inviolability of the person. No one may be subjected to arrest except upon the decision of a court or with the sanction of the prosecutor.

Article 128. The inviolability of the homes of citizens and the secrecy of correspondence are protected by law.

Article 129. The USSR grants the right of asylum to foreign citizens persecuted for defending the interests of the toilers or for their scientific activity or for their struggle for national liberation.

Article 130. Every citizen of the USSR is obliged to observe the constitution of the Union of Soviet Socialist Republics, to carry out the laws, observe labor discipline, honestly fulfill his social duties, and respect the rules of the socialist community.

Article 131. Every citizen of the USSR is obliged to safeguard and consolidate public, socialist property as the sacred and inviolable foundation of the Soviet system, as the source of wealth and might of the fatherland, as the source of the prosperous cultural life of all the toilers. Persons attempting to violate public socialist property are enemies of the people.

Article 132. Universal military service is the law.

Military service in the Workers' and Peasants' Red Army represents the honorable duty of the citizens of the USSR.

Article 133. The defense of the fatherland is the sacred duty of every citizen of the USSR. Treason to the fatherland: violation of oath, desertion to the enemy, impairing the military might of the state, espionage—is punishable with the full severity of the law as the most heinous crime.

ELECTORAL SYSTEM

Article 134. Deputies to all Soviets of toilers' deputies, the Supreme Council of the USSR, Supreme Councils of the Union republics, territorial and provincial Soviets of toilers' deputies, Supreme Councils of autonomous republics, Soviets of toilers' deputies of autonomous provinces, regional, district, city and village Soviets of toilers' deputies (including stanitsas, villages, khutors, kishlaks, auls), are elected by the electors on the basis of universal, equal and direct suffrage by secret ballot.

Article 135. Elections of the deputies are universal: all citizens of the USSR who have reached the age of 18, irrespective of race or nationality, religion, educational qualifications, residential qualifications, social origin, property status and past activity, have the right to participate in elections of deputies and to be elected, with the exception of the mentally deficient and persons deprived of electoral rights by the courts.

Article 136. Elections of deputies are equal: every citizen has one vote; all citizens participate in the elections on equal terms.

Article 137. Women have the right to elect and be elected on equal terms with men.

Article 138. Citizens serving in the ranks of the Red Army have the right to elect and be elected on equal terms with all other citizens.

Article 139. Elections of deputies are direct: elections to all Soviets of toilers' deputies from the village and city Soviets of toilers' deputies up to the Supreme Council of the USSR are affected by the citizens voting directly.

Article 140. Voting at elections of deputies is secret.

Article 141. Candidates are put forward for election according to electoral districts.

The right to put forward candidates is granted to social organizations and societies of the toilers: Communist Party organizations, trade unions, co-operatives, youth organizations and cultural societies.

Article 142. Every deputy is obliged to render account to the electors of his work and the work of the Soviet of toilers' deputies, and may at any time be recalled in the manner established by law on the decision of a majority of the electors.

Benito Mussolini

Benito Mussolini (1883–1945) was an Italian editor and political leader who spent most of his early life working for radical political movements. While still a young man he became interested in socialism, and it was because of its principles that he left his native land in 1902 in order to avoid military service. He spent some years in Switzerland, studying and participating in various working-class activities, but in 1904 he returned to Italy and for several years served on the editorial staff of various left-wing periodicals. In 1912 he established his own newspaper, Il Popolo d'Italia, which he used, strangely enough, to agitate for Italy's entrance into the First World War on the allied side. When she did, he served for two years in the army before returning to his editorial duties. In 1919 he formed a group of war veterans to oppose the Versailles treaty, which Mussolini characterized as a fraud perpetrated against the Italian people. This organization developed into the Fascist

Party, which in 1922 took advantage of the postwar economic and political unrest to seize control of the government in Rome. Thus began the fascist regime in Italy, and with it the gradual development of fascist doctrine. In 1932, Mussolini contributed to the Enciclopedia Italiana an article in which he described the philosophic basis of fascism. In reading this article note (1) Mussolini's description of his doctrine in 1919, (2) under what circumstances fascist doctrine emerged, (3) its attitude toward peace and war, (4) the Machiavellian attitude fascism assumed toward neighboring nations, (5) Mussolini's views on Marxian socialism, (6) his refutation of democracy, (7) the historical analysis he made of liberalism, (8) the eclectic and pragmatic aspects of fascism, (9) the foundation of fascism in the state, (10) the organic character of the fascist state, (11) the relation of the individual to the state, (12) fascist position on religion, and (13) the importance of imperialism to the strength of the fascist state.

From: THE POLITICAL AND SOCIAL DOCTRINE OF FASCISM

When, in the now distant March of 1919, I summoned a meeting at Milan through the columns of the *Popolo d'Italia* of the surviving members of the Interventionist Party who had themselves been in action, and who had followed me since the creation of the Fascist Revolutionary Party (which took place in the January of 1915), I had no specific doctrinal attitude in my mind. I had a living experience of one doctrine only—that of Socialism, from 1903–4 to the winter of 1914—that is to say, about a decade: and from Socialism itself, even though I had taken part in the movement first as a member of the rank and file and then later as a leader, yet I had no experience of its doctrine in practice. My own doctrine, even in this period, had always been a doctrine of action. A unanimous, universally accepted theory of Socialism did not exist after 1905, when the revisionist movement began in Germany under the leadership of Bernstein, while under pressure of the tendencies of the time, a Left Revolutionary movement also appeared, which though never getting further than talk in Italy, in Russian Socialistic circles laid the foundations of Bolshevism. Reformation, Revolution,

Centralization—already the echoes of these terms are spent—while in the great stream of Fascism are to be found ideas which began with Sorel, Peguy, with Lagerdelle in the "Mouvement Socialiste," and with the Italian trades-union movement which throughout the period 1904–14 was sounding a new note in Italian Socialist circles (already weakened by the betrayal of Giolitti) through Olivetti's *Pagine Libre,* Orano's *La Lupa,* and Enrico Leone's *Divenire Sociale.*

After the War, in 1919, Socialism was already dead as a doctrine: it existed only as a hatred. There remained to it only one possibility of action, especially in Italy, reprisals against those who had desired the War and who must now be made to "expiate" its results. The *Popolo d'Italia* was then given the subtitle of "The newspaper of ex-servicemen and producers," and the word producers was already the expression of a mental attitude. Fascism was not the nursling of a doctrine worked out beforehand with detailed elaboration; it was born of the need for action and it was itself from the beginning practical rather than theoretical; it was not merely another political

Benito Mussolini, "The Political and Social Doctrine of Fascism," in *International Conciliation,* January, 1935, no. 306, 5–17. Courtesy of the Hogarth Press, Ltd. and the Division of Intercourse and Education of the Carnegie Endowment for International Peace.

party but, even in the first two years, in opposition to all political parties as such, and itself a living movement. The name which I then gave to the organization fixed its character. And yet, if one were to re-read, in the now dusty columns of that date, the report of the meeting in which the *Fasci Italiana di combattimento* were constituted, one would there find no ordered expression of doctrine, but a series of aphorisms, anticipations, and aspirations which, when refined by time from the original ore, were destined after some years to develop into an ordered series of doctrinal concepts, forming the Fascists political doctrine—different from all others either of the past or the present day.

"If the bourgeoisie," I said then, "think that they will find lightning-conductors in us, they are the more deceived; we must start work at once. . . . We want to accustom the working-class to real and effectual leadership, and also to convince them that it is no easy thing to direct an industry or a commercial enterprise successfully. . . . We shall combat every retrograde idea, technical or spiritual. . . . When the succession to the seat of government is open, we must not be unwilling to fight for it. We must make haste; when the present régime breaks down, we must be ready at once to take its place. It is we who have the right to the succession, because it was we who forced the country into the War, and led her to victory. The present method of political representation cannot suffice, we must have a representation direct from the individuals concerned. It may be objected against this program that it is a return to the conception of the corporation, but that is no matter. . . . Therefore, I desire that this assembly shall accept the revindication of national trades-unionism from the economic point of view. . . ."

Now is it not a singular thing that even on this first day in the Piazza San Sepolcro that word "corporation" arose, which later, in the course of the Revolution, came to express one of the creations of social legislation at the very foundation of the régime?

The years which preceded the march to Rome were years of great difficulty, during which the necessity for action did not permit of research or any complete elaboration of doctrine. The battle had to be fought in the towns and villages. There was much discussion, but—what was more important and more sacred—men died. They knew how to die. Doctrine, beautifully defined and carefully elucidated, with headlines and paragraphs, might be lacking; but there was to take its place something more decisive—Faith. Even so, anyone who can recall the events of the time through the aid of books, articles, votes of congresses, and speeches of great and minor importance—anyone who knows how to research and weigh evidence—will find that the fundamentals of doctrine were cast during the years of conflict. It was precisely in those years that Fascist thought armed itself, was refined, and began the great task of organization. The problem of the relation between the individual citizen and the State; the allied problems of authority and liberty; political and social problems as well as those specifically national—a solution was being sought for all these while at the same time the struggle against Liberalism, Democracy, Socialism, and the Masonic bodies was being carried on, contemporaneously with the "punitive expedition." But, since there was inevitably some lack of system, the adversaries of Fascism have disingenuously denied that it had any capacity to produce a doctrine of its own, though that doctrine was growing and taking shape under their very eyes, even though tumultuously; first, as happens to all ideas in their beginnings, in the aspect of a violent and dogmatic negation, and then in the aspect of positive construction which has found its realization in the laws and institutions of the régime as enacted successively in the years 1926, 1927, and 1928.

Fascism is now a completely individual thing, not only as a régime but as a doctrine. And this means that today Fascism, exercising its critical sense upon itself and upon others, has formed its own distinct and peculiar point of view, to which it can refer and upon which, therefore, it can act in the face of all problems, practical or intellectual, which confront the world.

And above all, Fascism, the more it considers and observes the future and the development of humanity quite apart from political considerations of the moment, believes neither in the possibility nor the utility of perpetual peace. It thus repudiates the doctrine of Pacifism—born of a renunciation of the struggle and an act of cowardice in the face of sacrifice. War alone brings up to its highest tension all human energy and puts the stamp of nobility upon the peoples who have the courage to meet it. All other trials are substitutes, which never really put men into the position where they have to make the great decision—the alternative of life or death. Thus a doctrine which is founded upon this harmful postulate of peace is hostile to Fascism. And thus hostile to the spirit of Fascism, though accepted for what use they can be in dealing with particular political situations, are all the international leagues and societies which, as history will show, can be scattered to the winds when once strong national feeling is aroused by any motive—sentimental, ideal, or practical. This anti-pacifist spirit is carried by Fascism even into the life of the individual; the proud motto of the *Squadrista,* "Me ne frego," written on the bandage of the wound, is an act of philosophy not only stoic, the summary of a doctrine not only political—it is the education to combat, the acceptation of the risks which combat implies, and a new way of life for Italy. Thus the Fascist accepts life and loves it, knowing nothing of and despising suicide: he rather conceives of life as duty and struggle and conquest, life which should be high and full, lived for oneself, but above all for others—those who are at hand and those who are far distant, contemporaries, and those who will come after.

This "demographic" policy of the régime is the result of the above premise. Thus the Fascist loves in actual fact his neighbor, but this "neighbor" is not merely a vague and undefined concept, this love for one's neighbor puts no obstacle in the way of necessary educational severity, and still less to differentiation of status and to physical distance. Fascism repudiates any universal embrace, and in order to live worthily in the community of civilised peoples watches its contemporaries with vigilant eyes, takes good note of their state of mind and, in the changing trend of their interests, does not allow itself to be deceived by temporary and fallacious appearances.

Such a conception of life makes Fascism the complete opposite of that doctrine, the base of so-called scientific and Marxian Socialism, the materialist conception of history; according to which the history of human civilization can be explained simply through the conflict of interests among the various social groups and by the change and development in the means and instruments of production. That the changes in the economic field—new discoveries of raw materials, new methods of working them, and the inventions of science—have their importance no one can deny; but that these factors are sufficient to explain the history of humanity excluding all others is an absurd delusion. Fascism, now and always, believes in holiness and in heroism; that is to say, in actions influenced by no economic motive, direct or indirect. And if the economic conception of history be denied, according to which theory men are no more than puppets, carried to and fro by the waves of chance, while the real directing forces are quite out of their control, it follows that the existence of an unchangeable and unchanging class-war is also denied—the natural progeny of the economic conception of history. And above all Fascism denies that class-war can be the preponderant force in the transformation of society. These two fundamental concepts of Socialism being thus refuted, nothing is left of it but the sentimental aspiration—as old as humanity itself—towards a social convention in which the sorrows and sufferings of the humblest shall be alleviated. But here again Fascism repudiates the conception of "economic" happiness, to be realized by Socialism and, as it were, at a given moment in economic evolution to assure to everyone the maximum of well-being. Fascism denies the materialist conception of happiness as a possibility, and abandons it to its inventors, the economists of the first half of the nineteenth century: that is to say, Fascism denies the validity of the equation, well-being–happiness, which would reduce men to the level of animals, caring for one thing only—to be fat and well-fed—and would thus degrade humanity to a purely physical existence.

After Socialism, Fascism combats the whole complex system of democratic ideology, and repudiates it, whether in its theoretical premises or in its practical application. Fascism denies that the majority, by the simple fact that it is a majority, can direct human society; it denies that numbers alone can govern by means of a periodical consultation, and it affirms the immutable, beneficial, and fruitful inequality of mankind, which can never be permanently leveled through the mere operation of a mechanical process such as universal suffrage. The democratic régime may be defined as from time to time giving the people the illusion of sovereignty, while the real effective sovereignty lies in the hands of other concealed and irresponsible forces. Democracy is a régime nominally without a king, but it is ruled by many kings—more absolute, tyrannical, and ruinous than one sole king, even though a tyrant. This explains why Fascism, having first in 1922 (for reasons of expediency) assumed an attitude tending towards republicanism, renounced this point of view before the march to Rome; being convinced that the question of political form is not today of prime importance, and after having studied the examples of monarchies and republics past and present reached the conclusion that monarchy or republicanism are not to be judged, as it were, by an absolute standard; but that they represent forms in which the evolution—political, historical, traditional, or psychological—of a particular country has expressed itself. . . .

Fascism has taken up an attitude of complete opposition to the doctrines of Liberalism, both in the political field and the field of economics. There should be no undue exaggeration (simply with the object of immediate success in controversy) of the importance of Liberalism in the last century, nor should what was but one among many theories which appeared in that period be put forward as a religion for humanity for all time, present and to come. Liberalism only flourished for half a century. It was born in 1830 in reaction against the Holy Alliance, which had been formed with the object of diverting the destinies of Europe back to the period before 1789, and the highest point of its success was the year 1848, when even Pius IX was a Liberal. Immediately after that date it began to decay, for if the year 1848 was a year of light and hope, the following year, 1849, was a year of darkness and tragedy. The Republic of Rome

was dealt a mortal blow by a sister republic—that of France—and in the same year Marx launched the gospel of the Socialist religion, the famous Communist Manifesto. In 1851 Napoleon III carried out his far from Liberal *coup d'état* and reigned in France until 1870, when he was deposed by a popular movement as the consequence of a military defeat which must be counted as one of the most decisive in history. The victor was Bismarck, who knew nothing of the religion of liberty, or the prophets by which that faith was revealed. And it is symptomatic that such a highly civilized people as the Germans were completely ignorant of the religion of liberty during the whole of the nineteenth century. It was nothing but a parenthesis, represented by that body which has been called "The ridiculous Parliament of Frankfort," which lasted only for a short period. Germany attained her national unity quite outside the doctrines of Liberalism—a doctrine which seems entirely foreign to the German mind, a mind essentially monarchic—while Liberalism is the logical and, indeed, historical forerunner of anarchy. The stages in the achievement of German unity are the three wars of '64, '66, and '70, which were guided by such "Liberals" as Von Moltke and Bismarck. As for Italian unity, its debt to Liberalism is completely inferior in contrast to that which it owes to the work of Mazzini and Garibaldi, who were not Liberals. Had it not been for the intervention of the anti-Liberal Napoleon, we should not have gained Lombardy; and without the help of the again anti-Liberal Bismarck at Sadowa and Sedan it is very probable that we should never have gained the province of Venice in '66, or been able to enter Rome in '70. From 1870 to 1914 a period began during which even the very high priests of the religion themselves had to recognize the gathering twilight of their faith —defeated as it was by the decadence of literature and atavism in practice—that is to say, Nationalism, Futurism, Fascism. The era of Liberalism, after having accumulated an infinity of Gordian knots, tried to untie them in the slaughter of the World War—and never has any religion demanded of its votaries such a monstrous sacrifice. Perhaps the Liberal Gods were athirst for blood? But now, today, the

Liberal faith must shut the doors of its deserted temples, deserted because the peoples of the world realize that its worship—agnostic in the field of economics and indifferent in the field of politics and morals—will lead, as it has already led, to certain ruin. In addition to this, let it be pointed out that all the political hopes of the present day are anti-Liberal, and it is therefore supremely ridiculous to try to classify this sole creed as outside the judgment of history, as though history were a hunting ground reserved for the professors of Liberalism alone—as though Liberalism were the final unalterable verdict of civilization.

But the Fascist negation of Socialism, Democracy, and Liberalism must not be taken to mean that Fascism desires to lead the world back to the state of affairs before 1789, the date which seems to be indicated as the opening years of the succeeding semi-Liberal century: we do not desire to turn back; Fascism has not chosen De Maistre for its high-priest. Absolute monarchy has been and can never return, any more than blind acceptance of ecclesiastical authority.

So, too, the privileges of the feudal system "have been," and the division of society into castes impenetrable from outside, and with no intercommunication among themselves: the Fascist conception of authority has nothing to do with such a polity. A party which entirely governs a nation is a fact entirely new to history, there are no possible references or parallels. Fascism uses in its construction whatever elements in the Liberal, Social, or Democratic doctrines still have a living value; it maintains what may be called the certainties which we owe to history, but it rejects all the rest—that is to say, the conception that there can be any doctrine of unquestioned efficacy for all times and all peoples. Given that the nineteenth century was the century of Socialism, of Liberalism, and of Democracy, it does not necessarily follow that the twentieth century must also be a century of Socialism, Liberalism, and Democracy: political doctrines pass, but humanity remains; and it may rather be expected that this will be a century of authority, a century of the Left, a century of Fascism. For if the nineteenth century was a century of individualism (Liberalism always signifying individualism)

it may be expected that this will be the century of collectivism, and hence the century of the State. It is a perfectly logical deduction that a new doctrine can utilize all the still vital elements of previous doctrines.

No doctrine has ever been born completely new, completely defined and owing nothing to the past; no doctrine can boast a character of complete originality; it must always derive, if only historically, from the doctrines which have preceded it and develop into further doctrines which will follow. Thus the scientific Socialism of Marx is the heir of the Utopian Socialism of Fourier, of the Owens and of Saint-Simon; thus again the Liberalism of the eighteenth century is linked with all the advanced thought of the seventeenth century, and thus the doctrines of Democracy are the heirs of the Encyclopedists. Every doctrine tends to direct human activity towards a determined objective; but the action of men also reacts upon the doctrine, transforms it, adapts it to new needs, or supersedes it with something else. A doctrine then must be no mere exercise in words, but a living act; and thus the value of Fascism lies in the fact that it is veined with pragmatism, but at the same time has a will to exist and a will to power, a firm front in face of the reality of "violence."

The foundation of Fascism is the conception of the State, its character, its duty, and its aim. Fascism conceives of the State as an absolute, in comparison with which all individuals or groups are relative, only to be conceived of in their relation to the State. The conception of the Liberal State is not that of a directing force, guiding the play and development, both material and spiritual, of a collective body, but merely a force limited to the function of recording results: on the other hand, the Fascist State is itself conscious, and has itself a will and a personality—thus it may be called the "ethic" State. In 1929, at the first five-yearly assembly of the Fascist régime, I said:

"For us Fascists, the State is not merely a guardian, preoccupied solely with the duty of assuring the personal safety of the citizens; nor is it an organization with purely material aims, such as to guarantee a certain level of well-being and peaceful conditions of life; for a mere council of administration would be sufficient to realize such objects. Nor is it a purely political creation, divorced from all contact with the complex material reality which makes up the life of the individual and the life of the people as a whole. The State, as conceived of and as created by Fascism, is a spiritual and moral fact in itself, since its political, juridical, and economic organization of the nation is a concrete thing: and such an organization must be in its origins and development a manifestation of the spirit. The State is the guarantor of security both internal and external, but it is also the custodian and transmitter of the spirit of the people, as it has grown up through the centuries in language, in customs, and in faith. And the State is not only a living reality of the present, it is also linked with the past and above all with the future, and thus transcending the brief limits of individual life, it represents the immanent spirit of the nation. The forms in which States express themselves may change, but the necessity for such forms is eternal. It is the State which educates its citizens in civic virtue, gives them a consciousness of their mission and welds them into unity; harmonizing their various interests through justice, and transmitting to future generations the mental conquests of science, of art, of law and the solidarity of humanity. It leads men from primitive tribal life to that highest expression of human power which is Empire: it links up through the centuries the names of those of its members who have died for its existence and in obedience to its laws, it holds up the memory of the leaders who have increased its territory and the geniuses who have illumined it with glory as an example to be followed by future generations. When the conception of the State declines, and disunifying and centrifugal tendencies prevail, whether of individuals or of particular groups, the nations where such phenomena appear are in their decline."

From 1929 until today, evolution, both political and economic, has everywhere gone to prove the validity of these doctrinal premises. Of such gigantic importance is the State. It is the force which alone can provide a solution to the dramatic contradictions of capitalism, and that state of affairs which we call the crisis can only be dealt with by the State, as between other States. . . . Fascism desires the State to be a strong and organic body, at the same time reposing upon broad and popular support. The Fascist State has drawn into itself even the economic activities of the nation, and, through the corporative social and educational institutions created by it, its influence reaches every aspect of the national life and includes, framed in their respective organizations, all the political, economic and spiritual forces of the nation. A State which reposes upon the support of millions of individuals who recognize its authority, are continually conscious of its power and are ready at once to serve it, is not the old tyrannical State of the medieval lord nor has it any thing in common with the absolute governments either before or after 1789. The individual in the Fascist State is not annulled but rather multiplied, just in the same way that a soldier in a regiment is not diminished but rather increased by the number of his comrades. The Fascist State organizes the nation, but leaves a sufficient margin of liberty to the individual; the latter is deprived of all useless and possibly harmful freedom, but retains what is essential; the deciding power in this question cannot be the individual, but the State alone.

The Fascist State is not indifferent to the fact of religion in general, or to that particular and positive faith which is Italian Catholicism. The State professes no theology, but a morality, and in the Fascist State religion is considered as one of the deepest manifestations of the spirit of man, thus it is not only respected but defended and protected. The Fascist State has never tried to create its own God, as at one moment Robespierre and the wildest extremists of the Convention tried to do; nor does it vainly seek to obliterate religion from the hearts of men as does Bolshevism: Fascism respects the God of the ascetics, the saints and heroes, and equally, God as He is perceived and worshipped by simple people.

The Fascist State is an embodied will to power and government: the Roman tradition is here an ideal of force in action. According to Fascism, government is not so much a thing to be expressed in territorial or military terms as in terms of morality and the spirit. It must be thought of as an empire—that is to say, a nation which directly or indirectly rules other nations, without the need for conquering a single square yard of territory. For Fascism, the growth of empire, that is to say the expansion of the nation, is an essential manifestation of vitality, and its opposite a sign of decadence. Peoples which are rising, or rising again after a period of decadence, are always imperialist; any renunciation is a sign of decay and of death.

Fascism is the doctrine best adapted to represent the tendencies and the aspirations of a people, like the people of Italy, who are rising again after many centuries of abasement and foreign servitude. But empire demands discipline, the co-ordination of all forces and a deeply felt sense of duty and sacrifice: this fact explains many aspects of the practical working of the régime, the character of many forces in the State, and the necessarily severe measures which must be taken against those who would oppose this spontaneous and inevitable movement of Italy in the twentieth century, and would oppose it by recalling the outworn ideology of the nineteenth century—repudiated wheresoever there has been the courage to undertake great experiments of social and political transformation: for never before has the nation stood more in need of authority, of direction, and of order. If every age has its own characteristic doctrine, there are a thousand signs which point to Fascism as the characteristic doctrine of our time. For if a doctrine must be a living thing, this is proved by the fact that Fascism has created a living faith; and that this faith is very powerful in the minds of men, is demonstrated by those who have suffered and died for it.

Fascism has henceforth in the world the universality of all those doctrines which, in realizing themselves, have represented a stage in the history of the human spirit.

Adolf Hitler

Adolf Hitler (1889–1945) rose to political power largely because of the economic and social discontent in Germany after the First World War. He was born in an Austrian village, but when still a young man went to Vienna to study art. It was in the Austrian capital that Hitler developed many of his ideas and prejudices. He visited sessions of the Imperial parliament and became disgusted with the failure of this multi-national representative body to accomplish anything constructive. He developed an intense dislike for the Jews, and, because he associated Marxism with that race, for communism as well. On the other hand, he nourished an extreme admiration for the "Nordic" German race, both as citizens of the dual monarchy and in the German Empire. In 1912 he moved to Munich, and when the war broke out in 1914 he enlisted in the German army. After the defeat of the Central Powers, Hitler entered into German politics and was one of the seven men who established the Nazi Party in 1919. The Nazi program, like that of the Italian Fascists, was directed against the Treaty of Versailles and toward the strengthening of the "nation state," but for ten years it made little headway. Following the world-wide economic collapse of 1929, however, the Nazi movement gained rapidly in popular support, and in 1933, Von Hindenburg was forced to appoint Hitler Chancellor of the German Reich. The Nazi revolution was quickly launched, and by

1939 Germany's revival as a great nation was so far accomplished that Hitler dared to defy the western democracies, and the Second World War began. By the end of 1940 German industrial production and military strength had won impressive victories for the Reich, and in a speech to the German workers on December 10, 1940, Hitler proudly boasted of the Nazi revolution and its achievements. In reading it note (1) Hitler's analysis of world-wide imperialism, (2) his explanation for Germany's past weakness, (3) the first objective of the Nazi program, (4) Hitler's attitude toward the Treaty of Versailles, (5) his analysis of how democracy functioned under capitalism, (6) the Nazi position concerning the equality of men, (7) the basis for the German economic system contrasted with that of the western democracies, (8) the basic differences between the two worlds which were at war, (9) Hitler's expressed attitude toward armaments, and (10) his description of the Germany that would emerge when the war was over.

From: AN ADDRESS TO GERMAN ARMAMENT WORKERS, BERLIN, DECEMBER, 1941

Men and Women, My Fellow Countrymen, Workers of Germany: Nowadays I do not speak very often. First, I have little time for speaking, and second, I believe that this is a time for action rather than words. We are involved in a conflict in which more than the victory of one country or the other is at stake; it is rather a war of two opposing worlds. I shall try to give you, as far as possible in the time at my disposal, an insight into the basic reasons underlying this conflict. I shall, however, confine myself to Western Europe only. The peoples who are primarily affected—eighty-five million Germans, forty-six million Britishers, forty-five million Italians, and about thirty-seven million Frenchmen—are the nuclei of the states who were or still are opposed in war. If I make a comparison between the living conditions of these peoples the following facts become evident:

Forty-six million Britishers dominate and govern a complex of areas totaling sixteen million square miles of our globe. Thirty-seven million Frenchmen dominate and govern a combined area of approximately four million square miles. Forty-five million Italians possess, taking into consideration only those territories in any way capable of being utilized, an area of scarcely one hundred and ninety thousand square miles. Eighty-five million Germans possess as their living space scarcely two hundred and thirty-two thousand square miles. That is to say: eighty-five million Germans own only two hundred and thirty-two thousand square miles on which they must live their lives and forty-six million Englishmen possess sixteen million square miles.

Now, my fellow countrymen, this world has not been thus divided by Providence or God. This division has been made by man himself. The land was parcelled out for the most part during the last three hundred years, that is, during the period in which, unfortunately, the German people were helpless and torn by internal dissension. Split up into hundreds of small states in consequence of the Thirty Years' War and the Treaty of Muenster, our people frittered away their entire strength in internal strife. Princes and princelings, kings and high ecclesiastics, maintained the disunion amongst

As translated by the editors from Adolf Hitler, Discours . . . , Paris, 1941, 293–324.

our people. When it finally appeared as if this purely dynastic laceration of our country might come to an end, the dissension and confusion was perpetuated by political parties which appeared on the scene, and by false ideologies. While during this period the Germans, notwithstanding their particular ability among the people of Western Europe, dissipated their powers in vain internal struggles, the division of the world proceeded beyond their borders. It was not by treaties or by binding agreements, but exclusively by the use of force that Britain forged her gigantic Empire.

The second people that failed to receive their fair share in this distribution, namely the Italians, experienced and suffered a similar fate. Torn by internal conflicts, devoid of unity, split up into numerous small states, this people also dissipated all their energy in internal strife. Nor was Italy able to obtain even the natural position in the Mediterranean which was her due. Thus in comparison with others, these two powerful peoples have received much less than their fair share. The objection might be raised: "Is this really of decisive importance?"

My fellow countrymen, man does not exist on theories and phrases, on declarations or on systems of political philosophy; he lives on what he can gain from the soil by his own labor in the form of food and raw materials. This is what he can eat, this is what he can use for manufacture and production. If a man's own living conditions offer him too little, his life will be wretched. We see that within the countries themselves, fruitful areas afford better living conditions than poor barren lands. In the one case there are flourishing villages; in the other poverty-stricken communities. A man may live in a stony desert or in a fruitful land of plenty. Differences can never be fully overcome by theories, nor even by the will to work.

We see that the primary cause for the existing tensions lies in the unfair distribution of the riches of the earth. And it is only natural that evolution follows the same rule among the nations as it does in the case of individuals. Just as the tension existing between rich and poor within a country must be compensated for either by reason or often, if reason fails, by force, so in the life of a nation one cannot claim everything and leave nothing to others.

Providence did not place man on earth with the idea that one should claim for himself fifty or eighty times his neighbor's portion. Either he is reasonable and agrees to an equitable settlement, or the one who is oppressed and crushed by misfortune will sooner or later seize that to which he is entitled. That holds good for individuals as well as for nations.

The great task which I set myself in internal affairs was to bring reason to bear on this problem, to eliminate dangerous tensions by invoking the common sense of all, to bridge the gulf between excessive riches and excessive poverty. I recognized, of course, that such processes cannot be consummated overnight. It is always preferable to bring together widely separated classes gradually and by the exercise of reason, rather than to resort to a solution based on force.

The right to live is a common and equal right. Therefore, it is not fair for a people to say they are willing to let others go on shifting for themselves. It is the essence of any really socialist system to see, not that alms are distributed but that rights are established. It is not a question of giving alms as a matter of charity to nations who have not received their fair share, but of granting them their rights, just as men receive theirs in ordinary daily life. The claim to the right to live is not a request for charity, but a lawful and fundamental claim.

Therefore, the right to live is at the same time a just claim to the soil which alone is the source of life. When unreasonableness threatened to choke their development, nations fought for this sacred claim. No other course was open to them and they realized that even bloodshed and sacrifice are better than the gradual extinction of a nation. Thus, at the beginning of our National Socialist revolution in 1933, we set forth two demands. The first of these was the unification of our people, for without this unification it would not have been possible to mobilize the forces required to formulate and, particularly, to secure Germany's essential claims.

You all know the condition in which we found ourselves eight years ago. Our people were on the verge of collapse. Seven million were unemployed. About six and a half million were on part-time work; our economic system was threatened by disintegration; agriculture faced collapse; trade and industry were at a standstill and shipping was paralyzed. It was easy to foresee the time when the seven million unemployed would necessarily become eight, nine, or ten mililons. The number of working people became fewer and fewer, while on the other hand the number of unemployed—who had to be kept on relief—became greater and greater. In other words, even those who were still working could not benefit from the fruits of their labor to the fullest extent, for each had to support a non-worker besides himself. Whether this was done by social legislation or in the form of charity made no difference. When a worker has to nourish and support another who does not work, neither will have enough in the long run. There will be too little to live on, even though they do not starve.

National unity for us, therefore, was one of the essential conditions if we were to coordinate the powers inherent in the German nation properly, to make the German people conscious of their own greatness, realize their strength, recognize and present their vital rights, and seek national unity by an appeal to reason.

I know that I have not been successful everywhere. For nearly fifteen years of my struggle I was the target of two opposing sides. One side reproached me: "You want to drag us who belong to the intelligentsia and to the upper classes down to the level of the others. That is impossible. We are educated people. In addition to that, we are wealthy and cultured. We cannot accept this."

These people were incapable of listening to reason; even today there are some who cannot be converted. On the whole, however, the number of those who realize that the lack of unity in our national structure would sooner or later lead to the destruction of all classes, has become greater and greater.

I also met with opposition from the other side. They said: "We have our class consciousness." I was obliged, however, to take the stand that in the existing situation we could not afford to make experiments. It certainly would have been simple to eliminate the intelligentsia. Such a process could be carried out at once.

But we would have to wait fifty or perhaps a hundred years for the gap to refill—and such a period would mean the destruction of the nation. For how can our people, with its 360 persons per square mile, exist at all if they do not employ every ounce of brain power and physical strength to wrest from their soil what they need? This distinguishes us from the others. In Canada, for example, there are 2.6 persons per square mile; in other countries perhaps 16, 18, 20 or 26 persons. Well, my fellow countrymen, no matter how stupidly one managed one's affairs in such a country, a decent living would still be possible.

Here in Germany, however, there are 360 persons per square mile. The others cannot manage with 26 persons per square mile, but we must manage with 360. This is the task we face. That is why I expressed this view in 1933: "We *must* solve these problems and, therefore, we *shall* solve them." Naturally that was not easy; everything could not be done immediately. Human beings are the product of their education, and, unfortunately, this begins practically at birth. Infants are clothed in different ways. After this has been going on for centuries, someone suddenly comes along and says:—"I want to unwrap the child and remove all its clothing so that I may discover its true nature"—which, is, of course, the same in every case. You have only created the difference by the external wrappings; underneath these they are all alike.

It is not, however, easy to do this. Everyone resists being unwrapped. Everyone wishes to retain the habits he has acquired through his upbringing. But we will carry out our task just the same. We have enormous patience. I know that what has been done for three, four, or five centuries cannot be undone in two, three, or five years. The decisive point is to make a start. At that time I perceived what was essential: We must establish the people into a German community, if we want them to achieve anything at all. That this view was correct is evident from the fact that all our enemies vigorously opposed it. National unity was the first demand. It was realized, little by little, step by step. You know yourselves what we have abolished in the meantime. Much has happened in the space of those short six or seven years. What did Germany look like? Completely helpless; split up into parties, classes, ideologies, and religions. Then there came our dear friends, not natives of these parts but immigrants from the East. Finally, there were economic differences and then the traditional conceptions of the state—Prussia, on the one hand; Bavaria, Wuerttemberg, and so forth, on the other—until all their separate emblems were removed. We told them to put them away and replace them by a common national flag. Other countries did the same long ago, in fact, nearly three hundred years ago. It was only here in Germany that each one went about with his own particular badge in his buttonhole, imagining that this helped to strengthen his personality, but quite forgetting that his personality was only a part of the whole and that if this whole should break up there could be no other consequence than national collapse. I therefore endeavored to fulfill this national demand. A great deal has already been done. We have swept Germany clear of all this old rubbish. This development has spread into other spheres, where we had to make efforts to break with old traditions, dear to many. We quite understand that many were attached to the old symbols and colors, the old institutions and movements, their old class prejudices, and their own consciousness of rank and their pride of station. I understand that perfectly. Nevertheless all this must be gradually eliminated and will continue to be eliminated until we all are united in a single whole and our educational work is completed.

It has been a tremendous task. The establishment of a German community was the first item on the program in 1933. The second item was the elimination of foreign oppression as expressed in the Treaty of Versailles, which also prevented our attaining national unity, forbade large sections of our people to unite, and robbed us of our possessions in the world, our German colonies.

The second item on the program was, therefore, the struggle against Versailles. No one can say that I express this opinion for the first time today. I expressed it, my fellow countrymen, in the days following the Great War when, still a soldier, I made my first appearance in the political arena. My first address

was a speech against the collapse, against the Treaty of Versailles, and for the reestablishment of a powerful German Reich. That was the beginning of my work. What I have accomplished since then does not represent a new aim but the oldest aim. It is the primary reason for the conflict in which we find ourselves today. The rest of the world did not want our inner unity, because they knew that, once it was achieved, the vital claim of our masses could be realized. They wanted to maintain the dictate of Versailles in which they saw a second peace of Westphalia. However, there is still another reason. I have stated that the world was unequally divided. American and English observers have found a wonderful expression for this fact. They say there are two kinds of peoples—the haves and the have-nots. "We, the British, are the haves. It is a fact that we possess sixteen million square miles. And we Americans are also haves, and so are we Frenchmen. The others —they are simply the have-nots." He who has nothing receives nothing. He shall remain what he is. He who has is not willing to share it."

All my life I have been a have-not. At home I was a have-not. I regard myself as belonging to them and have always fought exclusively for them. I defended them and, therefore, I stand before the world as their representative. I shall never recognize the claim of the others to that which they have taken by force. Under no circumstances can I acknowledge this claim with regard to that which has been taken from us. It is interesting to examine the life of these rich people. In this Anglo-French world there exists, they say, democracy, which means the rule of the people by the people. Now the people must possess some means of giving expression to their thoughts or their wishes. Examining this problem more closely, we see that the people themselves have originally no convictions of their own. Their convictions are formed, of course, just as everywhere else. The decisive question is who enlightens the people, who educates them? In those countries, it is actually capital that rules; that is, nothing more than a clique of a few hundred men who possess untold wealth and, as a consequence of the peculiar structure of their national life, are more or less independent and free. They say: "Here we have liberty." By this they mean, above all, an uncontrolled economy, and by an uncontrolled economy, the freedom not only to acquire capital but to make absolutely free use of it. That means freedom from national control or control by the people both in the acquisition of capital and in its employment. This is really what they mean when they speak of liberty.

These capitalists create their own press and then speak of the "freedom of the press." In reality, every one of the newspapers has a master, and in every case this master is the capitalist, the owner. This master, not the editor, is the one who directs the policy of the paper. If the editor tries to write other than what suits the owner, he is ousted the next day. This press, which is the absolutely submissive and characterless slave of the owners, molds public opinion. Public opinion thus mobilized by them is, in its turn, split up into political parties. The distinction between these parties is as small as it formerly was in Germany. You know them, of course—the old parties. They were always one and the same. In Britain matters are usually so arranged that families are divided up, one member being a conservative, another a liberal, and a third belonging to the labor party. Actually, all three sit together as members of the family, decide upon their common attitude and determine it. A further point is that the "elected people" actually form a community which operates and controls all these organizations. For this reason, the opposition in England is really always the same, for on all essential matters in which the opposition has to make itself felt, the parties are always in agreement. They have one and the same conviction and through the medium of the press mold public opinion along corresponding lines. One might well believe that in these countries of liberty and riches, the people must possess an unlimited degree of prosperity. But no! On the contrary, it is precisely in these countries that the distress of the masses is greater than anywhere else. Such is the case in rich Britain.

She controls sixteen million square miles. In India, for example, a hundred million colonial workers with a wretched standard of living must labor for her. One might think perhaps, that at least in England itself every person must have his share of these riches. On the contrary! In that country class distinction is the crassest imaginable. There is poverty—incredible poverty—on the one side, and equally incredible wealth on the other. They have not solved a single problem. The workmen of that country which possesses more than one-sixth of the globe and of the world's natural resources dwell in misery, and the masses of people are poorly clad. In a country which ought to have more than enough bread and every sort of fruit, we find millions of the lower classes who have not even enough to fill their stomachs, and go about hungry. A nation which could provide work for the whole world must acknowledge the fact that it cannot even abolish unemployment at home. For decades this rich Britain has had two and a half million unemployed; rich America, ten to thirteen millions, year after year; France six, seven, and eight hundred thousand. . . .

It is self-evident that where this democracy rules, the people as such are not taken into consideration at all. The only thing that matters is the existence of a few hundred great capitalists who own all the factories and their stock and, through them, control the people. The masses of the people do not interest them in the least. They are interested in them just as were our bourgeois parties in former times—only when elections are being held, when they need votes. Otherwise, the life of the masses is a matter of complete indifference to them.

To this must be added the difference in education. Is it not ludicrous to hear a member of the British Labor Party—who, of course, as a member of the Opposition is officially paid by the government—say: "When the war is over, we will do something in social respects.". . .

It is the members of Parliament who are the directors of the business concerns—just as used to be the case with us. But we have abolished all that. A member of the Reichstag cannot belong to a Board of Directors, except as a purely honorary member. He is prohibited from accepting any emolument, financial or otherwise. This is not the case in other countries.

They reply: "That is why our form of government is sacred to us." I can well believe it, for that form of government certainly pays very well. But whether it is sacred to the mass of the people as well is another matter!

The people as a whole definitely suffer. I do not consider it possible in the long run for one man to work and toil for a whole year in return for ridiculous wages, while another jumps into an express train once a year and pockets enormous sums. Such conditions are a disgrace. On the other hand, we National Socialists equally oppose the theory that all men are equal. Today, when a man of genius makes some astounding invention and enormously benefits his country by his brains, we pay him his due, for he has really accomplished something and been of use to his country. However, we hope to make it impossible for idle drones to inhabit this country.

I could continue to cite examples indefinitely. The fact remains that two worlds are face to face with one another. Our opponents are quite right when they say: "Nothing can reconcile us to the National Socialist world." How could a narrow-minded capitalist ever agree to my principles? It would be easier for the Devil to go to church and cross himself with holy water than for these people to comprehend the ideas which are accepted facts to us today! But we have solved our problems.

To take another instance where we are reproached: They claim to be fighting for the maintenance of the gold standard as the currency basis. That I can well believe, for the gold is in their hands. We, too, once had gold, but it was stolen and extorted from us. When I came to power it was not malice which made me abandon the gold standard. Germany simply had no gold left. Consequently, quitting the gold standard presented no difficulties, for it is always easy to part with what one does not have. We had no gold. We had no foreign exchange. They had all been stolen and extorted from us during the previous fifteen years. But, my fellow countrymen, I did not regret it, for we have constructed our economic system on a wholly different basis. In our eyes, gold is not of value in itself. It is only an agent by which nations can be suppressed and dominated. When I took over the government, I had only one hope on which to build, namely, the efficiency and ability of the German nation and the German working man; the intelligence of our inventors, engineers, technicians, chemists, and so forth. I built on the strength which animates our economic system. One simple question faced me: Are we to perish because we have no gold; am I to believe in a phantom which spells our destruction? I championed the opposite opinion: Even though we have no gold, we have power to work.

The German capacity for work is our gold and our capital, and with this gold I can compete successfully with any power in the world! We want to live in houses which have to be built. Hence the workers must build them, and the raw materials required must be procured by work. My whole economic system has been built up on the conception of work. We have solved our problems while, amazingly enough, the capitalist countries and their currencies have suffered bankruptcy.

Sterling can find no market today. Throw it at anyone and he will step aside to avoid being hit. But our Reichsmark, which is backed by no gold, has remained stable. Why? It has no gold cover; it is backed by you and by your work. You have helped me to keep the mark stable. German currency, with no gold guarantee, is worth more today than gold itself. It signifies unceasing production. This we owe to the German farmer, who has worked from daybreak till nightfall. This we owe to the German worker, who has given us his whole strength. The whole problem has been solved in one instant, as if by magic.

If, my dear friends, I had stated publicly eight or nine years ago: "In seven or eight years the problem of how to provide work for the unemployed will be solved, and the problem then will be where to find workers," I should have harmed my cause. Everyone would have declared: "The man is mad. It is useless to talk to him, much less to support him. Nobody should vote for him. He is a fantastic creature." Today, however, all this has come true. Today, the only question for us is where to find workers. That, my fellow countrymen, is the blessing which work brings.

Work alone can create new work; money cannot create work. Work alone can create values, values with which to reward those who work. The work of one man makes it possible for another to live and continue to work. And when we have mobilized the working capacity of our people to its utmost, each individual worker will receive more and more of the world's goods.

We have incorporated seven million unemployed into our economic system; we have transformed another six millions from part-time into full-time workers; we are even working overtime. And all this is paid for in cash in Reichsmarks which maintained their value in peacetime. In wartime we had to ration its purchasing capacity, not in order to devalue it, but simply to earmark a portion of our industry for war production to guide us to victory in the struggle for the future of Germany. . . .

It is therefore understandable if an Englishman says: "We do not wish our world to be subject to any sort of collapse." That is reasonable; they realize that their Empire is not menaced by us. But they say quite truthfully: "If the ideas that are popular in Germany are not completely exterminated, they might become popular among our own people, and that is the danger. We do not want this." It would do no harm if they did become popular there, but these people are just as narrow-minded as many once were in Germany. In this respect they prefer to remain bound to their conservative methods. They do not wish to depart from them, and do not conceal the fact.

They say: "The German methods do not suit us at all."

And what are these methods? You know, my comrades, that I have destroyed nothing in Germany. I have always proceeded very carefully, because I believe—as I have already said—that we cannot afford to wreck anything. I am proud that the revolution of 1933 was accomplished without breaking a single windowpane. Nevertheless, we have wrought enormous changes.

I wish to put before you a few basic facts: The first is that in the capitalistic democratic world the most important principle of economy is that the people exist for trade and industry, and that these in turn exist for capital. We have reversed this principle and said capital exists for trade and industry, and trade and industry exist for the people. In other words, the people come first. Everything else is but a means to this end. When an economic system is not capable of feeding and clothing a people, then it is bad, regardless of whether a few hundred people say: "As far as I am concerned it is good, excellent; my dividends are splendid." However, the dividends do not interest me at all. Here we have drawn the line. They may then retort: "Well, look here, that is just what we mean. You jeopardize liberty."

Yes, certainly, we jeopardize the liberty to profiteer at the expense of the community, and, if necessary, we even abolish it. British capitalists, to mention only one instance, can pocket dividends of 76, 80, 95, 140 and even 160 per cent from their armament industry. Naturally they say: "If the German methods grow apace and should prove victorious, this sort of thing will stop."

They are perfectly right. I should never tolerate such a state of affairs. I believe a 6 per cent dividend is sufficient. Even from this 6 per cent we deduct one-half and, as for the rest, we must have definite proof that it is invested in the interest of the country as a whole. In other words, no individual has the right to dispose arbitrarily of money which ought to be invested for the good of the community. If he disposes of it sensibly, well and good; if not, the National Socialist state will intervene. . . .

In this state, the people, without doubt, decide their existence. They determine the principles of their government. In fact it has been possible in this country to incorporate many of the broad masses into the National Socialist Party, that gigantic organization embracing millions and having millions of officials drawn from the people themselves. This principle is extended to the highest ranks.

For the first time in German history, we have a state which has absolutely abolished all social prejudices in regard to political appointments as well as in private life. I myself am the best proof of this. Just imagine: I am not even a lawyer, and yet I am your Fuehrer! . . .

Opposed to this there stands an entirely different world. In that world the highest ideals are the struggle for wealth, for capital, for family possessions, for personal egoism; everything else is merely a means to such ends. Two worlds confront each other today. We know perfectly well that if we are defeated in this war it would not only be the end of our National Socialist work of reconstruction, but the end of the German people as a whole. For without its powers of co-ordination, the German people would starve. Today the masses dependent on us number 120 or 130 millions, of which 85 millions alone are our own people. We remain ever aware of this fact.

On the other hand, that other world says: "If we lose, our world-wide capitalistic edifice will collapse. For it is we who save hoarded gold. It is lying in our cellars and will lose its value. If the idea that work is the decisive factor spreads abroad, what will happen to us? We shall have bought our gold in vain. Our whole claim to world dominion can then no longer be maintained. The people will do away with their dynasties of high finance. They will present their social claims, and the whole world system will be overthrown."

I can well understand what they declare: "Let us prevent this at all costs; it must be prevented." They can see exactly how our nation has been reconstructed. They see it clearly. For example, there we see a state ruled by a numerically small upper class. They send their sons to their own schools, to Eton. We have Adolf Hitler Schools or national political educational establishments. On the one hand, the sons of plutocrats, financial magnates; on the other, the children of the people. There, only men of those schools rule; here, men of the people play the leading rôle in the State.

These are the two worlds. I grant that one of the two must succumb. Yes, one or the other. But if we were to succumb, the German people would succumb with us. If the other were to succumb, I am convinced that the nations will become free for the first time. We are not fighting individual Englishmen or Frenchmen. We have nothing against them. For years I proclaimed this as the aim of my foreign policy. We demanded nothing of them, nothing at all. When they started the war they could not say: "We are doing so because the Germans asked this or that of us." They said, on the contrary: "We are entering the war because the German system of government does not suit us; because we fear it might spread to our own people." That is the reason they are carry-

ing on this war. They wanted to shove our people way back to the time of Versailles, to the indescribable misery of those days. But they have made a singular mistake.

If in this war everything points to the fact that gold is fighting against work, capitalism against peoples, and reaction against the progress of humanity, then work, the peoples, and progress will be victorious. Even the support of the Jewish race will not avail them.

I have seen all this coming for years. What did I ask of the other world? Nothing but the right for Germans to reunite and the restoration of all that had been taken from them— nothing which would have meant a loss to the other nations. How often have I stretched out my hand to them? Ever since I came into power. I had not the slightest wish to rearm.

For what do armaments mean? They absorb so much labor. It was I who regarded work as being of decisive importance; I wished to employ the working capacity of Germany for other plans. And, my countrymen, you already know that, after all, I have some fairly important plans in my mind, vast and splendid plans for my people. It is my ambition to make the German people rich and to make the German homeland beautiful. I want the standard of living of the individual raised. I want us to have the most beautiful and the finest civilization. I should like the theatre—in fact, the whole of German civilization—to benefit all the people and not to exist only for the upper ten thousand, as is the case in England.

The plans which we had in mind were tremendous, and I needed workers in order to realize them. Armament only deprives me of workers. I have proposed to limit armaments. I was ridiculed. The only answer I received was "no." I proposed the limitation of certain types of armament. That was refused. I proposed that airplanes should be altogether eliminated from warfare. That also was refused. I suggested that bombers should be limited. That, they refused. They said: "That is just how we wish to force our regime upon you."

I am not a man who does things by halves. If it becomes necessary for me to defend myself, I defend myself with fanatical zeal. When I saw that the same old warmongers of the World War in Britain were mobilizing once more against the great new German revival, I realized that this struggle would have to be fought once more, that the other side did not want peace. . . . In the face of this I have armed the German people. . . .

When this war is ended, Germany will set to work in earnest, and a new reveille will sound throughout the country. Then the German nation will stop manufacturing cannon and will embark on peaceful occupations and the new work of reconstruction for the millions. Then we shall show the world for the first time who is the real master, capitalism or work. Out of this work will grow the great German Reich of which great poets have dreamed. It will be the Germany to which every one of her sons will cling with fanatical devotion, because she will provide a home even for the poorest. She will teach everyone the meaning of life.

Should anyone say to me: "These are mere fantastic dreams, mere visions," I can only reply that when I set out on my career in 1919 as an unknown, nameless soldier I built my hopes of the future upon a most vivid imagination. Yet all has come true.

What I am planning or aiming at today is nothing compared to what I have already accomplished and achieved. It will be achieved sooner and more definitely than everything already achieved. The road from an unknown and nameless person to Fuehrer of the German nation was harder than will be the way from Fuehrer of the German nation to creator of the coming peace.

I had to fight and struggle for fifteen years for your confidence. Today, thanks to your confidence, I fight and struggle for Germany. Some day we shall once more struggle together in confidence for this great Reich of peace, work, prosperity and culture which we intend to establish and shall establish. Once again, I thank you.

Contemporary Civilization

Germany, by 1939, had progressed so far along the path of national regeneration within the framework of national socialism, that it was ready to defy the other nations of Europe and seek to impose its will upon the continent. The democracies of the Western World, facing the alternative of war or eventual domination of their nations by Hitler, chose to fight, and for the second time within a generation the world was plunged into a bloody conflict. Before the struggle ended, mankind was introduced to atomic warfare, and thus was sharply confronted with the implications of twentieth-century science unchecked by an adequate system of ethics and an effective international organization. Before the war's end, the nations who had united in the common effort to defeat Germany, Japan, and their allies, met in San Francisco and drew up a charter for a new world organization to assure more certain international co-operation in the postwar era. The first world war exerted a profound moral shock upon the people of the West. The twentieth century had dawned as a century of hope, but the war, followed by the eclipse of idealism and the spread of materialism, quickly dispelled that hope. Some critics of contemporary civilization attacked the barrenness implicit in materialism, while others sought to re-evaluate the role of pragmatic realism in effecting society's reformation. In the confusion of aims and objectives produced by wars, economic dislocations, and moral insecurities, religious leaders re-examined the bases for their faith. Religious thought and conviction, especially among protestants, underwent modification in terms of a restatement of primary Christian dogma with its emphasis upon original sin and the necessity for the redemptive power of God. Although faith in capitalism and democracy suffered deflation in the modern world, defenders have appeared to remind the peoples of Western Civilization that there are some generalities that still glitter and that the means for a reinvigoration of democracy can be found in the democratic process itself.

Adolf Hitler

> Adolf Hitler (see p. 814) sent his mechanized hosts rolling into Poland on September 1, 1939, and within a month had brought that nation to its knees. England, after demanding a cessation of the Polish campaign, entered into war with Germany on September 3. Other nations quickly followed England and a second world war within a generation began. The fate of Danzig, a German city surrounded by Poland, served as the immediate cause of the war. On September 19, Hitler came to Danzig to receive the city back into the German Empire. The selection given here is from his speech to the people of Danzig and represents, in a measure, Hitler's explanation of Germany's attack upon Poland. In reading this selection note (1) Hitler's description of World War I and the Peace of Versailles, (2) his statement of Poland's maltreatment of Germans, (3) Hitler's review of his efforts to avoid conflict, (4) his explanation of Russia's attack upon Poland, (5) his renunciation of other territorial claims, (6) his review of overtures to Italy, France, and England, and (7) his prophecy for the future.

From: HITLER'S SPEECH TO THE PEOPLE OF DANZIG

My District Leader, My Dear Danzigers: . . .

The fate of this city, this beautiful land, is the fate of entire Germany. The World War, which was the most senseless struggle of all times, made also this city a victim; this World War which left neither victors nor vanquished; this World War which, after its finish, left all with the conviction that a similar fate should not be repeated, but which, alas, apparently has been forgotten by those who were the main agitators and main profiteers of this slaughter.

When this sanguinary struggle—into which Germany entered without any objective—was over, a peace was to be given to mankind that should be a renaissance of justice and abolition of all misery. This peace was given to our people at Versailles not through discussions, on an equal plane, but was imposed upon us by dictation. The authors of this peace saw in it the end of the German nation—at any rate, the beginning for new disturbances.

In one respect the authors of this peace erred, however; this peace did not solve problems but created numerous new ones, and it was only a question of time that the German nation would arise to bring about a solution of these problems. Because the most essential problem was then overlooked, namely, the fact that nations live and exist whether or not one or another of the warmongers likes it. The fact remains that 82,000,000 Germans are united in this Lebensraum, and these 82,000,000 want to live, and shall live, even if warmongers again do not like it.

The Versailles peace did the greatest injustice to Germany. If today a foreign statesman believes he may state that he has no confidence in the word of German statesmen or German people, then we Germans, above all, are entitled to say that we have no confidence whatsoever in the assurances of those who then broke their most solemn assurances.

I do not want to hear talk about the injustice of Versailles. The worst in the life of the nation is perhaps not this injustice but the senselessness and stupidity wherewith peace was then imposed upon a world which disregarded all historical, economic, ethnographical and political facts.

Then settlements were made, and it actually

Adolf Hitler, "Speech to the People of Danzig," from the New York *Times*, 20 September 1939.

may be doubted whether the men who made them really had their senses. Without any knowledge whatsoever of historical developments of these Lebensraume and without any consideration for economic necessities did these men tear apart estates in Europe, separate countries, oppress peoples and destroy cultures. . . .

The world, which immediately sheds tears when Germany expels a Polish Jew who only a few decades ago came to Germany, remained dumb and deaf toward the misery of those who, numbering not thousands but millions, were forced to leave their home country on account of Versailles—that is, if these unfortunates were Germans.

What was for us and also for me most depressing was the fact that we had to suffer all this from a State which was far inferior to us; for, after all, Germany is a great power, even though mad men believed the vital rights of a great nation could be wiped out by a crazy treaty or by dictation.

Germany was a big power and had to look on while a far inferior people of a far inferior State maltreated these Germans. There were two especially unbearable conditions: First, this city whose German character nobody could deny was not only prevented from returning to the Reich but in addition an attempt was made to Polonize it by all kinds of devices; second, the province [East Prussia] severed from the German Reich had no direct contact with the Reich, but traffic with this province was dependent upon all kinds of chicanery or upon the good-will of this Polish State.

No power on earth would have borne this condition as long as Germany. I do not know what England would have said about a similar "peace solution" at its expense or how America or France would have accepted it. I attempted to find a solution—a tolerable solution—even for this problem. I submitted this attempt to the Polish rulers in the form of verbal proposals. You know these proposals. They were more than moderate.

I attempted to find a solution between our desire to restore connection between East Prussia and the Reich and the Poles' wish to retain access to the sea. I attempted, above all, to find a synthesis between the German-character of the city of Danzig with its will to return to the Reich and Poland's economic demands.

I believe I may say that I was more than modest and that there were moments when I reviewed and thought over the question as to whether I would be able to justify before my own people my having made such proposals for the solution of the Polish question.

I did this only because I wanted to spare the German people and the Polish people the suffering of another conflict. I repeated this proposal early this year in the most concrete form: Danzig was to return to the German Reich, an extraterritorial road was to be built to East Prussia, of course, at our expense—Poland was to get free extraterritorial harbor rights in Danzig and the same extraterritorial access. I was ready to offer even to guarantee borders which were hardly tolerable for us, and lastly to offer Poland participation in the security of Slovakia.

I do not know what mental condition the Polish Government was in when it refused these proposals. I knew, however, that millions of Germans sighed with relief, since they felt I had gone too far. As an answer, Poland gave the order for the first mobilization. Thereupon wild terror was initiated, and my request to the Polish Foreign Minister to visit me in Berlin once more to discuss these questions was refused. Instead of going to Berlin, he went to London. For the next weeks and months there were heightened threats, threats which were hardly bearable for a small State but which were impossible for a great power to bear for any length of time. . . .

So, we have beaten Poland within eighteen days and thus created a situation which perhaps makes it possible one day to speak to representatives of the Polish people calmly and reasonably.

Meantime, Russia felt moved, on its part, to march in for the protection of the interests of the White Russian and Ukrainian people in Poland. We realize now that in England and France this German and Russian co-operation is considered a terrible crime. An Englishman even wrote that it is perfidious—well, the English ought to know. I believe England thinks this co-operation perfidious because the co-operation of democratic England with Bolshevist

Russia failed, while National Socialist Germany's attempt with Soviet Russia succeeded.

I want to give here an explanation: Russia remains what she is; Germany also remains what she is. About only one thing are both regimes clear: neither the German nor the Russian regime wants to sacrifice a single man for the interest of the western democracies. A lesson of four years was sufficient for both peoples. We know only too well that alternately, now one, then the other, would be granted the honor to fill the breach for the ideals of the western democracies.

We therefore thank both peoples and both States for this task. We intend henceforth to look after our interests ourselves, and we have found that we best have been able to look after them when two of the largest peoples and States reconcile each other. And this is made simpler by the fact that the British assertion as to the unlimited character of German foreign policy is a lie. I am happy now to be able to refute this lie for British statesmen. British statesmen, who continually maintain that Germany intends to dominate Europe to the Urals now will be pleased to learn the limits of German political intentions. I believe this will deprive them of a reason for war because they profess to have to fight against the present regime because it today pursues unlimited political goals. . . .

Firstly, Germany, by extensive yielding and renunciation in the west and south of the Reich, has accepted definite boundaries. Germany tried by these renunciations to attain lasting pacification. And we believe we would have succeeded were it not that certain warmongers could be interested in disturbing the European peace.

I have neither toward England nor France any war claims, nor has the German nation since I assumed power. I tried gradually to establish confidence between Germany and especially its former war enemies. I attempted to eliminate all tensions which once existed between Germany and Italy, and I may state with satisfaction that I fully succeeded.

That ever-closer and more cordial relations were established was due also to personal and human relations between Il Duce and myself. I went still further. I tried to achieve the same between Germany and France. Immediately after the settlement of the Saar question I solemnly renounced all further frontier revisions, not only in theory but in practice. I harnessed all German propaganda to this end in order to eliminate everything which might lead to doubt or anxiety in Paris.

You know of my offers to England. I had only in mind the goal of attaining the sincere friendship of the British people. Since this now has been repulsed, and since England today thinks it must wage war against Germany, I would like to answer thus: . . .

If peoples go to pieces it will not be the German people, who are fighting for justice, who have no war aims and who were attacked. . . .

England's goal is not "a fight against the régime" but a fight against the German people, women and children. Our reaction will be compatible, and one thing will be certain: This Germany does not capitulate. We know too well what fate would be in store for Germany. . . . A second Versailles, only worse. . . .

I was determined to come to Danzig only as a liberator. I now take Danzig into the great German community with a firm determination never to allow her to be taken away. Generations will come and generations will go. They all will look back on our twenty years of absence from this city as a sad period in our history. They not only will remember the year 1918, but will remember with pride the time of the resurrection and rise of the German Reich, that Reich which welds all real Germans together, which created unity, and which we are determined to defend to our last breath. . . .

All hail our Great German Reich.

Benito Mussolini

Benito Mussolini (see p. 807), after the rise to power of Adolf Hitler in Germany, tended to follow a more thoroughly chauvinist foreign policy than he had pursued in the 1920's. In July, 1936, Mussolini and Hitler announced the formation of the Rome-Berlin axis, which served as a mutual assistance pact against other powers. Italy failed to join the European war until June, 1940; by that time Hitler's mechanized forces were about to enter Paris in triumph. On June 10, 1940, Italy declared war against France and England, and the same day Mussolini spoke in Rome to his people, explaining Italy's action. In reading this selection note (1) Mussolini's description of Italy's enemies, (2) his statement of what was needed to avoid war, (3) his justification for entering the conflict, (4) how Mussolini placed the war in a larger setting, (5) Mussolini's declaration of intent concerning Italy's neighbors, (6) his order to the people of Italy, and (7) his prophecy for the future.

MUSSOLINI'S SPEECH, JUNE 10, 1940

Fighters of land, sea and air, Blackshirts of the revolution and of the legions, men and women of Italy, of the empire and of the Kingdom of Albania, listen!

The hour destined by fate is sounding for us. The hour of irrevocable decision has come. A declaration of war already has been handed to the Ambassadors of Great Britain and France.

We take the field against the plutocratic and reactionary democracies who always have blocked the march and frequently plotted against the existence of the Italian people.

Several decades of recent history may be summarized in these words: Phrases, promises, threats of blackmail, and finally, crowning that ignoble edifice, the League of Nations of fifty-two nations.

Our conscience is absolutely clear.

With you, the entire world is witness that the Italy of fascism has done everything humanly possible to avoid the tempest that envelops Europe, but all in vain.

It would have sufficed to revise treaties to adapt them to changing requirements vital to nations and not consider them untouchable for eternity.

It would have sufficed not to begin the stupid policy of guarantees, which proved particularly deadly for those who accepted them.

It would have sufficed not to reject the proposal the Fuehrer made last October 6 after the campaign in Poland ended.

Now all that belongs to the past.

If today we have decided to take the risks and sacrifices of war, it is because the honor, interests, and future firmly impose it since a great people is truly such if it considers its obligations sacred and does not avoid the supreme trials that determine the course of history.

We are taking up arms, after having solved the problem of our continental frontiers, to solve our maritime frontiers. We want to break the territorial and military chains that confine us in our sea because a country of 45,000,000 souls is not truly free if it has not free access to the ocean.

This gigantic conflict is only a phase of the logical development of our revolution. It is the conflict of poor, numerous peoples who labor against starvers who ferociously cling to a monopoly of all riches and all gold on earth.

Benito Mussolini, Speech, Rome, 10 June 1940, from the New York *Times*, 11 June 1940.

It is a conflict of fruitful, useful peoples against peoples who are in a decline. It is a conflict between two ages, two ideas.

Now the die is cast and our will has burned our ships behind us.

I solemnly declare that Italy does not intend to drag other peoples bordering on her by sea or land into the conflict. Switzerland, Yugoslavia, Greece, Turkey and Egypt, take note of these words of mine. It depends on them and only on them if these words are rigorously confirmed or not.

Italians, in a memorable mass meeting in Berlin, I said that according to the rules of Fascist morals when one has a friend one marches with him to the end. This we have done and will continue to do with Germany, her people and her victorious armed forces.

On this eve of an event of import for centuries, we turn our thoughts to His Majesty, the King and Emperor, who always has understood the thought of the country.

Lastly, we salute the new Fuehrer, the chief of great allied Germany.

Proletarian, Fascist Italy has arisen for the third time, strong, proud, compact as never before.

There is only one order. It is categorical and obligatory for every one. It already wings over and enflames hearts from the Alps to the Indian Ocean: Conquer!

And we will conquer in order, finally, to give a new world of peace with justice to Italy, to Europe and to the universe.

Italian people, rush to arms and show your tenacity, your courage, your valor.

Winston Churchill

W inston Churchill (1874–   ), English author, statesman, and orator, has been prominent in British life since 1899, when he went to South Africa as a reporter to cover the Boer War. In 1900 he was elected to Parliament as a Conservative, but by 1906 had joined the Liberal party as a supporter of free trade. During the First World War he served as head of the Admiralty and later in other important military posts. After the war Churchill returned to the Conservative party and was Chancellor of the Exchequer in the second Baldwin ministry (1924–1929). In May, 1940, after the Germans had successfully invaded Norway, Neville Chamberlain was forced to resign as prime minister, and the British people turned to the veteran Churchill to lead them through the dark days ahead. In June, 1940, he addressed the House of Commons and later the same speech was broadcast to the nation. His words came to the ears of the Empire at its darkest hour, but this famous speech, which has become known under the title, "Their Finest Hour," did much to calm his people and to steel them for the great task ahead. In reading the concluding section of this address note (1) the balance sheet of favorable and unfavorable factors which Churchill outlined, (2) the part he expected the Dominions and the United States to play in the struggle, (3) the parallel he drew with the First World War, (4) the war aims he stated, (5) his concept of what the Battle of Britain would mean for the future, and (6) the stirring admonition to the British people with which he concluded the passage.

From: A PARLIAMENTARY SPEECH BY WINSTON CHURCHILL

We may now ask ourselves: In what way has our position worsened since the beginning of the war? It has worsened by the fact that the Germans have conquered a large part of the coast line of Western Europe, and many small countries have been overrun by them. This aggravates the possibilities of air attack and adds to our naval preoccupations. It in no way diminishes, but on the contrary definitely increases, the power of our long-distance blockade. Similarly, the entrance of Italy into the war increases the power of our long-distance blockade. We have stopped the worst leak by that. We do not know whether military resistance will come to an end in France or not, but should it do so, then of course the Germans will be able to concentrate their forces, both military and industrial, upon us. But for the reasons I have given to the House these will not be found so easy to apply. If invasion has become more imminent, as no doubt it has, we, being relieved from the task of maintaining a large army in France, have far larger and more efficient forces to meet it.

If Hitler can bring under his despotic control the industries of the countries he has conquered, this will add greatly to his already vast armament output. On the other hand, this will not happen immediately, and we are now assured of immense, continuous and increasing support in supplies and munitions of all kinds from the United States; and especially of aeroplanes and pilots from the Dominions and across the oceans, coming from regions which are beyond the reach of enemy bombers.

I do not see how any of these factors can operate to our detriment on balance before the winter comes; and the winter will impose a strain upon the Nazi regime, with almost all Europe writhing and starving under its cruel heel, which, for all their ruthlessness, will run them very hard. We must not forget that from the moment when we declared war on the 3rd of September it was always possible for Germany to turn all her Air Force upon this country, together with any other devices of invasion she might conceive, and that France could have done little or nothing to prevent her doing so. We have, therefore, lived under this danger, in principle and in a slightly modified form, during all these months. In the meanwhile, however, we have enormously improved our methods of defense, and we have learned what we had no right to assume at the beginning, namely, that the individual aircraft and the individual British pilot have a sure and definite superiority. Therefore, in casting up this dread balance-sheet and contemplating our dangers with a disillusioned eye, I see great reason for intense vigilance and exertion, but none whatever for panic or despair.

During the first four years of the last war the Allies experienced nothing but disaster and disappointment. That was our constant fear: one blow after another, terrible losses, frightful dangers. Everything miscarried. And yet at the end of those four years the morale of the Allies was higher than that of the Germans, who had moved from one aggressive triumph to another, and who stood everywhere triumphant invaders of the lands into which they had broken. During that war we repeatedly asked ourselves the question: How are we going to win? and no one was able ever to answer it with much precision, until at the end, quite suddenly, quite unexpectedly, our terrible foe collapsed before us, and we were so glutted with victory that in our folly we threw it away.

We do not yet know what will happen in France or whether the French resistance will be prolonged, both in France and in the French Empire overseas. The French Government will be throwing away great opportunities and casting adrift their future if they do not continue the war in accordance with their Treaty obligations, from which we have not felt able to release them. The House will have read the historic declaration in which, at the

Winston Churchill, *Blood, Sweat and Tears*, G. P. Putnam's Sons, New York, 1941, 312–313. Courtesy of G. P. Putnam's Sons.

desire of many Frenchmen—and of our own hearts—we have proclaimed our willingness at the darkest hour in French history to conclude a union of common citizenship in this struggle. However matters may go in France or with the French Government, or other French Governments, we in this Island and in the British Empire will never lose our sense of comradeship with the French people. If we are now called upon to endure what they have been suffering, we shall emulate their courage, and if final victory rewards our toils they shall share the gains, aye, and freedom shall be restored to all. We abate nothing of our just demands; not one jot or tittle do we recede. Czechs, Poles, Norwegians, Dutch, Belgians have joined their causes to our own. All these shall be restored.

What General Weygand called the Battle of France is over. I expect that the Battle of Britain is about to begin. Upon this battle depends the survival of Christian civilization. Upon it depends our own British life, and the long continuity of our institutions and our Empire. The whole fury and might of the enemy must very soon be turned on us. Hitler knows that he will have to break us in this Island or lose the war. If we can stand up to him, all Europe may be free and the life of the world may move forward into broad, sunlit uplands. But if we fail, then the whole world, including the United States, including all that we have known and cared for, will sink into the abyss of a new Dark Age made more sinister, and perhaps more protracted, by the lights of perverted science. Let us therefore brace ourselves to our duties, and so bear ourselves that, if the British Empire and its Commonwealth last for a thousand years, men will still say, "This was their finest hour."

United States Strategic Bombing Survey

In November, 1944, the United States Secretary of War established the United States Strategic Bombing Survey to study the effects of aerial attacks upon Germany preparatory to planning strikes against Japan. In August, 1945, President Truman requested that a study be made of the effects of air attacks upon Japan. The Survey, thereupon, reconstructed much of wartime Japanese military planning, as well as Japan's over-all program and the background of her entry into the war. In addition, the Survey studied and reported upon the impact of the war on Japan. The Medical Division of the Survey, among other tasks, undertook to prepare a report on the effects of atomic bombs on health and medical services in Hiroshima and Nagasaki. A portion of this report, published in 1947, is reproduced here. In reading the selection note (1) the status of medical care before the attack, (2) the situation in Hiroshima immediately prior to the bombing, (3) the immediate effects of the raid, (4) the fate of medical facilities in the two cities, (5) the reaction of the population following the bombing, (6) the restoration of medical services following the disaster, (7) the efforts to deal with the dead, the wounded, the ill, and the essential sanitary services, (8) the effects on medical personnel in the two cities, and (9) the implications for civilization's future in this report.

From: REPORT OF THE EFFECTS OF ATOMIC BOMBS ON HEALTH AND MEDICAL SERVICES

In order to appreciate the effects of the atomic bombs on Hiroshima and Nagasaki one must realize something of the character and extent of medical institutions in the two cities. In addition, it is important for one to realize the magnitude of the destructive forces since they so completely surpass all previous concepts of destruction that one might have when thinking in terms of ordinary incendiary or high-explosive bombing.

STATUS OF MEDICAL CARE PRIOR TO BOMBING

Generally speaking, the Japanese are not accustomed to good medical care as one uses the term in light of practice in the Western world. Hospitals are usually available to only those who are able to pay and the average Japanese citizen has never been educated to the value and use of hospitals. Though the number of physicians per unit of population compares favorably with that in the United States, the average physician is poorly trained and the character of medicine which he practices is far below Western standards. Even the licensed physicians resort to unconventional and unscientific methods which have their origin in Far-Eastern religion and superstition. In addition, the government licenses a group of "persons engaged in the traditional methods of treatment," such as acupuncture, massage, and moxa. There are also a large number of unlicensed cultists who treat persons by means of faith healing. Both the licensed and unlicensed cultists have fairly large followings, particularly in the rural population and the lower classes.

The average Japanese hospital is a small private hospital which consists of 10 to 50 beds. Actually, the term "beds" is used loosely in this respect since few of them have western-style beds. The rooms in such hospitals are very much like rooms in Japanese homes with tatami floors and beds made by spreading bedding (Futon) upon the floor. It is thus impossible to give an accurate bed capacity, this figure actually representing the number that can be crowded into the available space. On the other hand, the larger city institutions and university hospitals are usually well equipped, of modern construction and use western beds throughout. Despite this fact, there are in every city large numbers of these small Japanese-style hospitals. Too, a large percentage of the population never go to hospitals, but are born, have their illnesses and babies, and die in their own homes. Most of the births in Japan are attended by midwives.

Hiroshima and Nagasaki did not differ from the usual medium-sized Japanese city. Hiroshima had two Army hospitals and an Army-Navy relief hospital in addition to the civilian institutions. The Red Cross Hospital and the Communications Hospital were modern structures and were the better institutions of the city. In addition there were many small Japanese hospitals scattered over the city. In the spring of 1945 a medical college was started in Hiroshima and the first class had matriculated. Though no school building was available they were being taught in one of the local hospitals at the time of the bombing. The supply of doctors and nurses seemed up to Japanese standards and it was thought that the city was well provided with medical care.

The situation in Nagasaki differed from Hiroshima in that it possessed one of the finest medical centers in Japan. The University Hospital was the pride of the city and was reputed to be second to none in Japan except the Imperial University Hospital in Tokyo. It was a large modern unit consisting of many buildings and contained about 500 beds. This number represented more than three-quarters of the hospital facilities in the city. The Medical College was located near the hospital and had a large staff of well-trained teachers. There were

"The Effects of Atomic Bombs on Health and Medical Services in Hiroshima and Nagasaki," in United States, *The United States Strategic Bombing Survey*, Washington, D. C., 1947, 2–4; 10; 19–21. Courtesy of the Department of the Air Force.

in adition a tuberculosis sanatorium and many small private and industrial hospitals. Here too, the number of physicians and nurses seemed to be adequate in comparison to other Japanese cities.

Since most of the other large cities of Japan had been subjected to demolition and incendiary raids during late 1944 and 1945 it was natural for Nagasaki and Hiroshima to expect similar treatment. Hiroshima contained no large war industries and had been bombed on one previous occasion only. At that time a single B-29 had dropped several demolition bombs on a suburban district, but there was little damage done. Nagasaki had experienced demolition bombing on several occasions but these raids were directed at key industrial plants. On 1 August 1945, 6 bombs were dropped on the University Hospital hitting the operating room and laboratories and resulting in the death of 3 students and 30–40 other casualties. Many patients were then evacuated as an air-raid precaution. The fact that Hiroshima had been so completely spared of bombing apparently gave rise to some rumors that the city was being saved for some "fantastic" weapon. Several survivors relate having heard such rumors. There was, however, no real reason to suspect that any fate other than that experienced by other cities was in store for it. Accordingly, the officials proceeded with the creation of large firebreaks. This work was started in March 1945 and continued until the time of the atomic bombing. Thousands of homes were thus destroyed and their occupants were required to leave the city. It was estimated by the Prefectural Health Officer that 150,000 people were evacuated from Hiroshima from March to August 1945, of whom probably 10,-000 had returned. Similar preparations were being carried out in Nagasaki but they appear to have been on a somewhat smaller scale.

THE ATOMIC BOMBING

It was upon the previously-described conditions that the atomic bombs were dropped on Hiroshima on 6 August and on Nagasaki three days later. In order to appreciate the conditions at the time of the blast and immediately thereafter it will be well to reconstruct the scene in Hiroshima as best it can be determined from talking with survivors.

The morning of 6 August 1945 began bright and clear. At about 0700 there was an air-raid alarm and a few planes appeared over the city. Many people within the city went to prepared air-raid shelters, but since alarms were heard almost every day the general population did not seem to have been greatly concerned. About 0800 an all-clear was sounded after the planes had disappeared. At this hour of the morning many people were preparing breakfast. This fact is probably important since there were fires in charcoal braziers in many of the homes at this time. Some of the laboring class were at work but most of the downtown business people had not gone to work. Consequently, a large percentage of the population was in their homes and relatively few were in the more strongly constructed business buildings.

After the all-clear sounded persons began emerging from air-raid shelters and within the next few minutes the city began to resume its usual mode of life for that time of day. It is related by some survivors that they had watched planes fly over the city. At about 0815 there was a blinding flash. Some described it as brighter than the sun, others likened it to a magnesium flash. Following the flash there was a blast of heat and wind. The large majority of people within 3,000 feet of ground zero were killed immediately. Within a radius of about 7,000 feet almost every Japanese house collapsed. Beyond this range and up to 15,000–20,000 feet many of them collapsed and others received serious structural damage. Persons in the open were burned on exposed surfaces, and within 3,000–5,000 feet many were burned to death while others received severe burns through their clothes. In many instances clothing burst into spontaneous flame and had to be beaten out. Thousands of people were pinned beneath collapsed buildings or injured by flying debris. Flying glass particularly produced many non-lethal injuries at greater distances from the center of the blast. Details relative to the nature of the injuries and the distances at which they occurred are discussed in the [following chapter], but the foregoing presentation was necessary for one to appreciate the state of the population immediately after the bomb exploded.

Shortly after the blast fires began to spring up over the city. Those who were able made a mass exodus from the city into the outlying hills. There was no organized activity. The people appeared stunned by the catastrophe and rushed about as jungle animals suddenly released from a cage. Some few apparently attempted to help others from the wreckage, particularly members of their family or friends. Others assisted those who were unable to walk alone. However, many of the injured were left trapped beneath collapsed buildings as people fled by them in the streets. Pandemonium reigned as the uninjured and slightly injured fled the city in fearful panic. Teams which had been previously organized to render first aid failed to form and function. Those closer to ground zero were largely demobilized due to injuries and death. However, there were physically intact teams on the outskirts of the city which did not function. Panic drove these people from the city just as it did the injured who could walk or be helped along. Much of the city's fire-fighting equipment was damaged beyond use so that soon the conflagrations were beyond control.

In Nagasaki a similar but slightly less catastrophic picture occurred. The blast was not centered over the main business section of the city but was up the valley about 2 miles. There were large industrial plants, hospitals, the medical school and partially built-up residential areas near the ground zero. The terrain in this area was uneven with large hills which shielded certain areas. Due to the shielding factor and the distance of the explosion from the center of the city, Nagasaki was less completely destroyed than Hiroshima and the panic was apparently less.

THE FATE OF MEDICAL FACILITIES

The fate of the hospitals in Hiroshima is particularly interesting in the light of this chaos and destruction. Many of the smaller hospitals and clinics were located in the center of the city and were of typical Japanese construction. For instance, the Shima Surgical Hospital was only 100 feet from ground zero. It was partly brick but largely wooden construction. The blast blew it flat, and it is believed that all of the occupants were killed immediately. The remains of the building burned, and the spot is now a mass of flattened rubble. The Tada Hospital was partly reinforced concrete and partly wooden construction. Located at 2,600 feet from ground zero it was completely demolished, and the only remnants were the concrete foundation and the gutted and broken concrete portions of the building. The exact fate of its occupants could not be definitely determined but it is believed that they were all killed by the blast and succeeding fire. Another building of medical nature which was located near the center of the blast was the Japan Red Cross Office Building. It was only 740 feet from ground zero and was almost completely demolished. The windows, window casements, and doors were blown out and even the concrete structure was broken by the downward thrust of the blast. The building was then gutted by fire and all occupants perished. The Hiroshima Army Hospitals No. 1 and No. 2 were located within 1,500–2,000 feet of ground zero. It is reported that 80 percent of the personnel and all of the patients (500 in No. 1 and 650 in No. 2) were killed. The ultimate fate of the surviving 20 percent of the personnel is not known, but on the basis of other experiences at this distance it is probable that a large percentage of them died of injuries or radiation effects. The hospital buildings collapsed and burned. The Red Cross Hospital, which was the city's largest and best hospital, was located 4,860 feet from ground zero. The basic structure of the building, which is reinforced concrete, remained virtually intact. However, steel window casements were blown out or twisted and torn on the side near the blast and the interior was seriously damaged by falling plaster, broken partitions, and falling ceilings. There were 90 percent casualties of the occupants of this building and the damage was so great that the hospital ceased operation for several weeks after the bombing. It did, however, serve as a first-aid station and out-patient clinic in the interim. Practically all instruments and supplies in this hospital were completely destroyed or damaged beyond repair. The Hiroshima Communications Hospital was located at a similar distance from the ground zero, 4,900 feet. It, too, was of reinforced-concrete construction. Though the concrete framework of the building remained intact it suffered even more severe damage than did the Red Cross Hospital. Steel window casements were blown out, partitions blown down, and all of the contents were damaged beyond repair. It was later reoccupied as were most of the buildings which were left standing. An example of a hospital located at greater distance from ground zero is the Army-Navy Relief Hospital. It was 10,400 feet from the ground zero and sustained considerable damage. The building was stucco and two floors in height. Though it did not collapse, it was seriously damaged. Most of the tile roof was broken and blown off, window frames were broken and blown out, and in a few places walls were crushed. The principal injuries to the occupants of this hospital were due to flying glass and other missiles. Many smaller hospitals and clinics were destroyed in similar manner, depending upon their distance from the center of the blast. Since practically all of these buildings were of wooden construction they were either blown down and/or burned shortly thereafter. There was little evidence of their existence to one who came into the area later. It has been impossible to trace the fate of their occupants but it is felt that it coincided to some extent with the fate of other persons in Japanese-type homes at similar distances from ground zero. Actually the incidence of flash burns was probably lower, since few of them would have been outdoors, but the secondary injuries were probably higher. Inasmuch as they were already ill and many no doubt were helpless, the mortality rate surely exceeded that of the general population at comparable distances.

Thus it may be said of Hiroshima that essentially all of the civilian hospitals and 2 large Army hospitals were located within 5,000 feet of ground zero and were functionally completely destroyed. Those within 3,000 feet were totally destroyed and the mortality rate of the occupants was practically 100 percent. Two large hospitals of reinforced concrete construction were located 4,860 and 4,900 feet from the ground zero. The basic structures remained erect but there was such severe interior damage that neither was able to continue operation as a hospital. The casualty rate in these 2 hospitals was approximately 90 percent. Hospitals and clinics beyond 7,000–10,000 feet often remained standing but were badly damaged and there were many casualties due to flying glass and other missiles.

The destruction of hospitals in Nagasaki was even more outstanding than that in Hiroshima. Since the Nagasaki University Hospital contained over three-quarters of the hospital beds in the city it represented the bulk of the city's hospital facilities. The center of the hospital grounds was only 2,400 feet from ground zero and from a functional standpoint the hospital was completely obliterated. Most of the buildings were of reinforced-concrete construction but a great deal of wood was used in interior construction and fittings. The basic structure of all these buildings remained essentially intact but there was severe damage otherwise. The blast effects were very severe and almost every building was gutted by fire. The mortality rate of occupants of this hospital was at least 80 percent, two-thirds being killed outright. The Nagasaki Medical College was located even closer to ground zero, being only 1,700 feet distant. A large portion of the buildings were of inflammable nature but a few small buildings were constructed of reinforced concrete. The wooden buildings were blown down and subsequently consumed by flames. The concrete structures remained erect but were completely gutted by fire. Of the 850 medical students present 600 were killed and 12 of the 16 professors were also lost. The third- and fourth-year medical students escaped by virtue of the fact that they were elsewhere at the time of the bomb blast. Almost all of the other occupants of the buildings were killed outright. All medical equipment and supplies in the medical college buildings were completely destroyed by blast and fire. The Nagasaki Tuberculosis Sanatorium was located across the valley from the college and the hospital but was only 2,600 feet from ground zero. Since the buildings were all of wooden construction they were completely destroyed by blast and fire. It was reported that all of the patients and other occupants of the sanatorium were killed. Except the 2 hospitals mentioned above there were no others of any size located within Nagasaki, although there were many small private hospitals and clinics of typical Japanese construction, scattered throughout the city. The fate of these buildings and their occupants corresponded in general to that of buildings of similar construction at comparable distances from the bomb in Hiroshima. However, there was an additional factor of the hills shielding some structures in Nagasaki. In Hiroshima the effective zone was entirely flat and hills on the outskirts of the city were so distant that they did not interfere with the effects of the bomb to any appreciable extent. On the other hand, in Nagasaki many structures that would otherwise have suffered much more severe damage were partially or completely protected from the bomb effects by hills.

In summary, it may be said of the hospital facilities in Nagasaki that over 80 percent of the hospital beds and the Medical College were located within 3,000 feet of ground zero and were completely destroyed. Reinforced-concrete buildings within this range remained standing but were completely gutted by fire; buildings of wooden construction were completely destroyed by fire and blast; the mortality rate of occupants of this group of buildings was about 75–80 percent.

RESTORATION OF HOSPITALS AFTER BOMBING

An amazing feature of the atomic bombings to one going into the areas later was the poor recuperative powers of the population towards the restoration of all types of facilities. Though this was probably less so in the medical field than in others it was still alarmingly apparent. The panic of the people immediately after the bombing was so great that Hiroshima was literally deserted. It was apparently less true of Nagasaki and this was probably due to the fact that the city was less completely destroyed, but the same apathy was there. The colossal effects of the bombs and the surrender following shortly thereafter seemed to have completely stunned the people. The effects of the typhoons of September and early October may have contributed to this psychological reaction.

Since the most outstanding feature of the atomic bombs was the high rate of human casualties, it was natural that this was the greatest problem in the areas following the bombing. But even in this regard the progress was astoundingly slow and haphazard. Other evidences of restoration were almost completely absent. For instance, at the time the Medical Division visited Hiroshima, 3 months after the bombing, the first street car was beginning operation, people wandered aimlessly about the ruins, and only a few shacks had been built as evidence of reoccupation of the city. No system for collection of night soil or garbage had been instituted. Leaking water pipes were seen all over the city with no evidence of any attention. It was reported that following the bombing several days were required for disposal of the dead and then they were simply piled into heaps and burned without attempts at identification or enumeration. Street cars were burned as a method of cremating the bodies within. All in all, there appeared to be no organization and no initiative.

The care of the wounded immediately after the bombing was essentially nil in Hiroshima. Beyond the sphere of family ties there seemed to be little concern for their fellow man. It is true that essentially all of the medical supplies were destroyed by the bombing, and that there were no hospitals and little with which to work. For the first 3 days there was no organized medical care. At the end of this time the Prefectural Health Department was successful in getting a portion of the surviving physicians together and to begin ministering to the wounded who remained in the city. Up until this time all nursing and medical care had been on an individual basis. The more seriously injured were placed in the few remaining public buildings on the outskirts of the city. Many of them died but many seriously burned cases remained. Small stocks of medical supplies which had been stored in caves outside the city were brought out but were soon exhausted. With all medical supplies gone and practically none being brought in the treatment of the injured seems to have consisted largely of offering a place of refuge. There is no doubt that many died who might have been saved by modern, competent medical care. As time elapsed many of the small hospitals and clinics were able to reopen and offer some help. Japanese medical authorities and other scientists visited the city in order to appraise the nature and extent of the damage but they did not contribute materially to the care of the sick and injured. Finally, medical teams consisting of medical students and physicians were sent into the area from the larger cities such as Tokyo, Osaka and Kyoto. They assisted materially in administering medical care but were handicapped by the overwhelming size of the task and the lack of supplies. The Red Cross Hospital was cleared of wreckage and finally reopened without any repair of the building. In many respects it was fortunate that such a large proportion of the injured fled to nearby towns and villages. Except for Kure which had been largely destroyed by incendiary bombing, the facilities in these areas were relatively intact.

Soon after American occupation forces entered the area some medical supplies were made available. A medical unit representing the Surgeon General of the United States Army was assigned to the project. The task of this unit was largely investigative in nature but they did assist the Japanese authorities in organizing and directing medical relief for the bomb victims. The American physicians did not treat any of the cases. In the first place they arrived so late (about 1 October) that deaths from radiation had practically ceased. Secondly, they did not have supplies and personnel to perform a thorough study of methods of treatment. Thirdly, it was apparently felt that investigation of the nature of the casualties was more important. And finally, with these facts in mind the Americans had a clear understanding with the Japanese that they would assume no responsibility for the treatment of cases but would merely consult with and advise the Japanese whenever necessary. In time a large rayon factory in Ujina and other buildings were taken over by the Japanese Government and utilized as hospitals. Some of the injured found their way to distant cities for treatment and other groups were officially transferred by the Japanese Government to medical centers in Osaka, Kyoto, and Tokyo for study and treatment.

Most of the fatalities due to flash burns and secondary injuries occurred within a few days after the bombing. The peak of deaths due to radiation effects was not reached until late August or the early part of September. Very few cases suffering from radiation died after 1 October and deaths due to other causes had practically ceased by this time. Thus during October the essential medical care was directed almost exclusively toward burn cases, most of which were flash burns. A large number were still in hospitals but the vast majority of these patients could be treated as out-patients. By 1 November adequate hospital space was available but it was still of emergency nature and medical supplies were inadequate. Many of the burns remained unhealed. Inadequate medical care, poor nutrition, and secondary infection were important factors in this delayed healing.

The effects of the atomic bombing of Nagasaki were very similar to those in Hiroshima. Even though it followed the bombing of Hiroshima by 3 days, wartime secrecy, general confusion and the short elapse of time did not allow the population of Nagasaki any particular advantage from the previous experience. The psychological reaction of the people was essentially the same and the chaos in the city seems to have been almost as great. A very important difference between the two cities was that Nagasaki was not so completely destroyed. Further, the bomb blast was centered over a more industrial area and the character of the buildings resulted in less extensive fires. But from the medical standpoint the bombing was particularly catastrophic because the bulk of the city's hospital facilities were located within a radius of 3,000 feet of the center of the explosion. The destruction of the University Hospital and the Medical College was so great that the buildings left standing could not be reoccupied even for emergency medical care. Other hospitals and clinics, including the Tuberculosis Sanatorium, had burned to a heap of ashes. The only remaining facilities were small private clinics and hospitals and many of them were seriously damaged. Essentially no organized medical care was carried out for several days after the bombing. The Shinkosen hospital was established in an old school building for the care of bomb victims, but it was woefully inadequate. At one time it harbored over 500 victims. Fortunately, there was a large medical depot at Omura, 20 miles away. Such large stocks of supplies were on hand here that Nagasaki did not suffer in this respect as did Hiroshima. Another school building was converted into an infectious disease hospital.

At the time the Allied Military Government entered Nagasaki, about 1 October, the population was found to be apathetic and profoundly lethargic. Even at this time the collection of garbage and night soil had not been reestablished, restoration of other public utilities was lacking and the hospital facilities were inadequate. Through the initiative of the Military Government, a system of reporting infectious diseases was instituted, the collection of garbage and night soil was reestablished, and attempts were made to increase the supply of safe water. A survey of the remaining hospitals and clinics at this time by Captain Horne of American Military Government revealed such obvious inadequacies that the survey was not even completed. A perusal of the incomplete report reveals that there were many small private hospitals remaining, most of which were damaged and without satisfactory potential value even if they were repaired. In the face of the inadequacy of the Shinkosen Hospital, and the absence of other facilities in Nagasaki, bomb victims were transferred to the Omura Naval Hospital where the conditions were much better. The Shinkosen Hospital has now been evacuated and abandoned.

When Nagasaki was visited by the Medical Division, about three months after the bombing, conditions were still very primitive. A visit to the Infectious Disease Hospital revealed that the school building in which it was located had been seriously damaged by bombing and no repairs had been made. The roof was partially destroyed, there were no window panes and the building was filthy. All of the patients, both male and female, were in adjacent beds in the same ward. Members of their families were present and were going in and out at will. The hospital had a capacity of 35 beds and contained 21 patients; 18 cases of dysentery and 3 cases of typhoid fever, at the time of the visit. There were no isolation precautions in practice. The only medicine and supplies were

those furnished by the Military Government. Because of these conditions the Military Government had taken over a Japanese Army hospital of 103 beds and 12 bassinets and was converting it for use as a Japanese civilian hospital. It was expected to be available very shortly thereafter. The Omura General Hospital (formerly a Naval hospital) was in excellent condition and was being used for the care of atomic bomb victims. Thus, it may be seen that by 1 November some semblance of medical care and sanitary procedures had been reestablished in Nagasaki but the facilities were still inadequate. The entire program had to be directed and forced by the Americans though they did not enter the area until nearly 2 months after the bombing.

The devastating effects of the atomic bombs upon medical facilities can be appreciated in the light of the foregoing presentation. Not only were the existing facilities almost completely destroyed but there was extreme apathy toward the restoration of hospitals and the care of the injured.

EFFECTS ON MEDICAL PERSONNEL

It was almost impossible to get any accurate information relative to the number of doctors, nurses and other medical personnel in the area prior to bombing, the number injured and killed, or even the number actually present at the time of the visit by the Medical Division. Data obtained from various sources showed extreme variation and were often unreliable. Naturally, the medical personnel in general met the same fate as others located at the same distances from the bomb. The number of casualties also probably bore a direct relationship to the fate of hospitals since medical personnel would be concentrated at those institutions and roughly in proportion to the size of the hospital or clinic.

The number of physicians in Hiroshima prior to the bombing has been variously estimated from 200 to 298. The former figure was supplied to the Medical Division by the Prefectural Health Officer and the latter figure was included in an address by the Prefectural Governor on 9 September 1945. The actual figures probably fall between these two extremes. Regardless of the total number it is known that the casualty rate among this group was very high. About 90 percent were casualties, and 60 of these physicians were killed. One month later only 30 physicians were able to perform their usual duties.

The Hiroshima Prefectural Medical College was started in the spring of 1945 and the first class had matriculated. As a result of the bombing the hospital was demolished and one member of the faculty was killed and another injured. The number of students killed and injured could not be determined.

Prior to the bombing there were 1,780 nurses in Hiroshima. Of these, 1,654 were killed or injured on 6 August. Consequently, the city suffered greatly because of the lack of nurses and many untrained volunteers had to be pressed into service in caring for the injured.

The experience in Nagasaki was very similar to that in Hiroshima. The exact number of physicians in the city prior to the bombing could not be determined but there were probably about 200–250 in 1944. This number may have decreased slightly in 1945 as a result of actual bombing and the effects of partial evacuation of the city in preparation for raids. Due to the different character of the two cities it would at first appear that the loss of medical personnel would have been proportionately less in Naga-saki. However, a factor which counterbalanced this fact to some extent was that the largest number and best of the medical personnel were concentrated in the medical school and the University Hospital, both of which were completely destroyed with a large percentage of their occupants. Actual investigation as of 1 November revealed that there were about 120 physicians in Nagasaki. So apparently the city did fare better than Hiroshima which had less than half that many physicians at about the same time.

The damage to the Nagasaki Medical College and University Hospital has already been described. Reports reveal that 600 of the 850 medical students were killed and some others may have died later. Of the survivors practically every one was injured and at least half had radiation sickness later. There were 16 of the 20 faculty members present at the time of the bombing and 12 of them were killed and the others injured.

The casualty rate among nurses in Nagasaki could not be accurately determined. There were 683 nurses in the city on 1 November but it is not known how many of those had come in after the bombing. The percentage of fatalities and injuries probably closely paralleled that of the physicians but no accurate figures are available to support this supposition. . . .

San Francisco Conference (1945)

The United Nations Charter (1945) was ratified at the San Francisco Conference in June, 1945, while the greatest war in the history of Western Civilization thundered to a close. Those leaders who hoped to avoid a repetition of failure marking peace efforts following the First World War, sought plans for a durable peace while the war yet continued. Preliminary steps for a world organization to supplant the defunct League of Nations were taken at the Dumbarton Oaks Conference in the fall of 1944. Representatives of the Big Four (The United States, Great Britain, Russia, and China) drafted a tentative United Nations Constitution and issued the call for the San Francisco meeting. Delegates from 50 nations and 200 representatives of every race and area met at San Francisco beginning in April, 1945, to iron out their differences and to ratify a new instrument of world organization. The San Francisco

Conference was not a peace conference; thus the issue of world organization was not complicated by the passions of the peace table as when the League of Nations was born. Moreover, the charter was not made part of any peace settlement or treaty. Rather, it extended into the era of peace an effective organization constructed during the war. The Statute of the International Court of Justice, although forming an integral part of the charter (as indicated in Article 92), is not included here. In reading this selection note (1) in the preamble the contrast between peoples and governments and the objectives to be attained by each, (2) the purpose and underlying principles of the United Nations, (3) the composition and powers of the General Assembly, (4) the composition and powers of the Security Council, (5) provisions for voting and the veto, (6) the measures for the peaceful settlement of disputes and for meeting threats to peace, (7) provisions for regional arrangements, (8) the measures and organization for the promotion of economic and social well-being, (9) the method devised to care for backward areas, (10) provisions for the International Court of Justice, (11) the organization and functions of the Secretariat, and (12) comparisons and contrasts with the Covenant of the League of Nations.

From: THE CHARTER OF THE UNITED NATIONS

We, the peoples of the United Nations, determined to save succeeding generations from the scourge of war, which twice in our lifetime has brought untold sorrow to mankind, and to reaffirm faith in fundamental human rights, in the dignity and worth of the human person, in the equal rights of men and women and of nations large and small, and to establish conditions under which justice and respect for the obligations arising from treaties and other sources of international law can be maintained, and to promote social progress and better standards of life in larger freedom, and for these ends to practice tolerance and live together in peace with one another as good neighbors, and to unite our strength to maintain international peace and security, and to ensure, by the acceptance of principles and the institution of methods, that armed force shall not be used, save in the common interest, and to employ international machinery for the pro-

motion of economic and social advancement of all peoples, have resolved to combine our efforts to accomplish these aims.

Accordingly, our respective Governments, through representatives assembled in the city of San Francisco, who have exhibited their full powers found to be in good and due form, have agreed to the present Charter of the United Nations and do hereby establish an international organization to be known as the United Nations.

CHAPTER I

PURPOSES AND PRINCIPLES

Article 1

The Purposes of the United Nations are:

1. To maintain international peace and security, and to that end: to take effective collective measures for the prevention and re-

Charter of the United Nations. . . . , Department of State, Publication 2353, Conf. series 74, n.p., n.d., 1–36.

moval of threats to the peace, and for the suppression of acts of aggression or other breaches of the peace, and to bring about by peaceful means, and in conformity with the principles of justice and international law, adjustment or settlement of international disputes or situations which might lead to a breach of the peace;

2. To develop friendly relations among nations based on respect for the principle of equal rights and self-determination of peoples, and to take other appropriate measures to strengthen universal peace;

3. To achieve international co-operation in solving international problems of an economic, social, cultural, or humanitarian character, and in promoting and encouraging respect for human rights and for fundamental freedoms for all without distinction as to race, sex, language, or religion; and

4. To be a center for harmonizing the actions of nations in the attainment of these common ends.

Article 2

The Organization and its Members, in pursuit of the Purposes stated in Article 1, shall act in accordance with the following Principles.

1. The Organization is based on the principle of the sovereign equality of all its Members.

2. All Members, in order to ensure to all of them the rights and benefits resulting from membership, shall fulfil in good faith the obligations assumed by them in accordance with the present Charter.

3. All Members shall settle their international disputes by peaceful means in such a manner that international peace and security, and justice, are not endangered.

4. All Members shall refrain in their international relations from the threat or use of force against the territorial integrity or political independence of any state, or in any other manner inconsistent with the Purposes of the United Nations.

5. All Members shall give the United Nations every assistance in any action it takes in accordance with the present Charter, and shall refrain from giving assistance to any state against which the United Nations is taking preventive or enforcement action.

6. The Organization shall ensure that states which are not Members of the United Nations act in accordance with these Principles so far as may be necessary for the maintenance of international peace and security.

7. Nothing contained in the present Charter shall authorize the United Nations to intervene in matters which are essentially within the domestic jurisdiction of any state or shall require the Members to submit such matters to settlement under the present Charter; but this principle shall not prejudice the application of enforcement measures under Chapter VII.

CHAPTER II

MEMBERSHIP

Article 3

The original Members of the United Nations shall be the states which, having participated in the United Nations Conference on International Organization at San Francisco, or having previously signed the Declaration by United Nations of January 1, 1942, sign the present Charter and ratify it in accordance with Article 110.

Article 4

1. Membership in the United Nations is open to all other peace-loving states which accept the obligations contained in the present Charter and, in the judgment of the Organization, are able and willing to carry out these obligations.

2. The admission of any such state to membership in the United Nations will be effected by a decision of the General Assembly upon the recommendation of the Security Council.

Article 5

A Member of the United Nations against which preventive or enforcement action has been taken by the Security Council may be suspended from the exercise of the rights and privileges of membership by the General Assembly upon the recommendation of the Security Council. The exercise of these rights and privileges may be restored by the Security Council.

Article 6

A Member of the United Nations which has persistently violated the Principles contained in the present Charter may be expelled from the Organization by the General Assembly upon the recommendation of the Security Council.

CHAPTER III

ORGANS

Article 7

1. There are established as the principal organs of the United Nations: a General Assembly, a Security Council, an Economic and Social Council, a Trusteeship Council, an International Court of Justice, and a Secretariat.

2. Such subsidiary organs as may be found necessary may be established in accordance with the present Charter.

Article 8

The United Nations shall place no restrictions on the eligibility of men and women to participate in any capacity and under conditions of equality in its principal and subsidiary organs.

CHAPTER IV

THE GENERAL ASSEMBLY

COMPOSITION

Article 9

1. The General Assembly shall consist of all the Members of the United Nations.

2. Each Member shall have not more than five representatives in the General Assembly.

FUNCTIONS AND POWERS

Article 10

The General Assembly may discuss any questions or any matters within the scope of the present Charter or relating to the powers and functions of any organs provided for in the present Charter, and, except as provided in Article 12, may make recommendations to the Members of the United Nations or to the Security Council or to both on any such questions or matters.

Article 11

1. The General Assembly may consider the general principles of co-operation in the maintenance of international peace and security, including the principles governing disarmament and the regulation of armaments, and may make recommendations with regard to such principles to the Members or to the Security Council or to both.

2. The General Assembly may discuss any questions relating to the maintenance of international peace and security brought before it by any Member of the United Nations, or by the Security Council, or by a state which is not a Member of the United Nations in accordance with Article 35, paragraph 2, and, except as provided in Article 12, may make recommendations with regard to any such questions to the state or states concerned or to the Security Council or to both. Any such question on which action is necessary shall be referred to the Security Council by the General Assembly either before or after discussion.

3. The General Assembly may call the attention of the Security Council to situations which are likely to endanger international peace and security.

4. The powers of the General Assembly set forth in this Article shall not limit the general scope of Article 10.

Article 12

1. While the Security Council is exercising in respect of any dispute or situation the functions assigned to it in the present Charter, the General Assembly shall not make any recommendation with regard to that dispute or situation unless the Security Council so requests.

2. The Secretary-General, with the consent of the Security Council, shall notify the General Assembly at each session of any matters relative to the maintenance of international peace and security which are being dealt with by the Security Council and shall similarly notify the General Assembly, or the Members of the United Nations if the General Assembly is not in session, immediately the Security Council ceases to deal with such matters.

Article 13

1. The General Assembly shall initiate studies and make recommendations for the purpose of:

a. promoting international co-operation in the political field and encouraging the progressive development of international law and its codification;

b. promoting international co-operation in the economic, social, cultural, educational, and health fields, and assisting in the realization of human rights and fundamental freedoms for all without distinction as to race, sex, language, or religion.

2. The further responsibilities, functions, and powers of the General Assembly with respect to matters mentioned in paragraph 1 (b) above are set forth in Chapters IX and X.

Article 14

Subject to the provisions of Article 12, the General Assembly may recommend measures for the peaceful adjustment of any situation, regardless of origin, which it deems likely to impair the general welfare or friendly relations among nations, including situations resulting from a violation of the provisions of the present Charter setting forth the Purposes and Principles of the United Nations.

Article 15

1. The General Assembly shall receive and consider annual and special reports from the Security Council; these reports shall include an account of the measures that the Security Council has decided upon or taken to maintain international peace and security.

2. The General Assembly shall receive and consider reports from the other organs of the United Nations.

Article 16

The General Assembly shall perform such functions with respect to the international trusteeship system as are assigned to it under Chapters XII and XIII, including the approval of the trusteeship agreements for areas not designated as strategic.

Article 17

1. The General Assembly shall consider and approve the budget of the Organization.

2. The expenses of the Organization shall be borne by the Members as apportioned by the General Assembly.

3. The General Assembly shall consider and approve any financial and budgetary arrangements with specialized agencies referred to in Article 57 and shall examine the administrative budgets of such specialized agencies with a view to making recommendations to the agencies concerned.

VOTING

Article 18

1. Each member of the General Assembly shall have one vote.

2. Decisions of the General Assembly on important questions shall be made by a two-thirds majority of the members present and voting. These questions shall include: recommendations with respect to the maintenance of international peace and security, the election of the non-permanent members of the Security Council, the election of the members of the Economic and Social Council, the election of members of the Trusteeship Council in accordance with paragraph 1 (c) of Article 86, the admission of new Members to the United Nations, the suspension of the rights and privileges of membership, the expulsion of Members, questions relating to the operation of the trusteeship system, and budgetary questions.

3. Decisions on other questions, including the determination of additional categories of questions to be decided by a two-thirds majority, shall be made by a majority of the members present and voting.

Article 19

A Member of the United Nations which is in arrears in the payment of its financial contributions to the Organization shall have no vote in the General Assembly if the amount of its arrears equals or exceeds the amount of the contributions due from it for the preceding two full years. The General Assembly may, nevertheless, permit such a Member to vote if it is satisfied that the failure to pay is due to conditions beyond the control of the Member.

PROCEDURE

Article 20

The General Assembly shall meet in regular annual sessions and in such special sessions as occasion may require. Special sessions shall be convoked by the Secretary-General at the request of the Security Council or of a majority of the Members of the United Nations.

Article 21

The General Assembly shall adopt its own rules of procedure. It shall elect its President for each session.

Article 22

The General Assembly may establish such subsidiary organs as it deems necessary for the performance of its functions.

CHAPTER V

THE SECURITY COUNCIL

COMPOSITION

Article 23

1. The Security Council shall consist of eleven Members of the United Nations. The Republic of China, France, the Union of Soviet Socialist Republics, the United Kingdom of Great Britain and Northern Ireland, and the United States of America shall be permanent members of the Security Council. The General Assembly shall elect six other Members of the United Nations to be non-permanent members of the Security Council, due regard being specially paid, in the first instance to the contribution of Members of the United Nations to the maintenance of international peace and security and to the other purposes of the Organization, and also to equitable geographical distribution.

2. The non-permanent members of the Security Council shall be elected for a term of two years. In the first election of the non-permanent members, however, three shall be chosen for a term of one year. A retiring member shall not be eligible for immediate re-election.

3. Each member of the Security Council shall have one representative.

FUNCTIONS AND POWERS

Article 24

1. In order to ensure prompt and effective action by the United Nations, its Members confer on the Security Council primary responsibility for the maintenance of international peace and security, and agree that in carrying out its duties under this responsibility the Security Council acts on their behalf.

2. In discharging these duties the Security Council shall act in accordance with the Purposes and Principles of the United Nations. The specific powers granted to the Security Council for the discharge of these duties are laid down in Chapters VI, VII, VIII, and XII.

3. The Security Council shall submit annual and, when necessary, special reports to the General Assembly for its consideration.

Article 25

The Members of the United Nations agree to accept and carry out the decisions of the Security Council in accordance with the present Charter.

Article 26

In order to promote the establishment and maintenance of international peace and security with the least diversion for armaments of the world's human and economic resources, the Security Council shall be responsible for formulating, with the assistance of the Military Staff Committee referred to in Article 47, plans to be submitted to the Members of the United Nations for the establishment of a system for the regulation of armaments.

VOTING

Article 27

1. Each member of the Security Council shall have one vote.

2. Decisions of the Security Council on procedural matters shall be made by an affirmative vote of seven members.

3. Decisions of the Security Council on all other matters shall be made by an affirmative vote of seven members including the concurring votes of the permanent members; provided that, in decisions under Chapter VI, and under paragraph 3 of Article 52, a party to a dispute shall abstain from voting.

PROCEDURE

Article 28

1. The Security Council shall be so organized as to be able to function continuously. Each member of the Security Council shall for this purpose be represented at all times at the seat of the Organization.

2. The Security Council shall hold periodic meetings at which each of its members may, if it so desires, be represented by a member of the government or by some other specially designated representative.

3. The Security Council may hold meetings at such places other than the seat of the Organization as in its judgment will best facilitate its work.

Article 29

The Security Council may establish such subsidiary organs as it deems necessary for the performance of its functions.

Article 30

The Security Council shall adopt its own rules of procedure, including the method of selecting its President.

Article 31

Any Member of the United Nations which is not a member of the Security Council may participate, without vote, in the discussion of any question brought before the Security Council whenever the latter considers that the interests of that Member are specially affected.

Article 32

Any Member of the United Nations which is not a member of the Security Council or any state which is not a Member of the United Nations, if it is a party to a dispute under consideration by the Security Council, shall be invited to participate, without vote, in the dis-

cussion relating to the dispute. The Security Council shall lay down such conditions as it deems just for the participation of a state which is not a Member of the United Nations.

CHAPTER VI

PACIFIC SETTLEMENT OF DISPUTES

Article 33

1. The parties to any dispute, the continuance of which is likely to endanger the maintenance of international peace and security, shall, first of all, seek a solution by negotiation, enquiry, mediation, conciliation, arbitration, judicial settlement, resort to regional agencies or arrangements, or other peaceful means of their own choice.

2. The Security Council shall, when it deems necessary, call upon the parties to settle their dispute by such means.

Article 34

The Security Council may investigate any dispute, or any situation which might lead to international friction or give rise to a dispute, in order to determine whether the continuance of the dispute or situation is likely to endanger the maintenance of international peace and security.

Article 35

1. Any Member of the United Nations may bring any dispute, or any situation of the nature referred to in Article 34, to the attention of the Security Council or of the General Assembly.

2. A state which is not a Member of the United Nations may bring to the attention of the Security Council or of the General Assembly any dispute to which it is a party if it accepts in advance, for the purposes of the dispute, the obligations of pacific settlement provided in the present Charter.

3. The proceedings of the General Assembly in respect of matters brought to its attention under this Article will be subject to the provisions of Articles 11 and 12.

Article 36

1. The Security Council may, at any stage of a dispute of the nature referred to in Article

33 or of a situation of like nature, recommend appropriate procedures or methods of adjustment.

2. The Security Council should take into consideration any procedures for the settlement of the dispute which have already been adopted by the parties.

3. In making recommendations under this Article the Security Council should also take into consideration that legal disputes should as a general rule be referred by the parties to the International Court of Justice in accordance with the provisions of the Statute of the Court.

Article 37

1. Should the parties to a dispute of the nature referred to in Article 33 fail to settle it by the means indicated in that Article, they shall refer it to the Security Council.

2. If the Security Council deems that the continuance of the dispute · is in fact likely to endanger the maintenance of international peace and security, it shall decide whether to take action under Article 36 or to recommend such terms of settlement as it may consider appropriate.

Article 38

Without prejudice to the provisions of Articles 33 to 37, the Security Council may, if all the parties to any dispute so request, make recommendations to the parties with a view to a pacific settlement of the dispute.

CHAPTER VII

ACTION WITH RESPECT TO THREATS TO THE PEACE, BREACHES OF THE PEACE, AND ACTS OF AGGRESSION

Article 39

The Security Council shall determine the existence of any threat to the peace, breach of the peace, or act of aggression and shall make recommendations, or decide what measures shall be taken in accordance with Articles 41 and 42, to maintain or restore international peace and security.

Article 40

In order to prevent an aggravation of the situation, the Security Council may, before making the recommendations or deciding upon the measures provided for in Article 39, call upon the parties concerned to comply with such provisional measures as it deems necessary or desirable. Such provisional measures shall be without prejudice to the rights, claims, or position of the parties concerned. The Security Council shall duly take account of failure to comply with such provisional measures.

Article 41

The Security Council may decide what measures not involving the use of armed force are to be employed to give effect to its decisions, and it may call upon the Members of the United Nations to apply such measures. These may include complete or partial interruption of economic relations and of rail, sea, air, postal, telegraphic, radio, and other means of communication, and the severance of diplomatic relations.

Article 42

Should the Security Council consider that measures provided for in Article 41 would be inadequate or have proved to be inadequate, it may take such action by air, sea, or land forces as may be necessary to maintain or restore international peace and security. Such action may include demonstrations, blockade, and other operations by air, sea, or land forces of Members of the United Nations.

Article 43

1. All Members of the United Nations, in order to contribute to the maintenance of international peace and security, undertake to make available to the Security Council, on its call and in accordance with a special agreement or agreements, armed forces, assistance, and facilities, including rights of passage, necessary for the purpose of maintaining international peace and security.

2. Such agreement or agreements shall govern the numbers and types of forces, their degree of readiness and general location, and the nature of the facilities and assistance to be provided.

3. The agreement or agreements shall be negotiated as soon as possible on the initiative of the Security Council. They shall be con-

cluded between the Security Council and Members or between the Security Council and groups of Members and shall be subject to ratification by the signatory states in accordance with their respective constitutional processes.

Article 44

When the Security Council has decided to use force it shall, before calling upon a Member not represented on it to provide armed forces in fulfillment of the obligations assumed under Article 43, invite that Member, if the Member so desires, to participate in the decisions of the Security Council concerning the employment of contingents of that Member's armed forces.

Article 45

In order to enable the United Nations to take urgent military measures, Members shall hold immediately available national air-force contingents for combined international enforcement action. The strength and degree of readiness of these contingents and plans for their combined action shall be determined, within the limits laid down in the special agreement or agreements referred to in Article 43, by the Security Council with the assistance of the Military Staff Committee.

Article 46

Plans for the application of armed force shall be made by the Security Council with the assistance of the Military Staff Committee.

Article 47

1. There shall be established a Military Staff Committee to advise and assist the Security Council on all questions relating to the Security Council's military requirements for the maintenance of international peace and security, the employment and command of forces placed at its disposal, the regulation of armaments, and possible disarmament.

2. The Military Staff Committee shall consist of the Chiefs of Staff of the permanent members of the Security Council or their representatives. Any Member of the United Nations not permanently represented on the Committee shall be invited by the Committee to be associated with it when the efficient discharge of the Committee's responsibilities requires the participation of that Member in its work.

3. The Military Staff Committee shall be responsible under the Security Council for the strategic direction of any armed forces placed at the disposal of the Security Council. Questions relating to the command of such forces shall be worked out subsequently.

4. The Military Staff Committee, with the authorization of the Security Council and after consultation with appropriate regional agencies, may establish regional subcommittees.

Article 48

1. The action required to carry out the decisions of the Security Council for the maintenance of international peace and security shall be taken by all the Members of the United Nations or by some of them, as the Security Council may determine.

2. Such decisions shall be carried out by the Members of the United Nations directly and through their action in the appropriate international agencies of which they are members.

Article 49

The Members of the United Nations shall join in affording mutual assistance in carrying out the measures decided upon by the Security Council.

Article 50

If preventive or enforcement measures against any state are taken by the Security Council, any other state, whether a Member of the United Nations or not, which finds itself confronted with special economic problems arising from the carrying out of those measures shall have the right to consult the Security Council with regard to a solution of those problems.

Article 51

Nothing in the present Charter shall impair the inherent right of individual or collective self-defense if an armed attack occurs against a Member of the United Nations, until the Security Council has taken the measures necessary to maintain international peace and security. Measures taken by Members in the exercise of this right of self-defense shall be immediately reported to the Security Council and shall not in any way affect the authority and responsibility of the Security Council under the present Charter to take at any time such action as it deems necessary in order to maintain or restore international peace and security.

Chapter VIII

REGIONAL ARRANGEMENTS

Article 52

1. Nothing in the present Charter precludes the existence of regional arrangements or agencies for dealing with such matters relating to the maintenance of international peace and security as are appropriate for regional action, provided that such arrangements or agencies and their activities are consistent with the Purposes and Principles of the United Nations.

2. The Members of the United Nations entering into such arrangements or constituting such agencies shall make every effort to achieve pacific settlement of local disputes through such regional arrangements or by such regional agencies before referring them to the Security Council.

3. The Security Council shall encourage the development of pacific settlement of local disputes through such regional arrangements or by such regional agencies either on the initiative of the states concerned or by reference from the Security Council.

4. This Article in no way impairs the application of Articles 34 and 35.

Article 53

1. The Security Council shall, where appropriate, utilize such regional arrangements or agencies for enforcement action under its authority. But no enforcement action shall be taken under regional arrangements or by regional agencies without the authorization of the Security Council, with the exception of measures against any enemy state, as defined in paragraph 2 of this Article, provided for pursuant to Article 107 or in regional arrangements directed against renewal of aggressive policy on the part of any such state, until such

time as the Organization may, on request of the Governments concerned, be charged with the responsibility for preventing further aggression by such a state.

2. The term enemy state as used in paragraph 1 of this Article applies to any state which during the Second World War has been an enemy of any signatory of the present Charter.

Article 54

The Security Council shall at all times be kept fully informed of activities undertaken or in contemplation under regional arrangements or by regional agencies for the maintenance of international peace and security.

Chapter IX

INTERNATIONAL ECONOMIC AND SOCIAL CO-OPERATION

Article 55

With a view to the creation of conditions of stability and well-being which are necessary for peaceful and friendly relations among nations based on respect for the principle of equal rights and self-determination of peoples, the United Nations shall promote:

a. higher standards of living, full employment, and conditions of economic and social progress and development;

b. solutions of international economic, social, health, and related problems; and international cultural and educational co-operation; and

c. universal respect for, and observance of, human rights and fundamental freedoms for all without distinction as to race, sex, language, or religion.

Article 56

All Members pledge themselves to take joint and separate action in co-operation with the Organization for the achievement of the purposes set forth in Article 55.

Article 57

1. The various specialized agencies, established by intergovernmental agreement and having wide international responsibilities, as defined in their basic instruments, in economic,

social, cultural, educational, health, and related fields, shall be brought into relationship with the United Nations in accordance with the provisions of Article 63.

2. Such agencies thus brought into relationship with the United Nations are hereinafter referred to as specialized agencies.

Article 58

The Organization shall make recommendations for the co-ordination of the policies and activities of the specialized agencies.

Article 59

The Organization shall, where appropriate, initiate negotiations among the states concerned for the creation of any new specialized agencies required for the accomplishment of the purposes set forth in Article 55.

Article 60

Responsibility for the discharge of the functions of the Organization set forth in this Chapter shall be vested in the General Assembly and, under the authority of the General Assembly, in the Economic and Social Council, which shall have for this purpose the powers set forth in Chapter X.

CHAPTER X

THE ECONOMIC AND SOCIAL COUNCIL

COMPOSITION

Article 61

1. The Economic and Social Council shall consist of eighteen Members of the United Nations elected by the General Assembly.

2. Subject to the provisions of paragraph 3, six members of the Economic and Social Council shall be elected each year for a term of three years. A retiring member shall be eligible for immediate re-election.

3. At the first election, eighteen members of the Economic and Social Council shall be chosen. The term of office of six members so chosen shall expire at the end of one year, and of six other members at the end of two years, in accordance with arrangements made by the General Assembly.

4. Each member of the Economic and Social Council shall have one representative.

FUNCTIONS AND POWERS

Article 62

1. The Economic and Social Council may make or initiate studies and reports with respect to international economic, social, cultural, educational, health, and related matters and may make recommendations with respect to any such matters to the General Assembly, to the Members of the United Nations, and to the specialized agencies concerned.

2. It may make recommendations for the purpose of promoting respect for, and observance of, human rights and fundamental freedoms for all.

3. It may prepare draft conventions for submission to the General Assembly, with respect to matters falling within its competence.

4. It may call, in accordance with the rules prescribed by the United Nations, international conferences on matters falling within its competence.

Article 63

1. The Economic and Social Council may enter into agreements with any of the agencies referred to in Article 57, defining the terms on which the agency concerned shall be brought into relationship with the United Nations. Such agreements shall be subject to approval by the General Assembly.

2. It may co-ordinate the activities of the specialized agencies through consultation with and recommendations to such agencies and through recommendations to the General Assembly and to the Members of the United Nations.

Article 64

1. The Economic and Social Council may take appropriate steps to obtain regular reports from the specialized agencies. It may make arrangements with the Members of the United Nations and with the specialized agencies to obtain reports on the steps taken to give effect to its own recommendations and to recommendations on matters falling within its competence made by the General Assembly.

2. It may communicate its observations on these reports to the General Assembly.

Article 65

The Economic and Social Council may furnish information to the Security Council and shall assist the Security Council upon its request.

Article 66

1. The Economic and Social Council shall perform such functions as fall within its competence in connection with the carrying out of the recommendations of the General Assembly.

2. It may, with the approval of the General Assembly, perform services at the request of Members of the United Nations and at the request of specialized agencies.

3. It shall perform such other functions as are specified elsewhere in the present Charter or as may be assigned to it by the General Assembly.

VOTING

Article 67

1. Each member of the Economic and Social Council shall have one vote.

2. Decisions of the Economic and Social Council shall be made by a majority of the members present and voting.

PROCEDURE

Article 68

The Economic and Social Council shall set up commissions in economic and social fields and for the promotion of human rights, and such other commissions as may be required for the performance of its functions.

Article 69

The Economic and Social Council shall invite any Member of the United Nations to participate, without vote, in its deliberations on any matter of particular concern to that Member.

Article 70

The Economic and Social Council may make arrangements for representatives of the specialized agencies to participate, without vote, in its deliberations and in those of the commissions established by it, and for its representatives to participate in the deliberations of the specialized agencies.

Article 71

The Economic and Social Council may make suitable arrangements for consultation with non-governmental organizations which are concerned with matters within its competence. Such arrangements may be made with international organizations and, where appropriate, with national organizations after consultation with the Member of the United Nations concerned.

Article 72

1. The Economic and Social Council shall adopt its own rules of procedure, including the method of selecting its President.

2. The Economic and Social Council shall meet as required in accordance with its rules, which shall include provisions for the convening of meetings on the request of a majority of its members.

CHAPTER XI

DECLARATION REGARDING NON-SELF-GOVERNING TERRITORIES

Article 73

Members of the United Nations which have or assume responsibilities for the administration of territories whose peoples have not yet attained a full measure of self-government recognize the principle that the interests of the inhabitants of these territories are paramount, and accept as a sacred trust the obligation to promote to the utmost, within the system of international peace and security established by the present Charter, the well-being of the inhabitants of these territories, and, to this end:

a. to ensure, with due respect for the culture of the peoples concerned, their political, economic, social, and educational advancement, their just treatment, and their protection against abuses;

b. to develop self-government, to take due account of the political aspirations of the peoples, and to assist them in the progressive development of their free political institutions, according to the particular circumstances of each territory and its peoples and their varying stages of advancement;

c. to further international peace and security;

d. to promote constructive measures of development, to encourage research, and to co-operate with one another and, when and where appropriate, with specialized international bodies with a view to the practical achievement of the social, economic, and scientific purposes set forth in this Article; and

e. to transmit regularly to the Secretary-General for information purposes, subject to such limitations as security and constitutional considerations may require, statistical and other information of a technical nature relating to economic, social, and educational conditions in the territories for which they are respectively responsible other than those territories to which Chapters XII and XIII apply.

Article 74

Members of the United Nations also agree that their policy in respect of the territories to which this Chapter applies, no less than in respect of their metropolitan areas, must be based on the general principle of good-neighborliness, due account being taken of the interests and well-being of the rest of the world, in social, economic, and commercial matters.

CHAPTER XII

INTERNATIONAL TRUSTEESHIP SYSTEM

Article 75

The United Nations shall establish under its authority an international trusteeship system for the administration and supervision of such territories as may be placed thereunder by subsequent individual agreements. These territories are hereinafter referred to as trust territories.

Article 76

The basic objectives of the trusteeship system, in accordance with the Purposes of the United Nations laid down in Article 1 of the present Charter, shall be:

a. to further international peace and security;

b. to promote the political, economic, social, and educational advancement of the inhabitants of the trust territories, and their progressive development towards self-government or independence as may be appropriate to the particular circumstances of each territory and its peoples and the freely expressed wishes of the peoples concerned, and as may be provided by the terms of each trusteeship agreement;

c. to encourage respect for human rights and for fundamental freedoms for all without distinction as to race, sex, language, or religion, and to encourage recognition of the interdependence of the peoples of the world; and

d. to ensure equal treatment in social, economic, and commercial matters for all Members of the United Nations and their nationals, and also equal treatment for the latter in the administration of justice, without prejudice to the attainment of the foregoing objectives and subject to the provisions of Article 80.

Article 77

1. The trusteeship system shall apply to such territories in the following categories as may be placed thereunder by means of trusteeship agreements:

a. territories now held under mandate;

b. territories which may be detached from enemy states as a result of the Second World War; and

c. territories voluntarily placed under the system by states responsible for their administration.

2. It will be a matter for subsequent agreement as to which territories in the foregoing categories will be brought under the trusteeship system and upon what terms.

Article 78

The trusteeship system shall not apply to territories which have become Members of the United Nations, relationship among which shall be based on respect for the principle of sovereign equality.

Article 79

The terms of trusteeship for each territory to be placed under the trusteeship system, including any alteration or amendment, shall be agreed upon by the states directly concerned, including the mandatory power in the case of territories held under mandate by a Member of the United Nations, and shall be approved as provided for in Articles 83 and 85.

Article 80

1. Except as may be agreed upon in individual trusteeship agreements, made under Articles 77, 79, and 81, placing each territory under the trusteeship system, and until such agreements have been concluded, nothing in this Chapter shall be construed in or of itself to alter in any manner the rights whatsoever of any states or any peoples or the terms of existing international instruments to which Members of the United Nations may respectively be parties.

2. Paragraph 1 of this Article shall not be interpreted as giving grounds for delay or postponement of the negotiation and conclusion of agreements for placing mandated and other territories under the trusteeship system as provided for in Article 77.

Article 81

The trusteeship agreement shall in each case include the terms under which the trust territory will be administered and designate the authority which will exercise the administration of the trust territory. Such authority, hereinafter called the administering authority, may be one or more states or the Organization itself.

Article 82

There may be designated, in any trusteeship agreement, a strategic area or areas which may include part or all of the trust territory to which the agreement applies, without prejudice to any special agreement or agreements made under Article 43.

Article 83

1. All functions of the United Nations relating to strategic areas, including the approval of the terms of the trusteeship agreements and of their alteration or amendment, shall be exercised by the Security Council.

2. The basic objectives set forth in Article 76 shall be applicable to the people of each strategic area.

3. The Security Council shall, subject to the provisions of the trusteeship agreements and without prejudice to security considerations, avail itself of the assistance of the Trusteeship Council to perform those functions of the United Nations under the trusteeship system relating to political, economic, social, and educational matters in the strategic areas.

Article 84

It shall be the duty of the administering authority to ensure that the trust territory shall play its part in the maintenance of international peace and security. To this end the administering authority may make use of volunteer forces, facilities, and assistance from the trust territory in carrying out the obligations towards the Security Council undertaken in this regard by the administering authority, as well as for local defense and the maintenance of law and order within the trust territory.

Article 85

1. The functions of the United Nations with regard to trusteeship agreements for all areas not designated as strategic, including the approval of the terms of the trusteeship agreements and of their alteration or amendment, shall be exercised by the General Assembly.

2. The Trusteeship Council, operating under the authority of the General Assembly, shall assist the General Assembly in carrying out these functions.

Chapter XIII

THE TRUSTEESHIP COUNCIL

COMPOSITION

Article 86

1. The Trusteeship Council shall consist of the following Members of the United Nations:

    a. those Members administering trust territories;

    b. such of those Members mentioned by name in Article 23 as are not administering trust territories; and

    c. as many other Members elected for three-year terms by the General Assembly as may be necessary to ensure that the total number of members of the Trusteeship Council is equally divided between those Members of the United Nations which administer trust territories and those which do not.

2. Each member of the Trusteeship Council shall designate one specially qualified person to represent it therein.

FUNCTIONS AND POWERS

Article 87

The General Assembly and, under its authority, the Trusteeship Council, in carrying out their functions, may:

a. consider reports submitted by the administering authority;

b. accept petitions and examine them in consultation with the administering authority;

c. provide for periodic visits to the respective trust territories at times agreed upon with the administering authority; and

d. take these and other actions in conformity with the terms of the trusteeship agreements.

Article 88

The Trusteeship Council shall formulate a questionnaire on the political, economic, social, and educational advancement of the inhabitants of each trust territory, and the administering authority for each trust territory within the competence of the General Assembly shall make an annual report to the General Assembly upon the basis of such questionnaire.

VOTING

Article 89

1. Each member of the Trusteeship Council shall have one vote.

2. Decisions of the Trusteeship Council shall be made by a majority of the members present and voting.

PROCEDURE

Article 90

1. The Trusteeship Council shall adopt its own rules of procedure, including the method of selecting its President.

2. The Trusteeship Council shall meet as required in accordance with its rules, which shall include provision for the convening of

meetings on the request of a majority of its members.

Article 91

The Trusteeship Council shall, when appropriate, avail itself of the assistance of the Economic and Social Council and of the specialized agencies in regard to matters with which they are respectively concerned.

CHAPTER XIV

THE INTERNATIONAL COURT OF JUSTICE

Article 92

The International Court of Justice shall be the principal judicial organ of the United Nations. It shall function in accordance with the annexed Statute, which is based upon the Statute of the Permanent Court of International Justice and forms an integral part of the present Charter.

Article 93

1. All Members of the United Nations are *ipso facto* parties to the Statute of the International Court of Justice.

2. A state which is not a Member of the United Nations may become a party to the Statute of the International Court of Justice on conditions to be determined in each case by the General Assembly upon the recommendation of the Security Council.

Article 94

1. Each Member of the United Nations undertakes to comply with the decision of the International Court of Justice in any case to which it is a party.

2. If any party to a case fails to perform the obligations incumbent upon it under a judgment rendered by the Court, the other party may have recourse to the Security Council, which may, if it deems necessary, make recommendations or decide upon measures to be taken to give effect to the judgment.

Article 95

Nothing in the present Charter shall prevent Members of the United Nations from entrusting the solution of their differences to other tribunals by virtue of agreements already in existence or which may be concluded in the future.

Article 96

1. The General Assembly or the Security Council may request the International Court of Justice to give an advisory opinion on any legal question.

2. Other organs of the United Nations and specialized agencies, which may at any time be so authorized by the General Assembly, may also request advisory opinions of the Court on legal questions arising within the scope of their activities.

CHAPTER XV

THE SECRETARIAT

Article 97

The Secretariat shall comprise a Secretary-General and such staff as the Organization may require. The Secretary-General shall be appointed by the General Assembly upon the recommendation of the Security Council. He shall be the chief administrative officer of the Organization.

Article 98

The Secretary-General shall act in that capacity in all meetings of the General Assembly, of the Security Council, of the Economic and Social Council, and of the Trusteeship Council, and shall perform such other functions as are entrusted to him by these organs. The Secretary-General shall make an annual report to the General Assembly on the work of the Organization.

Article 99

The Secretary-General may bring to the attention of the Security Council any matter which in his opinion may threaten the maintenance of international peace and security.

Article 100

1. In the performance of their duties the Secretary-General and the staff shall not seek or receive instructions from any government or from any other authority external to the Organization. They shall refrain from any action which might reflect on their position as international officials responsible only to the Organization.

2. Each Member of the United Nations undertakes to respect the exclusively international character of the responsibilities of the Secretary-General and the staff and not to seek to influence them in the discharge of their responsibilities.

Article 101

1. The staff shall be appointed by the Secretary-General under regulations established by the General Assembly.

2. Appropriate staffs shall be permanently assigned to the Economic and Social Council, the Trusteeship Council, and, as required, to other organs of the United Nations. These staffs shall form a part of the Secretariat.

3. The paramount consideration in the employment of the staff and in the determination of the conditions of service shall be the necessity of securing the highest standards of efficiency, competence, and integrity. Due regard shall be paid to the importance of recruiting the staff on as wide a geographical basis as possible.

CHAPTER XVI

MISCELLANEOUS PROVISIONS

Article 102

1. Every treaty and every international agreement entered into by any Member of the United Nations after the present Charter comes into force shall as soon as possible be registered with the Secretariat and published by it.

2. No party to any such treaty or international agreement which has not been registered in accordance with the provisions of paragraph 1 of this Article may invoke that treaty or agreement before any organ of the United Nations.

Article 103

In the event of a conflict between the obligations of the Members of the United Nations under the present Charter and their obligations under any other international agreement, their obligations under the present Charter shall prevail.

Article 104

The Organization shall enjoy in the territory of each of its Members such legal capacity as may be necessary for the exercise of its functions and the fulfillment of its purposes.

Article 105

1. The Organization shall enjoy in the territory of each of its Members such privileges and immunities as are necessary for the fulfillment of its purposes.

2. Representatives of the Members of the United Nations and officials of the Organization shall similarly enjoy such privileges and immunities as are necessary for the independent exercise of their functions in connection with the Organization.

3. The General Assembly may make recommendations with a view to determining the details of the application of paragraphs 1 and 2 of this Article or may propose conventions to the Members of the United Nations for this purpose.

CHAPTER XVII

TRANSITIONAL SECURITY ARRANGEMENTS

Article 106

Pending the coming into force of such special agreements referred to in Article 43 as in the opinion of the Security Council enable it to begin the exercise of its responsibilities under Article 42, the parties to the Four-Nation Declaration, signed at Moscow, October 30, 1943, and France, shall, in accordance with the provisions of paragraph 5 of that Declaration, consult with one another and as occasion requires with other Members of the United Nations with a view to such joint action on behalf of the Organization as may be necessary for the purpose of maintaining international peace and security.

Article 107

Nothing in the present Charter shall invalidate or preclude action, in relation to any state which during the Second World War has been an enemy of any signatory to the present Charter, taken or authorized as a result of that war by the Governments having responsibility for such action.

CHAPTER XVIII

AMENDMENTS

Article 108

Amendments to the present Charter shall come into force for all Members of the United Nations when they have been adopted by a vote of two thirds of the members of the General Assembly and ratified in accordance with their respective constitutional processes by two thirds of the Members of the United Nations, including all the permanent members of the Security Council.

Article 109

1. A General Conference of the Members of the United Nations for the purpose of reviewing the present Charter may be held at a date and place to be fixed by a two-thirds vote of the members of the General Assembly and by a vote of any seven members of the Security Council. Each Member of the United Nations shall have one vote in the conference.

2. Any alteration of the present Charter recommended by a two-thirds vote of the conference shall take effect when ratified in accordance with their respective constitutional processes by two thirds of the Members of the United Nations including all the permanent members of the Security Council.

3. If such a conference has not been held before the tenth annual session of the General Assembly following the coming into force of the present Charter, the proposal to call such a conference shall be placed on the agenda of that session of the General Assembly, and the conference shall be held if so decided by a majority vote of the members of the General Assembly and by a vote of any seven members of the Security Council.

CHAPTER XIX

RATIFICATION AND SIGNATURE

Article 110

1. The present Charter shall be ratified by the signatory states in accordance with their respective constitutional processes.

2. The ratifications shall be deposited with the Government of the United States of America, which shall notify all the signatory states of each deposit as well as the Secretary-General of the Organization when he has been appointed.

3. The present Charter shall come into force upon the deposit of ratifications by the Republic of China, France, the Union of Soviet Socialist Republics, the United Kingdom of Great Britain and Northern Ireland, and the United States of America, and by a majority of the other signatory states. A protocol of the ratifications deposited shall thereupon be drawn up by the Government of the United States of America which shall communicate copies thereof to all the signatory states.

4. The states signatory to the present Charter which ratify it after it has come into force will become original Members of the United Nations on the date of the deposit of their respective ratifications.

Article 111

The present Charter, of which the Chinese, French, Russian, English, and Spanish texts are equally authentic, shall remain deposited in the archives of the Government of the United States of America. Duly certified copies thereof shall be transmitted by that Government to the Governments of the other signatory states.

In Faith Whereof the representatives of the Governments of the United Nations have signed the present Charter.

Done at the city of San Francisco the twenty-sixth day of June, one thousand nine hundred and forty-five.

Thomas Stearns Eliot

T. S. Eliot (1888–   ) is one of the more influential poets and critics of the period following the First World War. He was born in St. Louis, Missouri, attended Harvard, the Sorbonne, and Oxford. In 1914, he became an expatriate, a practice common among artists and literary men during the first decades of the twentieth century. In 1927 he renounced his American citizenship to become a British subject. Eliot reacted with disgust against the sterility and sordidness of modern materialistic civilization, but he sought surcease in religion as a practical escape from materialism rather than follow some of his fellows into radical politics, sensualism in art, or retreat into the unconscious. His interest in religion helps to explain some of the symbolism so frequently found in Eliot's poetry. In reading these selections note (1) Eliot's tone of frustration and defeat, (2) his characterization of modern society, (3) what hopes he held out for contemporary society, and (4) his conclusions concerning man's ultimate destiny.

THE HOLLOW MEN

Mistah Kurtz—he dead.

A penny for the Old Guy.

I

We are the hollow men
We are the stuffed men

Leaning together
Headpiece filled with straw. Alas!
Our dried voices, when
We whisper together
Are quiet and meaningless
As wind in dry grass

T. S. Eliot, *Collected Poems of T. S. Eliot*, Harcourt, Brace and Company, Inc., New York, 1936, 99–105. Courtesy of Harcourt, Brace and Company, Inc.

Or rats' feet over broken glass
In our dry cellar

Shape without form, shade without colour,
Paralysed force, gesture without motion;

Those who have crossed
With direct eyes, to death's other Kingdom
Remember us—if at all—not as lost
Violent souls, but only
As the hollow men
The stuffed men.

II

Eyes I dare not meet in dreams
In death's dream kingdom
These do not appear:
There, the eyes are
Sunlight on a broken column
There, is a tree swinging
And voices are
In the wind's singing
More distant and more solemn
Than a fading star.

Let me be no nearer
In death's dream kingdom
Let me also wear
Such deliberate disguises
Rat's coat, crowskin, crossed staves
In a field
Behaving as the wind behaves
No nearer—

Not that final meeting
In the twilight kingdom

III

This is the dead land
This is cactus land
Here the stone images
Are raised, here they receive
The supplication of a dead man's hand
Under the twinkle of a fading star.

Is it like this
In death's other kingdom
Waking alone
At the hour when we are
Trembling with tenderness

Lips that would kiss
Form prayers to broken stone.

IV

The eyes are not here
There are no eyes here
In this valley of dying stars
In this hollow valley
This broken jaw of our lost kingdoms

In this last of meeting places
We grope together
And avoid speech
Gathered on this beach of the tumid river

Sightless, unless
The eyes reappear
As the perpetual star
Multifoliate rose
Of death's twilight kingdom
The hope only
Of empty men.

V

Here we go round the prickly pear
Prickly pear prickly pear
Here we go round the prickly pear
At five o'clock in the morning.

Between the idea
And the reality
Between the motion
And the Act
Falls the Shadow

                                   For Thine is the Kingdom

Between the conception
And the creation
Between the emotion
And the response
Falls the Shadow

                                   Life is very long

Between the desire
And the spasm
Between the potency
And the existence
Between the essence
And the descent
Falls the Shadow

                                   For Thine is the Kingdom

For Thine is

Life is

For Thine is the

This is the way the world ends
This is the way the world ends
This is the way the world ends
Not with a bang but a whimper.

Julian Huxley

Julian Huxley (1887–) is an eminent English biologist and brother of the novelist, Aldous Huxley. His
grandfather was the nineteenth-century scientist, Thomas
Huxley, friend, interpreter, and popularizer of the great
Charles Darwin. Julian Huxley accepts completely the philosophical and religious implications of modern science and
seeks to free men from dependence upon what he would
regard as the hampering presuppositions concerning the nature of truth and of life. The author prepared this essay as
an answer to a series of essays written by leading idealists
concerned with reinvigorating the spiritual life of western
peoples beset by crisis and war. In reading this selection
note (1) his statement of the apparent dilemma faced by
the contemporary world, (2) his views as to the possibilities
of reconciliation between these two ways of approaching
and thinking about the universe, (3) his step-by-step defense of science, (4) his attack upon dualism, (5) the
author's view of evolution, (6) man's position in the evolutionary process and man's relation to progress, (7) his
treatment of the problems of moral certitude, (8) how
modern psychology deals with ethics through the concept
of repression, (9) his description of the synthesis of relativism and absolutism in value judgments, and (10) Huxley's conclusions concerning the value of a scientifically
based philosophy.

THE BIOLOGIST LOOKS AT MAN

The Western world today, as all previous
contributors to this series have emphasized in
one way or another, is caught in an apparent
dilemma between two conflicting modes of
thought. The one thinks in terms of absolutes
—the absoluteness of truth, beauty, justice,
goodness, themselves all deriving from an Absolute of absolutes, which is God. The natural
world is complemented by the supernatural,
the body by the soul, the temporal by the eternal. This view gives an essentially static world
picture; the flux of events is merely change, in
which the only progress is a spiritual one, toward the perfection of eternal values. Empiri-
cism and the experimental method are alien to
it; the absolute of Revelation and the absolute
of pure Reason will between them answer all
the questions that can be answered. Man's
place in the universe is the place of an eternal
soul, created by God, and working out its destiny in terms of eternal values.

The other is the scientific method. It subjects

Julian Huxley, "The Biologist Looks at Man," in *Fortune,* December, 1942. Reprinted as "Philosophy in a World at War" in Julian Huxley, *On Living in a Revolution,* Harper and Brothers, New York, 1944. Courtesy of *Fortune* and Harper and Brothers.

the conclusions of reason to the arbitrament of hard fact to build an increasing body of tested knowledge. It refuses to ask questions that cannot be answered, and rejects such answers as cannot be provided except by Revelation. It discovers the relatedness of all things in the universe—of the motion of the moon to the influence of earth and sun, of the nature of the organism to its environment, of human civilization to the conditions under which it is made. It introduces history into everything. Stars and scenery have their history, alike with plant species or human institutions, and nothing is intelligible without some knowledge of its past. As Whitehead has said, each event is the reflection or effect of every other event, past as well as present. It rejects dualism. The supernatural is in part the region of the natural that has not yet been understood, in part an invention of human fantasy, in part the unknowable. Body and soul are not separate entities, but two aspects of one organization, and Man is that portion of the universal world stuff that has evolved until it is capable of rational and purposeful values. His place in the universe is to continue that evolution and to realize those values.

These two ways of approaching and thinking about the universe are irreconcilable—as irreconcilable as is magic with scientific agriculture, witch doctoring with preventive medicine, or number mysticism with higher mathematics. Because our thinking still contains elements from both, it and we are confused.

This is not the view of the previous contributors to this series. In different ways they have maintained that the two systems of thought are not mutually exclusive but complimentary. Though they all admit that the scientific or relativist approach is adequate and indeed essential so far as it goes, they agree in asserting that it cannot go all the way—that it is necessarily partial and needs to be supplemented by some elements derived from the alternative way of thinking. Professor Sperry says that we must supplement science with moral universals. Professor Maritain frankly finds the only chance of regeneration in a philosophy based on Christian theology. Professor Montague, more vaguely, postulates a tendency toward ideal good operating in nature—an omnipresent but not omnipotent Holy Spirit, strongly reminiscent of Matthew Arnold's "something, not ourselves, which makes for righteousness." Professor Montague calls this a god, without the capital letter. Professor Hocking is more definite: for him the truth of science needs to be supplemented by another truth: that the world is our absolute, in that it has a unity and a purpose, and is (if I understand him) the conscious purpose of God.

To me, this mixing of two totally different kinds of thinking can only lead to confusion. When men assert that the scientific approach is incomplete, it is because they have not been willing to follow it to its final conclusion, or because they are mistaking an early stage in its growth for full development.

Science inevitably began by trying its hand on the simpler phenomena of nature. Its first triumphs were in mechanics, including the spectacular celestial mechanics of Newton. It next proceeded to simple physics, like the gas laws or the decomposition of white light. Chemistry, even elementary chemistry, did not take real shape till a century later. The life sciences developed later than those of lifeless matter, for the sufficing reason that they deal with more complex phenomena. Physiology had to wait on physics and chemistry before it could become scientific. The central fact of biology, evolution, was not established until modern science had been in existence for over two hundred years; the mysteries of heredity did not become clear until well on in the present century. In the same way the science of mind developed later than biological science. What Newton was for mechanics and physics, and Darwin for biology, Freud was for psychology—the originator of a new and illuminating way of thinking about the subject matter of his science.

It is of some significance that none of the previous writers in this series have even mentioned Freud or taken the findings of modern psychology into consideration at all—not excluding Professor Montague, though he essays a psychological analysis of the development of conscience in the growing child.

This is one of the reasons for their claim that the scientific approach is insufficient. Of course it is insufficient if you leave out the latest stage of its development. You might just as well leave out physiology and evolution and then claim that the scientific approach as represented by classical physics and chemistry was insufficient. No, the only cure for the insufficiency of science is more science. The scientific approach, empirical and where possible experimental, refusing the absolute for the relative, and rejecting the deductions of pure reason except when based upon the inductions of raw fact, cannot be rejected as insufficient until it has been completely tried out on the analysis of human mind and human affairs as well as on that of nonliving matter. In these less complex fields its application has already revolutionized our way of thinking about the universe (not to mention producing the most spectacular practical results): there is no reason why it should not continue to do so as it consolidates its hold on the new areas it is now invading. Let us not forget that scientific method is extremely young: what are three centuries compared to the millenniums of civilization, the million years of man, or the thousand million years of evolving life?

Scientific method today has reached about as far in its understanding of human mind as it had in the understanding of electricity by the time of Galvani and Ampère. The Faradays and Clerk Maxwells of psychology are still to come; new tools of investigation, we can be sure, are still to be discovered before we can penetrate much further, just as the invention of the telescope and calculus were necessary precursors of Newton's great generalizations in mechanics.

However, even with the progress that science has already made, it is possible to give a reasonably coherent world picture based on the scientific approach; and this contains elements of the greatest importance to our philosophy and to our practical outlook. One is that the universe is not dualistic but monistic; another is the incorporation of values within the scientific picture, and a reconciliation of their absoluteness in principle with their relativity in practice; a third is the real existence of progress in evolution; a fourth is the complete and sole responsibility of man for achieving any further progress that may be made on this planet, and the falsity of all his attempts to

shift any of the burden of his responsibilities onto the shoulders of outside powers; and a fifth is the establishment of the developed human personality as the highest product of the universe (or at least the highest product of which we have any knowledge), with all the implications of this fact for our social and political philosophy.

DARWIN IS VINDICATED

Let me take these points one by one, to show their interconnection. The way of advance for truth is in general the same as the way of advance for existing life: of two alternatives, one dies out, not because the other destroys it directly, but because it is less fitted to survive. Even after Copernicus, the doctrine that the sun goes round the earth could still be logically maintained. But it demanded enormous complexity of epicycle upon epicycle. The rival theory that the earth goes round the sun was far simpler and more satisfying; in the climate provided by developing civilization it survived, the other simply died out of human thinking.

The monistic, unitary view of the universe will survive for the same kind of reason. Our scientific knowledge now permits us to assert definitely that there is no break in the continuity of phenomena. All matter, living or lifeless, is composed of the same units—all the millions of different lifeless substances, as well as of living species, are made of different combinations of the chemical elements, and these in turn of different combinations of still more elementary particles (or "wavicles"). In reproduction, there is no moment at which life enters; there is continuity of life between the offspring and its parent or parents. The offspring is merely a detached portion of the parental living substance. Nowhere in the transformation of microscopic ovum to adult human being is there a break at which one can say "here mind appears," or "there personality enters"; development is continuous.

It is the same with the vast process of organic evolution. Here too gradualness and continuity reign; there is no moment at which we can say that reptile ends or bird begins, no definite demarcation between man and not-man, no sharp line at which we must or indeed could postulate the sudden injection of thought or soul into evolving life. The ideas of evolution by brusque mutations of large extent have disappeared: with the new knowledge of the last twenty years the overwhelming consensus of biology has returned to support Darwin's original view of the extreme gradualness of all evolutionary change.

Nor is there the least reason for postulating any sudden injection of life into our world. Living matter is composed of the same elements as nonliving, and no trace of any special "vital energy" has been detected. The scientific view is that under the conditions obtaining during early history of the earth, the particular combination of matter that we call life was formed in the cosmic test tube, and once formed could maintain itself by its power of self-reproduction. Any other hypothesis is less simple: the onus of proof falls on those who would maintain it.

THE QUICK AND THE DEAD

What then becomes of the apparent dualism between matter and spirit? Many philosophers, including Professor Montague, persist in affirming that the only alternative is materialism, according to which mind is "a function of the body (matter), and depends upon it completely." This is an easy thesis to demolish; and having demolished it, they can conclude that the dualistic alternative is true. The real alternative to dualism they have conveniently omitted to mention.

The only logical alternative to dualism is monism—that matter and mind are two aspects of one reality, that there exists one world stuff, which reveals material or mental properties according to the point of view. Looked at from the outside, the world stuff has nothing but material properties; its operations appear as mind only to itself, from within. The first objection to this, that we have experience of the minds of other people, disappears when we remember that this experience is not direct, as is the experience of our own psychic processes, but indirect, deduced from other people's behavior (including expression and verbal behavior), combined with our knowledge of our own minds. The second objection, that a dead

man still has the same body as a live one, and therefore differs by the loss of a living soul, is still more easily disposed of. A dead body is *not* the same as a living body: the chemical conditions in it—for instance the presence of enough oxygen for the functioning of the tissues—are different. If you substitute oil for acid in the battery of your automobile, no current will pass. The interpretation of a primitive savage might well be that the living soul of the contraption had fled. But we know that the conditions have been altered: restore the old conditions and the battery becomes "live" again. It is the same with the body. The physicochemical conditions of the dead body are different from those of the living body: if you could restore the conditions found in the living body, the dead body would live again. This has been done by artificially restarting the heart; but owing to the rapidity with which irreversible changes take place in dying cells, this has so far proved possible only within a very short time after death (or, if you prefer, what otherwise would have been death) has occurred.

But if the world stuff is both matter and mind in one; if there is no break in continuity between the thinking, feeling adult human being and the inert ovum from which he developed; no break in continuity between man and his remote pre-amoebic ancestor; no break in continuity between life and not-life—why then mind or something of the same nature as mind must exist throughout the entire universe. This is, I believe, the truth. We may never be able to prove it, but it is the most economical hypothesis: it fits the facts much more simply than does any dualistic theory, whether a universal dualism or one that assumes that mind is suddenly introduced into existing matter at a certain state, and very much more simply than one-sided idealism (in the metaphysical sense) or one-sided materialism.

THE SIGNIFICANT ELECTRIC EEL

The notion that there is something of the same nature as human mind in lifeless matter at first sight appears incredible or ridiculous. Let us, however, illustrate its possibility by considering certain well-established biological facts concerning electricity. Apart from lightning, the only powerful electric phenomena known before the late eighteenth century were the electric shocks produced by the electric eel, the electric ray, and one or two other kinds of fish. The production of electricity by life might justly have appeared as something rare and sporadic. However, as physiology progressed, it was found that electric currents pass when a nerve is stimulated, when a muscle contracts, when a gland secretes; in fact we know that all vital activities, of whatever kind, from conscious thought to the fertilization of the egg, are accompanied by some electrical activity. The electrical charges are extremely minute and can be detected only by the most refined instruments; but they are always there. They are there because what we call electricity is one aspect of all matter (indeed, when we get down to the ultimate units of matter, such as electrons, their electric properties seem to be the most essential).

In the electric eel, certain muscles have been modified so that though they have lost their original function of contraction, their electric discharges are accumulated as in a galvanic pile, and the total voltage and current are quite respectable. Whereas in the great majority of cases the electrical properties of living matter play no special part in the life of the animal, they have become the specific function of the eel's electric organs: an accident of nature has become biologically significant.

One may suggest that the same sort of thing has happened with mind. All the activities of the world stuff are accompanied by mental as well as by material happenings; in most cases, however, the mental happenings are at such a low level of intensity that we cannot detect them; we may perhaps call them "psychoid" happenings, to emphasize their difference in intensity and quality from our own psychical or mental activities. In those organs that we call brains, however, the psychoid activities are, in some way, made to reinforce each other until, as is clearly the case in higher animals, they reach a high level of intensity; and they are the dominant and specific function of the brain of man. Until we learn to detect psychoid activities of low intensity, as we have learned to do with electrical happenings, we

cannot prove this. But already it has become the simplest hypothesis that will fit the facts of developmental and evolutionary continuity.

In evolution, science has not merely revealed the bridge that provides continuity between man and lifeless matter, but has also discovered what is perhaps the most important single biological fact yet known—the fact of evolutionary progress. A great deal of evolution is mere diversification. New species constantly arise, adapted to slightly different conditions, or produced by the biological accidents of isolation or hybridization. Through this frill of diversity, however, there can be perceived a series of long-range trends, whose course runs for millions or tens of millions of years. The great majority of these trends are specializations. They fit the existing type more closely to one mode of life, and in so doing cut it off from success in others. In the evolution of higher mammals, for instance, one line specialized as predators, and became the carnivores; another specialized in chewing and digesting foliage and herbage, and usually in swift running, to become the ungulates; a third in flying—the bats; a fourth in marine life—the whales and porpoises; and so on. It is a universal rule that one-sided specializations eventually come to a dead end. There is a point beyond which natural selection cannot push them. It is impossible to be more perfectly streamlined than a dolphin; when the horse stock had reduced its digits to one, it could go no further; elephants are close to the limit of weight that is possible for an efficient land animal. When a specialization has reached its biomechanical limit, it remains unchanged—unless new competition causes it to become extinct. Thus most mammals have not evolved in any important way for ten or twenty million years, birds not for twenty or twenty-five million, ants not for thirty million.

But besides these lines of specialization we find a few lines whose trend is toward all-round instead of one-sided improvement; and these are not doomed to come to a stop. It is this all-round and potentially unlimited advance that may legitimately be called progress. It is concrete and measurable. It consists in an increased control by life over its environment, an increased independence to the changes of that environment, an increase of knowledge, of harmonious complexity and self-regulation.

But it is not universal or inevitable. It occurs in a few only out of the tens of thousands of evolving types. It reveals itself not in any advance of life as a whole, but in a raising of the level reached by the type that is biologically dominant at any given time. The union of many cells to form a single individual was evolutionary progress. So was the formation of a central nervous system, of a head, of a blood circulation, of elaborate sense organs. Later on, emergence onto land, with its consequent increase of self-regulation, marked a step in progress; so did the self-regulation of temperature that we call warm blood, the nourishment of the mammalian young by its mother, and the steady development of intelligence and the power to profit by experience in the mammalian stock. The evolution by man of conceptual thought, of conscious reason and purpose, finally produced a dominant type with radically new biological characteristics.

EVOLUTION OF PERSONALITY

To assert that man is the highest product of evolution to date is a statement of simple biological fact. There are, however, some other points concerning man's position relative to evolutionary progress that are less obvious. First is the curious fact that the human species is now the sole repository of any possible future progress for life. When multicellular animals first appeared, they all had reached a new level of progress: later, some cut themselves off from further advance by entering on blind alleys, such as the fixed, vegetative existence of the polyps and corals or the headlessness and radial symmetry of the starfish and other echinoderms. The process of restriction has now gone so far that all future progress hangs on human germ plasm. It is a biological impossibility for any other line of life to progress into a new dominant type—not the ant, the rat, nor the ape.

Second, with the evolution of man, the character of progress becomes altered. With human consciousness, values and ideals appeared on earth for the first time. The criteria of further progress must include the degree to which those ideal values are satisfied. The quest for truth and knowledge, virtue, beauty and aesthetic expression, and its satisfaction through the channels of science and philosophy, mysticism and morality, literature and the arts, becomes one of the modes or avenues of evolutionary progress. A tendency in this direction had been manifested earlier in evolution. On the whole, biological progress in its later stages had been more concerned with independence of the environment than with control over it. The introduction of ideal values makes it possible for this tendency to go further. We may anticipate that in the remote future human control over the environment will become increasingly devoted to securing greater independence, greater freedom from material exigencies, and both of them together to securing a greater degree of self-realization and of the satisfaction of human values.

It is also important to note that biological progress demands no special agency. In other words, it does not require the intervention of a conscious Divine purpose, nor the operation of some mysterious life force or *élan vital:* like most other facts of evolution, it is the automatic result of the blind forces of reproduction, variation, and differential survival. Newton's great generalization of gravitational attraction made it possible and indeed necessary to dispense with the idea of God guiding the stars in their courses; Darwin's equally great generalization of natural selection made it possible and necessary to dispense with the idea of God guiding the evolutionary courses of life. Finally, the generalizations of modern psychology and comparative religion make it possible, and necessary, to dispense with the idea of God guiding the evolutionary courses of the human species, through inspiration or other form of supernatural direction.

The present culmination of the thousand-million-year sweep of biological progress is the human species, with all its defects and mistakes. Thus the highest and richest product of the cosmic process (or, again, the highest of which we have any knowledge) is the developed human personality. It is among individual men and women that we must search for our exemplars.

REPRESSION IS NORMAL

A corollary of the facts of evolutionary progress is that man must not attempt to put off any of his burden of responsibility onto the shoulders of outside powers, whether these be conceived as magic or necessity, as life force or as God. Man stands alone as the agent of his fate and the trustee of progress for life. To accept his responsibility consciously is itself an important step toward more rapid progress. Here is a field where a philosophy based on the scientific outlook is of the utmost practical importance.

But the problem that most perplexes our present age remains the question of moral certitude. As Dean Sperry says, it is the loss of the "ethical universals," with which Christianity has equipped Western civilization, that creates the "grave moral perplexities" of the present. This is where modern psychology enters the picture. For a justification of our moral code we no longer have to have recourse to theological revelation, or to a metaphysical Absolute; Freud in combination with Darwin suffice to give us our philosophic vision. The great contribution of Freud was the discovery of the unconscious mind. What matter if logicians assert that the phrase is a contradiction in terms? It is now firmly established that through the process known as repression, desires and ideas, emotions and purposes, can be forced out of consciousness, or at least out of contact with the main organization of consciousness that we call the self or ego. They are then "in the unconscious," but in the unconscious they continue operating just as if they were ordinary processes of the mind, and they are still able to influence the conscious life of the ego in the most varied ways.

Repression is the banishment from consciousness of desires and ideas that produce otherwise intolerable conflict. It is a special form of what psychologists and neurologists call inhibition. The repressed ideas are so intolerable that consciousness will not even recognize their existence or examine them rationally; yet they are so powerful that they dis-

tort consciousness itself. They may manage to enter, in suitably disguised forms, into the very forces of the mind that aid in their repression, and lead to a neurotic conflict that is indefinitely prolonged. They may emerge under the guise of perversions, sublimations, compulsions, or mere oddities of behavior. Most important for our purpose, since the conflict is never faced in the light of conscious reason, it has to be resolved by irrational methods; emotional force must be met by emotional force. This is accomplished by the development of what psychoanalysts call the superego, a mental construction embodying the repressive forces, and also the feelings of guilt engendered by the conflict. From another angle, the superego may be looked on as the injection of external authority into the infant's developing personality. There it takes root under the form of a sense of moral compulsion. To complete the story, we may add that it is often re-projected outward, so to speak, in the form of a jealous God, an absolute moral law, an infallible Führer, or some other externalization.

The superego is a rationalization of the conflict between primitive unregulated impulse and the deep infantile need for dependence. It can be equated with certain aspects of conscience; it gives the compulsive force to taboos, both ritual and ethical; it provides morality with its irrational certitudes, and sometimes with an unpardoning ruthlessness; primitively, its strength is bound up with cruelty, and this issues in the idea of punishment for sin, including expiatory self-torture. It is, in fact, the non-rational and emotional element in ethics.

It has not, I think, been sufficiently recognized that repression is normal in man. Man is the only organism whose mind is so constructed that conflict is inevitable. The young child is subjected to powerful conflicts even before it can talk and reason, and long before it has adequate experience to resolve a conflict rationally. Repression is thus an adaptation to conflict, especially to early conflict; in its absence, the degree of assurance necessary for action and adjustment would be impossible.

Undoubtedly the picture of human psychology given by psychoanalysis and other modern dynamic theories is crude and incomplete, but equally undoubtedly it is a first approximation to the truth. It is as great an improvement over older theories as was mid-nineteenth-century physiology, for all its crudity, over the medieval theory of humors, or Dalton's atomic theory of chemistry, for all its incompleteness, over alchemy.

Its importance for philosophy, and especially for ethics, is enormous, for it enables us to understand how ethical and other values can be absolute in principle while remaining obstinately relative in practice; and in conjunction with our knowledge of evolution, it enables us to reconcile absolutism and relativism by uniting them in the concept of right direction.

Values appear absolute for two reasons. The first is a result of the structure of language. The very existence of general and abstract terms like *true* and *truth* implies that an absolute Truth exists, and also that there is always an absolute difference between truth and falsehood. This, however, is not the case. Truth is only absolute when it deals with the incomplete, such as the abstractions from reality that form the basis of mathematics. The absolute difference between truth and falsehood only applies in a limited number of situations. The atomic theory of Dalton was true in giving a reasonably accurate picture of chemical fact. It was incorrect in ascribing indivisibility to atoms; but this does not make it false, only incomplete. The fact remains, however, that man's capacity for conceptual thought makes it more difficult for him to think in relative terms. The general and the abstract tend, almost automatically, to become invested with the intellectual halo of the absolute. The lesson of science is that this tendency should be resisted. Paradoxically, we find that we are enabled to accumulate a more complete and a more certain store of knowledge when, as in science, we reject the possibility of absolute completeness or absolute certainty, and are prepared to abandon our dearest theories in the face of new facts.

What holds for truth holds also for beauty and goodness. But in the case of goodness in particular, this predisposition to translate the particular into the general, the general into the abstract, and the abstract into the absolute, is reinforced by another effect—the sense of emotional certitude which in its origin is to be traced to the mental mechanisms growing out of the need for infantile repression. Thanks to repression, it is natural for us not only to think in absolute terms, but to feel in them. The inhibiting influences of the superego tend to produce an intolerant assurance of being right, because only through such an assurance could they have succeeded in repressing their opponents into the unconscious. In so far as they succeed, they acquire emotional certitude; and that emotional certitude, given the construction of the human mind, inevitably tends to rationalize itself by claiming absolute value.

THE ETHICAL CONFLICT

When, however, we come to practice, we find ourselves plunged back into the confusion of the relative. For instance, granted that we win this war, what will be the right way of treating Germany? The absolute principle of justice makes us feel the demand that crime should be punished. But, applied to the Germans, does this mean punishing Hitler, the Nazi leaders, all those directly guilty of cruelty and injustice, or the whole German people? Furthermore, the absolute principle of justice conflicts with the equally absolute principles of mercy and love. And finally these absolute emotional principles come in conflict with the frankly utilitarian principles like the greatest good of the greatest number, whose application must be decided rationally and relatively to circumstances. Clearly one course will prove to be more right than another; but in deciding which to adopt, the so-called absolute ethical and moral principles will only take us part way.

The same is true of the individual. As he grows up, he finds that his apparently absolute ethical values constantly need the assistance of relativism, in the shape of rational judgment in the light of experience, if they are to be applicable to particular situations. It is wrong to lie; but we all know circumstances where it is more wrong to tell the truth. It is wrong to take life; but it needs rational judgment to decide whether this applies to war, to certain cases of suicide and abortion, to euthanasia, to birth control.

In fact, one of the chief tasks before each individual is to make a rational and relative adjustment of the apparent absolute of his primitive ethics, derived from infantile repression, to the practical realities of life. To accomplish this, it may even be necessary that the original structure of repressed and repressing forces be destroyed, whether by some violent emotional or religious experience, or by the deliberate "mental operation" of psychoanalysis or other form of psychotherapy.

Looked at from the evolutionary point of view, both the individual ethical values of the superego and the collective ones of the current system of religion and morality are adaptations enabling human life to carry on without too great a degree of incertitude and inner conflict. This means that they must have some degree of external relevance to the environment in which they arise, and are bound to change as it changes. For instance, so long as infectious disease was supposed to be a punishment for sin, it was possible to regard sacrifice to the gods as an ethical duty in times of pestilence. Today our modern knowledge makes it ethical for us to compel the forcible isolation of sufferers from such diseases. Again, under the new conditions of Hitler's aggression and hateful methods of warfare, many convinced pacifists have changed their strong ethical belief that war is always wrong.

In the light of these facts, the dilemma of ethics begins to look rather different. The absoluteness of ethical values turns out to be apparent only, springing partly from the feeling of certitude or even compulsion associated with repression, partly from man's natural yearning for certitude, partly from his language habits. On the other hand, the inconstancy of ethical values revealed by history and anthropology, which is at first so confusing and distressing, turns out not to be wholly at random. Ethics is related, though incompletely and indirectly, to the solid facts of man's environment: it is a social adaptation.

The task before us, as ethical beings, now begins to take shape. It is to preserve the force of ethical conviction that springs up naturally out of infantile dependence and the need for inhibition and repression in early life, but to see that it is applied, under the correctives of reason and experience, to provide the most efficient and the most desirable moral frame-work for living. This will undoubtedly mean radical changes in the early upbringing of children, as well as in the methods of education and in accepted religions and codes of ethics. For instance, sociologists are beginning to realize that existing ethicoreligious systems often contain a large element of psychological compensation: they compensate for the miseries of this world with the bliss of a world to come, they compensate for ignorance of fact with certitude of feeling, they compensate for actual imperfections of ethical practice by setting up impossible ethical ideals. This is not merely hypocrisy; it is a primitive method of self-defense against a hard and difficult reality.

Again, it is becoming clear that harshness of punishment in early life tends to the development of a morally vindicative superego: other methods are required for the development of a character where the aggressive and sadistic impulses are kept subordinate. The most difficult lesson to learn is that irrational and intolerant certitude is undesirable. We have seen how this applies to truth: the lesson is difficult there also, but science has learned it. It will be even more difficult to learn in ethics: but it must be learned if we are to emerge from psychological barbarism. To cling to certitude is to prolong an infantile reaction beyond the period when it is necessary. To become truly adult, we must learn to bear the burden of incertitude.

Another serious difficulty is how to arouse strong ethical feeling on important moral issues. It is easy to feel strongly about sexual behavior, because almost inevitably certain components of the sexual impulse become repressed in early life—so easy, in fact, that "morality" is often used to mean sexual morality alone. But it is much harder to feel strongly about social problems such as malnutrition or unemployment because the connection with the repressive mechanism is not so automatic. Through education and general social attitude such problems can be linked with a strong feeling about the wrongness of cruelty, which in its turn is readily generated by the repression of the aggressive impulses. In addition, of course, the child's natural sense of sympathy can be appealed to and strengthened, and primitive feelings of aggression can be sublimated and canalized into constructive activities. But any strong emotional sense of absolute wrongness can only be introduced by utilizing the fact of repression, with its accompanying load of guilt. Society must make rational use of an irrational mechanism to create the system of values it wants.

MAN IS THE MEASURE OF PROGRESS

I would draw some such general and final conclusion as this. A scientifically based philosophy enables us in the first place to cease tormenting ourselves with questions that ought not to be asked because they cannot be answered—such as questions about a First Cause, or Creation, or Ultimate Reality. Secondly, it encourages us to think in terms of right direction and optimum speed in place of complete but static solutions. At the present moment, for instance, it is much more essential to know that we are moving with reasonable speed toward certain general types of supernational co-operation than to nail some elaborate blueprint of international organization to our masthead. Thirdly, it is capable of giving a man a much truer picture of his nature and his place in the universe than any other philosophic approach. Man is now the dominant biological type, and the developed human individual the highest product of the cosmic process that we know. That is a proud piece of knowledge. It is tempered by the reflection that very few human individuals realize a fraction of their possibilities, and that in a large proportion, passive or active evil predominates.

But the knowledge has important practical bearings. Once we realize that the development of individuals is the ultimate yardstick by which to measure human progress, we can see more clearly how to formulate our war aims.

The fact that we, all the human beings now in existence, are the exclusive trustees for carrying any further the progress already achieved by life is a responsibility which, if sobering, is also inspiring; as is the fact that we have no longer either the intellectual or the moral right to shift any of this responsibility from our own shoulders to those of God or any other outside power. Indeed, the problem that appears to be the most perplexing and distressing turns out, in the light of a thoroughgoing scientific approach, to be full of encouragement. I mean the problem of ethical and other values. We have been accustomed to think of these as a scaffolding for our morals, conveniently run up for us by some outside agency. Now that this is no longer possible, we feel bewildered, unable to conceive of any firm moral construction in which we can abide. The truth, however, as shown by the extension of scientific method into individual and social psychology, is that we create our own values. Some we generate consciously; some subconsciously; and some only indirectly, through the structure of the societies in which we live. Through a fuller comprehension of these mechanisms we shall be able to guide and accelerate this process of value creation, which is not only essential for our individual lives but basic to the achieving of true evolutionary progress in the future.

Reinhold Niebuhr

Reinhold Niebuhr (1892–   ) is an outstanding clergyman and theologian of contemporary America. He has for three decades played a conspicuous and contradictory role in American radical politics and in religion. Both as a clergyman and as a professor of the philosophy of religion and applied Christianity at Union Theological Seminary, Niebuhr has championed the lot of the common man, opposed the tyranny of dictatorships, and with a prophetic voice warned the modern world to give up its easy, optimistic ways of interpreting life and history. Following Hitler's rise to power, Niebuhr shifted from his earlier pacifist position and concluded that war was a lesser evil than totalitarian aggression. Although he struck boldly at totalitarianism, Niebuhr did not hesitate to apply the Hebraic-Christian theory of history to the problems of the twentieth century as manifest in the nontotalitarian world. The selection given below is a brilliant summary of Niebuhr's theological views as applied to totalitarianism and to the crisis of modern civilization. In reading this selection note (1) the author's survey of history's great crises and how Christianity reacted to them, (2) his analysis of the problem involved in each historical crisis, (3) his criticism of the shortcomings of the modern man's analysis of his own culture, (4) the weakness in laissez-faire philosophies and in reason in dealing with contemporary society, (5) his evaluation of history itself as a support for modern man, (6) the nature of the contemporary revolt against civilization, (7) what Niebuhr regards as the proper elements of an adequate religious faith, (8) why he thinks religion should transcend life, and (9) the advantages claimed for Christianity as a possible faith for "history's greatest crisis."

A FAITH FOR HISTORY'S GREATEST CRISIS

In our own Western history the crisis in which we stand is the third in a series. The first was the fall of the Roman Empire. The second was the decay of feudalism and the rise of our own bourgeois democratic society. A brief survey of what occurred in these crises may illumine our own situation.

The Roman Empire fell after Christianity had been made the official religion of the empire; but Christianity lost something of its profundity in the process of its domestication in the empire. The prestige of Rome had been so great, the Pax Romana had become one of the "eternal verities" to such a degree, that men were threatened with despair when they saw this great system of "law and order" crumbling before their eyes. Furthermore, they felt that Christianity had lost its meaning, because they assumed that Christian truth had validated itself by arresting the decay of Roman civilization and that its final inability to stop the decay had invalidated it.

This sense of despair and confusion prompted the greatest philosopher of Christian history, Augustine, to write one of the most important books of our spiritual history: *The City*

of God. In it he maintained that decay of Rome was not the end of all things, and certainly not a cause for despair. On the contrary he affirmed that the Christian religion contained an interpretation of life and history that made it possible to anticipate and to discount the periodic catastrophes of history. Every empire, every "city of this world," he declared, would have to break down ultimately because its "peace was based on strife." Which is to say that such social peace as is achieved in any civilization rests upon a precarious equilibrium of social forces. This equilibrium may degenerate into anarchy if there is no strong organizing center in it. And it may degenerate into tyranny if the organizing center destroys the vitality of the parts.

The new medieval society was, on the whole, built upon Christian presuppositions as defined by St. Augustine. But as medieval civilization finally integrated and organized the vast political and ethnic vitalities of Europe and achieved the social peace and equilibrium of the "golden" thirteenth century, it subtly compounded the complacency of a stable society with the profounder insights of Augus-

Reinhold Niebuhr, "A Faith for History's Greatest Crisis," in *Fortune*, July, 1942. Courtesy of *Fortune*.

tine. Augustine's conception of the tentativity of all historic achievements was lost. Medieval Christianity tended to define the characteristic social relations of a feudal-agrarian society as absolute and final. The invariable mistake of all cultures is that they tend to forget the relative character of such social justice and social peace as are achieved in a given civilization. And the greatest illusion of all historic cultures is that they mistake the precarious stability of their civilization for the final peace. They always fail to heed the warning: "If any man stand let him take heed lest he fall."

At the precise moment when medieval society celebrated its arangements as essentially final, it proved that it was unable to absorb a new factor into its life and law. That new factor was expanding commerce. The vital agent of that new factor was the businessman. The businessman found himself excluded from the political and economic organization of feudal society. By a series of evolutionary and revolutionary processes, including the Cromwellian revolution in England, the revolution in France, and our own American revolution, the businessman finally established a new society, capitalistic in economic form and, broadly speaking, democratic in political form.

It seems to me to be futile to attempt the solution of our contemporary problems by counseling a simple return to the "medieval synthesis" and the medieval unity of culture and civilization. I admit that it was more profoundly conceived than some of our modern substitutes. But the point is that it was not able to incorporate the new factor of world commerce, the rising nation and the rising business classes, into its political and economic equilibriums. These new factors destroyed its stability. And one reason, at least, why it could not adjust itself to the new was that a religious culture, which ideally should have transcended the particular perspectives of feudalism, did in fact give religious, which means absolute, sanctity to the relative forms of justice and injustice that characterized an agrarian society of landlords and serfs. In consequence, the bourgeois rebels against the feudal society expressed themselves in terms of either a secular or a Protestant culture.

The civilization that we are now defending against the attack of a synthetic barbarism (even while we are conscious of the fact that only internal weaknesses could have made that attack possible and allowed it to come so close to a triumph over us) is one that has developed largely under the leadership of the bourgeois classes. It has been supplanting feudalism, beginning with the fourteenth century. It rose to its greatest heights in the nineteenth and the early part of the twentieth century. And it finds itself in one of the deepest crises of world history in our own generation.

A CIVILIZATION DIFFERS FROM A CULTURE

Every great crisis in world history represents a breakdown both in the organization of civilization and in the life of a culture. It is a spiritual as well as a political and economic crisis. The two aspects of life may be distinguished, even though the distinction is slightly arbitrary, by the words "civilization" and "culture." Civilization is the body of a culture. Culture is the spirit of a civilization. Civilization means the political, economic, and social arrangements and mechanisms by which the life of men is ordered. Culture means the philosophical, esthetic, and religious ideas and presuppositions that inform the political organization and that in turn emerge from it.

Ideally an adequate culture would not be involved in the breakdown of a civilization. For an adequate culture would be an interpretation of the meaning of life and history, which would comprehend the periodic breakdowns of civilization as inevitable and would seek to appropriate the lessons to be learned from those breakdowns for the building of a better civilization. Actually this never quite happens for the reason that every culture tends to appropriate certain ideas and conceptions, which are the characteristic products and illusions of its own civilization, into its system of "eternal truths" and to imagine that life would be meaningless without them. It thus brings life fairly close to meaninglessness because the ideas that it regards as eternal are actually being destroyed in the crisis. Furthermore, this spiritual confusion tends to accentuate the political and social crisis; for in every great crisis confusion is worse confounded by the insistence of some that the very illusions that the crisis is challenging and destroying belong to the eternal verities, which cannot be destroyed.

The problem in every great historical crisis is therefore to find a philosophy of life sufficiently profound to be able to transcend both the political and moral confusion and to give a vantage point from which the errors, which brought it on, can be corrected.

From the standpoint of "civilization" rather than "culture," our own crisis is more complicated than that of either the Roman or the feudal decline. Like Rome, we are subject to external attack. But the external foe is not a "natural" but a "synthetic" barbarian. His barbarism has been generated out of the decay of our own unanswered problems. The decay within our own household is due not so much to the introduction of a new factor in the equilibrum of society as to the extension of the same factor that disturbed the Middle Ages. A commercial society has grown into an industrial one; and the industrial society has made use of technical instruments of communication and production of ever increasing power. Technics have altered every aspect of our existence. Their incredibly rapid extension has disturbed every established social equilibrium. In the international field they have created a potential world community through the economic interdependence of the nations and through the increased proximity fashioned by rapid means of communication. But a potential world community that lacks political instruments for the regulation of its economic interdependence, the arbitration of its various conflicts, and the mitigation of its various frictions is bound, in fact, to become a state of international anarchy. The false answer to the problem of this anarchy is the Nazi tyrannical unification of the world. The instruments of a technical civilization increased the anarchy of our world, made the tyrannical alternative to anarchy more cruel in its methods, and enhanced the possibility of success for its ambitions of world dominion.

Furthermore, the uncontrolled potencies of a technical society have also brought confusion into our domestic life. The units of industrial production have been consistently enlarged, the old checks and balances of competitive enterprise have been imperiled or become atrophied, economic power has become more and more centralized, and the fabulous productivity of the modern machine has created crises and unemployment rather than security and abundance. Eighteenth-century dreams of a simple automatic harmony of all economic forces, if only irrelevant political restraints were removed from the economic process, have been cruelly disappointed.

OUR ERROR WAS TOO MUCH OPTIMISM

It is not my province or purpose to analyze the political and economic maladjustments of contemporary civilization. I wish rather to call attention to the fact that *modern culture has no perspective from which it can view this confusion and plan a better world;* for all our cultural perspectives are themselves colored by the civilization that is involved. If, for instance, the optimistic assumption underlies a whole culture that the extension of technics inevitably makes for the advancement of the good life, such a culture can do little to save men from confusion and despair if the extension of technics actually aggravates domestic and foreign conflicts at a particular juncture of history.

The fact is that the tragic realities in which Western civilization is involved are really striking refutations of our characteristic credos. It is particularly significant that millions of rational and "idealistic" people refused to take the monstrous perils of totalitarianism seriously because, according to their interpretation of history, no great peril could arise in a mature period of civilization. Monsters belonged by definition in the dawn of human history. Highly developed civilization had presumably domesticated all their beasts of prey. If, nevertheless, the monster seemed to be real, it was assumed that he was no more than a hungry beast of prey. If he were fed he would subside. So these good people suggested new trade agreements for the monster. The mania and the fury of the monster were interpreted as merely the hunger of a have-not nation. Or perhaps his lust could be satisfied by territory.

Thus the sacrifice of Czechoslovakia was intended to bring "peace in our time." When all these devices failed, we talked about a "reversion to barbarism"; which means that we could imagine evil in history only as a return to a primitive past. We could not imagine that a mature civilization would produce in its decay, not the evils of nature or of primitive society, but terrible evils that are relevant to, and possible only in, maturity. We did not understand the difference between nature and history. In nature, beasts of prey lie down to go to sleep when their maws are crammed. In human history, no hunger is ever perfectly satisfied and grows by what it feeds on. Just as the desires of man are infinite so also are the possibilities for good and evil in history. But the possibilities for evil keep abreast of the possibilities for good. The delicate balances of a mature mind are more easily subject to disarrangement (insanity) than the simple psychic processes of a child; and a complex technical society can fall into more utter confusion than a simple agrarian economy. The cruelty of the Nazis is no more like "barbarism" than insanity is childishness. The persistent inclination of modern culture to minimize the monstrous evils against which we must contend, and to interpret them as reversions to nature or to a primitive past, reveals a false estimate of human history and a false confidence in its securities. The conflicts and catastrophes of our era have been the more terrible because we had no philosophy by which we could anticipate them, or understand them when they were upon us.

THE RENAISSANCE FATHERED OUR OPTIMISM

Our modern era, which followed the dissolution of the medieval culture and the feudal civilization was ushered in by two great movements, the Renaissance and the Reformation. We must understand the relation between these two movements to comprehend the shallowness of contemporary culture and its incapacity for profound historical analysis. Reformation and Renaissance are frequently interpreted as closely allied movements by which the freedom and individualism of modern civilization were established. Whatever the affinities

between them, they were actually diametrically opposed to each other in their main emphases. The Reformation regarded the medieval Catholic interpretation of life and history as too optimistic. Human history, according to the Reformation, never achieves such perfection, either individually or collectively, as the medieval era pretended to have achieved. The Reformation did not believe that there could ever be "Christian" societies, or governments, or economic arrangements in the exact ethical definition of the term. A civilization could be Christian only in the sense that it had a faith that would help it to understand, and contritely to admit, the inevitable egoistic and "sinful" corruption by which all human enterprises, including the church and religious institutions, were tainted.

The Renaissance criticized the Catholic ages from the very opposite point of view. It regarded the Christian interpretation of life as too pessimistic. It believed that the human mind had been fettered by religious authority and corrupted by religious superstition. It had great confidence that the "emancipated" mind would disclose the secrets of nature; penetrate into all the ultimate mysteries of life; exploit the buried treasures of the natural world and make them available for man; explore the complexities of human society and eliminate the social maladjustments that ignorance had perpetuated; finally turn its attention to man himself, to free him of the sorrows and pains, the frustrations and lusts by which he made himself and his fellows miserable.

These promises and hopes of the Renaissance, arising in the fourteenth century and achieving new forms and elaborations particularly in the seventeenth and eighteenth centuries, were sufficiently in accord with many actual achievements of history to defeat and overwhelm all the pessimistic scruples of the Reformation. The latter (partly indeed because they were too pessimistic and defeatist) maintained themselves only in the backwaters of modern civilization. All the basic beliefs of modern man about himself, his society, and his destiny were defined essentially by the Renaissance and by the various cultural movements that followed in its wake. Thinkers as diverse as Hegel and Marx participated in the general optimistic interpretation of human history. The latter did indeed believe that bourgeois society was moving toward catastrophe rather than triumph; but he was certain that an essentially perfect society would emerge from that catastrophe. Christianity itself, in its modern Protestant version, was strongly influenced by these optimistic interpretations of life and history. Some of the most stubborn and sentimental illusions about the possibilities of a simple and easy peace between the competing elements in human society have been fostered by modern churches. In America they contributed more possibly than any other influence to political and moral illusions, for they aggravated false estimates of man and history by compounding them with classical and pious conceptions.

The errors and illusions of our culture, which have made an estimate of the crisis of our civilization difficult if not impossible, are, almost without exception, various versions of a single error. They are all expressions of too great an optimism about the goodness of human nature; they all therefore underestimate the difficulties of relating life to life, will to will, interest to interest, in a harmonious social life. They regard the achievement of justice and social peace in human society as a comparatively easy task. It is, as a matter of fact, a very difficult task, which can be accomplished with tolerable success only if its difficulties are fully recognized.

Traditionalists are accustomed to criticize modern culture for the laxity of its moral standards. They think our primary sin is moral relativism and skepticism. Yet the moral relativism that denies the validity of all general norms of virtue and all universal standards of justice is really a subordinate note in modern culture. It has become dominant only in this latter day in Nazi philosophy and totalitarian politics. This philosophy proclaims unashamedly that there is no good but "my" good, and no standard of justice but the interest of "my" nation. This frank egoism, this cynical disregard of the interests of others, does indeed represent a final decay of moral standards. But it expresses itself as a revolt against our culture and civilization. It does not express the basic ideas of our culture.

Our culture in its dominant thought is neither skeptical nor cynical; neither relativist nor nihilistic. On the contrary, it has a touching confidence in the possibility of establishing "universal" standards of justice and general norms of value. It consistently underestimates the difficulties of achieving universal standards. It thinks that men can be beguiled from following their own interests and can be persuaded to espouse the general interest by some simple process of social reorganization or educational device.

HISTORY HAS NO NATURAL BALANCES OF POWER

Almost every version of modern culture has some futile and fatuous scheme for lifting men from selfish purposes as painlessly as possible. The simplest idea of all is that which underlies the laissez faire social philosophies of the eighteenth and nineteenth centuries. According to these philosophies all conflicting interests in human society, and all competing egoistic drives, would result in harmony rather than conflict if they were only left alone. If political society did not interfere with economic process, economic life would achieve a natural harmony. This idea, which obviates the necessity of either moral or political control upon selfish impulses, was a nice device for eating your cake and having it too. It justified unrestrained selfishness without justifying egoism morally; for it gave the assurance that "each man seeking his own would serve the commonweal." The only difficulty with the idea is that it is not true. The one element of truth in it is that there are indeed certain automatic harmonies in the economic process, and it is wise to maintain them. But on the whole, history, unlike nature, has no natural balances of power. Where power is disproportionate, power dominates weakness and injustice results. A technical civilization actually accentuates previous disproportions of power, so that the theory was less true for the growing technical society to which it was applied than for a more static agrarian society, to which it had not been applied.

The theory of the harmlessness of natural man, if only he is not controlled and regulated, is usually compounded with another theory, which is a little more profound. It is the theory that ignorant selfishness is dangerous to society, but that a wise and prudent selfishness knows how to relate the interests of the self to the interests of the whole; so that a wise egoist, while seeking his own pleasure, will finally serve "the greatest good of the greatest number." The confidence in the essential virtue of the intelligent man takes various forms. Sometimes intelligence supposedly restrains egoism in its narrow form and broadens it to include the interests of others. Sometimes it is assumed that the intelligence preserves a nice balance between egoistic and altruistic impulses. And sometimes reason throws the weight of its authority on the side of altruism as against egoism.

In the philosophy of Hegel, reason overcomes the narrow interests of the individual self by creating the state, as an expression of the broader interests of the collective self. Hegelian philosophy fails to consider, however, that human society is engulfed in conflict more frequently by competing collective wills than by conflicting individual wills and interests. The most tragic conflicts of history are between states, nations, classes, and races, and not between individuals.

The trust of the modern man in reason thus takes many forms. In all of them it assumes that reason is an organ of the universal and that in some way or other increasing reason will progressively remove conflict from human society and produce an ultimately perfect coincidence of interest with interest and a finally perfect conformity of will to will. Even Marxism, which is presumably a revolt against this trust in reason, is another version of the same faith. It assumes that nothing but the "class organization" of society tempts men to subordinate their reason to their passions and interests; and that the conflicts in human society will result in an ultimate catastrophe from which a new society will emerge in which there will be perfect harmony.

This trust in reason, as the organ of human virtue and as the guarantor of social peace and justice, underlies modern man's faith in history. For he conceives of history as a movement in which reason is progressively coming into control of all the vitalities, interests, and passions of life. If we are involved in conflict today we may therefore attribute it to the ignorance and the superstition of men; and look forward hopefully to the day when increasing education and advancing intelligence will have dispelled the bigotries of ignorant men and destroyed the parochialism of backward races and nations.

NAZISM PERVERTS PARTIAL TRUTHS

If the revolt against our civilization is to be understood profoundly and not merely attributed to the conspiracies of "bad" men, we must realize that totalitarian philosophy has in every case taken neglected portions of the total truth about man and history and fashioned them into perverse but potent instruments against a civilization that did not understand the nature and history of man. For the liberal faith in reason, Nazism substituted the romantic faith in vitality and force. For the simple faith that right creates its own might, it substituted the idea that might makes right. For the hope of liberal democracy that history was in the process of eliminating all partial, national, and racial loyalties and creating a universal community of mankind, it substituted a primitive loyalty to race and nation as the final end of life. In place of the sentimental idea that men could easily combine devotion to their own interests with loyalty to universal justice, it proclaimed the cynical idea that there is no justice but that which serves "my" or "our" purpose and interest.

It is wrong to worship force and to make power self-justifying. But such an error could not have arisen in a civilization that had not made the opposite mistake and assumed that men were in the process of becoming purely rational. It is perverse to make the interests of our nation the final end of life. But this error could not have achieved such monstrous proportions if our culture had not foolishly dreamed and hoped for the development of "universal" men, who were bereft of all loyalties to family, race, and nation. It is monstrous to glorify war as the final good. But that error could not have brought us so close to disaster if a comfortable civilization had not meanwhile regarded peace as a final good; and had not expected perfect peace to be an attainable goal of history. It is terrible to conduct the diplomacy and military strategy of nations upon the basis of "all or nothing" policies. But the fury expressed in such policies would have not come so close to success if it had not been met by the illusions of comfortable and fat nations in which the love of ease had been compounded with the caution of prudence, and the two together had resulted in an inability to act. If the lies embodied in the Nazi creed did not contain a modicum of truth and if that modicum of truth had not been directed against our weakness and our illusions, we would not have come so close to disaster.

NOT ALL PROGRESS IS MORAL PROGRESS

We have defined the error that underlies all the optimistic illusions of our culture as a too-simple confidence in man, particularly in rational man, and as a too-simple hope in the progressive achievement of virtue in history, by reason of the progressive extension of intelligence. This confidence that human history ultimately answers all its unsolved problems and overcomes all its earlier insecurities, that history is itself a kind of process of redemption, has gained such a strong hold upon modern man because it is actually partly true and because all the tremendous advances of science, technology, and intelligence seemed to justify the belief. The Renaissance, which trusted in history, triumphed over the Reformation, which had serious questions about history, because we were actually making progress in so many directions that it seemed plausible to assume that all these advances could be summed up as moral progress. But this final conclusion represents a grievous error. There is always progress in history in the sense that it cumulates wisdom, perfects technics, increases the areas of human co-operation, and extends the human control over nature. But this cannot be regarded as moral progress. There are morally ambiguous elements in human history on every new level of achievement. We ought to have known that. A person progresses from childhood to maturity, but it is not easy to compare the virtue of maturity with the innocency of a child, because mature life achieves higher unities and is subject to greater complexities than child life. It is in fact irrelevant to measure mature virtue with childish innocency because they are incommensurate. So it is with the history of mankind.

The advancement of knowledge may mitigate social conflict, but intelligence may also be the servant of imperial ambition. The applied sciences and technics may multiply human power and increase comfort. But the Nazis may use the power for destructive ends; and the democratic world may be beguiled by the comforts of bourgeois society into a false security. Modern means of communication may increase the breadth and extent of human communities, but they also enlarge areas of human conflict. Reason may serve as an arbitrator between my interest and those of my fellowmen. In that case, reason is a servant of justice. But reason may, as Bergson observed, also break the communities of primitive life by giving the egoistic urge a new instrument.

Whether one analyzes the advances of history in terms of technics or of intelligence, it is quite apparent that history is not so simple as we have believed. The morally ambiguous note remains in it on every level. The securities of its maturity save us from the insecurities of childhood; but they do not save us from the new insecurities of maturity. The wisdom of maturity is a cure for the ignorance of childhood; but it is no cure for the ignorance of maturity. It is because we have trusted history too much that we understand neither life nor history. History cannot be the answer to our problems, for history is itself our problems. History is, in short, an inadequate god. We have failed to gauge every contemporary problem in its true depth because of this false faith in history. Previous civilizations only made the mistake of misjudging their own history and estimating their own security too highly. We went one step beyond them in pride and pretension. We thought no evil could befall us because we trusted not "Roman civilization" nor medieval culture, but history itself. Yet our error was greater than previous errors, precisely because we believed that history's development of all human potencies also guaranteed the elimination of all human insecurities.

The very opposite is the truth. A highly dynamic technical society is more destructive in its decay than a simple agrarian society. The destruction dumped from the skies by modern airplanes is more awful than the lethal power of a bow and arrow.

And neither the further advance of science nor the mere return to religion will give us the perspective required. Neither return to a simpler piety nor advance from piety to a sophisticated scientific culture can solve our problem. Religious and scientific leaders may have been fighting each other, but they have shared the same common and erroneous faith. Neither were driven beyond the characteristic complacency of modern man in regard to history. The scientists may have regarded themselves as very sophisticated and thought of the religious people as very sentimental. But these superficial differences were insignificant. Scientists and pietists agreed in regarding human history as the answer to all human problems rather than as itself the great human problem.

RETURN TO FORMAL RELIGION IS NOT ENOUGH

If we seek for a cultural reconstruction in our day, we must look for something more fundamental than the mere extension of scientific knowledge, for science gives no answer to the ultimate problem of the meaning of life. Nor can we be satisfied with the conventional advice to return to religion. There must indeed be a return to religion in the sense that all final answers to ultimate problems are religious answers, whether clothed in the language and pretensions of science, philosophy, or religion. But a religious answer, per se, is no more adequate than a scientific answer. The Nazi answer to the problem of life is a religious answer; but Nazi religion is a primitive religion, which declares that the triumph of "my" nation fulfills the meaning of life and history. The Buddhist answer to the problem of life is a religious answer. But it declares that life is fulfilled by escape from history.

The primary significance of the Hebraic-Christian tradition, which underlies our Western culture, is that it regards historical existence as meaningful, but it sees no fulfillment of life's meaning in history, because it recognizes that history, on every level of achievement, contains ambiguities, problems, and insecurities that demand an answer. The answer to these problems given by the Christian faith is that history is borne by a divine reality that completes what remains incomplete in history and purges what is evil in history. This answer can be taken seriously only by those who recognize the seriousness of the problem to which it is an answer.

Our modern culture since the Renaissance has not taken the Christian faith seriously because it had a simpler answer to the problems of life. It agreed with Christianity in regarding human history as meaningful, but it assigned a simple meaning to history. The Reformation was meanwhile overwhelmed because it was too pessimistic about the possibilities of history.

An adequate faith for our day must again combine these broken fragments of the Christian tradition. Any culture or any religion that is deficient in the "tragic sense of life" is certainly inadequate to give us light and guidance in a day in which the very securities of a technical society have been transmuted into evil. We need a faith that throws light upon the importance of every historical task and responsibility. But it must on the other hand reveal the limits of all historical striving. Without such a faith, the modern man remains an inveterate utopian, disavowing all religious ultimates in one breath and in the next breath affirming his faith in some incredible utopia, some impossible heaven on earth.

An adequate religious culture must transcend the stabilities, securities, achievements of any given civilization. If faith is bound up with these too completely, life becomes meaningless when they break down. It must give people the resource to rebuild a civilization without illusions and yet without despair. We must, for instance, achieve a higher level of international organization after the war or our civilization will sink even lower. If we engage in the task of world reconstruction without a disavowal of the utopian illusion, which has informed our culture particularly since the eighteenth century, we shall ask for the impossible by way of world federation or some world superstate; we shall not get it, and then we shall be tempted again to despair and disillusionment. Furthermore, the utopians will always tempt the realists among us to become cynical in their reaction to utopianism. These cynics will be inclined to assert that history contains no new possibilities for good. They will seek to reconstruct the world on the basis of the old precarious balance of power, and they will not find a new level of international community compatible with our new economic interdependence.

All political and economic achievements must be informed by a religion and a culture, which know that history is a realm of infinite possibilities, and that each new level of maturity places new responsibilities upon us. But it must also be understood that all historic achievements are limited and precarious; that human egoism, individual and collective, can be transmuted and sublimated on many new levels, but that it cannot be eliminated from history. The faith that man as a particular force in history, contending against other particular forces, is in the process of becoming a universal force, has no historical evidence to justify it. The modern man regards himself as so sophisticated and is nevertheless incredibly credulous. Human existence is precarious and will remain so to the end of history. Human achievement contains a tragic element of frustration and corruption and will contain it to the end of history. There is an ultimate answer to these tragic aspects of human existence, but that answer can be known only to those who have stopped looking for some easy escape from tragedy.

The Christian religion regards history as meaningful but as having no fulfillment of its meaning within itself. In that sense Christianity is "otherworldly." For this reason all modern substitutes for the Christian faith, in which history is fulfilled in some kind of utopia, naturally find the Christian faith incredible because they have a simpler answer to the problems of life. The Christian faith becomes

credible only when those simpler answers are refuted by history, as indeed they are bound to be.

According to the Christian faith all finite and historical existence points to a ground and an end beyond itself. This divine end and ground is paradoxically defined as having a double relation to history. God judges the world because there are violations of the law of life on every level of human achievement. God "saves" the world because he has resources of mercy beyond this judgment. But mercy cannot express itself without taking justice seriously. Thus God is pictured as being able to be merciful only by taking the consequences of his judgment upon and into himself. These paradoxes of the Christian faith have sometimes been stated in terms of a wooden literalism that has made them offensive to human intelligence. But it is well to remember that they are a "stumbling block" and "foolishness" even when stated profoundly. The reason for this is that all men would like to believe that they have the power within themselves to complete their lives and their history. But this is exactly what all men lack.

A faith that is able to transcend the catastrophes of history must therefore be able to define both the possibilities of human creativity in history and the limits of human possibilities. It must also be able to clarify the fact that the evils of fanaticism, conflict, imperialism, and tyranny have their source in man's ambition to overleap his limitations and to seek unconditioned power, virtue, and security for his existence.

For this reason historical catastrophe seems to be nothing but chaos, which drives men to despair without the profundities of the Christian faith. And Christian faith becomes vapid and sentimental in periods of stability and peace. It recovers its own profoundest insights precisely in those periods of social chaos when all simpler interpretations of life break down and force men to seek for a profounder interpretation of existence.

Carl Becker

Carl Becker (1873–1945) was a distinguished American historian who as a teacher, lecturer, and author gave considerable attention to the study of ideas and institutions. He saw, as did many others, the basic issues involved in the crisis of liberalism, especially as it developed after 1919. Communism, fascism, and nazism each in its way sought to provide satisfying solutions to the central problem of the 20th century. Becker phrased well the question when he wrote: "How in practice to restrict the liberty of the individual in the economic realm so as to effect that measure of equality of possessions and opportunity without which democracy is an empty form, and at the same time to preserve that measure of individual liberty in political and intellectual life without which it cannot exist." In Modern Democracy, from which the following selection is taken, Becker attempted to provide an answer to this question which would be in harmony with the western traditions of liberal democracy. In reading this selection note (1) Becker's statement of the dilemma facing modern democracies, (2) his evaluation of laissez-faire, (3) the question he raised concerning government regulation as a solution, (4) his summary and criticism of communism and fascism, (5) upon what bases he thought the survival of democratic institutions depended, (6) the danger faced by contemporary democratic countries, (7) the suggested process for achieving the desirable goals, (8) his justification for waging war, (9) Becker's statement of the paradox faced by Western peoples, (10) the available resources for the solution of our problems, and (11) the condition he set for the survival of democracy.

From: MODERN DEMOCRACY

I

The problem of modern democracies as I have just defined it may be otherwise stated. Can the flagrant inequality of possessions and of opportunity now existing in democratic societies be corrected by the democratic method? If it cannot be so corrected the resulting discontent and confusion will be certain, sooner or later, to issue in some form of revolutionary or military dictatorship. This then is the dilemma which confronts democratic societies: to solve the economic problem by the democratic method, or to cease to be democratic societies.

It is obvious that the problem, intrinsically, is an economic one. At the present moment it takes the spectacular form of unemployment. For the past ten years, in the most prosperous democratic societies, from 10 to 20 per cent of the working population, for the most part willing but unable to find work, has been kept alive by public or private charity or by jobs created for that purpose by the government. Unemployment is no new thing, but never be-

Carl L. Becker, *Modern Democracy*, Yale University Press, New Haven, 1941, 67–100. Courtesy of the Yale University Press.

fore in democratic societies has it reached the proportions of a major social catastrophe.

The catastrophe cannot be explained as an act of God, cannot be attributed to destructive natural forces beyond human control. The people are famished, but there is no famine. On the contrary, there is wealth in abundance, or should be. Given our natural resources, manpower, and technical equipment, there could be produced, in this country at least, sufficient wealth to provide all the people with the necessities of life and many of the desired comforts and luxuries besides. Yet in spite of widespread and insistent human need, the technical equipment is used only in part, the manpower is not fully employed. In a land of plenty millions are destitute. Obviously the situation is one which arises not from lack of potential wealth, but from some defect in the method of producing and distributing wealth. That the defect is a serious one is indicated by a simple, ironic fact—the fact that in a world in which millions are destitute it is thought necessary, and under the prevailing system of production and distribution of wealth apparently is so, to limit the production of the necessities of life in order to keep people from starving.

The prevailing system for the production and distribution of wealth is variously denoted by the phrases capitalist system, competitive system, price system, system of free enterprise, system of *laissez-faire*. Its theoretical justification derives from the general assumption of the liberal-democratic ideology—the assumption that social welfare can best be achieved by reducing governmental interference with the freedom of the individual to a minimum. The assumption was never better stated than by John Stuart Mill in his famous essay *On Liberty*. Governmental interference with the activities of the individual, he maintained, is never justified except when manifestly necessary to prevent the activities of some individuals from injuring others. The principle is similarly, but more succinctly, formulated in the French Declaration of the Rights of Man: "Liberty is the right of everyone to do whatever does not injure others."

Applied to the economic realm, this principle was interpreted to mean the maximum freedom of the individual to choose his occupa-

tion or business, and to enter freely into contracts for the acquisition or disposal of private property and for the purchase or sale of personal services. It was assumed that the free play of individual initiative, stimulated by the acquisitive instinct, would result in the maximum production of wealth, and that the competitive instinct, operating through the law of supply and demand and the resulting price system, would result in as equitable a distribution of wealth as the natural qualities and defects of men would permit. In this system the function of the government was reduced to defining and guaranteeing the rights of private property, enforcing the rules of contract, and preserving social order. Having defined the rules of the game, the government would see that they were enforced, but would not otherwise interfere with the players. Let the game go on and the best man win. *Laissez-faire, laissez-passer!*

Contrary to a wide-spread belief, *laissez-faire* was never more than a theory imperfectly applied. The happy, imagined time when government did not interfere in the freedom of the individual by meddling in business never in fact existed. The institution of private property is itself a most drastic regulation of business enterprise, the law of contract a fundamental interference with the liberty of the individual. But assuming private property and the law of contract as part of the system, there never was a time when government did not find it necessary, according to Mill's famous definition, to interfere with the activities of some individuals in order to prevent those activities from injuring others.

In England the trend toward *laissez-faire* was reversed before it was completed. A decade before 1846, when the doctrine was officially adopted by the repeal of the corn laws, the government had found it necessary to restrict free enterprise by passing the first Factory Act for the protection of women and children. And from that day to this, in England and in every industrialized country, including the United States, the governmental regulation of private property, of free competition and free contract, of the price of commodities and of labor, of the inheritance of property and of the disposal of income from it, has steadily increased. This extension of governmental regulation, this trend toward what is called social legislation, was brought about by the pressure of labor unions supported by the humane sentiment of the community, and underlying it is the assumption, avowed or unavowed, that the system of *laissez-faire,* so eminently successful in stimulating the production of wealth, is incapable, without governmental regulation, of bringing about an equitable or even a tolerable distribution of it. It is far too late to ask whether government should interfere in business enterprise. It always has interfered in business enterprise. The only relevant question is in what ways and to what extent it should so interfere.

Nevertheless, in spite of increasing governmental regulation, the theory of *laissez-faire* was never abandoned. The prevailing assumption was, and still is, in democratic societies, that governmental regulation should be kept to a minimum, however high the minimum might in the event prove to be. It was taken for granted that the basic right and the assured foundation of the economic structure of society was private property in the means of production, free enterprise, and the competitive system. Social legislation was regarded as no more than a limited, if necessary, concession to adverse circumstances, a series of minor adjustments that would leave the system intact while enhancing its efficiency. In the optimistic decade before the Great War, social legislation came to be widely regarded, indeed, as in some sense an integral part of the system of free enterprise, a kind of insurance against the subversive doctrine of Socialism, a preordained and peaceful means of transforming that anomaly of progress and poverty which Henry George had so graphically described into that progress and prosperity which the prophets of democracy had so confidently predicted.

Since the Great War faith in social legislation as a means of validating the system of free enterprise has been much impaired. Surveying the history of a century of governmental regulation of business enterprise, it is obvious that while regulation has done much to correct minor evils it has as yet failed to solve the fundamental problem of an equitable distribution of wealth. On the contrary, the problem of the distribution of wealth is more serious and more insistent now than it was in the time of Henry George, so much so, indeed, that if the anomaly of progress and poverty is less glaring than it was, the only reason is that while the poverty is more patent the progress is less assured.

Inevitably, therefore, the question, long since raised, becomes every day more insistent: Can the problem of the production and distribution of wealth be solved, within the framework of the existing system of private property and free enterprise, by any amount of governmental regulation? In short, are the defects of the system of private property in the means of production incidental or inherent?

II

That the defects of the capitalist system are inherent is the contention of those ideologies known as Socialism and Communism. Socialism and Communism, taken in the generic sense of the words, are at least as old as Plato; but in their modern forms they derive from the doctrines formulated by Karl Marx in the middle of the last century.

Marxian Socialism, inspired by the failure of democratic institutions to effect an equitable distribution of wealth, was essentially a reinterpretation of the modern doctrine of progress, and as such it comprised a social theory and a philosophy of history. As a social theory it maintained that the social structure at any time is fundamentally determined by the methods of production and distribution of wealth, and that the prevailing institutions and ideas are those best adapted to maintain the interests of the class which, by ownership and control of the chief forms of wealth, dominates the social structure in its own interest. As a philosophy of history it maintained that social change, or progress, is the result, not of a conflict of ideas, but of economic forces, a conflict between the economic interests of the ruling and the dispossessed classes. Not by the persuasive force of ideas, but only by the impersonal pressure of economic conditions, could the ruling class ever be dispossessed, or the institutions and ideas through which its power operates ever be transformed.

Applying this theory to European history,

Marx found that the liberal-democratic revolution was the result of the conflict between the economic interests of the landed aristocracy and the rising capitalist class. So far from reflecting the triumph of true over false ideas, it reflected the triumph of capital over land as the predominant factor in production; and the superstructure of liberal-democratic ideas and institutions, so far from having a universal validity, had merely the relative and temporary value of being suited to the functioning of the capitalist system and the interests of the ruling bourgeois class. The liberal-democratic revolution could not, therefore, be regarded as the final term of the historic process. On the contrary, the capitalist system once established, there necessarily developed within it a new conflict between the interests of the ruling bourgeois class and the dispossessed proletariat which would inevitably issue in another social revolution.

The coming social revolution was inevitable, according to Marx, because the capitalist system, like the landed aristocratic system before it, contained within it the defects that would transform it—defects inherent in the institution of private property and the competitive system. The ruthless competition for profits would necessarily result in an increasing concentration of wealth in the hands of those who proved most able in the ruthless competition for profits, thereby reducing the laborers and the defeated capitalists to the level of a bare subsistence; and when this process reached a certain stage the system would collapse for the simple reason that there would be no profit in producing commodities when the underlying proletarian population was not longer able to purchase them at a price that would yield a profit. When this stage was reached, the proletariat, made class conscious by their misery, instructed in the dialectic of social change by their leaders, and united for the defense of their class interests, would by revolutionary action abolish private property in land and capital, and through a democratic government based upon a classless society, organize the production and distribution of wealth for the common good.

The Marxian doctrine provided a new and persuasive ideology for the oppressed working classes whose hopes were persistently defeated by liberal-democracy as a going concern. Its analysis of the capitalist system justified their grievances against their employers, while its philosophy of history promised them that all would be made right in the future, and assured them that in defending their class interests they could not fail since they were supported by the indefeasible forces that shaped the destiny of mankind.

Inspired by the Marxian faith, the industrial workers formed new political parties, for the most part called Socialist, and for the most part accepting the Marxian doctrine of the social revolution. But meantime, while waiting for the coming revolution, and as a preparation for it, the Socialist parties adopted a program of social legislation designed to benefit the masses at the expense of the classes. Attracted by this practical program, lower middle-class people, mostly timid folk who abhorred the idea of violence, voted in increasing numbers for Socialist candidates in the hope of benefiting from the legislation which the Socialist parties promised to support. One result of this trend in practical politics was that the Socialist parties derived their chief support from voters who were not Marxian socialists; another was that the leaders of the Socialist parties, in order to win and hold non-Marxian voters, found it necessary to soft-pedal the doctrine of imminent, catastrophic revolution. In the decade before the Great War the dominant Socialist parties had therefore virtually abandoned the Marxian conception of the revolution as a violent upheaval, and conceived of it as a slow and peaceful process in which the masses, by established political methods, would gain control of the government, and by normal legislative procedure within the existing democratic regime would abolish private property in land and capital and socialize the production and distribution of wealth.

During the Great War the influence of Socialism naturally declined, but the orthodox Marxian tradition, barely kept alive by minority groups within and without the dominant Socialist parties, was given a dramatic and world-wide significance by the Russian Revolution. As reinterpreted by Lenin and realized in the Soviet regime, neo-Marxianism took the name of Communism, and must be clearly distinguished from Socialism as understood by such prewar Socialists as Bernheim and Kautsky, and such present-day Socialists as Norman Thomas. Present-day Socialism and neo-Marxian Communism agree in one thing only—the necessity of abolishing private property in the means of production. In respect to the means for accomplishing this desired end they disagree radically. Socialism maintains that it can be accomplished by peaceful political methods within the framework of the existing democratic regime; Communism maintains that it can be accomplished only by violent revolutionary expropriation of the capitalist class, carried through for the masses by the dictatorship of a disciplined Communist party.

It was also an essential part of Communist theory that the establishment of Communism in one country would be the prelude to an international Communist revolution. So far, the prediction has not been realized. Revolutions there have been, in Italy, in Germany, in many European countries. But these revolutions, stimulated in part by the fear of Communism rather than by devotion to it, have taken the name of Fascist; and until recently at all events Communism and Fascism have been commonly regarded, especially by the Communists and Fascists themselves, as being fundamentally opposed to each other.

In respect to political theory there are certain differences between Communism and Fascism. In theory Communism maintains that the dictatorship, a drastic technique essential to the revolution but ending with it, will be replaced by a democratic government of free and equal individuals, while Fascism rejects the democratic ideal altogether in favor of the permanent dictatorship. In theory Communism professes to be international, while Fascism frankly accepts the doctrine of racial superiority and national egoism. In theory Communism recognizes the value of reason and science, while Fascism is essentially anti-intellectual in its subordination of reason to will.

In theory, yes; but the Soviet regime in Russia has failed, even more conspicuously than existing democratic societies, to harmonize theory and practice. Although the revolution has long since ended, the classless society has not emerged. The dictatorship is now more firmly established, the prospect for a democratic government is now more remote, than in the time of Lenin. The Stalin regime is no less nationalist and no more international than the regime of Hitler, and its regimentation of opinion and scholarship no less effectively subordinates reason to the will of the dictator. The revolution in Russia, as Trotsky said, has been betrayed; but it has been betrayed less by men and circumstances than by a radical contradiction in Communist theory. The rational and humane values proclaimed in Communist theory are frankly divorced from the means by which they can be realized; they are regarded as ideal ends projected into the future, but incapable of being attained except by the temporary resort to antirational and inhumane means. So far at least the result of this radical contradiction between ends and means has been, and as I think must under any circumstances have been, that the ideal ends were defeated by the very means employed to attain them.

It is in this fundamental discord between ends and means that Communism and Fascism, as they actually function, are alike—alike in the methods they employ and in the assumptions by which the methods are justified. The Communist and the Fascist revolutions were carried through by the same political technique and the same resort to naked force. The personal power of Mussolini and Hitler is no more arbitrary, more complete, or more ruthlessly employed than that of Stalin. Both Communism and Fascism assume that the welfare of the community and the progress of mankind are in some mystical fashion identified with an abstract entity, called in the one case the dialectic of history and in the other the totalitarian state. Both assume that this abstract entity is realized in the person of an inspired leader to whom the truth has been revealed and the direction of affairs committed. Both assume that the individual, in comparison with the state or the dialectic process, has no significance except as an instrument to be used, with whatever degree of brutality may be necessary, for realizing ends which the leader judges to be good. Both do in effect, whatever they may proclaim in theory, subordinate reason to will, identify right with naked force as an instrument of will, and accord value to the disinterested search for truth only in so far as the leader judges it to be temporarily useful for the attainment of immediate political ends.

Communism and Fascism claim to be theoretical formulations of a "new order" in the world. But as revealed in their works they are no more than the recurrence of old political forms, that is to say, the recurrence in practice of what is variously known as tyranny, dictatorship, absolute monarchy; the recurrence in theory of what is known as divine right. As such they are alike, and alike at war with the fundamental values and assumptions which liberal-democracy, if it is to retain any significance, must preserve.

III

The infinitely complicated process which we call history continuously gives rise to what are called social problems, and at the same time generates those political and intellectual trends which indicate the direction which the solution of those problems is likely to take. The term "solution," used in this connection, is misleading. It connotes a certain perfection or finality, comparable to the solution of a mathematical or a chemical problem, which is never possible in social relations. "The function of history," as J. B. Bury once remarked, "is not to solve problems but to transform them." In our time the historical process has given rise to the problem of the distribution of wealth, a problem which assumes the double form of social conflict within the nations and of diplomatic and military conflict between them. It would be naïve indeed to suppose that this problem, in either of its forms, will be "solved" with any notable degree of perfection or finality. It will be solved only in the sense of being transformed; and in looking for the direction which this transformation will take, we must consult, not merely our hopes or our preferences, but also the dominant political and intellectual trends which the history of our time discloses.

Those political and intellectual trends I have discussed and discriminated under the terms Liberal-Democracy, Socialism, Communism, and Fascism. The differences between them, both as ideological systems and as going concerns, are obvious and important; but underneath their differences we can note, in respect to what they propose to do and are doing to solve the problem of the distribution of wealth, an interesting and significant similarity. It is a similarity of direction: all these systems are carrying us, with or without our consent, toward an extension of governmental regulation of economic enterprise.

That this is the direction is evident. In all liberal-democratic countries, for the last hundred years, there has been a steadily increasing amount of such regulation of economic enterprise. Both Communism and Socialism propose to make the regulation complete by abolishing private property in the means of production, and the Communist regime in Russia has already accomplished this object. Fascism, no less than Communism, proposes to subordinate the individual to the state; and in the principal Fascist countries, although private property in land and capital has not been formally abolished, the national economy has been so far subjected to governmental direction that free economic enterprise has virtually disappeared. Like it or not, the complexities of a highly integrated technological civilization are carrying us in a certain direction, that is to say, away from freedom of the individual in economic enterprise and toward an extension of social control. This is therefore the direction which, in democratic as well as in other countries, the transformation of the problem of the distribution of wealth will surely take.

The question that chiefly concerns us is whether the necessary social regulation of economic enterprise can be effected by the democratic method, that is to say, without a corresponding social regimentation of opinion and political freedom. Can the possessors be sufficiently dispossessed and the dispossessed be sufficiently reinstated without resort to violence —to revolution and the temporary or the permanent dictatorship. The Communists say no —sooner or later the revolution. The Fascists say no—the totalitarian state is the only solution. They may of course be right. It is futile to suppose that democracy must survive because it accords with the law of nature or some transcendent increasing purpose. Nor can we dismiss the rise of dictatorship in half the world as a temporary aberration brought to birth by the ingenuity of sinister or psychopathic individuals. Common men, when sufficiently distressed, instinctively turn to the inspired leader; and dictatorship in our time, as in past times, is the normal price exacted for the failure of democracy to bind common men by their hopes and fears. The survival of democratic institutions thus depends, not upon the attractiveness or logical consistency of theories of government, but upon the possibility of effecting, by the pragmatic democratic method, a sufficient equalization of possessions and of opportunity to provide common men with what they will consent to regard as tolerable.

It may be said, it has often been said, that the most brilliant civilizations of the past have paid scant attention to the needs or desires of common men, that the oppression of common men was the price that had to be paid for those great and permanent achievements which we associate with the progress of mankind. It may be so, but it no longer matters. The very technology which gives peculiar form and pressure to the oppression of common men in our time has freed common men from the necessity of submitting to it. The time has gone by when common men could be persuaded to believe that destitution is in accord with God's will, or to rely upon the virtues of *noblesse oblige* to ease their necessities. Through education and the schools, through the press and the radio, common men are made aware of their rights, aware of the man-made frustration of their hopes, aware of their power to organize for the defense of their interests. Any civilization in our time, however brilliant or agreeable it may appear to its beneficiaries or to posterity, which fails to satisfy the desires of common men for decent living will be wrecked by the power of common men to destroy what seems to them no longer worth preserving. The ultimate task of democracy may be to establish a brilliant civilization; but its immediate task is the less exalted one of surviving in any form, and the condition of its survival is that it shall, even at the sacrifice of some of the freedoms

and amenities of civilization as we have known it, provide for the essential material need of common men.

Considered as a problem in scientific engineering, providing for the material needs of common men presents no insuperable difficulties: the necessary resources, equipment, man power, and knowledge are available. Given Plato's ruling class of philosopher-kings, and a docile population responding to suggestion as smoothly as molten iron yields to physical pressure, adequate wealth could be produced and equitably distributed. Unfortunately perhaps, there are no such philosopher-kings; fortunately, there are no such docile people. Government is much less a matter of knowing what is good to be done than of persuading average human beings, stubbornly rooted in conventional habits of thought and action, to do what fallible intelligence judges on incomplete data to be for the moment necessary or desirable. Democratic government is a matter of persuading them to do it voluntarily by registering their wishes in the form of ballots freely given. In democratic countries, therefore, the measures taken for effecting a more equitable distribution of wealth can never be based solely upon the best scientific knowledge available; they can be such only as the majority of citizens will voluntarily sanction and the minority voluntarily submit to.

It is as essential that the minority should voluntarily submit to the measures taken as it is that the majority should voluntarily approve them. Democratic government rests upon the principle that it is better to count heads than it is to break them. The principle is a good one, but unfortunately men will not, under certain conditions, so regard it. By and large the principle works well enough so long as the issues to be decided do not involve those interests which men will always fight for rather than surrender. By and large, democratic government, being government by discussion and majority vote, works best when there is nothing of profound importance to discuss, when the rival party programs involve the superficial aspects rather than the fundamental structure of the social system, and when for that reason the minority can meet defeat at the polls in good temper since it need not regard the decision as either a fatal or a permanent surrender of its vital interests. When these happy conditions disappear democratic government is always in danger.

The danger has already proved fatal in many countries. It exists, although it may not prove fatal, even in those countries where the democratic tradition is most strongly intrenched. For in these countries too the insistent problem of the distribution of wealth is beginning to involve those fundamental class interests which do not readily lend themselves to friendly discussion and mutual concession. The flagrant inequality of possessions and of opportunity is creating an ever sharper differentiation between the beneficiaries of private property in the means of production and the masses whose present circumstances and future prospects depend less upon individual character and talent than upon the hazards of the business cycle. Accompanying this differentiation there has been and is going on a confused but persistent realignment of political parties: on the Right, conservative parties representing the beneficiaries of the system of free enterprise; on the Left, radical parties representing the poor and the dispossessed. As the divergence between Right and Left becomes sharper and more irreconcilable, moderate and conciliatory parties tend to disappear, and the rival party programs of the extreme groups, no longer confined to the superficial aspects of policy within the framework of the traditional system, are increasingly concerned with the validity of the assumptions on which the system rests. Underlying the question of the equitable distribution of wealth is the more fundamental question of the validity of the institution of private property as a means of effecting it. The present power of the possessing classes rests upon the institution of private property; the present distress of the masses is somehow involved in it. If the present discords should be prolonged and intensified, the danger is that the masses will turn to revolution rather than submit to a system which fails to relieve them, that the classes will welcome forcible repression rather than surrender a system which guarantees their power.

The danger is not one to be lightly dismissed. It is certainly greater than many profess to think. But for all that we need not be browbeaten, by dogmatic assumptions, into believing that the discords in the capitalist system cannot under any circumstances be corrected by the democratic procedure. It is an article of Communist faith, which many advanced liberals seem to accept as a matter of course, that history offers no instance of a ruling aristocracy which has surrendered its power voluntarily, and that accordingly nothing short of violent revolutionary expropriation will induce the capitalist class to surrender the power which the institution of private property now confers upon it.

The premise is correct enough, but the conclusion is a *non sequitur*. True enough, no ruling class has ever surrendered its power voluntarily, but it does not follow that no ruling class has ever surrendered its power except under compulsion of naked force. The Roman Patricians did not surrender their power voluntarily, on demand; but they nevertheless surrendered it, gradually, under pressure, without incurring the destruction of republican institutions. The English aristocracy did not surrender its power voluntarily; but since the eighteenth century it has, under pressure exerted through the democratic political procedure, conceded one strategic position after another. And indeed in all those countries where democratic institutions still persist, the capitalist classes have, during the last fifty years or more, conceded bit by bit much of the control over private property which they formerly possessed and once thought indispensable. There is no compelling reason to suppose that, in those countries where the democratic tradition is strongly intrenched, this process of increasing governmental regulation of economic enterprise should not continue, even to the point, if that should prove necessary, of a virtual if not a formal socialization of certain basic industries, without incurring the destruction of democratic institutions.

It is not a question of keeping what we have or scrapping it for some untried ideal social system. At best it is a question of sufficiently improving what we have to avoid the intolerable distress which if unrelieved ends in despair and the resort to violence. No infallible panacea for accomplishing this end is available. The desired end can be accomplished, if at all, only by the method of trial and error, by employing the best knowledge available, so far as it can be employed by the democratic political method, to effect those adjustments which will put idle money to work in productive enterprises and idle men to work at a living wage. What particular measures are best adapted to do this I am incompetent to say. It is for the experts to suggest the particular measures. Since the experts disagree, the measures adopted, however carefully considered, will in the event no doubt be attended with unforeseen consequences calling for still further measures. That attempts to remedy the evil are not wholly successful is no reason for abandoning the task. Something must be done, and much must be attempted that a little may be gained. What is chiefly needed is time—time for experiment, for making mistakes and correcting them, time for the necessary adjustment in vested interests and the necessary psychological adaptation to new ideas, time for the slow crystallization of public opinion and for registering public opinion in legislative enactments by the cumbersome democratic technique.

It is true, of course, that there may not be time enough. There may not be time enough in any case. Technological advance has so accelerated the tempo and complicated the character of social change that present social ills can scarcely be properly diagnosed before they have been so far transformed that the proposed remedies are no longer adequate. But if time fails us, it will be less because of inherent defects in the capitalist system or the democratic procedure than because of the disastrous results of modern war in dislocating the national economy and in impairing the democratic morale.

IV

The ultimate cause of war is to be found no doubt in the nature of man. But the proximate cause is to be found in the particular conditions of time and place. Politically, the modern world is organized on the principle of the self-sufficiency and the self-determination of the sovereign state; economically, it is so far integrated that all countries are more or less interdepend-

ent. The result is that war in our time arises chiefly from the competitive political struggle for economic advantage—for land, markets, essential raw materials, and preferential opportunities for exploiting the undeveloped regions of the earth. A rational solution of the conflict would involve either complete freedom of trade and competitive industrial enterprise throughout the world, or the international allocation of commodities and industrial opportunities according to the legitimate needs of the several countries. A rational solution is impossible, however, because the rights of states are measured by the power they can exert, and the decisions of governments, and the attitudes of the people who support governments, are so largely determined by considerations of honor and prestige and deep-seated national fears and animosities. It is true that international conflicts may be, and often have been, mediated by friendly discussion and mutual concession. But such mediation is now more difficult than formerly. The profound divergence between the current ideologies makes friendly discussion between democratic countries on the one hand, and Communist and Fascist countries on the other, virtually impossible, and injects into their conflicts a fanatical and intransigent quality unknown since the religious wars of the sixteenth century. Thus in our time the perennial danger of war arising from economic conflict is at once increased and less easily obviated because of the fears and hatreds arising from the clash of discordant ideological systems.

War and the imminent danger of war may temporarily abate the social conflict in any country, but the ultimate effect can only be to diminish the possibility of resolving it by the democratic method. Political democracy is at best a slow and cumbersome method of managing the affairs of the community. In times of great emergency it is necessary to get things swiftly done, whether well done or not; and in the supreme emergency of war, when arms speak and laws are silent, the democratic liberties are inevitably subordinated to military efficiency. Nevertheless, the temporary eclipse of the democratic liberties is not what matters most. What chiefly matters is that war, by devoting the energies of the nation to destructive ends, disrupts the peacetime economy, impoverishes and demoralizes the people, and thereby intensifies the social conflict which tends to undermine the stability of democratic institutions.

In September, 1939, the imminent danger of war was replaced by war itself. The war is justified as a war for the defense of democracy and the restoration of social order in Europe. The last war was likewise justified: we were told, and at the time many of us confidently believed, that it was fought to make the world safe for democracy. We now know that an outstanding result of it was to make half of Europe safe for dictators. What the result of the present war may be no man can say; but it would be naïve indeed to suppose that it will do more than the last war did to strengthen democratic institutions throughout the world, or even in the countries where they still exist. On the contrary, if experience be any guide at all, we must suppose that the present war, like the last one, will intensify those economic and social conflicts which have already, in many countries, proved fatal to the democratic way of life.

This is not to say that war can or should always be avoided. If democratic institutions cannot be safeguarded by war, still less can they be safeguarded by submitting to aggressions designed to destroy them. It is not true that it takes two to make a quarrel. One can very easily make a quarrel if he gives a perverted mind to it; and a government as well as an individual can make a quarrel inevitable by deliberate and persistent aggression. In September, 1939, the choice presented to France and Great Britain was not between war or peace. They had to choose between making war at that time or sanctioning aggressions which there was every reason to think would be followed by still further aggressions, so that in the end the choice would be between submitting to conquest or fighting under less favorable conditions. In such a situation the relevant conclusion, it seems to me, is that although war, being the negation of the democratic idea, can in itself do nothing to safeguard democratic institutions, it may very well be the only means of safeguarding the independence of those countries where democratic institutions exist.

The essential condition for preserving democratic institutions is the political independence of the people who wish to preserve them. In this sense, therefore, if in this sense only, war may be a means of defending democracy. For although the chances for the survival of democratic institutions in Europe will be less at the end of the present war than they would have been if there had been no war, the chances will still be better in a Europe in which France and Great Britain retain their independence than they could be in a Europe dominated by the present Nazi regime in Germany. It is possible that democratic institutions may disappear in England as a result of the war even if Great Britain wins the war; they are certain to disappear if Germany wins the war. If then democratic institutions are to be destroyed in any case, it seems on the whole better that they should be destroyed by their friends than by their enemies.

When we consider the problem of preserving democratic institutions broadly, from both the national and the international point of view, we seem to be helplessly caught in a vicious circle. We know that democratic institutions are threatened by social discords within the nations, and still more by war between them. We know that if we could avoid war it would be much easier to resolve our social discords, and that if we could resolve our social discords it would be much easier to avoid war. If we could do either of these things without the other, the future of democracy would be fairly secure; if we could do both of them it would be altogether so. Yet we know that social discords are a major cause of war, and that war is the one thing that will make it impossible, if anything does, to resolve our social discords. It is in such situations that reason succumbs to force, in such situations that dictators flourish and democracy declines.

It is possible that the crisis which confronts the modern world involves something more serious even than the collapse of democratic institutions. The contradictions in the capitalist system may be no more than symbols of a discord more profound—the discord between the physical power at our disposal and our capacity to make a good use of it. It is obvious at all events that the history of the last two centuries presents us with a disturbing paradox: whereas the application of reason to the mastery of the physical world has proceeded with unanticipated success and mounting optimism, the persistent effort to shape the world of human relations to humane and rational ends has been so far unavailing that we are oppressed with a sense of frustration and defeat.

Long ago it was said that man can more easily take a city than govern himself. Never was the saying more true than now. Never before has the intelligence of man placed so much material power at his disposal: never before has he employed the power at his disposal for the realization of purposes more diverse or more irreconcilable. The hand of man is subdued to what it works in, and the mind admires what the hand can accomplish. Modern man is therefore enamored of mechanical force. Fascinated by the esthetic precision and sheer power of the instruments he has devised, he will use them for doing whatever by their aid can be done, in the confident expectation that what can be done with such clean efficiency must be worth doing. Thus the machines we have invented tend to enslave us. Compelling us to use them on their own terms, and to adjust our conduct to their virtues and limitations, they somehow generate social forces which, being too complex and too intangible to be easily understood, shape our lives to ends we do not will but cannot avoid.

In times past certain civilizations, long established, brilliant and prosperous and seemingly secure against mischance, slowly decayed and either disappeared altogether or were transformed past recognition and forgotten. What has happened many times in the history of mankind may happen again. There are no barbarian hosts without the gates, but there are plenty of potential barbarians within them. It is then within the range of possibility that the flagrant discord between the mechanical power at man's disposal and his capacity to make good use of it is carrying the world into another period of widespread and chronic confusion in which democracy will everywhere succumb to dictatorship, reason to naked force, and naked force prove to be the prelude to another dark age of barbarism.

I do not say that this will happen. I do not think it will. But it is futile to suppose that it cannot happen, futile to rely upon the saving grace of some transcendent increasing purpose (a law of nature, or dialectic of history, or totalitarian state) to bring us in spite of ourselves to a predestined good end. For the solution of our difficulties the only available purposes are our own, the only available intelligence such as we can command. If then democracy survives, if civilization in any tolerable form survives, it will be because, in some favored parts of the world the human mind remains unshackled and, aided by time and fortunate circumstances, proves capable of subordinating the unprecedented material power at its command to the achievement of rational and humane ends. More obvious now even than in the seventeenth century is the truth of Pascal's famous dictum: "Thought makes the whole dignity of man; therefore, endeavor to think well, that is the only morality."

The chief virtue of democracy, and in the long run the sole reason for cherishing it, is that with all its defects it still provides the most favorable conditions for the maintenance of that dignity and the practice of that morality.

Index

INDEX